Microsoft® Word 2016

by Jill Murphy, Custom Performance Solutions

LEVEL 1

LABYRINTH
LEARNING™

Microsoft Word 2016: Level 1

Copyright © 2017 by Labyrinth Learning

Labyrinth Learning
2560 9th Street, Suite 320
Berkeley, California 94710
800.522.9746
On the web at lablearning.com

Product Manager:
Jason Favro

Development Manager:
Laura Popelka

Senior Editor:
Alexandra Mummery

Junior Editor:
Alexandria Henderson

Assessment and Multimedia Content Development:
Ben Linford, Judy Mardar, Andrew Vaughnley

Production Manager:
Debra Grose

Compositor:
Happenstance Type-O-Rama

Indexer:
Valerie Perry

Interior Design:
Debra Grose

Cover Design:
Mick Koller

ebook only ITEM: 1-59136-836-7
            ISBN-13: 978-159136-836-6

ebook with printed textbook ITEM: 1-59136-837-5
            ISBN-13: 978-159136-837-3

Manufactured in the United States of America

GPP 10 9 8 7 6 5 4 3

Table of Contents

Preface

This textbook is part of our brand-new approach to learning for introductory computer courses. We've kept the best elements of our proven instructional design and added powerful, interactive elements and assessments that offer enormous potential to engage learners in a new way. We're delighted with the results, and we hope that learners and educators are, too!

Why Did We Write This Content?

In today's digital world, knowing how to use the most common software applications is critical, and those who don't are left behind. Our goal is to simplify the entire learning experience and help every student develop the practical, real-world skills needed to be successful at work and in school. Using a combination of text, videos, interactive elements, and assessments, we begin with fundamental concepts and take learners through a systematic progression of exercises to reach mastery.

What Key Themes Did We Follow?

We had conversations with dozens of educators at community colleges, vocational schools, and other learning environments in preparation for this textbook. We listened and have adapted our learning solution to match the needs of a rapidly changing world, keeping the following common themes in mind:

Keep it about skills. Our content focus is on critical, job-ready topics and tasks, with a relentless focus on practical, real-world skills and common sense as well as step-by-step instruction to ensure that learners stay engaged from the first chapter forward. We've retained our proven method of progressively moving learners through increasingly independent exercises to ensure mastery—an approach that has been successfully developing skills for more than 20 years.

Keep it simple. Our integrated solutions create a seamless and engaging experience built on a uniquely dynamic instructional design that brings clarity to even the most challenging topics. We've focused our content on the things that matter most and have presented it in the easiest way for today's learners to absorb it. Concise chunks of text are combined with visually engaging and interactive elements to increase understanding for all types of learners.

Keep it relevant. Fresh, original, and constantly evolving content helps educators keep pace with today's student and work environments. We have reviewed every topic for relevancy and have updated it where needed to offer realistic examples and projects for learners.

How Do I Use This Book?

We understand that we are in a time of transition and that some students will still appreciate a print textbook to support their learning. Our comprehensive learning solution consists of a groundbreaking interactive ebook for primary content delivery and our easy-to-use eLab course management tool for assessment. We want to help students as they transition to a digital solution. Our interactive ebook contains learning content delivered in ways that will engage learners. Students can utilize a print text supplement in conjunction with the ebook that provides all the textual elements from the ebook in a full-color, spiral-bound print format.

Our eLab platform provides additional learning content such as overviews for each chapter, automatically graded projects and other assessments that accurately assess student skills, and clear feedback and analytics on student actions.

Included with Your Textbook Purchase

▶ *Interactive ebook*: A dynamic, engaging, and truly interactive textbook that includes elements such as videos, self-assessments, slide shows, and other interactive features. Highlighting, taking notes, and searching for content is easy.

▶ *eLab Course Management System*: A robust tool for accurate assessment, tracking of learner activity, and automated grading that includes a comprehensive set of instructor resources. eLab can be fully integrated with your LMS, making course management even easier.

▶ *Instructor resources*: This course is also supported on the Labyrinth website with a comprehensive instructor support package that includes detailed lesson plans, PowerPoint presentations, a course syllabus, test banks, additional exercises, and more.

▶ *Learning Resource Center*: Files to accompany this textbook can be found within eLab or on the Learning Resource Center accessed from the ebook.

We're excited to share this innovative, new approach with you, and we'd love you to share your experience with us at www.lablearning.com/share.

Display Settings

Multiple factors, including screen resolution, monitor size, and window size, can affect the appearance of the Microsoft Ribbon and its buttons. In this textbook, screen captures were taken at the native (recommended) screen resolutions in Office 2016 running Windows 10, with ClearType enabled.

Visual Conventions

This book uses visual and typographic cues to guide students through the lessons. Some of these cues are described below.

Cue Name	What It Does
`Type this text`	Text you type at the keyboard is printed in this typeface.
Action words	The important action words in exercise steps are presented in boldface.
Ribbon	Glossary terms are highlighted with a light yellow background.
Note! *Tip!* *Warning!*	Tips, notes, and warnings are called out with special icons.
(!)	Videos and WebSims that are a required part of this course are indicated by this icon.
Command→Command→ Command→Command	Commands to execute from the Ribbon are presented like this: Ribbon Tab→Command Group→Command→Subcommand.
☰ **Design→Themes→Themes** 🅰	These notes present shortcut steps for executing certain tasks.

Acknowledgements

Many individuals contribute to the development and completion of a textbook. This book has benefited significantly from the feedback and suggestions of the following reviewers:

Pam Silvers, *Asheville-Buncombe Technical Community College*

Ramiro Villareal, *Brookhaven College*

Teresa Loftis, *Inland Career Education Center*

Kim Pigeon, *Northeast Wisconsin Technical College*

Lynne Kemp, *North Country Community College*

Tom Martin, *Shasta College*

Karen LaPlant, *Hennepin Technical College*

Kay Gerken, *College of DuPage*

Colleen Kennedy, *Spokane Community College*

1 | Creating and Editing Business Documents

The business letter is one of the most common business documents. It's different from sending a casual email, which tends to be more conversational. Business letters are formal; however, they shouldn't be stuffy. You want to engage the reader while maintaining a professional tone. Before you start writing, analyze your audience. Your readers want to know what's in it for them, so you need to tell them, and you need to convey the purpose clearly and succinctly. In this chapter, you will create business letters using proper formatting.

LEARNING OBJECTIVES

▸ Navigate in a document

▸ Create and save documents

▸ Enter and edit text

▸ Create numbered and bulleted lists

▸ Save documents as different file types

▸ Create envelopes

▸ Use document views

▸ Print documents

📁 Project: Creating a Well-Formatted Business Letter

School is over, and it's time to line up some interviews. You are seeking a retail computer sales position. You've scanned lots of computer company ads and websites, and now you're ready to write a cover letter in the proper format that states your desired position and highlights your educational and professional experience. Your goal is to create an impressive cover letter that gets you noticed right from the start.

Elements of a Professional Business Letter

There are several acceptable styles of business letters. All business letters contain similar elements but with varied formatting. The following block style is the most common business letter style. All elements are left aligned and single spaced, except for double spacing between paragraphs.

Date: two inches from top of page but may vary based on letterhead

Inside address: two to four lines below the date

Salutation: Followed by a colon

Body

Complimentary close: Followed by a comma

Signature

Enclosures notification

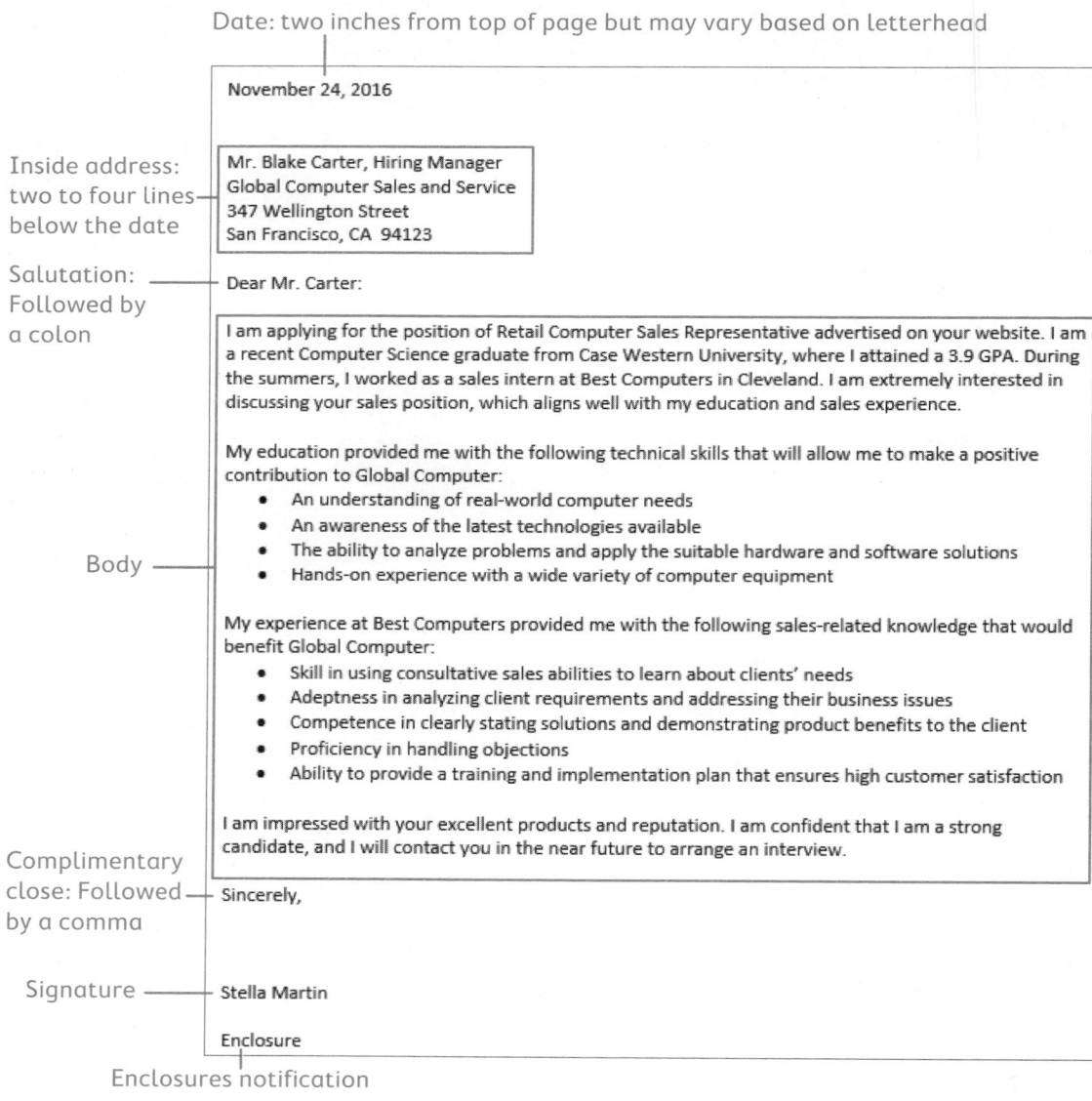

November 24, 2016

Mr. Blake Carter, Hiring Manager
Global Computer Sales and Service
347 Wellington Street
San Francisco, CA 94123

Dear Mr. Carter:

I am applying for the position of Retail Computer Sales Representative advertised on your website. I am a recent Computer Science graduate from Case Western University, where I attained a 3.9 GPA. During the summers, I worked as a sales intern at Best Computers in Cleveland. I am extremely interested in discussing your sales position, which aligns well with my education and sales experience.

My education provided me with the following technical skills that will allow me to make a positive contribution to Global Computer:
- An understanding of real-world computer needs
- An awareness of the latest technologies available
- The ability to analyze problems and apply the suitable hardware and software solutions
- Hands-on experience with a wide variety of computer equipment

My experience at Best Computers provided me with the following sales-related knowledge that would benefit Global Computer:
- Skill in using consultative sales abilities to learn about clients' needs
- Adeptness in analyzing client requirements and addressing their business issues
- Competence in clearly stating solutions and demonstrating product benefits to the client
- Proficiency in handling objections
- Ability to provide a training and implementation plan that ensures high customer satisfaction

I am impressed with your excellent products and reputation. I am confident that I am a strong candidate, and I will contact you in the near future to arrange an interview.

Sincerely,

Stella Martin

Enclosure

What's Important in a Cover Letter

Now that you know the fundamentals of a proper business letter, you will explore the best approach to creating a cover letter to go with your résumé. Keep the following points in mind:

▶ *Purpose:* Use a cover letter to introduce yourself and explain why you fit the job requirements.

▶ *Application Tracking System (ATS):* The first review of your application documents (cover letter and résumé) is likely to be done by an ATS software program. The software searches your documents for job-specific skills and keywords. You may wish to conduct an Internet search to become familiar with ATSs and how best to write your documents so that they will not be overlooked by an ATS.

▶ *File Types:* Some file types work better than others relative to an ATS, and some employers may request that you submit your documents using a specific file type. If you are not sure what file type to use, contact the prospective employer and ask if it has a preference.

▶ *Audience Awareness:* Study the job description and conduct an online search of the company to learn as much as you can. You need to know *what* your audience members are interested in so you'll know *how* to get their attention.

▶ *Beginning, Middle, and End:* Introduce yourself and include an attention grabber (I believe I could make an excellent contribution to your company); highlight, but don't duplicate, outstanding points from your résumé; close the letter expressing your enthusiasm for the company and position.

▶ *Importance of Fresh Eyes:* An error in your documents could eliminate you. Ask friends or colleagues to proof your documents with fresh eyes.

Navigating in a Document

If you are working in a multipage document, it's helpful to know various techniques for moving through it quickly. You can navigate using the scroll bar at the right side of the screen, or you can use keystrokes.

Navigating with the Scroll Bar

The scroll bar lets you navigate through documents; however, it does not move the insertion point. After scrolling, you must click in the document where you want to position the insertion point. There are several ways you can use the scroll bar. You can click the up and down arrows at the top and bottom of the scroll bar to scroll one line at a time. You can drag the scroll box to move quickly through a multipage document, and you can click below or above the scroll box to move up or down one screen at a time.

When the mouse pointer is in the text area, it resembles an uppercase "I" and is referred to as an I-beam. The insertion point is positioned at the location where you click the I-beam and it begins flashing. Wherever the insertion point is flashing is where the action begins.

 View the video "Using the Scroll Bar to Navigate."

Keyboard Navigation Tips

Whether you use the mouse or the keyboard to navigate is up to you. Navigating with the keyboard always moves the insertion point, so it will be with you when you arrive at your destination. Here are some handy keyboard navigations tips:

▶ Ctrl + End to move to the end of the document

▶ Ctrl + Home to move to the beginning of the document

▶ End to move to the end of the line

▶ Home to move to the beginning of the line

DEVELOP YOUR SKILLS: W1-D1

In this exercise, you will use the scroll bar and keyboard to navigate in a document. When you use the scroll bar, you have to position the insertion point. When you use the keyboard, the insertion point moves with you.

Before You Begin: *Be sure to visit the Learning Resource Center at labyrinthelab.com/lrc to retrieve the exercise files for this course before beginning this exercise.*

1. Click **Start**.
2. Type **Wo** and then choose **Word 2016** from the list of suggestions.
3. Click the **Blank Document** template on the Word start screen.
4. Make sure the Word window is **maximized** 🗗.

   When you hover the mouse pointer over the button, if the window is already maximized, the ToolTip will say Restore Down.

   Next you will open an existing document so you can practice navigating.

5. Choose **File→Open** to display the Open screen in Backstage view (which is what Microsoft calls the contents of the File tab).
6. Navigate to your **Word Chapter 1** folder and open **W1-D1-MyVirtualCampus**.
7. Move the mouse pointer in the body of the document and notice that it looks like an I-beam I .
8. Move the mouse pointer into the left margin area, and now the white selection arrow ⇗ is visible.

Navigate with the Scroll Bar and Keyboard

9. Click below the scroll box to move the document down one screen.

Notice that the insertion point has not moved.

10. Click the **I-beam** I in the document to position the insertion point.

The insertion point appears where you clicked. If the background is highlighted, you accidentally selected the text. Deselect by clicking the I-beam in the document background.

11. Drag the **scroll box** toward the bottom of the scroll bar until you see the end of the text and then position the insertion point at the end of the text.

12. Drag the **scroll box** to the top of the scroll bar and position the insertion point at the top of the document.

13. Position the insertion point at the beginning of the first paragraph.

14. Tap End to move the insertion point to the end of the line; tap Home to move the insertion point to the beginning of the line.

15. Press Ctrl + End to move the insertion point to the end of the document.

16. Choose **File→Close**, and if you are prompted to save changes, just click **Don't Save**.

The document screen is now a new blank document.

Entering Text

You always insert text at the flashing insertion point. Therefore, you must position the insertion point at the desired location before typing. When you insert text, existing text moves to the right as you type. You should not tap Enter at the end of each line. Text will automatically wrap to the next line when you reach the right-hand margin.

You use the Enter key to begin a new paragraph or to insert blank lines in a document. Anything that ends by tapping Enter is considered to be a paragraph. Thus, short lines such as a date line, an inside address, or even blank lines themselves are considered paragraphs.

Tapping Enter inserts a paragraph symbol in a document. These and other symbols are visible when you show formatting marks.

Showing and Hiding Formatting Marks

Although formatting marks appear on the screen, you will not see them in the printed document. Viewing these symbols can be important when editing a document. For example, you may need to see the formatting marks to determine whether the space between two words was created with the Spacebar or Tab.

Paragraph symbols appear when you tap Enter.

```
¶
¶
Mr.·Blake·Carter,·Hiring·Manager¶
Global·Computer·Sales·and·Service¶
347 Wellington·Street¶
San·Francisco,·CA··94123¶
¶
Dear·Mr.·Carter:¶
¶
I·am·applying·for·the·position·of·Retail·Computer·Sales·
```

Dots appear between words when you tap Spacebar.

DEVELOP YOUR SKILLS: W1-D2

In this exercise, you will turn on the Show/Hide button to show formatting marks and type a paragraph, allowing Word Wrap to end lines automatically at the right-hand margin. Then you will use the Enter *key to end the first paragraph and start another paragraph.*

1. If necessary, choose **File→New**.
2. Click the **Blank Document** template to start a new document.
3. Choose **File→Save As** and navigate to your **Word Chapter 1** folder.
4. Name the file **W1-D2-CoverLtrTips** and then click the **Save** button at the bottom of the dialog box.
5. Choose **Home→Paragraph→Show/Hide** ¶ to show formatting marks.

   All new documents contain a paragraph symbol; you won't see it if you don't turn on the Show/Hide feature. Paragraph symbols carry formatting in them. In this example, the Blank Document template formatting includes the default Calibri font and 1.08 line spacing.

 *Feel free to turn the Show/Hide button on and off as needed.*

6. Type the following text and let Word Wrap do its thing:

   Your cover letter may be the first impression a company has of you. You want to be certain it's a good impression. Research the company on its website before preparing a cover letter. The more you know about what a company is doing, the better you can explain how you can contribute to the company.

   If you make a typo, use Backspace *or* Delete *to remove it. Remember to position the insertion point next to the typo.*

7. Tap Enter.

   Notice the paragraph symbol ¶*. Also notice the extra space between the end of the paragraph and the insertion point. That is due to the default spacing of 1.08. You will learn more about spacing soon.*

8. Type the following text:

   Proofreading is critical. Errors in a cover letter will likely eliminate you. Don't go it alone. Ask others to proof your letter as well.

9. Save and close the file.

   The document window is now blank.

Spacing in Letters

The default line spacing in Word 2016 is 1.08 rather than the traditional 1.0 single spacing. It adds an extra 8% more space between lines than regular single spacing. It also adds 8 points of space after paragraphs. Therefore, rather than tapping Enter twice at the end of a paragraph, you just tap Enter once, and Word adds the extra spacing.

When you choose the Blank Document template on the Start screen or on the New screen in Backstage view, you are using the default spacing. Some documents, however, typically require single spacing, such as business letters, reports, and proposals. These methods are available for applying single spacing:

▶ Single Spaced (Blank) template

▶ Line and Paragraph Spacing button

Applying Traditional Spacing Using the Single Spaced (Blank) Template

Choosing the Single Spaced (Blank) template from the Start screen or from the New screen opens a single-spaced document. This is a good choice if the majority of your document will be single spaced. If you use single spacing in only part of your document, the Line and Paragraph Spacing button is a good choice.

Changing Spacing Using the Line and Paragraph Spacing Button

If you start a new document using 1.08 spacing and then decide to apply single spacing to a portion of the document, you can choose the 1.0 option in the Line and Paragraph Spacing button menu. You must select (highlight) the text to be single spaced or, at a minimum, position the insertion point in the paragraph before changing the spacing. If you wish to use other spacing such as double or triple spacing, the Line and Paragraph Spacing button is the place to go.

≡ Home→Paragraph→Line and Paragraph Spacing 📇 │ Right-click in the text→ Paragraph→Line Spacing

---

DEVELOP YOUR SKILLS: W1-D3

In this exercise, you will use the Single Spaced (Blank) template, and you will modify spacing in your cover letter.

1. Choose **File→New** to display the templates.
2. Click the **Single Spaced (Blank)** template to start a single-spaced document.

   A window appears describing the template.
3. Click the **Create** 🗋 button to start the document.

Tip! *If you double-click the template, the document will open immediately.*

   Now you will save the document in your student exercise folder.
4. Choose **File→Save As**, navigate to your **Word Chapter 1** folder, and save the file as **W1-D3-CoverLtr**.
5. Type **Nove**, but stop typing when AutoComplete displays a pop-up tip.
6. Tap ⎗Enter⎘ to automatically insert *November* in the letter.

   Word recognizes certain words and phrases, such as names of the months and days, and offers to complete them for you.
7. Finish typing the date as **November 24, 2016**.
8. Tap ⎗Enter⎘ three times to provide space between the date and the inside address.
9. If necessary, choose **Home→Paragraph→Show/Hide** ¶ to display formatting marks.

   Notice the paragraph symbols that were created when you tapped ⎗Enter⎘.

10. Type the following inside address and salutation, tapping ⎡Enter⎤ wherever you see a paragraph symbol.

If you catch a typo, you can tap ⎡Backspace⎤ *enough times to remove the error and then continue typing.*

> Mr.·Blake·Carter,·Hiring·Manager¶
> Global·Computer·Sales·and·Service¶
> 347·Wellington·Street¶
> San·Francisco,·CA··94123¶
> ¶
> Dear·Mr.·Carter:¶
> ¶
> ¶

11. Type the following body paragraphs, letting Word Wrap do its thing and tapping ⎡Enter⎤ twice the end of each paragraph.

Remember, you are using the single-spaced template now and there is no additional spacing when yo tap ⎡Enter⎤ *at the end of the paragraph. You have to tap* ⎡Enter⎤ *twice to create white space between paragraphs.*

> I·am·applying·for·the·position·of·Retail·Computer·Sales·advertised·on·your·website.·I·am·a·recent·Computer·Science·graduate·from·Case·Western·University,·where·I·attained·a·3.9·GPA.·During·the·summers,·I·worked·as·an·intern·in·the·sales·department·at·Best·Computers·in·Cleveland.·I·am·extremely·interested·in·discussing·your·sales·position,·which·aligns·well·with·my·education·and·sales·experience.¶
> ¶
> I·am·impressed·with·your·excellent·products·and·reputation.··I·am·confident·that·I·am·a·strong·candidate,·and·I·will·contact·you·in·the·near·future·to·arrange·an·interview.¶
> ¶
> ¶

Change Line Spacing

12. Position the insertion point anywhere in the first main paragraph.

13. Choose **Home→Paragraph→Line and Paragraph Spacing** 📄.

14. Slide the mouse pointer over the menu options and notice that Live Preview shows how the selected paragraph will look if the formatting is applied.

Notice the Add Space Before Paragraph and Add Space After paragraph options. These options add an extra 12 points of space before or after a paragraph.

15. Choose **3.0** (triple space).

Remembering that single spacing is appropriate for a business letter, you decide to change back to single spacing.

16. Choose **Home→Paragraph→Line and Paragraph Spacing** 📄 and choose **1.0**.

17. Save your letter.

Note! *Always leave the file open at the end of an exercise unless instructed to close it.*

Aligning Text Horizontally and Vertically

You can control how text aligns horizontally on the page using the paragraph alignment buttons in the Paragraph group on the Home tab. You can determine vertical alignment of text on a page using the Vertical Alignment feature in Page Setup.

TEXT ALIGNMENT OPTIONS

Horizontal Alignment	Vertical Alignment
• Align Left (default) • Center • Align Right • Justify (text distributed evenly between left/right margins)	• Top (default) • Center • Justified (text distributed evenly between top/bottom margins) • Bottom
☰ Home→Paragraph→Choose the desired alignment	☰ Layout→Page Setup ⌐ dialog box launcher→Layout tab→Page→Vertical Alignment

DEVELOP YOUR SKILLS: W1-D4

In this exercise, you will change the horizontal and vertical alignment in your letter.

1. Choose **File→Save As** and save your file as **W1-D4-CoverLtr**.

2. Position the insertion point anywhere in the date line.

3. Choose **Home→Paragraph→Center** ≡ to center the date between the margins.

   Notice that the Center button on the Ribbon is highlighted, indicating that center alignment is in effect at the insertion point.

4. Choose **Home→Paragraph→Align Right** ≡ to place the date at the right-hand margin.

   You've decided you prefer to have the date left-aligned.

5. Choose **Home→Paragraph→Align Left** ≡.

   Now you will type the complimentary close, the signature, and an enclosures notification.

6. Position the insertion point next to the last paragraph symbol in the document.

7. Type the end of the letter as shown, tapping [Enter] wherever you see a paragraph symbol.

   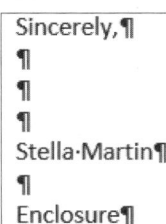

Center the Letter Vertically

8. Scroll down to the end of the page.

   There is too much white space at the bottom of the letter, so now you will center it vertically on the page.

9. Click the **Layout** tab on the Ribbon.

10. Click the **dialog box launcher** in the bottom-right corner of the Page Setup group to open the Page Setup dialog box.

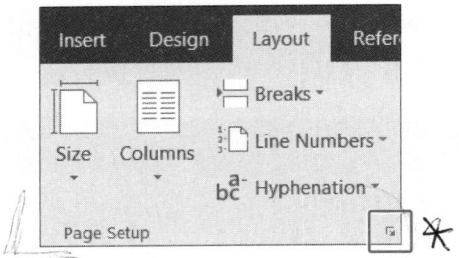

11. Follow these steps to center the letter vertically on the page:

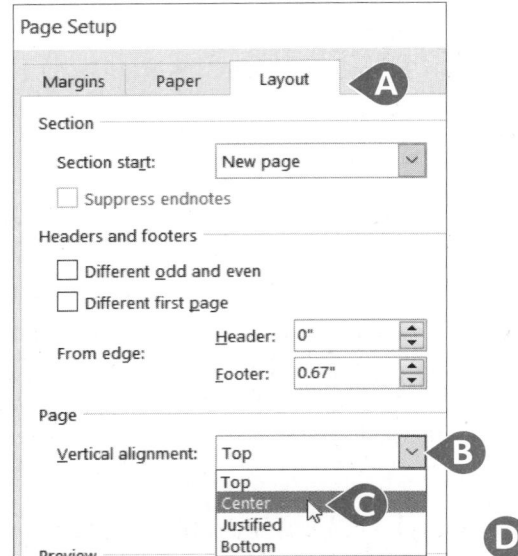

Ⓐ Click the **Layout** tab.

Ⓑ Click the **Vertical Alignment** field to display the menu.

Ⓒ Choose **Center** from the menu.

Ⓓ Click **OK** at the bottom of the dialog box to close it.

Now you will use the zoom controls to zoom out so you can see the entire page.

12. Click the **Zoom Out** button (at the bottom-right corner of the screen) enough times to see the entire page.

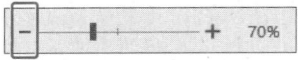

The letter is centered vertically on the page.

13. Click the **Zoom In** button enough times to return to 100%.

14. Save the letter.

Selecting Text

You must select (highlight) text if you wish to perform an action on it. Suppose you want to delete a line. You select the line first and then delete it. Whether you use the mouse or the keyboard to select text is up to you.

The Mini toolbar appears when you select text. It contains frequently used commands. You can choose a command or ignore the toolbar, and it will fade away.

View the video "Selecting Text with the Mouse."

Here are some handy mouse and keyboard selection tips:

▶ Use the shortcut click+⬚Shift⬚+click to select awkward amounts of text, such as the end of one line and the beginning of the next. It's as simple as clicking at the beginning of a text block, holding down ⬚Shift⬚, and clicking at the end of the text block.

▶ Press ⬚Ctrl⬚+click to select a sentence.

▶ Press ⬚Ctrl⬚+⬚A⬚ to select the entire document.

DEVELOP YOUR SKILLS: W1-D5

In this exercise, you will practice various selection techniques.

1. Follow these steps to select text using the left margin:

 Mr. Blake Carter, Hiring Manager
Global Computer Sales and Service
347 Wellington Street
San Francisco, CA 94123

 Dear Mr. Carter:

 I am applying for the position of Retail Computer Sales advertised on your website. I am a recent Computer Science graduate from Case Western University, where I attained a 3.9 GPA. During the summers, I worked as an intern in the sales department at Best Computers in Cleveland. I am extremely interested in discussing your sales position, which aligns well with my education and sales experience.

    Ⓐ Place the **selection arrow** in the margin to the left of the first line of the inside address; click to select the line. The Mini toolbar appears; you can ignore it for now.

    Ⓑ Use the **selection arrow** to select this line. (Notice that the previously selected line is no longer selected.)

    Ⓒ Select this paragraph by double-clicking the **selection arrow** in the margin to the left of the paragraph.

2. Using the selection arrow, drag down the left margin to select text.

3. Click anywhere in the body of the letter to deselect.

4. Triple-click with the selection arrow anywhere in the left margin to select the entire letter and then deselect it.

5. Double-click any word to select it.

6. Double-click a different word, notice that the previous word is deselected, and then deselect the latest selection.

Select Nonadjacent Text

You can select multiple locations simultaneously.

7. Double-click to select one word.

8. Press and hold ⬚Ctrl⬚ as you double-click another word; release ⬚Ctrl⬚.

Both selections are active. You can select as many nonadjacent areas of a document as desired using the ⬚Ctrl⬚ key.

9. Move the I-beam ⌶ to the start of the first main paragraph, click to position the insertion point and then hold down [Shift] and click after *Sales*.

> I am applying for the position of Retail Computer Sales advertised
> Computer Science graduate from Case Western University, where
> summers, I worked as an intern in the sales department at Best C
> interested in discussing your sales position, which aligns well with

10. Click to deselect.

Using Numbered and Bulleted Lists

Numbered and bulleted lists are effective in drawing your reader's attention to items of interest. You can turn them on before you begin typing or apply them after you typed the list. Numbered lists are automatically renumbered if you insert or delete an item. A good example of when to use a numbered list is when sequence is important, as in a series of steps in a procedure. Items in a bulleted list have no sequence.

 *Be sure to check whether the ATS used by a prospective employer can read numbered and bulleted lists.*

 View the video "Promoting and Demoting Lists."

≡ Home→Paragraph→Bullets ⊞

≡ Home→Paragraph→Numbering ⊞

DEVELOP YOUR SKILLS: W1-D6

In this exercise, you will create and format numbered and bulleted lists. Because correctness is important, you'll also work with proofreading tools.

1. Choose **File→Save As** and save your letter as `W1-D6-CoverLtr`.

2. If necessary, choose **Home→Paragraph→Show/Hide** ¶ to display formatting marks.

3. Position the insertion point at the end of the last line in the first body paragraph.

4. Tap [Enter] twice, type this paragraph, and then tap [Enter] once more.

> My·college·education·provided·me·with·the·following·technical·skills·that·will·allow·me·to·make·a·positive·contribution·to·Global·Computer:¶

Type a Numbered List

5. Choose **Home→Paragraph→Numbering** ⊞ to turn on numbers.

6. Type the following text, tapping [Enter] at the end of each item to generate the next number:

> 1.→ An·understanding·of·real-world·computer·needs¶
> 2.→ An·awareness·of·the·latest·technologies·available¶
> 3.→ The·ability·to·analyze·problems·and·apply·the·appropriate·hardware·and·software·solutions¶

Notice the arrow formatting marks following the numbers. They represent tabs, which were automatically generated by the numbering system.

7. Tap ⬚Enter⬚ at the end of the line to generate the next number.

8. Begin typing the last item, purposely misspelling *experience*, but don't tap ⬚Spacebar⬚ yet:

> 4.→ Hands-on·experence¶

9. Now, as you tap ⬚Spacebar⬚, watch how AutoCorrect fixes the misspelling for you.

This is another proofreading tool that makes corrections automatically. It also fixes common punctuation errors and capitalizes the names of days and months if you do not.

10. Finish typing the fourth item:

> 4.→ Hands-on·experience·with·a·wide·variety·of·computer·equipment¶

11. Tap ⬚Enter⬚ three times at the end of item 4: once to generate the next number, once to turn off numbering, and once again to add space between paragraphs.

12. Type the following paragraph and then tap ⬚Enter⬚ once:

> My·experience·at·Best·Computers·provided·me·with·the·following·sales-related·knowledge·that·would·benefit·Global·Computer:¶

Continue a Numbered List

13. Choose **Home→Paragraph→Numbering** ▤.

Notice that numbering restarted at 1. The system assumes you are starting a new list. There may be times when you want to continue numbering even though some regular text is entered within the list.

A smart tag pop-up appears next to the number.

14. Click the **AutoCorrect Options** ▤ smart tag and then click **Continue Numbering** to continue the previous list with the number 5.

Another smart tag appears.

15. Click the **AutoCorrect Options** ▤ smart tag and then choose **Restart Numbering**.

Remember that numbered lists are typically used when sequence is important. In this example, the items you type are not in sequence, so you will change to a bulleted list.

16. Choose **Home→Paragraph→Bullets** ▤.

17. Type the following list:

> •→ Skill·in·using·consultative·sales·skills·to·learn·about·clients'·needs¶
> •→ Adeptness·in·analyzing·client·requirements·and·addressing·their·business·issues¶
> •→ Competence·in·articulating·solutions·and·demonstrating·product·benefits·to·the·client¶
> •→ Proficiency·in·handling·objections¶
> •→ Ability·to·provide·a·training·and·implementation·plan·that·ensures·high·customer·satisfaction¶

Because numbering is typically used when sequence is important and in this case the list is not in sequential order, you decide to use bullets for the first list as well.

18. Move the mouse pointer to the left margin next to the first numbered item, press and hold down the **mouse button**, and drag down through the fourth item.

19. Choose **Home→Paragraph→Bullets** ▤ to apply bullets.

20. Click in the body to deselect the bullets and then save your letter.

Editing Text

There are many tools for editing documents, allowing you to insert and delete text. Remember, you must position the insertion point before you begin typing. You can use `Backspace` and `Delete` to remove one character at a time. If you select a block of text, you can use `Backspace` or `Delete` to remove the entire block, or you can type over the selected text to replace it.

Spell checker and grammar checker automatically help you edit text on the fly by placing a squiggly red line under words that might be misspelled and a squiggly blue line under words that may be grammatically incorrect. Right-clicking on underlined words presents possible options for correcting the potential error. Spell checker and grammar checker are only editing aids; you must use your own good judgment when deciding what action to take.

You can look up synonyms from within the document you are editing in order to enhance your word choice. You can view a list of synonyms by right-clicking a word and choosing Synonyms from the menu. For a more extensive list, choose Thesaurus from the submenu to open the Thesaurus task pane.

 View the video "Using the Thesaurus Task Pane."

DEVELOP YOUR SKILLS: W1-D7

In this exercise, you will insert and delete text, and you will use the pop-up menu to find synonyms.

1. Choose **File→Save As** and save your file as **W1-D7-CoverLtr**.
2. In the first line of the first main paragraph, click the **I-beam** `I` in front of *advertised* to position the insertion point.

> I·am·applying·for·the·position·of·Retail·Computer·Sales·advertised·
> Computer·Science·graduate·from·Case·Western·University,·where·

3. Type **Representative** `Spacebar`.
4. In the third line of the first paragraph, position the insertion point between the *a* and *n* in *an*.

> I am applying for the position of Retail
> a recent Computer Science graduate fr
> the summers, I worked as an intern in

5. Tap `Delete` to remove the *n* and then tap `Spacebar`.

   The a is underlined in blue indicating a grammar error, but you can ignore it, and it will eventually go away.

6. Type **sales**.
7. In the third line of the first paragraph, drag the mouse pointer across *in the sales department* to select (highlight) the words.

> I am applying for the position of Retail Computer Sales Representa
> a recent Computer Science graduate from Case Western University
> the summers, I worked as a sales intern in the sales department at

8. Tap `Delete` to remove the selected words.

9. In the first line of the second paragraph, double-click *college* to select it and then tap ⬚Delete⬚ to remove it.

10. In the third bullet point in the second bulleted list, double-click *articulating* to select it.

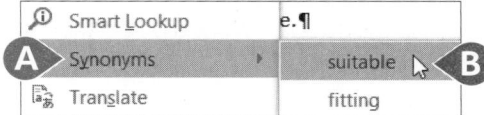

11. Type **clearly stating** in its place.

Work with Synonyms

12. In the third bullet point in the first bulleted list, right-click *appropriate* to display the pop-up menu.

13. Follow these steps to choose a synonym:

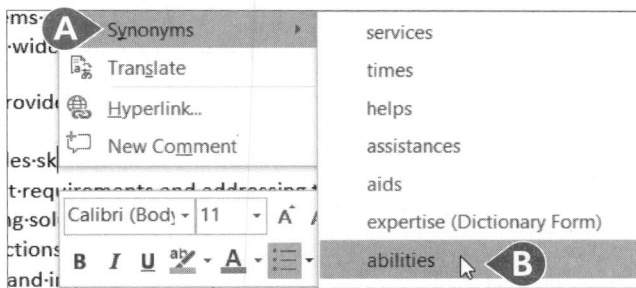

Ⓐ Drag the mouse pointer in the menu to **Synonyms**.

Ⓑ Drag over to the submenu and choose *suitable* from the list of synonyms.

The word Suitable *replaces* appropriate.

14. In the first bullet point in the second list, right-click *skills* and then follow these steps to choose a synonym:

Ⓐ Drag the mouse pointer to **Synonyms**.

Ⓑ Drag over to the submenu and choose *abilities* from the list.

15. Save your document.

Creating an Envelope

Creating envelopes is an easy task. When you type a business letter with the recipient's name and address at the top, it is recognized as the delivery address. You can choose to include a return address or not depending on whether there is a preprinted address on the envelope.

 *Word generates an envelope by pulling the recipient address from the letter exactly, including format and text case. The USPS recommends that addresses on envelopes appear in all caps and without punctuation.*

≡ Mailings→Create→Envelopes ▭

WORD

DEVELOP YOUR SKILLS: W1-D8

In this exercise, you will create an envelope and add it to your letter.

1. Choose **File→Save As** and save your file as **W1-D8-CoverLtr**.
2. Position the insertion point at the top of the document.
3. Choose **Mailings→Create→Envelopes** .

   Notice that the inside address of the letter displays as the delivery address. Remembering that the USPS prefers solid caps and no punctuation, you will now make those changes.
4. Click the **Options** button.
5. Click the **Font** button in the Delivery Address area.
6. In the Font tab, choose **All Caps** in the Effects area.

Effects

☐ Strikethrough   ☐ Small caps
☐ Double strikethrough   ☑ All caps
☐ Superscript   ☐ Hidden

7. Click **OK** twice.
8. Follow these steps to complete the envelope:

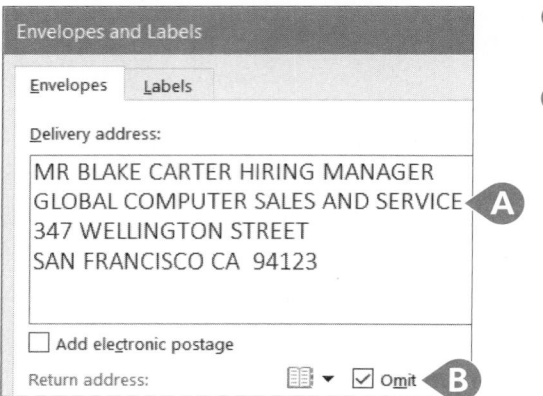

A Edit the delivery address to remove the punctuation.

B If necessary, check **Omit** to not include a return address on the envelope. (You would likely use this option when you have pre-printed envelopes that include the return address.)

9. Click the **Add to Document** button at the bottom of the dialog box and look over the envelope.

 *If the Show/Hide button is turned on, you will see a section break code at the top of the envelope. You can just ignore it for now.*

10. Save your document.

Working with Views

You can view your documents in several ways. Each view is optimized for specific types of work. The views change the way documents appear on the screen, but in most cases they have no impact on the appearance of printed documents. You can choose views from the View tab or from the status bar at the bottom right of the screen.

DOCUMENT VIEWS

View	Description
Read Mode (View tab) Read Mode (status bar)	This view provides a book-like reading experience with pages laid out side by side. The Ribbon disappears to display more of your document. You navigate horizontally as in a book.
Print Layout (View tab) Print Layout (status bar)	With this default view, your documents look similar to the way they will look when printed. You can see graphics, headers and footers, and multi-column layout.
Web Layout (View tab) Web Layout (status bar)	This view displays your document as it would look as a web page. It appears as one long page without page breaks.
Outline (View tab)	Outline view is useful for organizing long documents.
Draft (View tab)	This view simplifies page layout by eliminating elements such as headers and footers and graphic elements. This view is useful when you want to focus on content.

 View the video "Using Views."

DEVELOP YOUR SKILLS: W1-D9

In this exercise, you will try out various views.

1. If necessary, position the insertion point at the top of the document.
2. Locate and mouse over the View buttons on the status bar at the bottom right of the screen and notice the ToolTips that appear.

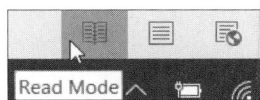

3. Click the first button, **Read Mode** , and notice how the look of your letter has changed.
4. Click the arrow at the right side of the window to move to the end of the document.

 *Depending on your screen's resolution, both pages may already be visible, in which case the arrow on the right side is not active.*

5. Click the **Print Layout** button on the status bar to return to the previous view.
6. Choose **View→Views** on the Ribbon to display all available views.

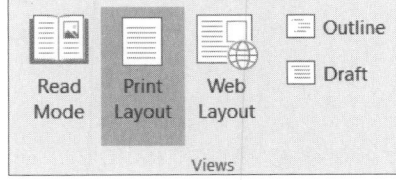

Notice that additional view options appear in the Views group.

WORD

Saving Your Work in a Different Format

You can save a document in many different formats. Prospective employers may ask you to send your application documents in one of several different formats. The format of a file is specified by the extension added at the end of the filename.

 *You may or may not see a file extension in your filenames. There is a Windows option to hide extensions.*

Document Files

Earlier versions of Word saved documents in the *.doc* file format. The current version uses the *.docx* file format. Users of earlier *.doc* formats may not be able to read files in the *.docx* format. However, you can choose to save your document in the older *.doc* format so users of earlier versions can read the document.

When you open a document created in earlier versions, the title bar displays *[Compatibility Mode]* next to the title. This means features not compatible with older versions are turned off while working in the document.

PDF Files

Using a PDF file (**.pdf*) is great when sharing files with others. If you're not sure what hardware and software the other person has, save as a PDF file, and the layout and fonts will look the same on various types of computers, software, and operating systems. A prospective employer may ask you to submit your employment application documents as PDF files.

Saving a Document for ATS Analysis

Text files (**.txt*) contain very little formatting, and thus they may be the best format when you are submitting employment application documents that are likely to be scanned into a computer. Text files can be read by ATS software. It's always a good idea to check with prospective employers if they haven't specified a particular file format.

DEVELOP YOUR SKILLS: W1-D10

It's great to have nicely formatted, paper-based documents to hand to an interviewer, if necessary. In addition, many prospective employers may ask to receive your documents electronically. In this exercise, you will assume the employer has asked to receive the document as a PDF file.

1. Choose **File→Save As** and navigate to your **Word Chapter 1** folder.

2. Click the **Save As Type** field toward the bottom of the dialog box to display the list of possible file formats.

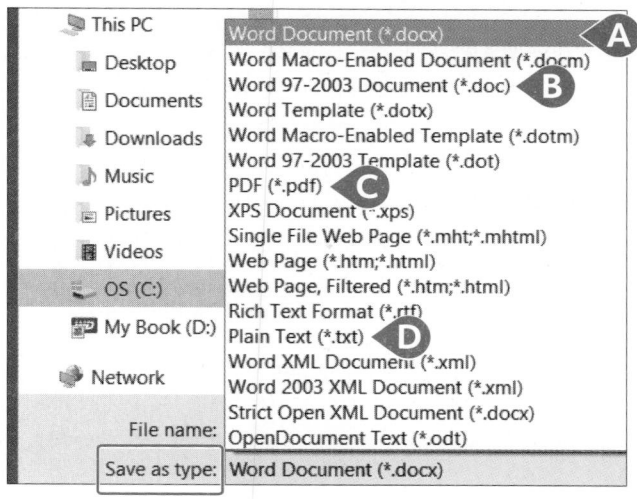

Ⓐ Default format

Ⓑ Older document versions

Ⓒ PDF format

Ⓓ Plain Text format

3. Choose **PDF (*.pdf)** from the menu.

   Notice that your file now has a .pdf file extension.

   Remember, you may or may not see a file extension in your filenames. There is a Windows option to hide extensions.

4. Change the filename to **W1-D10-CoverLtr.pdf** and then click the **Save** button at the bottom of the dialog box.

   Your document now appears in Adobe Acrobat Reader.

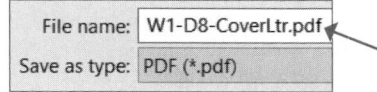

5. Click the **Close** ⊠ button in the upper-right corner of the Adobe screen.

   Your original .docx file is still open on the screen.

Working with Print and Print Preview

The Print command and Print Preview feature are available in Backstage view. Here you can choose various ways to print your document, and the Print Preview feature allows you to preview your document to see how it will look when printed.

 File→Print | Ctrl + P

DEVELOP YOUR SKILLS: W1-D11

In this exercise, you will work with the Print screen in Backstage view. You will explore printing options, and you will preview the document to see how it will look when it prints.

1. Choose **File→Print**.

   There are a number of options in the Settings area to help you control printing.

2. Take a moment to explore the options by clicking them to see what choices are available.

   Notice the top portion of the Print panel. You can choose the number of copies and any printer properties you want to modify.

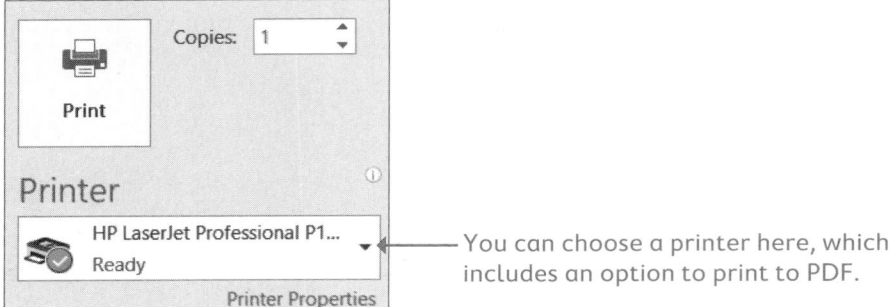

You can choose a printer here, which includes an option to print to PDF.

3. If directed, click the **Print** button. If you want to stay green and not print a page, you might print to PDF or simply click the **Back** button.

 If you printed to PDF, be sure to change back to your default printer the next time you print.

4. Exit Word.

Self-Assessment

 Check your knowledge of this chapter's key concepts and skills using the Self-Assessment in your ebook or eLab course.

Reinforce Your Skills

Create an Informal Letter

In this exercise, you will create a letter from Kids for Change to local residents, announcing an upcoming recycling pickup. Because this does not have to be a formal business letter, you will use a more casual style. You will also practice selection and navigation techniques.

1. Start Word.

2. Create a new document based on the **Blank Document** template and save it as **W1-R1-RecycleLtr**.

   Next you will center the return address at the top of the page.

3. Use the **Center** ☰ button on the <u>Ribbon</u>, type the return address, and then tap Enter twice:

Tab bar @ top of page.

4. Click the **Align Left** ☰ button on the Ribbon.

5. Type **Nove** to begin the date, use **AutoComplete** to finish entering the month, and then complete the date as **November 19, 2016**.

6. Tap Enter twice.

   Using the default 1.08 line spacing in the Blank Document template may cause the letter to be more than one page. Next you will change to single spacing.

7. Use two keystrokes to select the document and then use the **Line and Paragraph Spacing** ⌷ button to change to single spaced.

8. Use the **Line and Paragraph Spacing** ⌷ button again and choose **Remove Space After Paragraph**.

9. Complete the letter shown in the following illustration, tapping Enter wherever a paragraph symbol appears:

   Notice when you type the website address in the second paragraph that it is automatically recognized and formatted as a hyperlink.

WORD

Current·Resident¶
123·Peach·Blossom·Lane¶
Atlanta,·GA··30313¶
¶
Dear·Neighbor,¶
¶
I·am·the·recycling·representative·for·Kids·for·Change,·and·our·motto·is·Think·Globally,·Act·Locally.·We·know·that·recycling·large·objects·takes·extra·effort·since·they·do·not·fit·in·your·city-provided·recycle·cans.·We·would·like·to·give·you·a·hand.¶
¶
On·Tuesday,·November·22nd,·we·will·collect·recyclable·objects·in·your·neighborhood.·Visit·http://recycleatlanta.org·to·ensure·you·are·following·the·city's·recycling·guidelines.·Please·place·your·recyclables·at·the·curb·in·front·of·your·house·before·9:00·a.m.¶
¶
Thank·you·for·caring·about·our·planet!¶
¶
Sincerely,¶
¶
¶
¶
Tania·Tulip¶
Recycling·Representative¶

10. Use two keystrokes to position the insertion point at the top of the document.

11. Use the **selection arrow** in the margin to select the return address at the top of the page.

12. When the Mini toolbar appears, click the **Bold** [B] button to bold the return address.

    It might look nice to justify the body of the letter.

13. Select the first two body paragraphs and then click the **Justify** [≡] button on the Ribbon.

    The body of the letter now has a straight right-hand margin.

14. Click the **Zoom Out** button at the bottom right of the screen enough times to see the entire page.

    The letter is a little too high on the page.

15. Use the **Zoom In** button to return the screen to 100% and then click the **Layout** tab on the Ribbon.

16. In the Page Setup dialog box, click the **Layout** tab and choose **Center** in the Vertical Alignment field.

17. Use two keystrokes to position the insertion point at the bottom of the letter and then scroll down and notice that there is now less white space at the bottom.

18. Use two keystrokes to position the insertion point at the top of the letter.

19. Save and close your letter.

Edit a Document

In this exercise, you will edit a letter from Kids for Change to local residents inviting them to celebrate Mother Nature Day at Camp Cuyahoga. The group has planned many exciting activities. In the letter, you will create lists and use proofreading tools. You will create an envelope for your letter and then save the letter in an older version of Word.

1. Open the file **W1-R2-CuyahogaCamp** and save it as `W1-R2-CuyahogaCampRevised`.

   You can see the wavy red and blue lines indicating typos and grammar errors. There's a wavy blue line in the inside address indicating that there are two spaces between the state and zip. This is the format recommended by USPS guidelines.

2. Instruct the grammar checker to ignore the double space by right-clicking the underlined state and zip and choosing **Ignore Once**.

3. Correct the spelling of *leeding*.

4. In the second line of that paragraph, use the grammar checker to replace *receiving* with *receive*.

5. In the first line of the next paragraph, replace *convening* with *convene*.

6. Correct the spelling of *buug*.

7. In the second line of the next paragraph, right-click *accordingly* and then display the Thesaurus task pane.

8. In the Thesaurus task pane, hover the mouse pointer over *appropriately*, click the **drop-down arrow**, and choose **Insert** to replace *accordingly*. **Close** ⊠ the Thesaurus task pane.

Create a Bulleted List

9. In the second line of the first paragraph, delete the comma following *scheduled* and type a colon in its place.

10. Use an **arrow key** to position the insertion point in front of *including* and tap ⏎Enter.

11. Turn on the **Bullets** ⸬☰ feature.

12. Delete *including* and the space following it.

13. Delete the *h* in *hiking* and replace it with an uppercase **H**.

14. Delete the comma and space following *Hiking* and then tap ⏎Enter.

15. Continue editing the list of activities until it looks like the following illustration.

   - Hiking
   - Bird watching
   - Tree planting
   - Bug hunting

Create an Envelope

16. Position the insertion point at the top of the letter and create an envelope.

17. Modify the delivery information to conform with USPS guidelines and then add the envelope to the document.

18. If necessary, position the insertion point at the top of the document.

19. Display the document in **Read Mode** 📖 and then return to **Print Layout** 🖹 view.

Change Format and Print

Some recipients will get the letter as an email attachment. For those who may not have the latest version of Word, you will save the letter in an older format.

20. Choose the **Save As** option in Backstage view and navigate to your **Word Chapter 1** folder.

21. Use the *Save as Type* field to save the file in the Word 97-2003 Document (*.doc) format and then click **Save** at the bottom of the dialog box.

Notice [Compatibility Mode] in the title bar.

22. Position the insertion point in the envelope.

23. Choose the **Print** option in Backstage view and notice the Settings option Envelope #10.

How you print an envelope varies depending on the model of your printer.

24. If directed, click the **Print** 🖶 button. If you want to stay green and not print, you might print to PDF as a Printer option or simply click the **Back** ⬅ button.

 *If you printed to PDF, be sure to change back to your default printer the next time you print.*

25. Save and close the letter.

REINFORCE YOUR SKILLS: W1-R3

Edit a Letter and Navigate in a Three-Page Document

In this exercise, you will create a letter for Kids for Change members announcing a fundraiser to adopt a seal. Donations help to fund research and educate the public about ocean health. In the letter, you will work with line spacing, text alignment, lists, and proofreading tools. You will save your letter as a PDF file, and then you will navigate in a longer document.

1. Start a new single-spaced document and save it as **W1-R3-Fundraiser**.

2. Begin typing the letter.

Remember to use AutoComplete to help with the dates, and let Word Wrap do its thing.

> August·5,·2016¶
> ¶
> ¶
> ¶
> MEMBER·NAME¶
> STREET·ADDRESS¶
> CITY·STATE··ZIP¶
> ¶
> Dear·MEMBER:¶
> ¶
> Our·local·chapter·of·Kids·for·Change·will·hold·a·car·wash·fundraiser·to·collect·$300·to·adopt·a·
> seal·at·the·Center·for·Seals.··We·are·scheduling·the·car·wash·for·August·17ᵗʰ.·The·next·monthly·
> meeting·will·be·a·planning·session.·Here·are·some·things·to·think·about·before·the·meeting:·¶
> ¶
> ¶

Use Numbering and Bullets

3. Type the following list using the **Numbering** ⊞ feature:

> 1.→ Choose·a·location.·Our·options·are·the·parking·lots·at·the·following·businesses:·Jake's·Gas·
> Station,·Beulah's·Diner,·or·Dick's·Grocery·Store.¶
> 2.→ What·hours·can·you·volunteer·on·August·17ᵗʰ?¶
> 3.→ Let·me·know·if·you·can·supply·any·of·the·following:·hose,·vacuum,·soap,·brushes,·sponges,·or·
> rags.¶
> 4.→ Should·we·set·a·price·or·request·a·donation?¶
> 5.→ Can·you·design·a·flyer·for·the·car·wash?¶

Now you will demote, or indent, some of the items in the list.

4. In the first item, position the insertion point in front of *Jake's*, tap ⌈Enter⌉, and then demote the line by tapping ⌈Tab⌉.

5. Position the insertion point in front of *Beulah's* and tap ⌈Enter⌉ to generate the next item.

6. Continue modifying the list, deleting extraneous punctuation and words as shown.

> 1.→ Choose·a·location.·Our·options·are·the·parking·lots·at·the·following·businesses:·¶
>   a.→ Jake's·Gas·Station¶
>   b.→ Beulah's·Diner¶
>   c.→ Dick's·Grocery·Store¶

7. In item 3, position the insertion point in front of *hose*, tap ⌈Enter⌉, and then demote the line.

8. Organize the list as shown, deleting unnecessary punctuation and words.

> 3.→ Let·me·know·if·you·can·supply·any·of·the·following:·¶
>   a.→ hose¶
>   b.→ vacuum¶
>   c.→ soap¶
>   d.→ brushes¶
>   e.→ sponges¶
>   f.→ rags¶

Remembering that numbering is typically used when sequence is important, you decide to change to a bulleted list.

9. Select items 1 through 5 and apply **Bullets** ⊞ to the selected text.

10. Position the insertion point at the end of the last bulleted item and then tap ⌈Enter⌉ three times to turn off bullets and create a blank line.

11. Type the following sentence making the grammar error and typo as shown.

> ¶
> Were·looking·forward·to·a·great·planning·sassion.·See·you·at·the·meeting!¶

Proofread Your Letter

12. Correct the grammar and spelling errors.

13. Right-click the word *businesses* at the end of the first bullet point and display the **Thesaurus** task pane.

14. Use the task pane to replace *businesses* with *establishments* and then click the **Close** ⊠ button on the task pane.

Change Line Spacing and Vertical Alignment

Now you will add a little white space between the sub-bulleted items.

15. Select the three items in the first sublist, use the **Line and Paragraph Spacing** 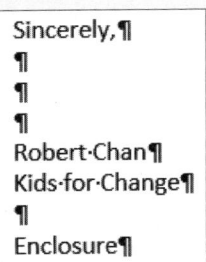 button to change to **1.15** spacing, and then use the same technique to add white space to the second sub-list.

16. Move the insertion point to the end of the document, tap ⌈Enter⌋ twice, and then type the letter closing:

Sincerely,¶
¶
¶
¶
Robert·Chan¶
Kids·for·Change¶
¶
Enclosure¶

17. Display the letter using the **Print** option in Backstage view and notice that the letter is a bit high on the page.

18. Return to the document window.

19. Click the **dialog box launcher** in the **Page Setup** group on the **Layout** tab on the Ribbon.

20. Change the Vertical Alignment to **Center** and then click **OK**.

Add an Envelope and Save the Letter in PDF Format

21. Position the insertion point at the top of the letter, create an envelope, and then add it to the document.

22. Save the file in PDF format and then close Adobe Acrobat Reader.

23. Save and close the Word file.

You've discovered a document that gives some helpful hints on car washing, and you plan to include it with the letter to the members.

24. Open the three-page document named **W1-R3-HowToWashACar**.

25. Using the following notes, navigate through this longer document.
   - Use **two keystrokes** to position the insertion point at the end of the document.
   - Use **two keystrokes** to move the insertion point to the top of the document.
   - Use an **arrow key** to move down one line.
   - Use **one keystroke** to move to the end of the line and then **use one keystroke** to move to the beginning of the line.

26. Use the following text selection techniques:
   - Position the insertion point at the top of the document and use mouse clicks to select **Introduction**.
   - With *Introduction* still selected, select **How** and **Wash** in the next heading and then click to deselect.
   - Use **two keystrokes** to select the entire document.

27. Use the following notes to observe the document in various views:

- Position the insertion point at the top of the document.
- Display the document in **Read Mode** 📖, using the status bar button, and then page through the document.
- Display the document in **Web Layout** 🖳 using the status bar button.
- Switch back to **Print Layout** 🗐 view using the status bar button.

28. Close the document and exit Word.

Apply Your Skills

Create a Business Letter

In this exercise, you will create a letter from a Universal Corporate Events representative inviting the sales winners at Reukert Enterprises to an orientation meeting for their Paris tour. You will work with proofreading tools and use navigation and text selection techniques.

1. Start Word, create a new single-spaced document, and save it as **W1-A1-LeeLtr**.

2. Create the following letter using AutoComplete with the dates and making the spelling and grammar errors indicated with wavy underlines:

   Note that in the company name, Reukert, is correctly spelled; it just is not in Word's dictionary. You can ignore it.

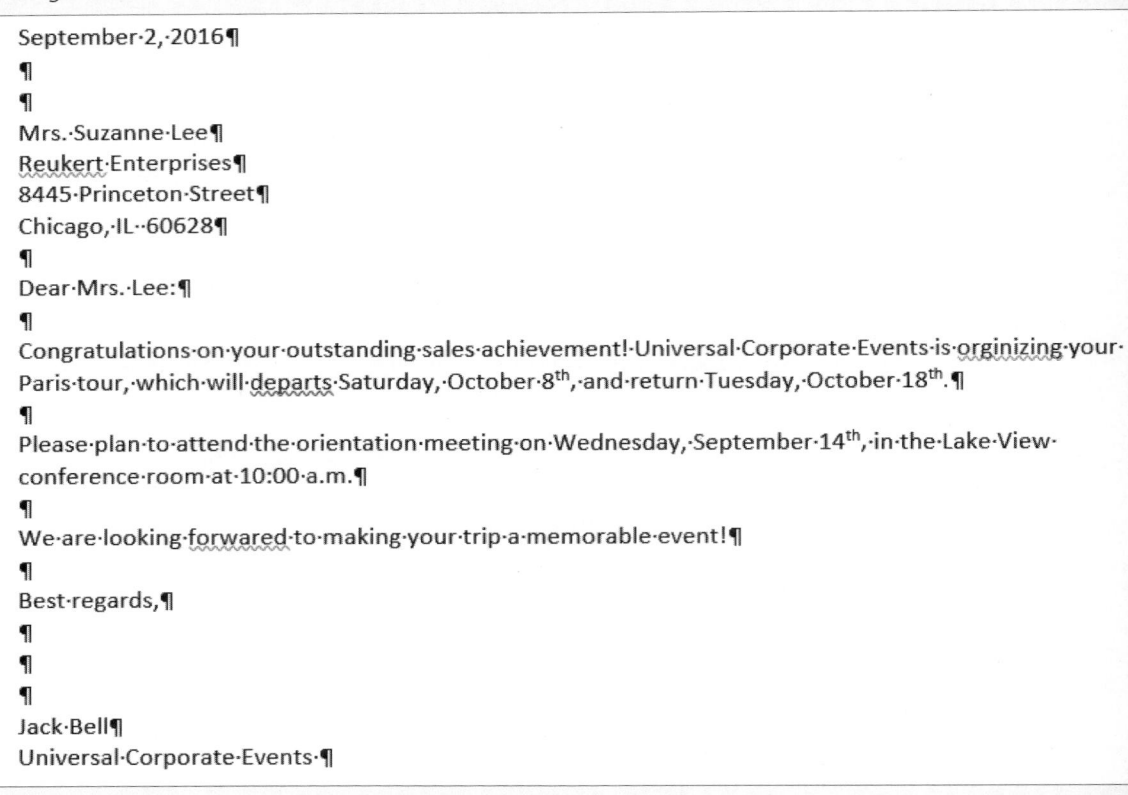

3. Correct the grammar and spelling errors.

4. In the first sentence, use the Synonyms feature to replace *achievement* with *attainment*.

5. Use the following navigation techniques:

Scroll Bar	Keyboard
• Move down one screen. • Move to the top of the document and then position the insertion point at the beginning of the first main paragraph.	• Use two keystrokes to move to the end of the document. • Use one keystroke to move to the beginning of the line. • Use one keystroke to move to the end of the line.

6. Use the following selection techniques:
   - Use the **white selection arrow** to select the first line of the first paragraph.
   - Use the **keyboard** to select the entire document and then deselect.
   - Use the **white selection arrow** to select the entire document and then deselect.
   - Select three nonadjacent words simultaneously and then deselect.

7. Save and close your letter.

APPLY YOUR SKILLS: W1-A2

Work with Lists and Make Editing Changes

In this exercise, you will create a letter from a Universal Corporate Events representative to a client suggesting ideas for side trips during its annual kickoff meeting in San Francisco. You will create a bulleted list and make line spacing and editing changes. Then you will save the letter in the older version .doc format.

1. Open **W1-A2-SFTours** and save it in the older .doc format as **W1-A2-SFToursRevised**.

2. Position the insertion point at the end of the letter and type the following bulleted list:

   - → Yacht·Charters¶
   - → Napa·Valley¶
   - → Sausalito¶

3. Tap Enter three times to turn off bullets and create a blank line.

4. Use cut and paste to rearrange the list in alphabetic order.

5. Position the insertion point after Napa Valley, generate a new bullet, and then demote the bullet one level.

6. Modify the list as shown.

   - → Napa·Valley¶
     - → Napa·Wine·Train¶
     - → Hot·air·balloon·rides¶
     - → Top-ranked·restaurants¶
   - → Sausalito¶
     - → Ferry·boat·ride·from·San·Francisco¶
     - → Docks·and·marinas¶
     - → Boutiques·and·art·galleries¶
   - → Yacht·Charters¶
     - → Sunset·cruise¶
     - → Sail·under·Golden·Gate·Bridge¶
     - → Alcatraz·and·Angel·Island¶

7. Position the insertion point at the end of the document and type the closing:

   Sincerely,¶
   ¶
   ¶
   ¶
   Geoff·Simons¶
   Universal·Corporate·Events¶

8. Make the following changes:
   - Center the letter vertically on the page.
   - In the first line of the first paragraph, select *needs regarding your* and replace it with **annual**.
   - In the second line of the same paragraph, insert **San Francisco** to the left of *meeting*.
   - In the first bullet point under Yacht Charters, insert **dining** between *Sunset* and *cruise*.

9. Change the line spacing for the sub-bulleted items to **1.15**.

10. Add an envelope to the top of the document, adjusting the delivery address to comply with USPS recommendations.

11. Display your letter in **Read Mode** 📖, page through to the end if your screen resolution allows it, and then return to **Print Layout** 📄 view.

12. Save and then close the file.

APPLY YOUR SKILLS: W1-A3

Edit and Format a Letter

In this exercise, you will draft a letter to a Universal Corporate Events employee detailing his responsibilities relative to the Vaughn Storage Device's Kauai event. You will use proofreading tools and the Thesaurus, work with alignment, and add a bulleted list to a letter. You will use navigation and selection techniques, work with line spacing, and save the document in PDF format. Finally, you will work with different views.

1. Open **W1-A3-WilliamsLtr**, save it as **W1-A3-WilliamsLtrRevised**, and then correct the spelling and grammar errors.

2. In the first line of the first paragraph, use the **Synonyms** feature to change *ambassador* to **representative**.

3. In the same line, select *Hawaiian* and replace it with **Kauai**.

4. At the beginning of the second paragraph, insert **and Martin** between *You* and *will*.

5. At the end of the second paragraph, change *entertainment* to **entertainers**.

Align Text and Complete the Letter

6. Use the keyboard to move the insertion point to the top of the letter and then tap Enter four times.

7. Move the insertion point to the top of the letter again and center-align the address:

   23 Park Ave.

   San Jose, CA 95119

8. Use the **selection arrow** in the margin to select the second paragraph and then deselect.

9. Use a keyboard and mouse combination, Ctrl +click, to select the first sentence in the first paragraph.

10. Use the **selection arrow** to select the entire document and then change the line spacing to **1.0**.

11. Move the insertion point to the end of the document and add the following text:

> The·side·tours·will·take·place·on·September·13ᵗʰ,·14ᵗʰ,·15ᵗʰ,·and·16ᵗʰ.·Here's·a·list·of·the·side·
> tours·that·attendees·will·sign·up·for·during·the·arrival·dinner.¶
>
> - → North·Shore·Bike·Tours¶
> - → Snorkeling·at·Salt·Pond·Beach·Park¶
> - → Catamaran·Tour·on·Na·Pali·Coast¶
> - → Surfing·at·Hanalei·Bay¶
> - → Kekaha·Beach·Luau¶
>
> ¶
> Sincerely,¶
> ¶
> ¶
> ¶
> Jose·Ramirez¶
> Universal·Corporate·Events¶

12. Center–align the letter vertically on the page.

Save the File in PDF and Print

Bill is on assignment out of the country, so to be sure the letter reaches him, you will send it as a PDF email attachment, but you will also create an envelope and send the letter to his snail mail address.

13. Save the file in **PDF format** and then close Adobe Acrobat Reader.

The .docx file is still open.

14. Create an envelope formatting the delivery address to conform with USPS recommendations and add the envelope to the top of the document.

15. Use the **View** tab on the Ribbon to view the document in **Read Mode** and then switch back to **Print Layout** view.

16. Move to **Backstage** view and choose the **Print** option.

17. If directed, click the **Print** button. If you want to stay green and not print, you might print to PDF as a Printer option or simply click the **Back** button.

 *If you printed to PDF, be sure to change back to your default printer the next time you print.*

18. Save and close the file and then exit Word.

 # Extend Your Skills

These exercises challenge you to think critically and apply your new skills. You will be evaluated on your ability to follow directions, completeness, creativity, and the use of proper grammar and mechanics. Save files to your chapter folder. Submit assignments as directed.

W1-E1   That's the Way I See It

You have decided to start your own landscaping business, and you are going to conduct online research to see what's involved. Your friend is studying for his MBA, and you will send him a letter containing the results of your research and ask him what he thinks of your idea.

Create a block-style, single-spaced letter, including a list of five landscaping tools that your research shows you will need to purchase. Then research what is involved in becoming a certified landscape professional and explain how you plan to earn your certification. Finally, list three tips for running a successful landscaping business. The letter should include at least three paragraphs (one to give an overview of the business, one or more to discuss certification, and one for the conclusion) and a list of three tips. Add an envelope using USPS-recommended formatting. Save the file in the older version *.doc* format, naming it **W1-E1-NewBusiness**.

W1-E2   Be Your Own Boss

You own Blue Jean Landscaping, a service that helps customers be their own landscapers. You provide the plans and directions and then the customer helps with the labor. A customer would like you to help her landscape her front yard. Use your imagination to decide on your business's location and climate. Conduct online research to determine what plants work well for the climate you chose. Send the client a block-style letter with traditional letter spacing to propose four plant options that would work well for the location and climate. The letter should contain both an introductory and concluding paragraph, as well as a list of four plant options, and each option should be associated with a sentence or two explaining why it is a good choice. Add an envelope to the document and save the file in PDF format as **W1-E2-NewClient**.

W1-E3   Demonstrate Proficiency

Stormy BBQ is a local BBQ restaurant featuring fresh, locally grown vegetables and local grass-fed pork and beef. As the marketing manager of Stormy BBQ, you've decided to hold a chili cook-off to attract new clients. Use online research to learn how to have a successful cook-off and also research rules for the chefs to ensure that they are competing on a level playing field.

Create a correctly formatted business letter to send to prospective chili chefs listing three important guidelines for a successful cook-off and three competition rules for your chefs. The letter should include both an introductory and concluding paragraph, as well as the rules that have been established. Make up the name and address for the first chef you want to invite. Create an envelope to go with the letter. Save your letter in Plain Text format as **W1-E3-ChiliChef**.

Creating a Résumé in a Table

A table is one of the most useful tools for organizing and formatting all sorts of information, from résumés to travel schedules. Tables are flexible and easy to use. There are many features that let you set up, modify, and format tables. In this chapter, you will merge and split table cells; align table text; apply table styles; and insert, delete, and resize rows and columns.

LEARNING OBJECTIVES

▸ Create a table

▸ Build an effective résumé in a table

▸ Select data in a table

▸ Format tables

▸ Apply table styles

▸ Use a template to create a résumé

📂 Project: Landing the Perfect Job

Your cover letter is complete, and now it's time for your résumé. You are pursuing a position in retail computer sales. You need to summarize your qualifications and experience, focusing on skills that target the position you are applying for. You also need to demonstrate that your skills fit the needs the employer has expressed. You decide to use a table for your résumé since it will make your résumé easy for a hiring manager to quickly read.

You also intend to make as many professional contacts as possible in the next few months, and using a table to track those contacts will be very helpful. You'll take advantage of the table's Sort feature to organize the data and apply formatting that will make it attractive and, more important, easy to read.

📖 What's Important in a Résumé?

The purpose of a résumé is to win an interview. Many hiring managers will take less than a minute to review a résumé; therefore, your résumé needs to immediately capture the reader. It needs to be dynamic, targeted, and designed to emphasize your experience, qualifications, and skills, particularly those that transfer to the job. Like the cover letter, one page is generally preferred.

There are three primary types of résumés: *chronological*, *functional*, and *combination*. A chronological résumé assumes you are continuing along a career path, listing your most recent position first. It is good for showing your growth within a profession. A functional résumé is skill and accomplishment based. It can be used by those just out of school, career changers, or those with gaps in their employment history. A combination résumé is a combination of chronological and functional, listing your skills and experience first, followed by your employment history.

Introducing Tables

Tables provide a convenient method for organizing and aligning data in an easy-to-read format, and they afford a nice way to break up a text-heavy document. Formatting with table styles adds flair to your documents, and tables draw your reader's attention to key items.

Just as with most actions on a computer, there are multiple ways to insert a table. You can use the Table button on the Ribbon, the Insert Table dialog box, and the Quick Tables gallery. You can even convert tabular columns to a table.

Contextual tabs appear in context with the task you are performing. A lot of features use contextual tabs. With tables, contextual tabs appear on the Ribbon when the insertion point is in a table.

 View the video "Creating Tables."

Tables are organized in columns and rows. Where columns and rows intersect, they form a rectangle known as a cell.

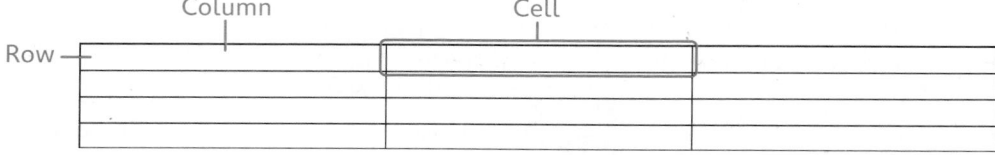

Navigating and Selecting Data in a Table

You can move the insertion point by clicking in a cell, or you can use keystrokes for navigating. Here are the keystrokes you are likely to use most often:

▸ `Tab` for moving to the next cell

▸ `Shift` + `Tab` for moving to the previous cell

Just as in a regular text document, if you want to format or modify something in a table, you select it first. The mouse pointer changes shape depending on whether you're selecting a cell, row, column, or the entire table.

 View the video "Selecting Data with the Mouse."

DEVELOP YOUR SKILLS: W2-D1

In this exercise, you will insert a table in a document and use selection and navigation techniques. Then you will enter data in your table.

1. Start Word and create a new document using the **Single Spaced (Blank)** template.

2. Navigate to your **Word Chapter 2** folder and save the document as **W2-D1-StellaResume**.

3. Choose **Home→Paragraph→Show/Hide** ¶ to display formatting marks.

4. Follow these steps to insert a **2×4** table from the Ribbon:

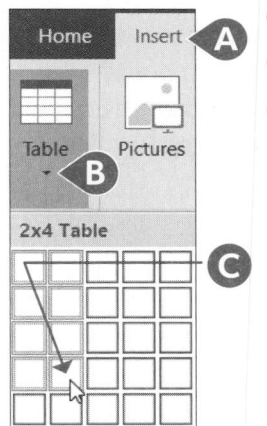

   Ⓐ Click the **Insert** tab.

   Ⓑ Click the **Table** button.

   Ⓒ Drag in the grid and click the fourth cell in the second column.

Notice that the insertion point is in the table and that the contextual Table Tools' Design and Layout tabs appear on the Ribbon.

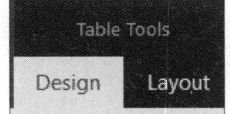

Select Table Elements and Navigate in a Table

Remember, the Mini toolbar appears when you select table data, just as when you select regular text.
It contains frequently used commands. You can choose a command or ignore the toolbar, and it will fade away.

5. Apply the following selection techniques:
   • Use the selection arrow to select a row.
   • Click the **move** handle ⊞ in the upper-left corner of the table to select the entire table. (The insertion point or the mouse pointer must be in the table for the move handle to appear.)
   • Use the down-pointing black mouse pointer to select a column.

WORD

6. Deselect by clicking anywhere in the table and then use the following notes to navigate in a table:

- Use ⏍Tab⏍ and ⏍Shift⏍+⏍Tab⏍ to move forward and back one cell at a time.
- Position the insertion point at the end of a row (not the last row) and tap ⏍Tab⏍ to move to the beginning of the next row.
- Press ⏍Alt⏍+⏍Page Up⏍ to move to the top of the column.
- Press ⏍Alt⏍+⏍Page Down⏍ to move to the end of the column.

Enter Data in a Table

7. Enter the following information:

Stella·Martin¶ 127·Stevens·Street¶ Cleveland,·OH··44113¶ 216-555-1212¶ SSMartin5@yahoo.com¤	¤
OBJECTIVE¤	¤
QUALIFICATIONS¤	¤
EXPERIENCE¤	¤

8. Save the document.

Modifying a Table

Whenever you click in a table or select cells, rows, or columns, the contextual Layout tab appears. All the features you'll need to modify your table's structure are located here. Also, some of these features are available in the pop-up menu when you right-click in a table.

Inserting Rows and Columns

You can insert new columns and rows in an existing table. If you want to insert multiple rows or columns, you must first select the same number of existing rows or columns as you want to insert. For example, to insert two new rows, select two existing rows first. You can also add a row to the bottom of a table with a tap of the ⏍Tab⏍ key when the insertion point is in the last table cell.

A quick and easy way to insert a single row or column is with the insert control that appears when the insertion point is in the table and the selection arrow is pointing between rows or columns.

≡ Table Tools→Layout→Rows & Columns │ Right-click in the table and choose Insert

Merging/Splitting Cells and Aligning Data

You can merge two or more adjacent cells in the same row or column into a single cell. The merge option is often used to create a heading row that spans the width of the table. You can also split a single cell into multiple cells.

You can split the entire table, if desired. The first step is to position the insertion point anywhere in the row that you want to become the first row of the second table. Then, execute the Split Table command. When formatting marks are visible, you will see a paragraph between the two tables. To rejoin the table, delete the paragraph symbol.

≡ Table Tools→Layout→Merge→Merge Cells *or* Split Cells │ Right-click in the table and choose Merge Cells *or* Split Cells

≡ Table Tools→Layout→Merge→Split Table

Aligning Table Data

You can align data horizontally or vertically, and you can change the direction of text. You can also modify the cell margins thereby customizing the spacing between cells.

≡ Table Tools→Layout→Alignment

DEVELOP YOUR SKILLS: W2-D2

In this exercise, you will use several techniques to insert and delete rows. You will also merge cells and align data within cells.

1. Choose **File→Save As** and navigate to your **Word Chapter 2** folder.
2. Name the file **W2-D2-StellaResume**.

Insert and Delete Rows

3. Make sure the insertion point is in the table.
4. Move the mouse pointer to the left edge of the table between the first and second rows until the insert control appears as shown.

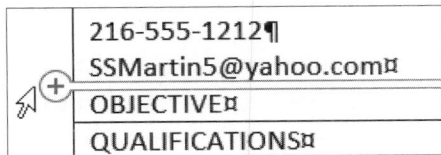

5. Click the **insert control** to add a row to the table.

   You will leave this row blank to add white space between the heading row and the rest of the table.

6. Position the insertion point in the last table cell (last column, last row) and then tap ⟦Tab⟧ to generate a new row.

   If you want to add several columns or rows at once, you must select the number of columns or rows that you want to add.

7. Use the selection arrow in the left margin to select the *QUALIFICATIONS* and *EXPERIENCE* rows.

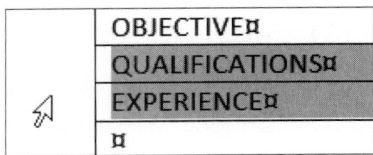

8. Follow these steps to insert two rows in the table:

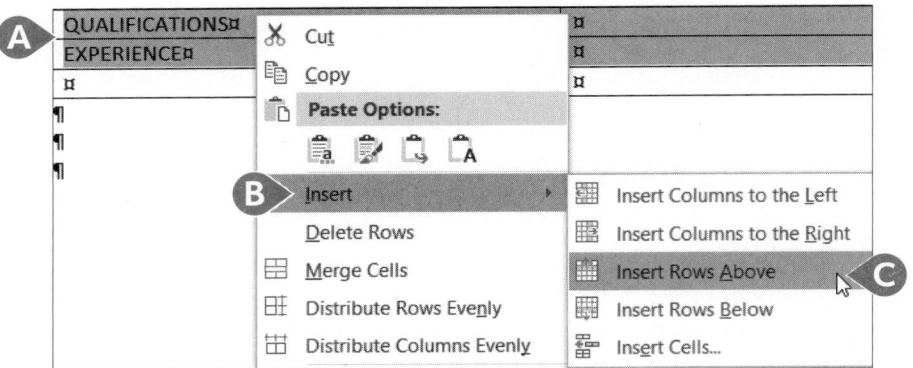

Ⓐ Position the mouse pointer within the selected rows and right-click to display the menu.

Ⓑ Drag the mouse pointer to the **Insert** command.

Ⓒ Choose **Insert Rows Above** from the submenu.

Two rows are inserted because two rows were selected. Now you will delete one of the rows.

9. Select the second blank row, position the mouse pointer in the selected row, and right-click to display the menu.

10. Choose **Delete Rows** from the menu.

Now you will insert another blank row.

11. Use the selection arrow to select the *EXPERIENCE* row and then click the right mouse button in the selected row.

12. Choose **Insert** from the menu and then choose **Insert Rows Above** from the submenu.

13. Use the **insert control** to insert another row at the bottom of the table.

Merge Cells and Align Data

14. Position the selection arrow to the left of the first row and click to select the row.

15. Choose **Table Tools→Layout→Merge→Merge Cells** 🔲 .

Row 1 is now one cell that spans the width of the table.

16. Choose **Table Tools→Layout→Alignment**.

The alignment options on the left of the Alignment group offer several ways of aligning data within the cells.

17. Follow these steps to center the heading data:

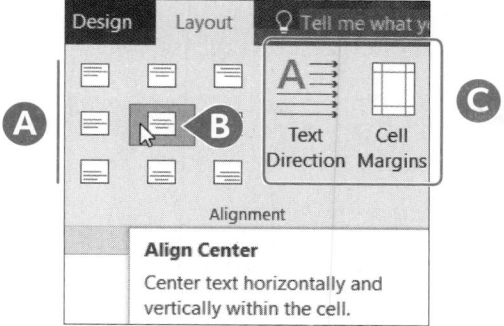

Ⓐ Hover the mouse pointer over the buttons in the group on the left and notice the ToolTips that describe the alignment options.

Ⓑ Choose the **Align Center** option.

Ⓒ Hover the mouse pointer over the two buttons on the right and read the ToolTips.

18. Save the file.

Sizing Columns and Rows

There are a number of techniques for resizing columns and rows. The adjust pointer, which is a double-headed arrow, appears whenever you position the mouse pointer on a row or column gridline. You can adjust the column width or row height by dragging the gridline. The Cell Size group in the contextual Table Tools' Layout tab provides handy tools for precise sizing.

☰ Table Tools→Layout→Cell Size

DEVELOP YOUR SKILLS: W2-D3

In this exercise, you will continue modifying the table by resizing columns and rows. Then you will finish entering data in the résumé.

1. Save your file as **W2-D3-StellaResume**.

The left column is wider than it needs to be.

2. Choose **View→Show→Ruler**.

3. Follow these steps to narrow the left column:

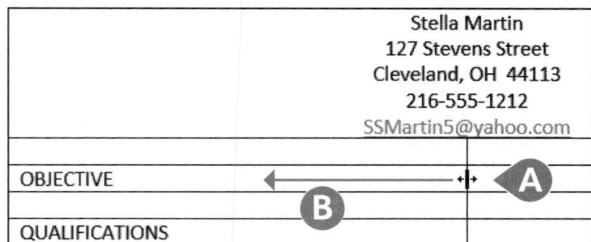

Ⓐ Position the mouse pointer on the center vertical gridline; it changes to the adjust pointer (a double-headed arrow).

Ⓑ Drag left until the column is approximately 1½" wide. You can use the ruler at the top of the page as a guide.

4. Position the mouse pointer on the bottom border of the *OBJECTIVE* row and notice the adjust pointer is a double-headed arrow pointing up and down.

5. Drag down a bit to increase the row height and then position the insertion point in the *OBJECTIVE* row.

6. Choose **Table Tools→Layout→Cell Size** and hover the mouse pointer over the buttons to observe their purpose.

   These buttons offer more precise sizing options. Notice the height of the OBJECTIVE *row in the Table Row Height field. (Your measurement may differ.)*

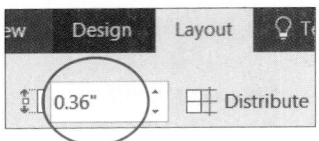

7. Position the insertion point in the next row and notice the default row height is 0.18".

   Now you will resize the OBJECTIVE *row to the same size as the other rows.*

8. Position the mouse pointer in the *OBJECTIVE* row, then click in the **Table Row Height** field, type **0.18**, and tap Enter .

Enter Data

9. Position the mouse pointer in the second cell of the *OBJECTIVE* row and type **Retail Computer Sales**.

10. Position the insertion point in the second cell of the *QUALIFICATIONS* row.

    Now you will type a bulleted list of Stella's qualifications.

11. Choose **Home→Paragraph→Bullets** and type **Hardware/Software** Enter .

    The next bullet will need to be demoted one level; however, inside a table, you cannot use the Tab *key to demote. Remember, using* Tab *in a table moves the insertion point to the next cell.*

12. Choose **Home→Paragraph→Increase Indent** .

13. Complete the list, including the last bullet:

    > • → Hardware/Software¶
    >   o → In-depth·knowledge·of·computer·hardware·and·peripherals¶
    >   o → Understanding·of·computer·operating·systems·and·end-
    >   user·applications,·including·Windows·and·Microsoft·Office·
    >   Suite¶
    >   o → Maintain·hardware·and·software·knowledge·via·blogs,·
    >   newsletters,·and·conventions¶
    >   o → ¤

    Now you need to promote the last bullet. This time you will decrease the indent.

14. Choose **Home→Paragraph→Decrease Indent** .

15. Type the following list, remembering to use the **Increase Indent** button to demote:

    > • → Sales¶
    >   o → Ability·to·build·good·customer·relations¶
    >   o → Good·presentation·skills¶
    >   o → Familiar·with·sales·proven·strategies¶
    >   o → Ability·to·close·the·sale¤

16. Position the insertion point in the second cell of the *EXPERIENCE* row and type **Sales Intern, Best Computers (Summers, 2013–2016)** Enter .

17. Type the remaining lists, remembering to use **Increase Indent** and **Decrease Indent** to demote and promote bullet points:

> Sales·Intern,·Best·Computers·(Summers,·2013–2016)¶
> > • → Presales¶
> > > o → Prepared·demonstrations·describing·hardware·and·software·features·and·benefits¶
> > > o → Prepared·proposals·and·sales·contracts¶
> > • → Sales¶
> > > o → Sold·various·brands·of·PCs,·tablets,·notebooks,·including·IBM,·Hewlett·Packard,·Compaq,·and·Macintosh¶
> > > o → Recommended·software·based·on·customer·needs¶
> > > o → Performed·follow-up·activities·necessary·to·close·sales¶
> > > o → Closed·difficult·deals·and·exceeded·sales·goals¶
> > > o → Assisted·in·promotional·events¶
> > > o → Recognized·as·Intern·of·the·Month·on·three·occasions¶
> > • → Post·Sales¶
> > > o → Scheduled·delivery·and·installation·and·implemented·training·schedules¶
> > > o → Followed·up·with·customers·to·ensure·satisfaction¤

18. Position the insertion point in the first cell of the last row and type **EDUCATION**.

19. In the second cell of the *EDUCATION* row, type **Computer Science Graduate, Case Western University**.

20. Choose **File→Print** to view your document in the Print screen.

Notice that the résumé is too high on the page.

21. Click **Back** to return to the Word screen.

22. Choose **Layout→Page Setup→dialog box launcher** , click the **Layout** tab, then choose **Center** from the Vertical Alignment field and click **OK**.

23. Save and close the file.

Formatting with Borders, Shading, and Styles

Borders, shading, and styles can enhance the readability of a table, and they add pizzazz. Whenever you click in a table or select cells, row, or columns, the contextual Design tab appears. The features you need to modify your table's formatting are located here.

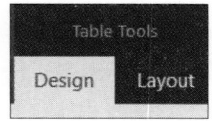

The Borders and Shading buttons have memory, meaning they reflect the last option chosen in the current session. This is handy if you want to apply the same effect multiple times.

Just like regular text, you can also format tables using the formatting tools on the Home tab. Or, use the Mini toolbar, which provides convenient formatting tools right at your mouse pointer when you select data.

DEVELOP YOUR SKILLS: W2-D4

In this exercise, you will open a table and apply formatting using borders, shading, and styles. Stella has started a list of hiring managers she plans to contact. Because she intends to make many contacts, a table is the perfect tool for staying organized.

1. Navigate to your **Word Chapter 2** folder, open **W2-D4-JobContacts**, and save it as **W2-D4-JobContactsRevised**.

2. Click the move handle in the upper-left corner of the table to select the entire table.

   Remember, the insertion point has to be in the table, or you have to hover the mouse pointer over the table for the move handle to appear.

3. Choose **Table Tools→Design→Borders→Borders** ⊞ **menu button** ▼ and choose **No Border**.

   You may see gridlines within the table, but they won't print; they are there just to guide you. The Borders menu button ▼ *on the Design tab provides the option to turn gridlines on or off.*

4. Select the first table row, choose **Table Tools→Design→Borders→Borders** ⊞ **menu button** ▼, and then choose **Outside Borders**.

5. Keep the first row selected and choose **Table Tools→Design→Table Styles→Shading** ⬚ **menu button** ▼.

6. Choose **Gray-25%, Background 2, Darker 10%**.

Use Table Styles

7. Make sure the insertion point is in the table and choose **Table Tools→Design→Table Styles**.

8. Click the **More** button to display the full gallery of styles.

9. Move the mouse pointer over several styles and notice that Live Preview displays the styles in the table.

10. Choose **Grid Table 5 Dark — Accent 1**.

    The style overrides your cell margin spacing, borders, and shading. In turn, you can override Table Styles formatting by applying direct formatting.

11. Select the first row of the table; choose **Home→Font→Font menu button** ▼ **→Century Gothic**.

12. Save the file but leave it open.

Remove Table Borders

Now that you know about table borders, you can remove the default borders on the résumé to give it a sleeker look.

13. Open **W2-D3-StellaResume** and save it as **W2-D4-StellaResume**.

14. Click the move handle to select the entire table.

15. Choose **Table Tools→Design→Borders→Borders** 🔲 **menu button** ▼.

16. Choose **No Border** from the menu and then deselect.

17. Choose **File→Print** to see how neat and professional the résumé looks.

18. Click **Back** ⬅ to return to the Word screen.

19. Save and close the résumé.

Sorting Data in a Table

Sorting Data in a Table

When sorting a table, you can choose to sort one or more columns in ascending or descending order and specify whether the first row of the table is a header row. You can sort a table by up to three levels. For example, say you have a table containing column headings for city, state, and zip. You can sort the table first by state, then by city within state, and then by zip code within city.

		Second sort level (City)	First sort level (State)	Third sort level (Zip)
Name	Address	City	State	Zip
Laurie Chu	61 Granger Road	Flagstaff	Arizona	86002
Martin Hernandez	45 Priscilla Court	Holbrook	Arizona	86025
Maria Valera	254 Part Street	Colorado Springs	Colorado	80840
Ella Goodspeed	32 Ash Lane	Denver	Colorado	80215
Adam Chaffee	51 Stony Lane	Denver	Colorado	80226

DEVELOP YOUR SKILLS: W2-D5

In this exercise, you will sort data in the Job Contacts file. You will want to sort the contacts table as it continues to grow so you can easily locate information. In this example, the table will be sorted by city and by company name within city. You could also sort the table by company name if you're looking for a particular company, or by contact date if you want to locate a company you contacted on a certain date.

Before You Begin: *The W2-D4-JobContactsRevised file should still be open on the screen.*

1. Save the file as **W2-D5-JobContactsRevised**.

2. With the insertion point in the table, choose **Table Tools→Layout→Data→Sort** 🔽 to open the Sort dialog box.

As the list grows longer, it will be convenient to have the cities sorted together so you can focus on one geographic area at a time.

3. In the **Sort By** field, click the drop-down arrow and choose **City** from the menu.

Notice the Ascending and Descending option buttons on the right. Because you won't change that option, the cities will be sorted in Ascending (A to Z) order.

4. In the **Then By** field, choose **Co Name**.

This will sort the company names alphabetically within city.

Notice the Header Row button in the bottom-left corner of the dialog box. This option indicates that the table has a header row, which prevents the row from being sorted in with the rest of the data.

5. Click **OK** and observe the sorted table.

 *As new rows are added to the bottom of the table, simply execute the sort again to re-establish the sort order.*

6. Save and close the file.

Using Templates

All documents are based on a template, which can include text, formatting, graphics, and other objects. The default template is Blank Document. The benefit of templates is that they do not change when documents *based on them* change. When you start a new document, you are opening a *copy* of the template. This lets you use templates repeatedly as the basis for new documents. Word provides a variety of ready-to-use templates, or you can create your own personal templates.

Templates are located in the Start screen or in Backstage view when you are starting a new file. Basing a new document on a template can save you a lot of time as much of the work is already included for you.

≡ File→New

DEVELOP YOUR SKILLS: W2-D6

In this exercise, you will search for a résumé template and use it as the basis for a new résumé file.

1. Choose **File→New** and then follow these steps to locate a résumé template:

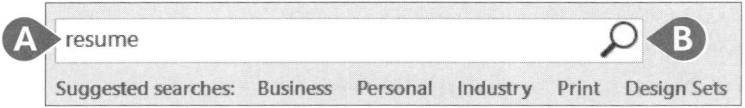

Ⓐ Type **resume** in the search field at the top of the screen.

Ⓑ Click the **Start Searching** button.

2. Scroll through the templates and locate a functional résumé of your choice.

You can open and close several until you decide which one you want.

3. Use data from Stella's résumé if you wish, or create your own data to complete the new résumé.

You can add or delete template elements and change formatting as desired.

4. Save the file as **W2-D6-MyResume** and then close it.

Saving Personal Templates

When you create a document containing specific formatting, you can save it to use later as a template. You should save the template in the Custom Office Templates folder unless instructed to do otherwise. This is what causes your templates to appear when you click the Personal link on the templates screen.

This Personal category refers to Word-supplied templates such as personal letterhead.

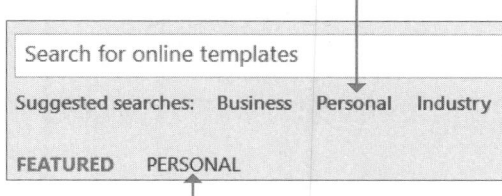

This PERSONAL category refers to templates you create yourself.

DEVELOP YOUR SKILLS: W2-D7

In this exercise, you will open a copy of a personal budget and save it as a template, so you can use it over and over every month. The variable text of the budget has been removed; however, other elements are still in place, including the expense items and the formatting.

1. Navigate to your **Word Chapter 2** folder, open **W2-D7-PersonalBudget**, and notice the elements that are in place that will be helpful each month when you create a new budget.

2. Choose **File→Save As**, navigate to any file storage location, and choose **Word Template (*.dotx)** from the Save As Type list at the bottom of the dialog box.

   Notice the file path that appears at the top of the Save As dialog box. Word defaults to the Custom Office Templates folder in the Documents folder as the file storage location.

3. Save the file.

4. Close the template file and then choose **File→New**.

5. Follow these steps to open a copy of your template:

   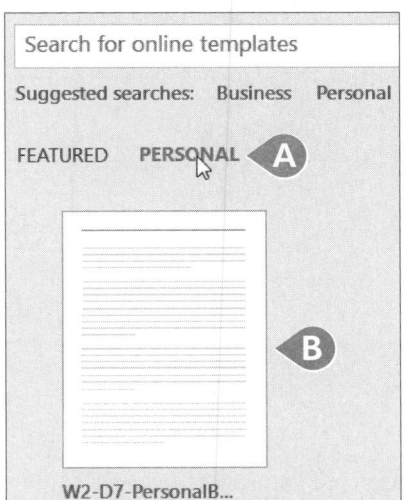

   (A) Click the **PERSONAL** link.

   (B) Click your template to open a copy.

   Notice the DocumentX filename in the title bar at the top of the window. This indicates that you are working on a copy of the template rather than the template itself.

6. Close the file and exit Word.

What to Do Before a Job Interview

Many job search sites, such as Monster.com and Careerbuilder.com, offer career advice including interviewing tips. Or do a web search of *interview tips*, and you'll get lots of tips to steer you in the right direction. Here are a few things to keep in mind:

▶ Anticipate the interviewer's questions and prepare your answers. You can even search for interview questions that are typical for a specific career, such as *interview questions for electrical engineers*.

▶ Practice, practice, practice. Get a friend or colleague to role play interviews with you. The more you practice, the more confident you will be during the interview.

▶ Think of questions you would like to ask the interviewer, especially those that demonstrate your interest in the job and company.

▶ Decide on your wardrobe. Conduct an Internet search for *how to dress for an interview*. Also, it's fine to ask the person scheduling the interview what the company dress code is. When in doubt, err on the side of conservatism.

▶ What to take with you: driving directions and contact information, folder/briefcase, paper copies of your résumé, pen, and notepad.

▶ What to not take with you: ear buds, cell phone that is not turned off, baseball cap, chewing gum, food or drink, distracting jewelry.

Self-Assessment

Check your knowledge of this chapter's key concepts and skills using the Self-Assessment in your ebook or eLab course.

Reinforce Your Skills

Insert Tables and Format Table Elements

Kids for Change is partnering with the local Center for Environmental Health to identify products in the home that present a risk to babies. In this exercise, you will create and enter data in a table. You will resize columns, rows, and cell margins and change alignment. You will use a Quick Table, convert a tabular document to a table, and split and merge cells.

1. Start Word and create a document using the **Single Spaced (Blank)** template saved as **W2-R1-RiskToBabies**.

2. Choose the **Insert→Tables→Table** button and create a **3×6** table.

3. Enter the data shown here, select the first row, and choose **Home→Font→Bold** B :

 Remember, you can add rows to the bottom of a table by tapping Tab when you reach the last table cell.

Member Name	School	Research Assignment
Stacey	Highland	Harmful chemicals
Jacob	Lincoln	Cribs
Noah	Tri-way	Baby slings
Emma	Blue Ridge	Bath seats
Olivia	Springville	Highchairs
Nanda	Arlington	Infant swings

Now you will resize the columns.

4. Position the mouse pointer on the border between *Member Name* and *School*.

5. When the mouse pointer changes to the adjust pointer, drag to the left about ¾".

6. Resize the second and third columns to be just as wide as they need to be to fit the data without allowing any text to wrap within the cell.

7. Position the adjust pointer on the bottom border of the top row and drag down until the row is about twice its original height.

8. Select the first row and choose **Table Tools→Layout→Alignment→Align Center** ▣ .

    Next you will insert a calendar Quick Table so you can keep track of meetings with the Center for Environmental Health.

9. Position the insertion point at the end of the document and tap Enter twice.

10. Choose **Insert→Tables→Table** ▦ , slide the mouse pointer down to **Quick Tables**, and insert **Calendar 2**.

    Now you will copy a tabular table from another file and paste it into your document.

Convert a Tabular Document to a Table

11. Open **W2-R1-FoodRisk** and then select the entire document.

12. Choose **Home→Clipboard→Copy** 🗈 and then close the file.

13. Position the insertion point at the end of the **Risk to Babies** document and tap Enter .

14. Choose **Home→Clipboard→Paste** 📋 and, if necessary, display formatting marks.

    Notice that the columns in this tabular table are separated by a single tab. Remember, there must be only one tab between columns for the conversion to work properly.

15. Select the entire tabular table and choose **Insert→Tables→Table** ▦ **→Convert Text to Table**.

16. Accept the defaults in the dialog box and click **OK**.

17. Use the mouse pointer to select the *Food* and *Risk Factor* columns.

18. Choose **Table Tools→Layout→Alignment→Align Center**.

19. Choose **Table Tools→Layout→Alignment→Cell Margins** ▦.

20. In the Table Options dialog box, change the top and bottom margins to **0.04** and click **OK**.

    This increases the vertical space between cells.

21. Click in the first table row.

22. Choose **Table Tools→Layout→Rows & Columns→Insert Above** ▦ and then position the insertion point in the first cell of the new row.

23. Choose **Table Tools→Layout→Merge→Split Cells** ▦.

24. In the Split Cells dialog box, change the number of columns to **4**; click **OK**.

25. Select the first row.

26. Choose **Table Tools→Layout→Merge→Merge Cells** ▦.

27. Click in the new row and type **Food Risk**.

28. Save and close the file.

REINFORCE YOUR SKILLS: W2-R2

Format and Sort a Table

Kids for Change members are planning a demonstration of safe cleaning products at the Community Center. They plan to distribute a table document that lists safe products you can use in the kitchen. In this exercise, you will use table formats to design a professional-looking table that is engaging and easy to read. Because you need to share this and other materials with other Kids for Change members, you will create a personal fax cover template to save time later.

1. Open **W2-R2-SafeClean** and save it as **W2-R2-SafeCleanRevised**.

2. Make sure the insertion point is in the table.

3. Choose **Table Tools→Design→Table Styles**, open the **Table Styles gallery**, and choose **Grid Table 4 — Accent 6**.

    Hint: It's a green style.

4. Select the table and choose **Table Tools→Design→Borders→Borders** ⊞ menu button ▼→ **Outside Borders**.

5. Select the first row and choose **Table Tools→Design→Borders→Borders** ⊞ menu button ▼→ **Bottom Border**.

6. With the first row still selected, choose **Table Tools→Design→Table Styles→Shading** 🖌 menu button ▼.

7. Choose **Green, Accent 6, Darker 50%** (last green color in the right column).

8. Select the entire table and choose **Home→Font→Font menu button ▾→Comic Sans MS**.

9. Select in the first column starting at *Clean coffee pot* through the end of the column.

10. Choose **Home→Font→Italic** $\boxed{I}$.

11. Save and close the file.

Sort a Data Table

Dylan, a Kids for Change member, volunteers at a green cleaning supply company so he can become familiar with safe cleaning products. He has been asked to take inventory this month, which is a good way to get to know the products. Dylan plans to sort the inventory list by Category and then by Sub-Category. This will make it easier to locate the items in the warehouse.

12. Open **W2-R2-Inventory** and save it as **W2-R2-InventoryRevised**.

13. Select the entire table and choose **Table Tools→Layout→Data→Sort** $\boxed{\text{A↓}}$; if necessary, choose the **Header Row** option in the bottom-left corner of the Sort dialog box.

14. Choose **Sort By menu button ▾→Category** and then choose **Then By→Sub-Category**; click **OK**.

    It will now be easier for Dylan to inventory the cleaning supplies.

15. Save and close the file.

Create a Table with a Template

16. Choose **File→New**, then type **table** in the search field at the top of the screen and tap $\boxed{\text{Enter}}$.

17. Scroll down the list of templates and choose **Fax Cover (Green Design)**.

 **Tip!** *Hover the mouse pointer over the fax cover thumbnail to see the full template name in a ToolTip. Some names are similar, so be sure to select the exact above description.*

18. Double-click the **thumbnail** to open a copy of the template and notice that it was created in a table.

    Notice [Compatibility Mode] *in the title bar, which indicates that the template was created in an earlier version of Word.*

19. Save it as **W2-R2-KidsFaxCover**.

    A message appears indicating that the document will be upgraded to the newest file format.

20. Click **OK** and notice that the filename in the title bar no longer includes the [Compatibility Mode] designation.

21. You will not include a logo in the fax cover, so click the **YOUR LOGO HERE** icon, and when you see small circles indicating the object is selected, tap $\boxed{\text{Delete}}$ to remove it.

22. In the second row, click the **Your Company Slogan** control and type **Think Globally, Act Locally**.

23. Scroll to the bottom of the page and fill in the following contact information, clicking each corresponding field:

    [Your Company Name]: **Kids for Change**

    [Street Address]: **159 Park Boulevard**

    [City, ST ZIP Code]: **Atlanta, GA 30313**

    Phone [000-000-0000]: **404-555-0100**

Fax [000-000-0000]: **404-555-0101**

[Email]: **Kids@Yahoo.com**

Now that you have customized the fax cover with Kids for Change information, you will save it as a personal template so you can use it over and over without typing the company slogan and contact information repeatedly.

24. Choose **File→Save As**, navigate to any file storage location, and choose **Word Template (*.dotx)** from the Save As Type list.

Notice that the file path at the top of the dialog box leads to the default Custom Office Templates. Unless instructed to do otherwise, you should use this folder if you want your template to appear whe you click the PERSONAL link on the templates screen.

25. Save the file and then close the template file.

Now you'll test your new template.

26. Choose **File→New**, click the **PERSONAL** link as shown, and then click your template.

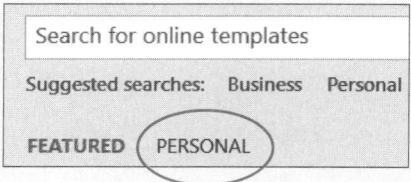

27. Click the **W2-R2-KidsFaxCover** thumbnail to open a copy of the template.

Notice that the default file name in the title bar is DocumentX, *indicating that this is a copy of your template.*

28. Close the file and choose **Don't Save** when prompted to save changes.

REINFORCE YOUR SKILLS: W2-R3

Insert and Format Tables

This holiday season Kids for Change members are working with the local fire department to collect toys for needy kids. The members will be assigned to different neighborhoods for collecting toys. In this exercise you will format a table that tracks how many toys each member collects. In preparation for sending out mailing lists and tracking additional donations, you will sort a table, insert a Quick Table, convert text to a table, and finally use a template.

1. Open **W2-R3-Toys** and save it as **W2-R3-ToysRevised**.

2. Select the second and third columns of the first table.

3. Choose **Table Tools→Layout→Alignment→Align Center** 🔲.

4. Select the entire table and choose **Table Tools→Layout→Alignment→Cell Margins** 🔲.

5. Change the top and bottom margins to **0.06** and then click **OK**.

Merge Cells, Format the Table, and Sort Data

6. Select the four *Sycamore* cells in the third column.

7. Choose **Table Tools→Layout→Merge→Merge Cells** 🔲 and then delete three of the *Sycamore* entries.

8. Use the same technique to merge the *Homestead Valley* and *Middle Ridge* cells and then delete three *Homestead Valley* and three *Middle Ridge* entries.

9. Select the entire table.

10. Choose **Table Tools→Design→Borders→Borders** ⊞ **menu button** ▾ →**No Border**.

   Only the gridlines, which do not print, are visible—unless they were turned off. (Remember, you can turn gridlines on and off via the Table Tools' Design tab and the Borders menu button ▾*.)*

11. Choose **Table Tools→Design→Table Styles→More** ▾ →**Grid Table 4 – Accent 5** style.

   Hint: It's a blue style.

   Several Kids for Change regional directors plan to meet following the toy collection to discuss plans for next year's collection. They compiled a mailing list of directors who will be notified of the meeting. Now you will sort the mail as presorted mail results in lower postage rates.

12. Scroll to the table on page 3 and position the insertion point in the table.

13. Choose **Table Tools→Layout→Data→Sort** ⫚.

14. Ensure that **Header Row** in the Sort dialog box is chosen and then choose to sort first by **State**, then by **City**, and finally by **Zip**. Click **OK**.

   The California cities sorted in ascending alphabetic order within State, and the Dallas Zip codes sorted in ascending numeric order within City.

Insert Rows and Resize Columns

15. Scroll to the table on page 4.

   Region 5 was accidentally omitted.

16. Position the mouse pointer to the left of, and between, the last two rows until the insert control appears.

Region
1
2
3
4
6

17. Click the **insert control** to insert a blank row between the last two rows and then enter the following data in the new row:

5	1,951	2,543

18. Select the entire table and choose **Table Tools→Layout→Cell Size→AutoFit** ▦ →**AutoFit Contents**.

Insert a Quick Table and Convert Text to a Table

Kids for Change members decided to take up a collection from friends and family to purchase additional toys. You will insert a Quick Table for tracking the donations.

19. If necessary, display formatting marks and then position the insertion point next to the last paragraph symbol on page 4.

20. Choose **Insert→Tables→Table** ▦ →**Quick Tables→Tabular List**.

21. Select the *ITEM* heading and type **MEMBER** in its place; select the *NEEDED* heading and type **AMOUNT** in its place.

22. Select the remaining rows, tap [Delete], and then enter the new data as shown.

MEMBER	AMOUNT
Ella	$20
Tom	$17
Roger	$32
Stella	$15
Jennifer	$22
Max	$29
Jose	$35
Albert	$40

23. Scroll to page 2 and select the rows in the tabular table.

24. Choose **Insert**→**Tables**→**Table** →**Convert Text to Table**.

25. When the Convert Text to Table dialog box appears, click **OK** and then save and close the file.

Use a Template

Kids for Change had a successful toy collection campaign, and now the employees are ready to celebrate. You have volunteered to create a flyer announcing the event.

26. Choose **File**→**New** and choose the **Event** category of templates.

Search for online templates	🔍
Suggested searches: Business Personal Industry Print Design Sets Education **Event**	

27. Double-click the **Winter Holiday Event Flyer** and save it as `W2-R3-HolidayFlyer`.

28. Use the following notes to complete the flyer.

What to select	What to type
Your Holiday Event	Celebration!
Date	December 17th
Time	7:00 p.m.
Address	159 Park Boulevard, Atlanta
Paragraph below address	Our toy collection was a great success, and we hope you'll join us to celebrate. Egg nog, hot cider, and munchies will be served. See you there!
Your Organization	Kids for Change

29. Save and close the file and then exit Word.

Apply Your Skills

APPLY YOUR SKILLS: W2-A1

Insert and Modify a Table

Universal Corporate Events is finalizing its schedule for the autumn cruises. You have been asked to complete the September cruise schedule for the Bahamas. In this exercise, you will insert a new table, align data, and resize columns and cell margins.

1. Start Word; open **W2-A1-CorpEvents** and save it as **W2-A1-CorpEventsRevised**.
2. If needed, display formatting marks and then position the insertion point on the first blank line below *Oceanic Cruise Lines*.
3. Insert a **4×4 table** and enter the data shown:

Date	Itinerary	Ship	From
09/02/16	4-night Bahamas Cruise from Miami	Oceanic Star	$560
09/09/16	3-night Bahamas Cruise from Miami	Oceanic Jewel	$600
09/30/16	7-night Bahamas Cruise from New York	Oceanic Odyssey	$1159

You accidentally overlooked the September 22 cruise, so you'll add that now.

4. Use the **insert control** to add a row between the last two rows and then enter this information:

09/22/16	7-night Bahamas Cruise from New York	Oceanic Star	$1120

5. Select the last two columns and then center-align the text.
6. Use the adjust pointer to resize the columns to the approximate width shown in the following figure.

Date	Itinerary	Ship	From
09/02/16	4-night Bahamas Cruise from Miami	Oceanic Star	$560
09/09/16	3-night Bahamas Cruise from Miami	Oceanic Jewel	$600
09/22/16	7 night Bahamas Cruise from New York	Oceanic Star	$1120
09/30/16	7-night Bahamas Cruise from New York	Oceanic Odyssey	$1159

7. Set the top/bottom margins to **0.08"**.
8. Insert a new row at the top of the table.
9. Merge the cells in the new row and type **Travel Special** as the table heading.

   Next, you will convert a table to text.

10. Scroll to page 2 and select the entire table.
11. Choose **Table Tools→Layout→Data→Convert to Text** and then click **OK**.
12. Save and close the file.

Format and Sort Tables

A Universal Corporate Events sales rep has asked you to prepare two tables of travel packages that he will present to two different clients. In this exercise, you will format the tables with borders, shading, and table styles and then you will sort the data. Finally, you will customize a template that you will use for gathering traveler information.

1. Open **W2-A2-Universal** from your **Word Chapter 2** folder and save it as **W2-A2-UniversalRevised**.
2. Remove the borders from the table on page 1.
3. Select the first row and use the **Borders** menu button ▾ to apply a bottom border.
4. Apply a bottom border to the last row of the table.
5. Select the first row and then choose **Table Tools→Design→Table Styles→Shading** menu button ▾→**Gold, Accent 4, Darker 25%**.
6. Select the third row and apply **Gold, Accent 4, Lighter 60%**.
7. Apply the same color you used in the third row to the fifth row.
8. Scroll to page 2, position the insertion point in the table, choose **Table Tools→Design→Table Styles**, and open the Table Styles gallery.
9. Choose **Grid Table 6 Colorful — Accent 4**; it's a yellow style.

Sort Data and Insert a Row

10. Using the page 2 table, specify that the table has a header row and sort by the **Travel Package** column in ascending order.
11. Using the page 1 table, insert a blank row at the top of the table, merge the cells in the first row, and type **Universal Corporate Events**.
12. Use **Align Center** to center the heading and then apply shading, **Gold, Accent 4, Lighter 40%**.
    The black print in the second row is a bit hard to read.
13. Change the Font Color **A** to **white**.
14. Save and close the file.

Use a Template

15. Choose **File→New** and use the search field to locate templates in the travel category.
16. Open a copy of the **Client Travel Planning Form** and save it as a template, naming it **W2-A2-TravelerInfo**.
17. Select *Travel Agency Name* and type **Universal Corporate Events** in its place.
18. Use your imagination to complete the two rows at the top of the form.
19. Scroll down and delete the rows at the bottom of the form, starting with *Tour Information*.
20. Save and close the file.

Create and Format Tables

The Universal Corporate Events marketing manager has asked you to create a list of the day tours from Paris. She also asks that you reformat the list of African trips and modify and reformat the Asian tour table. In this exercise, you will create a table, convert a table to text, and sort and reformat a table.

1. Open **W2-A3-Travel** from your **Word Chapter 2** folder, save it as **W2-A3-TravelRevised**, and, if necessary, display formatting marks.

2. Position the insertion point next to the first paragraph symbol at the top of the page.

3. Insert a **4×5 table** and enter the data as shown:

Day Tours	From	When	Duration
Versailles	$70	Daily except Mon	4 hrs.
Eiffel Tower	$75	Daily	3 hrs.
Louvre Museum	$65	Daily except Tue	2.5 hrs.
Moulin Rouge Show	$153	Daily	4.5 hrs.

4. Scroll to page 3 and select the table.

5. Convert the table to text; ensure that the *Tabs* option is chosen in the dialog box.

Sort a Table

6. Scroll to page 2 and position the insertion point in the table.

7. Open the **Sort** dialog box, indicate that the table has a header row, and sort by the **Dates** column in ascending order.

8. Delete the **Discount** column and use the **insert control** to add a column between *Dates* and *Duration*.

9. Enter the information shown in the following figure:

Departure
San Francisco
Los Angeles
Los Angeles
San Diego
San Francisco

10. Select **columns 2–5** and position the adjust pointer between two of the selected columns.

11. Double-click to autofit the columns to the width of the longest entry in each of the selected columns.

12. Insert a row at the top of the table and merge all cells in the row.

13. Type **Universal Corporate Events** in the row and center align the text.

14. Select the table and remove all borders.

15. Select the first row, apply outside borders, and apply a blue shading color of your choice.

16. Save and close the file; exit Word.

✈ Extend Your Skills

These exercises challenge you to think critically and apply your new skills. You will be evaluated on your ability to follow directions, completeness, creativity, and the use of proper grammar and mechanics. Save files to your chapter folder. Submit assignments as directed.

W2-E1   That's the Way I See It

You own a hardware store, and a few building contractors order from you in large quantities. Track their contact information in a ten-row table with column heads for Name, Address, City, State, and Zip. Your business covers four states: Utah, Arizona, New Mexico, and Colorado. Include each state and sort by State, then by City, then by Zip. Add a column at the end of the table for Phone and enter the new data. Add a header row centering your company name. Apply a table style and then save the file as **W2-E1-Contractors**.

You want to market to other contractors and will use a template to track them. Search for online **name and address list** templates. Open the Party Guest List template and modify it for your needs. For example, delete the image at the top and change the title. Change the column headings as needed and then apply a table style. Enter three new prospects. Save the file as **W2-E1-Prospects**.

W2-E2   Be Your Own Boss

Business is blooming at Blue Jean Landscaping; you need to get control of inventory. Decide how many landscapers work for you and the number of items needed to keep them supplied. Create a six-row table listing tools, such as spades and hoes. Note how many you have and how many you need to add. Include headings for Item, Location, Units Needed, Units in Stock, Units to Add, and Price. Add five rows of data, sort by item, and resize the columns as needed. Add a header row centering the company name. Add borders and shading for readability. Save the file as **W2-E2-Inventory**.

You've landed a big corporate client, and you'll need lots of plants to landscape the property. You will use an inventory template to help you keep track of plants to buy. Search for online **inventory** templates. Open a copy of the Physical Inventory Count Sheet template. Modify the title, column headings, and any other parts of the template to suit your needs. Start your list by entering five plants you'll need to purchase for the job. Save the file as **W2-E2-PlantsNeeded**.

W2-E3   Demonstrate Proficiency

The chef at Stormy BBQ will introduce a new dish. Decide on the dish and then create a document named **W2-E3-Order**. Set up a table for the food order including item, price, quantity, and cost and then enter five food items. Sort the table in an order you think most useful. Add a heading row and enter the restaurant name centered. Size the table so it's easy to read and apply a table style of your choice.

New dishes mean a new menu will be needed. Search for a menu template and modify it to include standard BBQ items as well as the new item you created the food order list for. Format it in a way that is attractive and will be easy for customers to read. Save your menu as **W2-E3-BBQMenu**.

WORD

3 | Creating a Promotional Brochure

In this chapter, you will add graphic elements, such as WordArt, to a brochure. SmartArt graphics provide a gallery of predesigned diagrams such as lists, processes, cycles, hierarchies, and relationships that help you communicate ideas clearly and vividly. Borders and page color add a polished look to your brochure. Live preview galleries allow you to quickly test many choices while deciding what looks best for your brochure. All these and more help you create materials that are both dynamic and informative.

LEARNING OBJECTIVES

▸ Create an eye-catching brochure

▸ Insert shapes in a document

▸ Add pictures, text boxes, and WordArt to a document

▸ Choose page setup features

▸ Communicate information with SmartArt

▸ Format the page background

🗁 Project: Promoting an Ergonomics Seminar

As the owner of Ergonomic Office Solutions, you have decided to create a presentation about the benefits of an ergonomic office. Your friend, Tommy Choi, owner of Green Clean, has provided you with his customer database. Knowing Tommy's customers are already interested in the environment, you believe they would be interested in your products. (You are already beginning the process of understanding who your audience is.) You decide to create a brochure to mail to local businesses promoting a seminar. You will use product pictures as well as shapes, WordArt, and SmartArt to create a brochure that is both informative and visually appealing.

📖 Designing an Engaging Brochure

Knowing your audience is the path to successful communication. This principal applies to almost everything you write. The readers want to know what's in it for them. Analyze them; walk in their shoes. What interests them? What would they want from you? What can you do for them? How can you engage them?

Design is critical. Use photos, shapes, and graphics that grab the audience's attention. And be sure to incorporate blank space. Without it, your page will look cluttered and hard to read. Space provides balance and symmetry. Don't get complicated. People tend to skim, so keep it simple. Your message should be clear, crisp, and concise. Decide which points are priorities and use bullets to focus the reader's attention. Limit the number of fonts to two or three and use fonts that are clean and easy to read.

Color is significant. Use a color scheme that reflects your photos and graphics. Color also conveys feeling and mood. Direct the reader's eye by highlighting important elements with prominent place-ment and distinctive colors. Take time to think about the colors you use; you may want to conduct an Internet search of the *psychology of color*.

Branding is important. Express your brand with a consistent logo, tagline, and color scheme that complement your company's other brand assets, such as packaging, your website, and media campaigns.

Working with Shapes

There is a large gallery of graphic shapes available to you, including lines, text boxes, rectangles, ovals, and many others. They can add interest to documents, such as flyers and brochures, and you can type text in most shapes. You can also rotate, resize, and move shapes. You insert shapes from the Shapes gallery. When a shape is selected (displays round handles), the contextual Drawing Tools and Format tabs appear, where you can choose many styles and designs for your shape.

≡ Insert→Illustrations→Shapes 🔲 │ Drawing Tools→Format→Insert Shapes

⚠ **View the video "Using Shapes."**

⚠ **View the video "Adding Text to and Formatting Shapes."**

In this exercise, you will draw, size, and move shapes. You'll maintain a shape's proportions with the Shift *key when resizing, and you'll see how the mouse pointer changes appearance based on various ways you work with shapes.*

1. Open **W3-D1-Brochure** and save it as **W3-D1-BrochureRevised** in your **Word Chapter 3** folder.

2. If necessary, turn on formatting marks.

   Notice that a number of paragraph symbols are already in the document. It can be easier to work with graphics if some spacing is already set up.

3. Choose **Insert→Illustrations→Shapes** 🔲 to display the Shapes gallery.

4. Choose the **Rounded Rectangle** from the Rectangles category.

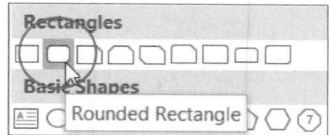

   After you choose a shape, the mouse pointer changes to a crosshair icon resembling a plus sign (+), which you click or drag in the document to create the shape.

5. Click and drag anywhere in the document to draw a rounded rectangle.

6. Choose **Insert→Illustrations→Shapes** 🔲 and then choose the **Rounded Rectangle** again.

7. Hold the Shift key and drag to draw another rounded rectangle.

   This time you drew a perfect square with rounded corners instead of an elongated rectangle, even though you started with the same shape. Holding down the Shift *key while drawing maintains the proportional relationship between the shape's width and height.*

Resize and Rotate Shapes

8. With the square shape selected (displaying round handles), follow these steps to resize the shape:

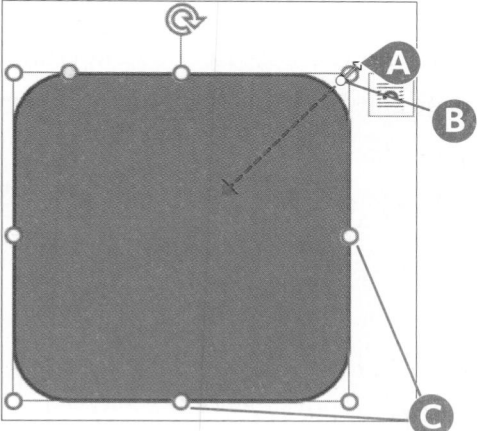

   Ⓐ Position the mouse pointer on the top-right corner sizing handle.

   Ⓑ Hold Shift and drag diagonally toward the center of the shape to resize while maintaining proportions.

   Ⓒ Drag from a side handle to change only the height or width of the object.

9. Follow these steps to rotate the shape:

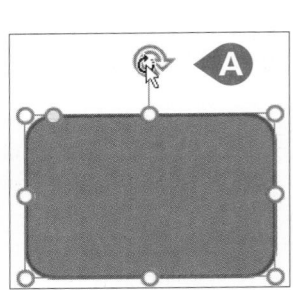 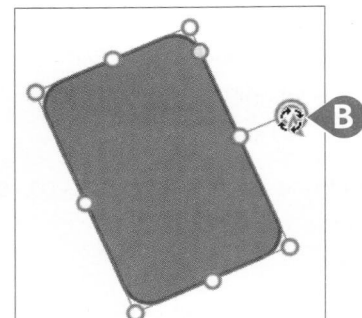

Ⓐ Position the mouse pointer on the rotation handle; the mouse pointer appears as a circular arrow.

Ⓑ Click and drag to the right about 45 degrees; the mouse pointer appears as four small arrows when rotating.

 *Holding* Shift *allows you to select multiple shapes at once. Then you can delete, move, or format them all at once.*

10. If necessary, click one of the shapes to display the handles and then hold Shift and click the other shape.

11. Tap Delete to remove both shapes.

    You can use the ruler to help align and size shapes and other graphic images. It may or may not be visible on your screen.

12. If necessary, choose **View→Show→Ruler**.

    Notice that there are two rulers: one at the top and one at the side of the screen. The margin areas (1" by default) are the gray areas at the left, right, top, or bottom ends of the rulers. The typing areas are white.

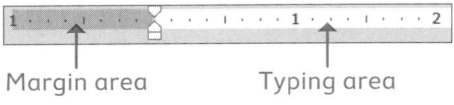

    Margin area   Typing area

13. Choose **Insert→Illustrations→Shapes** ⬦ and choose **Rounded Rectangle** again.

14. Starting about 1" from the top of the page and about 1" from the left-hand margin, draw a 1" tall rectangle that spans the page but remains within the margins.

15. Position the mouse pointer on the shape until the pointer appears as a four-headed arrow.

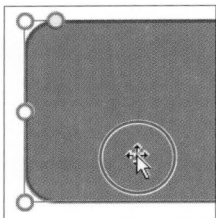

16. Practice dragging the shape to move it and then return it to its original position.

17. Save the file.

Adding Text and Formatting Shapes

You can add text to shapes you draw. This is handy if, for example, you want to create a flyer announcing an event. Just select the shape and begin typing the announcement. Text is automatically centered horizontally and vertically, and it wraps within a shape as you type.

The contextual Format tab contains many tools you can use to add pizzazz to a shape, including Shape Styles, Shadow effects, and 3-D effects. The contextual Format tab also has its own Shapes gallery in the Insert Shapes group. It contains the same shapes as the Shapes gallery located in the Illustrations group on the Insert tab.

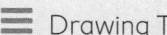 Drawing Tools→Format→Shape Styles

DEVELOP YOUR SKILLS: W3-D2

In this exercise, you will add text to a shape and format the text. Then you will format the shape using the Shape Styles gallery.

1. Save your file as **W3-D2-BrochureRevised**.
2. If necessary, select the rectangle shape at the top of the page by clicking anywhere on it.
3. Tap $\boxed{\text{Caps Lock}}$, type **ERGONOMIC OFFICE SOLUTIONS**, tap $\boxed{\text{Enter}}$, and type **PRESENTS**. Tap $\boxed{\text{Caps Lock}}$ once more to turn it off.

    Notice that the text was automatically centered in the shape.
4. Click the border of the shape, taking care not to drag.

 *Selecting a shape by clicking the border selects everything inside the shape. Thus, the text in the shape is selected, although it is not highlighted.*

5. Choose **Home→Font→Font menu button ▾ →Tahoma**.
6. Keep the shape selected and apply **Bold 22 pt** font.
7. If your shape is not big enough for the larger text, drag a sizing handle to enlarge it.

    Next, you will use the Shape Styles gallery to format the shape.
8. Make sure the object is selected so the contextual Format tab is available and then choose **Drawing Tools→Format→Shape Styles**.
9. Click the **More** button on the Shape Styles gallery to open the gallery.

10. Choose **Subtle Effect — Blue, Accent 1**.
11. Save the file.

Using WordArt and Inserting Pictures

WordArt is great for creating smart-looking text objects. It's wonderful for creating special effects such as logos and headings in newsletters, flyers, and brochures. You can use the built-in designs as they are, or you can customize them.

You can browse through your computer, or other computers, to locate pictures and other images for your document, or you can search online.

Search for pictures saved as files on a computer.

Search online for pictures and other images.

WordArt and pictures can be rotated, resized, and moved like other objects. The cropping tool can be used to remove any unwanted parts of a picture making portions of the image transparent, allowing anything under it to show through.

 View the video "Enhancing Pictures."

≡ Insert→Text→WordArt 🄰

≡ Insert→Illustrations→Pictures 🖼 *or* Online Pictures 🖼

Aligning Objects

You can manually drag and drop objects to align them, but using the Align feature on the contextual Format tab is more precise. Select the objects you want to align and then choose the desired alignment.

 *The terms object and image are both used when referring to graphical elements such as shapes, WordArt, and pictures.*

≡ Drawing Tools→Format→Arrange→Align 🄴

DEVELOP YOUR SKILLS: W3-D3

In this exercise, you will add a WordArt object and align it with a shape. You will insert and resize a picture and make its background transparent. Then you will format and move the table.

1. Save your file as **W3-D3-BrochureRevised**.
2. Click in the document below the rectangle.
3. Choose **Insert→Text→WordArt** 🄰.

4. Choose **Fill — Black, Text 1, Outline — Background 1, Hard Shadow — Accent1** from the menu that appears and then type **The Ergonomically Challenged Office**.

5. Place the mouse pointer on the border of the WordArt object and then drag to position it about 1" below the rectangle.

   Don't worry about centering it below the shape; you will center-align the objects in the next steps.

6. With the WordArt object still selected, hold down Shift and click the rounded rectangle above it that you created earlier.

   Both objects should be selected—handles appear on both.

7. Choose **Drawing Tools→Format→Arrange→Align** ▣**→Align Center**.

   This center-aligns the objects with each other.

8. If necessary, drag the selected objects so they are centered between the margins.

Insert a Picture

9. Scroll down and position the insertion point in the left cell of the table.

10. Choose **Insert→Illustrations→Pictures** ▣.

11. Navigate to your **Word Chapter 3** folder and double-click **ErgoChair.jpg** to insert it.

12. Hold the Shift and resize the picture using a corner handle until it matches the height of the text on the right.

   This picture has a white background. Later, you will add background color to your brochure and the picture's white background won't blend with the background color. Your chair would look like this when the background color is applied. Therefore, you will make it transparent, allowing the brochure's background color to show through.

   What: Luncheon Seminar
   Where: The Bakery Café
   When: September 27th at noon

13. With the chair image selected, choose **Picture Tools→Format→Adjust→Color** .

14. Choose **Set Transparent Color** at the bottom of the menu.

15. Click in the white background of the image.

   This makes the white background transparent, so when you add the page color to the brochure, the color will show through the picture's transparent background.

16. Click anywhere to deselect the image. Then position the mouse pointer on the line between the two cells and double-click to resize the cell.

   What: Luncheon Seminar
   Where: The Bakery Café
   When: September 27th at noon

17. Select the table using the move handle and then choose **Home→Paragraph→Center** ▣.

18. With the table still selected, choose **Home→Paragraph→Borders** ▣ **menu button** ▾.

19. Choose **No Border** to complete the page.

20. If gridlines appear in the table (although they won't print), follow these steps to remove them:
- Make sure the table is selected.
- Choose **Table Tools→Layout→Table→View Gridlines** .

21. Save your file.

Using Text Boxes and Page Setup Options

A text box is a special type of shape designed for inserting text or graphics. You may wonder how inserting a text box is different from drawing a shape and adding text inside it. It's because of the formatting. All documents are based on a theme, which contains a set of theme colors and theme fonts. The default theme for a new blank document is Office. When you originally created the rounded rectangles, they used a blue fill color that was the default fill color for *shapes*. Text boxes do not contain those formatting characteristics. You can format all of the text by selecting the text box itself or format only a portion of the text by selecting the part you want to change. The techniques for rotating, sizing, and moving are the same for text boxes as for other graphics.

≡ Insert→Illustrations→Shapes →Text Box | Insert→Text→Text Box

 View the video "Creating a Text Box."

Page Setup Options

Commonly used page setup options include page breaks, margins, page orientation, and paper size. All of these are located in the Page Setup group on the Layout tab. Some page setup options also appear in the Print screen in Backstage view.

≡ Layout→Page Setup

Tip! You can use ⎡Ctrl⎤+⎡Enter⎤ to quickly insert a *manual page break*.

 View the video "Page Setup Options."

DEVELOP YOUR SKILLS: W3-D4

In this exercise, you will insert a text box, align it with other objects, and format the text box border and the text within it. Then you will insert a page break to create a second page for your brochure.

1. Save your file as **W3-D4-BrochureRevised**.

2. Choose **Insert→Illustrations→Shapes**  and then choose **Text Box** from the Basic Shapes category in the Shapes gallery.

3. Position the mouse pointer below the WordArt object you created previously and then drag to draw a text box about **2" wide** and **½" tall**.

4. Type this text and size the box so the text wrapping is the same as shown:

> Email EOS@Yahoo.com or call
> 712-555-0123 to register.

5. If the email address appears as a hyperlink, right-click it and choose **Remove Hyperlink**.

6. Make sure the text box is selected and then choose **Home→Paragraph→Center** ☰.

7. Choose **Drawing Tools→Format→Shape Styles→Shape Outline** ✎ **menu button** ▾ and choose **Blue, Accent 1, Lighter 40%**.

8. With the text box still selected, hold down ⃞Shift and select the two objects above it.

9. Choose **Drawing Tools→Format→Arrange→Align** ⃞ and choose **Align Center**.

10. Click to deselect. If necessary, move the text box so it is well balanced on the page.

    Your brochure will be two pages in length, so you will now insert a page break to create a second page.

11. Position the insertion point at the bottom of the page.

12. Choose **Layout→Page Setup→Breaks** ⃞ **→Page**.

    Notice the other Page Setup options, including Margins, Orientation, and Size.

13. If necessary, display formatting marks and notice the page break symbol and the new second page.

    Now you will delete the page break and use keystrokes to re-insert a page break.

14. Position the insertion point in front of the page break symbol and tap ⃞Delete.

15. Press ⃞Ctrl+⃞Enter to insert another page break.

16. Save your file.

Working with SmartArt

It is often easier to grasp concepts if information is presented graphically rather than textually. The SmartArt gallery provides a large variety of graphics that you can add to documents. They make it easy to combine predesigned graphics with text to create sophisticated figures. SmartArt images are divided into the following categories.

Category	Purpose
⊞ List	Shows nonsequential data
⊶ Process	Use to show a progression, a timeline, or sequential steps in a task, process, or workflow.
⟳ Cycle	Shows a continual process
⛭ Hierarchy	Creates a hierarchical structure or shows a decision tree
⊞ Relationship	Illustrates associations
⊕ Matrix	Shows how parts relate to a whole
▲ Pyramid	Shows proportional relationships
⊡ Picture	Used when you want to convey your message with or without explanatory text, or when you want to use pictures to complement a list or process

☰ Insert→Illustrations→SmartArt ⊡

Inserting SmartArt Text and Modifying an Image

You can use the SmartArt text pane to add text to your image. Text placeholders in the image are replaced with text as you enter in the SmartArt text pane. The font size adjusts based on the amount of information you type. If you prefer, you can type directly in the text placeholders in the image.

If you cannot find the exact image you want, you can modify, add, and delete shapes within the graphic. SmartArt objects are formatted the same way as other graphic shapes.

 View the video "SmartArt Text and Bullets."

 View the video "Modifying SmartArt."

DEVELOP YOUR SKILLS: W3-D5

In this exercise, you will create two SmartArt graphics: one to list the seminar topics and one to list ergonomic products. Then, you will customize and resize the graphics.

1. Save your file as **W3-D5-BrochureRevised**.
2. If necessary, move the insertion point to the top of page 2.
3. Choose **Home→Paragraph→Center** 〓.

   This will center the SmartArt image that will be inserted next on the page.
4. Choose **Insert→Illustrations→SmartArt** 📇.
5. Follow these steps to insert a SmartArt graphic:

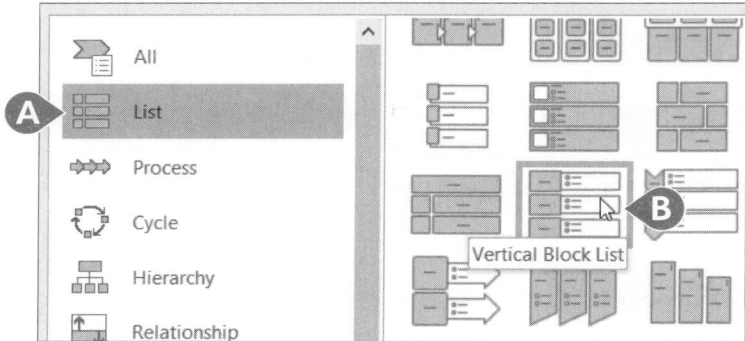

   Ⓐ Choose the **List** category.
   Ⓑ Scroll down and choose **Vertical Block List**.
6. Read the description in the bottom-right corner of the dialog box and then click **OK**.
7. If the text pane is not visible, click the tab.

Customize the Image

This image has three major text objects, but you will use only one.

8. Position the mouse pointer to the left of the first major bullet and then drag down to select the first six bullets.

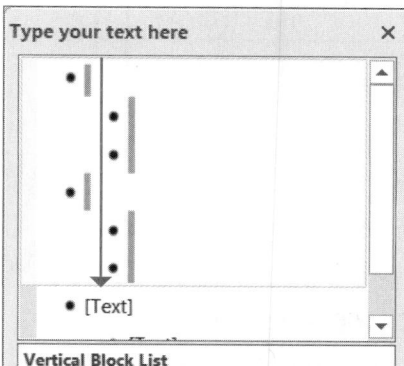

9. Tap Delete to remove the bullets.

10. Follow these steps to begin entering the seminar topics:

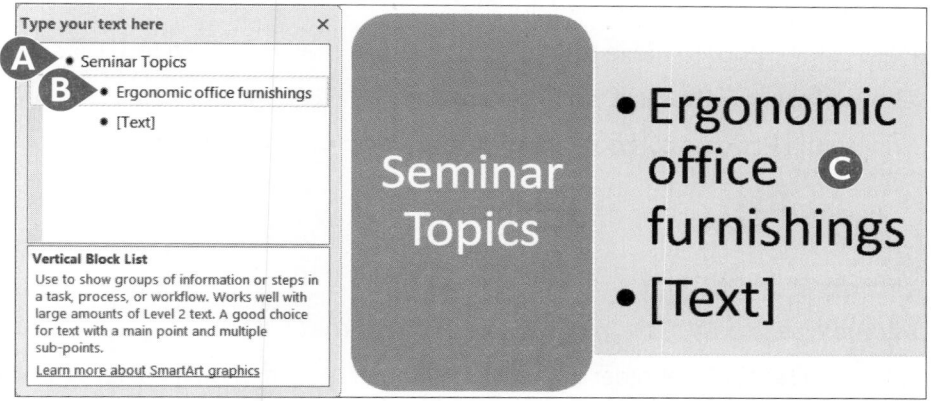

    A Position the insertion point to the right of the first bullet and type **Seminar Topics**.

    B Tap ↓ and type **Ergonomic office furnishings**.

    C Notice that the text appears in the graphic as you type.

11. Tap ↓ to go to the next line and type **Mobile workstations**.

12. Tap Enter to generate the next bullet and then type **Technology support**.

13. Tap Enter as needed and then type the following items to complete the list:
- **Personal lighting options**
- **Q&A**

14. Click **Close** × in the upper-right corner of the text pane.

15. Click the outside border frame to make sure the *entire* SmartArt image is selected.

You will resize the SmartArt object next. If an object within the main frame is selected, you could accidentally resize only a part of the SmartArt object. Clicking the outside border frame prevents that.

16. Drag the bottom-center sizing handle up until the image is approximately half as tall as the original image.

17. Save your file.

Changing a SmartArt Style

The SmartArt Styles gallery allows you to apply interesting variations of the original graphic. Live Preview lets you sample the effect of the various styles without actually applying them.

☰ SmartArt Tools→Design→SmartArt Styles

DEVELOP YOUR SKILLS: W3-D6

In this exercise, you will customize SmartArt graphics by applying colors and styles.

1. Save your file as **W3-D6-BrochureRevised**.
2. Make sure the outside border of the seminar topics image is selected.
3. Choose **SmartArt Tools→Design→SmartArt Styles→Change Colors** ⣿.
4. In the Accent 1 category, choose **Gradient Loop – Accent 1**.
5. Choose **SmartArt Tools→Design→SmartArt Styles→More** ⊡ to display the SmartArt Style gallery.
6. In the 3-D category, choose **Metallic Scene**.

   Next, you will add another SmartArt image.

7. Press ⌈Ctrl⌉+⌈End⌉ to move to the end of the document and then tap ⌈Enter⌉ twice.
8. Choose **Insert→Illustrations→SmartArt** 🖼.
9. Choose the **Process** category, then choose **Basic Chevron Process**, and then click **OK**.

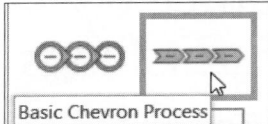

   You can type directly in the image without opening the text pane.

10. Click the **[Text]** placeholder in the first arrow on the left and type **Our Products**.
11. Click in each **[Text]** placeholder and enter the text as shown:

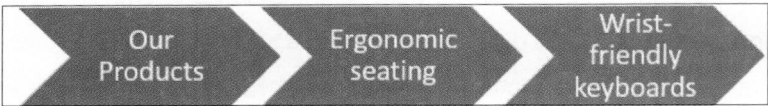

12. Click the outside border of the image and then follow these steps to add an arrow to the graphic:

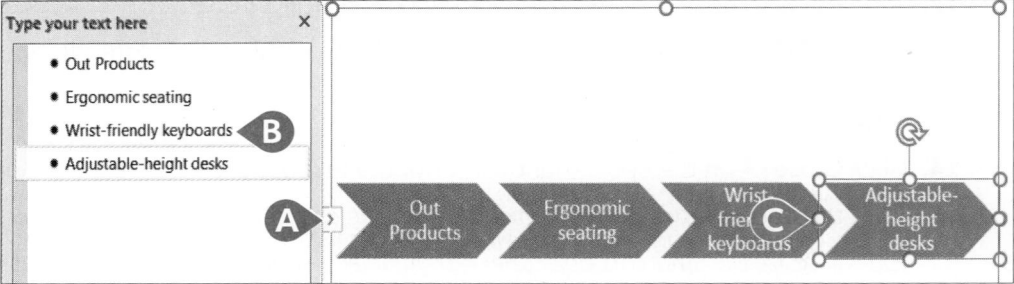

   Ⓐ Click the tab to open the text pane.
   Ⓑ Position the insertion point after the word *keyboards* and tap ⌈Enter⌉.
   Ⓒ Type **Adjustable-height desks** in the new arrow.

13. **Close** ⌈×⌉ the text pane.

Format the Image

14. Click the outside border of the shape.

15. Choose **SmartArt Tools→Design→SmartArt Styles→Change Colors** .

16. Choose the fourth item in the Accent 1 category, **Gradient Loop – Accent 1**.

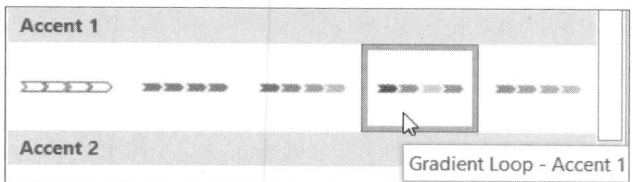

17. Click the **More** button on the SmartArt Styles gallery, and in the 3-D category, choose **Cartoon**.

18. Choose **SmartArt Tools→Format→Align→Align Center** →**Align Center**.

19. Save your file.

Formatting the Page Background

Page background formats add color and visual variety to your documents. Page colors and borders provide the finishing touches that add professional polish. For example, you can add colors from a gallery specifically designed to blend with a document's theme. Border colors are also designed to tastefully complement page colors.

Adding Page Colors and Page Borders

The Page Colors gallery is similar to other galleries you have worked with. The colors that appear in the Theme Colors section of the gallery, as the name implies, are based on the theme currently in effect in the document.

Page borders surround the outer edges of the entire page. You can adjust the color (again, based on the current theme), line thickness, and other features of the border.

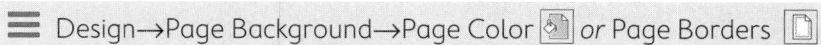

≡ Design→Page Background→Page Color or Page Borders

DEVELOP YOUR SKILLS: W3-D7

In this exercise, you will sample background colors using Live Preview. Then you will add a background color to your brochure and a border surrounding the pages.

1. Save your file as **W3-D7-BrochureRevised**.

2. Choose **Design→Page Background→Page Color** .

3. Hover the mouse pointer over several colors in the Theme Colors area of the gallery.

Live Preview displays the effects of the different colors.

4. Choose **Dark Blue, Text 2, Lighter 40%**.

Now you'll add a page border.

5. Choose **Design→Page Background→Page Borders** [icon].

6. Choose **Box** from the Setting area in the left-hand panel.

7. Follow these steps to format the page border:

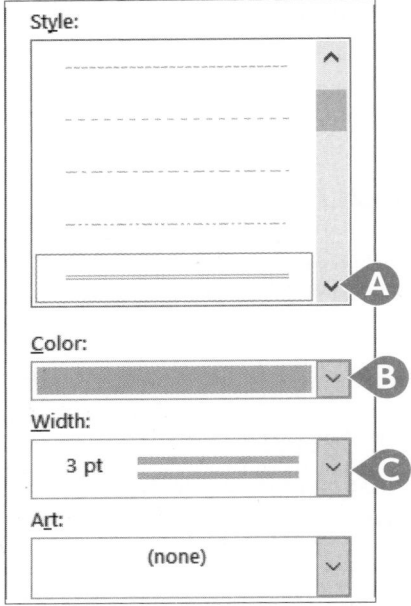

Ⓐ Choose the **double-line** Style.

Ⓑ Choose **Blue, Accent 1, Lighter 40%**.

Ⓒ Choose a Width of **3 pt** and then click **OK**.

8. Save and then close your file; exit Word.

Self-Assessment

Check your knowledge of this chapter's key concepts and skills using the Self-Assessment in your ebook or eLab course.

Reinforce Your Skills

Create a Flyer Recognizing an Outstanding Volunteer

Kids for Change has a volunteer program, and the person who volunteers the most hours in a quarter is recognized for his or her service. In this exercise, you will create a flyer announcing Janisha Robinson as the winner for this quarter. You will work with shapes, WordArt, pictures, and text boxes.

1. Start Word and create a new file based on the **Blank Document** template. Save it as **W3-R1-JanishaFlyer**.

2. Display formatting marks and tap ⌷Enter⌷ 20 times.

   It can be easier to work with graphics if some spacing is already set up.

3. If necessary, choose **View→Show→Ruler** to display the ruler.

4. Choose **Insert→Illustrations→Shapes** 〈⬡〉, and in the Stars and Banners category, choose **Down Ribbon**.

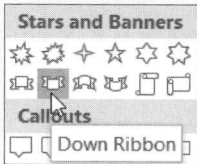

5. Position the crosshair mouse pointer next to the paragraph symbol at the top of the page.

6. Press and hold the mouse button and drag until the image is about **6½" wide** and **1½" tall**.

7. Type **Outstanding Member** in the image, then click the border to select the entire shape.

8. Choose **Home→Font→Font menu button** ▼ **→Comic Sans MS** and then apply **28 pt**, **Bold** 〈B〉.

9. Choose **Home→Font→Font Color** 〈A〉 **menu button** ▼ and choose **Red** in the Standard Colors category.

Insert and Crop a Picture

10. Position the insertion point a little below the graphic.

11. Choose **Insert→Illustrations→Pictures**, navigate to your **Word Chapter 3** folder, and double-click **Janisha.jpg**.

    Now you will resize the picture.

12. Press and hold ⌷Shift⌷ and then position the mouse pointer on the handle in the upper-right corner of the picture.

13. Drag diagonally toward the center until the picture is about **3" wide**.

    Next you will crop off the left side of the picture.

14. Make sure the picture is selected and then choose **Picture Tools→Format→Size→Crop** 〈⬚〉.

15. Follow these steps to crop the picture:

A Position the mouse pointer on the left-center cropping handle.

B Drag to the right to Janisha's right hand and then click in the document to deselect.

Next you will place a border on the picture to give it a finished look.

16. Select the picture, then choose **Picture Tools→Format→Picture Styles→Picture Border** ☒ **menu button** ▾ and pick a shade of blue that you think will blend well.

Now you will choose a layout option that will allow you to freely move the picture on the page.

17. Click the **Layout Options** ☒ smart tag at the upper-right side of the picture and choose **In Front of Text** (bottom-right).

18. Drag the picture to the center of the page.

Use WordArt

19. Position the insertion point a little below the picture.

20. Choose **Insert→Text→WordArt** ☒ and choose **Fill – Blue, Accent 1, Outline – Background 1, Hard Shadow – Accent 1**.

21. Type **Janisha Robinson** in the image and then click the outside border to select the entire image.

22. Choose **Drawing Tools→Format→WordArt Styles→Text Effects** ☒ **→Transform**.

23. In the Warp category, choose **Chevron Down**.

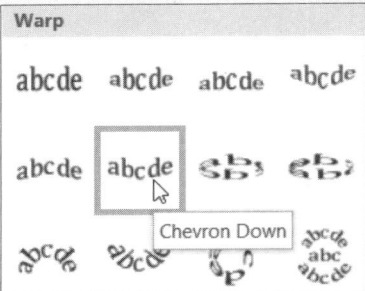

24. Center the WordArt on the page.

Add a Text Box

25. Choose **Insert→Illustrations→Shapes** ☒ **→Text Box**.

26. Below Janisha's name, draw a text box that is approximately **4" wide** and **2½" tall** and then type the following text:

Kids Helping Communities

• After-school tutor

- Schoolyard cleanup
- Meals for shut-ins
- Emergency relief food collection

27. Click the border of the text box, choose **Home→Font→Font menu button ▾→Comic Sans MS**, and apply **20 pt** font size; resize the text box if needed.

28. Hold down ⎢Shift⎥ and select all the images.

29. Choose **Drawing Tools→Format→Arrange→Align 🖿→Align Center**.

This center-aligns the images with each other.

30. Use the zoom control in the bottom-right corner of the screen to zoom out until you see the entire page.

31. If necessary, adjust the position of the images so they are well balanced on the page and then zoom back to **100%**.

32. Save and close the file.

REINFORCE YOUR SKILLS: W3-R2

Create a Flyer for Charity

Kids for Change is partnering with a local charity to collect clothing and household products for people with developmental disabilities. You have been asked to create a flyer to help in the collection process. In this exercise, you will change page orientation, work with graphic images, and add page color and a page border to the flyer.

1. Start a new document based on the **Blank Document** template and save it as **W3-R2-DonationsFlyer**.

2. If necessary, choose **View→Show→Ruler**.

3. Choose **Layout→Page Setup→Orientation 🖺→Landscape**.

4. Tap ⎢Enter⎥ 15 times to set up some spacing in advance and then position the insertion point at the top of the page.

5. Choose **Insert→Illustrations→Pictures 🖾** and then navigate to your **Word Chapter 3** folder and double-click **Donations.png**.

Now you will use a text-wrapping layout option so you can easily move the image.

6. Make sure the image is selected, then click the **Layout Options 🖻** smart tag at the upper-right corner of the image and choose **In Front of Text** (bottom-right).

7. Drag the image to center it between the margins.

8. Position the insertion point below the picture.

Add WordArt and SmartArt

9. Choose **Insert→Text→WordArt 🄰** and choose **Fill – Gray – 50%, Accent 3, Sharp Bevel**.

10. Type the following text in the WordArt image:
We need clothing, furniture, appliances, and household items.

11. Click outside the image to deselect.

12. Position the insertion point below the WordArt image.

13. Choose **Insert→Illustrations→SmartArt** 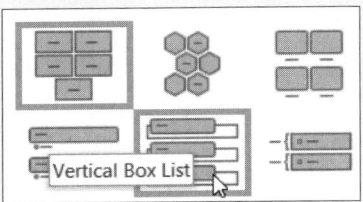; then click the **List** category, choose **Vertical Box List**, and click **OK**.

Now you will resize the SmartArt image so it fits on the first page.

14. Press and hold ⎵Shift⎵ and then position the mouse pointer on the handle in the upper-right corner of the image.

15. Drag diagonally toward the center of the image until it is about **3" wide**.

It should now be positioned on the first page.

16. Click the **Layout Options** ⬒ smart tag to the right of the image and choose **In Front of Text**.

Now you can move the image freely on the page.

17. Center the image between the margins.

Recolor the Image

18. Click the outside border to select the entire image.

19. Choose **SmartArt Tools→Design→Change Colors** ⬓ and choose **Colored Fill – Accent 3**.

20. Type the following in the three **[Text]** areas:

    Place boxes or bags by 8 a.m.

    Donations will be picked up by dark.

    Thank you for your contributions!

21. Click outside the image to deselect.

Change the Page Color and Add a Page Border

22. Choose **Design→Page Background→Page Color** ⬓ and then choose **White, Background 1, Darker 25%**.

Instead of using lines for the border, you will use an art border.

23. Choose **Design→Page Background→Page Borders** ▢.

24. Click the drop-down arrow in the **Art** field at the bottom of the dialog box and choose the **hot air balloons**.

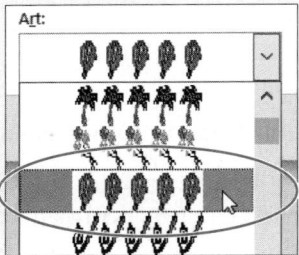

25. Click **OK** and turn off formatting marks.

26. Use the zoom controls at the bottom right of the screen to zoom out and see the entire page.

27. If necessary, adjust the position of the images so they are well balanced on the page and then zoom back to **100%**.

28. Save and close the file.

Create a Recycling Flyer

Kids for Change held a recycling campaign last month. Your cousin, Ingrid, is enjoying a semester studying at the Sorbonne in Paris. She saw the flyer you created, and she would like to implement a recycling program at the university. She asks that you create a copy of your flyer on standard European-size paper, A4. In this exercise, you will recreate the flyer using graphic images, a picture, a text box, as well as a page background and border.

1. Start a new document using the **Blank Document** template; save it as **W3-R3-RecycleFlyer**.

2. Choose **Layout→Page Setup→Size** 🗋 **→A4**.

3. Display the formatting marks and ruler, if necessary.

4. Tap [Enter] about twenty-five times to set up spacing in your flyer and then position the insertion point at the top of the page.

5. Choose **Insert→Text→WordArt** [A] and choose **Fill – Gray – 25%, Background 2, Inner Shadow**.

6. Type **Reduce, Reuse, Recycle** in the WordArt image and then click the outside border.

7. Choose **Drawing Tools→Format→WordArt Styles→Text Fill** [A] **menu button** ▾ **→Green, Accent 6**.

8. Choose **Drawing Tools→Format→Shape Styles→Shape Effects** [Q] **→Shadow**.

9. In the Outer category, choose **Offset Diagonal Top Left**.

10. Choose **Drawing Tools→Format→WordArt Styles→Text Effects** [A] **→Transform**.

11. In the Warp category, choose **Chevron Up**.

12. If necessary, drag the WordArt to center it between the margins, then position the insertion point a little below it.

Add a Picture to the Flyer

13. Choose **Insert→Illustrations→Pictures** 🖼, navigate to your **Word Chapter 3** folder, and double-click **World.jpg**.

14. Hold down [Shift] and resize the picture until it's about **3" wide**.

15. Click the **Layout Options** smart tag and choose **In Front of Text** and then drag the picture to center it on the page.

    Now you will place a border on the picture.

16. With the picture selected, choose **Picture Tools→Format→Picture Styles→Picture Border** [▱] **menu button** ▾ **→Weight→3 pt**.

17. Choose **Picture Tools→Format→Picture Styles→Picture Border menu button** ▾ **→Green, Accent 6, Darker 25%**.

WORD

Add a Text Box

18. Choose **Insert→Illustrations→Shapes** ▨**→Text Box**.

19. Draw a text box a little below the picture about **3½" wide** and **2" tall** and then type the following text in the text box:

- `Separate your trash`
- `Always look for recycle bins`
- `Reuse shopping bags`
- `If it's broken, fix it`
- `Buy recycled products`

20. Click the border of the text box and choose **Home→Font→18 pt**.

21. Resize your text box if needed; don't allow the text to wrap.

22. Click the border to select the object.

23. Choose **Drawing Tools→Format→Shape Styles→Shape Outline** ▨ **menu button** ▾ **→No Outline**.

24. Choose **Drawing Tools→Format→Shape Styles→Shape Fill** ▨ **menu button** ▾ and choose **Green, Accent 6, Lighter 60%**.

Use a Shape

25. Choose **Insert→Illustrations→Shapes** ▨, and in the Stars and Banners category, choose **6-Point Star**.

26. While holding down ⃞Shift⃞, draw a star about **2½" wide** below the text box and on the left side of the page.

27. Choose **Drawing Tools→Format→Shape Styles** and from the Shape Styles gallery choose **Colored Fill – Green, Accent 6**.

28. Type the following in the star:

`Be a star!`

`Do your part!`

Insert SmartArt

29. Position the insertion point a little below the text box.

30. Choose **Insert→Illustrations→SmartArt** ▨; then click the **Cycle** category, choose **Text Cycle**, and click **OK**.

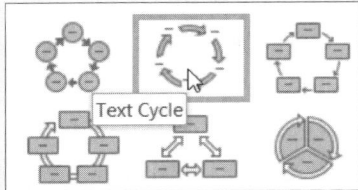

31. Type the following items in the [**Text**] boxes in any order:

```
Paper
Metal
Plastic
Hazardous Waste
Glass
```

32. Hold down ⎡Shift⎤ and resize the image until it's about **3½" wide**, then click the **Layout Options** smart tag and choose **In Front of Text**.

33. Arrange the star and SmartArt as needed so the star is on the left below the text box and the SmartArt is on the right below the text box.

34. Click the outside border of the SmartArt.

This image has an inside frame and an outside frame.

35. Click one of the arrows in the image, and you'll see both frames.

36. With both frames selected, choose **SmartArt Tools→Format→Shape Styles**; in the Shape Styles gallery, choose **Colored Fill — Green, Accent 6**.

This recolors that arrow that you originally clicked to display both frames. Also, notice that the Shape Styles gallery is now displaying the color you chose.

37. Click the next arrow (you won't see handles on the arrow) and click the green color that's visible in the gallery.

38. Continue until all arrows are recolored and then deselect the image.

39. Use the zoom controls to zoom out until you see the entire page.

40. If needed, rearrange the objects so they are balanced on the page to your satisfaction and zoom back to **100%**.

Add Page Color and a Page Border

41. Choose **Design→Page Background→Page Color** ▤ **→Green, Accent 6, Lighter 60%**.

42. Choose **Design→Page Background→Page Borders** ▯ and choose a line style, color, and width of your choice; click **OK**.

43. Save and close the file.

Apply Your Skills

Create a Services Flyer

The Universal Corporate Events marketing manager asked you to create a flyer highlighting services that Universal Corporate Events offers. You will use a picture and graphics to add zing to your flyer.

1. Start a new document using the **Blank Document** template and save it as **W3-A1-Services**.
2. Tap [Enter] enough times to position the insertion point close to the bottom margin and then move the insertion point to the top of the page.
3. Insert the **Horizontal Scroll** shape from the Stars and Banners category.
4. Drag in the document until the scroll is about **6½" wide** and **1" tall**.
5. Type **Take Off with Universal Corporate Events** and then change the font size to **24 pt**.
6. Resize the shape, if necessary, and then position the insertion point a bit below the shape.
7. Insert the **Plane.jpg** picture located in your **Word Chapter 3** folder.
8. Click the **Layout Options** smart tag and choose **In Front of Text**.
9. While maintaining the height/width proportions, resize the picture to about **3" wide**, then position the picture just below the Shapes image and center it between the margins.

   Now you'll add a border to the picture.

10. Choose **Picture Tools→Format→Picture Styles→Picture Border menu button ▼→Weight →3 pt**.
11. Change the picture border color to **Blue, Accent 1, Darker 25%**.

Add WordArt and a Text Box

12. Position the insertion point below the picture and insert a WordArt graphic using **Fill — Blue, Accent 1, Shadow**.
13. Type **Services We Offer**; center the graphic on the page.
14. Format the WordArt image by using the **Text Effects, Bevel** category, and choosing the **Circle**.
15. Then in the Text Effects, Transform category, choose **Arch Up** (first form in the Follow Path category).
16. Insert a text box shape below the WordArt image that is about **4" wide** and **1½" tall**.
17. Enter the following in the text box:
    - **Online itinerary**
    - **Online flight tracking**
    - **Travel insurance**
    - **Visa and passport services**
18. Remove the outline border from the text box.
19. Change the text to **22 pt** and then resize the text box if needed.

Align Images

20. Hold the [Shift] key and select all four images.

21. Use the **Align** feature to center-align the images with each other.

22. If necessary, drag the selected images to center them between the margins.

23. Zoom out to **Full Page View** and adjust the placement of the images as you deem necessary for the flyer to appear well balanced; then zoom back to **100%**.

24. Save and close the file.

APPLY YOUR SKILLS: W3-A2

Create a European Tours Flyer

A Universal Corporate Events sales rep has asked you to create a flyer for a corporate client who is planning an employee rewards plan. The client will be choosing among three options for the reward tour. In this exercise, you will change the page orientation, format the page background, and use SmartArt to highlight the details of the recommended tours.

1. Start a new file based on the **Blank Document** template and save it as `W3-A2-CorpTours`.

2. Use landscape orientation for the flyer, tap [Enter] until the insertion point is close to the bottom margin and then position the insertion point at the top of the page.

3. Apply the Page Color **Gold, Accent 4, Lighter 60%**.

4. Add a page border, making the formatting choices as shown. (Color is Gold, Accent 4, Darker 25%).

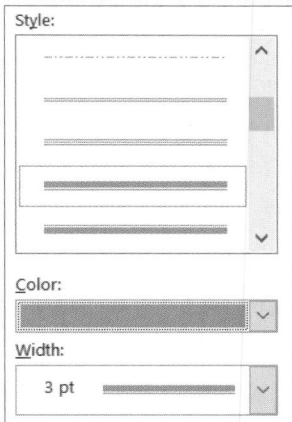

5. Use a WordArt image of your choice to add a **Universal Corporate Events** heading to the flyer; use a Text Fill color that blends well with the background color and a Text Effect of your choice.

6. Position the insertion point about 1" below the heading and insert the SmartArt graphic **Vertical Chevron List**, which is in the Process category.

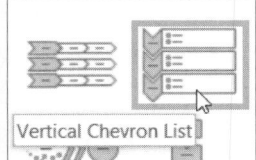

7. Resize the graphic, maintaining its proportions, to about **3" wide** and **3½" tall**.

8. Click the **Layout Options** smart tag and choose **In Front of Text**.

9. In the first blue *[Text]* box, type **London**; type **Berlin** and **Rome** in the next two blue *[Text]* boxes.

10. In the bulleted list to the right of *London*, enter **Stonehenge**, **Windsor Castle**, and **Tate Gallery**.

11. Enter **Dresden**, **Potsdam**, and **Rothenburg** for Berlin and **Pompeii**, **Tuscany**, and **Capri** for Rome.

Format the WordArt Graphic

12. Change the SmartArt color using the first color option in the Colorful category.

13. Select the white rectangle next to *London* and change the **Shape Fill** color to a color that you feel complements the London object.

14. Use the same technique to color the *Berlin* and *Rome* rectangles.

15. Arrange and size the objects in a balanced manner on the page.

16. Save and close the file.

APPLY YOUR SKILLS: W3-A3

Create a Mileage Awards Flyer

Universal Corporate Events provides car rentals for travelers, and the company is currently offering mileage awards. In this exercise, you will create a flyer highlighting the award offerings. You will use graphics for interest and format the flyer background for a polished, professional look.

1. Start a new document using the **Blank Document** template and name it **W3-A3-CarRental**.

2. Tap ⏎ Enter until the insertion point is close to the bottom margin and then move the insertion point to the top of the page.

   Next you will use WordArt to create a heading for the flyer.

3. Insert a new **WordArt** image, using the design in the third row, fifth column.

4. Enter the following text: **Universal Corporate Events**.

Add a Text Box and a Picture

5. Insert a text box below the WordArt about **3½" wide** and **1" tall** and then type the following lines in the text box.

   Get behind the wheel!

   Get more reward travel!

6. Change the font size to **22 pt**; resize the text box if necessary.

7. Change the font color to **Gray — 25%, Background 2, Darker 50%**.

   Later you will add page color, and removing the text box's white fill background and its outline will make the text box blend in better.

8. Change the Shape Fill to **No Fill** and change the Shape Outline to **No Outline**.

9. Position the insertion point a bit below the text box; then, insert the **Driver.jpg** file from your **Word Chapter 3** folder.

10. While maintaining the picture's proportions, resize the picture to about **2½" wide**.

11. Click the **Layout Options** smart tag and choose **In Front of Text**. Then center the picture between the margins.

12. With the picture selected, insert the **Center Shadow Rectangle** from the Picture Styles gallery.

13. Position the insertion point just below the picture and insert **Wave** in the Stars and Banners category of the Shapes gallery.

14. Draw the shape about **4½" wide** and **1" tall**, type `Book Now!` in the shape, and change the font size to **36 pt**.

15. With the shape selected, choose **Drawing Tools→Format→Shape Styles→Shape Fill→Gray – 25%, Background 2, Darker 25%**.

16. Change the shape outline to **white**.

17. Position the insertion point a bit below the shape.

18. Choose **Insert→Illustrations→SmartArt**, and in the List category, choose **Vertical Box List**.

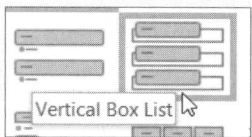

19. While maintaining its proportions, resize the shape to about **3" wide**.

20. Click the **Layout Options** smart tag, choose **In Front of Text** and then select all three **blue shapes**.

21. Choose **SmartArt Tools→Format→Shape Styles→Shape Fill** and then choose **Gray – 25%, Background 2, Darker 25%**.

22. Select all three white rectangles and then choose the same color for the **Shape Outline** ✎.

23. Center the SmartArt between the margins at the bottom of the page and then type the following in the three **[Text]** areas:

    ```
    100 award miles per day
    125 bonus miles per day
    150 miles for booking with us
    ```

24. Click to deselect, then zoom out to a full page view and, if needed, arrange the objects so they are well balanced on the page and then zoom back to **100%**.

Add a Page Color and a Page Border

25. Add the page color **Gray – 25%, Background 2, Darker 10%**.

26. Choose **Design→Page Background→Page Borders** and choose a line style that you prefer; then apply a **white** color and **3 pt** width.

    There is more white in the bottom half of the flyer. It may look better if the SmartArt heading were white.

27. Change the SmartArt Text Fill to **white**.

28. Save and close the file; exit Word.

 # Extend Your Skills

These exercises challenge you to think critically and apply your new skills. You will be evaluated on your ability to follow directions, completeness, creativity, and the use of proper grammar and mechanics. Save files to your chapter folder. Submit assignments as directed.

W3-E1   That's the Way I See It

You just completed your training as a dietician, and now you are ready to advertise your services by distributing a brochure throughout the area. Start a new document and save it as **W3-E1-GoodDiet**. Design a brochure using WordArt, a picture, and a text box and use page color and a page border to give your brochure a polished look. Create a tagline for your business and explain the services you offer and the benefits of eating well. Also include a suggestion that the reader schedule an appointment today.

W3-E2   Be Your Own Boss

As the owner of Blue Jean Landscaping, a Georgia company, you hope to increase sales as your customers get ready to spruce up their gardens with spring plants. Start a new document and save it as **W3-E2-Spring**. Create a flyer using landscape orientation and include graphics of your choice and a picture. Describe the services you provide and use upbeat verbiage about spring gardening in Georgia. Suggest plants that are appropriate for Georgia's climate. If needed, conduct an Internet search for information about plants that grow well in Georgia in the spring. Give your flyer a finished look by adding page color and a page border.

W3-E3   Demonstrate Proficiency

Stormy BBQ is expanding to include a catering department! You have been asked to create a brochure announcing this new venture. Start a new document and save it as **W3-E3-Catering**. Include pictures of food that would normally be found in a BBQ restaurant, formatting and cropping them as necessary. Use a SmartArt graphic to list the types of events that you provide catering for and format the image to blend well with the pictures you have chosen. Use one or more text boxes containing testimonials from test customers who have already enjoyed your catering services. Add page color and a page border to your brochure.

4 | Creating Reports

In this chapter, you will create a simple report. Reports are important documents often used in business and education to distribute information, communicate ideas, and share viewpoints and plans on a variety of topics. You will format your report using tabs, indents, margin changes, and headers and footers. You will also learn about research papers, a requirement for nearly every college student as well as professionally employed individuals. Your paper will include footnotes, citations, a bibliography, and a table of figures. Finally, you will explore Track Changes, a feature that allows for collaborative editing of a document.

LEARNING OBJECTIVES

▸ Work with columns and set margins

▸ Apply styles

▸ Insert headers and footers

▸ Add footnotes and endnotes

▸ Insert citations and a bibliography

▸ Incorporate captions and a table of figures

▸ Insert comments and explore Track Changes

📁 Project: Researching Social Media and Internet Commerce

My Virtual Campus is a social networking technology company. It sells web applications to colleges and universities. Your marketing manager, José Morales, has asked you to look into the latest trends in social media in schools. It is important to understand how the "always connected" generation is using technology in the pursuit of education. Your manager also wants you to download an online article regarding social media in education that he can distribute in the next staff meeting. And he wants you to make the article's dense text more readable by using heading styles, headers and footers, and white space.

You are also working on your masters in marketing, and your professor wants you to write a research paper about the origins and evolution of Internet commerce. You will use many sophisticated features, such as headers and footers, footnotes, citations, and bibliographies in creating this research paper.

Creating a Business Report

When writing a business report, you want it to be easy to read. Dense blocks of text are difficult to read, so break up your report with lists, headings/subheadings, and white space. Use a clear, easy-to-read font, such as Calibri (Word's default font), Arial, or Times New Roman. Here are some principles of communication you may want to keep in mind when writing a report:

- Plan before you write.
- Know your audience.
- Use active voice.
- Avoid wordiness.
- Use plain language; avoid overblown words.

- Don't use clichés.
- Use parallel structure.
- Edit out anything that doesn't add to your meaning.
- Chunk your writing into short sections.

Setting Margins

Margins determine the amount of white space around the edges of the page. You can set margins for the entire document, a section, or selected text. The default margins in the Blank Document and Single Spaced (Blank) templates, as well as many others, are one inch all around. You can choose from a gallery of preset margins, or you can set your own custom margins.

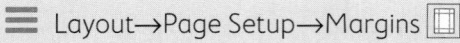 Layout→Page Setup→Margins

Indenting Text

Indents offset text from the margins. You can set indents by using the buttons on the Ribbon or by adjusting the indent markers on the ruler. The Increase and Decrease Indent buttons adjust the indent of an entire paragraph (or one or more selected paragraphs) and affect the left indent only. They adjust the indent based on the default tab stops, which are set at every half inch.

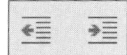

You can set custom indents by dragging the indent markers on the horizontal ruler.

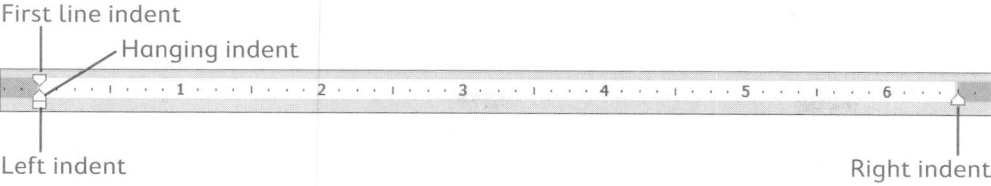

First line indent

Hanging indent

Left indent

Right indent

 View the video "Indent Markers."

Home→Paragraph→Increase Indent ⬛ *or* Decrease Indent ⬛

DEVELOP YOUR SKILLS: W4-D1

In this exercise, you will increase the margins in a report to provide a little more white space. You will use the Increase Indent button on the Ribbon to offset quotes in the report, and you will create your own custom indents using the indent markers on the ruler.

1. Open **W4-D1-SocMediaRpt** from your **Word Chapter 4** folder and save it as **W4-D1-SocMediaRptRevised**.

2. If necessary, choose **View→Show→Ruler**.

    Now you will increase the margin width to add more white space to the report.

3. Choose **Layout→Page Setup→Margins** ⬛ and notice the preset margin settings.

    You want a 1.5" left and right margin, and that is not available in the preset list, so you will customize your own settings.

4. Choose **Custom Margins** at the bottom of the menu.

5. On the Margins tab of the Page Setup dialog box, change the left and right margins to **1.5"** and then click **OK**.

    Notice the gray margin areas at the ends of the ruler; they have increased to 1.5".

    Now you will use the Increase Indent button to offset quotes in the report.

6. Below *The Net Generation* heading, select the second and third paragraphs, which are inside quotation marks.

7. Choose **Home→Paragraph→Increase Indent** ⬛.

    The paragraphs indent from the left a half inch based on the default tab settings; however, you want to indent the paragraphs from both the right and the left. So, now you will use the indent markers on the ruler to complete the job.

8. Follow these steps to adjust the left and right indents:

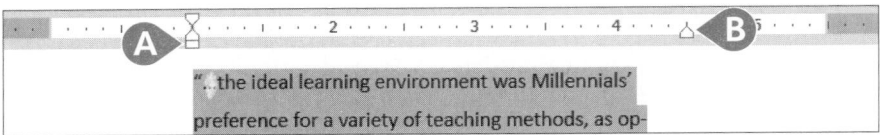

- **Ⓐ** Position the mouse pointer on the Left Indent marker (bottom rectangle) and drag to the **1"** mark.

- **Ⓑ** Drag the **Right Indent** marker to the **4½"** mark.

9. Save the report.

Setting Custom Tab Stops

Default tab stops are set every half inch, so the insertion point moves a half inch whenever you tap ⎡Tab⎦. You can customize tab stops if you want other settings.

 *Never use the ⎡Spacebar⎦ key to line up columns. Even if it looks right on the screen, it most likely will not print correctly.*

Using the Ruler to Set Custom Tabs

Word has four types of custom tab stops: left, right, center, and decimal. You can set all four types using the horizontal ruler. It is critical that you position the insertion point in the line where you plan to set tabs. Tab settings are carried inside the paragraph symbol to the next paragraph when you tap ⎡Enter⎦.

Use the Tabs box to choose the tab type. (ToolTips describe the symbols.)

You indicate the tab placement by clicking in the desired location on the ruler.

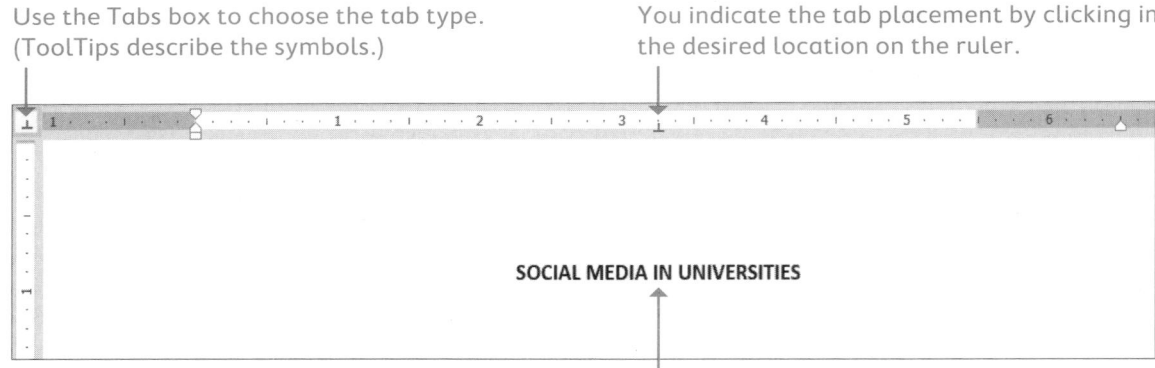

This heading is centered by a center tab.

 You can delete a custom tab by dragging it off the ruler with your mouse. When you release the mouse button, the tab disappears.

Using the Tabs Dialog Box to Set Custom Tabs

You can also set custom tab stops in the Tabs dialog box. You can specify precise positions for tabs, choose the type of tab (alignment), clear custom tab stops, and set dot leader tabs. A leader tab generates a row of dots when you tap ⎡Tab⎦. You often see dot leaders in a table of contents separating a topic from its page number.

You can change the default tab stops here.

You can enter a custom tab stop here.

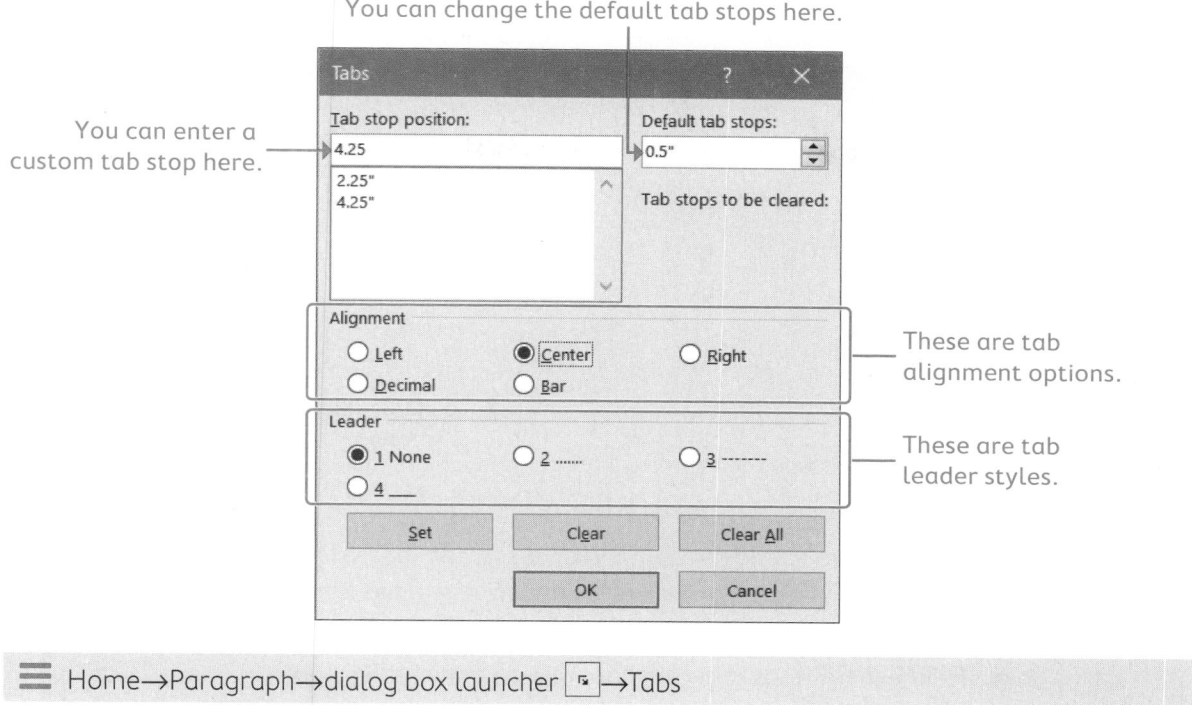

These are tab alignment options.

These are tab leader styles.

≡ Home→Paragraph→dialog box launcher 🖼 →Tabs

DEVELOP YOUR SKILLS: W4-D2

In this exercise, you will set custom tabs and create two tabbed tables.

1. Save your report as **W4-D2-SocMediaRptRevised**.

2. If necessary, display formatting marks.

3. Position the insertion point on the blank line below the section titled *Rapid Increase in the Use of Social Media*.

4. Follow these steps to set tabs for the first table:

 *If you accidentally click the tab in the wrong place, you can drag it to a new location with the mouse pointer, or you can drag it off the ruler and try again.*

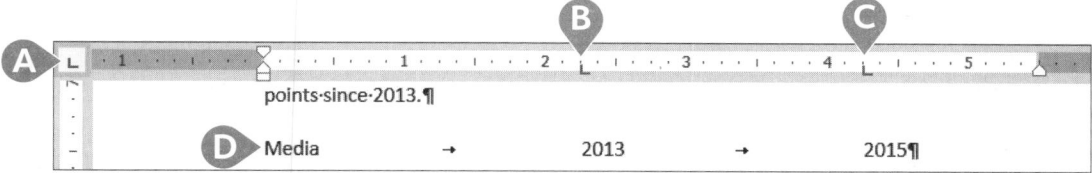

Ⓐ Verify that the Tabs box at the left of the ruler is set to a Left Tab. If not, click the box until it rotates around to Left Tab. (ToolTips describe the tab type.)

Ⓑ Click the ruler at the **2¼"** mark to set a tab.

Ⓒ Click the ruler at the **4¼"** mark for the second tab.

Ⓓ Type **Media** in the blank line and then type the next two entries, tapping ⌗Tab⌗ where you see the arrows and tapping ⌗Enter⌗ at the end of the line.

5. Type the rest of the table, tapping ⌷Tab⌷ and ⌷Enter⌷ where you see the arrows and paragraph symbols:

Media		2013		2015¶
Facebook	→	79%	→	84%¶
Twitter	→	35%	→	40%¶
Instagram	→	30%	→	36%¶
Snapchat	→	16%	→	23%¶

6. Select the first line of the table and choose **Home→Font→Bold** B .

Now you will type the second table.

7. Position the insertion point on the first blank line below the last paragraph of the document.

Look at the ruler and notice that the tabs you set for the first table have disappeared. The tab settings for the first table are carried in the paragraph symbols for that table only. Now you will set tabs for the second table.

8. Follow these steps to set the tabs and type the table:

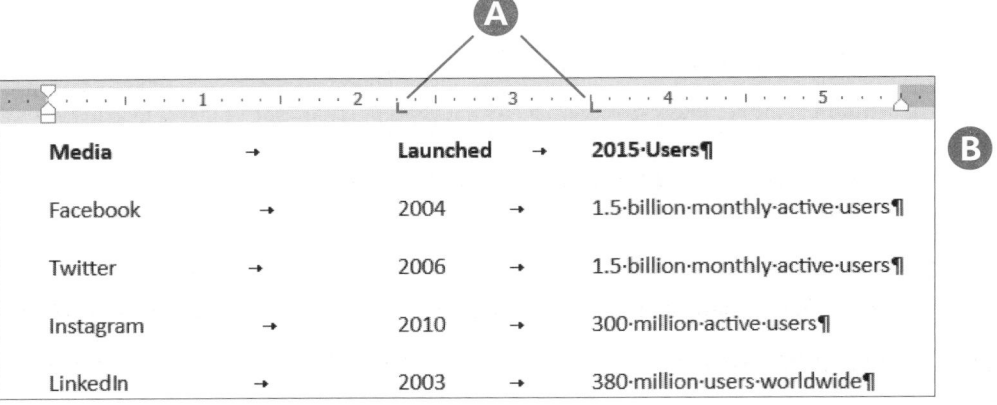

Ⓐ Set left tabs at the **2¼"** mark and the **3½"** mark.

Ⓑ Type the table as shown, applying **Bold** formatting to the first line of the table.

9. Save the file.

Formatting Text with Styles

A style is one of the most powerful formatting tools. It is a *group of formats* enabling you to apply multiple formats to a block of text all at once. Styles are based on the current template's theme, which is a set of colors, fonts, and graphic effects. There are styles for document elements, such as headings, titles, and special character formats, providing consistent formatting throughout a document.

Types of Styles

There are many built-in styles, and you are always working within a style. There are two basic types of styles: character and paragraph.

▶ Character styles: Character styles are applied to the word the insertion point is in or a selected group of words. Character styles contain only character formats, not paragraph formats. You can apply character styles *within* a paragraph that is formatted with a paragraph style.

▶ Paragraph styles: Paragraph styles are applied to all text in selected paragraphs or to the paragraph containing the insertion point. You can use any character or paragraph formats in a paragraph style. For example, you may want to format a heading with a large, bold font (character formatting) and apply paragraph spacing before and after the heading (paragraph formatting).

☰ Home→Styles→Styles Gallery │ Home→Styles→dialog box launcher ⌐

Collapsing Heading Topics

When you apply a heading style and the insertion point is in the heading, a small triangle marker appears at the left (whether formatting marks are displayed or not). You can click the marker to collapse and expand the text below it. In the following illustration, the text below *The Net Generation* is collapsed, allowing you to focus on certain parts of a document.

> ◢ ▷▪ The·Net·Generation¶
>   ▪ Rapid·Increase·in·the·Use·of·Social·Media¶
>   A·study·conducted·by·Harvard's·Institute·of·Politics·(iop.harvard.edu)·reports·use·of·

In this illustration, *The Net Generation* content is expanded.

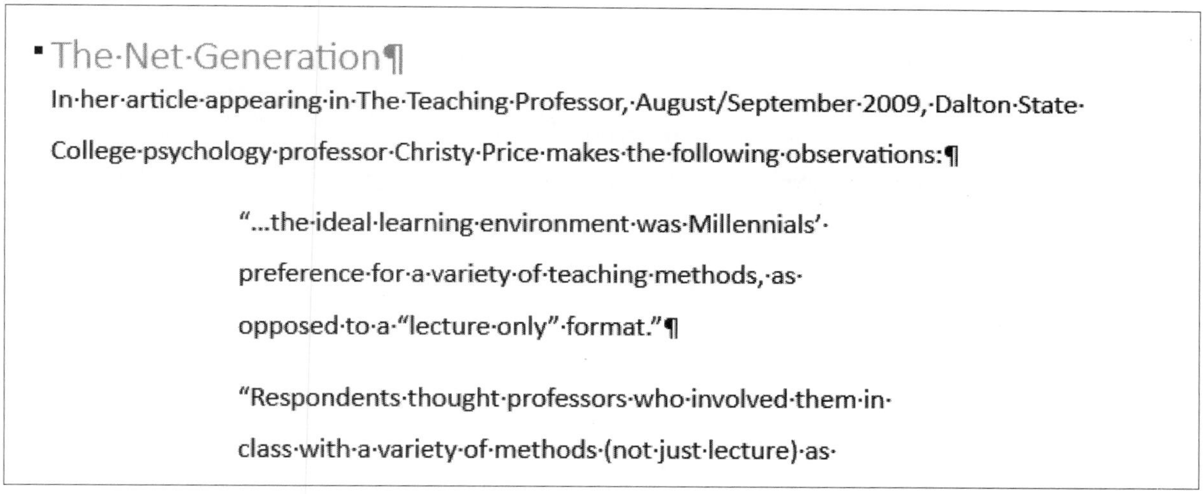

> ▪ The·Net·Generation¶
>   In·her·article·appearing·in·The·Teaching·Professor,·August/September·2009,·Dalton·State·
>   College·psychology·professor·Christy·Price·makes·the·following·observations:¶
>
>   "...the·ideal·learning·environment·was·Millennials'·
>   preference·for·a·variety·of·teaching·methods,·as·
>   opposed·to·a·"lecture·only"·format."¶
>
>   "Respondents·thought·professors·who·involved·them·in·
>   class·with·a·variety·of·methods·(not·just·lecture)·as·

ⓘ **View the video "Using the Styles Gallery and the Styles Task Pane."**

In this exercise, you will use Live Preview in the Styles gallery to find styles that will give your report a professional, polished look. You will apply the Title style to the report's main heading and the Heading 1 style to the headings within the report.

1. Save your file as **W4-D3-SocMediaRptRevised**.
2. Click anywhere in the report's main heading, *SOCIAL MEDIA IN UNIVERSITIES,* at the top of page 1.
3. Choose **Home→Styles** and then click the **More** button to open the Styles gallery.

4. Hover the mouse pointer over the Title style to see its effect on the heading and then click to apply the style.

   Now you'll open the Styles task pane. It includes all the styles that are in the Styles gallery.

5. Click the **dialog box launcher** in the bottom-right corner of the Styles group.

   Next you'll apply the Heading 1 style to the headings in the body of the report.

6. Position the insertion point in *The Net Generation* heading and then click the **Heading 1** style in the task pane to apply that style to the heading.

7. Use the same technique to apply the Heading 1 style to the remaining headings: *Rapid Increase in the Use of Social Media* and *University Recruiting Through Social Networking.*

8. Close the Styles task pane.

   Now you will collapse and expand the text below The Net Generation heading.

9. Scroll up and position the insertion point in *The Net Generation* heading to display the triangle marker to the left of the heading.

10. Click the **marker** to collapse the text below the heading.

    Collapsing parts of a document allows you to center your focus on the remaining parts.

11. Click the **marker** again to expand the text.

12. Save the report.

Inserting Headers/Footers and Comments

Headers and footers appear at the top and bottom of every page in a document, respectively, above and below the margins. You can place text, page numbers, dates, and other items in the header and footer areas. When you enter information in these areas, it is repeated on every page of the document. There is a variety of built-in header and footer formatting styles, or you can create your own.

The Comment feature is a great collaboration tool. It allows reviewers and originators to communicate about a document by posting comments to each other.

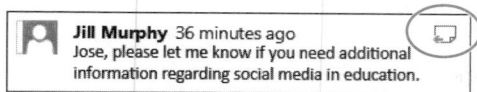

Jill Murphy 36 minutes ago
Jose, please let me know if you need additional
information regarding social media in education.

Clicking the reply button in the comments balloon allows threaded conversations between the originator and reviewers.

≡ Insert→Header & Footer→Header 🗋 *or* Footer 🗋 *or* Page Number 🗋

≡ Insert→Comments→Comment 🗩

DEVELOP YOUR SKILLS: W4-D4

In this exercise, you will add headers and page numbers to the report using the built-in formats. Then you will add a comment to your report.

1. Save your file as **W4-D4-SocMediaRptRevised**.
2. Choose **Insert→Header & Footer→Header** 🗋 and choose the **Sideline** format from the gallery.
3. Click **Document Title** and type **My Virtual Campus** in its place.
4. Double-click in the document to close the header.
5. Choose **Insert→Header & Footer→Page Number** 🗋 and slide the mouse pointer down the menu to **Bottom of Page**.
6. Scroll down in the gallery and choose **Large Color 3**.
7. Double-click in the document to close the page number footer.

   You can open the header/footer area by double-clicking anywhere in either the header or footer area.

8. Double-click the footer area to open it and then double-click in the document again to close it.
9. Scroll through the report and observe the headers and page numbers.

   It would look better to have at least two lines of the first table at the top of the second page.

10. Position the insertion point in front of *Instagram* in the first table and press Ctrl + Enter to insert a page break.

Add a Comment

Now you will add a comment for your marketing manager. He will see it when he reads your report.

11. Scroll to the top of the document and select the word *Universities* (the anchor point for the comment) in the title.
12. Choose **Insert→Comments→Comment** 🗩 and type the following in the comment balloon on the right:

    Jose, please let me know if you need additional information regarding social media in education.

13. Save and then close the report.

Arranging Text in Multiple Columns

You can use newspaper-style columns (also known as newsletter-style columns) to arrange text in multiple columns. In newspaper layout, text flows down one column and wraps to the top of the next column, as in a newspaper or magazine. Newspaper columns can enhance readability because shorter lines are easier to read, as the eye doesn't have to travel far across the page before reading the next line, and they break up dense text with random gaps. Columns are automatically reformatted as you add or delete text during editing cycles.

You can quickly set your text in columns with the Columns button on the Ribbon, or you can open the Columns dialog box where you can set up more sophisticated column layouts. For example, you can insert a line between columns and specify the width of each column.

These are commonly used column styles.

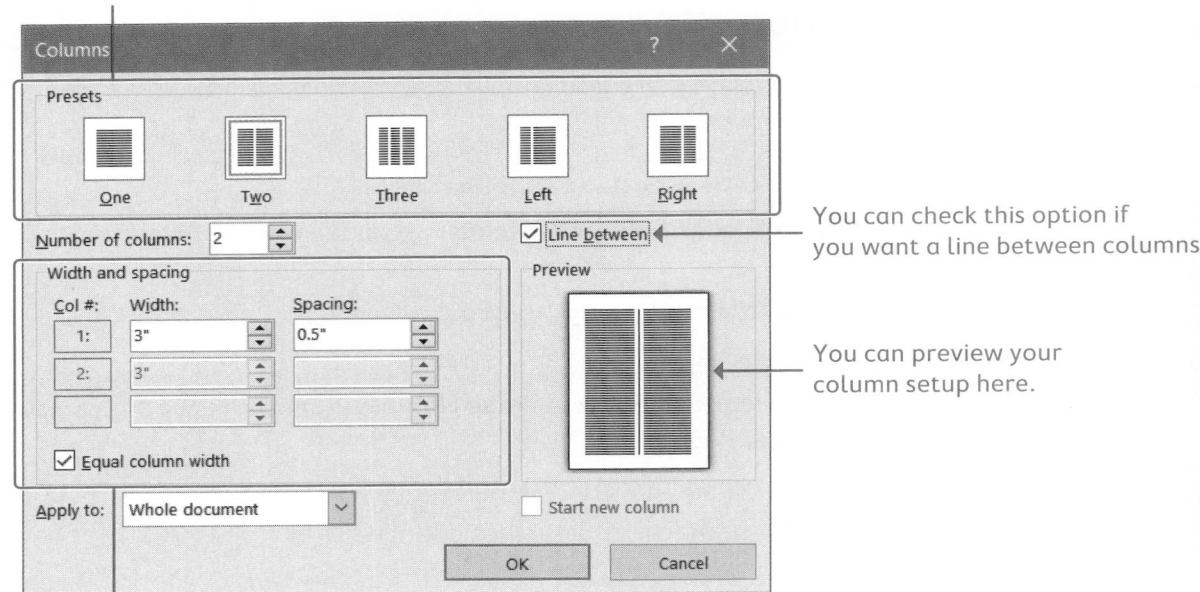

You can check this option if you want a line between columns.

You can preview your column setup here.

You can customize column widths and between-column spacing here.

≡ Layout→Page Setup→Columns 🗐

≡ Layout→Page Setup→Columns 🗐→More Columns

Column Breaks and Section Breaks

You can manually force a column to end by inserting a column break, thus moving the text at the break point to the top of the next column. This technique is often used to place headings at the top of columns and to balance columns on the last page of a multicolumn document.

Whenever you make a document-level formatting change that doesn't apply to the entire document, you need one or more section breaks to define the portion of the document affected by the change. For example, in a columnar magazine article, you may see a title line that extends across the page and then the body of the article is formatted in two columns. You need a section break to separate the one-column title from the two-column body of the article.

TYPES OF SECTION BREAKS

Section Break	Purpose
Next Page	Inserts a section break and starts the new section on the next page
Continuous	Inserts a section break and starts the new section on the same page
Odd Page	Inserts a section break and starts the new section on the next odd-numbered page; a blank page may be inserted to force the odd page section break
Even Page	Inserts a section break and starts the new section on the next even-numbered page; a blank page may be inserted to force the even-page section break

The following illustration shows the use of continuous section breaks that are sectioning off the two-column portion of a document.

The section above this break has one-column formatting, and the section below it has two-column formatting.

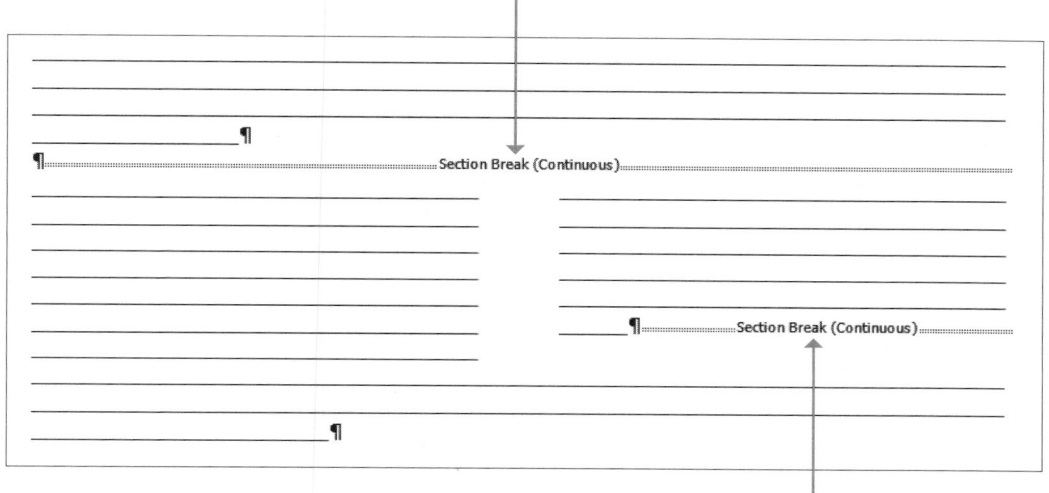

This section break ends the two-column section.

≡ Layout→Page Setup→Breaks ⊟→Page Breaks→Column

≡ Layout→Page Setup→Breaks ⊟→Page Breaks and then choose a Section Break type

DEVELOP YOUR SKILLS: W4-D5

Because the article your marketing manager wants to distribute at the next staff meeting consists of dense text, he wants you to set the article in newspaper columns to enhance readability. In this exercise, you will insert a section break after the introduction, and then you will layout the second section of the document in two columns.

1. Open **W4-D5-SocMedForStaff** from your **Word Chapter 4** folder and save it as **W4-D5-SocMedForStaffRevised**.

2. If necessary, display formatting marks.

   You want the introductory paragraph to span the page, so you will insert a section break before the social media article and then set the rest of the article in columns.

3. Position the insertion point in the second blank line following the first paragraph.

4. Choose **Layout→Page Setup→Breaks** 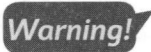**→Continuous**.

   This starts a new section on the same page.

5. Delete the blank line at the top of the second section.

6. Position the insertion point in the second section.

7. Choose **Layout→Page Setup→Columns** ▣**→Two**.

8. Scroll to page 2, and you'll see that the columns are not well balanced.

9. Position the insertion point at the beginning of the last paragraph in the left column beginning with *In the real world*.

10. Choose **Layout→Page Setup→Breaks** 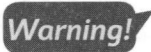**→Column**.

11. Save and close the file.

📖 Conducting Research

Research is the systematic investigation, analysis, and interpretation of data to confirm facts, answer questions, or solve problems. Students and professionals need to conduct research and effectively document findings and conclusions. Much is written on this topic, and an online search yields many results. Try this search phrase: *how to conduct research for a paper.*

Writing a Research Paper

There are a number of documentation styles for research papers, each with their own specific formatting requirements. For example, IEEE standards are used for research in computers and electronics; APA is used in psychology research; Turabian style is used for research in literature, history, and the arts; and MLA is primarily used for research in the humanities.

The Modern Language Association publishes the *MLA Handbook for Writers of Research Papers*. The MLA style has specific formatting requirements, *some* of which are already defaults within Word. For example, the default margins of one inch comply with the MLA requirement. However, Word does not comply with *all* MLA guidelines by default.

Warning! *This chapter does not presume to be a resource for MLA guidelines. Refer to the MLA handbook or the MLA website (http://mla.org) for guidance in complying with MLA requirements.*

Working with Footnotes, Endnotes, and Citations

Footnotes, endnotes, and citations are important elements of most research papers. You use them to comment on, or cite a reference to, a designated part of the text. Footnotes appear at the bottom of pages on which they are inserted; endnotes, as the name implies, appear at the end of a document or section; and citations appear on a separate Works Cited page at the end of the document. Works Cited is another name for a Bibliography. You can enter the source information when you create the citation or insert a placeholder and add the source data later.

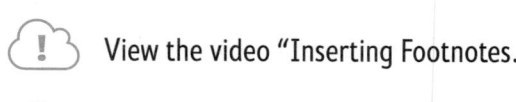 View the video "Inserting Footnotes."

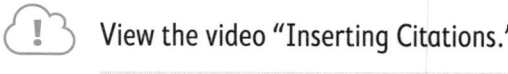 View the video "Inserting Citations."

≡ References→Footnotes→Insert Footnote AB¹ *or* Insert Endnote 🔟

≡ References→Citations & Bibliography→Insert Citation 📄

DEVELOP YOUR SKILLS: W4-D6

In this exercise, you will begin the research paper that your marketing professor requested. You will use footnotes and endnotes to clarify information and citations to support your premise.

1. Open **W4-D6-Internet** from your **Word Chapter 4** folder and save it as **W4-D6-InternetRevised**.

2. If necessary, choose **View→Views→Print Layout** 🔳.

   Footnotes may differ in appearance depending on the view you are using.

3. Position the insertion point at the top of the document and type the following four lines of text above the title, tapping ⎡Enter⎤ after each line, except the last:

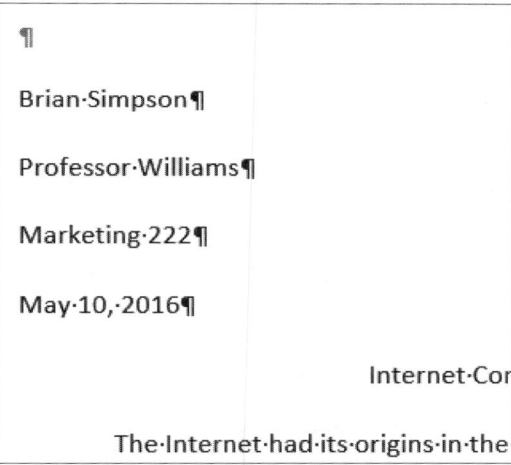

   Notice the paragraph text is double-spaced and the extra space after the paragraphs has been removed per MLA requirements. Now you will insert footnotes.

4. Position the insertion point to the right of the period at the end of the first paragraph.

5. Choose **References→Footnotes→Insert Footnote** AB¹.

   The footnote reference mark appears at the insertion point, and a corresponding footnote appears at the bottom of the page.

6. Follow these steps to complete the footnote:

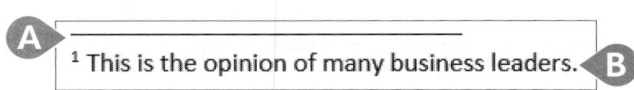

   Ⓐ Find a separator line and the footnote number.

   Ⓑ Type this text in the footnote area.

7. Use the same process to insert the footnote reference marks and the associated footnotes shown here.

> The commercial potential of the Internet stems from the fact that it is a global network with inexpensive access.[2] The Internet is also available 24x7. The multimedia capability to the Internet is important for marketing and advertising. Quick product delivery, automated order-taking, and low overhead are several more factors that are driving Internet commerce.[3]

> [1] This is the opinion of many business leaders.
> [2] Some nations still have high rates due to limited competition among Internet service providers.
> [3] These factors depend upon the capabilities of individual companies.

The default formatting of footnotes in Word does not adhere to MLA requirements. The text should use the same formatting as the body of the document (double-spaced, first line indented). You will format the footnotes later.

Now you will convert your footnotes to endnotes.

8. Choose **References→Footnotes→dialog box launcher** [⌐] and click **Convert**.

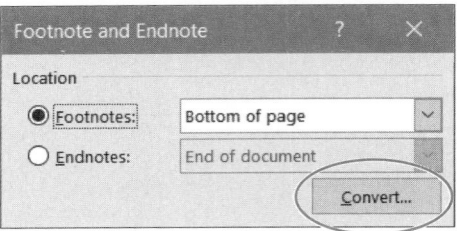

9. When the Convert Notes dialog box opens, click **OK** and then close the Footnote and Endnote dialog box.

10. Scroll through the document and notice that the footnotes are no longer at the bottom of page 1; they now appear as endnotes on the last page.

You decide that you prefer having the notes on the same page as the material they refer to, so you will convert the endnotes back to footnotes.

11. Choose **References→Footnotes→dialog box launcher** [⌐] and click **Convert**.

12. Click **OK** in the Convert Notes dialog box and then close the Footnote and Endnote dialog box.

Now you will choose the bibliography style for your paper and insert a citation.

13. Choose **References→Citations & Bibliography→Style ▾→MLA Seventh Edition**.

A citation should be placed inside the period at the end of a sentence.

14. At the end of the first paragraph on page 2, position the insertion point between the word *online* and the period and then tap [Spacebar].

15. Choose **References→Citations & Bibliography→Insert Citation** [⊡] and then choose **Add New Source**.

16. Follow these steps to create the new source to insert as the citation:

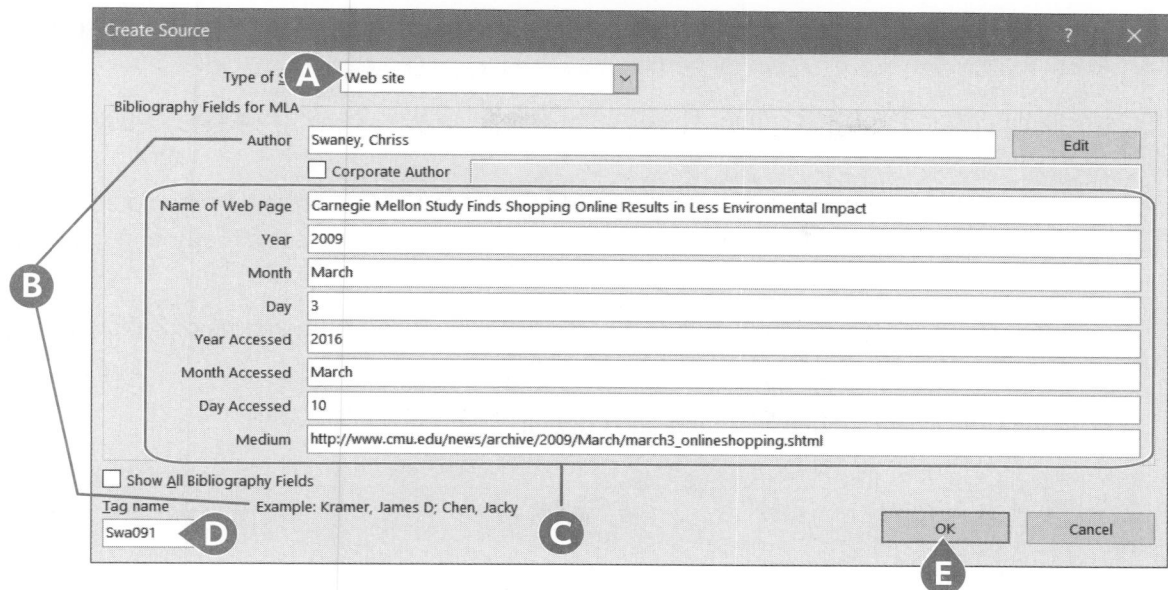

Ⓐ If necessary, choose **Web Site**.

Ⓑ Type the author's name as shown. Example text appears at the bottom of the window for each field.

Ⓒ Enter the remaining information.

Ⓓ The system uses tags internally to uniquely identify a source. The Tab Name you see may vary from this one.

Ⓔ Click **OK**.

 *Remember, Word does not follow all MLA guidelines. Refer to the MLA Handbook or website when writing academic papers.*

Insert Citation Placeholders

17. On page 2, position the insertion point at the end of the third bullet point between *themselves* and the period and tap ⌴Spacebar⌴.

18. Choose **References→Citations & Bibliography→Insert Citation** 🗐 and then choose **Add New Placeholder**.

19. Type **Fowler** in the Placeholder Name box and then click **OK**.

20. Position the insertion point at the end of the document between *years* and the period and tap ⌴Spacebar⌴.

21. Choose **References→Citations & Bibliography→Insert Citation** 🗐 and then choose **Add New Placeholder**.

22. Type **Mogg** in the Placeholder Name box and then click **OK**.

23. Save the file.

Editing and Formatting Footnotes and Citations

You can edit footnote text directly in the footnote area. In addition to editing the text of a footnote, you can also:

▸ Reposition: You can change the position of a footnote reference mark by dragging it to another location in the document.

▸ Format: You can change various formatting features of footnotes. For example, you can change the numbering scheme, change the starting number, or even replace a footnote number with a special character.

You can add source information to a citation placeholder by clicking the placeholder drop-down arrow and choosing the option to edit the source.

 View the video "Editing Footnotes and Citations."

DEVELOP YOUR SKILLS: W4-D7

In this exercise, you will format, edit, and delete footnotes and edit citation placeholders and sources.

1. Save your file as **W4-D7-InternetRevised**.

2. Position the insertion point at the beginning of the second paragraph on page 1 and scroll, if necessary, to see the three footnote reference marks and the footnotes at the bottom of the page.

3. Choose **References→Footnotes→dialog box launcher** ⬚ to display the Footnote and Endnote dialog box.

4. If necessary, at the top of the dialog box, choose **Footnotes**.

5. In the Number Format field, click the drop-down arrow and choose **A, B, C ...** and then click **Apply**.

   The footnote numbers change to alphabetic characters. You use the same technique to change the format of endnotes.

6. Choose **References→Footnotes→dialog box launcher** ⬚ ; change the Number Format back to the first option, numbers; and then click **Apply**.

7. If necessary, choose **View→Show→Ruler**.

8. Select the three footnotes at the bottom of the page and then follow these steps to format them:
   • Change line spacing to **double-space**.
   • Change the font size to **11 pt**.
   • On the ruler, drag the **First Line Indent** marker (top triangle) to the ½" mark.

Delete and Edit Footnotes and Edit Citation Placeholders

9. Select the reference mark following *marketplace* in the body of the document and tap Delete.

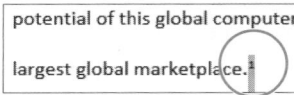

   The reference mark and the footnote are removed, and the remaining footnotes renumber.

10. Click **Undo** ⟲ to reinsert the footnote.

11. Position the insertion point between the last word and the period of the first footnote, tap Spacebar, and type **and economists**.

12. Scroll to the *Fowler* citation at the end of the third bullet on page 2.

13. Follow these steps to open the Edit Source dialog box:

Ⓐ Click the *Fowler* citation placeholder.

Ⓑ Click this drop-down arrow.

Ⓒ Choose **Edit Source**.

14. Enter the following information in the Edit Source dialog box in the order shown:
- Type of Source: **Web Site**
- Author: **Fowler, Geoffrey**
- Name of Web Page: **The Green Side of Online Shopping**
- Year: **2009**
- Month: **March**
- Day: 3
- Year Accessed: **2016**
- Month Accessed: **March**
- Day Accessed: 14
- Medium: **http://blogs.wsj.com/digits/2009/03/03/the-green-side-of -online-shopping/tab/article/**

15. Click **OK**.

16. Click **Yes** if a message appears asking if you want to update the master list and current document.

The citation may have picked up the name of the web page (title). If so, continue with step 17; otherwise, skip to step 18.

17. If necessary, click the drop-down arrow to the right of the Fowler citation and choose **Edit Citation**; then, check the **Title** box to suppress the title and click **OK**.

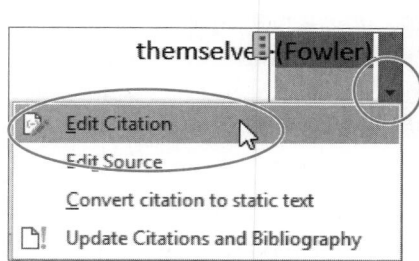

Now you will edit the Mogg placeholder.

18. Click the *Mogg* citation placeholder at the end of the document.

19. Click the drop-down arrow and choose **Edit Source**.

20. Enter the following information in the dialog box in the order shown:
- Type of Source: **Web Site**
- Author: **Mogg, Trevor**
- Name of Web Page: **Google says its drone delivery service could take flight in 2017**
- Year: **2015**
- Month: **November**
- Day: **3**
- Year accessed: **2016**
- Month Accessed: **March**
- Day Accessed: **14**
- Medium: **http://www.channelsellernews.com/shipping-tips-for -ecommerce/google-says-its-drone-delivery-service-could-take -flight-in-2017/**

21. Click **OK** and then save the file.

Working with Bibliographies

A bibliography is a list of the sources cited in the preparation of a document. Bibliographies are auto-matically generated based on the source information that you provide in the Create Source dialog box. The bibliography picks up the correct punctuation; however, certain formatting requirements are not defaults and must be addressed separately.

Tip! *The bibliography options may not format references as needed. Use the Insert Bibliography command to create citations more precisely.*

 View the video "Bibliography Options."

≡ References→Citations & Bibliography→Bibliography 📑

DEVELOP YOUR SKILLS: W4-D8

In this exercise, you will create a bibliography for the citations in your paper. You will title the page as Works Cited, as this chapter is following the MLA documentation style. Finally, you will edit an existing citation, update the bibliography, and format the paragraphs with double spacing.

1. Save your file as **W4-D8-InternetRevised**.

2. Position the insertion point at the end of the document and then press ⎡Ctrl⎤+⎡Enter⎤ to insert a new page for the bibliography.

3. Choose **Home→Paragraph→Center** ≡ and then type **Works Cited** and tap ⎡Enter⎤.

Insert and Update the Bibliography

4. Choose **References→Citations & Bibliography→Bibliography** 📑.

5. Choose **Insert Bibliography** at the bottom of the menu.

6. Scroll up to the second page, click the *Fowler* citation, and then click the **drop-down arrow**.

7. Choose **Edit Source** to open the dialog box.

8. Change the Day Accessed to **10** and click **OK**.

9. If the citation picked up the name of the web page, click the **drop-down arrow**, choose **Edit Citation**, check the **Title** checkbox, and click **OK**.

10. Scroll down to the Works Cited page and notice the date has not changed yet in the list.

11. Right-click anywhere in the list and choose **Update Field** from the menu that appears.

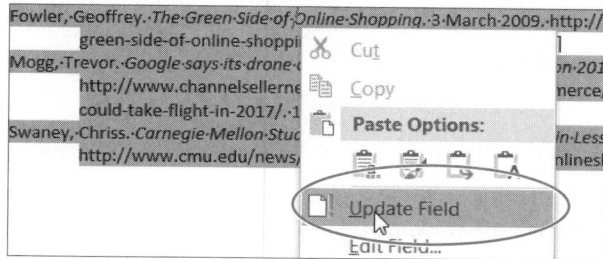

Notice the date accessed for the Fowler citation changed to 10 March 2016. Now you will format the list.

12. Select the bibliography list, but not the *Works Cited* title.

13. Choose **Home→Paragraph→Line and Paragraph Spacing** and then choose **2.0**.

14. Save the file.

Inserting Captions and a Table of Figures

You use captions to insert text associated with figures in a paper. The captions then become entries in the table of figures. Later, if you alter some of the captions, they will be updated when you regenerate the table of figures.

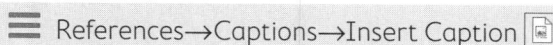 References→Captions→Insert Caption

View the video "Inserting Captions."

DEVELOP YOUR SKILLS: W4-D9

In this exercise, you will insert a file that contains PowerPoint slides from a presentation. You will add captions to the slides in preparation for creating a table of figures.

1. Save your file as **W4-D9-InternetRevised**.

2. Position the insertion point after the third footnote reference mark in the body of the document (not the footnote area) toward the bottom of the first page.

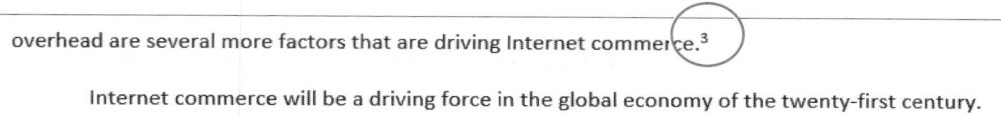

overhead are several more factors that are driving Internet commerce.[3]

Internet commerce will be a driving force in the global economy of the twenty-first century.

3. Tap [Enter] and then press [Ctrl]+[Enter] to insert a page break.

4. Choose **Insert→Text→Object** 🔲 **menu button** ▾→**Text from File**.

5. In the Insert File dialog box, navigate to your **Word Chapter 4** folder, choose **W4-D9-Evolution**, and click **Insert**.

6. If necessary, display formatting marks and then position the insertion point in the first blank line below the first slide.

7. Choose **References→Captions→Insert Caption** 🖼️.

The Caption dialog box should match the following illustration.

8. If *Figure 1* does not appear in the Caption text box, follow these steps; otherwise, go to the next step.

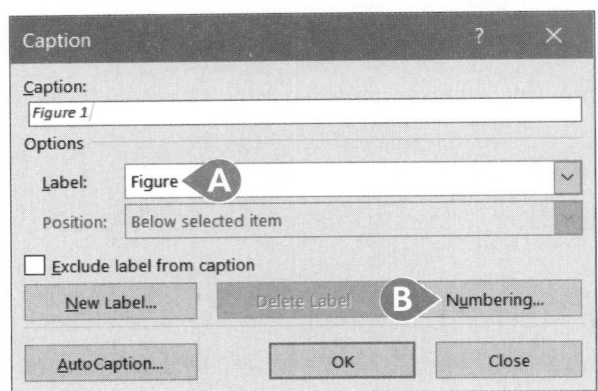
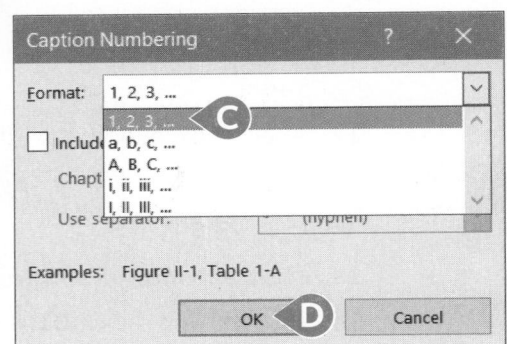

Ⓐ Click the **Label menu** button ▾ and choose **Figure**.

Ⓑ Click **Numbering** to open the Caption Numbering dialog box.

Ⓒ Click the **Format menu** button ▾ and then choose the **1,2,3, …** format.

Ⓓ Click **OK**.

9. If necessary, position the insertion point to the right of *Figure 1* in the Caption text box.

10. Tap [Spacebar], type **DOD and ARPANET**, and click **OK** to insert the caption.

The caption is placed at the left margin.

11. Choose **Home→Paragraph→Center** ≣.

12. Position the insertion point in the first blank line below the second slide.

13. Choose **References→Captions→Insert Caption** 🖼️.

14. Tap [Spacebar], type **NSF**, and click **OK**.

15. Center ≣ the caption.

16. Add these captions and center them:

Slide Number	Caption Text
3	MILNET and TCP/IP
4	First Graphical Browser
5	Netscape
6	Fourteen Years of Evolution
7	Delivery Drones?

Now you will edit a caption.

17. Return to **slide 2**, select *NSF*, and type **National Science Foundation** in its place.

18. Save the file.

Inserting a Table of Figures

Academic papers often include a table of figures at the front, which guides the reader to illustrations, charts, tables, and other figures. This is particularly helpful in long documents. The table entries conveniently function as hyperlinks if you are reading the document online.

≡ References→Captions→Insert Table of Figures 🗎

DEVELOP YOUR SKILLS: W4-D10

In this exercise, you will generate a table of figures from the captions you inserted earlier.

1. Save your file as **W4-D10-InternetRevised**.

2. Move the insertion point to the top of the document and press Ctrl + Enter to insert a page break.

3. Press Ctrl + Home to position the insertion point at the top of the new page and then type **Table of Figures** and tap Enter twice.

4. Format the heading you just typed with **Center, Bold, 16 pt**.

5. Place the insertion point in the blank line below the heading.

6. Choose **References→Captions→Insert Table of Figures** 🗎.

7. Follow these steps to complete the table:

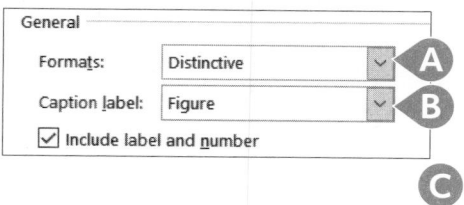

Ⓐ Choose **Distinctive** as the format.

Ⓑ If necessary, choose **Figure** as the caption label.

Ⓒ Click **OK**.

8. Save and then close the file.

Using Track Changes

The Track Changes feature is a useful tool when working with team members to collaborate on a report or other documents. You can electronically distribute copies to different members, and with Track Changes, the changes they make are marked. You can merge the changes from all copies into a single document, and then you can review each change and accept or reject it.

Turn Track Changes on or off.

Choose how you want changes to appear in the document.

Choose the types of revisions you want to see, such as formatting and insertions and deletions.

View all changes in a list.

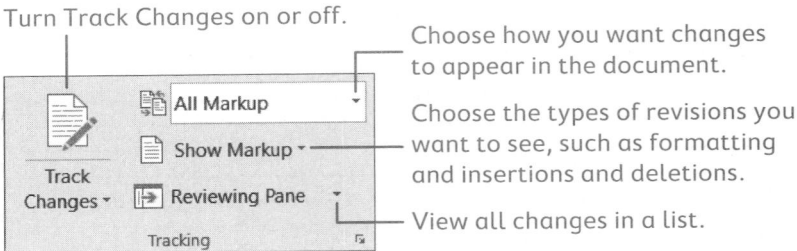

Reviewing Tracked Changes

It's easy to find and review changes to a document. When you review changes, you can jump from one change to the next, giving you the opportunity to accept or reject each change in order. You can also accept or reject all changes at once. After you accept or reject a change, the revision marks are removed.

This button accepts the currently selected change.

This button rejects the currently selected change.

These buttons navigate to the next or previous tracked change.

These options appear when you click the Accept menu button ▼. Similar choices are available on the Reject button.

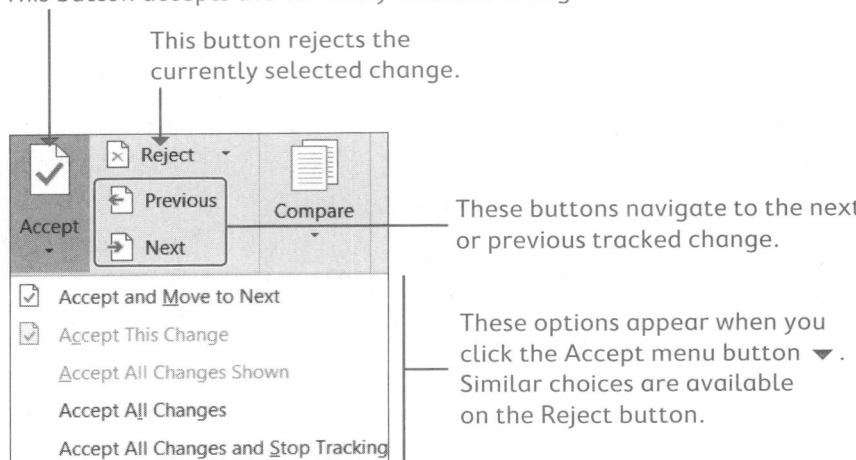

Self-Assessment

Check your knowledge of this chapter's key concepts and skills using the Self-Assessment in your ebook or eLab course.

Reinforce Your Skills

Format a Recycling Report

Kids for Change is planning a recycling fair, and you are creating a recycling report to be distributed during the fair. In this exercise, you will work with margins, indents, tabs, styles, and footers, and then you will format the body of the report into two columns. Finally, you will add a comment to the report.

1. Open **W4-R1-Recyc** from your **Word Chapter 4** folder and save it as **W4-R1-RecycRevised**.

   The document could use a little more white space in the left and right margins.

2. Choose **Layout→Page Setup→Margins** ▢ **→Normal**.

   This widens the left and right margins to 1". Now you'll indent the quote from the EPA to make it stand out on the page.

3. If necessary, choose **View→Show→Ruler**.

4. Position the insertion point in the **third paragraph**.

5. Place the mouse pointer on the **Left Indent** marker (the rectangle) and drag it to the **½"** mark and then place the mouse pointer on the **Right Indent** marker and drag it to the **6"** mark.

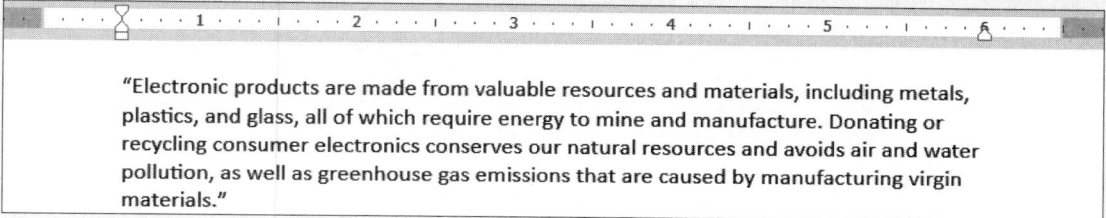

Now you will set tabs for a table indicating where people can drop off electronics they want to recycle.

6. Position the insertion point at the bottom of the document.

7. Type the following heading line using the default tab grid, tapping Tab where you see the arrows and tapping Enter at the end of the line:

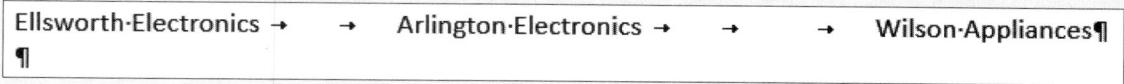

8. Select the heading line and choose **Home→Font→Bold** B .

9. Position the insertion point in the blank line below the heading line where you will set custom tabs.

10. Click the **tabs** box as many times as necessary to display the **Center Tab**. (It looks like an upside-down T.)

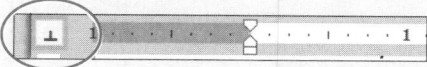

WORD

11. Perform these actions to set the following tab stops:
    - Click the **ruler** one tick mark to the right of **½"**.
    - Click one tick mark to the right of the **3"** mark.
    - Click at the **5½"** mark.

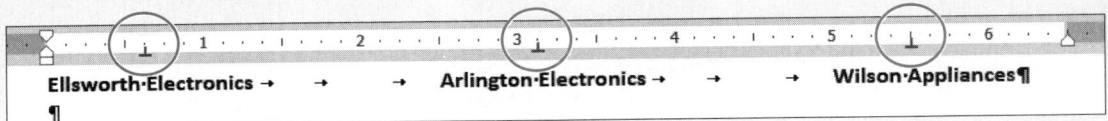

The center tab will cause the text to center around the tabs.

12. Type the following table, tapping [Tab] where you see the arrows and [Enter] where you see paragraph symbols.

Ellsworth·Electronics →	→	→	Arlington·Electronics →	→	→	Wilson·Appliances¶
→ Audio		→	Mobile·phones		→	Stoves¶
→ Car·&·GPS		→	Computers		→	Refrigerators¶
→ Mobile·phones		→	Digital·cameras		→	Freezers¶
→ Video·games		→	MP3·players		→	Washing·machines¶

Now you will adjust the last tab stop so it is better centered.

13. Select all lines to which the tab stop applies and drag the tab one tick mark to the right of **5½"**.

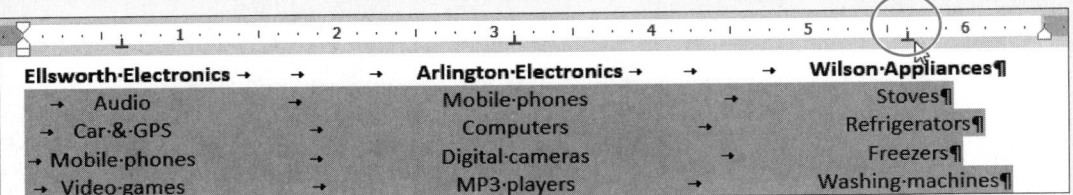

Now you will apply a style to the Report heading.

14. Position the insertion point in the heading line at the top of the page.

15. Choose **Home→Styles** and then click the **More** [▾] button to open the Styles gallery.

16. Choose **Title** from the gallery.

Add a Footer and a Comment

17. Choose **Insert→Header & Footer→Footer** [⬚] and choose **Edit Footer** at the bottom of the menu.

18. Type **Kids for Change** at the left side of the footer.

    Look at the ruler and notice that there are two custom tab stops: a center tab at 3¼" and a right tab at 6½".

19. Tap [Tab] twice.

    The insertion point is now aligned at a Right Tab.

20. Type **January, 2016** and then double-click in the body of the document to close the footer area.

Set the Document in Two Columns and Add a Comment

21. Select the body of the document from the first paragraph through the last bullet point.

22. Choose **Layout→Page Setup→Columns** 📊**→Two**.

   It might look better to keep the EPA quote together.

23. Position the insertion point in front of the line starting *The EPA provides*.

24. Choose **Layout→Page Setup→Breaks** 📑**→Column**.

   Now you will insert a comment.

25. Move to the top of the document and select *Recycling* in the heading.

26. Choose **Insert→Comments→Comment** 💬 and type the following in the comment balloon:

   `Jordan, please review and add any comments. I'll start on the`
   `Plastics Recycling section next.`

27. Save and close the file.

REINFORCE YOUR SKILLS: W4-R2

Create a Research Report

A Kids for Change volunteer has asked you to create another handout for the fair with an emphasis on acting locally. In this exercise, you will prepare the handout by inserting endnotes, footnotes, citations, a bibliography, and a table of figures.

1. Open **W4-R2-GlobalLocal** from your **Word Chapter 4** folder and save it as
   W4-R2-GlobalLocalRevised.

2. Position the insertion point after the period following *sales* in the second paragraph.

   > Kids for Change is a non-profit organization that helps minors in their
   >
   > social/community service within the mindset of "Think Globally, Act Locally."
   >
   > fundraisers, such as car washes, bake sales, and rain barrel sales. The kids are

3. Choose **References→Footnotes→Insert Endnote** 🔲.

   The insertion point jumps to the end of the document.

4. Type the following endnote text:

   `Proceeds go to organizations such as the local pantry.`

5. Position the insertion point after the comma following *construction* in the second to last line of the second paragraph.

   > fundraisers, such as car washes, bake sales, and rain barrel sales.
   >
   > community recycling drives, researching green construction, and
   >
   > garden program.

6. Choose **References→Footnotes→Insert Endnote** 🔲 and type the following endnote text:

   `Kids for Change successfully encouraged a local businessman to use`
   `green construction in a building addition.`

   You noticed a word is missing in the first endnote, so you will make that change now.

7. In the first endnote, position the insertion point to the left of *pantry*, type **food**, and tap Spacebar .

You've decided to convert the endnotes to footnotes so they will appear on the same page as the text they refer to.

8. Choose **References→Footnotes→dialog box launcher** ⌕ and then click the **Convert** button.

9. When the Convert Notes message appears, click **OK**; close the Footnote and Endnote dialog box.

Insert Citations

10. Choose **References→Citations & Bibliography** and then choose **MLA Seventh Edition** from the Style menu.

11. At the end of the fourth paragraph that begins with *The slogan*, position the insertion point between the word *activists* and the period and then tap Spacebar .

> practices – like environmental stewardship –
>
> of reference for some far-thinking activists.

12. Choose **References→Citations & Bibliography→Insert Citation** 🗊 and then choose **Add New Source**.

13. Enter the following information in the Create Source dialog box and then click **OK** when finished:
    - Type of Source: **Web Site**
    - Author: **Sathian, Sanjena**
    - Name of Page: **Think Locally, Act Globally**
    - Year: **2011**
    - Month: **July**
    - Day: **11**
    - Year Accessed: **2016**
    - Month Accessed: **September**
    - Day: **15**
    - Medium: **http://tyglobalist.org/onlinecontent/blogs /think-locally-act-globally/**

14. Position the insertion point following *Fluids* at the end of the fourth bullet point in the Jennifer King citation and then tap Spacebar .

> • Vehicle Fluids

15. Choose **References→Citations & Bibliography→Insert Citation** 🗊 and then choose **Add New Source**.

16. Enter the following information in the Create Source dialog box and then click **OK** when finished:
    - Type of Source: **Web Site**
    - Author: **King, Jennifer**
    - Name of Page: **How Does Car Pollution Affect the Environment & Ozone Layer?**
    - Year: (Leave blank.)
    - Month: (Leave blank.)
    - Day: (Leave blank.)

- Year Accessed: **2016**
- Month Accessed: **September**
- Day: **15**
- Medium: `http://homeguides.sfgate.com/car-pollution-affect`
  `-environment-ozone-layer-79358.html`

17. Position the insertion point at the end of the document between *Nations* and the period and then tap [Spacebar].

> ns (CFCs). And a treaty banning
>
> United Nations .

18. Choose **References→Citations & Bibliography→Insert Citation** ⬚ and then choose **Add New Source**.

19. Enter the following information in the Create Source dialog box and then click **OK** when finished:
- Type of Source: **Web Site**
- Author: `Trex, Ethan`
- Name of Page: `Whatever Happened to the Hole in the Ozone Layer?`
- Year: **2012**
- Month: **May**
- Day: **23**
- Year Accessed: **2016**
- Month Accessed: **September**
- Day: **15**
- Medium: `http://mentalfloss.com/article/30733/whatever`
  `-happened-hole-ozone-layer`

20. Position the insertion point at the end of the document, tap [Enter] twice, and then press [Ctrl]+[Enter] to insert a new page for the bibliography.

21. Choose **Home→Paragraph→Center** ☰, type `Works Cited`, and then tap [Enter].

22. Choose **References→Citations & Bibliography→Bibliography** ⬚.

23. Choose **Insert Bibliography** at the bottom of the menu.

Insert Captions

Now you will insert a document that contains slides from a PowerPoint presentation, and you will add captions to the slides.

24. If necessary, display the formatting marks and then position the insertion point on the blank line before the page break at the end of page 2 and tap [Enter].

25. Choose **Insert→Text→Object** ⬚ **menu button** ▾ **→Text from File**.

26. In the Insert File dialog box, navigate to your **Word Chapter 4** folder and double-click **W4-R2-YouCanHelp** to insert the file in your document.

27. Position the insertion point in the first blank line below the first slide.

28. Choose **References→Captions→Insert Caption** ⬚.

29. If *Figure 1* does not appear in the Caption text box, follow these steps; otherwise, go to the next step.
    - Click the **Label menu** button ▾ and choose **Figure**.
    - Click the **Numbering** button to open the Caption Numbering dialog box.
    - Click the **Format menu** button ▾ and then choose the **1,2,3, ...** format.
    - Click **OK**.

30. If necessary, position the insertion point to the right of *Figure 1* in the Caption text box, tap ⌷Spacebar⌷, type **Conduct a Home Survey**, and then click **OK**.

    Now you will center the caption.

31. Choose **Home→Paragraph→Center** ⊟ and then position the insertion point in the first blank line below the second slide.

32. Choose **References→Captions→Insert Caption** ▤.

33. Tap ⌷Spacebar⌷, type **Reduce Car Use**, and click **OK**.

34. **Center** ⊟ the caption.

35. Add the following captions and center them:
    - Slide 3: **Use Used**
    - Slide 4: **Think Before You Toss**

Insert a Table of Figures

36. Move the insertion point to the top of the document and insert a page break.

37. Move the insertion point to the top of the new page and type **Table of Figures** and tap ⌷Enter⌷ twice.

38. Format the heading with **Center**, **Bold**, **16 pt**.

39. Place the insertion point in the blank line below the heading.

40. Choose **References→Captions→Insert Table of Figures** ▤.

41. In the bottom-left of the Table of Figures dialog box, if necessary, change the format to **Distinctive**, ensure that the Caption Label says **Figure**, and then click **OK**.

42. Save and close the file.

REINFORCE YOUR SKILLS: W4-R3

Create an Organic Gardening Report

Kids for Change will host an organic gardening exhibition in the spring, and the planning is under way. You have already started a report about organic gardening for the exhibition. In this exercise, you will format the layout; apply styles; add a footer; and insert footnotes, endnotes, and citations. Then you will assign gardening duties to volunteers who will work in the Kids' garden starting in the spring. You will also create tabular columns and insert a comment.

1. Open **W4-R3-OrganicFood** from your **Word Chapter 4** folder and save it as **W4-R3-OrganicFoodRevised**.

    The left and right margins are a bit too wide in this document.

2. Choose **Layout→Page Setup→Margins** ▥ **→Normal**.

    Now you will apply Styles to the title and report headings.

3. Choose **Home→Styles→dialog box launcher** [⌐] to open the Styles task pane.

4. Apply the **Title** style to the document title and then apply the **Heading 1** style to the other two headings: *Plant Production* and *Support Organic Food*.

5. Close the Styles task pane.

   Next, you will format the first two main paragraphs in columns.

6. Select the text from the first paragraph through the *Plant Production* heading and its following paragraph.

7. If necessary, display the formatting marks.

8. Choose **Layout→Page Setup→Columns** [▤]→**Two**.

   When you select text and then apply columns, the section breaks are inserted automatically.

Insert Captions and a Table of Figures

9. Position the insertion point on the first blank line below the first picture.

10. Choose **References→Captions→Insert Caption** [▣].

11. Make sure **Figure** is in the Label field and the numbering format is **1,2,3, ...**.

12. If necessary, position the insertion point to the right of *Figure 1* in the Caption text box.

13. Tap [Spacebar], type **Build Healthy Soil**, click **OK**, and then center [≡] the caption.

14. Position the insertion point in the first blank line below the second picture.

15. Choose **References→Captions→Insert Caption** [▣].

16. Tap [Spacebar], type **Keep Chemicals Out of the Air, Water, Soil, and Our Bodies**, click **OK**, and then center [≡] the caption.

17. Follow the same process to place a caption titled **Taste Better and Truer Flavor** below the third picture.

18. Position the insertion point at the top of the document, press [Ctrl]+[Enter] to insert a page break, and then position the insertion point at the top of the new first page.

19. Type **Table of Figures**, tap [Enter] twice, and then apply **Center**, **Bold**, **16 pt** to the heading.

20. Position the insertion point on the blank line below the heading.

21. Choose **References→Captions→Insert Table of Figures** [▤].

22. In the dialog box, make sure **Distinctive** is the format style, ensure that the caption label is **Figure**, and click **OK**.

Add Footnotes and Citations

23. Position the insertion point to the right of the colon at the end of the first line below the *Support Organic Food* heading.

24. Choose **References→Footnotes→Insert Footnote** [AB¹] and type the following text in the footnote area:

    See Sustainable Plant Agriculture for details on growing organic plants.

    Now you will choose the style for citations.

25. Choose **References→Citations & Bibliography→Style menu button** ▾ and choose **MLA Seventh Edition**.

26. Position the insertion point between the period and the word *bay* at the end of the second paragraph following the *Plant Production* heading, and tap $\boxed{\text{Spacebar}}$.

> may conduct more sophisticated crop rotations and spread mulch or manure to keep weeds at bay .

27. Choose **References→Citations & Bibliography→Insert Citation** and then choose **Add New Source**.

28. Enter the following information and then click **OK** when finished:
- Type of Source: **Web Site**
- Author: **Mayo Clinic, Staff**
- Name of Web Page: **Nutrition and healthy eating**
- Year: (Leave blank.)
- Month: (Leave blank.)
- Day: (Leave blank.)
- Year accessed: **2016**
- Month Accessed: **October**
- Day Accessed: **15**
- Medium: **http://www.mayoclinic.org/healthy-lifestyle /nutrition-and-healthy-eating/in-depth/organic-food/art-20043880**

29. Position the insertion point at the end of the third bullet point below the *Support Organic Food* heading and tap $\boxed{\text{Spacebar}}$.

30. Choose **References→Citations & Bibliography→Insert Citation** and then choose **Add New Source**.

31. Enter the following information and then click **OK** when finished:
- Type of Source: **Web Site**
- Author: **Greene, Alan, Scowcroft, Bob, Tawse, Sylvia**
- Name of Web Page: **Top 10 Reasons to Support Organic in the 21st Century**
- Year: (Leave blank.)
- Month: (Leave blank.)
- Day: (Leave blank.)
- Year Accessed: **2016**
- Month Accessed: **October**
- Day Accessed: **15**
- Medium: **http://www.organic.org/articles/showarticle/article-206**

Insert a Bibliography and Add a Footer

32. Position the insertion point at the end of the document and press $\boxed{\text{Ctrl}}$+$\boxed{\text{Enter}}$ to insert a page break.

33. Choose **Home→Paragraph→Center** and then type **Works Cited** and tap $\boxed{\text{Enter}}$.

34. Choose **References→Citations & Bibliography→Bibliography** → and then choose **Insert Bibliography**.

35. Choose **Insert→Header & Footer→Footer**  and then scroll down and choose **Retrospect**.

36. Type **Kids for Change** in the author object (you may have to delete default text; print is automatically sets in all caps) and notice that the page number appears on the right side of the footer.

37. Double-click in the document to close the footer area.

38. Save and close the file.

Now you will finish creating the document for assigning gardening project duties.

39. Open **W4-R3-GardenProj** from your **Word Chapter 4** folder and save it as **W4-R3-GardenProjRevised**.

40. Position the insertion point at the end of the document and then type the following heading line, tapping ⬚Tab wherever you see an arrow and tapping ⬚Enter at the end of the line:

Volunteer	→	→	Vegetable	→	→	Assigned·Space·in·Feet¶
¶						

41. Format the heading line with **Bold** ⬚B.

Now you will set center tabs for the body of the table.

42. Position the insertion point on the blank line below the heading line.

43. Click the **tabs** box to display the **Center Tab** if necessary.

44. Place tabs in the following locations:

- Between the second and third tick marks from the left margin
- Between the second and third tick marks to the right of 1½"
- The first tick mark right of 3½"

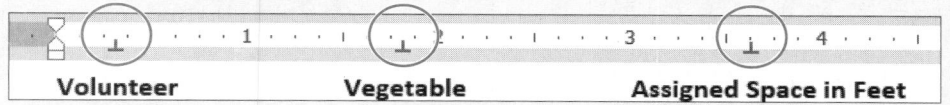

Remember, if you click a tab in the wrong position, you can drag it to the correct position or drag it down and off the ruler and try again.

45. Type the body of the table as shown, tapping ⬚Tab wherever you see an arrow and tapping ⬚Enter at the end of each line:

Volunteer	→	→	Vegetable	→	→	Assigned·Space·in·Feet¶
→ Kirk	→		corn	→		10·x·8¶
→Rachael	→		peas	→		8·x·4¶
→ Lena	→		green·beans	→		8·x·3¶
→ Bly	→		tomatoes	→		10·x·8¶
→Trevor	→		cauliflower	→		8·x·4¶
→ Neil	→		carrots	→		6·x·4¶

Now you will insert a comment.

46. Select the word *Change* in the heading, then choose **Insert→Comments→Comment** 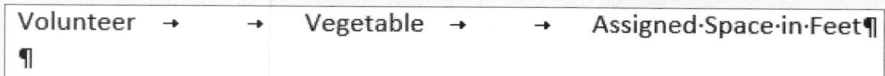 and type the following in the comment balloon: **Jeremy, please check the assigned spaces and make sure they are accurate.**

47. Save and close the file.

 Apply Your Skills

APPLY YOUR SKILLS W4-A1

Complete a Trip Report on Belize

You went on a familiarization trip to Belize for Universal Corporate Events and have written a trip report about the country. In this exercise, you will format the layout of the document, apply styles to headings, and insert footers and a comment.

1. Open **W4-A1-Belize** from your **Word Chapter 4** folder and save it as **W4-A1-BelizeRevised**.

    The text is pretty dense on this page. It needs to be lightened up to make it more readable. You will start by widening the margin areas.

2. Choose **Layout→Page Setup→Margins** 🔲**→Normal**.

    Headings allow the reader to scan a document for high-level concepts, adding to the document's readability. You will apply styles to the document's headings.

3. Apply the **Heading 2** style to the heading at the top of the document and then apply the **Intense Reference** style to the remaining headings: *Overview, Diving and Snorkeling, Ruins,* and *Artists.*

    Offsetting the text from the headings will also add to the document's readability.

4. Position the insertion point in the paragraph following the *Overview* heading.

5. Choose **Home→Paragraph→Increase Indent** 📇.

6. Use the same technique to indent the remaining paragraphs. (If you select all the paragraphs following the *Ruins* heading, you can indent them all at once.)

    Next you will set the document in columns. Shorter lines are easier to read because the eye doesn't have to travel far across the page before reading the next line.

7. Select the text starting with the *Overview* heading through the last paragraph following the *Ruins* heading. (Do not include the *Artists* paragraph.)

8. Format the selected text in a two-column layout.

    The Ruins *heading is at the bottom of the left-hand column. It would look better at the top of the right-hand column.*

9. Position the insertion point in front of the *Ruins* heading and insert a column break to move the heading to the top of the next column.

Insert a Footer

10. Add a footer using the **Ion (Dark)** option.

    You will use the objects in the footer for a different purpose than the labels specify.

11. Type **Universal Corporate Events** in the Document Title object and type **August, 2016** in the Author object. (The text will automatically convert to all upper case.)

12. Close the footer area.

Set Custom Tabs

Now you will add information about some of the talented local artists.

13. If necessary, turn on the ruler and display formatting marks.

14. Position the insertion point in the second blank line at the end of the document.

15. Type the following heading row, using the formatting marks as a guide; be sure to tap Enter at the end of the heading line:

16. **Bold** the heading row.

17. Position the insertion point in the line below the heading row and set custom **Center Tabs**.

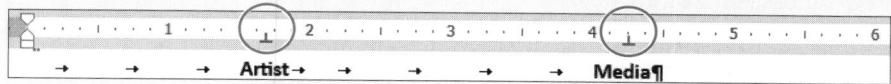

18. Type the rest of the table, using the formatting marks as a guide:

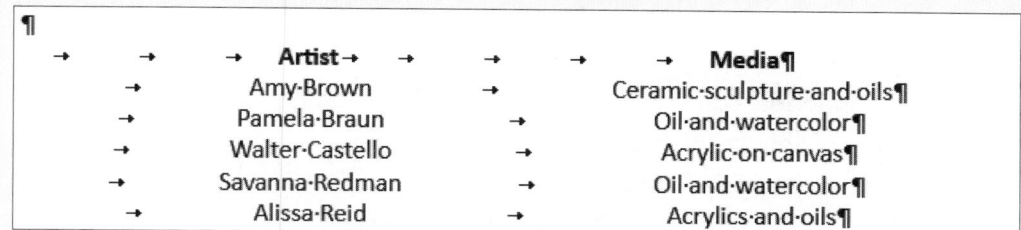

Now you'll add a comment to the document.

19. Select *Belize* in the document heading, insert a comment, and add the following text to the comment balloon:

> `Arrielle, since this is my first trip report, would you please check it out and add any comments you may have?`

20. Save and close the file.

APPLY YOUR SKILLS W4-A2

Report on Italian Tourist Sites

Because you used to live in Italy, Universal Corporate Events has asked you to create a report detailing some Italian tourist sites and providing tips on train travel in Italy. In this exercise, you will insert footnotes and citations and generate a bibliography for your report. Then you will add captions to pictures and create a table of figures.

1. Open **W4-A2-Italy** from your **Word Chapter 4** folder and save it as **W4-A2-ItalyRevised**.

2. Position the insertion point at the end of the first paragraph, after the period following *each*.

3. Insert this footnote: `Other major attractions are listed on this website`.

4. In the paragraph beginning *In the article*, position the insertion point after the period following the word *choices*.

5. Insert this footnote: `This article also offers advice on train schedules, buying tickets, and boarding your train.`

6. Set the report style to **MLA Seventh Edition** if necessary. (Hint: Go to the References tab.)

7. Position the insertion point after the *Colosseum* bullet point near the top of the document.

8. Tap Spacebar and enter the following source information:
   - Type of Source: **Web Site**
   - Author: **Rome Travel, Guide**
   - Name of Web Page: **Rome Italy travel guide**
   - Year: (Leave blank.)
   - Month: (Leave blank.)
   - Day: (Leave blank.)
   - Year Accessed: **2016**
   - Month Accessed: **May**
   - Day Accessed: **23**
   - Medium: **http://www.rome.info/**

9. Position the insertion point after *Pompeii* at the end of the fourth bullet point under the *Day Trips* heading.

10. Tap Spacebar and insert a citation with the following source information:
    - Type of Source: **Web Site**
    - Author: **Casura, Lily**
    - Name of Web Page: **Daytrips from Rome**
    - Year: (Leave blank.)
    - Month: (Leave blank.)
    - Day: (Leave blank.)
    - Year Accessed: **2016**
    - Month Accessed: **May**
    - Day Accessed: **23**
    - Medium: **https://www.tripadvisor.com.au/Guide-g187791-1296 -Rome _ Lazio.html**

11. Position the insertion point between *more* and the period at the end of the last paragraph.

12. Tap Spacebar and insert a citation with the following source information:
    - Type of Source: **Web Site**
    - Author: **Bakerjian, Martha**
    - Name of Web Page: **Italy Train Travel**
    - Year: (Leave blank.)
    - Month: (Leave blank.)
    - Day: (Leave blank.)
    - Year Accessed: **2016**
    - Month Accessed: **May**
    - Day Accessed: **23**
    - Medium: **http://goitaly.about.com/od/italytrainsportation/a /trains.html**

13. Position the insertion point at the end of the document, tap ⌷Enter⌷ twice, and insert a page break.

14. Type **Works Cited** as the heading and tap ⌷Enter⌷ twice.

15. Center the heading and then position the insertion point on the second blank line below the heading.

16. Insert a bibliography on the new page using the **Insert Bibliography** command.

17. Scroll to the top of the document, position the insertion point at the end of the *Colosseum* bullet point, and then tap ⌷Enter⌷ twice.

Next, you will insert pictures of Rome's major attractions.

18. Choose **Insert→Text→Object** ⬚ **menu button** ▾**→Text from File**.

19. Navigate to your **Word Chapter 4** folder and insert **W4-A2-RomePics**.

20. Positioning the insertion point on the first blank line below each picture, insert and center the following captions using the **1,2,3, ...** number format and the **Figure** label:
    - Picture 1 caption: **Trevi Fountain**
    - Picture 2 caption: **St. Peter's Square**
    - Picture 3 caption: **Spanish Steps**
    - Picture 4 caption: **Colosseum**

21. Insert a page break at the top of the document, and at the top of the new page, type **Table of Figures** and tap ⌷Enter⌷ twice.

22. Format the heading with **Center**, **Bold**, **16 pt**.

23. Position the insertion point on the blank line below the heading and generate the table of figures using the **Formal** format and **Figure** as the caption label.

24. Save and close the file.

APPLY YOUR SKILLS: W4-A3

Create Travel Reports

Universal Corporate Events is planning a Bangkok getaway for one of its clients, and you've been asked to research travel within Bangkok and interesting sites to see. In this exercise, you will format the layout of your report and add footnotes, citations, a bibliography, captions, and a table of figures. You have also been asked to write a sales report listing Universal Corporate Events' pending deals. You will work with margins and custom tabs, add header text, and insert a comment.

1. Open **W4-A3-Bangkok** from your **Word Chapter 4** folder and save it as **W4-A3-BangkokRevised**.

   The document needs some formatting to make it more readable. First you will add some styles to the document.

2. Select the title at the top of the document and apply the **Heading 1** style.

3. At the bottom of the page, apply the **Subtle Reference** style to the bulleted items.

4. If necessary, display the ruler and then position the insertion point in the second paragraph.

5. Position the mouse pointer on the Left Indent marker (the rectangle) on the ruler and drag it to the **½"** mark.

6. Drag the **Right Indent** marker to the **6"** mark.

7. Select text beginning with *Bangkok's Chao Praya Express Boats* down through *Myanmar* and then set the text in two columns.

   Next, you will insert pictures, add captions, and generate a table of figures.

8. Insert the **W4-A3-BNKPics** file at the end of the document.

9. Positioning the insertion point on the blank line below each picture and then insert and center the following captions using the **1,2,3, ...** number format and the **Figure** label:
   - Picture 1 caption: **Chatuchak Market**
   - Picture 2 caption: **Pak Klong Talat**
   - Picture 3 caption: **Bangkok Farmers Market**
   - Picture 4 caption: **Pratunam Market**

10. Insert a page break at the top of the document, and at the top of the new page, type **Table of Figures** and tap Enter twice.

11. **Center** and **Bold** the heading and then generate the table of figures on the blank line below the heading using the **Formal** format and **Figure** as the caption label.

Insert Footnotes and Citations

12. Position the insertion point in the first line of the first paragraph on page 2, to the right of *markets*, and insert this footnote:

    ---
    [1] Floating markets piled high with tropical fruits and vegetables provide an exciting shopping adventure.

13. Position the insertion point in the same line, this time to the right of *temples*, and insert this footnote:

    [2] Don't miss Wat Traimit's Golden Buddha or Wat Po's famous Reclining Buddha.

14. Choose the **MLA Seventh Edition** style for citations.

15. Insert a citation at the end of the indented paragraph at the top of the document and add the following source information:
    - Type of Source: **Web Site**
    - Author: **Thyberg, David**
    - Name of Web Page: **Bangkok Travel Tips**
    - Year: (Leave blank.)
    - Month: (Leave blank.)
    - Day: (Leave blank.)
    - Year Accessed: **2016**
    - Month Accessed: **September**
    - Day Accessed: **20**
    - Medium: **http://getawaytips.azcentral.com/bangkok-travel-tips -1945.html**

16. Insert a citation at the end of the second column next to *Myanmar* and add the following source information:
    - Type of Source: **Web Site**
    - Author: **Rowthorn, Chris**
    - Name of Web Page: **Take the boat out of Bangkok**
    - Year: **2012**
    - Month: **April**
    - Day: **13**
    - Year Accessed: **2016**
    - Month Accessed: **September**
    - Day Accessed: **20**
    - Medium: **http://www.bbc.com/travel/story/20120413-take-the-boat-out-of-bangkok**

17. Insert a citation at the end of the fourth bullet point at the end of page 2, and add the following source information:
    - Type of Source: **Web Site**
    - Author: **Hauglann, Maria Wulff**
    - Name of Web Page: **6 Markets in Bangkok You Should Not Miss**
    - Year: **2014**
    - Month: **July**
    - Day: **15**
    - Year Accessed: **2016**
    - Month Accessed: **September**
    - Day Accessed: **20**
    - Medium: **http://nerdnomads.com/6-markets-in-bangkok-you-should-not-miss**

    Now you will generate a Bibliography.

18. Insert a page break at the end of the document, type the title, **Works Cited**, center it on the page, and then tap Enter twice.

19. Generate the Bibliography on the first blank line below the title using the **Insert Bibliography** command.

20. Save and close the file.

Create a Sales Report

21. Open **W4-A3-SalesRpt** from your **Word Chapter 4** folder and save it as **W4-A3-SalesRptRevised**.

22. Change the margins to the preset **Normal** style.

23. Apply the **Title** style to *Sales Report* heading.

24. Position the insertion point on the second blank line at the end of the text, type **Pending Deals**, and format it with the **Heading 1** style.

25. Position the insertion point on the blank line below the *Pending Deals* heading and tap ⌈Enter⌉.

26. Use the ruler to set **Left** tabs at **2½"** and **4½"** and then type the following table, bolding the heading line:

Company	**Destination**	**Dates**¶
Rogers·Electronics	Hawaii	Oct·2·through·7¶
Wilson·Construction	Miami	Oct·11·through·17¶
Milltown·Mortgage	New·York·City	Oct·20·through·27¶

27. Select the entire table and move the 2½" tab to **2¼"** and the 4½" tab to **4¾"**.

Insert a Header and a Comment

28. Insert a header using the **Blank** style and type **Universal Corporate Events** as the header.

29. Select **Report** in the heading line and insert the following comment:

    Emma, do you have any prospects to add to the list?

30. Save and close the file.

 Extend Your Skills

These exercises challenge you to think critically and apply your new skills. You will be evaluated on your ability to follow directions, completeness, creativity, and the use of proper grammar and mechanics. Save files to your chapter folder. Submit assignments as directed.

W4-E1   That's the Way I See It

You are an intern working in the corporate offices of a major grocery store chain. Your manager has asked you to research the pros and cons of reusable shopping bags compared to plastic bags. Start a new document and name it **W4-E1-ShopBags**.

Type a creative title and an original introductory paragraph for the paper and include two footnote comments in the paragraph. Using an Internet search, find two sources who favor reusable shopping bags and two sources who do not. Pull information from these sources and compare the two sides of the issue using a two-column tabular table listing the pros and cons. Insert citations at the end of each source and generate a bibliography from the citations. Add a page number in the footer area. Insert two pictures you find on the Internet representing reusable bags and plastic bags. Add captions to the pictures and create a table of figures. Use styles and indenting, and widen the left and right margins to make your report more readable. Save the file.

W4-E2   Be Your Own Boss

As the owner of Blue Jean Landscaping, you plan to hold a rose-pruning seminar for your customers. Research pruning techniques and create a report of your research results to hand out to customers at the event. Start a new document and name it **W4-E2-RoseSeminar**. Type a creative title and an original introductory paragraph and include a footnote comment in the paragraph. Cite three different sources in your report and generate a bibliography of your citations. Insert a header that includes your company name. Use styles and indents, and increase the margin width to add to the paper's readability. Set the body of the report in a two-column format and insert a column break, if necessary, to balance the columns. Include a comment at the top of the document asking your partner to review the document and make any suggestions she likes. Save the file.

W4-E3   Demonstrate Proficiency

The owner of Stormy BBQ is proud to serve free-range beef. He wants his employees to understand the benefits of using natural, grass-fed beef so they can discuss the idea with customers. He has asked you to prepare a report that he can distribute to all employees. Start a new document and name it **W4-E3-GrassFed**.

Conduct online research on the benefits of using free-range, natural beef. Type a creative title and an original introductory paragraph that includes two commentary footnotes. Cite three sources who favor free-range beef. Generate a bibliography for the citations. Use indents and styles, and adjust the margins to make your paper more readable. Add a footer that includes the company name and page numbers.

Insert **W4-E3-Cattle** as a Text from File object into your report. Copy and paste the pictures into your report, insert creative captions for the pictures, and generate a table of figures. Create a two-column tabular table listing the disadvantages of feedlot cattle (fossil fuel–intensive, for example) versus the advantages of grass-fed cattle (higher in omega-3 fatty acids, for example). Include at least five rows in the table. Insert a comment at the top of the document asking your admin to look it over for spelling and grammar errors. Save the file.

Glossary

alignment Horizontal placement of text relative to the left and right margins of a cell or a page, where text is left-, right-, or center-aligned; or vertical placement of text relative to the top and bottom margins of a cell or page, where text is top-, middle-, or bottom-aligned

AutoComplete A feature that offers to complete the typing for you when it recognizes certain words or phrases

AutoCorrect Predefined text used for automatically correcting common spelling and capitalization errors; can be customized with user-defined entries

block style Letter style that aligns all parts of a letter with the left margin

captions Text added to a figure to describe or explain the figure; text formatted as captions can be used to create a table of figures

cell A box formed by the intersection of a row and column table, in which information is entered and displayed

character styles Styles used to format a single word or selected group of words with text formatting such as font, bold, font size, etc.; no paragraph formatting is included

citation(s) Reference to a source used in a document; contains information to locate the source

column break Manual break of a newsletter column at a specified location; moves text at the break point to the top of the next column

columns Vertical arrangement of cells in a table

Comment Electronic note attached to a document

contextual tab(s) Hidden Ribbon tabs that only appear when certain types of objects, such as pictures or tables, are selected

cropping Cutting off parts of a picture to make certain other elements stand out or to remove unwanted elements

demote To increase text indentation so it appears farther away from the left margin and, if numbered or bulleted, reduces the numbering or bulleting level to the next lower level

endnotes Notes that appear at the end of the document body in which the reference is made; numbered sequentially throughout a document

file format Type of method used for storing information in a file; each application normally has a special file format it uses by default

footer Text that usually, but not always, is located toward the bottom of a document and that repeats on all (desired) pages within a document

footnotes Notes that appear at the bottom of the page on which the reference is made; footnote numbers can start with 1 on each page or can be numbered sequentially throughout a document or individually

formatting marks Special characters such as spaces, tabs, and paragraph symbols made visible when the Show/Hide button is turned on

handles Small squares or circles on selected graphics that can be dragged to make the graphic larger or smaller

header Text that usually, but not always, is located toward the top of a document, slide, or handout and that repeats on all (desired) pages, slides, or handouts within a document or presentation

hyperlink A block of text or a graphic that jumps you to another location in a file, to another file, or to a web page when clicked

insert control Appears when the mouse pointer is outside the table, pointing between columns or rows; click the control to insert a new column or row at that location

line spacing Vertical space between lines of text

Live Preview Feature that allows you to you point at formatting commands on the Ribbon to show how the format would appear on selected text and objects without actually applying the format

manual page break Forced page break created by pressing [Ctrl]+[Enter] or choosing Insert→Pages→Page Break

MLA style *Modern Language Association Handbook for Writers of Research Papers*; shows how to work with sources in expository writing

object Refers to graphical images such as shapes, WordArt, and pictures

orientation Direction in which the page is turned for viewing and printing, either portrait (short edge on top) or landscape (long edge on top)

paragraph In Word, this is created anytime you tap Enter ; it can consist of several lines, a single line, or a blank line

paragraph style Style used to format a paragraph or selected group of paragraphs; may include character formatting

promote To reduce text indentation so it appears closer to the left margin and, if numbered or bulleted, to elevate the item to the next higher level of bullet

rows Horizontal groups of cells in a table

section break Position in a document where one section ends and another begins because page formatting is going to change, such as from single- to multiple-column layout

select To drag over the desired text with the mouse pointer or other techniques; used in preparation for tasks such as formatting and copying; also called *highlighting*

shapes Tool for drawing graphics in documents

Show/Hide button Feature that displays nonprinting characters such as tabs, spaces, and paragraph symbols onscreen for easy access.

smart tag Context-sensitive option button that appears on menus to provide easy access to commonly used tasks

SmartArt Predesigned graphic designs added to a document; categories include List, Hierarchy, Pyramid, and so forth

sort Process used to arrange data in a specific order, such as alphabetic, numeric, by date, or in ascending or descending order

split To create two or more table cells from a single table cell

style Group of formats that allows you to quickly apply multiple formats at once; when a style is modified, all text with the style applied is updated with the modification; also known as Quick Styles

tab stops Preset stops along the horizontal ruler set at every half inch to control and align text; can be customized

table styles Styles applied to table cells, rows, or columns to ensure formatting consistency

template A preformatted document or workbook layout used as the basis for new documents to maintain consistency among documents and save the user time and that usually contains text, paragraph, table, graphical, and other types of formatting

theme Preset formatting selections you can apply to a document or presentation; include colors, graphic elements, and fonts all designed to work well together and quickly achieve the look of a professional design

title bar Appears across the top of the application window, contains the name of the application and the name of the current file

Track Changes Feature that, when activated, marks each change to a document; the changes can then be reviewed and either accepted or rejected

view Onscreen layout of a document optimized for performing specific tasks or for determining how the document will look in final form

Word Wrap Automatic moving of text to a new line when it extends beyond the right margin of a paragraph; eliminates the need to tap Enter at the end of lines within a paragraph

WordArt Feature for creating stylized formatting of text; often used for headings

Index

Note: Index entries ending in "V" indicate that a term is discussed in the video referenced on that page.

NOTES

NOTES

NOTES

NOTES

NOTES

NOTES

TEACHER'S EDITION

WORLD
HISTORY

Elisabeth Gayor Ellis   **Anthony Esler**

PEARSON

Boston, Massachusetts   **Chandler, Arizona**   **Glenview, Illinois**   **New York, New York**

This work is protected by United States copyright laws and is provided *solely for the use of teachers and administrators* in teaching courses and assessing student learning in their classes and schools. Dissemination or sale of any part of this work (including on the World Wide Web) will destroy the integrity of the work and is *not* permitted.

PEARSON

ISBN-13: 978-0-13-330714-6
ISBN-10: 0-13-330714-X

INVESTIGATE! Step two of the Mastery System allows you to investigate the topic story through a number of engaging features as you learn the content.

>> **Active Classroom Strategies** integrated in the daily lesson plans help to increase in-class participation, raise energy levels and attentiveness, all while engaging in the story. These 5-15 minute activities have you use what you have learned to draw, write, speak, and decide.

>> **Interactive Primary Source Galleries:** Use primary source image galleries throughout the lesson to see, analyze, and interact with images that tie to the topic story content.

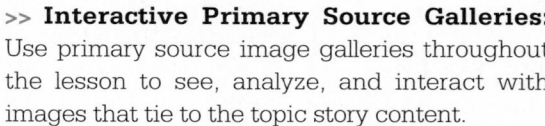

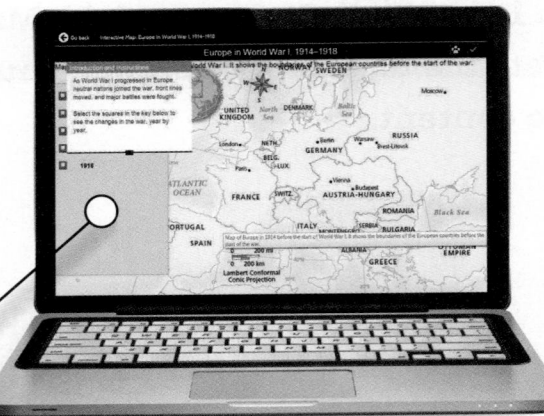

>> Feel like you are a part of the story with **interactive 3-D models**.

>> Continue to investigate the topic story through **dynamic interactive maps**. Build map skills while covering the essential standards.

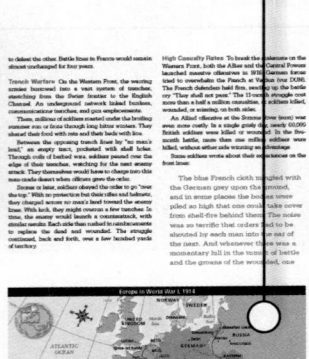

>> Learn content by reading narrative text online or in a printed Student Edition.

Synthesize: Practice Knowledge and Skills

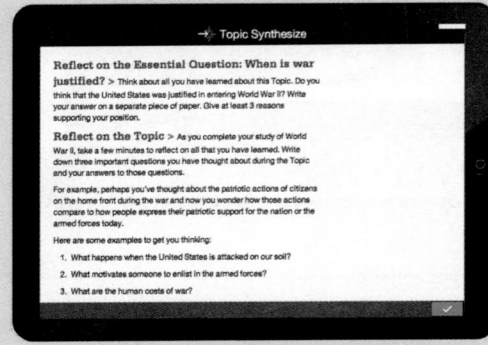

SYNTHESIZE!

In step three of the Mastery System, pause to reflect on what you learn and revisit an essential question.

DEMONSTRATE! The final step of the Mastery System is to demonstrate understanding of the text.

PEARSON
realize™

>> **The digital course on Realize!** The program's digital course on Realize puts engaging content, embedded assessments, instant data, and flexible tools at your fingertips.

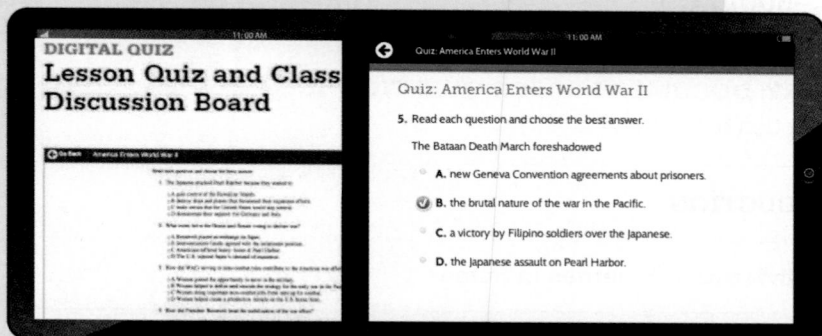

>> **Assessment**. At the end of each lesson and topic, demonstrate understanding through Lesson Quizzes, Topic Tests, and Topic Inquiry performance assessments. The System provides remediation and enrichment recommendations based on your individual performance towards mastery.

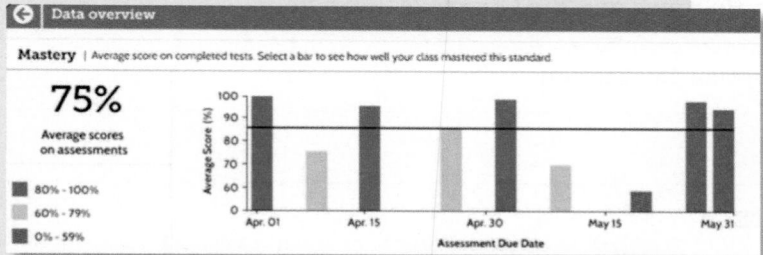

>> **Class and Data** features on Realize make it easy to see your mastery data.

Digital Course Content

Digital Course Content

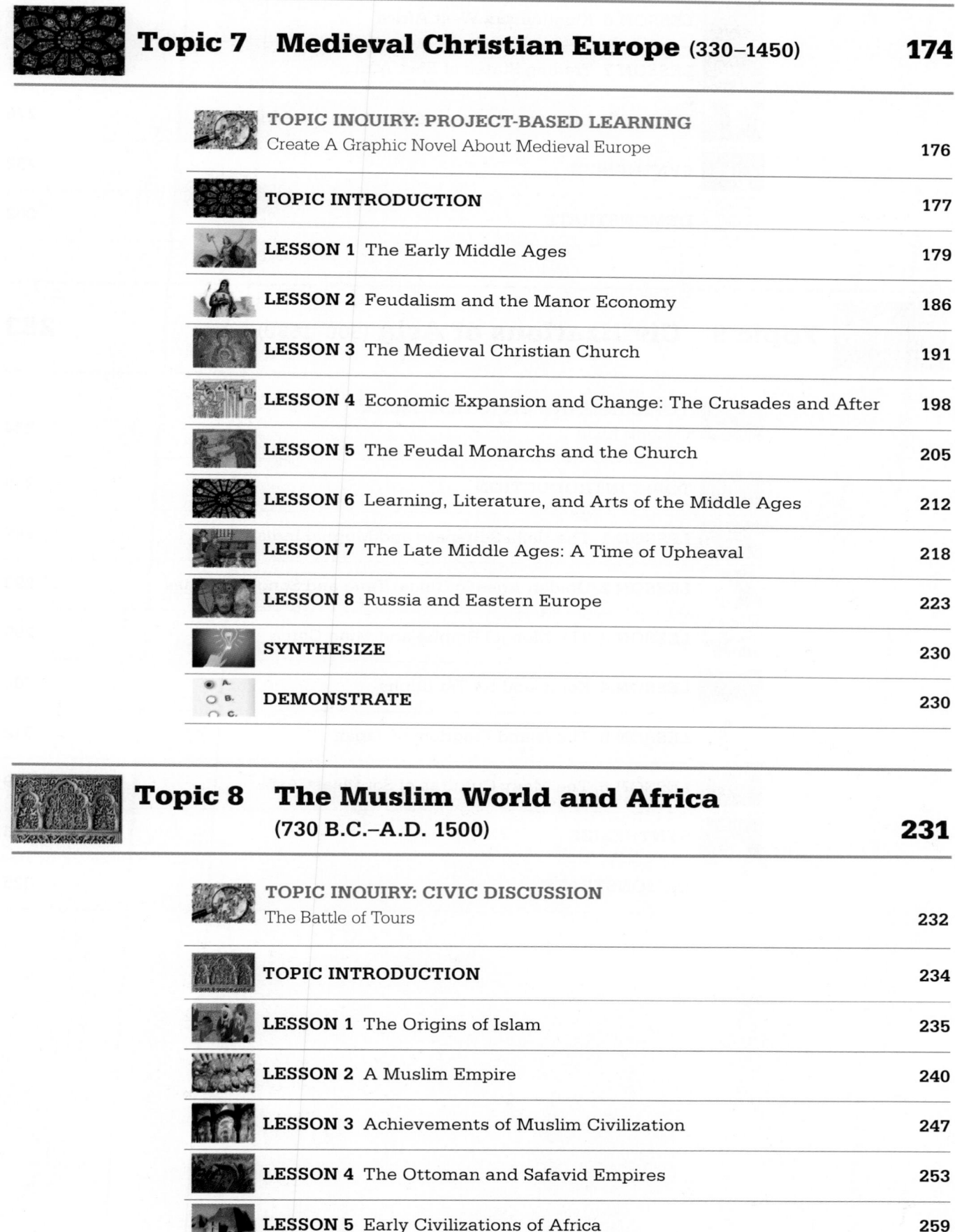

Digital Course Content

Digital Course Content

Digital Course Content

Topic 18 World War II (1930–1945)   694

Digital Course Content

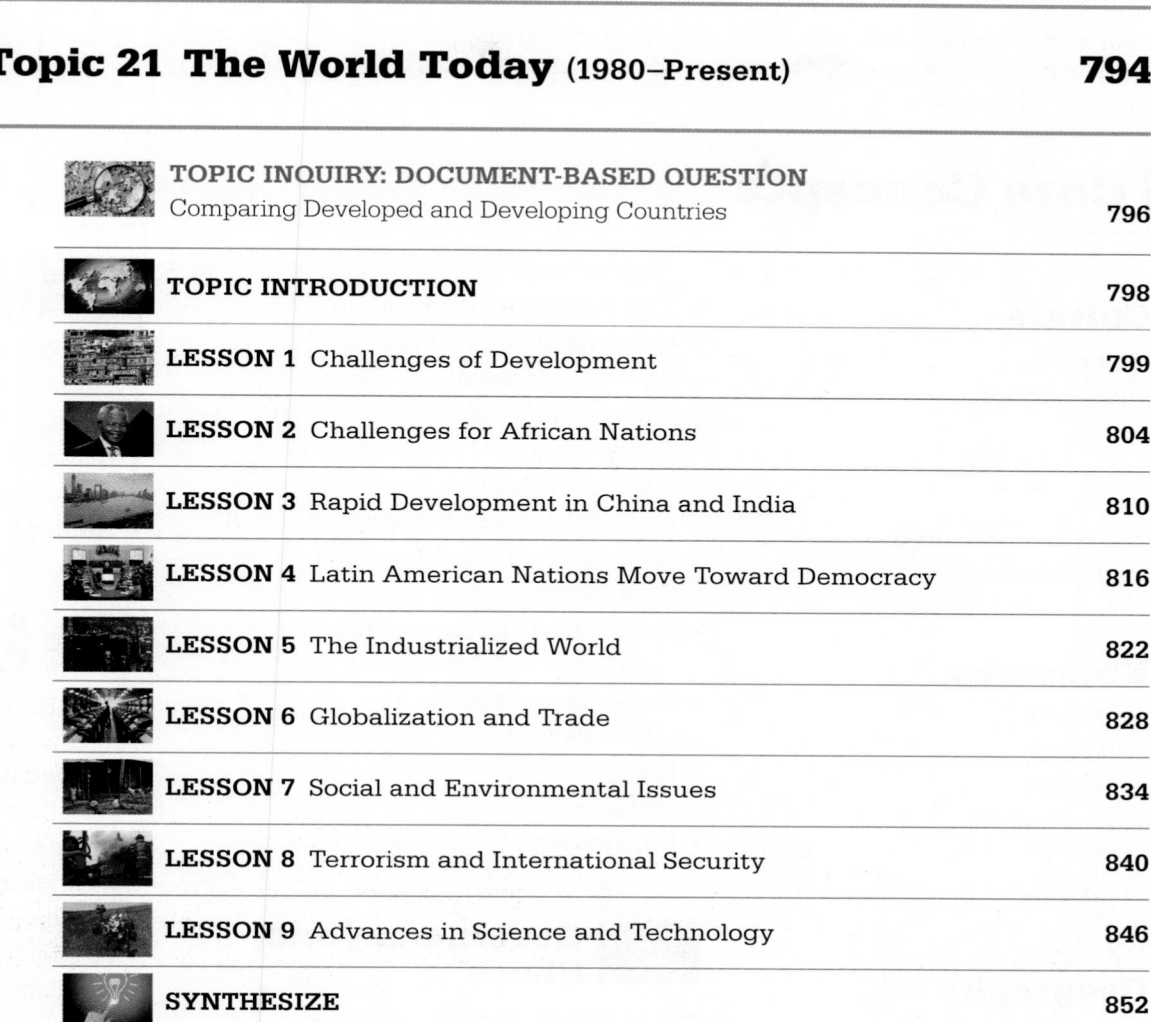

Digital Resources

Many types of digital resources help you investigate the topics in this course. You'll find biographies, primary sources, maps, and more. These resources will help bring the topics to life.

 ## Core Concepts

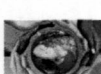 ### Culture
- What Is Culture?
- Families and Societies
- Language
- Religion
- The Arts
- Cultural Diffusion and Change
- Science and Technology

 ### Economics
- Economics Basics
- Economic Process
- Economic Systems
- Economic Development
- Trade
- Money Management

 ### Geography
- The Study of Earth
- Geography's Five Themes
- Ways to Show Earth's Surface
- Understanding Maps

- Earth in Space
- Time and Earth's Rotation
- Forces on Earth's Surface
- Forces Inside Earth
- Climate and Weather
- Temperature
- Water and Climate
- Air Circulation and Precipitation
- Types of Climate
- Ecosystems
- Environment and Resources
- Land Use
- People's Impact on the Environment
- Population
- Migration
- Urbanization

 ### Government and Civics
- Foundations of Government
- Political Systems
- Political Structures
- Conflict and Cooperation
- Citizenship

 ### History
- How Do Historians Study History?
- Measuring Time
- Historical Sources
- Archaeology and Other Sources
- Historical Maps

 ### Personal Finance
- Your Fiscal Fitness: An Introduction
- Budgeting
- Checking
- Investments
- Savings and Retirement
- Credit and Debt
- Risk Management
- Consumer Smarts
- After High School
- Taxes and Income

 ## Landmark Supreme Court Cases

- *Korematsu* v. *United States*
- *Marbury* v. *Madison*
- *McCulloch* v. *Maryland*
- *Gibbons* v. *Ogden*
- *Worcester* v. *Georgia*
- *Dred Scott* v. *Sandford*
- *Plessy* v. *Ferguson*
- *Schenck* v. *United States*
- *Brown* v. *Board of Education*
- *Engel* v. *Vitale*

- *Sweatt* v. *Painter*
- *Mapp* v. *Ohio*
- *Hernandez* v. *Texas*
- *Gideon* v. *Wainwright*
- *Wisconsin* v. *Yoder*
- *Miranda* v. *Arizona*
- *White* v. *Regester*
- *Tinker* v. *Des Moines School District*
- *Roe* v. *Wade*

- *Baker* v. *Carr*
- *Grutter* v. *Bollinger*
- *Edgewood* v. *Kirby*
- *Texas* v. *Johnson*
- *National Federation of Independent Businesses et al.* v. *Sebelius et al.*
- *Mendez* v. *Westminster* and *Delgado* v. *Bastrop*

Interactive Primary Sources

- Code of Hammurabi
- Psalm 23
- The Republic, Plato
- Politics, Aristotle
- Edicts, Asoka
- Analects, Confucius
- First Letter to the Corinthians, Paul
- The Quran
- The Magna Carta
- Travels, Ibn Battuta
- The Destruction of the Indies, Bartolomé de Las Casas
- Mayflower Compact
- English Petition of Right
- English Bill of Rights
- Two Treatises of Government, John Locke
- The Spirit of Laws, Baron de Montesquieu
- The Social Contract, Jean-Jacques Rousseau
- The Interesting Narrative of the Life of Olaudah Equiano
- "Give Me Liberty or Give Me Death," Patrick Henry
- "Remember the Ladies," Abigail Adams
- Common Sense, Thomas Paine
- Declaration of Independence
- Virginia Declaration of Rights
- Virginia Statute for Religious Freedom, Thomas Jefferson
- "To His Excellency, General Washington," Phillis Wheatley
- Articles of Confederation
- Anti-Federalist Papers
- The Federalist No. 10, James Madison
- The Federalist No. 39, James Madison
- The Federalist No. 51
- The Federalist No. 78, Alexander Hamilton
- Northwest Ordinance
- Iroquois Constitution
- Declaration of the Rights of Man and the Citizen
- Farewell Address, George Washington
- Mexican Federal Constitution of 1824
- State Colonization Law of 1825

- Law of April 6, 1830
- Debate Over Nullification, Webster and Calhoun
- Turtle Bayou Resolutions
- Democracy in America, Alexis de Tocqueville
- 1836 Victory or Death Letter from the Alamo, Travis
- Texas Declaration of Independence
- Declaration of Sentiments and Resolutions
- "Ain't I a Woman?," Sojourner Truth
- Uncle Tom's Cabin, Harriet Beecher Stowe
- "A House Divided," Abraham Lincoln
- First Inaugural Address, Abraham Lincoln
- Declaration of Causes: February 2, 1861
- Emancipation Proclamation, Abraham Lincoln
- Gettysburg Address, Abraham Lincoln
- Second Inaugural Address, Abraham Lincoln
- "I Will Fight No More Forever," Chief Joseph
- How the Other Half Lives, Jacob Riis
- The Pledge of Allegiance
- Preamble to the Platform of the Populist Party
- Atlanta Exposition Address, Booker T. Washington
- The Jungle, Upton Sinclair
- Hind Swaraj, Mohandas Gandhi
- The Fourteen Points, Woodrow Wilson
- Two Poems, Langston Hughes
- Four Freedoms, Franklin D. Roosevelt
- Anne Frank: The Diary of a Young Girl, Anne Frank
- Charter of the United Nations
- Universal Declaration of Human Rights
- Autobiography, Kwame Nkrumah
- Inaugural Address, John F. Kennedy
- Silent Spring, Rachel Carson
- "I Have a Dream," Martin Luther King, Jr.
- "Letter From Birmingham Jail," Martin Luther King, Jr.
- "Tear Down This Wall," Ronald Reagan
- "Freedom From Fear," Aung San Suu Kyi
- "Glory and Hope," Nelson Mandela

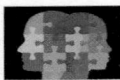 Biographies

- Abigail Adams
- John Adams
- John Quincy Adams
- Samuel Adams
- James Armistead
- Crispus Attucks
- Moses Austin
- Stephen F. Austin
- James A. Baker III
- William Blackstone
- Simón Bolívar
- Napoleon Bonaparte
- Chief Bowles
- Omar Bradley
- John C. Calhoun
- César Chávez
- Wentworth Cheswell
- George Childress
- Winston Churchill
- Henry Clay
- Bill Clinton
- Jefferson Davis
- Martin De León
- Green DeWitt
- Dwight Eisenhower
- James Fannin
- James L. Farmer, Jr.
- Benjamin Franklin
- Milton Friedman
- Betty Friedan
- Bernardo de Gálvez
- Hector P. Garcia
- John Nance Garner
- King George III
- Henry B. González
- Raul A. Gonzalez, Jr.
- Mikhail Gorbachev
- William Goyens

- Ulysses S. Grant
- José Gutiérrez de Lara
- Alexander Hamilton
- Hammurabi
- Warren Harding
- Friedrich Hayek
- Jack Coffee Hays
- Patrick Henry
- Adolf Hitler
- Oveta Culp Hobby
- James Hogg
- Sam Houston
- Kay Bailey Hutchison
- Andrew Jackson
- John Jay
- Thomas Jefferson
- Lyndon B. Johnson
- Anson Jones
- Barbara Jordan
- Justinian
- John F. Kennedy
- John Maynard Keynes
- Martin Luther King, Jr.
- Marquis de Lafayette
- Mirabeau B. Lamar
- Robert E. Lee
- Abraham Lincoln
- John Locke
- James Madison
- John Marshall
- George Marshall
- Karl Marx
- George Mason
- Mary Maverick
- Jane McCallum
- Joseph McCarthy
- James Monroe
- Charles de Montesquieu

- Edwin W. Moore
- Moses
- Benito Mussolini
- José Antonio Navarro
- Chester A. Nimitz
- Richard M. Nixon
- Barack Obama
- Sandra Day O'Connor
- Thomas Paine
- Quanah Parker
- Rosa Parks
- George Patton
- John J. Pershing
- John Paul II
- Sam Rayburn
- Ronald Reagan
- Hiram Rhodes Revels
- Franklin D. Roosevelt
- Theodore Roosevelt
- Lawrence Sullivan Ross
- Haym Soloman
- Antonio Lopez de Santa Anna
- Phyllis Schlafly
- Erasmo Seguín
- Juan N. Seguín
- Roger Sherman
- Adam Smith
- Joseph Stalin
- Raymond L. Telles
- Alexis de Tocqueville
- Hideki Tojo
- William B. Travis
- Harry Truman
- Lech Walesa
- Mercy Otis Warren
- George Washington
- Daniel Webster

- Lulu Belle Madison White
- William Wilberforce
- James Wilson
- Woodrow Wilson
- Lorenzo de Zavala
- Mao Zedong

21st Century Skills

- Identify Main Ideas and Details
- Set a Purpose for Reading
- Use Context Clues
- Analyze Cause and Effect
- Categorize
- Compare and Contrast
- Draw Conclusions
- Draw Inferences
- Generalize
- Make Decisions
- Make Predictions
- Sequence
- Solve Problems
- Summarize
- Analyze Media Content
- Analyze Primary and Secondary Sources
- Compare Viewpoints
- Distinguish Between Fact and Opinion
- Identify Bias
- Analyze Data and Models

- Analyze Images
- Analyze Political Cartoons
- Create Charts and Maps
- Create Databases
- Read Charts, Graphs, and Tables
- Read Physical Maps
- Read Political Maps
- Read Special-Purpose Maps
- Use Parts of a Map
- Ask Questions
- Avoid Plagiarism
- Create a Research Hypothesis
- Evaluate Web Sites
- Identify Evidence
- Identify Trends
- Interpret Sources
- Search for Information on the Internet
- Synthesize
- Take Effective Notes
- Develop a Clear Thesis
- Organize Your Ideas

- Support Ideas With Evidence
- Evaluate Existing Arguments
- Consider & Counter Opposing Arguments
- Give an Effective Presentation
- Participate in a Discussion or Debate
- Publish Your Work
- Write a Journal Entry
- Write an Essay
- Share Responsibility
- Compromise
- Develop Cultural Awareness
- Generate New Ideas
- Innovate
- Make a Difference
- Work in Teams
- Being an Informed Citizen
- Paying Taxes
- Political Participation
- Serving on a Jury
- Voting

Atlas

- United States: Political
- United States: Physical
- World Political
- World Physical
- World Climate
- World Ecosystems
- World Population Density
- World Land Use
- North Africa and Southwest Asia: Political
- North Africa and Southwest Asia: Physical
- Sub-Saharan Africa: Political
- Sub-Saharan Africa: Physical
- South Asia: Political
- South Asia: Physical
- East Asia: Political

- East Asia: Physical
- Southeast Asia: Political
- Southeast Asia: Physical
- Europe: Political
- Europe: Physical
- Russia, Central Asia, and the Caucasus: Political
- Russia, Central Asia, and the Caucasus: Physical
- North America: Political
- North America: Physical
- Central America and the Caribbean: Political
- Central America and the Caribbean: Physical
- South America: Political
- South America: Physical
- Australia and the Pacific: Political
- Australia and the Pacific: Physical

Creating an Active Classroom

This Social Studies program places a strong emphasis on

Inquiry in the form of

- Document-Based Questions
- Project-Based Learning
- Civic Discussions

Each inquiry strand requires students to formulate their own arguments based on evidence. To support this learning approach, the program integrates **Active Classroom strategies** throughout each lesson. These strategies encourage students to begin building their own arguments and collecting evidence about the past and present at even the earliest stages of a lesson.

You can use these strategies to help students participate in their own learning as you call upon them to

- draw
- write
- speak
- decide

You'll find a rich variety of these strategy suggestions throughout both the Teacher's Edition and online **Teacher Support** for each lesson.

ACTIVE CLASSROOM STRATEGIES

ACTIVITY NAME	HOW TO ACTIVATE
Quickdraw	· Pair students and give them 30 seconds to share what they know about a concept or Key Term by creating a symbol or drawing.
Graffiti Concepts	· Ask students to reflect on the meaning of a concept or idea and create a visual image and/or written phrase that represents that concept. Allow approximately 3–5 minutes. · Next ask students to post their "graffiti" on the board or on chart paper and ask students to look at all the various responses. · Next discuss similarities and differences in the responses as a group.
Word Wall	· Ask students to chose one of the Key Terms for the lesson and create a visual image with a text definition. Allow approximately 3–5 minutes. · Ask students to post their words on the board or on chart paper and ask students to look at all the various responses. · Discuss similarities and differences in the responses as a group. · Pick a few favorites and post them on the class "Word Wall" for the year.
Cartoon It	· Ask students to make a quick drawing of one compelling image from this lesson on a piece of paper. · Next ask students to turn their drawing into a political cartoon that illustrates a key concept or main idea from the lesson by adding a text caption or text "bubbles." · Ask students to share their cartoons with a partner or within small groups.
Wallpaper	· Ask students to review information they have learned in a topic and design a piece of "wallpaper" that encapsulates key learnings. · Then have students post their wallpaper and take a "gallery" walk noting what others have written and illustrated in their samples.
Quick Write	· Ask students to write what they know about a key idea or term in 30 seconds.
Make Headlines	· Have students write a headline that captures the key idea in a map, photo, timeline, or reading. · Ask students to share their headline with a partner.
Circle Write	· Break into groups and provide a writing prompt or key question. · Have students write as much as they can in response to the question or prompt for 1 minute. · Next have students give their response to the person on their right. That person should improve or elaborate on the response where the other person left off. · Continue to pass each response to the right until the original response comes back to the first person. · Each group then reviews all the responses and decides which is the best composition and shares that with the larger group.

Creating an Active Classroom

ACTIVE CLASSROOM STRATEGIES

ACTIVITY NAME	HOW TO ACTIVATE
Write 1-Get 3 (or Write 5-Get 4)	· Ask a question with multiple answers, such as: What are 4 key characteristics of _____ (a dictator)? What are the 5 key causes of _____? · Have students write down 1 response and then go around the room asking for 3 other responses. If they think a response is correct, ask them to write it down. · Have students keep asking and writing until they have 3 more responses on their page. · Have students share and discuss responses with the class.
Sticky Notes	· Ask students to spend three minutes jotting down their response to a critical thinking question on a sticky note. · Ask students to work in pairs and share their responses. · Next ssk students to post their sticky notes on the board or on chart paper and read all the notes. · Discuss similarities and differences in the responses as a group.
Connect Two	· Select 10 to 12 words or phrases you think are important for students to know prior to reading a selection. · List the words on the board. · Ask students to "Connect Two" or choose two words they think might belong together, and state the reason. "I would connect _____ and _____ because _____." Consider posting their Connect Two statements on the board. · As students read the text they should look for evidence to support or refute their Connect Two statements.
Conversation With History	· Ask students to choose one of the people mentioned or pictured in the text and write down a question they would like to ask that person if they could. · Next ask students to write what they think that person would say in response and then what they would say in response to that.
Walking Tour	· Post passages from a reading around the room. · Ask small groups to tour the room and discuss each passage. · Summarize each passage as a class. · Alternatively, assign each small group to a passage and have them summarize that passage for the rest of the class.
Audio Tour	· Ask students to work in pairs. Have the first student give the second a verbal "tour" of a map or graph or infographic. · Have the second student give the first an explanation of what the graphic shows.

ACTIVE CLASSROOM STRATEGIES

ACTIVITY NAME	HOW TO ACTIVATE
My Metaphor	· Post the following metaphor on the board: This (map, timeline, image, primary source) shows that _____ is like _____ because _____. · Ask students to fill in the metaphor prompt based on their understanding of the source.
Act It Out	· Choose an image in the lesson and ask students to think about one of the following questions as appropriate to the image: · What may have happened next in this image? · What may have happened just before this image? · What do you think the people in this image are thinking? · What do you think the people in this image are saying to each other?
If Photos/Images/Art Could Talk	· Ask the following questions about an image in the course: What do you think the person in this photo would say if they could talk? What's your evidence?
See-Think-Wonder	· Ask students to work in pairs. · Ask them to look at an image, map, or graph and answer these questions: · What do you see? · What does that make you think? · What are you wondering about now that you've seen this? · Have students share their answers with the class.
A Closer Look	· Project a map or image on the board and divide it into four numbered quadrants. · Have students count off from 1 to 4 into four small groups. Have each group look closely at the part of the image in their quadrant. · Have each small group report on what they observed and learned as a result of their focus on this part of the image.
Take a Stand	· Ask students to take a stand on a yes-or-no or agree/disagree critical thinking question. · Ask students to divide into two groups based on their answer and move to separate areas of the classroom. · Ask students to talk with each other to compare their reasons for answering yes or no. · Ask a representative from each side to present and defend the group's point of view. · Note: you can adapt this activity to have students take their place on a continuum line from 1 to 10 depending on how strongly they agree or disagree.

ACTIVE CLASSROOM STRATEGIES

ACTIVITY NAME	HOW TO ACTIVATE
Rank It	· List a group of items/concepts/steps/causes/events on the board. · Ask students to rank the items/steps . . . according to X criteria (which is most important, which had the greatest impact . . . most influential, essential, changed, affected). · Ask students to provide a justification for the ranking decisions they made. · Then ask students to work in pairs to share their rankings and justifications. · Poll the class to see if there is agreement on the ranking. OR · Place stickies on the board with key events from the lesson or topic. · Break students into small groups and ask each group to go up and choose the sticky with what they think is the most significant event. · Ask the group to discuss among themselves why they think it is most significant. · Ask one person from each group to explain why the group chose that event.
Sequence It	· Place key events from a lesson or topic on sticky notes on the board. · Ask students to place the events in chronological order. · You could do this activity with multiple groups in different parts of the classroom.
PMI Plus/Minus/Interesting	· Place students in groups and give each group a 3-column organizer with headings Plus/Minus/Interesting for recording responses. · Ask students to analyze a text or examine an issue and then answer these three questions in their organizer: 1. What was positive about this text/issue? 2. What was negative about this text/issue? 3. What was interesting about this text/issue?

Celebrate Freedom

■ PRINT STUDENT EDITION

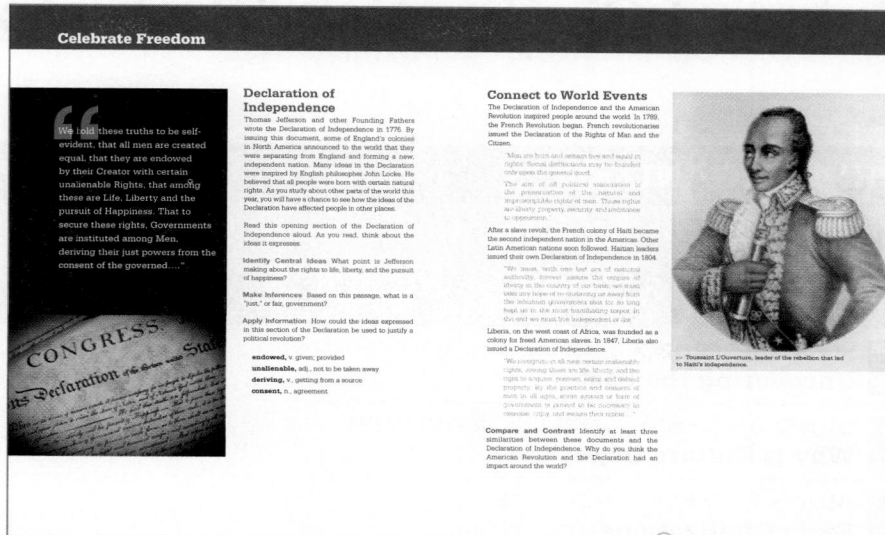

Objective 1: Understand the intent, meaning, and importance of the Declaration of Independence; 2: Recite the opening text from the Declaration of Independence

Quick Instruction

Using these materials, students can prepare for Celebrate Freedom Week by thinking about the importance of the Declaration of Independence. The materials will help you make links between the Declaration and your course of study.

Aa Vocabulary Development: Before students recite the words from the Declaration, review key terms such as "endowed," "unalienable," "deriving," and "consent." Ask students to compose a sentence using each word. Then have students paraphrase the excerpt from the Declaration, putting the ideas into their own words.

Have students recite the key section from the Declaration of Independence, "We hold these truths…" to each other or as a whole class.

Identify Central Ideas *that everyone is entitled to these rights*

Make Inferences *a government that is based on the will of the people*

Apply Information *Government gets its power from the people, so if it does not follow the wishes of the people, the people have the right to change the government, even if it means by revolution.*

Further Instruction
Connect to World Events

Plan Have students read the documents from France, Haiti, and Liberia. Ask them to look for phrases and terms that are similar in each of these documents, including the Declaration of Independence.

Explore Organize students into three groups and assign one historical document to each group. Have students paraphrase their document to be sure they understand it. Then have the groups share their understandings with the class.

Communicate Ask students to think about the rights mentioned in these documents. What does each right mentioned refer to? For example, what does the "right to security" mean? the "right to property?" Why do they think each of these is so important that it is specifically called out in these documents?

Compare and Contrast *Similarities include: government is based on mutual consent of the people and is charged with preserving their rights; people are free and equal, and are entitled to certain rights such as life, liberty, and property; people have the right to resist oppression.*

Possible answer: The Declaration inspired other people to recognize their rights and the idea that Americans could be successful in their revolution encouraged people around the world to gain these rights for themselves.

■ ADDITIONAL LESSON RESOURCES

- Print student text
- Declaration of Independence
- United States Constitution
- Pledge of Allegiance to the U.S. Flag
- Celebrate Freedom Resources

Origins of Civilization (Prehistory–300 B.C.)

TOPIC 1 ORGANIZER	PACING: APPROX. 6 PERIODS, 3 BLOCKS
	PACING
Connect	1 period
MY STORY VIDEO **Uncovering the Past**	10 min.
DIGITAL ESSENTIAL QUESTION ACTIVITY **Why is Culture Important?**	10 min.
DIGITAL TIMELINE ACTIVITY **Early Civilizations**	10 min.
TOPIC INQUIRY: PROJECT-BASED LEARNING **Create an Early Civilizations Video Game**	20 min.
Investigate	1–3 periods
TOPIC INQUIRY: PROJECT-BASED LEARNING **Create an Early Civilizations Video Game**	Ongoing
LESSON 1 Learning About Our Past	30–40 min.
LESSON 2 The Neolithic Revolution	30–40 min.
LESSON 3 Civilization Begins	30–40 min.
Synthesize	1 period
DIGITAL ACTIVITY **Reflect on the Essential Question and Topic**	10 min.
TOPIC INQUIRY: PROJECT-BASED LEARNING **Create an Early Civilizations Video Game**	20 min.
Demonstrate	1–2 periods
DIGITAL TOPIC TEST **Origins of Civilization**	10 min.
TOPIC INQUIRY: PROJECT-BASED LEARNING **Create an Early Civilizations Video Game**	20 min.

 TOPIC INQUIRY: PROJECT-BASED LEARNING

Create an Early Civilizations Video Game

In this Topic Inquiry, students will work in teams to create a video game that illustrates how culture impacted early peoples' progression through the stages of civilization. Learning about culture and its impact on each stage of development of early civilizations will deepen students' understanding of how the cultures of hunter-gatherers and Neolithic civilizations led to the establishment of complex river valley civilizations. It will also contribute to their understanding of the Topic Essential Question: Why is culture important?

STEP 1: CONNECT
Develop Questions and Plan the Investigation

Launch the Project and Generate Questions
Display the Entry Event, which is a fictional letter from an archaeological society. Direct students to critical points in the letter. Tell students that for this project, they will learn why culture is important, based on how early people shifted from simple nomadic bands to complex river valley civilizations.

Divide the class into teams of four to six students. Explain that each team will research, plan, and create a video game about the development of early cultures/civilizations. Tell students that their video games should include goals and a way for players to advance through each of the three stages. It must allow every player to perform as the leader of people at each of three stages, from hunter-gatherer bands, to Neolithic villages, to people of river valley civilizations. The choices will allow players and their team to either advance to the next stage or decline.

Then project and review with students, the bullet-point list of key features of the three stages of culture and civilizations that students will study. Point out that they can use the key features of each stage to design "worlds" or game environments for their video games.

Finally, provide time for teams to discuss the bullet-point list. Have them brainstorm ideas about features of Stone Age hunter-gatherer clans, Neolithic villages, and river valley civilizations that led them to advance, or establish the next stage.

Resources
- Project Tracker
- Entry Event
- Rubric for an Early Civilizations Video Game
- Need to Know Questions
- Work in Teams tutorial
- Student Instructions

STEP 2: INVESTIGATE
Apply Disciplinary Concepts and Tools

Collect Source Material
Prepare for Project Work Have students complete the 21st Century Skills Tutorial *Search for Information on the Internet* to review tips for finding information online. Then, guide a discussion of tips from the tutorial, emphasising key ideas. Project the list of possible sources and invite students to suggest why they might be useful. You may want to project one of the sites such as the Smithsonian National Museum of Natural History, Early Stone Age Tools, as an example of a site with information and features targeted to a particular stage of human development.

If time allows, have students begin researching early civilizations. Remind students to complete assigned tasks and fill in the Project Tracker as tasks are completed. Remind students that when searching online or in other sources, they should choose sources that are related to the features of the culture or civilizations that lead toward its development to the next level of civilization. Tell them to use the *Need to Know Questions* to help focus their research and notes. Encourage students to consult the readings and activities for this Topic, along with conducting research to try to answer all of the questions, or as many as possible with the information available.

Create and Edit Flowcharts and Content Charts
Project the first page of the *Information Organizer: Early Civilizations Video Game*. Explain that this flowchart will help them organize and design the structure, story, and mechanics of their video game. Tell students to add, delete, and rename shapes in the flowchart to fit their ideas.

Suggestion: To chunk the game design, encourage students to create a modified flowchart to design each of the three stages or levels, for which they will create "worlds" or environments that exemplify each of the three early culture/civilization(s) in their video games.

Resources
- 21st Century Skills Tutorial *Search for Information on the Internet*
- Information Organizer

STEP 3: SYNTHESIZE
Evaluate Sources and
Use Evidence to Formulate Conclusions

Build Your Video Game

Build Your Video Game Project the second page of the *Information Organizer: Early Civilization Video Game*. Explain that this chart will help guide their team to describe each part of their game. Tell students to complete one chart for each aspect of their video game, including its player goals and options, stories, mechanics, rules, and the media elements they will use. Once they have designed all aspects of their game, have them return to the flowchart(s) to begin building their video game. Stress that their video game should have options with rewards that lead to advancement through stages or levels to win the game and that there can be multiple ways to win. Remind them that their goal is to focus on the relationship between culture and the progression of early peoples, through stages, to the establishment of river valley civilizations.

Once students have finished researching, creating, and editing narratives and have planned how to design their video game using the chart, have them work as a team to build their video game with a free software program such as *Unity 3d* [https://unity3d.com/unity/download]. Remind students that they are not required to use Unity 3d and may use any video game building tool you approve to create their video game.

Suggestion: Before students get into these final stages, you may wish to show them some free video games with similar themes, such as *Civilization V*.

Write a Conclusion

Tell students they should write a thorough conclusion that clearly describes some of the important things they learned from creating a video game about the three stages of culture/civilization. Remind students that their conclusions should demonstrate an understanding of why culture is important. Project and discuss questions to help students focus their conclusions. Think about how the information you used in your game showed what made each culture distinctive, and helped the culture progress.

- Information Organizer

STEP 4: DEMONSTRATE
Communicate Conclusions
and Take Informed Action

Present Your Early Civilizations Video Game

Before students present their video game, suggest that they review the 21st Century Skills Tutorial: Give an Effective Presentation. Have students project their video game and invite their audience to observe as they demonstrate their video game and explain their findings and conclusions. Remind students to ask their audience to share their reactions to their video game work. Allow time for questions and answers, and if time allows, for teams to play each other's games.

Reflect on the Project

After students have finished creating and presenting their video games, provide your assessment, and help them identify what worked well and where improvements could be beneficial, so they can incorporate feedback to use for future projects. When all teams have completed their video games and presentations, schedule time for meetings to allow teams to reflect on what they have learned and how their group worked together as a team. Then, have all team members complete the **Self Assessment.**

Resources

- 21st Century Skills Tutorial: Give an Effective Presentation
- Self Assessment

Origins of Civilization (Prehistory–300 B.C.)

The cultural advances and development of early peoples led first to the establishment of farming villages, and later to prosperous river valley civilizations. Cultural features led early peoples to progress from less organized ways of life to prosper in complex civilizations. Eventually, advances in agriculture, technology, and other areas led to changes in culture, which led to the establishment of river valley civilizations. How did the cultures of river valley civilizations impact the world?

■ CONNECT

MY STORY VIDEO	DIGITAL ESSENTIAL QUESTION ACTIVITY	DIGITAL TIMELINE ACTIVITY
Uncovering the Past	**Why is Culture Important?**	**Early Civilizations**

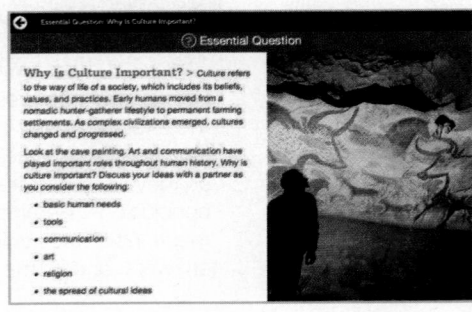

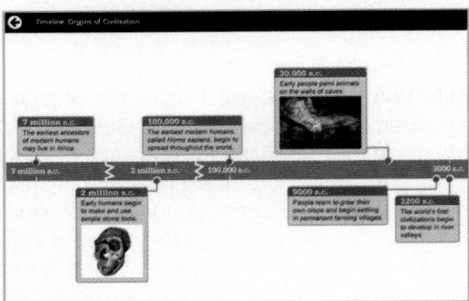

Watch a video about an archaeological dig.

Check Understanding Where are the archaeologists working? *(They are working in an ancient Mayan site in the Yucatan Peninsula of present-day Mexico.)*

Draw Conclusions What do the archaeologists in this video find rewarding about their profession? *The hard work notwithstanding, they enjoy learning about past human behavior and helping to connect the past with the present. They strive to help people today better understand their heritage.)*

⇅ FLIP IT!

Assign the My Story video

Ask students to think about the Essential Question for this Topic: Why is culture important? Have students share their ideas with the class.

Evaluate Impact How does this cave painting reflect the importance of culture? *(Sample answer: It shows that people took time to make art, felt a desire to communicate ideas, had religious beliefs, and developed tools to not only support basic needs, but to make paintings.)*

Predict Consequences How might farming change the lives and culture of hunter-gatherers? *(Sample answer: Farming might eliminate the need to roam to find food and result in permanent settlements. This might lead to more complex societies and culture as a result of new tools; technologies; economic, political, and religious structures.)*

Display the timeline showing the key periods of early human development. Students studying this Topic will learn about these periods and more, but this timeline will provide a framework into which they can compare early cultures and understand features that caused effects on other cultures.

D Differentiate: Extra Support How many years are there between when *Homo sapiens* began to spread throughout the world and when people learned to grow their own crops? *(91,000 years; Homo sapiens began to spread throughout the world around 100,000 B.C. and people learned to grow their own crops around 9,000 B.C.)*

Check Understanding What event on the timeline provides evidence that art has been important to humans since early times. *(Sample answer: The cave paintings found as early as 30,000 B.C.)*

Topic Inquiry
Launch the Topic Inquiry with students after introducing the Topic.

Learning About Our Past

Supporting English Language Learners

Use with Digital Text 1, **Studying Prehistory.**

Learning Strategies

Explain to students that connecting information they already know with new information they encounter can help them learn more easily. For this activity, tell students they will use prior knowledge to understand the meanings of the *Studying Prehistory* key terms in English. Then guide students through one of the following activities according to their English proficiency level.

Beginning Write and display the word *prehistory* for students. Ask students to think quietly for a moment about how the meanings of *pre-* and *history* combine to form the meaning of the target word, *prehistory*. Encourage students to share their understandings of both words with partners. Then read the first paragraph of *Studying Prehistory* aloud to students, focusing on the meaning of the term *prehistory*. Ask students to contribute any additional prior knowledge they have about the meaning of the word *prehistory*. Review the definition of *prehistory* with students.

Intermediate Write and display the word *prehistory* for students. Ask students to think about how the meanings of *pre-* and *history* combine to form the meaning of the target word, *prehistory*. Have students share their ideas with the class. Then have students keep their definition of *prehistory* in mind as you read *Studying Prehistory* aloud.

Advanced Have students brainstorm what they know about *prehistory*. Encourage students to explore the meaning of each word part, what part of human history to which it refers, and its meaning as it relates to the study of history. Working as a group, have students develop a basic definition of the term based on what they shared during the brainstorm. Write and display the definition for students' reference as they read *Studying Prehistory* silently.

Advanced High Have students work with a partner to brainstorm what they know about *prehistory*. Encourage students to explore the meaning of each word part, what part of human history to which it refers, and its meaning as it relates to the study of history. Then instruct each set of partners to share their ideas with another set, forming a group of four students. Following this activity, have students read *Studying Prehistory* silently.

Use with Digital Text 3, **Discoveries in Africa and Beyond.**

Learning Strategies

Read *Discoveries in Africa and Beyond* aloud to the class. Write and display the following words for students to use with the activities below. Have them complete one activity according to their level of English proficiency.

• humans, cities, countries, footprints, bones, tools

Beginning Write and display the words above. Have students copy them. Then provide students with a basic definition for each of the six words. Use each word in a simple but meaningful phrase. Write each phrase and ask students to copy them into their notebooks. Assign one phrase to each student and support students as they practice saying their phrase aloud.

Intermediate Write and display the words above. Have students copy them. Then instruct students to use bilingual dictionaries to find a basic definition for each word. Have students help develop simple but meaningful phrases using each word. Write each phrase and ask students to copy them into their notebooks. Have students take turns practicing saying the phrases aloud. Assist students with pronunciation as necessary.

Advanced Write and display the words above. Have students copy them. Then instruct pairs of students to work together to use English dictionaries to find a basic definition for each word. Have partners write simple but meaningful sentences using each word in their notebooks. Have students take turns speaking the sentences aloud to their partners. Assist students with pronunciation as necessary.

Advanced High Write and display the words above. Have students copy them. Then instruct students to use English dictionaries to find a basic definition for each word. Have students write simple but meaningful sentences using each word in their notebooks. Have students take turns speaking the sentences aloud to their partners. Assist students with pronunciation as necessary.

▣ Differentiate Instruction

Use the Differentiated Instruction notes throughout the lesson plan to support the varied skill sets, levels of readiness, and interests in the mixed-ability classroom.

Challenge These notes include suggestions for expanding the activity for advanced students.

On-Level These notes include suggestions for modifying the activity to address different interests or learning styles.

Extra Support These notes include ideas for providing more scaffolding or reading spuport.

Special Needs These notes provide ideas for adapting instruction to support the needs of various special needs students.

■ NOTES

Learning About Our Past

Objectives

Objective 1: Learn how scholars study the historical past.

Objective 2: Find out how anthropologists investigate the period of prehistory.

Objective 3: Understand how discoveries in Africa and beyond have influenced anthropologists' views about early humans and their ancestors.

LESSON 1 ORGANIZER		PACING: APPROX. 1 PERIOD, .5 BLOCKS			
				RESOURCES	
		OBJECTIVES	PACING	Online	Print
Connect					
DIGITAL START UP ACTIVITY **Learning About Our Past**			5 min.	●	
Investigate					
DIGITAL TEXT 1 **Studying Prehistory**		Objective 1	10 min.	●	●
INTERACTIVE GALLERY **Piecing the Past Together**			10 min.	●	
DIGITAL TEXT 2 **Investigating Prehistory**		Objective 2	10 min.	●	●
DIGITAL TEXT 3 **Discoveries in Africa and Beyond**		Objective 3	10 min.	●	●
INTERACTIVE MAP **Migrations of *Homo sapiens***			10 min.	●	
Synthesize					
DIGITAL ACTIVITY **Archaeologists at Work**			5 min.	●	
Demonstrate					
DIGITAL QUIZ **Lesson Quiz and Discussion Board**			10 min.	●	

CONNECT

INVESTIGATE

DIGITAL START UP ACTIVITY
Learning About Our Past

DIGITAL TEXT 1
Studying Prehistory

INTERACTIVE GALLERY
Piecing the Past Together

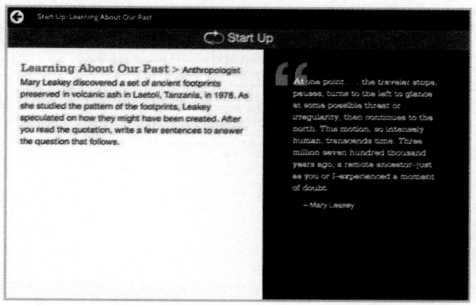

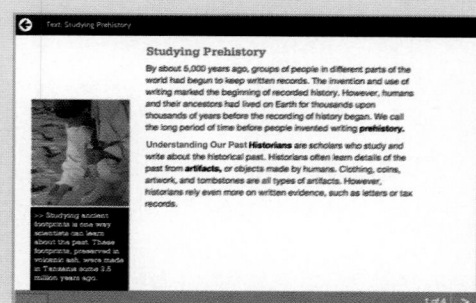

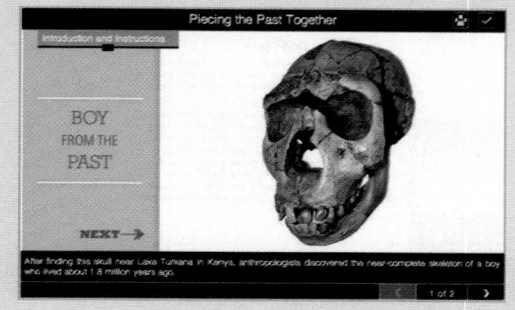

Project the Start Up Activity Ask students to answer this question as they enter and get settled: How do you think anthropologist Mary Leaky could study a series of footprints left in volcanic ash 3.7 million years ago and then guess that an early ancestor of modern humans "experienced a moment of doubt?" *(Students may say that Leaky was able to apply her knowledge of how a modern human would physically react while walking and then experiencing a "moment of doubt." The physical evidence allows her to reconstruct the mindset of an early human whose actions were similar.)*

Discuss Once students have answered the question, have them share their ideas with another student, either in class or through a chat room or blog.

Aa Vocabulary Development: Use the Interactive Reading Notepad to preview the Key Terms and Academic Vocabulary in the Lesson with students.

⇅ FLIP IT!
Assign the Flipped Video for this lesson.

■ STUDENT EDITION PRINT PAGES: 4–8

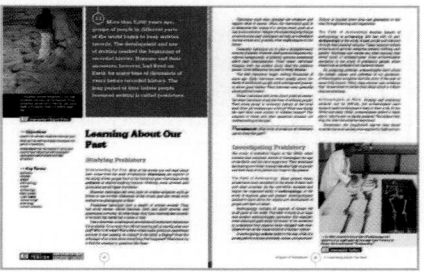

Objective 1: Learn how scholars study the historical past.

Quick Instruction
Interactive Gallery: Piecing the Past Together Project the digital activity on the whiteboard and click through the images. Introduce the activity by telling students that scientists rely on various methods to learn about our past. One method is to study the bones of early humans, such as the skeleton of Turkana Boy, a nearly complete 1.6 million-year-old fossil, buried for centuries. Explain to students that the historian's goal is to evaluate how early humans developed. To do this, historians examine sources and analyze their frame of reference, historical context, and point of view. This process helps them to interpret historical events. Such information also helps us to understand what might happen in the future.

👥 ACTIVE CLASSROOM
Ask students to choose one of these vocabulary words: prehistory, anthropology, archaeology, artifact, culture, and historian and tell them to create a visual image with a definition. Ask students to post their words and images on the board. Next, have students look at the various responses and allow them time as a group to discuss similarities and differences.

D Differentiate: Extra Support To better understand how historians work, ask students to write down the day-to-day details of what has happened to them in the past week. Next, ask students to think about why certain events took place, or why things happened as they did. Finally, ask students what lessons they learned that they can apply in the future.

ELL Use the ELL activity described in the ELL chart.

Further Instruction
Editable Presentation Use the Editable Presentation to present the main ideas for this Core Reading.

Project and go through the Interactive Reading Notepad questions and discuss the answers with the class.

Discuss Ask students to list, evaluate, and explain the different types of evidence historians use to study the past. *(Students should show they understand that historians study written records, artifacts, clothing, coins, artwork, and other relics. Students should also show an understanding that some types of evidence yield more information than others.)*

Learning About Our Past

DIGITAL TEXT 2

Investigating Prehistory

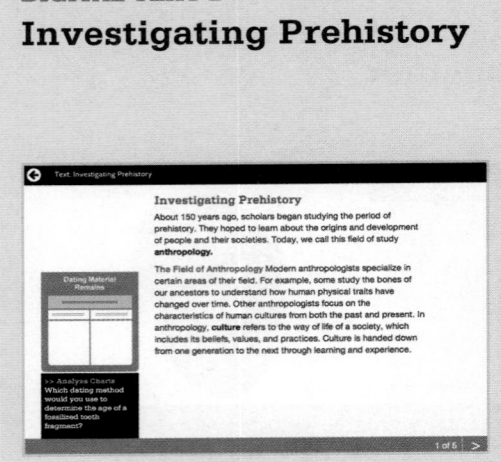

DIGITAL TEXT 3

Discoveries in Africa and Beyond

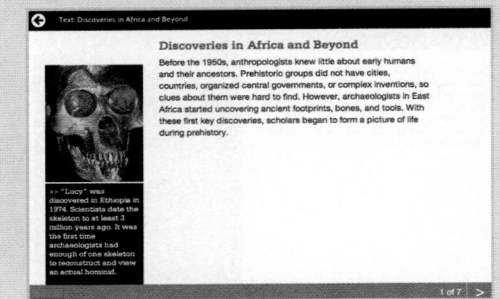

Objective 2: Find out how anthropologists investigate the period of prehistory.

Quick Instruction

Project the graphic Dating Material Remains on the whiteboard. Explain to students that accurately dating artifacts, relics, and bones is an important part of investigating prehistory. There are two ways that archaeologists and anthropologists can date bones and artifacts: Relative Dating and Absolute Dating. Relative dating allows scientists to create a chronology of artifacts based on the general fact that older artifacts are found deeper in the ground than newer artifacts. Absolute dating allows scientists to determine the age of a bone or some other organic material by measuring the decay of carbon-14, a radioactive element that decays at a set rate. Ask students to take a stand on the following question: Is it important for anthropologists and other scientists to investigate the past? Have students answer "yes" or "no." Divide the class into two groups based on their answers. Ask students to talk to each other to compare their reasons for answering the way they did.

Further Instruction

Project and go through the Interactive Reading Notepad questions and discuss the answers with the class.

Draw Inferences Ask students to evaluate the impact carbon-dating has had on archaeology and our understanding of the prehistory. *(Students might say that carbon-dating gives scientists an accurate way to determine the age of once-living, organic materials, including bones).*

Discuss Ask students to explain why studying prehistory is not just the responsibility of archaeologists, but of many other scientists including geologists, botanists, biologists, anthropologists, and others. *(Students might say that these other scientists provide vital, necessary information from their fields, to help archaeologists better understand how our ancient ancestors lived, worked, fought, farmed, and generally adapted to their environment.)* Ask students to describe at least one a geographer would contibute to the study of prehistory. *(Geographers can help determine the age of rocks and other natural features and can also help determine what the environment, including the climate, was like near an archaelogical site.)*

Objective 3: Understand how discoveries in Africa and beyond have influenced anthropologists' views about early humans and their ancestors.

Quick Instruction

Interactive Map: Migrations of *Homo sapiens* Project the hotspot map on the whiteboard. Explain to students that early humans migrated out of Africa and populated the world. Scientists and anthropologists have discovered evidence of many early human groups on each continent. The earliest group, Australopithecus, left their footprints in Africa some 7 million years ago. Scientists believe that modern humans emerged between 250,000 and 100,000 years ago.

Analyze Maps Have students study the Migrations of *Homo sapiens* map. Ask students why early humans migrated as they did. *(Students may say early humans moved as they did because they were following large herds of animals for food. They might also cite changing climate and other environmental conditions.)*

📖 ACTIVE CLASSROOM

Using the images and text associated with the Out of Africa Interactive Map, write a headline for each image that captures the most important aspects of that image. Pass your headline to a partner to review.

SYNTHESIZE

DEMONSTRATE

INTERACTIVE MAP
Migrations of *Homo sapiens*

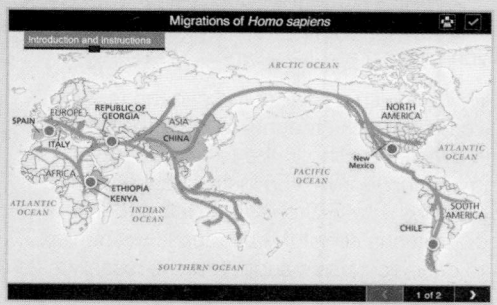

DIGITAL ACTIVITY
Archaeologists at Work

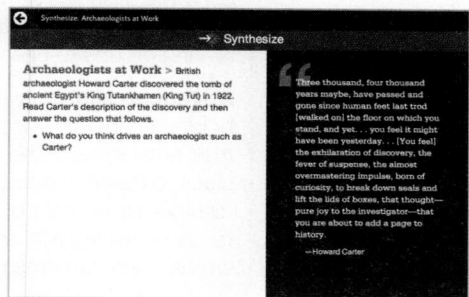

DIGITAL QUIZ
Lesson Quiz and Discussion Board

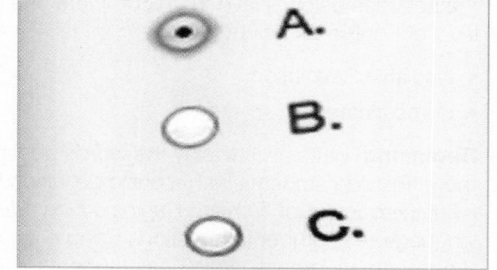

Further Instruction
Project and go through the Interactive Reading Notepad questions and discuss the answers with the class.

Draw Inferences What else did animals provide early humans with beside a source of food? *(Students should say that animals provided bones for tools and hides for clothing.)*

Identify Cause and Effect Analyze and describe how climate change might have impacted the migration routes of early humans. *(Students may say that people migrated towards climates that were more suitable for their survival.)*

Ask students to reread the quote from Howard Carter. Ask this key question: What methods does Carter, as an archaeologist use to analyze the past? Using the Circle Write strategy, have students write as much as they can for one minute on the key question then switch with the person on their right. That person should improve or elaborate the response. Have students continue to switch until that paper comes back to the first person. Have students share what they have written with the rest of the class.

Assign the online Lesson Quiz for this lesson if you haven't already done so. Students will be offered automatic remediation or enrichment based on their score.

Post these questions on the Discussion Board.

In "Understanding Our Past," you learned how scientists and scholars study the historical past. You also learned about some of the techniques anthropologists use to investigate prehistory, and how archaeological discoveries in Africa and elsewhere have influenced views about early humans and their ancestors.

Evaluate Why might someone devote his or her life to studying early humans? *(Students might say that those who devote their lives to studying early humans are curious as to how people in the past lived and are interested in the process of discovery. Students might also say that by studying our ancestors and how they adapted to changes, we can learn something about our world.)*

Topic Inquiry
Have students continue their investigations for the Topic Inquiry.

The Neolithic Revolution

Supporting English Language Learners

Use with Digital Text 2, **Farming Begins a New Stone Age.**

Learning Strategies
Read *Farming Begins a New Stone Age* aloud to the class. Write and display the following academic vocabulary words for students to use with the activities below. Have them complete one activity according to their level of English proficiency.

- Neolithic Revolution
- domesticate

Beginning Write and display the words above. Have students copy them. Provide students with a basic definition for each of the words. Then retell the content of *Farming Begins a New Stone Age* using accessible language. Ask students questions using each word, such as *What were the results of domestication*? Ask students leading questions to guide them to a complete answer to the discussion questions.

Intermediate Write and display the words above. Have students copy them. Provide students with bilingual dictionaries and guide them to find a basic definition for each word. Then retell the content of *Farming Begins a New Stone Age* using accessible language. Ask students discussion questions using each word, such as *How did domestication help humans*? Assist students as necessary as they work together to answer the discussion questions.

Advanced Have students work in small groups to scan the text for bolded academic vocabulary words and ask students to copy them into their notebooks. Provide students with dictionaries to look up the meaning of each word. Then instruct small groups to discuss the content of *Farming Begins a New Stone Age*. Tell students to focus on asking and answering questions about the academic vocabulary words. Circulate among groups to offer discussion support as necessary.

Advanced High Have students work with a partner to scan the text for bolded academic vocabulary words and ask students to copy them into their notebooks. Have students use information in the text and context clues to determine the meaning of each word. Then instruct pairs to discuss the content of *Farming Begins a New Stone Age*. Tell students to focus on asking and answering questions about the academic vocabulary words. Circulate among pairs to offer discussion support as necessary.

▣ Differentiate Instruction

Use the Differentiated Instruction notes throughout the lesson plan to support the varied skill sets, levels of readiness, and interests in the mixed-ability classroom.

Challenge These notes include suggestions for expanding the activity for advanced students.

On-Level These notes include suggestions for modifying the activity to address different interests or learning styles.

Extra Support These notes include ideas for providing more scaffolding or reading spuport.

Special Needs These notes provide ideas for adapting instruction to support the needs of various special needs students.

■ NOTES

Objectives

Objective 1: Describe the skills and beliefs that early modern humans developed during the Old Stone Age.

Objective 2: Analyze why the development of agriculture is considered the start of the New Stone Age and the Neolithic Revolution.

Objective 3: Explain how the Neolithic Revolution dramatically changed the way people lived.

LESSON 2 ORGANIZER		PACING: APPROX. 1 PERIOD, .5 BLOCKS			
				RESOURCES	
		OBJECTIVES	**PACING**	**Online**	**Print**
Connect					
	DIGITAL START UP ACTIVITY **The Neolithic Revolution**		5 min.	●	
Investigate					
	DIGITAL TEXT 1 **Old Stone Age Skills and Beliefs**	Objective 1	10 min.	●	●
	INTERACTIVE GALLERY **Paleolithic Cave Art**		10 min.	●	
	DIGITAL TEXT 2 **Farming Begins a New Stone Age**	Objective 2	10 min.	●	●
	DIGITAL TEXT 3 **Dramatic Change with the Neolithic Revolution**	Objective 3	10 min.	●	●
	INTERACTIVE GALLERY **Otzi—the Neolithic Ice Man**		10 min.	●	
Synthesize					
	DIGITAL ACTIVITY **Paleolithic Versus Neolithic**		5 min.	●	
Demonstrate					
	DIGITAL QUIZ **Lesson Quiz and Class Discussion Board**		10 min.	●	

The Neolithic Revolution

■ CONNECT

DIGITAL START UP ACTIVITY
The Neolithic Revolution

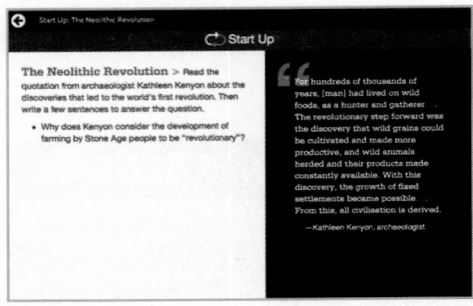

Project the Start Up Activity Ask students to answer this question as they enter and get settled: How was the introduction of farming a turning point in prehistory? *(Students should show an understanding that farming led to the development of permanent villages from which civilizations grew and flourished.)*

Discuss Once students have answered the question, have them share their ideas with another student, either in class or through a chat room or blog.

Aa Vocabulary Development: Use the Interactive Reading Notepad to preview the Key Terms and Academic Vocabulary in the Lesson with students.

↑↓ FLIP IT!
Assign the Flipped Video for this lesson.

■ STUDENT EDITION PRINT
PAGES: 9–13

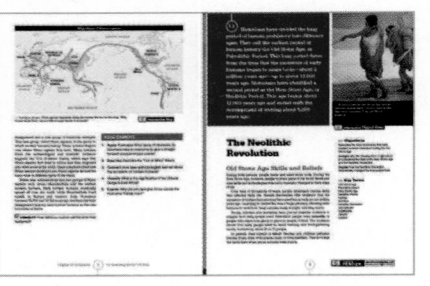

■ INVESTIGATE

 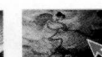

DIGITAL TEXT 1
Old Stone Age Skills and Beliefs

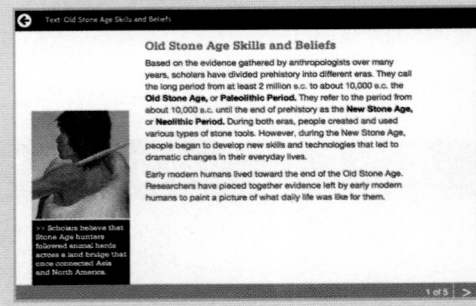

INTERACTIVE GALLERY
Paleolithic Cave Art

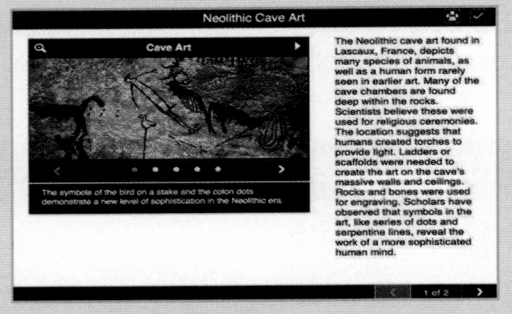

Objective 1: Describe the skills and beliefs that early modern humans developed during the Old Stone Age.

Quick Instruction
Interactive Gallery: Paleolithic Art Tell students that early peoples were nomads who depended on their environment for food, clothing, and shelter. They made tools from the materials available and developed spoken language, which broadened their ability to communicate and plan. Then project the digital activity on the whiteboard and click through the images. Introduce the activity by telling students that at the end of the Old Stone Age, people began leaving evidence of their beliefs in a spiritual world. They buried their dead with tools and weapons, indicating a belief in an afterlife. The Paleolithic cave art found in Lascaux, France, depicts some of their religious beliefs.

🖼 ACTIVE CLASSROOM
Ask students to study the images of the art carefully. Using the See-Think-Wonder strategy, have students pair with a partner. Ask them: What do you see? What does that make you think? What are you wondering about now that you've seen this? Have students share insights with the class.

D Differentiate: Extra Support Ask students to think about where they have seen pictures that communicate specific information, such as a handicapped sign in a parking lot, no smoking signs, and school bus stop signs. Ask students to think about why these pictures work well. Next, have them draw a picture that communicates something important without using words. Have the class try to guess what information the picture is trying to convey.

Further Instruction
Editable Presentation Use the Editable Presentation to present the main ideas for this Core Reading.

Project and go through the Interactive Reading Notepad questions and discuss the answers with the class.

Discuss Ask students to describe how scientists might go about analyzing, evaluating, and putting into historical context evidence of Neolithic religious beliefs. *(Students might say that by comparing evidence of religious activity [such as cave art and evidence of ceremonial rites] scientists can piece together how early religions developed and spread.)*

DIGITAL TEXT 2

Farming Begins a New Stone Age

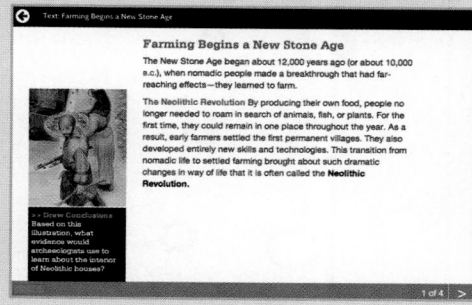

Objective 2: Analyze why the development of agriculture is considered the start of the New Stone Age and the Neolithic Revolution.

Quick Instruction

Explain to students that about 12,000 year ago, early humans scrapped their nomadic lifestyle and began to farm. Instead of searching for animals as a source of food, farming allowed people to settle in one area. As a result, permanent villages began to form as did new technologies and skills. People also began to domesticate animals and plants that were better suited for human use.

ELL Use the ELL activity described in the ELL chart.

Further Instruction

Project and go through the Interactive Reading Notepad questions and discuss the answers with the class.

Identify Central Issues How did agriculture and the domestication of plants and animals develop in different parts of the world? *(Students might say that evidence shows that the domestication of different plants and animals occurred at different times and different places.)*

Apply Concepts How did the development of farming contribute to permanent villages? *(Students might say that farming led to a more settled way of life, since humans could grow their own food, and did not need to roam to feed themselves. The result was the development of more permanent villages.)*

Discuss Explain the concept of revolution as it relates to farming and the Neolithic Revolution. *(Students should show an understanding that change is revolutionary when it is dramatic, all-encompassing, and requires great effort. The shift from a nomadic to a more settled way of life gave early humans greater control of their environment, creating a revolutionary change.)*

DIGITAL TEXT 3

Dramatic Change with the Neolithic Revolution

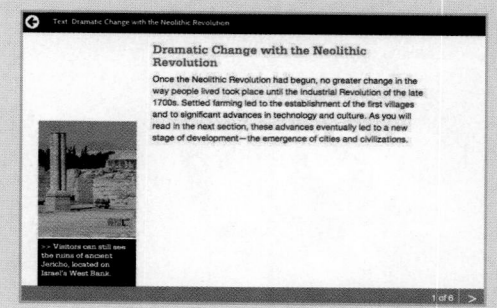

Objective 3: Explain how the Neolithic Revolution dramatically changed the way people lived.

Quick Instruction

Interactive Gallery: Otzi—the Neolithic Ice Man Project the digital activity on the whiteboard and click through the images. Introduce the activity by telling students that great changes came about during the Neolithic Revolution. Settled people changed their way of life by inventing new technologies that, among other things, helped them farm and measure time. Archaeologists know a lot about this period by studying finds such as Otzi, a Neolithic "Iceman" found preserved in the European Alps alongside various tools and other belongings.

🖳 ACTIVE CLASSROOM

Ask students to study the images of the "Iceman." Have students visualize that they are having a conversation with the Iceman as if he were alive. Have students write down a series of questions they would like the Iceman to answer, and what he would say to them.

D Differentiate: **Extra Support** Divide the class into two groups. One group will represent people who might be considered modern-day nomads, the other group will represent people who might be considered modern-day settlers. Have students create a photo collage of the characteristics of each group using photos pulled from the Internet or cut from magazines and newspapers. For example, to illustrate a modern-day nomad, a

The Neolithic Revolution

INTERACTIVE GALLERY
Otzi—the Neolithic Ice Man

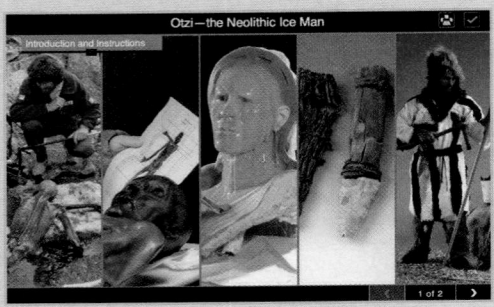

student might cut out a photo of a recreational vehicle traveling on a highway, or of a hiker. To illustrate a modern-day settler, a student might wish to use a photo of a house, or a farmer in the field.

Further Instruction
Project and go through the Interactive Reading Notepad questions and discuss the answers with the class.

Discuss with students how farming, especially in the river valleys, brought social, political, and economic change as urban civilizations and governments developed. For example, Neolithic peoples worked together and formed governments to direct projects such as the building of dikes and dams. When farming created surpluses of food, some farmers gained wealth, and in times of scarcity, hunters and warriors gained prestige. This marked the beginning of a social class system.

Draw Inferences How did farming encourage the development of new technologies? *(Students might say that early farmers had to develop new methods and tools to till the soil, protect their crops, make sure that they measured the right amount of seed, and know when to plant.)*

Discuss How did the development of farming contribute to the growth of civilizations? *(Students might say that farming led to he establishment of villages, which led to the creation of governments and significant advances in technology and culture.)*

DIGITAL ACTIVITY
Paleolithic Versus Neolithic

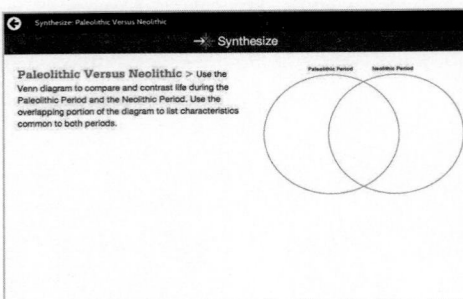

Project the graphic organizer on the whiteboard. Ask students to discuss Paleolithic Versus Neolithic. Using the PMI strategy, create three columns on the blackboard titled, Plus/Minus/Interesting. Discuss each point in the graphic organizer. Ask students to answer these three questions for each point: What are the positive aspects of this point? What are the negative aspects of this point? What is interesting about this point?

DIGITAL QUIZ
Lesson Quiz and Class Discussion Board

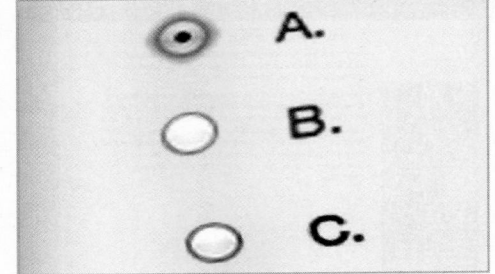

Assign the online Lesson Quiz for this lesson if you haven't already done so. Students will be offered automatic remediation or enrichment based on their score.

Post this questions on the Discussion Board:

In "The Neolithic Revolution," you learned how early modern humans lived toward the end of the Old Stone Age. You also learned how Neolithic peoples stopped being nomads and settled down in farming communities. You also learned how they developed their early religious beliefs, technologies, and how they domesticated plants and animals.

Determine Relevance How did the Neolithic Revolution impact the modern world? *(Students might say the world's modern civilizations might not have developed had it not been for the changes brought by the Neolithic Revolution.)*

Topic Inquiry
Have students continue their investigations for the Topic Inquiry.

Civilization Begins

Supporting English Language Learners

Use with Digital Text 2, **Features that Define Civilization.**

Learning Strategies
Read *Features that Define Civilization*. Identify one feature of civilization, such as organized governments, or job specialization to be the subject of a class discussion. As students discuss and answer questions about the chosen feature of civilization, focus on student responses. Then guide students through one of the following activities according to their English proficiency level.

Beginning Review *Features that Define Civilization* and use images, drawings, charts, maps, or the glossary to make sure that students understand the content. Then choose one of the seven features of civilizations to highlight in a guided discussion. Ask students basic questions about the content. When students respond, let them know if you understand their speech. Give specific feedback on their speech and provide opportunities for them to correct any speaking errors.

Intermediate Review *Features that Define Civilization* and use images, drawings, charts, maps, or the glossary to make sure that students understand the content. Then choose one of the seven features of civilizations to highlight in a guided discussion. Ask students basic questions about the content. When students respond, give specific feedback on their pronunciation, vocabulary, and fluency. Provide opportunities for them to correct any speaking errors.

Advanced Choose one of the seven features of civilizations to highlight in a student-led discussion. Provide student groups with discussion questions about the content and instruct each student in the group to contribute to the discussion. Spend time observing each group to give specific feedback on students' pronunciation, vocabulary, and fluency. Provide opportunities for them to correct any speaking errors.

Advanced High Choose one of the seven features of civilizations to highlight in a student-led discussion. Ask student groups to generate discussion questions about the content and instruct each student in the group to contribute to the discussion. Circulate among small groups to offer support as necessary. Encourage fellow students to share specific feedback on classmates' pronunciation, vocabulary, and fluency. Provide opportunities for them to correct any speaking errors.

Use with Digital Text 1, **The First Cities and Civilizations.**

Learning Strategies
Read *The First Cities and Civilizations* aloud to the class. Have them complete one activity according to their level of English proficiency.

Beginning Review the text with students to find, write, and display the bolded words. Say the words aloud and have students repeat them. Then provide students with a basic definition for each word. Use each word in a simple, meaningful sentence. Write each sentence and ask students to copy them into their notebooks. Then assist students in writing another simple sentence for each word and have students write those sentences in their notebooks, too.

Intermediate Review the text with students to find, write, and display the bolded words. Say the words aloud and have students repeat them. Then provide students with a basic definition for each word. Assist students in writing a simple sentence for each word and have students write those sentences in their notebooks, too.

Advanced Have pairs of students review the text to find the bolded words and write them in their notebooks. Instruct pairs to develop a basic definition for each word using context clues. Then ask pairs to write a meaningful sentence for each word. Pairs can share their work with the class when they are finished.

Advanced High Have students review the text to find the bolded words and write them in their notebooks. Instruct students to develop a basic definition for each word using context clues. Then ask them to write a meaningful sentence for each word. Students can share their work with a partner when they are finished.

▣ Differentiate Instruction

Use the Differentiated Instruction notes throughout the lesson plan to support the varied skill sets, levels of readiness, and interests in the mixed-ability classroom.

Challenge These notes include suggestions for expanding the activity for advanced students.

On-Level These notes include suggestions for modifying the activity to address different interests or learning styles.

Extra Support These notes include ideas for providing more scaffolding or reading spuport.

Special Needs These notes provide ideas for adapting instruction to support the needs of various special needs students.

■ NOTES

_____

_____

_____

_____

_____

_____

Civilization Begins

Objectives

Objective 1: Analyze the conditions under which the first cities and civilizations arose.

Objective 2: Outline the basic features that define civilization.

Objective 3: Understand the ways in which civilizations have changed over time.

LESSON 3 ORGANIZER		PACING: APPROX. 1 PERIOD, .5 BLOCKS			
		OBJECTIVES	**PACING**	**RESOURCES**	
				Online	**Print**
Connect					
DIGITAL START UP ACTIVITY **Civilization Begins**			5 min.	●	
Investigate					
DIGITAL TEXT 1 **The First Cities and Civilizations**		Objective 1	10 min.	●	
INTERACTIVE MAP **River Valley Civilizations**			10 min.	●	
DIGITAL TEXT 2 **Features That Define Civilization**		Objective 2	10 min.	●	
DIGITAL ACTIVITY **The Rise of River Valley Civilizations**			10 min.	●	
DIGITAL TEXT 3 **Civilizations Change**		Objective 3	10 min.	●	
Synthesize					
DIGITAL ACTIVITY **Cities and Civilizations Arise: Cause and Effect**			5 min.	●	
Demonstrate					
DIGITAL QUIZ **Lesson Quiz and Class Discussion Board**			10 min.	●	

■ CONNECT

DIGITAL START UP ACTIVITY
Civilization Begins

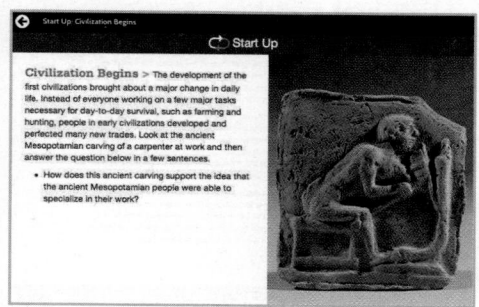

Project the Start Up Activity Ask students to answer this question as they enter and get settled: How did job specialization shape early civilizations? *(Students should show an understanding that as people settled into farming villages, a variety of new tasks emerged because one person could not master all the skills needed to make tools, weapons, or other goods. Some became artisans, weavers, metalworkers, merchants, or carpenters.)*

Discuss Once students have answered the question, have them share their ideas with another student, either in class or through a chat room or blog.

Aa Vocabulary Development: Use the Interactive Reading Notepad to preview the Key Terms and Academic Vocabulary in the Lesson with students.

⇕ FLIP IT!

Assign the Flipped Video for this lesson.

■ STUDENT EDITION PRINT PAGES: 14–19

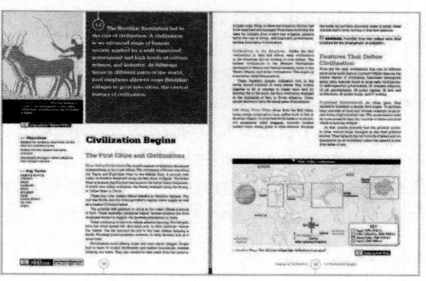

■ INVESTIGATE

DIGITAL TEXT 1
The First Cities and Civilizations

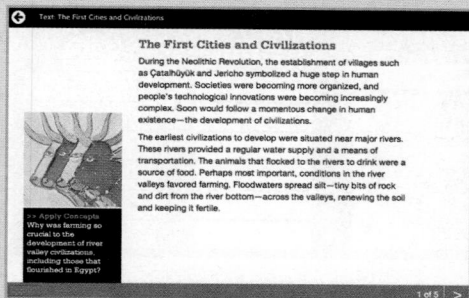

INTERACTIVE MAP
River Valley Civilizations

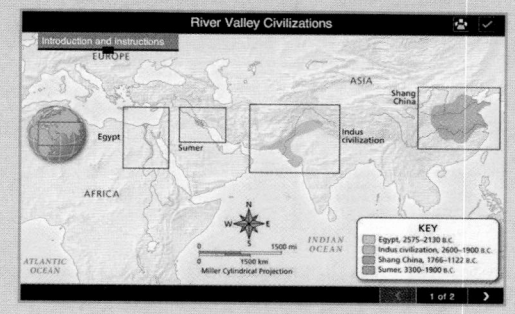

Objective 1: Analyze the conditions under which the first cities and civilizations arose.

Quick Instruction

Interactive Map: River Valley Civilizations Project the interactive map on the whiteboard and click through the hotspots. Explain to students that the world's first civilizations emerged near major rivers. The rivers provided ample food, as animals flocked to drink. Rivers were also superhighways, allowing people to travel. Perhaps the most important aspect of river valleys was the fertile soil that allowed farming to thrive. As agriculture grew, farmers were able to produce surpluses of food that allowed them to feed growing populations. As food surpluses grew, people could focus on work other than gathering food, or meeting basic survival needs. As a result, urban populations grew.

👥 ACTIVE CLASSROOM

Project the interactive map on the whiteboard and click through each of the hotspot maps. Divide the class by having students count off 1 to 4. Each number should correspond to a hotspot map. Next, have students look closely at their hotspot map and have them describe how geography played a role in the development of civilizations that flourished in each region.

D Differentiate: Challenge Have students research one of the areas where river valley civilizations thrived. Have them research and select an article from a current newspaper, Internet news site, or magazine, and use the content to analyze how geography continues to affect events and developments in their particular region.

ELL Use the ELL activity described in the ELL chart.

Further Instruction

Editable Presentation Use the Editable Presentation to present the main ideas for this Core Reading.

Project and go through the Interactive Reading Notepad questions and discuss the answers with the class.

Discuss Why were early civilizations in the Americas able to thrive away from river valleys? *(Students might say that people adapted to their environment by learning to farm on the sides of mountains or fill in swampy areas to farm.)*

Evaluate Impact How did civilizations that developed away from river valleys satisfy their need for water? *(Students might say that other civilizations developed by lakes or in climates where rain is plentiful. Others found ways to divert water to their farming settlements.)*

Civilization Begins

DIGITAL TEXT 2

Features That Define Civilization

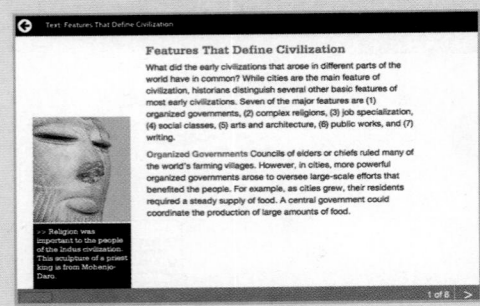

DIGITAL ACTIVITY

The Rise of River Valley Civilizations

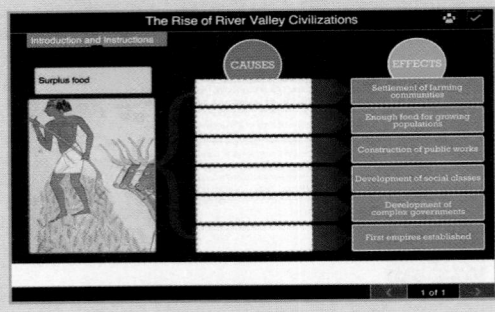

DIGITAL TEXT 3

Civilizations Change

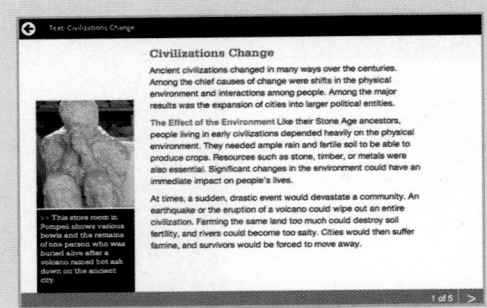

Objective 2: Outline the basic features that define civilization.

Quick Instruction

Project the digital activity on the whiteboard and explain to students that while early civilizations arose in different parts of the world, they had many things in common. They all formed organized governments, complex religions, job specialization, social classes, arts and architecture, public works, and systems of writing.

🔊 ACTIVE CLASSROOM

Using the Rank It strategy, Ask students to rank the seven features that define a civilization, from those that had the greatest impact, to those that had the least impact. Ask students to provide a justification for the ranking decisions they made. Then ask students to work in pairs to share their rankings and justifications. Poll the class to see if there is agreement on the ranking.

ELL Use the ELL activity described in the ELL chart.

Further Instruction

Project and go through the Interactive Reading Notepad questions and discuss the answers with the class.

Tell students that governments became more complex, and separate departments evolved to oversee different functions of government. In many early governments, priests probably had the greatest power. In a theocracy, the government was run by religious leaders. In other governments, warrior kings emerged as the main political leaders. Often, they claimed their right to rule came from the gods, and power was passed from father to son. Thus, many political rulers gained religious power as well.

Evaluate Impact How did governments help civilizations to thrive? *(Students might say that governments were able to oversee large-scale projects that aided the community, such as the building of dikes and irrigation systems, and coordinating the production and storage of large amounts of food. They also were able to rally citizens, not only for the common good, but for common defense.)*

Define What is the definition of a complex religion? *(Students might say that complex religions are religions that worship many gods or goddesses.)*

Evaluate Impact How did the development of a writing system aid in the development of civilization? *(Students should show an understanding that the development of ancient writing systems was the dividing line between prehistory and history. Writing allowed records to be kept and histories to be written. As a result, civilizations thrived as their citizens became literate.)*

Objective 3: Understand the ways in which civilizations have changed over time.

Quick Instruction

Explain to students that as the centuries passed, ancient civilizations changed in many ways. People interacted with each other differently; their physical environment changed; and cities expanded into large empires. Note that it was not only natural disasters, such as volcanic eruptions or earthquakes that affected cities and human migration patterns, but also factors created by humans, such as soil depletion and loss of timber sources. Migration, along with trade, contributed to cultural diffusion.

Further Instruction

Project and go through the Interactive Reading Notepad questions and discuss the answers with the class.

Identify Cause and Effect How did cultural diffusion impact civilizations over time? *(Students should show an understanding that cultural diffusion, which occurred as people traded, migrated, and fought one another, allowed ideas, customs, religions, and technologies to spread.)*

Identify Cause and Effect How did Earth's ever-changing environment facilitate the spread of ideas? *(Students should show an understanding that environmental disasters forced many people to migrate to other areas where they interacted with others from different cultures. As a result, people shared and adapted ideas and other aspects of life.)*

SYNTHESIZE

DIGITAL ACTIVITY
Cities and Civilizations Arise: Cause and Effect

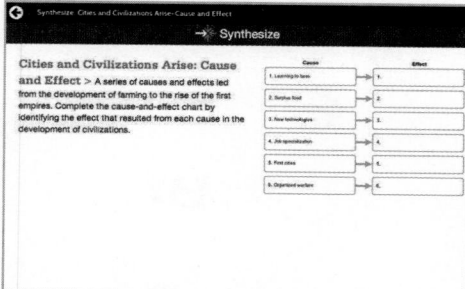

DEMONSTRATE

DIGITAL QUIZ
Lesson Quiz and Class Discussion Board

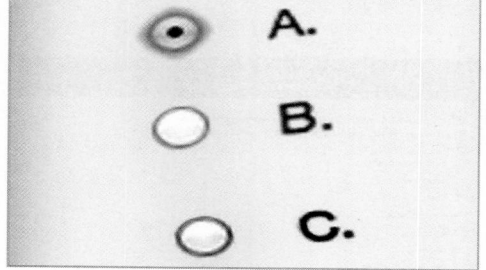

Evaluate Impact What was the impact of warfare on early civilizations? *(Students should say that as rival leaders battled for power, some were able to conquer many cities and villages, creating the first empires. Moreover, warfare sometimes brought benefits to the conquered, ending hostilities between neighboring communities and creating common bonds between people.)*

D **Differentiate: Extra Support** Organize students into groups of three or four. Give each group a card with a key term from the digital reading. Allow time for each group to brainstorm the meaning of the term and prepare a short presentation in which they will act out the term's meaning in front of the class. At the end of the skit, the rest of the class should be able to answer: "What did the term mean?"

Project the graphic organizer on the whiteboard. Using a version of the Rank It strategy, put sticky notes on the whiteboard for each "cause" listed on the graphic organizer. Next, have students work in groups and write down on separate sticky notes the "effect" for each "cause" they see on the board. Ask each group to go up to the board and pair the causes and the effects. When they are finished, have the students evaluate and discuss which group was more accurate.

Assign the online Lesson Quiz for this lesson if you haven't already done so. Students will be offered automatic remediation or enrichment based on their score.

Post the following questions on the Discussion Board:

In "Civilization Begins," you learned how early civilizations developed over time. You learned how the first civilizations grew and prospered along river valleys, while other groups flourished in other geographic regions. You also learned what the main features of civilization are.

Identify Cause and Effect How did religion influence the establishment of governments and social classes in early civilizations? *(Students might say that in many early civilizations, priests held great power in government, while religion created a social class system in which priests, along with nobles, were at the top of an increasing hierarchical society. Also, many rulers claimed that their right to rule came from the gods, and they passed their power to their sons, creating a government hierarchy.)*

Draw Conclusions Why would nomadic life not be classified as a civilization? *(Students might say that nomads did not exhibit any of the basic features that define civilization. They did not form governments, have job specialization or social classes, or excel in the arts and sciences.)*

Topic Inquiry
Have students continue their investigations for the Topic Inquiry.

Origins of Civilization (Prehistory–300 B.C.)

◼ SYNTHESIZE

DIGITAL ACTIVITY
Reflect on the Essential Question and Topic

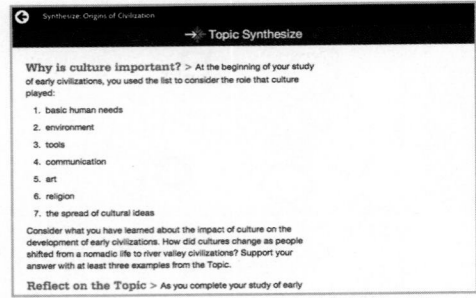

First ask students to reconsider the Essential Question for the Topic: Why is culture important? Remind students of the ideas they considered:

- basic human needs
- environment
- tools
- communication
- art
- religion

Have students consider those features again in light of what they've learned about the impact of culture on the development of early civilizations. Ask students to list three examples of cultural change. Discuss the examples as a class and/or ask students to post their examples on the Class Discussion Board.

Next, ask students to reflect on the Topic as a whole and jot down 1-3 questions they've thought about during the Topic. Share these examples if students need help getting started:

- How did dramatic changes in the cultures of early peoples affect the organization of societies?
- How did these changes affect migration habits, ways of adapting to the environment, and economic systems?
- On a scale of 1 to 5, with 5 being the highest, how much do you think culture affected the development of early civilizations?

You may ask students to share their questions and answers on the class discussion board.

Topic Inquiry
Have students complete Step 3 of the Topic Inquiry.

◼ DEMONSTRATE

DIGITAL TOPIC REVIEW AND ASSESSMENT
Origins of Civilization (Prehistory–300 B.C.)

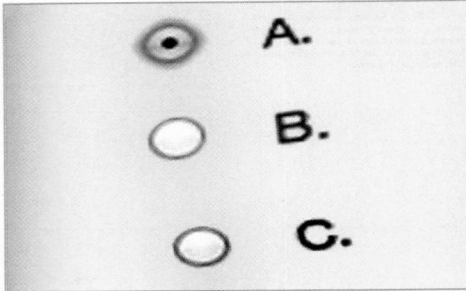

Students can prepare for the Topic Test by answering the questions in the Topic Review and Assessment online or the Assessment questions in the Print Student text. They can also prepare by reviewing their answers to the Interactive Reading Notepad questions or reviewing their notes in the Reading and Notetaking Study Guide.

DIGITAL TOPIC TEST
Origins of Civilization (Prehistory–300 B.C.)

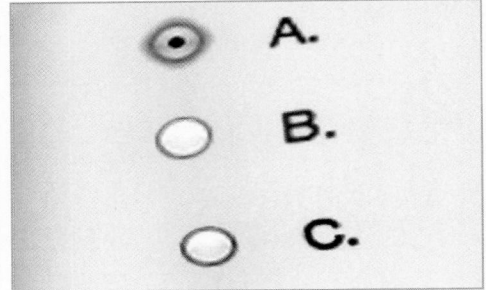

TOPIC TEST
Assign the Topic Test to assess students' understanding of topic content.

BENCHMARK TESTS
Assign these benchmark tests as you complete the relevant topics to monitor student progress toward mastering the course content and as preparation for the End-of-Course Test.

Benchmark Test 1: Topics 1–5
Benchmark Test 2: Topics 6–10
Benchmark Test 3: Topics 11–15
Benchmark Test 4: Topics 16–21

The Ancient Middle East and Egypt (3200 B.C.–500 B.C.)

TOPIC 2 ORGANIZER	PACING: APPROX. 7 PERIODS, 3.5 BLOCKS
	PACING
Connect	1 period
MY STORY VIDEO **Hatshepsut, The Woman Who Was King**	10 min.
DIGITAL ESSENTIAL QUESTION ACTIVITY **How Much Does Geography Affect People's Lives?**	10 min.
DIGITAL MAP ACTIVITY **The Ancient Middle East and Egypt**	10 min.
TOPIC INQUIRY: DOCUMENT-BASED QUESTION **What is the Function of Law?**	20 min.
Investigate	2–4 periods
TOPIC INQUIRY: DOCUMENT-BASED QUESTION **What is the Function of Law?**	Ongoing
LESSON 1 A Civilization Emerges in Sumer	30–40 min.
LESSON 2 Empires in Mesopotamia	30–40 min.
LESSON 3 The Hebrews and the Origins of Judaism	30–40 min.
LESSON 4 Egyptian Civilization	30–40 min.
Synthesize	1 period
DIGITAL ACTIVITY **Reflect on the Essential Question and Topic**	10 min.
TOPIC INQUIRY: DOCUMENT-BASED QUESTION **What is the Function of Law?**	20 min.
Demonstrate	1–2 periods
DIGITAL TOPIC TEST **The Ancient Middle East and Egypt**	10 min.
TOPIC INQUIRY: DOCUMENT-BASED QUESTION **What is the Function of Law?**	20 min.

What is the Function of Law?

In this Topic Inquiry, students work individually to analyze five documents, both primary and secondary sources, expressing ideas about the function of the law. Students will answer questions about each document, reflect on the ideas, draw their own conclusions, and then write an essay on the following question: **What is the function of the law?**

STEP 1: CONNECT
Develop Questions and Plan the Investigation

Launch the DBQ Writing Activity
Have students write their definitions of a law. Refer them to the bulleted list of questions to get them started. If necessary, ask students to think about laws they have been affected by in their own lives. Suggest they keep this definition in mind as they read the documents, answer the questions, and write their essays.

Suggestion: Have volunteers read their definitions and have the rest of the class discuss them. Ask: What are some different things laws can be designed to do?

Generate Questions
Divide the class into small groups and have them record their questions about the function of laws.

Professional Development
Document Based Questions
Be sure to view the Document Based Questions resources in the online course.

Resources
• Student Instructions • Need-to-Know Questions

⏻ PROFESSIONAL DEVELOPMENT

Document-Based Question
Be sure to view the Document-Based Question Professional Development resources in the online course.

STEP 2: INVESTIGATE
Apply Disciplinary Concepts and Tools

Read and Analyze Documents
Tell students that they will read and analyze five documents about some aspect of the law and its function in society. Then, they will write an essay and express their own opinions about what the function of the law is. Documents A and B are actual laws from two of the civilizations studied in this Topic. Document C is a discussion of the purpose and role of the law. Document D is a modern-day political cartoon. Document E is another actual law, but a modern one passed by the U.S. Congress.

At this time, discuss with students the differences between primary and secondary sources, a distinction that will be addressed frequently as students study world history. Share these definitions:

A **primary source** is a historical record produced at the time of the event or period that it describes, or soon thereafter. These sources may include written accounts, such as diaries, speeches, government records, law codes, religious texts, and period cartoons, photographs, and artifacts.

A **secondary source** is a document that describes, interprets, or analyzes an event or person. Secondary sources are removed from the event, but can be written at about the same time as the event.

When using both primary and secondary sources, students must keep in mind the author's frame of reference and point of view, as well as the context in which the document was created. Even if a soldier was on a particular battlefield, he was fighting for one side. His understanding and description of the battle may be colored by his feelings about the battle. His point of view will reflect his army's positions and values but not those of his enemy. His description of the battle will be limited to what he has experienced. Students need to take into account these specific limitations of all primary sources. Secondary sources, too, can be affected by the point of view and frame of reference of the writer, as well as by the context in which he or she is writing.

Suggestion: Have students offer examples of other primary and secondary sources they have read and used.

Check Understanding
After students finish reading each individual document, have them answer the questions attached to each document. Review the questions and discuss the answers after students have answered the questions.

Resources
• Information Organizer

STEP 3: SYNTHESIZE
Evaluate Sources and Use Evidence to Formulate Conclusions

Write Your Essay

Now have students write their essays to express their own opinion about the question: **What is the function of the law?**

Suggestion: Have volunteers review their definitions of the law as a reminder before students begin on their essays.

Edit Your Essay

Have students read over their first drafts. Suggest they ask themselves these questions: Does it accurately express my viewpoint? Does it need more details? Then have students proofread and edit their essays, revising as needed. If time allows, have students exchange essays for a peer edit.

Suggestion: Remind students to check spelling and grammar in their essays.

Resources

- 21st Century Skill Tutorials: Write an Essay
- Writing Rubric
- 21st Century Skill Tutorials: Develop a Clear Thesis

STEP 4: DEMONSTRATE
Communicate Conclusions and Take Informed Action

Present Your Essay

Have students make a neat, clean copy of their essays. Then ask volunteers to read their essays aloud to the class.

Suggestion: As an alternative, have students publish their essays on a class website, bulletin board, or other online vehicle.

Reflect on the Project

After students briefly discuss what they found challenging in their essays and what they feel they did well. Encourage them to use the lessons they learned writing this essay so they can write even more effectively in future writing projects.

Suggestion: As an extension activity, have students research the career of a leading American legal figure, focusing on his or her opinion about the function of law. Ask them to write a three-paragraph essay about the person's thoughts about the function of law. Suggest these jurists as starting points: John Marshall, Louis Brandeis, Oliver Wendell Holmes, Benjamin Cardozo, Felix Frankfurter, Thurgood Marshall, Sandra Day O'Connor, and Earl Warren. Ask students to share their essays with the class.

INTRODUCTION

The Ancient Middle East and Egypt (3200 B.C.–500 B.C.)

The world's first civilizations emerged about 4,000 years ago in the Middle East in a region called the Fertile Crescent. Nearby, in Egypt, another powerful and influential empire flourished, while at the eastern shore of the Mediterranean, the civilization of the ancient Israelites was born. All of these civilizations were powerful influences on those that came later, affecting the future development of science, economics, culture, religion, politics, and government.

◼ CONNECT

MY STORY VIDEO
Hatshepsut, The Woman Who Was King

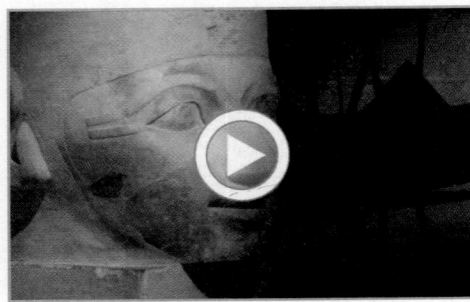

Watch a video showing the story of Hatshepsut, a ruler of ancient Egypt.

Check Understanding What about Hatshepsut was unprecedented in Egyptian history? *(She seized power and made herself king.)*

Hypothesize What does Hatshepsut's story reveal about the dangers of over-generalizing about history? *(Hatshepsut's story contradicts the assumption of most people that the rulers of ancient civilizations were always male.)*

⇅ FLIP IT!

Assign the My Story Video.

DIGITAL ESSENTIAL QUESTION ACTIVITY
How Much Does Geography Affect People's Lives?

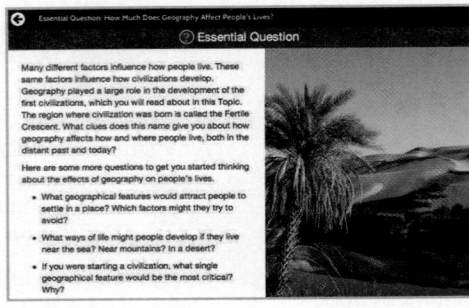

Ask students to think about the Essential Question for this Topic: How much does geography affect people's lives? Have a volunteer read each question. Discuss them as a class.

Identify Central Issues What geographical features might people settling in a place want to find? *(Answers may include a river, lake, or other source of clean water and for easy transportation, abundant wildlife for food, a climate that provides an adequate growing season for crops and is not extremely cold or hot, flat land for building on, access to building supplies such as timber or stone, and natural protection from invasions.)*

Classify What different ways of life would probably develop in different kinds of geographical areas? *(Sample response: People who live near the sea would probably become sailors and traders and depend on fish for much of their diet. People who live in a desert would have to trade for things they need and cannot produce, such as food. They might also become herders, since some animals can live in sparse climates.)*

DIGITAL MAP ACTIVITY
The Ancient Middle East and Egypt

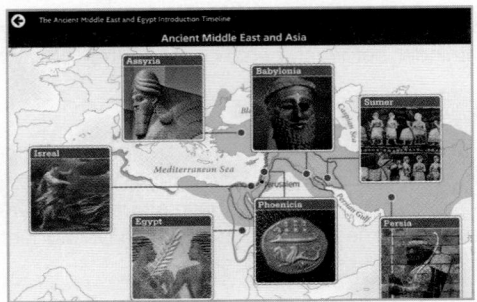

Display the map showing the civilizations of the Ancient Middle East and Egypt. During this Topic students will learn about all of these places, but this map will provide a framework into which they can place the civilizations and events they learn about. Ask students to use the map to point out how location and geographic features might affect the development of these civilizations and the ways the people live.

D Differentiate: **Extra Support** Have students locate Phoenicia on the map. Ask, what factor in Phoenicia's geography might have helped it develop into a trading civilization? *(It is located on the shore of a large sea, the Mediterranean, which meant it could easily sail to many different places to trade.)*

Analyze Maps What important geographical feature do Egypt and the civilizations of Mesopotamia have in common? *(a river)*

Topic Inquiry
Launch the Topic Inquiry with students after introducing the Topic.

A Civilization Emerges in Sumer

Supporting English Language Learners

Use with Digital Text 3, **Sumer's Legacy.**

Learning Strategies

Read *Sumer's Legacy* aloud to students. Then instruct students to complete one of the following writing activities based on their level of English proficiency.

Beginning Retell the content in *Sumer's Legacy* in accessible language for students. Explain the meaning of a *legacy* to students and use Sumer's civilization as an example. Then tell students that they will write one sentence to describe part of Sumer's legacy. Brainstorm parts of this legacy with students and write and display student responses. Then help students write one sentence about Sumer's legacy in their notebooks. Assist students by reviewing their sentences and helping them make any necessary corrections. Provide additional support as necessary, perhaps in the form of cloze sentences, such as:

- Later civilizations, like the Babylonians, used Sumerian knowledge of mathematics to develop _____.

Intermediate Retell the content in *Sumer's Legacy* in accessible language for students. Explain the meaning of a legacy to students and use Sumer's civilization as an example. Then tell students that they will write two or three sentences to describe part of Sumer's legacy. Brainstorm parts of this legacy with students and write and display student responses. Then work together with students to use the brainstormed ideas to write two or three sentences to describe Sumer's legacy. Review students' work, suggesting corrections and asking them to edit and improve their sentences before publishing their work.

Advanced Have students take turns retelling *Sumer's Legacy* to a partner. Then have pairs work together to brainstorm elements of this legacy. Students should work independently to write a short paragraph describing Sumer's legacy. Then have students trade paragraphs with their partners and review each other's work and make suggestions. Finally, have students make corrections to their paragraphs and prepare their own paragraphs for publishing.

Advanced High Have students review *Sumer's Legacy*. Then have them work independently to write a short paragraph describing Sumer's legacy. After writing, students should trade paragraphs with a partner and review each other's work and make suggestions. Finally, have students make corrections to their own paragraphs and prepare their paragraphs for publishing.

Use with Digital Text 2, **Sumerian Civilization Develops.**

Learning Strategies

Read *Sumerian Civilization Develops* aloud to the class. Have students complete one activity according to their level of English proficiency.

Beginning Examine the image of soldiers as it is displayed in *Sumerian Civilization Develops*. Ask students simple questions using accessible language about the picture to elicit descriptions of the image. Use student responses to build their understanding of the words *ruler* and *monarch*. As these words come up in the discussion, define them and use them in example sentences. Instruct students to write the definitions and sentences in their notebooks.

Intermediate Examine the image of soldiers as it is displayed in *Sumerian Civilization Develops*. Use accessible language to ask students to describe the image in their own words. Use students' responses to help build their understanding of the words *ruler* and *monarch*. After discussing the words, provide students with accurate definitions and use each word in an example sentence. Instruct students to write the definitions and sentences in their notebooks.

Advanced Have students work with a partner to examine the image of soldiers as it is displayed in *Sumerian Civilization Develops*. Ask pairs to discuss the image and make connections between the image and the information in the text. Then have pairs define the words *ruler* and *monarch* and write a sentence using each word. Finally, have each pair join with another pair to share their definitions and sentences. Circulate among students to provide feedback and support to as needed.

Advanced High Have students work with a partner to examine the image of soldiers as it is displayed in *Sumerian Civilization Develops*. Ask pairs to discuss the image and make connections between the image and the information in the text. Then have pairs define the words *ruler* and *monarch* and write a sentence using each word. Finally, have each pair join with another pair to share their definitions and sentences. Circulate among students to provide feedback and support to as needed.

▶ Differentiate Instruction

Use the Differentiated Instruction notes throughout the lesson plan to support the varied skill sets, levels of readiness, and interests in the mixed-ability classroom.

Challenge These notes include suggestions for expanding the activity for advanced students.

On-Level These notes include suggestions for modifying the activity to address different interests or learning styles.

Extra Support These notes include ideas for providing more scaffolding or reading spuport.

Special Needs These notes provide ideas for adapting instruction to support the needs of various special needs students.

■ NOTES

_____

_____

_____

_____

_____

A Civilization Emerges in Sumer

Objectives

Objective 1: Understand how geography influenced the development of civilization in the Fertile Crescent.

Objective 2: Outline the main features of Sumerian civilization.

Objective 3: Explain how the advances in learning made by the Sumerians left a lasting legacy for later peoples to build on.

LESSON 1 ORGANIZER			PACING: APPROX. 1 PERIOD, .5 BLOCKS		
				RESOURCES	
		OBJECTIVES	PACING	Online	Print
Connect					
	DIGITAL START UP ACTIVITY **The Fertile Crescent**		5 min.	●	
Investigate					
	DIGITAL TEXT 1 **Civilizations Arise in the Fertile Crescent**	Objective 1	10 min.	●	●
	INTERACTIVE MAP **Sumer and the Fertile Crescent**		10 min.	●	
	DIGITAL TEXT 2 **Sumerian Civilization Develops**	Objective 2	10 min.	●	●
	DIGITAL TEXT 3 **Sumer's Legacy**	Objective 3	10 min.	●	●
	INTERACTIVE GALLERY **Sumerian Civilization**		10 min.	●	
Synthesize					
	DIGITAL ACTIVITY **What is Civilization?**		5 min.	●	
Demonstrate					
	DIGITAL QUIZ **Lesson Quiz and Class Discussion Board**		10 min.	●	

■ CONNECT

DIGITAL START UP ACTIVITY
The Fertile Crescent

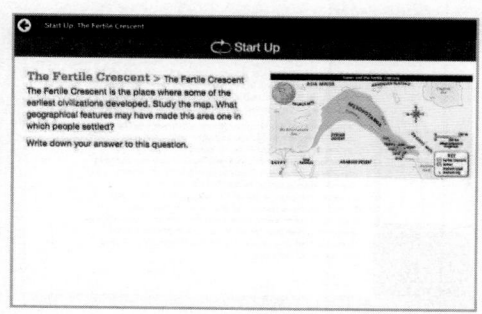

Project the Start Up Activity Ask students to look at the map and to think about what geographical features may have made this area one in which people settled.

Discuss Remind students that the area known as Mesopotamia was a river valley civilization because it grew between two rivers. As we learned previously, it was important for people to live near water sources in order to have access to drinking water as well as water for farming.

Aa Vocabulary Development: Use the Interactive Reading Notepad to preview the Key Terms and Academic Vocabulary in this Lesson with students.

⇄ FLIP IT!

Assign the Flipped Video for this lesson.

■ STUDENT EDITION PRINT
PAGES: 26–31

■ INVESTIGATE

DIGITAL TEXT 1
Civilizations Arise in the Fertile Crescent

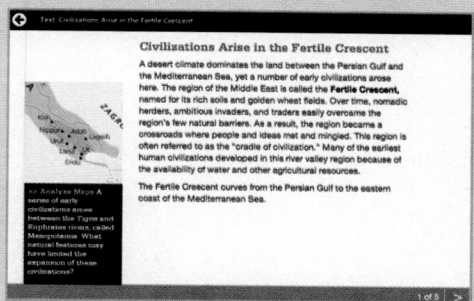

INTERACTIVE MAP
Sumer and the Fertile Crescent

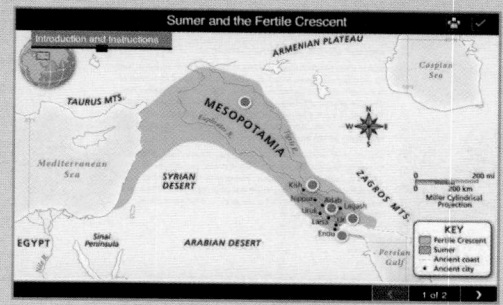

Objective 1: Understand how geography influenced the development of civilization in the Fertile Crescent.

Quick Instruction

The early civilizations of Mesopotamia depended on the region's two important rivers—the Tigris and the Euphrates. Mesopotamia means "between the rivers" in Greek and the fertile farmland allowed for the rise of civilizations. Hunter-gatherer groups first settled in Mesopotamia and these people learned how to plant crops and to grow their own food on the fertile farmland. Plentiful food led to population growth and the formation of villages, which eventually developed into city-states and the world's first civilization.

Interactive Map: Sumer and the Fertile Crescent Project the map. Look carefully at the purple area, Sumer, and discuss the importance of human factors as well as geography on the development of river valley civilizations. The early Sumerians faced the challenge of learning how to control the flow of river water to their fields during rainy and dry seasons. They learned to work together to control the waters, and over time city-states developed along with other features of river valley civilizations, such as government, social hierarchy, religion, and other features we will read about. What made civilization possible in Mesopotamia? *(The two rivers created fertile farmland, which provided people a place to settle and eventually led to the development of civilizations.)*

👥 ACTIVE CLASSROOM

Have students write a headline that captures the information displayed in the map. Instruct them to write a headline for this topic that captured the most important aspect that should be remembered. Allow time for them to share their headlines with a partner.

ELL Use the ELL activity described in the ELL chart.

Further Instruction

Editable Presentation Use the Editable Presentation to present the main ideas for this Core Reading.

Civilizations Develop in the Fertile Crescent: Core Text and Interactive Reading Notepad Project and discuss the questions and answers from the Interactive Reading Notepad.

Review the influence of geographic factors on the development of river valley civilizations, and discuss the influence of human factors on the development of civilizations.

Draw Conclusion Temple priests or royal officials would organize and provide leadership on large projects such as building dikes to hold back floodwaters and many other projects. How might running large projects prepare people for running a government? *(It would provide the leaders with organizational skills and ability to control a large group of people along with other necessary leadership skills.)*

A Civilization Emerges in Sumer

DIGITAL TEXT 2
Sumerian Civilization Develops

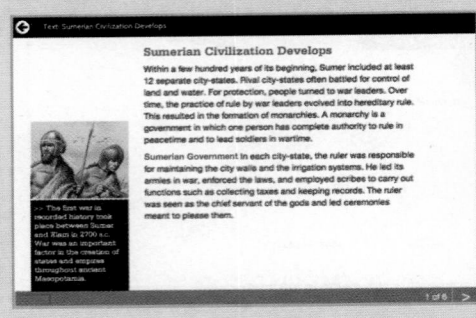

DIGITAL TEXT 3
Sumer's Legacy

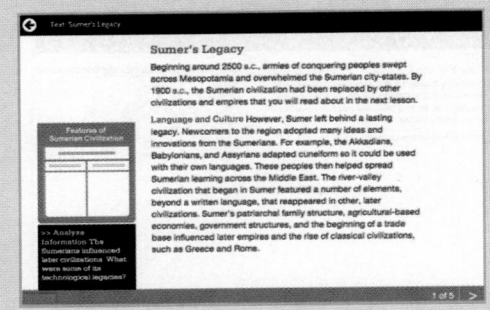

Objective 2: Outline the main features of Sumerian civilization.

Quick Instruction

The main features of Sumerian civilization included an organized government, a distinct social hierarchy, an organized religion, and a writing system. Ancient Sumerians used a system of writing known as cuneiform, which transformed pictorial drawings into signs that represented words. The famous *Epic of Gilgamesh*, a Sumerian tale of a man searching for eternal life, was written in cuneiform.

Analyze Images Project the infographic about cuneiform. Cuneiform recorded all important activities, from the sale of land to marriage and adoption contracts. By 3200 *B.C.*, the Sumerian written language was developed enough to record oral epic tales, such as the *Epic of Gilgamesh*. How did cuneiform writing allow Sumerians to communicate more effectively than they could using tokens and clay envelopes? *(It expanded their possibilities for more complex communication because it gave them options for not only economic transactions but also ideas.)*

Further Instruction

Sumerian Civilization Develops: Core Text and Interactive Reading Notepad Project and discuss the questions and answers from the Interactive Reading Notepad.

Review the features of Sumerian civilization, such as the formation of city-states leading to a government structure that consisted of an absolute monarchy with characteristics of theocracies, since the kings were seen as intermediaries between the human and the divine. Discuss the importance of a social structure within Sumerian society, again noting the highest class. Other features of Sumerian civilization were an organized religion and the cuneiform writing system.

Determine Relevance Sumerian scribes were in charge of keeping track of economic exchanges as well as social issues by recording details on clay tablets using cuneiform. How might the invention of cuneiform writing have strengthened Sumerian government and religious practices? *(It would have strengthened the government by allowing it to preserve its records, laws, and achievements. Sumerian religious practices were strengthened by allowing priests to preserve prayers, rituals, and beliefs about gods, goddesses, and the afterlife.)*

Objective 3: Explain how the advances in learning made by the Sumerians left a lasting legacy for later people to build on.

Quick Instruction

Discuss the development and diffusion of Sumerian ideas. Sumerian knowledge and advancements made in language, culture, astronomy, mathematics, and technology were eventually passed on to the classical civilizations of Greece and Rome through various conquerors and traders in the Middle East. Some inventions, such as the wheel, cuneiform, and the number system, created a foundation for developments that impacted the Western world of today.

Interactive Gallery: Sumerian Civilization Project the gallery. Look carefully at the photo of the handcrafted Sumerian jewelry and discuss the importance of trade on cultural diffusion of Sumerian inventions and ideas. The early Sumerians did not have a lot of natural resources, so they counted on trade to obtain the goods they needed and wanted. Through trade, goods, stories, and tales were exchanged, allowing other cultures to adopt the ways of life of others. How was it possible for the independent city-states to share a similar culture? *(Ideas, goods, and beliefs spread through trade as the traders brought products and ideas from other city-states and civilizations.)*

INTERACTIVE GALLERY
Sumerian Civilization

📷 ACTIVE CLASSROOM

Use the Write 1-Get 3 strategy. Ask a question with multiple possible answers, such as: What are some of Sumer's lasting legacies? Instruct students to fold a piece of paper into fourths, then write down one response in the first box. Then go around the room asking to hear student's responses. Instruct students to record a different correct response in each of their remaining boxes until they have four total responses. Share and correct responses with the class.

ELL Use the ELL activity described in the ELL chart.

Further Instruction

Sumer's Legacy: Core Text and Interactive Reading Notepad Project and discuss the questions and answers from the Interactive Reading Notepad.

Review how the lasting legacies of Sumer such as the writing system, cuneiform, understanding of planetary movements, and the creation of a number system, the wheel, irrigation systems, and advances in metalworking all lived on after Sumer's defeat. Explain that Sumer's advances diffused to other cultures through trade and conquerors. The Babylonians, for example, controlled Sumer and adapted many Sumerian technological advances and much culture allowing Sumer's legacy to grow and spread.

Determine Relevance Why was trade important to the ancient Sumerians? *(Trade allowed for Sumerians to have access to natural resources they lacked and allowed for the exchange of goods and ideas.)*

DIGITAL ACTIVITY
What is Civilization?

Ask students to consider the Topic Essential Question, "How much does geography affect people's lives?" Remind them of Mesopotamia's location and the importance of the Tigris and Euphrates rivers. Have them use the Think Pair strategy to answer the questions in the Digital Activity. Ask them to define civilization. Then have students explain how Sumer relates to this definition. Remind students to use details from the text to support their ideas. *(Civilization is when people can organize their society and place value on social welfare, art, science, religion, and other elements. Features of civilization in Sumer include: religion, social classes, art, culture, language, cities, writing, and government. Students should discuss the role of music in civilization.)*

Have partners think about the following question: Do you think geography is the most important factor for the development of early civilizations? *(Answers will vary, but many students may say yes, because it, in the case of river valleys, allowed people to stop living a nomadic lifestyle and to form structure and stability.)* Have pairs share their answers with the class.

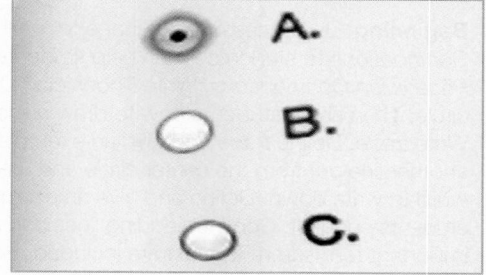

DIGITAL QUIZ
Lesson Quiz and Class Discussion Board

Assign the online Lesson Quiz for this lesson if you haven't already done so. Students will be offered automatic remediation or enrichment based on their score.

Pose the following question to the class on the Discussion Board:

In "Civilization Emerges in Sumer" you read about the events that led to the development of the river valley civilizations in Mesopotamia and the features of early civilizations.

Summarize Explain how geography influenced the development of Mesopotamian civilizations. *(Mesopotamia was the land "between rivers" which allowed for fertile farmland and provided trade routes. The fertile farmland provided people with a reason to stay in one place and form city-states, whereas trade routes allowed for the civilizations to share their advancements and natural resources).*

Evaluate Data Considering what you have learned in this lesson, do you think ancient civilizations would have prospered and grown without the access to trade? Why or why not? *(Answers will vary. Trade was important for ancient civilizations to grow because they needed access to other natural resources and adopted ideas from other city-states allowing each city-state to develop their ideologies and advancements in technology, mathematics, and astronomy.)*

Topic Inquiry
Have students continue their investigations for the Topic Inquiry.

Empires in Mesopotamia

Supporting English Language Learners

Use with Digital Text 4, **Phoenician Contributions.**

Learning Strategies
Read *Phoenician Contributions* aloud to students. Draw a concept map and ask students to complete it by drawing an illustration or writing words, phrases, or sentences on the map.

Beginning Use accessible language to retell the content in *Phoenician Contributions* to students. Then help students create a concept map for *Phoenician Contributions*. Write Phoenician Contributions in the center circle. Then show students how to draw a line out from the center circle. Write *trade*. Define *trade* and give an example from the text. Then draw another line out from the center circle and ask students to suggest a word to write down. Define and give an example for each correct term students suggest. Continue adding lines and words to the map until all the important terms from the text are included. Finally, have students copy the map into their notebooks. Ask students to draw an image with each term to provide hints about what the vocabulary means.

Intermediate Help students create a concept map for *Phoenician Contributions*. Write and display *Phoenician Contributions* in the center circle. Then have a student volunteer draw a line out from the center circle and suggest a key term to write here. Examples include *manufacturing, trade, colony,* and *alphabet*. Help students define each term and find examples of each in the text. Continue adding lines and words to the map until all the important terms from the text are included. Finally, have students copy the map into their notebooks.

Advanced Have students work with a partner to create a concept map for the information they learned from reading *Phoenician Contributions*. Instruct pairs to define the terms in their maps and find an example in the text for each. Review the maps with students to ensure that all important terms are included.

Advanced High Have students work independently to create a concept map for the information they learned from reading *Phoenician Contributions*. Instruct students to define the terms in their maps and find an example in the text for each. When students are finished with their maps, they should share their maps with a partner. Review the maps with students to ensure that all important terms are included.

Use with Digital Text 3, **Rise of the Persian Empire.**

Learning Strategies
Read *Rise of the Persian Empire* aloud to the class. Have students complete one activity according to their level of English proficiency.

Beginning Provide students with a list of formal and informal sentences about *Rise of the Persian Empire*. Read each sentence aloud and have students indicate whether the sentence is formal or informal. If time allows, help students write one formal and one informal sentence about the rule of Darius I.

Intermediate Provide students with a list of formal and informal sentences about *Rise of the Persian Empire*. Help student volunteers read each sentence aloud and indicate whether the sentence is formal or informal. If time allows, have students write one formal and one informal sentence about the rule of Darius I.

Advanced Have students work in small groups to write three formal and three informal sentences about *Rise of the Persian Empire*. Then have a volunteer from each group read the sentences aloud to the class.

Advanced High Have students work independently to write three formal and three informal sentences about *Rise of the Persian Empire*. Then have students convene in small groups of three or four to read the sentences aloud.

◘ Differentiate Instruction

Use the Differentiated Instruction notes throughout the lesson plan to support the varied skill sets, levels of readiness, and interests in the mixed-ability classroom.

Challenge These notes include suggestions for expanding the activity for advanced students.

On-Level These notes include suggestions for modifying the activity to address different interests or learning styles.

Extra Support These notes include ideas for providing more scaffolding or reading spuport.

Special Needs These notes provide ideas for adapting instruction to support the needs of various special needs students.

■ NOTES

PEARSON
realize™
www.PearsonRealize.com

Go online to access additional resources including:
Primary Sources • Biographies • Supreme Court cases •
21st Century Skill Tutorials • Maps • Graphic Organizers.

Objectives

Objective 1: Outline the achievements of the first empires that arose in Mesopotamia

Objective 2: Understand how conquests brought new empires and ideas into the Middle East.

Objective 3: Describe the major political, religious, and cultural influences of Persia.

Objective 4: Summarize the contributions the Phoenicians made to the ancient Middle East.

LESSON 2 ORGANIZER		PACING: APPROX. 1 PERIOD, .5 BLOCKS			
				RESOURCES	
		OBJECTIVES	PACING	Online	Print
Connect					
DIGITAL START UP ACTIVITY **The Spreading of Ideas**			5 min.	●	
Investigate					
DIGITAL TEXT 1 **Empires Emerge in Mesopotamia**		Objective	10 min.	●	●
DIGITAL TEXT 2 **New Empires and Ideas**		Objective 2	10 min.	●	●
INTERACTIVE GALLERY **Development of Civilizations**			10 min.	●	
DIGITAL TEXT 3 **Rise of the Persian Empire**		Objective	10 min.	●	●
DIGITAL TEXT 4 **Phoenician Contributions**		Objective 4	10 min.	●	●
INTERACTIVE GALLERY **Mesopotamian Empires**			10 min.	●	
Synthesize					
DIGITAL ACTIVITY **Persian Influences**			5 min.	●	
Demonstrate					
LESSON QUIZ **Lesson Quiz and Class Discussion Board**			10 min.	●	

Empires in Mesopotamia

■ CONNECT

DIGITAL START UP ACTIVITY
The Spreading of Ideas

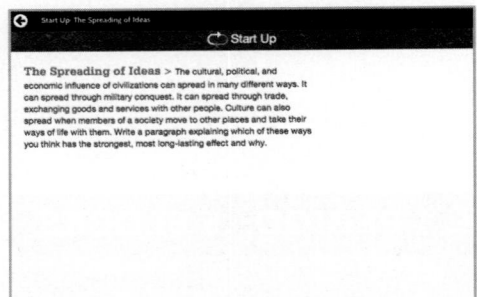

Project the Start Up Activity Ask students to answer the questions as they enter and get settled.

Discuss Remind students that one of the features of civilization is an organized government with laws. We will learn about a set of laws known as Hammurabi's Code, which gave rise to important political and legal ideas, such as the principle that government has a responsibility for what happens in society. These ideas strongly influenced Mesopotamian civilizations and future civilizations as well. Think about why laws are important and discuss the list of important laws the students listed.

Aa **Vocabulary Development:** Use the Interactive Reading Notepad to preview the Key Terms and Academic Vocabulary in this Lesson with students.

⤵ FLIP IT!
Assign the Flipped Video for this lesson.

■ STUDENT EDITION PRINT
PAGES: 32–39

■ INVESTIGATE

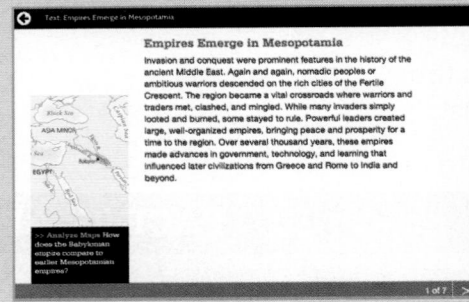

DIGITAL TEXT 1
Empires Emerge in Mesopotamia

Quick Instruction

Analyze Graphics Project the infographic from the text on the whiteboard. Introduce the infographic by reminding students that laws had been around since Sumerian times, but Hammurabi made them public by carving them on a stone pillar. Walk through a few of the laws listed on the infographic together, focusing on the impact of their political and legal ideas. Point out to students that there were laws against criminal acts. This part of the code was an advance because by setting out specific, usually harsh by our standards, punishments for specific offenses, Hammurabi's Code limited personal vengeance and encouraged social order and adherence to a legal process.

The civil law elements of the code were also influential. This branch of law deals with private rights and matters, such as business contracts, property inheritance, taxes, marriage, and divorce. Much of Hammurabi's civil code dealt with property rights, but some laws were designed to protect the powerless, such as slaves or women, although women's civil and legal rights lagged far behind men's. One key impact of Hammurabi's code was the idea the king did not have sole power over the people.

Analyze Maps The need for organization and law came from the growing size of the new empires. How does the extent of Sumer compare to the extents of the later Akkadian and Babylonian empires? *(The Akkadian and Babylonian empires were much larger than Sumer.)*

Further Instruction

Editable Presentation Use the Editable Presentation to present the main ideas for this Core Reading.

Empires Emerge in Mesopotamia: Core Text and Interactive Reading Notepad Project and discuss the Interactive Reading Notepad questions and answers.

Discuss that the river valley civilizations in Mesopotamia influenced the rise of later civilizations, such as Greece and Rome, in such ways as unifying cities and creating governmental structures. Be sure that students understand the importance of unified cities and a strong governmental structure to ruling large groups of people. Discuss the Babylonian empire, and the importance of established laws that maintained peace and stability within the empire.

Synthesize Explain a lasting legacy of Hammurabi's Code. *(the principle that government had a responsibility for what occurred in society)*

DIGITAL TEXT 2

New Empires and Ideas

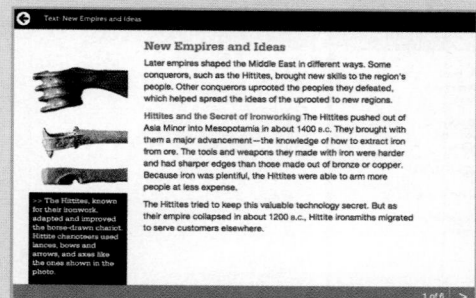

INTERACTIVE GALLERY

Development of Civilizations

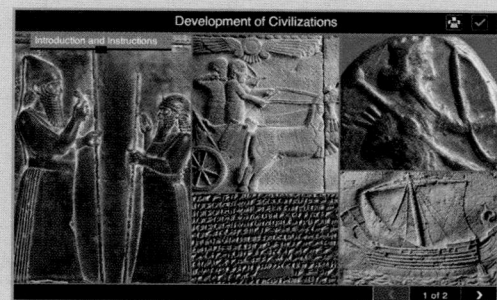

DIGITAL TEXT 3

Rise of the Persian Empire

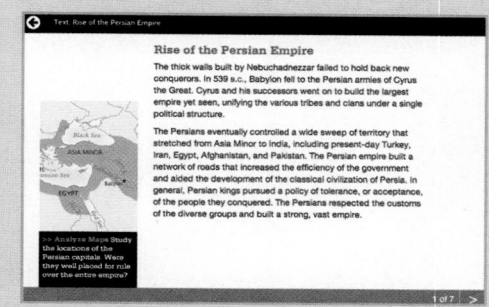

Objective 2: Understand how conquests brought new empires and ideas into the Middle East.

Quick Instruction

Hittites, Assyrians, and Babylonians all built strong empires with new ideas to the Middle East. The Hittites brought their advanced knowledge of ironworking, which eventually spread, across Asia, Africa, and Europe. The fierce Assyrian warriors created and maintained a well-ordered society. The new Babylonian empire was known for its vast size and impressive infrastructure. Each of these empires built on ideas from the preceding empire and introduced new ideas along the way.

Interactive Gallery: Development of Civilizations Project the gallery. Look carefully at the picture of the Assyrian ruins of the library. Discuss the cultural diffusion and how ideas were spread throughout the Middle East by conquering empires, trade, and written records. The diffusion of ideas eventually influenced the development of classical civilizations such as those in Persia, Greece, and Rome.

👥 ACTIVE CLASSROOM

Use the See-Think-Wonder strategy. Pair students with a partner. Then ask them: What do you see? What does that make you think? What are you wondering about now that you've seen this? Share insights with the class.

Further Instruction

New Empires and Ideas: Core Text and Interactive Reading Notepad Project and discuss the questions and answers from the Interactive Reading Notepad.

Discuss the diffusion of major ideas in technology, such as ironworking, throughout the Middle East, Africa, and Europe through conquering armies and trade. The Assyrians adopted the ironwork of the Hittites and used it to become a fearsome military power. Babylonians in turn adopted this technology from the Assyrians after they defeated them and established the New Babylonian Empire.

Summarize Each of the empires brought new ideas that were spread through conquest and trade. Describe a significant contribution made by the Hittites, Assyrians, and Babylonians. *(The Hittites introduced ironworking, the Assyrians introduced laws regulating life within the royal household, and Babylonians built one of the largest cities in ancient Mesopotamia.)*

Quick Instruction

Analyze Graphics Project the money economy chart from the text on the whiteboard. Introduce the chart by reminding students that the Persians eventually conquered Babylon and introduced many new ideas, including the revolutionary idea of a money economy. The money economy enabled the vast Persian empire to expand commerce and promote international trade.

ELL Use the ELL activity described in the ELL chart.

Further Instruction

Rise of the Persian Empire: Core Text and Interactive Reading Notepad Project and discuss the Interactive Reading Notepad questions and answers.

Discuss the major political influences of Persia including its system of government that became a model for later rulers. The large Persian empire was divided into departments and subdivisions, each administered by local officials who followed a set of procedures and rules. This bureaucracy allowed for the large empire to run smoothly in spite of the great diversity of its subjects.

Be sure that students understand that Zoroastrianism focused on two important elements: the struggle between good and evil, and the free will of the individual to choose one or the other.

Empires in Mesopotamia

DIGITAL TEXT 4
Phoenician Contributions

INTERACTIVE GALLERY
Mesopotamian Empires

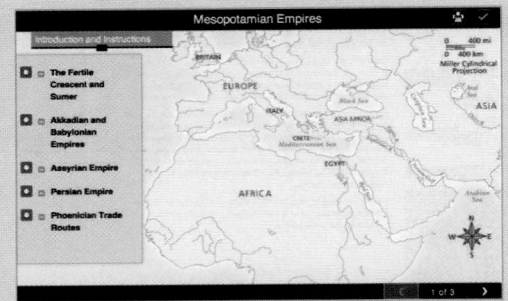

Synthesize Zoroastrian religious beliefs stressed the idea of an individual's free will to choose good or evil. Is this belief important in other religions you know of? Which ones? *(Three other religions, Judaism, Christianity, and Islam, also stressed the importance of individuals exercising their free will to choose between good or evil.)*

Objective 4: **Summarize the contributions the Phoenicians made to the ancient Middle East.**

Quick Instruction

The Phoenicians were from a string of cities along the eastern Mediterranean coast. Their location allowed them to develop manufacturing and trade. Phoenicians traded with people all around the Mediterranean Sea. They established colonies in North Africa, Sicily, and Spain as trading outposts, which also allowed them to spread ideas from Mesopotamia to faraway lands. As a result of their expansive trade routes, Phoenicians are known as "carriers of civilization" because they spread Middle Eastern ideas throughout the Mediterranean. Their most significant contribution to culture was the alphabet, which was later adapted by the Greeks and, with later adaptations, became the alphabet we use today.

Interactive Map: Mesopotamian Empires

Project the map. Look carefully at the map of the Phoenician trade routes. Discuss the extent of the Phoenician trade routes and their capabilities to learn and spread ideas and inventions through trade. The diffusion of ideas eventually influenced the development of classical civilizations such as Greece and Rome.

👥 ACTIVE CLASSROOM

Use the Closer Look strategy. Project the map of Persian lands onto the board and divide it into four numbered quadrants. Have students count off from one to four. Then have them look closely at the part of the image in their quadrant. Have them tell their group what they see and what they learned as a result of their focus on one part of the map. Share insights with the class.

ELL Use the ELL activity described in the ELL chart.

Further Instruction

Phoenician Contributions: Core Text and Interactive Reading Notepad Project and discuss the questions and answers from the Interactive Reading Notepad.

Discuss how major ideas spread throughout the Mediterranean as a result of Phoenician trade. Discuss how the diffusion of ideas through trade also impacted the development of classical civilizations.

Summarize Ideas, advancements in government, technology, and mathematics were spread through conquest and trade. Explain why the term "carriers of civilization" is used to describe Phoenicians. *(The Phoenicians traded goods and spread ideas throughout Mesopotamia and the Mediterranean reaching Sicily, Spain, and Britain.)*

■ SYNTHESIZE

■ DEMONSTRATE

DIGITAL ACTIVITY
Persian Influences

LESSON QUIZ
Lesson Quiz and Class Discussion Board

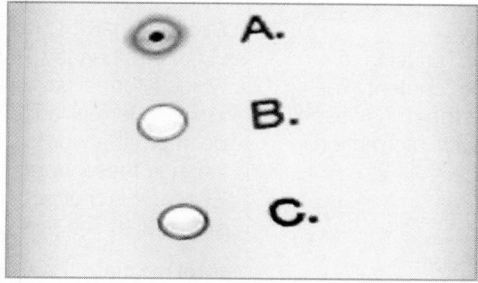

Ask students to recall Persian influences, especially on politics, religion, and culture. Have them use the Think Pair strategy to answer the questions in the Synthesize activity. Discuss that Persia became a strong and unified civilization because of their efficient government structure and by developing a money economy. Persia operated under a centralized government that was unified economically and applied the same laws to everyone.

Remind them that one feature of a classical civilization is the development of the idea that individuals have rights. Zoroastrian religious practices stressed the importance of the individual and his or her free will. Have students write two to three sentences describing how Zoroastrianism helped advance the importance of the individual. Remind students to use details from the text to support their ideas. *(Answers will vary. Civilizations developed the legal concept that individuals have natural rights, and Zoroastrianism was founded on the belief that individuals have free will and rights.)*

Have partners think about the following question: How did the size of the Persian empire strengthen its influence throughout the Middle East? *(Answers will vary, but many students will discuss Persia's willingness to accept and adapt ideas of the nations they conquered. Their government system also divided the large empire into manageable subdivisions that could effectively communicate through the use of the postal and roadway systems.)* Have pairs share their answers with the class.

Assign the online Lesson Quiz for this lesson, if you haven't already done so. Students will be offered automatic remediation or enrichment based on their score.

Pose the following question to the class on the Discussion Board:

In "Empires in Mesopotamia" you read about new empires and ideas that spread throughout ancient Mesopotamia, the Persian Empire, and the Mediterranean.

Summarize List three different influences of the Persian empire. *(The development of a roadway system leading to effective communication, the development of money economy that increased commerce and international trade, and the idea that individuals have free will and rights.)*

Topic Inquiry
Have students continue their investigations for the Topic Inquiry.

The Hebrews and the Origins of Judaism

 Supporting English Language Learners

Use with Digital Text 2, **The Ancient Israelites.**

Learning Strategies
Read *The Ancient Israelites* aloud to students. Then instruct students to complete one of the following activities based on their level of English proficiency.

Beginning Review *The Ancient Israelites* with students, pausing to demonstrate requesting assistance in understanding the content. Then read the following sentences and have students repeat them. Ask each student to read the sentences aloud and ask for help with information in the text.

- How do you say this word? (demonstrate pointing to challenging word in the text) Can you explain _____ again, please?

Intermediate Review the first paragraph of *The Ancient Israelites* with students, pausing to demonstrate requesting assistance in understanding the content. Divide students into small groups to generate their own questions to ask for assistance. Have groups choose three of their best questions to share with other groups.

Advanced Have students work with a partner to discuss why knowing how to ask for assistance is important for understanding the information in the reading assignment *The Ancient Israelites*. Then have pairs develop a list of questions and statements that can be used to request assistance in understanding the content in this section.

Advanced High Have students work independently to develop a list of questions and statements that can be used to request assistance in understanding the content in *The Ancient Israelites*. Have individuals turn to a partner to share their three best questions. Then engage students in a large group discussion about why knowing how to ask for assistance is an important skill when learning about history.

Use with Digital Text 3, **Judaism's Legacy.**

Learning Strategies
Read *Judaism's Legacy* aloud to the class. Have students complete one activity according to their level of English proficiency.

Beginning Provide students with several informal sentences about Judaism's Legacy. Read them aloud. Help students identify situations in which informal language is appropriate to use. Then identify situations in which formal language is best. Read the first sentence aloud and point out the words that make the sentence informal rather than formal. Change these words to reconstruct the sentence into a formal sentence. Repeat this procedure with the remaining informal sentences, encouraging students to suggest ways to make each sentence formal.

Intermediate Provide students with several informal sentences about Judaism's Legacy. Ask students to suggest situations in which informal language is appropriate to use. Then discuss situations in which formal language is best. Read the first sentence aloud and point out the words that make the sentence informal rather than formal. Change these words to reconstruct the sentence into a formal sentence. Then have small groups of students repeat this procedure with the remaining informal sentences. Circulate among student groups to offer support as necessary.

Advanced Provide student pairs with an informal e-mail message that describes the law of the ancient Israelites. Have pairs read the e-mail and make a list of situations in which such an e-mail is appropriate and another list of situations in which it would be inappropriate. Then instruct pairs to work together to transform the e-mail into a formal letter. Have pairs share their formal letters with the rest of the class. Circulate among students to offer support as necessary.

Advanced High Provide students with an informal e-mail message that describes the law of the ancient Israelites. Have students read the e-mail and create a list of situations in which such an email is appropriate and another list of situations in which it would be inappropriate. Then instruct students to work independently to transform the e-mail into a formal letter. Have students share their formal letters with the rest of the class. Circulate among students to offer support as necessary.

▣ Differentiate Instruction

Use the Differentiated Instruction notes throughout the lesson plan to support the varied skill sets, levels of readiness, and interests in the mixed-ability classroom.

Challenge These notes include suggestions for expanding the activity for advanced students.

On-Level These notes include suggestions for modifying the activity to address different interests or learning styles.

Extra Support These notes include ideas for providing more scaffolding or reading spuport.

Special Needs These notes provide ideas for adapting instruction to support the needs of various special needs students.

▮ NOTES

PEARSON
realize™
www.PearsonRealize.com

Go online to access additional resources including:
Primary Sources • Biographies • Supreme Court cases •
21st Century Skill Tutorials • Maps • Graphic Organizers.

Objectives

Objective 1: Understand what made the ancient Israelites' belief system unique from others at the time.

Objective 2: Outline the main events in the early history of the Israelites.

Objective 3: Analyze the central moral and ethical ideas of Judaism.

LESSON 3 ORGANIZER		PACING: APPROX. 1 PERIOD, .5 BLOCKS			
				RESOURCES	
		OBJECTIVES	**PACING**	**Online**	**Print**
Connect					
DIGITAL START UP ACTIVITY **The Hebrew Bible**			5 min.	●	
Investigate					
DIGITAL TEXT 1 **The Ancient Israelites' Unique Belief System**		Objective 1	10 min.	●	●
DIGITAL TEXT 2 **The Ancient Israelites**		Objective 2	10 min.	●	●
INTERACTIVE GALLERY **Origins of Judaism**			10 min.	●	
DIGITAL TEXT 3 **Judaism's Legacy**		Objective 3	10 min.	●	●
INTERACTIVE CHART **The Ten Commandments and Modern Laws**			10 min.	●	
Synthesize					
DIGITAL ACTIVITY **Origins of Judaism**			5 min.	●	
Demonstrate					
LESSON QUIZ **Lesson Quiz and Class Discussion Board**			10 min.	●	

The Hebrews and the Origins of Judaism

CONNECT

DIGITAL START UP ACTIVITY
The Hebrew Bible

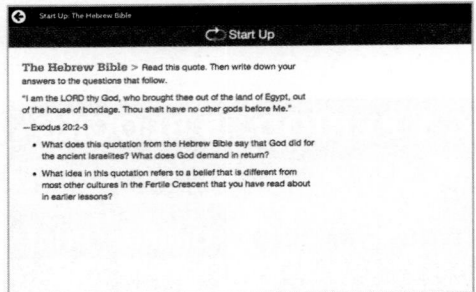

Project the Start Up Activity Ask students to read the quote from Exodus 20:2-3 then answer the questions as they enter and get settled.

Discuss Remind students that all of the other civilizations in ancient Mesopotamia were polytheistic; they believed in many gods. The ancient Mesopotamians built temples and statues in order to honor the gods. Discuss the different ideas of the ancient Israelites compared to the other cultures in the Fertile Crescent, highlighting monotheism as a central idea of Judaism. Reread the quote from Exodus and discuss the importance of one god for the ancient Israelites. Especially note that God expects the Israelites to only have one god and to worship only Him.

Aa Vocabulary Development: Use the Interactive Reading Notepad to preview the Key Terms and Academic Vocabulary in this Lesson with students.

⇅ FLIP IT!
Assign the Flipped Video for this lesson.

STUDENT EDITION PRINT PAGES: 40–45

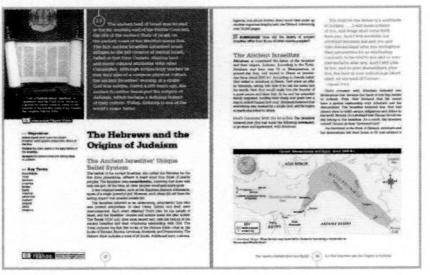

INVESTIGATE

DIGITAL TEXT 1
The Ancient Israelites' Unique Belief System

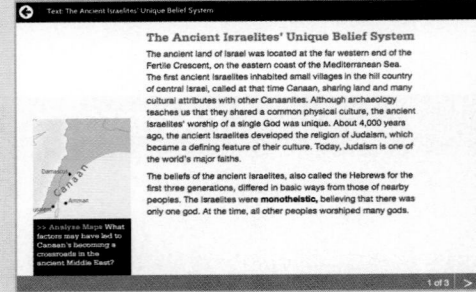

Objective 1: Understand what made the ancient Israelites' belief system unique from others at the time.

Quick Instruction

Analyze Maps Project the map from the Text on the whiteboard. Introduce the map by reminding students that every other group of people living in the same area believed in many gods, while the Israelites believed in one God. One of the central ideas of Judaism is the existence of one God who is all-knowing and all-powerful. Israelites believed their God was present everywhere and that he had a plan for the Israelites. Students will learn about what Jews believe are the origins of Judaism in the next Text: how the father of the Israelites and Judaism, Abraham, moved himself and his followers from the city-state Ur to the region of Canaan because he believed it was part of God's plan for him and his followers.

ELL Use the ELL activity described in the ELL chart.

Further Instruction

Editable Presentation Use the Editable Presentation to present the main ideas for this Core Reading.

The Ancient Israelites' Unique Belief System: Core Text and Interactive Reading Notepad Project and discuss the Interactive Reading Notepad questions and answers. Discuss the central ideas of Judaism, highlighting monotheism, as the Israelites were the only people of the time who believed in one god.

Synthesize Explain the central ideas of Judaism. *(Judaism was built around the belief in one god who is all-knowing and powerful. The Israelites believed their god was present everywhere and that he had a plan for the Israelites.)*

DIGITAL TEXT 2
The Ancient Israelites

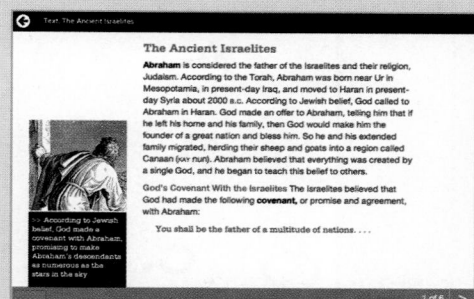

INTERACTIVE GALLERY
Origins of Judaism

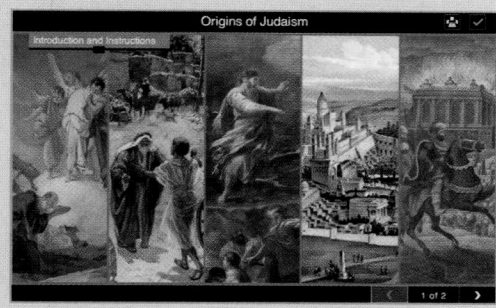

DIGITAL TEXT 3
Judaism's Legacy

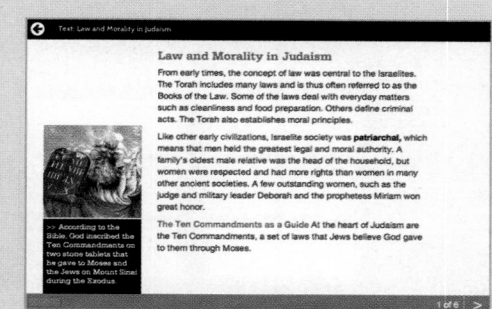

Objective 2: Outline the main events in the early history of the Israelites

Quick Instruction

According to Jewish belief, the origins of Judaism can be traced back to Abraham, who made a covenant with God. Abraham and his descendants moved to the land of Canaan, where Abraham had a son named Isaac. Isaac fathered Jacob who was believed to have been blessed by God and given the name Israel. Jacob had twelve sons and all his descendants are known as the children of Israel. The Israelites were eventually enslaved in Egypt, where they had fled during a famine. Moses led the Israelites back to their promised land. Eventually, Saul united the twelve tribes of Israel into the kingdom of Israel. The kingdom eventually divided into two separate entities until the Assyrians conquered the northern Kingdom of Israel, followed by the Babylonians and then the Persians. However, Israelites, or Jews, always kept their strong belief in one God, and Judasim developed into one of the world's major religions.

Interactive Drill-Down: Origins of Judaism
Project the drill-down interactivity. Look carefully at the fourth picture. Discuss the importance of the unification of the twelve tribes of Israel into the one kingdom of Israel. Then describe how the kingdom of Israel was divided into two and eventually conquered by the Assyrians, Babylonians, and Persians. Highlight that during the years of captivity, the Israelites kept their belief system.

🖥 ACTIVE CLASSROOM

Use the Sequence It strategy. Give students pieces of paper with the following events out of order: Abraham moves his descendants to Canaan, Jacob leads his family to Egypt, Moses receives the Ten Commandments, King David unites the twelve tribes of Israel and forms the kingdom of Israel, Assyrians defeat the kingdom of Israel. Allow students 3–5 minutes to put the events in the proper order.

Further Instruction

The Ancient Israelites: Core Text and Interactive Reading Notepad Project and discuss the questions and answers from the Interactive Reading Notepad.

Discuss how Judaism spread as a result of conquering nations. During the time of Babylonian occupation, Israelites were forced to leave Canaan and many settled back into Egypt and in the city of Babylon. Eventually, the Persian empire took control and allowed the Israelites to resettle in Canaan under Persian rule.

Summarize Moses led the Israelites back to the land of Canaan after they fled Egypt. Many Israelites returned to Canaan after the Persian empire took control. Why was Canaan a special location to the ancient Israelites? *(Canaan was considered the "promised land" because of God's covenant with Abraham.)*

Objective 3: Analyze the central moral and ethical ideas of Judaism

Quick Instruction

The concept of law was central to the way of life of the ancient Israelites. The Torah included many laws, from dealing with cleanliness to criminal and civil laws. The Ten Commandments also served as a foundation for laws, and Jews believe God gave these laws to them. Judaism became one of the world's major religions and its influences can be found in the ethical, political, and legal traditions of most western cultures, especially in the idea that all people are created equal.

Interactive Chart: The Ten Commandments and Modern Laws
Project the graphic organizer. In many of our laws today, you can see the influence of the Ten Commandments. Through the Diaspora, Judaism and its ideas spread throughout the world along with the values of justice, fairness, and compassion in society and government. These ideas influenced the classical civilizations of Greece and Rome, and many of the commandments are reflected in our legal and political systems today. One example is in a U.S. court of law, where people swear to tell the truth "so help me God," as in the Second Commandment.

🖥 ACTIVE CLASSROOM

Use the Quick Write strategy. Instruct students to write what they know about the influences of the Ten Commandments. Allow them 45 seconds to write, then instruct students to share with a partner.

The Hebrews and the Origins of Judaism

 **SYNTHESIZE**

 DEMONSTRATE

INTERACTIVE CHART
The Ten Commandments and Modern Laws

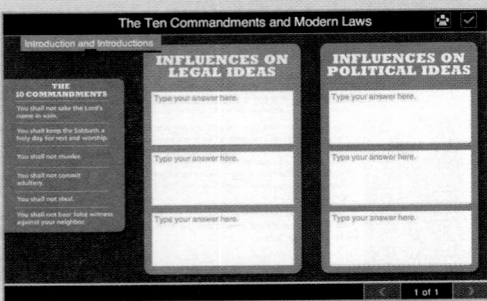

ELL Use the ELL activity described in the ELL chart.

Further Instruction
Law and Morality in Judaism: Core Text and Interactive Reading Notepad Project and discuss the questions and answers from the Interactive Reading Notepad.

Tell students that today, Judaism is numbered among the world's major religions for its contributions to religious thought as well as its strong influence on two later religions, Christianity and Islam. All three of these monotheistic faiths emerged in the Middle East and spread to other parts of the world.

Discuss how Judaism influenced the Judeo-Christian legal traditions, especially the right to a trial by jury and the assumption of "innocent until proven guilty." Some people have suggested that Judeo-Christian traditions had even more far-reaching impact on world history. They trace today's democratic-republican forms of government to the teachings of these religions, such as ideas about the worth of the individual, the importance of social responsibility, and the concept that all believers were equal before God.

Summarize During the Babylonian captivity, Israelites lived in Babylon and Egypt. Again, after Alexander the Great defeated the Persian empire, Jews were displaced. Describe the result of the Jewish Diaspora, the spreading of the Jews beyond their historic homeland. *(The influence of Jewish ideas and values were widely spread.)*

DIGITAL ACTIVITY
Origins of Judaism

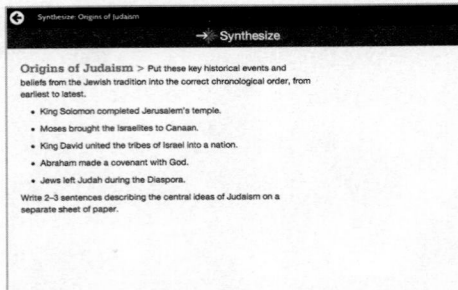

Ask students to recall the origins of Judaism. Have them use the Think Pair strategy to order the events on the Synthesize Activity into chronological order. Then have students write two to three sentences describing the central ideas of Judaism. Remind students to use details from the text to support their ideas. *(Answers will vary. The central ideas of Judaism include the belief in one all-knowing and all-powerful God, who has a plan for the Israelites and who, through his covenant, will guide them. Students may also cite the belief in the equality of all people, along with other values enshrined in modern legal and ethical systems.)*

Have partners think about the following question: What evidence did ancient Israelites have that God had a plan for them? *(Answers will vary. God's covenant with Abraham was part of his plan to establish Canaan as the land of the ancient Israelites as well as the exodus from Egypt led by Moses.)* Have pairs share their answers with the class.

LESSON QUIZ
Lesson Quiz and Class Discussion Board

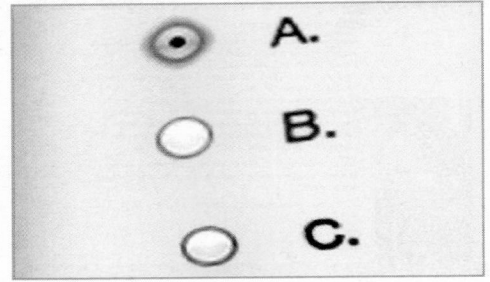

Assign the online Lesson Quiz for this lesson if you haven't already done so. Students will be offered automatic remediation or enrichment based on their score.

Pose the following question to the class on the Discussion Board:

In "The Hebrews and the Origins of Judaism" you read about the ancient Israelites' unique belief system and central ideas. You also learned how the political and legal ideas of Judaism influenced today's Judeo-Christian legal and ethical traditions.

Summarize How did the worship of only one God shape Judaism? *(The ancient Israelites were the only people at the time to worship only one god, which helped them to maintain close communities even when forced to relocate.)*

Topic Inquiry
Have students continue their investigations for the Topic Inquiry.

PEARSON
realize™

www.PearsonRealize.com
Access your Digital Lesson

Egyptian Civilization

Supporting English Language Learners

Use with Digital Text 4, **Religion Shapes Ancient Egyptian Life.**

Learning Strategies
Read *Religion Shapes Ancient Egyptian Life* aloud to students. Then instruct students to complete one of the following activities based on their level of English proficiency.

Beginning Display the following basic vocabulary words for students and have them copy the words into their notebooks: *gods, life, death*. Say the words aloud and have students repeat them. Use each word in a simple sentence to help describe Egyptian life.

Intermediate Display the following basic vocabulary words for students and have them copy the words into their notebooks: *gods, life, death*. Say the words aloud and have students repeat them. Help students use each word to develop a sentence that describes Egyptian life.

Advanced Display the following basic vocabulary words for students and have them copy the words into their notebooks: *gods, life, death*. Have students say the words aloud. Assist students with proper pronunciation as needed. Have students work with a partner to use each word to develop a sentence describing Egyptian life. Finally, have pairs share their sentences with the class.

Advanced High Display the following basic vocabulary words for students and have them copy the words into their notebooks: *gods, life, death*. Have students say the words aloud. Assist students with proper pronunciation as needed. Have students use each word to develop a sentence describing Egyptian life, then share their sentences with the class.

Use with Digital Text 5, **Organization of Egyptian Society.**

Learning Strategies
Use *Organization of Egyptian Society* to help students learn about deductive reasoning. Have students complete one activity according to their level of English proficiency.

Beginning Explain the concept of deductive reasoning to students using accessible language. Tell them that they will use deductive reasoning to predict specific facts about how Egyptian society was organized. Write and display the following deductive reasoning statements for students:

• *Humans live in organized groups. The ancient Egyptians were humans living together. This means that ancient Egyptians lived in organized groups.*

Read the first sentence of *Organization of Egyptian Society* aloud to students and explain how this information confirms the deductive reasoning that students just practiced. Then use the first sentence of the paragraph to demonstrate another round of deductive reasoning.

Intermediate Explain the concept of deductive reasoning to students using accessible language. Tell them that they will use deductive reasoning to predict specific facts about how Egyptian society was organized. Write and display the following deductive reasoning statements for students:

• *Humans live in organized groups. The ancient Egyptians were humans living together. This means that ancient Egyptians lived in organized groups.*

Read the first sentence of *Organization of Egyptian Society* aloud to students and explain how this information confirms the deductive reasoning that students just practiced. Then use the first sentence of the paragraph to help students develop another round of deductive reasoning.

Advanced Explain the concept of deductive reasoning to students using accessible language. Tell them that they will use deductive reasoning to predict specific facts about how Egyptian society was organized. Write and display the following deductive reasoning statements for students:

• *Humans live in organized groups. The ancient Egyptians were humans living together. This means that _____.*

Have students complete the sentence frame with a partner. Then have pairs read the first sentence of *Organization of Egyptian Society* and discuss how this statement confirms or denies the deductive reasoning that they just practiced. Then instruct pairs to use the first sentence of the paragraph to help students develop another round of deductive reasoning.

Advanced High Explain the concept of deductive reasoning to students using accessible language. Tell them that they will use deductive reasoning to predict specific facts about how Egyptian society was organized. Write and display the following deductive reasoning statements for students:

• *Humans live in organized groups. The ancient Egyptians were humans living together. This means that _____.*

Have students complete the sentence frame with a partner. Then have pairs read the first sentence of *Organization of Egyptian Society* and discuss how this statement confirms or denies the deductive reasoning that they just practiced. Then instruct pairs to use the first sentence of the paragraph to help students develop another round of deductive reasoning.

Egyptian Civilization

Objectives

Objective 1: Understand the ways in which geography helped shape ancient Egypt.

Objective 2: Explain how Egypt grew strong during the New Kingdom.

Objective 3: Describe the ways in which religious beliefs shaped the lives of ancient Egyptians.

Objective 4: Explain how the Egyptians organized their society.

Objective 5: Outline the advances that the Egyptians made in learning, the arts, science, and literature.

LESSON 4 ORGANIZER	PACING: APPROX. 1 PERIOD, .5 BLOCKS				
				RESOURCES	
		OBJECTIVES	**PACING**	**Online**	**Print**
Connect					
DIGITAL START UP ACTIVITY **The Nile River**			5 min.	●	
Investigate					
DIGITAL TEXT 1 **Geography Shapes Egypt**		Objective 1	10 min.	●	●
DIGITAL TEXT 2 **The Old Kingdom**			10 min.	●	●
DIGITAL TEXT 3 **Middle and New Kingdom Egypt**		Objective 2	10 min.	●	●
INTERACTIVE MAP **Ancient Egyptian Lands**			10 min.	●	
DIGITAL TEXT 4 **Religion Shapes Ancient Egyptian Life**		Objective 3	10 min.	●	●
3-D MODEL **Pyramids**			10 min.	●	
DIGITAL TEXT 5 **Organization of Egyptian Society**		Objective 4	10 min.	●	●
DIGITAL TEXT 6 **Egyptian Learning Advances**		Objective 5	10 min.	●	●
INTERACTIVE GALLERY **Hieroglyphics**			10 min.	●	
Synthesize					
DIGITAL ACTIVITY **Egypt's Kingdoms**			5 min.	●	
Demonstrate					
LESSON QUIZ **Lesson Quiz and Class Discussion Board**			10 min.	●	

CONNECT

DIGITAL START UP ACTIVITY
The Nile River

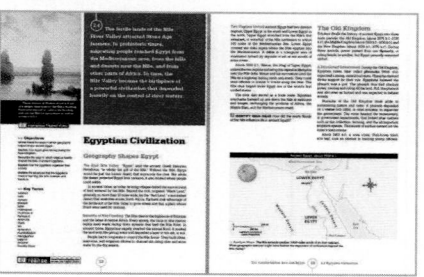

Project the Start Up Activity Ask students to answer the questions as they enter and get settled.

Discuss Remind students about the advantages and disadvantages of living in Mesopotamia because of the Tigris and Euphrates rivers. Although the rivers provided fertile farmland, they also brought flooding. Discuss with students how the Nile River impacted the lives of ancient Egyptians.

Aa **Vocabulary Development:** Use the Interactive Reading Notepad to preview the Key Terms and Academic Vocabulary in this Lesson with students.

⇅ FLIP IT!

Assign the Flipped Video for this lesson.

STUDENT EDITION PRINT
PAGES: 46–55

INVESTIGATE

DIGITAL TEXT 1
Geography Shapes Egypt

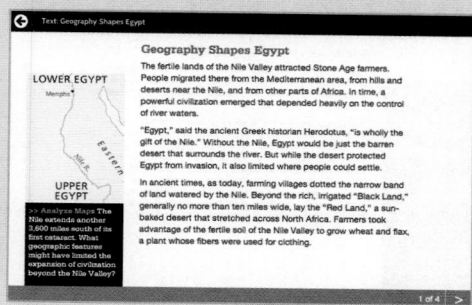

Quick Instruction

Analyze Maps Project the map from the text on the whiteboard. Introduce the map by reminding students of the limitations of living near bodies of water. Point out that Egypt is a barren desert except for the land near the Nile. Like ancient Mesopotamians, ancient Egyptians had to learn to control the flood waters by building dikes, reservoirs, and irrigation ditches. Menes, the king of Upper Egypt, was successful in uniting the two regions of Egypt by using the Nile as a highway to link the north and south. The Nile helped make Egypt one of the world's first unified states.

Further Instruction

Editable Presentation Use the Editable Presentation to present the main ideas for this Core Reading.

Geography Shapes Egypt: Core Text and Interactive Reading Notepad Project and discuss the Interactive Reading Notepad questions and answers.

Discuss the importance of geography on the development of the river valley civilization in Egypt. Besides the physical factors, humans also influenced the development of the Nile River valley by cooperating to control the Nile's floods. Be sure that students understand the importance of the unification of Upper and Lower Egypt. Remind students that it is necessary to have united states in order to have a strong governmental structure. Discuss the importance of the Nile for farming and trading and the development of a strong Egyptian civilization.

Synthesize How did the Nile influence life in ancient Egypt. *(It allowed people to have rich farmland and forced them to work together to control the waters.)*

Egyptian Civilization

DIGITAL TEXT 2

The Old Kingdom

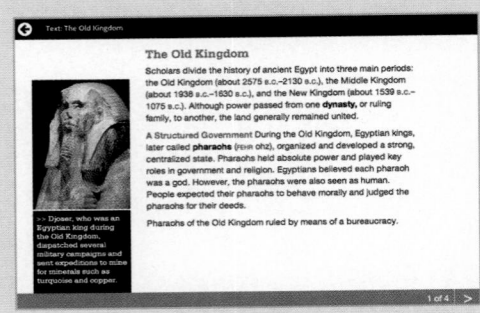

DIGITAL TEXT 3

Middle and New Kingdom Egypt

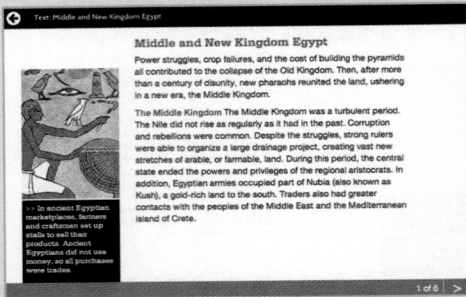

INTERACTIVE MAP

Ancient Egyptian Lands

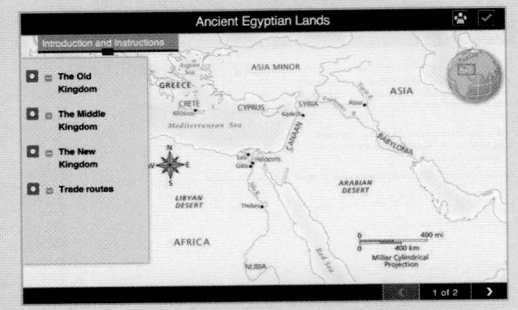

Objective 2: Explain how Egypt grew strong during the New Kingdom.

Quick Instruction

The history of ancient Egypt is divided into three main periods: the Old Kingdom, the Middle Kingdom and the New Kingdom. During the Old Kingdom, pharaohs, Egyptian monarchs, created, organized, and developed a strong centralized state. The Middle Kingdom was a turbulent time, as corruption and rebellion were common. During the Middle Kingdom, the Hyksos took over Egypt and adopted Egyptian customs and beliefs. Hyksos rule came to an end when the Egyptian leaders from the New Kingdom regained control over Egypt. The New Kingdom flourished and Egypt became a large empire. The heightened prosperity brought advances in medicine, hygiene, dentistry, and craftsmanship during this period.

Interactive Map: Ancient Egyptian Lands Project the map. Look carefully at the map of the New Kingdom. Discuss the importance of trade during the New Kingdom and the relationships Egyptians made with the Hittites. Discuss the importance of the Greeks eventually taking over Egypt: this was the primary source of cultural diffusion and how ancient Egyptian culture was able to influence the development of classical civilizations, such as Greece.

▥ ACTIVE CLASSROOM

Use the My Simile strategy. Give students the following prompt so they can create a simile based on the content of the New Kingdom text and map. This map shows that New Kingdom Egypt is like ____ because ____. Allow students time to write their simile and share with a partner.

Further Instruction

The Old Kingdom: New and Middle Kingdom Egypt: Core Text and Interactive Reading Notepad Project and discuss the questions and answers from the Interactive Reading Notepad.

Discuss how Old Kingdom Egypt helped to create a strong organized government structure, allowing Egyptian civilization to flourish as a monarchy. Middle Kingdom Egypt, despite social and political turbulence, was able to develop new areas of farmable land using the rich soil deposits from the Nile's flood water. The New Kingdom expanded the empire and brought about advances in mathematical and scientific ideas that reached later classical civilizations such as Greece.

Summarize Old Kingdom pharaohs set up bureaucracies to help administer a strong, organized central government. Describe the government bureaucracy of ancient Egypt. *(It was a monarchy with the pharaoh at the top; a chief administrator called a vizier who led various departments, followed by scribes who were below the vizier and carried out his directives.)*

DIGITAL TEXT 4

Religion Shapes Ancient Egyptian Life

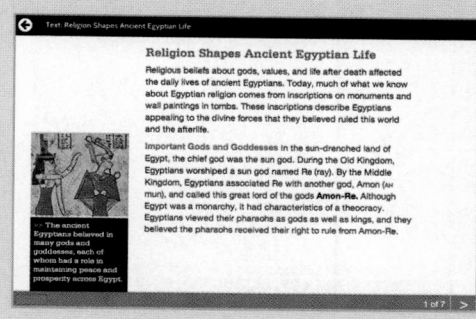

3-D MODEL

Pyramids

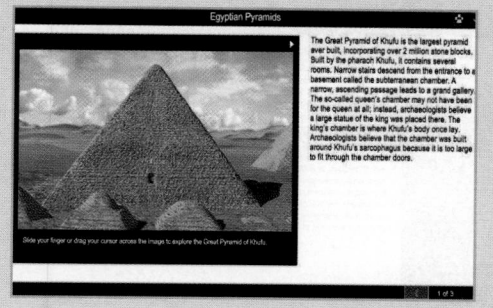

DIGITAL TEXT 5

Organization of Egyptian Society

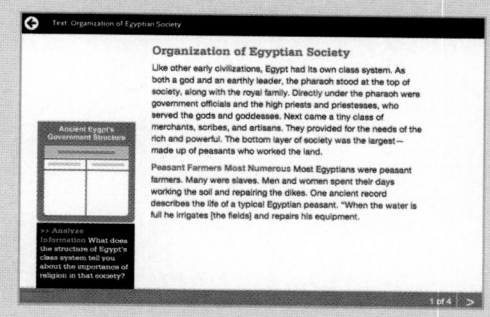

Objective 3: Describe the ways in which religious beliefs shaped the lives of ancient Egyptians.

Quick Instruction

Religion was an essential part of ancient Egyptian life. Ancient Egyptians believed in many gods and goddesses and that these divine forces ruled the world and the afterlife. Ancient Egypt was a monarchy and had characteristics of a theocracy, as ancient Egyptians viewed their pharaohs as gods as well as kings. Most of what we know about ancient Egyptian religion today comes from inscriptions on tombs or monuments, which depict the importance of the afterlife for ancient Egyptians. Mummification and pyramids reflect ancient Egyptian views of the afterlife.

3-D Model: Pyramids Project the 3-D model. Look carefully at the model of an ancient Egyptian pyramid. Discuss the importance Egyptians placed on the afterlife. Explain that ancient Egyptians wrote the Book of the Dead to help guide Egyptians into the afterlife successfully. Discuss the time it took to build pyramids, which is another indicator of the importance of religion in ancient Egypt's culture.

🖳 ACTIVE CLASSROOM

Use the See-Think-Wonder strategy. Pair students with a partner and have them select a part of the 3-D model to study closely. Ask them: What do you see? What does that make you think? What are you wondering about now that you've seen this? Share insights with the class.

ELL Use the ELL activity described in the ELL chart.

Further Instruction

Religion Shapes Ancient Egyptian Life: Core Text and Interactive Reading Notepad Project and discuss the questions and answers from the Interactive Reading Notepad.

Discuss how religion impacted the lives of ancient Egyptians. Tell students that ancient Egypt had characteristics of theocracies because pharaohs were seen as gods and as kings.

Summarize Describe how religion shaped the lives of ancient Egyptians. (*Ancient Egyptians believed that they would have eternal life after death, so they mummified people and built pyramids to protect the bodies of the dead and to give them a place to access their possessions after death. Ancient Egyptian pharaohs were also seen as gods as well as kings, which indicates the importance of religion in their lives.*)

Objective 4: Explain how the Egyptians organized their society.

Quick Instruction

Analyze Chart Project the chart about the Egyptian social hierarchy from the text on the whiteboard. Introduce the chart by reminding students that peasant farmers made up the largest part of the population. Explain that during the New Kingdom, social classes became more fluid as trade and warfare increased. Trade offered more opportunities for social advancement to a growing merchant class and also allowed for ancient Egyptian ideas to spread via the trade routes. Many skilled craftsmen emerged during the New Kingdom as the need for fine jewelry, furniture, and fabrics for the palaces and tombs of pharaohs and nobles grew.

Discuss the role of women in Egyptian society. Besides working in the fields, peasant women also spent much time raising children, collecting water, and preparing food. Egyptian women generally enjoyed a higher status and greater independence than women elsewhere in the ancient world. Women could inherit property, enter business deals, buy and sell goods, go to court, and obtain a divorce. Although there were often clear distinctions between the occupations of women and men, women's work was not confined to the home. Women manufactured perfume and textiles, managed farming estates, and served as doctors. Women could also enter the priesthood, especially in the service of goddesses.

ELL Use the ELL activity described in the ELL chart.

Egyptian Civilization

DIGITAL TEXT 6

Egyptian Learning Advances

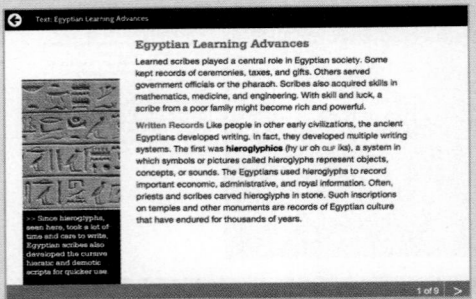

INTERACTIVE GALLERY

Hieroglyphics

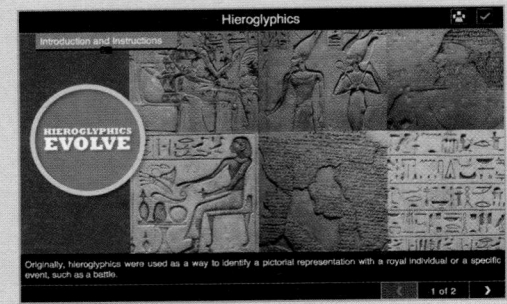

Further Instruction

Organization of Egyptian Society: Core Text and Interactive Reading Notepad Project and discuss the Interactive Reading Notepad questions and answers.

Discuss the importance of an organized social hierarchy in early civilizations. Stress how the middle class became more fluid and upwardly mobile as trade and warfare increased. Remind students that an organized social structure is a feature of early civilizations. Be sure that students notice the size of the lowest class and see the need for laborers in ancient Egypt, especially during the New Kingdom building booms.

Synthesize What does the much greater relative size of the lowest class tell you about the need for laborers in Egyptian society? *(Many workers were needed for such activities as building pyramids and other monuments and working in the farm fields.)*

Objective 5: Outline the advances that the Egyptians made in learning, the arts, science, and literature.

Quick Instruction

We know a lot about ancient Egypt today because of our ability to decipher ancient Egyptian writing, or hieroglyphics. The discovery of the Rosetta Stone allowed scholars to decipher the meaning of hieroglyphic passages. Discuss the advances ancient Egyptians made in mathematics and science and how they eventually influenced the classical civilization of Greece. Explain that Greek scholars traveled to Egypt to study and discuss ideas with Egyptian priests and scholars. The Greeks were impressed by Egyptian civilization and adapted many Egyptian ideas into their culture.

Interactive Gallery: Hieroglyphics Project the gallery. Look carefully at the Rosetta Stone. Discuss the importance of the discovery of the Rosetta Stone and how it unlocked many secrets about ancient Egypt. Explain that the Rosetta Stone was written in hieroglyphics, demotic text, and Greek. Describe how Egyptian culture was diffused into Greece after the Greek emperor Alexander the Great conquered Egypt.

Further Instruction

Egyptian Learning Advances: Core Text and Interactive Reading Notepad Project and discuss the questions and answers from the Interactive Reading Notepad.

Discuss how ancient Egyptians made advances in writing, through the use of hieroglyphics, in science, through their knowledge of the human body from mummification, and in mathematics, especially in geometry. Ancient Egyptian art in the forms of statues, paintings, sculptures, and architecture reflected its culture by emphasizing the importance placed on the gods, goddesses, and afterlife. Discuss how these advances in learning eventually influenced the classical civilizations of Greece and Rome through cultural diffusion.

Summarize Identify three important advances in learning made by the ancient Egyptians. *(Ancient Egyptians created hieroglyphics, advanced knowledge of the human body, and developed a sophisticated geometry.)*

🖭 ACTIVE CLASSROOM

Use the See-Think-Wonder strategy. Pair students with a partner and have them select a part of the gallery to study closely. Ask them: What do you see? What does that make you think? What are you wondering about now that you've seen this? Share insights with the class.

■ SYNTHESIZE

DIGITAL ACTIVITY
Egypt's Kingdoms

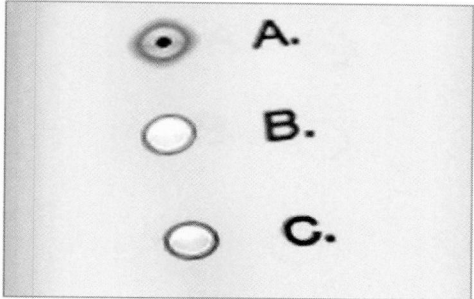

Ask students to recall the strengths and weaknesses of each of ancient Egypt's three kingdoms. Have them use the Think Pair strategy to answer the questions in the Synthesize Activity. Then have students write two or three sentences describing the importance of each kingdom. Remind students to use details from the text to support their ideas. *(Answers will vary. The Old Kingdom was important because it developed a strong centralized government and state, the Middle Kingdom expanded farmable land, while the New Kingdom expanded Egyptian territory and made important advances in learning.)*

Remind students how Greeks admired Egyptian civilization and that Greek scholars travelled to Egypt to study with Egyptian priests and scholars. Have partners think about the following question: What things and ideas of ancient Egypt do you think would have impressed visitors from other civilizations? *(Answers will vary, but many students will cite the impressive buildings, such as the pyramids, sphinx, and great temples, while others might point to the extensive agriculture, including the irrigation networks, the well-organized society and hierarchy, art, and other elements.)* Have pairs share their answers with the class.

■ DEMONSTRATE

LESSON QUIZ
Lesson Quiz and Class Discussion Board

Assign the online Lesson Quiz for this lesson if you haven't already done so. Students will be offered automatic remediation or enrichment based on their score.

Pose the following question to the class on the Discussion Board:

In "Egyptian Civilization" you read about the importance of geography on the development of ancient Egypt as well as the contributions of the three kingdoms. Eventually, Egyptian ideas in mathematics and science were adopted by the Greeks and other cultures through both trade and conquest.

Summarize Name an achievement of the ancient Egyptians in each of the following fields: medicine, astronomy, and mathematics. *(In medicine, knowledge of the human body, illnesses, and surgery developed. In astronomy, ancient Egyptians were able to map constellations and chart planetary movements, as well as develop a 365-day calendar. In mathematics, ancient Egyptians developed geometry.)*

Topic Inquiry
Have students continue their investigations for the Topic Inquiry.

The Ancient Middle East and Egypt (3200 B.C.–500 B.C.)

■ SYNTHESIZE

DIGITAL ACTIVITY

Reflect on the Essential Question and Topic

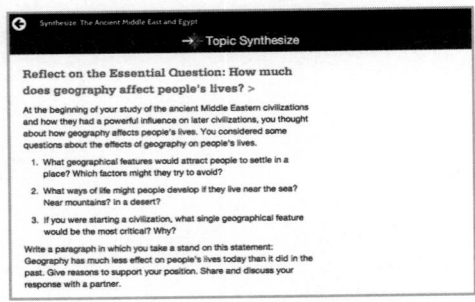

At the beginning of their study of the Ancient Middle East and Egypt and how these civilizations had a powerful influence on later people, students thought about how geography affects people's lives. They considered some questions about the effects of geography on people's lives.

- What geographical features would attract people to settle in a place? Which factors might they try to avoid?

- What ways of life might people develop if they live near the sea? Near mountains? In a desert?

- If you were starting a civilization, what single geographical feature would be the most critical? Why?

Have students write their paragraphs responding to the statement: Geography has much less effect on people's lives today than it did in the past. Suggest they start by making a list of things that may have influenced how geography has affected the way people live today.

Have volunteers read their paragraphs and discuss issues raised or ask students to post their responses on the Class Discussion Board.

Next ask students to reflect on the Topic as a whole, focusing on the cultures, governments, religions, scientific advances, and economic ideas of the civilizations studied. Have volunteers share the three elements they have chosen with the class and explain their choices. After discussing the choices and reasons, conclude by asking the class to vote on the three most important elements.

Topic Inquiry

Have students complete Step 3 of the Topic Inquiry.

■ DEMONSTRATE

DIGITAL TOPIC REVIEW AND ASSESSMENT

The Ancient Middle East and Egypt (3200 B.C.–500 B.C.)

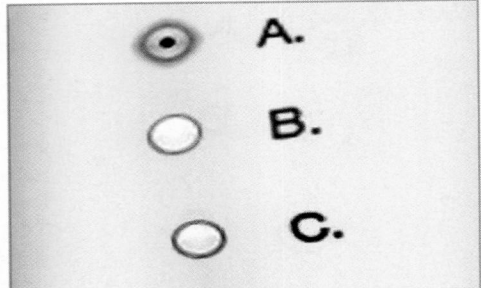

Students can prepare for the Topic Test by answering the questions in the Topic Review and Assessment online or the Assessment questions in the Print Student text. They can also prepare by reviewing their answers to the Interactive Reading Notepad questions or reviewing their notes in the Reading and Notetaking Study Guide.

DIGITAL TOPIC TEST

The Ancient Middle East and Egypt (3200 B.C.–500 B.C.)

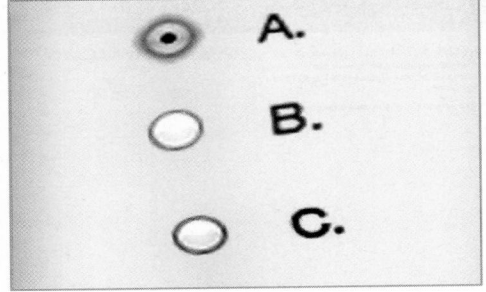

TOPIC TEST

Assign the Topic Test to assess students' understanding of topic content.

BENCHMARK TESTS

Assign these benchmark tests as you complete the relevant topics to monitor student progress toward mastering the course content and as preparation for the End-of-Course Test.

Benchmark Test 1: Topics 1–5

Benchmark Test 2: Topics 6–10

Benchmark Test 3: Topics 11–15

Benchmark Test 4: Topics 16–21

Ancient India and China (2600 B.C.–A.D. 550)

TOPIC 3 ORGANIZER	PACING: APPROX. 8 PERIODS, 4 BLOCKS
	PACING
Connect	1 period
MY STORY VIDEO **Shi Huangdi, First Emperor of a Unified China**	10 min.
DIGITAL ESSENTIAL QUESTION ACTIVITY **How Are Religion and Culture Connected?**	10 min.
DIGITAL TIMELINE ACTIVITY **Ancient India and China**	10 min.
TOPIC INQUIRY: DOCUMENT-BASED QUESTION **What Makes an Ordered Society?**	20 min.
Investigate	2–5 periods
TOPIC INQUIRY: DOCUMENT-BASED QUESTION **What Makes an Ordered Society?**	Ongoing
LESSON 1 Early Civilization in South Asia	30–40 min.
LESSON 2 The Origins of Hinduism and Buddhism	30–40 min.
LESSON 3 Powerful Empires Emerge in India	30–40 min.
LESSON 4 Rise of Civilization in China	30–40 min.
LESSON 5 Strong Rulers Unite China	30–40 min.
Synthesize	1 period
DIGITAL ACTIVITY **Reflect on the Essential Question and Topic**	10 min.
TOPIC INQUIRY: DOCUMENT-BASED QUESTION **What Makes an Ordered Society?**	20 min.
Demonstrate	1–2 periods
DIGITAL TOPIC TEST **Ancient India and China**	10 min.
TOPIC INQUIRY: DOCUMENT-BASED QUESTION **What Makes an Ordered Society?**	20 min.

 **TOPIC INQUIRY: DOCUMENT-BASED QUESTION**

What Makes an Ordered Society?

In this Topic Inquiry, students will analyze three primary source and two secondary source documents to draw their own conclusions on how Indian and Chinese religions contributed to the ordered structure of their society. The Topic Essential Question is "How are religion and culture connected?" This DBQ expands on that essential question and provides students an opportunity to consider some of the impact religion had on India and China's societal order.

STEP 1: CONNECT
Develop Questions and Plan the Investigation

Launch the DBQ Writing Activity
Show the flipped video on Shi Huangdi, First Emperor of Unified China. Lead a class discussion about the video, and then have students work together in partnerships to consider the following questions.
- What helps unify a society?
- How does a society govern itself?
- How does a society create a common purpose?

Generate Questions
Form small groups and have students record their questions about how religion affected the culture and society of India and China on the Need-to-Know Questions document.

Suggestion: Help students generate questions by referring to the 5 WQs and 1 H: Who? What? When? Where? Why? and How? Allot ten minutes for students to generate as many questions as possible. Select the questions that most target the DBQ question.

Professional Development
Document Based Questions
Be sure to view the Document-Based Questions resources in the online course.

Resources
- Need-to-Know Questions
- Student Instructions

STEP 2: INVESTIGATE
Apply Disciplinary Concepts and Tools

Analyze the Documents
Instruct students to analyze the five documents before responding to the question, What makes an ordered society? Before students read the selections, point out the distinction between primary and secondary sources. Explain that Documents A and B are primary sources about Confucianism, and Document C is an image of Buddha, which represents the religion of Buddhism. Documents D and E are secondary sources articles on the impact of the Hindu caste system and how Confucian teachings can affect a country's culture and government.

Check Understanding
Student should answer the multiple-choice and short answer questions at the conclusion of each document.

Resources
- Information Organizer

⏻ PROFESSIONAL DEVELOPMENT

Document-Based Question
Be sure to view the Document-Based Question Professional Development resources in the online course.

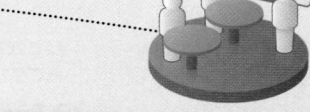

STEP 3: SYNTHESIZE
Evaluate Sources and
Use Evidence to Formulate Conclusions

Write Your Essay
Using the documents and their knowledge of history, have students write an essay on the following topic: What is an ordered society and which Indian and Chinese ideas contributed to such order?

Students should draw their own conclusions from reading the primary and secondary source evidence and viewpoints. Instruct students that their essays should have good organization and development, the criteria for which are found in their writing rubric. Remind students that they need to formulate clear topic sentences and use clearly identified supporting evidence from at least three of the documents. A conclusion should summarize the main concept and key points that provide proof of their hypothesis.

Suggestion: If students need assistance with organization, review the 5-paragraph essay: introduction of main idea, at least three paragraphs to develop key points, and a final paragraph to summarize the conclusion.

Edit Your Essay
Remind students that they should review the writing rubric and revise their first draft. Students should make necessary changes to the organization of their essay before turning it in. Peer editing may be an option before papers are finalized.

Resources
- Writing Rubric
- 21st Century Skill Tutorials: Draw Inferences

STEP 4: DEMONSTRATE
Communicate Conclusions
and Take Informed Action

Reflect on the Project
When students have completed their essays, explain that the DBQ study on how ancient Indian and Chinese ideas contributed to their social order will become a basis for their understanding of how religion and culture are connected. Emphasize that they may revise their thinking on religion's role in culture, but they will have the knowledge of how to analyze multiple sources and process varying viewpoints in order to establish an educated, informed opinion.

INTRODUCTION

Ancient India and China

In ancient India and China, complex civilizations developed with vast empires and powerful dynasties. They made great advances in the arts and sciences. In addition, the developing beliefs of Hinduism, Buddhism, Confucianism, and Daoism significantly affected ancient Indian and Chinese culture and governments. How did the religions and belief systems of this era help shape the way of life then and now?

◼ CONNECT

MY STORY VIDEO

Shi Huangdi, First Emperor of a Unified China

Watch a video showing the story of Shi Huangdi's efforts to unify China.

Check Understanding Why did Shi Huangdi seek to unify China? *(to end the warfare that was constantly breaking out among feudal warlords and rulers)*

Evaluate Data In what ways was Shi Huangdi great? What negative impact did he have? *(Shi Huangdi unified China for the first time, bringing stability. However, his harsh policies caused resentment among many Chinese.)*

⇅ FLIP IT!

Assign the My Story Video

DIGITAL ESSENTIAL QUESTION ACTIVITY

How Are Religion and Culture Connected?

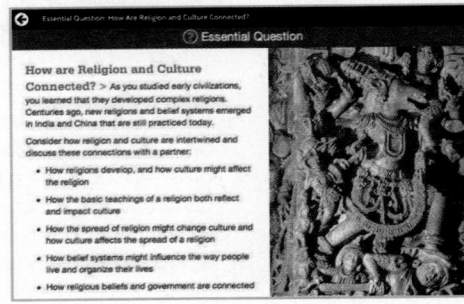

Ask students to consider the Essential Question for this Topic: How are religion and culture connected? Remind students of what they read in Topic 1 about the growth of complex religions as early civilizations developed. As a class, go over the ideas students discussed with their partners. Ask what other connections they added. Then, as a class, list and rank the five most important connections between religion and culture.

Support a Point of View with Evidence Why did you rank one of the connections as most important?

Identify Central Issues How might religion affect daily life? *(Sample response: the role of family members, devotion to prayers, dress, and ethical standards)*

Identify Cause and Effect How might religion affect government? *(Sample response: A religion might have ethical or moral codes that get incorporated into legal codes. There might also be a correlation between religious and political hierarchy.)*

DIGITAL TIMELINE ACTIVITY

Ancient India and China

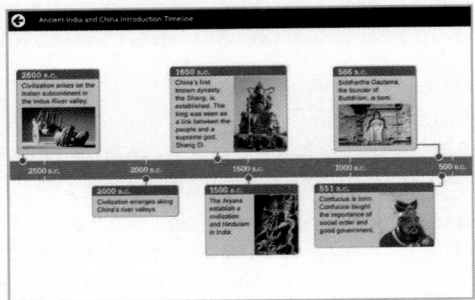

Display the timeline showing some of the major historical events in India and China between 2600 *B.C.* and *A.D.* 500. During this topic study, students will learn about these events and many more. The timeline will provide a framework into which they can place the events.

D Differentiate: Extra Support Explain that there is no "zero" year, but that *A.D.* immediately follows *B.C.* Ask the students to figure out the span of time between 2600 *B.C.* and *A.D.* 550. *(3,150 years)*

D Differentiate: Challenge Ask students to make a copy of the timeline and add entries as they read. After reading all of the lessons, invite the students to share their new entries.

Check Understanding Ask approximately how much time passed between when Hinduism was established in India and when the founder of Buddhism was born. *(around 900–934 years)*

Topic Inquiry

Launch the Topic Inquiry with students after introducing the Topic.

Early Civilization in South Asia

Supporting English Language Learners

Use with Digital Text 3, **Aryan Civilizations and the Vedas.**

Learning Strategies

Read *Aryan Civilizations and the Vedas* aloud to the class. Have them complete one activity according to their level of English proficiency.

Beginning Provide students with a short list of basic vocabulary words such as *cattle, horses,* and *mountain.* Write and display each word and its definition and have students copy these into their notebooks. Then ask students to choose one word and draw a picture to show its meaning. Support students as necessary.

Intermediate Provide students with a short list of basic vocabulary words such as *cattle, horses,* and *mountain.* Write and display each word. Have students help determine each word's definition. Then have students copy these definitions into their notebooks. Ask students to draw a picture to show the meaning of each word. Instruct students to write the word and its definition under the corresponding picture. Support students as necessary.

Advanced Have pairs of students review the text to find unfamiliar, basic words. Provide students with dictionaries and other resources to define each of the words on their lists. Then have pairs choose three words from their lists and write a sentence using each one. Finally, have each pair join with another pair to share their work and provide each other with feedback. Circulate among students to offer support as needed.

Advanced High Have students review the text to find and make a list of unfamiliar, basic words. Provide students with dictionaries and other resources to define each of the words on their lists. Then have students choose at least three words from their lists and write a sentence using each one. Finally, have students turn to a partner to share their work and provide each other with feedback. Circulate among students to offer support as needed.

Use with Digital Text 1, **Geography of the Indian Subcontinent.**

Listening

Remind students that careful listening is essential to learning any new language. Read *Geography of the Indian Subcontinent.* Then guide students through one of the following activities according to their English proficiency level.

Beginning Retell the content in *Geography of the Indian Subcontinent* in accessible language for students. Then choose a single sound in English to practice with students, such as -ing. Say the sound for students and write and display several examples of words with this sound from the text, such as *digging, startling,* and *towering.* Underline the -ing ending in each word, then have students repeat the words after you say them aloud.

Intermediate Retell the content in *Geography of the Indian Subcontinent* in accessible language for students. Then choose a single sound in English to practice with students, such as *-ing.* Say the sound for students and write and display several examples of words with this sound from the text, such as *digging, startling,* and *towering.* Underline the *-ing* ending in each word, then have students repeat the words after you say them aloud. Help students skim the text for additional words with the *-ing* ending. Write and display these words for students, then practice sounding them out together.

Advanced Choose a single sound in English for students to practice, such as *-ing.* Have students reread Geography of the Indian Subcontinent with a partner. Have students make a list of words with this sound, such as *digging, startling,* and *towering.* Instruct partners to write the words in their notebooks and underline the *-ing* ending in each word. After they finish reading, have pairs practice sounding out the words together. Circulate among students to offer support as necessary.

Advanced High Choose a single sound in English for students to practice, such as *-ing.* Reread Geography of the Indian Subcontinent aloud. Ask students to listen for and make a list of words from the text with this sound, such as *digging, startling,* and *towering.* Instruct students to write the words in their notebooks and underline the *-ing* ending in each word. After they finish reading, tell them to practice sounding out the words, then turn to a partner to take turns saying the words aloud. Circulate among students to offer support as necessary.

▣ Differentiate Instruction

Use the Differentiated Instruction notes throughout the lesson plan to support the varied skill sets, levels of readiness, and interests in the mixed-ability classroom.

Challenge These notes include suggestions for expanding the activity for advanced students.

On-Level These notes include suggestions for modifying the activity to address different interests or learning styles.

Extra Support These notes include ideas for providing more scaffolding or reading spuport.

Special Needs These notes provide ideas for adapting instruction to support the needs of various special needs students.

▮ NOTES

Topic ③ Lesson 1

Early Civilization in South Asia

Objectives

Objective 1: Describe the Indian subcontinent's geography.

Objective 2: Understand the clues archaeology has provided about the rise and fall of the Indus civilization.

Objective 3: Analyze the main characteristics of the Aryan civilization and the Vedic Age.

Objective 4: Explain what ancient Indian epics reveal about Aryan life.

LESSON 1 ORGANIZER		PACING: APPROX. 1 PERIOD, .5 BLOCKS			
				RESOURCES	
		OBJECTIVES	PACING	Online	Print
Connect					
DIGITAL START UP ACTIVITY **Ancient Civilizations, Modern Voices**			5 min.	●	
Investigate					
DIGITAL TEXT 1 **Geography of the Indian Subcontinent**		Objective 1	10 min.	●	●
INTERACTIVE MAP **Early Civilizations in South Asia**			10 min.	●	
DIGITAL TEXT 2 **The Forgotten Indus Civilization**		Objective 2	10 min.	●	●
INTERACTIVE GRAPHIC ORGANIZER **Technological Advances of the Indus Civilization**			10 min.	●	
DIGITAL TEXT 3 **Aryan Civilization and the Vedas**		Objective 3	10 min.	●	●
DIGITAL TEXT 4 **The Great Vedic Epics**		Objective 4	10 min.	●	●
Synthesize					
DIGITAL ACTIVITY **Ancient Civilizations of the Indian Subcontinent**			5 min.	●	
Demonstrate					
LESSON QUIZ **Lesson Quiz and Class Discussion Board**			10 min.	●	

PEARSON
realize™
www.PearsonRealize.com

Go online to access additional resources including:
Primary Sources • Biographies • Supreme Court cases •
21st Century Skill Tutorials • Maps • Graphic Organizers.

CONNECT

DIGITAL START UP ACTIVITY

Ancient Civilizations, Modern Voices

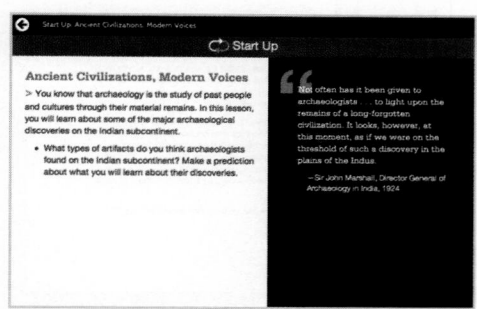

Project the Start Up Activity Ask students to read the quote and answer the questions as they enter and get settled: What types of items do you think archaeologists found on the Indian subcontinent? *(Answers will vary. Students should show an understanding that archaeologists would find ruins and relics from an ancient and previously undiscovered civilization.)*

Discuss What kinds of evidence of ancient civilizations have been found? Where did those civilizations arise? Why did they develop where they did? Help students understand that the Indus civilization arose along a river valley, as did many other ancient civilizations, and explain why this occurred.

Aa Vocabulary Development: Use the Interactive Reading Notepad to preview the Key Terms and Academic Vocabulary in this lesson with students.

⇵ FLIP IT!

Assign the Flipped Video for this lesson.

■ STUDENT EDITION PRINT PAGES: 62–67

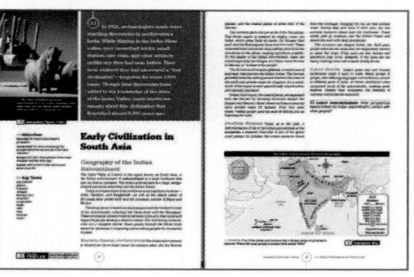

INVESTIGATE

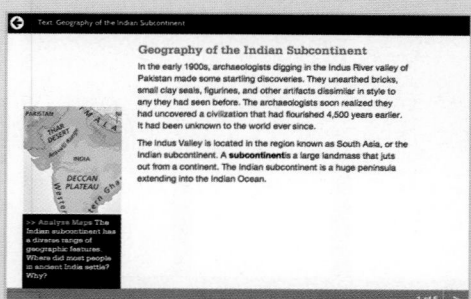
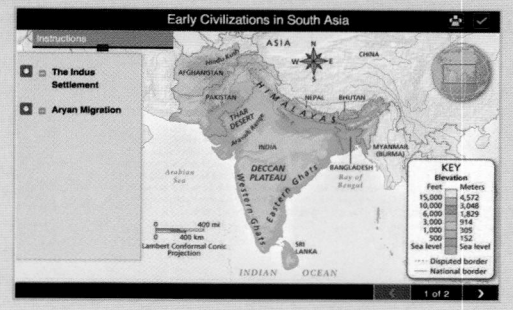

DIGITAL TEXT 1

Geography of the Indian Subcontinent

INTERACTIVE MAP

Early Civilizations in South Asia

Objective 1: Describe the Indian subcontinent's geography.

Quick Instruction

The Indian subcontinent juts into the Indian Ocean with the tallest mountains in the world forming natural boundaries to the north and west.

Interactive Map: Early Civilizations in South Asia Project the map on the whiteboard. Click through the key to show the physical geography of the Indian subcontinent, the area where the Indus civilization arose, and the path of the Aryan migration. Help students connect the physical geography of the subcontinent to the development of the Indus civilization *(It arose along the Indus River),* and the Aryan migration *(The Aryans came through passes of the Hindu Kush mountains in northwestern India.).*

🖧 ACTIVE CLASSROOM

Project the map and use a whiteboard tool to divide the physical geography layer into four main areas (northern mountains [Himalayas, Hindu Kush], Gangetic Plain, Deccan Plateau, Eastern and Western Ghats). Have students research images that depict the most important physical characteristics of these areas and present their findings to the class.

ELL Use the ELL activity described in the ELL chart.

Further Instruction

Editable Presentation Use the Editable Presentation to present the main ideas for this text.

Project the Interactive Reading Notepad questions and use student responses to discuss the physical geography of the Indian subcontinent and hypothesize about the effect of those factors on the development of Indian civilizations.

Identify Cause and Effect Ask students to think about the map and what they have read in the lesson to determine the effect of water on how and where people lived. *(People settled near oceans and rivers because they provided access to water and transportation, as well as food sources such as fish. River valleys provided fertile soil for farming.)*

Hypothesize Engage students in a discussion about how India's geography might have affected its development. Ask them to hypothesize based on the knowledge that the subcontinent is surrounded by water to the east and west, and by mountains to the north. *(Students should show an understanding that the oceans and mountains would limit migration into and out of the subcontinent. They should also understand how geography affected the development of Indian civilizations.)*

Early Civilization in South Asia

DIGITAL TEXT 2

The Forgotten Indus Civilization

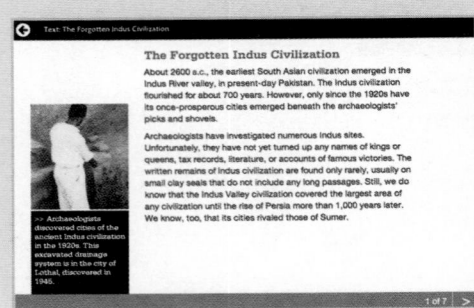

INTERACTIVE GRAPHIC ORGANIZER

Technological Advances of the Indus Civilization

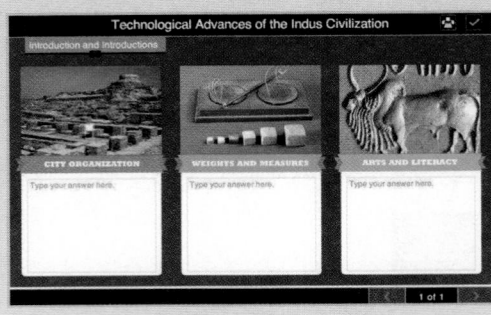

DIGITAL TEXT 3

Aryan Civilization and the Vedas

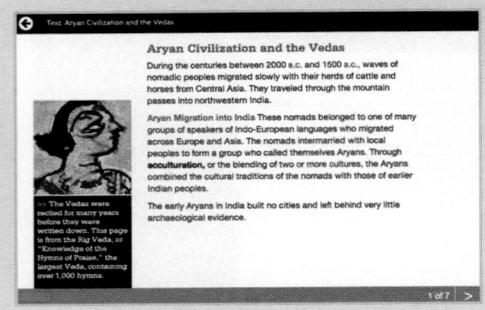

Objective 2: Understand the clues archaeology has provided about the rise and fall of the Indus civilization.

Quick Instruction

In the 1920s archaeologists found the remains of a great, complex civilization along the Indus River. This river valley civilization built impressive, carefully-planned cities, created beautiful and intricate objects, and traded with distant lands.

Interactive Graphic Organizer: Technological Advances of the Indus Civilization Project the graphic organizer on the whiteboard. Review the technological advances of the Indus civilization and how they might be categorized and entered into the graphic organizer. Discuss how these advances affected other cultures.

📹 ACTIVE CLASSROOM

Ask students to record the technological advances of the Indus civilization using two different criteria: 1) according to which had the greatest long-term impact and 2) which was most important to the civilization at the time. Ask students to provide a justification for their rankings. Then ask them to work in pairs to share their rankings and justifications. Poll the class to see if there is agreement on the rankings.

Further Instruction

Project the Interactive Reading Notepad questions and use student responses to discuss the Indus civilization of the Indian subcontinent.

Synthesize What other river valley civilizations have you read about? *(Students should note the river valley civilizations of Sumer, Mesopotamia, and Egypt.)*

Draw Conclusions Why would humans from such different areas of the world develop large civilizations along rivers? *(Students should understand that rivers provided access to a consistent water supply, fertile soil for farming, and transportation/trade routes, which helped people develop civilizations.)*

D **Differentiate: Extra Support** For students who are having difficulty connecting the various civilizations, show them a world map. Point out the rivers that are associated with each civilization. Then work with students to create a flow chart which can help students connect all of the benefits of living next to a river (access to drinking water, fertile river valley soil for farming, and a water source for irrigation) to the growth of civilization (stable food supplies allowed time to do other kinds of work, rivers provided the ability to travel and trade with others, etc.)

Objective 3: Analyze the main characteristics of the Aryan civilization and the Vedic Age.

Quick Instruction

Remind students that the text they just read introduced them to the Aryans, nomads who migrated to the Indian subcontinent and developed a society. Display the drawing of Purusha and lead students through a discussion about what it reveals about the Aryans and why the Aryans might have structured their society in this way.

Summarize What were the most important characteristics of the Aryan civilization? *(Students might point to various aspects of the Aryan civilization such as their religious beliefs, Aryan literature, or the way the society was organized into ranked groups based on occupation.)*

ELL Use the ELL activity described in the ELL chart.

Further Instruction

Project the Interactive Reading Notepad questions and use student responses to discuss the Aryan migration and settlement of the Indian subcontinent. Help students understand the political and cultural influence of the Aryan civilization on India.

DIGITAL TEXT 4
The Great Vedic Epics

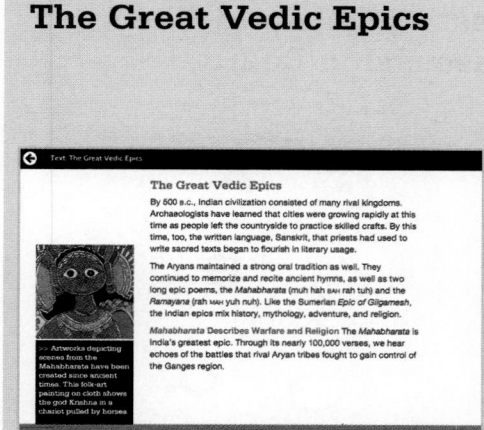

Make Connections Did the fact that the Aryans were herders influence their migration to the Indian subcontinent? *(Sample response: Herders are nomadic and always looking for new pastures. Therefore, they migrate to new territories.)* Why do you think the Aryans measured their wealth in cows and bulls? *(Sample response: As nomadic herders, they valued cattle, which provided them with food and clothing.)*

Objective 4: Explain what ancient Indian epics reveal about Aryan life.

Quick Instruction
Remind students that the Vedic epics, the *Mahabharata* and the *Ramayana,* are the major texts of the Aryan civilization. Review how these texts reveal important aspects of the civilization, including religious beliefs and the immortality of the soul, the value of performing one's duty, and warfare between rival tribes.

ELL Use the ELL activity described in the ELL chart.

Further Instruction
Project and discuss the Interactive Reading Notepad questions to cover more information about the Vedic epics. Be sure students understand the political and cultural influence of Vedic epics on the Aryan civilization.

Summarize What are the two main Vedic epics? How were they developed, and what are they about? *(Sample response: Both the Mahabharata and the Ramayana were epic poems, first recited orally by priests, then eventually written down. The Mahabharata tells the story of a struggle by five royal brothers to regain their kingdom. The Ramayana tells the story of Rama's rescue of his kidnapped wife Sita.)*

Draw Conclusions How do the Vedic epics reveal important information about the political, religious, and cultural life of the Aryans? *(Sample response: The stories of the Vedas reveal Aryan religious beliefs, and the importance of duty. They teach lessons about correct moral behavior and echo the history of wars between the different Aryan tribes.)*

D Differentiate: **Challenge/Gifted** Have students read and act out portions of the *Ramayana* or the *Mahabharata.* Then discuss the meaning and importance of the excerpts to ancient Indian society.

Early Civilization in South Asia

■ SYNTHESIZE

DIGITAL ACTIVITY
Ancient Civilizations of the Indian Subcontinent

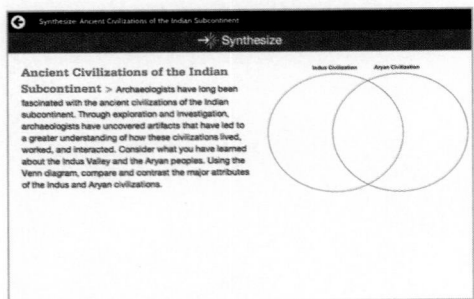

Remind students of the main issues connected to the lesson and the development of the early civilizations of India.

Identify Main Ideas What were the significant achievements of the Indus and Aryan civilizations? *(Answers may vary but students should be able to identify that technological advances; organized government; large, well-planned cities; and trade were among the most significant achievements of the Indus civilization. They should also identify that literature, religion, and societal and political structures were the significant achievements of the Aryan civilization.)*

Project the graphic organizer and help students complete it.

Compare and Contrast In what ways did the Indus civilization settlement patterns seem to differ from the Aryan civilizations. *(The Indus civilization built large cities and seemed to be a unified civilization. The Aryan civilization developed separate states.)* Why might they have developed differently? *(The Indus civilization might have been developed by farmers who settled along the Indus river. The Aryans were originally nomadic.)*

■ DEMONSTRATE

LESSON QUIZ
Lesson Quiz and Class Discussion Board

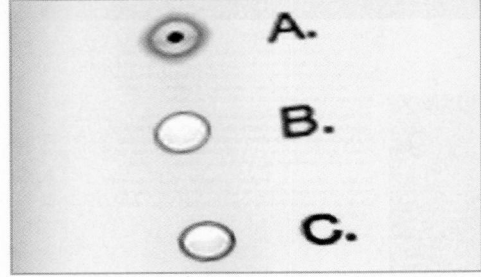

Assign the online Lesson Quiz for this lesson if you haven't already done so. Students will be offered automatic remediation or enrichment based on their score.

In this lesson you have read about the physical geography of the Indian subcontinent, the development of a river valley civilization along the Indus River, and the rise of the Aryan civilization, which had a major political and cultural influence on India. Pose these questions to the class on the Discussion Board.

Generate Explanations What discoveries by archaeologists in the Indus River valley led to the conclusion that they had found a previously unknown civilization? *(Sample response: They found the ruins of large, carefully-planned cities with complex plumbing, standardized bricks, weights and measures, and storage facilities. All of these elements showed that the Indus civilization had a well-organized government.)*

Topic Inquiry
Have students continue their investigations for the Topic Inquiry.

The Origins of Hinduism and Buddhism

Supporting English Language Learners

Use with Digital Text 2, **The Caste System Shapes India.**

Learning Strategies
Read *The Caste System Shapes India* aloud to the class. Have them complete one activity according to their level of English proficiency.

Beginning Provide students with a short list of basic vocabulary words from the text such as *jobs, eating,* and *pollution.* Write and display each word and its definition and have students copy these into their notebooks. Then ask students to choose one word and draw a picture to show its meaning. Help students say a sentence to describe their drawing. Support students as necessary.

Intermediate Provide students with a short list of basic vocabulary words from the text such as *jobs, eating,* and *pollution.* Write and display each word. Have students help determine each word's definition. Then have students copy these definitions into their notebooks. Ask students to draw a picture to show the meaning of each word. Instruct students to write the word and its definition under the corresponding picture. Finally, have students say one sentence to describe their picture. Support students as necessary.

Advanced Have pairs of students review the text to find unfamiliar, basic words. Provide students with dictionaries and other resources to define each of the words on their lists. Then have pairs choose three related words from their lists and describe an aspect of the text using the words. Finally, have each pair join with another pair to share their work and provide one another with feedback. Circulate among students to offer support as needed.

Advanced High Have students review the text to find and make a list of unfamiliar, basic words. Provide students with dictionaries and other resources to define each of the words on their lists. Then have students choose at least five related words from their lists and describe an aspect of the text using the words to a partner. Have students provide one another with feedback. Circulate among students to offer support as needed.

Use with Digital Text 1, **Hindu Beliefs Develop.**

Listening
Remind students that careful listening is essential to learning any new language. Read *Hindu Beliefs Develop.* Then guide students through one of the following activities according to their English proficiency level.

Beginning Choose two or three sentences from the text and read them aloud to students, focusing on proper intonation. Explain how placing the stress on a different word or phrase can alter the meaning of the sentence. Use the example sentences to demonstrate this. Then provide students with a simple sentence about the content and help them say it aloud with proper intonation.

Intermediate Choose two or three sentences from the text and read them aloud to students, focusing on proper intonation. Discuss how placing the stress on a different word or phrase can alter the meaning of the sentence. Use the example sentences to demonstrate this. Then provide students with a simple sentence about the content and listen as they say it aloud with proper intonation. Offer guidance, support, and correction as needed.

Advanced Choose two or three sentences from the text and read them aloud to students, focusing on proper intonation. Ask students to explain how placing the stress on a different word or phrase can alter the meaning of the sentence. Have students use the example sentences to demonstrate this. Then have students skim the text and choose another sentence with which to practice proper intonation. Have them say it aloud, then offer guidance, support, and correction as needed.

Advanced High Choose two or three sentences from the text and have students read them aloud, focusing on proper intonation. Ask students to explain how placing the stress on a different word or phrase can alter the meaning of the sentence. Have students use the example sentences to demonstrate this. Then have students skim the text and choose another sentence with which to practice proper intonation. Have them say it aloud to a partner. Instruct partners to offer guidance, support, and correction as needed. Circulate among students to give extra help.

▣ Differentiate Instruction

Use the Differentiated Instruction notes throughout the lesson plan to support the varied skill sets, levels of readiness, and interests in the mixed-ability classroom.

Challenge These notes include suggestions for expanding the activity for advanced students.

On-Level These notes include suggestions for modifying the activity to address different interests or learning styles.

Extra Support These notes include ideas for providing more scaffolding or reading spuport.

Special Needs These notes provide ideas for adapting instruction to support the needs of various special needs students.

▮ NOTES

The Origins of Hinduism and Buddhism

Objectives

Objective 1: Describe the origins and central beliefs of Hinduism.

Objective 2: Analyze and summarize how the caste system shaped India.

Objective 3: Describe the origins and central beliefs of Buddhism.

Objective 4: Explore how Buddhism grew and changed as it spread beyond India.

LESSON 2 ORGANIZER		PACING: APPROX. 1 PERIOD, .5 BLOCKS			
				RESOURCES	
		OBJECTIVES	**PACING**	**Online**	**Print**
Connect					
	DIGITAL START UP ACTIVITY **Religion and Society**		5 min.	●	
Investigate					
	DIGITAL TEXT 1 **Hindu Beliefs Develop**	Objective 1	10 min.	●	●
	INTERACTIVE GALLERY **The Origins of Hinduism**		10 min.	●	
	DIGITAL TEXT 2 **The Caste System Shapes India**	Objective 2	10 min.	●	●
	DIGITAL TEXT 3 **The Buddha's Key Teachings**	Objective 3	10 min.	●	●
	INTERACTIVE MAP **The Origins and Spread of Buddhism**		10 min.	●	
	DIGITAL TEXT 4 **Buddhism Spreads**	Objective 4	10 min.	●	●
Synthesize					
	DIGITAL ACTIVITY **Hinduism and Buddhism**		5 min.	●	
Demonstrate					
	DIGITAL QUIZ **Lesson Quiz and Class Discussion Board**		10 min.	●	

PEARSON
realıze
www.PearsonRealize.com

Go online to access additional resources including:
Primary Sources • Biographies • Supreme Court cases •
21st Century Skill Tutorials • Maps • Graphic Organizers.

■ CONNECT

DIGITAL START UP ACTIVITY
Religion and Society

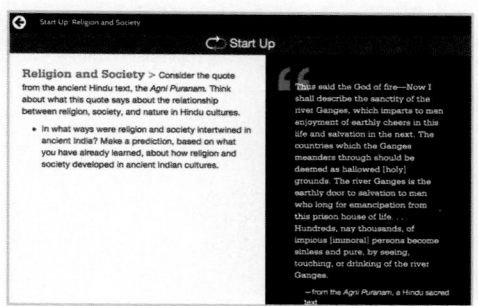

Project the Start Up Activity Ask students to answer the question as they enter and get settled. Then have them share their ideas with another student, either in class or through a chat or blog space.

Make Predictions Today in India, Hindus often bathe in the Ganges River. What would you predict is the connection between ancient Hindu beliefs about the Ganges and modern-day Hindu practices? *(Students can probably predict that ancient Hindu beliefs still influence modern-day Hindu practices. For example, the faithful still seek salvation, and also to become sinless and pure by touching or drinking water from the Ganges River.)*

Aa Vocabulary Development: Use the Interactive Reading Notepad to preview the Key Terms and Academic Vocabulary in this Lesson with students.

⇅ FLIP IT!

Assign the Flipped Video for this lesson.

■ STUDENT EDITION PRINT PAGES: 69–74

■ INVESTIGATE

DIGITAL TEXT 1
Hindu Beliefs Develop

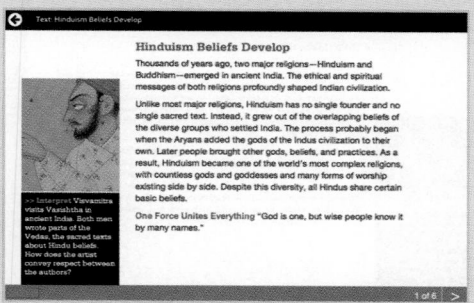

INTERACTIVE GALLERY
The Origins of Hinduism

Objective 1: Describe the origins and central beliefs of Hinduism.

Quick Instruction

Hinduism developed in ancient India from the religious beliefs of the diverse groups who settled there. A mixture of gods, beliefs, and practices overlapped and were recorded in sacred texts called the Vedas. A basic belief of Hinduism is an all-powerful spiritual force called Brahman. The goal of life for Hindus is to achieve moksha, or union with Brahman.

Interactive Gallery: The Origins of Hinduism Project the gallery. Have students examine the images, taking time to read captions and look at each picture.

▣ ACTIVE CLASSROOM

Use the See-Think-Wonder strategy with students working in partner pairs. Have each pair of students choose one image from the gallery. They should discuss with each other what they see in the image, what they think about it, and any questions they may have. Partners can then share highlights of their discussion with the class.

Cite Evidence Hinduism teaches that all life is interconnected. Find evidence from the text that Hindu gods were also considered to be interconnected. *(Answers may vary, but some textual evidence for this claim includes "God is one, but wise people know it by many names." "One Force Unites Everything." "... everything is part of the... spiritual force called brahman. Hindus worship a variety of gods who give concrete form to brahman." and "[Each god] represent(s) the various aspects of brahman with which he is associated.")*

ELL Use the ELL activity described in the ELL chart.

Further Instruction

Editable Presentation Use the Editable Presentation to present the main ideas for this text.

Hindu Beliefs Develop: Core Reading and Interactive Reading Notepad Project and discuss the Interactive Reading Notepad questions, including the graphic organizer asking students to record the most important principles of Hinduism. Fill in the graphic organizer on the whiteboard as you go.

Tell students that the development and spread of Hinduism differed from other major religions. Unlike most major religions, Hinduism has no single founder and no single sacred text. Instead, it grew out of the overlapping beliefs of the diverse groups who settled India. The process probably began when the Aryans added the gods of the Indus civilization to their own. Later people brought other gods, beliefs, and practices. As a result, Hinduism became one of the world's most complex religions, with countless gods and goddesses and many forms of worship existing side by side. Despite this diversity, all Hindus share certain basic beliefs.

Be sure students understand some other important principles of Hinduism, such as atman (an essential self), karma (one's actions that affect fate in the next life), dharma (the religious and moral duties of an individual), and ahimsa (nonviolence)

The Origins of Hinduism and Buddhism

DIGITAL TEXT 2

The Caste System Shapes India

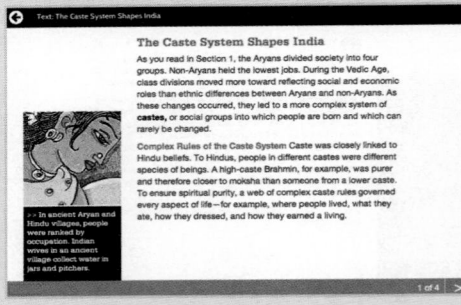

Compare and Contrast Compare and contrast the concepts of karma and moksha in Hinduism. *(Moksha is the goal of life for Hindus; it is the achievement of union with brahman, the all-powerful spiritual force. Karma are all actions a person takes that affect one's fate in the next life. Good karma earns rebirth at a higher level and gets one closer to moksha.)*

Topic Inquiry

Launch the Topic Inquiry with students after introducing the Topic.

Objective 2: Analyze and summarize how the caste system shaped India.

Quick Instruction

Hinduism contributed to the development of a caste system. To Hindus, people in different castes were different species and the law of karma determined caste. Higher castes were closer to moksha. The caste system also reflected and influenced social and economic roles; the "dirtiest" jobs were performed by the lowest castes. The caste system did ensure a stable social order, and castes were interdependent.

Project the Infographic from the text and have students read the diagrams. Ask students where was the first written record of a caste system? *(in the Vedas, ancient Aryan sacred texts)* What does this first written record of a caste system tell you about the system? *(It shows that the caste social system was used by other Indian groups, and probably only partially based on Hindu religious beliefs.)*

ELL Use the ELL activity described in the ELL chart.

Further Instruction

The Caste System Shapes India: Core Reading and Interactive Reading Notepad
Project and discuss the Interactive Reading Notepad questions.

Infer Why would a Hindu person labeled as a member of the lowest caste system most likely accept this label? *(Hindus believed that the law of karma determined caste level, and that good karma would lead to a better future reincarnation. They accepted that people were at different spiritual and social levels. The caste system gave a sense of identity, interdependence, and social order.)*

DIGITAL TEXT 3

The Buddha's Key Teachings

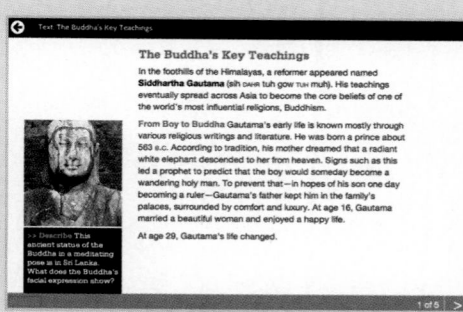

INTERACTIVE MAP

The Origins and Spread of Buddhism

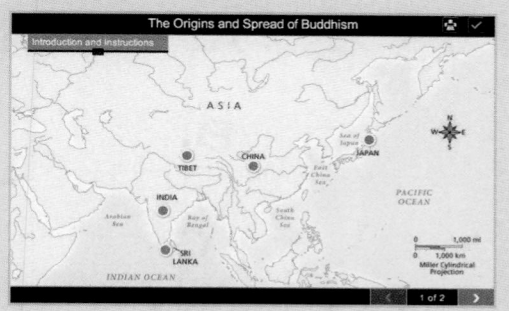

DIGITAL TEXT 4

Buddhism Spreads

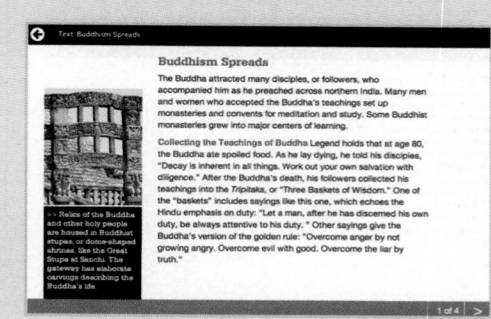

Objective 3: Describe the origins and central beliefs of Buddhism.

Quick Instruction

Siddhartha Gautama started life as a prince around 563 B.C. He renounced royal life when he discovered human suffering, and searched for "the realm of life where there is neither suffering nor death." He gained enlightenment and became the Buddha, teaching others about the Four Noble Truths and the Eightfold Path. The Truths describe that life is suffering, the cause of suffering is nonvirtue (negative acts and thoughts), and the cure is to overcome nonvirtue.

Interactive Map: The Origins and Spread of Buddhism Project the map. Have students click each country to learn about the origins and spread of Buddhism.

👥 ACTIVE CLASSROOM

Use A Closer Look strategy with small groups of students. Each group can be assigned to take a closer look at one country and the accompanying image. Have them tell you what they see and what they learned as a result of their focus on this part of the map. Collect insights from each group.

ELL Use the ELL activity described in the ELL chart.

Further Instruction

The Buddha's Key Teachings: Core Reading and Interactive Reading Notepad Project and discuss the Interactive Reading Notepad questions.

Be sure students understand that the Buddha taught an Eightfold Path as a way to overcome nonvirture and achieve nirvana, or union with the universe and release from the cycle of rebirth. The Path includes "right views, right aspirations, right speech, right conduct, right livelihood, right effort, right mindfulness, and right contemplation."

Compare How is nirvana in Buddhism similar to moksha in Hinduism? *(Nirvana and moksha are the ultimate goals in Buddhism and Hinduism, respectively. They are achieved through proper actions, and unite the faithful with higher powers while ending the cycle of rebirth, or reincarnation.)*

D Differentiate: Challenge/Gifted Have small groups of students prepare and present a skit on the life and philosophy of Siddhartha Gautama, the Buddha.

Objective 4: Describe how Buddhism grew and changed as it spread beyond India.

Quick Instruction

The Buddha's teachings were collected by followers in a series of texts. Missionaries and traders spread Buddhism to other parts of Asia. Buddhism eventualy split into two sects, or subgroups, known as Theraveda and Mahayana. Theraveda Buddhism spread to Sri Lanka and Southeast Asia. The Mahayana sect, in which people ask gods for help, spread even more widely across Asia. Meanwhile, Buddhism declined in India, absorbed by Hinduism.

Project the map from the text. According to this map, how many countries in Southeast Asia have follwers of Theraveda Buddhism today, and what are the names of those countries? *(Four countries: Myanmar (Burma), Laos, Thailand, and Cambodia)*

Further Instruction

Buddhism Spreads: Core Reading and Interactive Reading Notepad Project and discuss the Interactive Reading Notepad questions.

Identify Cause and Effect What features increased Mahayana Buddhism's popularity in places like China and Japan? *(This sect allowed followers to make appeals to compassionate gods for help with daily problems and to achieve salvation.)*

The Origins of Hinduism and Buddhism

■ SYNTHESIZE

DIGITAL ACTIVITY
Hinduism and Buddhism

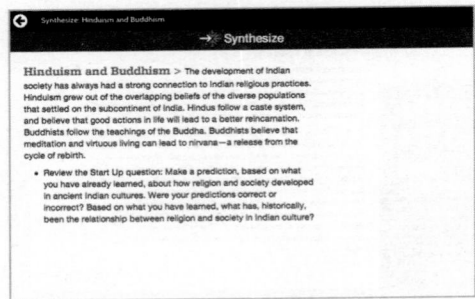

The development of society in India has been intertwined with the development of the religions of Buddhism and Hinduism.

Have students answer the questions in this activity, then share their answers with a partner. Have students discuss as a group the following question.

Identify Cause and Effect Re-read the last paragraph of this lesson's text. What were some causes of Buddhism's eventual decline in India? *(Hinduism eventually absorbed Buddhism and added Buddha to the pantheon of Hindu gods. In the 1100s some Muslim armies invaded India and destroyed some Buddhist temples, furthering the decline of Buddhism in India.)*

■ DEMONSTRATE

DIGITAL QUIZ
Lesson Quiz and Class Discussion Board

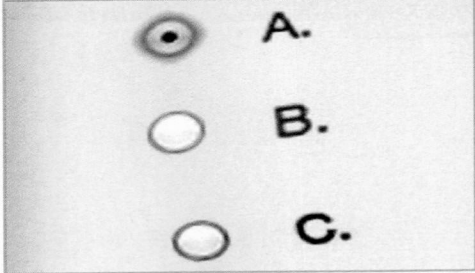

Assign the online Lesson Quiz for this lesson if you haven't already done so. Students will be offered automatic remediation or enrichment based on their score.

Pose these questions to the class on the Discussion Board: In "The Origins of Hinduism and Buddhism" you read about the development of two religions in ancient India. The religions had some similar characteristics but differences too; Buddhists did not endorse the caste system as Hindus did. Buddhism spread across Asia, but within India, it was mostly absorbed by Hinduism.

Summarize According to the Buddha, how can people escape worldly suffering? *(They can do this by understanding the Four Noble Truths, following the Eightfold Path, living a moral life, and meditating.)*

Draw Conclusions What is a main way that Hinduism influenced a social and economic order in ancient and modern India? *(Hinduism still brings spiritual guidance to Indians, but the main way it influenced a social and economic order in India is in the development and following of a caste system.)*

Topic Inquiry

Have students continue their investigations for the Topic Inquiry.

Powerful Empires Emerge in India

Supporting English Language Learners

Use with Digital Text 1, **The Maurya Empire Builds a Strong Government.**

Learning Strategies

Read *The Maurya Empire Builds a Strong Government* aloud to the class. Have them complete one activity according to their level of English proficiency.

Beginning Write and display one academic vocabulary word from the text *The Maurya Empire Builds a Strong Government*, such as *missionaries*. Define the word for students, then use it in a simple sentence that relates to the content. Have students write the word, definition, and sentence in their notebooks. Finally, have students draw a picture to demonstrate their understanding of the word. Invite them to describe their pictures using simple language. If time allows, repeat the process with anther academic vocabulary word from the text.

Intermediate Write and display the academic vocabulary words from the text: *missionaries* and *dissent*. Define the word for students and have them copy the definition into their notebooks. Then have groups of students work together to write a sentence for each vocabulary word in the list. Circulate among groups to monitor group progress and offer support as needed.

Advanced Instruct students to scan the text to find the two academic vocabulary words from the text: *missionaries* and *dissent*. Invite students to use classroom resources and context clues to define the words and have them copy the definition into their notebooks. Then have students write a sentence for each vocabulary word in the list. Circulate among students to monitor progress and offer support as needed.

Advanced High Instruct students to scan the text to find the two academic vocabulary words from the text: *missionaries* and *dissent*. Invite students to use classroom resources and context clues to define the words and have them copy the definition into their notebooks. Then have students work with a partner to use research materials to find and write a few sentences about additional historical examples of *missionaries* and *dissent*.

Use with Digital Text 4, **Family and Village Life Shape Indian Society.**

Listening

Read *Family and Village Life Shape Indian Society*. Then guide students through one of the following activities according to their English proficiency level.

Beginning Explain how the letter *y* operates in the English language. Make a distinction for students between the different sounds *y* can make at the end of a word. Slowly reread the first paragraph of *Family and Village Life Shape Indian Society* for students. Pause when you read the words *majority, society,* and *family*. Explain that all three of these words are examples of the letter *y* sounding like a long *e* at the end of a word. Scan the text or brainstorm other words that end in *y* and the long *e* sound.

Intermediate Say the word *family* aloud for students. Help them identify the sound made by the *y* at the end of the word. Slowly reread the first paragraph of *Family and Village Life Shape Indian Society* for students. Pause when you read the words *majority, society,* and *family*. Ask students to explain the similar sound at the end of these words. Help students scan the text or brainstorm other words that end in *y* and the long *e* sound.

Advanced Remind students of the sounds that the letter *y* can make. Have them work with a partner to review the text to find words that end in *y* and have the long *e* sound. Instruct pairs to make a list of these words and share them with the class to create a master list. Brainstorm other words that fit these requirements with students and add them to the list.

Advanced High Ask students to explain the different sounds that the letter *y* can make. Have them review the text to find words that end in *y* and have the long *e* sound. Instruct students to make a list of these words and share them with the class to create a master list. Brainstorm other words that fit these requirements with students and add them to the list.

▣ Differentiate Instruction

Use the Differentiated Instruction notes throughout the lesson plan to support the varied skill sets, levels of readiness, and interests in the mixed-ability classroom.

Challenge These notes include suggestions for expanding the activity for advanced students.

On-Level These notes include suggestions for modifying the activity to address different interests or learning styles.

Extra Support These notes include ideas for providing more scaffolding or reading spuport.

Special Needs These notes provide ideas for adapting instruction to support the needs of various special needs students.

■ NOTES

Powerful Empires Emerge in India

Objectives

Objective 1: Analyze how Mauryan rulers created a strong central government for their empire.

Objective 2: Explore the kingdoms that arose across the Deccan.

Objective 3: Explain why the period of Gupta rule in India is considered a golden age.

Objective 4: Understand how family and village life shaped Indian society.

LESSON 3 ORGANIZER		PACING: APPROX. 1 PERIOD, .5 BLOCKS			
				RESOURCES	
		OBJECTIVES	PACING	Online	Print
Connect					
	DIGITAL START UP ACTIVITY **Powerful Rulers and The Golden Age in India**		5 min.	●	
Investigate					
	DIGITAL TEXT 1 **The Maurya Empire Builds a Strong Government**	Objective 1	10 min.	●	●
	INTERACTIVE MAP **The Maurya and Gupta Empires**		10 min.	●	
	DIGITAL TEXT 2 **Deccan Kingdoms Arise**	Objective 2	10 min.	●	●
	DIGITAL TEXT 3 **A Golden Age Under Gupta Rule**	Objective 3	10 min.	●	●
	INTERACTIVE GALLERY **A Golden Age in the Arts**		10 min.	●	
	DIGITAL TEXT 4 **Family and Village Life Shape Indian Society**	Objective 4	10 min.	●	●
Synthesize					
	DIGITAL ACTIVITY **Maintaining Peace and Order**		5 min.	●	
Demonstrate					
	DIGITAL QUIZ **Lesson Quiz and Classroom Discussion Board**		10 min.	●	

■ CONNECT

DIGITAL START UP ACTIVITY

Powerful Rulers and The Golden Age in India

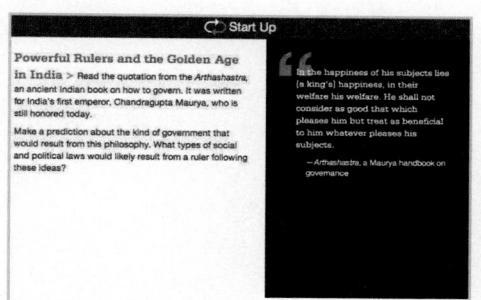

Project the Start Up Activity Ask students to answer the questions as they enter and get settled. Then have them share their responses with another student, either in class or through a chat or blog space.

Read the quotation from the *Arthashastra*, an Indian book on how to govern people. Make a prediction about the kind of government that would result from this philosophy. What types of social and political laws would likely result from a ruler following these ideas? *(Answers will vary. Students should consider the type of government that would result from a ruler who put the welfare of his people above his own welfare.)*

Aa Vocabulary Development: Use the Interactive Reading Notepad to preview the Key Terms and Academic Vocabulary in this Lesson with students.

⇅ FLIP IT!

Assign the Flipped Video for this lesson.

■ STUDENT EDITION PRINT PAGES: 75–80

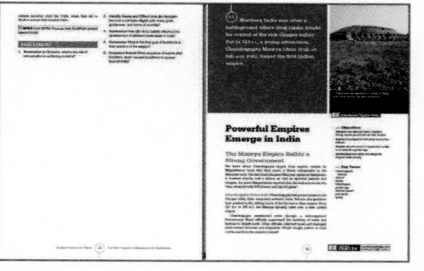

■ INVESTIGATE

DIGITAL TEXT 1

The Maurya Empire Builds a Strong Government

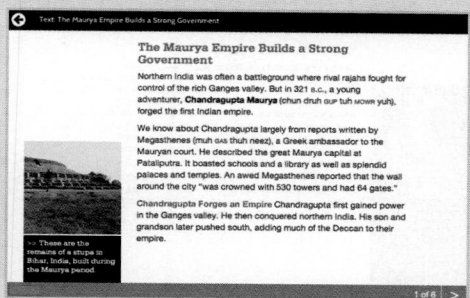

INTERACTIVE MAP

The Maurya and Gupta Empires

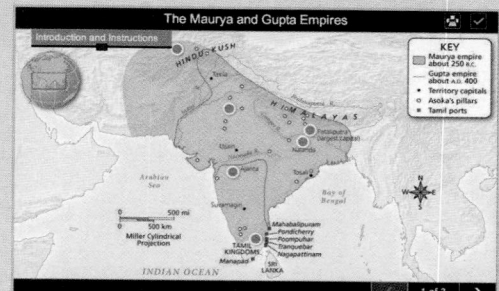

Objective 1: Analyze how Maurya rulers created a strong central government for their empire.

Quick Instruction

The Mauryan empire was one of the first major civilizations to develop in ancient India. As religion and government had shaped the Indus and Aryan civilizations before them, the Mauryan kings also relied on those two factors to shape their growing empire. However, the two greatest Maurya kings had quite different approaches to the roles of government and religion in their rule. Chandragupta, the first Mauryan king, built a strong central government and harshly enforced his policies. His grandson, Asoka, took a different path. He believed that rulers should lead by example and put the welfare of their subjects ahead of their own welfare. Asoka's reign also featured a strong government, but he promoted his policies much differently than his predecessors.

Interactive Map: The Maurya and Gupta Empires Project the map. Explain how the interaction works by clicking on one of the hotspots to demonstrate how it brings up a box with further information.

Explain to students that one of the most important achievements of the Mauryan empire was the unification of many warring states throughout India. A civilization cannot progress unless there is relative peace. Although the Gupta empire was smaller geographically, its stability encouraged other types of growth, such as in education and the arts.

🗪 ACTIVE CLASSROOM

Use the Conversation with History strategy and ask students to pretend they're having a conversation with either Chandragupta or Asoka. Have students write down a question they want to ask, then what that person would say and, finally, what the student would say in response. Discuss the results of the activity.

D Differentiate: Extra Support Help students better understand the achievements of Chandragupta and Asoka by asking students to create an illustrated timeline depicting and describing the key events and achievements of each king's reign. Each entry on the timeline should include an illustration as well as a concise description of the event or achievement.

ELL Use the ELL activity described in the ELL chart.

Further Instruction

Editable Presentation Use the Editable Presentation to present the main ideas for this text.

The Maurya Empire Builds a Strong Government: Core Reading and Interactive Reading Notepad Project and discuss the Interactive Reading Notepad questions.

Powerful Empires Emerge in India

DIGITAL TEXT 2

Deccan Kingdoms Arise

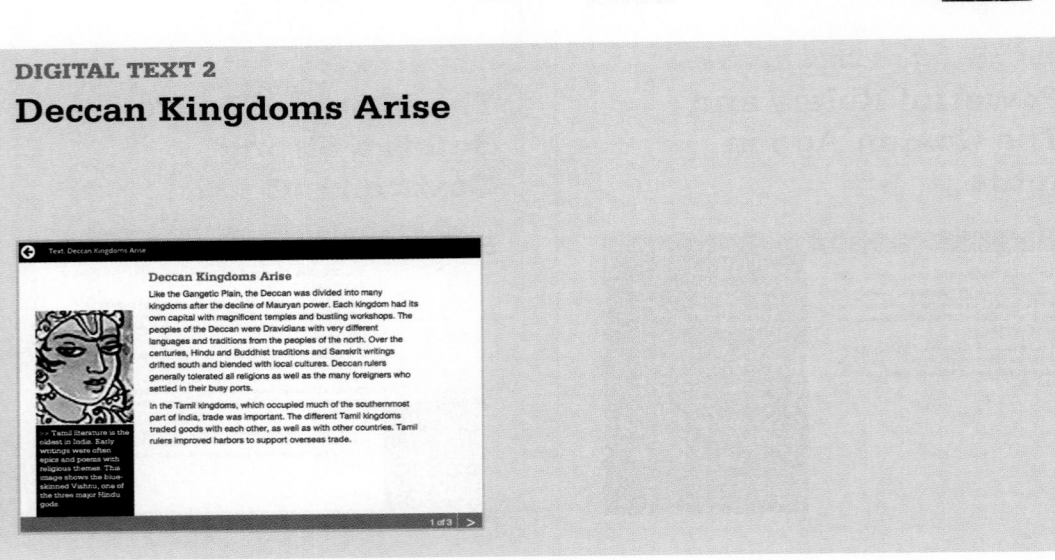

Explain that Chandragupta faced a formidable challenge in trying to create a cohesive empire out of a large geographic area. He chose to build a central government that maintained order by force and was supported by a well-organized bureaucracy. His efforts marked the beginning of the Mauryan empire that was eventually passed to his grandson, Asoka. Asoka chose a different method of maintaining a centralized government. Strongly influenced by his Buddhist beliefs, Asoka rejected violence and chose to lead by example while also maintaining the authority of a ruler. His approach was a form of contract between ruler and ruled that relied heavily on basic Buddhist teachings. Although different, both kings contributed to the political and cultural development of India's ancient civilization.

Identify Cause and Effect How would you describe the effects of Chandragupta's methods of government? *(Sample answer: Chandragupta used harsh methods to keep order in his centralized government. At the same time, his efficient bureaucracy maintained the infrastructure and allowed him to keep needed control over his far-flung lands.)*

Objective 2: Explore the kingdoms that arose across the Deccan.

Quick Instruction

With the fall of the Mauryan empire and the unity it had achieved, India once again divided into separate small kingdoms, each with its own capital city and ruler. Over time, cultural and religious influences from the northern parts of India filtered down to the Deccan. The Tamil kingdoms' strong trade network ensured lively trade both locally and overseas.

Further Instruction

Deccan Kingdoms Arise: Core Reading and Interactive Reading Notepad Project and discuss the Interactive Reading Notepad questions.

The Mauryan empire relied on a solid central government to unify the various peoples within the empire. When the empire fell, that unity was shattered. As a result, sometimes tenuous relationships became strained between regions within the empire. Ambitious leaders in these areas took the opportunity to form their own kingdoms and compete for territory. The Deccan area was Dravidian, which made it quite different from the Mauryan strongholds to the north. Despite the disunity, most of the Deccan rulers were tolerant of cultural and religious ideas that slowly filtered down from the north. This, plus the extensive trade system of the Tamil kingdoms, formed a kind of cohesion of its own. The Tamil, especially, traded with cultures as far away as Rome and China. It was inevitable that southern India would be exposed to goods and ideas from these areas.

Draw Inferences Why might the collapse of the Mauryan empire have been less of an upheaval to the Tamil than northern areas? *(The Tamil had an existing trade network that continued both locally and overseas, despite the loss of the stability provided by the Mauryan government system.)*

DIGITAL TEXT 3

A Golden Age Under Gupta Rule

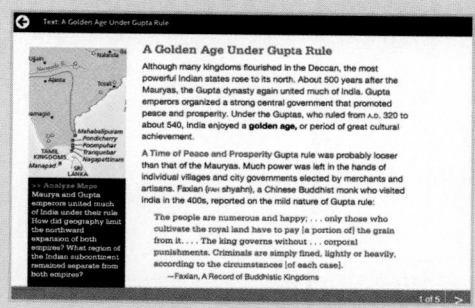

INTERACTIVE GALLERY

A Golden Age in the Arts

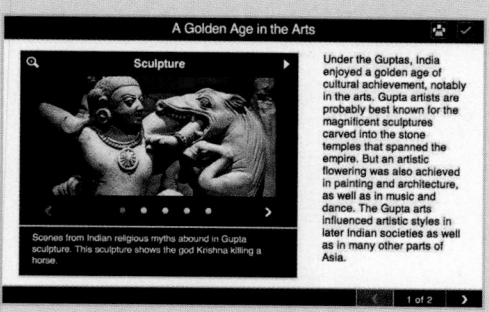

Objective 3: Explain why the period of Gupta rule in India is considered a golden age.

Quick Instruction

About 500 years after the Maurya empire fell, a dynasty formed in the north. It was built on the foundations of a strong central government and policies that promoted peace and prosperity. This dynasty was the Gupta, and for about 200 years the Gupta dynasty maintained power and ushered in a golden age of trade and cultural and technological advancements.

Interactive Gallery: A Golden Age in the Arts Project the activity. Explain how the interaction works by clicking on one of the images. The relative stability of the Gupta empire allowed people the time to explore the sciences and the arts. As a result, great discoveries were made that affect what we do today. Art and literature flourished, with many ancient plays continuing to entertain in modern settings.

🖳 ACTIVE CLASSROOM

Use the Quick Write strategy and give students 30 seconds to write what they know about the activity. They should write as if they were posting a Twitter statement. Therefore, their comment is limited to 140 characters. Ask students to share their statements.

ELL Use the ELL activity described in the ELL chart.

Further Instruction

A Golden Age Under Gupta Rule: Core Reading and Interactive Reading Notepad
Project and discuss the Interactive Reading Notepad questions and the graphic organizer comparing the Mauryan and Gupta empires. Review with the class the similarities and differences between the two eras and fill in the graphic organizer on the whiteboard as you go.

Like the Maurya before them, the Gupta relied on a strong central government with a well-organized bureaucracy. However, unlike the Maurya, the Gupta allowed more local self-government. The Gupta dynasty allowed people to prosper in an era of relative peace. As a result, trade flourished and farming expanded into new types of crops. Artisans produced everything from cloth to metal wares for both domestic and foreign markets. Gupta goods were traded in parts of Africa, the Middle East, and Southeast Asia.

Prosperity allowed the Gupta to turn their attention to education, the arts, and technology. Scholars and students attended schools that taught a wide variety of subjects such as mathematics, medicine, astronomy, literature, and other arts. One of these schools was the Buddhist monastery and university at Naranda, which attracted students from many parts of Asia. Advances in mathematics, such as Indian numerals, zero,and the decimal system, were carried to Europe and are used to this day. The advances in mathematics led to increased knowledge in the science of astronomy. Indian mathematicians greatly influenced the development of Islamic astronomy in Persia, which later influenced astronomy in Europe. Indian technological

advancements in the production of iron, copper, and zinc, cotton textiles, and shipbuilding were diffused through trade.

Gupta-era physicians used early forms of medical technology, including vaccinations and herbal medicines. Indian physicians often used a medical system called Ayurveda, which treats illness by addressing every part of the patient's life, from diet and exercise to herbal remedies. This method is still used in India.

Eventually, a combination of weak rulers, invasions, and fighting within the empire brought about the end of the Gupta empire. Both the Mauryan and Gupta empires helped to establish Indian civilization. Each empires' system of government encouraged trade and supported advancements in education in a variety of areas. This level of political and social organization would not be seen again in India for almost 1,000 years.

Draw Conclusions How did the stable government and economic prosperity of the Mauryan and Gupta empires encourage growth in other areas such as education and trade? *(Stability and prosperity provided the security people needed to explore other areas of growth. They had the time to innovate and advance their cultures.)*

Powerful Empires Emerge in India

DIGITAL TEXT 4

Family and Village Life Shape Indian Society

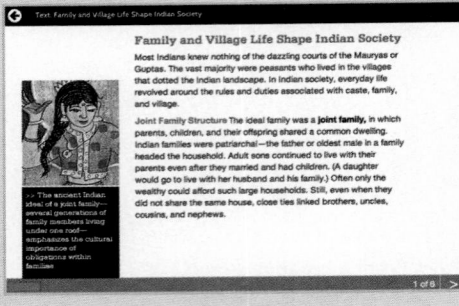

Objective 4: Understand how family and village life shaped Indian society.

Quick Instruction

Although the achievements of the Mauryan and Gupta empires left an indelible mark on Indian civilization, the vast majority of the population during these times were peasants who lived a structured life dictated by caste, family, and village. Joint families made up of several generations lived within the same household. The patriarchal system placed the father at the head of the household, with women and children fulfilling specific duties and responsibilities. Within the village, a headman and council made decisions that affected the whole community. People of different castes had duties and responsibilities to the village. The empire may have been ruled by kings and civil servants, but the villages were often left to manage their affairs on their own, developing cultural influences that have lasted to modern times.

ELL Use the ELL activity described in the ELL chart.

Further Instruction

Family and Village Life Shape Indian Society: Core Reading and Interactive Reading Notepad Project and discuss the Interactive Reading Notepad questions.

As with many developing civilizations, the vast majority of the population were not directly involved in the activities of kings and government. Instead, they were peasants whose world revolved around their daily lives and personal interactions. A clearly defined structure that included caste, family, and village outlined the specific responsibilities and duties of each person in the community.

The joint family, in which several generations shared a dwelling, was the ideal family. Each person in this patriarchal system had particular roles to play and duties to fulfill. As head of the household, the father or oldest male made the decisions for the rest of the family. Daughters went to live with their husband's family upon marriage and assumed the appropriate roles in that household. The higher status enjoyed by women during earlier Aryan civilization was replaced by a more restricted life centered on the home.

Families of different castes formed villages which were governed by a headman and an advisory council. This group would make the decisions that affected everyone in the community. These decisions might include calling on villagers to participate in community endeavors such as building irrigation systems or clearing fields for agriculture. People from one village routinely interacted with people from other villages for the purposes of trade, religious celebrations, and weddings. This interaction, generation after generation, helped develop the common ideas that have become a part of the Indian culture.

Analyze information What does the roles played by family and village in Indian life reveal about the needs of the individual versus the needs of the community? *(The needs of the community, or family, took precedence over the needs of the individual.)*

■ SYNTHESIZE

DIGITAL ACTIVITY

Maintaining Peace and Order

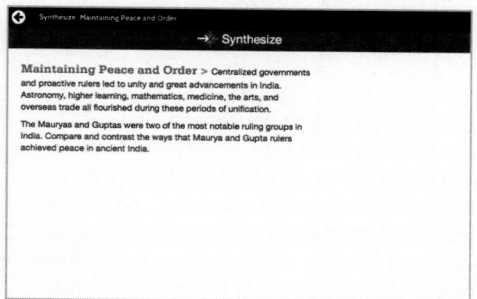

Ask students to share their responses to the Synthesize question. Discuss with students that there are modern examples of both leader's approaches to government. Have students try to think of examples that reflect the political influences of the ancient Mauryan and Gupta empires.

Describe the factors common to the governments of both Chandragupta and Asoka. *(both brought a period of peace and prosperity; both had strong central governments.)*

■ DEMONSTRATE

DIGITAL QUIZ

Lesson Quiz and Classroom Discussion Board

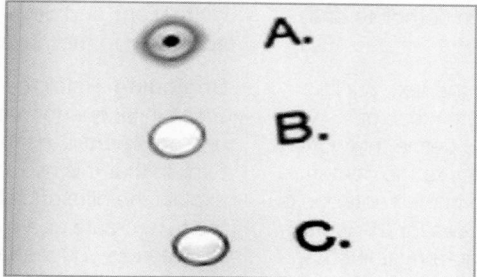

Assign the online Lesson Quiz for this lesson if you haven't already done so. Students will be offered automatic remediation or enrichment based on their score.

Pose these questions to the class on the Discussion Board:

In this lesson, you read about two of the earliest empires of India and their political and cultural influences on the development of civilization on the Indian subcontinent. At the time of the formation of the Mauryan and Gupta empires, India was a land of many separate and often warring kingdoms. Additionally, the kingdoms of northern India spoke different languages and had a different culture than the kingdoms in the Deccan.

Recognize Cause and Effect How did the formation of the Mauryan and Gupta empires contribute to the development of civilization in India? *(Both empires united warring kingdoms into one kingdom with a strong central government and an effective bureaucracy. The relative peace and prosperity encouraged advances in agriculture, education, technology, and the arts. With the Gupta, India experienced a golden age of significant cultural growth in many areas.)*

Draw Conclusions What are some factors that encourage the advance of civilizations? *(Some of the factors are a unifying government, a good civil service, peace, and economic prosperity where people no longer have to spend the majority of their lives simply trying to survive. A civilization has to have people who have the time to help it grow.)*

Topic Inquiry

Have students continue their investigations for the Topic Inquiry.

Rise of Civilization in China

Supporting English Language Learners

Use with Digital Text 5, **Two Major Belief Systems Take Root.**

Learning Strategies

Read *Two Major Belief Systems Take Root* aloud to the class. Students will use their language skills to learn new and essential language that explains the core ideas of Confucianism and Daoism. Have them complete one activity according to their level of English proficiency.

Beginning Write and display one essential word from the text, such as *education* or *responsibility*, that helps explain the core ideas of Confucianism and Daoism. Use accessible language to define the word for students, then use it in a simple sentence that relates to the content. Have students write the word, definition, and sentence in their notebooks. Finally, support students as they form their own sentences for the word, offering gentle feedback as needed to ensure correct grammar, fluency, and intonation.

Intermediate Write and display a few essential words from the text, such as *education* and *responsibility*, that helps explain the core ideas of Confucianism and Daoism. Use accessible language to define the word for students, and have them copy the definition into their notebooks. Then have groups of students work together to create and say a sentence for each essential word in the list. Circulate to monitor group progress and offer support as needed.

Advanced Instruct students to scan the text to find essential words from the text: words that they must know the meaning of in order to understand the core ideas of Confucianism and Daoism. Examples include *education*, *responsibility*, and *wisdom*. Invite students to use classroom resources and context clues to define the words and have them copy the definition into their notebooks. Then have students create and say a sentence to a partner for each vocabulary word. Tell students to work together to improve their pronunciation, fluency, and intonation. Circulate among students to monitor progress and offer support as needed.

Advanced High Instruct students to scan the text to find essential words from the text: words that they must know the meaning of in order to understand the core ideas of Confucianism and Daoism. Examples include *education*, *responsibility*, and *wisdom*. Invite students to use classroom resources and context clues to define the words and have them copy the definition into their notebooks. Then have students create and say a few sentences using these essential words. Tell students they will be sharing their sentences with the whole class. Encourage them to practice their pronunciation, fluency, and intonation before sharing with others. Offer support as needed.

Use with Digital Text 2, **The Shang Dynasty Begins to Form China.**

Listening

Read *The Shang Dynasty Begins to Form China* aloud to the class. Students will learn new language structures by listening to classroom instructions and other students. Have them complete one activity according to their level of English proficiency.

Beginning Retell the content in the *The Shang Dynasty Begins to Form China* in language that students easily understand. Write and display one of the red C-heads from the text, such as *Formation of Government*. Explain that this head, or subtitle, is a fragment. Students will listen as you explain the difference between a complete sentence and a fragment. Using the text, create and display a sentence that uses the fragment. Students will listen as you read the fragment, and then the sentence out loud. Finally, provide students with another fragment, and ask them to use the text to create a new sentence using that fragment.

Intermediate Retell the content in the *The Shang Dynasty Begins to Form China* in language that students easily understand. Write and display one of the red C-heads from the text, such as *Formation of Government*. Explain that this head, or subtitle, is a fragment. Students will listen as you explain the difference between a complete sentence and a fragment. Have students use the text to create a sentence using the fragment. Students will listen as others read their fragments, and then their sentences out loud. Finally, provide students with another fragment, and ask them to use the text to create a new sentence using that fragment. Have students listen as others read their fragments and completed sentences out loud.

Advanced Reread *The Shang Dynasty Begins to Form China* aloud for students. Instruct pairs of students to discuss the difference between a fragment and a complete sentence. Have pairs create 3 to 4 word fragments that describe the images in the reading. Have each student listen to the fragments created by their partner as they are read aloud. Then ask the pairs to work together to transform their new fragments into complete sentences using information from the text. Finally, combine pairs of students to form groups of four. Have them listen to each other's fragments and completed sentences as they are read out loud.

Advanced High Reread *The Shang Dynasty Begins to Form China* aloud for students. Instruct students to create 3 to 4 word fragments that describe the images in the reading. Then have each student turn to a partner to trade their fragments. After trading, students should use the text to turn their new fragments into complete sentences. Finally, ask students rejoin their partner. Have each partner listen as the other reads their fragments, and then their sentences out loud. Offer support as necessary.

PEARSON
realize™
www.PearsonRealize.com

Go online to access additional resources including:
Primary Sources • Biographies • Supreme Court cases •
21st Century Skill Tutorials • Maps • Graphic Organizers.

Objectives

Objective 1: Understand how geography influenced early Chinese civilization.

Objective 2: Analyze how Chinese culture took shape under the Shang and Zhou dynasties.

Objective 3: Describe the origins, central ideas, and spread of Confucianism and Daoism.

Objective 4: List some achievements made in early China.

LESSON 4 ORGANIZER   PACING: APPROX. 1 PERIOD, .5 BLOCKS

		OBJECTIVES	PACING	RESOURCES Online	Print
Connect					
	DIGITAL START UP ACTIVITY **Philosophy, Society, and Technology**		5 min.	●	
Investigate					
	DIGITAL TEXT 1 **Geography Influences Chinese Civilization**	Objective 1	10 min.	●	●
	DIGITAL TEXT 2 **The Shang Dynasty Begins to Form China**	Objective 2	10 min.	●	●
	DIGITAL TEXT 3 **The Zhou Dynasty**		10 min.	●	●
	DIGITAL TEXT 4 **Religious Beliefs in Early China**		10 min.	●	●
	DIGITAL TEXT 5 **Two Major Belief Systems Take Root**	Objective 3	10 min.	●	●
	INTERACTIVE CHART **Confucianism and Daoism**		10 min.	●	
	DIGITAL TEXT 6 **A Time of Achievements in Early China**	Objective 4	10 min.	●	●
	INTERACTIVE GALLERY **Silk Making in Ancient China**		10 min.	●	
Synthesize					
	DIGITAL ACTIVITY **Ancient Influences**		5 min.	●	
Demonstrate					
	DIGITAL QUIZ **Lesson Quiz and Classroom Discussion Board**		10 min.	●	

Rise of Civilization in China

■ CONNECT

DIGITAL START UP ACTIVITY
Philosophy, Society, and Technology

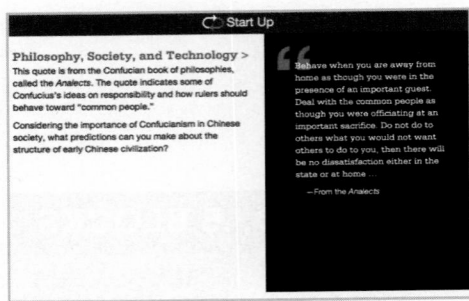

↻ Start Up

Philosophy, Society, and Technology >
This quote is from the Confucian book of philosophies, called the *Analects*. The quote indicates some of Confucius's ideas on responsibility and how rulers should behave toward "common people."

Considering the importance of Confucianism in Chinese society, what predictions can you make about the structure of early Chinese civilization?

"Behave when you are away from home as though you were in the presence of an important guest. Deal with the common people as though you were officiating at an important sacrifice. Do not do to others what you would not want others to do to you, then there will be no dissatisfaction either in the state or at home . . ."

— From the Analects

Project the Start Up Activity Ask students to answer the questions as they enter and get settled.

Have students carefully read the quote from the *Analects*. Explain that the quote is from a collection of Confucius' teachings on all facets of life and how it should be lived. In this particular quote, Confucius speaks about the responsibility of individuals as well as rulers, especially concerning the 'common people.'

Considering the importance of Confucianism in Chinese society, what predictions can you make about the structure of early Chinese civilization? *(Answers will vary. Students should discuss how the quote would reflect the ideals of early Chinese civilization.)*

Aa Vocabulary Development: Use the Interactive Reading Notepad to preview the Key Terms and Academic Vocabulary in this Lesson with students.

⚡ FLIP IT!
Assign the Flipped Video for this lesson.

■ STUDENT EDITION PRINT PAGES: 81–88

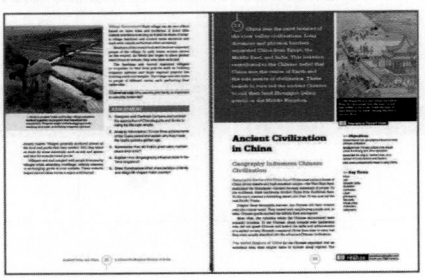

■ INVESTIGATE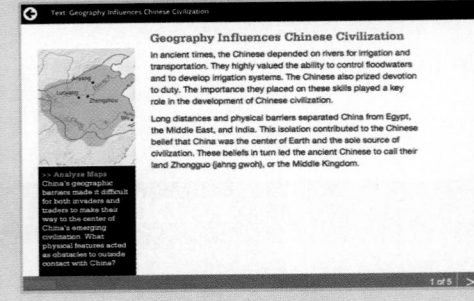

DIGITAL TEXT 1
Geography Influences Chinese Civilization

◄ Text: Geography Influences Chinese Civilization

Geography Influences Chinese Civilization
In ancient times, the Chinese depended on rivers for irrigation and transportation. They highly valued the ability to control floodwaters and to develop irrigation systems. The Chinese also prized devotion to duty. The importance they placed on these skills played a key role in the development of Chinese civilization.

Long distances and physical barriers separated China from Egypt, the Middle East, and India. This isolation contributed to the Chinese belief that China was the center of Earth and the sole source of civilization. These beliefs in turn led the ancient Chinese to call their land Zhongguo (jahng gwoh), or the Middle Kingdom.

>> Analyze Maps China's geographic barriers made it difficult for both invaders and traders to make their way to the center of China's emerging civilization. What physical features acted as obstacles to outside contact with China?

1 of 5 >

Objective 1: Understand how geography influenced early Chinese civilization.

Quick Instruction
Project the map of China. Tell students that vast distances and geographical barriers in the forms of high mountains, brutal deserts, and thick rainforests separated China from other areas of growing civilization, such as Egypt, the Middle East, and India. Although there was limited trade with neighboring peoples, the first Chinese civilization developed around the Huang River. The river provided much needed water for agriculture, but it also presented a deadly challenge when it rose over its banks. As Chinese civilization grew, it expanded its territory to include many different geographical regions.

ELL Use the ELL activity described in the ELL chart.

Further Instruction
Editable Presentation Use the Editable Presentation to present the main ideas for this text.

Geography Influences Chinese Civilization: Core Reading and Interactive Reading Notepad Project and discuss the Interactive Reading Notepad questions.

The geography of ancient China greatly influenced the development of Chinese civilization. Geographic barriers that included the Himalaya Mountains, the vast Gobi desert, and the thick rainforests of Southeast Asia all prevented easy access to the emerging Chinese civilization. Some trade did take place, however, with Chinese goods eventually ending up as far away as the Middle East.

The Huang River had a significant impact on the development of early Chinese civilization. It provided the water needed for the agricultural development that supported ancient China's growing population. At the same time, the Huang River presented a deadly hazard with its flooding. Controlling flooding required the work of entire communities. In time, this gave rise to the idea of centralized government as the most efficient way to enlist groups of people to build dikes, roads, and irrigation systems. Government also proved to be the most efficient way to create an army that could withstand invasion or act as a conquering force to expand Chinese lands.

Summarize How did the geography of ancient China affect the development of its early civilization? *(Geographic barriers like high mountains, deserts, and dense rainforests discouraged invaders, allowing the settlements along the Huang River to develop largely undisturbed. As China grew, it was able to absorb an increasing amount of territory into its country.)*

DIGITAL TEXT 2

The Shang Dynasty Begins to Form China

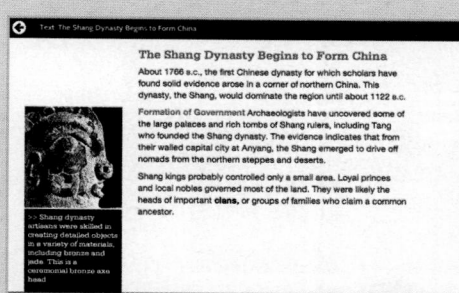

DIGITAL TEXT 3

The Zhou Dynasty

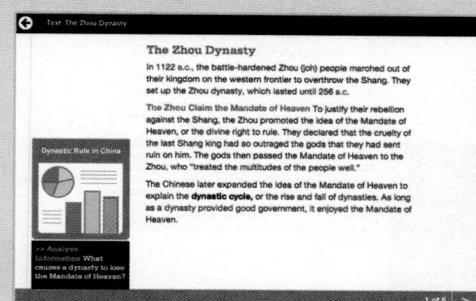

Objective 2: Analyze how Chinese culture took shape under the Shang and Zhou dynasties.

Quick Instruction

The Shang dynasty was the first dynasty for which solid archaeological evidence has been gathered. It ruled China for about 644 years. Its government began as a network of kings and loyal noblemen with the kings controlling a relatively small area, but depending on loyal noblemen to govern their clan areas. The Shang dynasty left behind artifacts that indicated the development of social classes. In 1122 *b.c.*, the Zhou overthrew the Shang rulers to form the Zhou dynasty. The Zhou established feudalism as their system of government. Feudalism relied on local lords governing their own lands, but owing military service to the Zhou emperors. During the Zhou dynasty, which lasted about 850 years, China made major advances in technology.

ELL Use the ELL activity described in the ELL chart.

Further Instruction

The Shang Dynasty Begins to Form China: Core Reading and Interactive Reading Notepad; The Zhou Dynasty: Core Reading and Interactive Reading Notepad Project and discuss the Interactive Reading Notepad questions. Review with the class the early structure of government and society that began to form under the Shang and how those basic ideas were expanded upon during the Zhou dynasty.

Tell students that the formation of a cooperative and somewhat centralized government first emerged in early China during the Shang dynasty. Although an emperor was recognized, he relied on loyal nobles or clan leaders to control their own areas. The Shang also established the beginnings of social classes, with the royal family at the top, followed by noblemen/warriors. However, the vast majority of people in Shang China were peasants who lived in farming villages.

Project the Infographic and note that the Zhou overthrew the Shang, citing the cruelty of the last Shang emperor. The Zhou claimed his poor behavior gave them the Mandate of Heaven, which justified the rebellion. The Zhou introduced the idea of the dynastic cycle, a naturally occurring cycle of dynasties based on how well they governed. If they governed well, they had the Mandate of Heaven. If they governed poorly, they would lose the gods' favor and dynastic power as well. This was a unique concept at the time because it holds the ruler to a standard of just government that benefits the ruled. For the Zhou dynasty, the stability of good government centered around feudalism. Their belief in keeping the Mandate of Heaven brought economic growth and advancements in ironworking technology that benefited the general populace as well as the ruling class.

Cause and Effect What are some of the contributions both the Shang and Zhou dynasties made to the growth of China's classical civilization? *(Answers will vary. The Shang established a system of cooperative government that produced enough stability to support artisans. The Zhou further solidified that government into feudalism. Introducing the idea of dynastic cycles and the Mandate of Heaven led to more attention being paid to good vs. bad government. That eventually brought economic prosperity and technological advances that benefited the civilization as a whole.)*

Rise of Civilization in China

DIGITAL TEXT 4

Religious Beliefs in Early China

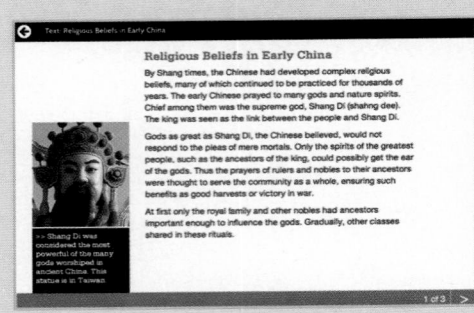

DIGITAL TEXT 5

Two Major Belief Systems Take Root

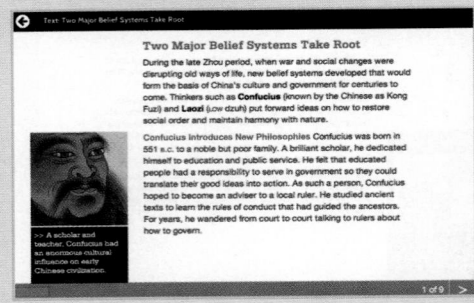

INTERACTIVE CHART

Confucianism and Daoism

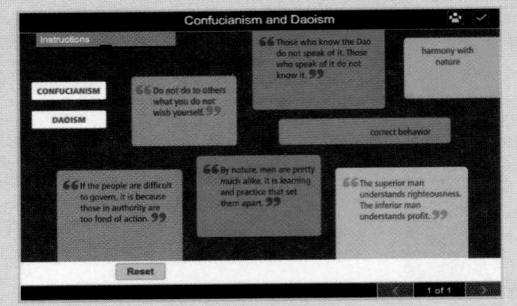

Objective 3: Describe the origins, central ideas, and spread of Confucianism and Daoism.

Quick Instruction

Interactive Chart: Confucianism and Daoism Tell students that Confucianism and Daoism were two religions that evolved from different philosophies on the meaning of life and the guidelines one should follow to ensure a properly lived life. Confucius promoted good government and a social order based on specific relationships. He spoke of the responsibilities and duties people had toward one another and toward their ruler, depending on their place in society. Daoists promoted the idea that people should step away from daily issues, live in harmony with nature, and pursue a more spiritual life. Go through the interactive chart with the students.

💬 ACTIVE CLASSROOM

Use the Wallpaper strategy and have students review what they have learned about Confucianism and Daoism. Ask each student to design a piece of "wallpaper" that encapsulates the key ideas they've learned. Each piece of wallpaper is then posted. Students take a gallery "wisdom" walk and note what others have written or illustrated. New ideas or notes that build on existing wallpaper content can be added during the tour.

ELL Use the ELL activity described in the ELL chart.

Further Instruction

Religious Beliefs Develop in Early China: Core Reading and Interactive Reading Notepad; Two Major Belief Systems Take Root: Core Reading and Interactive Notepad Project and discuss the Interactive Reading Notepad questions and the graphic organizer about the similarities and differences between Confucianism and Daoism. Fill in the graphic organizer on the whiteboard as you go.

Complex religious beliefs had developed by the time of the Shang dynasty. The early Chinese religions were built around many gods and nature spirits, with Shang Di being the most powerful of these and only reachable through the royal family and nobles. Although they did not worship ancestors, the Chinese would ask the ancestors for help or to bring good fortune. In turn, they honored their ancestors in special ways. The arrival of the Zhou was initially disruptive because of war and social change. New belief systems arose through the differing teachings of Confucius and Laozi. Confucianism had great appeal because it provided practical answers to a multitude of social questions. Confucianism also promoted the idea of maintaining a balance between yin—essentially Earth and darkness, and yang—light and heaven. Laozi, who founded the philosophy of Daoism, took a more removed and spiritual approach, promoting the importance of balance and harmony with nature. While Confucius encouraged involvement in life, Laozi discouraged it, believing that the ways of society were unnatural. Over time, people blended the two philosophies and often practiced both.

Compare and Contrast Describe the basic philosophies of Confucianism and Daoism. What is similar and what is different between the two beliefs? *(Shared characteristics: Both religions are based on the teachings of one individual, and both focus on the need for the correct balance or harmony in life. Confucianism: This religion has specific rules that govern behavior in all relationships, promotes involvement with life such as accepting one's place in the social order, and emphasizes the need to maintain balance and structure in all things. Daoism: This religion advocates that living in harmony with nature is most important, and that disengaging from social conflict and the unnatural structures of society is essential to spiritual growth.)*

D **Differentiate: Challenge/Gifted** Explain to students that this activity is called "Dear Confucius." After students have learned about Confucius and his teachings by reading the texts, ask them to apply the ideas of Confucius to modern-day situations. Students should write an advice column with questions for Confucius to respond to. Ask them to apply the ideas of Confucianism in crafting a plausible response that Confucius might have provided.

DIGITAL TEXT 6

A Time of Achievements in Early China

INTERACTIVE GALLERY

Silk Making in Ancient China

Objective 4: List some achievements made in early China.

Quick Instruction

Interactive Gallery: Silk Making in Ancient China Project the interactive gallery and click through the images that explain the secrets of making silk. Note that by 2640 *b.c.*, the Chinese had learned how to make silk thread from the cocoons of silkworms. It took a great deal of labor on the part of women who did everything from tending the silk worms to dyeing the finished cloth in brilliant colors. Silk was a fabric only royalty and nobles could afford, and the making of the fabric remained a closely guarded secret for hundreds of years.

ACTIVE CLASSROOM

Use the Rank It strategy to help students recognize the significance of key achievements made in early China. List the following on the board: silk-making, common written language, making books. Ask students to rank these achievements in order of greatest to least impact on the development of Chinese civilization. Then ask students to provide a justification for their ranking decisions. Group students in pairs to share their rankings and justifications. Poll the class to see if there is agreement on the ranking.

Further Instruction

A Time of Achievements in Early China: Core Reading and Interactive Reading Notepad Project and discuss the Interactive Reading Notepad questions.

Explain to students that advances in technology do not always have to be in areas of science. For the early Chinese, developing ways of farming silk worms, harvesting the silk, developing spinning and weaving looms, and the intricacies of fabric dyeing are all technological advances. Using a special tool, like a brush, to communicate a complex written language is also technology, as are the techniques needed to transform natural materials into books. These are three of the very significant advances made by a civilization thousands of years old. The language remains as does the essential silk-making. Books, of course, are made differently but the idea of creating a book has been sustained for centuries.

Identify What are some of the important technological advances made in early China? Why are they important? *(Silk making gave China a valuable trade item; a complex written language that was common to all who could read and write made it possible to communicate with people from all over China despite local dialects; and book-making allowed ideas and information to be documented as well as brought to other areas of China.)*

Rise of Civilization in China

■ SYNTHESIZE

DIGITAL ACTIVITY
Ancient Influences

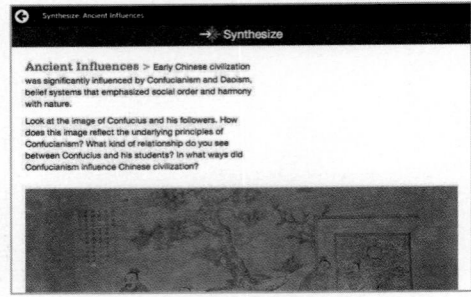

Ask students to share their predictions about how Chinese society would develop. Poll the students to see which predictions were correct. Ask: How did the quote from the *Analects* of Confucius help you predict information in the text? *(Answers will vary. Students should discuss which predictions from the beginning of the lesson were correct. Students should also discuss how the quote from the Analects of Confucius helped them predict the types of social structures that arose in early China.)*

Draw Conclusions Why might Confucianism appeal to many different kinds of people? *(Answers will vary but should include an understanding that Confucianism provides a firm structure for almost any facet of life, especially proper behavior and the core relationships among people regardless of whether they're rich or poor.)*

■ DEMONSTRATE

DIGITAL QUIZ
Lesson Quiz and Classroom Discussion Board

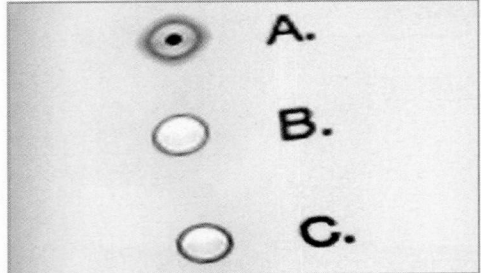

Assign the online Lesson Quiz for this lesson if you haven't already done so. Students will be offered automatic remediation or enrichment based on their score.

Pose these questions to the class on the Discussion Board:

In this lesson, you read about two powerful early Chinese dynasties. Their development as river valley civilizations demonstrate how early classical civilizations were established and grew. Both the Shang and Zhou had sophisticated systems of government. For the Zhou, the concept of a just government, the Mandate of Heaven, linked that idea to something greater than just the desires of the rulers. Philosophers such as Confucius and Laozi introduced religions that addressed the need for harmony and balance in one's life and, with Confucius, the importance of recognizing the duties and responsibilities people have towards each other regardless of their rank in society. Even though these civilizations are ancient, many of the innovations they launched are still in use today.

Describe Describe the major religious and philosophical influences of China's early classical civilization. *(Answers will vary, but should include an understanding of the impact on China's developing civilization by the types of government chosen by Shang and Zhou rulers, and of Confucianism and Daoism, the development of a common written language and the techniques of making silk. All of these things impacted China's later growth as a country.)*

Topic Inquiry
Have students continue their investigations for the Topic Inquiry.

Strong Rulers Unite China

Supporting English Language Learners

Use with Digital Text 2, **The Han Dynasty Creates a Strong China.**

Learning Strategies

Read *The Han Dynasty Creates a Strong China* aloud to the class. Have them complete one activity according to their level of English proficiency.

Beginning Explain to students that most of the information found in their texts is written in formal English. In addition, most interactions that students have with adults who are not members of their families or close friends should also use formal English. Demonstrate how students can tell another teacher what they are learning in history class. Remind students that such a conversation should be in formal English. Use the content from *The Han Dynasty Creates a Strong China* as the basis of your demonstration.

Intermediate Remind students that most of the information found in their texts is written in formal English. In addition, most interactions that students have with adults who are not members of their families or close friends should also use formal English. Tell students to pretend they are telling another teacher what they are learning in history class. Remind students that such a conversation should be in formal English. Have students use the content from *The Han Dynasty Creates a Strong China* as the basis of their conversations. Students can share their sentences ideas with the class. Write these sentences on the board and help students edit them as needed.

Advanced Have small groups of students identify situations in which formal and informal English should be used. Then tell student groups that they will be designing a conversation with another teacher to explain to him or her what they are studying in history class. Students should use *The Han Dynasty Creates a Strong China* for the content of their conversations. After students finish designing their conversations, have them share them with the rest of the class. Allow time for students to receive feedback on their formal conversations from others.

Advanced High Have students identify situations in which formal and informal English should be used. Then tell students that they will be designing a conversation with another teacher to explain to him or her what they are studying in history class. Students should use *The Han Dynasty Creates a Strong China* for the content of their conversations. After students finish designing their conversations, have them share them with a small group. Allow time for students to receive feedback on their formal conversations from others.

Use with Digital Text 1, **Shi Huangdi Unifies China.**

Listening

Explore the expression "You can't fight City Hall" with students. Read *Legalism Establishes Harsh Rule* aloud. As you read, have students listen for examples that reflect the idiom. Lead a discussion on legalism and the sentiment of this expression.

Beginning Write the idiom "You can't fight City Hall" on the board. Read it aloud and have students repeat it. Act it out to make sure students understand its literal meaning, then explain the idiom focusing on its figurative meaning. Read *Legalism Establishes Harsh Rule* aloud and have students listen for content that reflects the idiom. Have students share their examples with the group.

Intermediate Write the idiom "You can't fight City Hall" on the board. Read it aloud and have students repeat it. Have a volunteer act it out so students understand its literal meaning, then explain the idiom focusing on its figurative meaning. Read *Legalism Establishes Harsh Rule* aloud and have students listen for content that reflects the idiom. Discuss how legalism might have made the average Chinese person feel this way.

Advanced Write the idiom "You can't fight City Hall" on the board. Instruct students to work in groups to figure out its meaning. Have a volunteer in each group read *Legalism Establishes Harsh Rule* aloud as students listen for content that reflects the idiom. Then have groups discuss how legalism might have made the average Chinese person feel this way.

Advanced High Write the idiom "You can't fight City Hall" on the board. Instruct pairs to figure out its meaning. Have pairs take turns reading *Legalism Establishes Harsh Rule* aloud as their partner listens and takes note of content that reflects the idiom. Then have pairs share their ideas with the group and discuss how legalism may have made the average Chinese person feel this way.

Strong Rulers Unite China

Objectives

Objective 1: Understand how Shi Huangdi unified China and established a Legalist government.

Objective 2: Outline why the Han period is considered a Golden Age of Chinese civilization.

Objective 3: Analyze how the Silk Road facilitated the spread of ideas and trade in China.

Objective 4: Analyze why Buddhism spread through China.

LESSON 5 ORGANIZER		PACING: APPROX. 1 PERIOD, .5 BLOCKS		
	OBJECTIVES	PACING	**RESOURCES**	
			Online	Print
Connect				
DIGITAL START UP ACTIVITY **Strong Rulers, New Civilizations**		5 min.	●	
Investigate				
DIGITAL TEXT 1 **Shi Huangdi Unifies China**	Objective 1	10 min.	●	●
INTERACTIVE GALLERY **Terra Cotta Army of Shi Huangdi**		10 min.	●	
DIGITAL TEXT 2 **The Han Dynasty Creates a Strong China**	Objective 2	10 min.	●	●
INTERACTIVE GALLERY **The Silk Road Connects East and West**		10 min.	●	
DIGITAL TEXT 3 **The Han Golden Age**	Objective 3	10 min.	●	●
DIGITAL TEXT 4 **Buddhism Spreads in China**	Objective 4	10 min.	●	●
Synthesize				
DIGITAL ACTIVITY **Changing Systems of Government**		5 min.	●	
Demonstrate				
DIGITAL QUIZ **Lesson Quiz and Classroom Discussion Board**		10 min.	●	

PEARSON realize™
www.PearsonRealize.com

Go online to access additional resources including:
Primary Sources • Biographies • Supreme Court cases •
21st Century Skill Tutorials • Maps • Graphic Organizers.

CONNECT

DIGITAL START UP ACTIVITY
Strong Rulers, New Civilizations

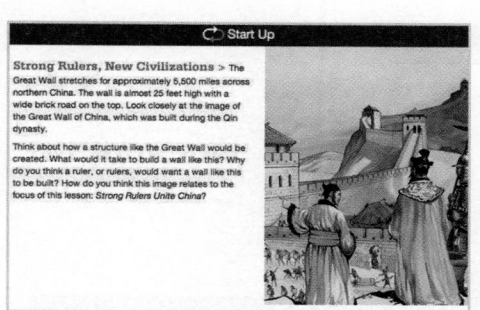

Project the Start Up Activity Ask students to answer the questions as they enter and get settled. Then have them share their responses with another student.

Have students study the image of the Great Wall. Explain that it is a picture of the Great Wall of China, built during the Qin dynasty. Ask: What would it take to build a wall like this? Make a prediction about the type of ruler who would have been able to get the Great Wall of China built. *(Answers will vary. Students should note that such a project would require massive manpower. Only a strong ruler would have been able to organize and successfully achieve this task. Students should predict that a ruler who achieved this had to be organized, powerful, focused, and determined.)*

Aa Vocabulary Development: Use the Interactive Reading Notepad to preview the Key Terms and Academic Vocabulary in this Lesson with students.

⇅ FLIP IT!
Assign the Flipped Video for this lesson.

■ STUDENT EDITION PRINT PAGES: 89–95

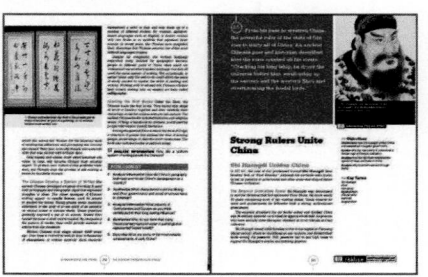

INVESTIGATE

DIGITAL TEXT 1
Shi Huangdi Unifies China

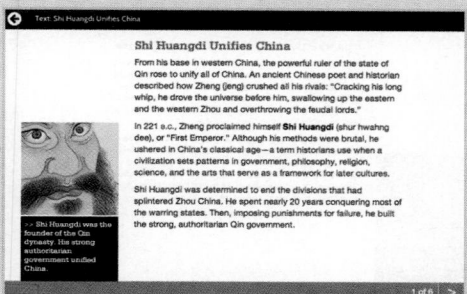

INTERACTIVE GALLERY
Terra Cotta Army of Shi Huangdi

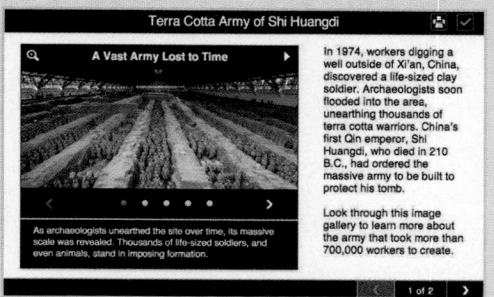

Objective 1: Understand how Shi Huangdi unified China and established a Legalist government.

Quick Instruction

Zheng was the powerful ruler of the state of Qin in China. Using harsh and often brutal methods, he unified parts of China. For the first time, there was one ruler and one government. Zheng called himself Shi Huangdi, which means First Emperor. He established the short-lived Qin dynasty and used Legalism as the governing structure of Qin China. Shi Huangdi also oversaw construction of the Great Wall of China. He is also famous as the Qin emperor who ordered a life-size army of terra cotta soldiers, including horses and chariots, to be built to guard him in his tomb.

Interactive Gallery: Terra Cotta Army of Shi Huangdi Project the activity. Explain how the interaction works by clicking on one of the hotspots to demonstrate the pop-up boxes. Step through the process as necessary so that students will be able to do the activity on their own.

Explain to students that the activity will introduce them to one of the most amazing Chinese archaeological finds of the modern era – an entire army made out of terra cotta, a type of baked clay. Uncovering this incredible piece of history took years of painstaking work to remove the soil surrounding the figures without damaging the figures themselves. As you will see, many more wonders were discovered as the Eternal Army once again saw the light of day.

■ ACTIVE CLASSROOM

Use the Act it Out strategy and have students act parts to bring to life the image in the lesson showing the initial building phase of the Great Wall. Have different students can play the overseers/soldiers, engineers, or laborers. Students should state what their characters are thinking about the endeavor in which they are involved.

D Differentiate: Challenge/Gifted Explain to students that the Great Wall of China is considered one of the wonders of the world, and that it is China's most recognizable landmark. Have students research aspects of the history of the wall, including the reasons for its construction, the building techniques and materials used, and its effectiveness in protecting China from invaders. Students should present their research to the rest of the class.

ELL Use the ELL activity described in the ELL chart.

Further Instruction

Editable Presentation Use the Editable Presentation to present the main ideas for this text.

Shi Huangdi Unifies China: Core Reading and Interactive Reading Notepad Project and discuss the Interactive Reading Notepad questions.

Strong Rulers Unite China

DIGITAL TEXT 2

The Han Dynasty Creates a Strong China

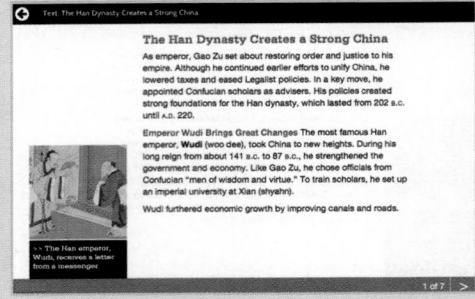

INTERACTIVE GALLERY

The Silk Road Connects East and West

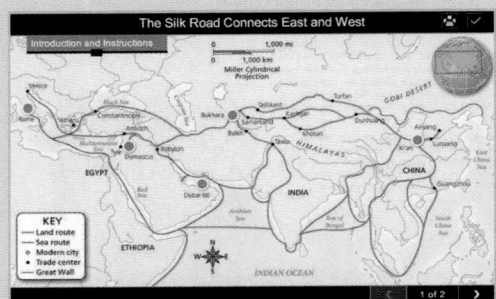

Along with the major achievement of unifying China for the first time, Shi Huangdi also introduced a political and governmental policy that was opposite of the generally accepted Confucian philosophy. The policy was called Legalism and its guiding principle was that the nature of man is evil. According to Legalism, strength, not goodness, was a ruler's greatest virtue. The only way to achieve order was through strict laws and harsh punishments for criminals. Those who opposed Shi Huangdi's rule were killed. Confucian ideas were violently repressed. Although Shi Huangdi's methods were effective, they depended greatly on his ability to enforce this structure. This is one of the reasons the Qin dynasty did not last long after Shi Huangdi's death.

Summarize How did Shi Huangdi unify China? *(He conquered the warring states and brought them under his rule. He replaced feudalism with military districts. Nobles were required to live in his capital. He promoted unity by standardizing weights and measures, replacing various coins with one currency, and creating uniformity in Chinese writing. He also improved transportation.)*

Objective 2: **Analyze how the Silk Road facilitated the spread of ideas and trade in China.**

Quick Instruction

Out of the chaos that followed Shi Huangdi's death, an illiterate peasant named Gao Zu took command. He defeated rival armies and established the Han dynasty. Easing the harsh Legalist system, he appointed Confucian scholars as government advisers. Later in the Han dynasty, the dynamic emperor Wudi created a network of trade routes later known as the Silk Road. It opened the gates for the exchange of goods and ideas with the West. The Silk Road stretched from China through deserts and mountains all the way to the Middle East. It included a sea route. The Silk Road delivered Chinese goods to the rest of the world, and brought goods and cultural influences from the West to China.

Interactive Gallery: The Silk Road Connects East and West Project the activity. Explain how the interaction works by clicking on one of the hotspots to demonstrate the pop-up boxes. Step through the process as necessary so that students will be able to do the activity on their own.

The Silk Road was a series of trade routes that stretched north, south, and west. As you will see, it facilitated the exchange of goods and ideas from places as far away as Rome. Each route presented its own perils and benefits, but it was a civilization-changing idea from a very enlightened ancient Chinese emperor, Wudi.

🖥 ACTIVE CLASSROOM

Use the Make Headlines strategy and have students write a headline that captures the adventure that was the Silk Road. Ask: If you were to write a headline for this topic right now that captured the most important aspect of the Silk Road that should be remembered, what would that headline be? The headline can be from the perspective of the Chinese or of one of the many trading partners represented on the map. Have students pass their headlines to partners for them to review.

ELL Use the ELL activity described in the ELL chart.

Further Instruction

The Han Dynasty Creates a Strong China: Core Reading and Interactive Reading Notepad Project and discuss the Interactive Reading Notepad questions and the graphic organizer comparing and contrasting the Qin emperor Shi Huangdi and the Han emperor Wudi. Review with the class the similarities and differences between the two rulers and fill in the graphic organizer on the whiteboard.

DIGITAL TEXT 3

The Han Golden Age

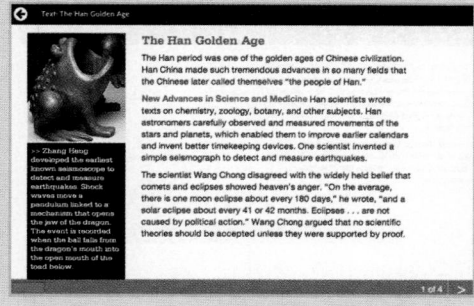

The Han Golden Age

The Han period was one of the golden ages of Chinese civilization. Han China made such tremendous advances in so many fields that the Chinese later called themselves "the people of Han."

New Advances in Science and Medicine Han scientists wrote texts on chemistry, zoology, botany, and other subjects. Han astronomers carefully observed and measured movements of the stars and planets, which enabled them to improve earlier calendars and invent better timekeeping devices. One scientist invented a simple seismograph to detect and measure earthquakes.

The scientist Wang Chong disagreed with the widely held belief that comets and eclipses showed heaven's anger. "On the average, there is one moon eclipse about every 180 days," he wrote, "and a solar eclipse about every 41 or 42 months. Eclipses . . . are not caused by political action." Wang Chong argued that no scientific theories should be accepted unless they were supported by proof.

>> Zhang Heng developed the earliest known seismoscope to detect and measure earthquakes. Shock waves move a pendulum linked to a mechanism that opens the jaw of the dragon. The event is recorded when the ball falls from the dragon's mouth into the open mouth of the toad below.

1 of 4

Both the Qin and Han dynasties made significant contributions to the development of a classical civilization in China. With Shi Huangdi, the Qin Dynasty was the first to successfully unite the warring Chinese territories under one ruler and government. The successful unification by the Qin set the stage for the Han dynasty and its more progressive political policies. One of the most successful Han emperors was Wudi. His achievements included strengthening the government and economy, and supporting education. His expansionist policy added as much territory as possible to the Han empire. Of his many achievements, establishing the network of trade routes called the Silk Road was one of the greatest. It opened up China to an exhange of goods and ideas with Western nations far from its borders, including the Middle East, Rome, and Persia. The Silk Road expanded and eventually stretched for 4,000 miles.

Cause and Effect Why might the Silk Road have been an opportunity for an exchange of ideas as well as goods? *(People from different cultures would travel the Silk Road. Even if they were traders, they would still bring their cultures, including religious beliefs, and technologies with them. Also, some travelers might have been scholars or priests from other countries.)*

Objective 3: Outline why the Han period is considered a Golden Age of Chinese civilization.

Quick Instruction

During the Han dynasty, China made tremendous advances in many fields. This political and cultural growth contributed to the development of China's classical civilization. The dynasty was also considered a golden age because of contributions in science, technology, government, and the arts. Many of the technological advances of the Han dynasty, such as the wheelbarrow and making paper from tree pulp, are still used today.

ELL Use the ELL activity described in the ELL chart.

Further Instruction

The Han Golden Age: Core Reading and Interactive Reading Notepad Project and discuss the Interactive Reading Notepad questions.

The Han dynasty is considered a golden age of China because there were advancements in several areas that included politics, culture, education, science, and technology. The stability of the Han government and the accessibility offered by the Silk Road created an environment that supported cultural and educational growth. The Chinese created a civil service system where government officials earned their positions through education and merit, rather than the accident of birth. Studies would include in-depth knowledge of the Five Classics, which included history, poetry, and Confucian conduct handbooks that served as a guide to conduct for about 2,000 years.

Identify Identify some of the technological advances made during the Han dynasty. *(compass, wheelbarrow, bronze and iron stirrups, boat rudder, suspension bridges, tree pulp to make paper)*

Summarize How did the Han dynasty culture influence China as it developed into a classical civilization? *(Answers will vary. Their acceptance of Confucian philosophy established firm roles for men and women, with women being subservient to men.)*

Strong Rulers Unite China

SYNTHESIZE

DEMONSTRATE

DIGITAL TEXT 4

Buddhism Spreads in China

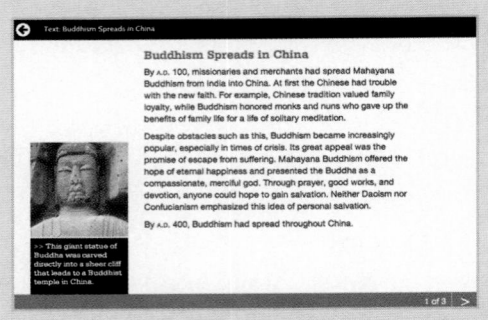

DIGITAL ACTIVITY

Changing Systems of Government

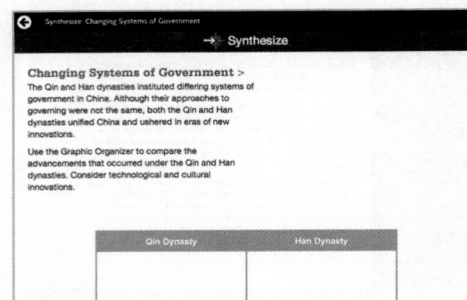

DIGITAL QUIZ

Lesson Quiz and Classroom Discussion Board

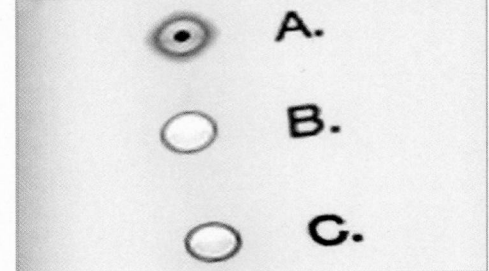

Objective 4: Analyze why Buddhism spread throughout China.

Quick Instruction

By 100 A.D, Buddhism had spread to China from India by missionaries and merchants traveling the Silk Road. Mahayana Buddhism was welcomed by Chinese who saw the religion as a source of hope for eternal happiness and salvation if one lived a good life. By the end of the Han dynasty, Buddhism had spread throughout China.

Further Instruction

Buddhism Spreads to China: Core Reading and Interactive Reading Notepad Project and discuss the Interactive Reading Notepad questions.

At first, Buddhism seemed like it would conflict with Confucian philosophy. Buddhism honored those who lived lives of solitude and prayer, while Confucianism stressed the importance of family loyalty. Eventually, though, many Chinese people embraced the merciful and hopeful premise of Buddhism. Buddhism had special appeal to those who were living through times of uncertainty. Buddhism promised a release from suffering and everlasting happiness if a person lived according to the tenets of the religion. Buddhist monasteries became centers of learning and the arts to which scholars and others would travel from all over the world.

Analyze information Why did Buddhism take solid root in China? *(It appealed to people who were living in uncertain times, because it promised escape from suffering and a path to eternal salvation. Buddhism represented mercy and compassion.)*

Ask students to share their graphic organizer results. Explain that both the Qin and Han dynasties had a profound impact on the development of classical civilization in China. Although the methods of the dynastic rulers differed, both contributed to the political, cultural, and technological advancements of their eras.

Draw Conclusions What are some of the key contributions made by the Qin and Han dynasties that had a long-lasting effect on China's development as a classical civilization?

Assign the online Lesson Quiz for this lesson if you haven't already done so. Students will be offered automatic remediation or enrichment based on their score.

Pose these questions to the class on the Discussion Board:

In this lesson, you read about the first and second dynasties of classical China. The Qin Dynasty was essentially one individual whose death so weakened the dynasty that it fell fairly quickly. The Han dynasty, on the other hand, lasted about 400 years with several effective emperors. The most memorable is Wudi, the founder of the Silk Road. It had an enormous impact on China's culture as well as its economy. As Buddhism was accepted throughout China, it provided evidence that China's culture was influenced by other cultures outside of its borders. It is likely that this influence came as part of the exchange of ideas that traveled the Silk Road along with products from other countries.

Describe Describe some of the ways China's development as a classical civilization affected other countries. *(Answers will vary but should include an understanding of the impact of the Silk Road in the exchange of ideas between China and the West. Some of the Chinese inventions such as wheelbarrows, compasses, and so on, had global effects on agriculture and land and sea travel. Chinese astronomers shared their discoveries as did Chinese physicians skilled in herbal medicine.)*

Topic Inquiry

Have students continue their investigations for the Topic Inquiry.

Ancient India and China (2600 B.C.–A.D. 550)

■ SYNTHESIZE

DIGITAL ACTIVITY

Reflect on the Essential Question and Topic

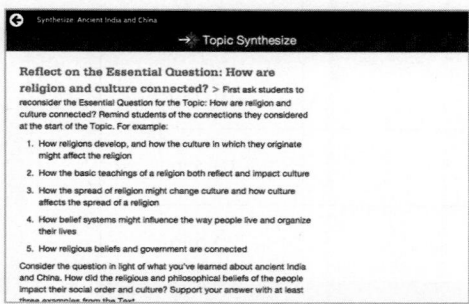

First ask students to reconsider the Essential Question for the Topic: How are religion and culture connected? Remind students of the criteria they considered at the start of the Topic

- how religions develop, and how the culture in which they originate might affect the religion

- how the basic teachings of a religion both reflect and impact culture

- how the spread of religion might change culture and how culture affects the spread of a religion

- how belief systems might influence the way people live and organize their lives

- how religious beliefs and government are connected

Ask students, "Which of these connections between religion and culture was the most significant in ancient India or China?" Have them support their answer with at least two examples from the Topic's lessons. Ask, "Did you learn anything that surprised you as you read about this Topic?" Have them identify at least one unexpected thing they learned in the Topic.

Reflect on the Topic

Next ask students to reflect on the Topic as a whole and jot down 1-3 questions they've thought about during the Topic. Share these examples if students need help getting started:

- Did culture reflect the development and spread of the religion?

- Did religion alter social structure?

- How did religion affect the lives of ancient Indians and Chinese?

Topic Inquiry

Have students complete Step 3 of the Topic Inquiry.

■ DEMONSTRATE

DIGITAL TOPIC REVIEW AND ASSESSMENT

Ancient India and China (2600 B.C.–A.D. 550)

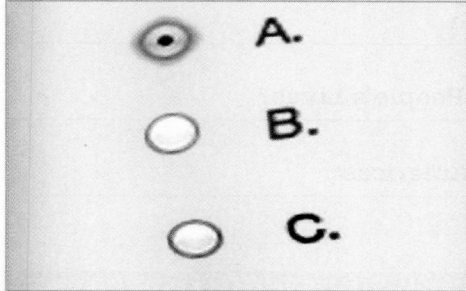

Students can prepare for the Topic Test by answering the questions in the Topic Review and Assessment online or the Assessment questions in the Print Student text. They can also prepare by reviewing their answers to the Interactive Reading Notepad questions or reviewing their notes in the Reading and Notetaking Study Guide.

DIGITAL TOPIC TEST

Ancient India and China (2600 B.C.–A.D. 550)

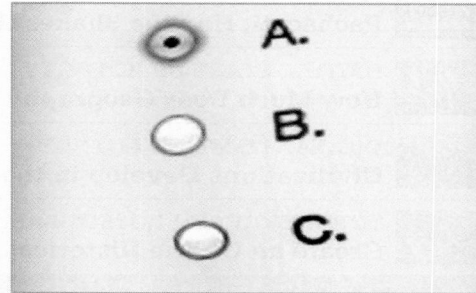

TOPIC TEST

Assign the Topic Test to assess students' understanding of topic content.

BENCHMARK TESTS

Assign these benchmark tests as you complete the relevant topics to monitor student progress toward mastering the course content and as preparation for the End-of-Course Test.

Benchmark Test 1: Topics 1–5

Benchmark Test 2: Topics 6–10

Benchmark Test 3: Topics 11–15

Benchmark Test 4: Topics 16–21

The Americas (Prehistory–A.D. 1570)

TOPIC 4 ORGANIZER	PACING: APPROX. 6 PERIODS, 3 BLOCKS	
		PACING
Connect		1 period
MY STORY VIDEO **Pachacuti, He Who Shakes the Earth**		10 min.
DIGITAL START UP ACTIVITY **How Much Does Geography Affect People's Lives?**		10 min.
DIGITAL TIMELINE ACTIVITY **Civilizations Develop in the Early Americas**		10 min.
TOPIC INQUIRY: PROJECT-BASED LEARNING **Create an Online Historical Atlas**		20 min.
Investigate		1–3 periods
TOPIC INQUIRY: PROJECT-BASED LEARNING **Create an Online Historical Atlas**		Ongoing
LESSON 1 Civilizations of Middle America		30–40 min.
LESSON 2 The World of the Incas		30–40 min.
LESSON 3 Peoples of North America		30–40 min.
Synthesize		1 period
DIGITAL ACTIVITY **Reflect on the Essential Question and Topic**		10 min.
TOPIC INQUIRY: PROJECT-BASED LEARNING **Create an Online Historical Atlas**		20 min.
Demonstrate		1–2 periods
DIGITAL TOPIC TEST **The Americas**		10 min.
TOPIC INQUIRY: PROJECT-BASED LEARNING **Create an Online Historical Atlas**		20 min.

Create an Online Historical Atlas

In this Topic Inquiry, students work in teams to create an online historical atlas that illustrates how geography impacted the lives and development of the Maya, Aztec, and Inca civilizations. Learning more about the impact of geography will deepen students' understanding of how the civilizations emerged and thrived and will contribute to the Topic Essential Question: How much does geography affect people's lives?

STEP 1: CONNECT
Develop Questions and Plan the Investigation

Launch the Project and Generate Questions

Display the *Entry Event*, which is a fictional assignment from a geographical society. Tell students that in this project they will learn about how geography affects human lives.

Divide the class into three groups, and assign each group one of the classical civilizations of the Americas: Maya, Aztec, or Inca. Explain that each group will research, plan, and create one section of an online historical atlas pertaining to their assigned civilization. Tell students that they must include and interpret at least one thematic map, one chart, and one graph to illustrate the relationship between the geography and historical development of their civilization. Then project and review the bullet-point list of additional components that they may include in their online atlases. If students are not familiar with atlases, you may want to project pages of an online atlas to help students better understand what they will be creating and how the elements work together.

Finally, allow students time to discuss the bullet-point list and begin to brainstorm ideas. Tell students to take notes as they brainstorm.

Prepare for Project Work

Before students begin researching, have them learn or review the essentials of working as a team by taking a tutorial and signing the *Project Contract*. Guide students as they complete the *Need to Know Questions* for their assigned civilization.

Suggestion: To control the length of this project, set parameters for how many pages each online atlas should include and how many days you will allow for the creation of the website.

Resources

- Entry Event
- Project Tracker and Project Roles
- Need to Know Questions
- Rubric for an Online Historical Atlas
- Project Contract
- Student Instructions

⏻ PROFESSIONAL DEVELOPMENT

Project-Based Learning
Be sure to view the Project-Based Learning Professional Development resources in the online course.

STEP 2: INVESTIGATE
Apply Disciplinary Concepts and Tools

Collect Source Material

Have students do the 21st Century Skills Tutorial *Search for Information on the Internet* to learn tips on how to find information online. Then project the list of possible sources and discuss why these sites might be helpful. You may want to project one of the sites, such as the University of Texas: Perry-Castaneda Library, Historical Map Website, to show students how to navigate the site and locate information and maps.

Suggest that students use the *Need to Know Questions* to help them focus their research. If time permits, allow students time to begin researching their civilizations. Tell students that they will need to continue researching outside of class. Remind students to complete the tasks that were assigned to them and to fill in the project tracker as each task is completed.

Create and Edit Content, Maps, Charts, and Graphs

Before students begin creating and editing maps, review the following map-making tools: Google Map Maker and Google Earth. Explain that both of these are robust authoring tools that will allow them to create maps with live GIS data. They will also be able to add and edit information on the maps. If time permits, project one of the sites and review how it works with students.

Then review the different types of graphs and charts, such as pie charts, line graphs, bar graphs, and tables. Help students understand what type of graph or chart might be the most suitable for the information and data they have collected. For example, a line graph is often used for average temperatures. A bar graph is often used for population statistics or average rainfall.

Project the *Information Organizer: Online Historical Atlas of the Americas*. Explain that the first page of the handout is a flowchart template that will help them determine what details to include in their section of the atlas and how to organize it. Stress that each box represents one page of their website and that each line indicates the way the pages will be linked.

Guide students as they write and edit their content, maps, charts, and graphs and as they complete their flowcharts.

Resources

- Information Organizer: Online Historical Atlas of the Americas

STEP 3: SYNTHESIZE
Evaluate Sources and
Use Evidence to Formulate Conclusions

Build Your Website

Project the second page of the *Information Organizer: Online Historical Atlas of the Americas*. Explain that this sketch will help students design each page. Provide each group with several copies of the page, or tell students to make additional copies so they can design each page of their website.

Once they have sketched each page, have them return to the flowchart they created and use the sketches and flowchart to begin building their website. Stress that their website should be easy to navigate. Remind them that their goal is to focus on the relationship between the geography and historical development of the civilization.

Remind students to review *Getting Started with WordPress* for information on building a website using WordPress. Tell students that they are not required to use this tool. They can use Weebly or other website building tools to create their online atlas.

Suggestion: Before students get into these final stages, you may wish to show them some finished websites created by your students of previous years.

Write a Conclusion

Tell students that they should write a powerful conclusion that clearly expresses what they learned about their civilization based on the maps, graphs, charts, and content they created. Project and review the questions to help students focus their conclusions.

Remind students that their conclusions should include an interpretation of the maps, graphs, and charts they created. They may also want to include any inferences they made.

Resources
• Getting Started with WordPress

STEP 4: DEMONSTRATE
Communicate Conclusions
and Take Informed Action

Present Your Online Historical Atlas

Before students present their website, suggest that they review the 21st Century Skills Tutorial: *Give an Effective Presentation*. Have students present their online atlases to the class or a larger audience. Allow time for comments, questions, and answers after each presentation.

Reflect on the Project

After students have finished creating and presenting their online atlases, provide your assessment, and help them go over what worked well and what did not work well so they can improve their results on the next project.

Resources
• 21st Century Skills Tutorial: Give an Effective Presentation
• Self Assessment

INTRODUCTION

The Americas (Prehistory–A.D. 1570)

While the classical civilizations of Greece and Rome dominated the Mediterranean world, complex civilizations developed in the Americas. The earliest arose in Mesoamerica, the region that lies between North America and South America. The Olmec, the Maya, and the Aztec built pyramids and cities there. Other parts of the Americas also saw the rise of civilizations, such as the Inca of South America and the Mississippians of North America. Each of these societies adapted to the landscape and climate of the places where they lived.

▉ CONNECT

MY STORY VIDEO
Pachacuti, He Who Shakes the Earth

Watch a video showing the story of Emperor Pachacuti.

Check Understanding What was the most powerful civilization in the Americas before the Europeans' arrival? *(Inca empire)*

Support a Point of View with Evidence Pachacuti's name meant "he who remakes the world." What evidence is there that his name was an appropriate one? *(He expanded the empire and strengthened it by building cities, roads, and bridges. He changed the Inca religion to focus on worship of the sun.)*

⟳ FLIP IT!

Assign the My Story video

DIGITAL START UP ACTIVITY
How Much Does Geography Affect People's Lives?

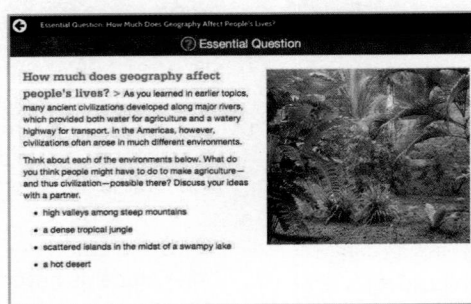

Ask students to think about the Essential Question for this Topic: How much does geography affect people's lives?

Remind students that they learned about how many ancient civilizations developed along major rivers, which provided both water for agriculture and a watery highway for transport. In the Americas, however, civilizations often arose in much different environments.

Have students think about each of the environments below. Ask students: What do you think people might have to do to make agriculture—and thus civilization—possible there? *(Answers will vary. Possible responses might include: create terraces in mountains, clear land in jungles, drain the swampy lake, and form an irrigation network in the desert.)*

- high valleys among steep mountains
- a dense tropical jungle
- scattered islands in the midst of a swampy lake
- a hot desert

Express Problems Clearly If a group of people wanted to farm in a desert, what do you think would be the main problem to overcome? *(Sample answer: getting enough water to grow crops)*

DIGITAL TIMELINE ACTIVITY
Civilizations Develop in the Early Americas

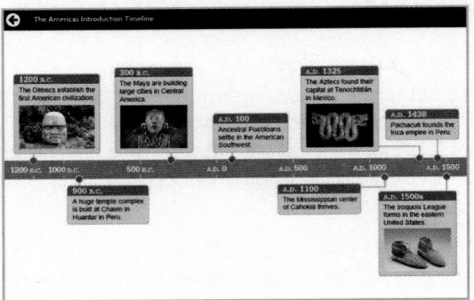

Display the timeline showing major events in the development of civilizations in the Americas. This timeline will provide a framework into which they can place the events they learn about.

D Differentiate: Extra Support Remind students that *B.C.* dates run backwards from the point at which dates change, while *A.D.* dates go forwards from that point. There is no year "zero"; 1 *A.D.* immediately follows 1 *B.C.* Then ask: How many years after the Maya built cities did the Puebloans settle in the American Southwest? *(400 years; the Maya built large cities around 300 B.C. and the Puebloans began to settle in the American Southwest around A.D. 100.)*

Sequence Events Place the following in chronological order: Cahokia thrives, the Maya build large cities, the Iroquois League forms, and the Aztecs found Tenochtitlán. *(Sample answer: The Maya build large cities, Cahokia thrives, the Aztecs found Tenochtitlán, the Iroquois League forms.)*

Topic Inquiry

Launch the Topic Inquiry with students after introducing the Topic.

Civilizations of Middle America

Supporting English Language Learners

Use with Digital Text 2, **The Maya.**

Learning Strategies

Read *The Maya* aloud to students. Then instruct students to complete one of the following activities based on their level of English proficiency.

Beginning Provide students with several examples of both formal and informal English on the topic of the Mayan civilization. Using these examples, explain the features of each type of writing. Then give students another example of writing about the Mayan civilization and ask them guiding questions to help them determine if the writing is formal or informal.

Intermediate Provide students with several examples of both formal and informal English on the topic of the Mayan civilization. Using these examples, ask students to point out the features of each type of writing. It may help to have students focus on what makes the examples different from one another. Then read aloud another example of writing about the Mayan civilization and ask them to identify the features of the writing that make it either formal or informal.

Advanced Instruct small groups of students to work together to use a variety of classroom resources to locate examples of formal and informal writing about the Mayan civilization. Circulate among groups to offer support and help students make the distinction between the two types of language as needed. Instruct each group to share one example of each type of writing with the rest of the class.

Advanced High Allow students to work together in pairs. Instruct them to use a variety of classroom resources to locate examples of formal and informal writing about the Mayan civilization. Finally, invite pairs to share at least two examples of each type of writing with the rest of the class.

Use with Digital Text 1, **Civilizations Develop in the Americas.**

Listening

Read *Civilizations Develop in the Americas* aloud. Then have students complete one activity according to their level of English proficiency.

Beginning Explain how to use context clues by modeling the process for students. Choose an unfamiliar word that students are unlikely to know, such as *scholars* or *migration*, and use a Think Aloud strategy to demonstrate how to use the surrounding words and phrases to support your understanding of the target word. Continue reading the text, pausing to identify other unfamiliar words, and use context clues to identify their meaning. If possible, have one or two student volunteers participate in the process.

Intermediate Review how to use context clues by modeling the process for students. Choose an unfamiliar word that students are unlikely to know, such as *scholars* or *migration*, and use a Think Aloud strategy to demonstrate how to use the surrounding words and phrases to support your understanding of the target word. Continue reading the text, pausing to identify other unfamiliar words. Ask students to use context clues to explain the meaning of the identified words.

Advanced Review context clues with students. Choose an unfamiliar word in the text, such as *scholars* or *migration*, or *evidence*, and ask student volunteers to demonstrate how they could use context clues to determine the meaning of the target word. Then have students continue reading the text with a partner. During their reading, pairs should pause to identify challenging words, then practice using context clues by speaking aloud with their partner until they determine the meaning of the word.

Advanced High Review context clues with students. Choose two unfamiliar words in the text, such as *scholars* or *migration*, *originally*, or *evidence*, and ask students to turn to a partner and demonstrate how they could use context clues to determine the meaning of the target word. Make sure each student demonstrates understanding with at least one of the target words. Then have students continue reading the text with their partners. Pairs should pause while reading to identify challenging words, then practice using context clues by speaking aloud with their partner until they determine the meaning of the word.

▣ Differentiate Instruction

Use the Differentiated Instruction notes throughout the lesson plan to support the varied skill sets, levels of readiness, and interests in the mixed-ability classroom.

Challenge These notes include suggestions for expanding the activity for advanced students.

On-Level These notes include suggestions for modifying the activity to address different interests or learning styles.

Extra Support These notes include ideas for providing more scaffolding or reading spuport.

Special Needs These notes provide ideas for adapting instruction to support the needs of various special needs students.

■ NOTES

_____

_____

_____

_____

_____

Civilizations of Middle America

Objectives

Objective 1: Explain when and where people first settled the Americas.

Objective 2: Analyze the rise of the Olmec civilization.

Objective 3: Describe the major developments of the Maya and Aztec civilizations.

Objective 4: Explain how prior civilizations influenced the Maya and Aztec.

LESSON 1 ORGANIZER		PACING: APPROX. 1 PERIOD, .5 BLOCKS			
		OBJECTIVES	PACING	RESOURCES	
				Online	Print
Connect					
DIGITAL START UP ACTIVITY **Civilizations in the Americas**			5 min.	●	
Investigate					
DIGITAL TEXT 1 **Civilizations Develop in the Americas**		Objectives 1, 2	10 min.	●	●
INTERACTIVE MAP **Settlements of Civilizations of Mesoamerica**			10 min.	●	
DIGITAL TEXT 2 **The Maya**		Objectives 3, 4	10 min.	●	●
DIGITAL TEXT 3 **Maya Cultural Life**		Objective 3	10 min.	●	●
INTERACTIVE GALLERY **The Religious Life of the Maya**			10 min.	●	
DIGITAL TEXT 4 **The Aztec**		Objective 3	10 min.	●	●
3-D MODEL **Aztec Temple**			10 min.	●	
Synthesize					
SYNTHESIZE ACTIVITY **The Rise of the Mesoamerican Civilizations**			5 min.	●	
Demonstrate					
DIGITAL QUIZ **Lesson Quiz and Classroom Discussion Board**			10 min.	●	

PEARSON **realize**™
www.PearsonRealize.com

Go online to access additional resources including:
Primary Sources • Biographies • Supreme Court cases •
21st Century Skill Tutorials • Maps • Graphic Organizers.

■ CONNECT

DIGITAL START UP ACTIVITY
Civilizations in the Americas

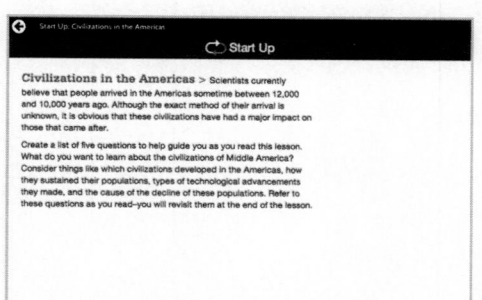

Project the Start Up Activity Ask students to answer the questions as they enter and get settled. Then have them share their ideas with another student in class or through a chat room or blog.

Discuss What would be the most influential item that an ancestor of a Mesoamerican who traveled from Asia to the Americas might carry to pass on to future generations? Explain. *(Answers will vary, but could include rituals, religious practices, carvings, a shell, or rock. The rituals and religious practices could be learned and carried on to future generations by oral tradition. Carvings, a shell, or a rock would be artifacts that would have scientific historical relevance.)*

Aa **Vocabulary Development:** Use the Interactive Reading Notepad to preview the Key Terms and Academic Vocabulary in this Lesson with students.

⇅ FLIP IT!
Assign the Flipped Video for this lesson.

■ STUDENT EDITION PRINT PAGES: 102–110

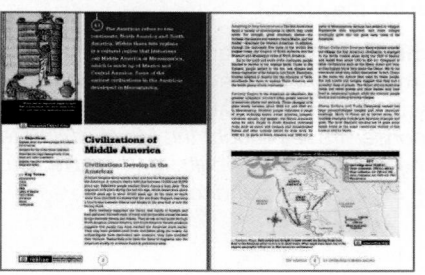

■ INVESTIGATE

DIGITAL TEXT 1
Civilizations Develop in the Americas

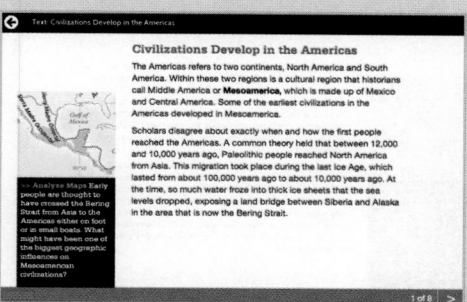

INTERACTIVE MAP
Settlements of Civilizations of Mesoamerica

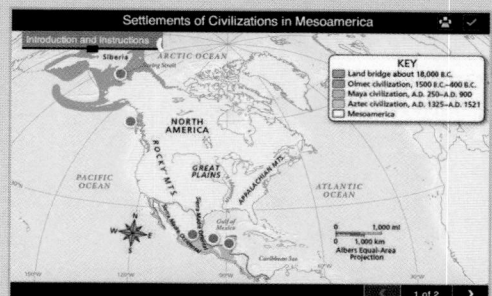

Objectives 1: **Explain when and where people first settled the Americas; 2:** **Analyze the rise of the Olmec civilization.**

Quick Instruction
Settlements of Civilizations in Mesoamerica: Interactive Map Project the interactive map on the whiteboard. Introduce the activity by explaining that scholars have different theories about how humans migrated and then settled in Mesoamerica. One of those theories proposes that people traversed a land bridge into North America and moved south, settling in North America and later moving to and settling in Mesoamerica. Some of these cultures included the Olmec, Maya, and Aztec. Click through the various hotspots on the map to familiarize students with geographical regions of settlement for the Mesoamerican civilizations.

Draw Comparisons Which civilizations were influenced by the Olmec, and how was this influence represented in the ways those later civilizations lived? *(There is evidence that both the Maya and the Aztec were influenced by the Olmec. The name Olmec is an Aztec name for that civilization, since the real name is unknown. The Olmec were the first to build the pyramid style of temples in Mesoamerica, a style later used by the Aztec and the Maya. The jaguars and serpents in Olmec art later appeared in the art of later Mesoamerican peoples.)*

👥 ACTIVE CLASSROOM
Use the Quickdraw strategy and pair students. Students have a short period to share what they know by writing with symbols or drawings. Have the first students tell their partners what they are going to draw or symbolize. Then, have the second students prepare the symbols or drawing. Use a document camera to scan drawings to add to the class blog.

D **Differentiate: Challenge/Gifted** While viewing the map, point out that, because of the migrations through the Americas, Mesoamericans developed advanced civilizations and settled in geographical regions that may have been quite different from the lands their predecessors inhabited. Ask students to list ways that Mesoamericans were able to survive in new, unfamiliar territory. *(Sample answer: People learned to use the resources of the land they inhabited. Some also relied upon the customs and beliefs of their predecessors.)*

ELL Use the ELL activity described in the ELL chart.

Further Instruction
Civilizations Develop in the Americas: Core Reading and Interactive Reading Notepad Project the questions provided in the notepad and have students answer as they move through the core text.

Civilizations of Middle America

DIGITAL TEXT 2

The Maya

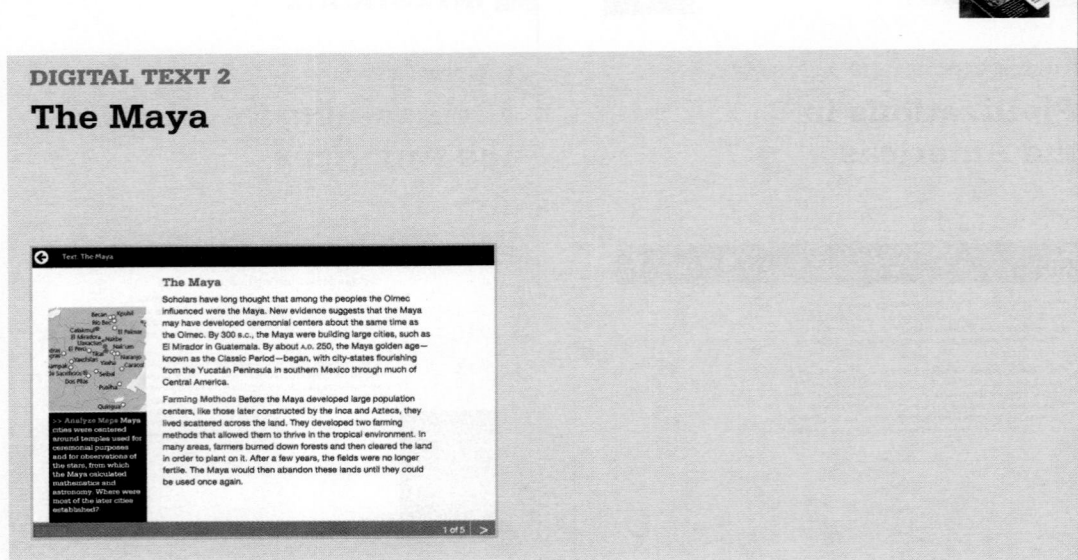

Settlements of Civilizations in Mesoamerica Project the interactive map of the migration and settlement of early people in the Americas. Ask students to describe how it is possible to understand what happened 12,000 to 10,000 years ago, and rebuild a history based on that information. Ask students to write two to three sentences about how knowledge has been gained about the settlements and cultures of the Olmec, Maya, and Aztec. *(Answers will vary, but may mention that archaeological excavations have provided historical insight. Artifacts found during the dig of a particular culture may provide evidence about that culture's time of existence, customs, religious practices, and agriculture. This information is shared globally and can help scholars form a solid theory about a civilization's way of life, which will be widely held until it is refuted by later scientific finds.)*

Make Generalizations The stone from which the Olmec carved their giant carved heads was not native to the area where the statues were found. What can you infer from that information? *(Sample answer: The stone carvings were moved into the area. The weight of each statue would mean that the Olmec were capable of organizing massive labor projects to move the stones or that they had advanced transportation technology.)*

Infer What was the significance of finding Olmec hieroglyphics carved into stone? *(The Olmec may have created a writing system.)*

Objectives 3: Describe the major developments of the Maya and Aztec civilizations; **4:** Explain how prior civilizations influenced the Maya and Aztec.

Quick Instruction

Project the map of Cities of the Maya Realm. Explain to students that these Maya cities, which flourished from 300 *B.C.* to *A.D.* 900, were hidden for centuries until archaeologists discovered some of them beneath tropical overgrowth. Through their excavations, archaeologists were able to piece together the history of powerful Maya rulers. Ask students the following: Since the Maya empire lay in ruins for so long, is it possible that other civilizations also existed and are now awaiting detection? Explain.

Make Generalizations Group students. Ask students to draw two columns, and to label one column Maya Developments and the other Aztec Developments. Then ask students to record responses to these questions in the column that corresponds. 1. How were the Maya and Aztec empires structured politically? *(Sample responses: Maya empire: a collection of city-states ruled independently by separate rulers; Aztec empire: a giant empire ruled by a single leader)* 2. What was the Maya and Aztec social hierarchy? *(Answer will vary, but should includes some of the following. Maya: Ruler of each city-state, Nobles (warriors, tax collectors, enforcers of law, leaders of pubic works, merchants), Scribes, Painters, Sculptors, less lucrative merchants, farmers, slaves; Aztec: Emperor of the empire, Council of Nobles (officials, judges, province governors), Priests,*

Warriors; Middle Class (long-distance traders), farmers, serfs, slaves)

ELL Use the ELL activity described in the ELL chart.

Further Instruction

The Maya Go through the Interactive Reading Notepad questions and discuss the answers with the class.

Discuss some of the major cultural and economic developments of the Maya and Aztec, including the long distance trade that brought the Maya city-states tremendous wealth. Items included honey, salt, and feathers. Much of the wealth for the Aztec came from the spoils of war and the tribute that conquered people had to pay the Aztec government.

Paraphrase Ask students to write brief answers to this question: How did prior civilizations influence the cultural developments of the Maya? *(Answers may vary. Students should mention that when Olmec artifacts were first found, they were thought to be Maya artifacts. They worshipped multiple gods as did the Maya. Their style of religious calendar was also used, in a different form, by the Maya.)*

Summarize What characteristics distinguish the major economic developments of the Maya and Aztec civilizations? *(Sampe response: Trade brought the Maya city-states tremendous wealth. Wealth for the Aztec came from the spoils of war and tribute.)*

DIGITAL TEXT 3
Maya Cultural Life

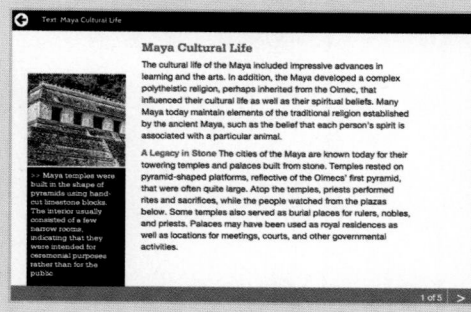

INTERACTIVE GALLERY
The Religious Life of the Maya

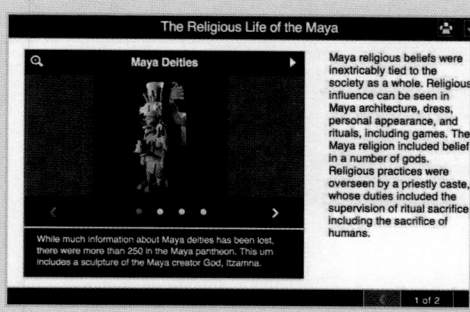

Objective 3: Describe the major developments of the Maya and Aztec civilizations.

Quick Instruction

The Religious Life of the Maya: Interactive Gallery Project the image gallery on the whiteboard and click through the hot spot images. Briefly introduce the gallery to the students by noting that archaeologists study the culture and daily life of Mesoamerican societies by examining artifacts found during scientific excavation. Tell students that Maya advances in astronomy were closely linked to mathematics. Maya priests needed to measure time accurately in order produce an accurate calendar. They developed a 365-day solar calendar as well as a 260-day religious calendar. Maya priests also invented a counting system based on three symbols: a dot to represent, a bar for five, and a shell for zero. With these three symbols, they could keep track of events. The Maya were one of the only early civilizations to understand the concept of zero.

Formulate Questions Have students explore the image gallery of the Common Culture of Mesoamerica. Ask students to pair with a partner, examine the gallery, then ask them: What do you see? What does that make you think? What are you wondering about now that you've seen these? Have students share their insights with the class. *(Answers will vary. Students should point out that the rituals of the Maya and Aztec cultures had some similarities. They each worshipped many gods and offered sacrifices. They also differed. The Maya studied astronomy and mathematics,*

used the stars for reference and created a calendar for agricultural use and religious events. The Aztec were warriors, interested in conquering. Aztec priests foretold the future using their knowledge of mathematics and astronomy. They also developed solar and ritual calendars.)

ACTIVE CLASSROOM

Pair activity in which students have a short period (typically 30 seconds) to share what they know by writing with symbols or drawings. Use a document camera to scan drawing to add to the class blog.

Further Instruction

Common Culture of Mesoamerica: Core Reading and Interactive Reading Notepad Go through the Interactive Reading Notepad questions and discuss the answers with the class.

Describe Maya architectural engineering, including Maya temples built in the shape of pyramids using hand-cut limestone blocks. Maya buildings were decorated with carvings and sometimes stucco and paint, and were often built on higher ground to avoid damp areas.

Draw Conclusions What is significant about the style of Maya architecture? *(Answers will vary and may include: The Maya temples, pyramids, walls, and residences were made of stone that remained for thousands of years. They decorated their stone work with carving and sometimes stucco and paint. Plazas were located in the middle of their cluster of buildings, and raised walkways connected*

residential areas. They built on higher, not necessarily level ground, to avoid the dampness associated with the environment of tropical forests. Because many structures are available today, they are artifacts that allow scientists to study and piece together Maya history.)

Summarize Ask students to explain the decline of the Maya civilization. *(Answers will vary. Students should note that in 900 B.C., the Maya began to disappear from their cities. Archaeologists do not have a solid explanation for this, but they do have theories. For example, warfare may have taken its toll on society, or the Maya may have exhausted their environment.)*

Paraphrase What purpose did scribes serve in the Maya society? *(The work of the Maya scribes preserved history. They wrote books made of bark. These books contained information on the Maya study of astronomy and religious matters.)*

Topic ④ Lesson 1

Civilizations of Middle America

DIGITAL TEXT 4

The Aztec

3-D MODEL

Aztec Temple

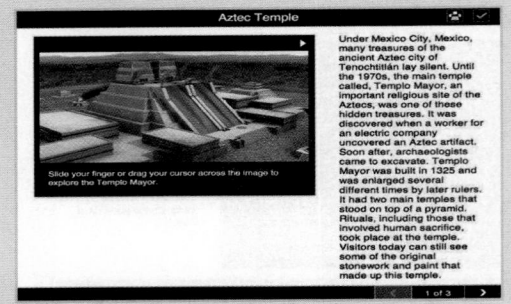

Objective 3: Describe the major developments of the Maya and Aztec civilizations.

Quick Instruction

Aztec Temple: 3-D Model Project the image of the Aztec temple on the whiteboard. Explain to students that they are looking at a cross-section of an Aztec temple. Tell students that rituals, and sometimes sacrifices, took place there. Architecturally, the temples were pyramid in shape and had stairs ascending from the foundation to the top. They had more than one worship area. Carvings found often included serpents.

📖 ACTIVE CLASSROOM

After completing the activity, ask students to break into groups to answer the following question: How did the structure of the Maya and Aztec temples differ? Have students write as much as they can for one minute then switch with the person on their right. The next person tries to improve or elaborate the response where the other person left off. Continue to switch until the paper comes back to the first person. The group then decides which is the best response and shares that with the entire class.

Further Instruction

Editable Presentation Use the Editable Presentation to present the main ideas for this Core Reading.

The Aztec: Core Reading and Interactive Reading Notepad Project the questions provided in the notepad and have students answer as they progress through the core text. Tell students that priests played an important role not only in Aztec religious rituals but also in education and in recording laws and historical events. Some priests used their knowledge of astronomy and mathematics to foretell the future. The Aztecs, like the Maya, developed a 260-day ritual calendar and a 365-day solar calendar.

Draw Inferences Have students review the text about the Olmec and how they contributed to the later Maya and Aztec civilizations. Ask students to point out what the influences were for each civilization. *(Response will vary, but should reflect the knowledge that the Olmec are considered leaders in the Mesoamerican cultures. The Olmec traded long-distance. They had elaborate ceremonial centers and worshipped many gods. They were great engineers, creating early aqueducts.)*

Compare Why was a social hierarchy important to both the Maya and the Aztec? *(The Maya had a vast culture of city-states with a ruler for each. To maintain this culture's economic, political, social and cultural well-being, their social hierarchy had designated responsibilities for each position. The Aztec were similar, though their extensive empire was ruled by a single leader.)*

■ SYNTHESIZE

SYNTHESIZE ACTIVITY
The Rise of the Mesoamerican Civilizations

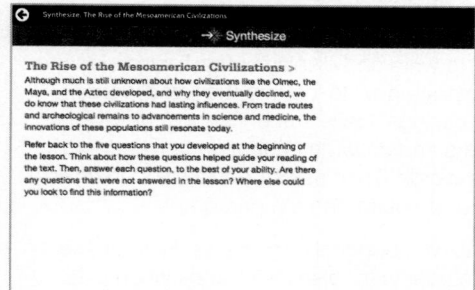

Ask students to recall the five questions that they created at the beginning of the class. Tell students they have five minutes to answer the questions in the The Rise of the Mesoamerican Civilizations activity. Then ask them to pair with a partner and share their responses.

Tell the pairs to collaborate on an answer for the following question: How were the early Maya and Aztecs able to carry their history with them over the extended period of centuries it took for them to settle in Mesoamerica? *(Answers may vary, but could include that they consistently practiced the traditions, rituals and religions of their ancestors and with them architecture, mathematics and astronomy.)*

■ DEMONSTRATE

DIGITAL QUIZ
Lesson Quiz and Classroom Discussion Board

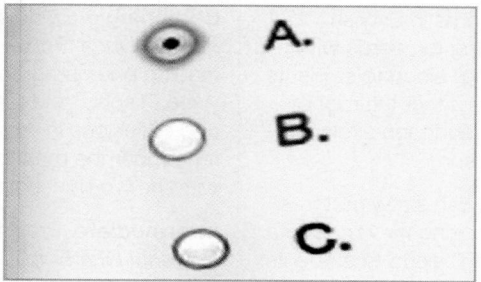

Assign the online Lesson Quiz for this lesson if you haven't already done so. Students will be offered automatic remediation or enrichment based on their score.

Pose these questions to the class on the Discussion Board:

In "The Aztecs" you read about how the Aztec empire expanded by conquest. Their immense wealth was used to build an infrastructure including networks of streets and canals, and elaborate cities with a worship center in the middle. As the empire expanded, the Aztecs incorporated some of the customs of the conquered peoples into their culture.

Recognize Cause and Effect How did the policies of the Aztec empire contribute to the success of the Spanish conquest? *(Many of the people conquered by the Aztec were not content with the harsh demands of Aztec rule. For example, the demand for tribute and the use of prisoners of war as sacrificial victims led to unrest. This discontent led to turmoil and a people who were ready for the change the Spanish offered.)*

Summarize What role did mathematics play in the life of the Maya and the Aztec? *(The Maya used mathematics to develop a method to hold their ceremonies at the appropriate times, and created a numbering system. The Aztec used mathematics in their engineering to develop a massive city laid out on a grid, and temples that lasted centuries.)*

Topic Inquiry
Launch the Topic Inquiry with students after introducing the Topic.

The World of the Incas

Supporting English Language Learners

Use with Digital Text 3, **Inca Life.**

Learning Strategies

Read *Inca Life* aloud to students. Then instruct students to complete one of the following activities based on their level of English proficiency.

Beginning Explain that related words can show patterns in English writing. Related words can often be identified by looking for words with the same root. Read the subsection "Terraced Farming" aloud to students. Write and display the words *farming* and *farmer*. Explain that the root of both of these words is *farm*. Define *farm* if necessary, and then explain to students that *farming* is an action, and *farmer* is a person.

Intermediate Explain to students that related words can show patterns in English. Related words can often be identified by looking for words with the same root. Read the subsection "Terraced Farming" aloud to students. Tell them to listen for words that are related to farm. Students should be able to identify *farming* and *farmer*.

Advanced As you read the subsection "Terraced Farming" aloud to students, have them follow along in their texts and identify any related words they hear. Students should be able to identify *farmer* and *farming*. Then have students tell what the root word of these related words. Challenge students to identify the part of speech for each of the three related words: *farm*, *farming*, and *farmer*.

Advanced High Have students read the subsection "Terraced Farming" and identify any related words they read. Students should be able to identify *farmer* and *farming*. Then have students identify the root word of these related words. Challenge students to identify the part of speech for each of the three related words: *farm*, *farming*, and *farmer*.

Use with Digital Text 2, **The Powerful Inca Empire.**

Listening

Read *The Powerful Inca Empire* aloud. Then have students complete one activity according to their level of English proficiency.

Beginning Provide students with bilingual dictionaries. Reread *The Powerful Inca Empire*, pausing to write and display unfamiliar words. After reading one paragraph, demonstrate how to look up the listed words. Write, display, and read their meanings. Have students copy the words and definitions in their notebooks and draw an illustration to help them remember the meanings of the words. Then ask students to listen again with the word meanings in mind as you reread the paragraph.

Intermediate Provide students with bilingual dictionaries. Reread *The Powerful Inca Empire* and ask students to raise their hands when they encounter unfamiliar words. Write and display these words. After reading one paragraph, assist students as they look up the listed words. Write, display, and read their meanings. Have students copy the words and definitions in their notebooks. Then ask students to listen again with the word meanings in mind as you reread the paragraph. Continue this activity with the rest of *The Powerful Inca Empire*.

Advanced Provide students with dictionaries. Ask students to work together in small groups to reread *The Powerful Inca Empire*. As one student reads out loud, the other students should write down any unfamiliar words. Instruct each group to write the words and their definitions in their notebooks. Groups should then reread the text and refer to their list of definitions as necessary to enhance their understanding of the text.

Advanced High Provide students with dictionaries. Ask students to work with a partner to reread *The Powerful Inca Empire*. As one student reads out loud, the other student should write down any unfamiliar words. Instruct each pair to write the words and their definitions in their notebooks. Partners should then reread the text and refer to their list of definitions as necessary to enhance their understanding of the text.

▣ Differentiate Instruction

Use the Differentiated Instruction notes throughout the lesson plan to support the varied skill sets, levels of readiness, and interests in the mixed-ability classroom.

Challenge These notes include suggestions for expanding the activity for advanced students.

On-Level These notes include suggestions for modifying the activity to address different interests or learning styles.

Extra Support These notes include ideas for providing more scaffolding or reading spuport.

Special Needs These notes provide ideas for adapting instruction to support the needs of various special needs students.

▪ NOTES

Objectives

Objective 1: Examine the early cultures of the Andes.

Objective 2: Understand how Inca emperors extended and maintained their empire.

Objective 3: Describe the major developments of Inca civilization.

LESSON 2 ORGANIZER	PACING: APPROX. 1 PERIOD, .5 BLOCKS			
			RESOURCES	
	OBJECTIVES	**PACING**	**Online**	**Print**
Connect				
DIGITAL START UP ACTIVITY **Government and Civilization**		5 min.	●	
Investigate				
DIGITAL TEXT 1 **Cultures of the Andes**	Objective 1	10 min.	●	●
INTERACTIVE MAP **Civilizations of the Andes**		10 min.	●	
DIGITAL TEXT 2 **The Powerful Inca Empire**	Objective 2	10 min.	●	●
DIGITAL TEXT 3 **Inca Life**	Objective 3	10 min.	●	●
INTERACTIVE GALLERY **Inca Culture**		10 min.	●	
Synthesize				
SYNTHESIZE ACTIVITY **Three Great American Civilizations**		5 min.	●	
Demonstrate				
LESSON QUIZ **Lesson Quiz and Class Discussion Board**		10 min.	●	

The World of the Incas

■ **CONNECT**

DIGITAL START UP ACTIVITY
Government and Civilization

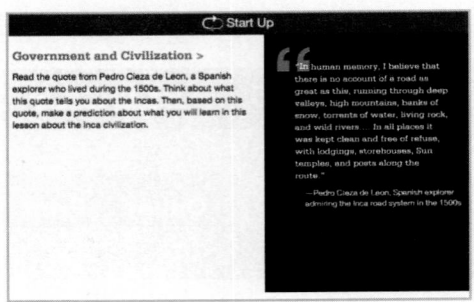

DIGITAL TEXT 1
Cultures of the Andes

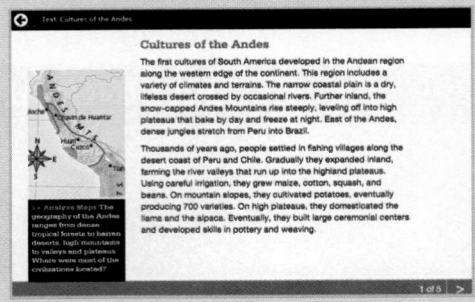

INTERACTIVE MAP
Civilizations of the Andes

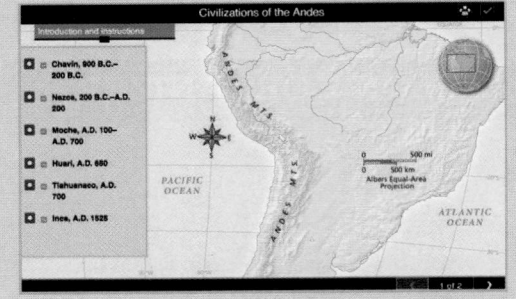

Project the Start Up Activity Ask students to answer the questions as they enter and get settled. Then have them share their ideas with another student in class or through a chat room or blog.

Discuss Consider what it was like to be a Spanish conquistador who had just ridden over the Andes Mountains and had his first view of an Inca city. What conclusions might he have drawn regarding the Inca competency in mathematics and engineering? *(Answers will vary, but may include amazement at the high level of skill involved in building the sophisticated architecture of an Inca city, and the organizational and mathematical skills required to govern the large and prosperous Inca empire.)*

Aa Vocabulary Development: Use the Interactive Reading Notepad to preview the Key Terms and Academic Vocabulary in this lesson with students.

⇅ FLIP IT!
Assign the Flipped Video for this lesson.

■ STUDENT EDITION PRINT PAGES: 111–115

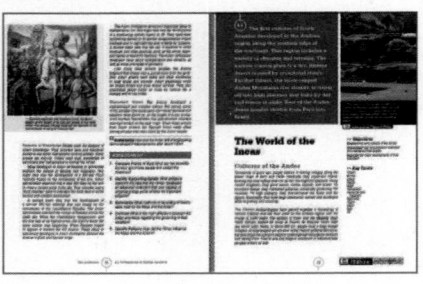

Objective 1: Examine the early cultures of the Andes

Quick Instruction
Civilizations of the Andes: Interactive Map Project the Civilizations of the Andes map on the whiteboard. Introduce the activity by explaining that the spread of civilization throughout the Andes was a gradual process with one civilization expanding upon another. Review the key to ensure students understand what the map displays. Then, click through the layers showing the students that they can review the geographical region of each civilization and the topography of the land they inhabited.

🎙 ACTIVE CLASSROOM
Put this question on the whiteboard: How did the cultures of the Andes use the resources in their geographical region? Ask students to spend three minutes writing a response to the question on sticky notes. Have students pair up and share their responses. Ask students to post their sticky notes on the board or on chart paper and then look at all the various responses. Finally, lead a class discussion on the similarities and differences in the individual responses. *(Sample responses: Those near the ocean fished; the ones in the river valleys used fresh water to irrigate maize and other crops; those who lived in colder mountain regions grew varieties of potatoes, a crop suitable to their climate, and domesticated llamas and alpaca.)*

D Differentiate: Extra Support While displaying the map, point out the region where each civilization resided. Ask students to list

the civilizations named in the key that reside in the coastal regions, rivers valleys, plateaus and mountains. *(coastal and river valley regions: Moche, Nazca; plateaus: Chavín; mountains: Huari; Tiahuanaco)*

Further Instruction
Editable Presentation Use the Editable Presentation to present the main ideas for this Core Reading.

Cultures of the Andes: Core Reading and Interactive Reading Notepad Project the questions provided in the notepad and have students answer as they move through the core text.

Project the image of the Chavín and tell students that it is believed that the culture's religion unified people in northern and central Peru. Its religion and arts continued to influence later civilizations. Explain to students how civilizations like the Moche influenced the later development, including the economy, of the Inca. The Moche developed methods for fertilizing the soil and used canals to irrigate the arid land. Tell students that the Inca agricultural economy was based on expanding step terraces built by earlier Andean peoples. The Moche also built roads and organized networks of relay runners to carry messages, ideas that influenced the organization of the Inca empire.

Discuss What contributions did the Chavín, Moche, and Nazca peoples make to the rise of Andean civilizations 2,000 years ago? Ask students to list one entry for each culture and then discuss their answers in class. *(Answers will vary, but may include Chavín: temple complex or uniting peoples of northern and central Peru; Moche: adobe structures, roads, irrigation canals, or ceramics, textiles and gold work; Nazca: animal geoglyphs in the desert.)*

DIGITAL TEXT 2

The Powerful Inca Empire

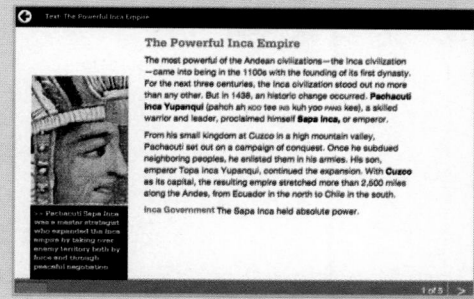

Objective 2: Understand how Inca emperors extended and maintained their empire.

Quick Instruction

Project the image of Pachacuti Sapa Inca from the Digital Text. Explain to students that he was the self-proclaimed and first emperor of the Incas. He and successor emperors expanded the Inca empire by conquest. Be sure students understand the major Inca ideas in mathematics and engineering and how these advances played an important role in maintaining the empire. To keep financial records, the Inca used quipu, which was a collection of colored strings that were knotted in different ways to represent various numbers. In this system, thin strings were looped around a large cord. Then colored knots made of thread were tied on the strings. The positioning of the colored knot symbolized its value. For example, the closer to the large cord, the higher the value. Modern knowledge of their use is derived from the few remaining quipa and from oral tradition, since the quipa are still in use today. The Inca then took the quipa and used it with the yupanas, a system of stone grids representing various mathematical values, to make complex calculations. To connect the empire, the Inca built over 14,000 miles of roads. This required great achievements in architectural engineering as they built hundreds of bridges to span rivers and gorges. Some bridges were pontoon style, floating on the water, while others were suspension bridges over deep valleys.

ELL Use the ELL activity described in the ELL chart.

Further Instruction

The Powerful Inca Empire: Core Text and Interactive Reading Notepad Project and discuss the questions from the Interactive Reading Notepad and discuss with the class.

Project the image of Machu Picchu, which was built at an elevation of more than 7,000 feet. Discuss the challenges this might have posed for architecture. Note that Inca builders designed structurally sound buildings that were so well made that they survived severe earthquakes. These buildings also reflected astronomical knowledge as the structures were often positioned to link them to the sun and moon.

Summarize Based on Text 1 and Text 2, summarize how prior Andean civilizations influenced the development of Inca civilization? *(Sample response: As the Inca expanded their empire, they conquered civilizations. They became a melting pot of cultures encompassing 13 million people and adopted their ideas. For example, they adopted the idea of engineering roads and using relay messengers from the earlier Moche. In addition, the Inca agricultural economy used farming methods, such as terracing and irrigation, developed by prior civilizations.)*

Summarize How did the Inca have an effective counting system when they did not have a method of writing? *(The Inca used quipa and yupanas to record and make calculations.)*

Paraphrase How do we know today that the Inca were exacting engineers? *(Structures of the Inca, such as Machu Picchu, have endured through the centuries. Their precision of building design has allowed the structures to survive earthquakes and be available for scientific exploration.)*

The World of the Incas

DIGITAL TEXT 3
Inca Life

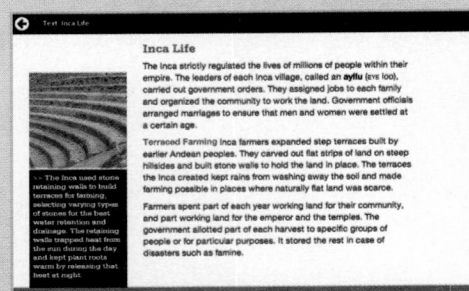

INTERACTIVE GALLERY
Inca Culture

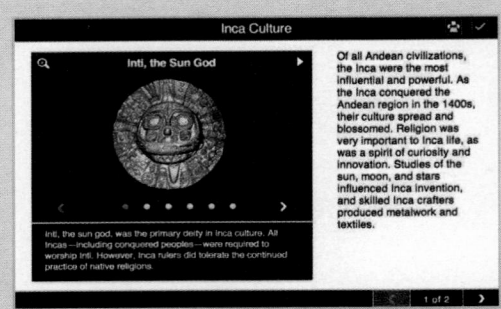

Objective 3: Describe the major developments of Inca civilization.

Quick Instruction

Inca Culture: Interactive Gallery Project the images of Inca cultural artifacts. Click through each image, and as you go through, discuss the major ideas in astronomy that developed in Inca civilization. Tell students the important role of the sun god, as well as the placement of buildings based upon astronomical observations and the organization of harvest festivals around moon cycles. The Inca used their high altitude cities and towns to make astronomy an important part of their society, including not only religious rites, but also as a way to plan the harvesting of crops. Also note that the Inca were masters of metalwork and skilled textile weavers.

Analyze Images Discuss the images as a class. Then ask students how the Inca were able to remain a civilization that dominated others during the time period and had no need to import or export goods. *(Answers will vary, but students may say that the Inca armies were always on the march. Their techniques to keep control of a large civilization included cooperation and subordination. They had a single ruler over a hierarchical bureaucracy that governed and was responsible for duties involving agriculture, food distribution, and taxation at a local level that fed into a larger system.)*

Summarize What significance did ideas in astronomy have in the Inca way of life? *(Inca knowledge of astronomy, the movement of the stars, helped them predict seasons, which in turn provided the timing for planting and harvesting crops. The stars in the heaven had a direct correlation to creatures on Earth.)*

🎬 ACTIVE CLASSROOM

Have students review the information they have learned. Each student should design a piece of "wallpaper" that encapsulates key learnings. The wallpaper is posted. Students then take a gallery/"wisdom" walk and note what others have written/illustrated. Students can jot down ideas as they occur. A video can be made of the wisdom walk and posted on YouTube.

D Differentiate: Challenge/Gifted The Inca offered incentives to those conquered. Have students research these incentives to create an advertisement convincing people to join the Inca empire. Advertisements should mention incentives and combine persuasive writing with maps or illustrations.

ELL Use the ELL activity described in the ELL chart.

Further Instruction

Inca Life: Core Reading and Interactive Reading Notepad Go through the Interactive Reading Notepad questions and discuss the answers with the class.

Have students compare the major social, economic, and cultural developments of the Maya, Inca, and Aztec civilizations. To help them, discuss the similarities and contrasts between these three great civilizations. The Maya, the Aztecs, and the Inca all had large-scale building projects, a clearly defined hierarchy, and a unified empire. Each of the three cultures adapted its environment to be able to farm more productively. All three

cultures were polytheistic. However, the Inca differed from the other two civilizations in significant ways. Because the emperor owned all property, trade was less important to the Inca than to the Maya and the Aztecs. Unlike the Maya and Aztec, the Inca did not develop a system of writing. Inca rulers kept their people fed and required them to labor for the empire. In contrast, the Maya farmers worked the land as an independent enterprise and a tax was imposed on them for food, while the Aztec required conquered people to pay a tribute.

Summarize How did the Inca communicate with one another? *(The Inca civilization used the language Quechua. All members of the civilization, including conquered people, were required to speak this language.)*

Compare and Contrast How do the Maya and Aztec civilizations contrast with the Inca civilization? *(Answers will vary, but could include that the Aztec and Inca were similar as warriors and determined conquerors of territories to expand their empires; Maya and Inca were dissimilar as traders. The Inca had no need for trade, as they were a self-supporting civilization. The Maya relied on trade. All three had a similar social hierarchy structure and were able to organize massive labor forces.)*

Paraphrase How were the Inca and Aztec empires impacted by European exploration? *(The Inca empire was destablized after the death of Huaya Capac leaving the empire ripe for European invasion. The Aztec conquering left many discontent. At the time of Spanish invasion, many Aztec became allies and the Spanish.)*

SYNTHESIZE

SYNTHESIZE ACTIVITY

Three Great American Civilizations

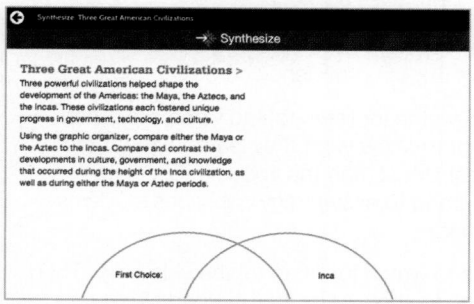

Project the Synthesize activity on the whiteboard. Introduce the activity by reviewing how to create a graphic organizer. Ask students to think about how the Inca, Maya, and Aztec compared. Students can complete the activity independently, in pairs, or in groups. When they have finished, hold a classroom discussion using student answers from their graphic organizers. Ask students to evaluate the similarities of the two civilizations they have chosen. How did they differ? Explain how these sililarities helped to create continuing traditions and ways of life that influenced that future generations in Mesoamerica.

Evaluate Ask students to list one way each of the three civilizations—the Inca, Maya and Aztec—still have a presence in modern society. *(Answers will vary, but possible answers may include: The Inca of Peru continue to speak in the ancient language of Quechua. The Maya, who live in much the same region as their ancestors, have continued with old traditions and still speak the Q'eqchi' language. Since Mexico City is built on top of Tenochititlan, it can be considered one of the oldest cities in the Americas. Nahuati, the language of the Aztecs, is still spoken by Mexican Indians.)*

DEMONSTRATE

LESSON QUIZ

Lesson Quiz and Class Discussion Board

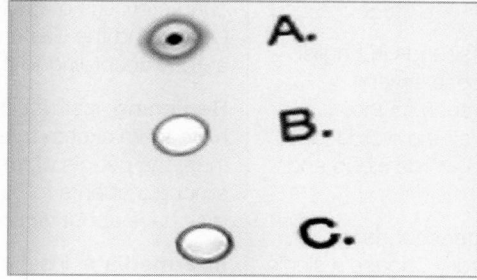

Assign the online Lesson Quiz for this lesson if you haven't already done so. Students will be offered automatic remediation or enrichment based on their score.

Pose these questions to the class on the Discussion Board:

Explain What medical contributions did the Inca offer society and how did this compare with the medicine of the Aztecs? *(Answers will vary, but may include that the Inca performed operations, cleaned the area prior to surgery, gave anesthesia, and mummified bodies. Similarly, the Aztecs set bones and prescribed medications for healing.)*

Draw Conclusions What were some benefits of the Inca road system? *(The Inca road system zigzagged across mountains, went through tunnels and across bridges throughout the expanse of the empire. Armies and runners carrying information were able to get to their destinations more easily and with reasonable speed on prepared surfaces.)*

Topic Inquiry

Have students continue their investigations for the Topic Inquiry.

Peoples of North America

Supporting English Language Learners

Use with Digital Text 1, **Cultures Develop in the Desert Southwest.**

Listening
Read *Cultures Develop in the Desert Southwest* aloud to students. Then instruct students to complete one of the following activities based on their level of English proficiency.

Beginning Explain that recognizing the different letter sounds in English can help students understand new English words. Choose several words in the text to illustrate a single sound in English, such as *the*, *with*, *Northwest*, *Southwest*, and *word*. Write and display the words for students. Underline the th sound in each word. Say the words aloud and have students repeat them.

Intermediate Explain that recognizing the different letter sounds in English can help students understand new English words. Choose a single sound in English, such as the th sound. Read *Cultures Develop in the Desert Southwest* and pause to write down each word with a th sound. Words should include *the*, *with*, *Northwest*, *Southwest*, and *word*. Have students copy the words into their notebooks and underline the th sound in each word. Say the words aloud and have students repeat them.

Advanced Remind students that recognizing the different letter sounds in English can help them understand new English words. Choose a single sound in English, such as the th sound. Then have small groups of students read *Cultures Develop in the Desert Southwest*. Instruct students to pause to write down each word they encounter with a th sound. Words should include *the*, *with*, *Northwest*, *Southwest*, and *word*. Have students underline the th sound in each word. Invite students in each group to say the words aloud. Circulate among students to support their pronunciation as needed.

Advanced High Remind students that recognizing the different letter sounds in English can help them understand new English words. Choose a single sound in English, such as the th sound. Then have students read *Cultures Develop in the Desert Southwest* independently. Instruct students to pause to write down each word they encounter with a th sound. Words should include *the*, *with*, *Northwest*, *Southwest*, and *word*. Have students underline the th sound in each word. Invite students to take turns saying the words aloud to the rest of the class. Provide pronunciation support as needed.

Use with Digital Text 3, **Distinct Cultures Develop in Different Geographic Regions.**

Listening
Have students watch [or listen to] the video clip depicting the various characteristics of the Native American cultures in the Arctic, the Northwest Coast, and the Eastern Woodlands. Then have students complete one activity according to their level of English proficiency.

Beginning Instruct students to watch [or listen to] the video clip. Then have them sketch three drawings to show what they learned about the Inuit, the people of the Northwest Coast, and the Iroquois. Circulate among students to offer support and to answer any questions students may have about what they learned.

Intermediate Instruct students to watch [or listen to] the video clip. Then have them sketch three drawings to show what they learned about the Inuit, the people of the Northwest Coast, and the Iroquois. After they've finished their drawings, have students write a single sentence to serve as a caption under each picture. Circulate among students to offer support and to answer any questions students may have about what they learned.

Advanced Instruct students to watch [or listen to] the video clip. Then have them sketch three drawings to show what they learned about the Inuit, the people of the Northwest Coast, and the Iroquois. After they've finished their drawings, have students write a short paragraph describing what they learned about each of the three cultures. Circulate among students to offer support as needed. Choose one or two student volunteers to share their work with the rest of the class.

Advanced High Instruct students to watch [or listen to] the video clip. Have students write a short paragraph describing what they learned about each of the three cultures. Then have them sketch three simple drawings to accompany their paragraphs. After they've finished their work, ask them to turn to a partner to share their finished products.

▣ Differentiate Instruction

Use the Differentiated Instruction notes throughout the lesson plan to support the varied skill sets, levels of readiness, and interests in the mixed-ability classroom.

Challenge These notes include suggestions for expanding the activity for advanced students.

On-Level These notes include suggestions for modifying the activity to address different interests or learning styles.

Extra Support These notes include ideas for providing more scaffolding or reading spuport.

Special Needs These notes provide ideas for adapting instruction to support the needs of various special needs students.

■ NOTES

Objectives

Objective 1: Understand how groups of people adapted to the desert environment of the Southwest.

Objective 2: Analyze the evidence from which we have learned about the emergence of culture in eastern North America.

Objective 3: Examine the cultures that developed in three very different geographic regions.

LESSON 3 ORGANIZER		PACING: APPROX. 1 PERIOD, .5 BLOCKS			
				RESOURCES	
		OBJECTIVES	**PACING**	**Online**	**Print**
Connect					
DIGITAL START UP ACTIVITY **Climate and Civilization**			5 min.	●	
Investigate					
DIGITAL TEXT 1 **Cultures Develop in the Desert Southwest**		Objective 1	10 min.	●	●
INTERACTIVE MAP **Native American Architecture**			10 min.	●	
DIGITAL TEXT 2 **Cultures Develop in the East**		Objective 2	10 min.	●	●
DIGITAL TEXT 3 **Distinct Cultures Develop in Different Geographic Regions**		Objective 3	10 min.	●	●
INTERACTIVE CHART **Native American Cultures**			10 min.	●	
Synthesize					
DIGITAL ACTIVITY **Ancient Civilizations in the Americas**			5 min.	●	
Demonstrate					
DIGITAL QUIZ **Lesson Quiz and Class Discussion Board**			10 min.	●	

Peoples of North America

■ CONNECT

DIGITAL START UP ACTIVITY

Climate and Civilization

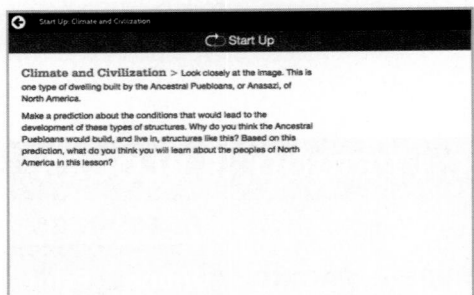

Project the Start Up Activity *Climate and Civilization*. Have students answer the questions as they enter and get settled. Then have them share their ideas with another student in class or through a chat or blog space.

Discuss Who were the Anasazi? *(The Anasazi were the Ancestral Puebloans who lived in what is now the Four Corners area of the United States.)* Why did they build their homes in the river valley cliffs? *(Answers will vary, but students may say that the Ancient Puebloans built homes in the hillside to protect themselves from invaders. Their homes were also high enough up the cliff hillside to protect them when rivers rose.)*

Tell students that in this lesson they will learn about early Native Americans that settled across North America.

Aa Vocabulary Development: Use the Interactive Reading Notepad to preview the Key Terms and Academic Vocabulary in the Lesson with students.

ⓘ FLIP IT!

Assign the Flipped Video for this lesson.

■ STUDENT EDITION PRINT PAGES: 116–120

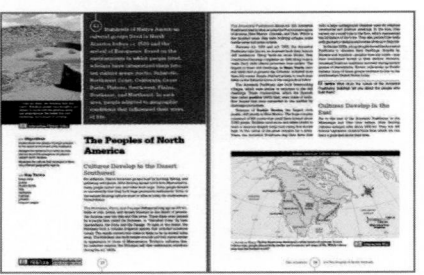

■ INVESTIGATE

DIGITAL TEXT 1

Cultures Develop in the Desert Southwest

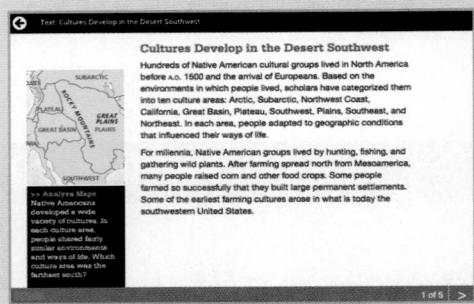

INTERACTIVE MAP

Native American Architecture

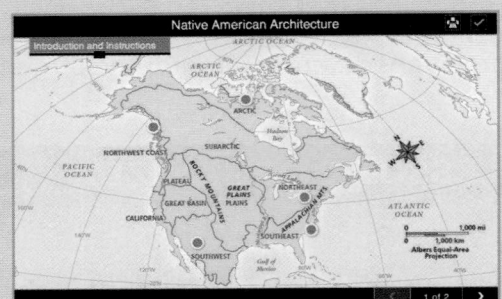

Objective 1: Understand how groups of people adapted to the desert environment of the Southwest.

Quick Instruction

Native American Architecture: Interactive Map Project the map on the whiteboard and click through the hotspots. Explain that Native Americans migrated across North America and settled in different geographical locations. To survive, these cultures had to learn to adapt to the climates of and the resources available in their new regions. To farm in the desert, the Hohokam built a complex irrigation system that included numerous canals. The canals carried river water to fields as far as several miles away.

📷 ACTIVE CLASSROOM

Put this question on the whiteboard: How did geography favor and frustrate the development of the North American Native American settlements? Ask students to spend three minutes writing their response to the question on sticky notes. Have students pair up and share their responses. Ask students to post their sticky notes on the board or on chart paper and then look at all the various responses. Finally, lead a class discussion on the similarities and differences in the individual responses. *(Responses will vary depending on which region students focused on, but could include the following: Native Americans of the Northwest lived in an environment of forest and ocean. Their access to these resources allowed them to flourish. The Inuit had a more limited selection of resources. They lived in an extreme climate and were able to use the ocean and animals to support themselves. The Desert Southwest Native Americans were able to develop agricultural crops using the river valley waters. Some cultures created cliff dwellings to protect themselves from invaders and extreme weather events such as flooding.)*

D Differentiate: Extra Support While displaying the map, point out the diverse geographical regions where Native Americans settled. Ask students to select three civilizations from the map and, for each one, list one resource or human-made artifact that was necessary for the creation of a successful

DIGITAL TEXT 2

Cultures Develop in the East

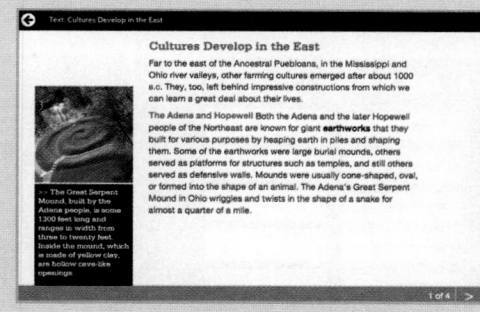

Cultures Develop in the East

Far to the east of the Ancestral Puebloans, in the Mississippi and Ohio river valleys, other farming cultures emerged after about 1000 B.C. They, too, left behind impressive constructions from which we can learn a great deal about their lives.

The Adena and Hopewell Both the Adena and the later Hopewell people of the Northeast are known for giant **earthworks** that they built for various purposes by heaping earth in piles and shaping them. Some of the earthworks were large burial mounds, others served as platforms for structures such as temples, and still others served as defensive walls. Mounds were usually cone-shaped, oval, or formed into the shape of an animal. The Adena's Great Serpent Mound in Ohio wriggles and twists in the shape of a snake for almost a quarter of a mile.

>> The Great Serpent Mound, built by the Adena people, is some 1300 feet long and ranges in width from three to twenty feet. Inside the mound, which is made of yellow clay, are hollow cave-like openings.

1 of 4 >

---

settlement. *(Answers will vary, but all civilizations needed water and fire. The Arctic cultures needed structures to protect them from the cold. The desert cultures needed water to grow crops. The Southeast cultures had access to the ocean, but needed fresh water for drinking.)*

ELL Use the ELL activity described in the ELL chart.

Further Instruction

Cultures Develop in the Desert Southwest: Core Reading and Interactive Reading Notepad Project and discuss the Interactive Reading Notepad questions and answers.

Make Generalizations What is significant about our present-day knowledge that the Hohokam grew corn, beans, and squash during the 300s *B.C.*? *(Answers will vary, but should include that agriculture was an organized event, these specific crops were used to sustain a civilization, and we can date the cultivation of these vegetables to at least 300 B.C.)*

Objective 2: Analyze the evidence from which we have learned about the emergence of culture in eastern North America.

Quick Instruction

Project the image of the serpentine earthwork on the whiteboard. Remind students that the actual purpose of earthworks such as this serpentine mound have been analyzed by scientists who studied artifacts. Explain to students that archaeologists believe the mounds were used as burial grounds, temple foundations, and defensive walls.

Analyze Images Ask students to review the serpentine mound. Discuss the image as a class. Then ask students how they believe a structure like the mound could have been built, and how the Adena came up with the idea to make their art in the shape of a snake. *(Answers will vary, but students may say that the Native Americans used the resources they had available—in this case dirt, rocks and shells. The mounds were constructed much like modern sand castles. The Adena, Hopewell, and other cultures created art that reflected what they knew. Most likely, they were familiar with snakes. Snakes also may have had religious significance for the cultures, as they did in Mesoamerica.)*

Further Instruction

Editable Presentation Use the Editable Presentation to present the main ideas for this Core Reading.

Cultures Develop in the East: Core Reading and Interactive Reading Notepad Project the questions provided in the notepad and have students answer as they progress through the core text.

Infer If the Mississippians left no written records, how have scientists been able to resurrect details of their history? *(Artifacts provided clues as to their settlements, and the Natchez people carried on their traditions.)*

Peoples of North America

DIGITAL TEXT 3

Distinct Cultures Develop in Different Geographic Regions

INTERACTIVE CHART

Native American Cultures

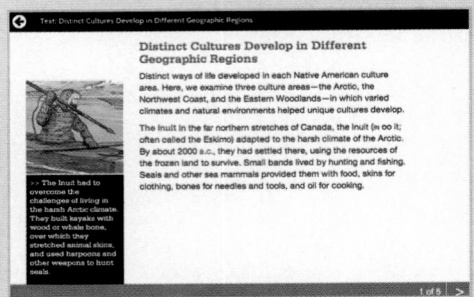

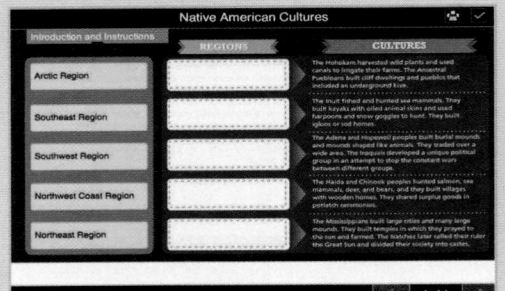

Objective 3: Examine the cultures that developed in three very different geographic regions.

Quick Instruction

Native American Cultures: Interactive Gallery Project the Drag and Drop activity on the whiteboard. Tell students that they must match the name of the region to the appropriate culture group that lived there by dragging a tile. Explain to students that different regions of North America provided Native American cultures differing life experiences that depended on what was naturally available in each locality.

⚃ ACTIVE CLASSROOM

After dragging the tiles to their appropriate positions in the interactive activity, ask students to pair up with a partner for a Circle Write. Ask students to answer the following questions: What did you discover? What does that make you think? What are you wondering about now that you've seen this? *(Sample responses: Some Native Americans survived by hunting salmon and hunting deer. These same activities were not available to the Ancestral Puebloans who lived in the desert. How the North American Native Americans survived was dependent on the resources available in their geographical region. For example, the Inuit built houses of ice and the Haida built homes of wood.)* After a few minutes of discussion, students should then share their insights with the class.

Further Instruction

ELL Use the ELL activity described in the ELL chart.

Distinct Cultures Develop in Different Geographic Regions: Core Reading and Interactive Reading Notepad Project the questions provided in the notepad and have students answer as they progress through the core text.

Draw Conclusions The Iroquois were a well-governed group of five to six tribes. What structures in their culture are similar to United States governance? *(Possible response: They operated as a democracy and abided by a constitution.)*

Paraphrase What environmental advantages did the people of the Northwest have over some other North American Native Americans? *(They lived in an environment of rivers, forests, and an ocean. The temperatures in this region were temperate, and it rained often. They were able to build villages, and they lived in a good location to trade the animals they trapped and the fish they caught. Building materials were as near as the closest forest.)*

PEARSON realize.™

www.PearsonRealize.com
Access your Digital Lesson

■ SYNTHESIZE

DIGITAL ACTIVITY

Ancient Civilizations in the Americas

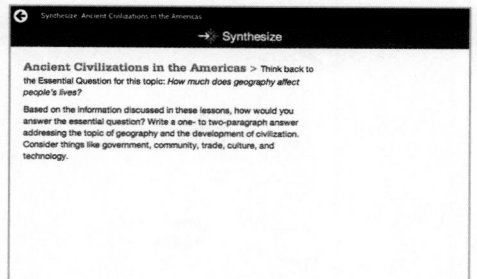

Ask students to recall the Topic Essential Question, "How much does geography affect people's lives?" Tell students they have five minutes to answer the questions in the Ancient Civilizations in the Americas activity. Then ask them to pair with a partner and share their responses.

Tell the pairs to collaborate on an answer for the following question: "How might the settlement of the Americas have varied if the ancient groups had not migrated across the land bridge in the Bering Strait or used small boats to cross from Asia into the Americas?" *(Answers may vary, but a sample answer may include that history may have to have been rewritten. The Americas were among the last group of continents to be inhabited by early people. Without the migration of ancient peoples described in the two theories, the Americas could have been void of Native Americans. The first settlers could very well have been the European colonists.)*

■ DEMONSTRATE

DIGITAL QUIZ

Lesson Quiz and Class Discussion Board

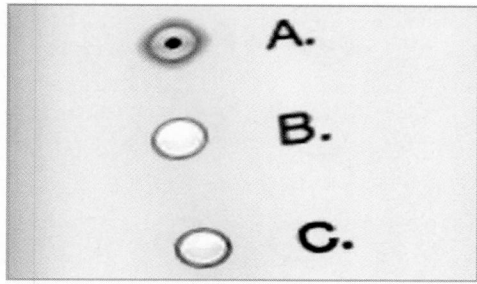

Assign the online Lesson Quiz for this lesson if you haven't already done so. Students will be offered automatic remediation or enrichment based on their score.

Pose the following question to the class on the Discussion Board:

In "Peoples of North America," you learned about cultures that built settlements across North America and the Native Americans resourcefulness in adapting to their geographical location.

Predict Consequences Consider what you have read about the civilizations of North America. What potential impact do you think the introduction of European explorers into North America would have on Native Americans? Explain your answer. *(The European explorers' interest in North America was largely for riches that would benefit their home country. They were well-funded and had powerful weapons and armies. Initially, the Native Americans might help the explorers learn to live off the land and act as guides. Ultimately, the Europeans could disrupt the Native American way of life to a point of permanent change or destruction.)*

Topic Inquiry

Have students continue their investigations for the Topic Inquiry.

The Americas (Prehistory–A.D. 1570)

■ SYNTHESIZE

DIGITAL ACTIVITY
Reflect on the Essential Question and Topic

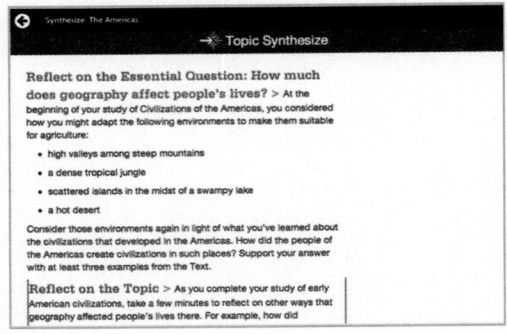

First ask students to reconsider the Essential Question for the Topic: How much does geography affect people's lives? Remind students that at the beginning of their study of Civilizations of the Americas, they considered how you might adapt the following environments to make them suitable for agriculture:

- high valleys among steep mountains
- a dense tropical jungle
- scattered islands in the midst of a swampy lake
- a hot desert

Have students consider those environments again in light of what they've learned about the civilizations that developed in the Americas. Ask students: How did the people of the Americas create civilizations in such places? Students should support their answers with at least three examples from the Text. *(Sample answer: The Inca, who lived in high valleys, practiced terrace farming by carving out flat strips of land on mountain slopes. The Maya burned down the tropical forests and then cleared the land to farm it. The Aztec built chinampas to be able to farm in their swampy lake environment. The peoples of the Southwest used irrigation to be able to farm in a desert.)*

Topic Inquiry
Have students complete Step 3 of the Topic Inquiry.

■ DEMONSTRATE

DIGITAL TOPIC REVIEW AND ASSESSMENT
The Americas (Prehistory–A.D. 1570)

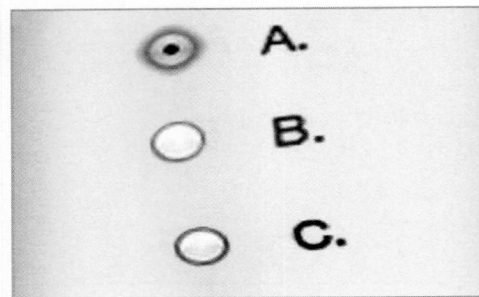

Students can prepare for the Topic Test by answering the questions in the Topic Review and Assessment online or the Assessment questions in the Print Student text. They can also prepare by reviewing their answers to the Interactive Reading Notepad questions or reviewing their notes in the Reading and Notetaking Study Guide.

DIGITAL TOPIC TEST
The Americas (Prehistory–A.D. 1570)

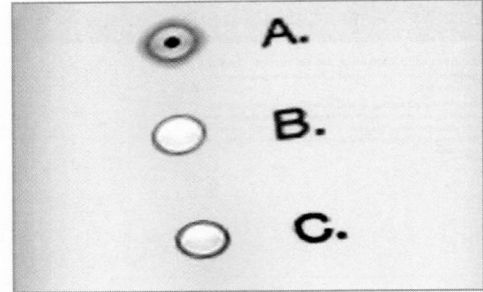

TOPIC TEST
Assign the Topic Test to assess students' understanding of topic content.

BENCHMARK TESTS
Assign these benchmark tests as you complete the relevant topics to monitor student progress toward mastering the course content and as preparation for the End-of-Course Test.

Benchmark Test 1: Topics 1–5

Benchmark Test 2: Topics 6–10

Benchmark Test 3: Topics 11–15

Benchmark Test 4: Topics 16–21

PEARSON realize.

www.PearsonRealize.com
Access your Digital Lesson

Ancient Greece (1750 B.C.–133 B.C.)

TOPIC 5 ORGANIZER	PACING: APPROX. 7 PERIODS, 3.5 BLOCKS
	PACING
Connect	1 period
MY STORY VIDEO **Pericles, The Golden Age of Athens**	10 min.
DIGITAL ESSENTIAL QUESTION ACTIVITY **How Much Power Should the Government Have?**	10 min.
DIGITAL TIMELINE ACTIVITY **Ancient Greece**	10 min.
TOPIC INQUIRY: CIVIC DISCUSSION **Athens or Sparta?**	20 min.
Investigate	2–4 periods
TOPIC INQUIRY: CIVIC DISCUSSION **Athens or Sparta?**	Ongoing
LESSON 1 Early Greece	30–40 min.
LESSON 2 The Greek City-States	30–40 min.
LESSON 3 Greek Thinkers, Artists, and Writers	30–40 min.
LESSON 4 Alexander the Great and the Legacy of Greece	30–40 min.
Synthesize	1 period
DIGITAL ACTIVITY **Reflect on the Essential Question and Topic**	10 min.
TOPIC INQUIRY: CIVIC DISCUSSION **Athens or Sparta?**	20 min.
Demonstrate	1–2 periods
DIGITAL TOPIC TEST **Ancient Greece**	10 min.
TOPIC INQUIRY: CIVIC DISCUSSION **Athens or Sparta?**	20 min.

TOPIC INQUIRY: CIVIC DISCUSSION

Athens or Sparta?

In this Topic Inquiry, students work in teams to examine different perspectives on this issue by analyzing several sources, arguing both sides of a Yes/No question, then developing and discussing their own point of view on the question: **Do you think it would have been better to live in Athens instead of Sparta?**

STEP 1: CONNECT
Develop Questions and Plan the Investigation

Launch the Civic Discussion

Divide the class into groups of four students. Students can access the materials they'll need in the online course or you can distribute copies to each student. Read the main question and introduction with the students.

Have students complete Step 1 by reading the Discussion Launch and filling in Step 1 of the Information Organizer. The Discussion Launch provides YES and NO arguments on the main question. Students should extract and paraphrase the arguments from the reading in Step 1 of their Information Organizers.

Next, students share within their groups the arguments and evidence they found to support the YES and NO positions. The group needs to agree on the major YES and NO points and each student should note those points in their Information Organizer.

Resources
- Student Instructions
- Information Organizer
- Discussion Launch

STEP 2: INVESTIGATE
Apply Disciplinary Concepts and Tools

Examine Sources and Perspectives

Students will examine sources with the goal of extracting information and perspectives on the main question. They analyze each source and describe the author's perspective on the main question and key evidence the author provides to support that viewpoint in Information Organizer Step 2.

Ask students to keep in mind:

- **Author/Creator:** Who created the source? An individual? Group? Government agency?
- **Audience:** For whom was the source created?
- **Date/Place:** Is there any information that reveals where and when the source was created?
- **Purpose:** Why was the source created? Discuss with students the importance of this question in identifying bias.
- **Relevance:** How does the source support one argument or another?

Suggestion: Reading the source documents and filling in Step 2 of the Information Organizer could be assigned as homework.

Resources
- Student Instructions
- Information Organizer
- Source documents

⏻ PROFESSIONAL DEVELOPMENT

Civic Discussion
Be sure to view the Civic Discussion Professional Development resources in the online course.

STEP 3: SYNTHESIZE
Use Evidence to Formulate Conclusions

Formulate Compelling Arguments with Evidence

Now students will apply perspectives and evidence they extracted from the sources to think more deeply about the main question by first arguing one side of the issue, then the other. In this way students become more prepared to formulate an evidence-based conclusion on their own.

Within each student group, assign half of the students to take the position of YES on the main question and the others to take the position of NO. Students will work with their partners to identify the strongest arguments and evidence to support their assigned YES or NO position.

Present Yes/No Positions

Within each group, those assigned the YES position share arguments and evidence first. As the YES students speak, those assigned NO should listen carefully, take notes to fill in the rest of the Compelling Arguments Chart (Step 3 in Information Organizer) and ask clarifying questions.

When the YES side is finished, students assigned the NO position present while those assigned YES should listen, take notes, and ask clarifying questions. Examples of clarifyin questions are:

- I think you just said [x]. Am I understanding you correctly?
- Can you tell me more about [x]?
- Can you repeat [x]? I am not sure I understand, yet.

Suggestion: You may want to set a 5 minute time limit for each side to present. Provide a two-minute warning so that students make their most compelling arguments within the time frame.

Switch Sides

The students will switch sides to argue the opposite point of view. To prepare to present the other position, partners who first argued YES will use the notes they took during the NO side's presentation, plus add any additional arguments and evidence from the reading and sources. The same for students who first argued the NO position.

STEP 4: DEMONSTRATE
Communicate Conclusions and Take Informed Action

Individual Points of View

Now the students will have the opportunity to discuss the main question from their own points of view. To help students prepare for this discussion, have them reflect on the YES/NO discussions they have participated in thus far and fill in Step 4 of their Information Organizers.

After all of the students have shared their points of view, each group should list points of agreement, filling the last portion of Step 4 on their Information Organizers.

Reflect on the Discussion

Ask students to reflect on the civic discussion thinking about:

- The value of having to argue both the YES and NO positions.
- If their individual views changed over the course of the discussion and why.
- What they learned from participating in the discussion.

Resources
- Student Instructions
- Information Organizer

INTRODUCTION

Ancient Greece (1750 B.C.–133 B.C.)

From its modest beginnings as a small society of seafaring traders and small farmers, Ancient Greece developed into one of the most influential civilizations in world history. The Ancient Greeks pioneered scientific and medical discoveries by examining nature, and they made important contributions in philosophy, history, and the arts. Democracy was born in the city-state of Athens, where citizens participated in lawmaking and in the courts. Alexander the Great conquered an empire stretching from Egypt to India, helping to spread Greek culture and learning across a wide area.

■ CONNECT

MY STORY VIDEO
Pericles, The Golden Age of Athens

Watch a video showing the story of Pericles.

Check Understanding How did Pericles change Athenian life? *(built stone monuments, reformed government, paid people who served on juries, emphasized freedom of speech, encouraged civic participation)*

Cite Evidence How do the ideals of Pericles live on today? *(His emphasis on civic responsibility and civic duty, as well as on freedom and equality, are values shared by modern-day democracies.)*

⇅ FLIP IT!
Assign the My Story Video.

DIGITAL ESSENTIAL QUESTION ACTIVITY
How Much Power Should The Government Have?

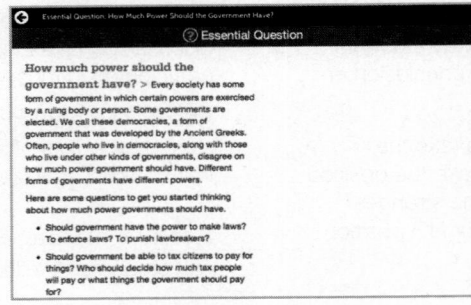

Ask students to think about the Essential Question: How much power should the government have? Have a volunteer read each bulleted suggestion. Discuss them as a class.

Predict Consequences What would happen if the government did not have the power to enforce laws? *(Students may predict chaos; others may argue that private police forces would take over law enforcement.)*

Generate Explanations Why do we pay taxes? What do our taxes pay for? How would we get these things if governments did not tax citizens? *(Students will recognize that taxes empower government to build roads or maintain an army. Others may argue that most tasks could be done more efficiently by private firms.)*

Analyze Is it government's responsibility to protect the disabled, old people, and children? Why or why not? *(Most students will accept some government role but will disagree on the extent of this duty.)*

Connect Why do people disagree about how much power a government should have? *(Students may say that one's opinion about government depends on faith in the government or on past experiences with government actions.)*

DIGITAL TIMELINE ACTIVITY
Ancient Greece

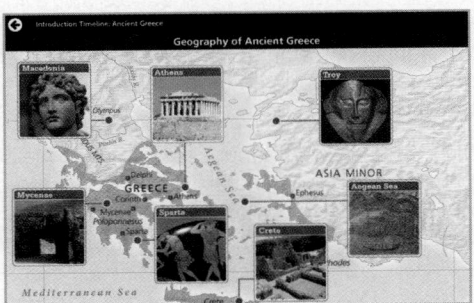

Display the map showing ancient Greece. Ask students to use the map to point out how location and geographic features might affect the development of this civilization.

D Differentiate: Extra Support Have students locate the Aegean Sea on the map. Ask in what way could the Aegean Sea be called the "Greek Lake"? *(Sample response: It is almost totally surrounded by Greek settlements, it was probably heavily traveled by Greek ships.)*

Analyze Maps How might the geography of ancient Greece have been an obstacle to unity? *(Sample response: The islands would have kept different peoples apart, more so than if they had lived on the same land mass, mountainous terrain would have made it harder to travel form place to place)*

Early Greece

Supporting English Language Learners

Use with Digital Text 1, **Minoans Prosper from Trade.**

Listening

Read *Minoans Prosper from Trade* aloud to students. Then instruct students to complete one of the following activities based on their level of English proficiency.

Beginning Explain the importance of understanding how to use intonation in English. Demonstrate the difference between statements (falling intonation at end) and yes/no questions (rising intonation at end) by using sentence examples based on the text, such as: Colorful frescoes describe Minoan society. Do you think the fresco in the text is pretty? Read the sentences aloud, focusing on proper intonation. Then have students repeat the sentences after you.

Intermediate Guide students in a discussion about the importance of proper intonation in English. Demonstrate the difference between statements (falling intonation at end), yes/no questions (rising intonation at end), *wh* - questions (falling intonation at end), and *either/or* questions (rising then falling intonation) by using sentence examples based on the text. Say each sentence and have students repeat after you. Then work with students to create four more sentences about the Minoans, one for each sentence type. Help students say each sentence, focusing on proper intonation for each one.

Advanced Guide students in a discussion about the importance of proper intonation in English. Ask student volunteers to demonstrate the difference between statements (falling intonation at end), yes/no questions (rising intonation at end), *wh* - questions (falling intonation at end), and *either/or* questions (rising then falling intonation) by creating sentence examples based on the text. Help students make corrections in their intonation as needed. Then have students work with a partner to create four more sentences about the Minoans, one for each sentence type. Have pairs practice saying each sentence, focusing on proper intonation for each one.

Advanced High Guide students in a discussion about the importance of proper intonation in English. Have students create four sentences about the Minoans, one for each sentence type (statement, yes/no question, *wh* - question, and *either/or* question). Have students practice saying each sentence, focusing on proper intonation for each one. Then invite all students to share their sentences in a small group to receive feedback on their use of intonation. Circulate among students to offer support as needed.

Use with Digital Text 3, **Homer and the Great Greek Legends.**

Listening

An audio recording of an excerpt of the *Iliad* or *Odyssey* is needed for this activity. Read *Homer and the Great Greek Legends* aloud to the class. Have students complete one activity according to their level of English proficiency.

Beginning After reading *Homer and the Great Greek Legends*, provide students with a transcript of the excerpt from the audio recording. Write and display challenging words for students. Begin by summarizing the recording to make the content easier to understand. Then play the recording. After listening, review the list of words: define them, say them aloud, and have students repeat them. If time allows, students can write the words and their meanings in their notebooks. Then play the recording again and ask students basic comprehension and language-attainment questions to gauge their understanding.

Intermediate After reading *Homer and the Great Greek Legends*, provide students with a transcript of the excerpt from the audio recording. Skim the transcript with students and underline each challenging word, say it aloud, and have students repeat the word. Then summarize the recording to make the content easier to understand. Play the recording and review the challenging words and their meanings. Then play the recording again and ask students basic comprehension and language-attainment questions to gauge their understanding.

Advanced After reading *Homer and the Great Greek Legends*, provide students with a transcript of the excerpt from the audio recording. Skim the transcript with students and underline each challenging word, say it aloud, and have students repeat the word. Play the recording and review the challenging words and their meanings. Then play the recording again and ask students to work in pairs to say three sentences to their partners using a challenging word from the list in each.

Advanced High After reading *Homer and the Great Greek Legends*, provide students with a transcript of the excerpt from the audio recording. Have students work with a partner to skim the transcript and underline any challenging words. Review students' lists, saying each word aloud, and have students repeat the word to ensure proper pronunciation. Play the recording and review the challenging words and their meanings. Then play the recording again and ask students to say three sentences to their partners using a challenging word from the list in each.

▣ Differentiate Instruction

Use the Differentiated Instruction notes throughout the lesson plan to support the varied skill sets, levels of readiness, and interests in the mixed-ability classroom.

Challenge These notes include suggestions for expanding the activity for advanced students.

On-Level These notes include suggestions for modifying the activity to address different interests or learning styles.

Extra Support These notes include ideas for providing more scaffolding or reading spuport.

Special Needs These notes provide ideas for adapting instruction to support the needs of various special needs students.

■ NOTES

_____

_____

_____

_____

_____

Topic (5) Lesson 1

Early Greece

Objectives

Objective 1: Identify the influences on Minoan culture and how the civilization prospered.

Objective 2: Summarize how the Mycenaeans ruled the sea trade and started the Trojan War.

Objective 3: Describe the works of Homer and their influence on Greek culture.

LESSON 1 ORGANIZER		PACING: APPROX. 1 PERIOD, .5 BLOCKS			
		OBJECTIVES	PACING	RESOURCES	
				Online	Print
Connect					
	DIGITAL START UP ACTIVITY **The Influence of Trade**		5 min.	●	
Investigate					
	DIGITAL TEXT 1 **Minoans Prosper From Trade**	Objective 1	10 min.	●	●
	DIGITAL TEXT 2 **Mycenaean Civilization**	Objective 2	10 min.	●	●
	DIGITAL TEXT 3 **Homer and the Great Greek Legends**	Objective 3	10 min.	●	●
	INTERACTIVE CHART **Values of Ancient Greek Culture**		10 min.	●	
Synthesize					
	DIGITAL ACTIVITY **Icarus Flying High**		5 min.	●	
Demonstrate					
	DIGITAL QUIZ **Lesson Quiz and Class Discussion Board**		10 min.	●	

■ CONNECT

DIGITAL START UP ACTIVITY
The Influence of Trade

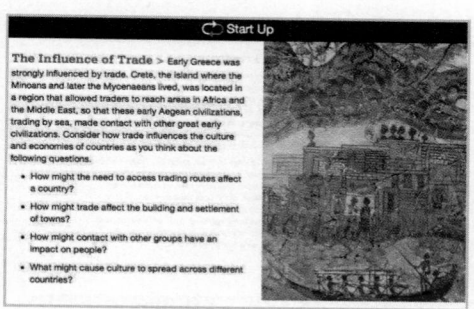

Project the Start Up Activity Ask students to answer the questions as they enter and get settled. Then have them share their ideas with another student.

Discuss How might the need to access trade routes affect a country? *(If one country wanted access to a route that another country controlled, conflict could result.)* How might trade affect the settlement of towns? *(People would build and live in towns close to trading routes to buy and sell goods.)* How might contact with other groups impact people? *(Contact might lead to learning new ways of doing things.)* What might cause culture to spread? *(Trade would spread new ideas, languages, and customs.)*

Tell students that in this lesson they will learn about ancient Greek civilizations and inspired Homer's epic poems.

Aa Vocabulary Development: Use the Interactive Reading Notepad to preview the Key Terms and Academic Vocabulary in this Lesson with students.

↕ FLIP IT!

Assign the Flipped Video for this lesson.

■ STUDENT EDITION PRINT PAGES: 126–130

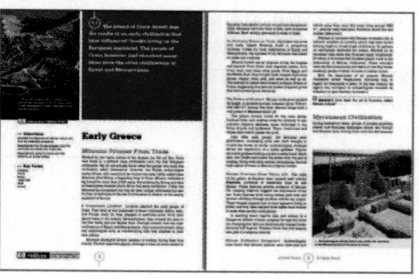

■ INVESTIGATE

DIGITAL TEXT 1
Minoans Prosper From Trade

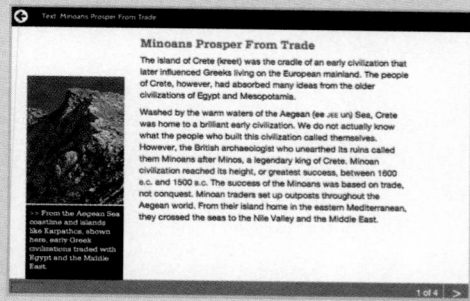

Objective 1: Identify the influences on Minoan culture and how the civilization prospered.

Quick Instruction

Aegean Sea Coast Project the photograph of the Aegean sea coast on the whiteboard. Look at each feature and then the photograph as a whole. Tell students that the brilliant Minoan civilization made its home on Crete, a rocky island in the Aegean Sea. The Minoan culture reached its greatest success between 1600 *B.C.* and 1500 *B.C.*

Analyze Images Tell students that early Aegean civilizations, such as the Minoans on Crete, began on coasts like these. Show students a map of the lands around the Mediterranean Sea and have them point out Crete. Ask: How do you think the people living on such a coast could survive and develop a civilization? *(Sample response: Because they probably have little and limited quality farmland, people living on such coasts would turn to the sea for food and trade with other lands.)* In which areas where you have studied early civilizations might the Greeks have made contact? *(Egypt or the Nile Valley, and Mesopotamia or the Middle East)*

ELL Use the ELL activity described in the ELL chart.

Further Instruction

Editable Presentation Use the Editable Presentation to present the main ideas of this text.

Minoans Trade and Prosper Project the Interactive Reading Notepad questions and discuss the answers with the class. Use the graphic organizer to record the main ideas relating to the Minoan civilization discussed in this text section.

Draw Conclusions Why do you think the Minoan civilization was important? *(Sample response: The Minoans traded with older civilizations in Egypt and the Middle East, absorbing and adapting important ideas and technology. Their brilliant civilization influenced later Aegean civilizations.)*

Hypothesize Archaeologists are uncertain how or why the Minoan civilization disappeared. How do you think the Minoan civilization might have ended? *(Sample response: A nearby volcanic eruption or earthquake destroyed the palace at Knossos. A little later, taking advantage of the devastation, another group attacked, conquered, and enslaved the Minoan survivors.)*

Early Greece

DIGITAL TEXT 2

Mycenaean Civilization

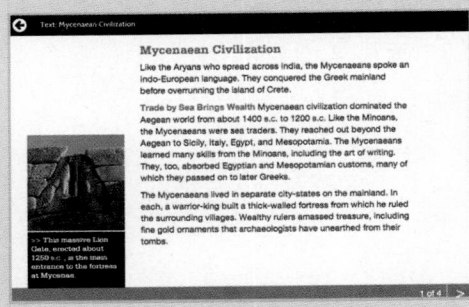

DIGITAL TEXT 3

Homer and the Great Greek Legends

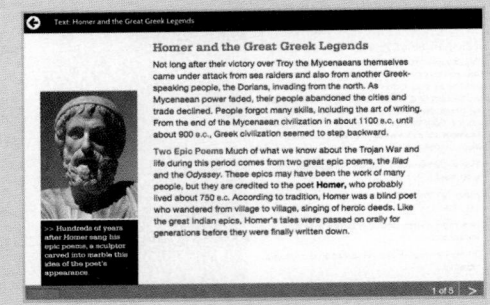

Objective 2: Summarize how Mycenaeans ruled the sea trade and started the Trojan War.

Quick Instruction

Tell students that by around 1400 *B.C.* the Minoan civilization ended and invading Mycenaeans helped destroy it. Also sea traders, the Mycenaeans learned skills from the Minoans and made contact with Sicily, Italy, Egypt, and Mesopotamia.

Mycenae: The Lion Gate Project the illustration of the Lion Gate at Mycenae on the whiteboard. Look at each feature of the walls and gate and then the photograph as a whole.

Analyze Images What main features of the Lion Gate and Mycenae do you observe? Why do you think Mycenae was built as shown in this photograph? *(Answers will vary but should include: tall and thick walls built of large stone blocks. Two lions face a pillar, or column, and rest their forepaws on a platform under it. Mycenae was built as a powerful fortress that could withstand attack by enemies and impress all who saw its massive construction.)*

Draw Inferences What factors do you think influenced how Mycenae was built? *(Answers will vary. Students should infer that Mycenae's solid fortress construction suggests the importance of showing strength and defending against attack in warlike times. Students may also mention the size and availability of the labor force required to build such masssive fortifications.)*

Further Instruction

Project the Interactive Reading Notepad questions provided in the notepad. Have students answer them as they progress through the core reading.

Infographic: In Search of Homer's Troy Project the infographic on the whiteboard. Look at the sections describing layers of cities discovered at Hisarlik, Turkey; what archaeologists found and have learned from their excavations; and then the whole infographic.

Identify Cause and Effect What do you think caused the Mycenaeans to go to war with Troy? *(Answers will vary but should include that Troy was a large and wealthy trading city. Its success and location, controlling the important straits between the Mediterranean and Black seas, likely made it a strong trade rival with the Mycenaean city-states and perhaps a tempting prize for conquest.)*

Compare and Contrast How are the reasons given for the Trojan War by Greek legend and by later scholars similar and different? Support your predictions with information from the text and infographic. *(Answers may vary. Sample answer: Both the Greek legend and later scholars describe the Trojan War as caused by rivalry between the Mycenaeans and the Trojans: over a kidnapped wife, Helen, or for control and dominance over trade. The Greek legend centers on personal insult to a Mycenaen king's honor, scholars focus on economic competition. The infographic shows that successful trade made Troy a very rich city.)*

Objective 3: Describe the works of Homer and their influence on Greek culture.

Quick Instruction

Tell students that the only Greek paintings to survive are on pottery. They offer glimpses of the daily lives of Greek men and women or tell stories from popular myths and legend, often from Homer's *Illiad* and *Odyssey*. To the ancient Greeks, the heroes of these epic poems became famous and familiar examples of honor, courage, and eloquence—and these heroes continue to inspire people today.

Values of Ancient Greek Culture Project the chart on the whiteboard and look at each detail in the image or images as well as the layout of the whole chart.

📷 ACTIVE CLASSROOM

Pair students to have a "Conversation with History." Have the first student assume the role of a famous Greek artist. Have the second student assume the role of his or her visiting patron *(supporter of the arts)* who has asked for a painting of a myth or legend. The artist gives his or her patron a verbal "tour" of what the painting shows. The patron makes comments and asks questions about the myth or legend presented by the painting. Ask students to record their conversation so others in class can access it.

INTERACTIVE CHART

Values of Ancient Greek Culture

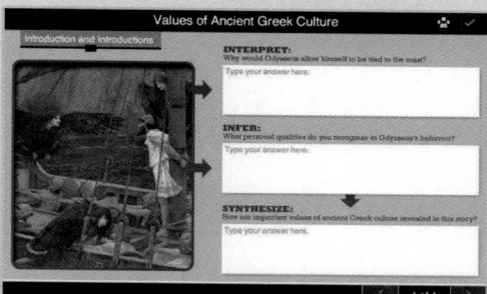

Cite Evidence What were the topics of the *Illiad* and the *Odyssey* and who wrote them? Cite evidence from the text. *(The Illiad tells the story of the Trojan War; the Odyssey tells of Odysseus' long voyage home after the war; both may have been the work of many people, though they are attributed to Homer, a blind poet.)*

ELL Use the ELL activity described in the ELL chart.

Further Instruction

Project the Interactive Reading Notepad questions for this text. Have students answer them as they progress through the text. Use the graphic organizer to record the main ideas relating to Homer and the Greek legends presented in his poems discussed in this text section.

Integrate Ask students to use the chart and text to explain what people today can learn about the ancient Greeks from images on pottery and stories of gods, goddesses, and heroes in Homer's epic poems. *(Sample response: From the scenes and activities we see in paintings and the stories Homer tells in his poems, we can get hints about daily life, ancient warfare, religious belief, and the values of the ancient Greeks.)*

Infer The *Illiad* begins with the mightiest Greek warrior, Achilles, refusing to fight because his commander has treated him unfairly and insulted him. What do you think this can tell us about the values of the ancient Greeks? *(Answers may vary but should include that an ancient Greek warrior's honor was extremely important to him. How others treated him, especially his commander, defined his importance and stature as a man. Achillles, as a great warrior, will not accept unfair treatment or allow insults without acting in response.)*

D Differentiate: Special Needs/Extra Support Tell students that much of what we know about the Trojan War is from reading the epic poems of Homer. Tell students that an epic is a long poem that tells the story of a hero or heroes. The term can also refer to a great story of heroic adventures. Then ask students to list stories of today that might be considered epics. Ask them what they can tell about the writer and the culture of the writer for each epic listed. Then tell them that the *Illiad* and the *Odyssey* give us clues about how the ancient Greeks lived and show us the values they thought were important, such as honor and courage.

Early Greece

■ SYNTHESIZE

DIGITAL ACTIVITY
Icarus Flying High

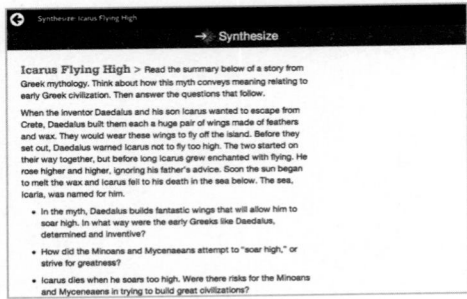

Have student form small groups to complete the "Icarus Flying High" activity. Ask them to read the description of a story from Greek mythology. Have them take five minutes to brainstorm and then write down brief answers to the following questions.

According to the myth, Daedalus builds fantastic wings that will allow him to soar high. In what way were the early Greeks like Daedalus, inventive and determined? How did the Minoans and Mycenaeans attempt to "soar high," or strive for greatness? Icarus dies when he soars too high. Were there risks for the Minoans and Mycenaeans in trying to build great civilizations? How do myths like this one communicate ideas across time?

Discuss Ask students to explain how myths like the story of Icarus and Daedalus reveal the values and culture of the ancient Greeks. How can myths reflect the history of the cultures in which they are produced yet hold meaning for other times and places? *(Answers may vary. Sample answer: This myth reveals that the ancient Greeks not only valued clever technology designed for difficult tasks, but were also aware that humans did not always patiently attend to limits and the dangers of overreaching. Daedalus invents—for its historical period—an almost magical device and, as a mature person, knows its use has limits. His son, fascinated by flying, ignores his father's warnings and crashes. The myth demonstrates the value of applied intelligence, contrasts the attitudes of sons and fathers, youth and age (eternal themes), and explains how a Greek sea was named.)*

■ DEMONSTRATE

DIGITAL QUIZ
Lesson Quiz and Class Discussion Board

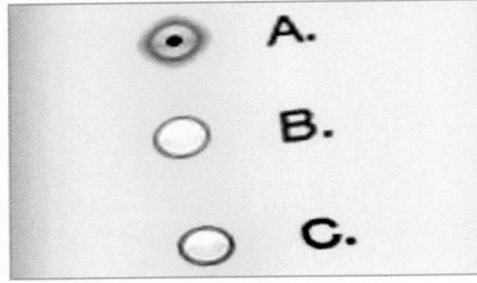

Assign the online Lesson Quiz for this lesson if you haven't already done so. Students will be offered automatic remediation or enrichment based on their score.

Pose these questions to the class on the Discussion Board:

In "Early Greece" you read about early civilizations that arose along the rocky Aegean sea coast and islands. The Minoans, based on Crete, traded with Egypt and Mesopotamia, adapting ideas and technologies into a lively culture that influenced later Greek civilizations. The Mycenaeans, also sea traders, learned skills (such as writing) from the Minoans. Ruled by warrior-kings, they established fortified city-states on the Greek mainland. Homer's epic poems, the *Illiad* and the *Odyssey*, tell us about them. Later, the Dorians, invaders from the north, conquered the Mycenaeans.

Compare and Contrast How were the Minoans and Mycenaeans alike and different? Explain. *(Sample response: Both the Minoans and Mycenaeans were far-ranging sea traders, adapting skills and technologies learned from Egypt and Mesopotamian civilizations. They both also passed along what they learned to later Greeks. As shown by frescoes at their Knossos palace, the Minoans developed a vital culture that honored gods and goddesses, and in which women probably played an active public role. The Mycenaeans by contrast built massive walled fortresses and, in Homer's poems, were led by warrior-kings in the Trojan War.)*

Draw Inferences How do you think literature reflects the history of the culture in which it is produced? (Sample response: Literature can reflect the history of a culture by describing people who lived then, important occurrences, and common daily activities. For example, in the *Illiad*, the Trojan War is described, reflecting how warrior-kings led Mycenaean city-states, warfare was conducted, and showing important values, such as honor, courage, and eloquence.

Topic Inquiry

Have students continue their investigations for the Topic Inquiry.

The Greek City-States

Supporting English Language Learners

Use with Digital Text 3, **Democracy Evolves in Athens.**

Listening

Read *Democracy Evolves in Athens* aloud to students. Then instruct students to complete one of the following activities based on their level of English proficiency.

Beginning Write and display the following words from the text: *Greek, Athens, chose, chief, wealth*, and *merchants*. Point to and say each consonant cluster in the displayed words. Then say each word aloud, emphasizing the consonant cluster, and have students repeat them. If possible, continue to scan the text for additional words with the consonant clusters *gr, ch*, and *th*. Repeat the procedure with the new words.

Intermediate Write and display the following words from the text: *Greek, Athens, chose, chief, wealth*, and *merchants*. Invite student volunteers to identify the consonant cluster in each word. Then say each word aloud, emphasizing the consonant cluster, and have students repeat them. If possible, have students scan the text for additional words with the consonant clusters *gr, ch*, and *th*. Repeat the procedure with the new words.

Advanced Tell students that they will be working with a partner to locate words with the following consonant clusters: *gr, ch*, and *th*. Instruct pairs to read the text and write down any words that contain one of the consonant clusters. Have pairs sound out each word on their list. Circulate among students to provide support as necessary.

Advanced High Tell students that they will be working independently to locate words with the following consonant clusters: *gr, ch*, and *th*. Instruct students to read the text and write down any words that contain one of the consonant clusters. Have students work with a partner to sound out each word on their list. Circulate among students to provide support as necessary.

Use with Digital Text 1, **Geography Shapes Greek City-States.**

Listening

Read *Geography Shapes Greek City-States* aloud to the class. Have students complete one activity according to their level of English proficiency.

Beginning Explain the concepts of main idea and details to students. Ask guiding questions to gauge students' understanding of the concepts. Then reread the subsection "Living by the Sea" aloud to students. Ask additional guiding questions to help students identify the main idea and at least two supporting details. To assess student understanding of the text, ask students to draw a picture depicting the content in "Living by the Sea."

Intermediate Guide students in a discussion of the main idea and details of a text. Ask guiding questions to make sure students understand the distinction between the two concepts. Then reread the subsection "Living by the Sea" aloud for students. Encourage students to listen for the main idea of the text as you read. After students listen to the text, lead a discussion to have students identify and discuss the main idea. Help students identify as many supporting details as they can.

Advanced Ask students to explain the concepts of main ideas and details in a text. Then reread the subsection "Living by the Sea" aloud for students. Encourage students to listen for the main idea of the text as you read. Encourage students to take notes. After students listen to the text, have small groups of students identify and discuss the main idea and as many supporting details as possible. Have groups share their ideas with the class.

Advanced High Reread the subsection "Living by the Sea" aloud for students. Encourage students to take notes. After students listen to the text, have them discuss the main idea and supporting details with a partner. Have pairs share their ideas with the class.

▣ Differentiate Instruction

Use the Differentiated Instruction notes throughout the lesson plan to support the varied skill sets, levels of readiness, and interests in the mixed-ability classroom.

Challenge These notes include suggestions for expanding the activity for advanced students.

On-Level These notes include suggestions for modifying the activity to address different interests or learning styles.

Extra Support These notes include ideas for providing more scaffolding or reading spuport.

Special Needs These notes provide ideas for adapting instruction to support the needs of various special needs students.

■ NOTES

The Greek City-States

Objectives

Objective 1: Understand how geography influenced the Greek city-states.

Objective 2: Explain how democracy and other forms of government developed in Ancient Greece.

Objective 3: Describe the influence of Ancient Greek concepts related to the rights and responsibilities of citizenship.

Objective 4: Identify the culture and values shared by Ancient Greeks.

Objective 5: Summarize how the Persian and Peloponnesian Wars affected Greece.

LESSON 2 ORGANIZER		OBJECTIVES	PACING	RESOURCES	
				Online	Print
Connect					
DIGITAL START UP ACTIVITY **By Mountains or the Sea**			5 min.	●	
Investigate					
DIGITAL TEXT 1 **Geography Shapes Greek City-States**		Objective 1	10 min.	●	●
INTERACTIVE CHART **Forms of Government**			10 min.	●	
DIGITAL TEXT 2 **Discipline and Warfare in Sparta**		Objective 2	10 min.	●	●
DIGITAL TEXT 3 **Democracy Evolves in Athens**			10 min.	●	●
DIGITAL TEXT 4 **Forces for Unity**		Objective 4	10 min.	●	●
DIGITAL TEXT 5 **Greek Wars With Persia**		Objective 5	10 min.	●	●
INTERACTIVE MAP **Persian Wars, 490 B.C.–479 B.C.**			10 min.	●	
DIGITAL TEXT 6 **Pericles, Democracy, and War**		Objectives 3, 5	10 min.	●	●
INTERACTIVE GALLERY **Athenian Democracy**			10 min.	●	
Synthesize					
DIGITAL ACTIVITY **Alliances: Cooperation for a Cause**			5 min.	●	
Demonstrate					
DIGITAL QUIZ **Lesson Quiz and Class Discussion Board**			10 min.	●	

PEARSON realize™
www.PearsonRealize.com

Go online to access additional resources including:
Primary Sources • Biographies • Supreme Court cases •
21st Century Skill Tutorials • Maps • Graphic Organizers.

CONNECT

DIGITAL START UP ACTIVITY
By Mountains or the Sea

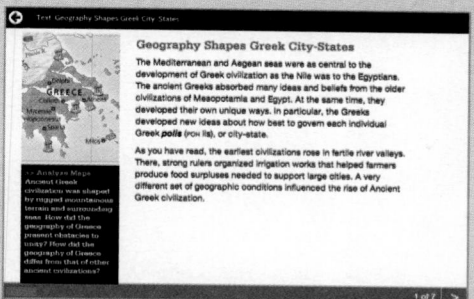

Project the Start Up Activity Ask students to read the introductory text and answer the questions as they get settled. Then have them share their ideas with another student.

Discuss How could access to the sea influence a country's trade, economy, and travel? (*Access to the sea would provide trading opportunities, since it is easier to ship large amounts of goods by sea. Trade provides work for those who make and sell goods, helping the economy. Travel by sea would be more common as the only available route.*) How might mountains impact trade and political unity? (*Mountains make overland trade more difficult. If mountains divide a country into separate regions, the people in those regions might have more difficulty working together.*)

Aa Vocabulary Development: Use the Interactive Reading Notepad to preview the Key Terms and Academic Vocabulary in this Lesson with students.

⇅ FLIP IT!
Assign the Flipped Video for this lesson.

STUDENT EDITION PRINT
PAGES: 131–141

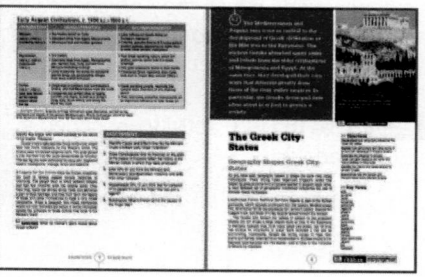

INVESTIGATE

DIGITAL TEXT 1
Geography Shapes Greek City-States

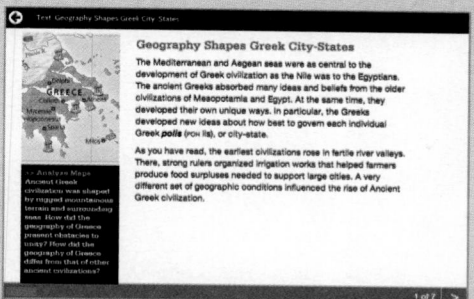

INTERACTIVE CHART
Forms of Government

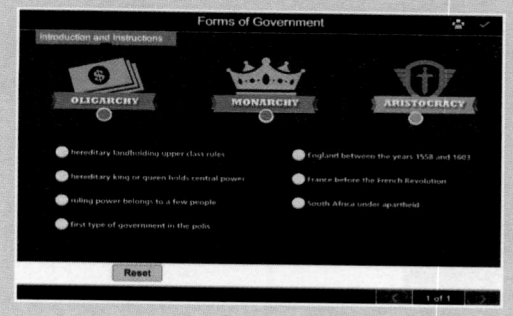

Objective 1: Understand how geography influenced the city-states.

Quick Instruction
Kings governed the early Greek city-states. The inherited central power of a monarch eventually shifted to noble landowners who won power for themselves and their families as military defenders. In time, as trade increased, a small elite of wealthy merchants, farmers, and artisans dominated some city-states forming oligarchies.

Interactive Chart: Forms of Government
Project the chart. Look at each description individually and then the layout of the chart as a whole. Which forms of government are directly based on noble birth? (*monarchy and aristocracy*) Which are based on wealth? (*oligarchy*) Which was the earliest form of govenrment in ancient Greece? (*monarchy*)

👥 ACTIVE CLASSROOM

Group students. Give each group a three-column organizer with the headings Plus/Minus/Interesting for recording responses to three questions about forms of government. Ask each group choose one form of government: monarchy, aristocracy, or oligarchy. Then have students answer these questions: 1. What are the positive ideas about the form of government you chose? 2. What are the negative ideas about it? 3. What is interesting about it? (*Sample response: Monarchy: positive ideas—one person clearly in charge, can make decisions and act right away; negative ideas—has total power, can be unfair or cruel, may not have intelligent or capable successors; interesting—how many countries were or are monarchies*)

ELL Use the ELL activity described in the ELL chart.

Further Instruction
Editable Presentation Use the Editable Presentation to present the main ideas of this text.

Go through the Interactive Reading Notepad questions and discuss the answers with the class. Have students create an outline to record the main ideas and supporting details described in this text section.

Analyze Images Project the "Geography of Ancient Greece" map on the whiteboard. Have students indicate the locations of Sparta, Mycenae, Corinth, Athens, and Ephesus. Ask: What do the locations of these cities have in common? (*They are all on a coast or very close to the sea.*) Point out that Greece itself is very mountainous and has limited natural resources, with the exception of marble.

Identify Cause and Effect What effect did the mountains and water have on Greek city-states? (*The Greeks were cut off from each other, developed their own systems of government, and fought frequently. Access to water helped Greeks become skilled sailors and traders.*)

D Differentiate: Special Needs/Extra Support Students may use the map above to learn more about Greece. Point out that Greece is made up of isolated valleys and small islands. Ask: How did its geography influence its economy? (*Because it was surrounded by the sea, the Greeks became great traders.*) How did its geography affect political divisions? (*It prevented the Greeks from building a large local empire. Instead they built small city-states.*)

The Greek City-States

DIGITAL TEXT 2

Discipline and Warfare in Sparta

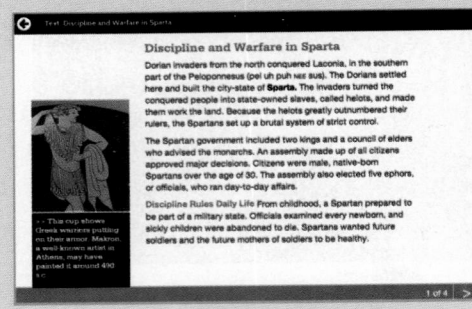

DIGITAL TEXT 3

Democracy Evolves in Athens

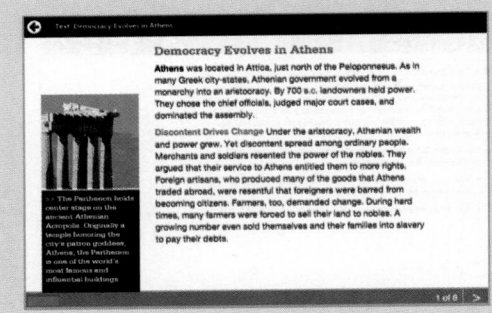

Objective 2: Explain how democracy and other forms of government developed in Greece.

Quick Instruction

Conquered and settled by Dorian invaders from the north, Sparta developed into a powerful military state that placed little emphasis on trade, wealth, new ideas, or the arts. Its conquered population became state-owned slaves who worked the land. Sparta was ruled by kings.

Summarize What form of government did Sparta have? What were the responsibilities of Sparta's citizens? *(Sparta was a dual monarchy: two kings ruled, advised by a council of elders and an assembly of citizens who approved major decisions. Male citizens trained from childhood to fight for Sparta; female citizens trained to produce healthy sons and sometimes to run the family estates.)*

D Differentiate: Extra Support Ask students to look up the definition of the word spartan. Then discuss how the definition reflects the philosophy of Sparta.

Further Instruction

Project the Interactive Reading Notepad questions for this text. Have students answer them as they progress through the text. Create an outline to record the main ideas and supporting details about Sparta. Discuss the life of young boys, who at the age of seven began training for military service. They moved into barracks, where they were toughened by a coarse diet, hard exercise, and rigid discipline. This strict and harsh discipline made Spartan youths excellent soldiers.

Infer What do you think daily life in Sparta was like? *(Sample response: Daily life was highly disciplined and difficult, with little or no time for personal freedom, contact between men and women, interests, leisure, or intellectual pursuits.)*

Predict Consequences How do you think Sparta's large enslaved population affected the daily life of its citizens? *(Sample response: Spartan citizens would always be aware that their slaves might rise up against their masters. Yet supplying the city-state's daily needs, especially food, depended on the reliable activity of this valuable underclass. I think that these factors would probably have made Sparta a tense place to live.)*

D Differentiate: Special Needs/Extra Support To help students learn how Sparta developed into a military society and Athens into a democracy, have them create a flowchart that shows the steps. *(For example, for Sparta the chart may read: (1) City-states emerge. (2) The kings lose power to the wealthy. (3) Changing technology means ordinary citizens can afford iron weapons. (4) The phalanx means more training an a greater sense of unity among citizens. (5) Spartans conquer Laconia and make its people helots. (6) The helots greatly outnumber the Spartans. (7) Spartans create a brutal system of strict control.)*

Objective 2: Explain how democracy and other forms of government developed in Greece.

Quick Instruction

Athens slowly moved from an aristocracy to a democracy. Popular discontent continued despite significant government reforms under Solon's leadership. By making reforms to help merchants and the poor, tyrants gained their support to seize power. Then the reformer Cleisthenes expanded citizens' role in government, made the assembly a lawmaking body, and Athens became a limited democracy.

Infographic: Steps to Democracy: Reformers and Tyrants Project the infographic on the whiteboard. Look at the sections describing Solon's reforms, the effects of a tyrant taking power in Athens, the reforms of Cleisthenes, and then the whole infographic.

Identify Steps in a Process Leaders favored the interests of which groups as government in ancient Athens gradually evolved into a democracy? *(Solon's reforms helped the poor, but the wealthy remain in power. Pisistratus helped farmers, merchants, and the poor. Cleisthenes worked with the popular assembly against the nobles, broadening the political role of ordinary citizens.)*

ELL Use the ELL activity described in the ELL chart.

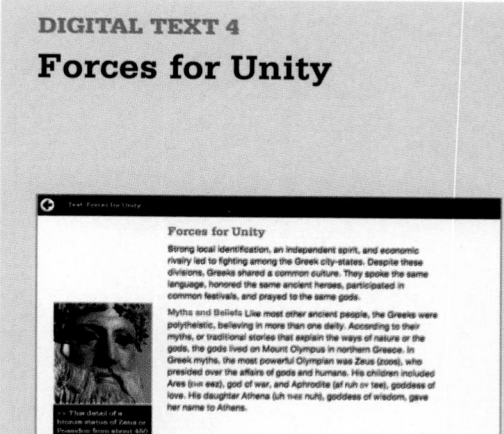

DIGITAL TEXT 4

Forces for Unity

Further Instruction

Athenian democracy, although limited by modern standards, did offer its citizens the opportunity to participate directly in the government of their polis. Remind students that more people were involved in decision making in Athens than in any other ancient civilization.

Discuss the role of families, including women and children in the society. Families played a vital role in ancient Greek culture, and women played their most significant public role in religion. Their participation in sacred processions and ceremonies was considered essential for the city's well-being. In well-to-do Athenian homes, women managed the entire household. They spun and wove, cared for their children, and prepared food, but lived a secluded existence and were rarely seen in public. Their slaves or children were sent to buy food and to fetch water from the public well. Only poor women went shopping alone in Athens. They worked outside the home, often beside their husbands.

Girls received little or no formal education, but boys attended school if their families could afford it. Besides learning to read and write, they studied music, memorized poetry, and studied public speaking because, as citizens in a democracy, they would have to voice their views. Although they received military training and participated in athletic contests, unlike Sparta, which put military training above all else, Athens encouraged young men to explore many areas of knowledge.

Classify Why is the democracy of ancient Athens considered a "limited one"? *(Though citizens had broad rights, few Athenians were actually citizens. Women and slaves were excluded from citizenship and thus any say in government, since only men could be citizens. Such a version of democracy was hardly representative of the population it ruled.)*

Draw Conclusions How do you think slavery may have contributed to the success of democracy in ancient Athens? *(Answers will vary and may include that many Athenians owned slaves, freeing them from spending time on daily chores or the routine work of commerce and manufacturing. Thus they had time they could dedicate to discussing public affairs in the marketplace, debating issues and voting on laws in the assembly, and holding public office.)*

Objective 4: Identify the culture and values shared by Greeks.

Quick Instruction

The Greek city-states shared a common culture—a language, ancient heroes, gods, and festivals—despite their fiercely independent spirit and economic rivalry. As trade and colonies increased, the Greeks met foreigners and borrowed many ideas. Yet the Greeks retained a sense of their own uniqueness and superiority.

Analyze Images Project the photo of the bronze statue of Zeus (or Poseidon) on the whiteboard. Remind students that Zeus was king of the Greek gods and his brother Poseidon was the god of the sea and earthquakes. Ask students to describe the main features of the statue and what feelings and understandings students feel it embodies. *(Sample response: The photo includes the head and shoulders of the god, perhaps he was holding a spear. He looks straight ahead with focused attention and strong, masterful energy.)*

Generate Explanations How do you think ancient Greek religion helped unify the Greeks and came to greatly influence later civilizations? *(Sample response: Having religious beliefs and practices in common, the ancient Greeks shared the same or similar values and could usually understand one another, even when they disagreed. Later civilizations absorbed the classical Greek religious values, embodied in traditional legends and myths, and through famous Greek works of art, such as poems, plays, and sculptures.)*

The Greek City-States

DIGITAL TEXT 5
Greek Wars With Persia

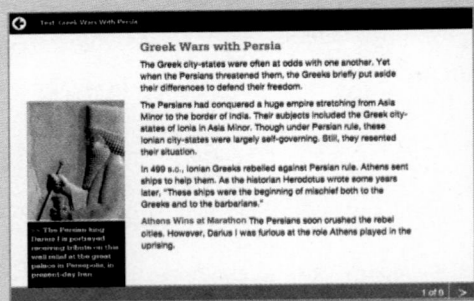

INTERACTIVE MAP
Persian Wars, 490 B.C.–479 B.C.

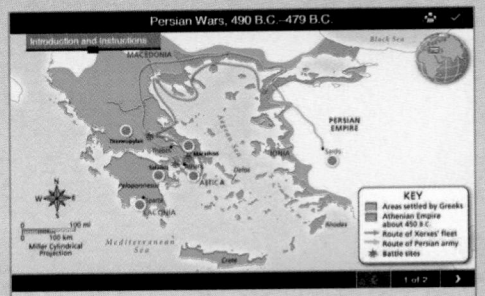

Further Instruction

Project the Interactive Reading Notepad questions for this text. Have students answer them as they progress through the text. Use an outline to record the main ideas about shared Greek culture and values.

Cite Evidence How did the ancient Greeks honor their gods? Ask students to provide evidence from the text that supports this idea. *(Sample response: The Greeks built temples and celebrated festivals to honor their gods. They held public processions, made sacrifices, and participated in feasts, plays, choral singing, and athletic competitions devoted to their gods.)*

Objective 5: Summarize how the Persian and Peloponnesian Wars affected Greece.

Quick Instruction

In 499 *B.C.*, Athens sent ships to help self-governing Greek city-states in Asia Minor fight against the Persian empire. This later led to the Persian Wars against Greece. The Greek city-states united to fight and ultimately defeat the Persians.

Interactive Map: Persian Wars, 490 *B.C.* –479 *B.C.* Project the map on the whiteboard and click through the hot spots on the map. Look at each battle site and route individually and then the map as a whole. Ask students: Where were the Athenian and Persian empires located? Compare their sizes. *(The Athenian empire was located along the eastern coast of Attica, the northern and eastern Aegean coasts, and included land around the Black Sea's southern entrance; the Persian empire stretched east from present-day western Turkey; the Athenian empire was much smaller than the Persian empire.)*

Infer Why do you think Xerxes' fleet hugged the Greek coastline instead of sailing directly across the Aegean Sea? *(Sample responses: Warships of the time were not built for deep-sea voyages; unpredictable weather or treacherous currents encouraged ships to travel near the coasts.)*

📖 ACTIVE CLASSROOM

Pair students to have a "Conversation with History." Ask the first student to assume the role of a Spartan king. Have the second student assume the role of a visiting official messenger from Athens. The Spartan king listens as the messenger from Athens provides a verbal "tour" of a map of the Aegean, describing the Persian threat to Greece and requesting Spartan military assistance. The Spartan king listens, then asks questions such as: How large is the Persian army? When will the Persians arrive? How many cities will join together to defend Greece? Have students record their conversation so others in class can access it.

Further Instruction

Greek Wars With Persia Project the Interactive Reading Notepad questions and discuss the answers with the class. Use the outline to record the main ideas and details about the Persian Wars discussed in this text section.

Sequence Events Describe the sequence of events leading to the Greek victory in the Persian Wars. *(Sample response: In 490 B.C., the greatly outnumbered Athenians defeated the Persians at Marathon. Athens then convinced Sparta and other city-states to band together for defense. In 480 B.C., despite the heroic Spartan defense at the pass of Thermopylae, the Persians burned Athens. However, the Athenians lured the Persian fleet into the straits of Salamis and destroyed it, ending the threat of Persian invasion.)*

DIGITAL TEXT 6

Pericles, Democracy, and War

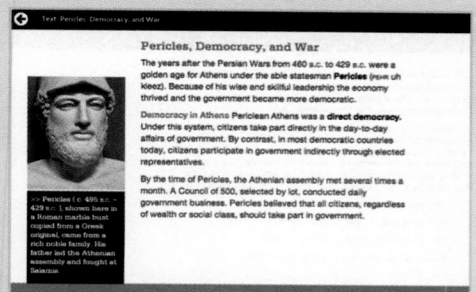

INTERACTIVE GALLERY

Athenian Democracy

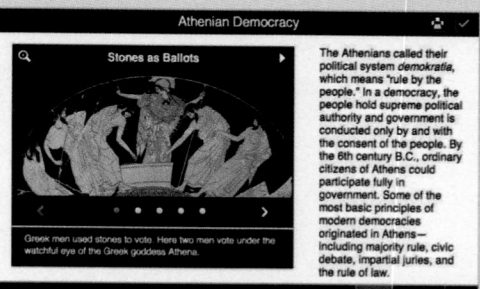

Identify Cause and Effect How did victory in the Persian Wars affect Athens? *(Sample response: Although the Persians burned Athens, the Athenians created the Delian League, a defensive alliance of Greek city-states, and led the Greeks to victory over a powerful empire. This success provided strong confirmation of Athens' importance and power. Thus encouraged, Athens continued to dominate other city-states in the Delian League and used force to create an Athenian empire.)*

Objectives 3: **Describe the influence of Greek concepts related to the rights and responsibilities of citizenship; 5:** **Summarize how the Persian and Peloponnesian Wars affected Greece.**

Quick Instruction

After the Persian Wars, Pericles led Athens in a golden age: its economy flourished and its government became more democratic. Athenian citizens from all social classes took part directly in their government's daily affairs. Greek concepts related to the rights and responsibilities of citizenship put into practice in Athens at this time set standards that influenced the laws and governments of many later societies.

Interactive Gallery: Athenian Democracy

Project the gallery. Click through the gallery, looking first at each image individually, and then consider how the collection of images as a whole describes Athenian democracy.

Cite Evidence What basic principles of modern democracies originated in Greece? Cite information from the gallery and the text. *(Sample response: majority rule, civic debate, impartial juries, trial by a jury of your peers, innocent until proven guilty, and the rule of law)*

Categorize List the three governmental bodies of ancient Athens. Which one do you think was the most important? Why? *(Sample response: The boule, or Council of 500; the ecclesia; and the courts and juries; I think the ecclesia was the most important because all the citizens of Athens met there to debate major issues, vote on laws, and exile citizens dangerous to Athens.)*

🖳 ACTIVE CLASSROOM

Grafitti Concepts: Ask students to reflect on the meaning of one of these concepts—"trial by a jury of your peers," "impartial juries," "innocent until proven guilty," and "the rule of law"—and create a visual image and/or phrase that represents that concept. Allow approximately 3 to 5 minutes. Have students post their "grafitti" on the board or on chart paper. Ask students to look at the various responses, then discuss similarities and differences in the responses as a group.

Compare How does Athenian democracy compare to the democratic system of the United States? *(Sample response: Athenian democracy was a direct democracy unlike the representative democracy of the United States; however, the U.S. system could be considered more democratic in that most adult Americans can vote and therefore have a voice in government.)*

D **Differentiate: Special Needs/Extra Support** To reinforce student understanding of the development of direct democracy in Pericles' Athens, have students scan this text section and find the Key Terms and People. Ask students to write a simple explanation of each by illustrating the word, sketching a map, writing a definition, or any combination of these.

Further Instruction

Project the Interactive Reading Notepad questions for this text. Have students answer them as they progress through the text.

The Greek City-States

■ SYNTHESIZE

■ DEMONSTRATE

DIGITAL ACTIVITY

Alliances: Cooperation for a Cause

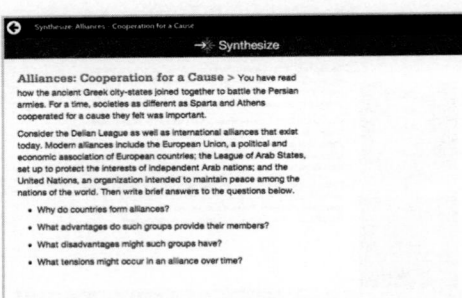

DIGITAL QUIZ

Lesson Quiz and Class Discussion Board

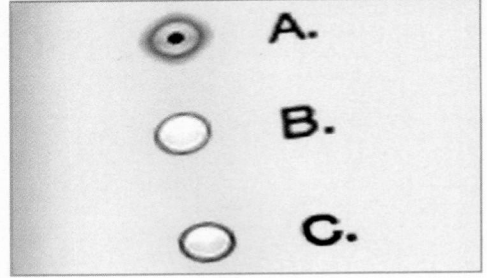

Identify Cause and Effect How were the outcomes of the Persian and Peloponnesian wars alike? How were they different? *(Sample response: Alike: very destructive wars, land battles, Persia involved, Athens captured, Greeks (though not the same Greek city-states) won. Different: no sea battles, Athens, allied with Sparta, emerged from the Persian wars as the most powerful and dominant city-state; Athens, defeated by Sparta, lost dominance in the Greek world after the Peloponnesian War.)*

Hypothesize Why do you think Sparta decided not to destroy Athens at the end of the Peloponnesian War? *(Sample answer: After 27 years of conflict, the Spartans had enough of the war's savagery, decided that their complete victory was enough, and did not feel the need to destroy a fellow Greek city-state.)*

Have students work in pairs to answer the questions in the "Alliances: Cooperation for a Cause" activity. Ask them to take five minutes to brainstorm and write down brief answers to the following questions.

Consider the Delian League as well as modern international alliances, such as the European Union, the League of Arab States, and the United Nations. Why do countries form alliances? What advantages do such groups provide their members? What disadvantages might such groups cause? What tensions might occur in an alliance over time?

Discuss Suppose the Persian Wars have just ended. Should your polis (parts of the class) join the Delian League? Divide the class into three groups: Delian League representatives, citizens wishing to join the league, and citizens who do not want to join. Have the groups meet to prepare their positions to debate the issue. First, the representatives of the Delian League should describe their recent achievements. Next the two sides present their positions in debate on the issue. Then, the citizens/students vote whether to join or not. *(Sample discussion: Delian League representatives describe their glorious victory over the Persians, arguing persuasively for the political and trading advantages of joining with them, perhaps hinting that those not with them will be against them. Citizens in favor of joining list advantages: support against enemies, closer relations with other city-states, favored alliance with Athens, cultural leader of the Greeks. Citizens against joining: point out that their polis has flourished quite well without such an alliance and will likely continue to do so, avoiding entanglement with the problems of other city-states and domination by the ambitious Athenians.)*

Assign the online Lesson Quiz for this lesson if you haven't already done so. Students will be offered automatic remediation or enrichment based on their score.

Pose these questions to the class on the Discussion Board:

In "The Greek City-States" you read about how isolated early Greek city-states turned to sea trading, borrowing and adapting ideas from other early civilizations. Greek forms of government developed from early monarchy and aristocracy to Athens' direct democracy. Greek concepts about the rights and responsibilities of citizens set important standards at this time that influenced later societies. After uniting under Athenian leadership to stop Persian invasions, the Greeks allied but later went to war against each other, and Sparta defeated Athens, ending Athenian political dominance.

Summarize How did the Persian Wars affect the Greek city-states? *(The Persian Wars united the Greek city-sates, increased the power and wealth of Athens, and led to the formatio of the Delian League.)*

Identify Cause and Effect How did the growth of Athenian power lead to war? *(Resentment of Athenian power encouraged Athens' rivals to set up their own alliances, and the rivalry eventually escalated into war.)*

Topic Inquiry

Have students continue their investigations for the Topic Inquiry.

PEARSON realize™
www.PearsonRealize.com
Access your Digital Lesson

Greek Thinkers, Artists, and Writers

Supporting English Language Learners

Use with Digital Text 1, **Philosophers and the Pursuit of Wisdom.**

Listening
Read *Philosophers and the Pursuit of Wisdom* aloud to students. Then instruct students to complete one of the following activities based on their level of English proficiency.

Beginning Explain the components of a complete sentence to students. Use example sentences about Greek philosophers and give examples of independent and dependent clauses. Say each sentence aloud and ask students to repeat. Then ask students to suggest a fact or term from the text. Model creating independent and dependent clauses using that fact. Say these clauses aloud and ask students to try to identify whether each is independent or dependent. Then have students say the clauses aloud.

Intermediate Explain the components of a complete sentence to students. Use one example sentence about Greek philosophers to give examples of independent and dependent clauses. Say the sentence aloud and ask students to repeat. Then have students work together to create independent and dependent clauses about a fact or a term from the text. Provide support and correction as needed. Write and display the sentences and ask students to try to identify the subject and verb of each. Then have students say the sentences aloud.

Advanced Review the difference between dependent and independent clauses. Have students silently reread *Philosophers and the Pursuit of Wisdom*. Then ask students to work with a partner to write four dependent clauses and four independent clauses about the Greek philosophers and their lives. Have pairs share their writing with another pair, forming a group of four. Students should take turns saying their clauses aloud, and the listeners will determine if they hear a dependent or an independent clause. After this, small groups should create complete sentences using all of their clauses and share their sentences with the class.

Advanced High Ask students to explain the difference between dependent and independent clauses and correct any misconceptions. Have students silently reread *Philosophers and the Pursuit of Wisdom*. Then ask students to write four dependent clauses and four independent clauses about the Greek philosophers and their lives. Have students share their writing with a partner. Each student should say their clauses aloud, and the listener will determine if they hear a dependent or an independent clause. After this, pairs should create complete sentences using all of their clauses and share their sentences with the class.

Use with Digital Text 3, **Greek Literature.**

Listening
Read *Greek Literature* aloud to the class. Have students complete one activity according to their level of English proficiency.

Beginning Explain to students that many topics they encounter in history overlap with information they learn in other classes in school. Point out that making connections between familiar and unfamiliar topics can make learning new information a little bit easier. Explain the concepts of tragedy and comedy; write and display their meanings for students to copy into their notebooks. Help students come up with modern examples of each genre. Then reread *Greek Literature* aloud to students and identify examples of each genre in the text.

Intermediate Guide students in a discussion to explore the ideas that many topics they encounter in history overlap with information they learn in other classes in school. Point out that making connections between familiar and unfamiliar topics can make learning new information a little bit easier. Write and display the terms *tragedy* and *comedy*; discuss their meanings with students and ask them to copy the terms and definitions into their notebooks. Brainstorm modern examples of each genre with students. Then reread *Greek Literature* aloud to students and have students identify examples of each genre in the text.

Advanced Ask students to brainstorm examples of how topics they encounter in history class overlap with information they learn in other areas of their lives or in other classes at school. Point out that making connections between familiar and unfamiliar topics can make learning new information a little bit easier. Then have students work together in small groups to generate working definitions for the concepts of *tragedy* and *comedy*. Encourage groups to identify examples of each genre. Then have small groups reread *Greek Literature* and identify examples of each genre from the text.

Advanced High Ask students to brainstorm examples of how topics they encounter in history class overlap with information they learn in other areas of their lives or in other classes at school. Ask students to discuss how making connections between familiar and unfamiliar topics can make learning new information a little bit easier. Then have students work individually to generate working definitions for the concepts of *tragedy* and *comedy*. Encourage students to identify examples of each genre. Then have students work with a partner to reread *Greek Literature* and identify examples of each genre from the text.

⊡ Differentiate Instruction

Use the Differentiated Instruction notes throughout the lesson plan to support the varied skill sets, levels of readiness, and interests in the mixed-ability classroom.

Challenge These notes include suggestions for expanding the activity for advanced students.

On-Level These notes include suggestions for modifying the activity to address different interests or learning styles.

Extra Support These notes include ideas for providing more scaffolding or reading spuport.

Special Needs These notes provide ideas for adapting instruction to support the needs of various special needs students.

■ NOTES

Greek Thinkers, Artists, and Writers

Objectives

Objective 1: Analyze the political and ethical ideas developed by ancient Greek philosophers.

Objective 2: Understand how balance and order governed ancient Greek art and architecture.

Objective 3: Identify the themes explored by ancient Greek writers and historians.

LESSON 3 ORGANIZER			PACING: APPROX. 1 PERIOD, .5 BLOCKS			
			OBJECTIVES	PACING	**RESOURCES**	
					Online	Print
Connect						
	DIGITAL START UP ACTIVITY **A Lasting Legacy**			5 min.	●	
Investigate						
	DIGITAL TEXT 1 **Philosophers and the Pursuit of Wisdom**		Objective 1	10 min.	●	●
	INTERACTIVE CHART **Understanding Greek Philosophers**			10 min.	●	
	DIGITAL TEXT 2 **Conveying Ideals in Art and Architecture**		Objective 2	10 min.	●	●
	INTERACTIVE GALLERY **Art and Architecture of Ancient Greece**			10 min.	●	
	DIGITAL TEXT 3 **Greek Literature**		Objective 3	10 min.	●	●
	DIGITAL TEXT 4 **Studying History**			10 min.	●	●
Synthesize						
	DIGITAL ACTIVITY **Remembering Greece**			5 min.	●	
Demonstrate						
	DIGITAL QUIZ **Lesson Quiz and Class Discussion Board**			10 min.	●	

PEARSON **realize**™
www.PearsonRealize.com

Go online to access additional resources including:
Primary Sources • Biographies • Supreme Court cases •
21st Century Skill Tutorials • Maps • Graphic Organizers.

■ CONNECT

DIGITAL START UP ACTIVITY
A Lasting Legacy

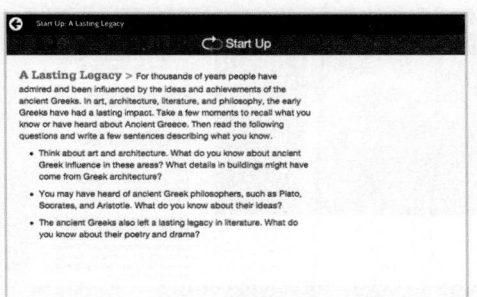

Project the Start Up Activity Ask students to read the introductory text and answer the questions as they get settled. Then have them share their ideas with another student.

Discuss What do you know about Greek art and architecture? *(Students may know the influence of Greek sculpture or that many buildings use Greek elements, such as columns.)* What do you know about Greek philosophers such as Socrates, Plato, and Aristotle? *(Students may cite the Socratic method of teaching.)* What do you know about the poetry and drama of ancient Greece? *(Students may know the poems of Homer or Greek playwrights such as Sophocles.)*

Tell students that in this lesson they will learn about cultural achievements in ancient Greece.

Aa Vocabulary Development: Use the Interactive Reading Notepad to preview the Key Terms and Academic Vocabulary in this Lesson with students.

↕ FLIP IT!

Assign the Flipped Video for this lesson.

■ STUDENT EDITION PRINT
PAGES: 142–147

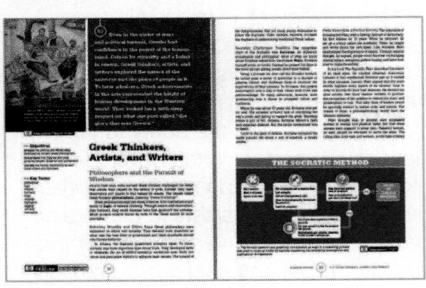

■ INVESTIGATE

DIGITAL TEXT 1
Philosophers and the Pursuit of Wisdom

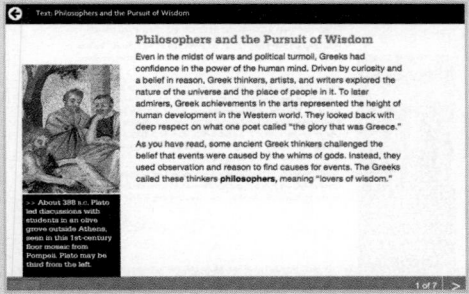

Objective 1: Analyze the political and ethical ideas developed by Greek philosophers.

Quick Instruction

Using observation and reasoning, Greek philosophers explored many subjects, including mathematics, music, ethics, and morality. Socrates, Plato, and Aristotle searched for laws that governed human behavior and the universe, seeking truth by questioning ideas and beliefs, including the authority of traditions. Plato and Aristotle established schools where they taught their ideas and examined many branches of knowledge.

Interactive Chart: Understanding Greek Philosophers Project the chart. Look at each description individually and then the collection of descriptions as a whole.

👥 ACTIVE CLASSROOM

Employ the Make Headlines Strategy with the interactive chart to explore the ideas and techniques of the ancient Greek philosophers. Ask: If you were to write a headline right now to capture the most important aspect that should be remembered about a Greek thinker, what would that headline be? Pass your headline to a partner for them to review— they can keep yours or ask for theirs back. *(Sample answers: "Socrates Seeks Truth With Questions," "Plato Describes Ideal State")*

INTERACTIVE CHART
Understanding Greek Philosophers

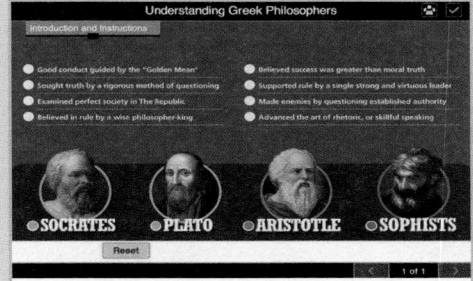

Contrast How did the aims and techniques of the Sophists differ from the goals and approach of Socrates and Plato? *(Answers may vary but should include that the Sophists taught rhetoric, the art of skillful and persuasive speaking. Unlike Socrates and Plato, they believed that success was more important than moral truth. Their teaching did not aim to find truths or develop self-knowledge by questioning and reasoning, unlike the approach taken by Socrates and Plato.)*

ELL Use the ELL activity described in the ELL chart.

Further Instruction

Editable Presentation Use the Editable Presentation to present the main ideas of this text.

Project the Interactive Reading Notepad questions for this text. Have students answer them as they progress through the text. Use the concept web to record the supporting details of the Greek achievements discussed in the section. Add circles as necessary.

Identify Steps in a Process Project "The Socratic Method" infographic on the whiteboard. Discuss with students the relationship between ideas in each text section as well as the layout of the infographic as a whole. Remind students that Socrates applied this method to many different subjects to uncover the underlying assumptions and implications in people's thinking. Ask: What steps did Socrates take to examine the answers people gave to his questions? *(Sample response: Socrates asked a question or had a person make a statement or express*

Greek Thinkers, Artists, and Writers

DIGITAL TEXT 2

Conveying Ideals in Art and Architecture

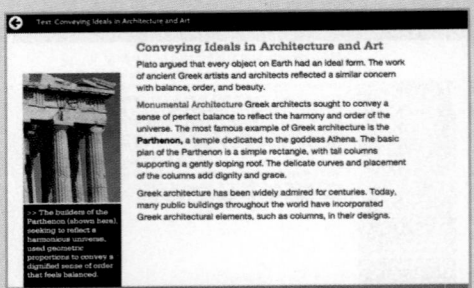

INTERACTIVE GALLERY

Art and Architecture of Ancient Greece

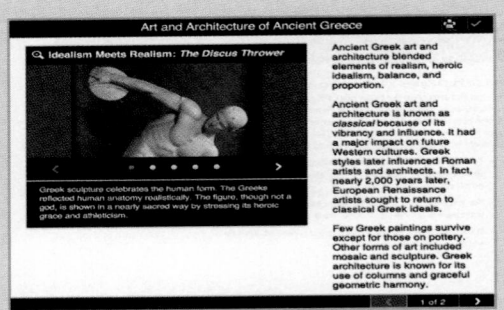

a raw idea. Next, he asked more questions to find premises or assumptions in the answers given. He looked for examples, to see if the premises were valid, and for exceptions, to see if the idea or statement was not always true. He would repeat this question-and-answer process until he arrived at a truth that had no false or imprecise premises or exceptions.)

Predict Consequences Divide students in groups and ask them to consider what they have learned about the Socratic method. What consequences do they predict would result from applying the Socratic method in everyday life? Why? *(Answers may vary. Students may predict that applying the Socratic method would encourage clearer thinking and therefore would encourage greater understanding and insight into many issues and fields of knowledge. Students may also foresee that repeated questioning of people's long-held beliefs could annoy them, causing resentment and resistance. Some people may refuse to examine the implications of their idea and actions.)*

Draw Conclusions Socrates said, "The unexamined life is not worth living." How did his actions support this idea? *(Sample response: Socrates questioned and examined everything in life. He expected others to do so as well. Although his constant questioning and examination brought public disapproval, he continued his questioning because without this, for Socrates, life would not be worth living.)*

D **Differentiate: Challenge/Gifted** Ask students to do additional research on the Sophists, working in a group to briefly jot down information about the ideas and techniques of two or three Sophists.

Objective 2: Understand how balance and order governed Greek art and architecture.

Quick Instruction

Greek architects and artists sought to express in created forms ideals of balance, order, and beauty. Reflecting the harmony and order of the universe, architects attempted to evoke a sense of perfect balance in buildings such as the Parthenon, which has been admired for centuries. Greek sculptors and painters also strived for the ideal by creating the most lifelike and graceful images of perfect human forms.

Interactive Gallery: Art and Architecture of Ancient Greece Project the gallery. Click through the gallery, looking at each image individually and then the collection of images as a whole.

Formulate Questions Have students explore the interactive gallery of ancient Greek art and architecture. Ask students to pair with a partner, examine the gallery hotspots, then ask them: What do you see? What does that make you think? What are you wondering about now that you've seen this? Have students share their insights with the class. *(Answers will vary. Students should observe the variety of images and objects and the elements of balance, order, and beauty they express, think about what kind of people and society produced them, and wonder how such impressive buildings and lifelike human forms could have been created.)*

Analyze Images Study the photograph of the Parthenon. What kinds of modern buildings were influenced by its architecture? Why do you think this is so? *(Sample response: Many buildings—including government buildings,*

financial institutions, and libraries—use the classical style of architecture. The style may have been chosen to emphasize the sense of power, success, timelessness, and equality that are affiliated with ancient Greece.)

⬛ ACTIVE CLASSROOM

Have students describe the Parthenon's history or the history of another object shown in the interactive gallery using the If Photos Could Talk Strategy. Ask: What do you think the Parthenon (or other object) would say about the rise of Athens and the evolution of democracy there if it could talk? What's your evidence? Have students present their responses to the class. *(Sample response: "As a temple dedicated to this city's patron goddess, I watched people pray for my help in their lives—for their children, for success in war, for changes in leadership—and saw the shifting fortunes of Athens.")*

Further Instruction

Go through the Interactive Reading Notepad questions and discuss the answers with the class.

Draw Conclusions Early Greek sculpture portrayed human figures in stylized images like those of ancient Egypt. Then, by the 400s *B.C.*, Greek sculptors began to create more realistic human forms at rest and in motion. Why do you think the ability to portray movement was important in the development of Greek art? *(Sample response: The ability to show movement allowed artists to capture an individual, an action, or an emotion rather than simply making a rigid and cold representation.)*

Summarize Ask students to use examples from the gallery and text to explain why today the art and architecture of ancient Greece is considered "classic"—a standard of excellence against which other art forms are measured. *(Answers may vary but should include discussion of illustrative examples of Greek architecture, sculpture, or painting that embody perfect human form or portray ideal forms of balance, order, and beauty.)*

D Differentiate: Special Needs/Extra Support For visual learners and students who need help with basic skills, direct attention to the "Art and Architecture of Ancient Greece" gallery. Explain that these visuals shows some of the finest examples of Greek art and architecture. Ask volunteers to explain how individual images demonstrate Greek ideals of beauty, balance, and order starting from the left-most image. *(For example, the image of the Parthenon shows a rectangular building with columns. It is built from simple geometric shapes—rectangles, a triangle—arranged in a graceful, orderly, and balanced way.)*

DIGITAL TEXT 3
Greek Literature

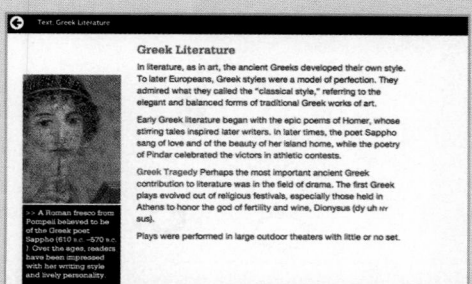

DIGITAL TEXT 4
Studying History

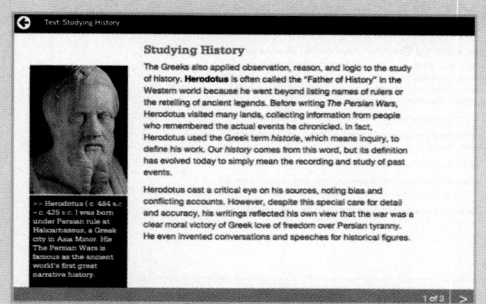

Objective 3: Identify the themes explored by Greek writers and historians.

Quick Instruction

The ancient Greek writers created the elegant and balanced "classical style" admired by later Europeans. Homer's epic poems inspired later Greek poets who sang of love, beauty, and victorious athletes. In tragedies, Greek playwrights explored universal dramatic conflicts between people and the gods, within families, and between individual duty and laws of the state. Comic writers probed current social issues and poked fun at foolish customs.

Analyze Information (a) How were Greek plays performed? (b) What were the topics of Greek poetry and plays? *([a] in outdoor theaters with little or no scenery by actors who wore elaborate costumes and masks [b] Familiar stories were used to explore moral and social issues or the relationship between people and the gods.)*

Infer Why do you think plays were performed in ancient Athens and other Greek cities? *(Answers may vary but should mention to honor and pay tribute to the gods. Students may also include to entertain and inform audiences, and to glorify and express pride in Greek cities.)*

ELL Use the ELL activity described in the ELL chart.

Further Instruction

Ancient Greek historians collected and recorded information about recent events from witnesses. They also carefully inquired and studied evidence from the past, traveling widely and sometimes taking part in the events they chronicled. Herodotus and Thucydides set critical standards in inquiry and presentation for future historians.

Identify Central Issues Why do you think research and avoiding bias is important to the writing of history? *(Without research, historians would lack knowledge of people and events from the past; biased histories would be inaccurate and one-sided, and therefore of very limited value.)*

Predict Consequences Thucydides lived through the Peloponnesian War and saw its effect on those involved in it. How do you think firsthand experience of these events might influence his writing about them? Why? *(Answers may vary. Students may predict that Thucydides' strong feelings would make him unavoidably one-sided and likely inaccurate when writing about events he experienced. Or students may predict his personal experience might powerfully motivate Thucydides to understand as much as he possibly could about all aspects and points of view before writing his history of this war.)*

D Differentiate: Challenge/Gifted Have students consider the importance of Herodotus' and Thucydides' advances in writing history. Then ask them to work in pairs to write a short history of this class period, by collecting information from firsthand observers and presenting it without bias. Have students present their histories to the class.

Greek Thinkers, Artists, and Writers

■ SYNTHESIZE

DIGITAL ACTIVITY
Remembering Greece

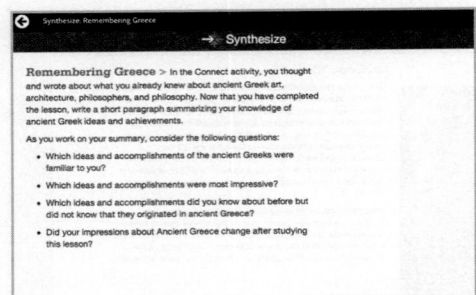

Have students use the Think Pair Share strategy to answer the "Remembering Greece" activity. Ask them to take five minutes to write down brief answers to the questions below, then share their answers with a talking partner. Ask partners to think about the following questions.

Which ideas and accomplishments of the ancient Greeks were familiar to you? Which were most impressive? Which did you know about before but did not know that they originated in ancient Greece? Did your impressions about Greece change after studying this lesson?

Discuss Have students use the Rank It strategy to explore the "Remembering Greece" activity. List the following areas of ancient Greek cultural accomplishments on the board: philosophy, arts (sculpture and painting), architecture, and literature (poetry, drama, history). Ask students to rank the areas according to which had the greatest impact. Have students write down a justification for the ranking decisions they made, citing examples. Then ask students to work in pairs to share their rankings and justifications. Poll the class to see if there is agreement on the ranking. *(Students should be aware that Greek achievements in these areas set standards for later ages. Sample response: Philosophy ranks greatest in impact because the use of reasoning by Socrates, Plato, and Aristotle provided a foundation for logical, clear, and effective thinking in all fields of knowledge since then. I rank literature, particularly drama, next for their deep and enduring insights into human character and motives that the great dramatists [Aeschylus, Sophocles, and Euripides] presented, and for their exploration of major social issues that continue to concern us. Then comes ancient Greek art, including lifelike sculpture and balanced architecture [the Parthenon], setting standards for quality and beauty by their inspiring ideal expressions of the human spirit.)*

■ DEMONSTRATE

DIGITAL QUIZ
Lesson Quiz and Class Discussion Board

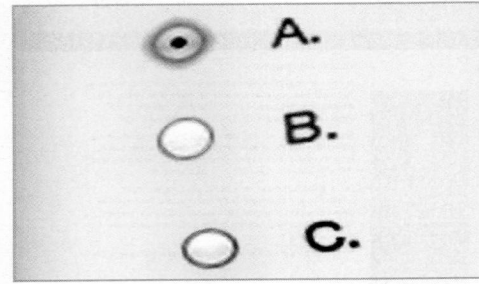

Assign the online Lesson Quiz for this lesson if you haven't already done so. Students will be offered automatic remediation or enrichment based on their score.

Pose these questions to the class on the Discussion Board:

In "Greek Thinkers, Artists, and Writers" you read about ancient Greek philosophers, artists, and writers exploring many subjects and creating "classic" works of art that set standards of excellence. Philosophers used observation and reason to discover moral truths. Greek architects and sculptors sought ideal balance, order, and beauty through elegant design and human beings portrayed in their most perfect graceful form. Greek poets, playwrights, and historians developed their own styles to sing of love and beauty, dramatize conflict, criticize society, and study recent and ancient events.

Cite Evidence How do the roots of modern science go back to the ancient Greek philosophers? Cite evidence from the text to support your answer. *(Sample response: The Greek philosophers believed that by observation and reasoning they could find the laws that governed the universe. These philosophers also studied mathematics and logic. Modern science continues to employ observation, mathematics, and logic to search for and explore such laws or principles.)*

Draw Inferences How do you think art reflects the history of the culture in which it is produced? *(Sample response: Art can reflect the history of a culture by depicting historical events or showing customary daily life. For example, the content and style of figures and scenes painted on vases surviving from ancient Greece reveal many details of everyday activities, including household life, athletic competitions, myths and legends, and religious practices. Such painted scenes also show or imply values that were important to ancient Greeks, such as honor and courage.)*

Topic Inquiry
Have students continue their investigations for the Topic Inquiry.

Alexander the Great and the Legacy of Greece

Supporting English Language Learners

Use with Digital Text 1, **The New Era of Alexander the Great.**

Listening
Read *The New Era of Alexander the Great* aloud to students. Then instruct students to complete one of the following activities based on their level of English proficiency.

Beginning Write and display the following expression from the text: *Alexander the Great.* Read the phrase aloud and have students repeat it. Then explain the meaning of this phrase to students. Tell students that Alexander was not born with the name "the Great"; it was given to him later. Tell students that they will listen as you read *The New Era of Alexander the Great* aloud. As you read, have students think about why Alexander was given this name. Guide a discussion to explore Alexander's leadership characteristics with students.

Intermediate Write and display the following expression from the text, *Alexander the Great.* Read the phrase aloud and have students repeat it. Then discuss the meaning of this phrase with students. Tell students that they will listen as you read *The New Era of Alexander the Great* aloud. As you read, have students think about the kind of leader Alexander the Great was. Discuss students' findings and opinions with the class.

Advanced Write and display the following expression from the text, *Alexander the Great.* Have students say this phrase aloud. Then ask small groups of students to discuss the meaning of this phrase. Each small group should share their explanation of the expression with other groups. Then, using the students' explanations, develop a single explanation students can use to read about Alexander the Great. Ask small groups to think about the kind of leader Alexander the Great was. Have groups discuss their findings and share their opinions with the class.

Advanced High Write and display the following expression from the text, *Alexander the Great*. Have students say this phrase aloud. Then ask pairs of students to discuss the meaning of this phrase and share their explanations with the class. Then, using the students' explanations, develop a single explanation students can use to read about Alexander the Great. Ask pairs to learn about and discuss the kind of leader Alexander the Great was. Facilitate a small group discussion about Alexander's characteristics to allow students to share their ideas with the class.

Use with Digital Text 3, **Hellenistic Arts and Sciences.**

Listening
Read *Hellenistic Arts and Sciences* aloud to the class. Have students complete one activity according to their level of English proficiency.

Beginning Provide students with a simple diagram of a right triangle and the Pythagorean theorem ($a^2 + b^2 = c^2$). Explain the basics of this math equation. Then reread the subsection "Math and Astronomy Advance" and focus on the information about Pythagoras. Explain that the Pythagorean theorem is named after the man who developed it. Help students use their understanding of math to make connections to the text.

Intermediate Provide students with a simple diagram of a right triangle and the Pythagorean theorem ($a^2 + b^2 = c^2$). Ask students to share what they already know about this math equation. Fill in any gaps as needed. Then reread the subsection "Math and Astronomy Advance" and focus on the information about Pythagoras. Ask students to make a connection between the term *Pythagorean theorem* and the name *Pythagoras.* Help students use their understanding of math to make connections to the text.

Advanced Provide students with a simple diagram of a right triangle and the Pythagorean theorem ($a^2 + b^2 = c^2$). Ask students to discuss the theorem in small groups and share what they already know about this math equation. Then have groups share a summary of their discussion with the class. Fill in any gaps as needed. Then instruct small groups to reread the subsection "Math and Astronomy Advance." Ask small groups to discuss any connection between the term *Pythagorean theorem* and the name *Pythagoras.* Ask students to use their understanding of math to make connections to the text.

Advanced High Provide students with a simple diagram of a right triangle and the Pythagorean theorem ($a^2 + b^2 = c^2$). Ask students to discuss the theorem with a partner and share what they already know about this math equation. Then have pairs share a summary of their discussion with another pair. Circulate among students to fill in any knowledge gaps as needed. Then instruct pairs to reread the subsection "Math and Astronomy Advance" and discuss any connection between the term *Pythagorean theorem* and the name *Pythagoras.* Encourage students to use their understanding of math to make connections to the text.

▷ Differentiate Instruction

Use the Differentiated Instruction notes throughout the lesson plan to support the varied skill sets, levels of readiness, and interests in the mixed-ability classroom.

Challenge These notes include suggestions for expanding the activity for advanced students.

On-Level These notes include suggestions for modifying the activity to address different interests or learning styles.

Extra Support These notes include ideas for providing more scaffolding or reading spuport.

Special Needs These notes provide ideas for adapting instruction to support the needs of various special needs students.

■ NOTES

Alexander the Great and the Legacy of Greece

Objectives

Objective 1: Explain how Alexander the Great built an extensive empire.

Objective 2: Describe the empire's cultural impact.

Objective 3: Identify major Hellenic Greek scientists and their discoveries and innovations.

LESSON 4 ORGANIZER		PACING: APPROX. 1 PERIOD, .5 BLOCKS		
				RESOURCES
	OBJECTIVES	PACING	Online	Print
Connect				
DIGITAL START UP ACTIVITY **The Golden Age**		5 min.	●	
Investigate				
DIGITAL TEXT 1 **The New Era of Alexander the Great**	Objective 1	10 min.	●	●
INTERACTIVE GALLERY **Alexander the Great's Conquests and Contributions**		10 min.	●	
DIGITAL TEXT 2 **Alexander's Legacy**	Objective 2	10 min.	●	●
DIGITAL TEXT 3 **Hellenistic Arts and Sciences**	Objective 3	10 min.	●	●
INTERACTIVE GALLERY **Math, Science, and Technology in the Hellenistic Age**		10 min.	●	
Synthesize				
DIGITAL ACTIVITY **Effects of Size**		5 min.	●	
Demonstrate				
DIGITAL QUIZ **Lesson Quiz and Class Discussion Board**		10 min.	●	

CONNECT

DIGITAL START UP ACTIVITY
The Golden Age

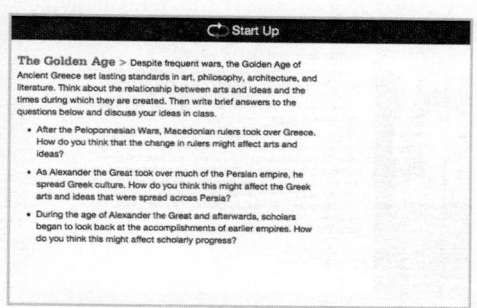

Project the Start Up Activity Ask students to read the introductory text and answer the questions as they get settled. Then have them share their ideas with another student.

Discuss After the Peloponnesian Wars, Macedonian rulers took over Greece. How might this change affect arts and ideas? *(New rulers might bring new ideas or customs that would affect Greek culture.)*

Tell students that in this lesson they will learn how Alexander the Great conquered vast territories and spread Greek culture. A new Hellenistic culture gradually emerged and led to important Greek works in the arts and sciences.

Aa Vocabulary Development: Use the Interactive Reading Notepad to preview the Key Terms and Academic Vocabulary in this Lesson with students.

⇅ FLIP IT!
Assign the Flipped Video for this lesson.

■ STUDENT EDITION PRINT
PAGES: 148–152

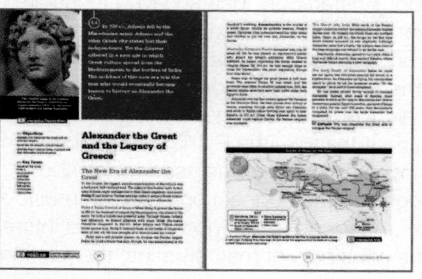

INVESTIGATE

DIGITAL TEXT 1
The New Era of Alexander the Great

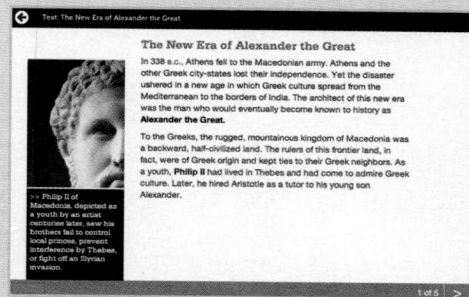

INTERACTIVE GALLERY
Alexander the Great's Conquests and Contributions

Objective 1: Explain how Alexander the Great built an extensive empire.

Quick Instruction
Interactive Gallery: Alexander the Great's Conquests and Contributions Project the gallery on the whiteboard. Click through the hot spots on the gallery and discuss Alexander's life and series of conquests. Remind students that Alexander, at age 20, unexpectedly became ruler of the backward kingdom of Macedonia when his father was assassinated. During the next 12 years, he led his army to conquer an empire that stretched from Greece to India.

💬 ACTIVE CLASSROOM
You are having a conversation with Alexander the Great. Write down a question you'd like to ask, then what that person would say to you, and what you would say in response. *(Possible answer: I ask Alexander, "Now that you've returned from India, what are you going to do next?" Alexander: "Conquer Africa and Asia and then set up cities and colonies there." Me: "So Greek civilization will continue to spread, influencing and blending with many more cultures.")*

ELL Use the ELL activity described in the ELL chart.

Further Instruction
Editable Presentation Use the Editable Presentation to present the main ideas of this text.

Project the Interactive Reading Notepad questions provided in the notepad. Have students answer them as they progress through the core reading. Make an outline to keep track of the important main ideas and supporting details of the empire of Alexander the Great.

Hypothesize After Darius was murdered and Alexander controlled much of the Persian empire, why do you think he continued his conquests? *(Possible answer: Defeating the Persians may have only intensified Alexander's restless drive to conquer the world. Perhaps he felt impelled by his personal destiny to conquer and rule all men. With Persia in his grasp, Alexander's armies could now expand the empire into Asia.)*

Infer What might be some of the unmentioned costs of Alexander's conquests? *(Sample responses: injuries and loss of many lives, destruction of the property and livelihoods of conquered peoples, loss of control of Greek politics)*

D Differentiate: Special Needs/Extra Support Because the earliest surviving sources about Alexander the Great were written three centuries after his exploits, modern historians must carefully sift through the evidence to separate the man from the myths that have grown up around him. Ask students what they know of more modern leaders, such as the president, and how they compare to Alexander. Ask students to discuss if Alexander fits with the title "the great."

Alexander the Great and the Legacy of Greece

DIGITAL TEXT 2

Alexander's Legacy

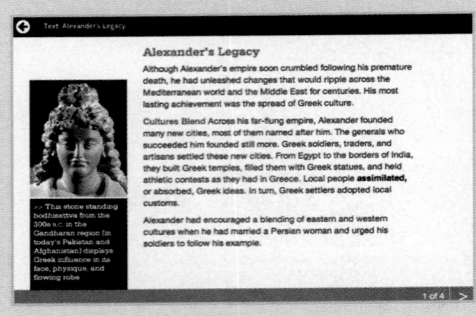

DIGITAL TEXT 3

Hellenistic Arts and Sciences

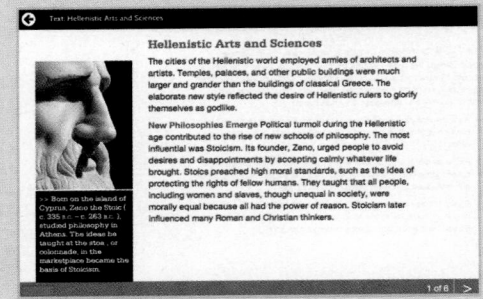

Objective 2: Describe the empire's cultural impact.

Quick Instruction

Project the image of the Pharos lighthouse, and tell students that it was one of the Seven Wonders of the World. Although Alexander's empire soon fell apart, his campaigns and conquests spread Greek culture from Persia to northern India. Greek soldiers, traders, and artisans settled in the newly founded cities, introducing Greek ideas and traditions. Over time, a new Hellenistic culture arose.

Identify Cause and Effect What factors shaped Hellenistic civilization? *(Alexander and his generals founded new cities settled by Greeks who brought their culture with them; local people assimilated Greek ideas; Greeks adopted local customs. This blending of influences created a new Hellenistic culture.)*

Infer Discuss the changing role of women, who were no longer restricted to their homes during the Hellenistic period. More women learned to read and write. Some became philosophers or poets. Royal women held considerable power, working alongside husbands and sons who were the actual rulers. Ask women began to play new roles during the Hellenistic period? *(Answers will vary. Sample response: The Hellenistic blending of ideas and customs from many cultures likely offered new social possibilities for men and women. During such a time, perhaps there was greater openness and tolerance for women to be educated and play more active roles beyond the household—in society and politics.)*

Further Instruction

Alexander's Legacy Project the Interactive Reading Notepad questions and discuss the answers with the class. Use details from students' note-taking outlines to trace the growth and cultural impact of Alexander the Great's empire.

Then project the photograph of the stone standing bodhisattva from Gandhara on the whiteboard. Look at each detail of the image and then the statue as a whole. Explain that a bodhisattva compassionately helps to save and enlighten others and is worshipped as a deity in Mahayana Buddhism.

Analyze Images Ask students which details of this bodhisattva show the influence of the classical Greek style? *(Answers will vary. Students should mention that the artist's treatment of the bodhisattva's face, muscular physique, and folds of clothing is similar to the style of classical Greek statues.)*

Draw Conclusions Why do you think Alexandria became the greatest of Hellenistic capitals? *(Answers will vary. Sample response: Alexandria's strategic location on sea lanes between Europe and Asia, great markets, mix of cultural resources and influences, and Alexander and his successors' encouragement of learning made it the greatest Hellenistic capital.)*

Objective 3: Identify major Greek scientists and their discoveries and inventions.

Quick Instruction

Interactive Gallery: Math, Science, and Technology in the Hellenistic Age Project the gallery on the whiteboard and look at each image individually as well as the collection as a whole and its layout. Review with students the ideas and inventions in the "Hellenistic Arts and Sciences" text, and identify the diffusion of major ideas in science, mathematics, and technology. Archimedes applied laws of physics (the lever and pulley) to devise practical inventions. The claw was type of crane that could be used in war to pick up attacking ships. The Archimedes screw, a mechanical pump used to lift water in irrigation, spread widely in ancient times and continues to be used in many places today. Eratosthenes showed Earth was round and used geometry to accurately estimate the size of the earth. Ancient writers preserved some of his calculations for later eras. Aristarchus argued that Earth rotated on its axis and orbited the sun (heliocentric solar system theory, recognized today). Although most scientists did not accept his heliocentric theory, Aristarchus' idea survived to inspire the major heliocentric theory presented by Polish astronomer Copernicus in the 1500s. The mathematician Pythagoras derived a formula to calculate the relationship between the sides of a right triangle (the Pythagorean Theorem). He invented math terms used today and recognized the connection between music and math. Although he left no writings, his interest in the principles of mathematics, the relations

INTERACTIVE GALLERY

Math, Science, and Technology in the Hellenistic Age

between numbers, and the idea of a proof influenced Plato, Aristotle, and through them, all of Western thought.

Analyze Images Identify major ideas in technology invented by Hellenistic Greeks shown and described in the gallery and text. Who invented these ideas? How did they influence later eras? Cite information to support your answer. *(Answers will vary but should identify Archimedes.)*

Summarize What major ideas in science did Hellenistic Greeks originate? Who discovered them? How did they spread to impact later societies? Cite information from the gallery and the text in your answer. *(Answers will vary but should identify Eratosthenes and/or Aristarchus.)*

Summarize Describe major ideas in mathematics originated by Hellenistic Greeks. Who discovered these ideas? How did they spread to influence later times? Cite information from the gallery and the text in your answer. *(Answers will vary but should identify Pythagoras.)*

ACTIVE CLASSROOM

Have students spend three minutes jotting down their response to this question on sticky notes: *Viewed as a whole, what does this gallery tell you about Hellenistic advances in science and technology?* Have students pair up and share their responses. Ask students to post their sticky notes on the board or chart paper and then have students look at all the various responses, discussing similarities and differences in the responses as a group. (Sample responses: During the Hellenistic period, Greek scientists made many important and useful advances. For example in medicine, a new theory proposed that illness had natural causes, rather than being caused by the gods, and so causes and cures of illnesses could be determined by observing patients.

Determine Relevance How did the vast expanse of Alexander's empire help promote advances in science and mathematics? *(Scientists and mathematicians could draw on the knowledge of many cultures, and in turn spread new ideas throughout the empire.)*

ELL Use the ELL activity described in the ELL chart.

Further Instruction

Project the Interactive Reading Notepad questions provided in the notepad. Have students answer them as they progress through the core reading.

Remind students that Hellenistic era thinkers, mathematicians, and scientists, such as Zeno,

Pythagoras, and Archimedes—who explored new ideas and devised useful inventions during the Hellenistic period—added their accomplishments to the important earlier Greek achievements students have already studied in politics, philosophy, the arts, architecture, and literature to form ancient Greece's legacy to later civilizations.

Infographic: The Greek Legacy Project the infographic on the whiteboard. Look at the sections describing the legacy of ancient Greece in government; culture; the arts; and mathematics, science, and technology. Then consider the infographic as a whole.

Categorize Which aspect of ancient Greece's legacy do you think is most important? Why? *(Answers will vary. Sample response: I think the Greek legacy in government, including citizens making laws, rule by majority vote, and trial by jury, is most important because it encourages people to participate in government, provides possibilities for change, and encourages fairness and justice.)*

Draw Conclusions Why do you think there were so many advances made during the Hellenistic Age? *(Sample response: The blending of cultures and ideas characteristic of this period greatly encouraged and stimulated people's thinking. This led to many discoveries and creative solutions in many fields of knowledge.)*

D Differentiate: Special Needs/Extra Support Students may use the examples of Hellenistic art and artifacts presented in this section to learn about Hellenistic civilization. Ask: What does each image show about the nature and achievements of the Hellenistic world? *(Sample response: They show the influence and spread of Greek culture, and the importance of science and technology throughout the Hellenistic world.)*

Alexander the Great and the Legacy of Greece

■ SYNTHESIZE

DIGITAL ACTIVITY
Effects of Size

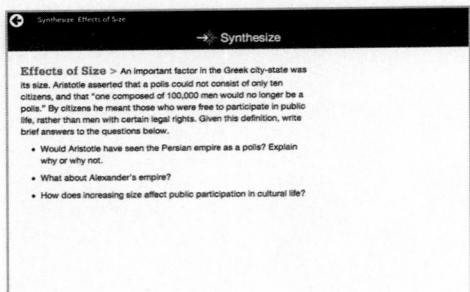

Have students form small groups to answer the questions in the "Effects of Size" activity. Ask them to take five minutes to brainstorm and write down brief answers to the following questions.

Aristotle asserted that a polis could not consist of only ten citizens, and that "one composed of 100,000 men would no longer be a polis." Would Aristotle have seen the Persian empire as a polis? Explain why or why not. What about Alexander's empire? How does increasing size affect public participation in cultural life?

Discuss In light of Aristotle's statement above, if he were alive today, what do you think he would say about the effects of size on a modern political state? Would modern electronic communication and present-day transportation influence his view? Why or why not? *(Sample response: Aristotle would think a modern political state (like Alexander's empire) was far too large to function as a polis—direct participation by citizens would be impossible, elected representatives would be necessary. Advanced modern communication and transportation would not influence his opinion that when a state grows beyond a certain point it cannot be a polis.)*

■ DEMONSTRATE

DIGITAL QUIZ
Lesson Quiz and Class Discussion Board

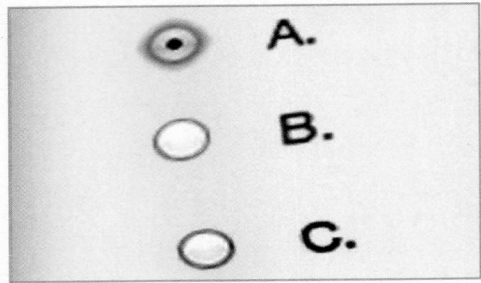

Assign the online Lesson Quiz for this lesson if you haven't already done so. Students will be offered automatic enrichment based on their score.

Pose these questions to the class on the Discussion Board:

In "Alexander the Great and the Legacy of Greece" you read about young Alexander conquering lands from Persia to the borders of India, founding cities, and spreading Greek culture. In time, a new Hellenistic civilization arose that blended Greek, Persian, Egyptian, and Indian influences. Building on earlier efforts from various cultures, important advances were made in mathematics, science, and technology. These Hellenistic achievements became part of the legacy of Greece, setting a standard for later Europeans.

Predict Consequences How do you think Alexander the Great's empire would have developed if he and his successors had not founded many Greek cities and encouraged Greek settlement? *(Answers may vary. Students may say such a large and varied empire was inherently unstable, and could not be held together for long—destined to split apart even sooner had Greek cities not been established. Other students may mention that the Hellenistic civilization's blending of Greek, Persian, Egyptian, and Indian influences may not have occurred or, if so, with far fewer creative outcomes.)*

Summarize What were some of the main achievements of mathematicians and scientists of the Hellenistic era? *(Answers may vary. Students may include: the mathematician Pythagoras derived a formula to calculate the relationship between the sides of a right triangle; the astronomer Eratosthenes showed that Earth was round and correctly computed its size; Aristarchus stated that Earth rotated on its axis and orbited the sun; Euclid created a textbook that became the basis for modern geometry; and Archimedes, mastering the lever and the pulley, made practical inventions by applying the laws of physics.)*

Topic Inquiry

Have students continue their investigations for the Topic Inquiry.

Ancient Greece (1750 B.C.–133 B.C.)

■ SYNTHESIZE

DIGITAL ACTIVITY
Reflect on the Essential Question and Topic

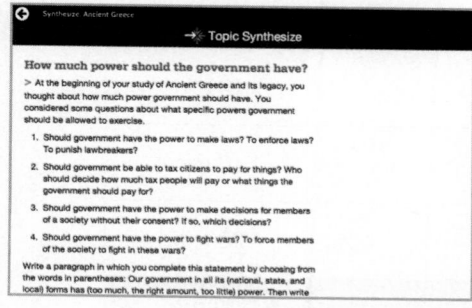

Ask students to reconsider the Essential Question: How much power should the government have? Remind students of the questions they discussed at the start of the Topic:

- Should government have the power to make laws? To enforce laws? To punish lawbreakers?

- Should government be able to tax citizens to pay for things? Who should decide how much tax people will pay or what things the government should pay for?

- Should government have the power to make decisions for members of the society? If so, which decisions?

- Should government have the power to fight wars? To force members of the society to fight in these wars?

Then have students write their paragraphs responding to the statement: Our government (national, state, and local) has (too much, the right amount, too little) power. Suggest they start by listing types of government power. Share these examples:

- maintaining an army
- building roads and bridges
- establishing public schools
- responding to natural disasters

Have volunteers read their paragraphs and discuss issues raised. Next ask students to reflect on the achievements and legacy of Ancient Greece. Conclude by asking the class to discuss this question: Could I have lived in Ancient Greece? Why or why not? You may ask student pairs to share their suggestions with the class.

Topic Inquiry
Have students complete Step 3 of the Topic Inquiry.

■ DEMONSTRATE

DIGITAL TOPIC REVIEW AND ASSESSMENT
Ancient Greece (1750 B.C.–133 B.C.)

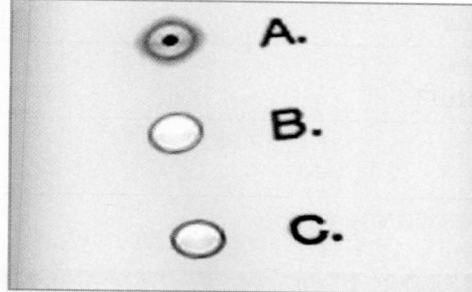

Students can prepare for the Topic Test by answering the questions in the Topic Review and Assessment online or the Assessment questions in the Print Student text. They can also prepare by reviewing their answers to the Interactive Reading Notepad questions or reviewing their notes in the Reading and Notetaking Study Guide.

DIGITAL TOPIC TEST
Ancient Greece (1750 B.C.–133 B.C.)

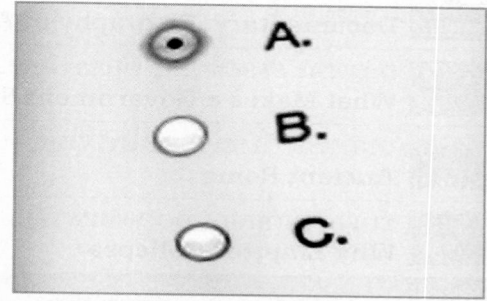

TOPIC TEST
Assign the Topic Test to assess students' understanding of topic content.

BENCHMARK TESTS
Assign these benchmark tests as you complete the relevant topics to monitor student progress toward mastering the course content and as preparation for the End-of-Course Test.

Benchmark Test 1: Topics 1–5

Benchmark Test 2: Topics 6–10

Benchmark Test 3: Topics 11–15

Benchmark Test 4: Topics 16–21

Ancient Rome and the Origins of Christianity (509 B.C.–A.D. 476)

TOPIC 6 ORGANIZER	PACING: APPROX. 7 PERIODS, 3.5 BLOCKS
	PACING
Connect	1 period
MY STORY VIDEO **Documentary: Biography of Augustus**	10 min.
DIGITAL ESSENTIAL QUESTION ACTIVITY **What Makes a Government Successful?**	10 min.
DIGITAL TIMELINE ACTIVITY **Ancient Rome**	10 min.
TOPIC INQUIRY: DOCUMENT-BASED QUESTION **Why Empires Collapse**	20 min.
Investigate	2–4 periods
TOPIC INQUIRY: DOCUMENT-BASED QUESTION **Why Empires Collapse**	Ongoing
LESSON 1 The Roman Republic	30–40 min.
LESSON 2 The Roman Empire: Rise and Decline	30–40 min.
LESSON 3 The Legacy of Rome	30–40 min.
LESSON 4 The Origins of Christianity	30–40 min.
Synthesize	1 period
DIGITAL ESSENTIAL QUESTION ACTIVITY **Reflect on the Essential Question and Topic**	10 min.
TOPIC INQUIRY: DOCUMENT-BASED QUESTION **Why Empires Collapse**	20 min.
Demonstrate	1–2 periods
ONLINE TEST **Ancient Rome and Early Christianity**	10 min.
TOPIC INQUIRY: DOCUMENT-BASED QUESTION **Why Empires Collapse**	20 min.

 TOPIC INQUIRY: DOCUMENT-BASED QUESTION

Why Empires Collapse

In this Topic Inquiry, students work in teams to research and create a multimedia presentation about the collapse of the Roman empire, Han dynasty, and Inca empire. Learning more about these empires and their collapse will contribute to students understanding of the Topic Essential Question: What makes a government successful?

STEP 1: CONNECT
Develop Questions and Plan the Investigation

Launch the Project and Generate Questions
Display the invitation from the Committee for Global Hotspots. Tell students they will have to research and create a multimedia presentation about the Roman empire, Han dynasty, or Inca empire focusing on its rise to power and the reasons for its collapse. Have them review the *Rubric for a Group Presentation* to establish expectations.

Suggestion: To get started, have students discuss and take notes about what they already know.

Plan the Investigation
Form students into teams. Have students sign the *Project Contract*, and assign team roles using the roles document in *Project Tracker*. Give students examples of how to break down the Driving Question to begin the *Need-to-Know Questions*.

Suggestion: You can control the length of the project by removing some of the elements, such as the timeline or cultural achievements image gallery. Similarly, if you prefer that each student do more research, form more than three teams.

Resources
- Project Contract
- Need-to-Know Questions
- Project Tracker
- Student Instructions

STEP 2: INVESTIGATE
Apply Disciplinary Concepts and Tools

Conduct Research
Before students begin their investigation, have them review the Skills Tutorial, *Work In Teams*.

Teams will learn how to assign tasks and monitor their work with the *Project Tracker*. They will brainstorm how to approach their subject, keeping in mind the Driving Question, What causes empires to collapse?

To guide their research, teams will create a list of *Need-to-Know Questions* about their empire or dynasty. Refer students to helpful resources within the core content of the topic to help answer their questions. For example, if they are researching cultural accomplishments, refer them to the readings and activities in Lesson 3. Help students begin to fill out the *Information Organizer*.

Suggestion: If your class has limited access to the Internet, you could make several books available to students, such as *The Ancient Romans* by Kathryn Hinds and *The Ancient Inca* by Patricia Calvert.

Write and Edit Presentation
The teams should plan how to present the information they have gathered. Next, students should write their presentation and create any visual elements, such as timelines and maps, that will be included in their presentation. When students do peer review of their work, remind them to offer detailed, constructive criticism.

Resources
- Project Tracker
- Information Organizer

⏻ PROFESSIONAL DEVELOPMENT

Document-Based Question
Be sure to view the Document-Based Question Professional Development resources in the online course.

STEP 3: SYNTHESIZE
Evaluate Sources and
Use Evidence to Formulate Conclusions

Create Your Presentation

Now have students get together to create their presentation. If students are having trouble sharing the work on this part of the project, remind them to review their *Roles for a Group Presentation* in the *Project Tracker*. Review each team's progress on their presentation to make sure they are on track. For students who are having trouble with their presentation, take a look at the Model Presentation as a class to get ideas.

Suggestion: For a less technology-dependent end product, have students assemble and organize the most important elements of their project and design a poster board to accompany their presentation. To take the technology a step further, have students incorporate audio or video into their presentation.

Review Your Presentation

Have students review one another's work and offer suggestions and edits to improve the text and visuals. Be prepared to offer advice on how to improve the teams' products.

Write a Conclusion

Have students write a conclusion about the Driving Question based on their work on the presentation. To help teams start, have each team member write down his or her answer to a different question listed in the *Student Instructions* and then share those answers with their team.

Resources

- 21st Century Skill Tutorials: Participate in a Dicussion or Debate
- 21st Century Skill Tutorials: Give an Effective Presentation

STEP 4: DEMONSTRATE
Communicate Conclusions
and Take Informed Action

Give Your Presentation

Have students prepare their collapse of empire presentations, then watch the team presentations. To help the teams structure their time, set up a clock in the back of the room and alert them when they have only a few minutes left.

Compare Conclusions

Lead a class discussion about each team's conclusions. First, have students compare common elements of each government's collapse. Then lead a discussion about modern nations that might be experiencing similar issues. Each team should use the *Information Organizer II* to record its thoughts.

Have students revise their presentation's conclusion by adding a comparison between the collapse of the Roman empire, Han dynasty, and Inca empire. Next, have students write a letter to the Committee for Global Hotspots detailing their conclusions.

Reflect on the Project

After students have finished their Team Assessments, help them go over what they thought went well and what did not, so they can be even more effective in the future.

Suggestion: As an extension activity, have students research a government today and compare its problems to the common elements of government collapse they uncovered in their project.

Resources

- Group Presentation Rubric   • Self-Assessment
- Information Organizer II

Ancient Rome and the Origins of Christianity (509 B.C.–A.D. 476)

The Roman civilization grew from a city on the Tiber to become a republic that spanned Europe and the Mediterranean. Many of the features of Rome's republican government would inspire Western democratic governments centuries later. Rome embraced Greek learning and beliefs, creating a Greco-Roman culture that is considered the basis of Western civilization. When Augustus took power, Rome became an empire and an era of prosperity began. Later, internal unrest and a relentless series of invasions led to the fall of the western empire. During the Roman empire, a new religion arose in the territory of Judea. Based upon the teachings of Jesus, Christianity spread throughout the empire until it became its official religion. What major influences does Rome have on our world today?

CONNECT

MY STORY VIDEO
Documentary: Biography of Augustus

Augustus, The Pax Romana Watch a video showing the story of Augustus.

Check Understanding Who was Augustus? *(the first emperor of Rome)*

Determine Point of View Augustus said, "I found Rome a city of bricks and left it a city of marble." What did he mean and how credible is his point of view? *(Augustus contributed to the growth of Rome's empire and to its prosperity. While it was in his interest to exaggerate his role, he is nevertheless viewed by scholars as one of the most significant figures in Roman history.)*

DIGITAL ESSENTIAL QUESTION ACTIVITY
What Makes a Government Successful?

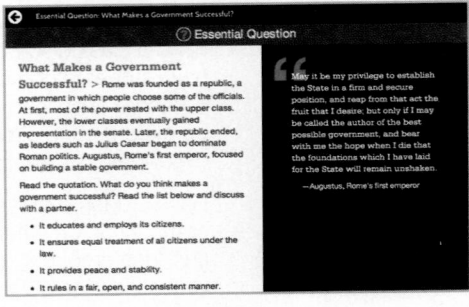

Ask students to think about the Essential Question for this Topic: What makes a government successful?

If students have not already done so, ask them to rank each of the criteria of good government in importance. Then go over the results as a class.

Support a Point of View with Evidence Why did you rank one of the criteria as most important?

Identify Central Issues What role does a citizen have in making government a success? *(Answers may vary. A citizen can vote, serve in the government or the military, obey the laws, pay taxes, serve on juries, and volunteer for community service.)*

Cause and Effect How would ensuring equal treatment of all citizens under the law contribute to a government's success? *(Answers may vary. Students might respond that citizens who perceive the law as fair would support the government and would be less likely to participate in civic unrest.)*

DIGITAL TIMELINE ACTIVITY
Ancient Rome

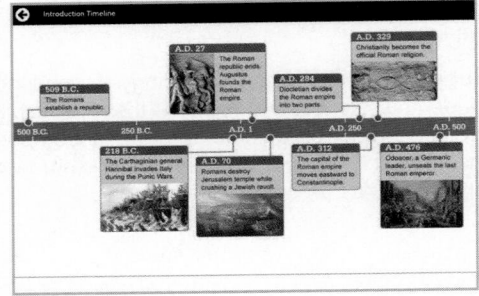

Display the timeline showing the major events of ancient Rome. While exploring this topic, students will learn about all of these events and many more, but this timeline will provide a framework into which they can place the events they learn about.

D **Differentiate: Extra Support** How many years are there between the establishment of the republic and when Augustus becomes the first Roman emperor? *(482; the republic was founded in 509 B.C.; Augustus became emperor in 27 B.C.)*

Check Understanding In what year did Christianity become the official Roman religion? *(A.D. 392)*

PEARSON
realize™
www.PearsonRealize.com
Access your Digital Lesson

The Roman Republic

Supporting English Language Learners

Use with Digital Text 2, **The Early Roman Republic.**

Listening
To help students learn basic vocabulary, tell them to listen carefully as others discuss vocabulary related to *The Early Roman Republic*. Then guide students in how to use these new terms as they explain aspects of government in the Roman republic.

Beginning Display the terms *republic* and *senate*. Read the terms and their definitions aloud. Ask students to listen carefully as you rephrase the definitions using words with which they are familiar. Then reread sentences in the text that contain these words aloud. Have students keep a log of new words, creating definitions in familiar English words, drawings, or in their native language.

Intermediate Display the words *senator, patrician, nominate,* and *consul*. Read the terms and their definitions aloud. Ask students to listen as volunteers describe the role of the senate in the Roman republic. Then have them complete these oral sentence frames: The role of the senate was _____. Senators were from the class of _____. Consuls were nominated by _____. Their job was _____.

Advanced Display the words *republic, senator, patrician, nominate, consul,* and *dictator*. Have student pairs take turns listening to each other explain each term as it relates to the Roman republic. Then have them work together to write a few sentences describing the government of the Roman republic. Ask volunteers to read their sentences aloud and answer questions from the group.

Advanced High Display the words *senator, patrician, consul, dictator, plebian* and *tribune*. Have pairs take turns listening to each other explain each term as it relates to the Roman republic. Then have them construct a graphic organizer explaining the different roles of a senator, a consul, and a dictator in the Roman republic. Ask them to share it with the group and answer questions.

Use with Digital Text 3, **Roman Society.**

Listening
To give students practice in understanding the main points of this reading, tell them to listen carefully to the reading and to the discussions that follow. Read aloud, or ask a volunteer to read, the introduction and the two sections, "The Role of Women" and "Roman Education" under the heading *Roman Society*. Then have students demonstrate their listening comprehension skills by completing the following tasks.

Beginning Ask students questions that can be answered by "Yes" or "No" or a few familiar words. Questions should be about the different roles of men and women in Roman society. Some examples: Was the mother or father the head of the family? Could women own shops? Did girls go to school?

Intermediate Have students describe the roles of women in Roman society. Have students complete these oral sentence frames: Women could _____ but they could not _____. Men usually _____ while women _____. These students can also work with advanced students to complete a Venn diagram as described under the Advanced instructions.

Advanced Have advanced and advanced high students meet in small groups with beginning and/or intermediate ELL classmates to discuss the roles of women and men in Roman society. Instruct advanced students to use the questions and oral sentence frames under the headings *Beginning* and *Intermediate*. Have the groups work together to fill in a Venn diagram showing the different roles of the genders and their overlapping, or similar, roles.

Advanced High Ask these students to work together to present an oral summary of the differences and similarities in the roles of men and women in Roman society. Tell them to use compare/contrast words such as *but, on the other hand,* and *instead*.

▶ Differentiate Instruction

Use the Differentiated Instruction notes throughout the lesson plan to support the varied skill sets, levels of readiness, and interests in the mixed-ability classroom.

Challenge These notes include suggestions for expanding the activity for advanced students.

On-Level These notes include suggestions for modifying the activity to address different interests or learning styles.

Extra Support These notes include ideas for providing more scaffolding or reading spuport.

Special Needs These notes provide ideas for adapting instruction to support the needs of various special needs students.

■ NOTES

_____

_____

_____

_____

_____

The Roman Republic

Objectives

Objective 1: Describe the development of the classical civilization of Rome.

Objective 2: Outline how the Roman republic was structured and governed.

Objective 3: Understand the rights and religious practices that characterized Roman society.

Objective 4: Explain how the Roman republic grew and used its political influence.

LESSON 1 ORGANIZER		PACING: APPROX. 1 PERIOD, .5 BLOCKS			
				RESOURCES	
		OBJECTIVES	**PACING**	**Online**	**Print**
Connect					
DIGITAL START UP ACTIVITY **From Humble Beginnings**			5 min.	●	
Investigate					
DIGITAL TEXT 1 **The Rise of the Roman Civilization**		Objective 1	10 min.	●	●
DIGITAL TEXT 2 **The Early Roman Republic**		Objective 2	10 min.	●	●
INTERACTIVE GALLERY **The Roman *Cursus Honorum***			10 min.	●	
DIGITAL TEXT 3 **Roman Society**		Objective 3	10 min.	●	●
DIGITAL TEXT 4 **The Roman Republic Expands**		Objective 4	10 min.	●	●
INTERACTIVE MAP **Growth of the Roman Republic, 500 B.C. to 44 B.C.**			10 min.	●	
Synthesize					
DIGITAL SYNTHESIZE ACTIVITY **Communication Is Key**			5 min.	●	
Demonstrate					
LESSON QUIZ **Lesson Quiz and Class Discussion Board**			10 min.	●	

PEARSON
realize™
www.PearsonRealize.com

Go online to access additional resources including:
Primary Sources • Biographies • Supreme Court cases •
21st Century Skill Tutorials • Maps • Graphic Organizers.

■ CONNECT

DIGITAL START UP ACTIVITY
From Humble Beginnings

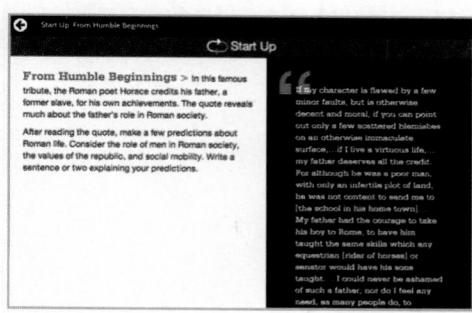

Project the Start Up Activity *From Humble Beginnings*. After reading the quote and looking at the image, have students make a few predictions about Roman life. Tell them to consider the role of men in Roman society, the values of the republic, and social mobility. Ask them to write a sentence or two explaining their response.

Discuss What do you think Horace meant, "my father was a poor man….my father had the courage to take his boy to Rome...taught the same skills which any...senator would have his sons taught...."? *(Roman Society emphasized education. His father, a former slave, understood how to advance through life and made sacrifices so his son could become accomplished.)*

Tell students they will be learning about the Roman republic's origin, structure, society, and evolution.

⇅ FLIP IT!
Assign the Flipped Video for this lesson.

■ STUDENT EDITION PRINT
PAGES: 158–162

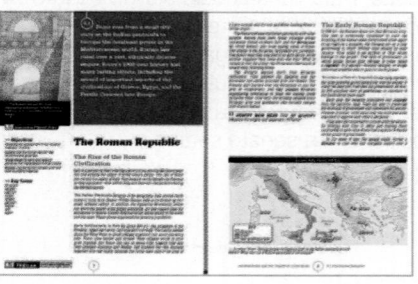

■ INVESTIGATE

DIGITAL TEXT 1
The Rise of the Roman Civilization

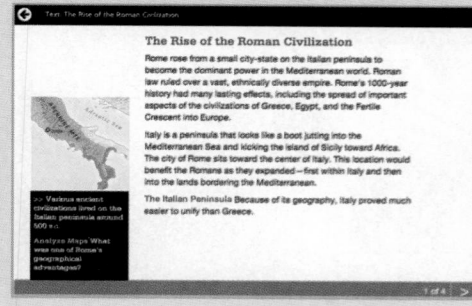

Objective 1: Describe the development of the classical civilization of Rome.

Quick Instruction

Remind students that Roman ancestors, the Latins, migrated to Italy by 800 B.C. According to legend, the twin brothers Romulus and Remus founded the city that would become the heart of the classical civilization of Rome.

Analyze Maps: Ancient Italy About 500 B.C. Project the map on the whiteboard. Have the class look at the legend and then the map. Have students identify which cultures lived on the Italian peninsula. *(The Etruscans controlled the area to the north of Rome's territory. Northern Africa, closest to Italy, was Carthaginian territory. The area on the southern side of Sicily and the toe and a small portion of the Italian boot belonged to the Greeks.)* Ask students to describe the role geography played in the rise of Rome. *(Sample response: The Italian peninsula is in the center of the Mediterranean Sea. The city of Rome is located toward the center of the peninsula at the mouth of the Tiber River. Rome has a prime location, with water access to the interior and a port for maritime trade. In times of war, Romans could move troops by land or by sea.)*

Further Instruction

The Rise of the Roman Civilization: Core Reading and Interactive Reading Notepad Project and discuss the Close Reading Notepad questions, including the graphic organizer asking students to categorize the different civilizations on the Italian peninsula and their contributions to Roman culture. Discuss the different groups with the class and fill in the graphic organizer on the whiteboard as you go.

Although the Greeks and Etruscans contributed to the development of Roman culture, they also stood in the way of Roman expansion.

Predict Consequences As Rome expands, what do you think its relationship will be with neighboring cultures? *(Sample response: Increased contact will create conflict, and Rome will want to conquer the Greeks and Etruscans.)*

Evaluate Impact How would the control of the Italian peninsula affect the development of Roman civilization? *(Sample response: Rome would have access to more ports, which would increase trade and bring it into more contact with other cultures. Rome might try to expand its rule beyond the Italian peninsula.)*

The Roman Republic

DIGITAL TEXT 2
The Early Roman Republic

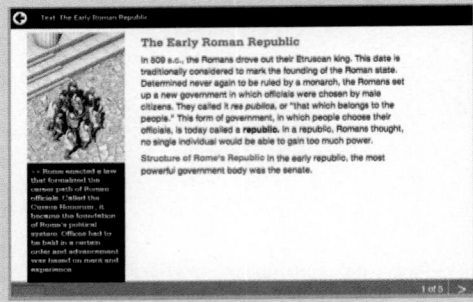

INTERACTIVE GALLERY
The Roman *Cursus Honorum*

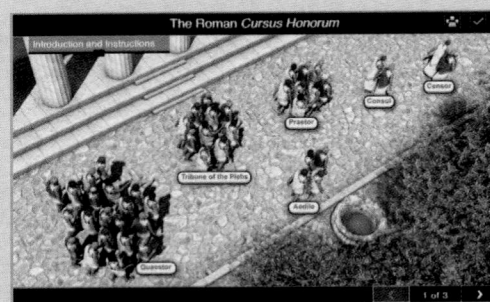

Objective 2: Outline how the Roman republic was structured and governed.

Quick Instruction

The Roman republic began when the Romans overthrew the Etruscan ruler in 509 B.C. Romans wanted a republic, a form of government in which the people choose some of the officials, to prevent any individual from gaining too much power. Romans structured the republic by creating a senate, initially comprised of upper class patricians, to make laws and control the government. Over time the plebeians gained more access to power and were able to serve in the senate. The structure of the Roman government created checks and balances on power. This idea was later adapted by the framers of the United States Constitution.

The Roman *Cursus Honorum*: Interactive Gallery Project the gallery on the whiteboard. It is organized in order of senate hierarchy. Each hotspot represents a position and details the career path of a senator. What was the main objective for creating a structured senate with term limits and veto powers? *(Romans believed this would prevent any one person or group from achieving too much power.)*

ELL Use the ELL activity described in the ELL chart.

📹 ACTIVE CLASSROOM

Use the Conversation with History strategy. Have students select a senatorial position that interests them. Tell them to imagine having a conversation with the senator they have selected. Have them write one question that they would like to ask the senator. Then ask them to jot down how they think the senator will respond and how they will reply. Suggest their dialogue be posted as a video conversation on YouTube.

Further Instruction

Go through the Interactive Reading Notepad questions and discuss the answers with the class. Have students re-examine the merits of a democratic-republican government.

Identify Cause and Effect How did Rome's government change over time and how did that affect its citizens? *(In the early years of the Republic, citizen patricians dominated the senate but only for the time limit of their office. Initially, citizen plebeians held little political influence. When they rallied as a group, they gained representation and more power, eventually serving in the senate. As a result, the senate represented more of the Roman people and more citizens had a voice in government.)*

Draw Inferences Why was this change significant? *(The common people achieved these gains without going to war or staging a revolution.)*

Analyze Information Consider that in the event of war, the senate could choose a dictator to rule for a maximum of six months. How does serving as a ruler for so little time help the republic? *(A ruler who has complete control over the government might abuse his power if allowed to reign for a longer period of time.)* Describe how this political restriction on a Roman dictator might have influenced aspects of the United States government. *(The United States Constitution set limits on the number of years a member of Congress could serve without being re-elected. There is also a two-term limit for presidents.)*

D **Differentiate: Challenge** Help students understand that the development of the Roman government was a matter of trial and error over extended time. Divide the class into two sections. Two-thirds of the class will be patrician senators grouped in their respective hierarchy of office. The second group will be the remainder of the class, who are the plebeians. Ask the plebeians to formulate an issue, based on the reading, that they want to present to the patrician senate. In advance of their presentation, have them write down the issue and give it to patrician students. Then have the plebeians gather to develop an outline for presentation of their issue to the senate. Patricians should subdivide into two groups, those who are for the plebeian plan and those who are against; each of these two groups should outline their positions. The plebeians and patricians will role-play their positions in a senate setting.

DIGITAL TEXT 3
Roman Society

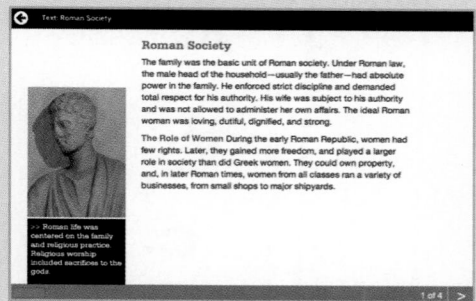

Objective 3: Understand the rights and religious practices that characterized Roman society.

Quick Instruction

Tell students that Roman society was centered on the family. The father was the authoritative figure, and the wife raised the family and usually worked at home. Discuss the role of women and children in Roman society. Romans placed a significant emphasis on education for both girls and boys.

Analyze Images Project the image of a Roman family on the whiteboard. Discuss the image as a class. Then ask students how the artist has depicted the role of the man in the family. *(Sample response: He appears to be in a position of authority. The focus of the child and the woman is on the man. He seems to be guiding or instructing them with his hand movement.)*

Further Instruction

Roman Society: Core Reading and Interactive Reading Notepad Project and discuss the Close Reading Notepad questions, including the graphic organizer that you filled out with class during the **The Rise of the Roman Civilization: Core Reading Extend**. Discuss the Greeks' contribution to Roman culture and finish filling in the graphic organizer on the whiteboard as you go.

Apply Concepts Describe religious worship and practice in ancient Rome. *(The worship of gods and goddesses was an important part of Roman society. Honoring them was thought to ensure divine favor. Roman citizens showed their loyalty by attending religious festivals that centered on paying homage to any one to a number of gods.)*

ELL Use the ELL activity described in the ELL chart.

DIGITAL TEXT 4
The Roman Republic Expands

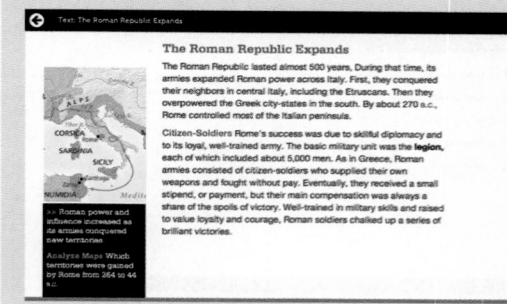

Objective 4: Explain how the Roman republic grew and used its political influence.

Quick Instruction

By 270 B.C., Rome controlled most of the Italian peninsula. Rome's loyal and well-trained legions, comprised of citizen-soldiers, battled and won many victories. The republic then used skillful diplomacy to control the conquered people. Rome allowed conquered persons to retain their customs, money, and local government. In return for retaining some autonomy, the conquered had to acknowledge the authority of Rome and contribute to the republic. For example, they paid taxes and supplied soldiers for the Roman army. Although most were non-citizens, some conquered groups were granted partial citizenship. A lucky few were granted full citizenship.

Growth of the Roman Republic, 500 B.C. to 44 B.C.: Interactive Map Project the map on the whiteboard. Each layer can be viewed as a separate map or as an overlay with other layers. Explain to students that each layer of the map reflects lands conquered by the Romans at the designated date. Does the map reflect an order in which the territories were conquered? Explain your answer. *(Yes. Rome was a small area in the center of Italy. From there, the Romans conquered most of Italy. In the next hundred years they branched into Macedonia, the southern side of the Alps and Spain. Finally, a hundred years later, they conquered Gaul, parts of Asia Minor, and territories from their victories over Carthage.)*

The Roman Republic

■ SYNTHESIZE

■ DEMONSTRATE

INTERACTIVE MAP
Growth of the Roman Republic, 500 B.C. to 44 B.C.

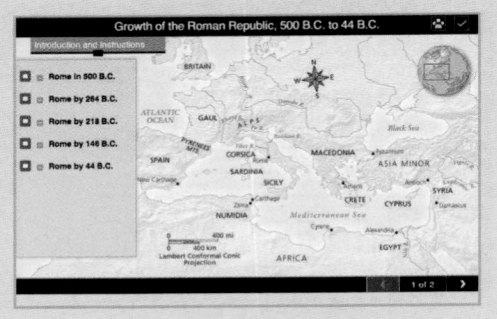

DIGITAL SYNTHESIZE ACTIVITY
Communication Is Key

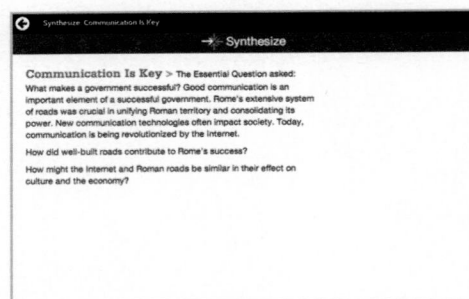

LESSON QUIZ
Lesson Quiz and Class Discussion Board

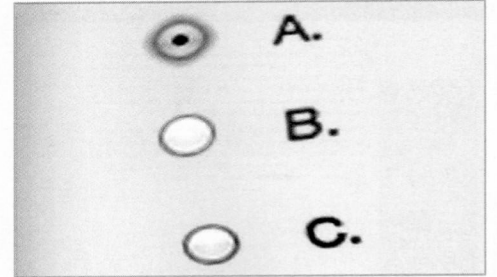

👥 ACTIVE CLASSROOM

Use the Make Headlines Strategy with the Interactive Map to explore the invasions' impact. Ask: If you were to write a headline right now to capture the most important aspect that should be remembered about any invasion, what would that headline be? Have students pass their headlines to a partner for them to review. Tell students they can post their ideas on Twitter.

Further Instruction
The Roman Republic Expands: Core Reading and Interactive Reading Notepad
Project and discuss the Interactive Reading Notepad questions and answers.

Interpret What steps did Rome take to govern its new territories? *(The senate instituted laws to determine how the conquered lands would be governed. Conquered persons could keep their customs, money, and local government. They had to acknowledge Rome's authority and contribute to the republic. For example, they paid taxes and served in the Roman army.)*

Analyze Information How did men, citizens, and noncitizens, serve the republic? *(They served in the army, initially using their own weapons, and fought without compensation.)*

Project the Synthesize Activity. Using Think Pair Share, suggest students briefly review the initial Synthesize Activity and answer the following questions. They should share their answers with their partner. How did well-built roads contribute to Rome's success? *(Roman roads improved communication and allowed faster movement of troops, which helped Rome conquer and then govern its distant territories.)* How might the Internet and Roman roads be similar in their effect on culture and the economy? *(The Internet and Roman roads improved the ability to share ideas. As travel increased with better roads, Rome's language, customs, and beliefs spread. The Internet and the road system both facilitate trade.)*

Discuss The partners should share and discuss their answers with the class. After hearing the responses of other students, ask if anyone would like to change their answer.

Assign the online Lesson Quiz for this lesson if you haven't already done so. Students will be offered automatic remediation or enrichment based on their score.

In "The Early Roman Republic" you read about the beginning of the republic's government, how it changed with challenges from the common people, which fundamental structures became a legacy for future generations, and how Rome expanded its control across the Italian peninsula.

Draw Inferences Do you think Rome will continue to conquer new territories? If so, where? Hint: Look at the map **Ancient Italy About 500 B.C.**

Predict Consequences Consider what you have read about Greece. What new challenges will the Roman republic face?

The Roman Empire: Rise and Decline

Supporting English Language Learners

Use with Digital Text 1, **Empire Building Through Conquest.**

Listening
Have students work with academic vocabulary from the text. As they listen to portions begin read aloud, have them respond to the use of the words. Guide students in their understanding of the meanings and usage of these terms.

Beginning Display the academic vocabulary: *conflict, distribute, expand,* and *series.* Read each word aloud and define it. As you read *Empire Building Through Conquest,* have students listen for each word and raise their hands at every instance they hear it used. Then provide students with sentence stems that allow them to use the academic word within the context of the Roman Empire.

Intermediate Display the academic vocabulary: *conflict, distribute, expand,* and *series.* Read each word aloud and help students define it. As you read *Empire Building Through Conquest,* have them listen for each word and raise their hands at every instance they hear it used. Then ask content-specific questions that allow students to use the academic word in their answer.

Advanced Work with students to review *Empire Building Through Conquest* to identify new academic words. Have partners use context clues and dictionaries to define each word on their list. Instruct them to write two content-specific sentences that each include one of the academic words. Have the group listen as pairs read their sentences aloud, omitting each academic word. Then have the group determine which academic words complete the sentences.

Advanced High Have pairs review *Empire Building Through Conquest* to identify new academic words and define each. Have them write a content-specific paragraph that includes at least four of their academic words. Instruct partners to turn to another pair to listen as they read their paragraph aloud, omitting the academic words. Have the new partners determine which academic words correctly complete the paragraph.

Use with Digital Text 2, **The Roman Republic Declines.**

Listening
To give students practice in understanding the main points of unfamiliar spoken language, tell them to listen for the most important points as you read aloud. Read, or ask a volunteer to read, the introduction and the first section, "I came, I saw, I conquered, " under the heading, *The Roman Republic Declines.* Then have students demonstrate their listening comprehension skills by completing the following tasks.

Beginning Model finding the main points about how Caesar became the ruler of Rome. Supply students with vocabulary such as *military commander, conquered, civil war, dictator.* Use the illustration of Caesar at war to clarify these terms. Provide sentence frames for a discussion of Caesar's actions, such as: Caesar conquered _____. Caesar fought _____ in a civil war. Caesar became _____ of Rome.

Intermediate Tell students to listen carefully as advanced students read a summary of how Caesar became the ruler of Rome. Encourage them to ask questions about unfamiliar language. Ask them to restate the main points using the following key words: *military commander, conquered, civil war, rebellion, dictator* and the sentence frame: Caesar became the ruler of Rome because _____.

Advanced and Advanced High These students can work together to summarize the text of how Caesar became ruler of Rome. Encourage them to find definitions of unfamiliar language and create a dictionary to put in the class library. Have them share their summary with the class and answer questions. Ask them to use a Think-Aloud to demonstrate how they created their summary.

▣ Differentiate Instruction

Use the Differentiated Instruction notes throughout the lesson plan to support the varied skill sets, levels of readiness, and interests in the mixed-ability classroom.

Challenge These notes include suggestions for expanding the activity for advanced students.

On-Level These notes include suggestions for modifying the activity to address different interests or learning styles.

Extra Support These notes include ideas for providing more scaffolding or reading spuport.

Special Needs These notes provide ideas for adapting instruction to support the needs of various special needs students.

■ NOTES

The Roman Empire: Rise and Decline

Objectives

Objective 1: Identify the events leading to the decline of the Roman republic.

Objective 2: Summarize the fundamental ideas and institutions of Western civilizations that originated in Rome.

Objective 3: Explain how and why the Roman empire divided.

Objective 4: Identify the factors that led to the decline and fall of Rome.

LESSON 2 ORGANIZER	PACING: APPROX. 1 PERIOD, .5 BLOCKS			
			RESOURCES	
	OBJECTIVES	**PACING**	**Online**	**Print**
Connect				
DIGITAL START UP ACTIVITY **Julius Caesar**		5 min.	●	
Investigate				
DIGITAL TEXT 1 **Empire Building Through Conquest**	Objective 1	10 min.	●	●
DIGITAL TEXT 2 **The Roman Republic Declines**		10 min.	●	●
DIGITAL TEXT 3 **The Roman Empire**	Objective 2	10 min.	●	●
INTERACTIVE TIMELINE **Roman Rulers Who Made History**		10 min.	●	
DIGITAL TEXT 4 **The Roman Empire Splits**	Objective 3	10 min.	●	●
DIGITAL TEXT 5 **Rome Faces Invasions**		10 min.	●	●
DIGITAL TEXT 6 **Why Did Rome Fall?**	Objective 4	10 min.	●	●
INTERACTIVE MAP **Invasions of the Roman Empire, A.D. 378–533**		10 min.	●	
Synthesize				
DIGITAL SYNTHESIZE ACTIVITY **When Did Rome Fall?**		5 min.	●	
Demonstrate				
LESSON QUIZ **Lesson Quiz and Class Discussion Board**		10 min.	●	

PEARSON realize.™
www.PearsonRealize.com

Go online to access additional resources including:
Primary Sources • Biographies • Supreme Court cases •
21st Century Skill Tutorials • Maps • Graphic Organizers.

CONNECT

DIGITAL START UP ACTIVITY
Julius Caesar

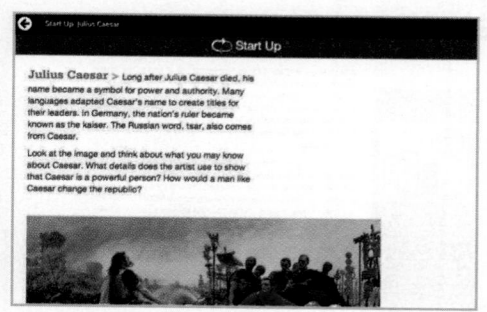

Project the Start Up Activity Ask students to review the image of Caesar, answer the questions, and share their ideas with another student.

Discuss What details does the artist use to show that Caesar is a powerful person? How do you think a man like Caesar will change the republic? *(Caesar is at the forefront of the painting and sits majestically on his horse as he points, giving direction to his men. His uniform and horse regalia are in color; his troops' uniforms are barely identifiable.)* *(Caesar was an ambitious military leader whose successes helped to expand the empire. As a result, he forced the senate to make him dictator.)*

⇅ FLIP IT!
Assign the Flipped Video for this lesson.

STUDENT EDITION PRINT
PAGES: 163–172

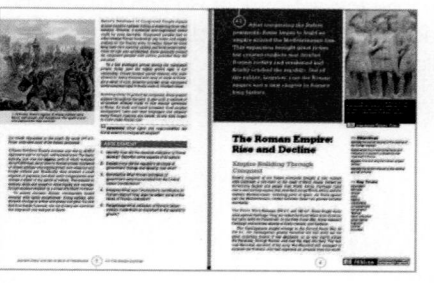

INVESTIGATE

DIGITAL TEXT 1
Empire Building Through Conquest

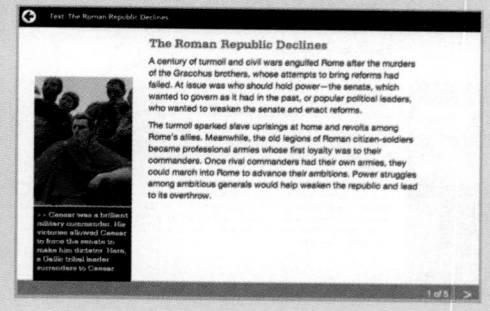

Objective 1: Identify the events leading to the decline of the Roman republic.

Quick Instruction
Remind students that once Rome controlled the Italian peninsula, it expanded westward and came into conflict with Carthage. After its victory in the Third Punic War, Roman conquest continued until Rome controlled most of the Mediterranean region. Rome had gained great power and wealth, but expansion created internal issues that threatened the republic. Small farmers could not compete with the latifundia. Unemployment and a growing gap between the rich and the poor led to social unrest.

Analyze Images Project the image of *Hannibal's Elephants* on the whiteboard. Tell students that after Rome won the First Punic War, Carthage sought revenge and invaded Italy. Led by the general Hannibal, the Carthaginian army left a path of destruction in the Second Punic War. Have the class look at the details of the picture. Note that the Roman army is in the forefront on foot and the Carthaginian army rides into battle with a front line of elephants. Then project the image of the praetorians. Explain that during the time of the late republic the praetorians, or bodyguards, began protecting army generals. Discuss how this reflects a decline in republican virtue as soldiers became loyal to the army commanders rather than the state. Also note that commanders used their own armies to advance their ambitions in Rome, which resulted in violent conflicts. Have students discuss what they know about Caesar from reading the text. Be sure they understand his significance in Roman history and the legacy of his reforms in Western civilization. Ask students to think about the image they looked at in the

DIGITAL TEXT 2
The Roman Republic Declines

Connect and then ask how these three images represent both the rise and the decline of the republic. *(Sample response: All images focus on the military. Two images are of battles and represent how Rome used its military in its policy of imperialism, which eventually weakened the republic internally. Caesar also used the army to take power, becoming the absolute ruler of Rome even though he maintained the senate.)*

Further Instruction
Empire Building Through Conquest and the Roman Republic Declines: Go through the Interactive Reading Notepad questions and discuss the answers with the class.

Draw Conclusions Why could the Punic Wars be considered a turning point for Rome? *(Sample response: They proved that Rome could challenge a powerful empire. The defeat of Carthage is the beginning of Rome's political and cultural domination of the Mediterranean region.)*

Evaluate Impact How did imperialism threaten the stability of the republic and foreshadow the decline of Rome? *(As it conquered more lands, Rome gained great wealth and more slaves. Small farmers could not compete with the latifundia. This led to unemployment and a growing gap between the rich and the poor. The disparity led to social unrest. Republican virtues declined as greed and corruption increased. These internal problems worsened as Rome expanded.)*

Analyze Information Which of Caesar's political reforms have influenced Western civilization? *(He created a program of public works to employ the jobless, a policy that many Western governments have implemented in times of economic hardship.)*

The Roman Empire: Rise and Decline

DIGITAL TEXT 3

The Roman Empire

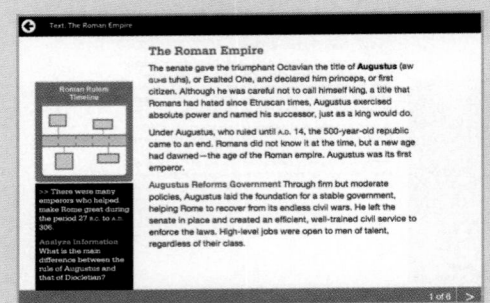

INTERACTIVE TIMELINE

Roman Rulers Who Made History

DIGITAL TEXT 4

The Roman Empire Splits

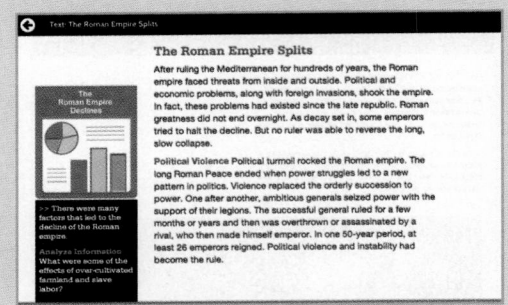

Objective 2: Summarize the fundamental ideas and institutions of Western civilizations that originated in Rome.

Quick Instruction

Augustus's reign marked the end of the Roman republic and the beginning of the Roman empire. The 200-year period of peace and prosperity that followed is known as the *Pax Romana.*

Roman Rulers Who Made History: Interactive Timeline Project the timeline on the whiteboard. Explain that it highlights some of the better-known Roman emperors and their accomplishments. The dates in red reflect the beginning of an emperor's rule and those in black designate the end. Each emperor's picture is a hotspot. Click through the hotspots and discuss some of the fundamental institutions or ideas of Western civilizations that originated during that emperor's rule of Rome.

Analyze Information Ask students to identify what they think is each emperor's most important achievement. *(Answers may vary. Augustus: civil service, self-government, census; Trajan: built aqueduct; Hadrian: codified Roman law; Marcus Aurelius: abolished the harshness in civil law; Diocletian: split the empire and slowed inflation; Constantine: supported tolerance for Christians.)*

Go over the answers with the class, and then take a poll on which emperor had the greatest role in the development of Roman civilization.

⚏ ACTIVE CLASSROOM

Use the Cartoon It activity to have students create a quick copy of one compelling emperor's image on a piece of paper. Then have them turn it into a political cartoon that illustrates a key concept or main idea of that emperor's accomplishments. Use a document camera to scan the political cartoons to add to a class blog.

ELL Use the ELL activity described in the ELL chart.

Further Instruction

The Roman Empire: Core Reading and Interactive Reading Notepad Review the Interactive Reading Notepad questions and answers with students.

Hypothesize Briefly review some of the fundamental principles of the Roman republic and the Interactive Timeline. Then ask students if they think the citizens of the republic would have viewed the Roman empire favorably or not. *(Answers will vary. Favorable: Some reforms made the government more fair, such as letting men of any class serve in high-level civil service jobs and creating a census for a better tax system. The prosperity of the empire increased the mobility of goods, people, and ideas. Unfavorable: The emperors had unlimited authority. Without the checks and balances of the republic, corrupt and incompetent emperors were able to rule Rome and contribute to its decline.)*

Objective 3: Explain how and why the Roman empire divided.

Quick Instruction

After the death of Marcus Aurelius, the empire entered a period of political violence and social unrest. The depth of the crisis is highlighted by the fact that in 50 years, there were 26 emperors.

Identify Cause and Effect Project the infographic, *The Roman Empire Declines*, on the whiteboard. Tell students to take a few minutes to review the categories listed for the causes of the empire's decline. Then discuss the reasons listed as causes and effects. Ask each student to look at all the categories and rank the causes of decline in importance with an explanation of the ranking. *(Possible answer: Political turbulence because civil war weakened the empire and negatively affected the economy, society, and military; Cause: high taxes; Effect: oppressive society.)*

Further Instruction

The Roman Empire Splits: Core Reading and Interactive Reading Notepad Project and discuss the Interactive Reading Notepad questions. Fill in the graphic organizer on the whiteboard as you go. Tell students to refer to the Interactive Timeline: Roman Rulers Who Made History if they need help answering the following questions.

DIGITAL TEXT 5
Rome Faces Invasions

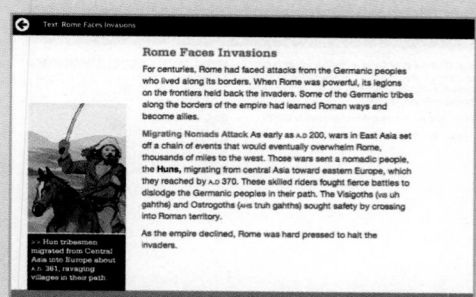

DIGITAL TEXT 6
Why Did Rome Fall?

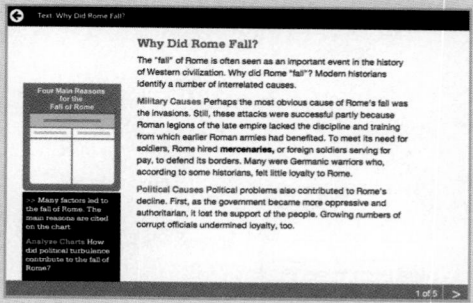

Identify Central Issues The Roman Empire was imploding in decay, corruption, and violence when Diocletian became emperor. Ask students to identify what steps Diocletian took to combat the empire's decline and the reason for each. *(Divided the empire in two for better management; appointed a co-emperor to split the responsibilities; fixed prices to slow inflation.)*

Evaluate Impact Constantine I continued Diocletian's reforms and made some of his own. What were the effects of these reforms? *(These two reforms changed European history. When Constantine I granted freedom of worship to Roman citizens, Christianity grew, as people could openly practice and preach their religion. Constantine I established a new capital, Constantinople, shifting the empire's center of power to the east.)*

D Differentiate: Extra Support Have students compare Diocletian to a modern day businessperson taking over a failing company. He had to assess the problems and came up with solutions. Write, Problem: the company (empire) was too large to administer effectively with one owner (emperor). Then ask students what they would write for Solution. *(Solution: divide the company (empire) and share ownership (power) with Maximian.)*

Objective 4: Identify the factors that led to the decline and fall of Rome.

Quick Instruction

The fall of Rome was a major turning point in the history of Western civilization. The empire's long decline is attributed to multiple causes that generally fit into four categories: military assaults, political turbulence, economic issues, and social decay.

Invasions of the Roman Empire, A.D. 378-533: Interactive Map Project the map on the whiteboard. Point out that Rome had faced attacks for centuries, but as the empire declined, its legions struggled to stop the invaders. Explain to students that each layer of the map shows the battles of that invader. Step through the layers on the map and discuss the impact that the invasions had on the Roman Empire.

⚎ ACTIVE CLASSROOM

Have students form an Opinion Line to answer the following question: Were invasions the major cause of the decline of Rome? Yes or no? *(Possible answers: Yes: the massive number of invasions drained resources from the empire to provide for its defense, disrupted trade, displaced people, and resulted in the loss of land. No: Rome had repelled attacks in the past, but the military began using mercenaries rather than citizen-soldiers. If the economy was strong and the government was unified and popular, Rome could have continued to successfully defend its borders.)*

Further Instruction

The Fall of the Roman Empire Project and review the Interactive Reading Notepad questions and answers for Rome Faces Invasions and Why Did Rome Fall?

Generate Explanations Review the text on the Roman defeat at Adrianople. What is the significance of Rome losing this battle? *(Adrianople was on the eastern edge of the Roman Empire. By the time invaders had pierced this border, the northern borders of Britain, France, and Spain had already been overrun. The invaders had now claimed the territories that surrounded Italy on the northern side of the Mediterranean and were pressing in on Rome.)*

Express Ideas Clearly Military assaults are considered to be one of the most obvious causes of the fall of Rome. What happened to the Roman army that made it incapable of defending the empire? *(It lacked discipline, training, and the sheer number of soldiers that were representative of the earlier legions. To bolster the number of soldiers, Rome hired mercenaries who may not have been loyal to Rome.)*

Paraphrase As the empire declined, there were increased numbers of political problems. How did they contribute to Rome's decline? *(The people lost faith in their leaders. Corruption was rampant, and the authoritative nature of the government was oppressive. As the reign changed from emperor to emperor, the stability of the empire eroded.)*

The Roman Empire: Rise and Decline

SYNTHESIZE

DEMONSTRATE

INTERACTIVE MAP
Invasions of the Roman Empire, A.D.

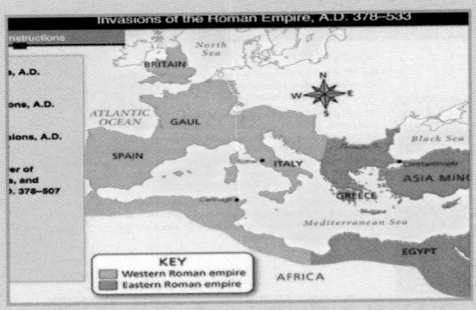

DIGITAL SYNTHESIZE ACTIVITY
When Did Rome Fall?

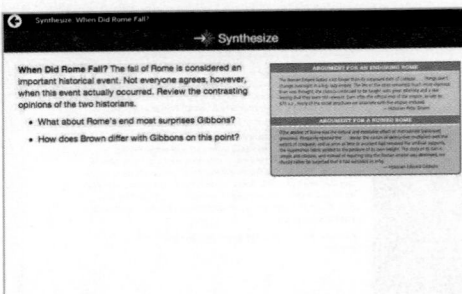

LESSON QUIZ
Lesson Quiz and Class Discussion Board

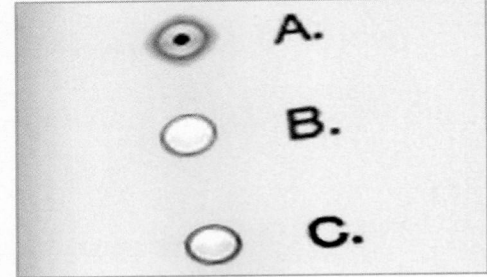

Evaluate Impact Diocletian divided the empire to help restore order and better govern it. How did this decision contribute the decline of Rome? *(It weakened the empire, and the wealthier eastern half did little to help the western half.)*

Project the Synthesize Activity Ask students to count off as 1 or 2. Then pair students. Ask one person to review the Brown quote and the other the Gibbons quote. Then direct students to write down their answer to the following questions.

What about Rome's end most surprises Gibbons? How does Brown differ with Gibbons on this point? *(Gibbons is surprised that the empire lasted as long as it did, while Brown states that the empire actually endured longer than its supposed date of collapse.)*

In a partner-to-partner dialogue, students should try and persuade their partner that their opinion is correct. *(Possible arguments: Brown supporters: The Roman Empire declined over a very long period of time. During the decline, people continued to live their daily life with little change. Gibbons supporters: On the surface the empire appeared affluent, but beneath it was in decay. What had brought the empire great wealth, its conquests, and vast territory, would inevitably lead to its collapse.)*

Discuss The partners should share and discuss their answers with the class. After hearing the responses of other students, ask if anyone would like to change their answer.

Assign the online Lesson Quiz for this lesson if you haven't already done so. Students will be offered automatic remediation or enrichment based on their score.

While the causes of the fall of the Roman Empire are still debated, it is certain that classical Rome had a lasting political influence on Western civilization.

Summarize What Roman institutions or ideas are incorporated into American culture and government? *(Possible answers: Institutions of the senate, the postal service, census, taxes, public works projects to employ the jobless, expanding citizenship, Julian calendar, civil service based on merit, codified law, and religious tolerance.)*

The Legacy of Rome

Supporting English Language Learners

Use with Digital Text 1, **Roman Literature, History, and Philosophy.**

Listening

Read aloud or have students read *Roman Literature, History, and Philosophy*. Encourage students to focus on how Greek culture influenced that of Rome. Then monitor students understanding of the vocabulary and content as they discuss the two cultures.

Beginning Read *Roman Literature, History, and Philosophy* aloud. Pause after each sentence to clarify any questions about unfamiliar vocabulary using drawings or gestures when necessary. Tell students to think about how the Romans learned from Greek culture. Then monitor their understanding by having them answer using a sentence frame such as: The Romans copied Greek _____.

Intermediate Read *Roman Literature, History, and Philosophy* aloud. Monitor student understanding by asking questions about key words and important points from the reading. For example, "What did the Romans admire about ancient Greek civilization?" Instruct students to use complete sentences when answering.

Advanced Have small groups read *Roman Literature, History, and Philosophy* aloud. Then have them discuss the quotation, "Greece has conquered her rude conqueror" and debate whether or not they agree with this statement. To monitor student understanding, circulate to correct mistakes and ask questions.

Advanced High Have students read *Roman Literature, History, and Philosophy*. Then have partners discuss the quotation, "Greece has conquered her rude conqueror" and debate whether or not they agree with this statement. To monitor student understanding, have partners summarize the results of their discussion.

Use with Digital Text 3, **Roman Achievements in Science and Engineering.**

Listening

To give students practice in understanding the main points of spoken language, provide support for a context that may be unfamiliar. Read, or have a volunteer read, the section "Science and Engineering." Then have students demonstrate their listening comprehension skills by completing the following tasks.

Beginning Preteach unfamiliar words such as *engineering* and *aqueduct*. Allow students time to study the photo of Roman aqueducts. Ask choice questions or questions that can be answered with familiar vocabulary. Examples: What were aqueducts used for? Were they made of stone or wood? Why?

Intermediate Help students use the photos to understand the contexts of engineering, medicine, and law. Use a Think-Aloud to model how to take notes on Roman achievements in engineering. Then have student pairs take notes on achievements in medicine and law.

Advanced Have students work in small groups to compare and contrast Roman laws with those of modern America. Each group will contribute to a Venn diagram to display for class use.

Advanced High Have students create a slide show of the achievements of Roman civilization in engineering and architecture with a script of information to accompany it.

▣ Differentiate Instruction

Use the Differentiated Instruction notes throughout the lesson plan to support the varied skill sets, levels of readiness, and interests in the mixed-ability classroom.

Challenge These notes include suggestions for expanding the activity for advanced students.

On-Level These notes include suggestions for modifying the activity to address different interests or learning styles.

Extra Support These notes include ideas for providing more scaffolding or reading spuport.

Special Needs These notes provide ideas for adapting instruction to support the needs of various special needs students.

■ NOTES

_____

_____

_____

_____

_____

The Legacy of Rome

Objectives

Objective 1: Summarize the works of Roman literary figures, historians, and philosophers.

Objective 2: Describe the art and architecture developed by the Romans.

Objective 3: Understand how the Romans applied science and mathematics for practical use.

Objective 4: Explain how Rome's rule of law influenced modern legal systems.

Objective 5: Summarize the Roman ideas and institutions that have influenced Western civilization.

LESSON 3 ORGANIZER		PACING: APPROX. 1 PERIOD, .5 BLOCKS			
				RESOURCES	
		OBJECTIVES	**PACING**	**Online**	**Print**
Connect					
	DIGITAL START UP ACTIVITY **Advances in Roman Culture**		5 min.	●	
Investigate					
	DIGITAL TEXT 1 **Roman Literature, History, and Philosophy**	Objective 1	10 min.	●	●
	DIGITAL TEXT 2 **Roman Art, Architecture, and Drama**	Objective 2	10 min.	●	●
	INTERACTIVE 3-D MODEL **The Pantheon**		10 min.	●	
	DIGITAL TEXT 3 **Roman Achievements in Science and Engineering**	Objective 3	10 min.	●	●
	INTERACTIVE GALLERY **Science and Technology in Ancient Rome**		10 min.	●	
	DIGITAL TEXT 4 **Roman Law Unites the Empire**	Objectives 4, 5	10 min.	●	●
	INTERACTIVE CHART **The Influence of Roman Law**		10 min.	●	
Synthesize					
	SYNTHESIZE ACTIVITY **Architecture in Ancient Rome**		5 min.	●	
Demonstrate					
	LESSON QUIZ **Lesson Quiz and Class Discussion Board**		10 min.	●	

PEARSON
realize™
www.PearsonRealize.com

Go online to access additional resources including:
Primary Sources • Biographies • Supreme Court cases •
21st Century Skill Tutorials • Maps • Graphic Organizers.

■ CONNECT

DIGITAL START UP ACTIVITY
Advances in Roman Culture

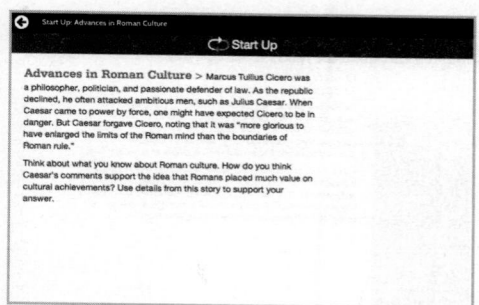

Project the Start Up Activity Ask students to answer the questions as they enter and get settled. Then have them share their ideas with another student, either in class or through a chat room or blog.

Discuss Think about what you know about Roman culture. Do you think Romans placed much value on cultural achievements? Use details from this story to support your answer. *(Sample Response: Despite provocation, Caesar forgave Cicero out of respect for his intellectual achievements in philosophy, politics, and the law. The quote places a higher value on enlightening the mind than expanding a nation.)*

Tell students that in this lesson they will be learning the origin, diffusion, and lasting influence of the Roman Empire.

⇅ FLIP IT!
Assign the Flipped Video for this lesson.

■ STUDENT EDITION PRINT
PAGES: 173–177

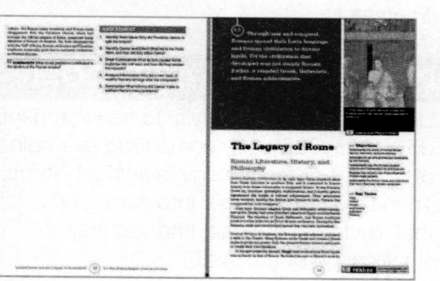

■ INVESTIGATE

DIGITAL TEXT 1
Roman Literature, History, and Philosophy

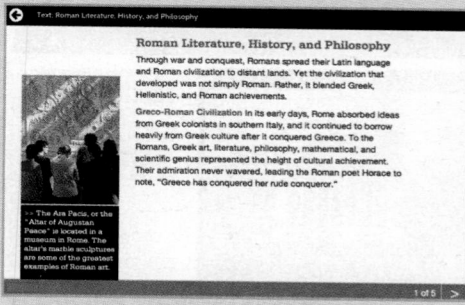

Objective 1: Summarize the works of Roman literary figures, historians, and philosophers.

Quick Instruction
Remind students that the Romans valued Greek culture and adapted Greek and Hellenistic ideas to create a Greco-Roman civilization. Have students think about the influence writers would have in a society that values their work. Then tell students many Roman poets, such as Virgil, and historians, such as Livy, used their writing to promote patriotism. In their literature, Roman writers focused on material that reflected on the greatness and heroism of Rome. The Hellenistic philosophy of Stoicism, which stressed the importance of duty and acceptance of one's fate, impressed Roman thinkers such as the emperor Marcus Aurelius. Stoics also showed concern for the well-being of all people.

Analyze Images Project the image of Virgil's *Aeneid* on the whiteboard. Point out that Aeneas is the central image of the picture. Note how Aeneas exhibits strength as people watch the fight. Ask students to think about what they have read and what the image depicts. Have students analyze how Virgil's *Aeneid* reflects the history of Rome.

ELL Use the ELL activity described in the ELL chart.

Further Instruction
Culture: The Arts: Literature Use The Arts: Literature to present ideas for this Core Reading.

Roman Literature, History, and Philosophy: Core Reading and Interactive Reading Notepad Project and discuss the Interactive Reading Notepad questions. Review the Roman achievements and the themes of Roman literature. Help students analyze how Roman literature reflected their admiration of the Greeks.

Be sure that students understand the Romans imitated Greek prose and borrowed Greek ideas. However, the greatest Roman literature was written in Latin. The use of satire was also popular with Roman poets.

Analyze Information Ask students how literature reflects the history of the culture in which it is produced. *(Writers often incorporate the values, opinions, and characteristics of the culture they are most closely associated with.)* Have students provide examples of modern literature, cinema, or television series that reflect characteristics of our culture.

The Legacy of Rome

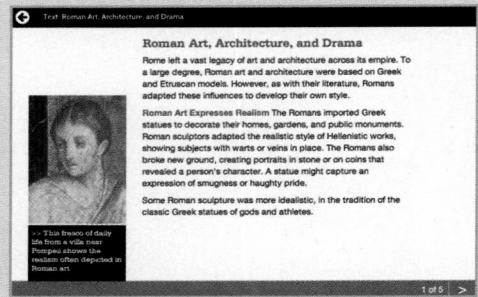

DIGITAL TEXT 2

Roman Art, Architecture, and Drama

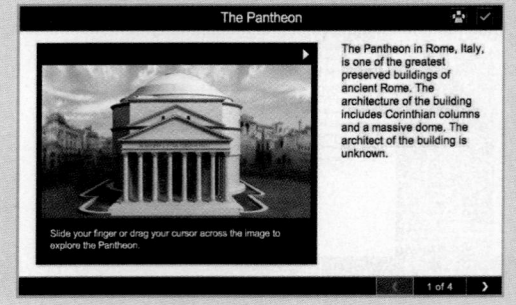

INTERACTIVE 3-D MODEL

The Pantheon

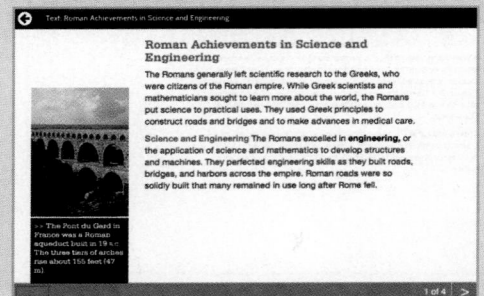

DIGITAL TEXT 3

Roman Achievements in Science and Engineering

Objective 2: Describe the art and architecture developed by the Romans.

Quick Instruction

Roman art, architecture, and drama all had Greek influences. Roman art and drama depicted idealism, daily life, and humor. Sometimes art and architecture reflected the history of Rome and its values. For example, a sculpture of Augustus did not try to achieve realism but instead focused on creating a symbol of power and leadership, reflecting his significance in Roman history. While the Greeks had a simple, elegant style of architecture, Roman architecture often reflected the majesty and grandeur of the Roman empire and history. The Colosseum and the Pantheon are good examples of imposing Roman architecture.

Interactive Flipbook: The Pantheon Project the Pantheon on the whiteboard. Introduce the activity by explaining some of the Roman advances in architecture. These innovations changed the face of Roman cities—immense buildings represented Roman power. Click through the hotspots on the Pantheon and discuss the Roman structural devices. Point out that some of the Roman contributions to architecture are visible in buildings in the United States.

👥 ACTIVE CLASSROOM

Have students complete a Closer Look activity. Project a visual of the interior of the Pantheon and use a whiteboard tool to divide it into four numbered quadrants. Have students count off 1 to 4. Then have them look closely at the part of the image in their quadrant. Have them tell you what they see and what they learned as a result of their focus on this part of the image. Collect insights for each quadrant.

D Differentiate: Extra Support Ask students to review the images in the reading and the achievements of Romans in various areas and nominate one person, invention, or idea for a Roman Culture Hall of Fame. Have each person explain the criteria he or she used to make the choice.

Further Instruction

Geography: Human Geography: Understanding Culture Use Understanding Culture to present ideas for this Core Reading.

Go through the Interactive Reading Notepad questions and discuss the answers with the class.

Analyze Information Ask students to analyze how art, drama, and architecture reflect Roman history. *(Art included both idealism in its statues and realism of daily Roman life. Some plays had Greek influences and were based on legends that focused on the glory of Rome. Others were written about the daily life of Romans. Roman architecture exemplified the expanse and power of the empire with its immense structures.)*

Objective 3: Understand how the Romans applied science and mathematics for practical use.

Quick Instruction

Remind students that many Roman ideas in science and mathematics originated from Greek ones. Roman engineers put Greek principles in mathematics and science to practical use in their technology. Romans are noted for their engineering projects. They built roads, bridges, harbors, and aqueducts throughout the empire that lasted for generations. Romans also compiled scientific encyclopedias that could be found centuries later in European libraries. Tell students that this transfer of information from one culture to another is called cultural diffusion.

Interactive Gallery: Science and Technology in Ancient Rome Project the gallery. Look at the collection as a whole and then each image individually.

Analyze Maps Look at the map of aqueducts in the first hotspot. What do you notice about the location of the aqueducts? *(They nearly surround the city.)* Why is this significant? *(Nearly all parts of the city could be supplied with water.)*

👥 ACTIVE CLASSROOM

Use the Cartoon It activity to have students do a quick copy of a compelling example of science or technology in ancient Rome. Then have them turn it into a cartoon that illustrates the use, importance, or significance of the item.

INTERACTIVE GALLERY

Science and Technology in Ancient Rome

DIGITAL TEXT 4

Roman Law Unites the Empire

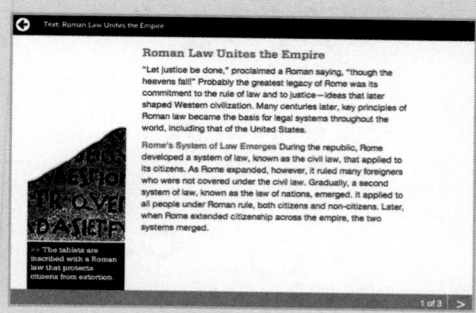

INTERACTIVE CHART

The Influence of Roman Law

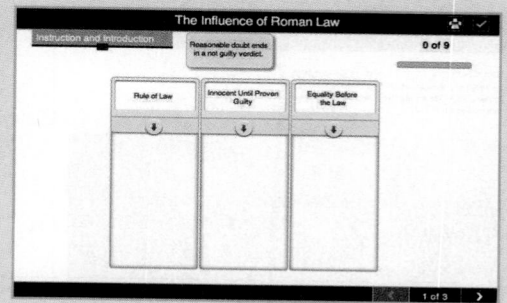

ELL Use the ELL activity described in the ELL chart.

Further Instruction

To extend the teaching of this objective, prompt students to identify some of the practical uses for science and engineering utilized by the Romans.

Roman Achievements in Science and Engineering: Core Reading and Interactive Reading Notepad Project and discuss the Interactive Reading Notepad question and discuss the answer with the class. Then ask students to read aloud and summarize the information under the heading "Science and Engineering."

Analyze Information What were some of the scientific accomplishments of Greek citizens of the Roman Empire? *(Ptolemy proposed an Earth-centered theory of the universe; Galen used experiments to prove a conclusion and compiled a medical encyclopedia.)*

Identify Central Issues How did the Romans put the Greeks' medical knowledge to practical use? *(They used the Greeks' medical knowledge and encyclopedias to improve public health.)*

Support Ideas with Examples Remind students that the transfer of ideas from one culture to another is called cultural diffusion. The expanse of Roman roads, trade, and travel fostered the diffusion of Roman ideas. Identify examples of the diffusion of Roman works. *(Roman roads were used long after the fall of the empire. Ptolemy's mistaken idea was accepted for nearly 1,500 years. Medical data and other scientific data were used by future civilizations.)*

Objectives 4: Explain how Rome's rule of law influenced modern legal systems; 5: Summarize the Roman ideas and institutions that have influenced Western civilizations.

Quick Instruction

The Influence of Roman Law: Interactive Chart Project the chart on the whiteboard and click through the topics. Introduce the chart activity by telling students that the Roman ideas and practices of law influenced many modern governments, including that of the United States. Once students have completed the activity, have them work with a partner and summarize the ideas in each column.

👥 ACTIVE CLASSROOM

Have students complete a Rank It activity. List the following on the board: rule of law, use of solid evidence, laws apply to citizens and non-citizens, the right to face the accuser, the right to offer a defense, and innocent until proven guilty. Ask students to rank the ideas according to what they think had the greatest influence on future civilizations. Have them support the ranking decisions they made. Then ask students to work in pairs to share their rankings and justifications. Poll the class to see if there is agreement on the ranking. Then tell students that these Roman ideas influenced many American legal principles, including the concept of innocent until proven guilty, and that judges interpret the laws and make fair decisions.

D Differentiate: **Extra Support** Have students reread the headings of the three columns in the Interactive Chart. Have them summarize the meaning of each heading and give one example of each.

Further Instruction

Go through the Interactive Reading Notepad questions and discuss the answers with the class.

Summarize Ask students to summarize the development of rule of law in ancient Rome. *(Rome developed civil law that only applied to its citizens. As more people became part of the empire, the law of nations emerged. It applied to all, citizens and non-citizens. In time, the two systems merged.)*

Analyze Information Ask students to read aloud and identify the basic concepts and principles in "Principles of Roman Law." Have them identify examples of Rome's ideas on the rights of people. *(An accused person is presumed innocent until proven guilty, the accused was allowed to face the accuser and offer a defense. Trial by jury is sometimes traced to Roman law practices.)* Ask students to summarize the influence of these ideas. *(People in the United States today are innocent until proven guilty: they have the right to a trial by jury. The idea of equality before the law is also supported in the United States.)*

The Legacy of Rome

■ SYNTHESIZE

■ DEMONSTRATE

SYNTHESIZE ACTIVITY
Architecture in Ancient Rome

Project the Synthesize Activity. Ask students to identify the image and take a few minutes to write down some of the ideas they think of when they see the image, keeping in mind the history of the Romans. Then have students share their responses with a partner.

Discuss Ask students to think about the Connect Activity at the beginning of this lesson. Ask if they can think of specific examples of how Romans valued cultural achievements.

LESSON QUIZ
Lesson Quiz and Class Discussion Board

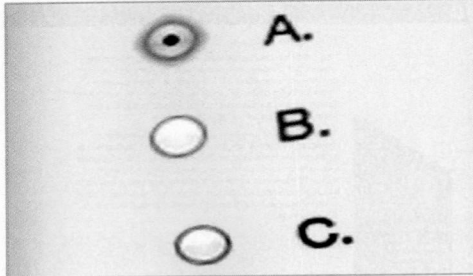

Assign the online Lesson Quiz for this lesson if you haven't already done so. Students will be offered automatic remediation or enrichment based on their score.

Pose these statements to the class on the Discussion Board:

In "The Legacy of Rome" you read about Roman culture and its influences on other cultures. Roman art, architecture, and basic principles continue to influence the modern world.

Draw Inferences With its Greco-Roman civilization, Rome demonstrated it could integrate other cultures. What were some other ways Romans demonstrated its adaptability?

Predict Consequences How do you think Roman civilization will affect the rest of Europe?

The Origins of Christianity

Supporting English Language Learners

Use with Digital Text 2, **The Teachings of Jesus.**

Listening
Read *The Teachings of Jesus* aloud. As the text is read, allow students to ask for clarification of vocabulary or content that they hear and do not understand. Encourage students to seek clarification whenever they need it during class.

Beginning Read *The Teachings of Jesus* aloud. As they listen, allow students to interrupt you with requests for clarification using the following: Could you explain what ____ means?. Answer each question using accessible language. Encourage students to seek clarification using this method as needed during class time.

Intermediate Read *The Teachings of Jesus* aloud. As they listen, allow students to interrupt you with requests for clarification using the following: I don't understand what you mean when you say _____. Does it mean ____? Answer each question. Encourage students to seek clarification using this method as needed during class time.

Advanced Read *The Teachings of Jesus* aloud. As they listen, allow students to interrupt you with requests for clarification by explaining what they understood and asking for confirmation or correction. Encourage students to seek clarification using this method as needed during class time.

Advanced High Read *The Teachings of Jesus* aloud. As they listen, allow students to interrupt you with requests for clarification by restating what they understood. Encourage students to seek clarification using this method as needed during class time.

Use with Digital Text 4, **The Growth of the Christian Church.**

Listening
Tell students that they will practice identifying important details that support the main idea as they listen to spoken language. Read, or ask a volunteer to read, "The Structure of the Christian Clergy" under the heading *The Growth of the Christian Church*. Present and discuss with students the chart that shows the structure of the early Christian church. Then have students demonstrate their listening comprehension skills by completing the following tasks:

Beginning Preteach the concept of a *hierarchy* and the content words *clergy*, *priests*, *bishops*, *patriarchs*. Tell students to draw a triangle as a symbol for the Christian Church. Have them work in pairs to label the hierarchy with the most powerful person(s) at the top and the least powerful at the bottom. Provide sentence frames for discussion, such as: The place for bishops in the hierarchy is _____. A patriarch has power over _____.

Intermediate Discuss with students the hierarchy of clergy in the early Christian Church. Have students use these sentence frames to debate the value of a hierarchy: A hierarchy is good for an organization because _____. A hierarchy might also be bad for an organization because _____.

Advanced Have students discuss the hierarchy of the early Christian Church. Have them work in small groups to complete an answer to the following question: What are the advantages and disadvantages of a hierarchy within a religious organization? Instruct them to support their answer with important details from the text. Then have groups share their answers.

Advanced High Have students role-play advocates for a hierarchy as the best way to run a large organization and advocates who oppose it. Have them present arguments and have classmates vote for the form of government they believe works best.

Ⓓ Differentiate Instruction

Use the Differentiated Instruction notes throughout the lesson plan to support the varied skill sets, levels of readiness, and interests in the mixed-ability classroom.

Challenge These notes include suggestions for expanding the activity for advanced students.

On-Level These notes include suggestions for modifying the activity to address different interests or learning styles.

Extra Support These notes include ideas for providing more scaffolding or reading spuport.

Special Needs These notes provide ideas for adapting instruction to support the needs of various special needs students.

■ NOTES

_____

_____

_____

_____

_____

The Origins of Christianity

Objectives

Objective 1: Understand the diverse religions included in the early Roman empire.

Objective 2: Describe the development and central ideas of Christianity.

Objective 3: Summarize the spread of Christianity.

Objective 4: Outline the development of the early Christian Church.

LESSON 4 ORGANIZER		PACING: APPROX. 1 PERIOD, .5 BLOCKS			
				RESOURCES	
		OBJECTIVES	**PACING**	**Online**	**Print**
Connect					
	DIGITAL START UP ACTIVITY **A Roman Emperor Accepts Christianity**		5 min.	●	
Investigate					
	DIGITAL TEXT 1 **Romans Accept Many Religions**	Objective 1	10 min.	●	●
	DIGITAL TEXT 2 **The Teachings of Jesus**	Objective 2	10 min.	●	●
	INTERACTIVE GALLERY **Christian Symbols**		10 min.	●	
	DIGITAL TEXT 3 **Christianity Spreads**	Objective 3	10 min.	●	●
	INTERACTIVE MAP **The Spread of Christianity**		10 min.	●	
	DIGITAL TEXT 4 **The Growth of the Christian Church**	Objective 4	10 min.	●	●
Synthesize					
	DIGITAL ACTIVITY **Key Roles in Early Christianity**		5 min.	●	
Demonstrate					
	LESSON QUIZ **Lesson Quiz and Class Discussion Board**		10 min.	●	

PEARSON
realize.
www.PearsonRealize.com

Go online to access additional resources including:
Primary Sources • Biographies • Supreme Court cases •
21st Century Skill Tutorials • Maps • Graphic Organizers.

■ CONNECT

DIGITAL START UP ACTIVITY

A Roman Emperor Accepts Christianity

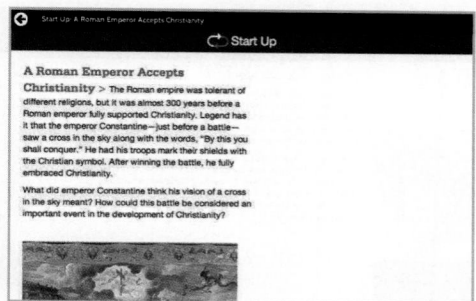

Project the Start Up Activity Ask students to answer the questions as they enter and get settled. Then have them share their ideas with another student, either in class or through a chat room or blog.

Discuss What did Constantine think his vision of a cross meant? *(It was a sign that his troops would win the battle if they marked their shields with a symbol of Christianity.)* How could this battle be considered an important event in the development of Christianity? *(Constantine was influential. When he accepted Christianity, the religion gained more followers.)* Why is this legend important? *(It shows the growing importance of Christianity in ancient Rome.)*

Tell students that in this lesson they will learn about the development of Christianity and how it spread throughout the Roman empire.

↕ FLIP IT!

Assign the Flipped Video for this lesson.

■ STUDENT EDITION PRINT
PAGES: 178–184

■ INVESTIGATE

DIGITAL TEXT 1

Romans Accept Many Religions

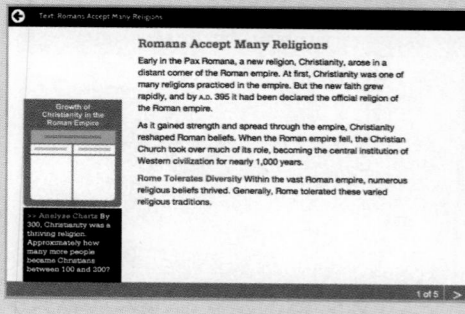

Objective 1: Understand the diverse religions included in the early Roman empire.

Quick Instruction

Remind students that the Romans were usually tolerant of other religious beliefs. Tell them this tolerance of local beliefs helped Rome govern its diverse territories. Point out that freedom of religion was not, however, a basic right for citizens like it is in the United States today.

Analyze Charts Project the chart of the Growth of Christianity in the Roman Empire. The chart shows Christianity grew rapidly from 300 to 350. Have students think about the different events that may have caused this dramatic increase as they read the text.

Describe Generally, as long as citizens showed loyalty by honoring Roman gods and acknowledging the divine spirit of the emperor, Roman subjects could worship other gods. Most people were polytheistic and were content to worship the Roman gods along with their own. Review the chart and the religions with students. Ask what do the terms *polytheism* and *monotheism* mean? *(Polytheism is the belief in many gods, and monotheism is the belief in one god.)* With this in mind, identify how religion in the empire changed over time as more people came to follow Christianity. *(Religion in the empire went from being polytheistic to monotheistic.)*

Further Instruction

Romans Accept Many Religions: Core Reading and Interactive Reading Notepad Project and discuss the Interactive Reading Notepad questions, including the graphic organizer asking students to explain the causes and effects of the Jewish revolt against Rome. Review the causes and effects with the class and fill in the graphic organizer on the whiteboard as you go.

Identify Cause and Effect Review the section under the heading "Divisions in Judea." Why were some Jews concerned that their religion was weakening? *(Many Jews absorbed Greek customs and ideas.)*

Analyze Information Ask students why the role of rabbis became more important after many Jews left Judea. *(Rabbis extended and preserved Jewish law since many Jews were scattered in communities around the Mediterranean.)*

The Origins of Christianity

DIGITAL TEXT 2

The Teachings of Jesus

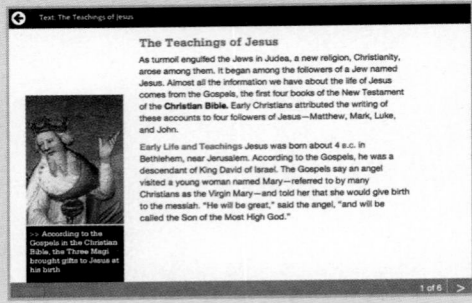

INTERACTIVE GALLERY

Christian Symbols

DIGITAL TEXT 3

Christianity Spreads

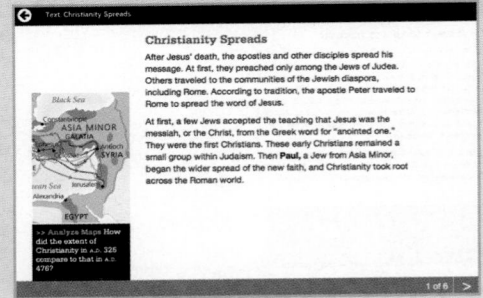

Objective 2: Describe the development and central ideas of Christianity.

Quick Instruction

Christianity emerged as a religion in the Roman territory of Judea. It started as people followed the teachings of a Jew named Jesus. His teachings reflect Jewish law and traditions. Jesus believed in one God and accepted the Ten Commandments and the teachings of the Jewish prophets. Echoing the teachings of Judaism, Jesus emphasized God's love and taught the need for justice, morality, and service to others. Jesus also preached new beliefs. According to his followers, he called himself the Son of God. Jesus said his mission was to bring spiritual salvation and eternal life to anyone who believed in him. Note that Shared Judeo-Christian beliefs about the just treatment of individuals and equality before the law would later influence Western legal systems as well as the governments of many Western democracies.

Interactive Gallery: Christian Symbols Project the gallery. Look at the collection as a whole then each image individually.

Analyze Images What does the image of the dove shown in the gallery represent in Christianity? *(The dove symbolizes the Holy Spirit. Doves are also associated with the birth and baptism of Jesus.)*

🔊 ACTIVE CLASSROOM

Have students complete a Walking Tour activity. Post images from the Interactive Gallery or passages from the text around the room. Have groups tour the room and discuss each image or passage. Have students describe the central idea of Christianity exhibited at each stop.

ELL Use the ELL activity described in the ELL chart.

Further Instruction

Go through the Interactive Reading Notepad questions and answers with the class. Record their responses on the whiteboard as you go through the questions.

Describe Ask students to describe the central ideas in Christianity. *(The belief in one god and the Ten Commandments. Jesus is the Son of God and will bring spiritual salvation and eternal life to his followers. A belief that mercy, sympathy, and forgiveness are all important traits.)*

D Differentiate: Challenge/Gifted After students finish reading and have completed the activity, have them write and perform a speech. The topic of the speech can be the development of Christianity, the development of monotheism, the central ideas in Christianity, or the historical origins of Christianity.

Objective 3: Summarize the spread of Christianity.

Quick Instruction

Remind students that the spread of Christianity took place as missionaries traveled the Roman empire and preached the teachings of Jesus. At first, the apostles preached only among the Jews, first in Judea and then in Jewish communities throughout the Roman world. When Paul decided to spread Jesus' teachings to non-Jews, it marked the beginning of Christianity becoming a world religion. Despite the persecution of Christians, the religion continued to draw followers with its message of love, teachings of equality, dignity, and the promise of a better life after death. Some missionaries used Greek philosophy to explain Jesus' message. Romans who had embraced Greek philosophy as their own were drawn to a religion that incorporated the discipline and moderation of this philosophy. Once Rome officially embraced Christianity, it grew in importance and in its number of followers.

Interactive Map: The Spread of Christianity Step through the spread of Christianity interactive map with students. Point out that it shows the spread of the religion from A.D. 325 through A.D. 476.

🔊 ACTIVE CLASSROOM

Use the See-Think-Wonder activity with students. Project the final map from the Interactive Map on the whiteboard. Ask students, What do you see? What does that make you think? What are you wondering about now that you've seen this? Ask volunteers to share their insights with the class.

INTERACTIVE MAP

The Spread of Christianity

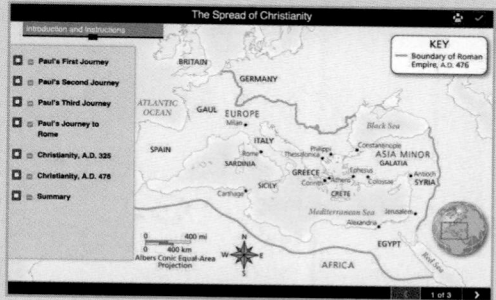

DIGITAL TEXT 4

The Growth of the Christian Church

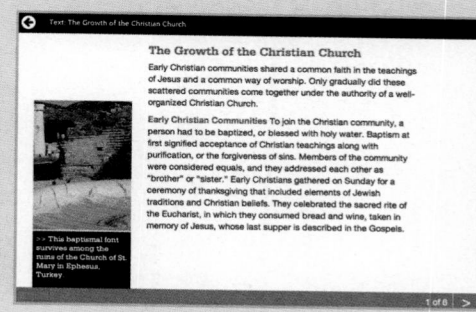

Draw Conclusions Prompt students to think about a map of the world today. Point out that today, Christianity is practiced on every continent. Ask students how Christianity may have continued to spread. (*Sample response: As people began to travel to other continents, missionaries had new opportunities to spread Christianity. When people migrated they brought their beliefs with them, introducing the religion into new lands.*)

Further Instruction

Go through the Interactive Reading Notepad questions and discuss the answers with the class.

Analyze Information How did Paul's actions contribute to Christianity becoming a world religion? (*He began preaching Jesus' teachings to non-Jews, established churches, and clarified Christian doctrine.*)

Ask students to read aloud and summarize the information under the heading "The Message Wins Converts."

Describe How did Christianity continue to spread during times when Christians were persecuted? (*The teachings of love, equality, dignity, and a promise of a better life appealed to people. In addition, Jesus had welcomed all people, especially the poor or oppressed. People also were drawn to the discipline and moderation of Greek philosophy that was part of the missionaries' message. The martyrs and the strength of their beliefs also impressed Romans.*)

Identify Cause and Effect Have students think about the actions of Theodosius. Then ask them to describe Rome's influence on Christianity. (*With Christianity the official religion of Rome, the religion grew and would likely continue to grow. The church would also gain more power as more churches were developed throughout the empire.*)

Objective 4: Outline the development of the early Christian church.

Quick Instruction

The Growth of the Christian Church: The Christian Clergy Project the chart on the whiteboard. Introduce the chart by telling students that as Christianity spread, the church became more organized and eventually became the central institution in the region.

ELL Use the ELL activity described in the ELL chart.

Further Instruction

The Growth of the Christian Church: Core Reading and Interactive Reading Notepad Call students' attention to the history and relevance of Christian traditions in the Core Reading. Then project the Interactive Reading Notepad questions on the whiteboard. Go through the questions and answer the questions with the class.

Analyze Information What was the history and relevance of the tradition of a baptism and the Eucharist in the Christian church? (*A baptism first signified acceptance of Christian teachings. Christians also believed that through the rite of baptism God forgave their sins. The Eucharist was done on Sunday, when Christians gathered for a ceremony of thanksgiving to God. The bread and wine was consumed in memory of Jesus, and his last supper, as described by the Gospels.*)

The Origins of Christianity

SYNTHESIZE

DEMONSTRATE

DIGITAL ACTIVITY
Key Roles in Early Christianity

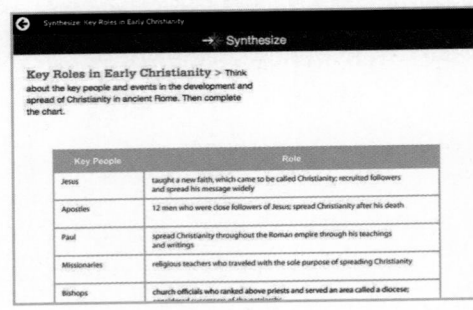

LESSON QUIZ
Lesson Quiz and Class Discussion Board

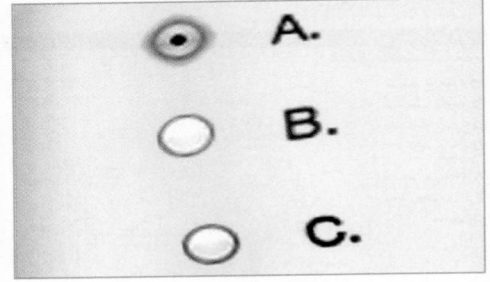

Summarize Discuss the roles of different members of the clergy. Ask students to summarize the role of women. *(At first women served as teachers and administrators. Later they were not allowed to serve in official roles; however, women could still carry on the tradition of missionary work.)* In the early Christian church, which officials were considered to be equal successors to the apostles? *(Bishops.)*

Identify Central Issues Why did church leaders seek a structure for the church? *(To ensure uniformity in beliefs, practices, and rituals so that local priests or bishops did not act independently, and to provide an orderly way to make decisions and settle conflicts over doctrine or practices.)*

ELL Use the ELL activity described in the ELL chart.

Project the Synthesize Activity Have students think about the key people and events in the development and spread of Christianity in ancient Rome. As students work through the chart, ask them to consider which of the key roles they would categorize as part of the central ideas in Christianity and which would fall into the category of the spread of Christianity. Ask them to make a quick list for each category, then as a class discuss the responses. *(Answers may vary. Central ideas in Christianity: Jesus and apostles; spread of Christianity: Jesus, apostles, Paul, and missionaries.)*

Discuss Ask students to think about the growth of the Christian church. Have them briefly summarize the development of Christianity, including its historical origins and the spread of Christianity. *(Sample response: Christianity began in Judea with the teachings of a Jew named Jesus. He gathered 12 disciples, called apostles, to help spread his message. After the death of Jesus, missionaries continued their work, traveling to most of the Roman empire. Christianity gained more followers, and Christian communities became more widespread. Christianity had become a major world religion with a structured church.)*

Assign the online Lesson Quiz for this lesson if you haven't already done so. Students will be offered automatic remediation or enrichment based on their score.

Pose these statements to the class on the Discussion Board:

In "The Origins of Christianity" you read about the different religions in Rome, the teachings of Jesus, and the development and spread of Christianity.

Predict Consequences How do you think the fall of Rome will affect the church and Western Europe? *(Answers may vary. Some students might respond that the church will lose power without the unity and organization that Rome brought to Western Europe. Other students might predict that the church, with its structure and widespread Christian communities, will have a chance to gain strength and fill the power vacuum left by the fall of Rome.)*

Draw Inferences What do you think will be the biggest challenge to the growth of Christianity? *(Answers may vary. Students might respond that as Christianity spreads its followers will come into conflict with those who hold different beliefs. Other students might note that the church, like the Roman empire, might become too large an institution to manage properly and will have an increase in internal divisions.)*

Ancient Rome and the Origins of Christianity (509 B.C.–A.D. 476)

■ SYNTHESIZE

■ DEMONSTRATE

DIGITAL ESSENTIAL QUESTION ACTIVITY

Reflect on the Essential Question and Topic

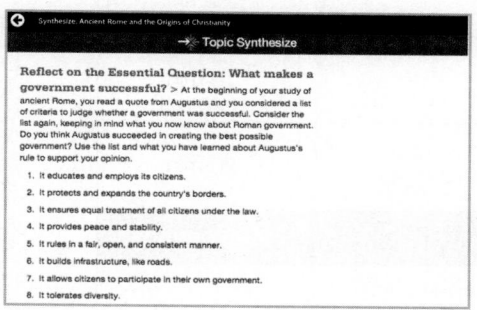

First, ask students to reconsider the Essential Question for the Topic: What makes a government successful? Remind students of the reasons they considered at the start of the topic. For example, does the government

- educate and employ its citizens?
- protect and expand its borders?
- ensure equal treatment of all citizens under the law?
- provide peace and stability?
- rule in a fair, open, and consistent manner?
- build infrastructure, like roads?
- allow citizens to participate in their own government?
- tolerate diversity?

Ask students, "Do you think the Roman government was successful?" Have them give at least three reasons to support their position. Discuss their answers on the Class Discussion Board.

Next, ask students to reflect on the topic as a whole and jot down 1-3 questions they've thought about during the topic. Share these examples if students need help getting started:

- How can governments broaden political participation?
- How did the Roman government try to meet the needs of its people, and what does your government do to help you?
- What were the rights and responsibilities of Roman citizens, and how do they compare to your rights and civic responsibilities today?

You may ask students to share their questions and answers on the Class Discussion Board.

DIGITAL TOPIC REVIEW AND ASSESSMENT

Ancient Rome and the Origins of Christianity (509 B.C.–A.D. 476)

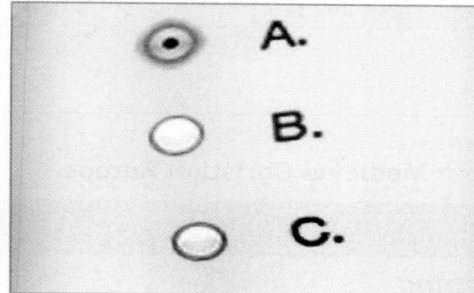

Students can prepare for the Topic Test by answering the questions in the Topic Review and Assessment online or the Assessment questions in the Print Student text. They can also prepare by reviewing their answers to the Interactive Reading Notepad questions or reviewing their notes in the Reading and Notetaking Study Guide.

DIGITAL TOPIC TEST

Ancient Rome and the Origins of Christianity (509 B.C.–A.D. 476)

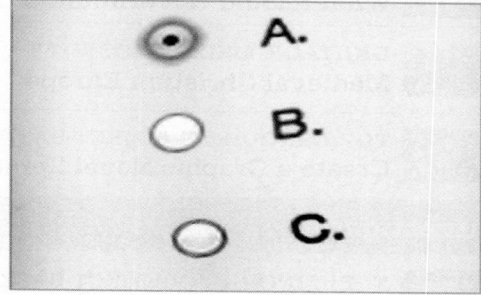

TOPIC TEST

Assign the Topic Test to assess students' understanding of topic content.

BENCHMARK TESTS

Assign these benchmark tests as you complete the relevant topics to monitor student progress toward mastering the course content and as preparation for the End-of-Course Test.

Benchmark Test 1: Topics 1–5
Benchmark Test 2: Topics 6–10
Benchmark Test 3: Topics 11–15
Benchmark Test 4: Topics 16–21

Topic 7

Medieval Christian Europe (330–1450)

TOPIC 7 ORGANIZER	PACING: APPROX. 11 PERIODS, 5.5 BLOCKS
	PACING
Connect	1 period
MY STORY VIDEO Guédelon, A Medieval Castle in the Making	10 min.
DIGITAL ESSENTIAL QUESTION ACTIVITY What Should Governments Do?	10 min.
DIGITAL TIMELINE ACTIVITY Medieval Christian Europe	10 min.
TOPIC INQUIRY: PROJECT-BASED LEARNING Create a Graphic Novel Spread About Medieval Christian Europe	20 min.
Investigate	4–8 periods
TOPIC INQUIRY: PROJECT-BASED LEARNING Create a Graphic Novel Spread About Medieval Christian Europe	Ongoing
LESSON 1 The Early Middle Ages	30–40 min.
LESSON 2 Feudalism and the Manor Economy	30–40 min.
LESSON 3 The Medieval Christian Church	30–40 min.
LESSON 4 Economic Expansion and Change: The Crusades and After	30–40 min.
LESSON 5 The Feudal Monarchs and the Church	30–40 min.
LESSON 6 Learning, Literature, and the Arts of the Middle Ages	30–40 min.
LESSON 7 The Late Middle Ages: A Time of Upheaval	30–40 min.
LESSON 8 Russia and Eastern Europe	30–40 min.
Synthesize	1 period
DIGITAL ESSENTIAL QUESTION ACTIVITY Reflect on the Essential Question and Topic	10 min.
TOPIC INQUIRY: PROJECT-BASED LEARNING Create a Graphic Novel Spread About Medieval Christian Europe	20 min.
Demonstrate	1–2 periods
ONLINE TEST Medieval Christian Europe	10 min.
TOPIC INQUIRY: PROJECT-BASED LEARNING Create a Graphic Novel Spread About Medieval Christian Europe	20 min.

NOTES

Topic ⑦

 **TOPIC INQUIRY: PROJECT-BASED LEARNING**

Create a Graphic Novel Spread About Medieval Christian Europe

In this Topic Inquiry, students work in teams to research and create an eight-panel graphic novel about life in Europe in the Middle Ages.

STEP 1: CONNECT
Develop Questions and Plan the Investigation

Launch the Project, Generate Questions, and Examine Graphic Novels

Tell students that they will research life in medieval Europe and use this knowledge, along with special software, to create a two-page spread from a graphic novel. Display the Project Launch and refer students to the bulleted list **What Makes a Graphic Novel Good?**

Suggestion: Have students describe favorite graphic novels and point out how they succeed in various categories such as characters, plot, setting, and text. Suggest they compare and contrast various graphic novels they have read and enjoyed.

Plan the Investigation

Form students into teams. Have them learn about working as a team by reviewing a skills tutorial. Then have each team sign the *Project Contract*, assign team roles using the *Project Tracker*, and begin the *Need to Know Questions*.

Suggestion: To spur discussion about various elements of a graphic novel and how they use visuals and text to present the author's ideas, ask team members to take turns describing a graphic novel they enjoy.

Resources
- Project Launch
- Project Contract
- Project Tracker
- Need-to-Know Questions
- Student Instructions
- Rubric for a Graphic Novel Skills Tutorial Search for Information on the Internet Skills Tutorial Work in Teams
- Skills Tutorial: Search for Information on the Internet
- Skills Tutorial: Work in Teams

⏻ PROFESSIONAL DEVELOPMENT

Project-Based Learning
Be sure to view the Project-Based Learning Professional Development resources in the online course.

STEP 2: INVESTIGATE
Apply Disciplinary Concepts and Tools

Identify Topic

Teams will learn how to assign tasks and monitor their work, then, with your help, choose a subject for their graphic novel spread. They will brainstorm how to approach their subject, keeping in mind the driving question, **What was life like in the Middle Ages for people at different economic and social levels?**

Suggestion: To ensure that a variety of subjects from different aspects of medieval life are portrayed, assign topics. Possible topics might include family life in either rural areas or cities, different kinds of work, the arts, kings and queens, the Church, science and technology, transportation, operating a manor, and the Crusades.

Conduct Research

There are two research tasks for this project: finding and learning how to use the graphic novel software to produce the spread and researching the Middle Ages to write the text and design the art. To guide their research, teams will create a list of *Need-to-Know Questions* about their subject and about the graphic novel software they plan to use. Refer students to helpful resources within the Topic to help answer their questions. If they are researching Gothic cathedrals, refer them to the text and activities in Lesson 6. Help students fill out the *Information Organizer*.

Suggestion: Preview some of the suggested graphic novel construction websites to make sure they fit students' needs. Also, see if your school has subscribed to any sites that might be appropriate for the project.

Write, Edit, and Storyboard Your Spread

Students write and edit their text and storyboard their visual ideas. Emphasize that the storyboard is a kind of draft where they can try out different visual elements before deciding on a final version.

Suggestion: Create a sample storyboard to show students how to create one.

Resources
- Skills Tutorial: Work in Teams
- Skills Tutorial: Search for Information on the Internet
- Need-to-Know Questions
- Project Tracking Sheet
- Information Organizing Worksheet

STEP 3: SYNTHESIZE
Evaluate Sources and Use
Evidence to Formulate Conclusions

Create the Graphic Novel Spread

Now have students get together to create their graphic novel spreads. If students are having trouble sharing the work on this part of the project, remind them to review their *Project Tracker* document to see how they planned to divide the work. Review each team's spread to make sure they are on track. For students who are having trouble, walk them through *Information Organizer: Plan Your Graphic Novel* as a class to get ideas.

Suggestion: For a less technology-dependent end product, have students use art materials to create a graphic novel spread by hand. To take the technology a step further, have students animate their spreads with audio or movement.

Review the Graphic Novel Spread

Have students edit each other's work and offer suggestions to improve the text and visuals. Be prepared to offer advice on how to improve the teams' products.

State Conclusion about the Guiding Question

Have students state a conclusion about the driving question based on their work with the graphic novel spread. They should produce a written paragraph to accompany their graphic novel spread.

Suggestion: Consider leading a short discussion on how the driving question relates to the teams' individual subjects.

Resources
• Information Organizer: Plan Your Graphic Novel Spread

STEP 4: DEMONSTRATE
Communicate Conclusions
and Take Informed Action

Present the Graphic Novel

Have students prepare their graphic novel spread presentations, then watch the team presentations. To help the teams structure their time, set up a clock in the back of the room, and alert them when they have only a few minutes left.

Reflect on the Project

After students have finished their Team Assessments, help them go over what they thought went well and what did not, so they can be even more effective in the future.

Suggestion: As an extension activity, have students create a "Then and Now" chart that compares aspects of life, including people's relationship with various governments, during the Middle Ages and today.

Resources
• Give an Effective Presentation Skills Tutorial
• Graphic Novel Spread Rubric
• Self-Assessment

Medieval Christian Europe (330–1450)

After the decline of Rome, Western Europe entered a period of political, social, and economic disorder as waves of invaders swept across the region. A decentralized political and economic structure known as feudalism developed, and the Church became powerful. Improvements in agriculture, growing towns and cities grew, and a new middle class helped plant the seeds of our modern world.

■ CONNECT

MY STORY VIDEO

Guédelon, A Medieval Castle in the Making

Watch a video that shows modern craftspeople building a castle using medieval techniques and materials.

Check Understanding What was the most essential element to building a medieval castle? *(stone)*

Hypothesize The video introduces viewers to a number of craftspersons. What does that say about the construction of a medieval castle? *(The work on a castle was highly specialized, with each craftsperson contributing skills that helped create an imposing building.)*

↳ FLIP IT!

Assign the My Story Video.

DIGITAL ESSENTIAL QUESTION ACTIVITY

What Should Governments Do?

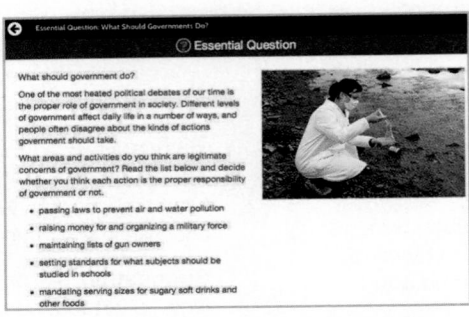

Ask students to think about the Essential Question for this Topic: What Should Governments Do?

Ask students to decide which of the six activities is an appropriate government activity. Then go over the results as a class.

Support a Point of View with Evidence Which activities did you consider to be an appropriate government activity? Why? What evidence did you use? *(historical records, facts about governmental and private efforts to perform the tasks, reasoned judgments of experts.)*

Identify Central Issues If not government, who should take on these responsibilities? Would nongovernmental groups do a better job in some cases than the government? *(Some students may cite nongovernmental groups as more cost-effective. Others may argue that some jobs are too big for anything but government to address.)*

Distinguish Among Fact, Opinion, and Reasoned Judgment Many people have strong opinions about the six responsibilities listed. What criteria can you use to separate facts from opinions? *(Criteria should include facts, historical records, and awareness of special interests that could affect someone's position.)*

DIGITAL TIMELINE ACTIVITY

Medieval Christian Europe

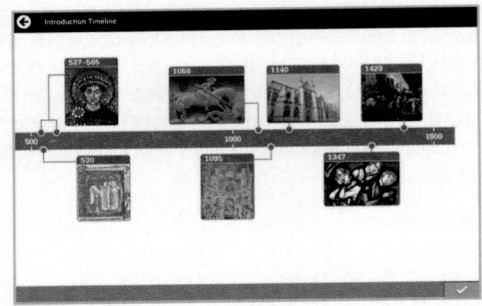

Display the timeline showing the major events of the Middle Ages. During this Topic students will learn about all of these events and many more, but this timeline will provide a framework into which they can place the events they learn about.

D Differentiate **Extra Support** Ask a volunteer to point out the time intervals on the timeline and the overall range of time covered by this timeline. Ask, how many years are there between the launching of the First Crusade and the election of Innocent III as pope? *(103; First Crusade began in 1095; Innocent III became pope in 1198)*

Check Understanding In what year did the Black Death first appear in Europe? *(1347)*

Topic Inquiry

Launch the Topic Inquiry with students after introducing the Topic.

The Early Middle Ages

Supporting English Language Learners

Use with Digital Text 2, **The Age of Justinian.**

Listening
Read *The Age of Justinian* aloud. Then have students complete one activity according to their level of English proficiency.

Beginning Explain that context clues are pieces of information in a text that help explain significant ideas, events, or people. Read *The Age of Justinian* aloud to students. Point out appositives in the text, explaining how information following the comma provides additional information. Then help students find the appositives in a section of the text, either highlighting them or copying them into a notebook. Help students identify the description and what is being described in the sentence. Finally, have students practice using appositives in conversation with the following sentence frames.

• My homework, _____, is always completed before I go to bed at night.

• I try to eat my favorite food, _____, at least once a week.

Intermediate Explain that context clues are pieces of information in a text that help explain significant ideas, events, or people. Read *The Age of Justinian* aloud to students. Point out one appositive in the text, explaining how information following the comma can explain the idea, event, or person before the comma. Then help students find the appositives in a section of the text, either highlighting them or copying them into a notebook. Ask students to identify which section of the sentence is the description and which section is being described. Finally, have students practice using appositives in conversation with the following sentence frames.

• My homework, _____, is always completed before I go to bed at night.

• I try to eat my favorite food, _____, at least once a week.

Advanced Ask student pairs to create a definition of context clues. Make sure that students understand that context clues are pieces of information in a text that help explain significant ideas, events, or people. Have student pairs read *The Age of Justinian*. Point out one appositive in the text, explaining how information following the comma can explain the idea, event, or person before the comma. Then have pairs find the appositives in the rest of the section, either highlighting them or copying them into a notebook. Finally, ask student pairs to practice using appositives as they discuss the text.

Advanced High Explain appositives to students, using an example from the text. Then have students read *The Age of Justinian* and identify the appositives. Have students choose 2 or 3 appositives and explain how the appositives enhance their understanding of the content. Finally, ask students to turn to a partner and practice using appositives as they discuss how Constantinople was rebuilt.

Use with Digital Text 6, **New Invasions Pound Europe.**

Listening
Have students identify and discuss any stereotypes they may have about the historical Vikings and their influence on Western Europe in the Early Middle Ages.

Beginning Write and display the word *Vikings* for students. Facilitate a discussion that allows students to identify what they think they already know about the Viking people. If necessary, provide visuals or use images from the text to help students make connections. Provide vocabulary for students as they work to describe this tribal group.

Intermediate Write and display the word *Vikings* for students. Ask students to identify what they think they already know about the Viking people. Encourage students to use bits of information that they have learned in other areas of life and apply it to this activity. Have students refer to the text or other images to help make connections. Provide vocabulary for students as they work to describe the Vikings. Then read the section aloud. After the section is read aloud, have students enhance their descriptions by adding details from the text.

Advanced Have students work in small groups. Write and display the word *Vikings* and ask students to identify what they already know about the Viking people. Encourage students to help each other identify bits of information that they have learned in other areas of life and apply it to this activity. Then ask each small group to read the section aloud. After reading, have students enhance their descriptions by making corrections or adding details from the text.

Advanced High Have students work in pairs to identify what they already know about the Viking people. Encourage pairs to help each other identify information that they have learned in other areas of life and apply it to this activity. Then ask students to read the section independently. After reading, have pairs enhance their descriptions by making corrections or adding details from the text.

▣ Differentiate Instruction

Use the Differentiated Instruction notes throughout the lesson plan to support the varied skill sets, levels of readiness, and interests in the mixed-ability classroom.

Challenge These notes include suggestions for expanding the activity for advanced students.

On-Level These notes include suggestions for modifying the activity to address different interests or learning styles.

Extra Support These notes include ideas for providing more scaffolding or reading spuport.

Special Needs These notes provide ideas for adapting instruction to support the needs of various special needs students.

■ NOTES

_____

_____

_____

_____

_____

The Early Middle Ages

Objectives

Objective 1: Summarize ways in which the Byzantine empire flourished after the decline of Rome.

Objective 2: Explain the impact of the fall of Rome on Western Europe.

Objective 3: Describe how Germanic tribes carved Europe into small kingdoms.

Objective 4: Explain how Charlemagne briefly reunited much of Western Europe and what happened to his empire after his death.

LESSON 1 ORGANIZER		PACING: APPROX. 1 PERIOD, .5 BLOCKS			
				RESOURCES	
		OBJECTIVES	PACING	Online	Print
Connect					
DIGITAL START UP ACTIVITY **A Sovereign City**			5 min.	●	
Investigate					
DIGITAL TEXT 1 **The Byzantine Empire Thrives**			10 min.	●	
DIGITAL TEXT 2 **The Age of Justinian**		Objective 1	10 min.	●	
INTERACTIVE GALLERY **Hagia Sophia**			10 min.	●	
DIGITAL TEXT 3 **Changes in Western Europe**		Objective 2	10 min.	●	
DIGITAL TEXT 4 **Germanic Kingdoms**		Objective 3	10 min.	●	
DIGITAL TEXT 5 **Charlemagne Builds an Empire**			10 min.	●	
DIGITAL TEXT 6 **New Invasions Pound Europe**		Objective 4	10 min.	●	
INTERACTIVE MAP **Invasions of Europe 700–1000**			10 min.	●	
Synthesize					
SYNTHESIZE ACTIVITY **Cooperation: The European Union**			5 min.	●	
Demonstrate					
LESSON QUIZ **Lesson Quiz and Class Discussion Board**			10 min.	●	

PEARSON realize.™
www.PearsonRealize.com

Go online to access additional resources including:
Primary Sources • Biographies • Supreme Court cases •
21st Century Skill Tutorials • Maps • Graphic Organizers.

■ CONNECT

DIGITAL START UP ACTIVITY

A Sovereign City

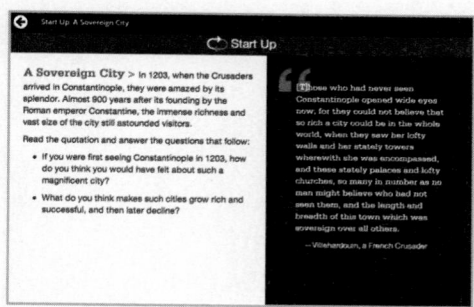

Project the Start Up Activity Ask students to read the quotation and answer the questions as they enter and get settled. Then have them share their ideas with another student, either in class or through a chat or blog space.

Discuss If you were first seeing Constantinople in 1203, how would you have felt about such a vast city? *(Answers may vary. Students should convey a powerful effect, positive or negative.)* Would you or did you feel that way when you first saw a big city? *(Answers may vary. Students should briefly describe their feelings.)* What makes such cities grow rich and successful, and then later decline? *(Sample Responses: location, access to natural resources, transportation, trade, and political power.)*

Tell students that in this lesson they will learn how Constantinople flourished.

⬆⬇ FLIP IT!

Assign the Flipped Video for this lesson.

■ STUDENT EDITION PRINT PAGES: 190–197

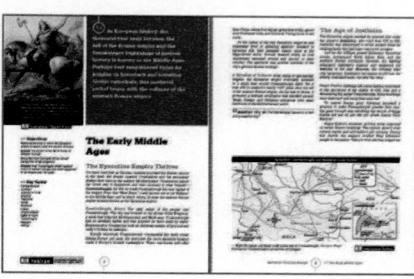

■ INVESTIGATE

DIGITAL TEXT 1

The Byzantine Empire Thrives

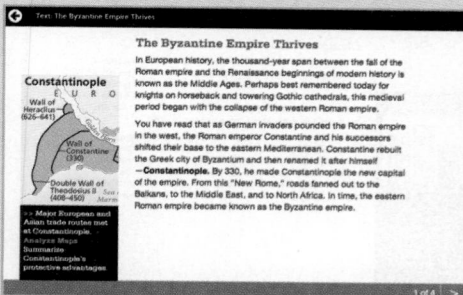

Objective 1: Summarize ways in which the Byzantine empire flourished after the decline of Rome.

Quick Instruction

Interactive Gallery: Hagia Sophia Project the gallery on the whiteboard. Explain that Constantine's magnificent rebuilding of Hagia Sophia and much of Constantinople provides an example of how the Byzantine empire flourished after the decline of Rome. Point out that the history of this building reflects the interactions between Christian and Muslim societies. Click through the hotspots on the gallery and discuss the building's important architectural features as a church and as a mosque.

🖼 ACTIVE CLASSROOM

Have students describe Hagia Sophia's history using the If Photos Could Talk strategy. Ask: What do you think Hagia Sophia (the exterior photo) would say about the flourishing Byzantine empire and the years that followed if it could talk? What's your evidence? Have students present their responses to the class. *(Sample Response: "As a church and mosque, I watched thousands of people from many different cultures praying, was destroyed and rebuilt luxuriously several times, and saw Constantinople's fortunes shift.")*

ELL Use the ELL activity described in the ELL chart.

DIGITAL TEXT 2

The Age of Justinian

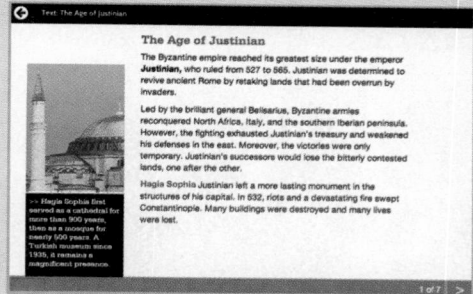

Further Instruction

The Age of Justinian Project the Close Reading Notepad questions and have students answer as they progress through the core reading.

The Impact of Justinian's Code: Infographic Project the infographic about Justinian's Code. Make sure students understand how Justinian's organization of Roman laws helped unify the Byzantine empire and the impact of the Code's political and legal ideas on later rulers and the development of systems of law.

Draw Inferences Have students review the text and Justinian's Code infographic. Ask: What was the impact of political and legal ideas contained in Justinian's Code of laws? *(Student answers may vary. Students should include that by gathering, organizing, and simplifying Roman laws, the Code helped unify Justinian's vast empire; its political and legal principles served as models for later Western European rulers' laws, helping leaders consolidate their power; and the Code became the main Roman law source, often borrowed from to develop civil and international legal systems in Western Europe, Latin America, Africa, and the United States.)*

The Early Middle Ages

INTERACTIVE GALLERY

Hagia Sophia

DIGITAL TEXT 3

Changes in Western Europe

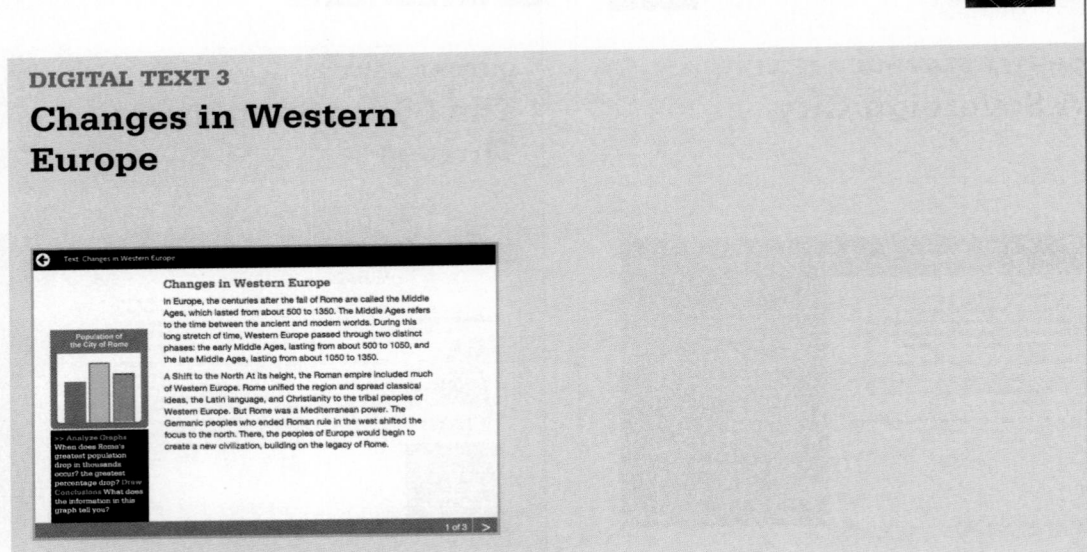

Objective 2: Explain the effects of the decline and the impact of the fall of Rome on Western Europe.

Quick Instruction

Project the bar graph of Rome's population on the whiteboard. Tell students that after the western Roman empire fell, the lack of a centralized Roman state and powerful army had a strong impact on Western Europe. Briefly introduce the bar graph to students, noting that the populations of many cities declined during the period following the collapse of the western Roman empire.

Formulate Questions Have students explore the bar graph of Rome's population. Ask students to pair with a partner and examine the graph. Then ask them: What do you see? What does that make you think? What are you wondering about now that you've seen this? Have students share their insights with the class. *(Answers will vary. Students should point out the large overall population drop, conclude that important events might have caused this, and wonder what drove so many people from the city.)*

Further Instruction

Changes in Western Europe: Core Reading and Close Reading Notepad Go through the Close Reading Notepad question and discuss the answer with the class.

Predict Consequences Have students imagine that a large country no longer has a centralized government or a strong army. What impact would that have on the country? Tell students to write three or four consequences that they predict would occur. List their predictions on the board. *(Sample Responses: regions become politically divided, become isolated from other regions, face rapid drops in trade, are threatened by invaders, and experience large declines in city populations.)*

Summarize Ask students to explain the impact of the fall of Rome on Western Europe. *(Answers will vary. Students should include that after the collapse of the western Roman empire, no centralized state backed by a strong army existed to maintain law and keep the peace in former Roman territories. Western Europe became politically divided, isolated, overrun by invaders, and experienced steep declines in trade and urban populations.)*

DIGITAL TEXT 4

Germanic Kingdoms

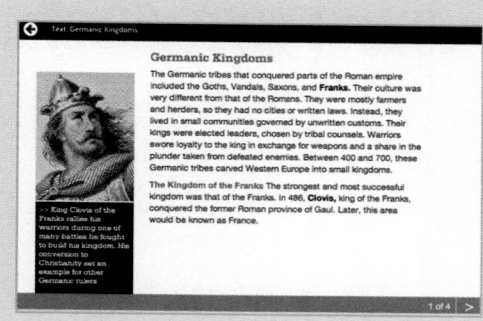

DIGITAL TEXT 5

Charlemagne Builds an Empire

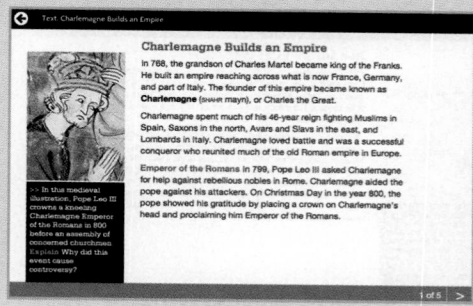

Objective 3: Describe how Germanic tribes carved Europe into small kingdoms.

Quick Instruction

Project the illustration of Clovis on the whiteboard. Have students look at the image. Tell students that early in the formation of medieval Europe, Germanic tribes, such as the Goths, Vandals, Saxons, and Franks, divided up Western Europe into many small kingdoms. The former Roman province of Gaul, for example, was conquered in 486 by Clovis, king of the Franks, a Germanic tribe. Clovis converted to Christianity but also followed Frankish and Roman customs.

Interpret Ask pairs of students to examine the illustration of Clovis again. Have them write a script about a conversation or a dramatic moment during the period of European decline after the fall of Rome, when the centralized Roman state and its mighty army no longer maintained the rule of law and kept the peace locally. Encourage students to consider what may have happened before or after the image shown, or what Clovis may have been thinking at the moment they see portrayed. Then have pairs of students act out their scripts. *(Sample Response [script idea]: Before a major battle, Clovis persuades the leader of a Frankish tribe to join with him and other Franks to defeat their mutual enemies. Together, he argues, they can defend and extend the lands the Franks hold.)*

D **Differentiate: Challenge/Gifted** Ask students to do additional research on Clovis, his conquest of Gaul, and his conversion to Christianity and present their findings.

Further Instruction

Germanic Kingdoms Project the Close Reading Notepad questions provided in the notepad. Have students answer them as they progress through the Core Reading.

Be sure that students understand that Clovis and the Franks represent only one among many small kingdoms that appeared in Western Europe after the fall of the western Roman empire.

Analyze Information Remind students that Clovis chose to change his religion to that of his subjects in Gaul. Ask students to discuss the reasons for his conversion to Christianity. Then have students form small groups to research Clovis and present their findings to the class. *(Answers will vary. Students should include Clovis's personal beliefs, family traditions, and his intentions to gain support for his leadership from his subjects and the pope.)*

Infer Point out that Frankish tribes in Gaul included both pagans and Christians. Ask: How did the conversion to Christianity by Clovis impact his efforts to politically and socially unite his kingdom? Students may wish to research Clovis's reign. *(Answers will vary. Students should understand Gaul was a formerly religiously diverse region that was undergoing Christian conversion. Clovis's conversion could both distance him from pagan leaders and their communities and bring him closer to Christian leaders and their groups.)*

Objective 4: Explain how Charlemagne briefly reunited much of Western Europe and what happened to his empire after his death.

Quick Instruction

Throughout his long rule, Charlemagne, king of the Franks, conquered tribes and fought off invaders to forge an empire unified by Christianity in what became present-day France, Germany, and Italy. He established a strong government, spread Christianity— allying with the pope—revived Latin learning, and built schools. After his death in 814, his sons vied for power, his grandsons divided his empire, and new invaders, the Magyars and Vikings, threatened Europe.

Interactive Map: Invasions of Europe, 700–1000 Project the map on the whiteboard. Point out that for three hundred years various groups both attacked and settled in Europe. Step through the layers on the map and discuss the impact that the invasions had on medieval society.

Analyze Images Ask: Where did the Magyars, Vikings, and Muslims come from? *(Magyars: west, south, and north from Hungary; Vikings: from Scandinavia across the ocean and to the British Isles, south along the coast of Europe and into the Mediterranean to Italy, east and south into Russia; Muslims: north from Africa and Spain, west from the Middle East)*

The Early Middle Ages

DIGITAL TEXT 6

New Invasions Pound Europe

INTERACTIVE MAP

Invasions of Europe 700–1000

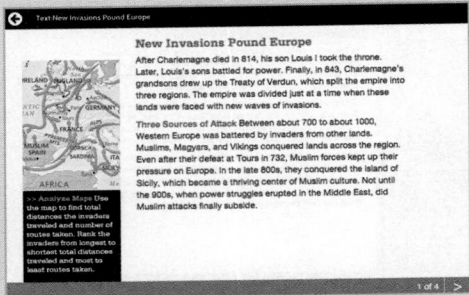

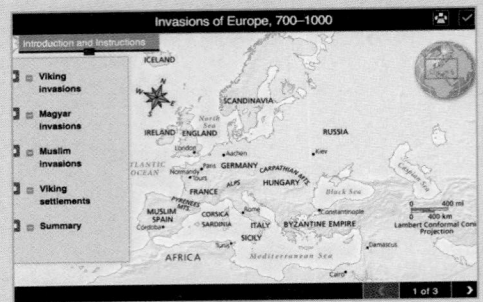

ACTIVE CLASSROOM

Employ the Make Headlines strategy with the interactive map to explore the invasions' impact. Ask: If you were to write a headline right now to capture the most important aspect that should be remembered about any invasion, what would that headline be? Pass your headline to a partner for review—that person can keep yours or ask for his or hers back. *(Sample Response: "Vikings Strike from the Sea! Some Stay to Settle.")*

Compare Have students consider how the collapse of Charlemagne's empire was similar to the collapse of the Roman empire. *(weakened when divided, then suffered attacks by outside plundering tribes)*

ELL Use the ELL activity described in the ELL chart.

D Differentiate: Extra Support Ask students to read "Charlemagne Builds an Empire" aloud. As they read, list Charlemagne's accomplishments on the board. Ask students to use the notes to write a short obituary commemorating Charlemagne. Follow up by discussing why Charlemagne was considered the greatest ruler of early medieval Europe.

Further Instruction

Charlemagne Builds an Empire: Core Reading and Close Reading Notepad
Project the questions provided in the notepad. Have students answer them as they progress through the Core Reading.

Identify Cause and Effect Why did Charlemagne support the creation of local schools and seek to revive Latin learning? *(Answers may vary, but should include that Charlemagne felt education would help unify his kingdom. To govern effectively, his officials would need to write reports and keep careful records. Charlemagne also hoped to revive Rome's glory at his court in Aachen, where he brought Europe's top scholars to his Palace School.)*

Compare and Contrast Ask: How did Clovis and Charlemagne spread Christianity and employ it as a unifying social and political force in their kingdoms? Write responses on the board under "Clovis" and "Charlemagne." *(Answers may vary. Clovis: converts to Christianity, thus unifying his Christian subjects, gains support of pope; Charlemagne: a Christian, allies with Church, crowned by Pope Leo III as Emperor of the Romans, sends out missionaries.)*

Draw Conclusions Why was Charlemagne important even though his empire collapsed after his death? *(He united and Christianized much of Western Europe, providing a model for future European leaders.)*

▇ SYNTHESIZE

SYNTHESIZE ACTIVITY
Cooperation: The European Union

Have students use the Think-Pair-Share strategy to answer the question in the Cooperation: The European Union activity. Ask them to take five minutes to write down some brief answers to the questions below, and then share their answers with a partner.

Ask partners to think about the following questions. What do you think were obstacles in unifying the nations in the European Union? How do you think these obstacles were similar to those Charlemagne encountered as he tried to unify his empire? Have pairs share their answers with the class.

Discuss Have students describe what they think governments should do to encourage cooperation as they try to unify diverse peoples into kingdoms or groups of nations, whether during the Middle Ages or today. *(Answers may vary. Students should mention such factors as the importance of establishing a strong central authority, accepting diverse religious and cultural traditions, and remaining aware of differences in political and economic structures between communities.)*

▇ DEMONSTRATE

LESSON QUIZ
Lesson Quiz and Class Discussion Board

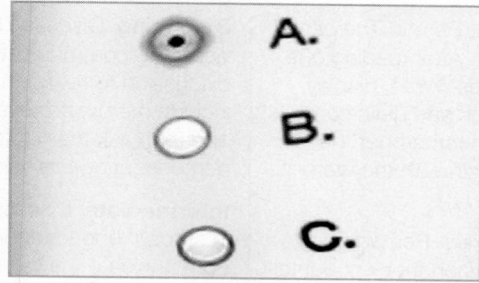

Assign the online Lesson Quiz for this lesson if you haven't already done so. Students will be offered automatic remediation or enrichment based on their score.

Pose these questions to the class on the Discussion Board:

In "The Early Middle Ages," you read about how the Byzantine empire flourished and Western Europe declined following the collapse of the western Roman empire. After the Germanic tribes established many small kingdoms in Europe, Charlemagne fought off invaders, expanded his Frankish kingdom, spread Christianity, and briefly reunified a large part of Western Europe into a Christian empire.

Recognize Cause and Effect Why did the collapse of the western Roman empire lead to the formation of medieval Europe? *(The lack of unifying forces—in the past provided by the centralized Roman state and army—led to turmoil and decline. These problems led to the development of the new political, social, and economic systems of medieval Europe.)*

Draw Conclusions Why do you think that Charlemagne encouraged the spread of Christianity in his empire? *(Christianity served as a unifying social and political factor that helped Charlemagne unify his empire by providing a common religion that different regions and groups could share.)*

Feudalism and the Manor Economy

Supporting English Language Learners

Use with Digital Text 2, **Nobles, Knights, and Warfare.**

Listening
Read *Nobles, Knights, and Warfare* aloud. Then have students complete one activity according to their level of English proficiency.

Beginning Provide students with bilingual dictionaries. Reread *The Life of a Knight,* pausing to write and display unfamiliar words. After reading one paragraph, demonstrate how to look up the listed words. Write, display, and read their meanings. Have students copy the words and definitions in their notebooks and draw an illustration to help them remember the meanings of the words. Then ask students to listen again with the word meanings in mind as you reread the paragraph.

Intermediate Provide students with bilingual dictionaries. Reread *The Life of a Knight* and ask students to raise their hands when they encounter unfamiliar words. Write and display these words. After reading one paragraph, assist students as they look up the listed words. Write, display, and read their meanings. Have students copy the words and definitions in their notebooks. Then ask students to listen again with the word meanings in mind as you reread the paragraph. Continue this activity with the rest of *Nobles, Knights, and Warfare.*

Advanced Provide students with dictionaries. Ask students to work together in small groups to reread *The Life of a Knight.* As one student reads out loud, the other students should write down any unfamiliar words. Instruct each group to write the words and their definitions in their notebooks. Groups should then reread the text and refer to their list of definitions as necessary to enhance their understanding of the text.

Advanced High Provide students with dictionaries. Ask students to work with a partner to reread *The Life of a Knight.* As one student reads out loud, the other student should write down any unfamiliar words. Instruct each pair to write the words and their definitions in their notebooks. Partners should then reread the text and refer to their list of definitions as necessary to enhance their understanding of the text.

Use with Digital Text 2, **Nobles, Knights, and Warfare.**

Listening
Read aloud, or have students read, the subsection entitled *The Code of Chivalry.* Then have students participate in the following activities.

Beginning Discuss *The Code of Chivalry* with students by providing visuals to communicate the values of a chivalrous knight. Guide the discussion to reveal that the values implicit in the practice of chivalry include *mercy, protection,* and *respect.* Define these terms for students and then ask them to choose one and draw a basic sketch of a knight demonstrating this value.

Intermediate Discuss *The Code of Chivalry* with students. To aid in student understanding, provide definitions of terms as needed to communicate the values of a chivalrous knight. Ask students to identify the ways knights must act to be considered chivalrous. Guide students to the realization that chivalrous knights show *mercy,* give *protection,* and demonstrate *respect.* Help students define these terms, and then ask them to choose one and write a sentence describing a knight exhibiting this value.

Advanced Discuss *The Code of Chivalry* with students. To aid in student understanding, provide dictionaries and other resources to students so they can define terms as needed to understand the values of a chivalrous knight. Facilitate a discussion that results in students' realization that chivalrous knights show *mercy,* give *protection,* and demonstrate *respect.* Provide resources for students to define these terms, and then ask them to write three sentences describing how a knight demonstrates these three values.

Advanced High Have students discuss *The Code of Chivalry* in small groups. Task each group with identifying the values of a chivalrous knight. If necessary, facilitate students' discussions to include the implicit understanding that knights should demonstrate *mercy, protection,* and *respect* to those in his care. Finally, have students write a short paragraph describing how a knight could demonstrate these three values in his actions toward others.

▣ Differentiate Instruction

Use the Differentiated Instruction notes throughout the lesson plan to support the varied skill sets, levels of readiness, and interests in the mixed-ability classroom.

Challenge These notes include suggestions for expanding the activity for advanced students.

On-Level These notes include suggestions for modifying the activity to address different interests or learning styles.

Extra Support These notes include ideas for providing more scaffolding or reading spuport.

Special Needs These notes provide ideas for adapting instruction to support the needs of various special needs students.

▮ NOTES

Objectives

Objective 1: Describe the development of the political and social system of feudalism.

Objective 2: Summarize the life of knights and nobles.

Objective 3: Analyze how the economic system of manorialism worked and how it affected peasants and nobles.

LESSON 2 ORGANIZER		PACING: APPROX. 1 PERIOD, .5 BLOCKS			
				RESOURCES	
		OBJECTIVES	PACING	Online	Print
Connect					
DIGITAL START UP ACTIVITY **Knighted on the Battlefield**			5 min.	●	
Investigate					
DIGITAL TEXT 1 **Feudalism Develops**		Objective 1	10 min.	●	
DIGITAL TEXT 2 **Nobles, Knights, and Warfare**		Objective 2	10 min.	●	
INTERACTIVE GALLERY **Defending a Castle**			10 min.	●	
DIGITAL TEXT 3 **Manorialism**		Objective 3	10 min.	●	
INTERACTIVE CHART **The Medieval Manorial System**			10 min.	●	
Synthesize					
SYNTHESIZE ACTIVITY **A Powerful Woman**			5 min.	●	
Demonstrate					
LESSON QUIZ **Lesson Quiz and Class Discussion Board**			10 min.	●	

Feudalism and the Manor Economy

CONNECT

DIGITAL START UP ACTIVITY
Knighted on the Battlefield

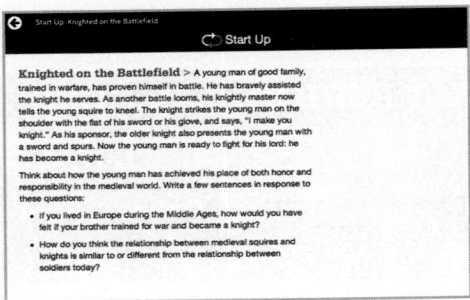

Project the Start Up Activity Ask students to answer the questions as they enter and get settled. Then have them share their ideas with another student in class or through a chat room or blog.

Discuss If you lived in Europe during the Middle Ages, how would you have felt if your brother or friend trained and became a knight? *(Sample Responses: respect, admiration, anger, fear, worry, acceptance)* How was the relationship between medieval squires and knights similar to or different from relationships between soldiers today? *(Sample Responses: similar—bonding in battle, recognition for bravery; different—unequal social backgrounds, very different times.)*

Tell students that in this lesson they will learn how knights prepared for warfare as a way of life.

⋈ FLIP IT!
Assign the Flipped Video for this lesson.

◼ STUDENT EDITION PRINT
PAGES: 198–202

INVESTIGATE

DIGITAL TEXT 1
Feudalism Develops

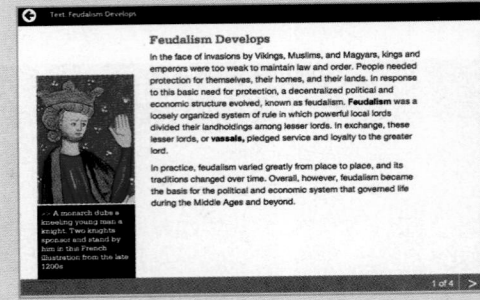

Objective 1: Describe the development of the political and social system of feudalism.

Quick Instruction
Explain to students that the political and social system of feudalism developed in response to the great need for protection Europeans felt during invasions by Vikings, Muslims, and Magyars. When kings and emperors could not maintain law and order, a loosely organized system of relationships arose between lords and vassals based on the exchange of land for loyalty and military service.

Infographic: How Does Feudalism Work? Project the infographic on the whiteboard. Look at each image and text individually and then the sequence of images as a whole.

Analyze Images How do knights fit into the feudal system? *(Knights are vassals of nobles and churchmen. Their lords grant them land in exchange for the knights' loyalty and military service.)*

Make Generalizations Group students. Give each group a three-column organizer with headings *Plus/Minus/Interesting* to record responses to these questions about the political/social system of feudalism: 1. What are positive characteristics of feudalism? *(Sample Responses: protects people, gives everyone a place within political/social structure)* 2. What are negative characteristics of feudalism? *(lords dominate, might abuse vassals; many peasants serve few nobles)* 3. What is interesting about feudalism? *(entire complex society can be linked by lord-vassal mutual obligations)*

D Differentiate: Extra Support After students have read the section, write the terms king, lord, knight, and peasant on the board. Write "Responsibilities" and "Privileges" under each. Have students share examples of responsibilities and privileges of each level of European feudal society. Write examples on the board and ask students to copy them into their notebooks.

Further Instruction
Feudalism Develops Go through the Interactive Reading Notepad questions and discuss the answers with the class.

Predict Consequences Ask students to write brief answers to this question: Do the major characteristics of the political and social system of feudalism encourage or discourage conflict? Have students form two panels and conduct a feudalism debate. *(Answers may vary. Students should mention that a vassal's sworn loyalty to a lord requires military service, which helps nobles gather supporters and form armies. Alternatively, the feudal bond represents mutual obligations that might also limit conflict among lords and vassals.)*

Draw Conclusions Why do you think land ownership became an increasing source of power for lords in the political and social system of feudalism? *(Sample Response: After the collapse of the western Roman empire, invasions in Europe led people to leave cities and move to rural areas. As agriculture became more important, owning land became a source of power. Local lords with large estates held the most power under the social and political system of feudalism.)*

DIGITAL TEXT 2

Nobles, Knights, and Warfare

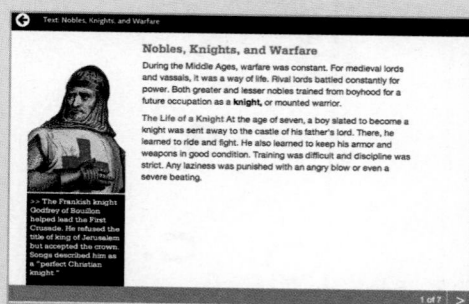

INTERACTIVE GALLERY

Defending a Castle

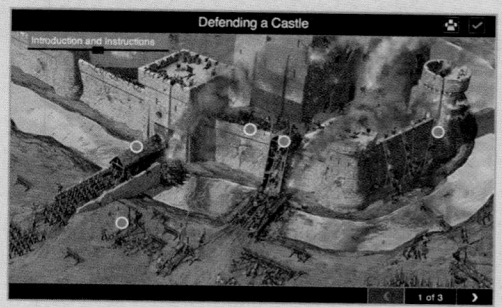

DIGITAL TEXT 3

Manorialism

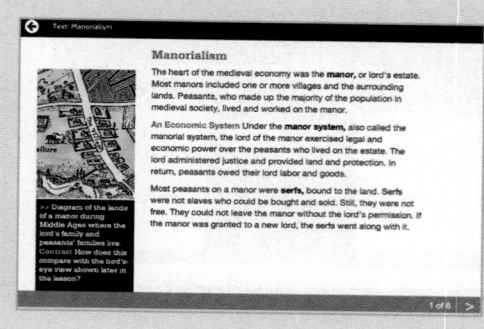

Objective 2: Summarize the life of knights and nobles.

Quick Instruction

Interactive Gallery: Defending a Castle Project the gallery on the whiteboard and click through the hotspots around the castle. Introduce the gallery by telling students that under the political system of feudalism, lords could summon vassals to join them on military campaigns. Warfare was a way of life for medieval nobles. From an early age, boys trained to fight and ride as knights. To protect their homes, powerful lords built castles to withstand attacks.

👥 ACTIVE CLASSROOM

Pair students for an Audio Tour of *Defending a Castle* gallery. Have the first student give the second a verbal "tour" of the castle—What does it show? Have the second student explain to the first what it means. *(Sample Responses: Moat, walls, towers, fire, and smoke. Attackers using catapult, battering ram, siege tower, arrows, spears, and ladders. Defenders replying with arrows [some flaming], swords, spears, hot oil, and poles with hooks to push away ladders.)*

ELL Use the ELL activity described in the ELL chart.

D **Differentiate: Challenge/Gifted** Have students use the text's *Defending a Castle* image and outside research to develop an attack plan for an invading army to take control of a fortified castle. Then ask them to create a defense plan that would enable a castle's occupants to successfully withstand an invasion.

Further Instruction

Nobles, Knights, and Warfare Go through the Interactive Reading Notepad questions and discuss the answers with the class.

Contrast How do you think the opportunities available to a noblewoman and a peasant woman differed within the political and social system of feudalism? *(Sample Response: A noblewoman could manage a manor for her husband, sometimes inherit land, and might even go to war or learn to read and write. None of these opportunities were available to a peasant woman; she worked with her family on a manor.)*

Make Generalizations Ask students: What positive effects do you think the code of chivalry might have had on the political and social system of feudalism? *(Sample Responses: taught boys about courtesy and honor; softened the brutality of a warlike society; provided guidelines for social behavior; promoted virtues of loyalty, faith, and bravery; inspired songs, epic stories, and poems)*

Objective 3: Analyze how the economic system of manorialism worked and how it affected peasants and nobles.

Quick Instruction

Interactive Chart: The Medieval Manorial System Project the chart on the whiteboard. Explain that during the Middle Ages, the economic system of manorialism supported the political and social structure of feudalism. On a lord's manor, or estate, mutual obligations tied together peasants and their lords. Point out that the tiles on the chart represent rights and responsibilities exchanged by lords and peasants in the manorial system. These rights and responsibilities helped to support nobles and to protect peasants.

👥 ACTIVE CLASSROOM

Have students imagine a conversation with a lord or peasant about shared rights and responsibilities on a manor. Ask students to write a question they would like to ask, what the lord or peasant would say, and what the student would say in response. *(Sample Response: Student: "How does your lord protect you?" Peasant: "When raiders come, his soldiers guard our fields. We can stay safe in his castle." Student: "That must be a great relief.")*

Feudalism and the Manor Economy

SYNTHESIZE

DEMONSTRATE

INTERACTIVE CHART
The Medieval Manorial System

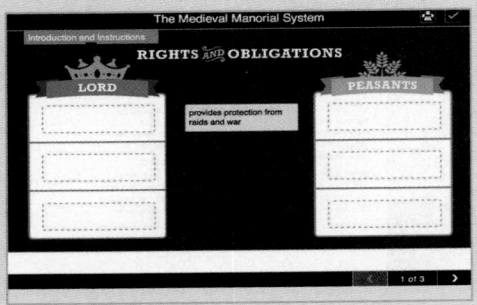

SYNTHESIZE ACTIVITY
A Powerful Woman

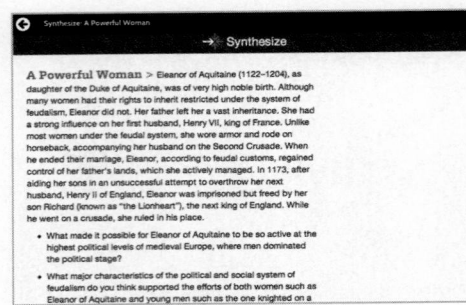

LESSON QUIZ
Lesson Quiz and Class Discussion Board

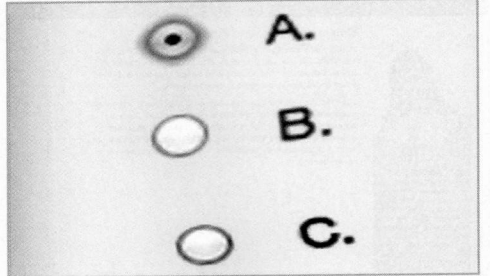

Further Instruction

Manorialism Go through the Interactive Reading Notepad questions and discuss the answers with the class.

Identify Cause and Effect How might the decline of trade during the early Middle Ages have contributed to the self-sufficiency of the economic system of manorialism? *(The limited amount of outside goods available during those times made it necessary for communities to produce everything they needed.)*

Analyze Information Ask: What benefits did the medieval economic system of manorialism provide to serfs living on a manor? What drawbacks were there? *(Answers will vary. Benefits: fulfilled basic food, shelter, and protection needs; offered security along with the feeling of belonging to a community; Drawbacks: limited freedom, exhausting labor, minimal awareness of the outside world, poor living conditions)*

Identify Steps in a Process Have pairs of students research why manors had plantings in the spring and fall, and why a field was left fallow. *(Spring and fall plantings produced food that was available all year. A field was left fallow to replenish its soil nutrients.)*

Have students form small groups to answer the questions in the A Powerful Woman activity. Ask them to take five minutes to brainstorm and write down brief answers to the following questions.

What made it possible for Eleanor of Aquitaine to be so active at the highest political levels of medieval Europe, where men dominated the political stage? What major characteristics of the political and social system of feudalism do you think supported the efforts of both women, such as Eleanor of Aquitaine, and young men, such as the one knighted on a battlefield in the lesson Connect activity, to achieve places of honor and responsibility in the medieval world? Have the groups present their answers to the class.

Draw Inferences Ask students to evaluate the roles available to medieval noblewomen, such as Eleanor of Aquitaine, and knights in the political and social system of feudalism. *(Answers may vary. Students should note that Eleanor of Aquitaine was a great exception. Most medieval noblewomen were limited to serving their husbands in customary roles of domestic support within the feudal structure. Noblewomen also generally neither managed their own estates nor were politically active. Knights, as men, had greater range of possible activity: supporting their lord and gaining personal glory in battle, ruling and enlarging their manors.)*

Assign the online Lesson Quiz for this lesson if you haven't already done so. Students will be offered automatic remediation or enrichment based on their score.

Pose these questions to the class on the Discussion Board:

In "Feudalism and the Manor Economy," you read about how the development of the political and social system of feudalism and the economic system of manorialism resulted in the characteristics of European society during the Middle Ages. Mutual obligations between lords and vassals provided a place for all nobles within the structure of power. At work on their lord's manor, peasants supported the nobility, making the feudal system possible.

Make Comparisons Compare the rights and obligations of noblemen and noblewomen during the Middle Ages. *(Noblemen owed military service and loyalty to their lord. They guided and protected their vassals. Noblewomen owed loyalty and obedience to their husbands, but performed some of the lord's duties if he was absent. They provided day-to-day management of the household and were expected to bear children.)*

Draw Conclusions How did the manor serve the needs of peasants during the early Middle Ages? *(Answers may vary. Students should include that it provided land to farm; necessary services, such as milling grain; and safety and security during raids and war.)*

www.PearsonRealize.com
Access your Digital Lesson

The Medieval Christian Church

Supporting English Language Learners

Use with Text 6, **The Christian Church is Divided.**

Listening

Read aloud, or have students read, *The Christian Church is Divided*. Then have students participate in the following activities.

Beginning Show students a video clip from the flipped video: *The Roman Catholic and Eastern Orthodox Churches* to give students a deeper understanding of Byzantine Christianity during the Middle Ages. Stop the video periodically to provide explanations and translations as appropriate. At the same time, highlight specific similarities and differences between the Roman and Byzantine churches. Have students practice speaking about the characteristics of the two Christian churches by repeating key words and phrases from the video and from the text.

Intermediate Show students a video clip from the flipped video: *The Roman Catholic and Eastern Orthodox Churches* to give students a deeper understanding of Byzantine Christianity during the Middle Ages. Stop the video periodically to highlight specific similarities and differences between the Roman and Byzantine churches. Have students practice speaking about the characteristics of the two Christian churches by identifying corresponding characteristics of each church and how they are similar and different.

Advanced Show students a video clip from the flipped video: *The Roman Catholic and Eastern Orthodox Churches* to give students a deeper understanding of Byzantine Christianity during the Middle Ages. Have students take notes on the characteristics of the Byzantine Empire while listening to the video. Then have students discuss these characteristics, using their notes as a guide.

Advanced High Show students a video clip from the flipped video: *The Roman Catholic and Eastern Orthodox Churches* to give students a deeper understanding of Byzantine Christianity during the Middle Ages. Have students take notes on the similarities and differences between the Roman and Byzantine churches while listening to the video. Then have students discuss the similarities and differences between the two churches, using their notes as a guide.

Use with Text 1, **The Church Shapes Everyday Life.**

Listening

Read *The Church Shapes Everyday Life* aloud. Then have students complete one activity according to their level of English proficiency.

Beginning Have students listen as *The Church Shapes Everyday Life* is read aloud. To help students identify the main idea and details of each subsection, create an outline form for students to complete. Read each subsection slowly, pausing frequently to allow for questions. Then review the content in each so that students may enter the appropriate information into their outlines. Provide assistance to students as they choose which details to include in their outlines. Students may also draw basic sketches as a way to supplement their understanding of the text.

Intermediate Have students listen as *The Church Shapes Everyday Life* is read aloud. Help students create an outline form to complete as the reading is shared aloud. Read each subsection slowly, allowing time for students to enter the appropriate information into their outline. Provide assistance to students as they choose which details to include in their outlines. Students may also use dictionaries and other references to enhance their understanding of the material.

Advanced Have students take turns reading aloud the subsections of *The Church Shapes Everyday Life*. Then ask students to create an outline form to complete, using the subsections as a guide. Instruct students to read each subsection slowly so that students can enter the appropriate information into their outlines. Provide dictionaries and other references to enhance students' understanding of the material.

Advanced High Have students work in small groups to read and outline the subsections of *The Church Shapes Everyday Life*. Instruct students to briefly discuss each subsection so that the appropriate information will be entered into their outlines. Provide dictionaries and other references to enhance students' understanding of the material.

▣ Differentiate Instruction

Use the Differentiated Instruction notes throughout the lesson plan to support the varied skill sets, levels of readiness, and interests in the mixed-ability classroom.

Challenge These notes include suggestions for expanding the activity for advanced students.

On-Level These notes include suggestions for modifying the activity to address different interests or learning styles.

Extra Support These notes include ideas for providing more scaffolding or reading spuport.

Special Needs These notes provide ideas for adapting instruction to support the needs of various special needs students.

■ NOTES

The Medieval Christian Church

Objectives

Objective 1: Explain how the Christian Church shaped medieval life.

Objective 2: Understand monastic life and the influence of medieval monks and nuns.

Objective 3: Analyze how the power of the Church grew during the Middle Ages and how reformers worked for change in the Church.

Objective 4: Describe the situation of Jews in medieval Europe.

Objective 5: Analyze how Christianity in the Byzantine empire differed from Christianity in the West.

LESSON 3 ORGANIZER		PACING: APPROX. 1 PERIOD, .5 BLOCKS			
				RESOURCES	
		OBJECTIVES	**PACING**	**Online**	**Print**
Connect					
DIGITAL START UP ACTIVITY **The Medieval Christian Church**			5 min.	●	
Investigate					
DIGITAL TEXT 1 **The Church Shapes Everyday Life**		Objective 1	10 min.	●	
INTERACTIVE MAP **Spread of Christianity in Europe**			10 min.	●	
DIGITAL TEXT 2 **Life in Monasteries and Convents**		Objective 2	10 min.	●	
INTERACTIVE 3-D MODEL **Medieval Monastery**			10 min.	●	
DIGITAL TEXT 3 **The Growth of Church Power**		Objective 3	10 min.	●	
DIGITAL TEXT 4 **The Church Faces Calls to Reform**			10 min.	●	
DIGITAL TEXT 5 **Jewish Communities in Medieval Europe**		Objective 4	10 min.	●	
DIGITAL TEXT 6 **The Christian Church Is Divided**		Objective 5	10 min.	●	
INTERACTIVE CHART **The Church Divides**			10 min.	●	
Synthesize					
SYNTHESIZE ACTIVITY **Role of the Church**			5 min.	●	
Demonstrate					
LESSON QUIZ **Lesson Quiz and Class Discussion Board**			10 min.	●	

■ CONNECT

DIGITAL START UP ACTIVITY
The Medieval Christian Church

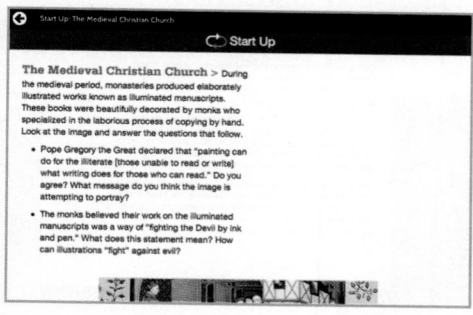

Project the image of an illuminated manuscript from the Start Up Activity Ask students to answer the questions as they get settled. Assign students on the left side of the room to answer question 1 and students on the right side to answer question 2. Then have them share their ideas with a partner. Each pair will present their answers to the class.

Discuss Do you agree with Pope Gregory's statement that "painting can do for the illiterate what writing does for those who can read"? How can illustrations "fight" evil? *(The images reinforced Christian beliefs, especially for those unable to read. This helped to spread Christianity and thus "fight evil.")*

Tell students that in this lesson they will learn that the Church played a vital role in the everyday lives of medieval Europeans.

⇅ FLIP IT!

Assign the Flipped Video for this lesson.

■ STUDENT EDITION PRINT
PAGES: 203–210

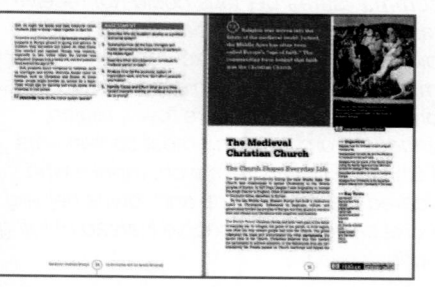

■ INVESTIGATE

DIGITAL TEXT 1
The Church Shapes Everyday Life

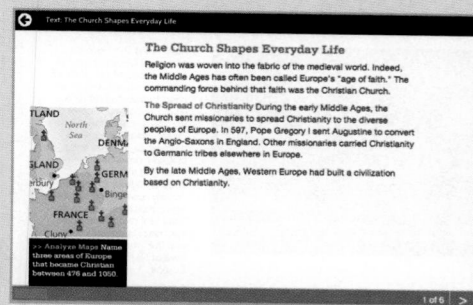

Objective 1: Explain how the Christian Church shaped medieval life.

Quick Instruction
Interactive Map: Spread of Christianity in Europe Project the map on the whiteboard. Introduce the activity by explaining that the spread of Christianity throughout medieval Europe was an important turning point in world history. Review the key to ensure students understand what the map is showing. Use the slider to view how Christianity spread across Europe between 476 and 1050.

Analyze Maps In what directions did Christianity spread? How did Christianity spread across Europe? *(Westward and northward; through the establishment of monasteries, by missionaries, and by monarchs deciding to become Christians)*

🖥 ACTIVE CLASSROOM

After viewing the interactive map, ask students to pair up with a partner for a Circle Write. Ask students to answer the following questions: What do you see? What does that make you think? What are you wondering about now that you've seen this? *(Sample Responses: Christianity spread to the east and north across medieval Europe. Christianity was an important part of people's lives. Why did so many people become Christians?)* After a few minutes of discussion, students should then share their insights with the class.

ELL Use the ELL activity described in the ELL chart.

INTERACTIVE MAP
Spread of Christianity in Europe

D Differentiate: Extra Support While viewing the map, point out that Christianity spread east and north. Ask students to list three areas of Europe named on the map that became Christian between 476 and 1050. *(Germany, Russia, Norway, Scotland, parts of England)*

Further Instruction
Editable Presentation Use the Editable Presentation to present the main ideas for this Core Reading.

Spread of Christianity in Europe: Core Reading and Interactive Reading Notepad Project the questions provided in the notepad and have students answer as they progress through the Core Text.

Spread of Christianity in Europe: Interactive Map Project the interactive map of the spread of Christianity and ask students to describe each change in the map. Be sure that students understand that the geography and cultural factors of Europe played a role in how quickly Christianity spread in Europe. Ask why Sweden, northern Scotland, and northwestern Russia around the Baltic Sea might have been the last areas to be Christianized. *(It was more difficult for missionaries to reach these areas; the people and/or their rulers may have been less inclined to become Christians.)*

Be sure students understand that the spread of Christianity was an important turning point in world history. Remind students of Charlemagne's vision of a united Christendom.

Predict Consequences Ask students to predict what they think the effects of the spread of Christianity in medieval Europe will be. *(Sample Response: The different people in various regions will be united by their faith and religious practices.)*

The Medieval Christian Church

DIGITAL TEXT 2

Life in Monasteries and Convents

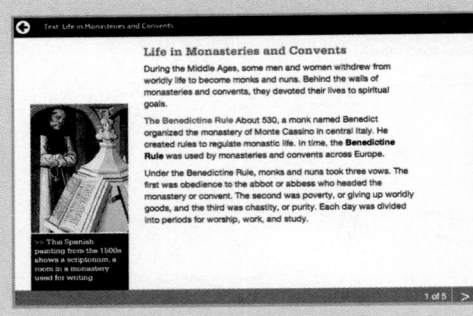

INTERACTIVE 3-D MODEL

Medieval Monastery

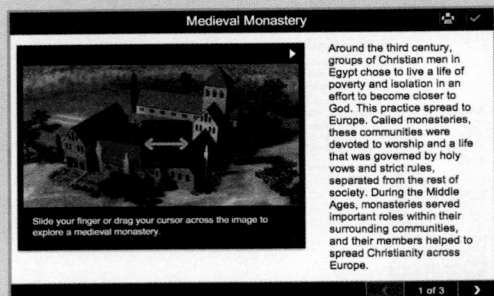

DIGITAL TEXT 3

The Growth of Church Power

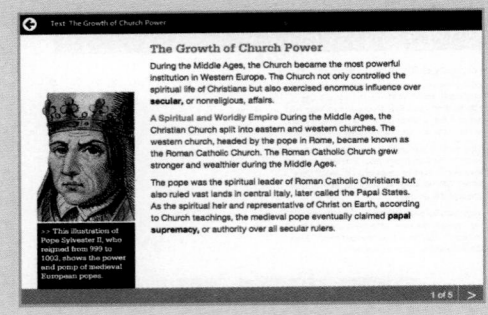

Objective 2: Understand monastic life and the influence of medieval monks and nuns.

Quick Instruction

Project the image of the Interactive 3-D Model "Medieval Monastery." Review the instructions and demonstrate to students how the model can be viewed from different angles. Click on the hotspots to learn more information about life in a monastery. Explain to students that the establishment of monasteries was a major force in the spread of Christianity. Monasteries also played an important role in medieval European villages by providing care for the sick and needy, forming schools, improving agricultural methods, and preserving knowledge.

📖 ACTIVE CLASSROOM

Ask students to break up into pairs and do an audio tour. Have the first student give the second a verbal "tour" of the monastery–what does it show? Have the second student give the first an explanation of what it means. *(Sample Response: First student points out the dormitory and explains that monks lived very humbly and were not allowed personal possessions. Second student describes the Benedictine Rule and how living humbly and devoting their lives to their faith set a moral example for the community.)*

Further Instruction

Project and discuss the Interactive Reading Notepad questions about convents and monasteries. Review the contributions monasteries and convents made to the general welfare of the community. Explain how these contributions helped to spread Christianity across Europe as more monasteries and convents were established. Make sure students understand that they were an important part of society and they were a unifying social factor in medieval Europe.

Draw Conclusions Monasteries and convents made important contributions to medieval society. Which contribution do you think was most useful to medieval society as a whole? Explain. *(Possible Response: They preserved and protected knowledge, copied manuscripts, and contributed their own scholarship. Without them, this knowledge could have been lost.)*

Compare How did convents and monasteries help to unify medieval Europe? *(The services they provided to surrounding communities attracted Christian converts. The people were unified by the vital roles the Church played in their daily lives.)*

Objective 3: Analyze how the power of the Church grew during the Middle Ages and how reformers worked for change in the Church.

Quick Instruction

Project the images of the pope and Saint Francis of Assisi from the Digital Text. Explain to students that as Christianity spread, the Church's social, economic, and political power expanded as well. Review the causes and effects of this growth in power.

Further Instruction

Project and discuss the questions from the Interactive Reading Notepad for Growth of Church Power and The Church Faces Calls to Reform. Ask students to think about the causes and effects of the Church's growth in power as you cover the material in the Digital Text. Explain how the spread of Christianity and the power of the Church affected one another. Review the problems of corruption and the role of reformers within the Church.

Compare and Contrast Ask students to explain the difference between interdict and excommunication. Then have them compare and contrast friars and monks. *(Excommunicated persons could not receive the sacraments or a Christian burial, which medieval Christians believed condemned them to hell for eternity, while an interdict was an order excluding an entire town, region, or kingdom from receiving most sacraments and Christian burial; friars were monks who wandered the countryside and towns helping and preaching to poor people instead of living in monasteries.)*

DIGITAL TEXT 4

The Church Faces Calls to Reform

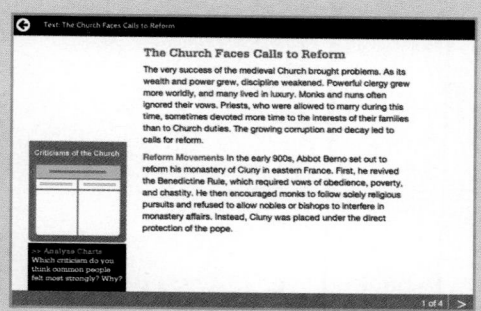

DIGITAL TEXT 5

Jewish Communities in Medieval Europe

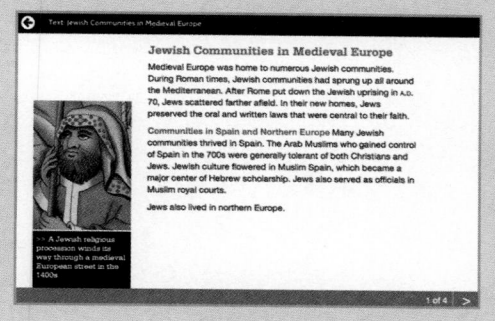

DIGITAL TEXT 6

The Christian Church Is Divided

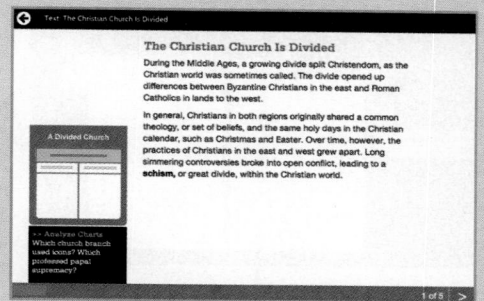

Make Generalizations In what ways were Church authority and secular authority intertwined? *(Feudal rulers appointed highly educated Church officials to government positions. Church officials were often relatives of secular rulers. High clergy were usually nobles and had their own territories and armies.)*

Paraphrase Why did reformers find it problematic for priests to live lives of luxury? *(Because it was at the expense of the majority of the people. Individual wealth was accumulated due to corruption and abuse of power.)*

Objective 4: Describe the situation of Jews in medieval Europe.

Quick Instruction

Project the image of the Jewish settlement from the Digital Text. Review how interactions between Jewish and Christian communities changed over time during the medieval period. Explain that Jews were treated differently in different geographic locations.

Further Instruction

Project the "Spread of Christianity" map and the questions found in the Interactive Reading Notepad. Ask what students know about anti-Semitism and discuss other kinds of religious, ethnic, and racial prejudice. Note the change in attitudes toward Jews in medieval Europe.

Summarize How were Jews treated in Muslim Spain? *(Muslim rulers were somewhat tolerant of other religions, and Jews flourished there.)*

Identify Central Issue Why might it have been difficult for Jews to celebrate their own religious holidays during the Middle Ages? *(Sample Response: Because they could be viewed as outsiders for celebrating holidays that were not part of the Christian religious calendar. Since the majority of people within a village were Christian, Jewish celebrations would be conspicuous and reinforce the idea that Jews were not a part of the social structure.)*

Objective 5: Analyze how Christianity in the Byzantine empire differed from Christianity in the West.

Quick Instruction

Introduce the lesson by explaining to students that, similar to Western Europe, Christianity was also a strong unifying political and social factor in the Byzantine empire. The Church was a significant influence in the daily lives of the majority of the people in Eastern Europe. They worshiped and celebrated holy days according to the Church's religious calendar and looked to the patriarch and ecumenical council, or heads of the Byzantine Church, for leadership. Many revered holy religious images, or icons. Also, most people spoke Greek, the language of the Eastern Church. The religious philosophies introduced in Western Europe following the fall of Rome were not adopted in the East. Instead, the Byzantine Church followed its own rituals and customs, which became as important to Eastern Christians as Roman Catholic practices were in the West.

The Church Divides: Interactive Graphic Organizer Project the interactive chart "The Church Divides" on the whiteboard. Remind students that the Great Schism divided the Church, creating the Roman Catholic Church in the West and the Orthodox Church in the East. Ask students to review the different beliefs, customs, and practices listed. Then drag and drop each one of the characteristics of Roman Catholicism and Eastern Orthodoxy into one of the two columns of the chart.

The Medieval Christian Church

The Church Divides

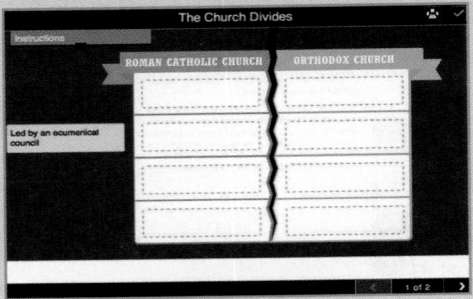

ACTIVE CLASSROOM

After completing the activity, ask students to break into groups to answer the following question: What are reasons the Eastern and Western Churches differed? Have students write as much as they can for one minute, and then switch with the person on their right. The next person tries to improve or elaborate the response where the other person left off. Continue to switch until the paper comes back to the first person. The group then decides which is the best response and shares that with the entire class.

D **Differentiate: Special Needs** Remind students that the use of icons was a significant factor in teaching about Christianity to an illiterate population. Ask students to draw a picture that conveys a message without using words. The final illustrations should be understood by anyone without prior understanding.

ELL Use the ELL activity described in the ELL chart.

Further Instruction

Project and discuss the Venn diagram and Interactive Reading Notepad questions about the characteristics of the Roman Catholic Church and the Eastern Orthodox Church. Review the similarities and differences between the two branches.

Draw Conclusions Ask students to explain why the development of Christianity unified medieval Europe. Then have them discuss how the schism divided different parts of Christian Europe. *(Almost all of the continent shared a theology and celebrated the same fasts and feasts according to identical religious calendars European Christians felt they were members of the same religious community; the schism was caused by, as well as reinforced, geographic, religious, cultural, and other differences.)*

SYNTHESIZE

SYNTHESIZE ACTIVITY
Role of the Church

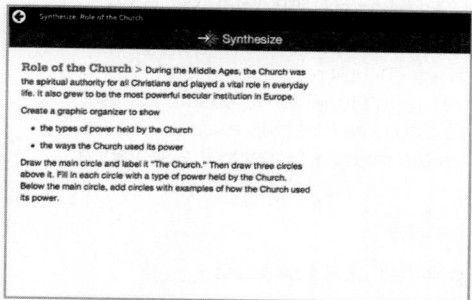

Project the Synthesize activity on the whiteboard. Introduce the activity by reviewing how to create a graphic organizer. Ask students to think about the types of power held by the Church and to consider the ways the Church used its power. Students can complete the activity independently, in pairs, or in groups. When finished, hold a classroom discussion using student answers from their graphic organizers. Ask students to evaluate the role of the medieval Church. How did it affect the everyday life of medieval Europeans? Explain how these events, as well as the Church's role in them, helped create unity in medieval Europe.

Evaluate Ask students to create a list of the different events in a person's life that were influenced by the Church. *(Sample Responses: marriage, baptism when a baby is born; festivals and fasting periods according to the religious calendar; marriage; death and burial)*

DEMONSTRATE

LESSON QUIZ
Lesson Quiz and Class Discussion Board

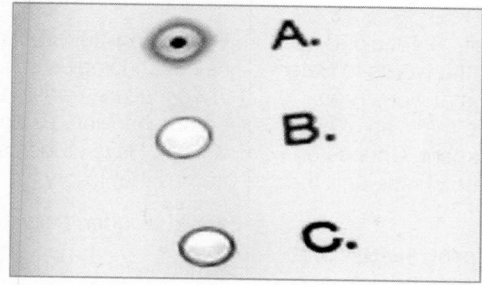

Assign the online Lesson Quiz for this lesson if you haven't already done so. Students will be offered automatic remediation or enrichment based on their score.

Pose these questions to the class on the Discussion Board:

In "The Medieval Christian Church," you read about how Christianity spread and the Church became a central part of life throughout Europe. The Church's power grew, both spiritually and politically, but many people were unhappy with the direction the Church was heading and called for reforms. The Christian Church eventually split, and two branches were formed: the Roman Catholic Church and the Eastern Orthodox Church.

Summarize What roles did the Church play in daily life? *(It had a central role; it dispensed moral guidance and help for the sick and needy, and its sacraments marked important life events.)*

Compare and Contrast What was one difference between the Roman and Byzantine Churches before the Great Schism? *(Sample Responses: Byzantine clergy could marry, unlike priests in the Roman Church; Greek, not Latin, was the language of the Byzantine Church; the head of the Byzantine Church was the patriarch of Constantinople, not the pope in Rome.)*

Draw Conclusions Ask students to discuss this question: What institution, if any, fills the same role for people today that the medieval Church filled for Europeans in the Middle Ages? Have them cite evidence to support their claims. *(Answer will vary. Some students may argue that no institution exists today with the far-reaching power and influence of the medieval Church, while others might point to the media, the Internet, various governments, religious organizations, or other social institutions.)*

Economic Expansion and Change: The Crusades and After

Supporting English Language Learners

Use with Digital Text 4, **A New Middle Class.**

Listening

Read aloud, or have students read, *A New Middle Class*. Then have students participate in the following activities.

Beginning Read the French apprenticeship agreement, 1248, aloud and with expression. First read as Peter Borre might speak the words to Peter Feissac as he gives his son to the weaver's care and instruction. Then reread the passage, helping students to understand the meaning of each phrase as well as the overall meaning of the legal document. Choose one sentence in the agreement and have students repeat the phrase until they are able to speak it with ease and fluency.

Intermediate Read the French apprenticeship agreement, 1248, aloud and with expression. First read as Peter Borre might speak the words to Peter Feissac as he gives his son to the weaver's care and instruction. Then reread the passage, helping students to understand the meaning of each phrase as well as the overall meaning of the legal document. Then have students practice repeating the agreement until they are able to speak it with ease and fluency.

Advanced Read the French apprenticeship agreement, 1248, aloud and with expression. First read as Peter Borre might speak the words to Peter Feissac as he gives his son to the weaver's care and instruction. Then have students reread the passage silently to identify any difficult words or phrases. Define any unfamiliar words and explain any unfamiliar concepts to students. Have students practice the agreement with a partner until they are able to speak it with ease and fluency.

Advanced High Have students read the French apprenticeship agreement, 1248, aloud and with expression. Then have students reread the passage silently to identify any difficult words or phrases. Define any unfamiliar words and explain any unfamiliar concepts to students. Finally, have each student speak the agreement aloud to the class as if he or she were Peter Borre, the father who entered into the apprenticeship agreement with Peter Feissac.

Use with Digital Text 1, **Changes in Agriculture Transform Europe.**

Listening

Read *Changes in Agriculture Transform Europe* aloud. Then have students complete one activity according to their level of English proficiency.

Beginning Tell students that they will be creating a summary of the new technologies that caused an agricultural revolution. Read *Changes in Agriculture Transform Europe* aloud to students. To ensure content comprehension, use pictures and diagrams that help explain the text visually. Have students summarize the material by using the sentence frames that follow.

• Old wooden plows were replaced by _____.

• Farmers could use horses to pull their plows because _____.

• The three-field system _____.

Intermediate Tell students that they will be creating a summary of the new technologies that caused an agricultural revolution. Read *Changes in Agriculture Transform Europe* aloud to students. To ensure content comprehension, define any difficult terms and concepts for students. Have students summarize the material by creating a list of key words and phrases to explain the changes and new technologies that led to the agricultural changes in Europe.

Advanced Tell students that they will be creating a summary of the new technologies that caused an agricultural revolution. Read *Changes in Agriculture Transform Europe* aloud to students. To ensure content comprehension, have students make note of any difficult terms and provide them with a dictionary or other resource to define them. Finally, have students summarize the material by writing one sentence about each of the three main developments that improved agriculture.

Advanced High Tell students that they will be creating a summary of the new technologies that caused an agricultural revolution. Read *Changes in Agriculture Transform Europe* aloud to students. To ensure content comprehension, have students make note of any difficult terms and provide them with a dictionary or other resource to define them. Finally, have students summarize the material by writing a short paragraph describing the new developments that improved agriculture.

◪ Differentiate Instruction

Use the Differentiated Instruction notes throughout the lesson plan to support the varied skill sets, levels of readiness, and interests in the mixed-ability classroom.

Challenge These notes include suggestions for expanding the activity for advanced students.

On-Level These notes include suggestions for modifying the activity to address different interests or learning styles.

Extra Support These notes include ideas for providing more scaffolding or reading spuport.

Special Needs These notes provide ideas for adapting instruction to support the needs of various special needs students.

◼ NOTES

PEARSON
realize™
www.PearsonRealize.com

Go online to access additional resources including:
Primary Sources • Biographies • Supreme Court cases •
21st Century Skill Tutorials • Maps • Graphic Organizers.

Objectives

Objective 1: Summarize how new technologies sparked an agricultural revolution, and the revival of trade led to the growth of towns and cities.

Objective 2: Explain how a commercial revolution changed society and how guilds led to the rise of the middle class.

Objective 3: Explain the causes and effects of the Crusades.

Objective 4: Summarize how Christians in Spain carried out the Reconquista.

LESSON 4 ORGANIZER		PACING: APPROX. 1 PERIOD, .5 BLOCKS			
				RESOURCES	
		OBJECTIVES	**PACING**	**Online**	**Print**
Connect					
DIGITAL START UP ACTIVITY **Power of the Church**			5 min.	●	
Investigate					
DIGITAL TEXT 1 **Changes in Agriculture Transform Europe**		Objective 1	10 min.	●	●
DIGITAL TEXT 2 **Trade Expands and Towns Grow**			10 min.	●	●
INTERACTIVE GALLERY **The Growth of Towns**			10 min.	●	
DIGITAL TEXT 3 **Economic Changes**		Objective 2	10 min.	●	●
DIGITAL TEXT 4 **A New Middle Class**			10 min.	●	●
DIGITAL TEXT 5 **The Crusades**		Objective 3	10 min.	●	●
INTERACTIVE MAP **The Crusades 1096–1204**			10 min.	●	
DIGITAL TEXT 6 **The Effects of the Crusades**			10 min.	●	●
DIGITAL TEXT 7 **The Reconquista**		Objective 4	10 min.	●	●
Synthesize					
SYNTHESIZE **Power of the Church**			5 min.	●	
Demonstrate					
LESSON QUIZ **Lesson Quiz and Class Discussion Board**			10 min.	●	

Economic Expansion and Change: The Crusades and After

CONNECT

DIGITAL START UP ACTIVITY
Power of the Church

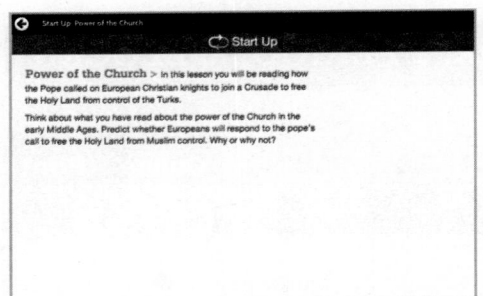

Project the Start Up Activity Ask students to answer the questions as they enter and get settled. Then have them share their ideas with another student.

Discuss The Crusades were a series of wars in which Christians battled Muslims for control of land in the Middle East. How did the Christian Church organize an international military campaign? *(The Church had power that exceeded religious doctrine. Christianity was a part of daily life for all Europeans. The Church's influence extended to recapturing Jerusalem with the military might needed to achieve that goal.)*

Predict Read the Connect question and poll the class to see what the predictions are. Note the results to use during the later Synthesize activity.

⚡ FLIP IT!
Assign the Flipped Video for this lesson.

▮ STUDENT EDITION PRINT
PAGES: 211–220

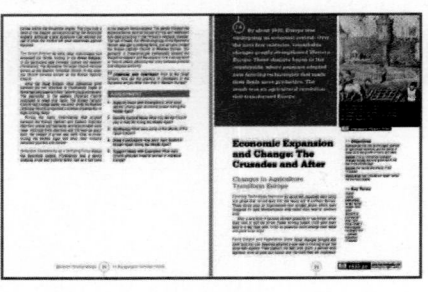

INVESTIGATE

DIGITAL TEXT 1
Changes in Agriculture Transform Europe

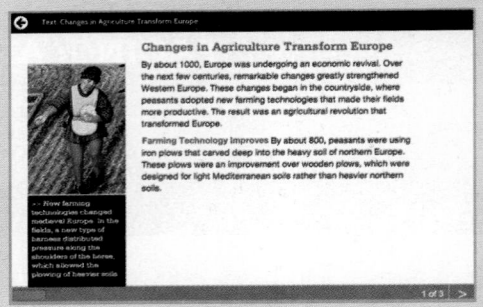

DIGITAL TEXT 2
Trade Expands and Towns Grow

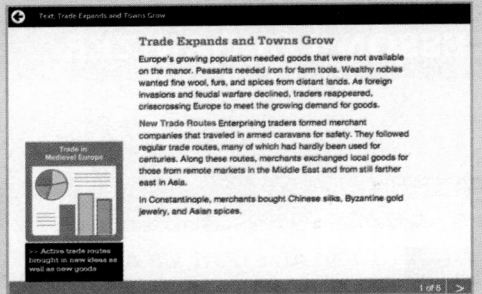

Objective 1: Summarize how new technologies sparked an agricultural revolution, and how the revival of trade led to the growth of towns and cities.

Quick Instruction
Introduce the activity by explaining that most towns and villages in the early Middle Ages were small, sparsely populated, and spread out over a fairly large geographic area.

The Growth of Towns: Interactive Gallery Project the gallery on the whiteboard.

Analyze Images Ask students to examine the before and after images. What has changed? Why? Ask students to think of instances where similar types of growth have taken place in their communities.

👥 ACTIVE CLASSROOM

Use the Word Wall strategy and ask students to choose one of the vocabulary terms for the lesson and create a visual image with a definition. Allow approximately three to five minutes. Then ask students to post their words on the board or on chart paper and look at all the various responses. As a group, discuss similarities and differences in the responses, pick a favorite, and post it on the Class Word Wall for the year.

ELL Use the ELL activity described in the ELL chart.

Further Instruction
Project and discuss the Interactive Reading Notepad questions and the graphic organizer identifying the causes and effects of the population growth in medieval Europe from 1000 *A.D.* to 1300 *A.D.*

Provide history background by pointing out that transportation was a major obstacle to trade in medieval Europe. Well-maintained concrete roads built at the height of the Roman empire had fallen into decay even though they remained in use. The lords who owned the lands through which the roads traveled were inconsistent in the roads' maintenance. They also could not provide adequate protection for merchant travelers from highwaymen. Travel by water was an alternative. Merchants from international ports such as Constantinople and Venice used sea routes, while other European merchants used rivers to transport goods.

INTERACTIVE GALLERY
The Growth of Towns

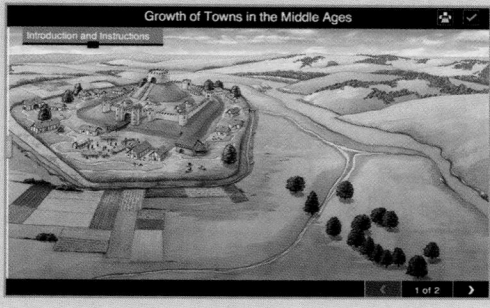

DIGITAL TEXT 3
Economic Changes

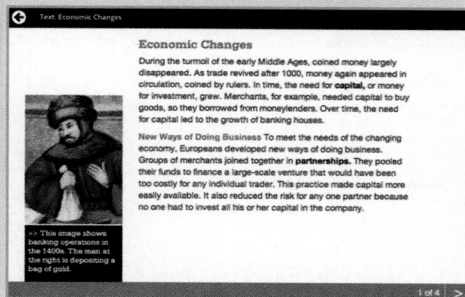

DIGITAL TEXT 4
A New Middle Class

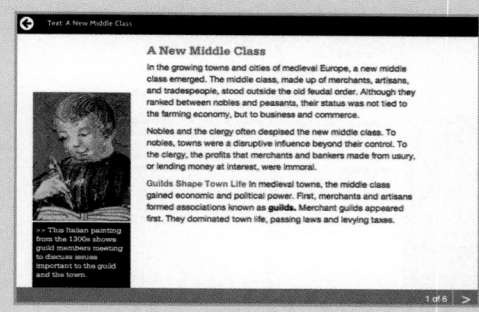

Draw Inferences What types of towns would be likely to attract the greatest variety of merchants? *(Towns with good transportation systems, adequate security against robbers, and a large enough population to make the trip profitable for the merchant.)*

Objective 2: **Explain how a commercial revolution changed society and how guilds led to the rise of the middle class.**

Quick Instruction

Introduce the activity by explaining that the growth of trade led to more people choosing to make trade the source of their livelihoods. This included people who produced goods, such as weavers, iron-workers, and goldsmiths. As tradespeople, these skilled individuals lived in towns where making goods or selling them would be part of each day rather than just a few trade fairs each year. The opportunities available in towns allowed some to earn more money than they had as farmers. They were not nobles, but they were not peasants either; they were in a new economic group – the middle class. This commercial revolution also affected women and children in families. Women and children often helped in what had become the family business. Some women were able to trade on their own. This was a dramatic change from life in the fields. Town life also presented educational opportunities for children.

Trade Goods: Infographic Project the Infographic on the whiteboard. Discuss the variety of goods represented. Ask students to think about the links between the producers of goods in Europe and producers of goods in other countries like Asia and the Byzantine empire. How did trade benefit everyone involved?

ELL Use the ELL activity described in the ELL chart.

Further Instruction

Project and discuss the Interactive Reading Notepad questions for this lesson.

Explain that medieval guilds served as models for today's trade unions. The first guilds, though, were merchant guilds, and they exerted a great deal of power over town life. The merchant guilds levied taxes and passed town laws. They also built bridges and paved roads within the towns. Artisan guilds also formed to protect the rights of workers in a particular occupation. To keep wages and prices favorable, the artisan guilds restricted membership. Guilds built hospitals and schools and tried to look after the needs of their members. Ask students to think about how guilds and modern unions are alike and how they differ.

Compare How are guilds similar to modern trade unions? *(Guilds made rules to ensure product quality, regular hours of labor, and set prices. They provided support for their members or for their widows and orphans.)*

Economic Expansion and Change: The Crusades and After

DIGITAL TEXT 5

The Crusades

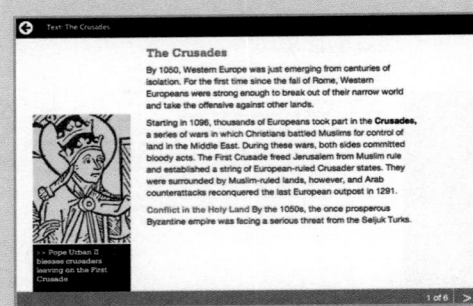

INTERACTIVE MAP

The Crusades 1096–1204

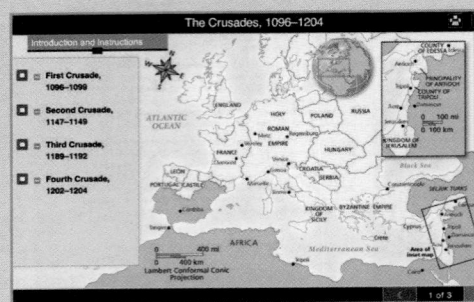

DIGITAL TEXT 6

The Effects of the Crusades

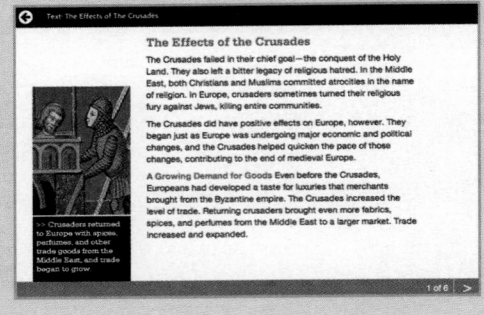

Objective 3: **Explain the causes and effects of the Crusades.**

Quick Instruction

The Crusades: Interactive Map Project the map on the whiteboard. Introduce the activity by explaining that there were four separate Crusades that took place over a period of 200 years. During this time, Western Europeans learned that the world was much larger than they had ever dreamed. The ideas brought back by crusaders accelerated change in Europe. By the end of the Fourth Crusade, social, economic, and political changes contributed to the end of medieval Europe. Trade with the Middle East increased, kings became stronger, and new ideas pushed Europe into a new era. Click on the button for each Crusade to present key information about that Crusade.

👥 ACTIVE CLASSROOM

Use the Audio Tour strategy and pair students who will tour the map. Have the first student give the second a verbal "tour" of the map – what does it show? Then have the second student give the first an explanation of what it means.

Draw Conclusions Why did the Fourth Crusade essentially "stall" in Constantinople? *(The crusaders ended up fighting the Byzantines in Constantinople because the Venetian merchants funding much of the Crusade wanted to control this important trading site.)*

D Differentiate: Extra Support The Church offered incentives to those who joined the Crusades. Have students research these incentives to create an advertisement convincing people to join the Crusades. Advertisements should mention incentives and combine persuasive writing with maps or illustrations.

Further Instruction

Project and discuss the Interactive Reading Notepad questions for this lesson.

Each of the Crusades was launched for different reasons. On the surface, the main reason for the Crusades was to regain control over lands in the Middle East under control of the Muslims. One of these areas was Jerusalem, or the Christian Holy Land, and the major roads that allowed Christian pilgrims to safely go there and return. However, the Crusades also had a political component. With the First Crusade, Urban hoped to reunite a divided Christian church. By the Fourth Crusade, kings had gained more power and securing profitable trading centers was as much a goal as securing safe passages for pilgrims. Trade increased with the Muslim nations in the Middle East and new ideas in science and medicine from Islamic countries traveled back with the crusaders as well.

Draw Comparisons What factors contributed to the vast difference in how the four Crusades were conducted? *(Answers should include at least two of the following: changing roles of monarchial power over 200 years, growing power and influence of Venetian traders, personalities of the individual nobles involved, weakening of the Byzantine empire, and changing role of the Church.)*

DIGITAL TEXT 7

The Reconquista

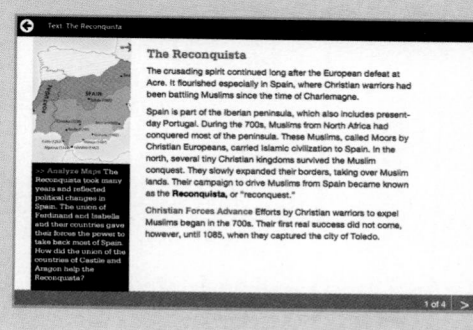

The Reconquista

The crusading spirit continued long after the European defeat at Acre. It flourished especially in Spain, where Christian warriors had been battling Muslims since the time of Charlemagne.

Spain is part of the Iberian peninsula, which also includes present-day Portugal. During the 700s, Muslims from North Africa had conquered most of the peninsula. These Muslims, called Moors by Christian Europeans, carried Islamic civilization to Spain. In the north, several tiny Christian kingdoms survived the Muslim conquest. They slowly expanded their borders, taking over Muslim lands. Their campaign to drive Muslims from Spain became known as the **Reconquista**, or "reconquest."

Christian Forces Advance Efforts by Christian warriors to expel Muslims began in the 700s. Their first real success did not come, however, until 1085, when they captured the city of Toledo.

>> Analyze Maps The Reconquista took many years and reflected political changes in Spain. The union of Ferdinand and Isabella and their countries gave their forces the power to take back most of Spain. How did the union of the countries of Castile and Aragon help the Reconquista?

1 of 4 >

Objective 4: Summarize how Christians in Spain carried out the Reconquista.

Quick Instruction

Project the map showing the Reconquista. Explain that most of Spain had been under Muslim control for more than 300 years. During this time, Spain had experienced the political, economic, and social impact of Islam. The early years of Muslim rule encouraged education in philosophy, medicine, and science. Different religions were tolerated, allowing people of different faiths to worship as they chose. Over time, though, Muslim control weakened. Christian kingdoms in the north of Spain took advantage of this to reconquer and return territory to Christian Spain. As the Reconquista progressed, it also led to the expulsion of Muslims and Jews from Spain.

Further Instruction

Project and discuss the Interactive Reading Notepad questions for this lesson.

The Reconquista ushered in enormous changes for Spain. This included political, economic, and social changes that affected the general population. To help students explore the effects of the Reconquista, have pairs of students write a news story that describes its effects in Spain. Encourage students to explore the different facets of the Reconquista. What specific things changed? What were the results of these changes? Ask student teams to read aloud their news stories.

Synthesize What did the Reconquista ultimately achieve? *(A more united Spain, but one that lost positive contributions from the cultural and religious diversity of its people.)*

Economic Expansion and Change: The Crusades and After

SYNTHESIZE

SYNTHESIZE
Power of the Church

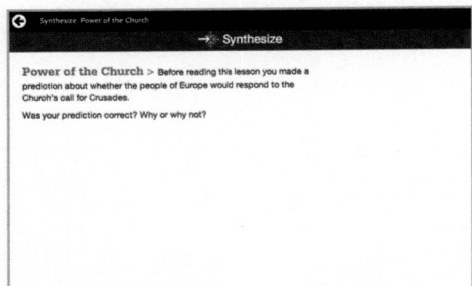

Ask students to share their responses to the Synthesize question. Take a poll to see how many students made the correct prediction. Ask these students to explain why they predicted as they did. Then, ask the students who predicted incorrectly why they believed that there would be no response to the Crusades.

Draw Conclusions What was the extent of the Church's power and influence during this time? *(The Church was very powerful in that it was able to persuade national leaders to conduct a war to reclaim the Holy Land.)*

DEMONSTRATE

LESSON QUIZ
Lesson Quiz and Class Discussion Board

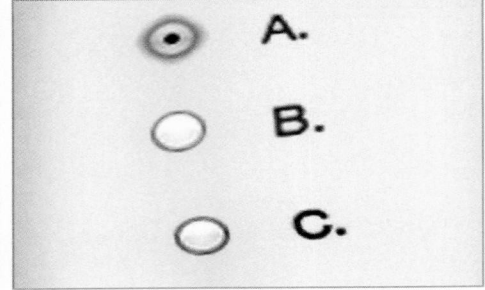

Assign the online Lesson Quiz for this lesson if you haven't already done so. Students will be offered automatic remediation or enrichment based on their score.

Pose these questions to the class on the Discussion Board:

Draw Conclusions What were some positive and negative effects of the Crusades? *(They were positive in that ideas and trade came back with the crusaders and negative in that a great deal of money and bloodshed was spent in a cause that ultimately failed to capture the Holy Land from Muslim control. Whether the Crusades were positive or negative also depends on which side one fought.)*

Summarize What factors influenced the growth of cities and towns? *(greater wealth, greater trade, safer trade routes, more productivity, and people leaving agriculture and moving into trades)*

The Feudal Monarchs and the Church

Supporting English Language Learners

Use with Digital Text 2, **English Kings Expand Their Power.**

Listening
Read aloud, or have students read, *English Kings Expand Their Power.* Then have students participate in the following activities.

Beginning Tell students the story of Thomas Becket. Use images to supplement students' understanding of the conflict between Henry II and the Church. Students may or may not be familiar with the terms *martyr*, *saint*, and *pilgrim*. Explain the meanings of the words using the story of Thomas Becket as an example.

Intermediate Tell students the story of Thomas Becket. Ask students to think about a time when they had a conflict with a good friend. Use this real-word example and images from the text to help students understand the conflict between Henry II and the Church. Students may or may not be familiar with the terms *martyr*, *saint*, and *pilgrim*. Explain the meanings of the words using Thomas Becket as an example. Students may use a bilingual dictionary to aid in their understanding.

Advanced Have students describe a time when they had a conflict with a close friend. Then have them use this experience for reference as they listen to the story of Henry II and Thomas Becket. Students may or may not be familiar with the terms *martyr*, *saint*, and *pilgrim*. Explain the meanings of the words using the story of Thomas Becket as an example.

Advanced High Have small groups of students discuss examples of conflicts they have had with a close friend or loved one. Then ask students to listen to the story of Henry II and Thomas Becket. After listening, have students return to their small groups to discuss the similarities and differences between their own experiences and the story of Henry II and Thomas Becket. Finally, have students define the terms *martyr*, *saint*, and *pilgrim*. Ask student groups to explain the meanings of the words using the story of Thomas Becket as an example.

Use with Digital Text 5, **The Holy Roman Empire.**

Listening
Read *The Holy Roman Empire* aloud. Then have students complete one activity according to their level of English proficiency.

Beginning Summarize aloud a short section of *The Holy Roman Empire* for students using simple sentences. Match each sentence with a visual aid. Then present written copies of the sentences for students and help them match each sentence with its corresponding visual aid. Assist students as necessary to ensure understanding of the spoken content.

Intermediate Summarize aloud a short section of *The Holy Roman Empire* for students using simple sentences. Then present written copies of the sentences to students. Display a set of visual aids that correspond to the section. Then have students match each sentence with its corresponding visual aid and arrange them in order. Assist students as necessary to ensure understanding of the spoken content.

Advanced Read a short section of *The Holy Roman Empire* aloud to students. Have students give a summary of the section using simple sentences. If necessary, have students supplement their summaries with visual aids that correspond to the section. Assist students as necessary to ensure understanding of the spoken content.

Advanced High Have students work in pairs and read different sections of *The Holy Roman Empire* independently. Then have students explain the sections they read to their partners. After the explanation, partners should summarize the information that they listened to. To check comprehension, have students read the sections read by their partners to make sure their summaries make sense.

▣ Differentiate Instruction

Use the Differentiated Instruction notes throughout the lesson plan to support the varied skill sets, levels of readiness, and interests in the mixed-ability classroom.

Challenge These notes include suggestions for expanding the activity for advanced students.

On-Level These notes include suggestions for modifying the activity to address different interests or learning styles.

Extra Support These notes include ideas for providing more scaffolding or reading spuport.

Special Needs These notes provide ideas for adapting instruction to support the needs of various special needs students.

■ NOTES

_____

_____

_____

_____

_____

The Feudal Monarchs and the Church

Objectives

Objective 1: Learn how monarchs gained power over nobles and the Christian Church, and how English kings strengthened their power.

Objective 2: Describe how traditions of government evolved under King John and later English monarchs.

Objective 3: Explain how strong monarchs unified France.

Objective 4: Describe the formation of the Holy Roman Empire and how some emperors struggled with the papacy to control specific religious and secular issues.

Objective 5: Analyze how the Church reached the height of its power under Pope Innocent III.

LESSON 5 ORGANIZER		PACING: APPROX. 1 PERIOD, .5 BLOCKS		
				RESOURCES
	OBJECTIVES	**PACING**	**Online**	**Print**
Connect				
DIGITAL START UP ACTIVITY **A Challenge to Power**		5 min.	●	
Investigate				
DIGITAL TEXT 1 **Feudal Monarchs Begin to Centralize Power**	Objective 1	10 min.	●	●
DIGITAL TEXT 2 **English Kings Expand Their Power**		10 min.	●	●
DIGITAL TEXT 3 **Developing New Traditions of Government**	Objective 2	10 min.	●	●
DIGITAL TEXT 4 **Growth of the French Monarchy**	Objective 3	10 min.	●	●
INTERACTIVE MAP **The Growth of France 987–1328**		10 min.	●	
DIGITAL TEXT 5 **The Holy Roman Empire**		10 min.	●	●
DIGITAL TEXT 6 **A Pope and Emperor Feud**	Objective 4	10 min.	●	●
DIGITAL TEXT 7 **The Battle for Italy**		10 min.	●	●
INTERACTIVE GALLERY **Battle for Power – Monarchs and Popes**		10 min.	●	
DIGITAL TEXT 8 **Church Power Reaches Its Peak**	Objective 5	10 min.	●	●
Synthesize				
SYNTHESIZE **Different Paths Develop Different Governments**		5 min.	●	
Demonstrate				
LESSON QUIZ **Lesson Quiz and Class Discussion Board**		10 min.	●	

PEARSON
realize™
www.PearsonRealize.com

Go online to access additional resources including:
Primary Sources • Biographies • Supreme Court cases •
21st Century Skill Tutorials • Maps • Graphic Organizers.

CONNECT

DIGITAL START UP ACTIVITY
A Challenge to Power

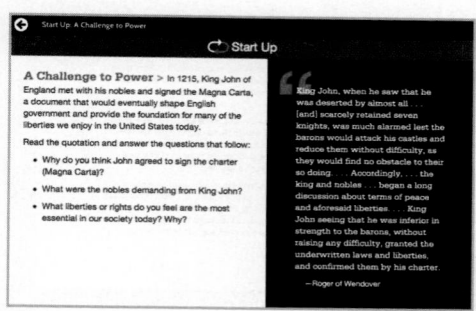

Project the Start Up Activity Ask students to answer the questions as they enter and get settled. Then have them share their ideas with another student, either in class or through a chat room or blog.

Discuss Why do you think John agreed to sign the charter (Magna Carta)? *(John agreed to sign the charter because he knew the nobles could seize power if he did not do what they asked.)*

What were the nobles demanding from King John? *(Sample Response: new laws and liberties for the nobles)*

What liberties or rights do you feel are the most essential in our society today? Why? *(Sample Response: The right to free speech and the right to elect our leaders are our most important rights today because they give us the opportunity to protest against or change the government if we don't like it. This controls the power of the government.)*

⇅ FLIP IT!
Assign the Flipped Video for this lesson.

STUDENT EDITION PRINT
PAGES: 221–230

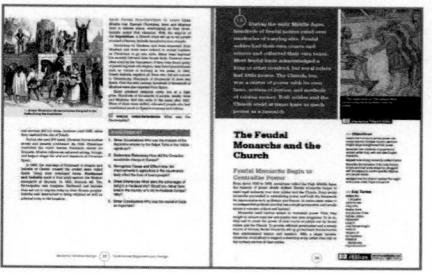

INVESTIGATE

DIGITAL TEXT 1
Feudal Monarchs Begin to Centralize Power

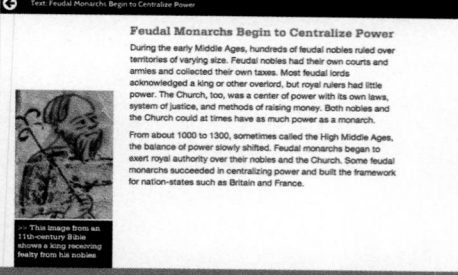

DIGITAL TEXT 2
English Kings Expand Their Power

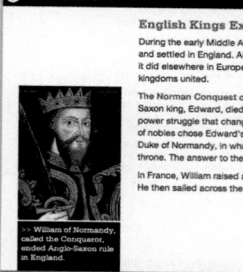

Objective 1: Learn how monarchs gained power over nobles and the Christian Church, and how English kings strengthened their power.

Quick Instruction

Introduce the text by explaining that strong monarchs who wanted to have total control over their domains would likely have a conflict with strong popes who wanted the Church to control as much as it could. This conflict included clerical issues, but also influenced secular issues that the Church felt would intrude on its authority.

Identify Central Issues What has to happen for one power to extend its authority over another power? *(The second power has to agree to give up authority or it has to be taken by force.)*

ELL Use the ELL activity described in the ELL chart.

Further Instruction

Project and discuss the Interactive Reading Notepad questions and the graphic organizer. Review the reigns of William the Conqueror and Henry II to start off the graphic organizer. Engage students in a discussion to decide if William's and Henry's efforts resulted in an increase or decrease in their power.

Support Ideas with Examples What events show that the Christian Church acted to politically unify medieval European nations? *(At this time, the ruling class and most citizens of European nations were Christian. As such, they were under the religious authority of the pope. That authority united the different kingdoms under Christianity.)*

The Feudal Monarchs and the Church

DIGITAL TEXT 3
Developing New Traditions of Government

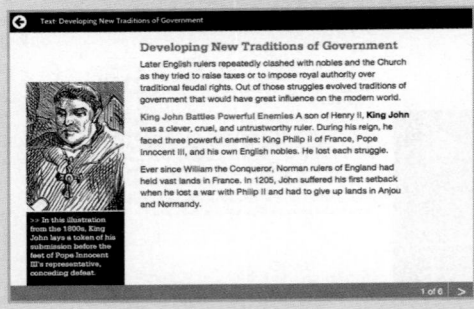

DIGITAL TEXT 4
Growth of the French Monarchy

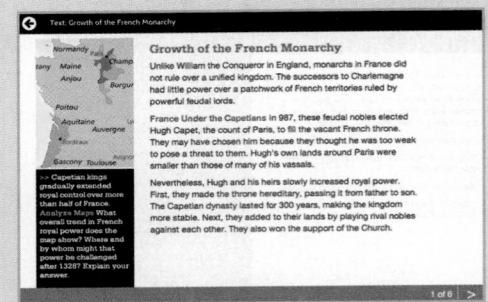

Objective 2: Describe how traditions of government evolved under King John and later English monarchs.

Quick Instruction

Introduce the text by explaining that the Magna Carta is one of the most important charters, or agreements, in European history. It was the first time noblemen successfully challenged the right of the king to rule as he chose. The Magna Carta spelled out some of what the nobles considered to be their basic rights. These "rights" would have been unheard of even a generation earlier, especially if the king disagreed. In centuries to come, the English people would frequently refer to the Magna Carta to support their efforts to establish a limited monarchy.

D **Differentiate: Extra Support** Explain that the British model of Parliament was a model for the United States Congress. Ask: How are the United States' legislature and Britain's Parliament alike? How are they different? *(Alike: both possess the exclusive power to tax, both are two-house bodies, both can limit the power of the monarch or president; Different: the House of Lords consists of nobles and clergy, while neither house of the United States Congress is for specific classes of people.)*

Further Instruction

Project and discuss the Interactive Reading Notepad questions for this lesson. Project the digital version of the Magna Carta on the whiteboard.

The political and legal ideas contained in the Magna Carta inspired future efforts to establish a representative government that ensured the rights of its citizens.

Draw Inferences What ideas in the Magna Carta have influenced the development of the U.S. legal and governmental systems? *(Many of the same rights, including habeas corpus and due process, are central to U.S. legal traditions. Other ideas in the Magna Carta, such as rulers must obey the law, people should have a voice in decisions about taxation, and all people have specific rights, have strongly influenced American ideas about government and what it should and should not do.)*

Objective 3: Explain how strong monarchs unified France.

Quick Instruction

The Growth of France 987–1328 Project the map on the whiteboard. Introduce the activity by explaining that while England was moving toward restrictions on the monarchy, France was moving in the other direction. During the period covered in this activity, France's monarchs consolidated their power along with their territory until more than half of France was under the control of one monarch.

📖 ACTIVE CLASSROOM

Use the Audio Tour strategy and pair students for this activity. Have the first student give the second a verbal "tour" of the map – what does it show? Have the second student give the first an explanation of what it means.

Determine Relevance Why is the Capetian kings' success at expanding their territory important to European history at this time? *(France was put on a different path than England in terms of how the country would be governed. This difference affected the future direction of both countries in everything from their relationship to the papacy to how wars were fought and paid for.)*

INTERACTIVE MAP

The Growth of France 987–1328

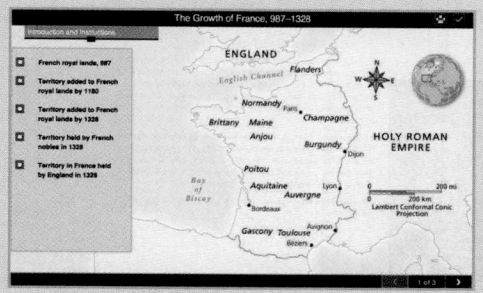

DIGITAL TEXT 5

The Holy Roman Empire

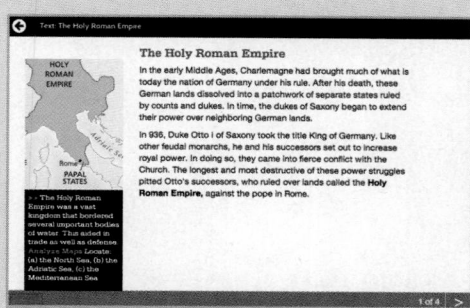

DIGITAL TEXT 6

A Pope and Emperor Feud

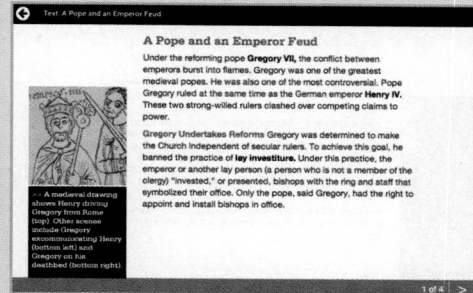

Further Instruction

Project and discuss the Close Reading Notepad questions for this lesson. Use the Close Reading Notepad questions to help students fill out the section on France in the graphic organizer at the beginning of the Notepad.

Draw Conclusions Why did the election of a French pope lead to a split in the papacy? *(The French pope was perceived as being more loyal to France than to the traditionally independent and powerful papacy. When the pope moved the papal court close to the French border, it angered other Church leaders, who then elected a different pope. The existence of the French papal court was a contributing factor to the Great Western Schism within the papacy.)*

Compare and Contrast What are some of the similarities and some of the differences between the development of the French monarchy and the development of the English monarchy? *(Sample Response: The English and French kings both developed centralized governments that took power away from the nobles while giving some power to common citizens. However, when the English monarch was weak, the nobles used the opportunity to secure more rights. The French monarchs never had to give up any power, even when they challenged the Church.)*

Objective 4: Describe the formation of the Holy Roman Empire and how some emperors struggled with the papacy to control specific religious and secular issues.

Quick Instruction

Interactive Gallery Battle for Power – Monarchs and Popes Project the gallery on the whiteboard. Explain that monarchs and popes were individuals who had absolute rule over their specific areas. The monarch ruled the secular activities of people, while the pope ruled the religious activities. At times, there was conflict regarding exactly where the boundaries were between the secular and religious worlds. When this happened, a struggle for power would ensue between a monarch and a pope.

👥 ACTIVE CLASSROOM

Use the Conversation with History strategy and ask students to pretend they are having a conversation with one of the people in the interactive gallery. Students should write down a question they'd like to ask their chosen historical person, then what the person would say to them and, finally, what the student would respond.

Discuss Ask students to share their conversations with the class. What types of responses did students get from the historical person to whom they posed their question?

The Feudal Monarchs and the Church

DIGITAL TEXT 7

The Battle for Italy

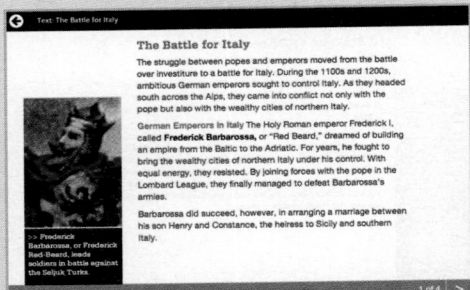

INTERACTIVE GALLERY

Battle for Power — Monarchs and Popes

DIGITAL TEXT 8

Church Power Reaches Its Peak

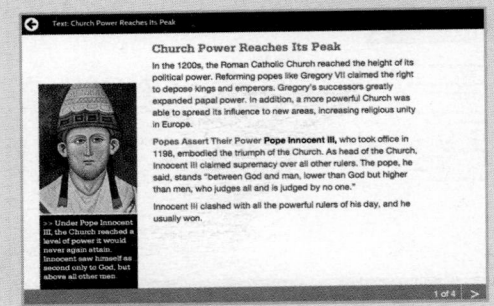

ELL Use the ELL activity described in the ELL chart.

Further Instruction

Project and discuss the Close Reading Notepad questions for this lesson. Use the Close Reading Notepad questions to help students fill out the section on the Holy Roman Empire in the graphic organizer at the beginning of the Notepad.

The actions of Pope Gregory VII made the political influence of the Church very clear. Although the initial issue with Emperor Henry IV appeared to be strictly concerned with Church doctrines and policies, it was more complicated because the clergymen involved held lands as royal fiefs and, therefore, owed allegiance to the emperor. The fact that the pope ultimately "won" because Henry IV was forced to humble himself is critical to what future popes expected from monarchs.

Draw Inferences Why was it important that Henry IV was finally forced to give in to Pope Gregory? *(It implied the pope had more power than even the Holy Roman Emperor. Other monarchs noticed this feud and its result, which likely affected how they would deal with future popes.)*

Objective 5: Analyze how the Church reached the height of its power under Pope Innocent III.

Quick Instruction

Introduce the reading by explaining that Pope Innocent III's claim that the pope was superior to all men and second only to God was a dramatic step to take. Other popes had not made such an explicit claim, and it angered many monarchs and some clergy. At the same time, others accepted it. Innocent's claim also opened the door for popes succeeding him to make the same claim. This added the potential for more conflict between future monarchs and popes.

Further Instruction

Project and discuss the Close Reading Notepad questions for this lesson. Use the Close Reading Notepad questions to help students fill out the section on the Holy Roman Empire in the graphic organizer at the beginning of the Notepad.

The popes reached the height of their political power during the 13th century under Pope Innocent III, one of the most powerful of all medieval popes. He introduced the controversial idea that the pope was the direct link to God, subordinate only to God and, therefore, under no temporal authority. In other words, the pope was the one individual on Earth above even the mightiest of kings. This led to Innocent's use of religious power, such as excommunication and interdict, to impose his will on kings who chose to challenge him.

■ **SYNTHESIZE**

■ **DEMONSTRATE**

SYNTHESIZE

Different Paths Develop Different Governments

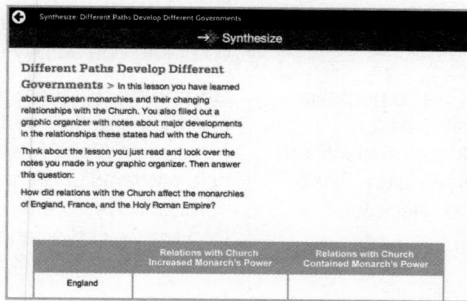

LESSON QUIZ

Lesson Quiz and Class Discussion Board

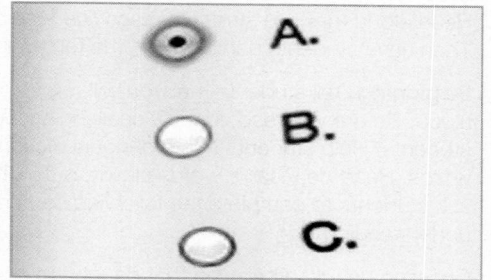

Draw Conclusions How did Innocent's claim that the pope judged all but was judged by no one reflect the Church's political power? *(He won in his clashes with King John of England over appointing bishops and with Philip of France over an annulment of a marriage. In both cases, he asserted the power of the pope over that of the monarch.)*

Ask students to share their responses to the Synthesize question. Explain that the Church developed enormous power in relation to European monarchies and that it was often the source of serious conflicts that affected the people of the countries, as well as the monarchs. For example, Pope Innocent III's interdict on the entire country of England punished regular citizens who were innocent of wrongdoing. The political power of the Church would continue to be a source of contention and spur efforts toward reform.

Assign the online Lesson Quiz for this lesson if you haven't already done so. Students will be offered automatic remediation or enrichment based on their score.

Pose these questions to the class on the Discussion Board:

Analyze Information How were nobles and the Church obstacles for monarchs who wanted more power? *(Nobles and popes fought for power. Nobles forced King John to sign the Magna Carta. Pope Innocent III forced King John to yield in regard to appointing bishops. In France, King Philip IV failed in his goal to tax clergy when the pope refused and said the pope was above "kings and kingdoms." Pope Gregory VII's clash with the Holy Roman Emperor Henry IV led nobles to take advantage of the situation to create further political unrest. The popes thus proved that they could, and would, get involved in political issues or use their religious authority to impose their will on kings.)*

Determine Relevance What was the significance of the conflict between Pope Gregory VII and Emperor Henry IV? *(It was central to the struggle for power between popes and secular rulers during the High Middle Ages.)*

Topic Inquiry

Have students continue their investigations for the Topic Inquiry.

Learning, Literature, and the Arts of the Middle Ages

Supporting English Language Learners

Use with Digital Text 1, **The Rise of Medieval Universities.**

Listening
Read aloud, or have students read, *The Rise of Medieval Universities.* Then have students participate in the following activities.

Beginning Tell students that you will read Christine de Pisan's quotation aloud. Before you read, identify challenging words and phrases for students. Help students use a bilingual dictionary to look up the identified words. Read de Pisan's words slowly, but with natural expression. Finally, ask students to complete the following sentence frame to check for understanding.

Christine de Pisan believed that daughters and sons _____.

Intermediate Tell students that you will read Christine de Pisan's quotation aloud. Before you read, identify challenging words and phrases for students. Direct students to use a bilingual dictionary to look up the identified words. Read de Pisan's words slowly, but with natural expression. Finally, ask students to explain, using simple sentences, de Pisan's ideas about education.

Advanced Tell students that you will read Christine de Pisan's quotation aloud. Before you read, have students skim the text to identify challenging words and phrases. Direct students to use a bilingual dictionary to look up the identified words. Read de Pisan's words slowly, but with natural expression. Finally, ask students to explain de Pisan's ideas about educating young women in their own words.

Advanced High Tell students that they will be reading Christine de Pisan's quotation aloud. Before reading, have students skim the text to identify challenging words and phrases. Direct students to use a bilingual dictionary to look up any difficult words. Have a student volunteer read de Pisan's words slowly and with natural expression. Finally, have students turn to a partner and explain de Pisan's ideas about educating young women in their own words. Circulate among students to offer linguistic support as needed.

Use with Digital Text 2, **New Knowledge Reaches Europe.**

Listening
Read *New Knowledge Reaches Europe* aloud. Then have students complete one activity according to their level of English proficiency.

Beginning Request that students find the section titled "Science and Mathematics" in the text *New Knowledge Reaches Europe*. Read the section aloud to students, using a variety of linguistic supports, help students understand the content. Ask students to identify two contributions from the Arabic world that improved the way European thinkers viewed science and mathematics. Students should point to or underline their selections.

Intermediate Request that students find the section titled "Science and Mathematics" in the text *New Knowledge Reaches Europe*. Read the section aloud to students, using a variety of linguistic supports, help students understand the content. Ask students to identify two contributions from the Arabic world that improved the way European thinkers viewed science and mathematics. Students should explain their selections using simple sentences.

Advanced Request that students find the section titled "Science and Mathematics" in the text *New Knowledge Reaches Europe*. Read the section aloud to students, explaining any terms that hinder student understanding of the content. Then ask students to identify two contributions from the Arabic world that improved the way European thinkers viewed science and mathematics. Students should discuss their selections with a small group of students.

Advanced High Request that students find the section titled "Science and Mathematics" in the text *New Knowledge Reaches Europe*. Read the section aloud to students, making sure students have an opportunity to ask any questions they may have about the language or the content of the section. Then ask students to identify two contributions from the Arabic world that improved the way European thinkers viewed science and mathematics. Students should explain their selections to the group.

▣ Differentiate Instruction

Use the Differentiated Instruction notes throughout the lesson plan to support the varied skill sets, levels of readiness, and interests in the mixed-ability classroom.

Challenge These notes include suggestions for expanding the activity for advanced students.

On-Level These notes include suggestions for modifying the activity to address different interests or learning styles.

Extra Support These notes include ideas for providing more scaffolding or reading spuport.

Special Needs These notes provide ideas for adapting instruction to support the needs of various special needs students.

▇ NOTES

_____

_____

_____

_____

_____

PEARSON
realize™
www.PearsonRealize.com

Go online to access additional resources including:
Primary Sources • Biographies • Supreme Court cases •
21st Century Skill Tutorials • Maps • Graphic Organizers.

Objectives

Objective 1: Explain the emergence of universities and their importance to medieval life.

Objective 2: Understand how newly translated writings from the past and from other regions influenced medieval thought.

Objective 3: Describe the literature, architecture, and art of the High and Late Middle Ages.

Objective 4: Examine the lasting heritage of the Byzantine Empire.

LESSON 6 ORGANIZER		OBJECTIVES	PACING	RESOURCES Online	RESOURCES Print
Connect					
DIGITAL START UP ACTIVITY **A Hero's Tale**			5 min.	●	
Investigate					
DIGITAL TEXT 1 **The Rise of Medieval Universities**		Objective 1	10 min.	●	●
DIGITAL TEXT 2 **New Knowledge Reaches Europe**		Objective 2	10 min.	●	●
INTERACTIVE GALLERY **Medieval Innovation in Europe**			10 min.	●	
DIGITAL TEXT 3 **Medieval Literature**			10 min.	●	●
DIGITAL TEXT 4 **Architecture and Art**		Objective 3	10 min.	●	●
INTERACTIVE GALLERY **A Gothic Cathedral**			10 min.	●	
DIGITAL TEXT 5 **The Byzantine Heritage**		Objective 4	10 min.	●	●
Synthesize					
SYNTHESIZE **Reach for the Sky**			5 min.	●	
Demonstrate					
LESSON QUIZ **Lesson Quiz and Class Discussion Board**			10 min.	●	

PACING: APPROX. 1 PERIOD, .5 BLOCKS

Learning, Literature, and the Arts of the Middle Ages

■ CONNECT

DIGITAL START UP ACTIVITY
A Hero's Tale

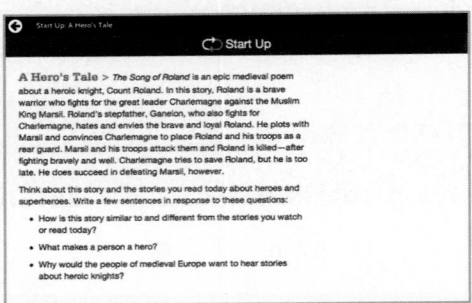

Project the Start Up Activity Ask students to answer the questions as they enter and get settled. Then have them share their ideas with another student.

Discuss Treachery and betrayal are often part of heroic stories. Why did Ganelon betray his king and cause Roland's death? *(Ganelon might have hoped for part of Charlemagne's kingdom if Charlemagne lost the war. Roland's death was a strike against Charlemagne.)* Why was betrayal, but with the just winning in the end, an important theme in medieval Europe? *(Warfare was almost constant. The Christian belief that the "good" cause would win eventually gave people hope.)*

Tell students that in this lesson they will learn how Christian churches and monasteries were the first centers of learning in medieval Europe.

⇅ FLIP IT!
Assign the Flipped Video for this lesson.

■ STUDENT EDITION PRINT
PAGES: 231–237

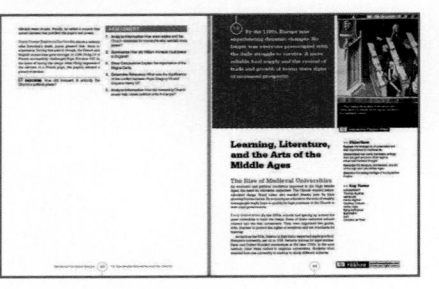

■ INVESTIGATE

DIGITAL TEXT 1
The Rise of Medieval Universities

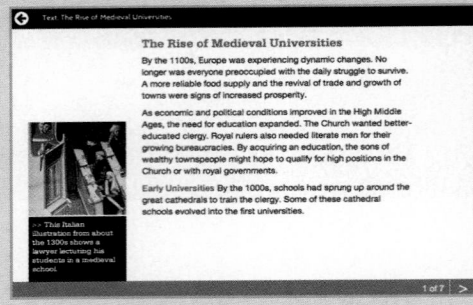

Objective 1: Explain the emergence of universities and their importance to medieval life.

Quick Instruction
Project the map. Introduce the activity by explaining that most schools and universities had their beginnings as church or monastery schools. These centers of learning were one of the ways medieval Christianity acted as a unifying social force. For a largely illiterate society, the Church and Christianity were the center of people's lives. The Christian faith provided the structure for daily life and the resource to which people turned not only for religious guidance, but also for help in dealing with secular issues. In most cases, the clergy were the only literate people for miles around. Literacy and education for common people resulted in greater independence. This would be especially true for women, most of whom were not allowed to attend schools.

Medieval Europe Centers of Learning Project the map on the whiteboard.

Draw Inferences Ask students for their opinions on why some of the earliest universities were in Italy. Point out that Rome was the center of the Church and that many busy trading centers were located in Italy. Boats carrying goods also carried ideas from other lands. This was especially true in the fields of medicine and astronomy.

D Differentiate: Challenge/Gifted Have students prepare a television interview with Christine de Pisan. Participating students should develop the script, act as videographers, interviewer, and Christine. Questions should reflect questions that explore Christine's

observations about her life and what she might have felt being one of very few literate women. Students could present the result as a video or as a live role-play to the rest of the class.

ELL Use the ELL activity described in the ELL chart.

Further Instruction
Project and discuss the Close Reading Notepad questions and the graphic organizer about the similarities and differences between higher education in the High Middle Ages and higher education today.

Historians now recognize that a new culture was emerging in the early Middle Ages. Education meant the introduction of new ideas from many different cultures, including ancient cultures such as the Greeks and Romans. Students studying medicine would become familiar with both Muslim and Greek writings. Those studying law would learn about the history of legal systems, as well as the local legal codes. With education, a broader world view started to emerge, especially in areas where foreign trade was common and ideas arrived along with trade goods.

Identify Cause and Effect Why did an improving economy lead to the growth of universities? *(As some people became wealthy, they looked for opportunities for their children in government bureaucracies and the Church, which required education.)*

Draw Inferences How did women get an education? *(Very few did. Of those, most would have gotten their education in convents or with private schools or tutors.)*

DIGITAL TEXT 2

New Knowledge Reaches Europe

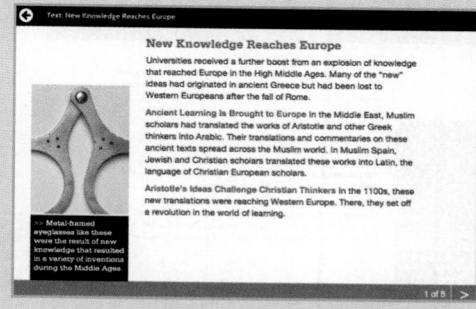

INTERACTIVE GALLERY

Medieval Innovation in Europe

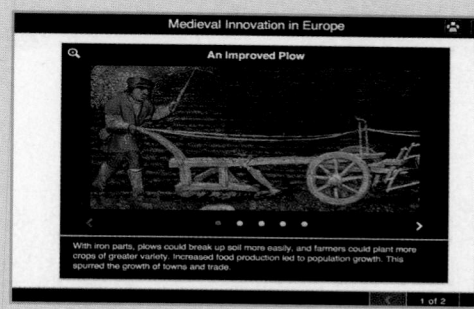

DIGITAL TEXT 3

Medieval Literature

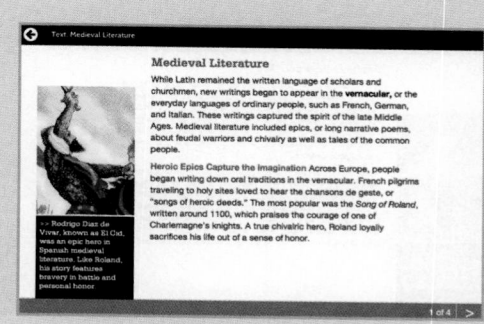

Objective 2: Understand how newly translated writings from the past and from other regions influenced medieval thought.

Quick Instruction

Introduce the activity by explaining that the High Middle Ages was a time of exciting ideas and inventions that changed how people lived.

Medieval Innovation in Europe: Interactive Gallery Project the gallery on the whiteboard. Click on each invention for a brief explanation of what it was and its impact on medieval life of the time. Discuss how seemingly minor innovations, such as an iron plow, could have far-reaching effects. Ask students for examples of modern inventions that impact their daily lives.

🖳 ACTIVE CLASSROOM

Use the Rank It strategy to have students decide which inventions had the greatest impact on medieval life. List the inventions on the board. Ask students to rank the inventions and provide a justification for ranking decisions they made. Then ask students to work in pairs to discuss their rankings and justifications. Poll the class to see if there is agreement on the rankings. Discuss any significant differences in poll results.

ELL Use the ELL activity described in the ELL chart.

Further Instruction

Project and discuss the Close Reading Notepad questions for this lesson.

Explain that the Greek philosopher, Aristotle, produced a work called *Ethics*. The main ideas of this work include: the importance of the soul in defining humans, finding the mean or middle between extremes, living a life of moderation, and the importance of developing virtue by maintaining positive behavior and habits. Other Greek philosophers emphasized the existence of natural and universal laws that are independent of laws passed by people. Christian scholars and philosophers, such as Thomas Aquinas, were often able to find common ground with these secular teachings.

Compare Where did Aquinas find the important similarities between Aristotle's philosophy and Christian religious beliefs? *(Answers will vary, but should include an understanding that the specific examples given of Aristotle's philosophy mirror basic Christian teachings concerning humans having a soul, adopting personal behaviors that are not indulgent or gluttonous, and the importance of living a virtuous life according to Church doctrine.)*

Objective 3: Describe the literature, architecture, and art of the High and late Middle Ages.

Quick Instruction

A Gothic Cathedral: Interactive Gallery Project the gallery on the whiteboard. Introduce the activity by explaining that along with dramatic changes in literature, the High Middle Ages was a time of both technical and artistic change in architecture. Builders used engineering skills to construct vast cathedrals that would have been structurally impossible even a generation earlier. Artisans were brought in from all over Europe to produce wondrous works of art in stained-glass windows. These windows reflected the power of the Church and portrayed Bible episodes for illiterate Christians. Italian stonemasons often traveled far from home to create the intricate statues of saints or fanciful gargoyles. Click on each hotspot to show students the amazing architectural and artistic skills represented by a Gothic cathedral.

Learning, Literature, and the Arts of the Middle Ages

DIGITAL TEXT 4
Architecture and Art

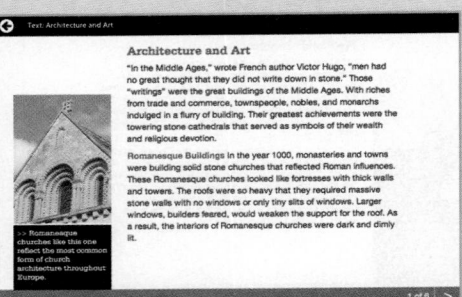

INTERACTIVE GALLERY
A Gothic Cathedral

DIGITAL TEXT 5
The Byzantine Heritage

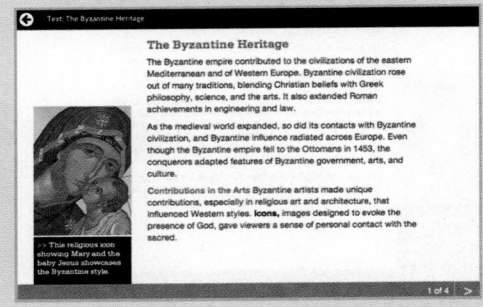

👥 ACTIVE CLASSROOM

Use the See-Think-Wonder strategy to have students take a closer look at the many architectural and artistic wonders present in a Gothic cathedral. Ask students: What do you see? What does that make you think? What are you wondering about now that you've seen this? Ask students to share their insights with the class.

Draw Conclusions Why was the flying buttress such an important architectural advance? *(It allowed for greater open spaces and light in cathedrals.)*

Further Instruction
Project and discuss the Close Reading Notepad questions for this lesson.

Medieval literature in the vernacular grew from several traditions. Traditional stories that had withstood the test of time were valued over original stories. Therefore, medieval authors often adapted themes and stories similar to those used by their Greek and Roman predecessors. Several of these works became the first examples of national literature, helping to define emerging European nations. These include the stories of King Arthur (Britain), The Song of Roland (France), and El Cid (Spain). However, there were also works that offered readers humor or a "slice of life" that opened a window on the lives of a wide variety of people.

Draw Comparisons How is a popular work like *The Canterbury Tales* like a medieval version of a modern-day TV reality show? *(Chaucer tried to represent different general types or categories of people as they actually were. Their opinions and actions reflect the reality of a person of that class or station in life.)*

Objective 4: Examine the lasting heritage of the Byzantine empire.

Quick Instruction
The Byzantine empire, especially Constantinople, was an important center of learning. Schools of law, philosophy, and religion attracted students from all over the known world. Heavily influenced by ancient Roman civilization, the Byzantines often integrated classical concepts with emerging Christian beliefs. This integration extended to Byzantine art and architecture, which reflected a strong Eastern influence drawing from many Middle Eastern cultures.

Draw Inferences Why is integrating different cultural influences a major factor in the development of art, literature, and architecture? *(The combination of different perspectives represented by the cultures creates a unique piece of art, literature, or architecture that reflects the time in which it is created.)*

Further Instruction
Project and discuss the Close Reading Notepad question for this lesson.

The modern Eastern Orthodox religions are still influenced by Byzantine art and architecture. For example, the priests' vestments are similar to what they were centuries ago and combine both an Eastern influence with a Western heritage. Eastern Orthodox churches feature mosaics and the unique Byzantine style religious pictures called icons. Even public buildings in places such as Russia bear a resemblance to the onion dome buildings of Constantinople (now Istanbul).

Draw Inferences Why do museums and libraries protect and share the art and literature of prior civilizations? *(public access, assistance to students and scholars, basis for cultural development)*

■ **SYNTHESIZE**

SYNTHESIZE
Reach for the Sky

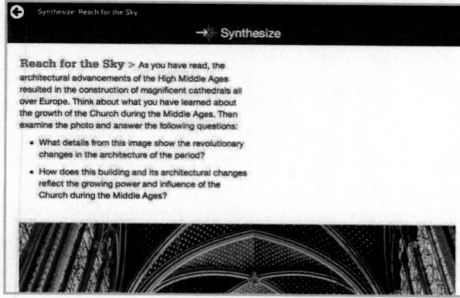

Have students use the Think-Pair-Share strategy to answer the questions in the Reach for the Sky activity. Ask them to take five minutes to write down some brief answers to the following questions and then share their answers with a partner.

How did increasing access to education affect architecture and art in the Middle Ages?

Discuss What is the role of government in providing education? *(Answers may vary. Students may argue that access to education is a human right that should not be limited to those who are wealthy or to specific genders and races. They may claim that education is a key to progress and, as such, it is the responsibility of government to ensure that there is equal access to quality education for all people.)*

■ **DEMONSTRATE**

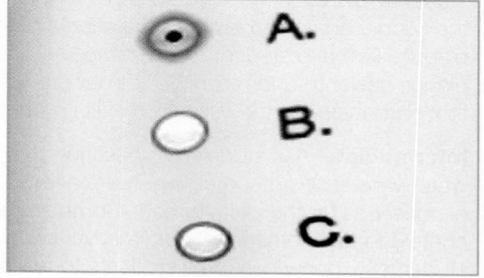

LESSON QUIZ
Lesson Quiz and Class Discussion Board

Assign the online Lesson Quiz for this lesson if you haven't already done so. Students will be offered automatic remediation or enrichment based on their score.

Pose these questions to the class on the Discussion Board:

In *Learning, Literature, and the Arts of the Middle Ages*, you learned how the rise of medieval universities and education had a profound effect on people of various social and economic backgrounds. Education led to a re-emergence of philosophical thought that challenged theologians. This inquiry led to greater intellectual growth within the Church. Education also influenced art and architecture, with both areas flourishing. Advanced techniques made it possible to build the Gothic cathedral, which had a major impact on Christian churches for many centuries. Finally, you learned about the influence of the Byzantine empire on educational growth in Europe. Byzantine scholars moved to Europe to teach, and there was a renewal of interest in classical thought. Ideas from the Middle East also influenced art and architecture.

Draw Conclusions How do art, literature, and architecture reflect the history of the cultures in which they are produced? *(The creativity that allows people to produce these works is a function of what they experience on a personal level. The cultures in which artisans live affect their views and, therefore, what and how they create.)*

Topic Inquiry
Have students continue their investigations for the Topic Inquiry.

The Late Middle Ages: A Time of Upheaval

Supporting English Language Learners

Use with Digital Text 1, **The Black Death Spreads Across Europe.**

Listening
Read aloud, or have students read, *The Black Death Spreads Across Europe*. Then have students participate in the following activities.

Beginning Ask students to consider a time when they were worried about something. Have one or two student volunteers offer their experiences for the class to hear. Some students will have a personal context for this, others will not. This variety is expected. Regardless of students' experiences, help students to feel empathy for the people of the Middle Ages who suffered the effects of the Black Death, or bubonic plague. To make students' understanding of the effects of the bubonic plague easier to understand, consider providing students with a video clip that demonstrates the difficulties of life during this time.

Intermediate Ask students to describe to a partner a time when they were worried about something. Have a few student volunteers offer their experiences for the class to hear. Some students will have a personal context for this, others will not. This variety is expected. Regardless of students' experiences, help students to feel empathy for the people of the Middle Ages who suffered the effects of the bubonic plague by asking them to identify words that describe how they would feel if they were living during this time. To make students' understanding of the effects of the bubonic plague easier to understand, consider providing students with a video clip that demonstrates the difficulties of life during the Middle Ages.

Advanced Ask students to turn to a partner and describe a time when they were worried about something. Then guide students to feel empathy for the people of the Middle Ages who suffered the effects of the bubonic plague. To make students' understanding of the effects of the bubonic plague easier to understand, consider providing students with a video clip that demonstrates the difficulties of life during this time. Finally, ask students to write one or two sentences to describe how people living during this time might feel about all the death and sadness around them.

Advanced High Ask students to share a time when they were worried about something. Then guide students to feel empathy for the people of the Middle Ages who suffered the effects of the bubonic plague. To make students' understanding of the effects of the bubonic plague easier to understand, consider providing students with a video clip that demonstrates the difficulties of life during this time. Finally, ask students to discuss in a small group how people living during the Middle Ages might feel about all the death and sadness around them.

Use with Digital Text 3, **The Hundred Years' War.**

Listening
Read *The Hundred Years' War* aloud. Then have students complete one activity according to their level of English proficiency.

Beginning Using linguistic aids, help students understand the story of Joan of Arc. Read aloud the section titled *Joan of Arc*. Have students work together to formulate opinions about Joan's participation in the Hundred Years' War. Have students identify other individuals, both historic and modern day, who took risks to support something in which they believed.

Intermediate After reading *The Hundred Years' War* with students, read aloud the section titled *Joan of Arc*. Ask students to work in pairs to identify the reasons that Joan of Arc was canonized a saint in the Church. Have students help each other with challenging vocabulary by providing them with resources to find word meanings. Finally, have students identify other individuals, both historic and modern day, who took risks to support something in which they believed.

Advanced Read aloud *Joan of Arc* to students. Guide a discussion of the sainthood of Joan of Arc. Students should discuss whether or not they think that the Church should have canonized Joan of Arc. Help students work together to develop the vocabulary to name reasons for and against Joan's canonization. Then have student volunteers read the lists to the group. Finally, have students identify and describe other individuals, both historic and modern day, who took risks to support something in which they believed.

Advanced High Read aloud *Joan of Arc* to students. Have small groups of students discuss the sainthood of Joan of Arc. Based on the text, groups should discuss and analyze why Joan of Arc was canonized. Finally, have students identify and describe other individuals, both historic and modern day, who took risks to support something in which they believed.

ⅅ Differentiate Instruction

Use the Differentiated Instruction notes throughout the lesson plan to support the varied skill sets, levels of readiness, and interests in the mixed-ability classroom.

Challenge These notes include suggestions for expanding the activity for advanced students.

On-Level These notes include suggestions for modifying the activity to address different interests or learning styles.

Extra Support These notes include ideas for providing more scaffolding or reading spuport.

Special Needs These notes provide ideas for adapting instruction to support the needs of various special needs students.

◼ NOTES

PEARSON
realize™
www.PearsonRealize.com

Go online to access additional resources including:
Primary Sources • Biographies • Supreme Court cases •
21st Century Skill Tutorials • Maps • Graphic Organizers.

Objectives

Objective 1: Understand how the Black Death caused social and economic decline.

Objective 2: Describe the problems facing the Church in the late Middle Ages and how the Church reacted.

Objective 3: Summarize the causes, turning points, and effects of the Hundred Years' War.

LESSON 7 ORGANIZER		PACING: APPROX. 1 PERIOD, .5 BLOCKS			
		OBJECTIVES	**PACING**	**RESOURCES**	
				Online	Print
Connect					
	DIGITAL START UP ACTIVITY **The Black Death Approaches**		5 min.	●	
Investigate					
	DIGITAL TEXT 1 **The Black Death Spreads Across Europe**	Objective 1	10 min.	●	●
	INTERACTIVE MAP **The Black Death**		10 min.	●	
	DIGITAL TEXT 2 **Crisis in the Church**	Objective 2	10 min.	●	●
	DIGITAL TEXT 3 **The Hundred Years' War**	Objective 3	10 min.	●	●
	INTERACTIVE MAP **The Hundred Years' War**		10 min.	●	
Synthesize					
	SYNTHESIZE **Epidemics: Science vs. Fears**		5 min.	●	
Demonstrate					
	LESSON QUIZ **Lesson Quiz and Class Discussion Board**		10 min.	●	

The Late Middle Ages: A Time of Upheaval

■ CONNECT

DIGITAL START UP ACTIVITY
The Black Death Approaches

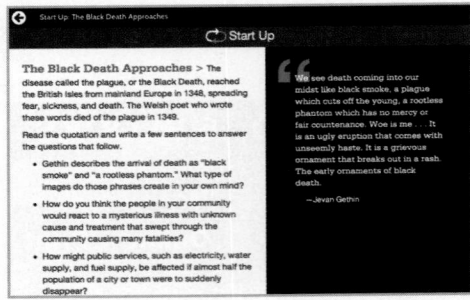

Project the Start Up Activity Ask students to answer the questions as they enter and get settled. Then have them share their ideas with another student, either in class or through a chat room or blog.

Discuss When Gethin describes the arrival of death as "black smoke" and "a rootless phantom," what types of feelings and images does that evoke in you? *(Sample Responses: mysterious, frightening, something uncontrollable)* How do you think your neighbors and friends would react to a mysterious, fatal illness that swept through the community? *(Sample Responses: fearfulness, chaos, blaming a person or group)* How might public services, such as electricity, water, and fuel, be affected if almost half the population of a city or town suddenly disappeared? *(Sample Responses: Services would stop because no one could run them.)*

⚑ FLIP IT!
Assign the Flipped Video for this lesson.

■ STUDENT EDITION PRINT PAGES: 238–242

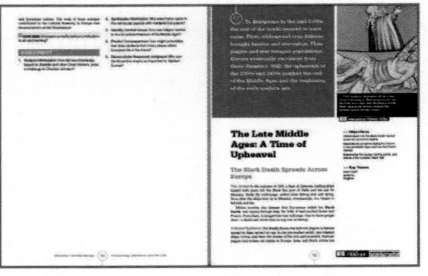

■ INVESTIGATE

DIGITAL TEXT 1
The Black Death Spreads Across Europe

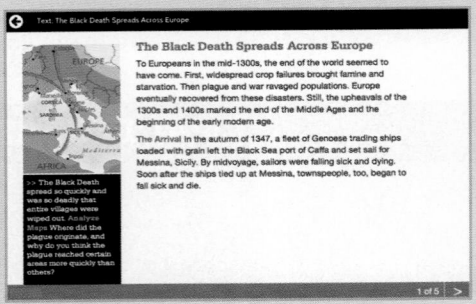

INTERACTIVE MAP
The Black Death

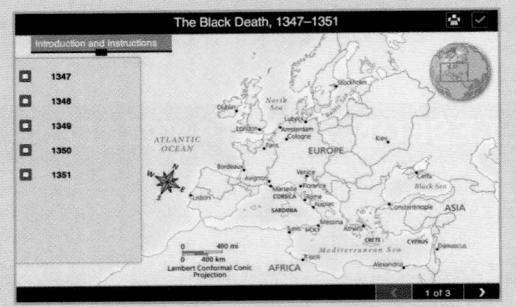

Objective 1: Understand how the Black Death caused social and economic decline.

Quick Instruction
Introduce the activity by explaining that the Black Death had an enormous impact on every aspect of medieval society. It spread far and fast, sometimes eradicating entire villages.

The Black Death: Interactive Map Project the map on the whiteboard. Click on each time period to show how fast and how far the Black Death spread. Discuss the effects of the Black Death on medieval society and how it contributed to the end of medieval Europe.

📷 ACTIVE CLASSROOM
Have students write a headline and then a three-sentence introduction to a television special on the Black Death. Ask for volunteers to present their introductions. Discuss which aspects of the Black Death contributed the most to the end of medieval Europe's social structure and economy.

D **Differentiate: Challenge/Gifted** After reviewing students' headlines and program introductions, have students complete the exercise by creating a script for a short documentary on the plague. Some students can write the script. Others can be the actors in a video presentation to the rest of the class.

ELL Use the ELL activity described in the ELL chart.

Further Instruction
Project and discuss the Close Reading Notepad questions on the whiteboard.

The significance of the plague is not solely in the outbreak of disease, but in the profound political, social, and economic consequences of high rates of mortality throughout Europe. Short-term consequences included an end to wars, a decline in trade, and a reduction in the amount of land under cultivation. All of this contributed to an economic depression. However, the long-term effects were even more far-reaching and permanent. This was especially true for peasants and former serfs.

Identify Cause and Effect How did the high mortality rate affect the feudal and manorial systems in medieval Europe? *(The medieval feudal and manorial systems began to collapse, giving serfs and peasants freedom to seek work where it was available.)*

Draw Inferences What might have happened to medieval Europe if the plague had been limited to Italy? *(The economy would have faltered due to Italy's trade role. Surrounding countries would likely have gone to war to gain control of Italy's trade routes and harbors. The social systems, including the feudal and manorial systems, would have continued for a longer period of time, thereby delaying the rise of the middle class.)*

DIGITAL TEXT 2
Crisis in the Church

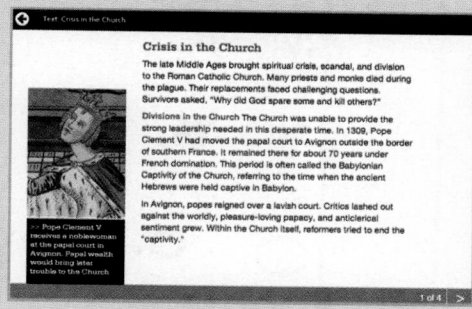

DIGITAL TEXT 3
The Hundred Years' War

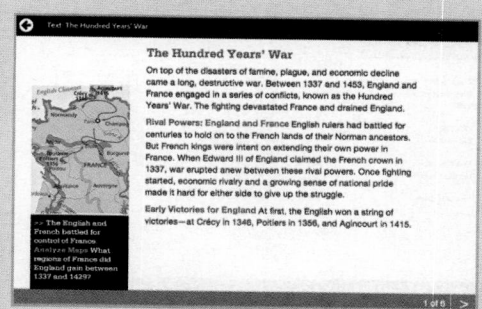

Objective 2: Describe the problems facing the Christian Church in the late Middle Ages and how the Church reacted.

Quick Instruction
After the devastation of the Black Death, survivors were asking difficult questions of their Church leaders. Strong Church leadership was sorely needed. However, the Church was dealing with serious internal conflicts. Opposing political forces influenced the papacy. Reformers resented the opulent lifestyle of the papal court. These conflicts and others contributed to the Great Schism, or split, within the Church. At one time, there were three different popes, each claiming he was the "true" pope. This strife contributed to the change in the Church's role in medieval Europe. Where once the Church represented social and religious cohesion, it now represented confusion. Questions were being asked about the Church's role in everyday life that would have been unthinkable in previous generations. The Church had been an integral foundation of medieval Europe. As that foundation broke apart, so did medieval Europe itself. Europe was leaving the Middle Ages behind and would be looking toward a different Europe.

Further Instruction
Project and discuss the Close Reading Notepad question for this lesson. Provide students with additional information regarding the Great Schism.

When the French monarchy forced the pope to move his court from Rome to Avignon in France, it began a period of intense rivalry and confusion within the Church. The pope finally moved the papal court back to Rome in 1377 and died a year later. The cardinals elected Pope Urban VI. However, Urban's policies were unpopular and he was considered mentally ill. The cardinals then elected another pope, Clement VII, who moved back to Avignon and French influence because Urban would not relinquish the papal throne. This began the Great Schism, also known as the Western Schism, with rival popes excommunicating each other and their followers. In 1409, a Church council in Pisa elected a third pope and added to the confusion.

Draw Inferences Why did the Church react so harshly to reformers like Wycliffe and Huss? *(Once the papacy was restored, the Church moved to regain the political and social control it had had before the Great Schism. Reformers like Wycliffe threatened the status quo.)*

Objective 3: Summarize the causes, turning points, and effects of the Hundred Years' War.

Quick Instruction
The Hundred Years' War: Interactive Map Project the map on the whiteboard. Introduce the activity by explaining that England and France battled each other over French territory from 1337 to 1453. During that time, weapons technology drastically changed, which greatly affected several key battles. Political changes also took place that set England and France on different political paths. Click through the key periods on the map and discuss how the results changed medieval Europe.

📹 ACTIVE CLASSROOM
Use the Ranking strategy to have students go through the key battles of the Hundred Years' War shown in the Interactive Map and rank the events that had the greatest impact on the course of the war. Ask students to provide a justification for their ranking decisions, and then ask students to work in pairs to share their rankings and justifications. Finally, poll the class to see if there is agreement on the rankings.

The Late Middle Ages: A Time of Upheaval

■ **SYNTHESIZE**

■ **DEMONSTRATE**

INTERACTIVE MAP
The Hundred Years' War

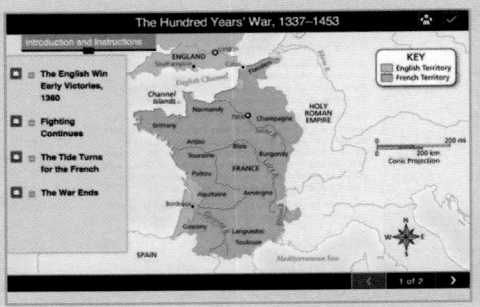

SYNTHESIZE
Epidemics: Science vs. Fears

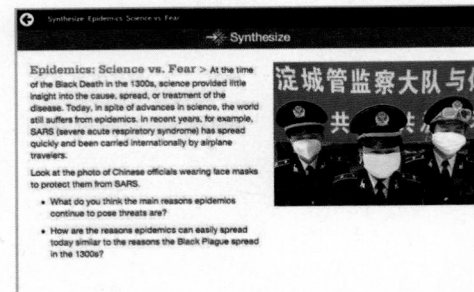

LESSON QUIZ
Lesson Quiz and Class Discussion Board

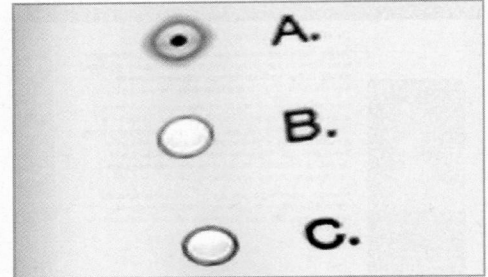

ELL Use the ELL activity described in the ELL chart.

Further Instruction

Project and discuss the Close Reading Notepad questions for this lesson.

The fourteenth century was a watershed for Europe. The century was marked by tremendous upheaval: The Hundred Years' War combined with the Black Death and the crisis in the Church led to a sense of pessimism and hopelessness that pervaded European society and culture. People lost confidence in their rulers and in the Church. In England, the people, in the form of Parliament, felt emboldened to restrict the war activities of the king through denying funds for war. Eventually, this would lead England to develop a strong parliamentary system with greater control over the monarchy.

Analyze While the Hundred Years' War led to greater parliamentary strength in England, it led to a stronger monarchy in France. The French people suffered a great deal during the constant fighting. Why do you think they continued to support a strengthened monarchy instead of pushing for a greater voice in government? *(After so many reverses, the French won back enormous amounts of territory. This inspired strong nationalistic feeling and, with it, a reinforced belief in the monarchy and established forms of government.)*

Have students use the Think-Pair-Share strategy to answer the questions in the A Challenge for Science: Epidemics activity. Ask them to take five minutes to write down some brief answers to the following questions and then share their answers with a partner.

What do you think are the main reasons epidemics continue to pose threats? How are the reasons epidemics can easily spread today similar to the reasons the plague spread in the 1300s?

Discuss What is the role of government in preventing epidemics? *(Answers may vary. Students should demonstrate an understanding that scientific cooperation between nations is essential to prevent dangerous epidemics and that governments often need to take the lead in scientific research to prevent diseases. Whenever possible, basic medical and sanitary standards should be in place, including access to clean water and food, basic vaccines, and education on preventing and treating communicable diseases.)*

Assign the online Lesson Quiz for this lesson if you haven't already done so. Students will be offered automatic remediation or enrichment based on their score.

Pose these questions to the class on the Discussion Board:

In *The Late Middle Ages: A Time of Upheaval*, you learned about three major crises facing the medieval world. These included the Black Death that wiped out almost 40 percent of Europe's population, the crisis in the Roman Catholic Church that led to the Great Schism, and the Hundred Years' War that brought bloodshed and hardship to the English and French forces and the people of France. The combination of these crises brought about the end of medieval Europe.

Recognize Cause and Effect In what specific ways did these crises bring about the end of medieval Europe? *(The Black Death changed the feudal and manorial system that was the basic structure of medieval life. The Hundred Years' War brought about changes in how war was conducted, with the emphasis being on larger, more temporary armies and weapons technology that reduced the importance of the medieval vassalage and personal fighting skills of a knight. The crisis in the Church led people to question the validity of the Church leadership and, eventually, to reform movements.)*

Topic Inquiry

Have students continue their investigations for the Topic Inquiry.

Russia and Eastern Europe

Supporting English Language Learners

Use with Digital Text 1, **The Geography of Russia.**

Listening
Read *The Geography of Russia* aloud. Then have students complete one activity according to their level of English proficiency.

Beginning Focus on the short section titled *Three Regions*. Before reading, describe the three regions of Russia to students. Use a visual aid to show the characteristics of each one. Then describe each zone with a few key words. Help students use linguistic aids, like bilingual dictionaries, to develop their understanding of the vocabulary used to describe the three areas.

Intermediate Focus on the short section titled *Three Regions*. Before reading, present three pictures to students; a separate picture should apply to each zone. Using simple sentences, describe the characteristics of each of the three regions of Russia. Allow students to use linguistic aids, like bilingual dictionaries, to help them develop their understanding of the three zones.

Advanced Focus on the short section titled *Three Regions*. Before reading, describe each of the three geographic zones to students. Then present students with three pictures, one for each zone. Have students identify which picture describes each zone. Then have students use simple sentences to describe the characteristics of each of the three regions of Russia. Allow students to use linguistic aids, like bilingual dictionaries, to help them develop their understanding of the three zones.

Advanced High Focus on the short section titled *Three Regions*. Before reading, describe each of the three geographic zones to students. Then present students with three pictures, one for each zone. Have students identify which picture describes each zone. Then have students describe the characteristics of each of the three regions of Russia to a partner. Encourage students to use each other as resources for understanding the meanings of any complex words or phrases.

Use with Digital Text 5, **The Geography of Eastern Europe.**

Listening
Read *The Geography of Eastern Europe* aloud. Then have students complete one activity according to their level of English proficiency.

Beginning Describe how geography has influenced the development of Eastern Europe. In order to improve student understanding, provide students with a list of key terms with bilingual definitions, including *migrating, plain, climate, hindered, fertile,* and *steppe.* Use visual aids, like maps, throughout the lecture to increase student engagement. Have students take notes on the topic during the discussion. Review students' notes after the lecture and correct any errors or areas of confusion before proceeding with the lesson.

Intermediate Describe how geography has influenced the development of Eastern Europe. In order to improve student understanding, provide students with a list of key terms with bilingual definitions, including *migrating, plain, climate, hindered, fertile,* and *steppe.* Use visual aids, like maps, throughout the lecture to increase student engagement. Have students take notes on the topic during the discussion. Have students review their notes after the lecture and make note of areas of concern. Revisit those areas with students and help them correct any errors or areas of confusion before proceeding with the lesson.

Advanced Give a lecture to describe how geography has influenced the development of Eastern Europe. In order to improve student understanding, provide students with a list of key terms, including *migrating, plain, climate, hindered, fertile,* and *steppe,* and bilingual dictionaries to use to find their definitions. Use visual aids, like maps, throughout the lecture to increase student engagement. Have students take notes during the discussion. Ask students to share their notes with a partner after the lecture to locate any errors or information gaps. Revisit those areas with students and help them correct any errors or areas of confusion before proceeding with the lesson.

Advanced High Give a lecture to describe how geography has influenced the development of Eastern Europe. Use visual aids, like maps, throughout the lecture to increase student engagement. Have students take notes during the discussion and make note of any confusing terms or concepts. After the lecture, focus on the confusing terms or concepts identified by students. Have students adjust their notes accordingly. Then ask students to share their notes with a partner to locate any errors or information gaps. Revisit those areas with students to correct any errors before proceeding with the lesson.

▣ Differentiate Instruction

Use the Differentiated Instruction notes throughout the lesson plan to support the varied skill sets, levels of readiness, and interests in the mixed-ability classroom.

Challenge These notes include suggestions for expanding the activity for advanced students.

On-Level These notes include suggestions for modifying the activity to address different interests or learning styles.

Extra Support These notes include ideas for providing more scaffolding or reading spuport.

Special Needs These notes provide ideas for adapting instruction to support the needs of various special needs students.

◼ NOTES

Topic 7 Lesson 8

Russia and Eastern Europe

Objectives

Objective 1: Describe how geography influenced the rise of Russia, and how Kiev grew to be the center of the first Russian state.

Objective 2: Explain how Mongol rule affected Russia.

Objective 3: Describe how Moscow took the lead in Russia and how its rulers developed authoritarian control.

Objective 4: Describe how geography influenced the development of Eastern Europe.

Objective 5: Understand how migration contributed to cultural diversity in Eastern Europe, and learn about three early Eastern European kingdoms.

LESSON 8 ORGANIZER		PACING: APPROX. 1 PERIOD, .5 BLOCKS			
				RESOURCES	
		OBJECTIVES	**PACING**	**Online**	**Print**
Connect					
DIGITAL START UP ACTIVITY **Clans and Factions**			5 min.	●	
Investigate					
DIGITAL TEXT 1 **The Geography of Russia**		Objective 1	10 min.	●	●
DIGITAL TEXT 2 **Early Russia**			10 min.	●	●
INTERACTIVE MAP **The Growth of Russia**			10 min.	●	
DIGITAL TEXT 3 **The Mongols Conquer Russia**		Objective 2	10 min.	●	●
DIGITAL TEXT 4 **Moscow Surpasses Kiev**		Objective 3	10 min.	●	●
DIGITAL TEXT 5 **The Geography of Eastern Europe**		Objective 4	10 min.	●	●
DIGITAL TEXT 6 **Migrations Increase Diversity**			10 min.	●	●
DIGITAL TEXT 7 **Early Kingdoms of Eastern Europe**		Objective 5	10 min.	●	●
INTERACTIVE MAP **Jewish Migrations and Expulsions 500–1650**			10 min.	●	
Synthesize					
SYNTHESIZE **The Impact of the Mongols**			5 min.	●	
Demonstrate					
LESSON QUIZ **Lesson Quiz and Class Discussion Board**			10 min.	●	

PEARSON
realize™
www.PearsonRealize.com

Go online to access additional resources including:
Primary Sources • Biographies • Supreme Court cases •
21st Century Skill Tutorials • Maps • Graphic Organizers.

CONNECT

DIGITAL START UP ACTIVITY
Clans and Factions

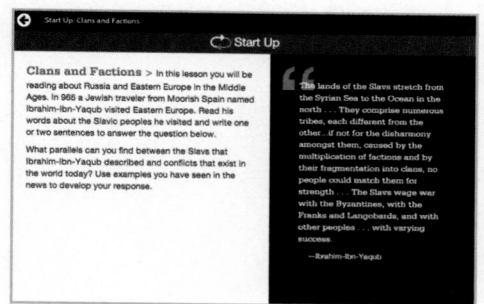

Project the Start Up Activity Ask students to answer the questions as they enter and get settled. Then have them share their ideas with another student, either in class or through a chat room or blog.

What parallels can you find between the Slavs that Ibrahim-Ibn-Yaqub described and the conflicts that exist in the world today? Use examples you have seen in the news to develop your response. *(Answers will vary. Students might refer to conflicts in the Middle East, such as the Arab Spring; conflicts in various nations regarding growing immigrant populations; or unrest in areas such as Africa, where different factions are fighting for control.)*

⇅ FLIP IT!

Assign the Flipped Video for this lesson.

STUDENT EDITION PRINT
PAGES: 243–250

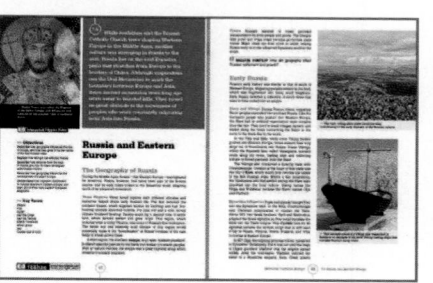

INVESTIGATE

DIGITAL TEXT 1
The Geography of Russia

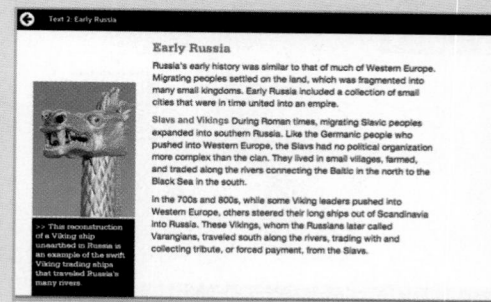

Objective 1: Describe how geography influenced the rise of Russia, and how Kiev grew to be the center of the first Russian state.

Quick Instruction
Introduce the activity by explaining that Russia as we know it today is far different from the Russia of the 14th century. Russia's growth was influenced by its geography, its early trading traditions, the Mongol invasion, and the influence of Byzantine culture.

Growth of Russia: Interactive Map Project the map on the whiteboard. Click on each period of time to show how Russia's boundary changed. Ask students what key events affected Russia's growth.

👥 ACTIVE CLASSROOM

Use the Walking Tour strategy. Post passages from the text on individual pages around the room. Form students into groups and ask the groups to tour the room, discuss each passage, and then summarize.

DIGITAL TEXT 2
Early Russia

D **Differentiate: Special Needs** "Steppe" is a key word in this text. Have pairs of students practice geographic terms by looking at a map of Russia. Ask pairs to locate each geographic feature mentioned in the text. After they have pointed out each feature, have them explain to their partner how each one influenced the rise of Russia.

ELL Use the ELL activity described in the ELL chart.

Further Instruction
Project and discuss the Close Reading Notepad questions and the concept web graphic organizer. Lead students in filling out the concept web. Use "reasons Russia developed differently from Western Europe" as the center concept.

The Byzantine empire established an early trading presence in Russia due to Russia's river geography and because, at the time, the Byzantine empire was more stable than Western Europe. This early relationship with the Byzantine world would have far-reaching effects on how Russia developed, including its eventual connections with Eastern Orthodox Christianity.

Topic (7) Lesson 8

Russia and Eastern Europe

  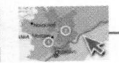

INTERACTIVE MAP

The Growth of Russia

DIGITAL TEXT 3

The Mongols Conquer Russia

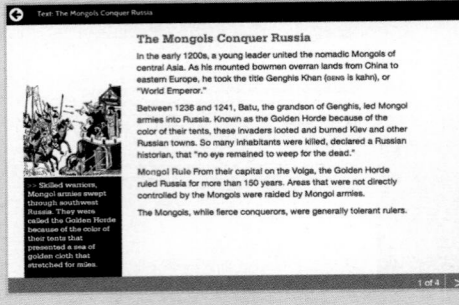

Draw Inferences How did the introduction of Cyrillic script influence Russian culture? *(As a written form of the Slavic language, Cyrillic provided a common link between people's everyday language and published laws and government documents. The translation of the Bible into Cyrillic made Christianity a more vivid presence in people's lives. Using a different script from that in Western Europe also helped to isolate Russia from the West.)*

Interpret Maps Which rivers link Russian territory with the Byzantine empire? *(Volga and Don Rivers, with the Dnieper giving access to the Black Sea and a sea route to Constantinople.)*

Objective 2: Explain how Mongol rule affected Russia.

Quick Instruction

Introduce the activity by explaining that the initial Mongol invasion swept through Russia like a firestorm. The extensive slaughter terrorized the inhabitants and gave the Mongol dynasty control of Russia for the next 150 years. However, once the system of tribute was established, the Mongols' general policies allowed the Russian nobility to grow in strength and eventually push out the Mongols and extend Russian territory.

Further Instruction

Project and discuss the Close Reading Notepad questions for this lesson.

Explain that once the Mongol forces were established in Russia, they were tolerant of diversity in religion and culture, as long as the Mongols profited from Russian growth through paid tributes. The Russians were left to develop their own authoritarian government and evolve in culture and religion. The Mongol army's presence ensured peace on trade routes, which encouraged Russia to establish even closer ties with Byzantium and other eastern markets.

Analyze Information How did the Russians benefit from the Mongol invasion? What did they forfeit? *(Gained stability, trade routes, freedom to develop their culture; they forfeited participation in scientific advances being made in Europe because of lack of contact through trade.)*

DIGITAL TEXT 4
Moscow Surpasses Kiev

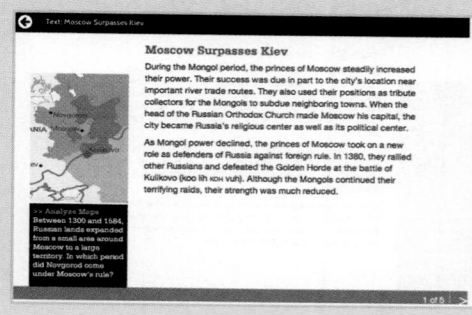

DIGITAL TEXT 5
The Geography of Eastern Europe

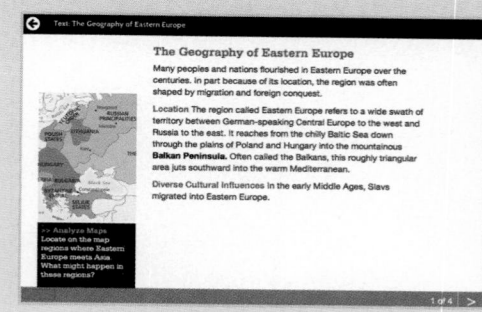

Objective 3: Describe how Moscow took the lead in Russia and how its rulers developed authoritarian control.

Quick Instruction
Project the image of Ivan the Terrible from the Text onto the whiteboard. Introduce the Text by explaining that although Ivan the Terrible is probably the more recognizable name, his grandfather Ivan III, or Ivan the Great, was a pivotal ruler in Russia's history. Between the two rulers, much of Russia was brought under the control of one ruler, which established Byzantine court rituals and an extreme absolute monarchy that defined Russia for centuries.

Further Instruction
Project and discuss the Close Reading Notepad question for this lesson.

Moscow's rise as the center of Russia was based on the strong leadership of Ivan the Great and Ivan the Terrible and the choice of Moscow to be the capital of the Russian Orthodox Church. With one city as the center of both religious and secular rule, Moscow was able to surge ahead of all other Russian cities. As power coalesced in Moscow, so did the Russian desire to rid itself of foreign rule. After a decisive victory against the Mongols, Russian rulers continued to consolidate their power and their form of government – absolute monarchy.

Draw Conclusions How were Ivan the Great and Ivan the Terrible able to wrest control from the Mongols and ensure the success of their regimes? *(They rallied Russians against foreign rule, limited the influences of competing factions, centralized royal power, and exercised total control.)*

Objective 4: Describe how geography influenced the development of Eastern Europe.

Quick Instruction
Project the map of the Balkans and explain that the geography of the area kept ethnic groups fairly isolated from each other for extended periods of time. The isolation was both caused by and reinforced by a wide diversity in local cultural influences. Some areas were more influenced by Europe, while other areas were influenced by the Byzantine world. The separately developing cultural identities contributed to a sense of clan or tribe that often impeded strong national feeling and unity.

ELL Use the ELL activity described in the ELL chart.

Russia and Eastern Europe

DIGITAL TEXT 6
Migrations Increase Diversity

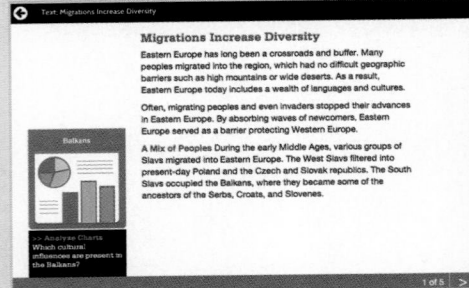

DIGITAL TEXT 7
Early Kingdoms of Eastern Europe

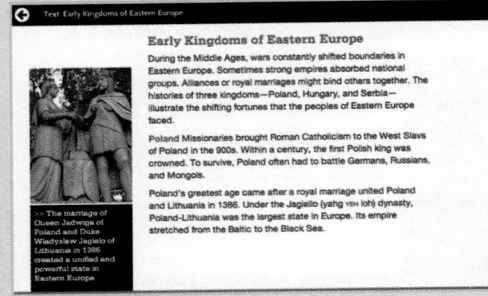

Further Instruction

Project and discuss the Close Reading Notepad question for this lesson.

The term *Balkanization* is used to describe the breaking up of an area into separate ethnic regions. The Balkan conflicts during the 1990s, following the breakup of Yugoslavia, pitted Eastern Orthodox Serbs, Bosnian Muslims, and Catholic Croats against each other. In 1998, Christian Serbs and Muslims of Albanian heritage clashed in Kosovo. These wars echo ethnic struggles that have existed for more than 600 years in the Balkans as different ethnic and religious groups have dispersed through the region. The conflicts had their beginnings during the time studied in this text, as the various areas were influenced by different cultural and religious factors.

Identify Supporting Details What influenced the development of different religious and cultural areas in the Balkans? *(The geography of the Balkans placed groups close to those areas that eventually influenced their religion and culture.)*

Objective 5: Understand how migration contributed to cultural diversity in Eastern Europe and learn about three early Eastern European kingdoms.

Quick Instruction

Project the "Jewish Migrations and Expulsions" map onto the whiteboard. Ask students to make generalizations about the information the map shows. *(Most of the places the Jews left are in Western Europe, while those they went to are in Eastern Europe; many of the routes they took are water routes, probably because it was easier and safer to travel by water.)*

🗣 ACTIVE CLASSROOM

Use the See-Think-Wonder strategy with the map. Pair students. Ask each pair: What do you see? What does that make you think? What are you wondering about now that you've seen this? Ask each pair to share insights with the class.

Further Instruction

Project and discuss the Close Reading Notepad question for this lesson.

A great variety of people migrated to Eastern Europe because of the lack of geographic barriers. These groups included Slavs from Belarus, several groups from Asia, Vikings, Germans, and Jews. Later migrations had political or religious incentives.

INTERACTIVE MAP

Jewish Migrations and Expulsions 500–1650

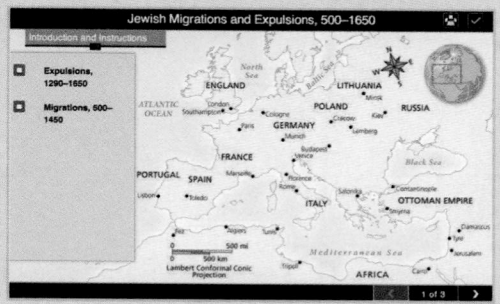

During the Middle Ages, Eastern Europe included many kingdoms and small states. Internal shifts in political power had an impact on a kingdom's ability to survive. While a monarch provided a central power able to act decisively, the movement toward assemblies of nobles holding power often resulted in fragmented government.

Draw Inferences How did the migration of many diverse peoples into Eastern Europe change the region? *(As different groups migrated into Eastern Europe, they brought their languages, cultures, and religions with them.)*

■ SYNTHESIZE

SYNTHESIZE

The Impact of the Mongols

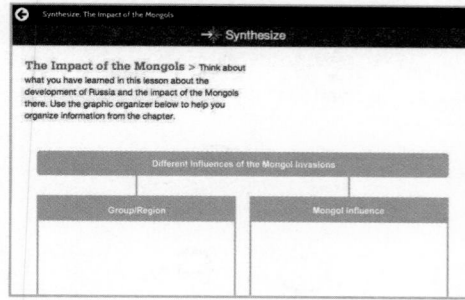

Ask students to share their responses to the Synthesize exercise.

Point out that the Mongol invasion and occupation of Russia and parts of Eastern Europe had far-reaching effects, such as the absolute monarchy model used by Russia and the de-stabilizing of Hungary when the invasion resulted in the death of about half of Hungary's population. Despite the devastation left in their wake, the Mongols also brought a controlled peace that allowed trade between Russia and Byzantium and a cultural exchange that continued into modern times.

■ DEMONSTRATE

LESSON QUIZ

Lesson Quiz and Class Discussion Board

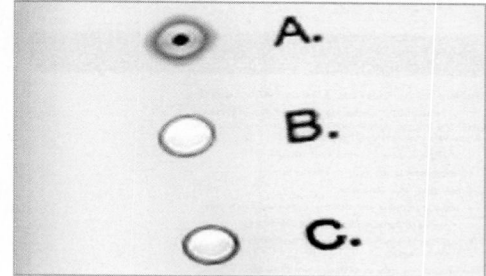

Assign the online Lesson Quiz for this lesson if you haven't already done so. Students will be offered automatic remediation or enrichment based on their score.

Pose these questions to the class on the Discussion Board:

Identify Key Steps in a Process How did the early Russian state develop? *(Trade routes that included Asian traders, Vikings, and Byzantine merchants plied the rivers throughout western Russia. Trading towns developed in the larger cities of Kiev and Moscow. After the Mongol invasion, Russian leaders paid tribute while they worked to push out the Mongols and extend Russia's borders.)*

Summarize How did the great diversity of migrating groups affect Eastern Europe? *(Each group brought its own culture, religion, and language along, with knowledge and skills.)*

Topic Inquiry
Have students continue their investigations for the Topic Inquiry.

Medieval Christian Europe (330–1450)

■ SYNTHESIZE

DIGITAL ESSENTIAL QUESTION ACTIVITY
Reflect on the Essential Question and Topic

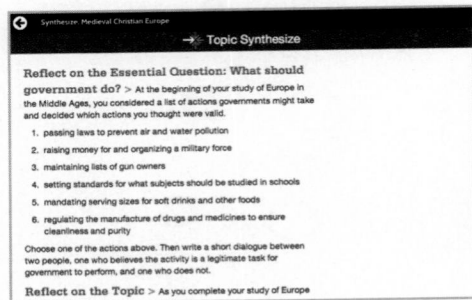

First ask students to reconsider the Essential Question: What should government do? Remind students of some reasons they considered at the start of the Topic:

- passing laws to prevent pollution
- raising money for and organizing an army
- setting standards for what subjects should be studied in schools
- regulating the manufacture of drugs

Then have students write their dialogues between two people, one who believes the activity is a legitimate task for government, and one who does not. Suggest they start by making two lists of reasons for supporting and opposing government's involvement in the particular activity. Share this example:

Reasons why government *should* set standards for what subjects should be studied in schools (*all students will have the same basic knowledge, it will be easier to evaluate schools*); Reasons why government *should not* set standards for what subjects should be studied in schools (*it will remove local control of schools, it gives government too much power*).

Have volunteers read their dialogues and discuss issues raised. Next ask students to describe communities they are a part of. Ask students which communities were relevant to people in the Middle Ages.

You may ask student pairs to share their conclusions with the class.

Topic Inquiry
Have students complete Step 3 of the Topic Inquiry.

■ DEMONSTRATE

DIGITAL TOPIC REVIEW AND ASSESSMENT
Medieval Christian Europe (330–1450)

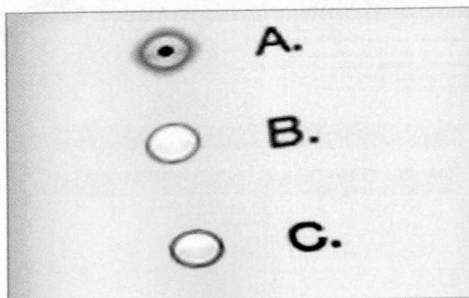

Students can prepare for the Topic Test by answering the questions in the Topic Review and Assessment online or the Assessment questions in the Print Student text. They can also prepare by reviewing their answers to the Interactive Reading Notepad questions or reviewing their notes in the Reading and Notetaking Study Guide.

DIGITAL TOPIC TEST
Medieval Christian Europe (330–1450)

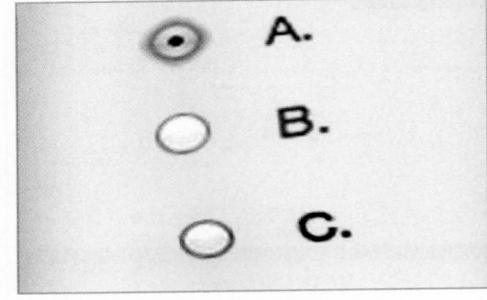

TOPIC TEST
Assign the Topic Test to assess students' understanding of topic content.

BENCHMARK TESTS
Assign these benchmark tests as you complete the relevant topics to monitor student progress toward mastering the course content and as preparation for the End-of-Course Test.

Benchmark Test 1: Topics 1–5
Benchmark Test 2: Topics 6–10
Benchmark Test 3: Topics 11–15
Benchmark Test 4: Topics 16–21

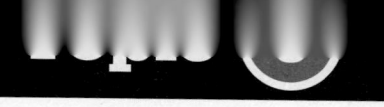
The Muslim World and Africa
(730 B.C.–A.D. 1500)

TOPIC 8 ORGANIZER	PACING: APPROX. 11 PERIODS, 5.5 BLOCKS
	PACING
Connect	1 period
MY STORY VIDEO **Ibn Battuta, Traveler**	10 min.
DIGITAL ESSENTIAL QUESTION ACTIVITY **How are religion and culture connected?**	10 min.
DIGITAL TIMELINE ACTIVITY **The Muslim World and Africa**	10 min.
TOPIC INQUIRY: CIVIC DISCUSSION **The Battle of Tours**	20 min.
Investigate	4–8 periods
TOPIC INQUIRY: CIVIC DISCUSSION **The Battle of Tours**	Ongoing
LESSON 1 The Origins of Islam	30–40 min.
LESSON 2 A Muslim Empire	30–40 min.
LESSON 3 Achievements of Muslim Civilization	30–40 min.
LESSON 4 The Ottoman and Safavid Empires	30–40 min.
LESSON 5 Early Civilizations of Africa	30–40 min.
LESSON 6 Kingdoms of West Africa	30–40 min.
LESSON 7 Trading States of East Africa	30–40 min.
LESSON 8 Diverse Peoples and Traditions in Africa	30–40 min.
Synthesize	1 period
DIGITAL ACTIVITY **Reflect on the Essential Question and Topic**	10 min.
TOPIC INQUIRY: CIVIC DISCUSSION **The Battle of Tours**	20 min.
Demonstrate	1–2 periods
DIGITAL TOPIC TEST **The Muslim World and Africa**	10 min.
TOPIC INQUIRY: CIVIC DISCUSSION **The Battle of Tours**	20 min.

 TOPIC INQUIRY: CIVIC DISCUSSION

The Battle of Tours

In this Topic Inquiry, students work in teams to examine different perspectives on this issue by analyzing several sources, arguing both sides of a Yes/No question, then developing and discussing their own point of view on the question: **Was the Battle of Tours the decisive event stopping the spread of Islam in Europe?**

STEP 1: CONNECT
Develop Questions and Plan the Investigation

Launch the Civic Discussion

Divide the class into groups of four students. Students can access the materials they'll need in the online course or you can distribute copies to each student. Read the main question and introduction with the students.

Have students complete Step 1 by reading the Discussion Launch and filling in Step 1 of the Information Organizer. The Discussion Launch provides YES and NO arguments on the main question. Students should extract and paraphrase the arguments from the reading in Step 1 of their Information Organizers.

Next, students share within their groups the arguments and evidence they found to support the YES and NO positions. The group needs to agree on the major YES and NO points and each student should note those points in their Information Organizer.

Resources
- Student Instructions
- Discussion Launch
- Information Organizer

STEP 2: INVESTIGATE
Apply Disciplinary Concepts and Tools

Examine Sources and Perspectives

Students will examine sources with the goal of extracting information and perspectives on the main question. They analyze each source and describe the author's perspective on the main question and key evidence the author provides to support that viewpoint in Information Organizer Step 2.

Ask students to keep in mind:

- **Author/Creator:** Who created the source? An individual? Group? Government agency?
- **Audience:** For whom was the source created?
- **Date/Place:** Is there any information that reveals where and when the source was created?
- **Purpose:** Why was the source created? Discuss with students the importance of this question in identifying bias.
- **Relevance:** How does the source support one argument or another?

Suggestion: Reading the source documents and filling in Step 2 of the Information Organizer could be assigned as homework.

Resources
- Student Instructions
- Source documents
- Information Organizer

⏻ PROFESSIONAL DEVELOPMENT

Civic Discussion

Be sure to view the Civic Discussion Professional Development resources in the online course.

STEP 3: SYNTHESIZE
Use Evidence to Formulate Conclusions

Formulate Compelling Arguments with Evidence
Now students will apply perspectives and evidence they extracted from the sources to think more deeply about the main question by first arguing one side of the issue, then the other. In this way students become more prepared to formulate an evidence-based conclusion on their own.

Within each student group, assign half of the students to take the position of YES on the main question and the others to take the position of NO. Students will work with their partners to identify the strongest arguments and evidence to support their assigned YES or NO position.

Present Yes/No Positions
Within each group, those assigned the YES position share arguments and evidence first. As the YES students speak, those assigned NO should listen carefully, take notes to fill in the rest of the Compelling Arguments Chart (Step 3 in Information Organizer) and ask clarifying questions.

When the YES side is finished, students assigned the NO position present while those assigned YES should listen, take notes, and ask clarifying questions. Examples of clarifying questions are:

- I think you just said [x]. Am I understanding you correctly?
- Can you tell me more about [x]?
- Can you repeat [x]? I am not sure I understand, yet.

Suggestion: You may want to set a 5 minute time limit for each side to present. Provide a two-minute warning so that students make their most compelling arguments within the time frame.

Switch Sides
The students will switch sides to argue the opposite point of view. To prepare to present the other position, partners who first argued YES will use the notes they took during the NO side's presentation, plus add any additional arguments and evidence from the reading and sources. The same for students who first argued the NO position.

STEP 4: DEMONSTRATE
Communicate Conclusions and Take Informed Action

Individual Points of View
Now the students will have the opportunity to discuss the main question from their own points of view. To help students prepare for this discussion, have them reflect on the YES/NO discussions they have participated in thus far and fill in Step 4 of their Information Organizers.

After all of the students have shared their points of view, each group should list points of agreement, filling the last portion of Step 4 on their Information Organizers.

Reflect on the Discussion
Ask students to reflect on the civic discussion thinking about:

- The value of having to argue both the YES and NO positions.
- If their individual views changed over the course of the discussion and why.
- What they learned from participating in the discussion.

Resources
- Student Instructions
- Information Organizer

INTRODUCTION

The Muslim World and Africa
(730 B.C.–A.D. 1500)

A new major world religion emerged in the Arabian Peninsula with the teachings of Muhammad. As Arabs united under Islam, a Muslim empire arose and expanded. Under the caliphates, and then later the Ottoman and Safavid empires, Muslim civilization developed a rich and diverse culture. Arab traders in the flourishing gold and salt trade routes in Africa helped spread Islam to the region. The kingdoms and trading states of Africa, influenced by the continent's wide range of climate, vegetation, and terrain, had a variety of unique cultures and societies. While there were some isolated but flourishing smaller societies, areas with abundant resources and access to trade routes grew into vast and wealthy empires.

■ CONNECT

MY STORY VIDEO
Ibn Battuta, Traveler

Watch a video about the travels of Ibn Battuta.

Check Understanding Why is Ibn Battuta's journey considered one of the greatest in history? *(In the 14th century, he visited the lands of every Muslim ruler at the time.)*

Hypothesize What impact might the news of Ibn Battuta's travels have had on people of the time? *(a desire to travel, a desire to learn more about other lands, eagerness to exchange ideas and goods with other peoples)*

⚑ FLIP IT!
Assign the My Story Video.

DIGITAL ESSENTIAL QUESTION ACTIVITY
How Are Religion and Culture Connected?

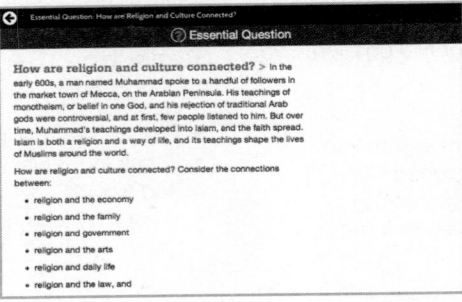

The relationship between religion and culture can vary depending on the society and can change over time. Ask students to think about the Essential Question for this Topic: How are religion and culture connected? If students have not already done so, ask them to list which of the connections has the most influence on society. Then go over the results as a class.

Identify Central Issues Why does religion often play a central role in the cultural development of a society? *(Answers may vary. Religion can affect many aspects of a society, ranging from the most personal, the beliefs of the individual, family roles, and daily life, to the broadest, such as law, economics, and government.)*

Cause and Effect How might religion be a unifying force? *(Answers may vary. Students might respond that if most members of a society practice the same religion, then they might share similar cultural values.)*

DIGITAL TIMELINE ACTIVITY
The Muslim World and Africa

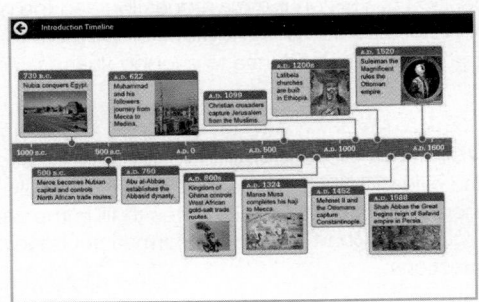

Display the timeline showing some of the major events in Muslim civilization and Africa. These are just some of the events that students will learn about while exploring this Topic. The timeline will provide a framework into which students can place the events they learn about. How many years are there between the establishment of the Abbasid dynasty and the reign of Shah Abbas in the Safavid empire? *(838; Abu al-Abbas establishes the Abbasid dynasty in 750; Shah Abbas begins reign in 1588.)*

D **Differentiate: Extra Support** How many years are there between the establishment of the Abbasid dynasty and the reign of Shah Abbas in the Safavid empire? *(838; Abu al-Abbas establishes the Abbasid dynasty in 750; Shah Abbas begins reign in 1588.)*

Check Understanding How many years after the hijra did Mansa Musa complete his haji to Mecca. *(702, Mohammad traveled to Medina in 622 and Mansa finished his haij in 1324.)*

The Origins of Islam

Supporting English Language Learners

Use with Digital Text 2, **Teachings of Islam.**

Listening

Read aloud, or have students read, *Teachings of Islam*. Then have students participate in the following activities, which focus on the subsection "The Five Pillars of Islam."

Beginning Slowly and clearly read each sentence in the subsection "The Five Pillars of Islam" aloud to students. Pause to explain any difficult vocabulary. Then have the students draw a simple picture for each of the five pillars to demonstrate their understanding of the content.

Intermediate Read the subsection "The Five Pillars of Islam" aloud to students. Pause as needed to explain any difficult vocabulary. Ask students to explain each of the five pillars using short phrases. Support their verbal descriptions as necessary. Finally, have students draw a picture and write a descriptive caption for each of the five pillars.

Advanced Have students work with a partner to read "The Five Pillars of Islam" aloud. Circulate among student pairs to support their understanding and define any difficult vocabulary. Then have pairs take turns describing each of the five pillars. Pairs should use these descriptions to create a chart that describes the characteristics and requirements of each of the five pillars. Finally, have pairs share their charts with the whole class to ensure their understanding of the content.

Advanced High Have students listen as you read "The Five Pillars of Islam" aloud. Students can take notes on the reading if they choose to. After listening to the text, students should create a chart that describes the characteristics and requirements of each pillar. Have students share their work with a partner. Partners should work together to check their work for accuracy and correct understanding of the content.

Use with Digital Text 1, **Muhammad and Early Islam.**

Speaking

Before beginning this activity with students, read the text *Muhammad and Early Islam* aloud to the class. Then have students complete one of the following activities.

Beginning Choose two or three sentences in the introductory paragraph of the text. Write and display these sentences for students. Then slowly read each sentence aloud. As you read, underline each consonant cluster you encounter. Then explain the definition of a consonant cluster. Review each of the underlined words by saying them aloud and having students repeat them. Continue this process for each consonant cluster, focusing on correct pronunciation and fluency.

Intermediate Review consonant clusters with students and provide them with a few examples from the first few sentences of the text. Then, as you read the next two or three sentences aloud to students, ask them to raise their hands when they hear you say a word containing a consonant cluster. Make and display a list of all the words students indicate. Review the words and have students identify the consonant cluster in each one. Help students sound out the words on the list to ensure correct pronunciation of consonant clusters.

Advanced Review consonant clusters with students and have them brainstorm several examples of words that contain consonant clusters. Then have small groups of students work together to read and review one paragraph from *Muhammad and Early Islam*. Students should look for words with consonant clusters in the text and create a list of these words. Finally, ask students to circle the consonant clusters in each of their chosen words. Groups should share their lists with the class to ensure accuracy and understanding.

Advanced High Have pairs of students develop a basic definition for consonant clusters. Then have them take turns reading parts of a paragraph from *Muhammad and Early Islam* to each other. As one student reads, the other student should listen and write down words that contain consonant clusters. Then the partners switch tasks. Finally, pairs should revisit the text they read to compare their responses against the words in the paragraph. Circulate among students and support them as needed.

▣ Differentiate Instruction

Use the Differentiated Instruction notes throughout the lesson plan to support the varied skill sets, levels of readiness, and interests in the mixed-ability classroom.

Challenge These notes include suggestions for expanding the activity for advanced students.

On-Level These notes include suggestions for modifying the activity to address different interests or learning styles.

Extra Support These notes include ideas for providing more scaffolding or reading spuport.

Special Needs These notes provide ideas for adapting instruction to support the needs of various special needs students.

■ NOTES

Topic 8 Lesson 1

The Origins of Islam

Objectives

Objective 1: Understand how Muhammad spread Islam.

Objective 2: Describe the central ideas of Islam.

Objective 3: Explain how Islam helped shape the way of life of its believers.

LESSON 1 ORGANIZER		PACING: APPROX. 1 PERIOD, .5 BLOCKS			
				RESOURCES	
		OBJECTIVES	PACING	Online	Print
Connect					
	DIGITAL START UP ACTIVITY **Mecca**		5 min.	●	
Investigate					
	DIGITAL TEXT 1 **Muhammad and Early Islam**	Objective 1	10 min.	●	●
	INTERACTIVE GALLERY **The Origins of Islam**		10 min.	●	
	DIGITAL TEXT 2 **Teachings of Islam**	Objective 2	10 min.	●	●
	INTERACTIVE GALLERY **The Five Pillars of Wisdom**		10 min.	●	
	DIGITAL TEXT 3 **Islam as a Way of Life**	Objective 3	10 min.	●	●
Synthesize					
	DIGITAL ACTIVITY **Foundations of Islam**		5 min.	●	
Demonstrate					
	DIGITAL QUIZ **Lesson Quiz and Class Discussion Board**		10 min.	●	

PEARSON realize™
www.PearsonRealize.com

Go online to access additional resources including:
Primary Sources • Biographies • Supreme Court cases •
21st Century Skill Tutorials • Maps • Graphic Organizers.

CONNECT

DIGITAL START UP ACTIVITY
Mecca

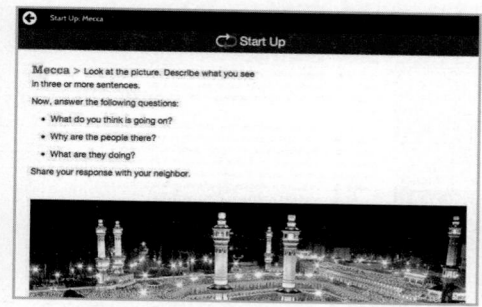

Project the Start Up Activity Ask students to look at the image of the crowds at the Kaaba in Mecca and answer the questions as they enter and get settled. Then have them share their ideas with another student.

Discuss Have students look again at the image of the pilgrims at Mecca. Ask them what the image might reveal about the role of pilgrimage and the significance of Mecca in Islam. *(Sample Response: Given the large crowds, pilgrimage likely plays an important part in Islam, and Mecca is probably an important religious site for Muslims.)*

Tell students that in this lesson they will study the origins, beliefs, and spread of Islam.

Aa **Vocabulary Development:** Use the Interactive Reading Notepad to preview the Key Terms and Academic Vocabulary in this lesson with students.

↑↓ FLIP IT!
Assign the Flipped Video for this lesson.

■ STUDENT EDITION PRINT
PAGES: 256–260

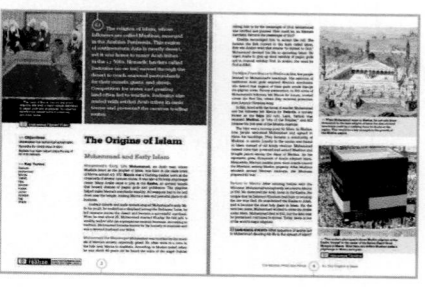

INVESTIGATE

DIGITAL TEXT 1
Muhammad and Early Islam

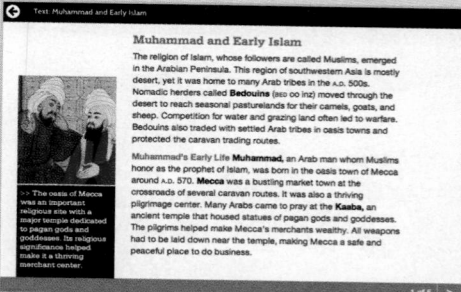

INTERACTIVE GALLERY
The Origins of Islam

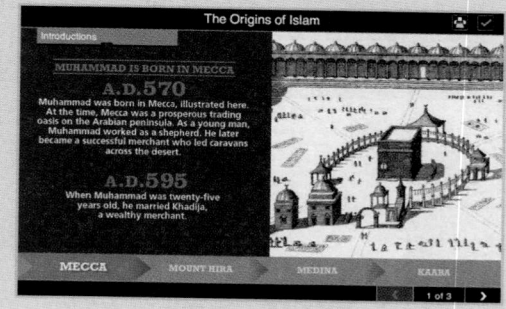

Objective 1: Understand how Muhammad spread Islam.

Quick Instruction

Interactive Gallery: The Origins of Islam
Project the Hijra gallery on the whiteboard and click through the hot spots that describe the origins and spread of Islam on the Arabian peninsula. As you begin, note that Mecca was an important pilgrimage site, home to the Kaaba, an ancient pagan temple, and was a thriving merchant town. Tell students that Muhammad, a successful merchant troubled by the moral ills of Mecca, went to meditate in a cave on Mount Hira. There, according to Islamic belief, he was called to be the messenger of God. In Mecca, people rejected Muhammad's call to worship Allah—the Arabic word for *God*—instead of their pagan gods. Fearing for his life, Muhammad travelled to Medina, a journey called the Hijra. In Medina, Muhammad gathered many followers to Islam and helped unite Arabs into a larger Muslim community. He triumphantly returned to Mecca and rededicated the Kaaba to Allah, making it the most holy site in Islam. Over time, Islam spread throughout the region, becoming one of the world's largest religions.

Ask students to reflect on the Connect and Hijra activities, and then look at their Connect answer and reconsider why a pilgrimage to Mecca might be an important part of Islam. *(Sample Response: According to Islam, Mecca was the site of Muhammad's calling as a messenger and where he returned in triumph after his journey to Medina and back, and a pilgrimage by other Muslims might honor the Hijra, which was a turning point in Islam.)*

■■ ACTIVE CLASSROOM

Have students complete a See-Think-Wonder activity as they look at the images of the Hijra. With a partner, students should think about these questions: What do you see? What does it make you think about? What are you wondering about now that you have seen this?

D Differentiate: Challenge/Gifted Ask students to do extra research on the Hijra and present their findings to the class. Suggest they also think about the geography of the region and the role it played in Muhammad's life, as well as the economics and culture of the area. Challenge them to present their findings in a multimedia format.

ELL Use the ELL activity described in the ELL chart.

Further Instruction

Editable Presentation Use the Editable Presentation to present the main ideas for this Core Reading.

Muhammad and Early Islam: Core Reading and Interactive Reading Notepad Go through the Interactive Reading Notepad questions and discuss the answers with the class.

Review with students Muhammad's actions in Medina, particularly the initial acceptance of his teachings, the unification of the Arab community there, the thousands who came to adopt Islam, and the role it played in conquering Mecca.

The Origins of Islam

DIGITAL TEXT 2

Teachings of Islam

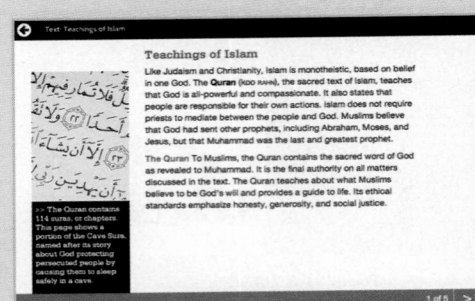

INTERACTIVE GALLERY

The Five Pillars of Wisdom

DIGITAL TEXT 3

Islam as a Way of Life

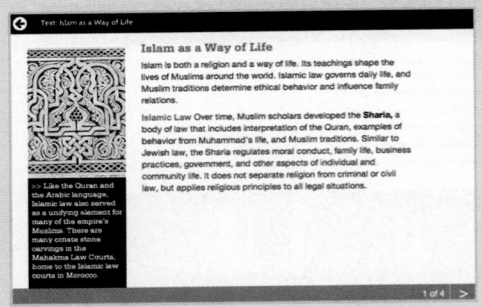

Objective 2: Describe the central ideas of Islam.

Quick Instruction

Be sure students understand the central ideas of Islam. Remind them that Islam is a monotheistic religion, that the Quran is the sacred text that preaches that God is all powerful and compassionate, and that Muslims perform five duties, called the Five Pillars of Wisdom.

Interactive Gallery: The Five Pillars of Wisdom Project the Five Pillars of Wisdom activity on the whiteboard and click through the hot spots that describe the five duties central to Islam: the declaration of faith, prayer five times daily, alms for the poor, fasting during Ramadan, and the Hajj.

ACTIVE CLASSROOM

Ask the following question using the Sticky Note strategy: Viewed together, what do these images tell you about an important aspect of Islam? *(Sample Response: Many of these images show group activities, which demonstrate the strong community ties in Muslim traditions.)*

ELL Use the ELL activity described in the ELL chart.

Further Instruction

Editable Presentation Use the Editable Presentation to present the main ideas for this Core Reading.

Central Ideas of Islam: Core Reading and Interactive Reading Notepad Go through the Interactive Reading Notepad questions and discuss the answers with the class.

Tell students that for Muslims the Quran is the sacred word of God as revealed to Muhammad. It is the final authority, teaches God's will, and sets ethical standards.

Draw Conclusions How might the importance of the Quran inspire Muslims to learn Arabic, and how might that affect the Muslim community? *(Sample Response: Because it is considered the sacred word of God, many Muslims learn Arabic, which provides a unifying language for Muslims.)*

Objective 3: Explain how Islam helped shape the way of life of its believers.

Quick Instruction

Tell students that Islam is both a religion and a way of life, having both a political and social impact. Islam, through its law and codes of ethics, shapes daily and family life for Muslims throughout the world. Go over how the Sharia is a body of law that interprets the Quran and provides guidance for Muslims in conducting all aspects of their life, from community to business to government to family life.

Summarize How do the Quran and the Sharia unify Muslims? *(Sample Response: The Quran unifies Muslim beliefs while the Sharia provides a unifying legal framework for Muslims throughout the world.)*

SYNTHESIZE

DEMONSTRATE

DIGITAL ACTIVITY
Foundations of Islam

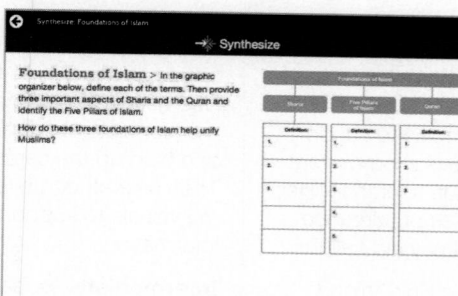

DIGITAL QUIZ
Lesson Quiz and Class Discussion Board

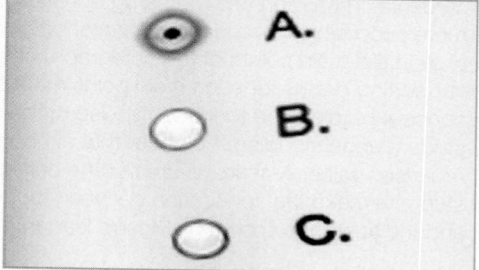

Further Instruction

Editable Presentation Use the Editable Presentation to present the main ideas for this Core Reading.

Islam as a Way of Life: Core Reading and Interactive Reading Notepad Go through the Interactive Reading Notepad questions and discuss the answers with the class.

Review the role of women in Islam with students. Note that while women had certain rights, such as the right to inherit or to reject a marriage offer, women and men had different rights and roles in Muslim society. Then read students the following quote from the Quran, "Whoever does right, whether male or female, and is a believer, all such will enter the Garden."

Cite Evidence What does this quote suggest about the spiritual role of women in the Islamic faith? *(Sample Response: It suggests that men and women are spiritually equal.)*

Project the Synthesize Activity on the whiteboard. Have students work through it with a partner and compare their answers. Then go over the graphic organizer as a class and discuss these three important aspects of the Islamic faith—the Quran, the Sharia, and the Five Pillars of Wisdom— and the role they play in unifying Muslims.

Assign the online Lesson Quiz for this lesson if you haven't already done so. Students will be offered automatic enrichment or remediation based on their score. Pose these questions to the class on the Discussion Board:

Make Predictions How might Islam spread beyond the Arabian peninsula? *(Sample Response: With its rules, legal traditions, and common language, it might provide a unifying element and appeal to people as it is introduced through trade and conquest to other regions.)*

Topic Inquiry
Have students continue their investigations for the Topic Inquiry.

A Muslim Empire

Supporting English Language Learners

Use with Digital Text 3, **Umayyad Caliphs Create an Arab Empire.**

Listening

Read aloud, or have students read, *Umayyad Caliphs Create an Arab Empire*. Then have students participate in the following activities. Discuss the concept of tolerance with students.

Beginning Reread "Conquered People Under Islamic Rule" aloud to students. Then rephrase the paragraph in basic language to make it more accessible for students. Using short phrases, write, display, and explain the main points of the paragraph for students to see. Point out the supporting details for each main point in the paragraph. Then explain the concept of tolerance to students. Use modern-day examples to support student understanding. Point out that although tolerance is an important American value, Americans are not the only group to value tolerance. Help students make the connection between modern examples of tolerance and the tolerance shown by Muslim leaders under the Umayyad caliphs.

Intermediate Reread "Conquered People Under Islamic Rule" aloud to students. Demonstrate for students how to locate a main point and a detail to support it in the subsection. Then have small groups of students identify the remaining main points and supporting details in the subsection. Circulate among students to provide support as needed. Finally, review the concept of tolerance with students. Facilitate a discussion to help students make connections between modern examples of tolerance and the ways that Muslim leaders showed tolerance to the people they ruled.

Advanced Have small groups of students read "Conquered People Under Islamic Rule" aloud and identify the main points and supporting details of this subsection. Have one representative from each group share one main point and detail from their lists with the class. Then ask small groups to discuss an example of modern-day tolerance. Finally, facilitate a class discussion in which students make connections between their examples of tolerance and the ways in which Umayyad caliphs demonstrated tolerance towards the groups they ruled.

Advanced High Have students independently reread "Conquered People Under Islamic Rule" and identify the main points and supporting details in this subsection. Have students turn to a partner to describe the main points and supporting details in their own words. Then ask partners to discuss how the way Muslim leaders demonstrated tolerance toward the groups they ruled during the Umayyad reign is similar or different to how tolerance is demonstrated in modern times. Finally, ask student pairs to share their ideas in a whole-class discussion.

Use with Digital Text 1, **Islam Faces Challenges.**

Speaking

Before beginning this activity, explain and give examples of high-frequency words to students. Then read the text *Islam Faces Challenges* aloud to the class. Have students complete one of the following activities according to their level of English proficiency.

Beginning Tell a simple version of the events that occurred following Muhammad's death through the Sunni and Shi'ite division. Make sure to use as many high-frequency words in your description as possible. Use visuals to support student understanding, such as large cards with names, pictures, and illustrations of leaders and groups. Tell the story and hold up the cards as you talk about each relevant person or group. Then help students retell the story in their own words. Have them use the visuals to support their understanding and ability to convey the information.

Intermediate Reread *Islam Faces Challenges* aloud to students, pausing frequently to explain the events described in the text. Use visuals for each of the leaders and groups to support student understanding. Then, as a group, have students organize the visuals in the correct order in which they occur in the story. Finally, have students utilize the visuals to retell the events as they are described in the text.

Advanced Reread *Islam Faces Challenges* aloud to students. Then have students work together in small groups to practice retelling the events and describe the challenges that Muslims experienced following Muhammad's death.

Advanced High Have students reread *Islam Faces Challenges* independently. Then have them work with a partner to retell the events and describe the challenges that Muslims faced following Muhammad's death.

⧉ Differentiate Instruction

Use the Differentiated Instruction notes throughout the lesson plan to support the varied skill sets, levels of readiness, and interests in the mixed-ability classroom.

Challenge These notes include suggestions for expanding the activity for advanced students.

On-Level These notes include suggestions for modifying the activity to address different interests or learning styles.

Extra Support These notes include ideas for providing more scaffolding or reading spuport.

Special Needs These notes provide ideas for adapting instruction to support the needs of various special needs students.

■ NOTES

PEARSON
realize.
www.PearsonRealize.com

Go online to access additional resources including:
Primary Sources • Biographies • Supreme Court cases •
21st Century Skill Tutorials • Maps • Graphic Organizers.

Objectives

Objective 1: Describe the spread of Islam.

Objective 2: Identify the divisions that emerged within Islam.

Objective 3: Describe the rise of Umayyad and Abbasid dynasties.

Objective 4: Explain why the Abbasid empire declined.

LESSON 2 ORGANIZER		PACING: APPROX. 1 PERIOD, .5 BLOCKS			
		OBJECTIVES	PACING	RESOURCES	
				Online	Print
Connect					
DIGITAL START UP ACTIVITY **Nomadic Raids**			5 min.	●	
Investigate					
DIGITAL TEXT 1 **Islam Faces Challenges**		Objective 1	10 min.	●	●
DIGITAL 3-D **The Dome of the Rock**			10 min.	●	
DIGITAL TEXT 2 **Divisions Split Islam**		Objective 2	10 min.	●	●
DIGITAL TEXT 3 **Umayyad Caliphs Create an Arab Empire**			10 min.	●	●
INTERACTIVE MAP **Spread of Islam**			10 min.	●	
DIGITAL TEXT 4 **New Rule Under the Abbasid Dynasty**		Objectives 1, 3	10 min.	●	●
INTERACTIVE TIMELINE **Rise and Decline of an Arab Empire**			10 min.	●	
DIGITAL TEXT 5 **Decline of the Arab Empire**		Objective 4	10 min.	●	●
Synthesize					
DIGITAL ACTIVITY **The Umayyad and Abbasid Caliphates**			5 min.	●	
Demonstrate					
DIGITAL QUIZ **Lesson Quiz and Class Discussion Board**			10 min.	●	

A Muslim Empire

■ CONNECT

DIGITAL START UP ACTIVITY
Nomadic Raids

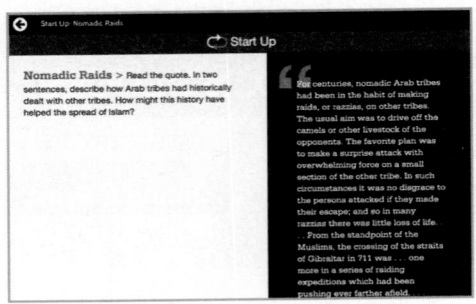

Project the Start Up Activity Ask students to write their sentences about the quote as they enter and get settled. Have them then share their sentences with another student, either in class or through a chat or blog space.

Discuss Have students share their sentences about how Arab tribes dealt with other tribes. How did new alliances affect the spread of Islam? *(Answers may vary. Most students will say something about surprise raids and subduing the other tribes so they eventually became allies; over time, many tribes decided to convert to Islam.)*

Tell students that in this lesson they will learn about how the Arab empire grew and about the divisions within Islam.

Aa Vocabulary Development: Use the Interactive Reading Notepad to preview the Key Terms and Academic Vocabulary in this Lesson with students.

⇅ FLIP IT!

Assign the Flipped Video for this lesson.

■ STUDENT EDITION PRINT PAGES: 261–268

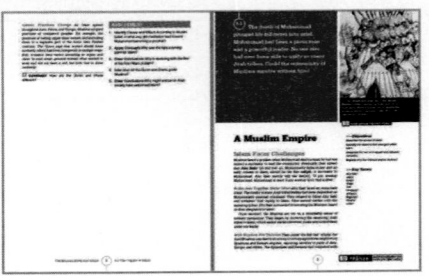

■ INVESTIGATE

DIGITAL TEXT 1
Islam Faces Challenges

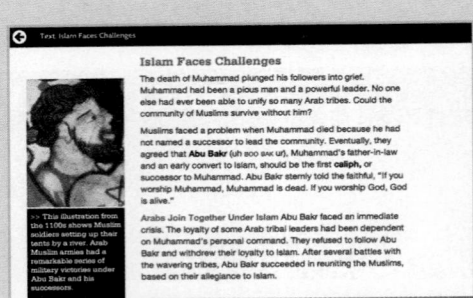

DIGITAL 3-D
The Dome of the Rock

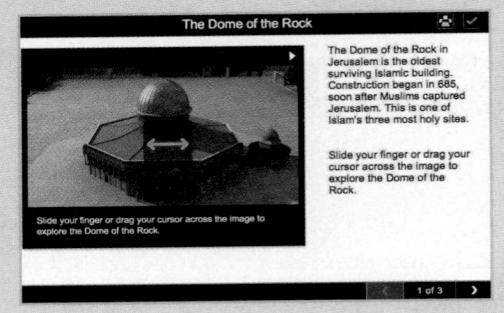

Objective 1: Describe the spread of Islam.

Quick Instruction

After Muhammad died, his successor needed to unite Arab tribes who had been dependent on Muhammad's personal command. They did this through military campaigns and converting tribes to Islam. Abu Bakr, Muhammad's father-in-law, was Islam's first caliph after Muhammad died.

Dome of the Rock Project the 3D model of the Dome of the Rock. As students study the model, have them identify different components of the building. Tell students that the Dome of the Rock was built around 691 after the Muslims captured Jerusalem to mark the site of Muhammad's ascent into heaven. Be sure they understand the importance of the building to both Muslims and Jews.

👥 ACTIVE CLASSROOM

Use the See-Think-Wonder strategy with students as they view images of the Dome of the Rock. Ask them: What do you see? What does it make you think? What are you wondering about now that you've seen this? *(Possible answer: "I see a very ornate building, colorful and large. It makes me think that it would have taken a lot of people a lot of time to build it. I wonder how long it took to build, where the materials came from and how was it accomplished.")*

D Differentiate: On-Level Have students research the history of the Dome of the Rock and develop a written report or digital presentation with the information they find. They should include topics such as, how it was built and how long it took.

ELL Use the ELL activity described in the ELL chart.

Further Instruction

Editable Presentation Use the Editable Presentation to present the main ideas for this Core Reading.

Islam Faces Challenges: Core Reading and Interactive Reading Notepad Go through the questions and discuss the answers with the class.

Ask students to find the word *caliph* in the text. Ask them to predict what criteria Muslims might have used to select a caliph.

Draw Conclusions Why was it important that Muslims accepted Abu Bakr as Muhammad's successor? *(Possible answer: It was important to keep Muslims unified and to ensure that Muhammad was seen as a messenger of God and a leader rather than be worshipped himself.)*

Determine Central Ideas What was the purpose of the early raids on Arab tribes? *(Possible Response: The purpose of the raids was to take livestock from other tribes and to push into new lands.)*

Remind students that when the Arabs united they were able to win victories against the Byzantine and Persian empires, which had been weakened from fighting each other.

DIGITAL TEXT 2
Divisions Split Islam

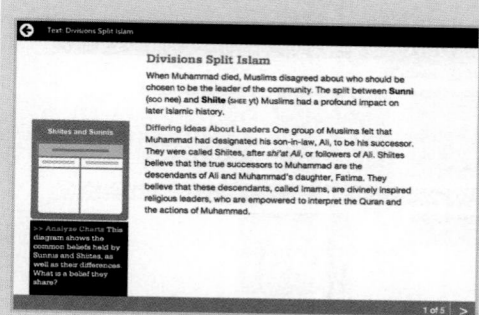

Divisions Split Islam

When Muhammad died, Muslims disagreed about who should be chosen to be the leader of the community. The split between **Sunni** (SOO nee) and **Shiite** (SHEE yt) Muslims had a profound impact on later Islamic history.

Differing Ideas About Leaders One group of Muslims felt that Muhammad had designated his son-in-law, Ali, to be his successor. They were called Shiites, after ah'at Ali, or followers of Ali. Shiites believe that the true successors to Muhammad are the descendants of Ali and Muhammad's daughter, Fatima. They believe that these descendants, called imams, are divinely inspired religious leaders, who are empowered to interpret the Quran and the actions of Muhammad.

DIGITAL TEXT 3
Umayyad Caliphs Create an Arab Empire

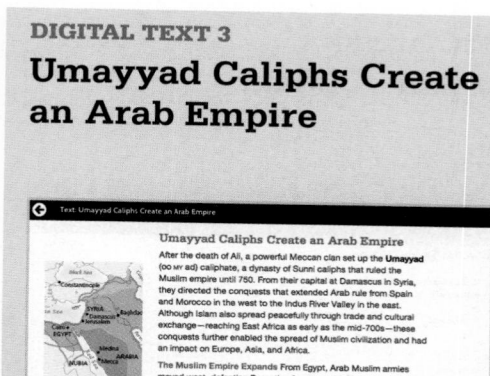

Umayyad Caliphs Create an Arab Empire

After the death of Ali, a powerful Meccan clan set up the **Umayyad** (oo MY ad) caliphate, a dynasty of Sunni caliphs that ruled the Muslim empire until 750. From their capital at Damascus in Syria, they directed the conquests that extended Arab rule from Spain and Morocco in the west to the Indus River Valley in the east. Although Islam also spread peacefully through trade and cultural exchange—reaching East Africa as early as the mid-700s—these conquests further enabled the spread of Muslim civilization and had an impact on Europe, Asia, and Africa.

The Muslim Empire Expands From Egypt, Arab Muslim armies moved west, defeating Byzantine forces across North Africa.

Objective 2: Identify the divisions that emerged within Islam.

Quick Instruction

Tell students that divisions emerged within Islam, forming the Sunni and Shiite branches. The Sunnis wanted a caliph who was a political leader. The Shiites wanted a caliph who was a descendent of Muhammad's daughter Fatima and son-in-law Ali, and a religious leader. Later on, the two groups developed different practices and laws. One group, the Sunnis, compromised around a leader who would be a political leader of the religious community and not a prophet. Project the Venn Diagram on the whiteboard and go over the points on which Sunni and Shiite Muslims agree and differ.

Further Instruction

Project the **Interactive Reading Notepad** on the whiteboard and go through the questions and discuss the answers with the class.

Identify Main Ideas Describe the Sufis. To which branch of Islam do they belong? How do they differ from other Muslims? *(Sample Response: Sufis are Muslim mystics that can belong to either the Sunni or Shiite branch of Islam. Sufis differ in some beliefs and practices. They helped spread Islam by traveling, preaching, and being good examples to others. They blended local traditions and beliefs into Muslim culture.)*

Predict Consequences Ask students to predict long-term issues that might arise from the division within Islam. *(Possible answer: Continued conflict could result in discrimination and regional conflicts.)*

Objectives 1: Describe the spread of Islam; 3: Describe the rise of Umayyad and Abbasid dynasties.

Quick Instruction

Interactive Map: Spread of Islam Project the map and click through the layers. Tell students that in less than 150 years, Muslim rule spread from Arabia across southwest Asia and North Africa and into Europe. Be sure students can point out Damascus, Baghdad, Persia, Cairo, Constantinople, Cordoba, and Tours on the map.

Make Predictions Muslim armies conquered Spain and remained in control there until 1492. Frankish forces defeated Muslims at the battle of Tours in France and Muslim forces advanced no further into Europe. If Muslim forces had been successful in France, where might they have advanced next? What might the advancement of Muslims further into Europe have meant for the area? *(Sample Response: The Muslim armies may have moved into more areas around the Mediterranean and Black seas, thus giving them control of all areas surrounding the Mediterranean.)*

Identify Central Ideas How might the spread of the Muslim empire have contributed to an increase in trade? *(Possible answer: Muslim control of the land around the Mediterranean allowed merchants to travel safely through the region. Many Muslims learned Arabic, making communication easier.)*

A Muslim Empire

INTERACTIVE MAP
Spread of Islam

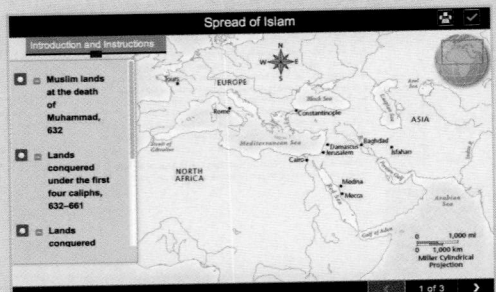

DIGITAL TEXT 4
New Rule Under the Abbasid Dynasty

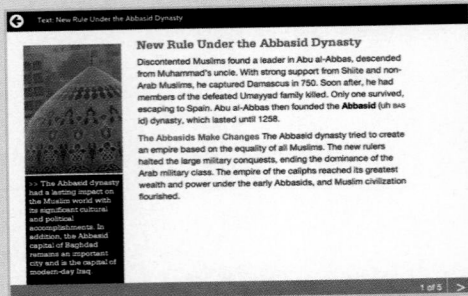

INTERACTIVE TIMELINE
Rise and Decline of an Arab Empire

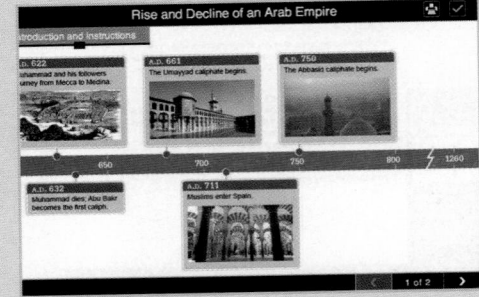

📷 ACTIVE CLASSROOM

Use the See-Think-Wonder strategy with students as they examine the Interactive Map: Spread of Islam. Ask them: What do you see? What does it make you think? What are you wondering about now that you've seen this?

ELL Use the ELL activity described in the ELL chart.

Further Instruction

Editable Presentation Use the Editable Presentation to present the main ideas for this Core Reading.

Project the **Interactive Reading Notepad** on the whiteboard and go through the questions and discuss the answers with the class.

Interactive Timeline: Rise and Decline of an Arab Empire Step through the timeline of Islamic History 622–1258 with students. Point out the changes from Sunni to Shiite rule. Tell students that after the death of Ali, a powerful clan set up the Umayyad caliphate, a dynasty of Sunnis that ruled the Muslim empire until 750. This caliphate extended the Muslim world into Spain and farther into Central Asia and

North Africa, where they built many mosques. Many of the peoples of North Africa quickly converted to Islam. The Umayyads were successful because they unified the tribes and created an empire with an orderly system of administration. In their territory in Europe, North Africa, and Asia, they treated conquered peoples well, placing certain restrictions and a special tax on non-Muslims but allowing Christians, Jews, and Zoroastrians to practice their own faiths and follow their own religious customs within those restrictions. They prevented the looting and destruction of conquered lands. The Umayyads faced problems in governing their large territories, including criticism of their rule and the lavish lifestyles of the caliphs. Abu al-Abbas, a descendent from Muhammad's uncle, won strong support from Shiite and non-Arab Muslims who were discontented with Uamyyad rule. He captured Damascus in 750 and founded the Abbasid dynasty that lasted until 1258. The Abbasid dynasty developed an empire based on the equality of all Muslims. The capital was moved from Damascus to Baghdad, where the court became a sophisticated center of trade and learning.

📷 ACTIVE CLASSROOM

Quick Write–Have students write what they know about the timeline of Islamic History for 30 seconds. Challenge them to keep the length to 140 characters.

Create a chart on the whiteboard with two columns, labeled *Advantages of Umayyed Rule* and *Disadvantages of Umayyed Rule*. Create 4 rows for Sunni Arabs, Shiite Arabs, non-Arab Muslims, and non-Muslims. Have students volunteer information to fill in the chart. Be sure they include reasons for the decline of the caliphate.

Have students look at the map and discuss why al-Mansur chose Baghdad as his capital. *(Sample Response: It was more centrally located, on a river.)* Ask how his choice symbolized one of the key differences between the Abbasids and the Umayyads. *(Sample Response: symbolized the move away from Arab domination and allowed Persian traditions to influence the caliphate)*

DIGITAL TEXT 5

Decline of the Arab Empire

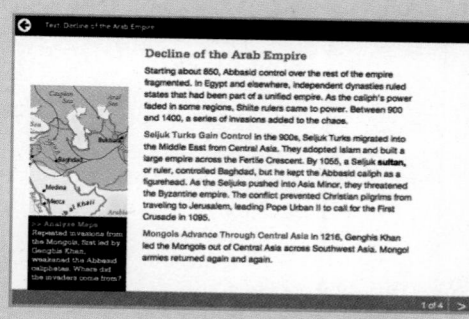

Decline of the Arab Empire

Starting about 850, Abbasid control over the rest of the empire fragmented. In Egypt and elsewhere, independent dynasties ruled states that had been part of a unified empire. As the caliph's power faded in some regions, Shiite rulers came to power. Between 900 and 1400, a series of invasions added to the chaos.

Seljuk Turks Gain Control In the 900s, Seljuk Turks migrated into the Middle East from Central Asia. They adopted Islam and built a large empire across the Fertile Crescent. By 1055, a Seljuk **sultan**, or ruler, controlled Baghdad, but he kept the Abbasid caliph as a figurehead. As the Seljuks pushed into Asia Minor, they threatened the Byzantine empire. The conflict prevented Christian pilgrims from traveling to Jerusalem, leading Pope Urban II to call for the First Crusade in 1095.

Mongols Advance Through Central Asia In 1216, Genghis Khan led the Mongols out of Central Asia across Southwest Asia. Mongol armies returned again and again.

>> Analyze Maps Repeated invasions from the Mongols, first led by Genghis Khan, weakened the Abbasid caliphates. Where did the invaders come from?

1 of 4

Objective 4: Explain why the Abbasid empire declined.

Quick Instruction

Project the map of the Mongol invasions on the whiteboard. Point out to students that the Abbasids never ruled Spain and began to lose control over the rest of the Muslim empire starting around 850. The caliph's power began to fade in some areas, and Shiite rulers came to power. Invasions by the Seljuk Turks weakened the Abbasid rule of Central and Southwest Asia. Genghis Khan and other Mongol leaders led a number of Mongol invasions of Southwest Asia, seeking to expand their lands. In the invasions, they destroyed Baghdad and killed the last Abbasid caliph. Later Mongol rulers, such as Tamerlane, converted to Islam and helped restore influence to Muslims, and mosques were built throughout the empire.

Identify Cause and Effect Why did the empire of the Abbasid caliphs decline and eventually break up? *(Sample Response: The Abbasid empire became fragmented into many small states and was further weakened by invasions from Seljuk Turks, crusaders, and Mongols.)*

Further Instruction

Project the **Interactive Reading Notepad** on the whiteboard and go through the questions and discuss the answers with the class.

Cite Evidence What strategies did the Seljuk Turks and the Mongols use to gain control in Central Asia? Why was their strategy important? *(Sample Response: They adopted Islam as they mingled with local inhabitants to build trust and unity.)*

A Muslim Empire

■ SYNTHESIZE

DIGITAL ACTIVITY
The Umayyad and Abbasid Caliphates

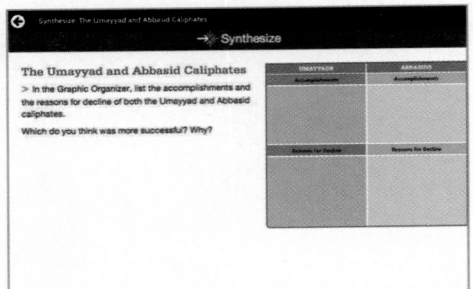

Have students work in pairs to complete the Graphic Organizer comparing the Umayyed and Abbasid caliphates. Have them think about the type of leadership structure and economic development during each caliphate as they think about which one was more successful. *(Responses will vary; students should use the information from their graphic organizer as their reasons. Umayyad Accomplishments • Expanded Islam (North Africa and Spain; Southwest Asia) • Created unified state • Treated non-Muslims well; but taxed them; Reasons for Decline • Too large a territory to control • Too much reliance on local non-Arabs • Tensions between Arabs and non-Arab Muslims • Luxurious lifestyle of caliphs; Abbasid Accomplishments • Arab and non-Arab Muslims treated equally • Encouraged learning • Baghdad as capital city; Reasons for Decline • Seljuk Turks invaded • Mongols invaded)*

■ DEMONSTRATE

DIGITAL QUIZ
Lesson Quiz and Class Discussion Board

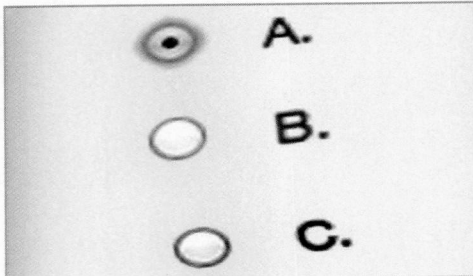

Assign the online Lesson Quiz for this lesson if you haven't already done so. Students will be offered automatic enrichment or remediation based on their score. Pose these questions to the class on the Discussion Board.

Cause and Effect What were some of the effects of the Shiite and Sunni divisions? *(Sample Response: While Islam was a strong unifying force among Muslims, the split created unrest and divisions within the Arab empire that eventually weakened it and contributed to its decline.)*

Identify Main Ideas How did Muslims treat Christian and Jewish peoples in conquered lands? *(Sample Response: They generally tolerated conquered peoples who followed monotheistic religions, but they taxed them and did not provide equal rights or opportunities.)*

Topic Inquiry
Have students continue their investigations for the Topic Inquiry.

Achievements of Muslim Civilization

Supporting English Language Learners

Use with Digital Text 1, **Economic and Social Changes.**

Listening

Read *Economic and Social Changes* aloud to students. Then have students participate in the following activities, which focus on understanding supporting details.

Beginning Explain the purpose of supporting details to students by creating and displaying a simple outline that demonstrates how details support main points. Explain that supporting details are used in speaking, not just in writing. Retell the main points and supporting details of *Economic and Social Changes* in your own words. Then work with students to create a simple outline of the information you explained that clearly shows the details that support the main points in this section.

Intermediate Review the relationship between main points and supporting details with students. Then reread *Economic and Social Changes* aloud. Have small groups retell the information from the text to one another. Then have small groups identify the details that support the main points in *Economic and Social Changes*.

Advanced Have pairs of students discuss the relationships between supporting details and main points with each other. Then ask each pair to talk about the information they learned from reading *Economic and Social Changes* by identifying the details that support the main ideas in this section of text.

Advanced High Facilitate a brief discussion in which students explain the purpose of important details in spoken language. Make sure students understand that important details support and explain main ideas. Then change the focus of the discussion to the main points and important details of *Economic and Social Changes*. Have students talk about which main points are supported by the important details from this section of text.

Use with Digital Text 3, **An Emphasis on Knowledge.**

Speaking

Before beginning this activity, read *An Emphasis on Knowledge* aloud to the class. Have students complete one of the following activities according to their level of English proficiency.

Beginning After reading *An Emphasis on Knowledge* aloud, turn students' attention to the image depicting Hindu-Arabic numerals. Model using new English vocabulary, like the words *numerals* and *traders*, as you explain the importance of these numerals. Have students use simple words and phrases to retell the information shown in this visual in their own words.

Intermediate Reread *An Emphasis on Knowledge* aloud to students, pausing frequently to model retelling the meaning of the text in your own words. Have students examine the visual depicting Hindu-Arabic numerals. Ask students to explain what they have learned from studying the visual in their own words.

Advanced Have students reread *An Emphasis on Knowledge* aloud in small groups. Remind students to pause frequently to check their understanding of the text by retelling what they have read in their own words. Then have small groups focus on the visual showing Hindu-Arabic numerals. Ask each group to explain what information is communicated by the visual.

Advanced High Have pairs of students focus on the visual showing Hindu-Arabic numerals. Ask each pair to retell the information they see in the image. Ask each pair to discuss how a universal set of numbers improves trade and communication across cultures. Have pairs report on their discussion to the group to share what they have learned.

▣ Differentiate Instruction

Use the Differentiated Instruction notes throughout the lesson plan to support the varied skill sets, levels of readiness, and interests in the mixed-ability classroom.

Challenge These notes include suggestions for expanding the activity for advanced students.

On-Level These notes include suggestions for modifying the activity to address different interests or learning styles.

Extra Support These notes include ideas for providing more scaffolding or reading spuport.

Special Needs These notes provide ideas for adapting instruction to support the needs of various special needs students.

■ NOTES

_____

_____

_____

_____

_____

Achievements of Muslim Civilization

Objectives

Objective 1: Describe the role of trade in Muslim civilization.

Objective 2: Identify the traditions that influenced Muslim art, architecture, and literature.

Objective 3: Describe the major ideas in mathematics, science, and technology that occurred in Muslim civilization.

LESSON 3 ORGANIZER		PACING: APPROX. 1 PERIOD, .5 BLOCKS			
				RESOURCES	
		OBJECTIVES	PACING	Online	Print
Connect					
DIGITAL START UP ACTIVITY **Inspiration from Aristotle**			5 min.	●	
Investigate					
DIGITAL TEXT 1 **Economic and Social Changes**		Objective 1	10 min.	●	●
DIGITAL TEXT 2 **Literature, Art, and Architecture**		Objective 2	10 min.	●	
INTERACTIVE GALLERY **Islamic Art and Architecture**			10 min.	●	
DIGITAL TEXT 3 **An Emphasis on Knowledge**		Objective 3	10 min.	●	●
INTERACTIVE GALLERY **Muslim Advances in Technology, Math, and Science**			10 min.	●	
Synthesize					
DIGITAL ACTIVITY **Accomplishments in Medicine, Literature, History, and Mathematics**			5 min.	●	
Demonstrate					
DIGITAL QUIZ **Lesson Quiz and Class Discussion Board**			10 min.	●	

PEARSON
realize™
www.PearsonRealize.com

Go online to access additional resources including:
Primary Sources • Biographies • Supreme Court cases •
21st Century Skill Tutorials • Maps • Graphic Organizers.

CONNECT

DIGITAL START UP ACTIVITY
Inspiration from Aristotle

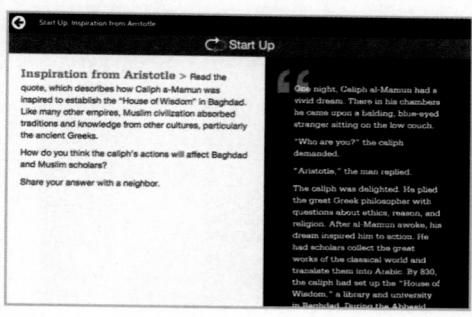

Project the Start Up Activity Ask students to answer the questions as they enter and get settled. Then have them share their ideas with another student either in class or through a chat or blog sequence.

Discuss What fields of study do you think the caliph might have in his "House of Wisdom"? *(Answers will vary. They could include: art, architecture, literature, (including drama), history, medicine, philosophy, and democracy.)*

Tell students that in this lesson they will learn about the social and economic advances made by the Muslim civilization as well as their advances in art, architecture, and literature.

Aa Vocabulary Development: Use the Interactive Reading Notepad to preview the Key Terms and Academic Vocabulary in this Lesson with students.

⇅ FLIP IT!
Assign the Flipped Video for this lesson.

STUDENT EDITION PRINT
PAGES: 269–275

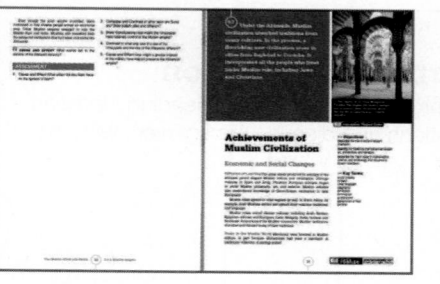

INVESTIGATE

DIGITAL TEXT 1
Economic and Social Changes

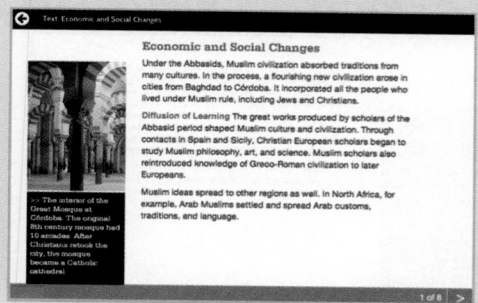

Objective 1: Describe the role of trade in Muslim civilization.

Quick Instruction

Muslim civilization blended many traditions from the various cultures in the empire including Arab, Persian, Egyptian, African, and European. Merchants were honored because Muhammad had been a merchant. Between 750 and 1350, merchants built a vast trading network across Muslim lands in Europe, Asia, and Africa. Trade among these regions spread products, technologies, knowledge, and culture. Arabic grew as a common language, and many people converted to Islam. Banking grew as a new industry. Manufactured goods such as carpets became highly valued, and agricultural production increased with more projects such as draining swamps and irrigating lands. People had more social mobility during this period, and many were able to move up in social class.

ELL Use the ELL activity described in the ELL chart.

D Differentiate: Extra Support Preview the Lesson Objective and the vocabulary for this section with students, then have them write the section heads and vocabulary in their notebooks. Students should add definitions and thoughts about each topic as they read the text. Definitions should be in student's own words-not from the glossary.

Further Instruction

Editable Presentation Use the Editable Presentation to present the main ideas for this Core Reading.

Go through the Interactive Reading Notepad questions and discuss the answers with the class.

Discuss with students the social and economic impact of Islam as the Muslim empire spread across Europe, Asia, and Africa. Brainstorm a list of advances with students and list on the board. Describe the significance of each. (**Trade:** *Between 750 and 1350 a vast trading network was built across Muslim lands. This trade spread products, technologies, knowledge and culture along the routes.* **Arabic numerals** *common number system allowed for easier business transactions* **New business practices** *formed banks, sought and sold on credit, this allowed for a wider trade system.* **Manufactured goods** *quality products developed for sale and trade, steel swords, leather goods, textiles and carpets– all from different areas in the Muslim world, Europe, Asia and Africa and were bought and sold.* **Growth of agriculture** *irrigation increased food output and crops were sold in far away markets.* **Social mobility** *people had the ability to move up in social class, allowed them more freedom. Slaves had the ability to gain their freedom.*)

Achievements of Muslim Civilization

DIGITAL TEXT 2
Literature, Art, and Architecture

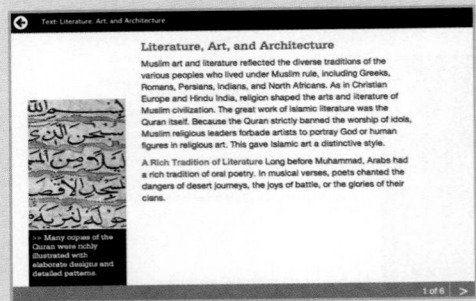

INTERACTIVE GALLERY
Islamic Art and Architecture

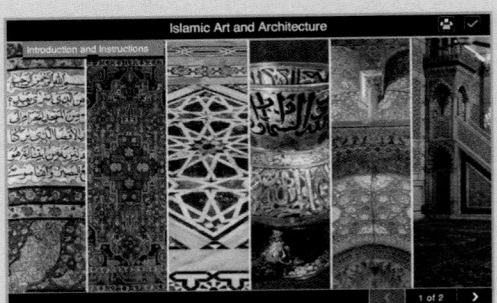

Be sure students understand the significance of the economic and social advances made during this period. Merchants, workers, and farmers could all prosper due to increase in trade and improved farming practices. Slavery was discouraged and people had the ability to improve their social class. There was the acceptance of a variety of different groups of people in society.

Draw Conclusions How did the start of a banking system have a positive economic impact on merchants? *(Possible Response: It standardized currency, and it protected merchants on long journeys for carrying large sums of money that cold be stolen.)*

Identifying Supporting Details Detail an example of social mobility in Muslim society in the eighth and ninth centuries. *(Possible answers: slaves could be freed as an act of charity, a child born of a slave mother but a free father was considered freeborn, and slave-soldiers loyal to the caliph could rise to high government positions)*

Objective 2: Identify the traditions that influenced Muslim art, architecture, and literature.

Quick Instruction

In Muslim cultures, religion shaped the arts, architecture, and literature of the civilization. The great work of Islamic literature was the Quran, which banned the worship of idols. Artists were forbidden to portray God or human figures in religious art pieces. This made Muslim artists perfect geometric designs and calligraphy. Human and animal figures appeared in nonreligious art and in science illustrations. Arabs and Persians also had a rich history of oral poetry and tales of adventure including stories such as "Aladdin and his Magic Lamp" and "Ali Baba and the Forty Thieves." Arab writers were great storytellers and their writing included romances, fables, adventures, and humorous writings. Domed mosques and tall minarets became symbols of Muslim architecture. Nonreligious art included human and animal figures in scientific works as well as intricate miniatures painted to illustrate stories and poems.

Interactive Gallery: Islamic Art and Architecture Project the gallery. Look at each image individually, and then the collection as a whole. Included in the gallery are examples of Muslim art and architecture including domes, minarets, horseshoe arches, geometric patterns, calligraphy, and arabesques. Be sure students identify the scrolling and interlacing leaf patterns and scrolling stems in the arabesques. They should also be able to identify the minarets—tall spires topped with domes used to call people to prayer. The style

and architecture of minarets differs by region and time period. Tell students that arabesques and mosaics showed the infinity of God and the unity of Islam—many small diverse pieces contributing to a whole. Calligraphy was often used to illustrate passages from the Quaran as decoration.

Analyze Images Examine each of the images and identify the aspects of Muslim art and architecture that you see. *(Answers will vary. Students should identify aspects such as domes, minarets, horseshoe arches, geometric patterns, calligraphy, and arabesques.)*

D **Differentiate: Challenge/Gifted** Have students research different styles of minarets built at different mosques around the world. Have them choose one that interests them and research its history. Their information can be posted on the class Web page.

🔲 ACTIVE CLASSROOM

Ask students to review information they have learned in this lesson and design a piece of wallpaper that encapsulates key learnings. Post the wallpaper and have students take a gallery/"wisdom" walk and note what others have written/illustrated.

Further Instruction

Go through the Interactive Reading Notepad questions and discuss the answers with the class.

DIGITAL TEXT 3

An Emphasis on Knowledge

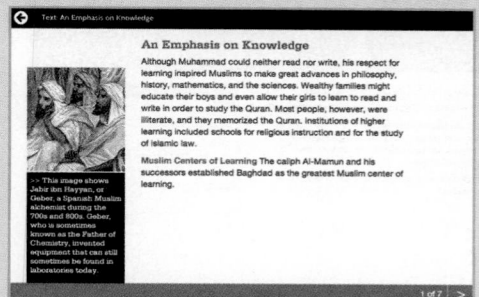

INTERACTIVE GALLERY

Muslim Advances in Technology, Math, and Science

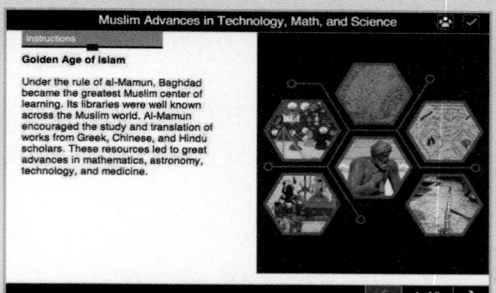

Construct An anecdote is a brief, often amusing story. What kind of anecdotes might a caliph enjoy? Describe one or create one. *(Students' answers will vary. Anecdote topics would be entertaining and typically historical.)*

Summarize What is calligraphy, and where can it be found? *(beautiful writing that can be found in books and on buildings)*

Distinguish Between Fact and Opinion Is the statement "Muslim art, literature, and architecture is the most original in the world" a fact or an opinion? Support your answer. *(Sample Response: Students should identify the statement as an opinion. Muslim art, literature, and architecture have all been influenced by the traditions of the people who have lived under Muslim rule. This includes Greeks, Romans, Persians, and Indians.)*

Objective 3: Describe the major ideas in mathematics, science, and technology that occurred in Muslim civilization.

Quick Instruction

Although Muhammad could not read or write, he inspired Muslims to respect learning, and great advances were made in philosophy, history, mathematics, and the sciences. Boys and girls attended school, where reading and writing were emphasized, so Muslims could study the Quran. Many advances were made in the field of astronomy by advancing tools designed by the Greeks. Medicine advanced and included improvements in the area of public heath. Medical texts written by two Muslim doctors became standards in European schools. Mhuammad al-Razi, the head physician at Baghdad's chief hospital, wrote a medical book including a pioneering study of measles and smallpox. A Muslim surgeon developed a way to treat cataracts. A Muslim mathematician wrote an algebra book that became the standard in Muslim areas and Europe when translated to English. This mathematician, al-Khwarizmi, also developed a set of astronomical tables based on Greek and Indian discoveries.

Interactive Gallery Muslim Advances in Technology, Math, and Science Click through the images representing the accomplishments of Muslims in science, technology, and math with students. Have students study the images and descriptions and think about how the advancements in these areas contributed to the rest of the world.

📖 ACTIVE CLASSROOM

Have students form groups and generate a response to this prompt, "Summarize the scientific contributions of Muslim civilization." Have students write as much as they can for one minute then switch with the person on their right. The next person tries to elaborate on where the other person left off. Continue to switch until the paper comes back to the first person. The group then decides which is the best response and shares with the class.

ELL Use the ELL activity described in the ELL chart.

Further Instruction

Project and discuss the Interactive Reading Notepad questions. Have students focus on the importance of preserving the learning of earlier civilizations. As you review the rest of the questions, have students reflect on how things may have been different if Muslims had disregarded the learning of the past.

The Muslim physician Muhammad al-Razi changed the way doctors treated patients. He believed in treating the mind as well as the body. Modern medicine rediscovered and proved the importance of treating both the mind as well as the body. Have students discuss other advances in medicine still in practice today.

Muslim scholars translated many Persian, Sanskrit, and Greek texts into Arabic and housed them in large libraries. Some Greek classics were destroyed in other areas by invaders and only survived in their Arabic translations.

Achievements of Muslim Civilization

 **SYNTHESIZE**

 DEMONSTRATE

DIGITAL ACTIVITY
Accomplishments in Medicine, Literature, History, and Mathematics

DIGITAL QUIZ
Lesson Quiz and Class Discussion Board

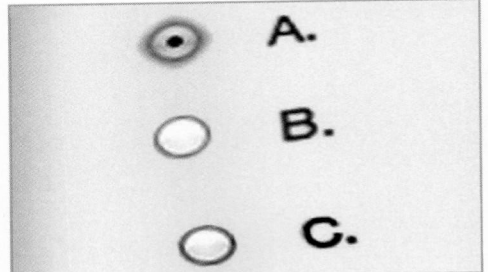

Evaluate Data Muslims made advances in medicine and public health in part by building on the knowledge of the ancient Greeks. What does this tell you about their acceptance of information from different sources? *(Sample Response: Muslim scholars had tremendous respect for the works of scholars from earlier civilizations.)*

Cite Evidence How did Muslim scholars preserve and build on the learning of earlier civilizations? *(Sample Response: They collected writings into libraries, translating them into Arabic, and expanding on the ideas contained in them.)*

Make Predictions Under the caliphs, physicians and pharmacists had to pass a test to practice. How might the advances in medicine made by the Muslims been different if this had not been a rule? *(Sample Response: By having physicians and pharmacists pass a test, medicine was standardized, and more advancements could be made. If it had not been standardized, there could have been many different ideas on how to treat patients and no single pool of knowledge developed.)*

Ask students to complete the Graphic Organizer identifying the accomplishments of the Muslim civilization in medicine, history, literature, and mathematics.

Discuss Have students compare answers and share with the class. What do the accomplishments reveal about the Muslim civilization? *(Answers will vary. Students should comment on the importance of reason and innovation; willingness to change; and promotion of religious tolerance.)*

Assign the online Lesson Quiz for this lesson if you haven't already done so. Students will be offered automatic remediation or enrichment based on their score.

Pose these questions to the class on the Discussion Board.

In "Achievement of Muslim Civilization," you learned about how trade and commerce benefited Muslim civilization. Traditions from many cultures were absorbed into Muslim civilization. Muslims also made many advances in art, economics, literature and science.

Cite Evidence Describe the advances in medicine that were made by Muslim physicians. *(Sample Response: They set up hospitals and rural health care, learned and wrote about diagnoses and treatments of disease, improved medical practices, developed prescriptions and a way to treat cataracts.)*

Draw Conclusions Muhammad taught that "the ink of the scholar is holier than the blood of the martyr." What do you think he meant? How might this attitude have contributed to the development of Muslim civilization? *(Possible answer: Knowledge was more important than sacrificing one's life in battle. Muslim scholars pursued learning.)*

Topic Inquiry
Have students continue their investigations for the Topic Inquiry.

The Ottoman and Safavid Empires

Supporting English Language Learners

Use with Digital Text 1, **Growth of the Ottoman Empire.**

Listening

Read *Growth of the Ottoman Empire* aloud to students. Then have students participate in the following activities, which focus on understanding important details despite unfamiliar language.

Beginning Provide students with the following list of challenging words from *Growth of the Ottoman Empire*: *weapons, warfare, treaty, conquer, invasion, edicts*. Then retell the main points and important details of the text in simple, accessible language. Pause when you mention one of the vocabulary terms from the list and explain its meaning to students. Use examples from the text and make connections to students' prior knowledge to promote understanding.

Intermediate Provide students with the following list of challenging words from *Growth of the Ottoman Empire*: *weapons, warfare, treaty, conquer, invasion, edicts*. Then retell the main points and important details of the text and ask students to raise their hands when they hear one of the words from the list. Pause and help students use context clues and prior knowledge to define each word.

Advanced Provide students with the following list of challenging words from *Growth of the Ottoman Empire*: *weapons, warfare, treaty, conquer, invasion, edicts*. Have students reread the text. Then have small groups of students retell what they learned from reading the section. Instruct groups to define the six terms provided and to identify and define any other challenging language in the text. Groups should develop definitions for challenging language using context clues and their prior knowledge. Discuss students' words and definitions as a large group to ensure correct understanding.

Advanced High Have students take turns retelling what they learned from the text to a partner. Instruct pairs to identify any challenging language and develop a working definition for each term using context clues and prior knowledge. Then have partners share their results with another pair.

Use with Digital Text 2, **Ottoman Society.**

Speaking

Before beginning this activity, read *Ottoman Society* aloud to the class. Have students complete one of the following activities according to their level of English proficiency.

Beginning Display the following directions for students:

- Locate the heading "Ottoman Society."
- Underline each of the four divisions of Ottoman Society.
- Draw a sketch to show your understanding of each of the four divisions.

Read these directions one at a time and help students as necessary by demonstrating what each direction tells them to do. Allow time between each direction for students to accomplish the tasks described.

Intermediate Display the following directions for students:

- Locate the heading "Ottoman Society."
- Underline each of the four divisions of Ottoman Society.
- Draw a sketch to show your understanding of each of the four divisions.

Have student volunteers read these directions one at a time. Help students as necessary by having volunteers demonstrate what each direction tells them to do. Allow time between each direction for students to accomplish the tasks described. When the tasks are complete, have students share their final sketches with the whole group.

Advanced Display the following directions for students:

- Locate the heading "Ottoman Society."
- Underline each of the four divisions of Ottoman Society.
- Draw a sketch and write a caption to show your understanding of each of the four divisions.

Instruct students to read each task and follow the directions. Circulate among students to support their understanding as needed. When the tasks are complete, have students share their final sketches and captions with the group.

Advanced High Display the following directions for students:

- Locate and underline each of the four divisions of Ottoman Society in the text.
- Draw a sketch and write a caption to show your understanding of each division.
- Be prepared to share your work with the group.

Instruct students to read and follow the directions. Circulate among students to support their understanding as needed. When the tasks are complete, have students share their final sketches and captions with the group.

The Ottoman and Safavid Empires

Objectives

Objective 1: Explain the impact of the Ottoman empire on Eastern Europe.

Objective 2: Describe the characteristics of Ottoman culture.

Objective 3: Explain how Abbas the Great strengthened the Safavid empire.

LESSON 4 ORGANIZER		PACING: APPROX. 1 PERIOD, .5 BLOCKS			
		OBJECTIVES	PACING	RESOURCES	
				Online	Print
Connect					
DIGITAL START UP ACTIVITY **Constantinople Falls**			5 min.	●	
Investigate					
DIGITAL TEXT 1 **Growth of the Ottoman Empire**		Objective 1	10 min.	●	●
INTERACTIVE GALLERY **Ottoman Empire under Suleiman**			10 min.	●	
DIGITAL TEXT 2 **Ottoman Society**		Objective 2	10 min.	●	●
DIGITAL TEXT 3 **The Rise of the Safavids**		Objective 3	10 min.	●	●
INTERACTIVE MAP **Growth of the Ottoman and Safavid Empires**			10 min.	●	
Synthesize					
DIGITAL ACTIVITY **The Ottoman and Safavid Empires**			5 min.	●	
Demonstrate					
DIGITAL QUIZ **Lesson Quiz and Class Discussion Board**			10 min.	●	

PEARSON
realize™
www.PearsonRealize.com

Go online to access additional resources including:
Primary Sources • Biographies • Supreme Court cases •
21st Century Skill Tutorials • Maps • Graphic Organizers.

■ CONNECT

DIGITAL START UP ACTIVITY
Constantinople Falls

Project the Start Up Activity Ask students to read the text on the fall of Constantinople and the rise of the Ottoman empire, and then answer the following question. They can share their answer with another student either in class or through a chat or blog space.

Discuss Why was the fall of Constantinople a powerful symbol? *(Sample Response: It meant the capture by Muslims of a major Christian city—once the capital of the eastern Roman empire—in a strategic location at the doorway of Europe.)*

Aa **Vocabulary Development:** Use the Interactive Reading Notepad to preview the Key Terms and Academic Vocabulary in this Lesson with students.

⇅ FLIP IT!

Assign the Flipped Video for this lesson.

■ STUDENT EDITION PRINT
PAGES: 276–280

■ INVESTIGATE

DIGITAL TEXT 1
Growth of the Ottoman Empire

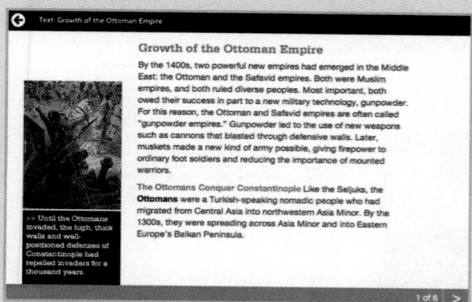

INTERACTIVE GALLERY
Ottoman Empire under Suleiman

Objective 1: Explain the impact of the Ottoman empire on Eastern Europe.

Quick Instruction

Ottoman Empire under Suleiman: Interactive Gallery Project the Interactive Gallery on the whiteboard and click through the hotspots. Explain to students that Suleiman's power came through diplomacy as well as war, expanding the empire from the Balkan peninsula into Eastern Europe, including much of Hungry. He modernized the army and used cannons and muskets to extend Ottoman rule.

Tell students that the Ottoman empire controlled major trade routes between Europe, Africa, and Asia. As a result, Istanbul became one of the great trading capitals of the world. The Ottoman empire strengthened its trading position by bringing merchants into Istanbul, particularly European Jewish traders. French merchants, through a treaty, were allowed to travel and trade throughout the Ottoman empire—unlike traders from other European countries. In 1533, Suleiman created an enormous fleet that dominated all trade in the eastern Mediterranean. The Portuguese and other European countries looked for new trade routes, and their navies eventually commanded new trade routes around Africa and ended Ottoman control of both land and sea routes

👥 ACTIVE CLASSROOM

Have students create a political cartoon from one image in this lesson to include in a class blog. The caption should provide detail about the image. *(Possible example: Students may choose the image of a member of one social class such as a merchant. Caption should describe the life of a merchant in the Ottoman social structure.)*

ELL Use the ELL activity described in the ELL chart.

D **Differentiate: Extra support** Ask students to make a table identifying key characteristics of the Ottoman and Safavid empires. *(The tables should be constructed so students find characteristics for the Ottomans and Safavids for the following, Capital, Dates, Strongest Ruler, Extent of Empire, Branch of Islam, and Relationship with Europe.)*

Further Instruction

Editable Presentation Use the Editable Presentation to present the main ideas for the Core Reading.

Growth of the Ottoman Empire: Core Reading and Interactive Reading Notepad Go through the Interactive Reading Notepad question and discuss the answers with the class.

The Ottoman and Safavid Empires

DIGITAL TEXT 2

Ottoman Society

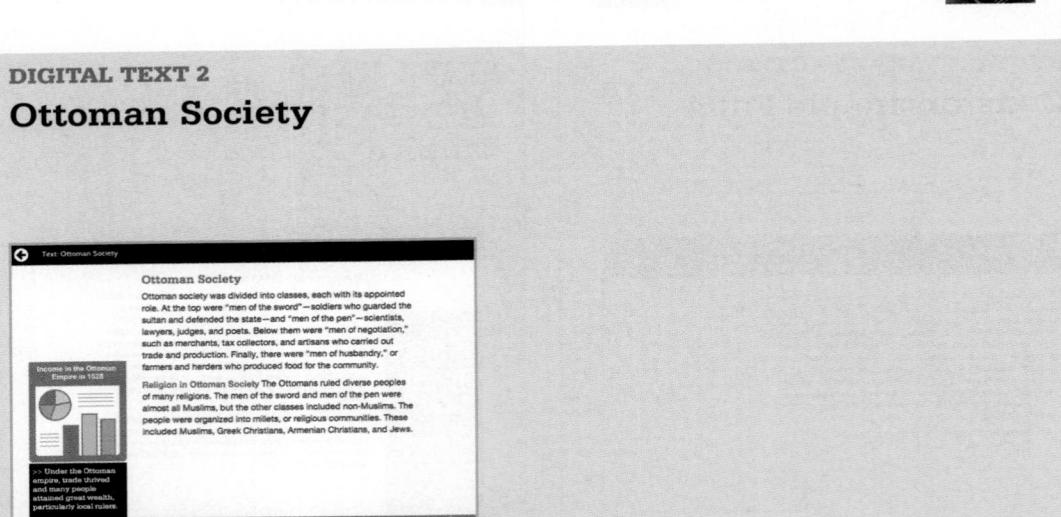

The Ottomans captured Constantinople and renamed it Istanbul. Be sure students understand Europeans feared the Ottomans because they were getting very close to Western Europe, and they were very powerful. They were also Muslim, not Christian. Review the map of the Ottoman and Safavid empires, 1452–1629.

Identify Supporting Details Find details in the text supporting the statement that new weapon technology allowed the Ottomans to successfully expand their empire. *(Possible answer: Ottoman cannons blasted gaps in the defensive walls of Constantinople. Muskets gave greater firepower to foot soldiers reducing the need for mounted warriors.)*

Objective 2: Describe the characteristics of Ottoman culture.

Quick Instruction

Project the image of the Income in the Ottoman Empire. Discuss the organization of the empire and how it was governed. Tell students that Ottoman society was organized into classes, each with its own role. The soldiers who guarded the sultan and defended the state held the top role in the society. The farmers held the bottom role. The Ottoman empire began to decline after Suleiman's death in 1566.

ELL Use the ELL activity described in the ELL chart.

D **Differentiate: Challenge/Gifted** Have students use Internet sources to find examples of detailed miniatures and illuminated manuscripts produced by Ottoman painters or research the work of the royal architect Sinan, a who designed hundreds of mosques and palaces. Students should write a sentence or two analyzing how the art or architecture reflects the history of the Ottoman empire. Have them share their findings with the class with a digital poster or slide show. They can also post their findings on the class Web site or blog.

Further Instruction

Ottoman Society: Core Reading and Interactive Reading Notepad Go through the Interactive Reading Notepad questions and discuss the answers with the class.

Be sure students understand that the Ottomans organized religious groups into millets—Muslims, Greek Christians, Armenian Christians, and Jews. The millets each had their own leaders and brought ideas and connections to the Ottoman empire. Many of these ideas and connections allowed the Ottoman empire to expand.

Cite evidence The Ottomans ruled people of many religions. How did Islam grow in the Ottoman empire? *(Possible answer: The Ottomans required Christian families to turn over their young sons for government service and often converted them to Islam.)*

DIGITAL TEXT 3
The Rise of the Safavids

INTERACTIVE MAP
Growth of the Ottoman and Safavid Empires

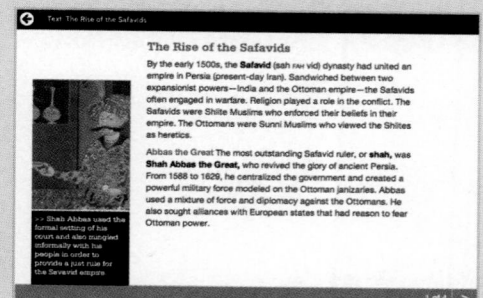

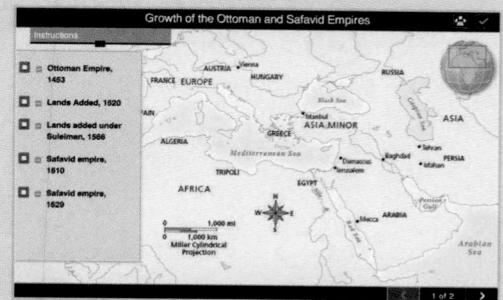

Objective 3: Explain how Abbas the Great strengthened the Safavid empire.

Quick Instruction
Growth of the Ottoman and Safavid Empires: Interactive Map Project the map on the whiteboard and click through the hot spots on the map. Introduce the map by telling students that at its greatest extent, the Ottoman empire stretched across three continents. The Savavid empire controlled most of what is modern day Iran.

👥 ACTIVE CLASSROOM

Use the headline strategy. Have students write a headline that captures the essence of the interactive map. Ask: If you were to write a headline for this topic or issue right now that captured the most important aspect that should be remembered, what would that headline be? Exchange headlines with a partner and review. *(Possible answers: "Heading toward Europe," "Prosperity Increases Size of Kingdom," "Gaining Ground Quickly")*

Further Instruction
Editable Presentation Use the Editable Presentation to present the main ideas for this Core Reading.

The Rise of the Safavids: Core Reading and Interactive Reading Notepad Go through the Interactive Reading Notepad questions and discuss the answers with the class.

The Safavid empire flourished under the reign of Shah Abbas. He tolerated non-Muslims and valued their economic contributions. During the reign of the Shah Abbas, a new capital was built at Isfahan and it became the center of the international silk trade. The arts also flourished during this time.

Draw Conclusions Most people in the Safavid and Ottoman dynasties were Muslims. How did religion divide these empires? *(Possible answer: The Savafids were Shiites and the Ottomans were Sunnis. The Shiites enforced their beliefs in their empire, the Sunni Muslims viewed the Shiites as heretics.)*

Summarize How did the Savafid empire decline? *(Possible answer: Shiite scholars challenged the shah's authority and persecuted religious minorities, causing the Sunnis to rebel. This ultimately led to a new dynasty, the Qajars taking control of the area.)*

The Ottoman and Safavid Empires

SYNTHESIZE

DIGITAL ACTIVITY
The Ottoman and Safavid Empires

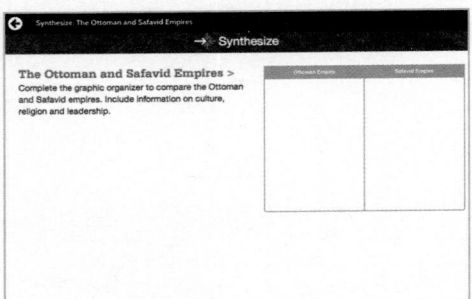

Ask students to complete the Graphic Organizer comparing the Ottoman and Safavid empires. They should then compare with a partner. Have them discuss what differences in rule may have made a difference in the fate of each of the empires. **Ottoman Empire** • *Ruled by Suleiman the Magnificent, modernized the army and extended the kingdom, strengthened government, improved system of justice* • *Class system, with the men of the sword at the top and farmers at the bottom.* • *Poetry, painting, and architecture grew under Suleiman* • *Primary religion - Islam (Sunni)* **Safavid Empire** • *Shah Abbas rules from 1588 to 1629. Centralized government and created a powerful military. Sought alliances with European states* • *Isfahan, the capital, became a center for art and architecture. The city produced paintings, metalworks, textiles, and rugs. The city was the center of international silk trade.* • *Major religion - Islam (Shiite)*

Discuss Ask students to share their ideas on what differences in rule may have made a difference in the fates of each of the empires.

DEMONSTRATE

DIGITAL QUIZ
Lesson Quiz and Class Discussion Board

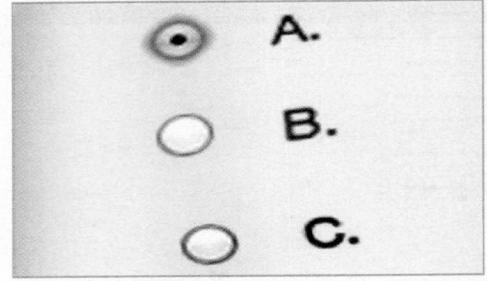

Assign the online Lesson Quiz for this lesson if you haven't already done so. Students will be offered automatic enrichment or remediation based on their score.

Pose these questions to the class on the Discussion Board:

In "The Ottoman and Safavid Empires" you read about the rise and fall of both the Ottoman and Safavid empires. Each empire made contributions to the belief system, culture, and arts of their respective empires.

Draw Conclusions Why do you think Ottoman and Safavid rulers had some tolerance of other religious groups? *(Possible answer: The successful rulers realized that non-Muslim groups made important economic and cultural contributions to their empires.)*

Predict consequences How do you think Safavid shahs might have been able to halt or slow the decline of their empire after the reign of Abbas the Great? *(Possible answer: by strengthening the army, centralizing political and religious authority, and/or practicing tolerance of religious minorities.)*

Topic Inquiry
Have students continue their investigations for the Topic Inquiry.

Early Civilizations of Africa

Supporting English Language Learners

Use with Digital Text 2, **Migration of People and Ideas.**

Listening
Read *Migration of People and Ideas* aloud to students. Then have students participate in the following activities, which focus on the creating a context for the concept of desertification.

Beginning To help students understand the meaning and effects of desertification on African people, show visuals and discuss examples of great geographic change. Examples could include a powerful earthquake or a significant climate change like the end of the Ice Age or currently proposed concept of global warming. Use visuals that help you demonstrate what the geography looked like before and after these significant changes. Help students choose words and phrases to describe the changes they see in the visuals provided.

Intermediate Show students before and after visuals to represent the changes experienced in the Sahara because of desertification. Guide a brief discussion in which students are assisted in making connections between the desertification of the Sahara and other great geological changes that occur on Earth.

Advanced Facilitate a group discussion on desertification. Ask students to define the concept based on what they read in the text. Then guide the discussion to help students make connections between desertification of 2500 B.C. and geological or ecological events in recent history.

Advanced High Have small groups of students discuss the connections between the desertification experienced in Africa in 2500 B.C. and geological and ecological events in recent history. Then have small groups share the main points of their discussion with the rest of the class.

Use with Digital Text 3, **Egypt and Nubia Flourish.**

Speaking
Before beginning this activity, read *Egypt and Nubia Flourish* aloud to the class. Then have students practice saying different types of sentences according to their level of English proficiency.

Beginning Write and display the following short, simple sentence about *Egypt and Nubia Flourish*:

Nubians copied Egyptian pyramids.

Read the sentence aloud and have students repeat it. Listen to make sure that students are pronouncing each word correctly and help them make corrections as needed. Then ask students to say their own simple sentence about what they learned from reading *Egypt and Nubia Flourish*. Help students as needed.

Intermediate Instruct students to write then say two simple sentences to a partner about what they learned from reading *Egypt and Nubia Flourish*. Provide examples and assistance to students as needed.

Advanced Instruct students to write then say three sentences aloud to a partner about the information they learned from reading *Egypt and Nubia Flourish*. Have students include at least one phrase in each sentence. Assist students with sentence structure and pronunciation as needed.

Advanced High Have students write then say four sentences to the class about what they learned from reading *Egypt and Nubia Flourish*. Make sure students use a variety of phrases and clauses that include descriptive words and active verbs in each sentence.

▣ Differentiate Instruction

Use the Differentiated Instruction notes throughout the lesson plan to support the varied skill sets, levels of readiness, and interests in the mixed-ability classroom.

Challenge These notes include suggestions for expanding the activity for advanced students.

On-Level These notes include suggestions for modifying the activity to address different interests or learning styles.

Extra Support These notes include ideas for providing more scaffolding or reading spuport.

Special Needs These notes provide ideas for adapting instruction to support the needs of various special needs students.

■ NOTES

_____

_____

_____

_____

_____

Early Civilizations of Africa

Objectives

Objective 1: Understand how geography affected migration, cultural development, and trade in Africa.

Objective 2: Describe the rise and decline of Nubia.

Objective 3: Explain how outside influences led to change in North Africa.

LESSON 5 ORGANIZER		PACING: APPROX. 1 PERIOD, .5 BLOCKS			
				RESOURCES	
		OBJECTIVES	PACING	Online	Print
Connect					
	DIGITAL START UP ACTIVITY **Danger in the Desert**		5 min.	●	
Investigate					
	DIGITAL TEXT 1 **The Geography of Africa**		10 min.	●	●
	INTERACTIVE MAP **Africa's Vegetation Regions**	Objective 1	10 min.	●	
	DIGITAL TEXT 2 **Migration of People and Ideas**		10 min.	●	●
	DIGITAL TEXT 3 **Egypt and Nubia Flourish**		10 min.	●	●
	INTERACTIVE GALLERY **Nubian Art and Culture**	Objective 2	10 min.	●	
	DIGITAL TEXT 4 **North Africa in the Ancient World**	Objective 3	10 min.	●	●
Synthesize					
	DIGITAL ACTIVITY **Revisit the Essential Question**		5 min.	●	
Demonstrate					
	DIGITAL QUIZ **Lesson Quiz and Discussion Board**		10 min.	●	

CONNECT

DIGITAL START UP ACTIVITY
Danger in the Desert

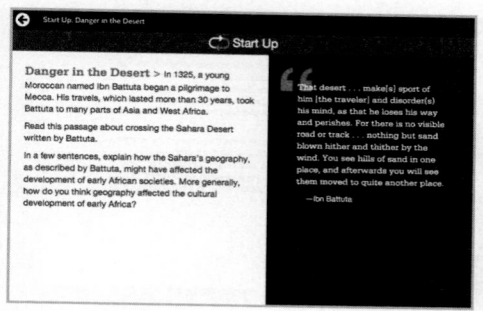

Project the Start Up Activity Ask students to answer these questions as they enter and get settled: How might Africa's climate and geography have affected the development of early North African societies? How might the Sahara's environment have influenced trade? Answer these questions in four to five sentences. *(Students may note that geography and environment affected how people lived and made a living, and that the desert acted as a barrier to movement.)*

Discuss Once students have answered the questions, have them share their ideas with another student, either in class or through a chat room or blog.

Aa **Vocabulary Development:** Use the Interactive Reading Notepad to preview the Key Terms and Academic Vocabulary in the Lesson with students.

⇅ FLIP IT!
Assign the Flipped Video for this lesson.

■ STUDENT EDITION PRINT
PAGES: 281–285

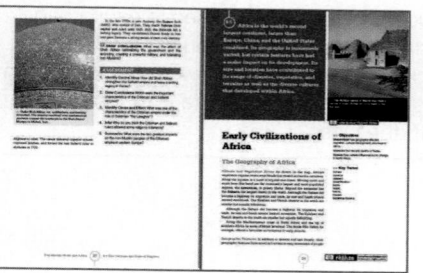

INVESTIGATE

DIGITAL TEXT 1
The Geography of Africa

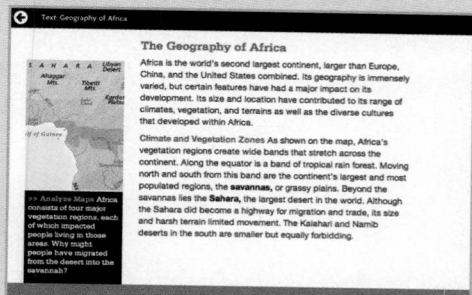

INTERACTIVE MAP
Africa's Vegetation Regions

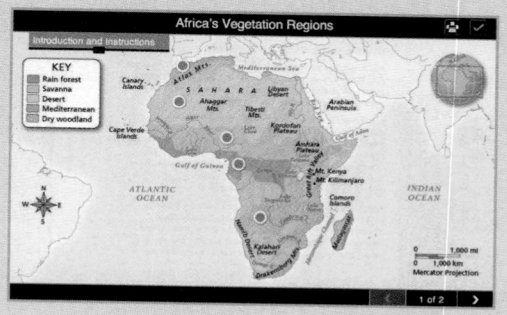

Objective 1: Understand how geography affected migration, cultural development, and trade in Africa.

Quick Instruction
Africa's Vegetation Regions: Interactive Map Project the map on the whiteboard and click through the hotspots. Introduce the map activity by telling students that Africa's early civilizations were diverse and formed in part because of the continent's geography and climate. Tell students that Africa's geographic features not only acted as barriers to trade and cultural development, but also as passageways linking many kingdoms and villages.

■ ACTIVE CLASSROOM
Think of yourself as a merchant living on the Mediterranean coast just north of the Libyan Desert. A trader from the Great Rift Valley wants to do business with you. Write down a series of questions that you'd like ask the trader about the products he or she wants to trade and what life in that particular part of Africa is like. Next, write down what they would say in response.

D **Differentiate: Extra Support** Point out that traders provide goods that people need by bringing them from other areas including different countries. Ask students to list three modern examples of products from a different region or country.

Further Instruction
Project and go through the Interactive Reading Notepad questions and discuss the answers with the class.

Discuss Ask students to evaluate and explain the influence of camels on trade in the Sahara Desert. *(Students may say that camels allowed traders to move a vast amount of goods over great distances, often with very little water.)*

Apply Concepts Ask students to explain how each of the following geographic features influenced ways of life: desert; rain forest; savanna. *(Students may say: in the desert, the lack of rainfall prevented farming and herding; in the rain forest, diverse plants and animals allowed for a variety of ways of life to flourish; in the savanna, fertile soil permitted farming and herding.)*

Early Civilizations of Africa

DIGITAL TEXT 2

Migration of People and Ideas

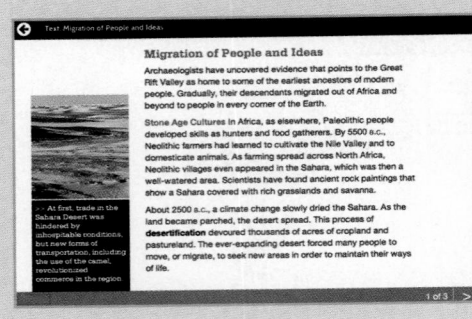

DIGITAL TEXT 3

Egypt and Nubia Flourish

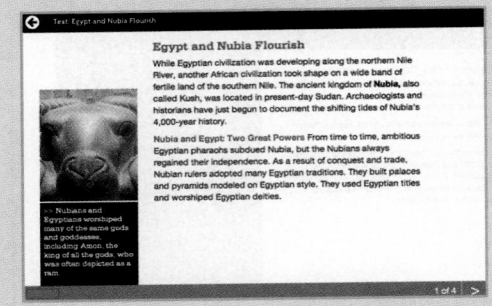

Objective 1: Understand how geography affected migration, cultural development, and trade in Africa.

Quick Instruction

Tell students that Neolithic people, skilled as hunter-gathers, began to cultivate the Nile Valley. This farming led to the development of villages along the river valley and the Sahara, which was then a well-watered area. Project the Bantu Migration map on the whiteboard. Explain to students how desertification prompted migration, which contributed to the rich diversity of cultures in Africa, and that Bantu-speaking people migrated south and east spreading their culture.

Analyze Maps Have students study the Bantu Migration map. Ask students why they think Bantu-speakers migrated south in the pattern described on the map as opposed to migrating north. *(Students may say that the Bantu migrated south because the area's geography allowed for easy travel and that vegetation allowed for easy access to food and water.)*

ELL Use the ELL activity described in the ELL chart.

Further Instruction

Go through the Interactive Reading Notepad and discuss the answers with the class.

Discuss Ask students to evaluate and explain the impact that farming had on Neolithic culture and trade in Africa. *(Students may say farming resulted in the production of surplus food, which led to trade and the establishment of villages and trading centers along routes of that trade.)*

Draw Inferences What impact did the Bantu migration have on language in southern Africa? *(Students may say that as the Bantu migrated south, many cultures absorbed the Bantu language.)*

Objective 2: Describe the rise and decline of Nubia.

Quick Instruction

Explain that Nubia, located to the south of Egypt along the Nile river valley, was one of the great kingdoms of ancient Africa. Its culture and religion were influenced heavily by Egypt. After invasions from the Assyrians, Nubians moved their capital to Moroë, where it commanded vital trade routes and had great natural resources. There it thrived until it was overwhelmed by Axum's armies.

Interactive Gallery: Nubian Art and Culture Project the images. Tell students to look at each image individually and then the collection of images as a whole. Analyze and explain how these artifacts and paintings illustrate the cultural relationship between Egypt and Nubia.

Analyze Images Analyze and explain how these images illustrate the relationship between Egypt and Nubian religious beliefs.

> **📷 ACTIVE CLASSROOM**
>
> Use the See-Think-Wonder strategy and pair students and ask them to review all the images in the photo gallery. Ask students: What do you see in each image? What does that make you think? What are you wondering about now that you've seen this? Have students share their insights with the class.

INTERACTIVE GALLERY

Nubian Art and Culture

ELL Use the ELL activity described in the ELL chart.

Further Instruction

Project the questions in the Interactive Reading Notepad and have students answer them as they progress through the text.

Identify Cause and Effect Analyze and describe how Egypt's geographic location influenced Nubia. *(Students may say that Egypt's proximity led to trade and the sharing of ideas. As a result, the Nubians adapted many Egyptian traditions including religion.)*

DIGITAL TEXT 4

North Africa in the Ancient World

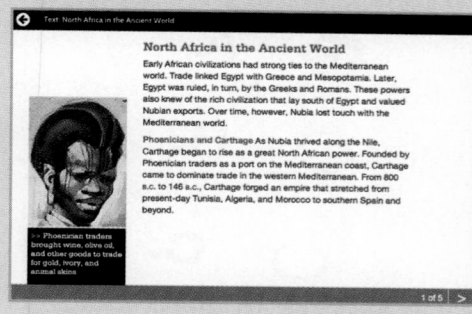

Objective 3: Explain how outside influences led to change in North Africa.

Quick Instruction

Project the image of the map, Islam, Christianity, and Judaism in Africa (A.D. 1000) on the whiteboard. Remind students that early Africa had strong ties to the regions across the Mediterranean and the Red seas. Explain that the Phoenicians, Romans, and Muslim Arabs all affected African history.

Analyze Maps After studying the map, in which area(s) do you think Muslims, Jews, and Christians might have interacted? Which religion had expanded into the largest geographic location by *a.d.* 1000? *(Students may say that Muslims, Jews, and Christians would have interacted along the Mediterranean coast. Students may also say that by a.d. 1000, Islam had the greatest geographical influence of all three religions.)*

Further Instruction

To extend the teaching of this objective, have students answer the following question: In what ways did outside influences contribute to the spread of Islam, Christianity, and Judaism in North Africa? *(Answers may vary, but students should show an understanding that Early African civilizations had strong ties to regions across the Mediterranean, and that these outside influences, including the interactions with Romans and Muslim Arabs, brought changes in religion and other aspects of life.)*

Early Civilizations of Africa

■ SYNTHESIZE

DIGITAL ACTIVITY

Revisit the Essential Question

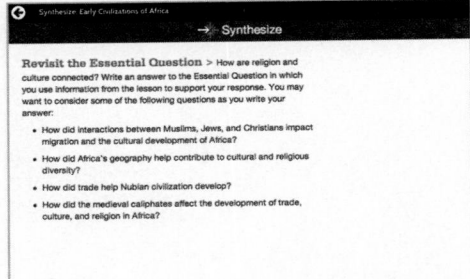

First ask students to reconsider the Essential Question for the Topic: How are religion and culture connected? Using the Rank It strategy, ask students to rank *(from most important to least important)* the interaction of religion, trade, and geography on African culture. Ask students to provide a justification for their ranking decisions. Then ask students to work in pairs to share their rankings and justifications. Poll the class to see if there is any agreement of the ranking.

■ DEMONSTRATE

DIGITAL QUIZ

Lesson Quiz and Discussion Board

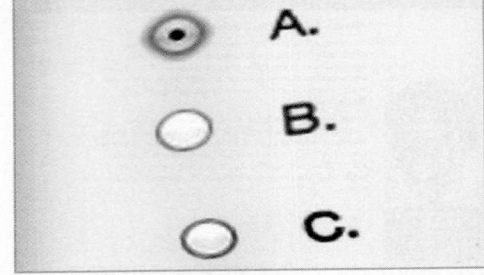

Assign the online Lesson Quiz for this lesson if you haven't already done so. Students will be offered automatic remediation or enrichment based on their score.

Post these questions on the Discussion Board.

In "Early Civilizations of Africa," you read about the influence of physical geographic factors on Early Africa; you studied the interactions among Muslim, Christian, and Jewish societies; and you read how art reflects the history of the cultures in which it is produced.

Describe: What effect did trade have on the cities of North Africa? *(Students may answer that success in trade allowed the Carthaginians to build a mighty empire, but led to war. Trade with Rome helped spur the adoption of Christianity. Later, trade promoted the development of Muslim culture and the adoption of Islam.)*

Topic Inquiry

Have students continue their investigations for the Topic Inquiry.

PEARSON realize
www.PearsonRealize.com
Access your Digital Lesson

Kingdoms of West Africa

Supporting English Language Learners

Use with Digital Text 1, **Trade Grows Across the Sahara.**

Listening

Read *Trade Grows Across the Sahara* aloud to students. Then have students participate in the following activities, which focus on identifying implicit ideas.

Beginning Have students listen as *Trade Grows Across the Sahara* is read aloud twice. During the first reading, have students listen carefully. Before the second reading, tell them that they will listen for explicit information, or facts that are clearly stated. After reading, guide the students to share the factual information they heard: that the Neolithic people left the Sahara once the desert developed. Now introduce and explain implicit information to students. Using sentence frames like the ones below, help students understand that implicit ideas are ideas that are suggested by the facts in a text.

- _____ caused the Neolithic people to move from the Sahara. [Desertification]
- Most plants _____ grow in the desert. [do not]
- Implicit information: Deserts are not good for farming.

Intermediate Have students listen as *Trade Grows Across the Sahara* is read aloud twice. During the first reading, have students listen carefully. Before the second reading, tell them to listen for and write down explicit information in the text. If necessary, review the meanings of explicit and implicit. Review explicit information that students noted, then guide them to determine the implicit information from the text.

Advanced Have students listen as *Trade Grows Across the Sahara* is read aloud. Instruct students to write down the explicit information they hear in the text. Then have students use the explicit information they heard to determine the implicit information in the section. Finally, have students turn to a partner to share their findings. Circulate among students to offer support as needed.

Advanced High Have students work in small groups to determine the explicit and implicit ideas in *Trade Grows Across the Sahara*. Have one student in each group read the text aloud while the others take notes on the explicit information. Then instruct the groups to discuss and identify the implicit ideas in the text. Finally, have each group share their findings with the entire class.

Use with Digital Text 5, **Small Societies and Kingdoms of West Africa.**

Speaking

Before beginning this activity, read *Small Societies and Kingdoms of West Africa* aloud to the class. Then have students practice saying sentences of different lengths according to their level of English proficiency.

Beginning Write and display the following short, simple sentences about *Small Societies and Kingdoms of West Africa*:

- Benin City was enclosed with a wall.
- The Hausa also had walled city-states.
- Farming and trading were important to the success of these societies.

Read the sentences aloud and have students repeat them. Listen to make sure that students are pronouncing each word correctly and help them make corrections as needed. Then ask students to say their own simple sentence about what they learned from reading *Small Societies and Kingdoms of West Africa*. Help students add length to their sentences to provide additional challenges as needed.

Intermediate Instruct students to say two short and one long sentence to a partner about what they learned from reading *Small Societies and Kingdoms of West Africa*. Provide examples and assistance to students as needed.

Advanced Instruct students to say three shorter and two longer sentences aloud to a partner about the information they learned from reading *Small Societies and Kingdoms of West Africa*. Encourage students to speak using increasingly complex sentences. Assist students as needed.

Advanced High Have pairs of students take turns saying longer sentences about what they learned about *Small Societies and Kingdoms of West Africa*. Circulate among students to challenge or assist them in their efforts.

▣ Differentiate Instruction

Use the Differentiated Instruction notes throughout the lesson plan to support the varied skill sets, levels of readiness, and interests in the mixed-ability classroom.

Challenge These notes include suggestions for expanding the activity for advanced students.

On-Level These notes include suggestions for modifying the activity to address different interests or learning styles.

Extra Support These notes include ideas for providing more scaffolding or reading spuport.

Special Needs These notes provide ideas for adapting instruction to support the needs of various special needs students.

■ NOTES

Kingdoms of West Africa

Objectives

Objective 1: Analyze how the gold and salt trade in Africa facilitated the spread of ideas and trade.

Objective 2: Describe how the rulers of Ghana, Mali, and Songhai built strong kingdoms.

Objective 3: Summarize how other West African societies developed.

LESSON 6 ORGANIZER		PACING: APPROX. 1 PERIOD, .5 BLOCKS			
				RESOURCES	
		OBJECTIVES	PACING	Online	Print
Connect					
	DIGITAL START UP ACTIVITY **Trade in Mali**		5 min.	●	
Investigate					
	DIGITAL TEXT 1 **Trade Grows Across the Sahara**	Objective 1	10 min.	●	●
	INTERACTIVE MAP **Trans-Saharan Trade (750 B.C.)**		10 min.	●	
	DIGITAL TEXT 2 **Ghana**		10 min.	●	●
	DIGITAL TEXT 3 **Mali**	Objective 2	10 min.	●	●
	DIGITAL TEXT 4 **Songhai**		10 min.	●	●
	INTERACTIVE GALLERY **Artifacts from West Africa's Great Kingdoms**		10 min.	●	
	DIGITAL TEXT 5 **Small Societies and Kingdoms of West Africa**	Objective 3	10 min.	●	●
Synthesize					
	DIGITAL ACTIVITY **Reflect on the Essential Question**		5 min.	●	
Demonstrate					
	DIGITAL QUIZ **Lesson Quiz and Class Discussion Board**		10 min.	●	

■ CONNECT

DIGITAL START UP ACTIVITY
Trade in Mali

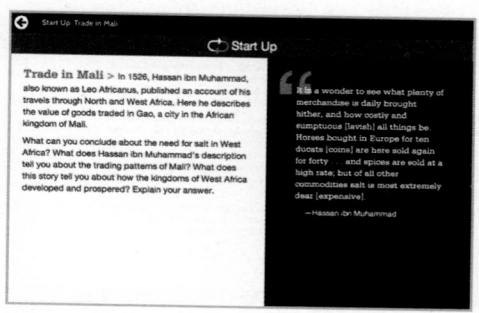

Project the Start Up Activity Ask students to answer the questions as they enter and get settled.

Discuss What can you conclude about the need for salt in West Africa? What does Hassan ibn Muhammad's description tell you about the trading patterns of Mali? *(Students' responses should include the idea that salt was very important in West Africa, and that the city of Gao had a trade route directly to Europe.)*

Tell students that in this lesson they will be learning about how the gold and salt trade influenced various cultures in West Africa and how leaders of those kingdoms built strong societies. They'll also be learning how other smaller African societies developed.

Aa Vocabulary Development: Use the Interactive Reading Notepad to preview the Key Terms and Academic Vocabulary in the Lesson with students.

⚡ FLIP IT!
Assign the Flipped Video for this lesson.

■ STUDENT EDITION PRINT
PAGES: 286–291

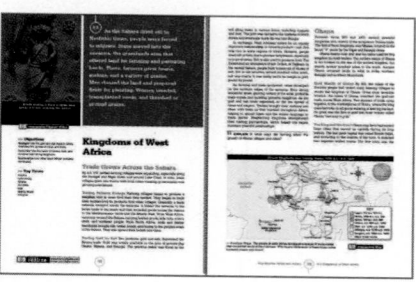

■ INVESTIGATE

 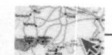

DIGITAL TEXT 1
Trade Grows Across the Sahara

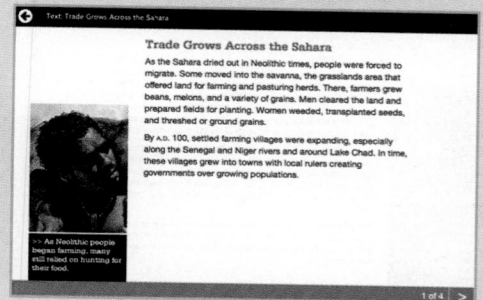

INTERACTIVE MAP
Trans-Saharan Trade (750 B.C.)

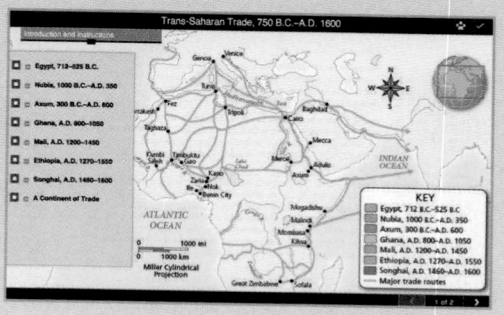

Objective 1: Understand why gold and salt were important to early Africa.

Quick Instruction
Remind students that salt is important to human health, and while abundant in the Sahara, it was rare in many other regions of Africa. In West Africa, gold was widely available. Trade networks that originally dealt in surplus agriculture expanded and became dominated by these two commodities.

Trans-Saharan Trade (750 B.C.–A.D. 1600): Interactive Map Project the map on the whiteboard and click through the boxes. Introduce the map activity by telling students that in West and East Africa a series of kingdoms developed as trade extended beyond village borders. Some of the cities along trade routes became wealthy international commercial centers.

👥 ACTIVE CLASSROOM
Using A Closer Look Strategy, use the whiteboard tool to divide the map into four numbered quadrants. Have students count off from 1 to 4. Next, have them look closely at the part of the image in their quadrant. Have them discuss what they see. Ask students why the trade routes in their quadrant are shaped as they are. Have them explain how these trade routes facilitated the spread of ideas and goods. Ask students what geographic factors might have impeded or helped spur trade.

D Differentiate: Challenge Pair students and explain to them they are going to assume the role of traders. Have the students negotiate for about five minutes with each other over goods that they have and that the other trader might want, such as pencils, erasers, books, pens, etc. When the time is up, ask each pair of students whether they were able to successfully complete a deal. Ask them to explain the problems they encountered and the benefits of the trade.

ELL Use the ELL activity described in the ELL chart.

Further Instruction
Project and go over Interactive Reading Notepad questions.

Evaluate Ask students to explain how trade might have allowed Islam to spread among the kingdoms of West Africa and what impact Islam had on those kingdoms. *(Students might say that Muslim merchants brought their Islamic faith with them to many West African kingdoms, and as a result, their ideas impacted the political, economic, and social fabric of those communities.)*

Kingdoms of West Africa

DIGITAL TEXT 2
Ghana

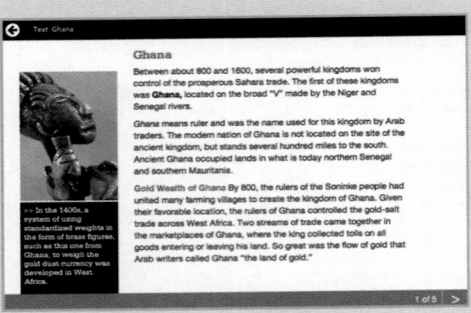

DIGITAL TEXT 3
Mali

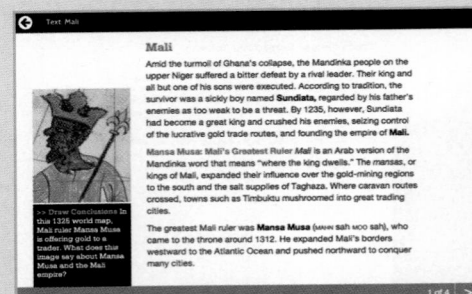

DIGITAL TEXT 4
Songhai

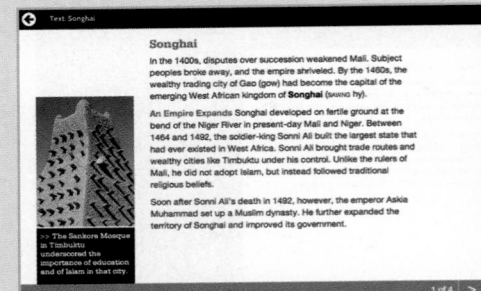

Objective 2: Describe how the rulers of Ghana, Mali, and Songhai built strong kingdoms.

Quick Instruction

Tell students that the control of gold-salt trade routes across West Africa made the kingdom of Ghana very wealthy. Its capital was divided into two walled towns, one dominated by the court, the other with prosperous Muslim merchants. Muslim traders brought the Arabic language and writing, coinage, and new business methods. While Muslims introduced their culture to Ghana and were influential in court as counselors and officials, Islam was slow to spread. The Almoravid caliphate overwhelmed Ghana around 1050 but was unable to maintain control of the region. The kingdom of Mali emerged in the region, and its greatest ruler, Mansa Musa, converted to Islam.

Project the image of details of Mansa Musa's hajj and note the role he played promoting Mali's reputation and helping Timbuktu become a center of learning. Discuss how the Songhai empire arose in the region after the kingdom of Mali weakened. Draw comparisons to the importance Islam played in both kingdoms and the ties it forged to the Muslim world.

Artifacts from West Africa's Great Kingdoms: Image Gallery Project the image gallery on the whiteboard and go through each image as it appears. Tell students that trade made the kingdoms of West Africa rich and that evidence of their prosperity and culture can be found in the art, textiles, ideas, and literature that each society left behind.

Analyze Images What do you think the fourth image in the gallery, Gold Art from Ghana, says about trade and the kingdom's wealth? *(Answers will vary. Students might say that Ghana's gold lured merchants from a variety of places, making the kingdom a bustling center of trade and power.)*

🎥 ACTIVE CLASSROOM

In 1324, Mansa Musa made a hajj, or pilgrimage, to Mecca. People at the time said that his traveling caravan was one of the most wondrous sights they had ever seen. Let's say that you were a reporter traveling with Mansa Musa. Write down a series of questions you'd like to ask him and what you would expect him to say to you.

Further Instruction

Project and go over the Interactive Reading Notepad questions.

Discuss Explain how Sonni Ali made Songhai a wealthy kingdom after Mali's empire shriveled. *(Students might say that Sonni Ali made Songhai a powerful kingdom by bringing trade routes and wealthy cities under his control.)*

INTERACTIVE GALLERY

Artifacts from West Africa's Great Kingdoms

Gold made Ghana wealthy, but iron weapons made the kingdom powerful. Iron was strong and helped Ghana defeat its enemies.

DIGITAL TEXT 5

Small Societies and Kingdoms of West Africa

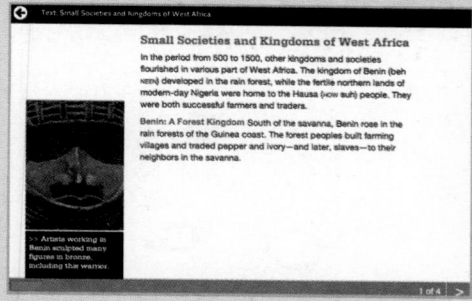

Objective 3: Summarize how other West African societies developed.

Quick Instruction

Remind students that smaller kingdoms flourished in West Africa in the period from 500 to 1500. They included the forest kingdom of Benin, and the city-states of the Hausa. Tell students that a three-mile long wall surrounded the capital of Benin and that their king was a political, judicial, and religious leader. The queen mother and a council of chiefs were also important. Discuss the impact Ife artisans had on the development of brass and bronze sculptures in Benin. The walled cities of the Hausa, built for protection from invaders, expanded into thriving commercial centers with vast trade networks. Some of the city-states had kings who were Muslims, resulting in an Islamic influence on the region. Some of the cities were ruled by women.

Summarize Ask students to explain how the walled cities of the Hausa impacted trade. *(Students might say the walled cities provided merchants and traders protection, which allowed cities to expand and thrive.)*

ELL Use the ELL activity described in the ELL chart.

Compare and Contrast Compare the influence of Islam on the political and economic life in Mali and Songhai. *(Students might say that in Mali, Islam was important to forging economic and political ties with other Muslim nations, although the country's rulers did not impose Islam on the population. In Songhai, the kingdom did not at first follow Islam, but traditional religious beliefs. However, as time went on, Islam greatly influenced the kingdom's government and economy.)*

Further Instruction

Project the Interactive Reading Notepad questions. Ask students to analyze the interaction between Ife and Benin and how this relationship impacted Benin. *(Students might say Ife taught Benin how to cast bronze and brass, which allowed Benin sculptors to develop their own unique style.)*

Kingdoms of West Africa

■ SYNTHESIZE

DIGITAL ACTIVITY
Mansa Musa's Pilgrimage

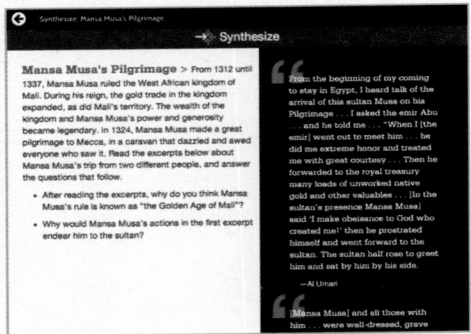

Ask students to recall the Topic Essential Question: How are religion and culture connected? Ask students to spend three minutes writing down a response to this question on a sticky note. Have students post their sticky notes on the board. Ask students to look at all the various responses from other students then discuss similarities and differences in the responses as a group.

Explain to students that Mansa Musa's journey demonstrated the wealth and religious connections of the kingdom. Next, have them draw a compelling image of one of the scenes in the story.

Discuss When the students are finished, ask them to discuss the image they created. Ask them to describe the impact of the journey. *(Students might say Mansa Musa showed the wealth of the kingdom, the relationship of trade in Africa, and the importance of Islam.)*

■ DEMONSTRATE

DIGITAL QUIZ
Lesson Quiz and Class Discussion Board

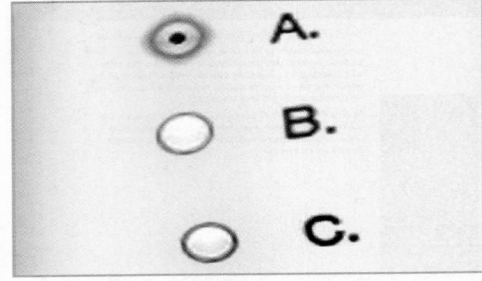

Assign the online Lesson Quiz for this lesson if you haven't already done so. Students will be offered automatic remediation or enrichment based on their score. Pose these questions to the class on the Discussion Board:

In "Kingdoms of West Africa," you read about how the gold and salt trade allowed many African nations to prosper. You also read how the rulers of Ghana, Mali, and Songhai built strong kingdoms and how other West African societies developed.

Predict Consequences Do you think West Africa would have developed differently had Muslim traders not dominated trade on the continent? *(Students might say that many African societies might have been more influenced by other outsiders, such as those from Europe, had Muslim traders not brought Islam to Africa. Islam dominated the educational, political, economic, and social institutions of many West African kingdoms.)*

Identify What impact did Islam have on education, government, and economics in West Africa? *(Students might say that in many West African kingdoms, Islamic schools were built; new ideas about governments were introduced; and Islam helped many nations forge trading ties with other Muslim lands.)*

Topic Inquiry
Have students continue their investigations for the Topic Inquiry.

Trading States of East Africa

Supporting English Language Learners

Use with Digital Text 1, **Axum.**

Listening

Read *Axum* aloud to students. Then have students participate in the following activities, which focus on identifying implicit information.

Beginning Before beginning, explain explicit and implicit information to students. Have students listen as *Axum* is read aloud twice. During the first reading, have students listen carefully. Before the second reading, tell them to listen for explicit information. After reading, guide the students to share the factual information they heard, for example, Geez was the unique written and spoken language of the Axum. Using a sentence frame like the one below, help students understand that implicit information is sometimes suggested by several pieces of explicit information in the text.

- Geez was the unique written and spoken _____ of the Axum. [language]
- Implicit information: The Axum used tools to write, like we use paper and pencils.

Intermediate Before reading, review explicit and implicit information with students. Have students listen as *Axum* is read aloud twice. During the first reading, have students listen carefully. Before the second reading, tell them to listen for and write down explicit information in the text. Have students share the explicit information they found, and then guide them to determine the implicit information from the text.

Advanced Have students listen as *Axum* is read aloud. Instruct students to write down the explicit information they hear in the text. Then have students use the explicit information they heard to determine the implicit information in the section. Finally, have students turn to a partner to share their findings. Circulate among students to offer support as needed.

Advanced High Have students work in small groups to determine the explicit information and implicit information in *Axum*. Have one student in each group read the text aloud while the others take notes on the explicit information. Then instruct the groups to discuss and identify the implicit information in the text. Finally, discuss each group's findings with the entire class.

Use with Digital Text 2, **Ethiopia.**

Speaking

Before beginning this activity, read *Ethiopia* aloud to the class. Then have students practice saying different types of sentences according to their level of English proficiency.

Read the following examples based on *Ethiopia.*

- Ethiopia was separated from other cultures by mountains.
- Why did Ethiopian Jews leave the mountains in the late 1900s?
- Look at the photos of medieval Ethiopia.
- Lalibela's churches were built down into the ground!

Beginning Review the four types of sentences with students. Then read the sentences above and have students repeat them. Listen to make sure that students are pronouncing each word correctly and help them make corrections as needed. Then ask students to say one declarative sentence about what they learned from reading *Ethiopia.* Assist them as needed.

Intermediate Provide students with the four sentence types listed above. Instruct students to say two declarative and two interrogative sentences to a partner about what they learned from reading *Ethiopia.* Provide additional examples and assistance to students as needed.

Advanced Have pairs of students work together to identify each of the four sentence types as the examples above are read aloud. Then instruct students to say three declarative, three interrogative, and three imperative sentences about the information they learned from reading *Ethiopia.* Encourage students to speak using increasingly complex sentences.

Advanced High Have students identify each of the four sentence types as the examples above are read aloud. Then have students work with a partner to take turns saying several sentences of each type. The sentences should relate to the information students learned from reading *Ethiopia.*

▶ Differentiate Instruction

Use the Differentiated Instruction notes throughout the lesson plan to support the varied skill sets, levels of readiness, and interests in the mixed-ability classroom.

Challenge These notes include suggestions for expanding the activity for advanced students.

On-Level These notes include suggestions for modifying the activity to address different interests or learning styles.

Extra Support These notes include ideas for providing more scaffolding or reading spuport.

Special Needs These notes provide ideas for adapting instruction to support the needs of various special needs students.

■ NOTES

Trading States of East Africa

Objectives

Objective 1: Explain how religion influenced the development of Axum and Ethiopia.

Objective 2: Understand how trade affected the city-states in East Africa.

Objective 3: Describe the economy of Great Zimbabwe.

LESSON 7 ORGANIZER		PACING: APPROX. 1 PERIOD, .5 BLOCKS			
				RESOURCES	
		OBJECTIVES	**PACING**	**Online**	**Print**
Connect					
DIGITAL START UP ACTIVITY **Trading States of East Africa**			5 min.	●	
Investigate					
DIGITAL TEXT 1 **Axum**		Objective 1	10 min.	●	●
DIGITAL TEXT 2 **Ethiopia**			10 min.	●	●
DIGITAL TEXT 3 **City-States of East Africa**		Objective 2	10 min.	●	●
INTERACTIVE MAP **Journeys of Ibn Battuta**			10 min.	●	
DIGITAL TEXT 4 **Great Zimbabwe**		Objective 3	10 min.	●	●
INTERACTIVE GALLERY **Architecture of the African Kingdoms**			10 min.	●	
Synthesize					
DIGITAL ACTIVITY **Kingdoms and Trading States of East Africa**			5 min.	●	
Demonstrate					
DIGITAL QUIZ **Lesson Quiz and Class Discussion Board**			10 min.	●	

PEARSON realize. www.PearsonRealize.com

Go online to access additional resources including:
Primary Sources • Biographies • Supreme Court cases •
21st Century Skill Tutorials • Maps • Graphic Organizers.

CONNECT

DIGITAL START UP ACTIVITY
Trading States of East Africa

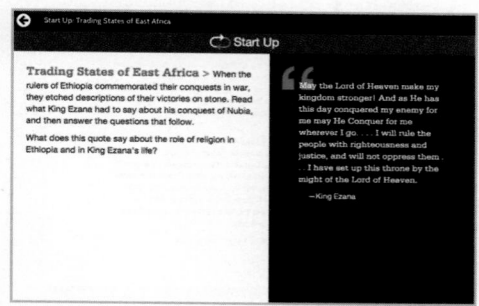

Project the Start Up Activity As they get settled, ask students to read the passage and answer the question that follows. What does this quote reflect about the role of religion in Ethiopia and in King Ezana's life? Have students share their ideas with another student, either in class or through a chat or blog.

Discuss How can religion and other beliefs influence and unify a society? *(Students might say that members of a group often share common beliefs and values, including religion. Such beliefs provide a strong sense of identity.)*

Tell students that in this lesson they will be learning about how religion influenced the development of Axum and Ethiopia. They'll also be learning how trade affected many East African societies.

Aa Vocabulary Development: Use the Interactive Reading Notepad to preview the Key Terms and Academic Vocabulary in the Lesson with students.

⇡ FLIP IT!
Assign the Flipped Video for this lesson.

■ STUDENT EDITION PRINT PAGES: 292–297

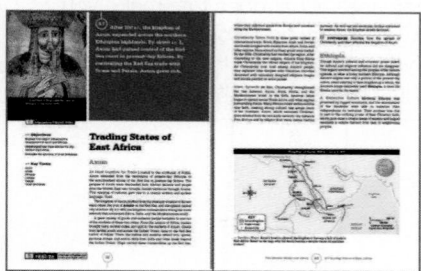

INVESTIGATE

DIGITAL TEXT 1
Axum

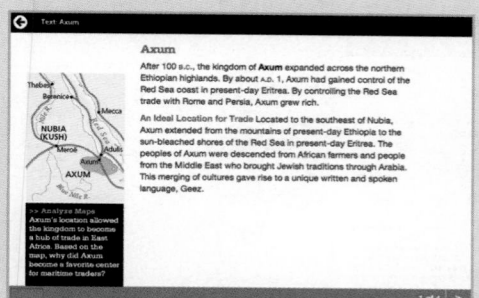

Objective 1: Explain how religion influenced the development of Axum and Ethiopia.

Quick Instruction
Introduce the readings by explaining to students that Axumite kings frequently called Axum, Ethiopia, a term the Greeks used for the region. Tell students that Axum was a major center of trade that allowed the kingdom to grow and prosper. Greek, Egyptian, Arab, and Jewish merchants interacted with one another. Eventually, Christianity would greatly influence the region, even after Axum's political and economic power faded. Note that Christianity, which had once strengthened Axum's ties to its trading partners, isolated it as Islam spread to much of the region. In medieval Ethiopia, which was protected by mountains, the descendants of Axumites maintained their independence for centuries. Their Christian faith was a unifying force, creating a cultural identity different from those of neighboring peoples. Project the image of the Axum Trade Route map (A.D. 300–700) on the whiteboard and allow students to study it.

ELL Use the ELL activity described in the ELL chart.

Further Instruction
Draw Conclusions What was it about Axum's location that allowed religion to influence the region? *(Students may say that Axum's location allowed trade routes to develop that brought people from different cultures and different religions to the region.)*

DIGITAL TEXT 2
Ethiopia

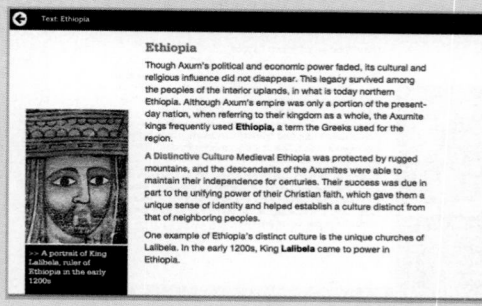

Identify Cause and Effect Explain how Islam influenced Ethiopia's development. *(Sample response: Ethiopia, which was a Christian kingdom, grew isolated from its own trade network as its trading partners began to embrace Islam.)*

D Differentiate: Challenge Ask students to name three examples of how religion has influenced their community. *(Students might say that churches help the poor; feed the homeless; provide meeting spaces for local groups, etc.)*

Trading States of East Africa

DIGITAL TEXT 3
City-States of East Africa

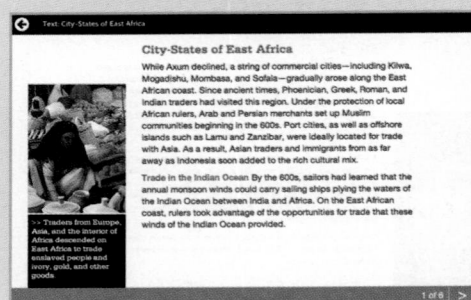

INTERACTIVE MAP
Journeys of Ibn Battuta

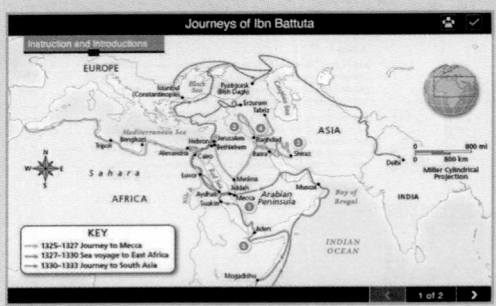

DIGITAL TEXT 4
Great Zimbabwe

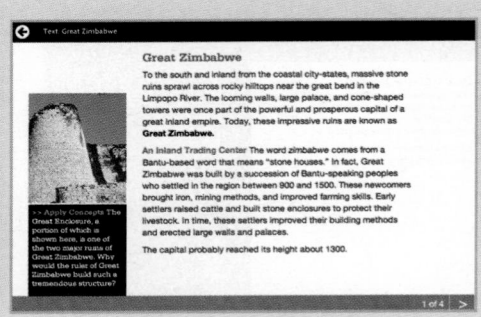

Objective 2: **Understand how trade affected the city-states of East Africa.**

Quick Instruction

Tell students that the city-states along the coast of East Africa reflected the diversity of the merchants who traded there, such as the Muslim communities that were established. Point out that the monsoon winds were critical to the shipping between Africa and India across the Indian Ocean, leading to trade that stretched from the interior of Africa to India, Southeast Asia, and China. Discuss the emergence of Swahili as a culture and language, including the contributions of traders from the Middle East and Asia who settled in the coastal cities.

Journeys of Ibn Battuta: Interactive Map Project the hotspot map on the whiteboard and click through each hotspot. Introduce the map activity by telling students that Ibn Battuta was a Muslim man who at the age of 21 decided to make a pilgrimage to Mecca in Saudi Arabia. During his journey, Battuta visited much of Southwest Asia, East Africa, and other regions.

ACTIVE CLASSROOM

Let's say you were traveling with Ibn Battuta on his trip. After studying the hotspots on the map, do additional research on all of the regions and write a travel blog that you can either post online or print out for your classmates to read. In your blog, explain what life was like in each location, and what you might have seen had you actually traveled with Battuta.

Compare and Contrast Compare the travels of Ibn Battuta with the travels of Mansa Musa from the previous lesson. Are there any similarities? Are there any differences? *(Sample response: Similarities: Both men were Muslim. Both showed their devotion to Islam by making a pilgrimage to Mecca. Differences: Mansa Musa traveled mostly in North Africa and Saudi Arabia; Battuta traveled not only across Saudi Arabia, but throughout Asia and East Africa. Mansa Musa traveled with a great caravan that showed Mali's wealth.)*

Further Instruction

Go through the Interactive Reading Notepad questions and discuss the answers with the class.

Describe Describe the impact Islam had on the city-states of East Africa. *(Sample response: Arab and Persian traders descended on the East African city-states and set up Muslim communities in those areas. Local culture, such as language and architecture, also reflects Arabic influence.)*

Objective 3: **Describe the economy of Great Zimbabwe.**

Quick Instruction

Architecture of the African Kingdoms: Image Gallery Project the image gallery on the whiteboard and go through each image as they appear. Tell students that the various architectural forms in Africa differed greatly from society to society and from geographic region to geographic region. In some places, architecture reflected a community's culture or wealth, while in other cases, it showcased the influence of religion.

Analyze Images Study the photo of the Gede Ruins and the image of Ethiopia's Sculpted Churches of Lalibela. How did religion influence the design of these buildings? *(Sample responses: In Gede, the ancient mosques underscored the importance of Islam in that prosperous Swahili community, while Ethiopia's sculpted churches reflected Christianity's influence on that kingdom.)*

ACTIVE CLASSROOM

Using the See-Think-Wonder strategy, pair students and ask them to review each image in the photo gallery. Ask them: What do you see? What does that make you think? What are you wondering about now that you've seen this? Have students share their insights with the class.

■ SYNTHESIZE

■ DEMONSTRATE

INTERACTIVE GALLERY
Architecture of the African Kingdoms

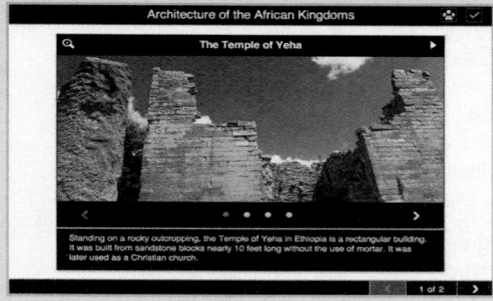

DIGITAL ACTIVITY
Kingdoms and Trading States of East Africa

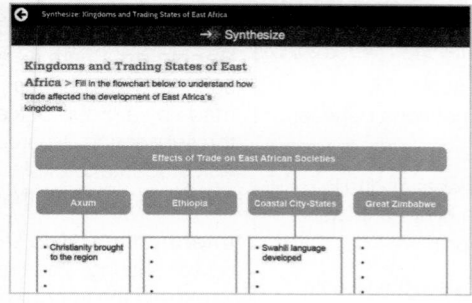

DIGITAL QUIZ
Lesson Quiz and Class Discussion Board

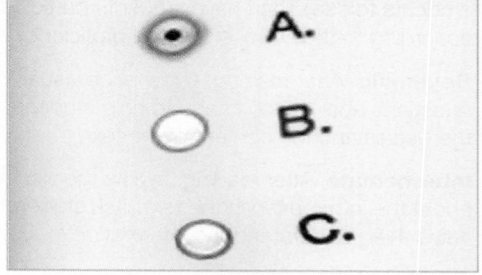

Further Instruction

Go through the Interactive Reading Notepad questions and discuss the answers with the class.

To extend the teaching of this objective, ask students to analyze how people lived, worked, and played in Great Zimbabwe by doing additional research on the kingdom. Have students print out pictures of any relics that they might have found that underscore the importance of Great Zimbabwe as a trading center.

D **Differentiate: Challenge** Ask students to create and perform a fictional reader's theater based on the society of Great Zimbabwe. The parts for the reader's theater can include: a narrator; a king; a Muslim merchant; a trader from China; a skilled artisan; and member of Zimbabwe's community. The play should revolve around Great Zimbabwe as a hub of trade in East Africa.

Ask students to recall the Topic Essential Question: How are religion and culture connected? Ask students to create a Concept Web to show the relationship.

Identify Cause and Effect Project the Synthesize flow chart, Kingdoms and Trading States of East Africa, on the whiteboard. Explain to students trade was essential to the development of many East African societies, including Axum, Ethiopia, the Coastal City-States, and Great Zimbabwe. As you discuss the causes and effects with students, have them fill in the chart.

Assign the online Lesson Quiz for this lesson if you haven't already done so. Students will be offered automatic remediation or enrichment based on their score. Pose these questions to the class on the Discussion Board:

In "Trading States of East Africa," you read about how trade and religion influenced the cultural, political, economic, and social fabric in many East African nations.

Predict Consequences Do you think Ethiopia would have developed differently had the nation embraced Islam as opposed to Christianity? *(Students might say that if Ethiopia had embraced Islam, it would not have found itself isolated from its one-time trading partners, many of whom were influenced by Islam.)*

Compare and Contrast Describe any similarities between the trade routes in East Africa and the trade routes in West Africa. *(Sample Response: Each region had trade routes that linked Africa to the Mediterranean world; both connected the interior to coastal regions; both traded in gold.)*

Topic Inquiry

Have students continue their investigations for the Topic Inquiry.

Diverse Peoples and Traditions in Africa

Supporting English Language Learners

Use with Digital Text 4, **Art and Literature.**

Listening

Read *Art and Literature* aloud as students listen without looking at their texts. As you read, display corresponding visuals (included in the text) for students to see. Then have students participate in the following activities according to their level of English proficiency.

Beginning After reading, show each visual to students again. Ask questions about each image to help students make connections between the visuals and the content of the text.

Intermediate After reading, review the visuals with students and talk about the information in the text. Ask students to explain how each visual helps them understand the information in *Art and Literature*.

Advanced After reading, instruct pairs of students to review the visuals and identify ways that each visual helped them understand the information in *Art and Literature*.

Advanced High After reading, instruct students to review *Art and Literature* independently. Have students choose a piece of information or concept from the text that does not have a corresponding visual. Students should sketch a visual that helps explain that piece of information or concept and share it with the class.

Use with Digital Text 2, **Government and Power.**

Listening

Before beginning this activity, read *Government and Power* aloud to the class. Then have students complete one of the following activities depending on their level of English proficiency.

Beginning Share an everyday example of power-sharing with students, such as decisions that are made together by parents or a decision made by a group of friends. Then summarize the important details in the subsection "Shared Power" for students using simple sentences. Ask students to explain similarities between their everyday examples of power-sharing and those of smaller medieval African societies.

Intermediate Help students generate examples of modern, everyday power-sharing. Then read "Shared Power" aloud and ask students to explain the important details of power-sharing described in this subsection. Help students explain how the power-sharing described in the text is similar to the examples generated at the beginning of the activity.

Advanced Facilitate a large group discussion of power-sharing examples in modern, everyday life. After students identify several examples of power-sharing, have them summarize the important details from the passage and make connections between the everyday examples of power-sharing and the examples described in the subsection "Shared Power."

Advanced High Have small groups of students generate examples of power-sharing in modern, everyday life. Then instruct groups to summarize the important details of what they learned about power-sharing among medieval African societies from listening to "Shared Power." Finally, ask small groups to make connections between the way these African groups shared power and the way modern people share power. Ask small groups to share the important details of their discussions with the large group.

▣ Differentiate Instruction

Use the Differentiated Instruction notes throughout the lesson plan to support the varied skill sets, levels of readiness, and interests in the mixed-ability classroom.

Challenge These notes include suggestions for expanding the activity for advanced students.

On-Level These notes include suggestions for modifying the activity to address different interests or learning styles.

Extra Support These notes include ideas for providing more scaffolding or reading spuport.

Special Needs These notes provide ideas for adapting instruction to support the needs of various special needs students.

▮ NOTES

PEARSON
realize™
www.PearsonRealize.com

Go online to access additional resources including:
Primary Sources • Biographies • Supreme Court cases •
21st Century Skill Tutorials • Maps • Graphic Organizers.

Objectives

Objective 1: Identify the different ways that the family influenced medieval African cultures.

Objective 2: Describe the variety of forms of medieval African governments.

Objective 3: Understand the role of religion and art in medieval societies.

LESSON 8 ORGANIZER — PACING: APPROX. 1 PERIOD, .5 BLOCKS

		OBJECTIVES	PACING	Online	Print
				RESOURCES	
Connect					
DIGITAL START UP ACTIVITY **The Dama**			5 min.	●	
Investigate					
DIGITAL TEXT 1 **Many Cultures and Patterns of Life**		Objective 1	10 min.	●	●
INTERACTIVE CHART **Family Patterns in African Society**			10 min.	●	
DIGITAL TEXT 2 **Government and Power**		Objective 2	10 min.	●	
DIGITAL TEXT 3 **Religion**			10 min.	●	●
DIGITAL TEXT 4 **Art and Literature**		Objective 3	10 min.	●	●
INTERACTIVE GALLERY **African Art and Culture**			10 min.	●	
Synthesize					
DIGITAL ACTIVITY **African Society**			5 min.	●	
Demonstrate					
DIGITAL QUIZ **Lesson Quiz and Class Discussion Board**			10 min.	●	

Diverse Peoples and Traditions in Africa

■ CONNECT

DIGITAL START UP ACTIVITY
The Dama

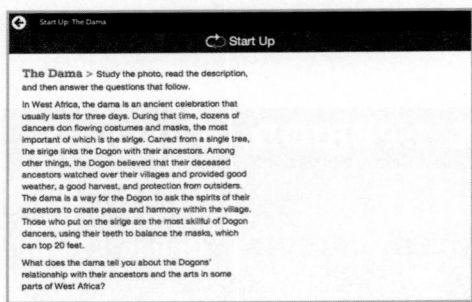

Project the Start Up Activity Ask students to read the passage and answer the questions as they enter and get settled. Identify in two or three sentences what the dama tells you about ancestral relationships in some parts of West Africa. *(Sample response: The dance reflects the importance the Dogon placed on their deceased ancestors. This ancestor worship meant that the Dogon valued family relationships above all else.)*

Tell students that in this lesson they will be learning about different ways that family patterns influenced medieval African cultures; the different forms of medieval African governments; and how religion and art impacted African society.

Aa Vocabulary Development: Use the Interactive Reading Notepad to preview the Key Terms and Academic Vocabulary in the Lesson with students.

↳ FLIP IT!

Assign the Flipped Video for this lesson.

■ STUDENT EDITION PRINT
PAGES: 298–302

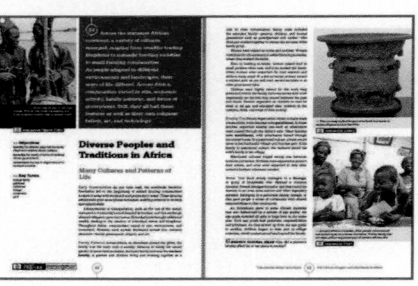

■ INVESTIGATE

DIGITAL TEXT 1
Many Cultures and Patterns of Life

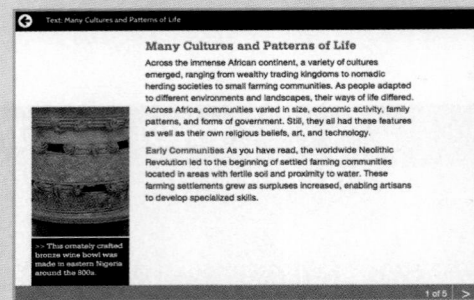

INTERACTIVE CHART
Family Patterns in African Society

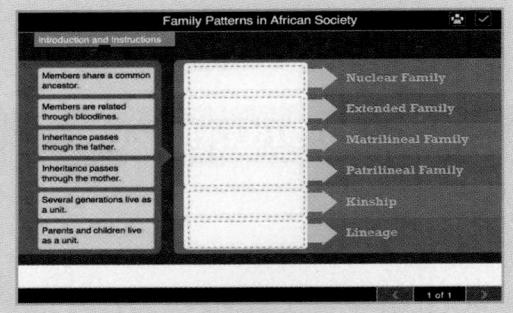

Objective 1: Identify the different ways that the family influenced medieval African cultures.

Quick Instruction

Family Patterns in African Society: Interactive Chart Project the Interactive Chart on the whiteboard. Introduce the activity by telling students that there were several types of family relationships in African society. Explain that patterns of family life varied greatly depending on the culture of the group. In some communities, the nuclear family was the main family unit, while in other cultures, extended families dominated society.

▦ ACTIVE CLASSROOM

Using the Graffiti Concept strategy, have students reflect on each of the family relationships in African society. Next, have students create a visual image that represents each concept. Allow 3 to 5 minutes. When time is up, ask students to post their "graffiti" on the board. Have the class look at the various responses, and discuss any similarities or differences between each family relationship.

D Differentiate: Challenge Have students learn about their own families by creating a time line of their family's history. Have students interview family members and record such things as marriages, immigration dates, births, deaths, and divorces.

Further Instruction

Project and go over Interactive Reading Notepad questions.

Identify Ask students to describe the roles of children in some medieval African cultures. *(Sample response: In some cultures, an individual's place was determined by a system of age grades that included all the children born in a particular year. Those age grades determined a child's responsibilities in that society.)*

DIGITAL TEXT 2

Government and Power

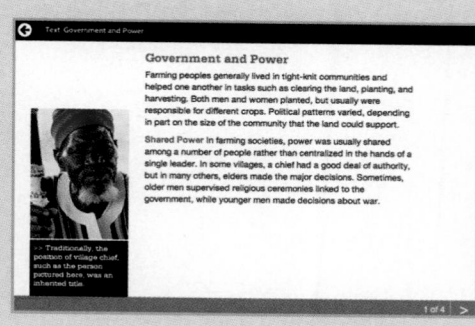

DIGITAL TEXT 3

Religion

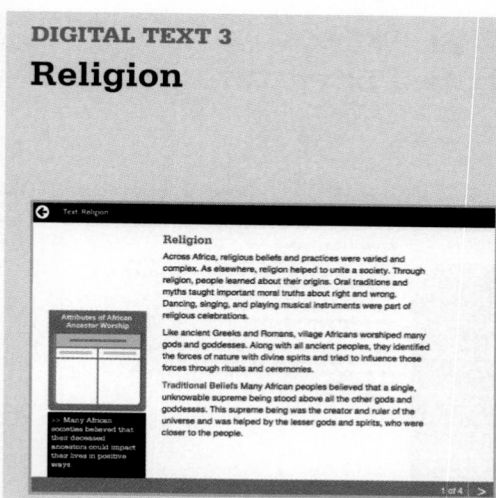

Objective 2: Describe the variety of forms of medieval African governments.

Quick Instruction

Remind students that in larger kingdoms, villages had to obey decisions and pay taxes and provide soldiers to a centralized, and often distant, court. In some kingdoms, a monarch's power was somewhat limited. Unlike larger African kingdoms, the governments of smaller medieval African societies were often organized through power-sharing arrangements rather than centralized in the hands of a single leader. While in some societies a chief had a good deal of authority, most decisions were made collectively. Explain that consensus was a common method of decision-making, with the wisdom of older men and women carrying the most weight in many village decisions.

ELL Use the ELL activity described in the ELL chart.

Further Instruction

Project and discuss Interactive Reading Notepad questions.

Summarize How does a power-sharing government in Africa work? *(Answers may vary. Students should have an understanding that in a power-sharing system, members of a village, rather than a single leader, would make decisions based on consensus.)*

Draw Inferences Why might the opinions of older individuals carry more weight than the opinions of younger people? *(Answers may vary. Some students may say that the experience and wisdom of older people carried the greatest weight.)*

Compare and Contrast What differences existed between the form of government found in an African kingdom and the form of government found in a smaller village? *(Answers may vary. Students should have an understanding that in a kingdom, taxes were collected through local governors, and the king had to rule according to traditional laws. The governments of smaller villages were led generally by a chief with limited power, and the main decision-making body was often a group of village elders. Villages did not have standing armies as in a kingdom.)*

Objective 3: Understand the role of religion and art in medieval societies.

Quick Instruction

African Art and Culture: Interactive Gallery Project the Interactive Gallery on the whiteboard. Introduce the activity by telling students that art's important role in the culture of many communities can be seen in African jewelry, dance, music, and literature. Click through the images in the gallery. Then explain to students that religion and art were important to the development of medieval African societies. Tell students that the religious beliefs that existed before the arrival of Islam and Christianity were often complex and varied. Some Africans worshiped multiple gods and goddesses; others believed, as Muslims and Christians did, of one supreme being. In other African cultures, ancestor worship dominated.

▶ ACTIVE CLASSROOM

After reviewing all the images in the Interactive Gallery, use the Act it Out strategy to make the images come to life. Have students choose one of the images and create a story around that image.

Diverse Peoples and Traditions in Africa

DIGITAL TEXT 4

Art and Literature

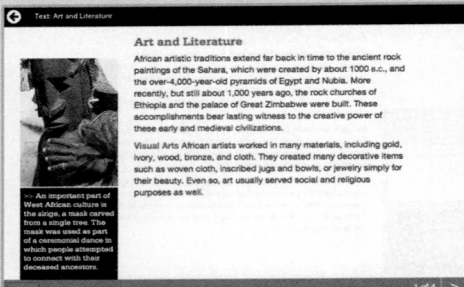

INTERACTIVE GALLERY

African Art and Culture

Describe Explain how literature, art, and religion influenced medieval African society. *(Answers may vary. Students should have an understanding that literature, religion, and art encouraged a sense of community and common values with medieval African societies.)*

Determine Relevance How was art connected to religion in African cultures? *(Sample response: Statues and other objects were used in religious rights and ceremonies.)*

D Differentiate: Challenge Have students connect to the past by creating their own oral histories. Encourage students to record interviews with older family members about a specific event in their lives, such as living through a war or some other event. Students can also interview family members about family history. When the assignment is completed, call on students to talk about what they learned about their family's history.

ELL Use the ELL activity described in the ELL chart.

Further Instruction

Project and discuss Interactive Reading Notepad questions. Also, project the info graphic on African ancestor worship.

Draw Inferences Why do you suppose many African societies believed that their deceased ancestors could impact the lives of those living on Earth? *(Answers may vary. Students should show an understanding that family relationships were very important to many Africans, and as a result, deceased family members could positively influence their lives by bringing them good luck, protection, and fortune.)*

Determine Central Ideas Why were Christianity and Islam able to absorb some of the beliefs of many African religions? *(Sample response: Some students might say that those who adopted these religions often associated the God of Christians and Muslims with their traditional supreme being.)*

SYNTHESIZE

DEMONSTRATE

DIGITAL ACTIVITY

African Society

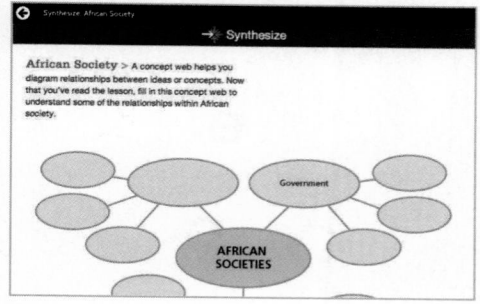

Project the Synthesize activity on the whiteboard. Introduce the activity by reviewing how to create a content web. Students can complete the activity independently, in pairs, or in groups.

Ask students to list the different ways families, government, and religion were connected to African society. Next, have them rank which concept they believe was the most important. Have them explain their reasons for the ranking. *(Answers will vary. Students' answers should reflect an understanding of the various family, religious, and governmental relationships discussed in the lesson.)*

DIGITAL QUIZ

Lesson Quiz and Class Discussion Board

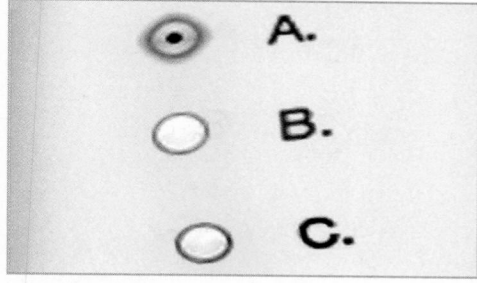

Assign the online Lesson Quiz for this lesson if you haven't already done so. Students will be offered automatic remediation or enrichment based on their score. Pose these questions to the class on the Discussion Board:

In "Diverse Peoples and Traditions in Africa," you learned about the role that families, government, and religion played in medieval African societies. You also read about the importance of art, literature, and music.

Evaluate How did kinship ties influence daily life in medieval Africa? *(Sample response: Kinship ties were an important factor in determining the people that an individual identified with, lived with, worked with, and supported and could expect support from.)*

Summarize How can artistic traditions identify a community and its environment? *(Sample response: Art was created using locally available materials, and often illustrated the community's beliefs.)*

Topic Inquiry

Have students continue their investigations for the Topic Inquiry.

The Muslim World and Africa (730 B.C.–A.D. 1500)

SYNTHESIZE

DIGITAL ACTIVITY

Reflect on the Essential Question and Topic

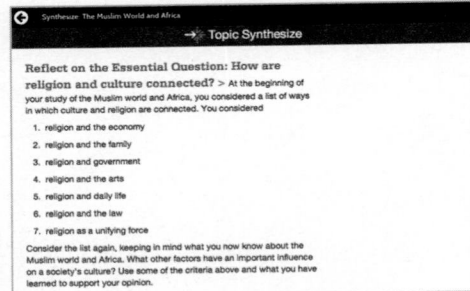

First ask students to reconsider the Essential Question for the Topic: How are religion and culture connected? Remind students of the connections they considered at the start of the Topic. For example, - religion and the economy - religion and the family - religion and the government - religion and the arts - religion and daily life - religion and the law - religion as a unifying force. Ask students to consider the list again, keeping in mind what they now know about the Muslim world and Africa. Have them write down other factors that have an important influence on a society's culture, giving at least three other examples. Discuss their answers on the Class Discussion Board.

Next, ask students to reflect on the Topic as a whole and jot down 1–3 questions they've thought about during the Topic. Share these examples if students need help getting started: - How did Islam affect peoples' perception of family and daily life? - How did Islam affect the regions' arts, economy, and law? - In what ways did Islamic traditions influence government?

DEMONSTRATE

DIGITAL TOPIC REVIEW AND ASSESSMENT

The Muslim World and Africa (730 B.C.–A.D. 1500)

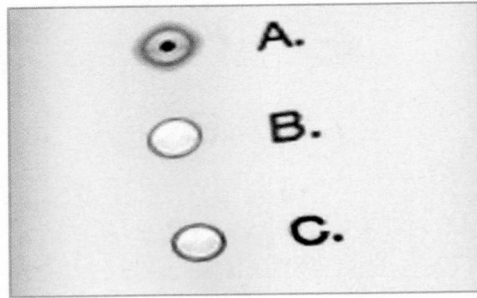

Students can prepare for the Topic Test by answering the questions in the Topic Review and Assessment online or the Assessment questions in the Print Student text. They can also prepare by reviewing their answers to the Interactive Reading Notepad questions or reviewing their notes in the Reading and Notetaking Study Guide.

DIGITAL TOPIC TEST

The Muslim World and Africa (730 B.C.–A.D. 1500)

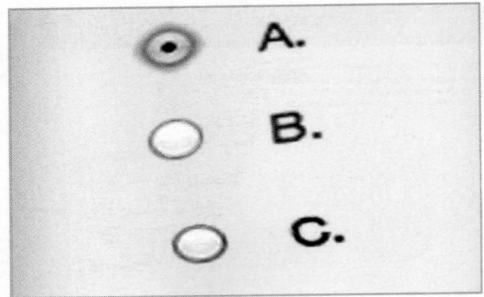

TOPIC TEST
Assign the Topic Test to assess students' understanding of topic content.

BENCHMARK TESTS
Assign these benchmark tests as you complete the relevant topics to monitor student progress toward mastering the course content and as preparation for the End-of-Course Test.

Benchmark Test 1: Topics 1–5

Benchmark Test 2: Topics 6–10

Benchmark Test 3: Topics 11–15

Benchmark Test 4: Topics 16–21

Civilizations of Asia (500–1650)

TOPIC 9 ORGANIZER	PACING: APPROX. 9 PERIODS, 4.5 BLOCKS
	PACING
Connect	1 period
MY STORY VIDEO Genghis Kahn, Conqueror	10 min.
DIGITAL ESSENTIAL QUESTION ACTIVITY What Distinguishes One Culture from Another?	10 min.
DIGITAL MAP ACTIVITY Civilizations of Asia	10 min.
TOPIC INQUIRY: CIVIC DISCUSSION Genghis Khan	20 min.
Investigate	3–6 periods
TOPIC INQUIRY: CIVIC DISCUSSION Genghis Khan	Ongoing
LESSON 1 The Delhi Sultanate and Mughal India	30–40 min.
LESSON 2 Golden Ages in China: Tang and Song Dynasties	30–40 min.
LESSON 3 The Mongol Empire and Ming China	30–40 min.
LESSON 4 Korea and Its Traditions	30–40 min.
LESSON 5 The Island Kingdom of Japan	30–40 min.
LESSON 6 The Many Cultures of Southeast Asia	30–40 min.
Synthesize	1 period
DIGITAL ACTIVITY Reflect on the Essential Question and Topic	10 min.
TOPIC INQUIRY: CIVIC DISCUSSION Genghis Khan	20 min.
Demonstrate	1–2 periods
DIGITAL TOPIC TEST Civilizations of Asia	10 min.
TOPIC INQUIRY: CIVIC DISCUSSION Genghis Khan	20 min.

TOPIC INQUIRY: CIVIC DISCUSSION

Genghis Khan

In this Topic Inquiry, students work in teams to examine different perspectives on this issue by analyzing several sources, arguing both sides of a Yes/No question, then developing and discussing their own point of view on the question: **Does Genghis Khan deserve to be known primarily for his cruelty and ruthlessness?**

STEP 1: CONNECT
Develop Questions and Plan the Investigation

Launch the Civic Discussion
Divide the class into groups of four students. Students can access the materials they'll need in the online course or you can distribute copies to each student. Read the main question and introduction with the students.

Have students complete Step 1 by reading the Discussion Launch and filling in Step 1 of the Information Organizer. The Discussion Launch provides YES and NO arguments on the main question. Students should extract and paraphrase the arguments from the reading in Step 1 of their Information Organizers.

Next, students share within their groups the arguments and evidence they found to support the YES and NO positions. The group needs to agree on the major YES and NO points and each student should note those points in their Information Organizer.

Resources
• Student Instructions • Information Organizer • Discussion Launch

STEP 2: INVESTIGATE
Apply Disciplinary Concepts and Tools

Examine Sources and Perspectives
Students will examine sources with the goal of extracting information and perspectives on the main question. They analyze each source and describe the author's perspective on the main question and key evidence the author provides to support that viewpoint in Information Organizer Step 2.

Ask students to keep in mind:
• **Author/Creator:** Who created the source? An individual? Group? Government agency?
• **Audience:** For whom was the source created?
• **Date/Place:** Is there any information that reveals where and when the source was created?
• **Purpose:** Why was the source created? Discuss with students the importance of this question in identifying bias.
• **Relevance:** How does the source support one argument or another?

Suggestion: Reading the source documents and filling in Step 2 of the Information Organizer could be assigned as homework.

Resources
• Student Instructions • Information Organizer • Source documents

⏻ PROFESSIONAL DEVELOPMENT

Civic Discussion
Be sure to view the Civic Discussion Professional Development resources in the online course.

STEP 3: SYNTHESIZE
Use Evidence to Formulate Conclusions

Formulate Compelling Arguments with Evidence
Now students will apply perspectives and evidence they extracted from the sources to think more deeply about the main question by first arguing one side of the issue, then the other. In this way students become more prepared to formulate an evidence-based conclusion on their own.

Within each student group, assign half of the students to take the position of YES on the main question and the others to take the position of NO. Students will work with their partners to identify the strongest arguments and evidence to support their assigned YES or NO position.

Present Yes/No Positions
Within each group, those assigned the YES position share arguments and evidence first. As the YES students speak, those assigned NO should listen carefully, take notes to fill in the rest of the Compelling Arguments Chart (Step 3 in Information Organizer) and ask clarifying questions.

When the YES side is finished, students assigned the NO position present while those assigned YES should listen, take notes, and ask clarifying questions. Examples of clarifying questions are:

- I think you just said [x]. Am I understanding you correctly?
- Can you tell me more about [x]?
- Can you repeat [x]? I am not sure I understand, yet.

Suggestion: You may want to set a 5 minute time limit for each side to present. Provide a two-minute warning so that students make their most compelling arguments within the time frame.

Switch Sides
The students will switch sides to argue the opposite point of view. To prepare to present the other position, partners who first argued YES will use the notes they took during the NO side's presentation, plus add any additional arguments and evidence from the reading and sources. The same for students who first argued the NO position.

STEP 4: DEMONSTRATE
Communicate Conclusions and Take Informed Action

Individual Points of View
Now the students will have the opportunity to discuss the main question from their own points of view. To help students prepare for this discussion, have them reflect on the YES/NO discussions they have participated in thus far and fill in Step 4 of their Information Organizers.

After all of the students have shared their points of view, each group should list points of agreement, filling the last portion of Step 4 on their Information Organizers.

Reflect on the Discussion
Ask students to reflect on the civic discussion thinking about:

- The value of having to argue both the YES and NO positions.
- If their individual views changed over the course of the discussion and why.
- What they learned from participating in the discussion.

Resources
- Student Instructions
- Information Organizer

INTRODUCTION

Civilizations of Asia (500–1650)

Various civilizations developed in Asia, including those in India, China, Korea, and Japan. Each civilization developed its own unique culture and institutions, but each was also strongly influenced by outside forces. As a result, there was a blending of ideas and knowledge that revealed itself in the artistic, scientific, social, and religious elements of each civilization.

■ CONNECT

MY STORY VIDEO

Genghis Kahn, Conqueror

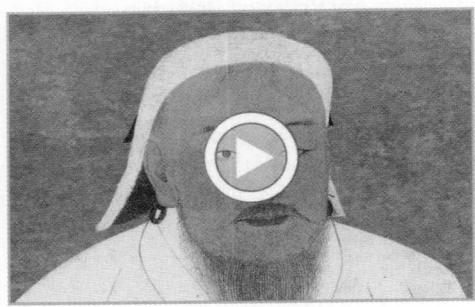

Watch a video about the life of Genghis Kahn.

Check Understanding From what part of the world did Genghis Kahn come? *(from the remote grasslands of Mongolia)*

Identify Central Issues Genghis Kahn's name means "Universal Ruler." Why is that an appropriate name? *(Genghis Kahn conquered and ruled a vast empire, stretching from the Pacific to the Caspian Sea.)*

⇅ FLIP IT!
Assign the My Story video.

DIGITAL ESSENTIAL QUESTION ACTIVITY

What Distinguishes One Culture from Another?

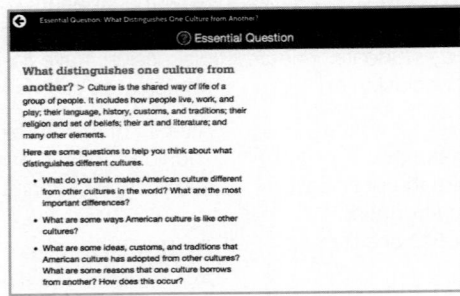

Ask students to think about the Essential Question for this Topic: What distinguishes one culture from another? Have a volunteer read each bulleted suggestion. Discuss them as a class.

Contrast What do you think makes American culture different from other cultures in the world? What are the most important differences? *(Students may point to American history, religion, popular culture; possible differences might include the importance of individual liberties, free enterprise, or equal opportunity.)*

Compare What are some ways American culture is like other cultures? *(Answers will vary. Possible examples include the importance of family values and relationships or strong religious beliefs.)*

Analyze What are some ideas, customs, and traditions that American culture has adopted from other cultures? What are some reasons that one culture borrows from another? How does this occur? *(Answers may include religions, ideas about government, and customs and traditions involving food, languages, dress, music and other arts.)*

Make Generalizations Are some values, beliefs, or ideas shared by all cultures? *(Answers will vary. Most students will agree that elements such as family love, patriotism, and desire to be useful are shared by all cultures.)*

DIGITAL MAP ACTIVITY

Civilizations of Asia

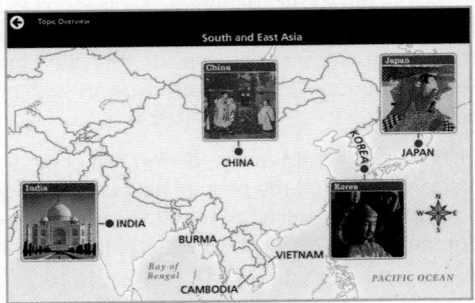

Display the map showing the civilizations of Asia that will be discussed during this Topic. Ask students to use the map to point out how location and geographic features might affect the development of these civilizations.

D Differentiate: Extra Support Have students locate Japan on the map. Ask, what factor in Japan's location might have helped it remain isolated from influences from other countries? *(It is an island.)*

Analyze Maps From what other countries might cultural influences on Cambodia and Vietnam come? Why? *(Possible answers: from China because it is the closest civilization to Cambodia and Vietnam; from India because it would have been easy to sail across the Bay of Bengal)*

Topic Inquiry

Launch the Topic Inquiry with students after introducing the Topic.

PEARSON realize™

www.PearsonRealize.com
Access your Digital Lesson

The Delhi Sultanate and Mughal India

Supporting English Language Learners

Use with Digital Text 1, **The Delhi Sultanate.**

Listening
Have students practice following directions below according to their level of English proficiency.

Beginning Explain that understanding and following directions is an important skill for school success. Then model how to follow directions for students. Write and display "Find and read *The Delhi Sultanate*." Tell students that the directions are to find this heading in the text and read the text that follows it. Model how to do this for students by locating the heading and reading the first paragraph of the text aloud. Then write and display "Find and read 'Struggles for Power' and 'Muslim Invaders Triumph.'" Help students locate these headings and read the first paragraph of the subsections.

Intermediate Remind students of the importance of following directions for school success. Write, display, and read aloud "Find and read *The Delhi Sultanate*." Ask a student volunteer to follow these directions for the group. Assist the student as needed until the directions are followed correctly. Then write and display "Find and read 'Struggles for Power' and 'Muslim Invaders Triumph.'" Have students locate these headings and then read each subsection aloud for students.

Advanced Ask students to explain the importance of following directions for school success. Then write, display, and read these directions: "Work with a partner to find and read *The Delhi Sultanate*. Take turns reading the text with your partner and take notes as you listen." Have students follow the directions as they are displayed. Support students as needed.

Advanced High Instruct students to follow these directions: "Read and take notes on *The Delhi Sultanate*. When you are finished, turn to a partner to check your notes and share two new facts that you learned from reading this section." Circulate among students to ensure comprehension.

Use with Digital Text 2, **The Meeting of Islam and Hinduism.**

Speaking
Before beginning this activity, read *The Meeting of Islam and Hinduism* aloud to the class. Then have students complete one of the following activities depending on their level of English proficiency.

Beginning Say the following sentences aloud and have students repeat them after you.

- The Muslim conquest of Northern India resulted in disaster for Hindus and Buddhists. Some sultans even left rajahs, or local Hindu rulers, in place.

- Muslims believed that all people were equal before God, but Hindus accepted differences in caste status.

Explain when to use the conjunctions *and*, *but*, and *or* to students. Instruct the students to say one sentence on their own using *and*, *but*, or *or*.

Intermediate Help students scan the text for sentences that include *and*, *but*, and *or*. Then help them say each of the sentences using correct pronunciation and increased fluency. Ask students to generate a short summary sentence using the word *and*.

Advanced Instruct pairs of students to scan the text for sentences with connecting words and phrases like *and*, *or*, *but*, *in fact*, *for example*, and *however*. When they find a sentence, have students pause and take turns saying them aloud to their partner.

Advanced High Instruct pairs of students to scan the text for sentences with connecting words and phrases like *and*, *or*, *but*, *in fact*, *for example*, and *however*. Then have students write and say three sentences about the information in *The Meeting of Islam and Hinduism* using connecting words in each one.

▶ Differentiate Instruction
Use the Differentiated Instruction notes throughout the lesson plan to support the varied skill sets, levels of readiness, and interests in the mixed-ability classroom.

Challenge These notes include suggestions for expanding the activity for advanced students.

On-Level These notes include suggestions for modifying the activity to address different interests or learning styles.

Extra Support These notes include ideas for providing more scaffolding or reading spuport.

Special Needs These notes provide ideas for adapting instruction to support the needs of various special needs students.

■ NOTES

Topic ⑨ Lesson 1

The Delhi Sultanate and Mughal India

Objectives

Objective 1: Describe the effects of the Delhi sultanate on India.

Objective 2: Explain how Muslim and Hindu civilizations interacted in India.

Objective 3: Describe the historical origins and central ideas of Sikhism.

Objective 4: Summarize the policies of Akbar that strengthened Mughal India.

LESSON 1 ORGANIZER		PACING: APPROX. 1 PERIOD, .5 BLOCKS			
				RESOURCES	
		OBJECTIVES	**PACING**	**Online**	**Print**
Connect					
DIGITAL START UP ACTIVITY **Akbar the Great Speaks on Religion**			5 min.	●	
Investigate					
DIGITAL TEXT 1 **The Delhi Sultanate**		Objective 1	10 min.	●	●
INTERACTIVE MAP **The Delhi Sultanate and Mughal Empire**			10 min.	●	
DIGITAL TEXT 2 **The Meeting of Islam and Hinduism**		Objective 2	10 min.	●	●
DIGITAL TEXT 3 **Sikhism Emerges**		Objective 3	10 min.	●	●
DIGITAL TEXT 4 **Mughal India**		Objective 4	10 min.	●	●
INTERACTIVE GALLERY **The Art of the Mughal Empire**			10 min.	●	
Synthesize					
DIGITAL ACTIVITY **Cultures Meet in India**			5 min.	●	
Demonstrate					
DIGITAL QUIZ **Lesson Quiz and Class Discussion Board**			10 min.	●	

PEARSON realize™
www.PearsonRealize.com

Go online to access additional resources including:
Primary Sources • Biographies • Supreme Court cases •
21st Century Skill Tutorials • Maps • Graphic Organizers.

CONNECT

DIGITAL START UP ACTIVITY
Akbar the Great Speaks on Religion

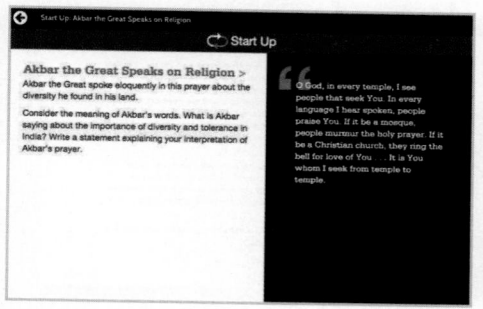

Project the Start Up Activity Ask students to answer the questions as they enter and get settled. Then have them share their ideas with another student, either in class or through a chat or blog space.

Discuss Does Akbar recognize that his subjects are a diverse group of people with different beliefs about seeking God? *(yes)* What else does he understand abut their religious beliefs? *(Sample Response: Students should note that he understood that the different religions in his kingdom all sought the same basic thing, even though the forms of their worship and religious practices differed.)*

Tell students that in this lesson they will be learning about a region of the world where cultural, political, and religious currents have mingled for thousands of years, creating diverse civilizations.

Aa Vocabulary Development: Use the Interactive Reading Notepad to preview the Key Terms and Academic Vocabulary in this Lesson with students.

⇅ FLIP IT!

Assign the Flipped Video for this lesson.

■ STUDENT EDITION PRINT PAGES: 308–313

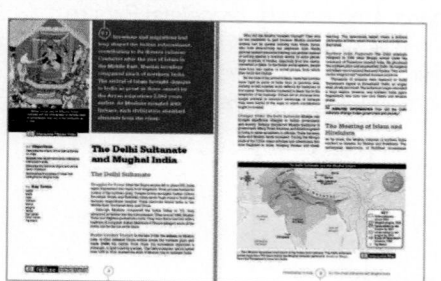

INVESTIGATE

DIGITAL TEXT 1
The Delhi Sultanate

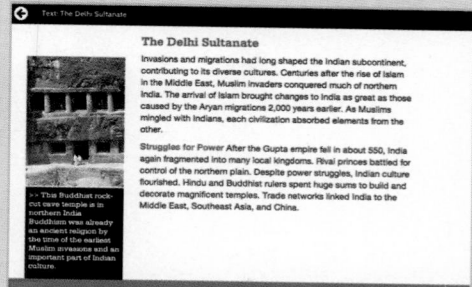

Objective 1: Describe the effects of the Delhi sultanate on India.

Quick Instruction

Interactive Map: The Delhi Sultanate and Mughal Empire Project the map on the whiteboard. Explain that two Muslim dynasties ruled much of India. The first, the Delhi Sultanate, held power for more that 300 years, when it was replaced by the Mughal dynasty, founded by the famous Mongol general Tamerlane. Click through the hot spots on the map and discuss the various images.

📷 ACTIVE CLASSROOM

Use the Write Headlines Strategy. Ask students to write a headline that captures the main focus of the map. Ask: If you were to write a headline for this topic or issue right now that captured the most important aspect that should be remembered, what would that headline be? Pass your headline to a partner for them to review. They can keep yours or ask for theirs back.

ELL Use the ELL activity described in the ELL chart.

INTERACTIVE MAP
The Delhi Sultanate and Mughal Empire

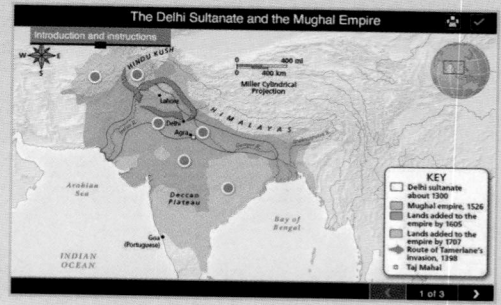

Further Instruction

The Delhi Sultanate Project the Interactive Reading Notepad questions and have students answer as they progress through the core reading.

Identify Cause and Effect Ask students to work with a partner to identify causes and effects of the Mongol invasion of India. Taking turns, have one student list a cause and the other provide an effect. Share this example: Cause: Muslim archers rode swift horses, while Hindu defenders rode slow-moving elephants. Effect: Muslim invasions were successful. *(Other possible causes and effects: Hindu princes battled each other/ it was easier for Muslim invaders to triumph; Hindus believed that people were born into castes they could not change/lower-caste Hindus converted to Islam; Turks, Persians, and Arabs migrated to India/trade between Indian and Muslim areas increased)*

Map: Tamerlane Invades India Project the map of Tamerlane's invasion and ask: From what direction did Tamerlane invade India? *(northwest)* What geographic features may have made this invasion route a good choice? *It avoided mountainous areas south of the Hindu Kush; it partly followed river valleys.)*

The Delhi Sultanate and Mughal India

The Meeting of Islam and Hinduism

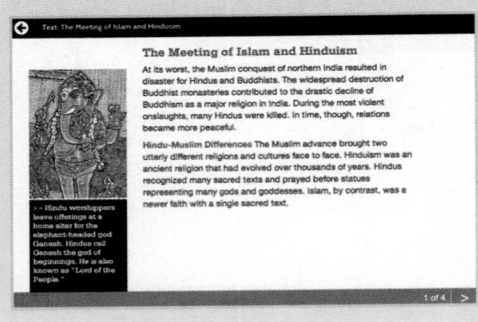

Objective 2: **Explain how Muslim and Hindu civilizations interacted in India.**

Quick Instruction

Project the illustration of Akbar the Great riding on the elephant. Explain that Akbar was the grandson of Babur, the Mughal, or Mongol, conqueror of India. Tell students that Babur and Akbar, like other Mongol conquerors they have read about, became tolerant of other religions after an initial period of violent conflict. Interactions between Muslims and Hindus in the Indian subcontinent resulted in important exchanges of cultural, political, religious, social, and artistic ideas. These exchanges have led to the multicultural India we know today.

ELL Use the ELL activity described in the ELL chart.

Further Instruction

The Meeting of Islam and Hinduism Project the Interactive Reading Notepad questions and have students answer as they progress through the core reading.

Make Generalizations Ask pairs of students to examine the illustration of the rajah holding court. Have them make generalizations about the court based on the image. *(Sample responses: the rajah was wealthy; he lived like a noble or monarch in Western countries; he enjoyed luxurious clothing and furnishings, music, and dancing.)*

Infer Why did some Hindus convert to Islam during the Delhi Sultanate? *(Some lower-caste Hindus preferred Islam because it rejected the caste system. Other converts came from higher castes. They chose to adopt Islam either because they accepted its beliefs or because they served in the Muslim government. Indian merchants were attracted to Islam in part because of the strong trade network with Muslim lands.)* Why do you think it was less common for Muslims to convert to Hinduism? *(The rulers of India at that time were Muslims, while Hindus were the people ruled, Muslims had fewer incentives to become Hindus in a society ruled by Muslims.)*

D Differentiate: Extra Support Discuss
Use these and similar questions to differentiate instruction for students who need extra support when discussing Muslim and Hindu interactions: What does the text say about the ages of Islam and Hinduism? *Hinduism was an ancient religion that had evolved over thousands of years. Islam, by contrast, was a newer faith.)* What does the text say about the sacred texts of the two religions? *(Hindus recognized many sacred texts. Islam had a single sacred text.)* What does the text say about how Muslims and Hindus celebrated religious occasions? *(Hindus celebrated religious occasions with music and dance, a practice not found in Muslim worship.)*

Sikhism Emerges

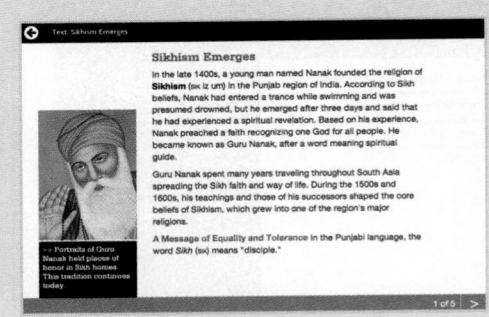

Objective 3: **Describe the historical origins and central ideas of Sikhism.**

Quick Instruction

Project the illustration of the Sikh parade in New York City. Have students look at the image. Tell students that the Sikh religion has its historical origins in the Punjab, a region that includes northwestern India and part of Pakistan today. It was founded in the 1400s by a man named Nanak, who after a religious experience spent many years traveling throughout South Asia spreading the Sikh faith and way of life. During the 1500s and 1600s, his teachings and those of his nine successors shaped the core beliefs of Sikhism, which spread throughout the region and developed into a major religion. Sikhism teaches a faith in one God for all people.

In addition to the belief in one God for all humanity, the basic Sikh beliefs include the equality of all people in the eyes of God, regardless of their race, gender, social class, or religion. Sikhs also strive to actively practice the values of truthfulness, trust, loyalty, productive labor, sharing, integrity, and spirituality. Today, Sikhs express their belief in equality before God by certain symbolic items that show all people are equal. Ask students what some of these symbols might be, based on the image of the Sikh parade in New York. *(turbans, long beards, bracelets)* Explain that in this section, students will learn about Sikhism, which has spread to become the world's fifth-largest religion.

DIGITAL TEXT 4
Mughal India

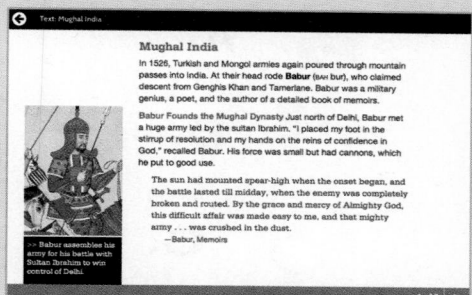

INTERACTIVE GALLERY
The Art of the Mughal Empire

Further Instruction

Sikhism Emerges Project the Interactive Reading Notepad questions and have students answer as they progress through the core reading.

Synthesize Why was Sikhism a radical set of ideas in the early 1500s? What ideas made it different from most customs and traditions of the time? *(Sample response: Most people at the time, in both the East and West, believed in some kind of hierarchy of society, rigid social classes with some people on top and most on the bottom; they did not believe in social equality; they did not consider women equal to men; belief in one God for all people.)*

Support Ideas with Examples Project the image of the Sikh symbols and have students identify and explain the importance of each one based on the text. Then ask them to identify symbols that could stand for other religions in the same way these items reflect Sikh beliefs. *(Answers will vary; most students will identify familiar symbols such as the cross, star and crescent, star of David, wheel [Buddhism], and om [Hinduism]. Students may also describe certain colors and articles of clothing associated with various religions.)*

Transfer Information Have students work with a partner to write a dialogue between a Sikh and a Muslim or Hindu, set either in the 1500s or today, based on information in this lesson. Ask volunteers to share their dialogues with the class and discuss issues they raise.

Objective 4: Summarize the policies of Akbar that strengthened Mughal India.

Quick Instruction

Project the illustration of Akbar the Great. Tell students Akbar's grandfather Babur led Mongol and Turkish armies into India in the 1500s. Babur overthrew the Delhi Sultanate and established the Mughal empire, which lasted until 1857. During Akbar's long reign (1556–1605), he built a strong central government, using paid officials in place of hereditary officeholders, and modernized the army, encouraged international trade, standardized weights and measures, and introduced land reforms.

Use Context Clues Have students look at the image and identify elements that show Akbar was considered a great and powerful ruler. *(Sample response: He is wearing expensive clothes; he is sitting under a fancy tent; he is being attended by many servants; he is in the center of the picture.)*

Interactive Gallery: The Art of the Mughal Empire Project the gallery on the whiteboard, and as you click through the images, discuss their significance and how the art reflects Mughal India.

👥 ACTIVE CLASSROOM

Employ the See-Think-Wonder strategy with the interactive gallery. Pair students with a partner. Have them take turns explaining. What do you see? What does that make you think? What are you wondering about now that you've seen this? Have volunteers share insights with the class.

Further Instruction

Mughal India Project the Interactive Reading Notepad questions and have students answer as they progress through the core reading.

Identify Main Ideas How did Akbar promote religious and cultural diversity in his kingdom? What effect did this decision have on the strength of his rule? *(Although a Muslim, he won the support of Hindu subjects through his policy of tolerance. He opened government jobs to Hindus of all castes and treated Hindu princes as his partners in ruling the vast empire. Akbar ended the tax on non-Muslims, and he married a Hindu princess. By promoting religious harmony through tolerance and recognizing India's diversity, Akbar placed Mughal power on a firm footing.)*

Support Ideas with Evidence Why was the Taj Mahal built? In what ways does it reflect the Islamic culture of the Mughal ruler Shah Jahan? *(It was built as tomb for the wife of the Mughal ruler Shah Jahan; it was designed by a Persian architect with domes and minarets, or prayer towers, and has verses from the Quran on its walls.)*

The Delhi Sultanate and Mughal India

■ SYNTHESIZE

DIGITAL ACTIVITY
Cultures Meet in India

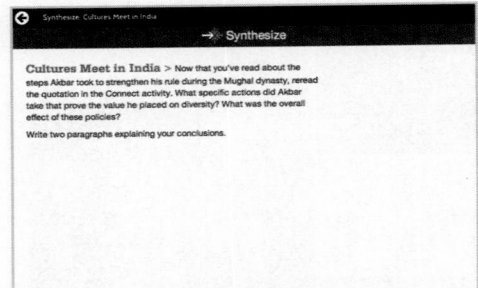

Have students list steps Akbar the Great took to unify and strengthen his rule. *(Sample response: He removed the taxes on non-Muslims, invited Hindus to become government officials, worked with the Hindu rajas to govern, and married a Hindu princess. He also paid government officials instead of relying on the traditional inheritance of government posts. He increased trade and put land reforms into place.)*

Discuss Ask students to recall the quotation from the beginning of this lesson by Akbar the Great about the religious diversity of his subjects and his understanding of the common elements in all religions. Ask what Akbar did to show that he valued this religious and cultural diversity. *(Answers will vary but may include introduction of Islam into greater Indian society, conversion of lower caste Hindus to Islam, centralized government, greater trade opportunities, blending of cultures, and advanced art and architecture that reflected the blended culture.)*

■ DEMONSTRATE

DIGITAL QUIZ
Lesson Quiz and Class Discussion Board

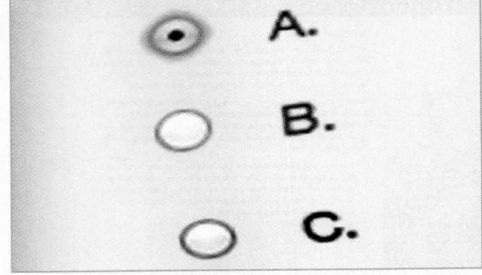

Assign the online Lesson Quiz for this lesson if you haven't already done so. Students will be offered automatic remediation or enrichment based on their score.

Pose the following question to the class on the Discussion Board:

Predict Consequences After learning about India, what can you predict about how it will change?

Topic Inquiry
Have students continue their investigations for the Topic Inquiry.

Golden Ages in China: Tang and Song Dynasties

Supporting English Language Learners

Use with Digital Text 2, **The Song Dynasty.**

Listening
Have students practice retelling and summarizing the information they learn from reading *The Song Dynasty* according to their level of English proficiency.

Beginning Slowly and clearly read aloud each sentence from the subsection "The Growth of Trade." After each sentence, pause to retell what was read using simple, accessible language for students. Ask students to draw a picture to summarize this subsection. When they are finished, help them create a simple sentence to describe the picture. Then have them speak the sentence aloud. Assist them as needed with pronunciation.

Intermediate Slowly and clearly read aloud each sentence from the subsection "The Growth of Trade." After the first few sentences, pause to retell what was read using simple, accessible language for students. Then ask students to retell the remaining sentences in the subsection. Finally, have students draw a picture and write a descriptive caption to summarize this subsection. Have them explain their picture and speak the caption aloud.

Advanced Instruct students to listen and take notes as each subsection of *The Song Dynasty* is read aloud. Pause after each subsection so students can summarize the text to a partner. When each of the sections has been read, ask students to work with their partners to write and share a few sentences to summarize the entire text.

Advanced High Instruct students to listen and take notes as *The Song Dynasty* is read aloud. Then have them turn to a partner to summarize the text. Ask pairs to write and share a few sentences to summarize the entire text.

Use with Digital Text 4, **The Rich Culture of Tang and Song China.**

Speaking
Before beginning this activity, remind students that special words used in history class are history vocabulary words. Explain that knowing these words can help improve understanding of the topics. Then have students complete one of the following activities depending on their level of English proficiency.

Beginning Provide students with several examples of vocabulary words from the study of history in this section. These could include *culture, scholar, architecture,* and *gentry.* Model using a bilingual dictionary to define these terms for students. Then read *The Rich Culture of Tang and Song China* aloud. Pause to highlight any vocabulary terms. Help students use the bilingual dictionary to define the terms aloud and help students understand them in the context of the section.

Intermediate Read *The Rich Culture of Tang and Song China* aloud. Ask students to raise their hands when they encounter an unfamiliar history vocabulary word. Also pause to highlight any vocabulary terms in the text. Assist students as they use the bilingual dictionary to define the terms, then read their definitions aloud. Guide them to a contextual understanding of the terms as they are used in the section.

Advanced Instruct pairs of students to scan the text to make a list of at least four grade-level content vocabulary words. Then have pairs create a list of words with their definitions and read the definitions to each other. Encourage students to reread the text while using their list of definitions as a reference.

Advanced High Instruct students to scan the text for grade-level content vocabulary words. Have students create a glossary for their words. Glossaries should include a definition, the part of speech, and an example sentence for each word. Then have students read their glossary to a partner.

▣ Differentiate Instruction

Use the Differentiated Instruction notes throughout the lesson plan to support the varied skill sets, levels of readiness, and interests in the mixed-ability classroom.

Challenge These notes include suggestions for expanding the activity for advanced students.

On-Level These notes include suggestions for modifying the activity to address different interests or learning styles.

Extra Support These notes include ideas for providing more scaffolding or reading spuport.

Special Needs These notes provide ideas for adapting instruction to support the needs of various special needs students.

■ NOTES

_____

_____

_____

_____

_____

Golden Ages in China: Tang and Song Dynasties

Objectives

Objective 1: Summarize how the Tang dynasty reunified China.

Objective 2: Explain how the Song dynasty grew rich and powerful despite military setbacks.

Objective 3: Understand how China created an ordered society.

Objective 4: Describe the major cultural developments in the Tang and Song dynasties.

LESSON 2 ORGANIZER	PACING: APPROX. 1 PERIOD, .5 BLOCKS		RESOURCES	
	OBJECTIVES	PACING	Online	Print
Connect				
DIGITAL START UP ACTIVITY **Fireworks and Gunpowder**		5 min.	●	
Investigate				
DIGITAL TEXT 1 **The Tang Dynasty Restores China to Glory**	Objective 1	10 min.	●	●
DIGITAL TEXT 2 **The Song Dynasty**	Objective 2	10 min.	●	●
INTERACTIVE GALLERY **Technology in the Tang and Song Dynasties**		10 min.	●	
DIGITAL TEXT 3 **An Ordered Society**	Objective 3	10 min.	●	●
DIGITAL TEXT 4 **The Rich Culture of Tang and Song China**	Objective 4	10 min.	●	●
INTERACTIVE GALLERY **Chinese House and Compound**		10 min.	●	
Synthesize				
DIGITAL ACTIVITY **Tang China**		5 min.	●	
Demonstrate				
DIGITAL QUIZ **Lesson Quiz and Class Discussion Board**		10 min.	●	

Go online to access additional resources including:
Primary Sources • Biographies • Supreme Court cases •
21st Century Skill Tutorials • Maps • Graphic Organizers.

CONNECT

DIGITAL START UP ACTIVITY
Fireworks and Gunpowder

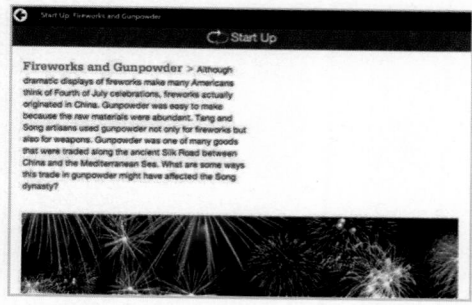

Project the Start Up Activity Ask students to look at the photo of a modern fireworks display and read the text and question as they enter and get settled. Then have them share their ideas with another student, either in class or through a chat or blog space.

Discuss How has gunpowder changed the history of the world? Overall, do you think this Chinese invention has had a positive or negative influence on the world? *(Answers will vary, but should show evidence of careful thought and the examination of gunpowder's effects.)*

Tell students that in this lesson they will learn about a period in Chinese history of technological and cultural achievements.

Aa Vocabulary Development: Use the Interactive Reading Notepad to preview the Key Terms and Academic Vocabulary in this lesson with students.

⇄ FLIP IT!
Assign the Flipped Video for this lesson.

■ STUDENT EDITION PRINT
PAGES: 314–320

INVESTIGATE

DIGITAL TEXT 1
The Tang Dynasty Restores China to Glory

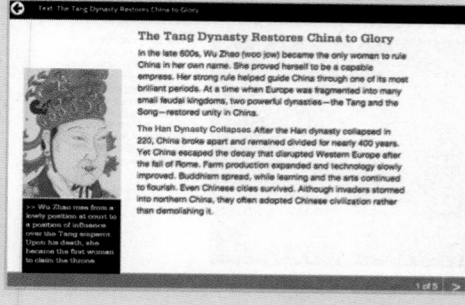

Objective 1: Summarize how the Tang dynasty reunified China.

Quick Instruction

After the Han dynasty collapsed in 220, China broke apart and remained divided for nearly 400 years. The Tang dynasty was founded in 618 and ushered in a period of stability. Tang rulers strengthened their rule by centralizing power, rebuilding the bureaucracy, and enlarging the civil service system. They undertook a series of land reforms designed to redistribute land to peasants, increase tax revenues, and weaken the power of large landowners. The Tang rulers also sent their armies into neighboring countries, forcing them to become tributary states, those that remain self-governing but must acknowledge Chinese dominance and pay tribute to China.

Draw Conclusions Ask students to think about why some governments are able to rule well, while others are not. What factors contribute to a well-run government such as the Tang? Which factors can a government control? Which factors can it not control? *(Answers will vary. Students may cite the innate ability, education, and training of rulers and government officials, external factors such as threats of invasion and climate issues, organization of society, the economy, and the willingness of the people to be ruled or not.)*

Further Instruction

Go through the Interactive Reading Notepad questions and discuss the answers with the class.

Editable Presentation Use the Editable Presentation to present the main ideas for this Core Reading.

Analyze Images Project the illustration of the Western market. What signs of prosperity and a well-run government and society can you see in this image? *(Possible response: lots of goods for sale, different classes of people interacting peacefully, some people expensively dressed, fine horses, market seems organized)*

Identify Cause and Effect What factors led to the decline of the Tang dynasty? *(loss of territory in central Asia, corruption, high taxes, drought and resulting famine, rebellions*

Golden Ages in China: Tang and Song Dynasties

DIGITAL TEXT 2
The Song Dynasty

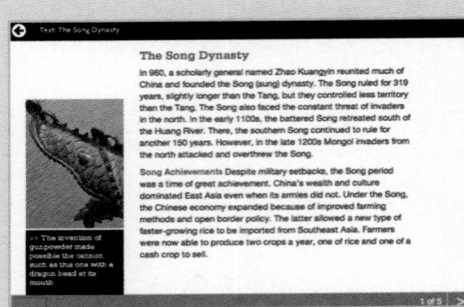

INTERACTIVE GALLERY
Technology in the Tang and Song Dynasties

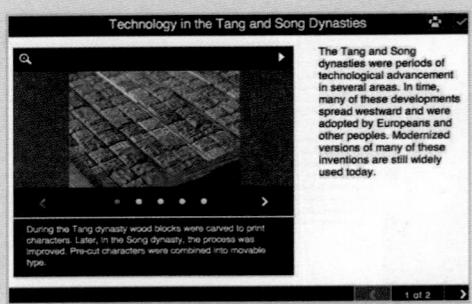

Objective 2: Explain how the Song dynasty grew rich and powerful despite military setbacks.

Quick Instruction

After the fall of the Tang dynasty in 907, a short period of disorder was ended by the founding of the Song dynasty in 960. In spite of suffering military defeats and controlling less territory than the Tang, Song rulers were able to create a society of great wealth, cultural achievement, and economic and political influence.

Project the slideshow. Tell students that the Tang and Song dynasties were periods of technological, science, and mathematical advancement in several areas. Trade spread ideas as well as goods and technology. Merchants traveled in both directions along the 4,000-mile Silk Road, which linked China to India, Persia, and the Middle East. They helped spread technologies, religious beliefs, music, and artistic styles. Advances made in China slowly were slowly carried westward to the Mediterranean world.

The Chinese made breakthroughs in astronomy, agriculture, medicine, and military technology. They produced accurate star maps and calendars and developed irrigation and flood control projects. The human-operated water wheel was invented as well as new plows and rice-growing technologies.

By the mid-800s, the Chinese had discovered the chemistry of making explosives. Gunpowder was first used for fireworks, but was soon used for military purposes for canons and other firearms. The Chinese

pioneered the use of movable type to print books. The invention made printed books, which enabled the more rapid spread of learning, especially medical knowledge. The magnetic compass invented in China helped sailors at sea. The Chinese also developed mechanical clocks to tell exact time.

Click through the images and look at each image individually and then the collection of images as a whole.

Support Ideas with Examples What would have made these inventions attractive to people in other countries? *(Sample response: Inventions such as block type would appeal to other countries because it would make possible the printing of many more books and other documents.)*

ELL Use the ELL activity described in the ELL chart.

🖥 ACTIVE CLASSROOM

Use the Rank It Strategy. Ask students to rank the inventions according to which had the greatest impact on world civilizations. In a class discussion, ask students to provide a justification for the ranking decisions they made. Then poll the class to see if there is agreement on the ranking. Make a tally of the top inventions.

Further Instruction

Identify Main Ideas How did trade benefit Song China? *It allowed new ideas and products, such as the new type of rice to come into China; it also helped China gain economic, political, and cultural influence in other countries.)*

Synthesize Point out that the Chinese government built the Grand Canal, which helped improve China's economy by making trade and transportation easier. Explain that, in the 1950s, the U.S. government built the interstate highway system for many of the same reasons. Ask students to identify some pluses and minuses in government-sponsored public improvement programs such as the Grand Canal and interstate highway system. Have them evaluate the reasons for and against such government participation in the economy and decide in what cases it is justified. *(Responses will vary. Some students will support large-scale public improvement programs because only the government has the resources to undertake such large projects. Others may object on principle, arguing that a free-market approach to public improvements encourages private-sector solutions and benefits free enterprise.)*

D Differentiate: Challenge/Gifted Ask students to research the modern-day effects of food production on economic development, focusing on one less-developed country. (Refer students to the 21st Century Skills Tutorial: Search for Information on the Internet.) You may want to offer this list of possible countries to research: India, Pakistan, Bangladesh, North Korea, Sudan, Mali, Niger, and Chad. Have students answer this question: How has the lack or availability of food helped or hindered economic development in this country? Ask students to share their research with the class.

DIGITAL TEXT 3

An Ordered Society

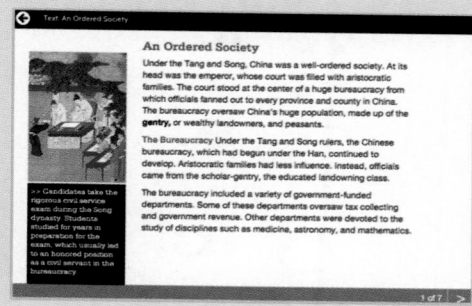

An Ordered Society

Under the Tang and Song, China was a well-ordered society. At its head was the emperor, whose court was filled with aristocratic families. The court stood at the center of a huge bureaucracy from which officials fanned out to every province and county in China. The bureaucracy oversaw China's huge population, made up of the **gentry**, or wealthy landowners, and peasants.

The Bureaucracy Under the Tang and Song rulers, the Chinese bureaucracy, which had begun under the Han, continued to develop. Aristocratic families had less influence. Instead, officials came from the scholar-gentry, the educated landowning class.

The bureaucracy included a variety of government-funded departments. Some of these departments oversaw tax collecting and government revenue. Other departments were devoted to the study of disciplines such as medicine, astronomy, and mathematics.

>> Candidates take the rigorous civil service exam during the Song dynasty. Students studied for years in preparation for the exam, which usually led to an honored position as a civil servant in the bureaucracy.

1 of 7 >

DIGITAL TEXT 4

The Rich Culture of Tang and Song China

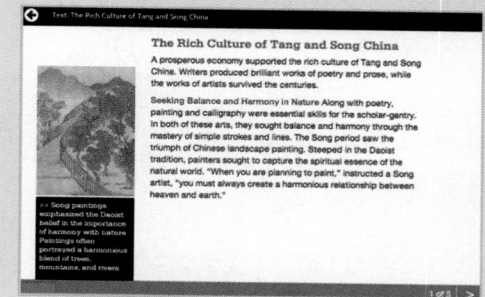

The Rich Culture of Tang and Song China

A prosperous economy supported the rich culture of the Tang and Song China. Writers produced brilliant works of poetry and prose, while the works of artists survived the centuries.

Seeking Balance and Harmony in Nature Along with poetry, painting and calligraphy were essential skills for the scholar-gentry. In both of these arts, they sought balance and harmony through the mastery of simple strokes and lines. The Song period saw the triumph of Chinese landscape painting. Steeped in the Daoist tradition, painters sought to capture the spiritual essence of the natural world. "When you are planning to paint," instructed a Song artist, "you must always create a harmonious relationship between heaven and earth."

>> Song paintings emphasized the Daoist belief in the importance of harmony with nature. Paintings often portrayed a harmonious blend of trees, mountains, and rivers

1 of 5 >

Objective 3: Understand how China created an ordered society.

Quick Instruction

Ask students to identify and describe other highly ordered societies they have read about (medieval Europe, ancient Egypt, ancient Rome) and ask what they have in common *(strictly arranged hierarchy with a few monarchs, nobles, and religious leaders at the top and the vast majority of peasants and other laborers at the bottom)* Explain that Tang and Song China were similarly ordered societies, with one key difference from some other highly ordered societies. Challenge students to look for this difference as they read through this text.

Transfer Information Ask students to create a chart, diagram, or other graphic that shows the four levels of Chinese society. *(emperor, gentry, peasants, merchants)*

Further Instruction

Identify Patterns Direct students' attention to the key term *gentry* in the text and explain that people in this class were not expected to do hard, physical labor and were considered more polite and fashionable than those who did. Ask students to discuss whether modern American society makes a similar social distinction.

Compare and Contrast Ask students to describe how the rigid social hierarchy could be overcome. *(If a peasant boy received an education and was able to pass the difficult civil service exams, he could rise in the social hierarchy, bringing his family up with him.)* Ask if this idea is still honored today in our country. Have students explain their answers.

Identify Central Issues How did the status of women change from Tang and early Song times to the later Song dynasty. *(Their status was higher during the earlier times.)* Then have students explain the connection between foot binding and Chinese society's ideas about the role and value of women.) *(Chinese society valued women who were delicate and subordinate, and foot binding locked women into a subservient role. It reinforced the idea that women should stay inside the home, since many were unable to walk without assistance after their feet were deformed.*

Pose and Ask Have pairs of students write a dialogue/interview between a modern news reporter and a Chinese woman of the Song dynasty gentry, based on what they have learned in this text. Have volunteers read their dialogues to the class. Discuss issues raised.

Objective 4: Describe the major cultural developments in the Tang and Song dynasties.

Quick Instruction

A prosperous economy made possible the rich cultural achievements of the Tang and Song dynasties. Various influences, including Daoism, Buddhism, admiration of nature, and respect for older traditions shaped the art and literature of this rich period. In turn, art influenced everyday life, as Chinese gentry chose to live in beautiful homes that reflected their artistic values.

Interactive Gallery: Chinese House and Compound Project the images. Look at each image individually and then the collection of images as a whole.

Analyze Images How does the Chinese house reflect ideas about art, nature, and respect for traditions? *(Answers will vary. Students may cite the space set aside for ancestor worship as reflecting respect for traditions, the many garden spaces as reflecting the love of nature, and the careful arrangement of all the rooms and spaces as reflecting the love of harmony.)*

☐ ACTIVE CLASSROOM

Use the Audio Tour Strategy. Pair students. Have the first student give the second a verbal "tour" of the house—what does it show? Have the second student give the first an explanation of what it means. If you have suitable technology, have students make an mp3 of their audio tour and share it with other students.

Golden Ages in China: Tang and Song Dynasties

  **SYNTHESIZE** **DEMONSTRATE**

INTERACTIVE GALLERY
Chinese House and Compound

ELL Use the ELL activity described in the ELL chart.

Further Instruction

Apply Concepts Ask students to review the major themes of the three poets discussed in the text and to look at the images of artworks. Then have half the students choose one of the themes and write a poem. Have the other half read one of the poems and make a drawing to accompany it. Display the poems and drawings as you continue to study the civilizations of Asia.

Synthesize Share with students the Latin aphorism "ars longa, vita brevis" (art is long, life is short). Ask them how this saying might apply to the art, architecture, and literature of the Tang and Song dynasties. *(Sample response: The lives of the people who created the art of the Tang and Song ended long ago, but their artistic creations live on and are still considered beautiful today.)*

DIGITAL ACTIVITY
Tang China

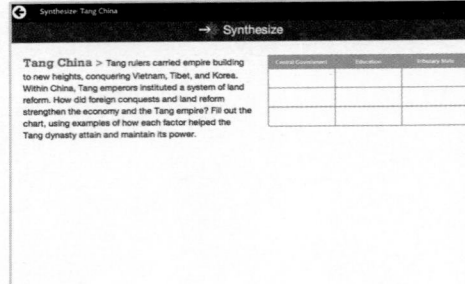

The Tang rulers took specific steps to maintain and extend their control over China. Foreign conquests and land reform strengthen the economy and the central government. Point out that, in filling out the chart, they have added details that support the main ideas: education and foreign conquests helped the Tang rulers maintain and extend their control over China. After students have filled out the chart, discuss examples of how each factor helped the Tang dynasty reach and maintain its power.

Discuss Rulers of the Tang dynasty placed a high value on a strong central government. Do you agree that strong central government offers the best possibility of a well-run country and provides the most benefit to citizens of the country? Why or why not? What other possibilities exist? *(Responses will vary. Some students will argue that a strong central government offers the best chance for an ordered society, while others may cite a federal system with more localized control as providing more freedom for decision-making to fit local conditions.)*

DIGITAL QUIZ
Lesson Quiz and Class Discussion Board

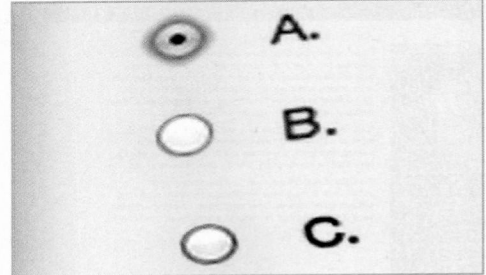

Assign the online Lesson Quiz for this lesson if you haven't already done so. Students will be offered automatic remediation or enrichment based on their score.

Pose these questions to the class on the Discussion Board:

In "Golden Ages in China: Tang and Song Dynasties" you read about two golden ages of China. Exciting advances in science and technology were accompanied by new approaches to art, literature, and architecture. Traditional ideas about government and society were adapted to meet new situations.

Support a Point of View with Evidence The Song dynasty survived despite military setbacks in part because it encouraged innovation in technology and agriculture and supported an extensive trading system. Do you think countries can be strong without maintaining a powerful army? Why or why not? *(Answers will vary. Some students may argue that a strong military is necessary to defend a nation's vital interests if necessary, while others might point out that economic power can be a powerful weapon as well.)*

Categorize The Chinese placed a high value on a well-ordered social structure. Make a list of advantages and disadvantages of such a belief. *(Possible response: advantages: promotes social stability, all jobs/tasks are fulfilled; disadvantages: people can become dissatisfied, important talents and abilities are wasted, incompetence is rewarded)*

Topic Inquiry

Have students continue their investigations for the Topic Inquiry.

The Mongol Empire and Ming China

Supporting English Language Learners

Use with Digital Text 2, **Mongols Rule China.**

Listening

Students will listen as *Mongols Rule China* is read aloud. As the selection is read, pause and ask *How* questions about the text. Students will respond to the questions using single words, phrases, and sentences.

Beginning Reread *Mongols Rule China* aloud to students, pausing frequently to explain challenging vocabulary and concepts. Ask students to listen to each of the following questions before completing the sentence frames below: How did Kublai Khan keep Mongols and Chinese separated? What was the Chinese name of Kublai Khan's dynasty? How did Kublai Khan show tolerance for many cultures?

- Kublai Khan kept Mongols and Chinese separate by _____.
- The Chinese name of Kublai Khan's dynasty was _____.
- Kublai Khan showed tolerance for many cultures by _____.

Intermediate Reread *Mongols Rule China* aloud to students. Pause after each paragraph to retell the content in more accessible language. Ask students to complete the sentence frames below.

- Kublai Khan kept Mongols and Chinese separate by _____.
- The Chinese name of Kublai Khan's dynasty was _____.
- Kublai Khan showed tolerance for many cultures by _____.

Advanced Have students reread *Mongols Rule China* aloud to a partner, alternating speakers after each paragraph. Have pairs demonstrate their listening comprehension by summarizing each paragraph after it is read. Then ask student pairs to answer the following questions:

- How did Kublai Khan keep Mongol and Chinese cultures from merging?
- How did Kublai Khan do show tolerance for many cultures?

Advanced High Have students listen as student volunteers reread *Mongols Rule China* aloud. Have students summarize each subsection and discuss the answers to the following questions with their classmates:

- How did Kublai Khan keep Mongol and Chinese cultures from merging?
- How did Kublai Khan do show tolerance for many cultures?

Use with Digital Text 3, **Chinese Rule Restored by the Ming.**

Speaking

Before beginning this activity, read *Chinese Rule Restored by the Ming* aloud to the class. Then review a few content area vocabulary words with students by providing examples like *mathematical achievements* and *technological achievements*. Explain that it helps to study new vocabulary words when learning new concepts in history. Then have students complete one of the following activities depending on their level of English proficiency.

Beginning Write and display the words *mathematical achievements* for students. Say the phrase aloud and ask students to repeat it. Then define the phrase for students. Have students whisper-read the section *Ming Math, Science, and Technology* as you read it aloud. Ask students to identify information about Ming mathematical achievements using one- or two-word responses. Help students say one sentence to show that they understand the effect of Chinese developments in mathematics.

Intermediate Write and display the words *technological achievements* for students. Have students define the phrase using classroom resources and then say the phrase and definition aloud to a partner. Instruct pairs to identify how the Chinese used astronomy and technology during the Ming dynasty. Finally, have pairs write, then say, one or two sentences to summarize Chinese technological advancements during the Ming dynasty.

Advanced Have students define *astronomy* and *technology* using classroom resources. Instruct students to review the text and identify how the Chinese used astronomy and technology during the Ming dynasty. Then have students analyze how these advances allowed them to connect with Western cultures in Europe. Finally, have students turn to a partner to share their ideas.

Advanced High Have students summarize Ming *mathematical achievements* and *technological achievements* using classroom resources. Instruct students to review the text and identify how the Chinese used astronomy and technology during the Ming dynasty. Then have students analyze how these advances allowed them to connect with Western cultures in Europe. Finally, have students share their ideas with the group. Circulate among students to offer support as necessary.

▷ Differentiate Instruction

Use the Differentiated Instruction notes throughout the lesson plan to support the varied skill sets, levels of readiness, and interests in the mixed-ability classroom.

Challenge These notes include suggestions for expanding the activity for advanced students.

On-Level These notes include suggestions for modifying the activity to address different interests or learning styles.

Extra Support These notes include ideas for providing more scaffolding or reading spuport.

Special Needs These notes provide ideas for adapting instruction to support the needs of various special needs students.

■ NOTES

_____

_____

_____

_____

_____

_____

_____

The Mongol Empire and Ming China

Objectives

Objective 1: Summarize how Mongol armies built an empire.

Objective 2: Describe China under Mongol rule.

Objective 3: Understand how the Ming restored Chinese rule.

Objective 4: Explain why the Ming explored the seas for only a brief period.

LESSON 3 ORGANIZER		PACING: APPROX. 1 PERIOD, .5 BLOCKS			
		OBJECTIVES	**PACING**	**RESOURCES**	
				Online	**Print**
Connect					
DIGITAL START UP ACTIVITY **Warriors on Horseback**			5 min.	●	
Investigate					
DIGITAL TEXT 1 **Mongols Build an Empire**		Objective 1	10 min.	●	●
INTERACTIVE MAP **The Mongol Empire**			10 min.	●	
DIGITAL TEXT 2 **Mongols Rule China**		Objective 2	10 min.	●	●
INTERACTIVE GALLERY **Marco Polo and Life Under the Mongols**			10 min.	●	
DIGITAL TEXT 3 **Chinese Rule Restored by the Ming**		Objective 3	10 min.	●	●
3-D MODEL **Ming Vase**			10 min.	●	
DIGITAL TEXT 4 **Chinese Fleets Explore the Seas**		Objective 4	10 min.	●	●
Synthesize					
DIGITAL ACTIVITY **Timeline of Mongol Empire in China**			5 min.	●	
Demonstrate					
DIGITAL QUIZ **Lesson Quiz and Class Discussion Board**			10 min.	●	

Go online to access additional resources including:
Primary Sources • Biographies • Supreme Court cases •
21st Century Skill Tutorials • Maps • Graphic Organizers.

CONNECT

DIGITAL START UP ACTIVITY
Warriors on Horseback

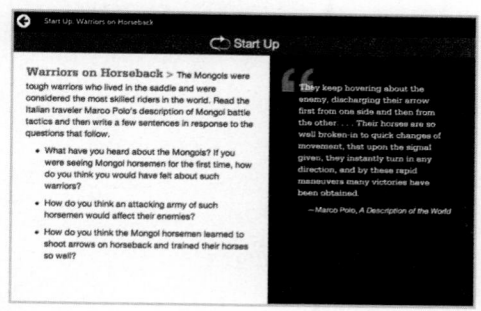

Project the Start Up Activity Ask students to read the quotation and answer the questions as they enter and get settled. Then have them share their ideas with another student, either in class or through a chat or blog space.

Discuss What have you heard about the Mongols? If you were seeing Mongol horsemen for the first time, how do you think you would have felt about such warriors? *(Possible answer: wild barbarian hordes. Students should briefly convey their feelings.)*

Tell students that in this lesson they will learn how the Mongols conquered a vast empire and ruled China.

Aa Vocabulary Development: Use the Interactive Reading Notepad to preview the Key Terms and Academic Vocabulary in this Lesson with students.

⇅ FLIP IT!

Assign the Flipped Video for this lesson.

STUDENT EDITION PRINT
PAGES: 321–327

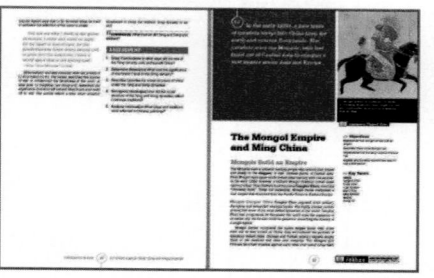

INVESTIGATE

DIGITAL TEXT 1
Mongols Build an Empire

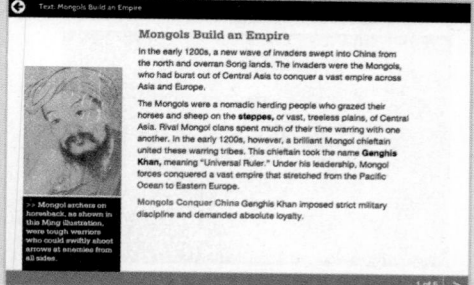

Objective 1: Summarize how Mongol armies built an empire.

Quick Instruction
Interactive Map: The Mongol Empire
Project the map on the whiteboard. Point out that in less than a hundred years the Mongols swept across the Central Asian steppe lands, conquering vast territory and attacking China. Step through the layers on the map and discuss how the Mongol armies built an empire that stretched from eastern Europe to the Pacific.

Analyze Images Ask: From where did Genghis Khan's conquests begin? In which directions did he lead his armies? *(from northeastern Asia, in present-day Mongolia; he led his armies west, southwest, south, and southeast.)*

👥 ACTIVE CLASSROOM

Employ the Make Headlines Strategy with the interactive map to explore the Mongol invasions' impact. Ask: If you were to write a headline right now to capture the most important aspect that should be remembered about any invasion, what would that headline be? Pass your headline to a partner for them to review—they can keep yours or ask for theirs back. *(Possible answer: "Mongol Horsemen Strike from the Steppes!")*

INTERACTIVE MAP
The Mongol Empire

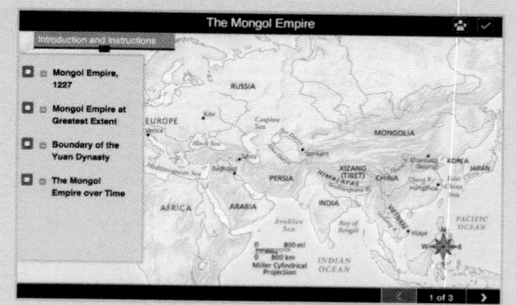

Draw Conclusions Why did Genghis Khan impose strict discipline and demand absolute loyalty from his armies? *(Possible answer: Strong discipline and absolute loyalty kept his warriors, who came from many different clans, focused on conquering enemy forces rather than fighting among themselves to settle old feuds.)*

D Differentiate: Extra Support Ask students to read "Mongols Build an Empire" aloud. As they read, list on the board the steps the Mongols took to create their empire. Have students use the notes to write a paragraph describing the formation of the Mongol empire. Follow up by discussing why the Mongols' achievement is considered one of the world's greatest empires.

Further Instruction
Mongols Build an Empire: Core Reading and Interactive Reading Notepad Project the questions provided in the notepad. Have students answer them as they progress through the core reading.

Contrast How did the impact of Mongol armies on China differ from their impact on India? *(Sample Response: When Mongol armies arrived in China, they devastated the province of Sichuan and destroyed Chengdu, its capital city. In contrast, steep mountain ranges protected India from Mongol invasion.)*

Categorize What was Genghis Khan's most important legacy to his successors? *(Possible answer: He set an example by ruling conquered lands with toleration and justice.)*

The Mongol Empire and Ming China

DIGITAL TEXT 2
Mongols Rule China

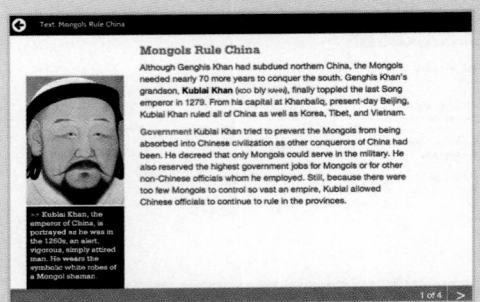

INTERACTIVE GALLERY
Marco Polo and Life Under the Mongols

Objective 2: Describe China under Mongol Rule.

Quick Instruction

Interactive Gallery: Marco Polo and Life Under the Mongols Project the gallery on the whiteboard. Explain that Marco Polo was among many foreign visitors to the court of Kublai Khan during the Yuan dynasty. Important contact between Europe and Asia continued during this prosperous and peaceful time. Click through the hot spots on the gallery and discuss Marco Polo's visit and life under the Mongols.

🗣 ACTIVE CLASSROOM

Use the Conversation with History Strategy. Have students think about having a conversation with Marco Polo or Kublai Khan. Write down a question you'd like to ask, then what that person would say to you, and what you would say in response. *(Possible answer: I ask Marco Polo, "What did people in Venice say when you told them about China?" Polo: "They thought I made everything up or was crazy." Me: "So then you wrote it all down in your book.")*

D **Differentiate: Challenge/Gifted** Organize a small group of students to act as Marco Polo's publisher. They are undecided about whether to publish his book. A second small group debates the first group in class—praising Polo and the strong effect his descriptions of China are having on people—and arguing that he should be believed and published. Tell students to support their arguments with details from the text.

ELL Use the ELL activity described in the ELL chart.

Further Instruction

Mongols Rule China Project the Interactive Reading Notepad questions and have students answer them as they progress through the core reading.

Infer Point out that the Mongols conquered huge territories and dominated many different groups. Ask students why they think the Mongols did not oppress conquered peoples and allowed them to live much as they did before. *(Possible answer: The Mongols were nomads organized by clans, not city-dwellers or administrators. They wanted to receive tribute, not change beliefs or cultural traditions. Also, there were not enough Mongols to control fully all the areas they had conquered.)*

Predict Consequences Have students consider the ways an empire such as that of the Mongols can change over time. Tell students to write three or four consequences that they predict would occur. List their predictions on the board. *(Possible answers: empire expands (perhaps too far), leadership weakens, corruption occurs, internal conflicts arise, rival groups fight for power, external enemies attack, territory becomes divided up)*

DIGITAL TEXT 3

Chinese Rule Restored by the Ming

3-D MODEL

Ming Vase

Objective 3: Understand how the Ming restored Chinese rule.

Quick Instruction

Project the photo of the Ming vases on the whiteboard. Have students look at the image. Tell them that the Ming restored Chinese rule in a period of economic expansion and cultural achievement. Making fine porcelain reached a peak of great artistry. Such pottery was in high demand both within China and in Asia, Africa, and Europe. Porcelain production was an important part of the growing Ming economy.

By strictly limiting Chinese trade with Europeans and accepting only gold and silver in payment for goods, the Ming had a significant impact on world trade. To purchase highly valued Ming porcelain, silk, and other trade goods, European traders brought huge quantities of precious metals to China.

Formulate Questions Have students look at the photo of the Ming vases. Ask students to pair with a partner, examine the photo, then ask them: *What do you see? What does that make you think? What are you wondering now that you've seen this?* Have students share their insights with the class. *(Answers will vary. Students may observe the patterns and images on the vases, their colors and shapes, and then wonder how such ceramics were made and then traded around the world.)*

Interpret Ask pairs of students to examine the photo of the Ming vases again. Have them write a script about a conversation or a dramatic moment during the early Ming period when, after years of Mongol rule, leaders strove to show China's greatness. Encourage students to consider what may have happened

before or after the image shown—the making, viewing, or trading of the vases—or what people may have thought or felt when they saw the vases. Then have pairs of students act out their scripts. *(Possible answer (script idea): The vases are from an order made for the emperor's family. Summoned to court, the supervisor of the imperial porcelain workshops presents the vases as samples. He is terrified the emperor may be displeased; however, the emperor, knowing superb work when he sees it, makes intelligent remarks about the vases' design and workmanship, praising them as fine examples of true Chinese beauty.)*

D **Differentiate: Challenge/Gifted** Ask students to do additional research on major Ming Chinese trade goods, such as porcelain, silk, or tea and present their findings.

ELL Use the ELL activity described in the ELL chart.

Further Instruction

Explain that major ideas in mathematics, science, and technology—such as abacus calculation, gunpowder, and the magnetic compass—originated and were first applied in China long before diffusing through Asia and beyond. At this time, use of the abacus rapidly spread inside and beyond China. In addition, Chinese scholars reformed China's calendar by combining ideas from Western science and technology (learned from Jesuit missionaries) with traditional Chinese astronomy.

Chinese Rule Restored by the Ming Project the Interactive Reading Notepad questions provided in the notepad. Have students answer them as they progress through the core reading.

Analyze Information Remind students that as part of their restoration of Chinese rule, Ming leaders brought back the civil service system and repaired the canal system. Ask students to discuss how the revival of arts and literature at this time also contributed to and reflected the Chinese restoration. Then have students form small groups to research Ming arts and literature and present their findings to the class. *(Answers will vary. Students should include that the revival of arts and literature both contributed to and reflected Chinese culture by reminding and encouraging people to take pride in China's rich traditions and to continue its long history of great achievement. Student groups should present examples of Ming developments in art and literature.)*

Compare Ask students: How did Ming China compare with Europe in science and technology in the late 1400s? Have students cite evidence from the text mentioning major ideas that originated in China and spread widely. List these ideas on the board. Then have students describe an example of how the Chinese applied European science to solve one of their problems. *(Answers may vary. Students may mention that China was the richest civilization in the world at this time—far more advanced than Europe in science and technology. Technologies originating and used earliest in China include gunpowder, papermaking, the magnetic compass, horse collars, cast iron, and textile machinery. Chinese scholars applied Western astronomy and technology (including telescopes) to gather information they used to improve the accuracy of their calendar.)*

The Mongol Empire and Ming China

DIGITAL TEXT 4

Chinese Fleets Explore the Seas

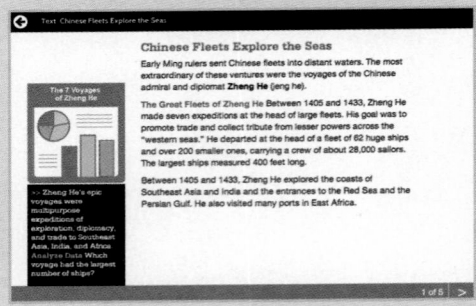

Objective 4: **Explain why the Ming explored the seas for only a brief period.**

Quick Instruction

Make sure that students understand that extensive voyages of exploration and trade such as Zheng He's took place during the early part of the long Ming dynasty (1368–1644), when China's rulers sought to reaffirm the greatness of their country. The aim of these voyages was to show the glory of the Ming government, to collect tribute from lesser foreign powers, as well as to promote trade.

Infographic: The Seven Voyages of Zheng He Project the infographic on the whiteboard. Look at the section for each voyage and the sequence of voyages as a whole. Remind students that soon after the fleet's final voyage the Ming ruler stopped the building of seagoing ships, ending overseas trading and exploration expeditions. His reasons are unknown but may have included cost, lack of profits, or opposition from Confucian scholars at court who, lacking interest in such activities, felt their civilization was superior to all others and wanted to preserve China's ancient traditions.

Evaluate Data What do Zheng He's huge treasure ships and great numbers of ships and men suggest about the Chinese economy and its seafaring technology at this time? Why? *(China's economy was very strong and its seafaring technology advanced. To plan, build, supply, and navigate such large fleets on numerous long voyages required great resources and advanced naval technology.)*

Draw Inferences In what ways do you think Zheng He's voyages affected the places he visited? Cite information from the text and infographic to support your answer. *(Answers may vary. Students should mention that Zheng He's voyages had a significant impact wherever his fleets visited. He often provided the first contact with the powerful nation of China and its valuable trade goods, such as silk and porcelain. After his voyages, Chinese merchants established their permanent presence in the trading centers of Southeast Asia and India. He also helped open diplomatic relations with foreign nations by attending an Indian king's inauguration, visiting heads of state, and transporting ambassadors to and from China.)*

Further Instruction

Chinese Fleets Explore the Seas Project the Interactive Reading Notepad questions provided in the notepad. Have students answer them as they progress through the core reading.

Make Generalizations Divide students into small groups. Give each group a 3-column organizer with headings Plus/Minus/Interesting to record responses to these questions about Zheng He's overseas expeditions: 1. What are positive characteristics of the voyages? *(Sample responses: glory of China shown, tribute gained, trade promoted)* 2. What are negative characteristics of the voyages? *(costly, no or not enough profits, new ideas conflict with Chinese traditions)* and 3. What is interesting about the voyages? *(huge ships and fleets, encountering distant places and exotic animals, unknown reasons why*

overseas exploration and trade were shut down in 1435)

Predict Consequences Ask students what they think the long-term effects on global trade would have been if China had not closed down its overseas exploration and trade in 1435. Tell students to write three or four consequences that they predict would occur. List their predictions on the board. *(Sample answers: Chinese goods and influence would have been greater and more widespread earlier; European and African goods and influence in China would have been greater; Chinese explorers and traders might have reached and colonized Australia, the Pacific islands, and the Americas; if they reached the Americas, Chinese might have mined the great silver and gold deposits in the Americas, causing very different world trade patterns.)*

■ SYNTHESIZE

DIGITAL ACTIVITY

Timeline of Mongol Empire in China

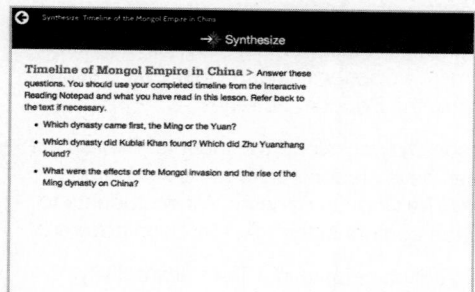

Have students use the Think Pair Share strategy along with their completed timelines from the Interactive Reading Notepad to answer the questions in the Reading Skill: Recognize Sequence activity. Ask them to take five minutes to write down some brief answers to the questions below, then share their answers with a talking partner.

Ask partners to think about the following questions. How do timelines help you keep track of events as you read about historical periods? Why is knowing the order in which events occurred important when studying the history of China? What can you learn about a dynasty from the life of its founder? Have pairs share their answers with the class.

Discuss Have students explain why keeping track of the sequence of events is important for understanding a historical period. *(Answers may vary. Students should mention that knowing the order in which given events happened can make it possible to trace connections between those events. Recognizing sequence is necessary to determine whether past events have or have not influenced or directly caused events that occur after them).*

■ DEMONSTRATE

DIGITAL QUIZ

Lesson Quiz and Class Discussion Board

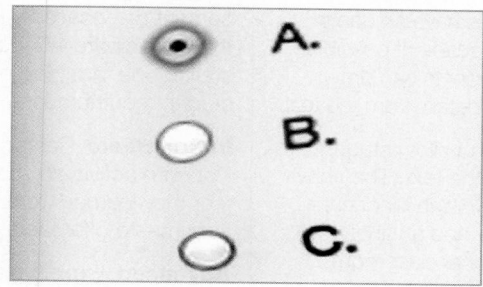

Assign the online Lesson Quiz for this lesson if you haven't already done so. Students will be offered automatic enrichment based on their score.

Pose these questions to the class on the Discussion Board:

In "The Mongol Empire and Ming China" you read about how the Mongol armies built their vast conquests into an empire that included China. Although their Yuan dynasty established order and peace while tolerating diverse beliefs and customs, most Chinese despised foreign rule. During the Ming dynasty's restoration of Chinese rule, the country's economy expanded and its arts and literature revived.

Predict Consequences When Kublai Khan established his capital in what is now Beijing, he decreed that only Mongols could serve in the military. If he had allowed Chinese soldiers to serve, what do you think might have been the outcome? *(Answers will vary. Students should mention that if Chinese soldiers were admitted into the military, they may have shared their culture with the Mongols. Such interactions may have lessened Chinese resentment of Mongol rule.)*

Draw Inferences How do you think the contact that Zheng He's fleets made with distant lands affected Ming China? *(Answers will vary. Students should mention that initial contact from these distant cultures came from accounts of such voyages, tribute, and trade goods. Chinese merchants in South and Southeast Asia trade centers may have provided longer-term interaction and influence.*

Some students may suggest Zheng He's voyages did not greatly impact most of Ming China during this flourishing period. Other students, however, may infer there could have been enough potential foreign influence to disturb Confucian scholars at court, as some historians speculate, causing them to oppose further seagoing ventures.)

Topic Inquiry

Have students continue their investigations for the Topic Inquiry.

Korea and Its Traditions

Supporting English Language Learners

Use with Digital Text 1, **The Geography of Korea.**

Listening
Have students demonstrate their listening comprehension by collaborating with classmates to produce a detailed drawing of Korean geography and its attributes.

Beginning Retell aloud the information in *The Geography of Korea* in accessible language for beginning English students. Then have students work with a partner to draw a picture of the Korean landscape. If possible, provide students with a basic map of Korea in which students can draw details. Help students label their drawings or maps with details from the text.

Intermediate Read aloud *The Geography of Korea* and allow students to ask any clarifying questions that they may have about the text. Then have students work with a partner to draw a picture of the Korean landscape. If possible, provide students with large sheets of paper and a variety of drawing implements. Allow student pairs to use additional classroom resources to improve their understanding of Korea's geography. Help students write a few sentences to serve as captions that describe their drawings.

Advanced Have a student volunteer read *The Geography of Korea* aloud. Instruct student pairs to use the information they heard in *The Geography of Korea* to develop a drawing of the country's various geographical attributes. If possible, provide students with large sheets of paper and a variety of drawing implements. Allow students to use additional classroom resources if they need more information. Encourage students to include as many details as possible in their drawings. Have pairs write a brief description of their drawings to share with the rest of the group.

Advanced High Instruct student pairs to take turns reading paragraphs from *The Geography of Korea* aloud. Then have them use the geographical descriptions of Korea to develop three drawings of the country's various geographical areas: mountains, farmland, and coastal regions. If possible, provide students with large sheets of paper and a variety of drawing implements. Allow students to use additional classroom resources if they want to research Korea's geography more deeply. Finally, have each pair write a brief description of each geographic region to share with the rest of the group.

Use with Digital Text 3, **The Choson Dynasty.**

Speaking
Before beginning this activity, read *The Choson Dynasty*. Then have students complete one of the following activities depending on their level of English proficiency.

Beginning Reread *The Choson Dynasty* aloud to students and retell the content as necessary to ensure comprehension. Then support students as they participate in a Popcorn activity. Tell students that they will take turns stating one fact they learned from *The Choson Dynasty*. Make sure each student contributes at least once to the Popcorn activity.

Intermediate Reread *The Choson Dynasty* aloud to students. Explain the Popcorn activity to students. Then have students take turns stating one fact they learned from listening to *The Choson Dynasty*. Allow students to continue to offer facts until all of the content in the text has been covered.

Advanced Explain that students will participate in a Tea Party activity. Have students face one another in two concentric circles. Students will hear a question, then discuss it with their partner. After a minute, have students in the outside circle rotate to the left. Students will discuss a new question with their new partner for the next minute. Repeat the procedure until all three questions have been discussed by student pairs.

- Why is General Yi Song-gye important to Korean history?
- Discuss the differences between written Chinese and Korean languages. Which language is easier to learn and why?
- How did the Japanese invasion of the 1590s damage Korea and its culture?

Advanced High Explain that students will participate in a Tea Party activity. Have students face one another in two concentric circles. Students will hear a question, then discuss it with their partner. After a minute, have students in the outside circle rotate to the left. Before continuing, students should give their new partners a brief summary of their previous discussion. Then students will discuss a new question with their new partner for the next minute. Repeat the procedure until all three questions have been discussed by student pairs.

- Why is General Yi Song-gye important to Korean history?
- Discuss the differences between written Chinese and Korean languages. Which language is easier to learn and why?
- How did the Japanese invasion of the 1590s damage Korea and its culture?

◻ Differentiate Instruction
Use the Differentiated Instruction notes throughout the lesson plan to support the varied skill sets, levels of readiness, and interests in the mixed-ability classroom.

Challenge These notes include suggestions for expanding the activity for advanced students.

On-Level These notes include suggestions for modifying the activity to address different interests or learning styles.

Extra Support These notes include ideas for providing more scaffolding or reading spuport.

Special Needs These notes provide ideas for adapting instruction to support the needs of various special needs students.

◼ NOTES

PEARSON
realize™
www.PearsonRealize.com

Go online to access additional resources including:
Primary Sources • Biographies • Supreme Court cases •
21st Century Skill Tutorials • Maps • Graphic Organizers.

Objectives

Objective 1: Describe how geography affected life on the Korean peninsula.

Objective 2: Understand the influence of China and Buddhism on Korea.

Objective 3: Explain the major achievements of the Choson dynasty.

LESSON 4 ORGANIZER		PACING: APPROX. 1 PERIOD, .5 BLOCKS			
				RESOURCES	
		OBJECTIVES	PACING	Online	Print
Connect					
DIGITAL START UP ACTIVITY **Korea and Its Traditions**			5 min.	●	
Investigate					
DIGITAL TEXT 1 **The Geography of Korea**		Objective 1	10 min.	●	●
DIGITAL TEXT 2 **The Silla and Koryo Dynasties Develop**		Objective 2	10 min.	●	●
INTERACTIVE MAP **Korea's Three Kingdoms**			10 min.	●	
DIGITAL TEXT 3 **The Choson Dynasty**		Objective 3	10 min.	●	●
INTERACTIVE CHART **Silla, Koryo, and Choson Dynasties**			10 min.	●	
Synthesize					
DIGITAL ACTIVITY **Korean Civilization**			5 min.	●	
Demonstrate					
DIGITAL QUIZ **Lesson Quiz and Class Discussion Board**			10 min.	●	

Korea and Its Traditions

■ CONNECT

DIGITAL START UP ACTIVITY
Korea and Its Traditions

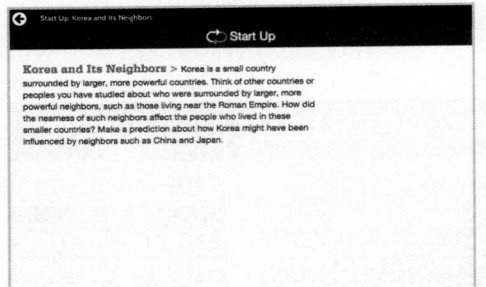

Project the Start Up Activity Ask students to answer the question as they enter and get settled. Then have them share their answer with another student either in class or through a chat or blog space. *(Sample response: Smaller countries near the Roman empire adopted many Roman customs, including language and religion, along with ideas about government, social order, education, and the military. Students might predict Korea will also adopt these elements from China.)*

Tell students that in this lesson they will be learning about Korea, a smaller but influential civilization that grew up in the shadow of the larger countries China and Japan. Ask them to look for ways Korea not only was influenced by its larger neighbors, but also how it affected them.

Aa Vocabulary Development: Use the Interactive Reading Notepad to preview the Key Terms and Academic Vocabulary in this Lesson with students.

⇅ FLIP IT!

Assign the Flipped Video for this lesson.

■ STUDENT EDITION PRINT
PAGES: 328–331

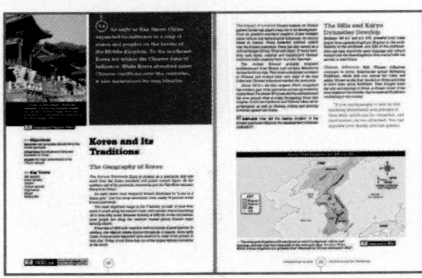

DIGITAL TEXT 1
The Geography of Korea

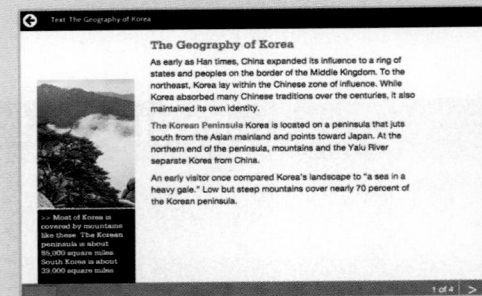

Objective 1: Describe how geography affected life on the Korean peninsula.

Quick Instruction

Korea's geography has played an important role in its development. Almost 70 percent of the Korean peninsula is covered by mountains, mostly running north and south. Because it was difficult to farm these mountainous areas, most Koreans lived and live on the coastal plains and depend on the sea for food. Equally influential is Korea's location. Its northern neighbor China has exerted many cultural, religious, political, and technological influences on Korea. Because it lies between China and its other larger neighbor, Japan, Korea has often served as a bridge linking China and Japan.

Analyze Images Project the photograph of the mountainous Korean landscape. What kinds of economic activities would people living in this type of geographical area take part in? *(Sample response: hunting, lumbering, possibly mining)* Why would early Koreans have preferred to settle in a different geographical area? *(Sample response: It would be easier to farm, build homes and towns, travel, fish, and do other activities in a flatter region.)*

Analyze Graphs Project the Infographic about the way Korea, China, and Japan have influenced one another. What generalization can you make about the influences among these three countries and the direction that most of the influences moved? *(Sample response: Most influences were on Korea from China.)*

ELL Use the ELL activity described in the ELL chart.

Further Instruction

The Geography of Korea Go through the Interactive Reading Notepad questions for this text and discuss the answers with the class.

Identify Central Issues Ask students to define "cultural bridge." *(Sample response: a geographic location that allows people, ideas, trade, armies, and other elements to pass easily from one country or civilization to another)* Ask why Korea meets this definition. *(Sample response: It is a peninsula that juts out into the sea only a short distance from the island nation of Japan; it also has China as its immediate neighbor to the north.)* Then ask them to identify other geographic places they have read about that might also be considered cultural bridges and why. *(Possible responses include southern England and northern France and the Low Countries because they are separated only by the English Channel, which could be crossed easily; north Africa/Sicily/Italy; Constantinople; Greece/Turkey/Anatolia; eastern Mediterranean area; the Nile River.)*

Predict Consequences Ask students to make a prediction about Korea's relationship with China over the thousand years covered in this lesson. Have them explain on what they base their prediction. *(Sample response: Korea will be strongly influenced, even dominated at some points, by China because of its nearness to China and the great difference in the countries' size and power.)*

DIGITAL TEXT 2

The Silla and Koryo Dynasties Develop

INTERACTIVE MAP

Korea's Three Kingdoms

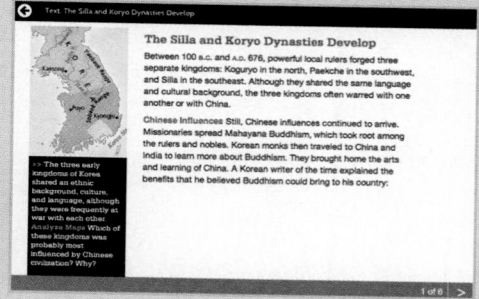

Objective 2: Understand the influence of China and Buddhism on Korea.

Quick Instruction

Tell students that in this reading, they will learn about Korea's two early dynasties and the way that China, Confucian ideas, and Buddhism shaped Korean life, culture, politics, religion, and technology. Confucian China had a strong influence on the political, religious, philosophical, and cultural development of Korea, and it also exchanged technologies with its smaller neighbor. Korean culture reflected the Confucian emphasis on the family, and the Silla set up a Confucian academy to train young men. Buddhism, founded in India and brought to Korea from China, became the dominant religion in Korea.

Three Early Kingdoms: Interactive Map

Project the map on the whiteboard and click through the hotspots on the map. Have volunteers read each description. Ask students to look for evidence in the images of the influences of China and of Buddhism.

Analyze Context Ask students to click through the map hotspots and choose one of the images. Have them explain to a partner how the image represents the time and place when it was created. For example, the Silla-period Buddha shows the importance of Buddhism in the Silla kingdom when it became the official religion of the monarchy. Encourage them to think about how the image reflects religious, artistic, or cultural ideas of the time.

ACTIVE CLASSROOM

Pair students and have them compile an Audio Tour of the map of Korea's Three Kingdoms. Have the first student give the second a verbal "tour" of the map—what does it show? Have the second student give the first an explanation of what it means. If technology allows, have the students make an mp3 file of their tour and share it with others.

D **Differentiate: Extra Support** Explain that students can build their reading skills by linking visuals to the text. For example, the map shows that Korea consisted of three separate kingdoms in the years 100 *B.C* to *A.D.* 676. The written text states the same information, but the map shows the kingdoms' locations and their relative sizes. Point out that they can use both text and visual sources to gain information about a subject.

Further Instruction

The Silla and Koryo Dynasties Develop

Go through the Interactive Reading Notepad questions for this text and discuss the answers with the class.

Identify Bias Have students read the quotation about bringing Buddhism to Korea. Review the claims that Gihwa makes for adopting Buddhism. Then ask students why Gihwa thought these were valid reasons for a country adopting a specific religion. *(Answers will vary, but should reflect understanding of the social role Gihwa expected Buddhism to play.)*

Determine Central Ideas Ask a group of students to review the information in the text and write a one-minute TV news report about the influence of China on Silla Korea. Have them specify an image to accompany the report. Then have another group of students do the same for Buddhism. *(News reports and images will vary, but should show understanding of the powerful cultural influence of both China and Buddhism on Korea.)*

Apply Concepts Ask students to role-play the following scenarios, using information from the text: 1. A Koryo dynasty salesperson is trying to interest a Chinese businessperson in buying a moveable type machine; 2. A scientist from another Asia country is trying to convince a Korean potter of the Koryo dynasty to reveal the secret of making celadon. *(Dialogues will vary. They should show understanding of the text information about the ingenuity of Korean artisans in adopting and improving Chinese techniques.)*

Sequence Events After students have read this text, have pairs work together to make a list, with dates from the text and a short description, of the important events in Korean history. Share this example: 668: Silla kingdom defeats Paekche and Koguryo to unite Korea.

Korea and Its Traditions

DIGITAL TEXT 3

The Choson Dynasty

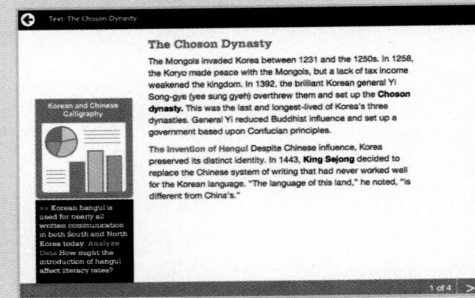

INTERACTIVE CHART

Silla, Koryo, and Choson Dynasties

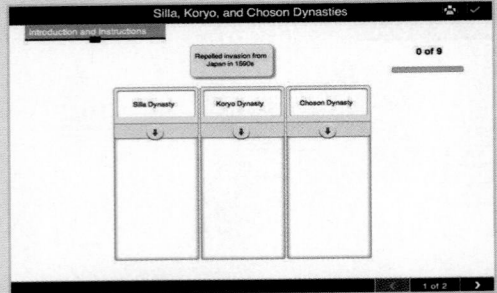

Objective 3: Explain the major achievements of the Choson dynasty.

Quick Instruction

Tell students that, as they did to many other cultures, the Mongols invaded Korea between 1231 and the 1250s. Their rule and influence were short-lived, however, as Koreans had thrown off Mongol rule by the late 1300s. Korea's longest-lived dynasty, the Choson, lasted from 1392 until the early 1900s. Ask students to identify qualities a dynasty needs to survive for over 500 years. *(Possible responses include: competent and just rulers, a way to create civil harmony, a strong military, and the ability to keep the good will of the people it rules)*

Make Generalizations As a class, complete the interactive chart activity. After sorting these tiles about Korean dynasties, what general statements can you make about Korean civilization? *(Possible generalizations include: it was strongly influenced by China; Buddhism was an important influence on Korean culture, art, and architecture; Koreans are clever and capable at adapting technologies; Koreans are proud of their civilization and language and wanted to stress its unique aspects by creating their own alphabet)*

ACTIVE CLASSROOM

Ask students to Take a Stand on the following question: Has the influence of China on Korean civilization been mostly positive or negative? Why? *(Answers will vary. Students should note that China has been an important influence on Korean culture, politics, art, and architecture, and other areas. Those arguing that China's influence has been mostly positive may cite the transfer of technology and ideas about good government, efficient civil service, and religion; those claiming a mostly negative influence may note frequent military and political dominance that stifled Korea's independent development.)*

D Differentiate: Construct: Gifted/ Challenge Ask students to review the discussion of hanja and hangul and how each writing system translates spoken language into written language. Then have them choose a common English compound word (a word made up by combining two or more shorter words). Give as examples butterfly, airplane, football, earthquake, grasshopper, and moonlight. Then have them create two writing systems, one, like hangul, based on the sounds in the word, and one, like hanja, to represent the ideas that make up the word. Have them write the word both ways or post them to the class discussion board and explain how they invented the language and how the written words represent the original word.

ELL Use the ELL activity described in the ELL chart.

Further Instruction

Silla, Koryo, and Choson Dynasties Go through the Interactive Reading Notepad questions for this text and discuss the answers with the class.

Contrast After students have read the account in the text about the creation of Korea's writing system, project the Infographic comparing Chinese characters (hanja) and hangul, the system created under King Sejon in the 1400s. Ask students to explain how hangul is different from hanja. *(Sample response: Hangul uses symbols to represent the sounds of the Korean language; hanja characters represent ideas or things)*

SYNTHESIZE

DIGITAL ACTIVITY
Korean Civilization

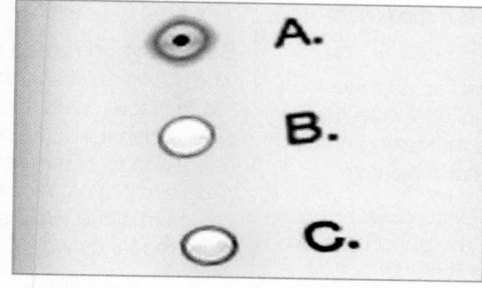

Ask students to take out the graphic organizer with predictions about how Korea might be influenced by its larger neighbors. After they have had time to fill in the middle and right-hand columns, have volunteers read a prediction to the class, state whether it was accurate or not, and share the text evidence they found to support or disprove the prediction.

Discuss Ask the class to briefly discuss this question: What was the most important outside influence on Korean civilization? Why? *(Responses will vary. Many students will cite China because of its geographical nearness and strong influence on the culture, politics, religion, and society of Korea.)*

DEMONSTRATE

DIGITAL QUIZ
Lesson Quiz and Class Discussion Board

Assign the online Lesson Quiz for this lesson if you haven't already done so. Students will be offered automatic remediation or enrichment based on their score.

Pose the following question to the class on the Discussion Board:

Predict Consequences After learning about medieval Korea and its relationship with China, what can you predict about the two countries' relationship in the years after 1500? *(Sample response: Because China will always be near and large, its influence on Korea will continue to be strong, unless China decides to isolate itself.)*

Support Ideas with Evidence Choose either movable metal type for printing or celadon pottery and explain how it illustrates Koreans' talent for improving on foreign inventions. *(Sample response: Koreans adapted Chinese printing blocks, which were designed for the Chinese language and system of writing, into movable metal type, better suited to the simpler hangul system of Korea. This led to a sharp rise in the literacy rate and number of books printed.)*

Make Decisions In earlier texts about Asian civilizations you learned that some rulers decided to restrict foreign influences and contact. What advice would you give to a ruler of the Koryo or Choson dynasty in Korea who asked you if he should limit Korea's contact with foreign countries? *(Answers will vary. Some students may argue that foreign influences, especially improved technologies, are mostly beneficial if carefully monitored. Others might claim that foreign influences, such as new religious or social ideas, can cause unrest and discord.)*

Topic Inquiry
Have students continue their investigations for the Topic Inquiry.

The Island Kingdom of Japan

Supporting English Language Learners

Use with Digital Text 4, **Japanese Culture in the Heian Period.**

Listening
Tell students that they will be taking notes in this activity. Remind them that note-taking is a good way to improve their listening skills. Then tell students to listen carefully as you read *Japanese Culture in the Heian Period* aloud.

Beginning Reread *Japanese Culture in the Heian Period* aloud, pausing after each important detail to give students the opportunity to write down any main ideas and important details. Remind students that taking notes is not the same as copying every piece of information that they hear.

Intermediate Reread *Japanese Culture in the Heian Period* aloud, pausing after reading a few sentences to give students the opportunity to write down any main ideas and important details. Remind students that taking notes is not the same as copying every piece of information that they hear.

Advanced Reread *Japanese Culture in the Heian Period* aloud. Instruct students to take notes on the main idea and important details in the text as you read. Remind students that taking notes is not the same as copying every piece of information that they hear. Encourage them to use abbreviations and shorter phrases when possible. Then have students revisit their notes and work with a partner to fill in any missing information or make any necessary corrections.

Advanced High Reread *Japanese Culture in the Heian Period* aloud. Instruct students to take notes on the text as you read. Remind students that taking notes is not the same as copying every piece of information that they hear. Encourage them to use abbreviations and shorter phrases when possible. Then have students revisit their notes and work with a partner to fill in any missing information or make any necessary corrections. Finally, have students write a one- or two-sentence summary of their notes to share with the larger group.

Use with Digital Text 1, **Japan's Geography.**

Speaking
Before beginning this activity, read *Japan's Geography* aloud to the class. Then have students complete one of the following activities depending on their level of English proficiency.

Beginning Write and display several high-frequency world history words and expressions for students. Examples include *trade routes, mountainous, civilization,* and *geography.* Point to each word and say it aloud, then ask students to repeat it. Model forming simple questions about *Japan's Geography* with each word, such as *How did Japan's geography affect farming?* Have students repeat the questions after you say them aloud. Help students formulate their own question using one high-frequency word.

Intermediate Write and display several high-frequency world history words and expressions for students. Examples include *trade routes, mountainous, civilization,* and *geography.* Say each word aloud and ask students to repeat it. Model forming simple questions with one or two of the example words. Have students repeat the questions after you say them aloud. Have students write three simple questions about *Japan's Geography* using one high-frequency word in each question.

Advanced Have students review *Japan's Geography* to look for content-based vocabulary words such as *archipelago* and *tsunami.* Students should generate questions using these vocabulary words. Then have students work with a partner to ask and answer their questions.

Advanced High Have students reread *Japan's Geography.* Then have students ask their classmates questions about the text. One student should pose a question to the group using content-based vocabulary and call on another student to answer the question. The student who answers the question should ask the next one, calling on another student to provide the answer. Have students continue with this pattern until every student has asked and answered a question.

ⅅ Differentiate Instruction

Use the Differentiated Instruction notes throughout the lesson plan to support the varied skill sets, levels of readiness, and interests in the mixed-ability classroom.

Challenge These notes include suggestions for expanding the activity for advanced students.

On-Level These notes include suggestions for modifying the activity to address different interests or learning styles.

Extra Support These notes include ideas for providing more scaffolding or reading spuport.

Special Needs These notes provide ideas for adapting instruction to support the needs of various special needs students.

■ NOTES

PEARSON
realize™
www.PearsonRealize.com

Go online to access additional resources including:
Primary Sources • Biographies • Supreme Court cases •
21st Century Skill Tutorials • Maps • Graphic Organizers.

Objectives

Objective 1: Explain how geography set Japan apart.

Objective 2: Understand how China influenced Japan, and describe the Heian period.

Objective 3: Summarize the Japanese feudal system.

Objective 4: Explain how the Tokugawas united Japan.

Objective 5: Identify how Zen Buddhism shaped culture in Japan.

LESSON 5 ORGANIZER		PACING: APPROX. 1 PERIOD, .5 BLOCKS			
				RESOURCES	
		OBJECTIVES	PACING	Online	Print
Connect					
DIGITAL START UP ACTIVITY **Devastating Tsunamis**			5 min.	●	
Investigate					
DIGITAL TEXT 1 **Japan's Geography**		Objective 1	10 min.	●	●
DIGITAL TEXT 2 **Early Japan**			10 min.	●	●
DIGITAL TEXT 3 **Chinese Influence in Japan**		Objective 2	10 min.	●	●
DIGITAL TEXT 4 **Japanese Culture in the Heian Period**			10 min.	●	●
DIGITAL TEXT 5 **Japan's Feudal Age**			10 min.	●	●
INTERACTIVE CHART **Feudal Society in Japan**		Objective 3	10 min.	●	
DIGITAL TEXT 6 **A United Japan**		Objective 4	10 min.	●	●
DIGITAL TEXT 7 **Japanese Feudal Culture Evolves**			10 min.	●	●
INTERACTIVE GALLERY **Japanese Art and Theater**		Objective 5	10 min.	●	
Synthesize					
DIGITAL ACTIVITY **Japan During the Heian and Tokugawa Periods**			5 min.	●	
Demonstrate					
LESSON QUIZ **Lesson Quiz and Class Discussion Board**			10 min.	●	

The Island Kingdom of Japan

■ CONNECT

DIGITAL START UP ACTIVITY
Devastating Tsunamis

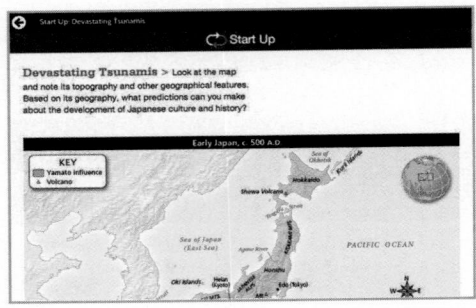

Project the Start Up Activity Ask students to look at the map of Japan and answer the question as they enter and get settled. Then have them share their ideas with another student, either in class or through a chat or blog space.

Discuss Geography, such as mountainous terrain, proximity to the sea, or fertile river valleys, affected the development of other regions. Ask students to compare one aspect of Japan's geography to another region they've studied. (Sample response: Rome used its sea power to conquer and trade in the Mediterranean region.)

Aa Vocabulary Development: Use the Interactive Reading Notepad to preview the Key Terms and Academic Vocabulary in this Lesson with students.

⇅ FLIP IT!

Assign the Flipped Video for this lesson.

■ STUDENT EDITION PRINT PAGES: 332–340

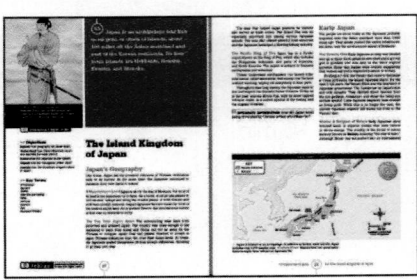

■ INVESTIGATE

DIGITAL TEXT 1
Japan's Geography

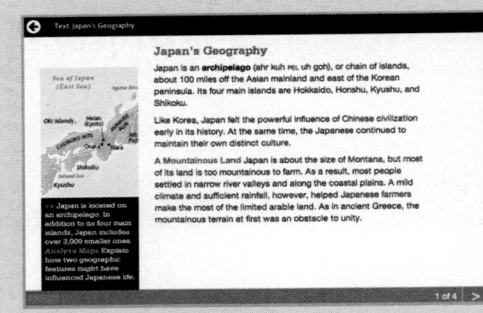

Objective 1: Explain how geography set Japan apart.

Quick Instruction

Project the map of Early Japan on the whiteboard. Ask students to list ways Japan's geography might have shaped its development. *(The islands of Japan were close enough to the mainland to be influenced by Asian countries, but separated enough by the Sea of Japan to remain as isolated as it wished to be.)* Be sure students understand that Japan is located in an area of the Pacific Ocean that has many earthquakes and where many volcanoes are located. The ocean provides many resources and protection as well as many dangers.

D Differentiate: Extra Support Have students practice map skills. 1. Have students locate the following on the map (a) Edo (b) Mt Fuji (c) Honshu (d) Kyushu 2. Explain to students how the geographic features of large mountain ranges and the seas influenced Japanese life. *(The mountain ranges on Honshu made farming difficult and forced most people to live on the coasts. The seas provided many food resources and the Japanese developed a thriving fishing industry.)* 3. Which city was more likely to feel the influence of the Yamoto clan— Osaka or Edo? Why? *(Osaka: because the map shows it was in the area of Yamato influence.)*

ELL Use the ELL activity described in the ELL chart.

Further Instruction

Editable Presentation Use the Editable Presentation to present the main ideas for this core reading.

Japan's Geography: Core Reading and Interactive Reading Notepad Project and discuss the Interactive Reading Notepad Questions.

Identify Cause and Effect Ask students to explain what tsunamis are and how they are formed. Why are they more common in Japan than in many other parts of the world? How were these events significant in Japan's history? *(Possible answer: Tsunamis are large tidal waves that form after underwater earthquakes. They are more common around Japan because it is located in the "Ring of Fire", an area in the Pacific Ocean with a lot of volcanic activity and earthquakes. Tsunamis prevented several invasions by foreign armies.)*

DIGITAL TEXT 2
Early Japan

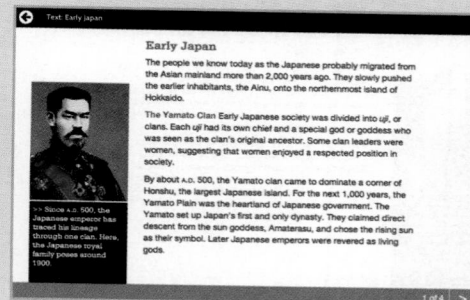

DIGITAL TEXT 3
Chinese Influence in Japan

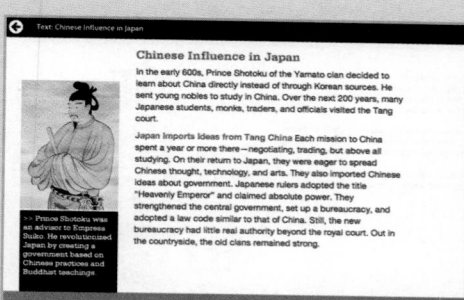

DIGITAL TEXT 4
Japanese Culture in the Heian Period

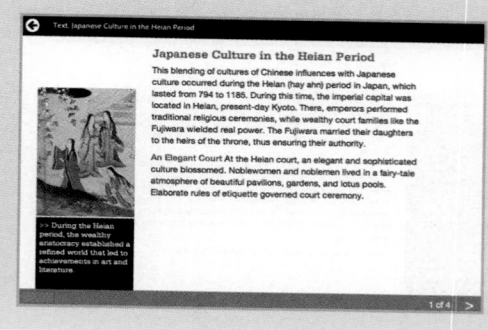

Objective 2: Understand how China influenced Japan, and describe the Heian period.

Quick Instruction

Chinese culture was introduced to Japan by Korea. In the early 600s, Japanese students, monks, traders, and officials visited China and brought back Chinese customs, architecture, government, and bureaucracy. The Japanese continued to selectively borrow elements of Chinese culture and modified them to produce their own civilization. During the Heian period (794 to 1185), wealthy families, not the emperor, dominated Japan. Elegance and sophistication were the norm at the Heian court. Heian women produced important works of literature. One, Lady Murasaki, wrote the world's first full-length novel.

Draw Conclusions What are some of the benefits and disadvantages of borrowing traditions from other cultures? *(Technology from another culture can make work more productive and efficient, but people sometime resent the influence of foreign ideas.)*

D **Differentiate: Special Needs** Write the following questions on the board: What did I read about in this text? What did I learn from the text? What do I not understand? What conclusions can I draw from the text? Have students apply these questions to the text readings in this Topic to help them increase their understanding. ELPS Use the ELPS activity described in the Texas Standards pages.

ELL Use the ELL activity described in the ELL chart.

Further Instruction

Editable Presentation Use the Editable Presentation to present the main ideas for this Core Reading.

Early Japan: Core Reading and Interactive Reading Notepad Go through the Interactive Reading Notepad questions and discuss the answers with the class.

Identify Supporting Details Early Japanese clans honored Shinto gods called kami. Describe kami. What was their connection to nature? Provide details from the text. *(Kami were superior powers that were natural or divine. The worship of the forces of nature became known as Shinto, The Japanese built Shinto shrines in natural settings. Each shrine is dedicated to a special natural site such as a mountain, waterfall, ancient tree, or unusual rock.)*

Make Generalizations Ask students to explain how Korea and China influenced the Japanese culture. *(Continuous contact with Korea early in Japan's history allowed the adoption and modification of many Korean ways. Korea introduced Buddhism to Japan as well as Chinese writing and culture.)*

Make Predictions Think about the early influences of China on Japanese society. What do you think might have happened if the Japanese did not practice selective borrowing of Chinese ways? *(Possible answers may include that the Japanese government would have been different, the Japanese might have maintained the Chinese writing system, and the Japanese may not have developed their own style of art.)*

Analyze Images Have students study the images of the Heian period in this text. Discuss the style of dress and hairstyles shown. Ask students if these clothing styles probably made it easy or difficult for a person to work. *(Lead students to infer that the people who wore these clothes did not engage in manual labor but lived lives of elegant leisure.)*

Support Ideas with Evidence Women were very important in court in Japan during the Heian period. Identify two examples that support this statement. *(Women wrote important literary works during this time period. Sei Shonagon wrote the Pillow Book, and Lady Murasaki wrote The Tale of Genji.)*

The Island Kingdom of Japan

DIGITAL TEXT 5
Japan's Feudal Age

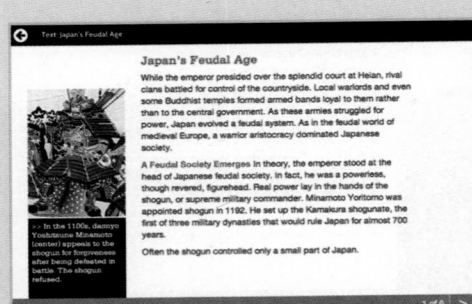

INTERACTIVE CHART
Feudal Society in Japan

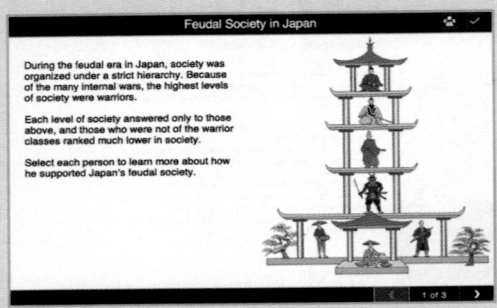

DIGITAL TEXT 6
A United Japan

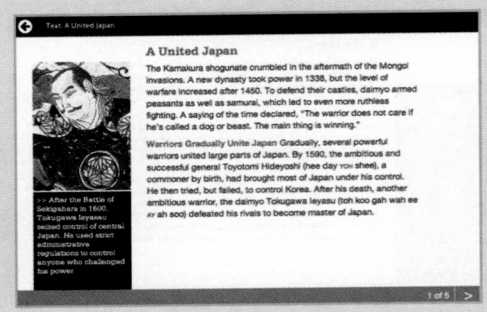

Objective 3: Summarize the Japanese feudal system.

Quick Instruction

Project the feudal pagoda activity on the whiteboard and click through the different levels of Japanese society. Introduce the activity by telling students that in the 1400s, warfare swept Japan, and social disorder continued through the following century. Despite the turmoil, a new Japanese feudal social system arose. As in the feudal world of medieval Europe, a warrior aristocracy dominated Japanese society during this time. Remind students that the emperor remained at the head of the feudal society, but he was a mostly powerless figurehead. The shogun, or supreme military commander, was the true ruler. He had the obedience of powerful vassals called daimyo, who were, in turn, supported by local warrior lords called samurai. Far below the samurai in the social hierarchy were the peasants and artisans, with merchants at the bottom.

📹 ACTIVE CLASSROOM

Employ the Conversation with History strategy with the interactive chart. Have students imagine they are having a conversation with one of the people in the interactive chart about Japanese feudalism. Ask them to write down a question they'd like to ask, then what that person would answer, and what they would say in response. Have volunteers share their questions and responses with the class.

Further Instruction

Japan's Feudal Age: Core Reading and Interactive Reading Notepad Go through the Interactive Reading Notepad questions and discuss the answers with the class.

Editable Presentation Use the Editable Presentation to present the main ideas for this core reading.

Predict As an introduction to this subject, ask students to describe feudalism in medieval Europe. They should identify key elements such as the loyalty between lord and vassal and the importance of knights. Ask them to predict the structure of feudalism in Japan. They should set up a chart to compare and contrast once they learn the structure in Japan.

Compare and Contrast Have students compare and contrast the positions and roles of feudal society in Japan. *(Answers should reflect information from the chart of Feudal Society in Japan.)* What role did the samurai play? *(They were warriors granted land by the daimyo in return for loyalty.)* Be sure students understand the hierarchy of the feudal age in Japan. Point out that the only way to move up in society was to be a warrior able to rise through the ranks to become a samurai. Review the terms *feudalism* and *vassal* with students. *Vassal* refers to a person granted land in exchange for service and loyalty to a greater lord. *Feudalism* is a loosely organized system of government in which local lords governed their own lands but owed military service and other support to a greater lord.

Objective 4: Explain how the Tokugawas united Japan.

Quick Instruction

Tell students that after years of unrest, several powerful warriors united large parts of Japan. In 1600 the daimyo Tokugawa Ieyasu defeated all rivals to become master of Japan. He was named shogun and his dynasty would rule Japan until 1868. The Tokugawas maintained the outward forms of feudal society but imposed central government control on all Japan and created a unified, orderly society. A strict moral code was enforced, transportation improved, trade flourished, and the economy grew.

Summarize the changes in Japanese society during the Tokugawas' rule. *(The Tokugawas ended feudal warfare, imposed a central government on Japan replacing a weak government and country overrun with fighting warlords, the position of women declined, and the economy boomed after the fighting ended.)*

Further Instruction

A United Japan: Core Reading and Interactive Reading Notepad Go through the Interactive Reading Notepad questions and discuss the answers with the class.

DIGITAL TEXT 7

Japanese Feudal Culture Evolves

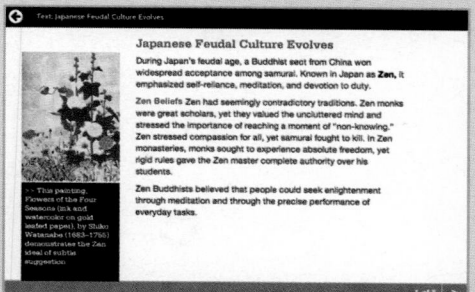

INTERACTIVE GALLERY

Japanese Art and Theater

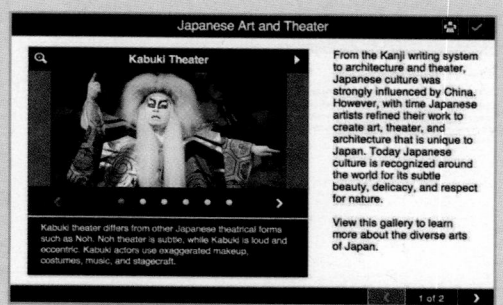

Identify Cause and Effect How did the end of warfare allow the economy of Japan to grow? *(Possible answer: Men worked on farms and in businesses rather than fighting wars.)* Be sure students understand the concept of centralized feudalism. The feudal society still existed with people assigned to a position in the hierarchy, but the government was centralized. Have students discuss the differences between this type of feudalism and the feudalism in place before the Tokugawa rule. *(The positions of the people in the hierarchy stayed the same, but the daimyos had less power and were subjected to more controls.)*

Objective 5: Identify how Zen Buddhism shaped culture in Japan.

Quick Instruction

Interactive Gallery: Japanese Art and Theater Project the gallery on the whiteboard and click through the hot spots in the gallery. Introduce the gallery by telling students that Zen Buddhism became widespread in Japan during the feudal age. Zen emphasized self-reliance, meditation, and devotion to duty. Some Zen teachings were contradictory, but the love of beauty and nature powerfully influenced the development of art and drama.

> ### 👥 ACTIVE CLASSROOM
>
> Employ the See-Think-Wonder strategy with the interactive gallery. Pair students with a partner. Have them take turns explaining. What do you see? What does that make you think? What are you wondering about now that you've seen this? Have volunteers share insights with the class.

Further Instruction

Japan's Feudal Culture Evolves: Core Reading and Interactive Reading Go through the Interactive Reading Notepad questions and discuss the answers with the class.

Identifying Supporting Details Zen Buddhism had contradictory traditions. Have students identify some of these contradictions in a chart format. *(Sample response: Zen monks were great scholars, yet they valued the uncluttered mind and the importance of "not-knowing"; Zen stressed compassion for all, yet the samurai fought to kill; Zen monks wanted absolute freedom yet lived with strict rules.)* Explain to students that the samurai were a group most likely to embrace Zen Buddhism because the religion's values were already important to the samurai culture.

Identify Main Ideas Have students summarize the new art and theater traditions that developed during this period. *(Possible answer: A new form of drama called Kabuki was developed that appealed to more middle-class tastes. Wood block printing became very popular.)*

Identify Cause and Effect New drama and art forms that appealed to the middle class developed. Why do you think this happened? *(The economy improved so that more people had access to these things. The culture changed and nobles and the middle class mixed together more.)*

The Island Kingdom of Japan

■ SYNTHESIZE

DIGITAL ACTIVITY
Japan During the Heian and Tokugawa Periods

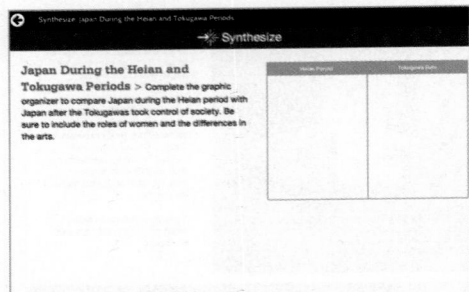

Ask students to go over their answers to the Synthesize graphic organizer and discuss the cultural and political changes between the Heian period and the Tokugawa rule.

Discuss Then have students look at the Connect activity and how the geography of Japan influenced the main aspects of its cultural and political development. How might Japan have developed differently if it were connected to the mainland near India or China? How did Japan's geography influence these two Japanese eras?

■ DEMONSTRATE

DIGITAL QUIZ
Lesson Quiz and Class Discussion Board

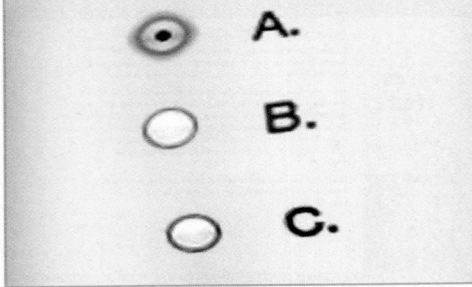

Assign the online Lesson Quiz for this lesson if you haven't already done so. Students will be offered automatic enrichment or remediation based on their score. Pose the questions below to the class on the Discussion Board: In "The Island Kingdom of Japan" you read about how the geography of Japan allowed it to remain isolated and to develop its own traditions. China had an influence on Japan early in the civilization, but Japan selected which Chinese ways they wanted to adopt or revise. Japan adopted a feudal societal structure with shoguns, powerful warriors, in the most influential position. Japan was unified during the reign of the Tokugawas and the economy grew. Zen Buddhism grew in popularity and in the larger cities the arts and theater grew in importance.

Determine Central Ideas How did life in Japan change under the Tokugawas? *(The central government strengthened and the social order became rigidly fixed. Merchants improved their social status, but women faced greater restrictions.)*

Identify Cause and Effect A new form of drama developed in the 1600s called Kabuki. Why was this new form of drama so popular? *(Kabuki appealed to the middle class as well as the upper class. It was popular as it had a wider audience.)*

Topic Inquiry

Have students continue their investigations for the Topic Inquiry.

The Many Cultures of Southeast Asia

Supporting English Language Learners

Use with Digital Text 1, **The Geography of Southeast Asia.**

Speaking

Before beginning this activity, read *The Geography of Southeast Asia* aloud to students. Then have students complete the following activities according to their English proficiency.

Beginning Write and display the following words, with underlined letters, for students: *Singapore, separate, seaborne, island,* and *elsewhere.* Explain that each of these words includes one or more silent letters. Then read the words aloud, pointing at the silent letters as you say them. Have students repeat each word after you. Have each student take turns saying each word aloud to practice proper pronunciation.

Intermediate Review *The Geography of Southeast Asia* with students to look for words that contain silent letters. Then write the following list of words on the board and help students identify the silent letters in each word: *comb, write, where, knowledge,* and *sign.*

Advanced Have student pairs review *The Geography of Southeast Asia* to look for words that contain silent letters. Have pairs write down their list and underline the silent letters. Finally, have them write three sentences using at least one word with silent letters per sentence.

Advanced High Have students review *The Geography of Southeast Asia* and write down a list of words that contain silent letters. Ask students to underline the silent letters in each word. Finally, instruct students to write one sentence for each word they found in the text and share their sentences with a partner.

Use with Digital Text 2, **Indian Culture Spreads.**

Speaking

Before beginning this activity, read *Indian Culture Spreads* aloud to the class. Then have students complete one of the following activities depending on their level of English proficiency.

Beginning Write and display several high-frequency world history words and expressions for students. Examples include *merchants, port, traders,* and *products.* Point to each word and say it aloud, then ask students to repeat it. Model answering simple questions about how Indian culture spread, using each word. Have students repeat the answers after you say them aloud. Help students formulate their own answers using one high-frequency word in a sentence.

Intermediate Write and display several high-frequency world history words and expressions for students. Examples include *merchants, port, traders,* and *products.* Say each word aloud and ask students to repeat it. Model answering simple questions with one or two of the example words. Have students repeat the answers after you say them aloud. Have students write three simple questions and answers about *Indian Culture Spreads* using one high-frequency word in each question.

Advanced Have students review *Indian Culture Spreads* to look for content-based vocabulary words like *monks, scholars,* and *pilgrims.* Ask students to read the information and work with a partner to provide three pieces of information they have learned about how Indian culture spread. Have partners give their information to other pairs within the group.

Advanced High Have students reread *Indian Culture Spreads.* Then have students ask their classmates questions about the text. One student should pose a question to the group using content-based vocabulary such as *monks, scholars,* or *pilgrims.* The student asking the question should call on a different student to answer the question. The student who answers the question should ask the next one, calling on another student to provide the answer. Have students continue with this pattern until every student has asked and answered a question.

Ⓓ Differentiate Instruction

Use the Differentiated Instruction notes throughout the lesson plan to support the varied skill sets, levels of readiness, and interests in the mixed-ability classroom.

Challenge These notes include suggestions for expanding the activity for advanced students.

On-Level These notes include suggestions for modifying the activity to address different interests or learning styles.

Extra Support These notes include ideas for providing more scaffolding or reading spuport.

Special Needs These notes provide ideas for adapting instruction to support the needs of various special needs students.

◼ NOTES

_____

_____

_____

_____

_____

Topic ⑨ Lesson 6

The Many Cultures of Southeast Asia

Objectives

Objective 1: Describe the geography of Southeast Asia.

Objective 2: Understand the impact of India on the history of Southeast Asia.

Objective 3: Summarize the characteristics of the new kingdoms and empires in Southeast Asia.

Objective 4: Explain the emergence of Vietnam.

LESSON 6 ORGANIZER	PACING: APPROX. 1 PERIOD, .5 BLOCKS			
			RESOURCES	
	OBJECTIVES	PACING	Online	Print
Connect				
DIGITAL START UP ACTIVITY **Geography of Southeast Asia**		5 min.	●	
Investigate				
DIGITAL TEXT 1 **The Geography of Southeast Asia**	Objective 1	10 min.	●	●
INTERACTIVE MAP **Topography of Southeast Asia**		10 min.	●	
DIGITAL TEXT 2 **Indian Culture Spreads**	Objective 2	10 min.	●	●
DIGITAL TEXT 3 **Kingdoms and Empires**	Objective 3	10 min.	●	●
INTERACTIVE GALLERY **Angkor City and Angkor Wat**		10 min.	●	
DIGITAL TEXT 4 **The Rise of Vietnam**	Objective 4	10 min.	●	●
Synthesize				
DIGITAL ACTIVITY **The Impact of Geography**		5 min.	●	
Demonstrate				
DIGITAL QUIZ **Lesson Quiz and Class Discussion Board**		10 min.	●	

CONNECT

DIGITAL START UP ACTIVITY

Geography of Southeast Asia

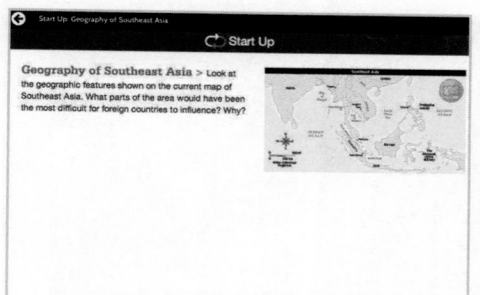

Project the Start Up Activity Ask students to look at the maps of the ancient kingdoms of Southeast Asia and current Southeast Asia and answer the question as they enter and get settled. Then have them share their ideas with another student, either in class or through a chat or blog space. Have students look at the location of Southeast Asia in relation to other important Asian civilizations. Ask them to predict which culture—India or China—had the greater influence on Southeast Asia. *(Possible answer: India may have had better access via land and sea routes.)*

Aa **Vocabulary Development:** Use the Interactive Reading Notepad to preview the Key Terms and Academic Vocabulary in this Lesson with students.

📏 FLIP IT!

Assign the Flipped Video for this lesson.

STUDENT EDITION PRINT PAGES: 341–345

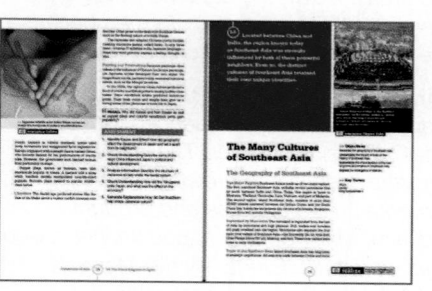

INVESTIGATE

DIGITAL TEXT 1

The Geography of Southeast Asia

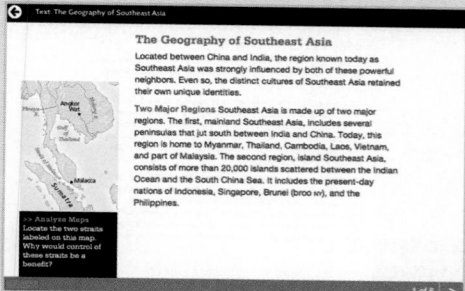

INTERACTIVE MAP

Topography of Southeast Asia

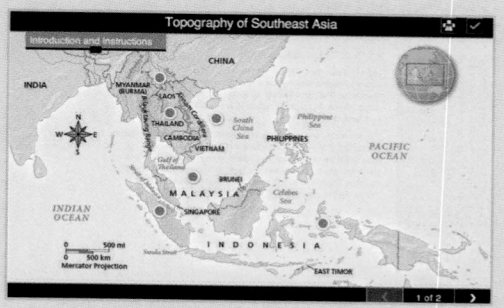

Objective 1: Describe the geography of Southeast Asia.

Quick Instruction

Topography of Southeast Asia: Interactive Map Project the map on the whiteboard and click through the hot spots on the map. Ask students to give their initial impressions of the area. *(Possible answer: The area covers a very large area and contains many island groupings.)* Then ask them to make predictions about how the geography of the region will influence its development. *(Possible answer: people, trade, and ideas will move easily across water, but not so easily across land barriers.)*

🖼 ACTIVE CLASSROOM

Use the strategy called A Closer Look. Project the map of Southeast Asia and use a whiteboard tool to divide it into four numbered quadrants. Have students count off 1 to 4. Then have them look closely at the part of the map in their quadrant. Have them tell you what they see and what they learned as a result of their focus on this part of the image. Collect insights for each quadrant.

ELL Use the ELL activity described in the ELL chart.

Further Instruction

Editable Presentation Use the Editable Presentation to present the main ideas for this core reading.

The Geography of Southeast Asia: Core Reading and Interactive Reading Notepad Go through the Interactive Reading Notepad questions and discuss the answers with the class.

Review the geography of Southeast Asia with students. Ask how location and climate affected the way the region developed. *(Trade routes through the islands gave straits enormous strategic value. While waiting for the monsoon winds to stop, trading ships remained in Southeast Asian ports. As the ships waited, cultural, religious, and economic exchange took place.)*

Identify Cause and Effect Ask students to explain how culture developed on some of the more isolated islands and villages in Southeast Asia. *(Because of their isolation, many developed and followed their own religious and cultural patterns, less influenced by Chinese and Indian models. For example, in some places, women had greater equality in Southeast Asia than elsewhere in Asia. In addition, matrilineal descent was an accepted custom in Southeast Asia in contrast to Chinese and Indian customs.)*

The Many Cultures of Southeast Asia

DIGITAL TEXT 2

Indian Culture Spreads

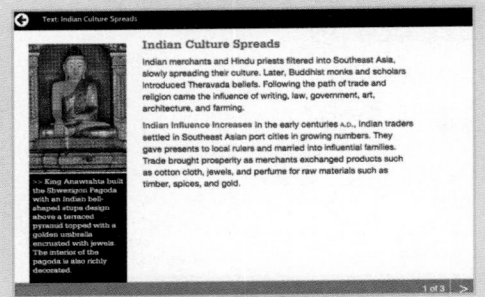

DIGITAL TEXT 3

Kingdoms and Empires

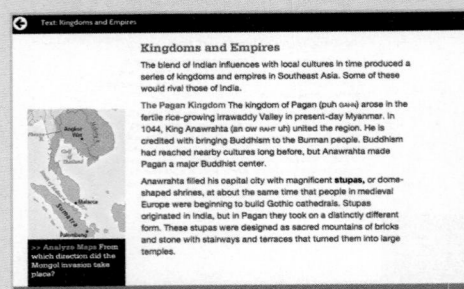

INTERACTIVE GALLERY

Angkor City and Angkor Wat

Objective 2: Understand the impact of India on the history of Southeast Asia.

Quick Instruction

Indian culture came to Southeast Asia by way of trade and religion. Indian merchants and Hindu priests came first followed by Buddhist monks and scholars. Indian influence was seen in writing, law, government, art, architecture, and farming. Indian influence reached its peak between 500 and 1000. Along with Hinduism and Buddhism, Indians brought Islamic beliefs and Muslim culture to the area.

ELL Use the ELL activity described in the ELL chart.

Further Instruction

Indian Culture Spreads: Core Reading and Interactive Reading Notepad Go through the Interactive Reading Notepad questions and discuss the answers with the class.

Support a Point of View with Evidence *"Southeast Asia would not be the same today without the influence of Indian culture."* Write a paragraph agreeing or disagreeing with this statement. Explain your reasoning with evidence from the text. *(Possible answer: Indians brought Islam and Muslim culture to the area. Indonesia has the largest Muslim population in the world.)*

Objective 3: Summarize the characteristics of the new kingdoms and empires in Southeast Asia.

Quick Instruction

Interactive Gallery: Angkor City and Angkor Wat Project the Angkor City and Angkor Wat map on the whiteboard and click through the hotspots. Introduce the activity by telling students that Angkor was the capital of the Khmer empire for more than 500 years. Angkor Wat was built by the Khmer civilization between 802 and 1220. The buildings remaining today are just a small part of the original complex that included palaces, houses, public buildings, and temples. Explain to students that King Suryavarman II built the temple at Angkor Wat. The temple included many works of art including sculptures. The interior walls of each room are decorated with reliefs that illustrated elements of Hindu mythology. Angkor Wat was built to honor the Hindu god Vishnu.

📷 ACTIVE CLASSROOM

Have students complete a See-Think-Wonder activity as they look at the images of Angkor Wat. With a partner, students should think about these questions: What do you see? What does it make you think about? What are you wondering about now that you have seen this? *(Possible answer: Angkor Wat was so extensive that it suggests that the civilization that built it had many resources and a strong ruler.)*

D Differentiate: Challenge/Gifted Ask students to do extra research on Angkor Wat and present their findings to the class. Challenge them to present their findings in a multimedia format.

Further Instruction

Editable Presentation Use the Editable Presentation to present the main ideas for this Core Reading.

Kingdoms and Empires: Core Reading and Interactive Reading Notepad Go through the Interactive Reading Notepad questions and discuss the answers with the class.

Project the map of the Empires and Kingdoms of Southeast Asia. As you review the map, tell students that the blend of Indian influences and local cultures produced a series of kingdoms and empires in Southeast Asia. Hinduism and Buddhism also spread to the region.

Draw Conclusions Ask students to explain how culture developed on some of the more isolated islands and villages in Southeast Asia. *(Possible answer: The area of Southeast Asia is large and contains many mainland and island areas. Isolated groups with different customs and ideas gradually formed because of the geographic barriers to easy travel.)*

Summarize the history of the Pagan kingdom. What factors influenced its rise and fall? *(Possible answer: The Irrawaddy Valley was a fertile rice-growing area. King Anawrahta united the area and brought Buddhism. Many dome-shaped shrines called stupas were built. Eventually the Mongols conquered the Pagan civilization.)*

DIGITAL TEXT 4

The Rise of Vietnam

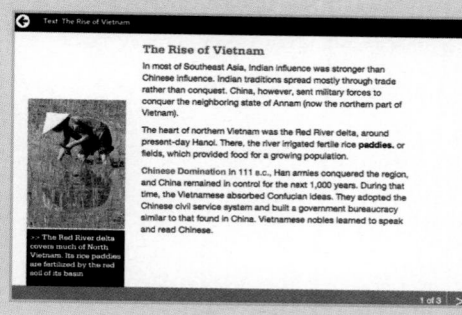

Objective 4: Explain the emergence of Vietnam.

Quick Instruction

Tell students that in most of Southeast Asia, Indian influence outweighed the Chinese influence. That was not the case in Vietnam. Chinese armies conquered and dominated the area. The Vietnamese adopted many Confucian ideas and adopted the Chinese civil service system and Chinese governmental structure. The Vietnamese became free of China in 939 when the Tang dynasty collapsed. China tried to re-conquer the area but was not successful.

Further Instruction

The Rise of Vietnam: Core Reading and Interactive Reading Notepad Go through the Interactive Reading Notepad questions and discuss the answers with the class.

Draw Conclusions Unlike the rest of Southeast Asia, Vietnam was influenced by China more than India. Provide several reasons why this occurred. *(Possible answer: Vietnam borders China and China sent in military forces to take control of the area.)*

Summarize the history of the Pagan kingdom. What factors influenced its rise and fall? *(Possible answer: The Irrawaddy Valley was a fertile rice-growing area. King Anawrahta united the area and brought Buddhism. Many dome-shaped shrines called stupas were built. Eventually the Mongols conquered the Pagan civilization.)*

The Many Cultures of Southeast Asia

■ SYNTHESIZE

DIGITAL ACTIVITY
The Impact of Geography

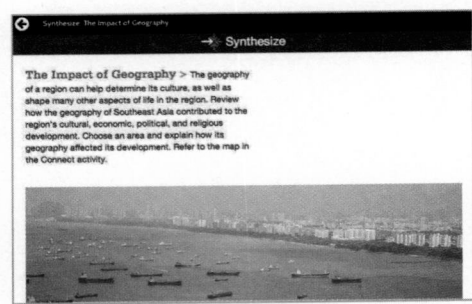

Ask students to look at the map of Southeast Asia from the Connect activity with a partner. Have each partner choose a country, kingdom, or empire and explain, using the text information and map key information, how geography affected the place's cultural, economic, political, and religious development. Have them take five minutes for this activity.

Discuss Then have volunteers share their specific insights with the class. Have the class sort the responses into four categories: cultural, economic, political, and religious. *(Sample responses: religious: Indian traders crossed the Indian Ocean and spread Islamic beliefs and Muslim culture throughout the islands of Indonesia and as far east as the Philippines; religious, cultural, and political: The Khmer people adapted Indian writing, mathematics, architecture, and art. Khmer rulers became pious Hindus. Like the princes and emperors of India, they saw themselves as god-kings. Most ordinary people, however, preferred Buddhism; economic: Indian traders settled in Southeast Asian port cities in growing numbers. They gave presents to local rulers and married into influential families. Trade brought prosperity as merchants exchanged products such as cotton cloth, jewels, and perfume for raw materials such as timber, spices, and gold.)*

■ DEMONSTRATE

DIGITAL QUIZ
Lesson Quiz and Class Discussion Board

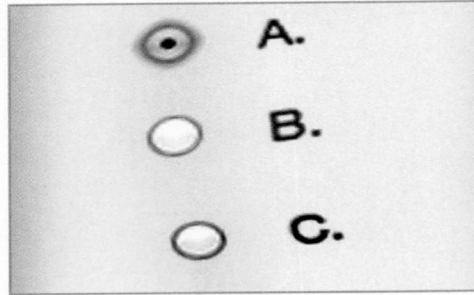

Assign the online Lesson Quiz for this lesson if you haven't already done so. Students will be offered automatic enrichment or remediation based on their score. Pose these questions to the class on the Discussion Board: In "Many Cultures of Southeast Asia" you read that the geography of Southeast Asia had a large effect on how the cultures of the area developed. India and China both had an impact on the area, and India was the most influential. New kingdoms and empires arose, each adopting their own traditions and religions. Vietnam was the area most influenced by China.

Compare and Contrast How were the kingdoms of Southeast Asia similar and different? *(Sample answer, Similar: the kingdoms and empires of Southeast Asia were influenced by other civilizations—India in the case of most, but China in the case of Vietnam; women had more influence than in other Asian cultures. Different: some were more heavily involved in trade than others; Svrijaya adopted Islam, which the others did not, and Vietnam adopted a different form of Buddhism than the other islands.)*

Support Ideas with Evidence Architectural advances were made in civilizations with strong leaders. Where is this evident in Southeast Asia? *(Sample answer: King Suryavarman built the temple complex at Angkor Wat, King Anawrahta built a capital city and many stupa shrines.)*

Topic Inquiry
Have students continue their investigations for the Topic Inquiry.

Civilizations of Asia (500–1650)

■ SYNTHESIZE

DIGITAL ACTIVITY
Reflect on the Essential Question and Topic

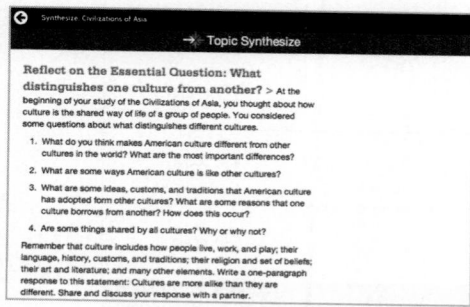

First ask students to reconsider the Essential Question for the Topic: What distinguishes one culture from another? Remind students of the questions they discussed at the start of the Topic:

- What do you think makes American culture different from other cultures in the world? What are the most important differences?

- What are some ways American culture is like other cultures?

- What are some ideas, customs, and traditions that American culture has adopted form other cultures? What are some reasons that one culture borrows from another? How does this occur?

- Are some values, beliefs, or ideas shared by all cultures?

Then have students write their paragraphs responding to the statement: cultures are more alike than they are different. Suggest they start by making two lists of ways cultures are similar and different.

Have volunteers read their paragraphs and discuss issues raised or ask students to post their responses on the Class Discussion Board. Next, ask students to reflect on the Topic as a whole, focusing on examples of the cultures of the civilizations studied. Have volunteers share their lists with the class and explain their choices. After discussing the choices, conclude by asking the class to suggest similar cultural elements that could represent American culture today. You may ask student pairs to share their suggestions with the class or on the Class Discussion Board.

Topic Inquiry
Have students complete Step 3 of the Topic Inquiry.

■ DEMONSTRATE

DIGITAL TOPIC REVIEW AND ASSESSMENT
Civilizations of Asia (500–1650)

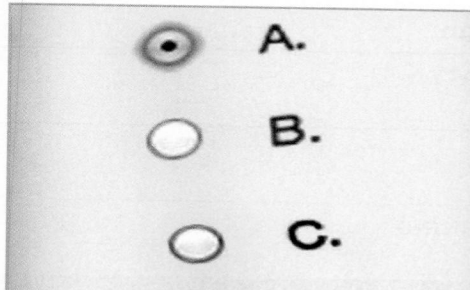

Students can prepare for the Topic Test by answering the questions in the Topic Review and Assessment online or the Assessment questions in the Print Student text. They can also prepare by reviewing their answers to the Interactive Reading Notepad questions or reviewing their notes in the Reading and Notetaking Study Guide.

DIGITAL TOPIC TEST
Civilizations of Asia (500–1650)

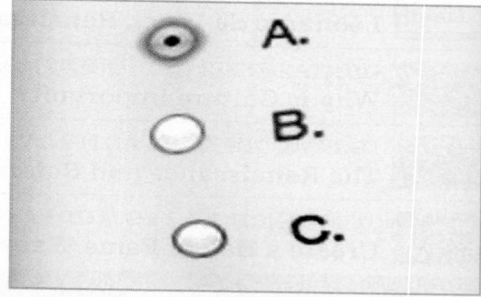

TOPIC TEST
Assign the Topic Test to assess students' understanding of topic content.

BENCHMARK TESTS
Assign these benchmark tests as you complete the relevant topics to monitor student progress toward mastering the course content and as preparation for the End-of-Course Test.

Benchmark Test 1: Topics 1–5

Benchmark Test 2: Topics 6–10

Benchmark Test 3: Topics 11–15

Benchmark Test 4: Topics 16–21

The Renaissance and Reformation (1300–1650)

TOPIC 10 ORGANIZER	PACING: APPROX. 8 PERIODS, 4 BLOCKS
	PACING
Connect	1 period
MY STORY VIDEO **Leonardo da Vinci, Renaissance Man**	10 min.
DIGITAL ESSENTIAL QUESTION ACTIVITY **Why is Culture Important?**	10 min.
DIGITAL TIMELINE ACTIVITY **The Renaissance and Reformation**	10 min.
TOPIC INQUIRY: PROJECT-BASED LEARNING **Create a Hall of Fame Website**	20 min.
Investigate	2–5 periods
TOPIC INQUIRY: PROJECT-BASED LEARNING **Create a Hall of Fame Website**	Ongoing
LESSON 1 The Italian Renaissance	30–40 min.
LESSON 2 The Renaissance in Northern Europe	30–40 min.
LESSON 3 The Protestant Reformation	30–40 min.
LESSON 4 Reformation Ideas Spread	30–40 min.
LESSON 5 The Scientific Revolution	30–40 min.
Synthesize	1 period
DIGITAL ACTIVITY **Reflect on the Essential Question and Topic**	10 min.
Demonstrate	1–2 periods
DIGITAL TOPIC TEST **The Renaissance and Reformation**	10 min.
TOPIC INQUIRY: PROJECT-BASED LEARNING **Create a Hall of Fame Website**	20 min.

 **TOPIC INQUIRY: PROJECT-BASED LEARNING**

Create a Hall of Fame Website

In this Topic Inquiry, students work in teams to research the lives of important figures of the Renaissance and the Scientific Revolution and build a Hall of Fame website honoring their lives and the significance of their work. Learning about these individuals will contribute to students' understanding of the Topic Essential Question: Why Is Culture Important?

STEP 1: CONNECT
Develop Questions and Plan the Investigation

Launch the Project and Generate Questions
Display the letter from the European Museum of Culture and Science. Tell students that for their project, each team will need to research, nominate, and select ten inductees for a Renaissance Hall of Fame. They will then write Hall of Fame profiles for these key figures of the Renaissance and Scientific Revolution. They will build a Hall of Fame website that will include the inductee profiles, as well as additional material on the era.

Plan the Investigation
Form students into teams. Have them learn about working as a team by taking a tutorial, signing the *Project Contract*, and beginning the *Need to Know Questions*.

Suggestion: You can control the length of the project by assigning either fewer or more inductees. Similarly, if you prefer that each student research and write an inductee entry as well as doing some of the other roles, either form groups of three or have larger groups research more inductees.

Resources
- Entry Event
- Rubric for a Group Website
- Student Instructions
- Need to Know Questions
- Project Contract

⏻ PROFESSIONAL DEVELOPMENT

Project-Based Learning
Be sure to view the Project-Based Learning Professional Development resources in the online course.

STEP 2: INVESTIGATE
Apply Disciplinary Concepts and Tools

Identify Potential Hall of Fame Inductees
Teams will work together to decide the criteria for admittance to the Hall of Fame, who should be nominated, and who should be inducted into their website. Help students to determine the significance of a nominee's work in the Renaissance or Scientific Revolution if they are having trouble choosing their inductees. You can also direct them to other Hall of Fame websites, such as the Baseball or Rock-n-Roll Hall of Fame, if students need more examples.

Suggestion: If your class has limited access to the Internet, you could make several books available to students, such as *Leonardo and His Times* by Dorling Kindersley and *William Shakespeare: Playwright and Poet* by Compass Point Books.

Conduct Research on the Inductees
Have students research their inductees. To guide their research, teams will create a list of *Need-to-Know Questions* about the people they have chosen for the Hall of Fame. Refer students to helpful resources within the core content of the Topic to help answer their questions. Help students begin to fill out the *Information Organizer*.

Write and Edit the Hall of Fame Profiles
The teams should plan how to present the information they have gathered.

Next, students should write their inductees' entries and do some peer review of one another's writing. Remind students to offer detailed, constructive criticism of one another's work.

Resources
- Project Tracker
- Information Organizer

STEP 3: SYNTHESIZE
Evaluate Sources and
Use Evidence to Formulate Conclusions

Build Your Website
Now have students get together to build their websites. If students are having trouble sharing the work of this part of the project, remind them to review their *Project Tracker and Project Roles* document to make sure they are on track. For students who are having trouble, walk them through *Plan Your Website* to get ideas.

Suggestion: For a less technology-dependent end product, have students write their inductees' Hall of Fame profiles and create a Hall of Fame exhibit with the information they have gathered. To take technology a step further, have students set up a mock blog and conduct discussions using their inductees as online personas.

Write a Conclusion
Ask teams to review their websites and draw conclusions about what they have learned. To help teams start, have each team member write down their answer to a different question listed in the *Student Instructions* and then share those answers with the group. Have students work their conclusions into the selection criteria of the website.

STEP 4: DEMONSTRATE
Communicate Conclusions
and Take Informed Action

Present Your Hall of Fame Website
Have students prepare their website presentations, then watch the team presentations. To help the teams structure their time, set up a clock in the back of the room and alert them when they have only a few minutes left.

Reflect on the Project
After students have finished their Team Assessments, help them go over what they thought went well and what did not, so they can be even more effective in the future.

Resources
- Website Rubric
- Self Assessment

The Renaissance and Reformation (1300–1650)

The Renaissance was an era marked by a new way of thinking and a burst of artistic creativity. It spread from Italy to northern Europe, where a remarkable number of artists and writers produced great works. The invention of the printing press not only helped spread Renaissance ideas but also made the Bible widely available. When Martin Luther challenged some practices of the Catholic Church, it marked the beginning of the Protestant Reformation. It spread throughout Europe, often sparking bloody religious wars, and forever broke the unity of the Church in Europe. The Catholic Reformation stemmed the spread of Protestantism and reasserted its power in much of Europe. The Church faced other challenges as scientists, spurred by a new approach called the scientific method, made exciting new discoveries.

■ CONNECT

MY STORY VIDEO
Leonardo da Vinci, Renaissance Man

Watch a video about one of the leading figures of the Renaissance, Leonardo da Vinci.

Check Understanding Why did Renaissance artists use the new technique of perspective? *(To show depth and distance on a flat surface, perspective introduced new levels of realism to art.)*

Apply Concepts Leonardo da Vinci said "The knowledge of all things is possible." How did this statement reflect Renaissance thinking? *(The Renaissance was a time when people in Europe took great interest in art, literature, and learning.)*

> **⚡ FLIP IT!**
> Assign the Flipped Video for this topic.

DIGITAL ESSENTIAL QUESTION ACTIVITY
Why is Culture Important?

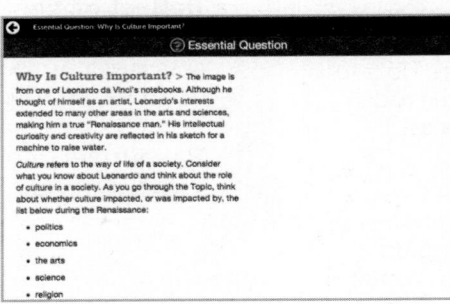

Ask students to think about the Essential Question for the Topic: Why Is Culture Important? Culture touches on almost every aspect of our lives.

If students have not already done so, ask them to list which of the cultural connections is most important. Rank them in order of importance. Then go over the results as a class.

Support a Point of View with Evidence
Why did you rank this cultural impact, or impact upon, as most important? *(Answers will vary. Students should understand the impact that changes in thinking during the Renaissance affected not only the arts but also the politics, religion, and science of the time, which in turn affected European society.)*

Identify Cause and Effect Why might new scientific discoveries significantly impact culture? *(Sample response: If a new scientific discovery challenges commonly held beliefs, it will require people to reevaluate how they think about their world.)*

DIGITAL TIMELINE ACTIVITY
The Renaissance and Reformation

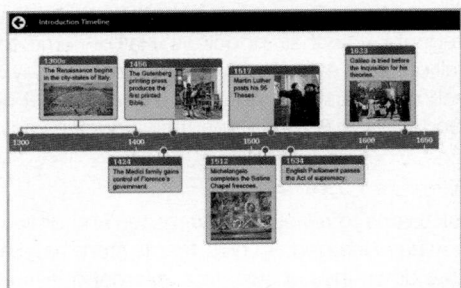

Display the timeline showing major events of the Renaissance and Reformation, as well as the Scientific Revolution. These are just some of the events that students will learn about while exploring this Topic. The timeline will provide a framework into which students can place the events they learn about.

D **Differentiate: Extra Suppor** How many years passed between the Gutenberg printing press producing the first printed Bible and Martin Luther posting his 95 Theses? *(61, Bible printed in 1456; 95 Theses posted in 1517)*

Check Understanding How many years was it after Martin Luther posted his Theses that the English Parliament passed the Act of Supremacy? *(17; Theses posted in 1517; Act of Supremacy was 1534)*

Topic Inquiry
Launch the Topic Inquiry with students after introducing the Topic.

PEARSON realize™

www.PearsonRealize.com
Access your Digital Lesson

The Italian Renaissance

Supporting English Language Learners

Use with Digital Text 1, **The Italian Renaissance.**

Speaking
Read *The Italian Renaissance* aloud to students. Then have students practice retelling by completing the following activities according to their level of English proficiency.

Beginning Model retelling for students by reading the first few sentences of *The Italian Renaissance* to students and retelling the information in your own words. Continue reading and retelling through the first subsection, "A New World View." For the second and third subsections, support students as they retell the information that you read aloud. Define any challenging vocabulary and simplify any complex sentence structure to help students understand the content.

Intermediate Model retelling for students by reading the introduction of *The Italian Renaissance* to students and retelling the information in it in your own words. Then continue reading the text, pausing every few sentences to help students practice retelling the content. Correct and guide students to an accurate retelling of the information as necessary. Assist students by defining any difficult vocabulary and clarifying any complex sentence structures.

Advanced Have students work together in cooperative groups of four. Have students count off, using numbers one through four. Students assigned to the number one will read the introductory paragraph of *The Italian Renaissance* Number twos will read "A New World View," number threes will read "A Spirit of Adventure and Curiosity," and number fours will read "Renaissance Humanism." After students read their assigned section of the text, they will retell what they learned from reading to the rest of the group. Circulate among students to assist with pronunciation or comprehension as necessary.

Advanced High Instruct student pairs to divide *The Italian Renaissance* into two sections: the introduction and "A New World View" in the first section and "A Spirit of Adventure and Curiosity" and "Renaissance Humanism" in the second section. One student in each pair should read the first section of the text silently while the other student in each pair reads the second section of the text silently. After reading, have students retell the section they read to their partner. Circulate among students to help them with pronunciation or comprehension as necessary.

Use with Digital Text 2, **Art Flourishes in the Renaissance.**

Speaking
Have students examine the images of Renaissance art in the text. Allow students time to establish an opinion about the artist or his work. Then have them select a favorite or least favorite and share their opinions.

Beginning Ask students to examine the images in the text. Display each image and have students describe what they see. Then ask students to choose a favorite piece. Have them express their opinion using the following sentence stem: My favorite piece is _____ because _____.

Intermediate Ask students to examine the images in the text. Display each image and have students describe what they see. Have students choose a favorite piece or favorite artist. Then have them express their opinion using a short sentence that explains their choice.

Advanced Direct students' attention to the images in the text. Allow them time to examine the art and choose a favorite piece. Then have them turn to a partner and share their opinion on the piece that they chose. Encourage students to use varied and rich language to describe their opinions to their partner.

Advanced High Direct students' attention to the images in the text. Allow them time to examine the art and choose a favorite and least favorite piece. Then have them express their opinions on the pieces and explain their reasoning to the group. Encourage students to use varied and rich language as they share their opinions.

▣ Differentiate Instruction

Use the Differentiated Instruction notes throughout the lesson plan to support the varied skill sets, levels of readiness, and interests in the mixed-ability classroom.

Challenge These notes include suggestions for expanding the activity for advanced students.

On-Level These notes include suggestions for modifying the activity to address different interests or learning styles.

Extra Support These notes include ideas for providing more scaffolding or reading spuport.

Special Needs These notes provide ideas for adapting instruction to support the needs of various special needs students.

■ NOTES

_____

_____

_____

_____

_____

_____

The Italian Renaissance

Objectives

Objective 1: Describe the characteristics of the Renaissance and understand why it began in Italy.

Objective 2: Identify Renaissance artists and explain how new ideas affected the arts of the period.

Objective 3: Understand how writers of the time addressed Renaissance themes.

Objective 4: Explain the impact of the Renaissance.

LESSON 1 ORGANIZER		PACING: APPROX. 1 PERIOD, .5 BLOCKS			
				RESOURCES	
		OBJECTIVES	PACING	Online	Print
Connect					
	DIGITAL START UP ACTIVITY **Michelangelo's *David***		5 min.	●	
Investigate					
	DIGITAL TEXT 1 **The Italian Renaissance**		10 min.	●	●
	DIGITAL TEXT 2 **The Renaissance Begins in Italy**	Objective 1	10 min.	●	●
	INTERACTIVE MAP **Renaissance Italy's City-States**		10 min.	●	
	DIGITAL TEXT 3 **Art Flourishes in the Renaissance**		10 min.	●	●
	BEFORE AND AFTER **The Discovery of Perspective**	Objectives 2, 4	10 min.	●	
	3-D MODEL **Duomo in Florence**		10 min.	●	
	DIGITAL TEXT 4 **New Books Reflect Renaissance Themes**	Objective 3	10 min.	●	●
Synthesize					
	DIGITAL ACTIVITY **Sistine Chapel**		5 min.	●	
Demonstrate					
	LESSON QUIZ **Lesson Quiz and Class Discussion Board**		10 min.	●	

PEARSON realize.™
www.PearsonRealize.com

Go online to access additional resources including:
Primary Sources • Biographies • Supreme Court cases •
21st Century Skill Tutorials • Maps • Graphic Organizers.

■ CONNECT

DIGITAL START UP ACTIVITY
Michelangelo's *David*

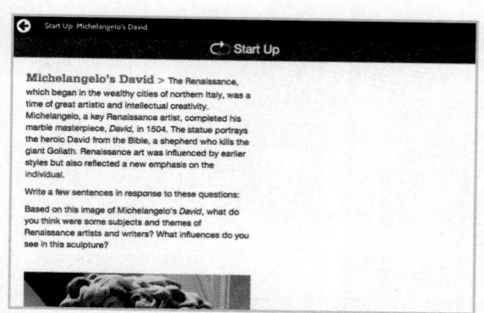

Project the Start Up Activity Ask students to answer the question as they enter and get settled. Then have them share their ideas with another student, either in class or through a chat or blog space.

Discuss Based on the subject that Michelangelo chose for this sculpture, what might be predicted as subjects or topics of interest for Renaissance artists? (*Possible answers: realistic portrayals of humans, religious themes, individual achievement, and classical Greek and Roman subjects*)

Aa Vocabulary Development: Use the Interactive Reading Notepad to preview the Key Terms and Academic Vocabulary in this Lesson with students.

⇅ FLIP IT!
Assign the Flipped Video for this lesson.

■ STUDENT EDITION PRINT PAGES: 350–356

■ INVESTIGATE

DIGITAL TEXT 1
The Italian Renaissance

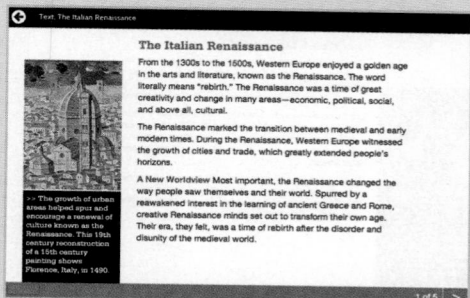

DIGITAL TEXT 2
The Renaissance Begins in Italy

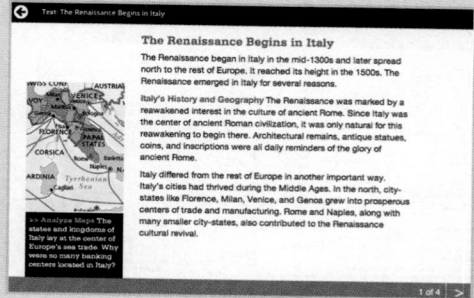

Objective 1: Describe the characteristics of the Renaissance and understand why it began in Italy.

Quick Instruction

Tell students that the Renaissance was a time of rebirth for the arts and culture in Europe, beginning in Italy in the 1300s. During the Renaissance, Western Europe witnessed the growth of cities and trade. There was renewed interest in classical learning and arts from Greece and Rome, along with technological innovations, an interest in humanism, and realism in the arts. Italy was a fertile ground for the Renaissance, with its classical Roman history and its location for trade with Muslim countries, which brought not only wealth but also the access to scholarship and translations of preserved classical works. In Italy, wealthy merchants and the powerful Catholic Church helped the arts flourish by their patronage of artists, architects, and writers.

Interactive Map: Renaissance Italy's City-States Project the interactive map. Click each hotspot to bring up images and text about the various city-states, artists, and sea trade. Tell students that the city-states had some similarities. They were often led by powerful merchant families, and most had famous artists from their area. The Catholic Church, with its control of the Papal States and the churches of the city-states, was a great patron of the arts and commissioned some of the most important works of the Renaissance.

■ ACTIVE CLASSROOM

Use the strategy A Closer Look and explain that students will be studying the role of arts in various Italian city-states or along a trade route. Divide the class into six groups. Project the Interactive Map. Have each group focus on one hotspot area of the map. Have them tell you what they learned as a result of their focus on this section. Collect insights for each map section.

ELL Use the ELL activity described in the ELL chart.

Further Instruction

While the Interactive Map focuses on visual arts, writers also benefited from the wealth and flourishing culture in Italy. Renaissance writers like Francisco Petrarch were pious Christians who focused on worldly subjects and emphasized humanism. Petrarch valued education and the classics in his work as a scholar, poet, and humanist.

Identify Causes Based on the Interactive Map and texts, why did the Renaissance develop in Italy before other European countries? (*Possible answer: The Renaissance developed first in Italy because merchants from wealthy city-states, rich from trade, financed and supported artists, as did the Roman Catholic Church; there were also art and artifacts from ancient Rome; and the knowledge of that era from trade with Muslims, who had preserved the classic works of Greece and Rome.*)

The Italian Renaissance

INTERACTIVE MAP
Renaissance Italy's City-States

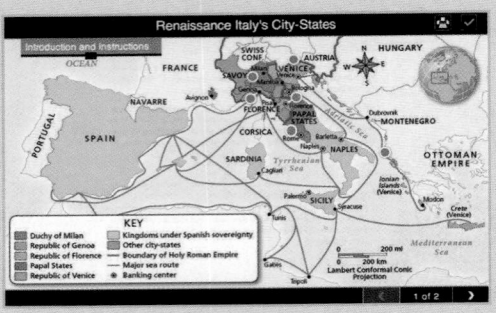

DIGITAL TEXT 3
Art Flourishes in the Renaissance

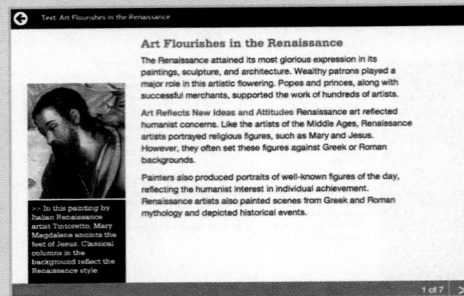

BEFORE AND AFTER
The Discovery of Perspective

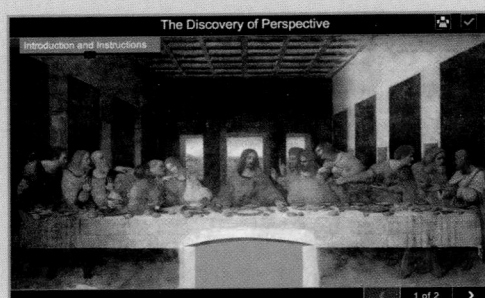

Predict Consequences The Interactive Map shows how the location of Italy helped the Renaissance to begin there. Based on the map, where might Renaissance ideas spread to next? *(Possible answer: Other countries in Europe would be impacted by the Italian Renaissance.)*

Project and discuss the Interactive Reading Notepad questions with the class.

Compare What were some characteristics of the Renaissance that can be seen in Francesco Petrarch and his work? *(Possible answer: Petrarch was multi-talented and had varied interests, a characteristic of Renaissance men. He stressed education and valued the classics, both Renaissance characteristics. He advocated humanism, also typical of the Renaissance.)*

Identify Causes What were some economic causes of the Italian Renaissance? *(Possible answer: Italy's location allowed sea trade, which made Italian merchants and merchant families wealthy. Wealthy families like the Medicis became arts patrons, helping the arts to flourish. The Roman Catholic Church also gave financial support to artists and scholars.)*

Objectives 2: **Identify Renaissance artists and explain how new ideas affected the arts of the period; 4: Explain the impact of the Renaissance.**

Quick Instruction

Remind students that even today, some of the world's most famous and influential artists— like Leonardo da Vinci, Michelangelo, and Raphael—are from the Italian Renaissance. These artists represented the ideals of their time: reviving classical forms, using innovative techniques, and focusing on humanism and realism in addition to religious themes. One example of Renaissance impact is Michelangelo's dome design for St. Peter's Cathedral, which, centuries later, was an inspiration for the United States Capitol's dome.

Before and After: The Discovery of Perspective Project the Interactive Art. Explain how the Italian Renaissance architect Brunelleschi is credited with inventing perspective; other Renaissance artists then started refining and using the technique to convey realism. Look at each image individually and view the transition between the two images. The activity describes vanishing lines used to create perspective. Let students know that another way artists added perspective to drawings was to make distant objects in the picture smaller than those closest to the viewer.

ACTIVE CLASSROOM

Use the Quickdraw strategy with students working in pairs. Give students a short period to share what they understand about perspective by trying to create their own sketches that show perspective.

Analyze Visuals Look again at the finished painting of *The Last Supper*. What Renaissance themes do you think are included in this painting? *(Possible answer: Student might find humanism in the portrayal of people and emotions, a religious theme, and realism.)*

Summarize Why was the development of perspective such an influential and important event in art history? *(Possible answer: The development of perspective allowed artists to create more realistic scenes. They could paint scenes that appeared three-dimensional for the first time. Architects also used the technique in sketches for buildings.)*

Interactive 3-D Model: Duomo in Florence Project the Interactive 3-D Model. Look at the model from various views and at the interactive aspects of the cathedral dome. Note that Brunelleschi, the dome's architect, was a Renaissance man in that he designed the dome, invented perspective, and built some machines used in the dome's construction.

3-D MODEL
Duomo in Florence

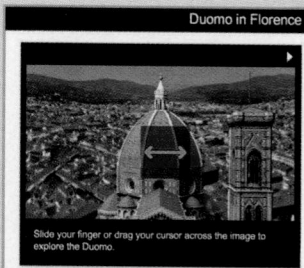

Duomo in Florence

The Italian Renaissance architect Filippo Brunelleschi designed this majestic dome ("Duomo") for the cathedral in Florence. He modeled it on the dome over the Pantheon, built in ancient Rome. Brunelleschi is credited with inventing perspective, which he used in his design. The Duomo, completed in 1436, was the largest domed structure built since A.D. 125.

Slide your finger or drag your cursor across the image to explore the Duomo.

1 of 3

⚡ ACTIVE CLASSROOM

Use the See-Think-Wonder strategy and have each student pair with a partner. Ask them: What do you notice about the dome? What does that make you think? What are you wondering about now that you've seen this? Share insights with the class.

ELL Use the ELL activity described in the ELL chart.

Further Instruction

Renaissance Art Flourishes: Core Reading and Interactive Reading Notepad Project and discuss the Interactive Reading Notepad questions, including the graphic organizer, asking students to chart artists, architects, and their accomplishments. Review the names of Renaissance artists and architects and their accomplishments and fill in the graphic organizer on the whiteboard as you go.

Summarize How did the new Renaissance worldview shape the work of Italian Renaissance artists and writers? *(Artists and writers adopted a new realism and a new emphasis on humanity.)*

D **Differentiate: Challenge** Have students research the design and look of the United States Capitol. Also have them research Michelangelo's design for (and find an image of) the St. Peter's Cathedral dome in Rome. Have students compare the two buildings, since the Capitol was modeled on Michelangelo's dome. Students may wish to draw a picture of one or both buildings to illustrate similarities.

DIGITAL TEXT 4
New Books Reflect Renaissance Themes

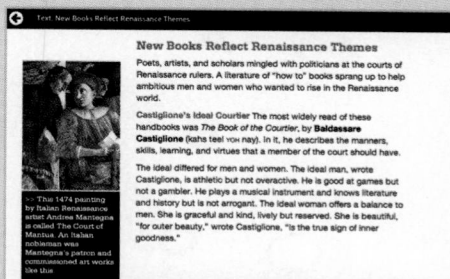

Text: New Books Reflect Renaissance Themes

New Books Reflect Renaissance Themes

Poets, artists, and scholars mingled with politicians at the courts of Renaissance rulers. A literature of "how to" books sprang up to help ambitious men and women who wanted to rise in the Renaissance world.

Castiglione's Ideal Courtier The most widely read of these handbooks was *The Book of the Courtier*, by **Baldassare Castiglione** (kahs teel yoн nay). In it, he describes the manners, skills, learning, and virtues that a member of the court should have.

The ideal differed for men and women. The ideal man, wrote Castiglione, is athletic but not overactive. He is good at games but not a gambler. He plays a musical instrument and knows literature and history but is not arrogant. The ideal woman offers a balance to men. She is graceful and kind, lively but reserved. She is beautiful, "for outer beauty," wrote Castiglione, "is the true sign of inner goodness."

>> This 1474 painting by Italian Renaissance artist Andrea Mantegna is called *The Court of Mantua*. An Italian nobleman was Mantegna's patron and commissioned art works like this

1 of 4

Objective 3: Understand how writers of the time addressed Renaissance themes.

Quick Instruction

Like Italian Renaissance artists, the writers of the time also showed curiosity, creativity, scholarship, and humanism. For example, Machiavelli and Castiglione both wrote "how-to" type books that were designed to help their fellow men. Some writers like Machiavelli had an impact beyond their own generation, influencing politicians for centuries.

Further Instruction

New Books Reflect Renaissance Themes: Interactive Reading Notepad Project and discuss the Interactive Reading Notepad questions.

Draw Conclusions What Renaissance idea appears in writing by Castiglione? *(Possible answer: He wrote about the ideal man having multiple talents and skills, which was a popular idea in the Renaissance.)*

Identify Effects How did Machiavelli's book *The Prince* have political impact many years after Machiavelli's life? *(Possible answer: The term "Machiavellian" came to refer to the use of deceit in politics. Later students of government argued that Machiavelli provided a realistic look at politics. His work is still read today for its study of government and power.)*

The Italian Renaissance

▌ SYNTHESIZE

DIGITAL ACTIVITY
The Sistine Chapel

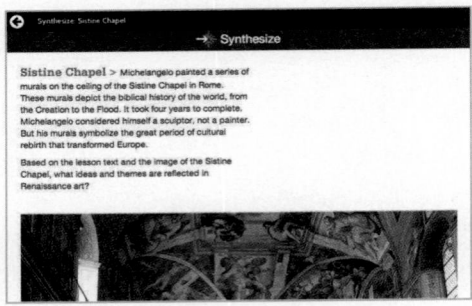

Tell students the enormous project of painting the Sistine Chapel ceiling still impresses artists today. The Italian Renaissance had a lasting impact on art and architecture.

Have students answer the questions in this activity, then discuss their answers with a partner.

Have partners think about the following question: Why is culture important? Have pairs share their answers with the class.

Discuss The Sistine Chapel painting was commissioned by a pope for a church. Wealthy merchant families in Renaissance Italy were patrons of the arts, sometimes purchasing art for their own homes or palaces. In today's modern American culture, where can you find examples of important art and architecture? *(Possible Answer: Churches today still sometimes display art and interesting architecture. Private galleries, public monuments, and public buildings like libraries and state capitols also house art or have unique architecture.)*

▌ DEMONSTRATE

LESSON QUIZ
Lesson Quiz and Class Discussion Board

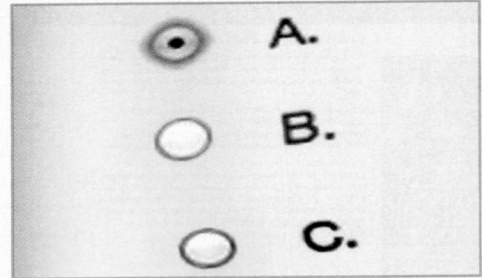

Assign the online Lesson Quiz for this lesson if you haven't already done so. Students will be offered automatic remediation or enrichment based on their score.

Pose these questions to the class on the Discussion Board: In "The Italian Renaissance" you read that Italy's ancient history, geography, and thriving city-states contributed to the development of a new age and a new way of thinking. The Italian Renaissance and its artists, writers, and architects shared some characteristics such as an emphasis on humanism, realism, and multiple talents. They also all had an impact on later time periods.

Predict Consequences What would you predict for where Renaissance ideas might have spread to next, after Italy? Students may refer back to the Interactive Map of political Europe to remember how Italy's location helped spark the Renaissance and to help predict where ideas might spread to next after Italy. *(Possible answer: Other countries in Europe would be a good prediction for the impact of the Italian Renaissance.)*

Predict Consequences How might the Renaissance world view and characteristics such as humanism eventually influence other areas, such as religion? *(Possible Answer: A student might predict correctly that a focus on humanism could lessen the power and influence of organized religion and the Catholic Church.)*

Topic Inquiry
Have students continue their investigations for the Topic Inquiry.

PEARSON realize www.PearsonRealize.com Access your Digital Lesson

The Renaissance in Northern Europe

Supporting English Language Learners

Use with Digital Text 3, **The Printing Revolution.**

Speaking
mass production

Beginning Read the subsection "Impact of the Printed Book" aloud to students and have them look at the associated image. Help them retell the information by using these sentence stems: The printing revolution ______ Europe. The changes that the printing revolution caused include ______.

Differentiate Instruction

Use the Differentiated Instruction notes throughout the lesson plan to support the varied skill sets, levels of readiness, and interests in the mixed-ability classroom.

Challenge These notes include suggestions for expanding the activity for advanced students.

On-Level These notes include suggestions for modifying the activity to address different interests or learning styles.

Extra Support These notes include ideas for providing more scaffolding or reading spuport.

Special Needs These notes provide ideas for adapting instruction to support the needs of various special needs students.

NOTES

The Renaissance in Northern Europe

Objectives

Objective 1: Describe the themes that northern European artists, humanists, and writers explored.

Objective 2: Explain how the printing revolution shaped European society.

LESSON 2 ORGANIZER		PACING: APPROX. 1 PERIOD, .5 BLOCKS			
				RESOURCES	
		OBJECTIVES	**PACING**	**Online**	**Print**
Connect					
DIGITAL START UP ACTIVITY **An Expanding World**			5 min.	●	
Investigate					
DIGITAL TEXT 1 **Artists of the Northern Renaissance**			10 min.	●	●
DIGITAL TEXT 2 **Northern Renaissance Humanists and Writers**			10 min.	●	●
INTERACTIVE GALLERY **Realism in Northern Europe Renaissance Art**		Objective 1	10 min.	●	
INTERACTIVE GALLERY **Shakespeare: "For All Time"**			10 min.	●	
DIGITAL TEXT 3 **The Printing Revolution**		Objective 2	10 min.	●	●
Synthesize					
DIGITAL ACTIVITY **Erasmus**			5 min.	●	
Demonstrate					
LESSON QUIZ **Lesson Quiz and Class Discussion Board**			10 min.	●	

Go online to access additional resources including:
Primary Sources • Biographies • Supreme Court cases •
21st Century Skill Tutorials • Maps • Graphic Organizers.

■ CONNECT

DIGITAL START UP ACTIVITY
An Expanding World

Project the Start Up Activity Ask students to answer the questions as they enter and get settled. Then have them share their ideas with another student, either in class or through a chat or blog space.

Discuss Why does Rabelais compare his time to that of Plato and Cicero? *(Sample Response: Renaissance humanists measured their own time against that of the classical period.)*

Aa **Vocabulary Development:** Use the Interactive Reading Notepad to preview the Key Terms and Academic Vocabulary in the Lesson with students.

⇅ FLIP IT!
Assign the Flipped Video for this lesson.

■ STUDENT EDITION PRINT
PAGES: 357–361

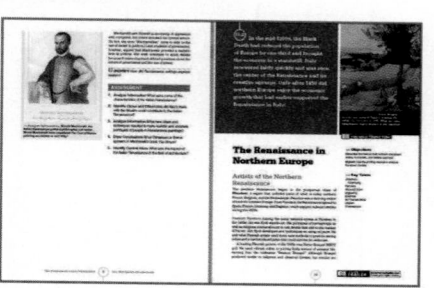

■ INVESTIGATE

DIGITAL TEXT 1
Artists of the Northern Renaissance

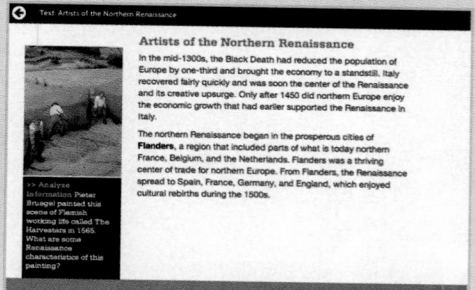

Objective 1: Describe the themes that northern European artists, humanists, and writers explored.

Quick Instruction
Tell students that the northern Renaissance began in the trading cities of Flanders in northern Europe. Artists who had traveled to Italy also helped Renaissance ideas move north. Like the Italians, northern European artists explored realism and humanism. Northern writers also examined these themes, and some were often critical of organized religion. The works of playwright William Shakespeare exemplified the Renaissance and had a lasting cultural impact.

Interactive Gallery: Realism in Northern Europe Renaissance Art Project the gallery. Look at and discuss each image individually. Explain how northern European artists like Jan van Eyck pioneered the technique of oil painting to reflect light, achieve depth, and create realistic details in their works. Northern Renaissance artists brought new realism to paintings of peasant life, religious scenes, and landscapes.

👥 ACTIVE CLASSROOM
Use the Quickdraw strategy with students working in pairs. Have each pair work on a sketch to show an understanding of realism. One student can research an Internet image of an animal or something else from nature; the other student can try to realistically recreate that image in a sketch.

DIGITAL TEXT 2
Northern Renaissance Humanists and Writers

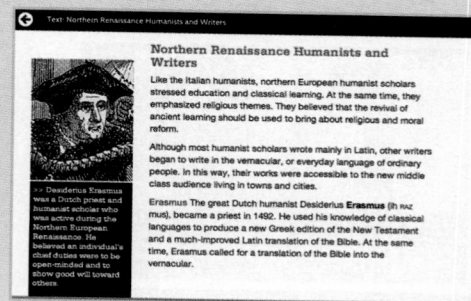

Interactive Gallery Project the Globe Theater. Click each hotspot individually to bring up images and text. Explain how Shakespeare's plays reflected their own Renaissance time period. For example, they often included some religious characters. His plays also transcend time by addressing universal themes such as family, power, and love. Shakespeare has had a lasting impact on language and culture.

👥 ACTIVE CLASSROOM
Use the Act It Out strategy with students working in small groups. Have each group choose one of the hotspot images to act out. Their choice might include lines from *Hamlet*, a short biography of Shakespeare, or an image from his other plays. They can find scenes from his plays online to enhance the model's text and get more lines to enact.

ELL Use the ELL activity described in the ELL chart.

The Renaissance in Northern Europe

INTERACTIVE GALLERY
Realism in Northern Europe Renaissance Art

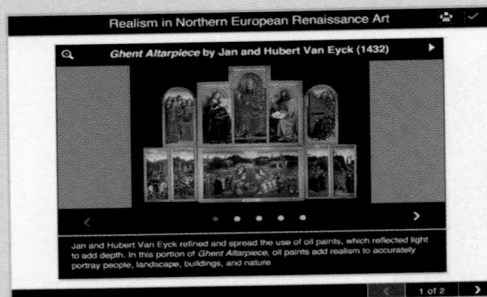

INTERACTIVE GALLERY
Shakespeare: "For All Time"

DIGITAL TEXT 3
The Printing Revolution

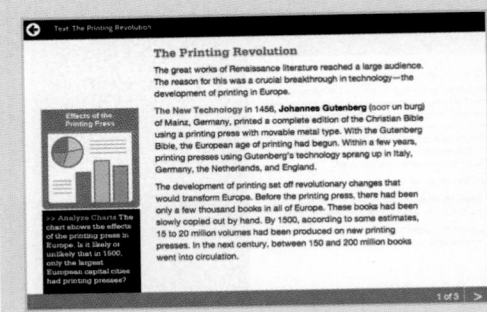

Further Instruction

Besides Shakespeare, other northern European Renaissance writers included Sir Thomas More, Desiderius Erasmus, and François Rabelais. These three writers were humanists, addressing society's problems and advocating for social reforms and better education.

Artists of the Northern Renaissance: Core Reading and Interactive Reading Notepad Project and discuss the Interactive Reading Notepad questions.

Analyze Images What realistic images appear in van Eyck's paintings, as seen in the accompanying text and Interactive Gallery? *(Possible answer: The people look true to life, and there are scenes of nature and animals that look realistic. The settings are natural, there are everyday objects, and the colors and lighting are realistic.)*

Analyze Information How did northern Renaissance artists blend Italian Renaissance ideas with their own? *(Dürer used Italian painting techniques along with his own ideas for engraving. Flemish artists used oil paintings to achieve depth, create realistic details, and express humanist themes.)*

Northern Renaissance Humanists and Writers: Interactive Reading Notepad Project and discuss the Interactive Reading Notepad questions, including the graphic organizer asking students to chart universal themes addressed by northern European writers. Fill in the graphic organizer on the whiteboard as you go.

Compare How did More's vision of utopia fit with some ideas of Erasmus? *(Possible answer: More's utopia included education for all, and Erasmus put a high value on education. Both writers also wanted social reforms.)*

Summarize How did popular writers like Shakespeare help spread humanist ideas? *(Possible answer: They wrote in the vernacular so everyday people could read their works. They focused on stories about individuals and their human problems and emotions.)*

D Differentiate: Challenge/Gifted Have students search online to find the words to a monologue from a Shakespeare play. Each student can practice and then perform their speech. Students can also research to find a video clip of a performance from the same play and write a short paragraph describing why they think that play still has relevance to people today.

Objective 2: Explain how the printing revolution shaped European society.

Quick Instruction

Tell students that around 1455, Johann Gutenberg invented a printing press in Germany. The first book he printed was a Bible. Many Bibles soon followed; the press allowed books to be produced at a much faster rate than medieval handwriting methods. The Italian Renaissance, already spreading to northern Europe, expanded quickly throughout Europe due to the increased knowledge and education nurtured by the printing revolution and books.

ELL Use the ELL activity described in the ELL chart.

SYNTHESIZE

DIGITAL ACTIVITY
Erasmus

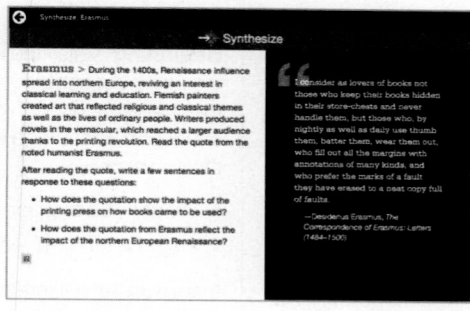

Ask students to think about why culture was important to northern Europeans like Erasmus. Why did artists like Dürer travel to Italy? Have students think about and discuss how the printing revolution helped spread culture throughout Europe.

Have students complete the questions in the Digital Activity and share their answers with partners.

Discuss Why did humanists like Erasmus call for translating the Bible into the vernacular? *(He believed that all people should have access to religious and classical learning.)*

DEMONSTRATE

LESSON QUIZ
Lesson Quiz and Class Discussion Board

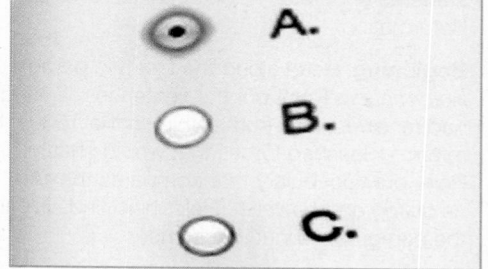

Assign the online Lesson Quiz for this lesson if you haven't already done so. Students will be offered automatic remediation or enrichment based on their score.

Pose these questions to the class on the Discussion Board: In "The Renaissance in Northern Europe" you read about the printing revolution and its effect on helping spread Renaissance ideals such as humanism and education. You also learned about northern European Renaissance artists and writers, the techniques they used, and the themes they explored.

Identify Effects What political impacts did writers like More, Rabelais, and Erasmus hope to achieve in their own time and for future generations? *(Possible Answer: They wanted to reform societies to be more fair and just, with widespread literacy and education. More envisioned an ideal utopian society. They challenged the political power of the Church by critiquing corruption in organized religion.)*

Predict Consequences What impact might the printing press have had on religious reform movements of the 1500s? *(Possible Answer: Religious reformers could use the printing press to spread their ideas to a large number of people quickly and cheaply.)*

Topic Inquiry
Have students continue their investigations for the Topic Inquiry.

Further Instruction
The Printing Revolution: Interactive Reading Notepad Project and discuss the Interactive Reading Notepad questions.

Infer Why was the Christian Bible the first book that Gutenberg printed? *(Possible Answer: It was the most widely used book of the time, and even Renaissance humanists were still influenced by Christianity and religious themes.)*

Predict Consequences Do you think that the Renaissance would have spread as quickly throughout northern Europe if the presses printed only Bibles? *(Answers may vary, but the best prediction is probably no. Through other books, readers gained access to a broad range of knowledge, from medicine and law to mining. Other printed books exposed educated Europeans to new ideas and places, including Renaissance ideas from Italy.)*

The Protestant Reformation

Supporting English Language Learners

Use with Digital Text 1, **Causes of the Reformation.**

Speaking
Have students explore terms commonly used to indicate contrasts, especially over time, such as *during, by, since,* and *however.* Help students understand how changes over time contributed to the Reformation.

Beginning Read aloud the first two paragraphs of *Causes of the Reformation.* Point out the sentences "During the Middle Ages, the Church had renewed itself from within. In the 1500s, however, the movement for reform unleashed forces that would shatter Christian unity in Europe." Point out vocabulary that compares the Middle Ages to the 1500s, such as *during* and *however.* Help them find similar word use later in the text in the paragraph about indulgences.

Intermediate Read aloud the first two paragraphs of *Causes of the Reformation.* Ask students to identify a passage that contrasts the Middle Ages and the 1500s. Have them identify words used that show the two periods are being compared. Then, ask them to find similar word usage later in the text.

Advanced Ask pairs of students to read *Causes of the Reformation* to one another. Tell them to identify words and phrases that compare the Middle Ages to the era of the Reformation. Then, have them construct complex sentences of their own using such words and phrases such as *since, by the time of,* and *before then.*

Advanced High Ask groups of students to read *Causes of the Reformation.* Have them construct complex sentences that explain changing conditions that led to the Reformation. Tell them their sentences should include connecting words and phrases used for comparison and contrast.

Use with Digital Text 1, **Causes of the Reformation.**

Speaking
Before beginning this activity, read *Causes of the Reformation* aloud to the class. Then have students complete one of the following activities depending on their level of English proficiency.

Beginning Retell the information in *Causes of the Reformation* using language accessible for beginning English learners. Have students complete the questions using information from the text. Explain challenging words and concepts. Encourage students to point to information in the text to support their answers.

- Would you support the Reformation?
- How would you feel about authority if you lived during this time?

Intermediate Reread *Causes of the Reformation* aloud to students. Have students discuss the text using the questions below as a guide. Explain any challenging words and concepts. Encourage students to refer to information in the text to support their answers.

- Would you support the Reformation?
- How would you feel about authority if you lived during this time?

Advanced Have students reread the text. Discuss the text using the questions below as a guide. Help students work together to explain challenging words and concepts. Encourage students to refer to information in the text to support their answers.

- How would you feel if you lived during the Reformation?
- Would you support the efforts of reformers? Why or why not?

Advanced High Have students reread the text. Instruct small groups of students to share their feelings about the text using the questions below as a guide. Remind students to work together to explain challenging words and concepts to one another. Encourage students to refer to information in the text to support their answers and circulate to provide support.

- How would you feel if you lived during the Reformation?
- Would you support the efforts of reformers? Why or why not?

◨ Differentiate Instruction

Use the Differentiated Instruction notes throughout the lesson plan to support the varied skill sets, levels of readiness, and interests in the mixed-ability classroom.

Challenge These notes include suggestions for expanding the activity for advanced students.

On-Level These notes include suggestions for modifying the activity to address different interests or learning styles.

Extra Support These notes include ideas for providing more scaffolding or reading spuport.

Special Needs These notes provide ideas for adapting instruction to support the needs of various special needs students.

◼ NOTES

PEARSON
realize
www.PearsonRealize.com

Go online to access additional resources including:
Primary Sources • Biographies • Supreme Court cases •
21st Century Skill Tutorials • Maps • Graphic Organizers.

Objectives

Objective 1: Summarize the factors that encouraged the Protestant Reformation.

Objective 2: Explain the impact of the printing press on the Reformation.

Objective 3: Analyze Martin Luther's role in shaping the Protestant Reformation.

Objective 4: Explain the teachings and impact of John Calvin.

LESSON 3 ORGANIZER			PACING: APPROX. 1 PERIOD, .5 BLOCKS		
		OBJECTIVES	**PACING**	**RESOURCES**	
				Online	**Print**
Connect					
DIGITAL START UP ACTIVITY **Launching the Protestant Reformation**			5 min.	●	
Investigate					
DIGITAL TEXT 1 **Causes of the Reformation**		Objective 1	10 min.	●	●
DIGITAL TEXT 2 **Martin Luther's Protests Bring Change**		Objectives 2, 3	10 min.	●	●
BEFORE AND AFTER **Illuminated Manuscripts to Printed Pages**			10 min.	●	
INTERACTIVE GALLERY **Reformation Art**			10 min.	●	
DIGITAL TEXT 3 **John Calvin Challenges the Church**		Objective 4	10 min.	●	●
Synthesize					
DIGITAL ACTIVITY **Technology: The Communications Revolution**			5 min.	●	
Demonstrate					
DIGITAL QUIZ **Lesson Quiz and Class Discussion Board**			10 min.	●	

Topic ⑩ Lesson 3

The Protestant Reformation

CONNECT

DIGITAL START UP ACTIVITY
Launching the Protestant Reformation

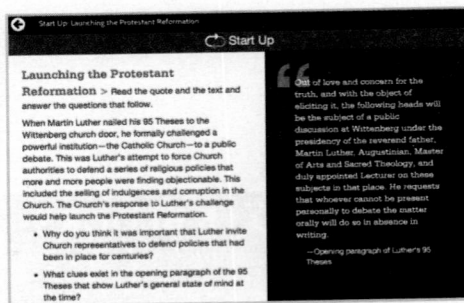

Project the Start Up Activity Ask students to answer the questions as they enter and get settled. Then have them share their ideas with another student.

Discuss Why do you think it was important that Luther invite Church representatives to defend its policies? *(It showed that Luther was willing to work for change within the Church and that the purpose of the debate was to reform the existing Church, not create a new church.)* What clues in the opening paragraph show Luther's general state of mind? *(Luther uses the word "request". This makes the debate an invitation. Luther also identifies himself as a master of theology to make clear that he is qualified to debate these issues.)*

Aa Vocabulary Development: Use the Interactive Reading Notepad to preview the Key Terms and Academic Vocabulary in this Lesson with students.

⇅ FLIP IT!

Assign the Flipped Video for this lesson.

■ STUDENT EDITION PRINT PAGES: 362–367

INVESTIGATE

DIGITAL TEXT 1
Causes of the Reformation

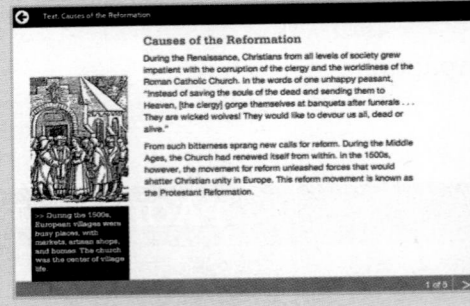

Objective 1: Summarize the factors that encouraged the Protestant Reformation.

Quick Instruction

Remind students that, as in Renaissance Italy, life for most people in northern Europe was filled with uncertainty. The changing economy and uncertain times led society to begin to embrace the idea of social and religious reform. The humanist stress on education resulted in people questioning traditional ways of doing things. Renaissance humanist ideas added to a spirit of reform. This was especially true of religious traditions, as abuses within the Church became common. All of these factors encouraged protests and calls for reform.

ELL Use the ELL activity described in the ELL chart.

Further Instruction

Causes of the Reformation: Core Reading and Interactive Reading Notepad Project and discuss the Interactive Reading Notepad questions.

Be sure students understand that the economic changes to a market economy resulted in an unequal distribution of wealth, which, in turn, contributed to Renaissance ideas of social reform.

Tell students that the Church's involvement in secular and political matters, as well as the papal wealth and lavish lifestyle, began to draw criticism. When the Church began to condone the selling of indulgences for money instead of awarding them for good works, many people began to think that the Church was corrupt and was losing its moral authority. Some people questioned why they should follow the practices of such a Church instead of the simpler practices of the early Christian church.

Analyze Information Popes had led lavish lifestyles for centuries. Why would people find that lifestyle objectionable at this point in history? *Sample response: Renaissance ideas promoted the concepts of social reform and the return of the Church to its simpler Christian roots. Most people at the beginning of the Reformation were poor. The great wealth of the popes and lavish spending made them appear to be more like secular nobles than religious leaders.*

DIGITAL TEXT 2

Martin Luther's Protests Bring Change

BEFORE AND AFTER

Illuminated Manuscripts to Printed Pages

INTERACTIVE GALLERY

Reformation Art

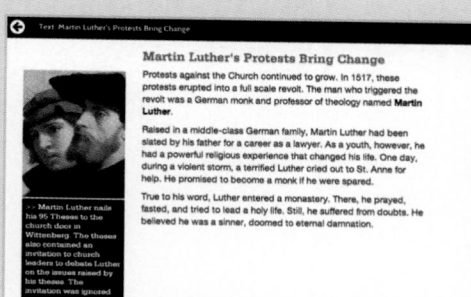

Objectives 2: Explain the impact of the printing press on the Reformation; 3: Analyze Martin Luther's role in shaping the Protestant Reformation.

Quick Instruction

Interactive Gallery: Reformation Art
Project the Lucas Cranach painting. Explain that Protestant art was another means of communicating Protestant ideas. Look at the images surrounding the labeled hotspots. Demonstrate how a hotspot works. Click on one of the hotspots for an explanation of what that area of the painting is communicating. Ask students to examine the different parts of the painting before they click on the hotspot. Tell students that the Protestant Reformation was a response to several conditions that existed in northern Europe. Martin Luther was at the forefront of the Protestant Reformation and was greatly aided in his goals by the printing press. Luther's objections to Church practices sparked a full scale revolt, leading to his excommunication. One of his important teachings was that people have access to God through faith and the Bible, which was more readily available as a result of the printing press. Reformation ideas were also expressed through the visual medium of the arts, with painters expressing Reformist ideas on canvas.

📷 ACTIVE CLASSROOM

Use the See-Think-Wonder strategy and have students pair with a partner. Students should study the Cranach painting. Ask them: What do you see? What does it make you think? What are you wondering about now that you've seen this? Have the student pairs share their insights with the class.

ELL Use the ELL activity described in the ELL chart.

D Differentiate: Extra Support Help students understand why someone who had dedicated his life to the Church would then decide to protest against it. First, ask students to think about groups that they belong to. Then ask them to think of a time when they disagreed with the group's decision. How did they feel about the group? Did they speak out? If so, what was their motivation? *Sample response: to bring about change* Reinforce that Luther's goal was not to bring down the Church but, rather, to change it because he did not agree with some of its practices.

Further Instruction

Martin Luther—Catalyst for Change: Core Reading and Interactive Reading Notepad Project and discuss the Interactive Reading Notepad questions.

Before and After: Illuminated Manuscripts to Printed Pages Project the slider image. Explain how the interaction works by demonstrating the slider feature that allows students to compare a hand-written, illuminated text with a similar text produced by a printing press from the 1500s. Make sure students understand the importance of the printing press to the success of the Protestant Reformation. Whereas earlier reform movements were more localized, the printing press allowed Martin Luther and other reformers to publish their views throughout northern Europe and beyond, in a relatively short period of time. Printed versions of Luther's 95 Theses made the critical questions and challenges to Church authority accessible to many people. This gave people an opportunity to discuss these new ideas and, often, support reform movements.

📷 ACTIVE CLASSROOM

Use the Make Headlines strategy and ask students to write a headline that captures the most important aspect about the printing press and its impact on the Protestant Reformation. Have students share their headlines with the rest of the class.

Draw inferences How did the Renaissance and Reformation emphasis on greater education help the Protestant Reformation? *The Renaissance humanists encouraged education and Luther, along with other reformers, strongly promoted education for all. The printing press provided affordable books and other writings that allowed people to read about these issues.*

The Protestant Reformation

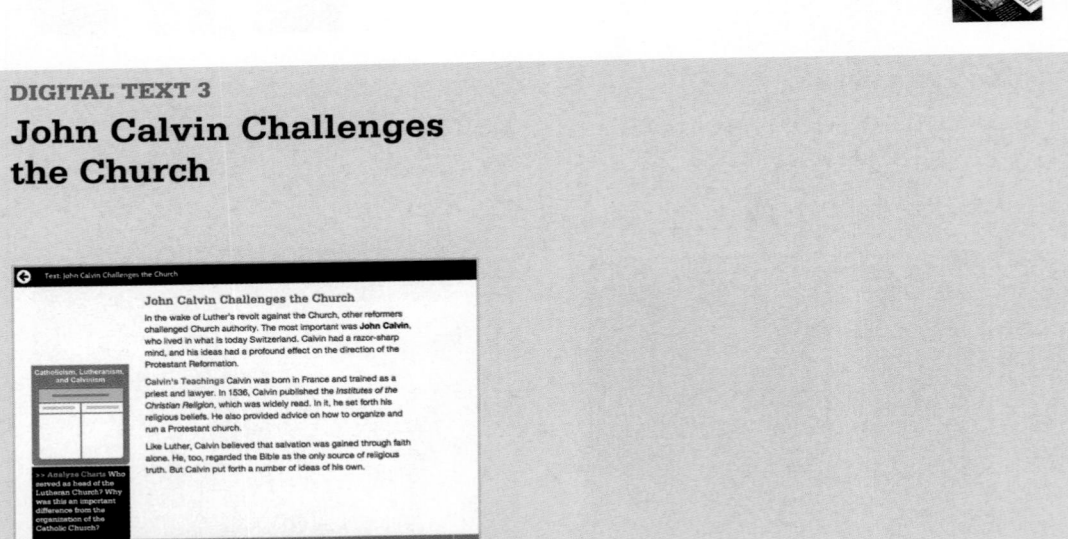

DIGITAL TEXT 3

John Calvin Challenges the Church

Objective 4: Explain the teachings and impact of John Calvin.

Quick Instruction

Tell students that the Reformation included the founding of many different Protestant sects. Calvinism became one of the largest. John Calvin and his followers established a theocracy in Geneva. A theocracy is a government run by religious leaders. It was the only political system of this type in Europe. Along with this theocratic political system, the Calvinist belief in predestination set them apart from the other main Protestant faiths.

Further Instruction

The Reformation in Switzerland: Core Reading and Interactive Reading Notepad Project and discuss the Interactive Reading Notepad questions.

Tell students that Calvinism and the doctrine of predestination appealed to many people because it provided a pre-ordained structure in a time of uncertainty. If people lived good lives, it was evidence that they had attained salvation because only those chosen would live good lives in the first place. Calvinism presented a very simple and direct approach to the question of salvation. While Calvinism had a strong following, it faced a great deal of opposition from both Catholics and Lutherans, which led to religious wars throughout Europe.

Draw Conclusions Why might Calvin's belief in a theocracy as the ideal form of government lead to persecution of Calvinists? *Sample response: The secular leaders of other European countries would see a theocracy as a threat because it suggests that a secular government would prevent a truly Christian society.*

SYNTHESIZE

DIGITAL ACTIVITY

Technology: The Communications Revolution

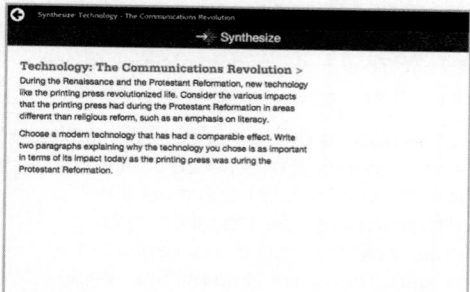

Project the Synthesize activity. Have students work in pairs to exchange ideas on the technology they chose. Ask a talking partner to share their ideas with the rest of the class.

Discuss How is the impact of the modern technology chosen similar to the impact of the printing press? *Sample response: Communication over large areas is much quicker than it was in the past. The printing press was as revolutionary in this regard as television, cell phones, computers, or the Internet.* What basic skills or abilities do users of the modern technology need to have compared to the users of the printing press? *Sample response: Those who use modern technology need to know how to read. Printing press operators had to learn how to set type, properly ink the type, and work the press. Authors had to be able to read and write well enough to produce text that would be understandable by most people.*

DEMONSTRATE

DIGITAL QUIZ

Lesson Quiz and Class Discussion Board

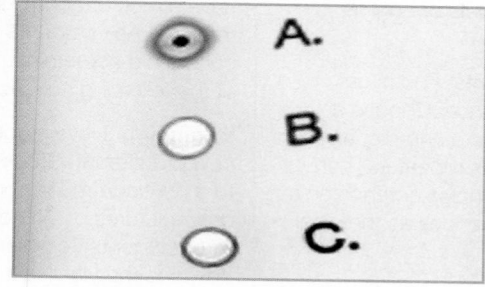

Assign the online Lesson Quiz for this lesson if you have not already done so. Students will be offered automatic remediation or enrichment based on their score.

Pose these questions to the class on the discussion board.

Analyze Main Idea What were the causes of the Protestant Reformation?

Summarize What impact did the printing press have on the Protestant Reformation?

Topic Inquiry

Have students continue their investigations for the Topic Inquiry.

Reformation Ideas Spread

Supporting English Language Learners

Use with Digital Text 3, **The Catholic Reformation.**

Speaking

Read *The Catholic Reformation* aloud to students. Then have students practice recognizing and using different grammatical structures by completing the following activities according to their levels of English proficiency.

Beginning Review grammatical structures with students. Focus on the subject and verb necessary for formulating a sentence. Choose a simple sentence from *The Catholic Reformation* and write and display it for students. Then slowly read it aloud. Have students repeat it. Then have students say their own sentences, using the example sentence as a model. Encourage students to add details to their sentences as they feel able to do so.

Intermediate Review different grammatical structures with students. Choose two or three sentences from *The Catholic Reformation* to use as examples. Show students which sentences have phrases and which have dependent and independent clauses. Then ask students to write and say two or three of their own sentences, using the example sentences as a model.

Advanced Have students review dependent and independent clauses with a partner. Then ask them to reread *The Catholic Reformation* to look for examples of different types of sentences. Then have pairs write and speak four sentences, two with dependent and independent clauses and two with just independent clauses. Circulate among students to offer support as needed.

Advanced High Have students write a paragraph about *The Catholic Reformation* using a variety of sentence types. Then have students speak their paragraph aloud to the class. Help students make grammatical corrections when necessary.

Use with Digital Text 1, **An Explosion of Protestant Sects.**

Speaking

Before beginning this activity, read *An Explosion of Protestant Sects* aloud to the class. Explain to students that groups of people throughout history have struck out on their own to form new communities for many different reasons. Ask students to think of stories they know in which a group or culture did something new or different. Then have students complete one of the following activities depending on their level of English proficiency.

Beginning Have students tell a story about a group that does something new or different. Students can use their personal experience of moving to a new community or a story from their native culture. Instruct them to draw pictures of different parts of their story and arrange them in order. After students complete each picture, help them develop a caption to describe the images they have created. Then have students use simple words and phrases to tell their story to a partner or to the class.

Intermediate Have students tell a story about a group that does something new or different. Students can use their personal experience of moving to a new community or a story from their native culture. Instruct them to write then speak simple sentences to tell their stories. Students may draw pictures and write captions to enhance their stories. Then have students tell their stories to the class using the most detailed language possible.

Advanced Have students tell a story about doing something differently from others. Students can use their personal experience of moving to a new community or a story from their native culture. Instruct them to organize their stories by writing down key phrases. Then have students share their stories with a partner. Encourage students to use descriptive details and action verbs as they tell their stories. Partners should ask clarifying questions as needed. Circulate among students to offer assistance as necessary.

Advanced High Have students tell a personal story about doing something differently from others. Students can use their personal experience of moving to a new community or a story from their native culture. Have students think about and plan their stories before sharing them with the whole class. Encourage students to use vivid language and descriptive details. Listening students should ask clarifying questions as needed.

◨ Differentiate Instruction

Use the Differentiated Instruction notes throughout the lesson plan to support the varied skill sets, levels of readiness, and interests in the mixed-ability classroom.

Challenge These notes include suggestions for expanding the activity for advanced students.

On-Level These notes include suggestions for modifying the activity to address different interests or learning styles.

Extra Support These notes include ideas for providing more scaffolding or reading spuport.

Special Needs These notes provide ideas for adapting instruction to support the needs of various special needs students.

◼ NOTES

PEARSON
realize™
www.PearsonRealize.com

Go online to access additional resources including:
Primary Sources • Biographies • Supreme Court cases •
21st Century Skill Tutorials • Maps • Graphic Organizers.

Objectives

Objective 1: Describe the new ideas that Protestant sects embraced.

Objective 2: Understand why England formed a new church.

Objective 3: Analyze how the Catholic Church reformed itself.

Objective 4: Explain why many groups faced persecution during the Reformation.

Objective 5: Explain the impact of the Reformation.

LESSON 4 ORGANIZER

PACING: APPROX. 1 PERIOD, .5 BLOCKS

		OBJECTIVES	PACING	RESOURCES Online	RESOURCES Print
Connect					
DIGITAL START UP ACTIVITY **Reformation Ideas Reach England**			5 min.	●	
Investigate					
DIGITAL TEXT 1 **An Explosion of Protestant Sects**		Objectives 1, 5	10 min.	●	●
DIGITAL TEXT 2 **The English Reformation**			10 min.	●	
INTERACTIVE TIMELINE **Timeline of the English Reformation**		Objectives 2, 5	10 min.	●	
DIGITAL TEXT 3 **The Catholic Reformation**			10 min.	●	●
INTERACTIVE MAP **Major European Religions, About 1600**		Objectives 3, 5	10 min.	●	
DIGITAL TEXT 4 **Religious Persecution Continues**		Objective 4	10 min.	●	●
Synthesize					
DIGITAL ACTIVITY **Spread and Impact of the Protestant Reformation**			5 min.	●	
Demonstrate					
LESSON QUIZ **Lesson Quiz and Class Discussion Board**			10 min.	●	

Reformation Ideas Spread

■ CONNECT

DIGITAL START UP ACTIVITY

Reformation Ideas Reach England

Project the Start Up Activity Ask students to answer the question as they enter and get settled. Then have them share their ideas with another student.

Discuss What does the image suggest about Henry VIII's attitude toward the Roman Catholic Church and the fate of the Reformation in England? *(Sample answer: Henry has rejected the authority of the Church and the Reformation will change England.)*

Aa Vocabulary Development: Use the Interactive Reading Notepad to preview the Key Terms and Academic Vocabulary in this Lesson with students.

⚑ FLIP IT!
Assign the Flipped Video for this lesson.

■ STUDENT EDITION PRINT PAGES: 368–373

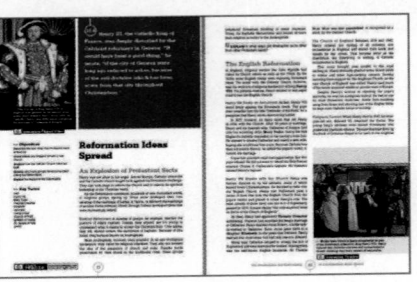

■ INVESTIGATE

DIGITAL TEXT 1

An Explosion of Protestant Sects

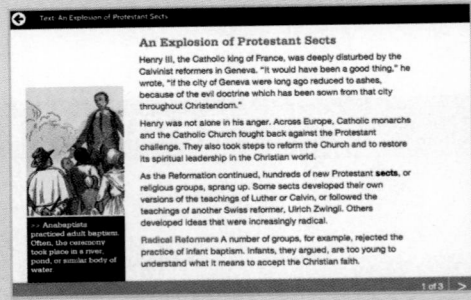

Objectives 1: Describe the new ideas that Protestant sects embraced; **5:** Explain the impact of the Reformation.

Quick Instruction

Tell students that as the Reformation spread from northern Germany, different Protestant sects emerged throughout Europe. Some of these sects, like the Anabaptists, were considered quite radical even by other Protestants. While most of the new Protestant movements were peaceful, some spurred violence as reformers clashed with other reformers.

⬛ **ELL** Use the ELL activity described in the ELL chart.

Further Instruction

An Explosion of Protestant Sects: Core Text and Interactive Reading Notepad
Project and discuss the Interactive Reading Notepad questions.

Explain to students that during this period of change, groups protesting traditional Catholic authority took the opportunity to develop a religious system that fit their specific needs and change what the sect believed was wrong about traditional doctrine or forms of worship.

Among these early sects, those who opposed infant baptism were considered the most radical by Catholics and other Protestants. The Anabaptists, as they were called, also had more radical groups within their own sect that sought sweeping social change as well as religious change. Disagreement over religion erupted into violence in some places and earned the condemnation of Reformation leaders like Martin Luther.

Identify Cause and Effect What was one of the effects of the Protestant Reformation on religion in Europe? *(Europe had more religious diversity as a variety of religious sects developed.)*

Compare What belief did all Protestant reformers share, regardless of sect? *The Catholic Church had no spiritual or moral authority over Christians.*

DIGITAL TEXT 2
The English Reformation

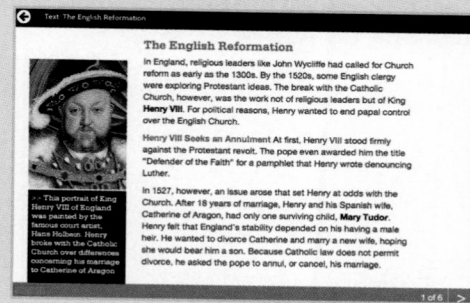

INTERACTIVE TIMELINE
Timeline of the English Reformation

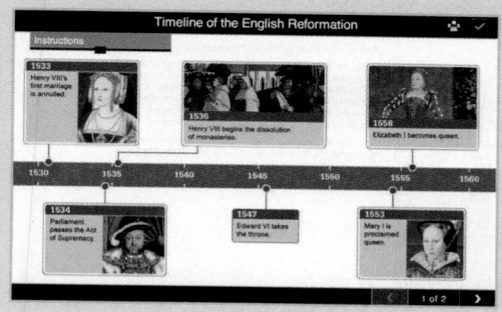

DIGITAL TEXT 3
The Catholic Reformation

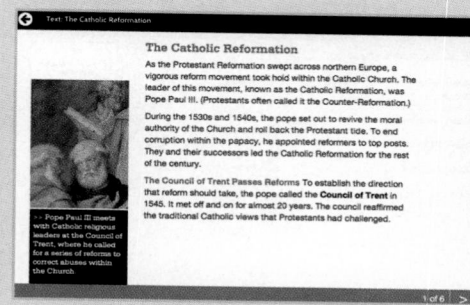

Objectives 2: Understand why England formed a new church; 5: Explain the impact of the Reformation.

Quick Instruction

Interactive Timeline: Timeline of the English Reformation Project the timeline. Look at each image individually and then view the timeline as a whole. Remind students that the English Reformation was a relatively long process. It ended with a compromise and a Protestant England with a state church that was similar to the Catholic Church in terms of hierarchy. The differences between the two churches, though, were substantial enough to cause conflict through the reigns of four consecutive English monarchs.

🖳 ACTIVE CLASSROOM

Use the Ranking Strategy to have students go through the events in the timeline and rank which ones had the greatest impact on the English Reformation.

Draw Conclusions Look at the rankings. What are the most important influences on the English Reformation? (*Answers will vary. Some students will see Henry's break from the Church as the most important influence, as it is questionable whether an English Reformation would have taken place without Henry's break from the Church. Other students may point out that it was Elizabeth's settlement that made England a truly Protestant country.*)

Further Instruction

The Reformation in England: Core Text and Interactive Reading Notepad Project

and discuss the Interactive Reading Notepad questions.

Read aloud Henry VIII's statement to the pope and give students a few minutes to think about it. ". . . we believe that no duty is more incumbent on a Catholic sovereign than to preserve and increase the Catholic faith. . . so when we learned that the pest of Martin Luther's heresy had appeared in Germany and was raging everywhere. . . we bent all our thoughts and energies on uprooting (those heresies) in every possible way."

Explain to students that Henry VIII considered himself a staunchly Catholic monarch of a Catholic country. Explore with students how Henry's actions could be so different from his earlier words.

Predict Would Henry have still broken with the Church if Luther's teachings had not become as popular as they were? (*Possible answer: It's not likely he would have broken away from the Church, as he would have been the first to do so and would likely have faced a revolt from his Catholic subjects. Luther's teachings were gaining popularity in England as well as Europe, and this gave Henry a foothold for the break.*)

Point out to students that Henry's Church of England had many similarities to the Catholic Church in terms of the basic hierarchy and in many of the religious rituals. For example, bishops and archbishops remained, while Henry essentially took the place of the pope as the supreme head of the church.

Infer How did Henry gain support for his Anglican church? (*He kept some forms of Catholic worship to appease those who wanted reform, but maybe not to the extent that Luther chose.*)

Objectives 3: Analyze how the Catholic Church reformed itself; 5: Explain the impact of the Reformation.

Quick Instruction

Interactive Map: Major European Religions, About 1600 Project the interactive map. Note that despite the spread of Protestantism, Europe remained mostly Catholic. Explain that the Catholic Reformation is also called the Counter-Reformation because it was driven by the Church's desire to counter the Protestant Reformation that had spread so quickly throughout parts of Europe. There had long been Catholic reformers in the Church who wanted to effect change. The challenge of the Protestant Reformation gave impetus to these internal reform efforts and the goal of stopping Protestantism from spreading further.

🖳 ACTIVE CLASSROOM

Use the Audio Tour strategy and pair students to work with the map. Have the first student give the second a verbal "tour" of the map—what does it show? Have the second student give the first an explanation of what it means.

D Differentiate: Challenge/Gifted Ask challenge students to compare how the Protestant Reformation and the Catholic Reformation responded to the growing problems within the Church. Ask them to make a three-column chart, listing the problems in the Church, the Protestant reform movement, and the Catholic reaction.

Reformation Ideas Spread

INTERACTIVE MAP

Major European Religions, About 1600

DIGITAL TEXT 4

Religious Persecution Continues

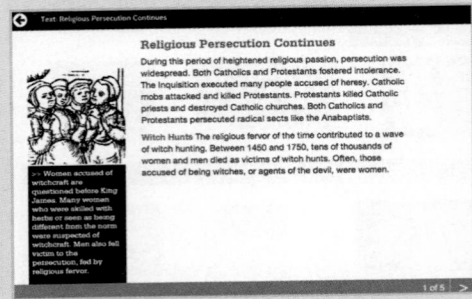

Then ask students to write a short answer to the following question: In what ways can the Catholic Reformation be considered a Counter-Reformation?

ELL Use the ELL activity described in the ELL chart.

Further Instruction

The Catholic Reformation: Core Text and Interactive Reading Notepad Project and discuss the Interactive Reading Notepad questions.

Remind students that many elements of the Catholic Reformation were a response to the rapid spread of Protestantism. The Catholic Reformation's goals included not only stopping that spread but also bringing those who had left the Church back into the faith as well as reforming the Church itself. Empowering the Inquisition to root out Protestant heretics, a reaffirmation of religious piety, and an active support of humanist and Catholic education were three major efforts of the Catholic Reformation.

Draw Conclusions What does the term Counter-Reformation imply about the causes of the Catholic Reformation? *(that it was a specific response to the Protestant Reformation)*

Objective 4: Explain why many groups faced persecution during the Reformation.

Quick Instruction

Tell students that a dramatic increase in religious persecution followed the rise in religious fervor among Catholics and Protestants. Throughout Europe, witch hunts were common, with tens of thousands of men and women perishing. Jews in Europe were forced to live in ghettos, separate, segregated parts of a town or city, even in regions that had been relatively tolerant.

Further Instruction

Religious Persecution Continues: Core Text and Interactive Reading Notepad Project and discuss the Interactive Reading Notepad questions.

Students should understand that the religious intolerance that spread throughout Europe was a direct result of heightened tensions between Protestants and Catholics. Protestantism was strengthening in certain parts of Europe, and Catholicism was attempting to stem the tide and win back some who had converted. Intense religious feelings tended to result in harsh actions toward those who appeared different or who were of a non-Christian faith. Many of the victims of witch hunts were simply men or women who used herbs to heal. Those skills were suddenly perceived as being a tool of the devil, with violent consequences following.

Draw Inferences Why was persecution of Jews and "witches" especially harsh? *(In a time of insecurity, people looked for others to blame, especially those most unlike themselves.)*

Compare Ask students to define the word "ghetto." Then ask them where they have heard the term used and how it was used. Ask them to compare what they understand the word to mean to what it meant during this period in history. *Possible answer: A ghetto is an area where everyone is the same race, religion, and/or social status. The word may have a negative connotation. The same definition applies to the Jewish ghettoes during the Reformation. People of the same religion lived in a specific area. In the case of the historical time period, it was often forced. In modern times, it may be by choice or necessity.*

■ **SYNTHESIZE**

DIGITAL ACTIVITY

Spread and Impact of the Protestant Reformation

Ask students to review their flowchart on the spread and impact of the Protestant Reformation. Have them use the Think Pair Share strategy to compare their graphic organizers.

Have partners think about the following question: What are three causes/effects that you believe made the greatest impact on the Protestant or Catholic Reformation movements? Have them share their answers with the class.

Discuss What characteristics did the two reformation movements share? What were the most important differences? Could the Catholic Church have done anything to prevent the Protestant Reformation in Germany and in England? Call on students to offer their opinions. Ask for evidence to support those opinions. Explain that both movements were a result of a situation that existed that one or more people wanted to change. That is essentially what it means to reform something.

■ **DEMONSTRATE**

LESSON QUIZ

Lesson Quiz and Class Discussion Board

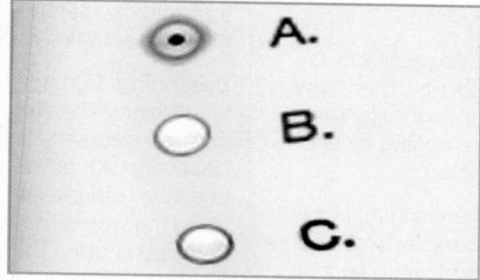

Assign the online Lesson Quiz if you have not already done so. Students will be offered automatic remediation or enrichment based on their score.

Pose these questions to the class on the Discussion Board.

Analyze Main Idea How did Reformation ideas take root in England? Why did the Church respond with its Catholic Reformation?

Topic Inquiry

Have students continue their investigations for the Topic Inquiry.

The Scientific Revolution

Supporting English Language Learners

Use with Digital Text 3, **Breakthroughs in Medicine and Chemistry.**

Speaking

Read *Breakthroughs in Medicine and Chemistry* aloud to students. Then have students practice recognizing and speaking sentences of different lengths by completing the following activities according to their levels of English proficiency.

Beginning Choose a short, simple sentence from *Breakthroughs in Medicine and Chemistry* and write and display it for students. Then slowly read it aloud. Have students repeat it. Then find another, slightly longer sentence from the text. Repeat the procedure. Continue looking for short sentences in the text and helping students read them aloud.

Intermediate Choose two or three sentences of different lengths from *Breakthroughs in Medicine and Chemistry* to use as examples. Point out the subject and verb in each sentence. Then have students read each sentence aloud. Assist with pronunciation as needed. Then ask students to write and say two or three of their own sentences about the text, using the example sentences as a model.

Advanced Have students find several sentences of various lengths in the text. Then ask students to examine the characteristics of the longer and shorter sentences to determine what is added to make sentences longer. Have pairs write and speak a single short sentence. After this, instruct students to add clauses or descriptive phrases to make the sentence longer, then say the sentence aloud. Have them lengthen their sentences one more time and say the whole sentence aloud to the class. Circulate among students to offer support as needed.

Advanced High Ask students to examine the characteristics of the longer and shorter sentences to determine what is added to make sentences longer. Then have individual students write and speak a single short sentence. After this, instruct students to build upon their sentences three more times, adding clauses or descriptive phrases to make the sentences longer. Finally, have students share their whole sentences with the class. Circulate among students to offer support as needed.

Use with Digital Text 1, **Changing Views of the Universe.**

Speaking

Read *Changing Views of the Universe* aloud to the class. Explain that a good description of an event includes words that help the reader see the event as they listen. Ask students to listen to the text and imagine a picture of what they hear. Then have students complete one of the following activities depending on their level of English proficiency.

Beginning Reread "The Church Rejects Galileo's Discoveries" aloud to students. Then tell students that they will work together to describe Galileo's discovery and what happened to him after he shared his discovery with others. Ask students to offer words and phrases to describe Galileo's situation. Then model describing what was read by using the words provided by students. Have students formulate their own description using the same group of words and phrases.

Intermediate Reread "The Church Rejects Galileo's Discoveries" aloud to students. Then tell students that they will work together to describe Galileo's discovery and what happened to him after he shared his discovery with others. Ask students to offer words and phrases to describe Galileo's situation. Then instruct them to create descriptive sentences based on the words and phrases they provided. Make sure each student has a chance to develop at least one descriptive sentence.

Advanced Have students reread "The Church Rejects Galileo's Discoveries." Then tell students that they will work together in small groups to describe Galileo's discovery and what happened to him after he shared his discovery with others. Have small groups brainstorm descriptive words and phrases to describe Galileo's situation. Then instruct groups to create descriptive sentences based on the words and phrases they provided. Make sure to challenge students to make their sentences as descriptive as possible. Consider creating a contest for the most descriptive sentences.

Advanced High Have students reread "The Church Rejects Galileo's Discoveries." Then ask students to describe what they read in as much detail as possible to a partner. Make sure to challenge students to make their sentences as descriptive as possible. If time allows, have students share their sentences with their classmates. Then have classmates vote on the most descriptive sentences in this activity.

▶ Differentiate Instruction

Use the Differentiated Instruction notes throughout the lesson plan to support the varied skill sets, levels of readiness, and interests in the mixed-ability classroom.

Challenge These notes include suggestions for expanding the activity for advanced students.

On-Level These notes include suggestions for modifying the activity to address different interests or learning styles.

Extra Support These notes include ideas for providing more scaffolding or reading spuport.

Special Needs These notes provide ideas for adapting instruction to support the needs of various special needs students.

■ NOTES

PEARSON
realize™
www.PearsonRealize.com

Go online to access additional resources including:
Primary Sources • Biographies • Supreme Court cases •
21st Century Skill Tutorials • Maps • Graphic Organizers.

Objectives

Objective 1: Explain how new discoveries in astronomy changed the way people viewed the universe.

Objective 2: Understand the new scientific method and how it developed.

Objective 3: Identify the contributions that Galileo, Copernicus, Newton, and other scientists made to the Scientific Revolution.

LESSON 5 ORGANIZER			PACING: APPROX. 1 PERIOD, .5 BLOCKS		
		OBJECTIVES	PACING	**RESOURCES**	
				Online	Print
Connect					
DIGITAL START UP ACTIVITY **A New Way of Thinking**			5 min.	●	
Investigate					
DIGITAL TEXT 1 **Changing Views of the Universe**		Objective 1	10 min.	●	●
INTERACTIVE GALLERY **Changing Views of the Universe**			10 min.	●	
DIGITAL TEXT 2 **A New Scientific Method**		Objective 2	10 min.	●	●
DIGITAL TEXT 3 **Breakthroughs in Medicine and Chemistry**		Objective 3	10 min.	●	●
INTERACTIVE GALLERY **A Scientific Revolution in Medicine**			10 min.	●	
Synthesize					
DIGITAL ACTIVITY **Important People of the Scientific Revolution**			5 min.	●	
Demonstrate					
DIGITAL QUIZ **Lesson Quiz and Class Discussion Board**			10 min.	●	

The Scientific Revolution

■ CONNECT

DIGITAL START UP ACTIVITY
A New Way of Thinking

Project the Start Up Activity Ask students to read the quote and then answer the questions as they enter and get settled. Then have them share their ideas with another student.

Discuss Galileo's discovery set him on a path of direct conflict with the Church and its traditional teachings. What might your reaction have been had you been in Galileo's place? *(Answers should reflect an understanding of how thrilling such a discovery must have been, along with frustration at the Church's opposition.)*

Aa Vocabulary Development: Use the Interactive Reading Notepad to preview the Key Terms and Academic Vocabulary in the Lesson with students.

⚡ FLIP IT!

Assign the Flipped Video for this lesson.

■ STUDENT EDITION PRINT
PAGES: 374–378

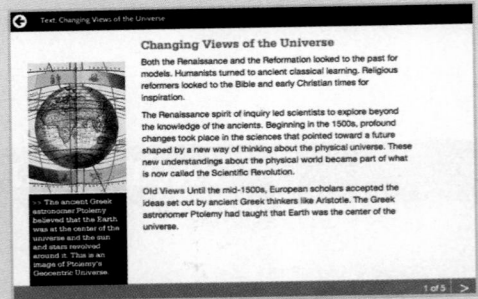

■ INVESTIGATE

DIGITAL TEXT 1
Changing Views of the Universe

INTERACTIVE GALLERY
Changing Views of the Universe

Objective 1: Explain how new discoveries in astronomy changed the way people viewed the universe.

Quick Instruction

Introduce the activity by explaining that changes in science happened at the same time as the social, political, and artistic changes of the Renaissance. The Scientific Revolution was spurred by scientists' interest in the natural world and their desire to know more about it. The invention of the telescope allowed astronomers to examine the moon and identify planetary bodies invisible to the naked eye. This ability to observe eventually changed the way people viewed the universe.

Changing Views of the Universe: Interactive Gallery Project the activity. Point out that each scientist included in the activity made discoveries that would have been considered earth-shattering for the time. Collectively, they challenged traditional beliefs people had held unquestioningly for more than a thousand years. Show students that clicking on each photo will open a box that contains key information about each man.

🎬 ACTIVE CLASSROOM

Use the Make Headlines strategy and have students write a headline about one of the scientists covered in the interactive activity. Ask: If you were to write a headline capturing the most important aspect of this person's discovery, what would that headline be? Have students pass their headline to a partner to review.

ELL Use the ELL activity described in the ELL chart.

Further Instruction

Changing Views of the Universe: Core Text and Interactive Reading Notepad Project and discuss the Interactive Reading Notepad questions.

Summarize Tell students that each scientist's discoveries were more than just scientific discoveries. The discoveries represented a search for a truth that often contradicted traditional thought and led even non-scientists to change how they viewed the universe and their place in it. For these people, changing the way they thought would affect every part of their lives.

Tell students that the seed for this change in thinking was planted during the Renaissance with its emphasis on rational thought and inquiry. The Reformation extended Renaissance ideas and encouraged the questioning of traditional beliefs. The astronomers of the Scientific Revolution were some of the first to actively explore a new approach to conventionally accepted truths.

Infer Why would Galileo's discovery that the universe is heliocentric threaten the Catholic Church? *After the sweeping changes of the religious Reformation, it was one more challenge to the Church's authority and traditional teachings.*

Analyze Interactions Why would changing a person's view of the universe possibly affect other parts of their lives? *If their traditional view of the universe was wrong, then there were likely other beliefs they held that were equally in error.*

DIGITAL TEXT 2

A New Scientific Method

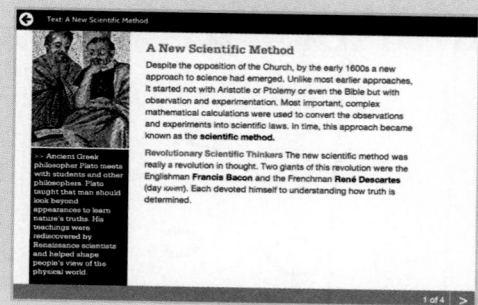

Objective 2: Understand the new scientific method and how it developed.

Quick Instruction

The development of a structured, step-by-step process of inquiry into the physical world grew from the belief of the philosophers Francis Bacon and René Descartes that truth isn't found at the beginning of an inquiry, but at the end. The scientific method that eventually developed incorporates this belief as well as Bacon's emphasis on experimentation and observation.

INFOGRAPHIC—Scientific Method Project the Infographic on the whiteboard. Review each of the steps in the scientific method. Discuss why each step is needed and the importance of the sequence of each step.

Further Instruction

A New Method of Inquiry: Core Text and Interactive Reading Notepad Project and discuss the Interactive Reading Notepad questions.

Be sure that students understand that a method of inquiry that relies on experimentation and observation would have to have some type of structure in order to have lasting value.

Analyze How do the repeating steps of the scientific method reflect Bacon's philosophy on finding truth? *A series of steps that are specific and follow a particular order means that the experiment's results and the observations of the scientist can be repeated by another person. When the same process gets the same results, a "truth" is created. This is the core of Bacon's philosophy and the thrust of the scientific method. According to Bacon, there can be no truth without testing and observing.*

Compare How did the scientific method differ from traditional methods of finding truth? *Traditional methods relied on people just accepting what they were told to be truth. The scientific method relies on personal experimentation and observation.*

DIGITAL TEXT 3

Breakthroughs in Medicine and Chemistry

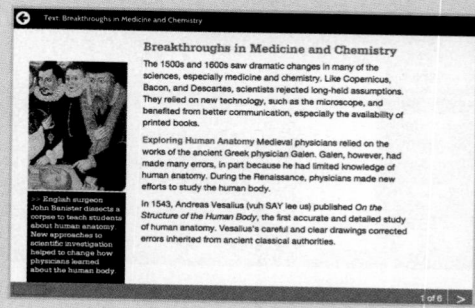

Objective 3: Identify the contributions that Galileo, Copernicus, Newton, and other scientists made to the Scientific Revolution.

Quick Instruction

Introduce the activity by explaining that changes in science extended to the new science of chemistry and to real exploration of how the human body functions.

A Scientific Revolution in Medicine: Interactive Gallery Project the activity. Explain that the human body and how it functions was as big a mystery as any other in nature. These medical trailblazers helped people to better understand anatomy, chemistry, and microorganisms. Click on one of the images to demonstrate how doing so brings up additional information about each scientist.

👥 ACTIVE CLASSROOM

Use the Conversation with [History] strategy and have students pretend they are having a conversation with one of the scientists featured in the Interactive Gallery. Ask students to write down a question they'd like to ask and then how that person would respond to the students. Students would also offer a response.

ELL Use the ELL activity described in the ELL chart.

The Scientific Revolution

INTERACTIVE GALLERY

A Scientific Revolution in Medicine

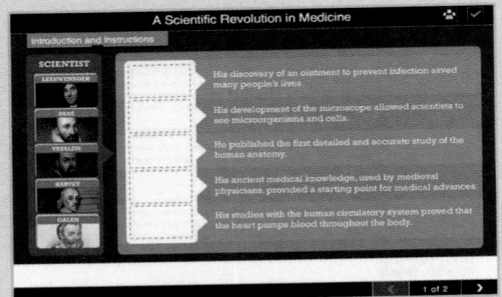

Further Instruction

Knowledge Expands in Other Sciences: Core Text and Interactive Reading Notepad Project and discuss the Interactive Reading Notepad questions.

Isaac Newton put his considerable intellect to the study of a variety of scientific disciplines. He specialized in mathematics and physics but also studied alchemy, the precursor to chemistry. Robert Boyle's discoveries in chemistry and his formulas expressing the relationship between gases and pressure are still used today. The discoveries of anatomists like Andreas Vesalius and William Harvey forever changed how people viewed the human body.

Test Conclusions The discoveries of Galileo, Newton, and other leaders of the Scientific Revolution are often described as evidence of human progress. Evaluate whether this is an accurate description. *Answers may agree with this description because the discoveries made by these scientists and others of the period advanced human knowledge of the natural world. Other answers may suggest that most people did not benefit greatly from the period's progress and still lived in poverty.*

■ SYNTHESIZE

DIGITAL ACTIVITY

Important People of the Scientific Revolution

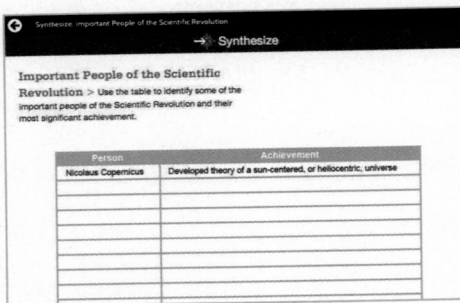

Ask students to recall the section focus question: How did discoveries in science lead to a new way of thinking for Europeans? Have them use the Think Pair Share strategy to compare how they filled out the chart of important people of the Scientific Revolution and then answer the focus question. Ask them to take five minutes to write down some brief answers to the question, then share their answers with a talking partner.

Have partners think about the following question: What are three discoveries that you believe made the greatest impact on society? Have pairs share their answers with the class.

■ DEMONSTRATE

DIGITAL QUIZ

Lesson Quiz and Class Discussion Board

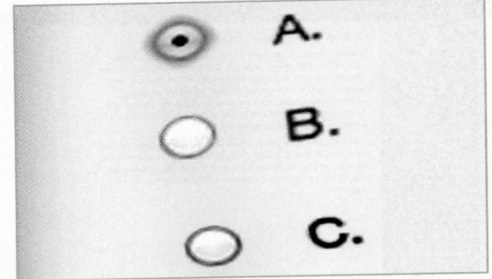

Assign the online Lesson Quiz for this lesson if you have not already done so. Students will be offered automatic remediation or enrichment based on their score.

Pose these questions to the class on the Discussion Board:

Analyze the Main Idea How did the Scientific Revolution build on the spirit of the Reformation? *The Reformation was a time of challenging long-held religious beliefs and the authority of the Church on these matters. The Scientific Revolution also challenged traditional beliefs about the natural world and challenged Church authority in the process.* Would the Scientific Revolution have taken place had the Reformation not occurred? *Answers will vary. Likely answers would include that the Scientific Revolution would have taken place anyway, but might have taken place later in human history.*

Draw Conclusions The title of this section is "The Scientific Revolution." Why was it a revolution? *It brought about a totally new way of viewing the natural world, including the body, that was based on observation and experimentation instead of just acceptance of traditional beliefs.*

Topic Inquiry

Have students continue their investigations for the Topic Inquiry.

PEARSON
realize™

www.PearsonRealize.com
Access your Digital Lesson

The Renaissance and Reformation (1300–1650)

■ SYNTHESIZE

DIGITAL ACTIVITY
Reflect on the Essential Question and Topic

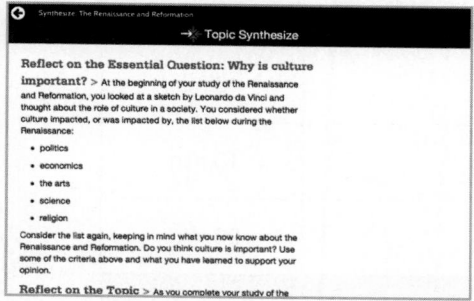

First ask students to reconsider the Essential Question for the Topic: Why Is Culture Important? Remind students that they discussed the role of culture in a society at the start of the Topic. For example, they considered whether culture impacted, or was impacted by

- politics
- economics
- the arts
- science
- religion

Have students consider the list again, keeping in mind what they now know about the Renaissance and Reformation. Ask students "Do you think culture is important?" Ask them to give at least three reasons to support their answer. Discuss their answers as a class or ask students to post their answers on the Class Discussion Board.

Next ask students to reflect on the Topic as a whole and jot down 1-3 questions they've thought about during the Topic. Share these examples if students need help getting started:

- How did Renaissance thinking affect politics, the arts, and economics?
- How did the Renaissance influence the Reformation?
- In what ways did the Renaissance spark a shift in scientific thinking and contribute to the Scientific Revolution?

You may ask students to share their questions and answers on the Class Discussion Board.

Topic Inquiry
Have students complete Step 3 of the Topic Inquiry.

■ DEMONSTRATE

DIGITAL TOPIC REVIEW AND ASSESSMENT
The Renaissance and Reformation (1300–1650)

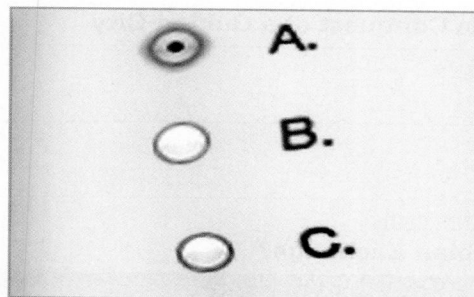

Students can prepare for the Topic Test by answering the questions in the Topic Review and Assessment online or the Assessment questions in the Print Student text. They can also prepare by reviewing their answers to the Interactive Reading Notepad questions or reviewing their notes in the Reading and Notetaking Study Guide.

DIGITAL TOPIC TEST
The Renaissance and Reformation (1300–1650)

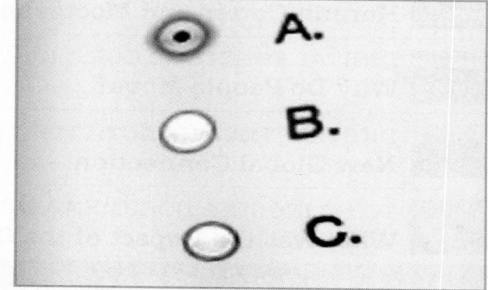

TOPIC TEST
Assign the Topic Test to assess students' understanding of topic content.

BENCHMARK TESTS
Assign these benchmark tests as you complete the relevant topics to monitor student progress toward mastering the course content and as preparation for the End-of-Course Test.

Benchmark Test 1: Topics 1–5
Benchmark Test 2: Topics 6–10
Benchmark Test 3: Topics 11–15
Benchmark Test 4: Topics 16–21

Topic 11

New Global Connections (1415–1796)

TOPIC 11 ORGANIZER	PACING: APPROX. 9 PERIODS, 4.5 BLOCKS
	PACING
Connect	1 period
MY STORY VIDEO **Hernán Cortés and Moctezuma, The Conquest of a Golden City**	10 min.
DIGITAL ESSENTIAL QUESTION ACTIVITY **Why Do People Move?**	10 min.
DIGITAL TIMELINE ACTIVITY **New Global Connection**	10 min.
TOPIC INQUIRY: DOCUMENT-BASED QUESTION **What was the Impact of the Columbian Exchange?**	20 min.
Investigate	3–6 periods
TOPIC INQUIRY: DOCUMENT-BASED QUESTION **What was the Impact of the Columbian Exchange?**	Ongoing
LESSON 1 Europeans Explore Overseas	30–40 min.
LESSON 2 Europeans Gain Footholds in Asia	30–40 min.
LESSON 3 European Conquests in the Americas	30–40 min.
LESSON 4 European Colonies in North America	30–40 min.
LESSON 5 The Slave Trade and Its Impact on Africa	30–40 min.
LESSON 6 Effects of Global Contact	30–40 min.
Synthesize	1 period
DIGITAL ACTIVITY **Reflect on the Essential Question and Topic**	10 min.
TOPIC INQUIRY: DOCUMENT-BASED QUESTION **What was the Impact of the Columbian Exchange?**	20 min.
Demonstrate	1–2 periods
ONLINE TEST **New Global Connections**	10 min.
TOPIC INQUIRY: DOCUMENT-BASED QUESTION **What was the Impact of the Columbian Exchange?**	20 min.

What was the Impact of the Columbian Exchange?

In this Topic Inquiry, students analyze six primary and secondary source documents to draw their own conclusions on how the Columbian Exchange had a lasting impact on Europe and the Americas. This DBQ on the Columbian Exchange expands on that essential question and provides students an opportunity to consider some of the consequences of human migration, which address the Topic Essential Question: "Why do people move?"

STEP 1: CONNECT
Develop Questions and Plan the Investigation

Launch the DBQ Writing Activity
Show the flipped video "Cortés and Moctezuma" which deals with early encounters between Europeans and Native Americans and the resulting Columbian Exchange. Use the questions to lead a class discussion about the video, or have students work in pairs to answer the questions.

Suggestion: Give more context for the video by explaining that Mexico City is built upon the ruins of the Aztec capital of Tenochtitlan. In its people and culture, today's Mexico City reflects the enduring impact of the Columbian Exchange.

Generate Questions
Divide the class into small groups and have them use the Need-to-Know Questions document to record their questions about how the Columbian Exchange affected Europe and how it affected the Americas.

Suggestion: Help students generate questions by reminding them of the five Ws and one H used by journalists: *Who? What? When? Where? Why?* and *How?* Suggest that students take ten minutes to brainstorm as many questions as possible and then select the ones most relevant to the broader DBQ question.

Resources
- Need-to-Know Questions
- Student Instructions

STEP 2: INVESTIGATE
Apply Disciplinary Concepts and Tools

Analyze the Documents
Have students analyze the six documents to start building their response to the question "How did the Columbian Exchange affect both Europe and the Americas?" Before students read the material, you may wish to point out that Documents A through D are all secondary sources, while Documents E and F are primary sources. Another distinction is that Documents A and C are both charts that provide data on the migration of people, plants, and animals, while the other documents all express a viewpoint on the effects of these migrations. Remind students that as they analyze these, they should be aware of any biases that the authors might have.

Suggestion: Document E contains some words that the translator left in the original Spanish. You may wish to help students use context to understand the meaning of these words. Or you might use a Spanish dictionary to provide English translations for these words.

Check Understanding
Students should answer the multiple choice and short answer questions that follow each document.

⏻ PROFESSIONAL DEVELOPMENT

Document-Based Question
Be sure to view the Document-Based Question Professional Development resources in the online course.

STEP 3: SYNTHESIZE
Evaluate Sources and
Use Evidence to Formulate Conclusions

Write Your Essay

Have students consider all of the evidence and viewpoints and draw their own conclusions. Using the documents and their knowledge of history, have them write an essay on the following topic: **How did the Columbian Exchange affect both Europe and the Americas?**

Remind students that their essays should have the following characteristics: a topic sentence that states their view; evidence from at least *three* of the documents, clearly identified; relevant facts; an explanation and rebuttal of at least one opposing viewpoint; logical organization, including an introduction and a conclusion. Be sure that students use social studies terminology correctly and use standard grammar, spelling, sentence structure, and punctuation.

Suggestion: If students struggle with organization, review the structure of a five-paragraph essay. The first paragraph is the introduction. The body consists of three paragraphs, each of which explores a key point. The conclusion should restate the main idea and summarizes the key points.

Edit Your Essay

Remind students that they should revise their first draft and create a final draft of their essay before turning it in. You may want to suggest that they ask a classmate to peer edit their essay.

Resources
• Writing Rubric

STEP 4: DEMONSTRATE
Communicate Conclusions
and Take Informed Action

Reflect on the Project

After students have finished their essays, explain that the work they did on this DBQ on the Columbian Exchange will serve as a foundation for their understanding of human migration and the variety of effects that can result from it. In the future, they may refine or revise ideas they developed here on migration, but they can use a similar process for considering multiple sources of evidence and points of view to form an educated and carefully reasoned opinion.

Suggestion: Help students connect this inquiry project to their world today by reminding them that the impact of human migration is still a significant global issue. For example, in our own country, citizens and government leaders are often concerned with the issue of immigration. Throughout the world, the movement of people affects the region from which they move and the region to which they move.

INTRODUCTION

New Global Connections (1415–1796)

Beginning in the 1400s, European voyages of exploration ushered in an era of new global connections. Migration and commerce across the Indian and Atlantic Ocean led to European expansion, the Columbian Exchange, and the Atlantic slave trade. These and other developments affected people in Europe, Africa, Asia, and the Americas. As a result, some civilizations increased in power and wealth, while others declined. How did the movement of people during this era of global connections shape the world we live in today?

■ CONNECT

MY STORY VIDEO
Hernán Cortés and Moctezuma, The Conquest of a Golden City

Watch a video about the Spanish conquest of Mexico.

Check Understanding What factors helped the Spanish defeat the Aztecs? *(alliances with other native peoples, the death of Moctezuma, disease)*

Hypothesize How might history have been different if Moctezuma had not believed Cortes to be the god Quetzalcoatl? *(He might not have welcomed the strangers but, with his superior numbers, have driven them out of his land.)*

⬆ FLIP IT!
Assign the My Story Video.

DIGITAL ESSENTIAL QUESTION ACTIVITY
Why Do People Move?

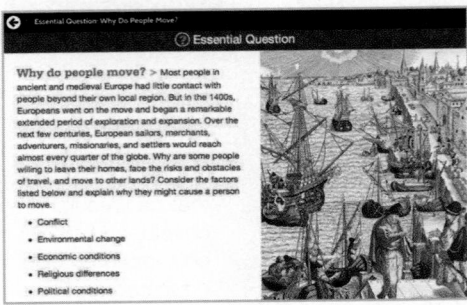

Ask students to think about the Essential Question for this Topic: Why do people move? If students have not already done so, ask them to jot down explanations as to how the various factors listed in the activity might cause people to move.

Express Ideas Clearly Invite volunteers to share their ideas with the class, expressing clearly how one or more of the factors cause movement of people.

Express Problems Clearly What problems might people have to overcome in order to successfully move? *(Sample responses: long distance, cost of travel, harsh weather and geography, attacks along the way)* After they have moved, what new problems might arise? *(Sample responses: conflict with native inhabitants, inadequate supplies, unfamiliar territory, need to establish new home)*

Hypothesize Based on what they have learned about European civilization around the 1400s, why do they think Europeans began to move beyond their own continent? *(Sample responses: Renaissance spirit of curiosity, to flee harsh rulers, to find more profitable work, to trade with other regions)*

DIGITAL TIMELINE ACTIVITY
New Global Connection

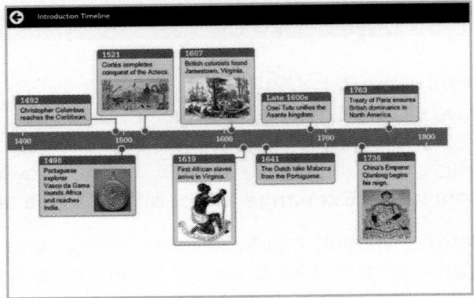

Display the timeline showing some major events of the era of new global connections. During their work on this Topic, students will learn about all of these events and many more, but this timeline will provide a framework into which they can place the events they learn about.

D Differentiate: Challenge/Gifted Suggest that students copy the timeline onto their own paper and add entries to it as they read the chapter. Have them make a final, clean copy after they read all six lessons, and discuss the new entries as a class.

Check Understanding About how much time passed between the arrival of Europeans in the Caribbean and Britain's establishment of dominance in North America? *(about 270 years)*

Topic Inquiry
Launch the Topic Inquiry with students after introducing the Topic.

Europeans Explore Overseas

Supporting English Language Learners

Use with Digital Text 3, **Columbus Searches for a Route to Asia.**

Speaking

Read *Columbus Searches for a Route to Asia* aloud to students. Then have students practice recognizing and speaking different types of sentences by completing the following activities according to their levels of English proficiency.

Beginning Choose a short declarative sentence from *Columbus Searches for a Route to Asia* and write and display it for students. Then slowly read it aloud and have students repeat it. Modify the sentence in order to turn it into an interrogative sentence. Repeat this procedure once more. Then write and display an interrogative sentence, read it, and have students repeat it. Finally, turn this question into a declarative sentence for students and have them repeat it after you.

Intermediate Choose several short declarative sentences from *Columbus Searches for a Route to Asia.* Write and display them for students. Assist students as they practice saying the sentences aloud. Help students turn each declarative sentence into an interrogative sentence. Write and display these questions for students to see. Point out the similarities and differences between the declarative sentences and their interrogative counterparts. Then have students choose a declarative sentence from the text and modify it to create an interrogative sentence on their own. Support students as needed.

Advanced Have student pairs choose and write down three declarative sentences from *Columbus Searches for a Route to Asia.* Have partners say each sentence aloud together. Instruct partners to modify each declarative sentence into an interrogative sentence, an imperative sentence, and an exclamatory sentence. Support pairs as needed. Finally, have each pair choose their favorite set of sentences and share them with the class.

Advanced High After reading *Columbus Searches for a Route to Asia,* have students discuss the text with a partner. During their discussions, students should use at least one declarative, one interrogative, one imperative, and once exclamatory sentence. Remind students to use rich and varied vocabulary. Support student pairs as needed. Finally, have each pair choose their favorite sentence(s) from their discussion to share with the class.

Use with Digital Text 2, **Portugal Explores the Seas.**

Speaking

Read *Portugal Explores the Seas* aloud to the class. Tell students that explaining what they learn is one way to show that they have learned about a topic. Ask students listen to the text and then have students complete one of the following activities depending on their level of English proficiency.

Beginning Reread *Portugal Explores the Seas* aloud to students. Then tell students that they will explain how Portuguese explorers came to control Africa. Ask students to use words and phrases from the text to explain how Portuguese explorers influenced the East African trade network. If necessary, have students point to words and phrases that help explain their ideas. Then model creating a sentence or two from the words and phrases students point out. If possible, have students create their own sentences to explain how Portuguese explorers influenced Africa.

Intermediate Reread *Portugal Explores the Seas* aloud to students. Instruct students to explain how Portuguese explorers influenced the East African trade network. Remind students that they can use vocabulary from the text and paraphrase what they read to help them explain the topic.

Advanced Have students take turns rereading *Portugal Explores the Seas* aloud to a partner. Then ask students to work with a partner to develop an explanation of why the Portuguese empire in Africa declined after the 1600s. Challenge students to use accurate, specific, and detailed information in their explanations. Circulate among pairs to offer support as needed.

Advanced High Have students reread *Portugal Explores the Seas.* Then ask students to explain why the Portuguese empire in Africa declined after the 1600s. Challenge students to use accurate, specific, and detailed information in their explanations.

▶ Differentiate Instruction

Use the Differentiated Instruction notes throughout the lesson plan to support the varied skill sets, levels of readiness, and interests in the mixed-ability classroom.

Challenge These notes include suggestions for expanding the activity for advanced students.

On-Level These notes include suggestions for modifying the activity to address different interests or learning styles.

Extra Support These notes include ideas for providing more scaffolding or reading spuport.

Special Needs These notes provide ideas for adapting instruction to support the needs of various special needs students.

▬ NOTES

_____

_____

_____

_____

_____

_____

Topic 11 Lesson 1

Europeans Explore Overseas

Objectives

Objective 1: Understand the major causes of European exploration.

Objective 2: Analyze early Portuguese and Spanish explorations and expansion.

Objective 3: Describe how the Portuguese established footholds on Africa's coasts.

Objective 4: Describe European searches for a direct route to Asia.

LESSON 1 ORGANIZER	PACING: APPROX. 1 PERIOD, .5 BLOCKS				
				RESOURCES	
		OBJECTIVES	PACING	Online	Print
Connect					
	DIGITAL START UP ACTIVITY **The Search for Spices**		5 min.	●	
Investigate					
	DIGITAL TEXT 1 **Causes of European Exploration**	Objective 1	10 min.	●	●
	DIGITAL TEXT 2 **Portugal Explores the Seas**	Objectives 2, 3	10 min.	●	●
	INTERACTIVE MAP **Early Voyages of European Exploration, 1487–1522**		10 min.	●	
	DIGITAL TEXT 3 **Columbus Searches for a Route to Asia**	Objectives 2, 4	10 min.	●	●
	3-D MODEL **Explorer's Ship**		10 min.	●	
	DIGITAL TEXT 4 **The Search for a Route to the Pacific**	Objective 4	10 min.	●	●
	INTERACTIVE GALLERY **Navigating the World**		10 min.	●	
Synthesize					
	DIGITAL ACTIVITY **The Wealth of Asia**		5 min.	●	
Demonstrate					
	LESSON QUIZ **Lesson Quiz and Class Discussion Board**		10 min.	●	

PEARSON
realize™
www.PearsonRealize.com

Go online to access additional resources including:
Primary Sources • Biographies • Supreme Court cases •
21st Century Skill Tutorials • Maps • Graphic Organizers.

■ CONNECT

DIGITAL START UP ACTIVITY

The Search for Spices

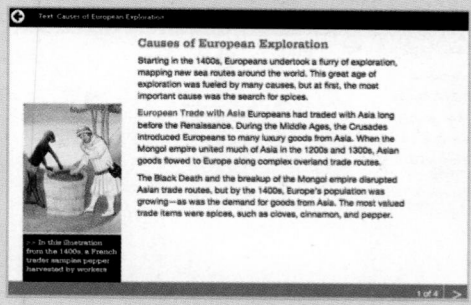

Project the Start Up Activity Ask students to answer the questions as they enter and get settled. Then have them share their ideas with another student, either in class or through a chat or blog space.

Discuss If you were a king or queen in Europe during the 1400s, how do you think you would respond when an explorer asked for your help to pay for a voyage to find a direct route to the Asian source of spices? *(Answers may vary. Students may predict that despite the great expense and high risks, the potential prestige and profits might outweigh the costs and risks.)*

Aa Vocabulary Development: Use the Interactive Reading Notepad to preview the Key Terms and Academic Vocabulary in this Lesson with students.

⚡ FLIP IT!

Assign the Flipped Video for this lesson.

■ STUDENT EDITION PRINT
PAGES: 384–389

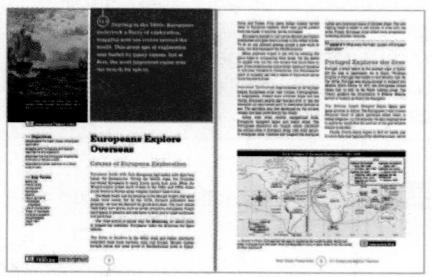

■ INVESTIGATE

DIGITAL TEXT 1

Causes of European Exploration

Objective 1: Understand the major causes of European exploration.

Quick Instruction

Tell students that there were several causes of European exploration in the 1400s. Europeans wanted to find a direct sea route to access the valuable spices of East Asia. Other causes were the Renaissance spirit of curiosity, the desire to spread Christianity, and competition with other European powers for glory and wealth.

Analyze Maps Have students view the map "Early Voyages of European Exploration." In Southeast Asia, identify the Moluccas, islands which were a main source of spices. Ask students to use the text and map to describe the spice trade route that Arab and Italian merchants dominated. *(overland across Asia to the Middle East and Ottoman empire; from there, overland or across the Mediterranean Sea to Europe)* Ask: Which European countries sent explorers into the Atlantic Ocean? *(Portugal, Spain, England, France, Netherlands)* Why? *(They were looking for new trade routes to Asia, ones not controlled by the Italians and Arabs.)*

D Differentiate: Challenge/Gifted

Further Instruction

Editable Presentation Use the Editable Presentation to present the main ideas for this text.

Causes of European Exploration Project the Interactive Reading Notepad questions provided in the notepad. Have students answer them as they progress through the text.

Identify Supporting Details Project image of harvesting pepper. Ask students to identify details that explain why Europeans valued spices so highly. *(They wanted spices to flavor and preserve food and to make medicines and perfumes.)*

Infer Why do you think Arab and Italian traders were able to retain control of the spice trade? *(Answers may vary. Students may infer that Arabs controlled the overland routes to the Middle East and that Italian merchant ships controlled trade across the eastern Mediterranean Sea. European maps and naval technology had not advanced enough to make practical exploration for a direct sea route.)*

Europeans Explore Overseas

DIGITAL TEXT 2

Portugal Explores the Seas

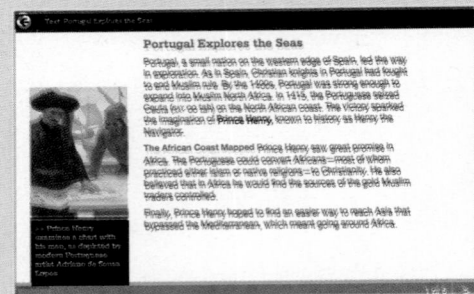

INTERACTIVE MAP

Early Voyages of European Exploration, 1487–1522

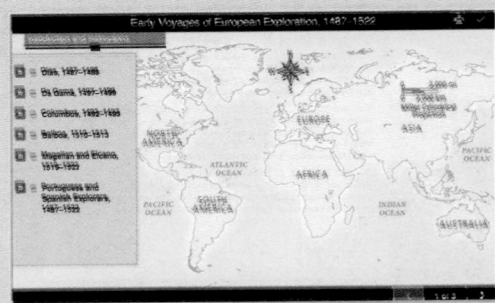

DIGITAL TEXT 3

Columbus Searches for a Route to Asia

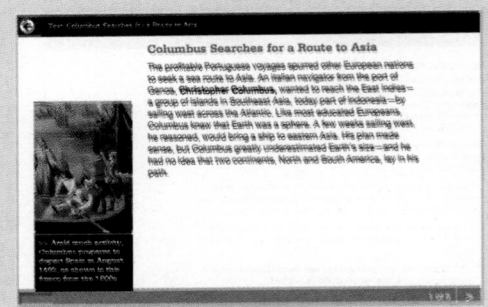

Objectives 2: **Analyze early Portuguese and Spanish explorations and expansion; 3: Describe how the Portuguese established footholds on Africa's coasts.**

Quick Instruction

Tell students that Portuguese ships under Prince Henry's sponsorship were the first Europeans to venture far out into the Atlantic Ocean. They were soon followed by the Spanish. The Portuguese applied their growing naval knowledge and technology to exploration. They built forts and trading posts along the African coast, sailed across the Indian Ocean to India, and gained control of the spice trade.

ACTIVE CLASSROOM

Have students write several headlines that capture the action in the interactive map "Early Voyages of European Discovery." Ask: If you were to tweet news headlines that captured the most important events of this topic, what would those headlines be? Exchange your headlines with a partner to review and improve. *(Sample headlines: Prince Henry gathers navigation and technology experts. Portuguese explore west coast of Africa. Bartholomeu Dias reaches southern tip of Africa. Vasco da Gama reaches India. Portuguese seize control of Indian Ocean spice trade.)*

D **Differentiate: Extra Support** Ask students to create a chart with two columns labeled "Explorer" and "Accomplishments." Ask students to complete the chart with the names of Portuguese explorers and their major

accomplishments. Then discuss how each person's accomplishments were based on the previous accomplishments.

ELL Use the ELL activity described in the ELL chart.

Further Instruction

Go through the Interactive Reading Notepad questions and discuss the answers with the class.

Remind students that the Portuguese continued to explore the African coasts for two centuries and established many military and commercial footholds during that time.

Analyze Images Project the illustration of Elmina Castle on the whiteboard. Ask students to examine carefully the image of Elmina Castle, built in 1482, an early Portuguese foothold on the West African coast. Ask: How did the architecture and design of the castle help the Portuguese achieve their goals? *(Sample response: The castle's massive size and tall walls protected the Portuguese who stopped here on their way to India. Also, from this fortress, Portuguese traders and soldiers were able to trade with Africans of the region and gain control over coastal trade networks.)*

Draw Conclusions Why do you think the Portuguese limited their footholds in Africa to coastal forts and trading posts and did not explore much into the interior? *(Sample response: The Portuguese were only interested in trading profitably in Africa. They had little desire to settle or colonize the interior. African groups resisted Portuguese efforts to explore the interior and take control of the gold trade.)*

Objectives 2: **Analyze early Portuguese and Spanish explorations and expansion; 4: Describe European searches for a direct route to Asia.**

Quick Instruction

Project the illustration of Columbus embarking from Spain on the whiteboard. Explain to students that Columbus believed the world was round and that he could reach the spices of the East Indies by sailing west. Spain financed his voyage, hoping to gain riches and glory. Columbus landed not in the Indies, but in the Americas. Soon after, Spain and Portugal agreed to a treaty dividing the newly-discovered lands into two zones, one for Spain and one for Portugal.

ACTIVE CLASSROOM

Pair students. Have the first student give the second a verbal "tour" of the 3-d model showing the design and structure of an explorer's sailing ship. Have the second student give the first an explanation of the challenges that Columbus's crew faced on its long voyage across the Atlantic. *(Sample challenges: storms, damage to ship, cramped quarters, inadequate or spoiling food, uncertainty about location and destination)* Suggest that students record their conversation for use in a class presentation.

ELL Use the ELL activity described in the ELL chart.

3-D MODEL
Explorer's Ship

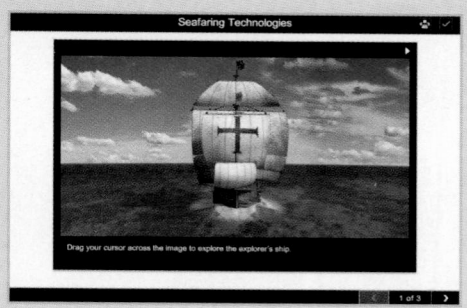

DIGITAL TEXT 4
The Search for a Route to the Pacific

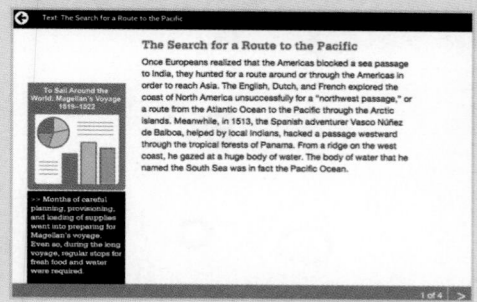

INTERACTIVE GALLERY
Navigating the World

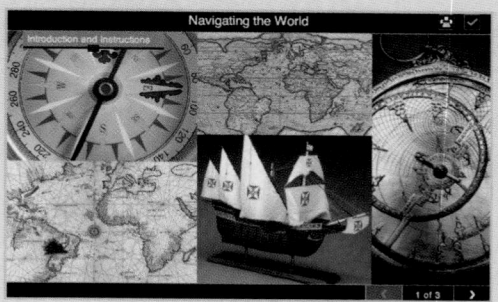

Further Instruction

Editable Presentation Use the Editable Presentation to present the main ideas of this text.

Generate Explanations Why do you think Portugal refused to sponsor Columbus but Spain did? *(Answers may vary. Sample response: The Portuguese did not feel the need. They had already explored the coast of Africa. They hoped to reach the spice trade by sailing around Africa into the Indian Ocean. One year after Columbus reached the Americas, da Gama sailed across the Indian Ocean and reached India.)*

Hypothesize If Spain's rulers had known of the existence of the Americas and the actual size of the world, would they still have financed Columbus's voyage? Why or why not? *(Sample response: Even if they knew that Columbus would have to find a way through or around the Americas to get to East Asia, they still might have paid for the riskier and longer voyage. They were eager to gain direct access to the spice trade, to gain wealth and glory for Spain, and to spread Christianity.)*

Objective 4: Describe European searches for a direct route to Asia.

Quick Instruction

Explain to students that the search for direct water routes to Asia continued. European explorers looked for ways through or around the Americas. Ferdinand Magellan led an expedition that sailed from Spain, around South America, and on to Asia. Meanwhile, Britain, France, and the Netherlands also joined the search and began developing their own trade networks.

Interactive Gallery: Navigating the World Project the gallery on the whiteboard. Click through the hotspots on the gallery, looking at each image individually, and then consider the collection of images as a whole. Discuss how such improvements in naval technology affected European exploration and expansion.

🗣 ACTIVE CLASSROOM

Tell students that they are explorers in the late 1400s or early 1500s. Ask them to rank the items from the Interactive Gallery according to which they think will be most useful on a voyage to find a route to the Pacific. Have students provide a justification for the ranking decisions they make. Then ask students to work in pairs to share their rankings and justifications. Poll the class to see if there is agreement on the rankings.

Further Instruction

Infographic: To Sail Around the World: Magellan's Voyage, 1519–1522 Project the infographic on the whiteboard. Look at the data included in each section. Ask: Judging from the items and amounts shown on this infographic, what skills and resources would be needed to assemble these materials? *(Sample response: They needed project organization and management skills, vast amounts of supplies, food that would keep long, and money to pay for it all.)*

Identify Cause and Effect Ask: How did the need to replenish supplies and make repairs on the long voyages to Asia cause European expansion? *(Answers may vary. Sample response: European countries established outposts along the routes of the long journeys. They built forts and outposts along the coasts of Africa and the Americas, and eventually on islands in the Pacific.)*

Compare and Contrast Ask: How were the efforts of other European powers to enlarge their trade networks in Africa similar to or different from the Portuguese approach to expansion? *(Like the Portuguese, the British, French, and Dutch constructed forts on the coast of Africa to protect their trade networks. Unlike the Portuguese, the Dutch outposts became more permanent and attracted immigrants from Europe.)*

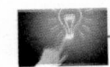
Europeans Explore Overseas

■ SYNTHESIZE

DIGITAL ACTIVITY
The Wealth of Asia

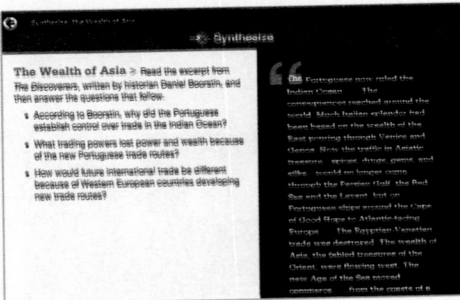

Have students form small groups to answer the questions in the Synthesize Activity: "The Wealth of Asia." Have them read the Daniel Boorstin quotation and discuss its meaning. Ask them to take five minutes to then write down brief answers to each of the three questions. Ask selected students to read their answers to the class. Invite students to agree, disagree, or build on the response.

According to Boorstin, why did the Portuguese establish control over trade in the Indian Ocean? What trading powers lost power and wealth because of the new Portuguese trade routes? How would future international trade be different because of Western European countries developing new trade routes? Have the groups present their answers to the class.

Discuss Direct students to the opening sentence of the Boorstin quote: "The Portuguese now ruled the Indian Ocean.... The consequences reached around the world." Ask students what they think Boorstin meant by this. (*Sample response: Europeans countries, especially ruling and merchant classes, became wealthy. Europeans expanded their power, building outposts in Africa, Asia, and the Americas. European nations competed for wealth and power around the world.)* Ask students to identify and describe changes in trade networks today that might have great consequences in the future. (*Answers will vary. Students may mention the European Union, NAFTA, the rapid economic growth of China, and more. Changes in trade patterns can have long-term global effects, such as the redirected flow of raw materials, goods, and wealth and power, favoring some countries and regions, while weakening others.*)

■ DEMONSTRATE

LESSON QUIZ
Lesson Quiz and Class Discussion Board

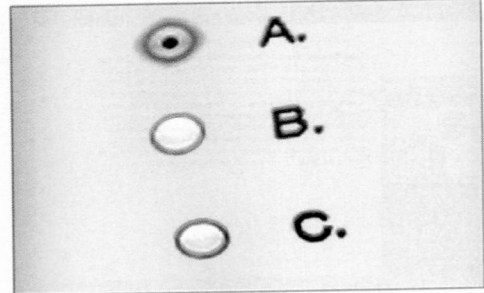

Assign the online Lesson Quiz for this lesson if you haven't already done so. Students will be offered automatic remediation or enrichment based on their score.

Pose this question to the class on the Discussion Board:

In "Europeans Explore Overseas," you learned how Portuguese navigators explored the seas, sailed around Africa to India, and established a trading empire around the Indian Ocean. Seeking other water routes to Asia, Columbus and other Spanish explorers sailed westward. Soon, England, France, and the Netherlands were also exploring and expanding their interests in Africa, Asia, and the Americas.

Predict Consequences How will European exploration and expansion during this time affect much of the world in the centuries that follow? (*Answers will vary. Students may mention European colonization in Africa, Asia, and the Americas, expansion of the African slave trade, increased European power and wealth, the decline of states in Asia, Africa, and the Americas, an exchange of goods around the world, or a blending of cultures around the world.*)

Topic Inquiry

Have students continue their investigations for the Topic Inquiry.

Europeans Gain Footholds in Asia

Supporting English Language Learners

Use with Digital Text 4, **Ming China and Europe.**

Speaking

Read *Ming China and Europe* aloud to students. Then have students practice using a variety of connecting words as they speak about the topic.

Beginning Write and display the following sentences for students, making sure to underline the connecting word:

- European interest in China and other parts of East Asia continued to grow.
- The Portuguese wanted Chinese silks and porcelains but had little to offer in exchange.

Explain that connecting words, called conjunctions, are words that connect ideas within a sentence. Tell students that conjunctions include *and*, *but*, and *or*. Read each sentence above and have students repeat it. Explain how *and* connects ideas, while *but* shows contrast.

Intermediate Have partners skim the text for sentences that use connecting words. Remind students that connecting words like *and*, *but*, and *or* are conjunctions that connect ideas within a sentence. Have partners to use the example sentences they find to say their own sentences about the text with *and*, *but*, and *or*.

Advanced Have students reread *Ming China and Europe* and write and say four sentences to a partner about the text using connecting words and transitional phrases. If necessary, give students examples of transitional words and phrases, such as *in fact*, *however*, *by the way*, and *for example*.

Advanced High Have students reread *Ming China and Europe* and write and say to the group eight sentences about the text using connecting words and transitional phrases. If necessary, give students examples of transitional words and phrases, such as *in fact*, *however*, *by the way*, and *for example*. Remind students to use details from the text in their sentences.

Use with Digital Text 2, **Rise of the Dutch and the Spanish.**

Speaking

Read *Rise of the Dutch and the Spanish* aloud to the class. Tell students that formal language is used in certain important situations, such as interviewing for a job or presenting a report to class. Ask students to listen to the text and then have them complete one of the following activities depending on their level of English proficiency.

Beginning Reread *Rise of the Dutch and the Spanish* aloud to students. Then model using formal language to summarize the information presented in the text. Help students formulate complete, formal sentences about the ways the Dutch and Spanish controlled trade in Asia and East Asia. Then have students say their sentences aloud.

Intermediate Reread *Rise of the Dutch and the Spanish* aloud to students. Have students explain why and how the Spanish were able to conquer the Philippines. Remind students to use formal language when they speak and provide them with examples to help them understand the difference between formal and informal language.

Advanced Have students reread *Rise of the Dutch and the Spanish* and then discuss what they learned with a partner. Then ask pairs to work together to develop a formal summary of the text for the class. Remind students to use formal language in their summaries. Then have pairs present their summaries to the class.

Advanced High Have students reread *Rise of the Dutch and the Spanish* and then prepare a mini presentation to explain how the Dutch gained power across the Indian Ocean. Remind students to use formal language in their reports. Ask students to present their reports to the class.

Challenge students to use accurate, specific, and detailed information in their explanations.

D Differentiate Instruction

Use the Differentiated Instruction notes throughout the lesson plan to support the varied skill sets, levels of readiness, and interests in the mixed-ability classroom.

Challenge These notes include suggestions for expanding the activity for advanced students.

On-Level These notes include suggestions for modifying the activity to address different interests or learning styles.

Extra Support These notes include ideas for providing more scaffolding or reading spuport.

Special Needs These notes provide ideas for adapting instruction to support the needs of various special needs students.

▮ NOTES

Europeans Gain Footholds in Asia

Objectives

Objective 1: Summarize how Portugal built a trading empire in South and Southeast Asia.

Objective 2: Analyze the rise of Dutch and Spanish dominance in Asia and the Indian Ocean.

Objective 3: Understand how the decline of Mughal India affected European traders in the region.

Objective 4: Describe European contacts with Ming and Qing China.

Objective 5: Summarize Korea's and Japan's attitudes toward contact with the outside world.

LESSON 2 ORGANIZER		OBJECTIVES	PACING	RESOURCES Online	Print
Connect					
	DIGITAL START UP ACTIVITY **Gunfire Over Malacca**		5 min.	●	
Investigate					
	DIGITAL TEXT 1 **Portugal Builds an Empire in Asia**	Objective 1	10 min.	●	●
	DIGITAL TEXT 2 **Rise of the Dutch and the Spanish**	Objective 2	10 min.	●	●
	DIGITAL TEXT 3 **European Trade in Mughal India**	Objectives 1, 2, 3	10 min.	●	●
	INTERACTIVE CHART **European Footholds in the Eastern Hemisphere**		10 min.	●	
	DIGITAL TEXT 4 **Ming China and Europe**	Objective 4	10 min.	●	●
	DIGITAL TEXT 5 **The Manchus Conquer China**		10 min.	●	●
	INTERACTIVE MAP **Trade Among Europe, Africa, and Asia**		10 min.	●	
	DIGITAL TEXT 6 **Korea and Japan Choose Isolation**	Objective 5	10 min.	●	●
Synthesize					
	DIGITAL ACTIVITY **International Trade: Different Approaches**		5 min.	●	
Demonstrate					
	LESSON QUIZ **Lesson Quiz and Class Discussion Board**		10 min.	●	

LESSON 2 ORGANIZER — PACING: APPROX. 1 PERIOD, .5 BLOCKS

PEARSON
realize.
www.PearsonRealize.com

Go online to access additional resources including:
Primary Sources • Biographies • Supreme Court cases •
21st Century Skill Tutorials • Maps • Graphic Organizers.

CONNECT

DIGITAL START UP ACTIVITY
Gunfire Over Malacca

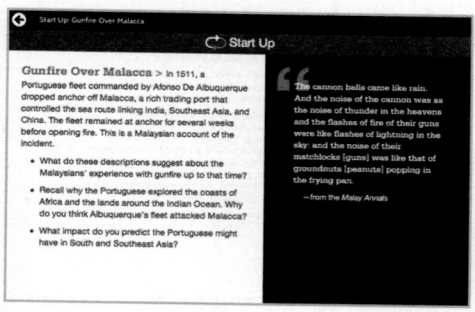

Project the Start Up Activity Ask students to read the quotation and answer the questions as they enter and get settled. Then have them share their ideas with another student, either in class or through a chat or blog space.

Discuss What do these descriptions suggest about the Malaysians' experience with gunfire up to that time? *(Sample response: Malaysians had not experienced gunfire before.)* Recall why the Portuguese explored the coasts of Africa and the geography of the lands around the Indian Ocean. Why do you think Albuquerque's fleet attacked Malacca? *(Sample response: The Portuguese wanted to take control of the spice trade from Arab traders, and Malacca was an important trading port strategically located in Southeast Asia.)*

Tell students that in this lesson they will learn how Europeans built trading empires and established footholds in Asia.

⇅ FLIP IT!

Assign the Flipped Video for this lesson.

■ STUDENT EDITION PRINT
PAGES: 390–396

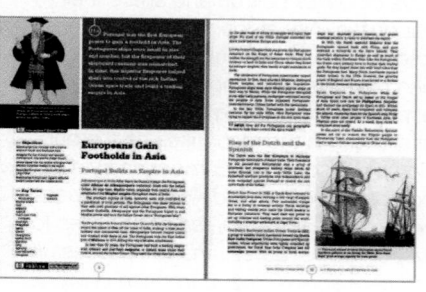

■ INVESTIGATE

DIGITAL TEXT 1
Portugal Builds an
Empire in Asia

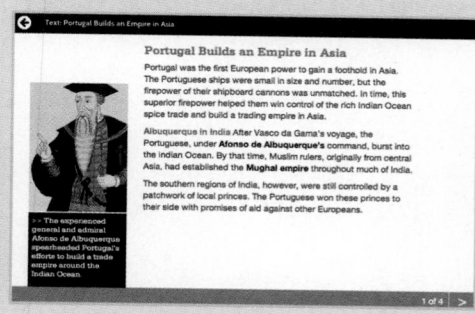

Objective 1: Summarize how Portugal built a trading empire in South and Southeast Asia.

Quick Instruction

Explain that Afonso de Albuquerque continued the exploration and expansion begun by Vasco da Gama. He used diplomacy and violence to grow and solidify the Portuguese trading empire in coastal India and around the Indian Ocean. He then led the Portuguese into Southeast Asia, where they overpowered rival Arab fleets and in 1511 captured the East Indies port of Malacca.

Analyze Images Project the image of Malacca on the whiteboard. Ask: What main features of Malacca do you observe? Why do you think the Portuguese developed it this way? *(Sample response: Malacca was built on top of a cliff and had fortified walls enclosing many areas, with houses inside the fort. Malacca seems laid out with military protection in mind.)*

Draw Inferences Project the Interactive Gallery that accompanies text 5 of this lesson. Show students the location of Malacca. Ask why Malacca was so important to the Portuguese. *(Sample response: Malacca had an ideal East Indies location as a trading and supply outpost for Portuguese ships traveling the trade route between the Indian and Pacific Oceans.)*

Further Instruction

Portugal Builds an Empire in Asia Go through the Interactive Reading Notepad questions and discuss the answers with the class. Use the graphic organizer to trace the causes and effects of Portuguese exploration in South and Southeast Asia.

Compare How did Vasco da Gama's achievements compare with those of Afonso de Albuquerque? *(They were quite similar. Da Gama pioneered the route to India, forced a treaty on Calicut's ruler, and made highly profitable voyages. Albuquerque increased Portuguese power in India, went on to Southeast Asia, attacked coastal towns, destroyed Arab fleets, and seized the port of Malacca. Da Gama and Albuquerque built a Portuguese trading empire around the Indian Ocean and Southeast Asia.)*

Europeans Gain Footholds in Asia

DIGITAL TEXT 2

Rise of the Dutch and the Spanish

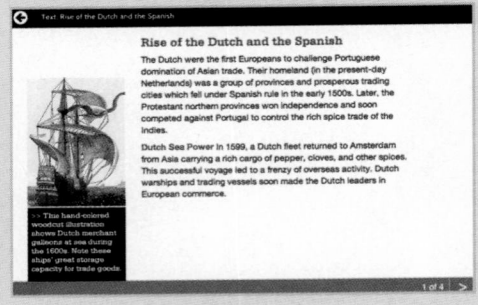

DIGITAL TEXT 3

European Trade in Mughal India

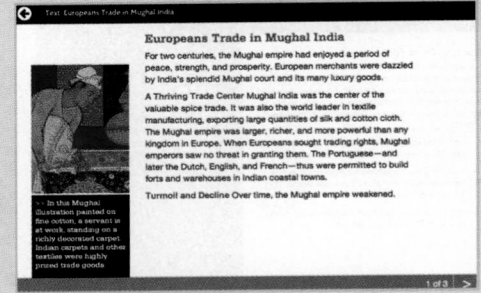

Objective 2: Analyze the rise of the Dutch and Spanish dominance in Asia and the Indian Ocean.

Quick Instruction

Tell students that Portugal's dominance of trade with Asia ended due to stiff competition. After Dutch warships defeated the Portuguese and seized Malacca, the Dutch East India Company dominated the spice trade. Meanwhile, Spain seized the Philippine Islands in the Pacific and established a trade network from the Americas through the Philippines to China.

Infer Project the Dutch painting of Jacob Mathieusen and his wife. Describe the Dutch East India Company of which Mathieusen was a senior official. Ask students what advantages Dutch East India officials might have had over their Portuguese rivals who were directed by the Portuguese monarchy. *(Sample response: The Dutch had the power to wage war, make treaties, and govern colonies. They were working for private profit. The Portuguese were under royal direction. Advantages for the Dutch: their independent authority enabled them to act more quickly, the private profit motive made them more determined to achieve personal rewards.)*

D **Differentiate: Special Needs/Extra Support** Have students imagine that they are going shopping in a busy store during the holiday shopping season when there are big special deals. Ask them to list the challenges they might encounter and the actions they

could take to beat out other shoppers and get the best deals. Ask them how this experience is a bit similar to the European competition for the spice trade. *(Sample similarities: the need to get to the market early, to bring lots of helpers, to negotiate, and occasionally to bump and push to get the products you want)*

ELL Use the ELL activity described in the ELL chart.

Further Instruction

Editable Presentation Use the Editable Presentation to present the main ideas for this text.

Distinguish Ask students: What were key differences between the Portuguese presence in India and the Spanish presence in the Philippines? *(Sample response: The Portuguese had a limited impact on India. They did not move far beyond the coast and did not leave a strong cultural influence on most of India. The Spanish conquered the Philippines and brought Catholic missionaries to convert people to Christianity.)*

Identify Steps in a Process Ask students to draw a diagram identifying the steps in the Spanish trade system that linked the Spanish colonies in the Americas, the Spanish Philippines, and China. *(Sample response: step 1: mine silver and gold in Americas; step 2: ship precious metals to Philippines; step 3: go to China and use gold and silver to buy goods; step 4: ship Chinese goods to Spain, its colonies, and other countries for a profit.)*

Objectives 1: Summarize how Portugal built a trading empire in South and Southeast Asia; **2:** Analyze the rise of the Dutch and Spanish dominance in Asia and the Indian Ocean; **3:** Understand how the decline of Mughal India affected European traders in the region.

Quick Instruction

Interactive Chart: European Footholds in the Eastern Hemisphere Project the chart on the whiteboard and look at each country, foothold, and reason, as well as the layout of the whole chart. Remind students that a series of European powers gained Asian footholds from the 1500s through the 1700s. Many, but not all, footholds were achieved and held by force. Diplomacy during changes in local political power also played an important role.

🖳 ACTIVE CLASSROOM

Have students spend three minutes jotting down their response to this question on sticky notes: *Viewed as a whole, what does this chart tell you about European expansion in the Eastern Hemisphere?* Have students pair up and share their responses. Ask students to post their sticky notes on the board or chart paper and then have students look at all the various responses, discussing similarities and differences in the responses as a group. *(Sample responses: Europeans established footholds in Africa and Asia. The causes were to gain trade, to establish bases to support trade routes, and to successfully compete against rival European powers.)*

INTERACTIVE CHART

European Footholds in the Eastern Hemisphere

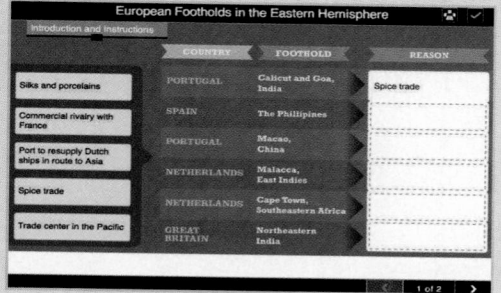

DIGITAL TEXT 4

Ming China and Europe

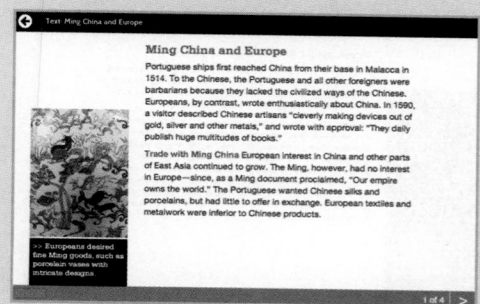

DIGITAL TEXT 5

The Manchus Conquer China

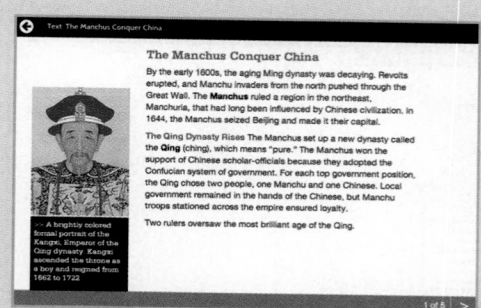

Further Instruction

Project the Interactive Reading Notepad questions provided in the notepad. Have students answer them as they progress through the core reading.

Identify Cause and Effect Why were European merchants strongly attracted to trade with the Mughal empire? *(Mughal India, during a long era of peace and prosperity, had acquired many luxury goods. It was the center of a valuable spice trade and the world leader in textile manufacturing, especially silk and cotton cloth. All this greatly attracted European merchants.)*

Draw Inferences Discuss the military sepoy system. Ask: Why do you think the East India companies hired armies of sepoys? *(Sample response: Because of Indian disunity, Indians were willing to fight against other Indians. The European East India companies felt it was easier to hire soldiers in India than bring soldiers from Europe.)*

Sequence Events Ask students to create a time line identifying when individual European powers acquired their footholds in the Eastern Hemisphere. *(Portugal first: Goa, 1510; and Malacca, 1511; then Spain: the Philippines, claimed in 1521; next the Netherlands: Malacca, taken from the Portuguese, 1641; and Cape Town, 1652; finally the British and French in India during the 1700s)*

Objective 4: Describe European contacts with Ming and Qing China.

Quick Instruction

Explain to students that European merchants desired Chinese trade goods. The Chinese economy thrived under the Ming and Qing Dynasties, but both dynasties limited trade with Europeans. The Ming demanded payment in gold or silver, which They allowed the Portuguese to set up a trading post at Guangzhou. They later permitted Europeans to trade with Chinese merchants only at Canton, supervised by imperial officials, and only during a yearly trading season.

Interactive Gallery: Trade Among Europe, Africa, and Asia Project the gallery. Have students look at each image individually and then the collection of images as a whole. Ask students to pair with a partner and then ask them: *What do you see? What does that make you think? What are you wondering about now that you've seen this?* Have students share their insights with the class. *(Answers will vary. Students should observe the far-flung trading locations and variety of items, from spices to clothes to porcelain, and conclude that a very strong demand drove all this trade. They should wonder, for example, who purchased and finally acquired these valued goods.)*

ACTIVE CLASSROOM

For this "Act it Out" activity, divide the class into four groups (Portugal, Spain, the Netherlands, and Great Britain). Have each group select a spokesperson. The group's job is to role play explorers and merchants of the late 1400 through the 1700s. They will write a short speech to convince others to invest in their profit-seeking voyage to Asia. The spokesperson should then deliver the speech. *(Students should describe where they plan to go and what goods they plan to trade for.)*

ELL Use the ELL activity described in the ELL chart.

Further Instruction

Go through the Interactive Reading Notepad questions and discuss the answers with the class.

Identify Steps in a Process What steps did the Ming take to limit trade with European merchants? *(The Ming demanded payment in gold or silver. They allowed the Portuguese to set up a trading post at Guangzhou. They later permitted Europeans to trade with Chinese merchants only at Canton, supervised by imperial officials, and only during a yearly trading season.)*

Draw Conclusions What effects do you think Ming restrictions had on global trade? *(Sample response: a large flow of gold and silver into China; because of the limited supply, there was probably increased worldwide demand and higher prices for Chinese goods, and hence intense competition among European merchants.)*

Europeans Gain Footholds in Asia

INTERACTIVE MAP

Trade Among Europe, Africa, and Asia

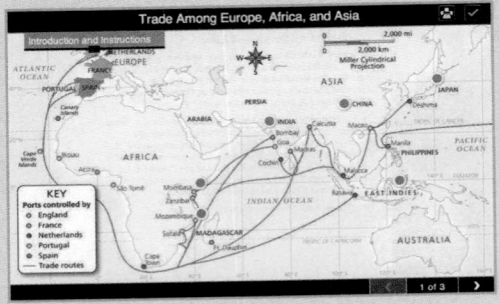

DIGITAL TEXT 6

Korea and Japan Choose Isolation

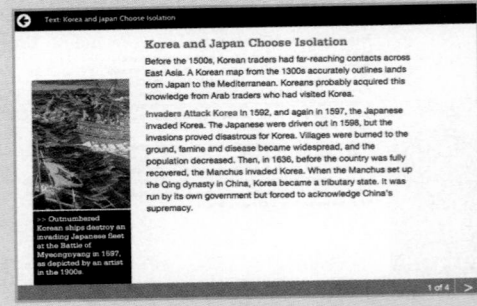

Infographic: The Chinese Tribute System Project the infographic on the whiteboard. Look at the sections for every step, the information about Lord Macartney's 1793 mission to the Qing court, and the whole infographic.

Predict Consequences What do you think would have resulted in China and Britain if Lord Macartney had performed the required kowtow before the Qing emperor Qianlong? *(Sample response: Having shown the required subservience to the emperor, Britain would then have been granted trading privileges in China. In Britain, however, I think that Lord Macartney's behavior probably would not have been acceptable. He might have been permanently disgraced and forced to retire from diplomatic service.)*

Objective 5: Summarize Korea and Japan's attitudes toward contact with the outside world.

Quick Instruction

Tell students that Korea, after invasion by Japan and conquest by China, did not welcome many foreigners. From the 1500s on, it preferred a policy of isolationism. Japan at first welcomed contact with Portuguese, Spanish, and Dutch traders, and even showed interest in Christianity. However, after Spanish conquest of the Philippines and a rise in conversion to Christianity, Japanese rulers began to fear foreigners and turned to isolationism.

Analyze Images Project the illustration of the battle of Myeongnyang (1597) between Korean and Japanese warships. Have students carefully review the scene. Explain that the outnumbered Korean fleet defeated the Japanese at Myeongnyang, but that Korea was once again invaded and then came under Chinese domination. Ask: How do you think dramatic images of invasion such as this would impact Korea's and Japan's interest in increased contact with foreigners? *(Answers may vary. Sample response: Korea and Japan would most likely be fearful that their relatively small nations might be overpowered by more powerful and aggressive countries. They would therefore avoid or limit contact with foreigners.)*

D Differentiate: Challenge/Gifted Ask two students or two small groups of students to conduct a class presentation debating the positives and negatives of Japan choosing a policy of isolationism.

Further Instruction

Editable Presentation Use the Editable Presentation to present the main ideas for this text.

Identify Steps in a Process What actions did the Tokugawas take against foreign influences on Japan? *(Answers may vary. Students may include many of the following: they expelled foreign missionaries, persecuted Japanese Christians, barred European merchants, forbade Japanese to travel abroad, and outlawed the building of large ships, which effectively closed off foreign trade.)*

Identify Supporting Details Tell students that in many ways Japan thrived despite its policy of isolationism. Ask them to identify details from the text that support this statement? *(Sample response: Japanese arts flourished, internal trade thrived, cities grew in population, and a merchant class grew in wealth.)*

Topic Inquiry

Launch the Topic Inquiry with students after introducing the Topic.

SYNTHESIZE

DIGITAL ACTIVITY

International Trade: Different Approaches

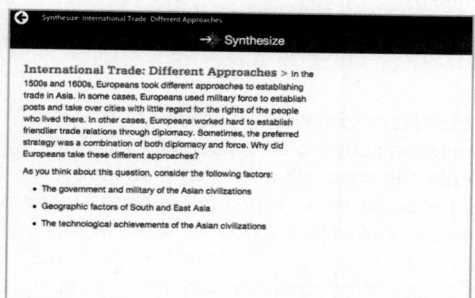

Have students form small groups to consider the issue in the "International Trade: Different Approaches" activity. Ask them to take five minutes to brainstorm and write down brief answers to the following question.

Why did Europeans take different approaches—including military force and diplomacy—to establishing trade in Asia? As they brainstorm, they should consider the government and military of the Asian civilizations, geographic factors of South and East Asia, and the technological achievements of the Asian civilizations.

Discuss In light of the factors mentioned above, why did the British and Spanish take different approaches to establishing trade in India and the Philippines? *(Sample response: Mughal India had a strong government and military when the British first sought trade there, so the British pursued diplomacy. Later, when the Mughals fell into decline, the British applied military force to oust rivals and take control. The Spanish seized the Philippines by force. Diplomacy was not required because the Filipinos were not united, and were therefore easier to conquer. Both India and the Philippines were far from Europe: a long distance to send and supply troops. Neither country was more advanced technologically than Britain or Spain.)*

DEMONSTRATE

LESSON QUIZ

Lesson Quiz and Class Discussion Board

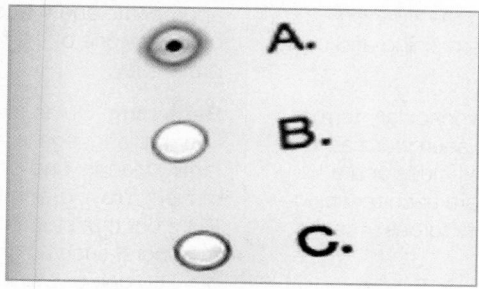

Assign the online Lesson Quiz for this lesson if you haven't already done so. Students will be offered automatic enrichment based on their score.

Pose these questions to the class on the Discussion Board:

In "Europeans Gain Footholds in Asia," you read about how the Portuguese, followed by the Dutch, British, and French, won footholds in Asia through diplomacy, force, and sometimes both. Over time, European powers established forts, trading posts, resupply stations, and colonies around the Indian Ocean, in India, and in Southeast Asia. However, European trade with China was limited. Korea and Japan pursued isolationism.

Predict Consequences How do you think European policies in Asia at this time would affect future relations between Europe and Asia? *(Answers may vary. Students may think that in the short-term European influence and trade in Asia will grow and bring wealth to Europe and China. However, in the long-term, governments and people of Asia may resent the violence and force that Europeans used to expand their interests in Asia. This may damage relations between the two regions.)*

Analyze Information Which European country do you think was most successful in establishing a trade empire and good long-term relationships with people in Asia? Why? *(Sample response: The Dutch. They drove out the Portuguese. They set up successful trading posts and colonies across South and Southeast Asia that lasted until the 1900s in Indonesia. I think their closer relationships with local people led to this long-term success for the Dutch. They not only built forts and traded profitably, but also established settlements, formed ties with local leaders, and many Dutch traders married Asian women.)*

Topic Inquiry

Launch the Topic Inquiry with students after introducing the Topic.

European Conquests in the Americas

Supporting English Language Learners

Use with Digital Text 4, **Governing the Spanish Empire.**

Speaking
Explain that content area vocabulary is specific to each academic discipline. There are certain words that are used in history that are not typically used in math or the sciences. Read *Governing the Spanish Empire* aloud to students. Then have students practice defining and using content area vocabulary as they speak about the topic.

Beginning Provide students with a few content area vocabulary terms from the text, such as *empire*, *colony*, and *settler*. Say each word and have students repeat it. Then model how to use context clues and a dictionary to determine the meaning of each word. Share each meaning with students and help them read it aloud. Ask students to describe the meaning of one term in a word or two.

Intermediate Help pairs of students find three grade-level content area vocabulary terms from the text. Then help them use dictionaries, context clues, and glossaries to create a definition for each word. Ask pairs to use the words in phrases or simple sentences to describe the text.

Advanced Instruct students to find six grade-level content area terms from the text. Have them use dictionaries, context clues, and glossaries to create a definition for each word. Ask pairs to use the terms in complete sentences in a discussion about the text.

Advanced High Instruct students to find six grade-level content area terms from the text. Have them use dictionaries, context clues, and glossaries to create a definition for each word. Then have students write a sentence using each term correctly and share their sentences aloud with a partner. Ask pairs to have a discussion about the text using the terms in complete sentences.

Use with Digital Text 5, **Society and Culture in Spanish America.**

Speaking
Read *Society and Culture in Spanish America* aloud to the class. Ask students to think about situations in which informal language is appropriate and welcome. After students listen to the text, have them complete one of the following activities depending on their level of English proficiency.

Beginning Guide students to brainstorm situations in which using informal language is appropriate. Make sure the list includes talking with family, friends, and peers. Students can share situations such as family dinners, playing with friends, and activities with siblings or cousins. Point out that students may even use formal language with some family members, such as grandparents or aunts and uncles. Then help students develop one or two informal sentences to describe "A Society of Unequal Classes" that students can use in an informal conversation with family. Have students practice saying those sentences aloud.

Intermediate Ask students to work in pairs to role-play a conversation with a friend in which they use informal language to talk about the social classes of Spanish America in "A Society of Unequal Classes." Circulate among student pairs to help them as needed.

Advanced Ask students to work together in small groups to role-play a conversation among friends. Students should use informal language to talk about the social classes of Spanish America in "A Society of Unequal Classes." Circulate among groups to offer support as needed.

Advanced High Ask students to work together in small groups to role-play a conversation among friends. Students should use informal language to talk about the social classes of Spanish America in "A Society of Unequal Classes." Instruct students to reflect on how and why the mixing of social groups can change the structure of a society over several generations. Encourage students to think about and share their own ethnic backgrounds during this discussion. Circulate among groups to offer support as needed.

◨ Differentiate Instruction

Use the Differentiated Instruction notes throughout the lesson plan to support the varied skill sets, levels of readiness, and interests in the mixed-ability classroom.

Challenge These notes include suggestions for expanding the activity for advanced students.

On-Level These notes include suggestions for modifying the activity to address different interests or learning styles.

Extra Support These notes include ideas for providing more scaffolding or reading spuport.

Special Needs These notes provide ideas for adapting instruction to support the needs of various special needs students.

◼ NOTES

Objectives

Objective 1: Analyze the results of the first encounters between the Spanish and Native Americans.

Objective 2: Explain how the Aztec and Inca empires were impacted by Spanish conquistadors and European colonization.

Objective 3: Describe how Portugal and other European nations challenged Spanish power.

Objective 4: Analyze the major features of Spanish colonial government, society and culture.

Objective 5: Describe the impact of Spanish colonization of the Americas.

LESSON 3 ORGANIZER — PACING: APPROX. 1 PERIOD, .5 BLOCKS

		OBJECTIVES	PACING	RESOURCES Online	RESOURCES Print
Connect					
	DIGITAL START UP ACTIVITY **Moctezuma Is Filled with Terror**		5 min.	●	
Investigate					
	DIGITAL TEXT 1 **First Encounters**	Objective 1	10 min.	●	●
	DIGITAL TEXT 2 **Cortés Conquers the Aztecs**	Objective 2	10 min.	●	●
	DIGITAL TEXT 3 **The Incan Empire and Beyond**	Objectives 2, 3	10 min.	●	●
	INTERACTIVE MAP **Spanish and Portuguese Colonies in the Americas**		10 min.	●	
	DIGITAL TEXT 4 **Governing the Spanish Empire**	Objective 4	10 min.	●	●
	DIGITAL TEXT 5 **Society and Culture in Spanish America**		10 min.	●	●
	DIGITAL TEXT 6 **The Impact of Spanish Colonization**	Objective 5	10 min.	●	●
	INTERACTIVE CHART **Causes and Effects of Spanish Colonization**		10 min.	●	
Synthesize					
	DIGITAL ACTIVITY **Unexpected Impacts**		5 min.	●	
Demonstrate					
	DIGITAL QUIZ **Lesson Quiz and Class Discussion Board**		10 min.	●	

European Conquests in the Americas

■ CONNECT

DIGITAL START UP ACTIVITY
Moctezuma Is Filled with Terror

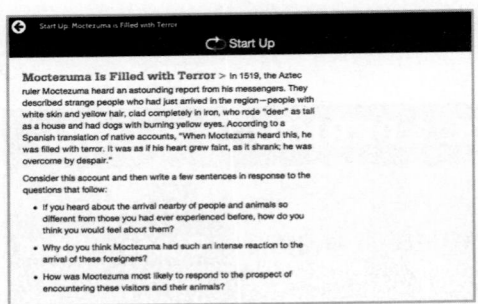

Project the Start Up Activity Ask students to read the account and answer the questions as they enter and get settled. Then have them share their ideas with another student, either in class or through a chat or blog space.

Discuss Why do you think Moctezuma had such an intense reaction to the arrival of these foreigners? *(Sample response: He feared them because they seemed so very different and might harm him and his people.)*

Tell students that in this lesson they will learn about European conquests and colonization in the Americas and the effects of this expansion on both Europeans and Native Americans.

Aa Vocabulary Development Use the Interactive Reading Notepad to preview the Key Terms and Academic Vocabulary in this lesson with students.

⇅ FLIP IT!
Assign the Flipped Video for this lesson.

■ STUDENT EDITION PRINT
PAGES: 397–405

■ INVESTIGATE

DIGITAL TEXT 1
First Encounters

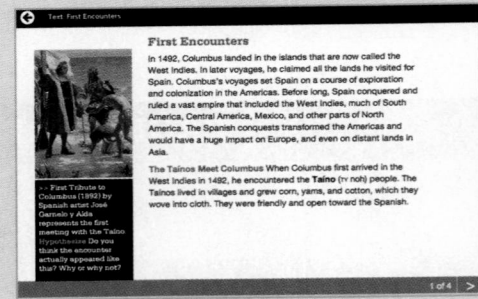

Objective 1: Analyze the results of the first encounters between the Spanish and Native Americans.

Quick Instruction
Explain to students that Columbus's first encounters with the Taíno people began a pattern of interaction that would have many far-reaching effects for both Europeans and Native Americans. Spanish conquistadors conquered Native Americans, seized their gold and other valuables, and urged or forced them to accept Christianity.

Analyze Images Project the "First Tribute to Columbus" illustration on the whiteboard. Tell students that a Spanish artist painted this illustration hundreds of years after Columbus's landing. Ask: What do you think the artist wants viewers to know and feel about this meeting? How does he use images to convey this viewpoint? *(Sample response: The artist portrays the scene in a positive way as a great and heroic event. He wants viewers to feel pride in Spain's power and Christianity. Columbus, formally dressed with a large wooden cross right behind him, is placed near the center of the picture. Spanish flags are flying and his ships are close by. An Indian kneels subserviently before Columbus and another presents a gift, while others watch, excited or fascinated. A soldier shows a Native American his sword.)*

Further Instruction
Go through the Interactive Reading Notepad questions and discuss the answers with the class. Use the graphic organizer to track the encounters and order of events that resulted in European empires in the Americas.

Compare and Contrast Direct students to compare Columbus's first meeting with the Taínos with his relations with them. How do they compare? *(They differed. At first, Columbus was welcomed and Columbus noted their generosity. But afterwards, Columbus imprisoned some of them and claimed their land for Spain.)*

Generate Explanations Remind students that the early conquistadors were greatly outnumbered by the Native Americans. Even so, they conquered the Native Americans. Ask students to explain why the conquistadors were so successful. *(Students should explain that the Spanish had horses, guns, and other superior weapons that Native Americans did not have. Also, many Native Americans died from European diseases that they had no immunity against.)*

Digital Text 2

Cortés Conquers the Aztecs

DIGITAL TEXT 2

Cortés Conquers the Aztecs

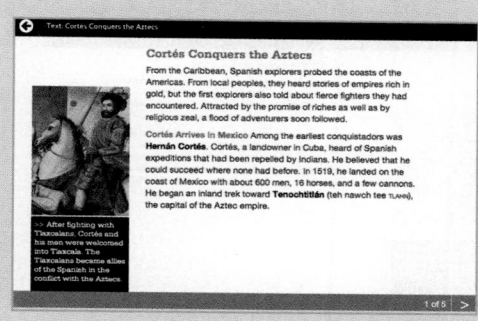

Cortés Conquers the Aztecs

From the Caribbean, Spanish explorers probed the coasts of the Americas. From local peoples, they heard stories of empires rich in gold, but the first explorers also told about fierce fighters they had encountered. Attracted by the promise of riches as well as by religious zeal, a flood of adventurers soon followed.

Cortés Arrives in Mexico Among the earliest conquistadors was **Hernán Cortés**. Cortés, a landowner in Cuba, heard of Spanish expeditions that had been repelled by Indians. He believed that he could succeed where none had before. In 1519, he landed on the coast of Mexico with about 600 men, 16 horses, and a few cannons. He began an inland trek toward **Tenochtitlán** (teh nawch tee TLAHN), the capital of the Aztec empire.

>> After fighting with Tlaxcalans, Cortés and his men were welcomed into Tlaxcala. The Tlaxcalans became allies of the Spanish in the conflict with the Aztecs

1 of 5 >

Objective 2: Explain how the Aztec and Incan empires were impacted by Spanish conquistadors and European colonization.

Quick Instruction

In 1519, Hernán Cortés and his soldiers landed in Mexico and marched to Tenochtitlán, the Aztec capital. After friendly first encounters, the Spanish tried to convert the Aztecs to Christianity and take their riches. They imprisoned the emperor Moctezuma, battled the Aztecs, and demolished Tenochtitlán.

Analyze Maps Project the map of Cortés's route to Tenochtitlán on the whiteboard. Ask students to describe the route. (*He traveled by sea from Cuba to the Yucatán Peninsula of Mexico. His ships then hugged the coast until reaching Veracruz. From there, they marched inland to Tenochtitlán.*) Ask students to explain how this route benefited Cortés. (*Sample response: The Spanish could travel more quickly and safely by sea. They avoid marching a long distance over rough terrain and fighting Native Americans along the way.*)

Draw Inferences Why do you think Cortés thought he could conquer the Aztecs? (*Sample response: Cortés was a very determined and courageous person. Although greatly outnumbered, he thought his men with their armor, guns, swords, and horses could terrify and dominate the Aztecs.*)

Further Instruction

Editable Presentation Use the Editable Presentation to present the main ideas of this text.

Compare How were the character and impact of Cortés and Columbus alike? (*Sample response: Both Cortés and Columbus were very courageous and determined and led successful expeditions. Despite being at first welcomed by Native Americans, they both used force against them, claimed their land, and sought to convert them to Christianity.*)

Support Ideas with Evidence Tell students that Cortés was flexible and used both peaceful diplomacy and military force to achieve his goals. Ask students to provide evidence from the text that supports this idea. (*Cortés used force against the Aztecs but cooperated with Malinche and formed alliances with other Native American groups.*)

DIGITAL TEXT 3

The Incan Empire and Beyond

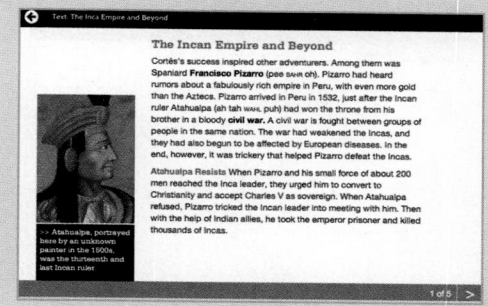

The Incan Empire and Beyond

Cortés's success inspired other adventurers. Among them was Spaniard **Francisco Pizarro** (pee SAHR oh). Pizarro had heard rumors about a fabulously rich empire in Peru, with even more gold than the Aztecs. Pizarro arrived in Peru in 1532, just after the Incan ruler Atahualpa (ah tah WAHL puh) had won the throne from his brother in a bloody **civil war**. A civil war is fought between groups of people in the same nation. The war had weakened the Incas, and they had also begun to be affected by European diseases. In the end, however, it was trickery that helped Pizarro defeat the Incas.

Atahualpa Resists When Pizarro and his small force of about 200 men reached the Inca leader, they urged him to convert to Christianity and accept Charles V as sovereign. When Atahualpa refused, Pizarro tricked the Incan leader into meeting with him. Then with the help of Indian allies, he took the emperor prisoner and killed thousands of Incas.

>> Atahualpa, portrayed here by an unknown painter in the 1800s, was the thirteenth and last Incan ruler

1 of 5 >

Objectives 2: Explain how the Aztec and Incan empires were impacted by Spanish conquistadors and European colonization; 3: Describe how Portugal and other European nations challenged Spanish power.

Quick Instruction

The success of Cortés in Mexico inspired the Spanish and other Europeans to pursue conquests and colonization. In South America, the Spanish conquistador Francisco Pizarro conquered the Incas, killed their ruler, and captured Peru. From Peru, the Spanish added much of South America to their empire. Meanwhile, the Portuguese developed a large colony in Brazil. The English, French, and Dutch made some small efforts to challenge Spanish and Portuguese dominance in the region.

Interactive Gallery: Spanish and Portuguese Colonies in the Americas, About 1700 Project the gallery. Look at each image individually and then the collection of images as a whole. Where were the Spanish and Portuguese colonies in the Americas located? Which nation claimed the most territory? (*Spain: Viceroyalty of New Spain consisted of Florida, Cuba, and other Caribbean islands, as well as Mexico, Central America, and a northern portion of South America. Viceroyalty of Peru: much of the west coast of South America; parts of today's Chile and Argentina; all of Peru, Ecuador, and Bolivia; and part of Columbia, Paraguay, and Uruguay. Portugal's Brazil: the northern and eastern coastal regions of present-day Brazil. Spain claimed the most territory.*)

European Conquests in the Americas

INTERACTIVE MAP

Spanish and Portuguese Colonies in the Americas

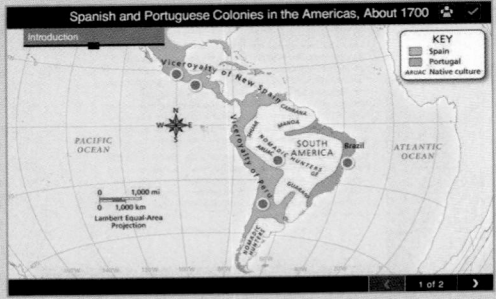

DIGITAL TEXT 4

Governing the Spanish Empire

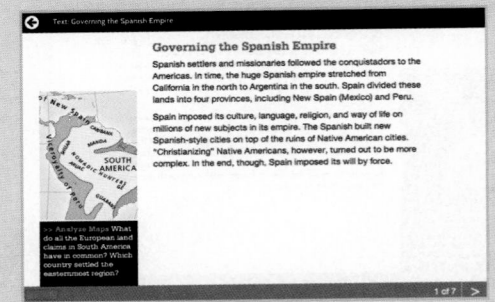

📷 ACTIVE CLASSROOM

Pair students to have a "Conversation with History." Have the first student assume the role of a Spanish colonial official. Have the second student assume the role of a visiting royal official from Spain. The colonial official gives the official from Spain a verbal "tour" of the map—what does it show? The official from Spain makes comments and asks questions about the benefits and challenges for Spain. Ask students to record their conversation so others in class can access it.

Further Instruction

Project the Interactive Reading Notepad questions for this text. Have students answer them as they progress through the text. Use the graphic organizer chart to follow the order of events and impact of the Spanish conquistadors on the Incan empire.

Integrate Ask students to use the gallery and text to explain how the Portuguese empire in the Americas differed from the Spanish empire. *(Sample response: The Portuguese empire was much smaller, limited to coastal areas of Brazil. The Portuguese colony did not have much gold and silver. But they developed a profitable colony. Settlers cut and exported brazilwood, established plantations, and raised cattle.)*

Summarize Ask students to use the gallery and text to explain how Britain, France, and the Netherlands competed with the Spanish and Portuguese in South America. *The French and Dutch had very small colonies in northeastern South America. Pirates and privateers preyed on treasure ships from the Americas. All three European nations sent explorers to search the Americas' coasts for riches.)*

D Differentiate: Special Needs/Extra Support Ask students to work in a group to briefly jot down three or more similarities between the actions of Cortés and Pizarro. *(Both conquered Native American civilizations, killed their rulers, claimed their land, and took their riches.)*

Objective 4: Analyze the major features of Spanish colonial government, society, and culture.

Quick Instruction

The Spanish monarchy sent royal officials to direct the government and economy of its American colonies. Catholic missionary priests spread Christianity and Spanish culture. Under the encomienda system, Native Americans were forced to work under brutal conditions. The Spanish brought enslaved Africans to work in mines and on plantations. Cultural blending occurred, but there was a layered society of unequal classes based on ethnicity and wealth.

Analyze Images Have students quickly view all the images and captions for this lesson. Ask: What were four key characteristics of Spain's colonies in the Americas? Have students take a piece of paper and fold it into quarters, write down one response in the first box, and then go around the room asking other students for their responses. If they think a response is correct, they should write it in another one of their boxes until they have four different responses on their page. Ask volunteers to read their responses to the class and post them on the whiteboard.

D Differentiate: Special Needs/Extra Support Have students make a graphic organizer, such as a concept web with four circles, and then jot down characteristics of Spanish colonial government in one circle, and so forth, for economy, culture, and society.

ELL Use the ELL activity described in the ELL chart.

DIGITAL TEXT 5

Society and Culture in Spanish America

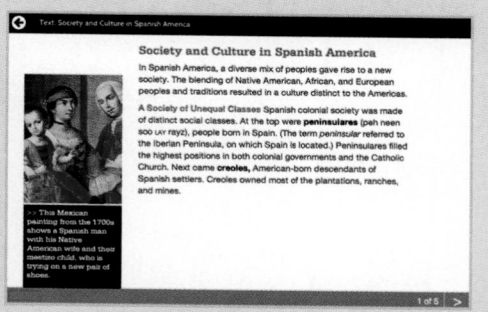

DIGITAL TEXT 6

The Impact of Spanish Colonization

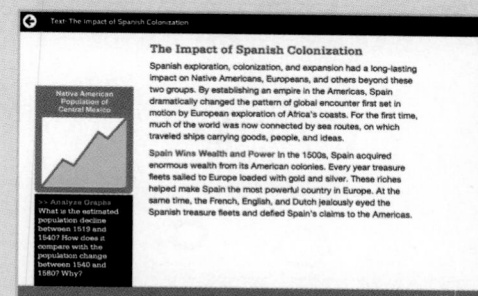

INTERACTIVE CHART

Causes and Effects of Spanish Colonization

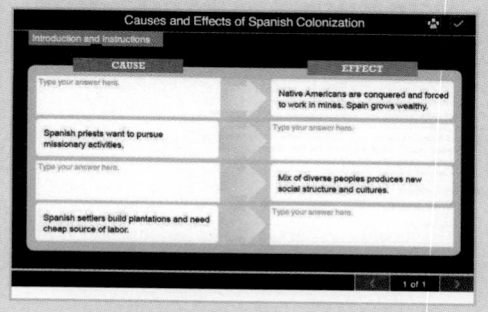

Further Instruction

A new social structure and culture arose in Spanish America as Native American, African, and European peoples and traditions interacted. Various crops, foods, farming methods, cooking styles, religions, and artistic expressions blended together. Spanish colonial society consisted of distinct social classes: peninsulares, creoles, mestizos, mulattoes, Native Americans, and people of African descent.

Editable Presentation Use the Editable Presentation to present the main ideas for this text.

Identify Steps in a Process Project the infographic on the Potosí mines on the whiteboard. Show students the images and information in each section and the layout of the infographic as a whole. Remind students that the encomienda system was used in mines such as Potosí. Ask: What steps did workers take to remove silver from the Potosí mines? *(Sample response: Carrying candles, miners walked into the mines, climbed down hundreds of feet, dug out silver ore, and then carried it out, climbing back up and walking out of the mines to deposit the ore in piles. Please note: This answer may need revision to match infographic content.)*

Predict Consequences Divide students into groups and ask them to consider what they have learned about Spanish colonial life. Do they predict that there will be social and political stability in the future or social and political conflict? Why? *(Answers may vary. Students may predict rebellion and revolution as colonists try to be free of the strict rule of the Spanish monarchy or change the unequal society where only a few have the most freedom, power, and wealth.)*

Objective 5: Describe the impact of Spanish colonization of the Americas.

Quick Instruction

Spanish exploration, colonization, and expansion in the Americas had far-reaching effects. Ships carried people, goods, and ideas to and from distant places throughout the Spanish empire and beyond. Sea routes now connected many parts of the world for the first time. Spain grew in wealth and became Europe's leading power. However, Native American civilizations and populations declined greatly.

Interactive Chart: Causes and Effects of Spanish Colonization Have students work individually or in small groups to complete the chart. Then review with students. Discuss the overall impact of Spanish colonization.

📖 ACTIVE CLASSROOM

Group students. Give each group a three-column organizer with headings "Plus/Minus/Interesting" to record responses to questions about the impact of Spanish colonization: 1. What are positive ideas about the impact of Spanish colonization? *(Sample responses: brings new animals, European ideas and technologies)* 2. What are negative ideas about the impact of Spanish colonization? *(plunders and destroys cultures, brings lethal diseases, exploits and enslaves Native Americans and Africans)* 3. What is interesting about the impact of Spanish colonization? *(interaction of Native Americans, African, and European traditions creates a new society and culture)*

Further Instruction

As Spain profited from the resources and goods taken from the Americas, Native Americans suffered and resisted. The Maya, Incas, and other Native Americans fought and resisted Spanish rule for centuries, preserving as much as they could of their own cultures.

Editable Presentation Use the Editable Presentation to present the main ideas for this text.

Analyze Graphs Discuss the population graph with the class. Ask: During which interval did the Native American population of Central Mexico decline the most? Why? *(1500–1540; war and diseases)* the least? *(1580–1620)* What is the estimated total population decline between about 1520 and 1600? *(about 25 million people)*

European Conquests in the Americas

■ SYNTHESIZE

DIGITAL ACTIVITY
Unexpected Impacts

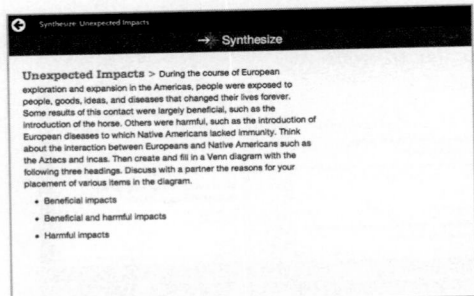

Have students use the Think Pair Share strategy to work on the Synthesis Activity titled "Unexpected Impacts." Then ask them to create their Venn diagram on the impacts of European exploration and expansion in the Americas. Invite volunteers to present their diagram showing beneficial impacts, harmful impacts, and impacts that were both beneficial and harmful.

Discuss Ask students to consider the United States and Latin America today. How is the impact of conquest and colonization by the Spanish and other Europeans still visible today? *(Answers will vary. Students may mention the prevalence of Spanish and English traditions, cultures and languages, the poverty of many Native Americans, ethnic and cultural diversity, and continuing efforts to reform social inequalities.)*

■ DEMONSTRATE

DIGITAL QUIZ
Lesson Quiz and Class Discussion Board

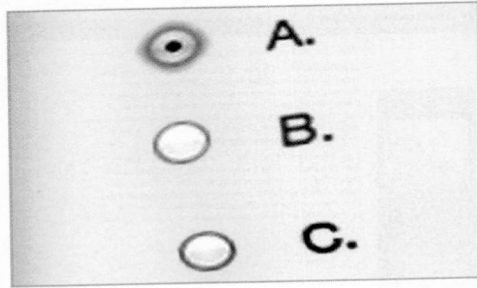

Assign the online Lesson Quiz for this lesson if you haven't already done so. Students will be offered automatic remediation or enrichment based on their score.

Pose these questions to the class on the Discussion Board:

In "European Conquests in the Americas," you read about the profound impact European exploration, expansion, and colonization had on the Americas. Encounters with Columbus, Cortés, Pizarro, and other conquistadors had drastic and destructive effects on Native American civilizations. The Spanish governed the Americas strictly, closely monitoring trade and allowing forced labor of Native Americans and enslaved Africans to ensure their empire's profitability. Native Americans suffered and resisted. In time, Native American, African, and European traditions blended into a new Spanish colonial society and culture in the Americas.

Compare and Contrast How were the ways the Spanish treated Native Americans and Africans alike or different? Explain. *(Sample response: The Spanish used both Native Americans and Africans as forced laborers on plantations and in mines, often mistreating them and seeking to convert them to Christianity. Spanish explorers and conquistadors assaulted and killed Native Americans who did not bring gold on demand, destroyed the Aztec and Incan civilizations, and disrupted or destroyed other Native American cultures. In contrast, Africans were taken from their cultures, sold as slaves, and brought to the Americas. Some were eventually able to buy their freedom.)*

Draw Inferences Why do you think rebellion attempts by the Maya, the Incas, and other Native American groups usually failed? *(Sample response: The strength and circumstances of Native American groups varied. Many were decimated by disease and warfare and did not have the strength to face European soldiers. Their leaders were killed and their political and military systems destroyed.)*

Topic Inquiry
Launch the Topic Inquiry with students after introducing the Topic.

European Colonies in North America

Supporting English Language Learners

Use with Digital Text 1, **Britain and France in a Global Struggle.**

Speaking

Read *Britain and France in a Global Struggle* aloud to students. Then have students partner up and ask pairs to explain the rivalry between Britain and France in their own words. Have students discuss with their partner why the countries struggled and give examples of how that struggle affected North America.

Beginning Ask students to use short sentences to respond. Provide them with model sentence starters: *Britain and France struggled because _____. This struggle affected North America when _____.* Have students name or draw illustrations to show their examples.

Intermediate Ask students to give three examples of how the struggle between Britain and France affected North America. Encourage open-ended discussion. Provide a sentence starter: *The struggle between Britain and France affected North America when _____.*

Advanced Encourage students to have an open-ended discussion about the struggle between Britain and France during the 1700s. Encourage them to use complex sentences with connecting words such as *and, but,* and *because* in their examples.

Advanced High After students discuss the rivalry between Britain and France, ask them to discuss the impact of the Treaty of Paris on the rivalry. Ask them to give examples to support their statements.

Use with Digital Text 2, **The 13 English Colonies.**

Speaking

Read *The 13 English Colonies* aloud to the class. Remind students that using visuals can improve their understanding of concepts and ideas. After students listen to the text, have them complete one of the following activities depending on their level of English proficiency.

Beginning Review the chart that describes self-government in the English colonies. Explain how a chart can provide quick, easy-to-understand access to information presented in a text. Read and explain each section of the chart, making connections to the text whenever possible. Assist students in summarizing what they have learned from the chart using language that is accessible to their English proficiency level.

Intermediate Work with students to review the chart that describes self-government in the English colonies. Ask students to explain the benefits of presenting information in a chart (a chart can provide quick, easy-to-understand access to information presented in a text). Have students read each section of the chart and then collaborate with them to explain the information presented, making connections to the text whenever possible. Have students summarize what they have learned from the chart using language that is accessible to their English proficiency level.

Advanced Ask students to work together in small groups to discuss the benefits of presenting information in a chart. Then instruct small groups to read and explain each section of the chart, making connections to the text whenever possible. Have small groups create a summary to share what they have learned from the chart with the rest of the class. Circulate among groups to offer support as needed.

Advanced High Ask students to work together in small groups to discuss the benefits of presenting information in a chart. Then instruct students to examine each section of the chart individually, making connections to the text whenever possible. Have students rejoin their small groups to share what they learned and create a summary of information presented in the chart. Circulate among groups to offer support as needed.

▶ Differentiate Instruction

Use the Differentiated Instruction notes throughout the lesson plan to support the varied skill sets, levels of readiness, and interests in the mixed-ability classroom.

Challenge These notes include suggestions for expanding the activity for advanced students.

On-Level These notes include suggestions for modifying the activity to address different interests or learning styles.

Extra Support These notes include ideas for providing more scaffolding or reading spuport.

Special Needs These notes provide ideas for adapting instruction to support the needs of various special needs students.

■ NOTES

European Colonies in North America

Objectives

Objective 1: Explain why the colony of New France grew slowly.

Objective 2: Analyze the establishment and growth of the English colonies.

Objective 3: Understand why Europeans competed for power in North America and how their struggle affected Native Americans.

LESSON 4 ORGANIZER		PACING: APPROX. 1 PERIOD, .5 BLOCKS			
				RESOURCES	
		OBJECTIVES	PACING	Online	Print
Connect					
	DIGITAL START UP ACTIVITY **Competing for a Continent**		5 min.	●	
Investigate					
	DIGITAL TEXT 1 **New France**	Objective 1	10 min.	●	●
	INTERACTIVE MAP **European Colonization of North America, About 1700**		10 min.	●	
	DIGITAL TEXT 2 **The 13 English Colonies**	Objective 2	10 min.	●	●
	DIGITAL TEXT 3 **A Power Struggle Begins**	Objective 3	10 min.	●	●
	INTERACTIVE CHART **Characteristics of French and English Colonies**		10 min.	●	
Synthesize					
	DIGITAL ACTIVITY **A Conquest of the Greatest Importance**		5 min.	●	
Demonstrate					
	DIGITAL QUIZ **Lesson Quiz and Class Discussion Board**		10 min.	●	

CONNECT

DIGITAL START UP ACTIVITY
Competing for a Continent

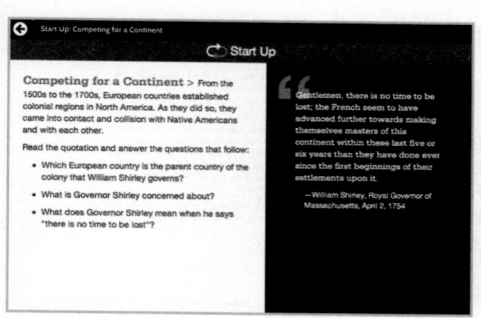

Project the Start Up Activity *Competing for a Continent.* Ask students to answer the questions as they enter and get settled. Then have them share their ideas with another student in class or through a chat or blog space.

Discuss Ask students to predict how the colonization of North America will be similar to and different from the colonization of Latin America. *(Sample response: Similarities will be European competition and conflict with Native Americans. One difference will be that France and England will engage in more conflict with each other than Spain and Portugal did.)*

Tell students that in this lesson they will learn about French and English competition for colonies in North America and how their struggle affected Native Americans.

Aa Vocabulary Development: Use the Interactive Reading Notepad to preview the Key Terms and Academic Vocabulary in this lesson with students.

FLIP IT!
Assign the Flipped Video for this lesson.

STUDENT EDITION PRINT
PAGES: 406–410

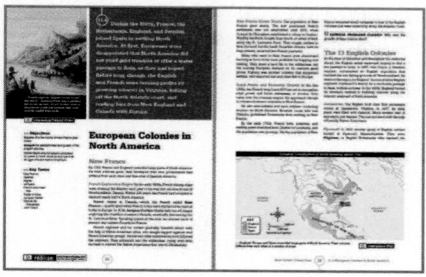

INVESTIGATE

DIGITAL TEXT 1
New France

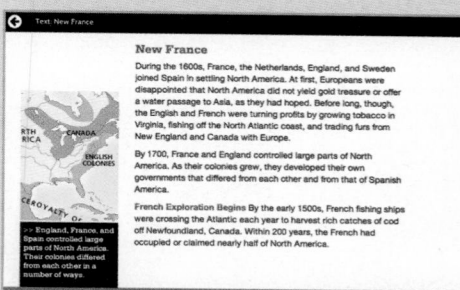

Objective 1: Explain why the colony of New France grew slowly.

Quick Instruction

European Land Claims in North America, About 1700: Interactive Map Project the map on the whiteboard and click through the hotspots. Explain that France and England colonized large parts of North America, but that their colonies were very different from each other and from Spanish colonies. They differed in geography, government, economy, and culture.

📖 ACTIVE CLASSROOM

Put this question on the whiteboard: How did geography benefit and hinder the development of New France? Ask students to spend three minutes writing their response to the question on sticky notes. Have students pair up and share their responses. Ask students to post their sticky notes on the board or on chart paper and then look at all the various responses. Finally, lead a class discussion on the similarities and differences in the individual responses. *(Sample responses: Cold winters limited farming and kept population down; abundant wildlife supported fishing and fur industries; rivers and lakes aided hunters, trappers, and missionaries; large geographic area made it difficult to govern.)*

INTERACTIVE MAP
European Colonization of North America, About 1700

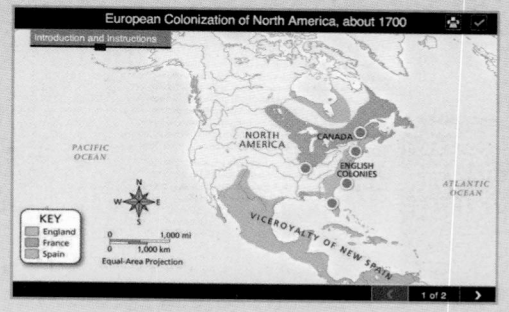

Further Instruction

Go through the Interactive Reading Notepad questions and discuss the answers with the class.

Draw Inferences How did the policies of the French king Louis XIV benefit and hinder the development of New France? *(Sample response: Louis XIV helped development by sending more soldiers, settlers, and women to new France. He hindered development by prohibiting Protestants from settling in New France.)*

D Differentiate: Challenge/Gifted Have students work in small groups and ask them to assume the role of advisors to King Louis XIV. Assign them to write up a proposed plan on what the king can do to solve the problem of New France's slow growth. *(Sample plan: lower taxes, send more settlers and soldiers, allow non-Catholics, make more alliances with Native Americans, take better land from the English and Spanish)*

European Colonies in North America

DIGITAL TEXT 2

The 13 English Colonies

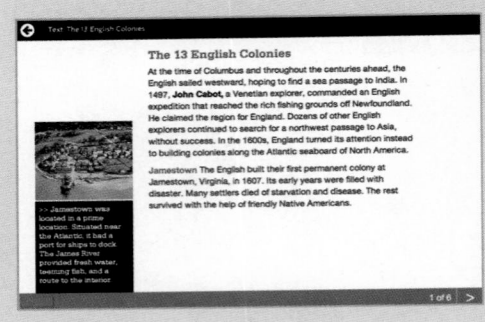

DIGITAL TEXT 3

A Power Struggle Begins

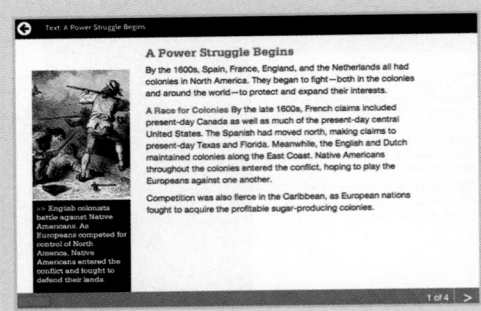

Objective 2: Analyze the establishment and growth of the English colonies.

Quick Instruction

Use the interactive map from the previous text to showcase the geography of the 13 English colonies. Explain that the English colonies had a variety of climates and that economic activities therefore varied by region. English colonists enjoyed some self-government based on English traditions and rights.

Analyze Images What does the picture of the Jamestown settlement reveal or suggest about colonial life in Virginia? *(Sample response: Colonists engaged in farming. They relied on ships for imports and exports. They located settlements along rivers and coasts for access to water and ease of travel. They needed a stockade to defend themselves from attack.)*

Analyze Charts Direct students to the charts on the Mayflower Compact and the roots of democracy in English colonial government. Ask them to identify the influences that contributed to self-government in the English colonies. *(Sample response: Judeo-Christian ideals, Greco-Roman models, English tradition of rights, English parliamentary tradition.)*

ELL Use the ELL activity described in the ELL chart.

Further Instruction

Direct students to the Interactive Reading Notepad and ask them to work through the questions on English colonial government and regional economies.

Editable Presentation Use the Editable Presentation to present the main ideas of this text.

Compare How did the economies of New England and the South differ? *(New England's economy relied on shipbuilding, fishing, and timber. Southern colonies developed a plantation economy based on cash crops such as rice and tobacco.)*

D Differentiate: Extra Support To help students remember the regional variations of the English colonies, ask them to write down one unique fact about each of the three regions.

Objective 3: Understand why Europeans competed for power in North America and how their struggle affected Native Americans.

Quick Instruction

European countries frequently clashed over colonial territories and trade in North America. In the mid-1700s, the British battled the French in the French and Indian War. Some Native American groups fought on the French side, while others fought on the British side. The British won the war, and the French had to give up Canada, leaving much of North America to the British.

Characteristics of French and British Colonies: Interactive Chart Project the chart on the whiteboard and click through each tile individually. Tell students to drag the tiles into their appropriate place on the chart.

Hypothesize Have students consider the interactive chart as it applies to the French and Indian War. Ask them to hypothesize how the differences between the French and British colonies might have helped the British win. *(Sample response: The British colonies had: a larger population and therefore a larger fighting force; a long coast and therefore easier access to aid shipped from Britain; a more compact territory that was easier to defend.)*

SYNTHESIZE

DEMONSTRATE

INTERACTIVE CHART

Characteristics of French and English Colonies

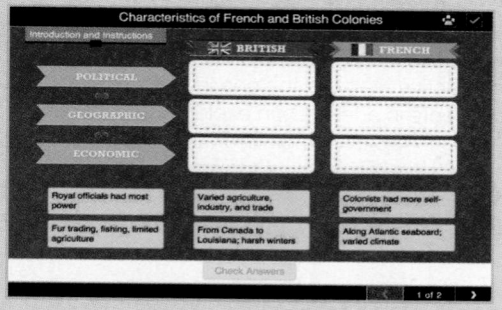

ACTIVE CLASSROOM

Imagine that you are having a conversation with one of the people in the visuals or text covered in this lesson. Write down a question you'd like to ask, then what that person would say to you, and what you would say in response. Post a video of the conversation on YouTube.

ELL Use the ELL activity described in the ELL chart.

Further Instruction

Editable Presentation Use the Editable Presentation to present the main ideas of this text.

Direct students to the Interactive Reading Notepad and ask them to work through the questions on British colonial government and regional economies.

Analyze Maps Direct students to the maps of North America in 1700 and 1763. Pair students. Have the first student give the second a verbal "tour" of the map–what does it show? Have the second student give the first an explanation of what it means.

DIGITAL ACTIVITY

A Conquest of the Greatest Importance

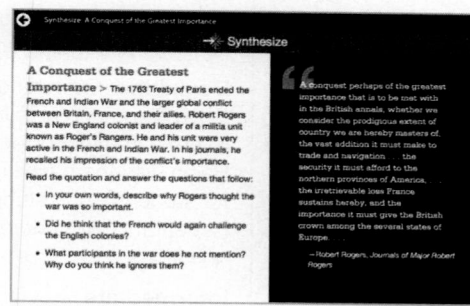

Ask students to recall the Topic Essential Question, "Why do people move?" Tell students they have five minutes to answer the questions in the A Conquest of Great Importance activity. Then ask them to pair with a partner and share their responses.

Tell the pairs to collaborate on an answer for the following question: "How might the outcome of the French and Indian War cause movement among French colonists, British colonists, and Native Americans?" (Answers may vary. Sample response: French colonists might move back to France or to other French colonies; British colonists might move west and north into the French territories that they gained in the war; as British settlers advance, Native Americans might have to move away.)

DIGITAL QUIZ

Lesson Quiz and Class Discussion Board

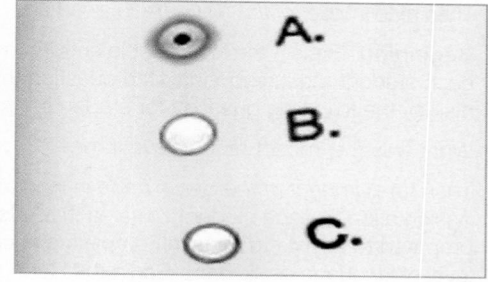

Assign the online Lesson Quiz for this lesson if you haven't already done so. Students will be offered automatic remediation or enrichment based on their score.

Pose the following question to the class on the Discussion Board:

In "European Colonies in North America," you learned about French and British competition for colonies in North America, their struggle for dominance, and how that struggle affected Native Americans.

Draw Inferences How does the British victory in the French and Indian War have a lasting impact on North America today? (Sample response: The primary language of Canada and the United States is English. Both countries have democratic governments based on British traditions. A French-speaking population remains in Canada, especially in the province of Quebec, Native American populations in the eastern United States are much smaller than they used to be.)

Topic Inquiry

Have students continue their investigations for the Topic Inquiry.

The Slave Trade and Its Impact on Africa

Supporting English Language Learners

Use with Digital Text 4, **Impact of the Slave Trade.**

Speaking

Arrange students in small groups of four to participate in a Roundtable activity. Give each student a job: timekeeper, reader, discussion leader, and scribe. Then read *Impact of the Slave Trade* aloud and begin the following activities.

Beginning Explain the Roundtable activity to students. Tell them that each student must respond to the question that is asked. Write and display the following question for students:

What was the impact of the slave trade?

Then retell *Impact of the Slave Trade* in language accessible to students. Assign a job to each student. Give each student one of these jobs but be prepared to assist students in completing each job, depending on their level of language proficiency. Begin the Roundtable activity by working with each student as he or she answers the above question. Make sure that each student in each group gives a different answer to the question. Then review answers with the cooperative group and help them choose their two best answers to share with the class.

Intermediate Explain the Roundtable activity to students. Tell them that each student must respond to the question that is asked. Write and display the following question for students:

What was the impact of the slave trade?

Then reread *Impact of the Slave Trade* to students. Begin the Roundtable activity by assigning a job to each student. Then have students share their answers to this question one at a time. Make sure that each student in each group gives a different answer to the question. Then have each cooperative group review their answers and choose their three best answers to share with the class.

Advanced Explain the Roundtable activity to students. Tell them that each student must respond to the question that is asked. Write and display the following question for students:

What was the impact of the slave trade?

Have students reread *Impact of the Slave Trade*. Begin the Roundtable activity by assigning a job to each student. Then have students share their answers to this question one at a time. The discussion leader should ensure that each student in each group gives a different answer to the question. Then have the scribe from each group review answers and guide the group in writing a summary of their three best answers to share with the class.

Advanced High Explain the Roundtable activity to students. Tell them that each student must respond to the question that is asked. Write and display the following questions for students:

• What was the impact of the slave trade?

• How did the slave trade affect the development of the economies in the Americas?

Have students reread *Impact of the Slave Trade*. Begin the Roundtable activity by assigning a job to each student. Then have students share their answers to the questions one at a time. The discussion leader should ensure that each student in each group gives a different answer to each question. Then have the scribe from each group review answers and guide the group in writing a summary of the best answers to share with the class.

Use with Digital Text 2, **The Atlantic Slave Trade.**

Speaking

Read *The Atlantic Slave Trade* aloud to the class. Discuss how electronic media can enhance students' understanding of concepts and ideas. After students listen to the text, have them complete one of the following activities depending on their level of English proficiency.

Beginning Explain how an interactive map like the one in *The Atlantic Slave Trade* can help clarify concepts in a text. Then explore the different layers of the triangular trade map in *The Atlantic Slave Trade* with students. Begin with the base layer and explain each element in accessible language for students. Ask students simple questions to ensure comprehension. Repeat this procedure for each layer of the map, pausing to answer any questions.

Intermediate Ask students to explain how an interactive map like the one in *The Atlantic Slave Trade* can help clarify the triangular trade routes of the slave trade. Then explore the different layers of the triangular trade map one at a time with students. Discuss each layer with students. Ask different student volunteers to use the map to explain each leg of the triangular trade route.

Advanced Ask students to examine the interactive map on triangular trade in *The Atlantic Slave Trade*. Have students work together with a partner to discuss each layer of the triangular trade map one at a time. Instruct pairs to identify which goods were traded on each leg of the route.

Advanced High Ask students to examine the interactive map on triangular trade in *The Atlantic Slave Trade*. Have students take turns explaining which goods were traded on each leg of the routes. Then facilitate a discussion on the many effects of the triangular trade routes in Europe, Africa, and the Americas.

PEARSON
realize™
www.PearsonRealize.com

Go online to access additional resources including:
Primary Sources • Biographies • Supreme Court cases •
21st Century Skill Tutorials • Maps • Graphic Organizers.

Objectives

Objective 1: Summarize the expansion of the African slave trade.

Objective 2: Explain how triangular trade worked.

Objective 3: Understand the nature of the Middle Passage and describe its effects.

Objective 4: Analyze the impact of the Atlantic slave trade on West Africa and the Americas.

LESSON 5 ORGANIZER		PACING: APPROX. 1 PERIOD, .5 BLOCKS			
				RESOURCES	
		OBJECTIVES	**PACING**	Online	Print
Connect					
DIGITAL START UP ACTIVITY **Slave Ships From West Africa**			5 min.	●	
Investigate					
DIGITAL TEXT 1 **The African Slave Trade Expands**		Objective 1	10 min.	●	●
DIGITAL TEXT 2 **The Atlantic Slave Trade**		Objective 2	10 min.	●	●
INTERACTIVE MAP **Triangular Trade Routes**			10 min.	●	
DIGITAL TEXT 3 **Horrors of the Middle Passage**		Objective 3	10 min.	●	●
DIGITAL TEXT 4 **Impact of the Slave Trade**		Objective 4	10 min.	●	●
INTERACTIVE CHART **Effects of Slavery**			10 min.	●	
Synthesize					
SYNTHESIZE ACTIVITY **Trade**			5 min.	●	
Demonstrate					
DIGITAL QUIZ **Lesson Quiz and Class Discussion Board**			10 min.	●	

The Slave Trade and Its Impact on Africa

CONNECT

DIGITAL START UP ACTIVITY
Slave Ships From West Africa

Project the Start Up Activity Ask students to answer the questions as they enter and get settled. Then have them share their ideas with another student, either in class or through a chat or blog space.

Determine Author's Point of View Based on this writer's words, what was his opinion of slave trading? *(Answers may vary. Students might say that the author did not think highly of slave trading because he reports in detail the sorrow and suffering of the slaves, including women and children. His description tells of the abuses and cruelty that enslaved Africans endured.)*

Tell students that in this lesson they will be learning about the expansion of the African slave trade and its impact on the people of Africa and the Americas.

Aa Vocabulary Development: Use the Interactive Reading Notepad to preview the Key Terms and Academic Vocabulary in this lesson with students.

⇅ FLIP IT!
Assign the Flipped Video for this lesson.

■ STUDENT EDITION PRINT PAGES: 411–416

■ INVESTIGATE

DIGITAL TEXT 1
The African Slave Trade Expands

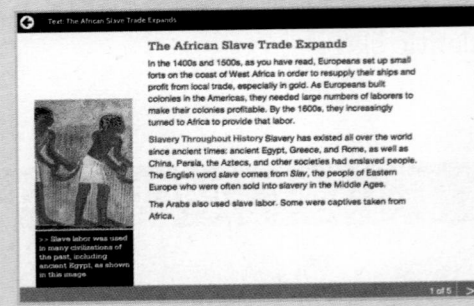

Objective 1: Summarize the expansion of the African slave trade.

Quick Instruction
The African slave trade expanded because of a high European demand for cheap slave labor, at first in European households, but later in far greater numbers for plantations in the Americas. Some African leaders tried to resist the slave trade. But the profits for slave traders and American plantation owners were high, and the demand for slaves grew.

Identify Steps in a Process Ask students to create a flowchart describing the process by which Africans were enslaved and shipped to plantations in the Americas. *(African traders seized captives in the interior, transported them to the coast, and traded slaves for European goods; European traders shipped slaves across the Atlantic to plantations in the Americas.)*

Further Instruction
Project the Interactive Reading Notepad questions provided in the notepad. Have students answer them as they progress through the text. Be sure students understand that some African leaders tried to resist the transatlantic slave trade.

Compare Ask students to compare the African slave trade before and after the involvement of the Portuguese and other Europeans. What differences do they note? *(Sample response: before European involvement: Arab and African traders, lower volume of trade; After European involvement: European, Arab, and African traders, greater volume of trade, slaves transported across Atlantic, slaves in Americas had little hope of improving their status.)*

D Differentiate: Challenge/Gifted Tell students that slavery and slave trading are still problems in the world today. Ask them to do some quick online research on this topic and share their findings with the class.

DIGITAL TEXT 2

The Atlantic Slave Trade

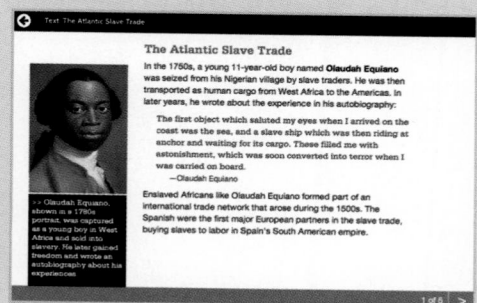

INTERACTIVE MAP

Triangular Trade Routes

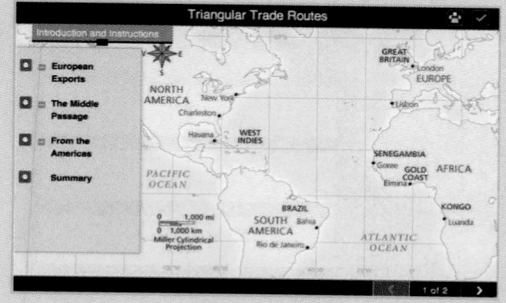

DIGITAL TEXT 3

Horrors of the Middle Passage

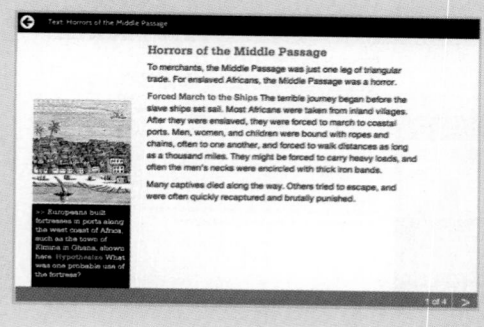

Objective 2: Explain how triangular trade worked.

Quick Instruction

Starting in the 1500s, a triangular trade system linked Europe, Africa, and the Americas. Ships went from Europe to Africa carrying trade items such as guns, cloth, and cash, which were exchanged for slaves. Ships then took African slaves to the Americas, where they were exchanged for cash, sugar, molasses, cotton, and rum or other goods. These American products were then shipped to Europe and sold for profit.

Interactive Map: Triangular Trade Routes
Project the map and bring up the different layers showing each of the three legs of the triangular trade. Examine each route individually.

ACTIVE CLASSROOM

Use the "A Closer Look" strategy with the interactive map. Have students divide into three groups. Each group should more closely investigate one leg of the triangular trade map, and then share what they learned about that part of the map with the class.

ELL Use the ELL activity described in the ELL chart.

Further Instruction

Editable Presentation Use the Editable Presentation to present the main ideas for this text.

Project and discuss the Interactive Reading Notepad questions, including the graphic organizer asking students to fill in the general sequence of events in triangular trade. Review triangular trade's general sequence of events and fill in the graphic organizer on the whiteboard as you go.

Identify Cause and Effect Be sure students understand that the triangular trade connected Europe, Africa, and the Americas. Ask: Which social classes and regions within continents profited the most from the triangle trade? *(Answers may vary. Sample response: shipping merchants, plantation owners, manufacturers and merchants in port towns and cities)*

Synthesize What role did each of the following play in triangular trade: a New England merchant, an enslaved African person, and a Southern plantation owner? *(Sample response: An enslaved African person was brought unwillingly from Africa to the Americas and forced to provide labor. A Southern plantation owner benefited from the labor. A New England merchant may have built the ship, unloaded the ship, or traded goods to Europe in exchange for the slaves to be sent to Southern plantations.)*

Objective 3: Understand the nature of the Middle Passage and describe its effects.

Quick Instruction

The Middle Passage was the central leg of the triangular trade route. Enslaved Africans were transported from Africa to the Americas on slave ships. Middle Passage conditions were terrible, causing up to half the Africans aboard the ships to die from diseases or mistreatment.

Generate Explanations Why did so many enslaved Africans die over the course of the Middle Passage? *(Disease was the biggest threat to people aboard the crammed slave ships. Most victims of diesease died from dysentery or smallpox. Many other people died from physical mistreatment.)*

Further Instruction

Editable Presentation Use the Editable Presentation to present the main ideas for this text.

Project the Interactive Reading Notepad questions provided in the notepad. Have students answer them as they progress through the core reading.

Identify Supporting Details Remind students of some details of the Middle Passage journey that made it a horror for Africans aboard slave ships. What were some ways that Africans tried to resist the Middle Passage? *(Sample response: While being marched from inland Africa to the coast, slaves were bound with chains, but some still tried to escape. While on the ships, slaves sometimes tried to join in mutinies or take over the ships to return to Africa.)*

The Slave Trade and Its Impact on Africa

DIGITAL TEXT 4
Impact of the Slave Trade

INTERACTIVE CHART
Effects of Slavery

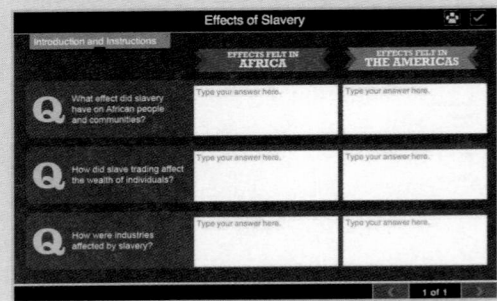

Objective 4: Analyze the impact of the Atlantic slave trade on West Africa and the Americas.

Quick Instruction

The Atlantic slave trade had immediate and long-term effects on Africa and on the Americas. Some African kingdoms participated in slavery and used their wealth to conquer weaker states. But slavery also destroyed many African states. Millions of Africans died or lived in the terrible conditions of slavery. In the Americas, plantation owners and merchants in port cities and towns profited from slavery. Eventually, slavery was one of the leading causes of the American Civil War.

Interactive Chart: Effects of Slavery Project the chart and discuss the questions on the chart. Work as a group to fill in answers for the chart's questions on the whiteboard.

ACTIVE CLASSROOM

Use the "Make Headlines" strategy with the chart. Have each student choose one cell of the chart and write a headline based on information filled in on that chart area. The headline might discuss the effects of slavery in Africa or in the Americas, either on African people, African states, individual wealth, or industries. Ask: If you were to write a headline for this topic that captured the most important aspect to be remembered, what would that headline be? Pass your headline to a partner for review.

ELL Use the ELL activity described in the ELL chart.

Further Instruction

Editable Presentation Use the Editable Presentation to present the main ideas for this text.

Compare and Contrast Compare and contrast some short-term effects of slavery on West African states with some longer-term effects of slavery in the Americas. *(Sample response: Short-term effects on West African states included the disappearance of some states as their population was removed. But some other states profited from the slave trade and used new wealth to build and maintain power. Longer-term effects of slavery in the Americas included that it was one of the causes of a civil war in the United States and eventual abolition in Brazil. There was growth in African-American populations in the Americas due to the slave trade, as contrasted to the decline in West Africa's population.)*

Analyze Data Ask students to examine the infographic on the Atlantic Slave Trade. For each set of data, have students write one sentence summarizing a key idea supported by the data. *(Sample response: The slave trade volume peaked in the 1780s. Eleven million enslaved Africans were transported to the Americas. The vast majority went to South America and the Caribbean. The transatlantic slave trade ended in the 1800s.)*

D Differentiate: Special Needs/Extra Support Have students work in pairs to identify and write three words in the text they do not fully understand and three questions that they have about the effects of the slave trade. Provide guidance or student volunteers to help them with these questions.

SYNTHESIZE

SYNTHESIZE ACTIVITY
Trade

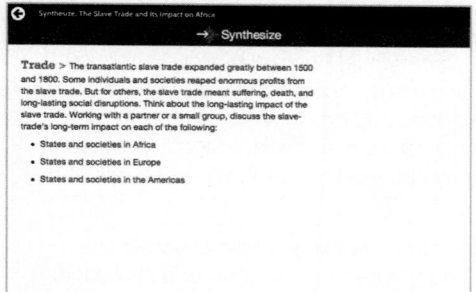

The Essential Question for this topic is: "Why do people move?" Ask students to take five minutes to write down some brief answers to the questions below, and then share their answers with a partner.

Have partners think about the following questions: Why did Europeans go to Africa? Why did Africans go to the Americas? Have pairs share their answers with the class.

Hypothesize After existing for centuries, the transatlantic slave trade's volume peaked in the 1780s, just a few decades before the United States and Britain passed laws abolishing it. Why do you think there was such a short amount of time between the slave trade's peak and abolition? *(Answers will vary. Sample response: The period of high volume made the slave trade and its horrors very visible, and increased calls to abolish it. The ideals of the American and French revolutions increased abolitionism. Slave traders anticipated the abolition laws and increased their volume to make more money and provide customers with more slaves.)*

DEMONSTRATE

DIGITAL QUIZ
Lesson Quiz and Class Discussion Board

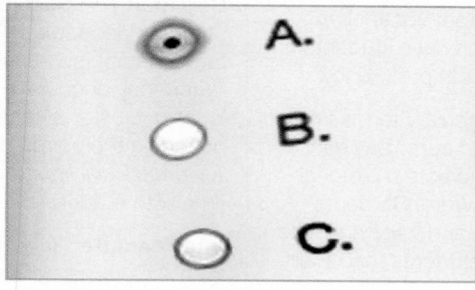

Assign the online Lesson Quiz for this lesson if you haven't already done so. Students will be offered automatic remediation or enrichment based on their score.

Pose this question to the class on the Discussion Board: In this lesson, you read about the expansion of the African slave trade, how triangular trade worked, and the impact of the slave trade on the people of Europe, Africa, and the Americas.

Identify Causes and Effects How has the transatlantic slave trade affected the history, society, and culture of the United States from the 1700s to today? *(Answers will vary. Students may mention the plantation culture of the American South, the Civil War, the struggle for civil rights, the ethnic diversity of the United States, or the African influence on American culture)*

Topic Inquiry
Have students continue their investigations for the Topic Inquiry.

Effects of Global Contact

 ## Supporting English Language Learners

Use with Digital Text 1, **The Columbian Exchange.**

Speaking

Explain that an understanding of both concrete and abstract vocabulary is necessary to ensure comprehension of topics in history. Explain the differences between concrete and abstract vocabulary to students. Beginning and Intermediate students will focus on concrete vocabulary, while Advanced and Advanced High will focus on abstract vocabulary. Read *The Columbian Exchange* aloud to students. Then have students complete the following activities according to their English proficiency.

Beginning Provide students with a few concrete vocabulary terms from the text, such as *tomatoes*, *pumpkins*, *plants*, *pigs*, and *corn*. Say each word and have students repeat it. Then have students create a pictorial dictionary to demonstrate their understanding of each word. Students should write each word, draw a picture of its meaning, and write a simple interrogative sentence using the word correctly. Have students read their sentences to a partner.

Intermediate Have students identify several concrete vocabulary terms from the text, such as *tomatoes*, *pumpkins*, *plants*, *pigs*, and *corn*. Instruct each student to create a pictorial dictionary to demonstrate their understanding the words they identified. Students should write each word and its definition, draw a picture, and write an interrogative sentence using the word correctly. Have students use the terms in conversation with a partner.

Advanced Provide students with a few abstract vocabulary terms from the text, such as *global exchange* and *migration*. Instruct students to locate these terms in the text and develop a definition for each using context clues. Then have students turn to a partner to share, ask questions, correct, and improve their definitions. Finally, have pairs discuss their definitions with the whole group, using the information from the text as a framework for understanding the larger concepts present in the text.

Advanced High Instruct students to identify a few abstract vocabulary terms from the text, such as *global exchange* and *migration*. Have students develop a definition for each term using context clues and a dictionary. Have students bring their working definitions to a large group discussion. Finally, facilitate a discussion in which students ask and answer questions about these concepts, using the information in the text as a framework for understanding.

Use with Digital Text 2, **A Commercial Revolution.**

Reading

Read *A Commercial Revolution* aloud to the class. After students listen to the text, have them complete one of the following activities depending on their level of English proficiency.

Beginning Explain that being able to sound out unfamiliar words will help students decode and understand new English words. Have students take turns reading sentences from *A Commercial Revolution* aloud after you. When they encounter a challenging word, model how to sound out each letter or cluster of letters. As students practice, they will be able to try decoding the words on their own. Continue practicing decoding words in *A Commercial Revolution* until they can read two or three sentences at a time with moderate fluency.

Intermediate Have students take turns reading individual sentences from *A Commercial Revolution* aloud. When they encounter a challenging word, have students pause to carefully sound out the word. Offer support as needed. Point out similarities among words that share similar characteristics, such as *inflation*, *revolution*, and *production*.

Advanced Ask students work in small groups to review *A Commercial Revolution*. Invite students to read aloud to each other. When the reader encounters a challenging word, the listeners should assist in sounding it out. Groups should make a list of challenging words. When they have completed the text, small groups should review the lists of challenging words and practice pronouncing them correctly. Circulate among students to offer support as needed.

Advanced High Ask students work in pairs to review *A Commercial Revolution*. Invite pairs to read aloud to each other. When the reader encounters a challenging word, the listener should assist in sounding it out. Pairs should make a list of challenging words. When they have completed the text, each pair should join with another pair to make a group of four students. This small group should review the lists of challenging words and practice pronouncing them correctly. Circulate among students to offer support as needed.

▣ Differentiate Instruction

Use the Differentiated Instruction notes throughout the lesson plan to support the varied skill sets, levels of readiness, and interests in the mixed-ability classroom.

Challenge These notes include suggestions for expanding the activity for advanced students.

On-Level These notes include suggestions for modifying the activity to address different interests or learning styles.

Extra Support These notes include ideas for providing more scaffolding or reading spuport.

Special Needs These notes provide ideas for adapting instruction to support the needs of various special needs students.

■ NOTES

PEARSON
realize™
www.PearsonRealize.com

Go online to access additional resources including:
Primary Sources • Biographies • Supreme Court cases •
21st Century Skill Tutorials • Maps • Graphic Organizers.

Objectives

Objective 1: Explain how European exploration led to the Columbian Exchange.

Objective 2: Explain new economic factors and principles that contributed to the success of the commercial revolution.

Objective 3: Understand the impact of mercantilism on European and colonial economies.

LESSON 6 ORGANIZER		PACING: APPROX. 1 PERIOD, .5 BLOCKS			
		OBJECTIVES	**PACING**	**RESOURCES**	
				Online	Print
Connect					
	DIGITAL START UP ACTIVITY **Uniting Distant Parts of the World**		5 min.	●	
Investigate					
	DIGITAL TEXT 1 **The Columbian Exchange**	Objective 1	10 min.	●	●
	INTERACTIVE MAP **The Columbian Exchange**		10 min.	●	
	DIGITAL TEXT 2 **A Commercial Revolution**	Objective 2	10 min.	●	●
	INTERACTIVE CHART **Economic Concepts**		10 min.	●	
	DIGITAL TEXT 3 **Mercantilism**	Objective 3	10 min.	●	●
Synthesize					
	DIGITAL ACTIVITY **Capitalism and Mercantilism**		5 min.	●	
Demonstrate					
	DIGITAL QUIZ **Lesson Quiz and Class Discussion Board**		10 min.	●	

Effects of Global Contact

CONNECT

DIGITAL START UP ACTIVITY
Uniting Distant Parts of the World

Project the Start Up Activity Ask students to answer the questions as they enter and get settled. Then have them share their ideas with another student, either in class or through a chat or blog space.

Determine Point of View Ask students to summarize Adam Smith's viewpoint on the Columbian Exchange. Do they agree with his conclusion? Why or why not? (*Answers will vary. Students may cite the benefits of trade and exchanged goods. They also might cite negative aspects such as diseases that were introduced to Native Americans.*)

Tell students that in this lesson they will learn about the effects of increased global contact and new economic ideas.

Aa Vocabulary Development: Use the Interactive Reading Notepad to preview the Key Terms and Academic Vocabulary in this lesson with students.

⇅ FLIP IT!
Assign the Flipped Video for this lesson.

STUDENT EDITION PRINT PAGES: 417–421

INVESTIGATE

DIGITAL TEXT 1
The Columbian Exchange

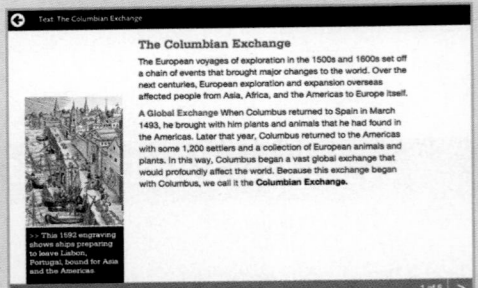

INTERACTIVE MAP
The Columbian Exchange

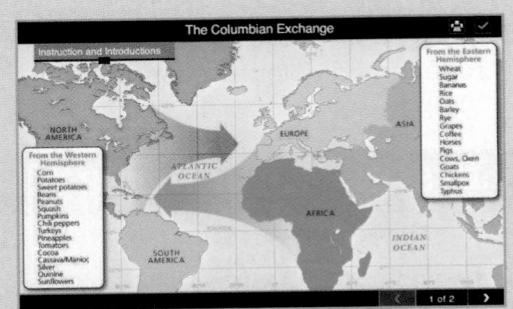

Objective 1: Explain how European exploration led to the Columbian Exchange.

Quick Instruction
Christopher Columbus's voyage to the Americas in 1492 started a global exchange of people, plants, animals, ideas, and technology. This exchange had a profound impact on the people of the Americas, Europe, Africa, and Asia. Because it started with Columbus, it is called the Columbian Exchange.

Interactive Gallery: The Columbian Exchange Project the Interactive Gallery for the class to see. Explain how ships going back and forth across the Atlantic carried all these products to new areas of the world. Then bring up each hotspot image and text and discuss it with students.

👥 ACTIVE CLASSROOM
Use the "Audio Tour" strategy, starting by assigning each student a partner. For each student pair, have one student give the other a verbal "tour" of the map and hotspots. What do they show? Have the second student give the first an explanation of the lasting impact associated with each hotspot area. Pairs may want to audio record their tours to share with the class.

ELL Use the ELL activity described in the ELL chart.

Further Instruction
Project the Interactive Reading Notepad questions, including the graphic organizer, asking students to fill in causes and effects of the Columbian Exchange. Discuss the exchange's causes and effects, filling in the graphic organizer on the whiteboard as you do.

Identify Main Ideas Ask students to differentiate between positive and negative effects of the Columbian Exchange. What were some positive effects? (*Sample response: New foods enriched diet.*) Negative effects? (*Sample response: Diseases spread.*)

Draw Inferences Choose an item that was transported as part of the Columbian Exchange. Explain how life in the hemisphere it traveled to might be different if the Columbian Exchange hadn't happened. (*Answers will vary. Sample response: Many people in the Eastern Hemisphere would have died from malaria without quinine, which originated in the Western Hemisphere and is used to treat malaria.*)

D Differentiate: Extra Support Have students identify three items that moved from one hemisphere to another. Ask them to trace their movement on the interactive gallery, and explain how the items were good or bad for the people in the hemisphere to which it moved.

DIGITAL TEXT 2

A Commercial Revolution

INTERACTIVE CHART

Economic Concepts

DIGITAL TEXT 3

Mercantilism

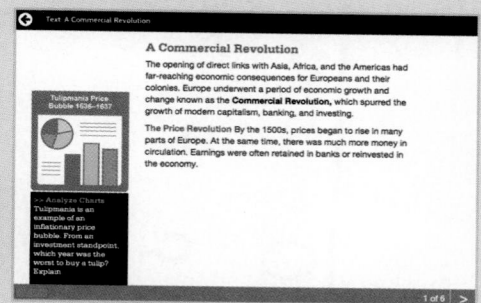

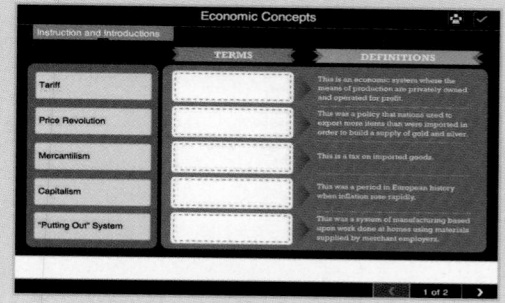

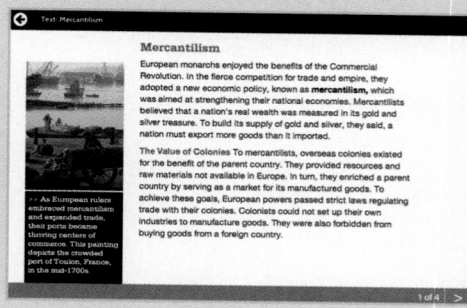

Objective 2: Explain new economic factors and principles that contributed to the success of the Commercial Revolution.

Quick Instruction

Increased trade between Europe, Asia, Africa, and the Americas brought economic consequences. Europe underwent a period of economic growth, expansion, and colonialism known as the Commercial Revolution. This period lasted from about the 1500s until the early 1700s and included the growth of capitalism, banking, and investing.

Interactive Chart: Economic Concepts Work through the Interactive Chart with students, helping them to match economic terms with correct definitions. Use this chart with this digital text, as well as the next on mercantilism.

👥 ACTIVE CLASSROOM

Use the "Sticky Notes" strategy. Have each student choose an economic term and spend three minutes writing responses to this question on sticky notes: "What were some effects of this particular economic event or system?" Students can post their Sticky Notes on a chart, grouped under each economic term. Compare and contrast the responses as a group.

ELL Use the ELL activity described in the ELL chart.

Further Instruction

Editable Presentation Use the Editable Presentation to present the main ideas of this text.

Project the Interactive Reading Notepad questions for this text. Have students answer them as they progress through the text.

Identify Main Ideas Point out that the capitalist free enterprise system provided new economic freedoms that stimulated business and trade, increased people's wealth, and broadened access to a greater variety of goods. Have students consider the economic freedoms that are part of the free enterprise system. Ask them to name some of the benefits of capitalism. *(Answers will vary. Sample response: consumers and producers can make free choices; prices are not set but determined by free market conditions; individuals have investment opportunities to assume risks and realize profits; competition among entrepreneurs creates innovation, jobs, and wealth.)*

D Differentiate: Extra Support For students who have trouble understanding some of the economic terms in this text and activity, help them list some modern-day examples of capitalism, entrepreneurs, inflation, and cottage industries. Examples could come from their own business experience. *(Sample response: Examples of capitalism are the stock market and companies competing for consumers. Local entrepreneurs include babysitters, lawn service providers, and people who own and operate stores. Rising gas prices is an example of inflation. Modern-day cottage industries include people who sell their crafts online or sell flowers at farmers' markets.)*

Objective 3: Understand the impact of mercantilism on European and colonial economies.

Quick Instruction

European countries adopted the policy of mercantilism. This policy sought to increase national wealth by exporting more than importing. Colonies supplied the parent country with raw materials and served as a market for the parent country's exports. Tariffs, or taxes on imported goods, were used to limit imports.

Compare Ask students to compare capitalism and mercantilism. How was mercantilism consistent or inconsistent with capitalist principles? How so? *(Answers may vary. Sample response: Mercantilism is inconsistent with capitalism in that mercantilist governments regulated trade and used tariffs to limit free trade.)*

Further Instruction

Editable Presentation Use the Editable Presentation to present the main ideas of this text.

Project the Interactive Reading Notepad questions for this text. Discuss the steps that governments took to impose mercantilism. Lead students in discussion of their evaluation of whether or not the Commercial Revolution was beneficial to society.

Effects of Global Contact

SYNTHESIZE

DIGITAL ACTIVITY
Capitalism and Mercantilism

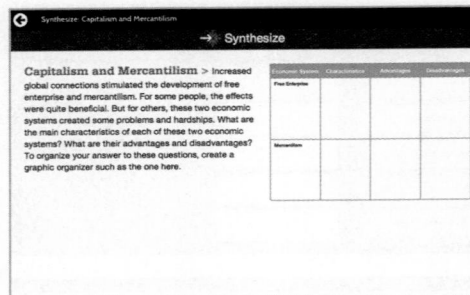

DEMONSTRATE

DIGITAL QUIZ
Lesson Quiz and Class Discussion Board

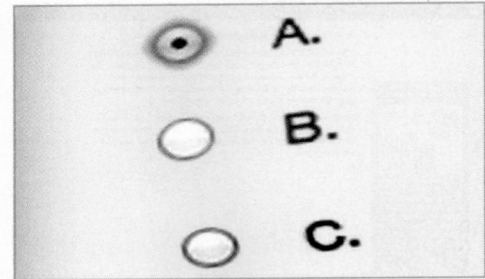

Predict Consequences Why might mercantilist policies be a reason for colonies to rebel against parent countries? *(Sample response: Mercantilist laws limited the economic freedoms of colonies. They prevented colonies from starting their own industries to manufacture goods. Colonies had to provide resources and raw materials to parent countries. They were forbidden to buy goods from a foreign country. Only ships from the parent country or colonies could be used to send goods.)*

Apply Concepts Have students consider mercantilist policies and economic policies today. Ask them which mercantilist policies are still pursued by some countries today. Ask if students think these policies are beneficial today. *(Answers will vary. Sample response: Most countries still try to export more than they import. Many countries still use tariffs on imports to achieve that goal. The tariffs do reduce imports. But they raise prices and limit free trade.)*

Some effects of global contact included the development of free enterprise and mercantilism. For many people, these developments were quite beneficial. But some people experienced problems and hardships as a result of these new economic developments.

Have students complete the chart in this activity, and then share their chart with a partner and discuss their answers.

Discuss Based on your chart showing advantages and disadvantages of free enterprise and mercantilism, who were some people that benefited from those economic developments? Who were some people who experienced problems because of the economic developments? *(Sample response: Middle and upper class entrepreneurs profited the most. Their hired laborers earned wages, but were often poorly paid. Nobles may not have profited much because their wealth was based on land and not business ventures.)*

Assign the online Lesson Quiz for this lesson if you haven't already done so. Students will be offered automatic remediation or enrichment based on their score.

Pose these questions to the class on the Discussion Board:

In "Effects of Global Contact," you learned about the Columbian Exchange and the economic principles and effects of the Commercial Revolution, capitalism, and mercantilism.

Identify Cause and Effect What were some of effects of the the Columbian Exchange on Native Americans? *(Sample response: Positives include the introduction of horses to help with transportation and labor, and the introduction of new food sources like chickens and goats that improved nutrition. Negatives would include the imposition of European culture over Native American culture and diseases brought by Europeans.)*

Apply Concepts How does the free enterprise system operate in the U.S. economy today? What are some benefits and problems of the American free enterprise system? *(Answers will vary: Students might include private property, individual profit, free competition, prices set by market conditions, stock market, banking, limited government regulations; benefits include economic freedoms, innovation, business and investment opportunities, social mobility; problems may include excessive regulations, high prices, unbalanced distribution of wealth, poverty for some.)*

Topic Inquiry
Have students continue their investigations for the Topic Inquiry.

New Global Connections (1415–1796)

 SYNTHESIZE

DIGITAL ACTIVITY
Reflect on the Essential Question and Topic

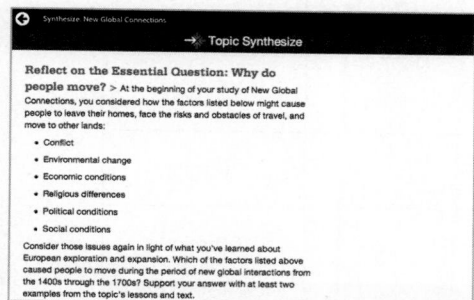

Ask students to reconsider the Essential Question for the Topic: Why do people move? Remind students of the factors they considered at the start of the Topic. For example,

- Conflict
- Environmental change
- Economic conditions
- Religious differences
- Political conditions
- Social conditions

Ask students, "Which of these factors caused people to move during the period of new global interactions from the 1400s through the 1700s? Have them support their answer with at least two examples from the Topic's lessons. Ask, "Did you learn anything that surprised you as you read about this Topic?"

Next, ask students to reflect on the era of new global connections as a whole. Have them consider these questions as well as others that you or they might come up with:

- How did European colonization affect Native Americans?
- What was the impact of the slave trade?
- How did the Commercial Revolution and the free enterprise system affect Europe and the Americas?
- How does the movement of people, culture, goods, plants, animals, and ideas from the 1400s through the 1700s still shape the world you live in today?

Topic Inquiry
Have students complete step 3 of the Topic Inquiry.

 DEMONSTRATE

DIGITAL TOPIC REVIEW AND ASSESSMENT
New Global Connections (1415–1796)

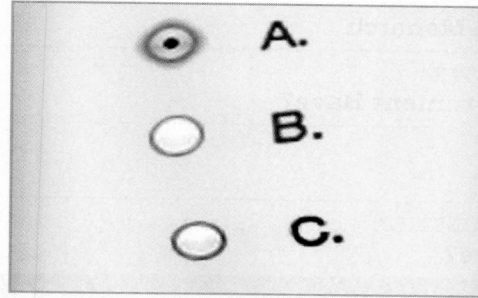

Students can prepare for the Topic Test by answering the questions in the Topic Review and Assessment online or the Assessment questions in the Print Student text. They can also prepare by reviewing their answers to the Interactive Reading Notepad questions or reviewing their notes in the Reading and Notetaking Study Guide.

DIGITAL TOPIC TEST
New Global Connections (1415–1796)

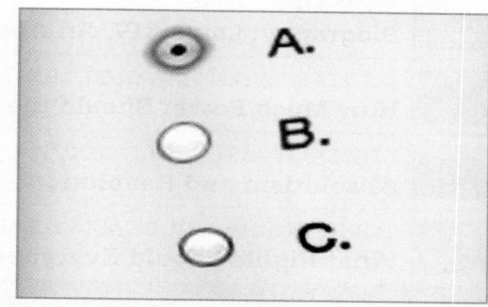

TOPIC TEST
Assign the Topic Test to assess students' understanding of topic content.

BENCHMARK TESTS
Assign these benchmark tests as you complete the relevant topics to monitor student progress toward mastering the course content and as preparation for the End-of-Course Test.

Benchmark Test 1: Topics 1–5

Benchmark Test 2: Topics 6–10

Benchmark Test 3: Topics 11–15

Benchmark Test 4: Topics 16–21

Absolutism and Revolution

TOPIC 12 ORGANIZER	PACING: APPROX. 11 PERIODS, 5.5 BLOCKS
	PACING

Connect		1 period
MY STORY VIDEO **Biography: Louis XIV, An Absolute Monarch**		10 min.
DIGITAL ESSENTIAL QUESTION ACTIVITY **How Much Power Should the Government Have?**		10 min.
DIGITAL TIMELINE ACTIVITY **Absolutism and Revolution**		10 min.
TOPIC INQUIRY: DOCUMENT-BASED QUESTION **What Rights Should Everyone Have?**		20 min.
Investigate		4–8 periods
TOPIC INQUIRY: DOCUMENT-BASED QUESTION **What Rights Should Everyone Have?**		Ongoing
LESSON 1 Absolute Monarchy in Spain and France		30–40 min.
LESSON 2 Rise of Austria, Prussia, and Russia		30–40 min.
LESSON 3 Triumph of Parliament in England		30–40 min.
LESSON 4 The Enlightenment		30–40 min.
LESSON 5 The American Revolution		30–40 min.
LESSON 6 The French Revolution Begins		30–40 min.
LESSON 7 A Radical Phase		30–40 min.
LESSON 8 The Age of Napoleon		30–40 min.
Synthesize		1 period
DIGITAL ACTIVITY **Reflect on the Essential Question and Topic**		10 min.
TOPIC INQUIRY: DOCUMENT-BASED QUESTION **What Rights Should Everyone Have?**		20 min.
Demonstrate		1–2 periods
DIGITAL TOPIC TEST **Absolutism and Revolution**		10 min.
TOPIC INQUIRY: DOCUMENT-BASED QUESTION **What Rights Should Everyone Have?**		20 min.

What Rights Should Everyone Have?

In this Topic Inquiry, students work individually to analyze six documents expressing ideas about the rights of people. Students will reflect on the six viewpoints, draw their own conclusions, and then write an essay on the following question: **What rights should everyone have?** Learning about different philosophies on human rights will contribute to students' understanding of the Topic Essential Question: How much power should the government have?

STEP 1: CONNECT
Develop Questions and Plan the Investigation

Launch the DBQ Writing Activity
Have students watch the video of President Barack Obama talking about human rights, and then discuss the video in class or have students discuss it with a partner. Have students address the questions from the Student Instructions about the video. Make sure they understand that China has often been criticized for restricting individual rights, which is why President Obama refers to Americans' belief in the universality of some rights.

Generate Questions
Have students use the *Need-to-Know Questions* document to record their questions about the rights of individuals.

Resources
- Need-to-Know Questions
- Student Instructions

⏻ PROFESSIONAL DEVELOPMENT

Document-Based Question
Be sure to view the Document-Based Question Professional Development resources in the online course.

STEP 2: INVESTIGATE
Apply Disciplinary Concepts and Tools

Read and Analyze Documents
Tell students that they will read and analyze six documents about human rights. Then, they will write an essay and express their own opinions about human rights. Documents A and D express the views of absolute monarchs. Documents B and C express the views of Enlightenment thinkers. Document E is taken from the Bill of Rights of the U.S. Constitution, and Document F is a modern-day political cartoon.

Help students begin to fill out the *Information Organizer.* Point out that the organizer will help them keep track of the various views about the rights of people in the documents they read. Suggest that students paraphrase or summarize the information as they fill out the organizer.

Suggestion: Review each student's *Information Organizer* as he or she is completing it to make sure students are on track.

Check Understanding
After students finish reading each individual document, have them answer the multiple-choice and short-answer questions attached to each document. Review the questions and discuss the answers after students have answered the questions for all the documents.

Resources
- Information Organizer

STEP 3: SYNTHESIZE
Evaluate Sources and Use Evidence to Formulate Conclusions

Write Your Essay

Now have students write their essays to express their own opinion about the question: **What rights should everyone have?** If students are having trouble getting started, remind them to review their *Information Organizer* and reflect on the information.

Suggestion: Review each student's essay as he or she is writing it to make sure students are on track.

Edit Your Essay

Have students read over their first drafts. Suggest they ask themselves these questions: Does it accurately express my viewpoint? Does it need more details? Then have students proofread and edit their essays, revising as needed. If time allows, have students exchange essays for a peer edit.

Suggestion: Have students use a thesaurus to better describe their viewpoint and to make the essay more interesting.

Resources
- Writing Rubric

STEP 4: DEMONSTRATE
Communicate Conclusions and Take Informed Action

Present Your Essay

Have students make a neat, clean copy of their essays. Then ask volunteers to read their essays aloud to the class.

Suggestion: As an alternative, have students read one or more of their classmates' essays on their own.

Reflect on the Project

After students have finished their essays, help them go over what they thought went well in their essays and what did not so they can be even more effective in the future.

Suggestion: As an extension activity, have students research human rights issues around the world today. Ask them to write a three-paragraph essay in which they compare the limitations on rights during the period of absolute monarchies versus those in modern-day countries. Ask students to share their comparisons with the class.

INTRODUCTION

Absolutism and Revolution (1550–1850)

After feudalism died out in Europe, strong nation states emerged. Most of these were absolute monarchies, where strong rulers held complete power over their nations and people. However, by the 1700s, Enlightenment thinkers introduced new ideas about liberty and human rights. What role did the Enlightenment have in the government we have in the United States today?

CONNECT

MY STORY VIDEO
Biography: Louis XIV, An Absolute Monarch

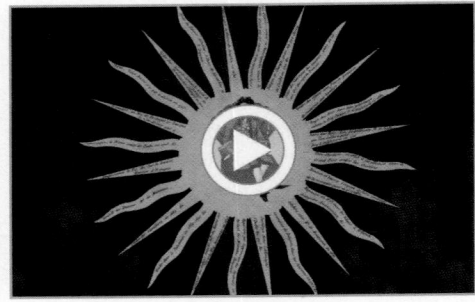

Watch a video about Louis XIV, the greatest of the absolute monarchs.

Check Understanding What is the meaning of the expression "divine right of kings"? *(the right to rule comes from God, not from people)*

Generate Explanations Why did Louis XIV build Versailles? *(He built the lavish palace at Versailles as a symbol of his kingdom's wealth and power.)*

⇅ FLIP IT!

Assign the My Story video.

DIGITAL ESSENTIAL QUESTION ACTIVITY
How Much Power Should the Government Have?

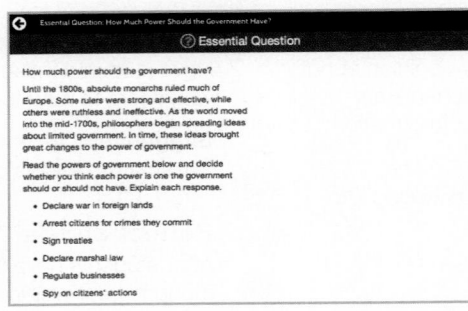

Ask students to think about the Essential Question for this Topic: How much power should governments have? Governments around the world have different levels of power. How much power is enough?

Allow volunteers to share their opinions with the class.

Identify Central Issues What level of government power do you think might be problematic? *(Sample response: too much power, too little power)*

Predict Consequences What do you think might be some unintended negative consequences of a government having too much or too little power? Explain. *(Sample Response: Too much power might lead to oppression of the people; too little power might make society unorganized and dangerous.)*

Infer Why do you think the period of governments having too much power in Europe was followed by revolutions? *(Sample response: because people became tired of social inequality and limited rights)*

DIGITAL TIMELINE ACTIVITY
Absolutism and Revolution

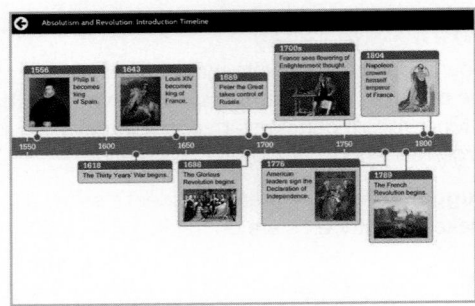

Display the timeline showing the major events in the age of absolutism and revolution. During the Topic, students will learn about all of these events and many more, but this timeline will provide a framework into which they can place the events they learn about.

D Differentiate: Challenge/Gifted Suggest that students copy the timeline onto their own paper and add entries to it as they read the chapter. If they want, they can make a final, clean copy after they read all eight lessons to share with the class.

Check Understanding How many years after Louis XIV became king of France did the French Revolution begin? *(146 years)*

Topic Inquiry
Launch the Topic Inquiry with students after introducing the Topic.

Absolute Monarchy in Spain and France

Supporting English Language Learners

Use with Digital Text 3, **Philip II Becomes an Absolute Monarch.**

Speaking

Beginning Tell students to think about the actions of King Philip as you read *Philip II Becomes an Absolute Monarch* aloud. Then write the following sentence on the board and read it to students: *King Philip II of Spain was a good king who ruled every part of his empire fairly and justicely.* Have students use the following sentence stem to express their opinions: I agree/disagree with this statement because _____.

Intermediate Tell students to think about the actions of King Philip as you read *Philip II Becomes an Absolute Monarch* aloud. Allow students time to think about his reign and to determine whether or not they think he was a good or bad king. Then have students turn to a partner to express their opinion, making sure to include one reason to support it.

Advanced Have students read *Philip II Becomes an Absolute Monarch*. Then have them work in small groups to discuss the benefits and drawbacks of having a king who rules with the intensity and focus of Philip II. Members should share their opinions about Phillip's reign. Then have the group make a final statement, based on its discussion, expressing its opinion of the reign of Philip II.

Advanced High Have students work in small groups to discuss Philip II's reign. Within each group, each student should take on one of the following personas: a resident of Madrid, a Roman Catholic priest, a Spanish colonist, and a Dutch Protestant. Then, based on the information in the text, have group members express their persona's opinion of Philip II and his tactics to expand the Spanish empire.

Use with Digital Text 7, **The Royal Palace at Versailles.**

Reading

Tell students that they will be reading the first paragraph from the text *The Royal Palace at Versailles*. Have students demonstrate their understanding of how to recognize and read English sentences from left to right and from the top of a paragraph to the bottom by completing the following tasks:

Beginning Ask students to point at the word in the paragraph that they will read first. Then have them point at the word in the paragraph that they will read last. Then have students read the first sentence of the paragraph aloud to you while running their finger along below the words as they read them. If students need a reminder, you can draw an arrow above the first line of the paragraph from left to right and another on the left side of the paragraph from the top to the bottom.

Intermediate Have students point at the first word in each sentence in the paragraph. Then have them read the first three sentences in the paragraph aloud as they run their fingers along below the words.

Advanced Have students explain to a partner where the paragraph begins and ends. Then have students take turns reading the paragraph aloud to each other.

Advanced High Have students write and read aloud a sentence to explain the directionality of English reading. Then ask students to read the paragraph aloud to a small group. Other members of the small group should offer pronunciation and vocabulary support as necessary.

ⓓ Differentiate Instruction

Use the Differentiated Instruction notes throughout the lesson plan to support the varied skill sets, levels of readiness, and interests in the mixed-ability classroom.

Challenge These notes include suggestions for expanding the activity for advanced students.

On-Level These notes include suggestions for modifying the activity to address different interests or learning styles.

Extra Support These notes include ideas for providing more scaffolding or reading spuport.

Special Needs These notes provide ideas for adapting instruction to support the needs of various special needs students.

▮ NOTES

Topic (12) Lesson 1

Absolute Monarchy in Spain and France

Objectives

Objective 1: Identify the characteristics of absolute monarchy, including the concept of divine right.

Objective 2: Explain how Spanish power grew under Charles V and Philip II.

Objective 3: Understand how France built a centralized monarchy after the wars of religion.

Objective 4: Evaluate Louis XIV as an absolute monarch.

Objective 5: Describe how the arts flourished in Spain and France.

LESSON 1 ORGANIZER		PACING: APPROX. 1 PERIOD, .5 BLOCKS			
				RESOURCES	
		OBJECTIVES	PACING	Online	Print
Connect					
DIGITAL START UP ACTIVITY **Defining Absolute Monarchy**			5 min.	●	
Investigate					
DIGITAL TEXT 1 **Ruling with Absolute Power**		Objective 1	10 min.	●	●
DIGITAL TEXT 2 **Spain and the Hapsburg Empire**		Objective 2	10 min.	●	●
DIGITAL TEXT 3 **Philip II Becomes an Absolute Monarch**			10 min.	●	●
DIGITAL TEXT 4 **Arts and Literature of Spain's Golden Century**		Objective 5	10 min.	●	●
INTERACTIVE IMAGE GALLERY **Art of Spain's Golden Century**			10 min.	●	
DIGITAL TEXT 5 **Royal Power Expands in France**		Objective 3	10 min.	●	●
DIGITAL TEXTS 6, 7, AND 8 **Louis XIV, an Absolute Monarch, The Royal Palace at Versailles, The Legacy of Louis XIV**		Objective 4	10 min.	●	●
INTERACTIVE IMAGE GALLERY **The Palace of Versailles**			10 min.	●	
Synthesize					
DIGITAL ACTIVITY **Graphic Organizer: Techniques of Absolutism**			5 min.	●	
Demonstrate					
LESSON QUIZ **Lesson Quiz and Class Discussion Board**			10 min.	●	

CONNECT

DIGITAL START UP ACTIVITY
Defining Absolute Monarchy

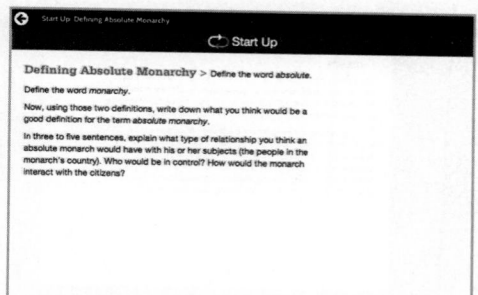

Project the Start Up Activity Ask students to answer the questions as they enter and get settled. If you think it necessary, provide either definition to students. *(absolute: total, complete; monarchy: rule by a leader who gains his or her position through heredity [being born to it]. The two words combine to create something like "complete rule by a hereditary leader.")*

Discuss After students have answered individually, have them share their ideas with another student, either in class or through a chat room or blog. Possible follow up questions: What would it be like to live under an absolute monarchy? Is an absolute monarchy fair to the people living in it?

Aa Vocabulary Development: Use the Interactive Reading Notepad to preview the Key Terms and Academic Vocabulary in this Lesson with students.

ℕ FLIP IT!
Assign the Flipped Video for this lesson.

■ STUDENT EDITION PRINT PAGES: 426–434

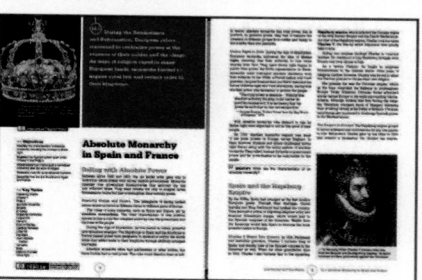

INVESTIGATE

DIGITAL TEXT 1
Ruling with Absolute Power

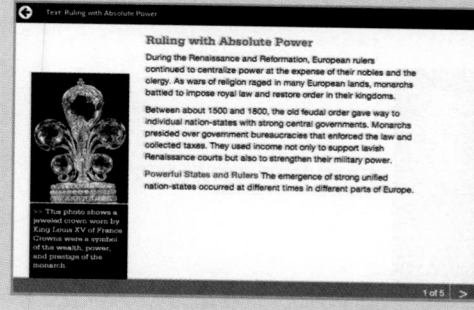

Objective 1: Identify the characteristics of absolute monarchy, including the concept of divine right.

Quick Instruction
Project the image of Louis XIV. Read (or project on the whiteboard) this quote from Bishop Bossuet, 17th century French cleric, about the divine right of kings: "all strength and all perfection are united in God, so all the power of individuals is united in the person of the prince [king]." Ask: according to Bossuet, what is the role of the king? What are the limits on his power? *(to rule absolutely over his people; there are no limits to his power.)* Ask students to share their responses with a neighbor and then discuss answers as a class.

Further Instruction
Project the Interactive Reading Notepad questions. Go through them and discuss the answers with the class.

Break students into groups of four. Then, ask students what kind of government we have in the United States. *(democratic republic)* Ask them to write a definition of a democratic republican form of government. Allow some time for students to research the definition, if necessary. Have students compare this definition to that of an absolute monarchy from the Start Up activity. Discuss the differences as a class.

After the discussion, have students write a short essay explaining the differences between our system of government and an absolute monarchy. Have students exchange their essays with a partner.

Absolute Monarchy in Spain and France

DIGITAL TEXT 2

Spain and the Hapsburg Empire

Spain and the Hapsburg Empire

By the 1500s, Spain had emerged as the first modern European power. Through their marriage, Queen Isabella and King Ferdinand had unified the country. They pursued a policy of imposing religious unity and financed Columbus's voyage, which would lead to the Spanish conquest of the Americas. Wealth from the Americas would help Spain to become the most powerful nation in Europe.

Charles V Wears Two Crowns In 1516, Ferdinand and Isabella's grandson, Charles I, became king of Spain, and thereby ruler of the Spanish colonies in the Americas as well. When his other grandfather died in 1519, Charles I also became heir to the sprawling **Hapsburg empire**, which included the German states of the Holy Roman Empire and the Dutch Netherlands. As ruler of the Hapsburg empire, Charles took the name **Charles V**, the title by which historians now usually refer to him.

Ruling two empires involved Charles in constant warfare. He continued a long Hapsburg struggle with France over rival claims in Italy.

>> In the early 1500s, Charles V became ruler over both the Spanish and the Hapsburg empires. He faced constant warfare, particularly against the Ottomans

1 of 3 >

DIGITAL TEXT 3

Philip II Becomes an Absolute Monarch

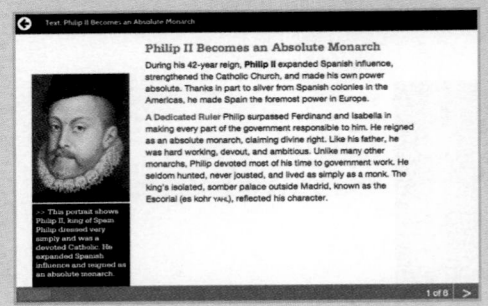

Philip II Becomes an Absolute Monarch

During his 42-year reign, **Philip II** expanded Spanish influence, strengthened the Catholic Church, and made his own power absolute. Thanks in part to silver from Spanish colonies in the Americas, he made Spain the foremost power in Europe.

A Dedicated Ruler Philip surpassed Ferdinand and Isabella in making every part of the government responsible to him. He reigned as an absolute monarch, claiming divine right. Like his father, he was hard working, devout, and ambitious. Unlike many other monarchs, Philip devoted most of his time to government work. He seldom hunted, never jousted, and lived as simply as a monk. The king's isolated, somber palace outside Madrid, known as the Escorial (es kohr YAHL), reflected his character.

>> This portrait shows Philip II, king of Spain. Philip dressed very simply and was a devoted Catholic. He expanded Spanish influence and reigned as an absolute monarch.

1 of 6 >

DIGITAL TEXT 4

Arts and Literature of Spain's Golden Century

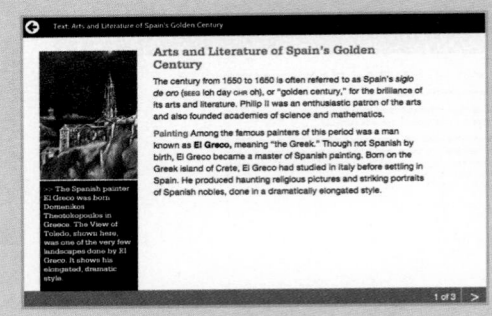

Arts and Literature of Spain's Golden Century

The century from 1550 to 1650 is often referred to as Spain's *siglo de oro* (SEEG loh day OHR oh), or "golden century," for the brilliance of its arts and literature. Philip II was an enthusiastic patron of the arts and also founded academies of science and mathematics.

Painting Among the famous painters of this period was a man known as **El Greco**, meaning "the Greek." Though not Spanish by birth, El Greco became a master of Spanish painting. Born on the Greek island of Crete, El Greco had studied in Italy before settling in Spain. He produced haunting religious pictures and striking portraits of Spanish nobles, done in a dramatically elongated style.

>> The Spanish painter El Greco was born Domenikos Theotokopoulos in Greece. This View of Toledo, shown here, was one of the very few landscapes done by El Greco. It shows his elongated, dramatic style.

1 of 3 >

Objective 2: Explain how Spanish power grew under Charles V and Philip II.

Quick Instruction

Project the map "The Wars of Philip II, 1571–1588" in Text 3. Ask students the following questions: With whom did Philip II go to war? *(the Netherlands, Ottoman Empire, England)* What were the main reasons for these wars? *(religion, extension of territory)* Ask students why they think religion mattered so much to Philip II? *(Sample response: His father was very religious and became a monk, and the Reformation was a threat to his country's stability.)*

Tell students that by the 1580s, Philip saw England's Queen Elizabeth I as his chief Protestant enemy. She sided with the Dutch against Spain and encouraged English captains, known as sea dogs, to plunder Spanish treasure ships and loot Spanish cities in the Americas. Philip eventually sent the armada to attack England, only to be humbled by defeat.

D Differentiate: Challenge/Gifted Have students research the defeat of the Spanish Armada (1588) and produce a sequence of four to five basic maps showing where the ships were at each stage. Ask students to address the effect that the weather played in the defeat in a caption for the map series. If students are able, have them scan the maps to create a stop-action animation of the battle, which could be narrated and posted online.

ELL Use the ELL activity described in the ELL chart.

Further Instruction

Project the Interactive Reading Notepad questions, and go over them as a class.

Ask the question: Is it ever a good idea to go to war over religion? To extend territory? Why or why not? *(Answers will vary but students might mention that religious wars typically put one religion over another and don't respect people's differences, and wars over territory affect not only control over land but also the people who live on it.)* Students should first share their answers with their neighbor. Then, have pairs participate in a full-group discussion.

Objective 5: Describe how the arts flourished in Spain and France.

Quick Instruction

Interactive Image Gallery: Art of Spain's Golden Century Project the gallery on the whiteboard. Introduce the activity by explaining that the culture of each society reflects its history and values. Give examples from American 21st century culture (or ask students to supply examples). Click through the images in the gallery, reading (or having student volunteers read) the captions. Ask students how the history and values of 16th century Spain are reflected in its art. *(royalty, religion, expansion/war)* Students' answers can be written individually, shared with a neighbor, or shared on the board.

ACTIVE CLASSROOM

Ask students to write a headline that captures the most important aspect that should be remembered about 16th century Spanish culture. Post a quick print of one of the images from the gallery on the whiteboard or elsewhere in the room. Have students write their headline on a sticky note, and place it the image. Alternatively, students could tweet their responses. Discuss the similarities and differences in responses.

INTERACTIVE IMAGE GALLERY
Art of Spain's Golden Century

Art of Spain's Golden Century

Diego Velázquez

Spain's Golden Century
By the middle of the 16th century, Spain was the foremost power in Europe and controlled a large overseas empire. Spanish leaders' support of the arts led to Spanish influence in literature, painting, sculpture, architecture, and the decorative arts. The images in this gallery show works produced during Spain's Golden Century. As you view them, consider how these pieces reflect the cultural values of Spain.

As a young artist, Diego Velázquez (1599–1660) painted everyday scenes including *Old Woman Cooking Eggs*. Later, as a painter for the Hapsburg court, he produced mainly portraits of the king and his family.

1 of 2

DIGITAL TEXT 5
Royal Power Expands in France

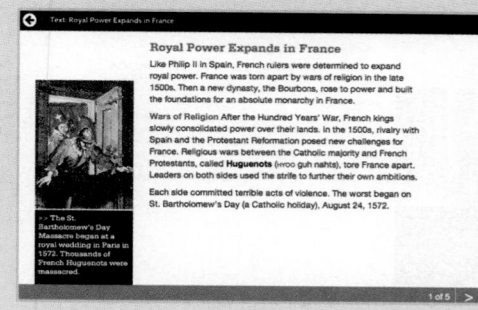

Text: Royal Power Expands in France

Royal Power Expands in France

Like Philip II in Spain, French rulers were determined to expand royal power. France was torn apart by wars of religion in the late 1500s. Then a new dynasty, the Bourbons, rose to power and built the foundations for an absolute monarchy in France.

Wars of Religion After the Hundred Years' War, French kings slowly consolidated power over their lands. In the 1500s, rivalry with Spain and the Protestant Reformation posed new challenges for France. Religious wars between the Catholic majority and French Protestants, called **Huguenots** (HYOO guh nahts), tore France apart. Leaders on both sides used the strife to further their own ambitions.

Each side committed terrible acts of violence. The worst began on St. Bartholomew's Day (a Catholic holiday), August 24, 1572.

>> The St. Bartholomew's Day Massacre began at a royal wedding in Paris in 1572. Thousands of French Huguenots were massacred.

1 of 5

D Differentiate: Extra Support Have students list three individuals who contributed to arts and literature during Spain's golden century and write two to three sentences describing how their works reflect the times. *(Some works reflect religion; others reflect absolutism.)* Discuss how arts and literature reflect the times.

Further Instruction

Project the Interactive Reading Notepad questions. Go through them and discuss the answers with the class.

List two of Philip II's goals ("Expansion of Territory" and "Strengthening Catholic Religion") on the whiteboard. Have students go through the images in the gallery and decide which of these motivations is evident in each (some works can feature in both lists). Ask students if they see any other cultural value represented in the art. You could also ask them: Can a culture as a whole value something that its leader does not? *(Answers will vary, but some students may say that it can, while others may say it cannot. Some may point to governments in which dictators control the state as an example of a culture with a leader who does not value what his or her people value.)* Discuss as a class.

Objective 3: Explain how France built a centralized monarchy after the wars of religion.

Quick Instruction

Project the image of the St. Bartholomew's Day Massacre. Ask students to re-read the statistics on this massacre. *(Three thousand Huguenots were killed initially, and a few thousand more were killed in the days that followed.)* Then project an image of Henry IV and discuss his conversion. You may want to refer to the quote, "Paris is well worth a mass." Ask students: Did Henry IV do the right thing by converting? Why or why not? *(Some students may respond that compromise led to less conflict, while others may say that it's best to stick with your beliefs.)*

D Differentiate: Extra Support After asking students to take a stand, ask them to think of a time when they had to compromise to get what they wanted. Why is it sometimes a good idea to compromise? What can be gained by compromise? Have students work in groups to create a list of compromises and share the list with the class.

Further Instruction

Project the Interactive Reading Notepad questions. Go through them and discuss the answers with the class.

Ask students: How did Henry IV's attitude toward religion differ from Philip II's? *(Henry IV was more tolerant of different religions than Philip II was.)* What did Philip gain from his attitude toward religion? *(He was a devout Catholic, so he defended the Catholic Reformation, and strengthened his power to rule by claiming divine right.)* What did Henry gain? *(He was able to protect Protestants and unite France.)* List these responses on the whiteboard.

Then, ask students to write a letter from Henry IV to a Huguenot supporter (who is upset by his conversion) explaining his reasons for conversion. *(Students' letters will vary but should include that Henry IV converted to Catholicism to end conflict with Catholics. They might also mention that he issued the Edict of Nantes in order to protect Protestants.)*

Absolute Monarchy in Spain and France

DIGITAL TEXT 6

Louis XIV, an Absolute Monarch

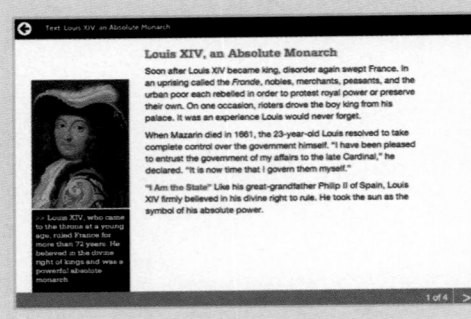

DIGITAL TEXT 7

The Royal Palace at Versailles

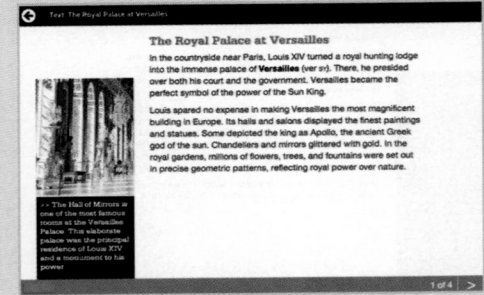

DIGITAL TEXT 8

The Legacy of Louis XIV

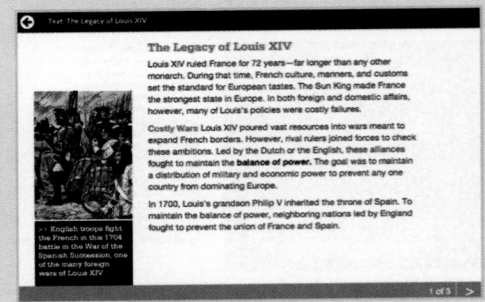

Objective 4: Evaluate Louis XIV as an absolute monarch.

Quick Instruction

Interactive Image Gallery: The Palace of Versailles Ask students to make a graphic organizer using a piece of paper, with the paper divided into five sections. Project the Interactive Image Gallery: The Palace of Versailles. Click each hotspot, without stopping to read the captions. Ask students to write a one-word response to each image and record it on the graphic organizer. Ask students to share their responses with a neighbor. Click through the images again, this time reading (or having student volunteers read) the captions. Ask students to answer (for each slide) the question: What does this image say about Louis XIV and his goals? *(Sample one-word responses—Versailles: huge; Hall of Mirrors: amazing; Royal Chapel: religion; Court Theater: ornate; Grand Apartments: grand; Salon of Hercules: dramatic; Geometric Garden: patterned. For the second part, students are in general likely to say that Louis XIV wanted the biggest, best, and most expensive of everything in order to show his power as the absolute monarch.)* Record and discuss answers.

📖 ACTIVE CLASSROOM

Speaking: Audio Tour Pair students. Have one student give the other a verbal "tour" of the interior of Versailles. Have the second student give the first an explanation of how the interior of the palace reflects absolutism. Then, have the second student give the first a verbal "tour" of the exterior of Versailles. Ask the first student to give the second an explanation of how the exterior of the palace reflects absolutism.

D Differentiate: Challenge/Gifted Break students into groups. Have them write a set of questions for Louis XIV about his tactics and motivations for controlling the nobles and unifying religion. Ask the students to then conduct an interview of Louis (one student should write the questions, the other should play Louis). This activity could involve costumes and could be performed in front of the class or recorded and posted to YouTube.

D Differentiate: Extra Support Project the image of Louis XIV as "Sun King." Write on the whiteboard: "I am the state." What do the image and the statement have in common? *(Everything revolves around the sun; If you ARE the state, everything revolves around you.)* Introduce three of the "techniques" of absolutism from the Synthesize activity *(control the nobles, unify religion, build monuments)*, and discuss how Louis accomplished these.

ELL Use the ELL activity described in the ELL chart.

■ SYNTHESIZE

 ■ DEMONSTRATE

INTERACTIVE IMAGE GALLERY
The Palace of Versailles

DIGITAL ACTIVITY
Graphic Organizer: Techniques of Absolutism

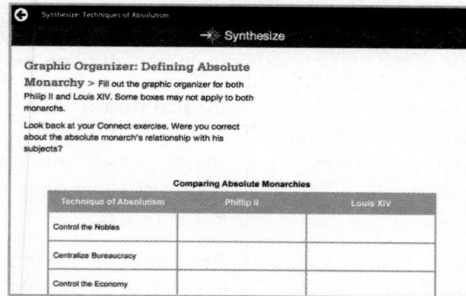

LESSON QUIZ
Lesson Quiz and Class Discussion Board

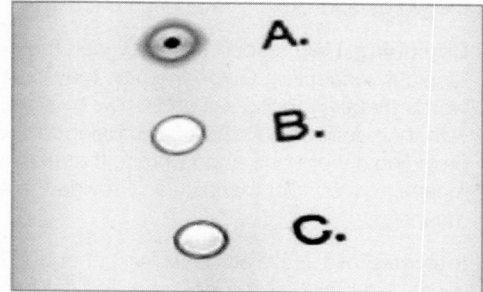

Further Instruction

Ask the class, "What are some possible consequences of Louis XIV's skills as an absolute monarch?" *(These can be positive or negative.)* List some of the principles of absolutism on the whiteboard and have students brainstorm possible consequences of each. This could be broken up by topic, assigning one topic to each of up to 6 groups. List results on the whiteboard. Discuss.

Ask students to recall the Topic Essential Question, "How much power should government have?" First, have students fill out the graphic organizer for Louis XIV. His accomplishments will fit into all six areas. Then, have them fill out the chart for Philip II, whose accomplishments do not fit all six. Discuss the differences.

Compare and Contrast Have students use evidence from the chart to write a two-paragraph essay comparing and contrasting the two leaders. *(Students' essays should include both how the two leaders were alike and different; similarities include persecution of Protestants, wars, monuments; differences include how they handled the nobles and the economy.)*

Assign the online Lesson Quiz for this lesson if you haven't already done so. Students will be offered automatic remediation or enrichment based on their score.

Post the following to the class on the Discussion Board:

Remind students that in "Absolute Monarchy in Spain and France" they read about the characteristics of absolute monarchy and how different absolute monarchs sought to gain and keep power. They also read about some of their accomplishments and some of their failures.

Main Ideas Identify three characteristics that helped solidify the power of absolute monarchs. *(Possible answers: claimed divine right, controlled nobles, controlled economy, organized bureaucracy, unified religion, expanded territory, formed alliances.)* Now list some general failures. *(Overly ambitious, fought too many wars and used too many resources to fight them, taxed too heavily, expelled different groups.)* What were some of their accomplishments? *(Patronizing the arts, literature, architecture, and music; at times bringing stability.)*

Topic Inquiry

Have students continue their investigations for the Topic Inquiry.

Rise of Austria, Prussia, and Russia

Supporting English Language Learners

Use with Digital Text 1, **The Thirty Years' War.**

Reading
Instruct students to look at the red headers of select portions of the text *The Thirty Years' War* for sight vocabulary. Ask students to create a list of the words and explain what each means.

Beginning Help students as they look through *The Thirty Years War* for sight vocabulary. Guide them as they look at all the red headings for words that they recognize and know by sight. Write the list of the words with their definition on the board. Using this list, have partners take turns providing a word or a short phrase that explains what each sight word means (e.g. *conflict* means *war*) Provide the sentence frame: _____ means _____.

Intermediate Have students look through *The Thirty Years War* for sight vocabulary. Tell them to look at all the red headings for words that they recognize and know by sight. Write the list of words on the board. Then have partners define each of the sight words and work together to write sentences using each word.

Advanced Have students look through the red headings in Lesson 2 *Rise of Austria, Prussia, and Russia* for sight vocabulary. Instruct students to make flash cards of each of their sight words. Ask them to write the word on the front of an index card and write a short definition and a sentence on the back. Have students quiz each other on the meaning of each word.

Advanced High Have students look through the red headings in Lesson 2 *Rise of Austria, Prussia, and Russia* for sight vocabulary. Have them define each sight word and write sentences using each word. Ask them to exchange lists and sentences with another pair and peer edit their work. Have students explain their edits to each other and revise their sentences as needed.

Use with Digital Text 6, **Catherine the Great.**

Speaking
Beginning Read *Catherine the Great* aloud. Help students identify positive and negative aspects of her reign, supporting them with simple phrases and words to help them formulate and communicate their ideas. Have students use sentences frames to express their ideas, such as: The reign of Catherine the Great was good/bad for Russia because _____.

Intermediate Read *Catherine the Great* aloud. Have partners create a list of words to describe Catherine the Great and her reign. Then ask the pairs to discuss whether these words describe Catherine's reign as positive or negative. Have pairs share their ideas with supporting details from the text to the group.

Advanced Have students work together in small groups. Instruct them to discuss the life of Catherine the Great and develop a list of positive and negative outcomes that define her reign. Using their list of outcomes, have students discuss their ideas of the how Catherine's reign affected Russia and its people.

Advanced High Divide students into two groups. Have students in each group discuss the influence of Catherine the Great. Then have one group develop a list of positive outcomes of her reign, and have the other develop a list of negative outcomes. Then have groups debate their positions, supporting their ideas with evidence from the text.

▣ Differentiate Instruction

Use the Differentiated Instruction notes throughout the lesson plan to support the varied skill sets, levels of readiness, and interests in the mixed-ability classroom.

Challenge These notes include suggestions for expanding the activity for advanced students.

On-Level These notes include suggestions for modifying the activity to address different interests or learning styles.

Extra Support These notes include ideas for providing more scaffolding or reading spuport.

Special Needs These notes provide ideas for adapting instruction to support the needs of various special needs students.

■ NOTES

_____

_____

_____

_____

_____

PEARSON
realize™
www.PearsonRealize.com

Go online to access additional resources including:
Primary Sources • Biographies • Supreme Court cases •
21st Century Skill Tutorials • Maps • Graphic Organizers.

Objectives

Objective 1: Outline the causes and results of the Thirty Years' War.

Objective 2: Understand how Austria and Prussia emerged as great powers.

Objective 3: Explain the steps Peter the Great took to modernize Russia.

Objective 4: Describe how Russia grew under Peter the Great and Catherine the Great.

Objective 5: Describe how European nations tried to maintain a balance of power.

LESSON 2 ORGANIZER		OBJECTIVES	PACING	RESOURCES Online	RESOURCES Print
Connect					
DIGITAL START UP ACTIVITY **Experiencing the Thirty Years' War**			5 min.	●	
Investigate					
DIGITAL TEXT 1 **The Thirty Years' War**		Objective 1	10 min.	●	●
DIGITAL TEXTS 2 AND 3 **Hapsburg Austria Expands, Prussia Emerges**		Objective 2	10 min.	●	●
INTERACTIVE MAP **Maps of Europe, 1648 and 1700**			10 min.	●	
DIGITAL TEXT 4 **Peter the Great Modernizes Russia**		Objective 3	10 min.	●	●
INTERACTIVE GALLERY **The Achievements of Peter the Great**			10 min.	●	
DIGITAL TEXT 5 **Expanding Russia's Borders**		Objective 4	10 min.	●	●
DIGITAL TEXT 6 **Catherine the Great**			10 min.	●	●
DIGITAL TEXT 7 **Five Great European Powers**		Objective 5	10 min.	●	●
Synthesize					
DIGITAL ACTIVITY **Lesson Synthesize: Mini DBQ**			5 min.	●	
Demonstrate					
LESSON QUIZ **Lesson Quiz and Class Discussion Board**			10 min.	●	

PACING: APPROX. 1 PERIOD, .5 BLOCKS

Rise of Austria, Prussia, and Russia

■ CONNECT

DIGITAL START UP ACTIVITY
Experiencing the Thirty Years' War

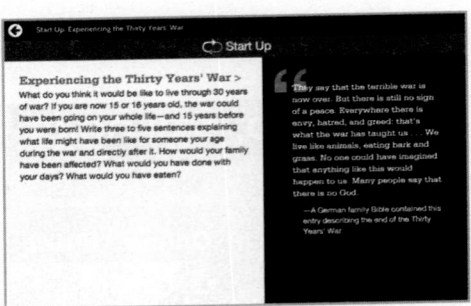

Project the Start Up Activity Ask students to read the primary source and answer the questions as they enter and get settled: What do you think it would be like to live through 30 years of war? Write three to five sentences explaining what life might have been like for someone your age during the war and directly after it.

Discuss When the Thirty Years' War ended, the German states were decimated. Farmland was destroyed, and people had lost their faith. Discuss the possible effects of loss of population, loss of economic security, and loss of faith of the people.

Aa Vocabulary Development: Use the Interactive Reading Notepad to preview the Key Terms and Academic Vocabulary in this Lesson with students.

> ↯ **FLIP IT!**
> Assign the Flipped Video for this lesson.

■ STUDENT EDITION PRINT
PAGES: 435–443

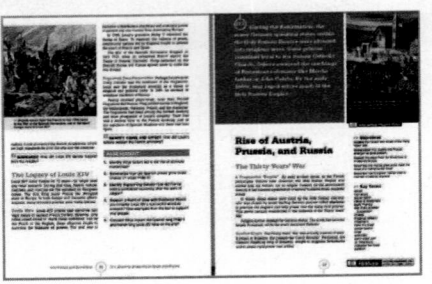

■ INVESTIGATE

DIGITAL TEXT 1
The Thirty Years' War

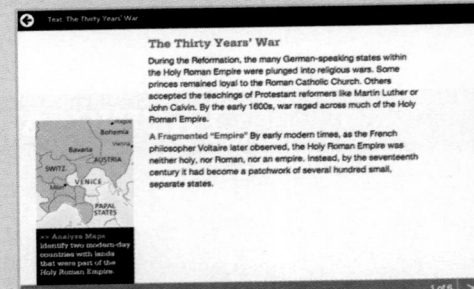

Objective 1: Outline the causes and results of the Thirty Years' War.

Quick Instruction

Project the map of the Holy Roman Empire in 1600 (before the Thirty Years' War). Ask students what three religions are represented in the region. (*Roman Catholic, Lutheran, Calvinist*) Now, project the map of Europe in 1648 (after the Thirty Years' War). Ask students to identify which two states became independent after the Thirty Years' War. (*Dutch Netherlands, Swiss Confederation*) Next, have them look back at the 1600 (religious) map. What was the religion of these two regions? (*Protestant and Catholic*)

D Differentiate: Extra Support Help students use word roots and associates to learn definitions. *Elector*, like *elect*, comes from the Latin word, *electus*, meaning *chosen*. *Defenestration* comes from the Latin *fenestra*, or *window*. *Depopulation* comes from the Latin *populous*, or *people*. (Ask students what other English word might come from *populous*? [example: *popular*]) Have students write a definition of each word using a root or related word.

ELL Use the ELL activity described in the ELL chart.

Further Instruction

The Thirty Years' War: Core Reading and Interactive Reading Notepad Project and discuss the Interactive Reading Notepad questions. Go through the questions, and call on students to provide answers.

For over 200 years, the German states were extremely divided. Two strong states—Prussia and Austria—emerged to fill the void, but many other German states remained independent until the middle of the 19th century.

D Differentiate: Challenge Break students into small groups and assign each group one of the larger states—Bavaria, Saxony, Hesse-Kassel, Wurttemberg, Hanover, and Baden—and ask them to research the history of that state from 1648 to 1800 and the type of government in each. Presentations can be a PowerPoint or could use digital media and be posted on a website. Follow with a discussion of the similarities and differences of the stories from each state.

DIGITAL TEXT 2

Hapsburg Austria Expands

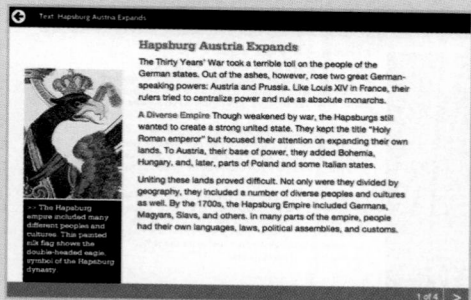

DIGITAL TEXT 3

Prussia Emerges

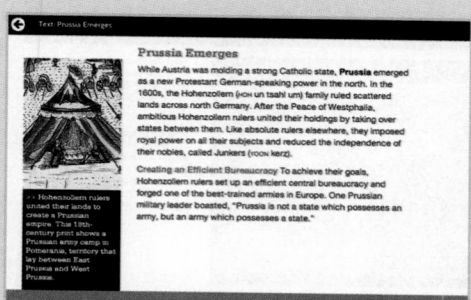

INTERACTIVE MAP

Maps of Europe, 1648 and 1700

Objective 2: Understand how Austria and Prussia emerged as great powers.

Quick Instruction

Interactive Map: Maps of Europe, 1648 and 1700 Project the 1648 map and focus students' attention to the area of the Holy Roman Empire. Slide to the 1700 map, asking students to keep their eyes on the same region. Which two states grew the most from 1648 to 1700? *(Austria and Prussia)* On the whiteboard, draw a T-chart (students could also construct their own graphic organizer) and list Maria Theresa and Frederick William I on the chart. Ask students to list how both Maria Theresa and Frederick William I consolidated their power. *(Maria Theresa: reorganized bureaucracy, taxed nobles and clergy, used German-speaking officials to help unify; Frederick William I: built up army, gave Junkers positions in Army, created an efficient bureaucracy.)*

🖳 ACTIVE CLASSROOM

Speak: A Close Look Part I: Project the 1648 map on the whiteboard and use a whiteboard tool to divide it into four numbered quadrants. Have students count off 1 to 4. Ask them to look closely at the part of the map in their quadrant. Ask students to list what they see. Part 2: Repeat with the 1700 map. Part 3: Ask students to focus on any changes they see in their quadrant and list them. Collect insights and list them on the board or charting paper.

D Differentiate: Extra Support Have students look closely at the 1648 map and identify the Dutch Netherlands, Spanish Netherlands, Hungary, and Westphalia. Then ask: 1) What is controlled by Spain? *(Spain, Spanish Netherlands, Sardinia, Sicily, boot of Italy, regions in north of Italy and Holy Roman Empire)* 2) Which state has land on the coast of Poland? *(Prussia)*

Slide map to reveal the 1700 map. Ask students: 1) Have Spain's lands decreased, increased, or stayed the same? *(stayed the same))*; 2) Which other state (besides Spain, Austria, and Prussia) has land in the Holy Roman Empire? *(Sweden)*

Further Instruction

Project the Interactive Reading Notepad questions and discuss the answers with the class.

Ask students to look again at the 1700 map. Which states have the most coastline? *(Spain, France, England, Sweden)* Why would this be a benefit to the state? *(more ports, more shipping, more trade)* Which states have the least coastline? *(Austria, Poland, Russia)* What do you think they might do to increase their access to the sea? *(invade other countries, develop alliances)*

Rise of Austria, Prussia, and Russia

DIGITAL TEXT 4

Peter the Great Modernizes Russia

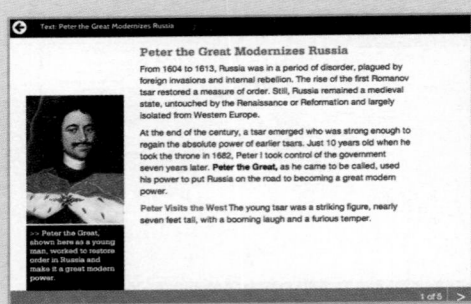

INTERACTIVE GALLERY

The Achievements of Peter the Great

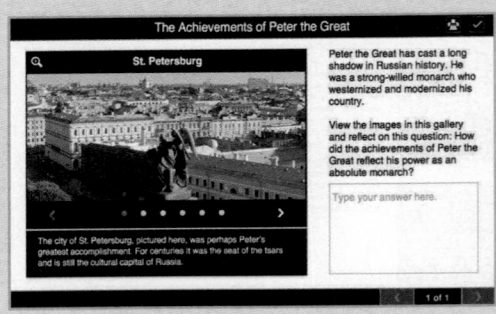

DIGITAL TEXT 5

Expanding Russia's Borders

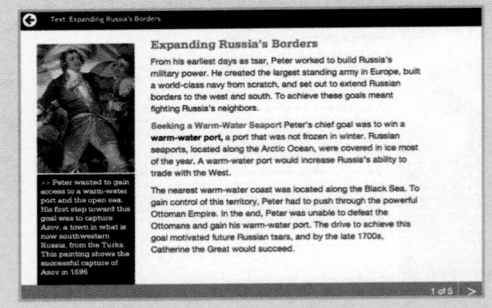

Objective 3: **Explain the steps Peter the Great took to modernize Russia.**

Quick Instruction

Interactive Gallery: The Achievements of Peter the Great Project the images from the Interactive Image Gallery. Read (or have student volunteers read) caption copy as you click through the images. Remind students about the techniques of absolutism (control nobles, control economy, centralize bureaucracy, unify religion, increase military strength/expand territory, build monuments to self) Ask students: How did the achievements of Peter the Great reflect his strength as an absolute monarch? Cite at least three pieces of specific information from the images and captions. (*Improved trade, regulated churches, built St. Petersburg, strengthened navy*)

👥 ACTIVE CLASSROOM

Group students. Give each group a three-column organizer with the headings Plus/Minus/Interesting for recording responses to three questions. 1. What were the positive effects of Peter the Great's achievements? 2. What were the negative effects? 3. What is interesting about them? Each column must have at least one entry. Record students' responses on the whiteboard or on charting paper. Discuss the answers as a class.

D **Differentiate: Challenge** Group students, and give each group a copy of the image of Peter the Great cutting off the beards of the Boyars. Ask students to create a political cartoon using this image about the tactics Peter used to westernize Russia. Groups will need to write 1) a title; 2) a caption; and 3) word bubbles for Peter and the Boyars.

Further Instruction

Ask students to answer the following questions: 1) How did Peter the Great westernize Russia? Cite three pieces of evidence from the text. (*modernized the military, forced the Boyars to westernize their dress, improved education, built western city [St. Petersburg]*) 2) What challenges did Peter the Great face when he tried to westernize Russia? Cite three pieces of evidence from the text. (*building a world class navy from nothing, the resistance of the Boyars, the difficulties building St. Petersburg*)

Objective 4: **Describe how Russia grew under Peter the Great and Catherine the Great.**

Quick Instruction

Project the map of Russia's Expansion, 1689–1796. Ask students to locate Sweden, the Baltic Sea, St. Petersburg, Siberia, and the Bering Sea. Ask them: 1) Why do you think Peter the Great wanted to improve his navy? (*It would help him expand Russia's borders.*) 2) How might this map look different if Peter the Great had not developed a modern navy? (*Sample response: Russia might look smaller.*) 3) What do the lands that were added during Catherine's reign have in common? (*Catherine succeeded in gaining a warm-water port that Peter wanted badly.*)

D **Differentiate: Challenge/Gifted** Project the image of Serfs in Russia during the reign of Catherine the Great (Text 6). Break the students into groups. Ask them to write dialogue for the people in the picture. They will need to determine: 1) Who are these people? 2) What is their relationship to one another? 3) What are they doing? Ask students to answer the questions using the reading and additional research, if necessary.

DIGITAL TEXT 6

Catherine the Great

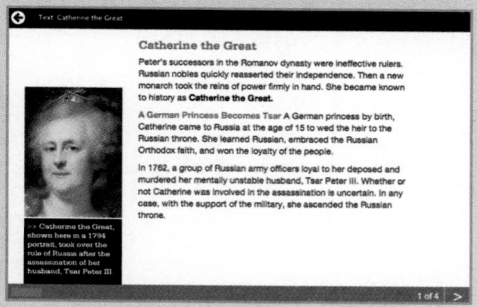

ELL Use the ELL activity described in the ELL chart.

Further Instruction

Catherine the Great continued Peter the Great's efforts to westernize Russia but was also a ruthless leader in the old Russian mold. Give examples of both her reforms and her ruthlessness in a paragraph where you assess Catherine's achievements as an absolute monarch. *(Answers will vary. Examples of westernizing: French language and customs, education for both boys and girls, reorganizing government, making the laws more clear/systematic—"codifying" them; Examples of ruthlessness: harsh treatment of serfs; giving more rights to nobles [Boyars], and exempting nobles from taxation.)*

DIGITAL TEXT 7

Five Great European Powers

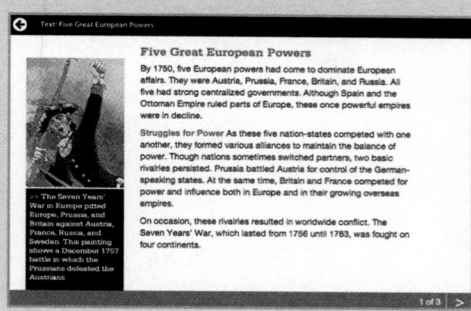

Objective 5: Describe how European nations tried to maintain a balance of power.

Quick Instruction

Project the second map in the Interactive Map Activity from this lesson (Europe, 1700). Ask students what they remember about the relationship between Prussia and Austria. *(They were great rivals for territory and power.)* Discuss the concept of an alliance. Who might Prussia ally with? *(England)* Who might Austria ally with? *(France)* What role might shared borders play in rivalries between states? *(States that share borders can become rivals for territory and power.)* How might Russia's relationship with Austria change after the Partition of Poland? *(As they became neighbors, their competition increased.)*

D **Differentiate: Extra Support** Ask students: What is an ally? *(a person/country who will fight your battles with you if you are attacked)* Ask them to give an example from their lives when they needed an ally. Ask them: Why are allies important in world politics? *(If a country has allies, it doesn't need to fight wars all alone.)* What might happen to a country without any allies? *(It could lose many wars, especially if all the surrounding countries had allies.)*

Further Instruction

In the 1740s, the alliances between the major European powers shifted. England and France were in opposition, as were Austria and Prussia. The Seven Years' War was fought between these powers, and it was the first European war to be fought on four continents.

Five Great European Powers: Core Reading and Interactive Reading Notepad Project and discuss the Interactive Reading Notepad questions. Then, ask students to review the reading and answer the questions independently.

D **Differentiate: Challenge/Gifted** Break students into four groups. Assign two groups to research the Seven Years' War as fought on the European continent; assign one group to research the war as fought in North America (where it was known as the French and Indian War); and assign another group to research the war as fought on the Indian subcontinent. Presentations could be made in PowerPoint and could include maps and descriptions of battles.

Rise of Austria, Prussia, and Russia

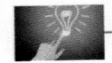

SYNTHESIZE

DIGITAL ACTIVITY

Lesson Synthesize: Mini DBQ

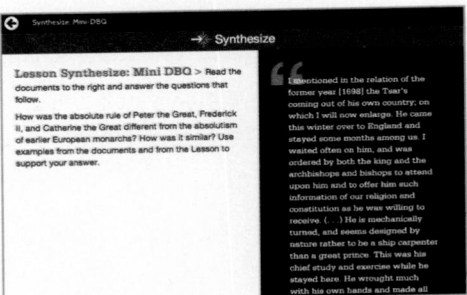

Remind students of the Topic Essential Question: How much power should the government have? Tell them that the absolute power of monarchs can be viewed from different perspectives. Have the students read the three documents in the Mini-DBQ: Absolutism in Prussia and Russia, and answer the question: How was the absolute rule of Peter the Great, Frederick II, and Catherine the Great different from earlier European absolute monarchs? How was it similar? Encourage them to highlight any text that answers the questions. Ask students to use examples from the documents (and the lesson) to support their answers. *(Answers will vary based on students' ability to structure a DBQ. Sample answer: Document 1 [Peter the Great]: Different from earlier monarchs: interested in working with his hands and admired the British constitution and religion. Document 2 [Frederick II]: Different from earlier monarchs: Leader is the head/ eyes/brain of the state [not the state itself as Louis XIV said]; Ruler should be active, honest, upright, hardworking; must be worthy. No mention of divine right. Document 3 [Catherine the Great]: Similar: Decree itemizes ways to keep down the serfs; stresses obedience to authority. Expectation that all will go to church on Sunday assumes religious unity.)*

DEMONSTRATE

LESSON QUIZ

Lesson Quiz and Class Discussion Board

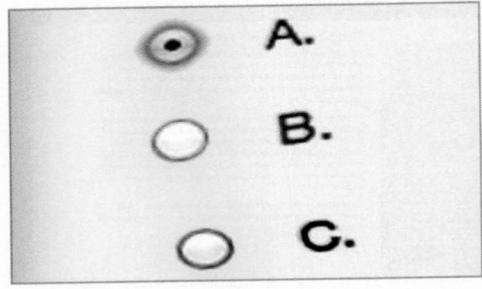

Assign the online Lesson Quiz for this lesson if you haven't already done so. Students will be offered automatic remediation or enrichment based on their score.

Remind students that in "Rise of Austria, Prussia, and Russia" they read about the Thirty Years' War, how Austria and Prussia emerged as powers, the reigns of Peter the Great and Catherine the Great, and the five great European powers that existed by 1750.

How did Austria, Prussia, and Russia expand their power and territory to become three of the most powerful countries in 18th century Europe? *(Their leaders ruled as absolute monarchs, expanded their armies, and in some cases, formed alliances. In addition, both Peter the Great and Catherine the Great modernized and westernized their countries.)* In your opinion, which country was most successful and why? *(Answers will vary but students should provide support for their opinions. Some students might mention economic or military success, while others might mention territorial gain or social reform.)*

Topic Inquiry

Have students continue their investigations for the Topic Inquiry.

PEARSON realize™

www.PearsonRealize.com
Access your Digital Lesson

Triumph of Parliament in England

Supporting English Language Learners

Use with Digital Text 2, **Stuart Monarchs Clash with Parliament.**

Speaking
Point out that all people, leaders included, are affected by their emotions about a subject when they are making decisions. Instruct students to act as if they are members of the English Parliament during the time of King James I. Then, read aloud the excerpt of James I's speech to Parliament on the divine right of kings.

Beginning Facilitate students' expression of their emotional reactions by providing them with sentence frames. Support students with simple phrases and words to help them formulate and communicate their emotions. If necessary, provide students with visual expressions of various emotions, such as happy, angry, sad, frustrated, relaxed, and uninterested. Remind students to listen to the speech as if they are members of Parliament. Use the following sentence frames to support students' ideas.

King James' speech makes me feel _____.

I _____ (agree/disagree) with the idea that the monarch's power comes from God.

Intermediate Provide sentence frames for students to express their feelings about James' belief in the divine right of kings. Provide linguistic support in the form of word meanings and visual expressions of various emotions to support students' understanding of the task.

I felt _____ when King James I said _____.

I _____ (agree/disagree) with the idea that the monarch's power comes from God.

Advanced Arrange students in small groups. Explain that they should act as if they are members of Parliament and have assembled a committee to share their feelings on King James' speech. To support students' discussions, provide linguistic support in the form of word meanings and visual expressions of various emotions.

Advanced High Arrange students in small groups. Explain that they should take the roles of members of Parliament and have assembled a committee to share their feelings on King James' speech. Instruct students to link their emotions about the speech to specific phrases from the speech. Then have each small group share a summary of their discussion with the whole class.

Use with Digital Text 6, **England's Constitutional Government Evolves.**

Reading
Write down *Environmental Print* and ask students to read it out loud. Remind them that *environmental print* means printed materials that are part of everyday life, including signs, billboards, labels, and business logos. Explain to students that in order to gain an understanding of what constitutes environmental print, they will create their own environmental print based on *England's Constitutional Government Evolves.*

Beginning Have students examine the image of the 18th century market scene in London. Then have each student make a list of any environmental print they can identify in the photograph. After they've completed their lists, have students trade with a partner and read their partner's list. Support student understanding by defining any unfamiliar terms and helping students identify any items they may have overlooked in the image.

Intermediate Have students reread the last paragraph of *An Unequal Society.* Point out that the middle class included merchants, craftspeople, and manufacturers. Have students work in pairs to design a business sign, including a name and a logo or symbol, for one of the three categories.

Advanced Have students reread the section, *Political Parties.* Then, working in small groups, have students make text-only campaign signs of England's two political parties—Tories and Whigs—in the style of political party signs in the United States today.

Advanced High Have students reread the section, *Political Parties.* Then, working in small groups, assign students to design a political party logo for one of England's two political parties—Tories or Whigs. Have the groups show and explain their completed logos and how they might be used as environmental print in London.

D Differentiate Instruction

Use the Differentiated Instruction notes throughout the lesson plan to support the varied skill sets, levels of readiness, and interests in the mixed-ability classroom.

Challenge These notes include suggestions for expanding the activity for advanced students.

On-Level These notes include suggestions for modifying the activity to address different interests or learning styles.

Extra Support These notes include ideas for providing more scaffolding or reading spuport.

Special Needs These notes provide ideas for adapting instruction to support the needs of various special needs students.

■ NOTES

Triumph of Parliament in England

Objectives

Objective 1: Describe the relationship between Parliament and the monarchy under the Tudors and Stuarts.

Objective 2: Explain how English government developed after the English Civil War.

Objective 3: Identify the causes of the Glorious Revolution and the ideas contained in the English Bill of Rights.

Objective 4: Identify the characteristics of limited monarchy and constitutional government in England.

LESSON 3 ORGANIZER		OBJECTIVES	PACING	RESOURCES	
				Online	Print
Connect					
	DIGITAL START UP ACTIVITY **Compare Rulers**		5 min.	●	
Investigate					
	DIGITAL TEXT 1 **Tudor Monarchs Work with Parliament**	Objective 1	10 min.	●	●
	DIGITAL TEXT 2 **Stuart Monarchs Clash with Parliament**		10 min.	●	●
	DIGITAL TEXTS 3 AND 4 **The English Civil War, Cromwell and the Commonwealth**	Objective 2	10 min.	●	●
	INTERACTIVE TIMELINE **England Divided: The Monarchy and Parliament Fight for Power**		10 min.	●	
	DIGITAL TEXT 5 **From Restoration to Glorious Revolution**	Objective 3	10 min.	●	●
	INTERACTIVE GALLERY **Protections of the English Bill of Rights**		10 min.	●	
	DIGITAL TEXT 6 **England's Constitutional Government Evolves**	Objective 4	10 min.	●	●
Synthesize					
	DIGITAL ACTIVITY **Steps Toward Liberty**		5 min.	●	
Demonstrate					
	LESSON QUIZ **Lesson Quiz and Class Discussion Board**		10 min.	●	

PACING: APPROX. 1 PERIOD, .5 BLOCKS

PEARSON realize™
www.PearsonRealize.com

Go online to access additional resources including:
Primary Sources • Biographies • Supreme Court cases •
21st Century Skill Tutorials • Maps • Graphic Organizers.

CONNECT

DIGITAL START UP ACTIVITY
Compare Rulers

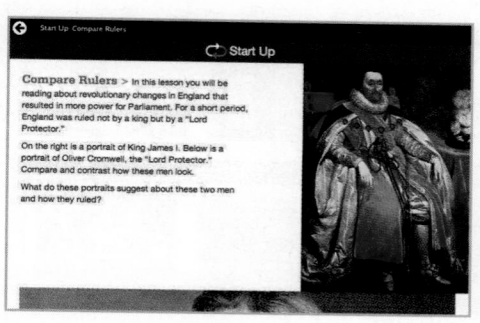

Project the Start Up Activity Ask students to answer the question below as they enter and get settled. Then have them share their ideas with another student, either in class or through a chat room or blog.

Discuss What do these portraits suggest about these two men and how they ruled? *(Sample response: King James is wearing an elaborate robe, expensive clothing, and jewels. He sits on a throne. All of these are symbols of his power as king. He probably rules as an absolute monarch. Cromwell is dressed much more simply. His dress does not display either wealth or power but shows a more military focus.)*

Aa **Vocabulary Development:** Use the Interactive Reading Notepad to preview the Key Terms and Academic Vocabulary in this Lesson with students.

⇌ FLIP IT!

Assign the Flipped Video for this lesson.

STUDENT EDITION PRINT
PAGES: 444–451

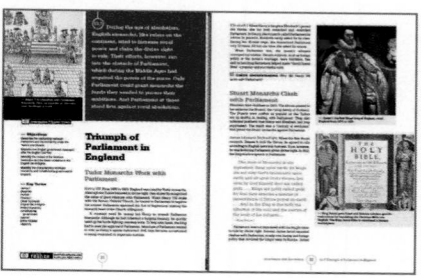

INVESTIGATE

DIGITAL TEXT 1
Tudor Monarchs Work with Parliament

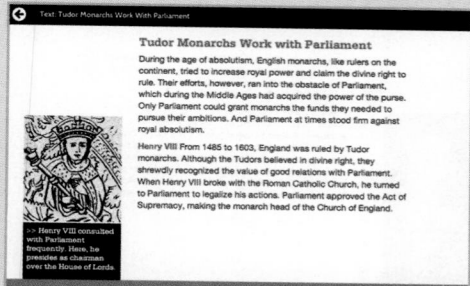

DIGITAL TEXT 2
Stuart Monarchs Clash with Parliament

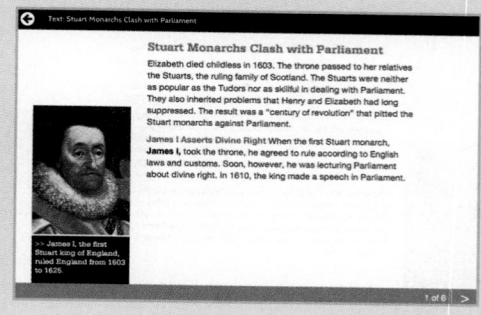

Objective 1: Describe the relationship between Parliament and the monarchy under the Tudors and Stuarts.

Quick Instruction
The tradition of the English Parliament set England apart from other European nations with absolute monarchs. English monarchs had to work with Parliament, and each had developed his or her own method for dealing with its members. When James Stuart ascended the English throne, he brought with him strong views about the power of the monarchy, which did not sit well with Parliament.

Analyze Images Project the image of Henry VIII and Parliament. What does the image suggest about the relationship between the king and Parliament? *(That the king and Parliament are one governing body; they act in concert with each other.)*

Predict Consequences What might be a likely outcome when an absolute monarch clashes with a Parliament that is growing in strength? *(One or the other would have to back down. If both refuse, a civil war or other armed conflict might result.)*

D **Differentiate: Challenge/Gifted** Ask students to research and prepare a short presentation about English political philosopher Thomas Hobbes, who favored an absolute monarchy. Have students concentrate on why Hobbes believed that an absolute monarchy was the correct system of government. Part of the presentation should include a comparison of Hobbes's beliefs and those who supported a much more limited monarchy.

ELL Use the ELL activity described in the ELL chart.

Further Instruction
Project the Interactive Reading Notepad questions and discuss the answers.

Elizabeth's deft handling of Parliament did not continue with James Stuart. The radical difference between Elizabeth's approach to working with Parliament and James's insistence on his right to rule without interference set the monarchy up against Parliament. When Charles I ascended the throne, he was committed to ruling as his father had. This attitude brought him into continued direct conflict with Parliament, resulting in the Long Parliament and, eventually, the English Civil War.

Identify Cause and Effect What could Charles have done to avoid a war? *(He could have been more willing to work with Parliament instead of constantly overriding it and treating the members of Parliament as enemies.)*

Triumph of Parliament in England

DIGITAL TEXT 3
The English Civil War

DIGITAL TEXT 4
Cromwell and the Commonwealth

INTERACTIVE TIMELINE
England Divided: The Monarchy and Parliament Fight for Power

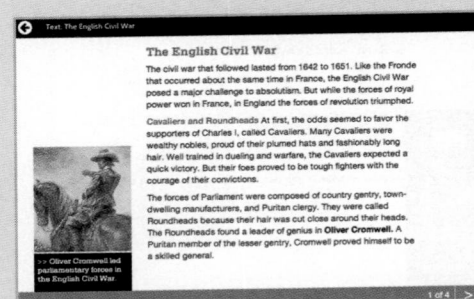

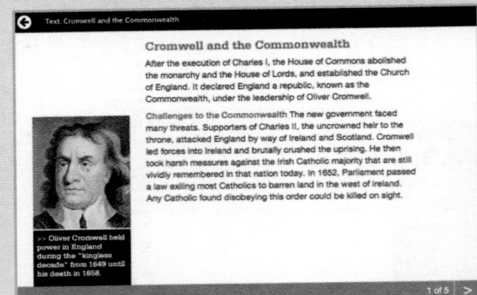

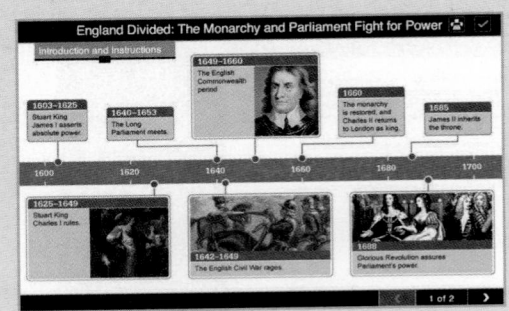

Objective 2: Explain how English government developed after the English Civil War.

Quick Instruction

Introduce the activity by explaining that the English Civil War was the result of years of conflict between the Stuart monarchy and Parliament.

Interactive Timeline: England Divided: The Monarchy and Parliament Fight for Power Project the timeline on the whiteboard. Review the events presented on the timeline. Click on the hotspots for information on especially important points. Ask students to think about the stages at which a war might have been avoided. What actions would each side have had to take?

🖳 ACTIVE CLASSROOM

Use the Wallpaper strategy to have students review what they have learned. Ask each student to design a piece of "wallpaper" that encapsulates the key items they have learned. Then post each piece of the wallpaper. Invite students to take a "wisdom" walk and note what others have written or illustrated.

Further Instruction

Project and discuss the Interactive Reading Notepad questions and the graphic organizer flowchart for this lesson. Use a whiteboard tool to fill in the first event in the graphic organizer to give students an idea of where they might start.

Explain that there was a specific sequence of events that led to the English Civil War. The Cavaliers expected a quick and easy victory. When the Roundheads rallied and eventually won, it was a shock not only to the Cavaliers but also to the absolute monarchs in Europe.

Analyze Information Why did the Cavaliers expect a quick victory? *(They were well-trained and experienced soldiers who saw themselves as far superior to the Roundheads in military ability.)*

Infer Why did Cromwell and the Roundheads decide to execute Charles instead of just imprisoning him or sending him into exile? *(As long as Charles was alive, there would be supporters who would encourage him to try to win back his crown. This would have led to constant warfare. Also, his execution made a clear statement that no one, not even a king, was above the law established by the people.)*

Identify Cause and Effect Explain how the English Civil War led to the development of a democratic-republican government. *(Limiting the authority of the monarch and giving greater authority to a partially elected body such as Parliament led to a representative system of government.)*

DIGITAL TEXT 5

From Restoration to Glorious Revolution

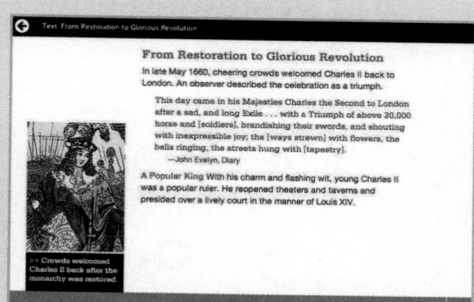

INTERACTIVE GALLERY

Protections of the English Bill of Rights

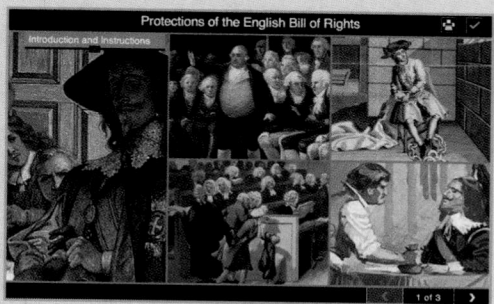

DIGITAL TEXT 6

England's Constitutional Government Evolves

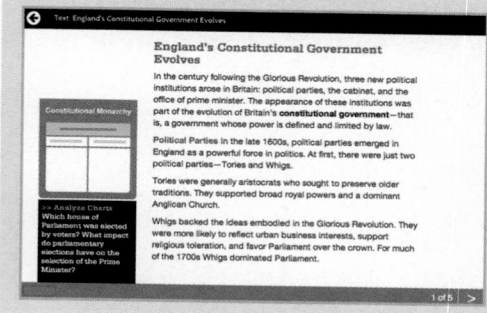

Objective 3: **Identify the causes of the Glorious Revolution and the ideas contained in the English Bill of Rights.**

Quick Instruction

Introduce the activity by having students identify the main characteristic of a limited monarchy. *(A legislative body or written constitution limits the powers of the monarch.)* Explain that the Glorious Revolution and English Bill of Rights created a limited monarchy in England. Have students identify the impact of the political and legal ideas contained in the English Bill of Rights. Tell students that the document gave citizens certain civil rights that could not be abridged by anyone, regardless of social rank. The English Bill of Rights was also the foundation of the U.S. Bill of Rights.

Interactive Gallery: Protections of the English Bill of Rights Project the gallery on the whiteboard. Click on each image to give students more information on the English Bill of Rights.

👥 ACTIVE CLASSROOM

Use the Make Headlines strategy and have students write a headline that captures the impact of the ideas in the English Bill of Rights. Ask: If you were to write a headline right now for this topic that captured the most important aspect to be remembered, what would that headline be? Pass your headline to a partner for him or her to review. Ask your partner if he or she agrees or disagrees with your headline, and why.

Draw Conclusions Apart from the rights it ensures, why was the English Bill of Rights such an important document? *(It was an important step in forming a representative government. The Bill of Rights was developed by Parliament with the intention of giving citizens equal protection under the law. This revolutionary concept influenced citizens of other nations to follow suit.)*

Further Instruction

Project the Interactive Reading Notepad questions for this lesson, and discuss the answers.

Habeas corpus is one of the rights included in the English Bill of Rights and in our own U.S. Constitution. Habeas corpus is Latin for "you may have the body," and requires that a prisoner must be brought before a judge and charged with a crime or be released. In the United States, like other nations, there are provisions for suspending this right in times of rebellion or war. President Abraham Lincoln suspended habeas corpus during the American Civil War.

Analyze Information Can a "right" be a "right" if it can be legally taken away? *(Some students may argue that rights cannot be taken away under any circumstances. Others may argue that the authority given to the president or other governing body to restrict a "right" comes from the will of the people. The people agree that certain circumstances may take precedence over a legal "right.")*

Objective 4: **Identify the characteristics of limited monarchy and constitutional government in England.**

Quick Instruction

Project on the whiteboard the organizational chart for the British constitutional monarchy. Introduce the concepts of limited monarchy and constitutional government. Briefly review the organizational chart to ensure students understand what it shows about the British government. Point out that the institutions of the cabinet and the prime minister were part of the evolution of Britain's constitutional government that includes a limited monarchy.

Draw Conclusions What are the characteristics of an oligarchy? Since Britain's constitutional government provided for a House of Commons as well as a House of Lords, how could the government be an oligarchy? *(An oligarchy is a government ruled by a small group of people. Even though the Commons was intended to represent the "common" person, it was still largely the wealthy, non-titled individuals who were representatives. Therefore, the British government remained a government by the privileged few.)*

ELL Use the ELL activity described in the ELL chart.

Triumph of Parliament in England

SYNTHESIZE

DEMONSTRATE

DIGITAL ACTIVITY
Steps Toward Liberty

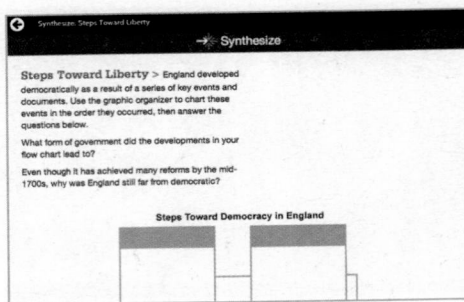

LESSON QUIZ
Lesson Quiz and Class Discussion Board

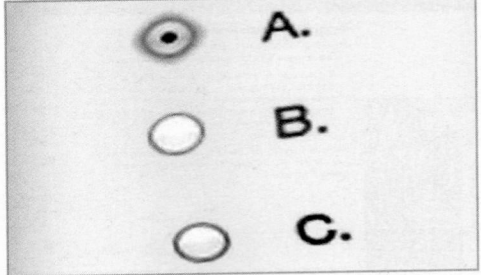

Further Instruction

Project and discuss the Interactive Reading Notepad questions and the marketplace image.

The first model for a parliament was Rome's senate, a council of the elite. Throughout England's history, councils advising the king were made up of the nobility. With the development of a constitutional monarchy, the government was one of laws. The evolution into a parliamentary democracy ensured a voice for more people. However, not everyone could vote. It took many more years before England's system of government was truly a parliamentary democracy.

Infer Why would the wealthy English "commoners" try to prevent the less wealthy from having an equal say in government? *(The wealthy Commons representatives were interested in preserving and promoting laws that would most benefit them. Although they were not nobility, they were still of a higher class than most, and they tended to look down on the poor.)*

Have students use the Think-Pair-Share strategy to answer the questions in the Steps Toward Liberty activity. Ask them to take five minutes to write down some brief answers to the following questions and then share their answers with a talking partner.

What form of government did the developments listed in your flow chart create?

Discuss Remind students of the Topic Essential Question: How much power should the government have? Ask them to respond to the question while considering the outcome of the English Civil War. *(Answers may vary. Students should demonstrate an understanding that whatever power a government has must come from the people who elected that government. At times, the governed can choose to give the government a great deal of power. However, the governed have the same right to remove that power if they choose. In the English Civil War, the power of the monarchy lessened, while the power of the more-representative Parliament grew.)*

Assign the online Lesson Quiz for this lesson if you haven't already done so. Students will be offered automatic remediation or enrichment based on their score.

Pose these questions to the class on the Discussion Board:

In the lesson *Triumph of Parliament in England*, you learned about how the English government evolved from a near-absolute monarchy to a constitutional monarchy and, eventually, to a parliamentary democracy. This process included key events like the Glorious Revolution and the development of the English Bill of Rights.

Draw Conclusions Why do you think the people didn't immediately try to set up a constitutional monarchy with houses of Parliament after Cromwell's death? *(Answers will vary, but should demonstrate an understanding that the English Civil War was a time of upheaval as well as progress. Many people wanted stability and were willing to re-establish a system of government with which they were familiar, like the monarchy under Charles II. However, during this time, people took advantage of relative peace to coalesce and reaffirm what they had achieved with the Commonwealth. They put these ideas into practice as soon as they could with William and Mary.)*

Topic Inquiry
Have students continue their investigations for the Topic Inquiry.

PEARSON realize

www.PearsonRealize.com
Access your Digital Lesson

The Enlightenment

Supporting English Language Learners

Use with Digital Text 1, **Scientific Revolution Leads to the Enlightenment.**

Speaking
Explain to students that when people study the ideas of others, they often discover that they have interesting ideas to share, too. That is one way that ideas spread throughout Europe during the Scientific Revolution. Read the text *Scientific Revolution Leads to the Enlightenment*, and complete the activities below.

Beginning Have students point to words and phrases in the text that show an understanding of how the Scientific Revolution gave rise to the Enlightenment. Then help students put those words and phrases into a logical order that shows the progression from the Scientific Revolution to the Enlightenment. Finally, help students say their lists aloud, focusing on correct pronunciation and fluency.

Intermediate Help students create a list of ideas that shows how the Scientific Revolution led to the Enlightenment. Students can use words and phrases that appear in the text to create their lists. Then help student develop two or three simple sentences from the words and phrases on their lists. Finally, have students practice speaking their sentences aloud, focusing on pronunciation and fluency.

Advanced Have students review the section with a partner and create a list of ideas that show how the Scientific Revolution led to the Enlightenment. Then have two pairs of students form a small group to share their lists with each other. Finally, have each group develop a paragraph that narrates the progression of European thought from the Scientific Revolution to the Enlightenment. Have small groups use their prepared paragraphs to narrate this progression for the class.

Advanced High Have students review the text individually. Then ask students to create a list of ideas and events that demonstrate how the Scientific Revolution led to the Enlightenment. Ask each student to prepare a creative way to "tell the story" of how the Scientific Revolution gave rise to the Enlightenment. For example, students can use poetry or a metaphor to tell the story. Then have them narrate their stories aloud to the class.

Use with Digital Text 2, **Hobbes and Locke on the Role of Government.**

Reading
Read the text with students, and point out the following frequently used social studies terms.

- government
- laws
- revolution
- society
- political

Beginning Have students reread the text. Then point to each vocabulary term. Say each word aloud and have students repeat the word after you. Then define the words for students using images and context to support their understanding.

Intermediate Have students reread the text. Then have students point to and say each vocabulary term. Correct students' pronunciation when necessary. Help students define each word by establishing contextual support from the text and using visual images if necessary.

Advanced Have students reread the text. Then have students identify and define each of the five vocabulary terms. Provide students with print or electronic dictionaries to assist them in learning the definitions. Remind students to use context clues from the text to support their understanding of each term.

Advanced High Have students reread the text and locate each vocabulary term in the text. Then have them define each term and explain how the terms relate to one another using context clues from the text.

▶ Differentiate Instruction

Use the Differentiated Instruction notes throughout the lesson plan to support the varied skill sets, levels of readiness, and interests in the mixed-ability classroom.

Challenge These notes include suggestions for expanding the activity for advanced students.

On-Level These notes include suggestions for modifying the activity to address different interests or learning styles.

Extra Support These notes include ideas for providing more scaffolding or reading spuport.

Special Needs These notes provide ideas for adapting instruction to support the needs of various special needs students.

■ NOTES

The Enlightenment

Objectives

Objective 1: Describe how science led to the Enlightenment.

Objective 2: Explain the political philosophies of Hobbes, Locke, Voltaire, Montesquieu, and Rousseau.

Objective 3: Summarize the economic ideas of the physiocrats and Adam Smith.

Objective 4: Describe how Enlightenment ideas spread and influenced the arts.

Objective 5: Understand the role of enlightened despots.

LESSON 4 ORGANIZER		OBJECTIVES	PACING	RESOURCES	
	PACING: APPROX. 1 PERIOD, .5 BLOCKS			Online	Print
Connect					
	Digital Start Up Activity **Salons Spread Ideas**		5 min.	●	
Investigate					
	DIGITAL TEXT 1 **Scientific Revolution Leads to the Enlightenment**	Objective 1	10 min.	●	●
	DIGITAL TEXTS 2 AND 3 **Hobbes and Locke on the Role of Government, The Philosophes**	Objective 2	10 min.	●	●
	INTERACTIVE GALLERY **Thinkers of the Enlightenment**		10 min.	●	
	DIGITAL TEXT 4 **New Economic Ideas**	Objective 3	10 min.	●	●
	DIGITAL TEXT 5 **Spread of Enlightenment Ideas**	Objective 4	10 min.	●	●
	DIGITAL TEXT 6 **Arts and Literature of the Enlightenment**		10 min.	●	●
	INTERACTIVE GALLERY **Music of the Enlightenment**		10 min.	●	
	DIGITAL TEXT 7 **The Enlightened Despots**	Objective 5	10 min.	●	●
Synthesize					
	DIGITAL ACTIVITY **Enlightenment Ideas: Then and Now**		5 min.	●	
Demonstrate					
	LESSON QUIZ **Lesson Quiz and Class Discussion Board**		10 min.	●	

■ CONNECT

DIGITAL START UP ACTIVITY
Salons Spread Ideas

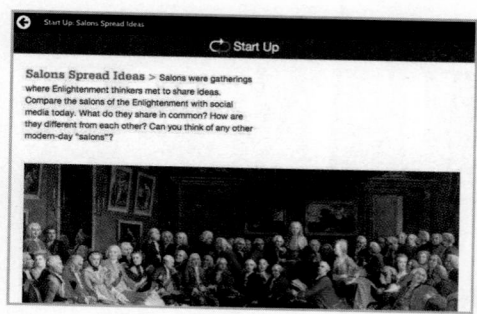

Project the Start Up Activity Ask students to answer the questions as they enter and get settled: Compare, contrast, and develop connections between the salons of the Enlightenment with social media today. How are they similar to and different from each other? *(Answers will vary, but students may point out that salons and social media are alike in that people share ideas and opinions in both. They are different in that salons were gatherings of Enlightenment thinkers but social media can include anyone.)*

Aa Vocabulary Development: Use the Interactive Reading Notepad to preview the Key Terms and Academic Vocabulary in this Lesson with students.

⇅ FLIP IT!

Assign the Flipped Video for this lesson.

■ STUDENT EDITION PRINT
PAGES: 452–459

■ INVESTIGATE

DIGITAL TEXT 1
Scientific Revolution Leads to the Enlightenment

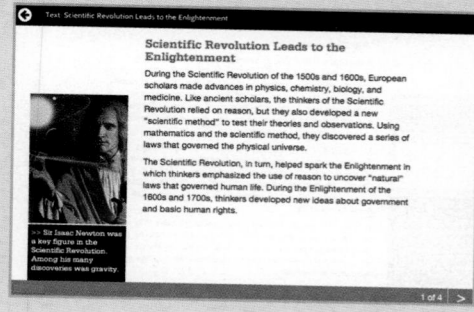

Objective 1: Describe how science led to the Enlightenment.

Quick Instruction

Project the image from the text of Isaac Newton. Identify for students the major causes for the Enlightenment. Explain the key term **natural law** in the text and that a belief in natural law and the use of the scientific method was a significant change from the past.

ELL Use the ELL activity described in the ELL chart.

Further Instruction

Scientific Revolution Leads to the Enlightenment: Core Text and Interactive Reading Notepad Project and discuss the Interactive Reading Notepad questions, and go through the answers as a class. Then, explain to students that reason is thought based on logic. Previously, people accepted things based on faith or unquestioning beliefs. Students should understand that scientific successes convinced many educated Europeans to accept the power of reason. Many people's long-held beliefs were challenged.

Infer Through the Renaissance, Scientific Revolution, and Enlightenment, European thinkers increasingly relied on principles of natural law rather than religious authority to social, economic, and political problems. Thinkers also placed greater emphasis individual achievement and rights. How might the relationship among Christianity, individualism, and growing secularism influence subsequent political developments? *(Possible answer: The Enlightenment caused people to question many areas of their lives. The idea of divine right was challenged by new notions of natural rights. Church influence in government declined as governments became more secular.)*

Infer Who might have objected to people using reason to challenge long-held ideas? *(Possible answers: the Church, noblemen, political leaders)*

The Enlightenment

DIGITAL TEXT 2

Hobbes and Locke on the Role of Government

DIGITAL TEXT 3

The Philosophes

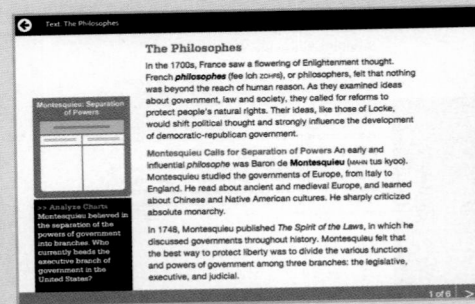

INTERACTIVE GALLERY

Thinkers of the Enlightenment

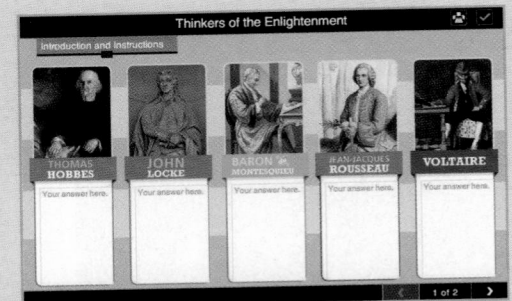

Objective 2: Explain the political philosophies of Hobbes, Locke, Voltaire, Montesquieu, and Rousseau.

Quick Instruction

Interactive Chart: Thinkers of the Enlightenment Project the chart of Enlightenment thinkers on the whiteboard. Introduce the activity by reviewing the contributions of each of the men listed. Be sure students understand and can explain the contributions of their political philosophies to the development of democratic-republican government. Students should use the chart to list the key ideas of each man.

ACTIVE CLASSROOM

Ask students to have a Conversation with History with one of the Enlightenment thinkers listed in the interactive chart. Have students write down a question they would like to ask, what that person would say in response, and how they would reply to the thinker's response.

ELL Use the ELL activity described in the ELL chart.

Further Instruction

Editable Presentation Use the Editable Presentation to present the main ideas for this Core Reading.

Project and discuss the Interactive Reading Notepad questions from the texts. Then, compare Hobbes's and Locke's political philosophies. Discuss the meanings of a social contract *(an agreement by which people gave up their freedom to a powerful government in order to avoid chaos)* and a natural right *(right that belongs to all humans from birth, such as life, liberty, and property)*. Be sure students understand that Hobbes believed that the government needed to impose order and force obedience, while Locke thought governments should have limited power and be sanctioned by all citizens.

Draw Conclusions How did Locke's ideas shift political thought in Europe? *(His theory of natural rights contradicted the theory of divine rights.)*

Make Predictions What might be the long-term effect of these ideas? *(They influenced revolutions across the globe.)*

D **Differentiate: Extra Support** Complete the interactive chart as a group or class. Provide students with the ideas and achievements. Then, ask them to sort the list into the appropriate column according to the Enlightenment thinker for which it corresponds.

Summarize Ask students how the political philosophies of the *philosophes* helped to shift political thought by creating new assumptions about the proper use of power and the attributes of a just government. *(Possible answer: They proposed that a government's power was dependent upon the consent of the governed, that government should have limited power and that its power should be separated by a system of checks and balances, that the goal of government was material well-being and social justice, that the purpose of government was to protect natural rights, and that the people have the right to overthrow the government when it fails.)*

DIGITAL TEXT 4
New Economic Ideas

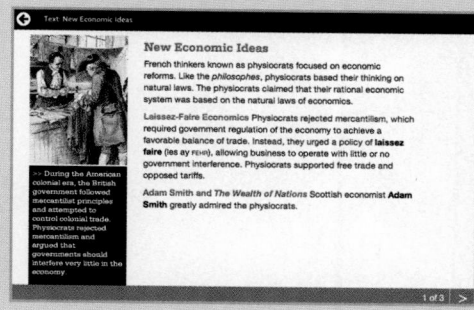

DIGITAL TEXT 5
Spread of Enlightenment Ideas

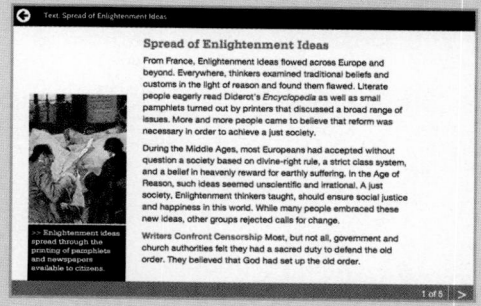

Objective 3: Summarize the economic ideas of the physiocrats and Adam Smith.

Quick Instruction

Project the image of the 1700s marketplace from the Text. Explain to students that natural law could be applied to economics. Introduce the lesson by asking students to predict how natural law could apply to economics. Explain that mercantilists favored government regulation and believed in building wealth through trade, while physiocrats opposed government regulation and believed in building wealth through land productivity. Economist Adam Smith built upon these ideas with his ideas about the **free-enterprise system**. *(economic system in which the free market regulates business activity with minimal government interference)*

Further Instruction

Project and discuss the questions from the Interactive Reading Notepad for New Economic Ideas. Help students identify the contributions of Adam Smith and the characteristics of the free enterprise system. Discuss how Adam Smith believed that the free market should be allowed to regulate business activity with minimal government interference, and that the economy should be ruled by the market forces of supply and demand. Review Smith's argument from *The Wealth of Nations* that the market will create a balance between supply and demand that affects the quantity of products and services available as well as their prices.

Summarize What are the characteristics of the free enterprise system? *(a free market in which the government has minimal interference with business activity)*

Apply Concepts According to Smith, a characteristic of the free enterprise system is that the quantity and prices of goods and services are dependent upon demand. Smith argued that as the supply of a product increases but demand remains unchanged, prices fall. What will happen if supply decreases but demand increases? *(The price will rise.)*

Objective 4: Describe how Enlightenment ideas spread and influenced the arts.

Quick Instruction

Project the image of the woman handing out pamphlets from the Text. Discuss how information and ideas have spread throughout history thus far. Ask students how the spread of ideas during the Enlightenment challenged preexisting institutions.

The Enlightenment

DIGITAL TEXT 6

Arts and Literature of the Enlightenment

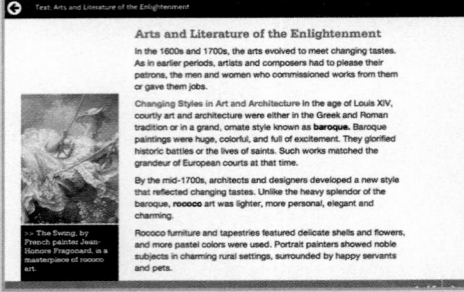

INTERACTIVE GALLERY

Music of the Enlightenment

Further Instruction

Project the questions in the Interactive Reading Notepad and discuss answers as a class. Ask students to predict why the government and church authorities would want to censor the new ideas of the Enlightenment. Explain the ways in which Enlightenment ideas spread. Review how government restricted access to information by banning books and imprisoning writers. Discuss how the *philosophes* disguised their ideas in works of fiction and exchanged ideas in private at salons to try to avoid censorship.

Summarize Why would people defend the old order? *(Many government and Church officials felt they had a sacred duty to defend the old order that God had established.)*

Objective 4: Describe how Enlightenment ideas spread and influenced the arts.

Quick Instruction

Interactive Gallery: Music of the Enlightenment Project the interactive gallery on the whiteboard. Introduce the activity by explaining that music reflects the history of the cultures in which it is produced. Ask students to listen to the audio selections. Discuss the characteristics of the music and how it differed from the heavy, ornamental music of the Baroque period. Ask students to identify an example of music from this period that transcended Enlightenment culture and expressed universal themes. *(Possible answer: All these composers remain popular. Handel's Messiah reflects universal themes of joy and celebration.)*

Further Instruction

After completing the activity, project and discuss the Interactive Reading Notepad questions from the text, Arts and Literature of the Enlightenment. Discuss how people's taste in art changed as the ideas of the Enlightenment spread. Explain the differences between baroque and rococo styles. *(Rococo art moved away from religion and, unlike the heavy splendor of the baroque, was lighter, elegant, and charming.)* Point out that the middle class emerged as a new audience for the arts because they could now afford to attend operas and commission works of music and art. Their tastes were different than that of the royal court, and the music and art reflected this new influence.

ACTIVE CLASSROOM

After completing the activity, ask students to break into pairs to discuss the music selections. Have students each do a Quick Write activity in which they take 30 seconds to write their observations about the music they listened to. Once they are finished, ask them how the music reflected the Enlightenment period. *(There was a transition in music from the baroque style to rococo. An elegant style of music known as "classical" followed. Also, music was accessible to more of the general public.)* Then have them compare it to popular music today. *(Answers will vary, but could compare instruments used or the fact that classical music is typically instrumental in nature.)*

DIGITAL TEXT 7

The Enlightened Despots

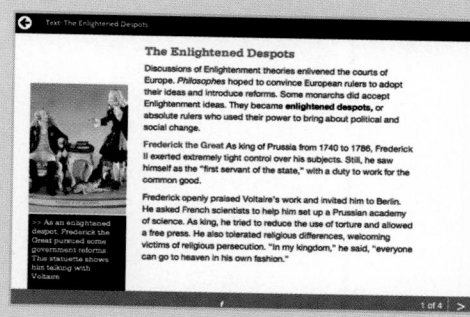

Text: The Enlightened Despots

The Enlightened Despots

Discussions of Enlightenment theories enlivened the courts of Europe. *Philosophes* hoped to convince European rulers to adopt their ideas and introduce reforms. Some monarchs did accept Enlightenment ideas. They became **enlightened despots**, or absolute rulers who used their power to bring about political and social change.

Frederick the Great As king of Prussia from 1740 to 1786, Frederick II exerted extremely tight control over his subjects. Still, he saw himself as the "first servant of the state," with a duty to work for the common good.

Frederick openly praised Voltaire's work and invited him to Berlin. He asked French scientists to help him set up a Prussian academy of science. As king, he tried to reduce the use of torture and allowed a free press. He also tolerated religious differences, welcoming victims of religious persecution. "In my kingdom," he said, "everyone can go to heaven in his own fashion."

>> As an enlightened despot, Frederick the Great pursued some government reforms. This statuette shows him talking with Voltaire

1 of 4

Objective 5: Understand the role of enlightened despots.

Quick Instruction

Project the image of Catherine the Great from the Text on the whiteboard. Introduce the section by discussing the absolute rulers who used their power to bring about political changes. Review the reforms enacted by enlightened despots and their goals in affecting change. *(Frederick the Great of Prussia, reduced the use of torture, allowed free press, made government more efficient, tolerated religious differences; Catherine II of Russia, limited reforms in law and government, abolished torture, established religious tolerance, granted nobles a charter of rights; Maria Theresa of Austria, improved peasants' way of life; and Joseph II of Austria, supported religious equality for Protestants and Jews, sold the property of monasteries and gave funds to those who helped the poor or sick, abolished serfdom.)*

Further Instruction

Explain to students that some rulers who believed in absolute power also saw value in political and social reform. Because the *philosophes* wanted reform, they tried to persuade rulers to accept their ideas, and the rulers had the power to effect change. Ask students to offer speculations on the rulers' motivations for accepting the philosophes' ideas. *(Answers will vary, but students may say that rulers might be motivated toward reform because they believed it would keep them in power. Others might respond that the rulers believed in a more just society.)*

Analyze Information What did Fredrick the Great mean when he said, "In my kingdom, everyone can go to heaven in his own fashion"? *(He was referring to freedom of religion.)*

Predict Consequences What actions might peasants take as they learn more about ideas such as equality? *(Possible answer: Peasants might begin to desire or expect more equality or perhaps protest or revolt to fight for equality.)*

The Enlightenment

▊ SYNTHESIZE

DIGITAL ACTIVITY
Enlightenment Ideas: Then and Now

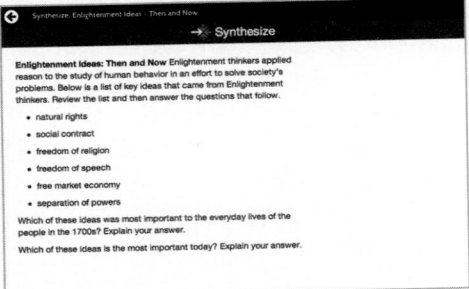

Remind students of the Topic Essential Question: How much power should the government have? Then, project the Synthesize activity on the whiteboard. Introduce the activity by pointing out that each of the bullet points can be related to the power of government. Review the key ideas in the list. Ask students to discuss their opinions regarding the importance of each. Then have volunteers give their opinions on which one is the most important in the list.

Draw Conclusions How did ideas of a "just society" change during the Enlightenment? How might these ideas lead to the development of a new form of government? *(Enlightenment thinkers said a just society should ensure justice before the law and happiness for the people. This was not true of the old governmental and social system, which was based on divine-right rule and a strict class structure.)*

▊ DEMONSTRATE

LESSON QUIZ
Lesson Quiz and Class Discussion Board

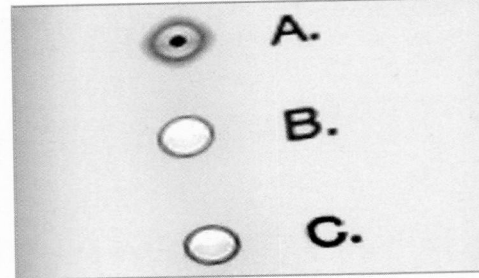

Assign the online Lesson Quiz for this lesson if you haven't already done so. Students will be offered automatic remediation or enrichment based on their score.

Pose these questions to the class on the Discussion Board:

In The Enlightenment, you learned about how new scientific methods inspired thinkers to apply natural law to human behavior. Both political philosophers and economists took the concept of natural law and used it to explain what they saw as problems in government and the economy. As people questioned old ways of thinking about society, changes in the arts took place as well.

Predict Consequences How might Enlightenment thinkers later inspire revolutionaries? *(By introducing new ideas on liberty and government, Enlightenment thinkers inspired revolutionaries to question what existed and strive for a better, more just, society and system of government.)*

Compare and Contrast Salons originated in the 1600s with a group of noblewomen and a few friends. How had salons changed by the 1700s, and why was this change significant? *(Possible answers: By the 1700s, middle-class citizens began to attend salons. They were now able to meet and discuss ideas with the nobility on equal footing and became a major force in the spread of Enlightenment ideas.)*

Topic Inquiry
Have students continue their investigations for the Topic Inquiry.

PEARSON realize™

www.PearsonRealize.com
Access your Digital Lesson

The American Revolution

Supporting English Language Learners

Use with Digital Text 1, **Britain Becomes a Global Power.**

Reading

Tell students that they will be using the third paragraph from the text *Britain Becomes a Global Power* for this activity. This section is titled "George III Takes Power." Have students demonstrate their understanding of how quotation marks are used in the context of this paragraph.

Beginning Begin by explaining the role of quotation marks in printed text. Ask students to skim the paragraph and point to the two quotation marks that frame the sentence, *"George, go be a king!"* Once students are able to identify the quotation marks, expressively read the paragraph to demonstrate how the quotation marks affect the reading of the text. Instruct students to listen to the paragraph with their eyes closed and to raise their hands when they think the quotation has begun, and to lower them when they believe the quotation has ended. Then ask each student to read the sentence containing the quotation aloud for the instructor.

Intermediate Have students skim the paragraph and point out the location of the quotation marks. Explain that quotation marks are used to indicate a word, phrase, or statement spoken by a specific person. Then have students read the paragraph aloud to a partner, paying special attention to the quotation.

Advanced Have students read the paragraph silently to themselves first, then aloud to a partner. Before students begin reading, explain the role of quotation marks in this paragraph. Explain that the quotation marks indicate that another voice, separate from the narrator, is speaking.

Advanced High Have students read the paragraph aloud to the group. Before reading, have students work together with a partner to discuss the role of quotation marks in this paragraph. Students should understand that the quotation marks indicate that another voice, one separate from the narrator, is speaking.

Use with Digital Text 3, **Discontent in the Colonies.**

Speaking

Tell students that many changes that occurred throughout history were the result of a group of people who were unhappy about their circumstances. The American colonists were no different. Many colonists felt that they were not being properly represented in Parliament. Eventually, this discontent led to a revolution.

Beginning Read the text aloud to students. Then ask students to identify phrases and sections of the text that describe the complaints of American colonists. Support students as needed with visual supports and definitions of unfamiliar words.

Intermediate Read the section with students. Ask students to identify phrases in the text that describe the complaints of American colonists. Then, using those phrases, students should turn to a partner and describe those complaints in a brief conversation.

Advanced Have a student volunteer read the text aloud to the group. Provide support to aid in student understanding as necessary. Then have students describe the complaints of the American colonists to a partner, using information from the text to support their descriptions.

Advanced High Have students read the section individually. Then have each student describe one complaint to the rest of the class. Students should be prepared to describe this complaint in detail and answer any questions posed by other students.

▣ Differentiate Instruction

Use the Differentiated Instruction notes throughout the lesson plan to support the varied skill sets, levels of readiness, and interests in the mixed-ability classroom.

Challenge These notes include suggestions for expanding the activity for advanced students.

On-Level These notes include suggestions for modifying the activity to address different interests or learning styles.

Extra Support These notes include ideas for providing more scaffolding or reading spuport.

Special Needs These notes provide ideas for adapting instruction to support the needs of various special needs students.

■ NOTES

The American Revolution

Objectives

Objective 1: Describe how Britain became a global power.

Objective 2: Understand the events and ideas leading up to the American Revolution, including the impact of the Enlightenment.

Objective 3: Summarize key events of the American Revolution.

Objective 4: Identify the political and legal ideas in the Declaration of Independence and the United States Constitution.

LESSON 5 ORGANIZER		PACING: APPROX. 1 PERIOD, .5 BLOCKS			
				RESOURCES	
		OBJECTIVES	**PACING**	**Online**	**Print**
Connect					
	DIGITAL START UP ACTIVITY **The Unalienable Rights of Citizens**		5 min.	●	
Investigate					
	DIGITAL TEXT 1 **Britain Becomes a Global Power**	Objective 1	10 min.	●	●
	DIGITAL TEXT 2 **The British Colonies in America**		10 min.	●	●
	DIGITAL TEXT 3 **Discontent in the Colonies**	Objective 2	10 min.	●	●
	INTERACTIVE IMAGE **From Words to Action—Ideology in the American Revolution**		10 min.	●	
	DIGITAL TEXT 4 **The American Revolution**	Objective 3	10 min.	●	●
	DIGITAL TEXT 5 **The United States Constitution**	Objective 4	10 min.	●	●
	INTERACTIVE CHART **Checks and Balances**		10 min.	●	
Synthesize					
	DIGITAL ACTIVITY **The United States Constitution**		5 min.	●	
Demonstrate					
	LESSON QUIZ **Lesson Quiz and Class Discussion Board**		10 min.	●	

■ CONNECT

DIGITAL START UP ACTIVITY
The Unalienable Rights of Citizens

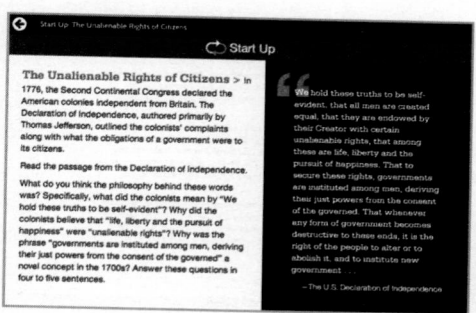

Project the Start Up Activity Ask students to answer these questions as they enter and get settled: What did the colonists mean by "We hold these truths to be self-evident"? Why did the colonists believe that "life, liberty and the pursuit of happiness" were "unalienable rights"? Why was the phrase "governments are instituted among men, deriving their just powers from the consent of the governed" a novel concept in the 1700s? *(Answers will vary but should point out that these words reflect their belief that the purpose of government is to protect its citizens' basic rights and that government gets its power from the people who create it.)*

Aa **Vocabulary Development:** Use the Interactive Reading Notepad to preview the Key Terms and Academic Vocabulary in this Lesson with students.

⇅ FLIP IT!
Assign the Flipped Video for this lesson.

■ STUDENT EDITION PRINT PAGES: 460–465

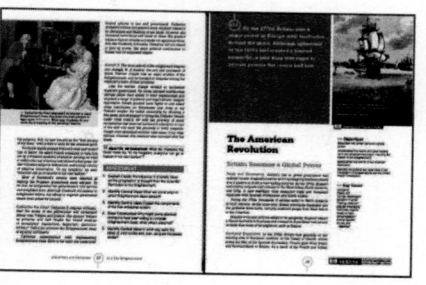

■ INVESTIGATE

DIGITAL TEXT 1
Britain Becomes a Global Power

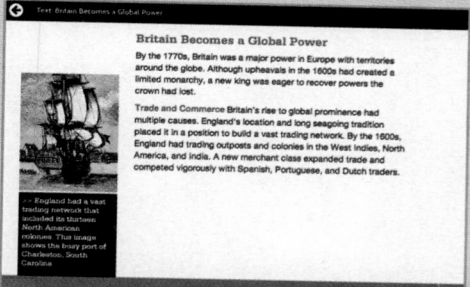

Objective 1: Describe how Britain became a global power.

Quick Instruction
Explain to students that Britain was a world power on the eve of the American Revolution. Its king, George III, was eager to recover the powers the monarchy had lost during the Glorious Revolution. With the help of his friends in Parliament, George III began introducing polices that would prove disastrous to Britain, especially in relation to its North American colonies. Colonists eventually sought rights that were equal to those of British citizens.

D **Differentiate: Challenge/Gifted** After asking students to describe the impact Great Britain had on the world, have them write a letter to George III explaining their views on Britain's status as a world power and its impact on its overseas colonies. Remind students that their letters should show evidence from the Text that illustrates the causes of the American Revolution.

ELL Use the ELL activity described in the ELL chart.

DIGITAL TEXT 2
The British Colonies in America

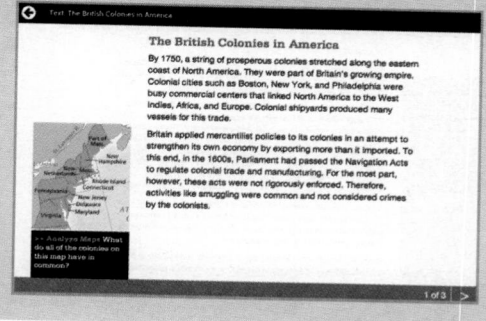

Further Instruction
Point out to students that by the mid-1700s, the colonies were home to diverse religious and ethnic groups. Wealthy landowners and merchants dominated government and society, but class differences were less rigid than those in Europe. Colonists felt free to discuss politics and other topics. Their colonial assemblies had a great deal of control over local affairs. Colonists began to feel entitled to the rights of English citizens.

Hypothesize How might having more local control over colonial affairs have changed colonists' ideas about their rights compared with those of British citizens? *(Sample response: Colonists probably began to feel that they should have the same rights as those of British citizens because they were part of the British colonies. Having local control over affairs gave them direct experience with making decisions about government.)*

Discuss Have students evaluate the impact of Britain's rise as a global power. Ask them to identify how its policies might have affected the ideas of equality and liberty in the American colonies. *(Students might say that Americans felt that their rights and liberties as English citizens were being violated because of England's colonial policies.)*

The American Revolution

DIGITAL TEXT 3

Discontent in the Colonies

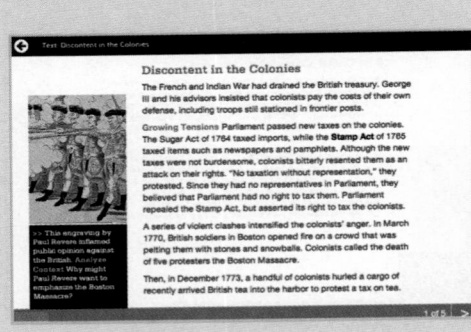

INTERACTIVE IMAGE

From Words to Action— Ideology in the American Revolution

DIGITAL TEXT 4

The American Revolution

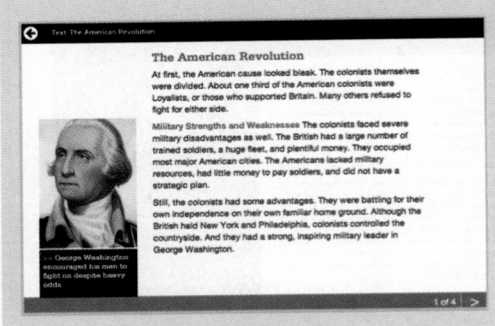

Objective 2: Understand the events and ideas leading up to the American Revolution and the Declaration of Independence.

Quick Instruction

Interactive Image: From Words to Action—Ideology in the American Revolution Project the Interactive Image on a whiteboard, and click through all the hotspots so students can read about the philosophical beliefs of several of the country's founders. Explain how the ideas of the Enlightenment, coupled with the background of each individual, gave rise to American independence and the formation of a government that derives its power from the people.

ACTIVE CLASSROOM

Ask students to reflect on the meaning of "liberty" and create a collage of images that depict the concept. Have students post their "graffiti" on the board so they can discuss similarities and differences as a group.

ELL Use the ELL activity described in the ELL chart.

Further Instruction

Project the questions in the Interactive Reading Notepad and have students answer as they progress through the text.

Explain how the political philosophies of individuals, such as Thomas Jefferson, impacted the political and legal ideas contained in the Declaration of Independence. *(Students might answer that Jefferson and others believed that it was important to put in the Declaration the philosophy that people are by nature equally free and independent with inherent political and legal rights. They also believed governments existed only through the will of the people. When a government fails to protects its citizens' rights, such as the right to have a say in government or the right to trial by jury, the people have a right to change their government.)*

Apply Concepts How did the Enlightenment concept of popular sovereignty influence the American Revolution? *(Students might answer that the founders were influenced by John Locke's idea that citizens have the right to alter or abolish unjust governments because governments derived their power from the people.)*

Objective 3: Summarize key events of the American Revolution.

Quick Instruction

Remind students that times were often bleak for the American army during the Revolution. However, George Washington's leadership held the army together until the French ultimately came to America's aid.

D Differentiate: Challenge/Gifted Have students create a storyboard to represent key military events in the American Revolution. Ask them to either sketch the storyboard by hand or use a computer program.

Further Instruction

Project the Interactive Reading Notepad questions. Review the questions and answers with students.

Ask: How did such ideas as human rights, liberty, and equality influence the American patriots? *(Students might say that American patriots believed that British policies, especially as they related to trade and taxes, were unfair.)*

DIGITAL TEXT 5

The United States Constitution

INTERACTIVE CHART

Checks and Balances

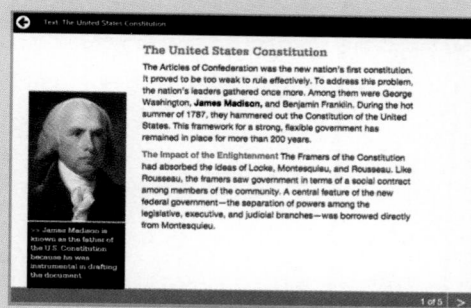

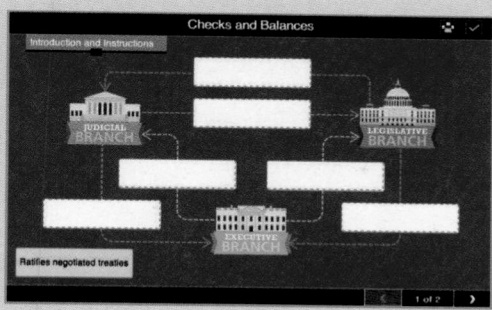

Objective 4: Identify the political and legal ideas in the United States Constitution, including the impact of the Enlightenment.

Quick Instruction

Interactive Chart: Checks and Balances Project the drag and drop activity onto a whiteboard. Remind students that the U.S. Constitution was written because the Articles of Confederation were weak. The framers replaced the system under the Articles with a federal republic in which power was divided between the federal, or national, government and the states. Explain to students that one of the central political ideas in the new Constitution was the idea separation of powers among the legislative, executive, and judicial branches, with checks and balances to limit the power of each branch. Have students study the role each branch of government plays in the U.S. government by participating as a group to complete the activity.

📷 ACTIVE CLASSROOM

Ask students to assume the role of reporters covering the Constitutional Convention. Have them write headlines that capture the outcome. Tell them to make sure that their headlines identify the impact of the convention's proceedings, such as the creation of the three branches of government. Then, have them pass their headlines to a partner for him or her to review.

Further Instruction

The United States Constitution Core Reading and Interactive Reading Notepad Project the Interactive Reading Notepad questions. Review the questions and answers with students.

Then tell students that the Declaration of Independence and the Constitution put forth the idea that everyone holds certain rights. The Bill of Rights states that citizens have basic rights that the government must protect, including freedom of religion, speech, and the press. It also protects the right to trial by jury. Point out that in 1789, most countries in Europe were ruled by hereditary absolute monarchs who did not give people these rights. The United States became an inspiration to Europeans, who took up the cry for liberty and freedom.

Ask: How did the ideals of democracy and human rights put forth in the Declaration and the Constitution impact people in other parts of the world outside of the United States? *(The idea that government is created by people, who by nature have certain basic human rights, spread to other parts of the world, including France and Latin America. People overthrew oppressive regimes and tried to form their own constitutional governments.)*

Discuss How did the ideas of the Enlightenment impact the creation of the Bill of Rights? *(Students might answer that the ideals of the Enlightenment centered on individual rights, freedom, and liberty. As a result, the U.S. Constitution eventually contained the Bill of Rights, which guaranteed to U.S. citizens certain rights that the government could not abridge.)*

Tell students that in addition to the ideas of Locke, Montesquieu, and Rousseau, the framers were influenced by the ideas of English jurist Sir William Blackstone. Blackstone's ideas about law played a foundational role in the American legal system.

Express Ideas Clearly Describe why a system of law is important in a democracy. *(Students might say that laws help protect the rights and freedoms of citizens and punish those who violate others' rights and freedoms.)*

Finally, tell students that U.S. citizens also have many responsibilities. They are expected to vote, sit on juries, and keep informed on important local and national issues. Noncitizens who reside in the United States also enjoy its constitutional rights and protections and have responsibilities such as paying taxes and abiding by local, state, and federal laws.

Ask: Why would noncitizens be protected by American constitutional rights? *(Answers will vary but students may mention that because American constitutional rights are those that the framers believed everyone by nature should have, those rights are applied to anyone who lives in this country.)*

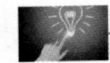

The American Revolution

■ SYNTHESIZE

DIGITAL ACTIVITY
The United States Constitution

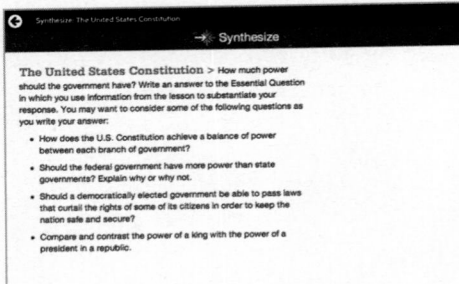

Ask students to recall the Topic Essential Question, "How much power should the government have?" Using the Take a Stand strategy, break students into equal groups of four or five people. Tell students they are going to debate the powers of the federal government. Half of the groups will debate the merits of a strong federal government; the other half will debate the merits of a weak federal government. Tell them to consider these questions: Should the government be able to pass laws curtailing a person's civil rights in a national emergency? Should state governments be allowed to nullify, or not follow, federal laws that the states think unfair? Should the federal government dictate policy when it is in the national interest?

■ DEMONSTRATE

LESSON QUIZ
Lesson Quiz and Class Discussion Board

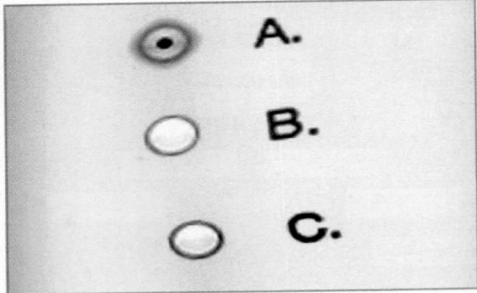

Assign the online Lesson Quiz for this lesson if you haven't already done so. Students will be offered automatic remediation or enrichment based on their score.

Pose these questions to the class on the Discussion Board:

In "The American Revolution," you read about why the Americans sought to break ties with Britain. You also read how the ideals of the Enlightenment fueled the rebellion and influenced the Declaration of Independence, the U.S. Constitution, and the Bill of Rights.

Predict Consequences Do you think the American Revolution was inevitable, or do you think it could have been avoided? *(Students might say that had Britain taken a more moderate approach to running its North American colonies, the rebellion might never have happened. Others might say that America was so far removed from Britain [culturally and economically], that the war was inevitable.)*

Express Ideas Clearly What were some of the motivating factors behind the framers' decision to divide equally the power of the government between the three branches of government? *(Students might say that by separating the government's powers it would be impossible for one person or group to rule with absolute power.)*

Topic Inquiry
Have students continue their investigations for the Topic Inquiry.

The French Revolution Begins

Supporting English Language Learners

Use with Digital Text 1, **The Old Regime in France.**

Reading
Have students pre-read the red headings in *The Old Regime in France* and examine a political cartoon to identify the three estates and the groups that belong to each. Have students create a chart depicting their findings and instruct them to read the text to check and correct their work.

Beginning Have students read each red heading in *The Old Regime in France*. Then help them examine the political cartoon and identify the social classes represented. On the board, write *First Estate, Second Estate, Third Estate* in one column and *nobility, bourgeoisie, peasants,* and *clergy in another*. Then have students match each group with the estate to which it belongs.

Intermediate Have small groups read each red heading in *The Old Regime in France*, and examine the political cartoon to determine the different social classes depicted. On the board, write *First Estate, Second Estate, Third Estate* in one column and *nobility, bourgeoisie, peasants,* and *clergy* in another. Have students match each group with the estate to which it belongs.

Advanced Have students skim each red heading in *The Old Regime in France*, and examine the political cartoon to identify the three different social classes depicted. Have students create a graphic organizer that lists the estates and the groups that belong to each. Ask students to reread *The Old Regime in France* and to check their work and add details to their graphic organizer.

Advanced High Have students examine the political cartoon, and use it to identify and name the three different social classes depicted by the cartoon. Have students create a graphic organizer that lists the estates and the groups that belong to each. Ask students to reread *The Old Regime in France* to check their work.

Use with Digital Text 3, **Louis XVI Calls the Estates-General.**

Speaking
Read aloud or have students read *Louis XVI Calls the Estates-General*. Have students explain to the group the events that led up to and occurred during the meeting.

Beginning After reading *Louis XVI Calls the Estates-General* to students, ask students to explain the Tennis Court Oath using the following sentence frames.

The Third Estate wanted to meet as a single body because _____.

The Tennis Court Oath was taken to make sure that _____.

Intermediate After reading *Louis XVI Calls the Estates-General* to students, ask students to explain the Tennis Court Oath using the following sentence frames.

The Third Estate wanted _____.

The Tennis Court Oath was _____.

Advanced Have students read *Louis XVI Calls the Estates-General*. Then have students work in small groups to discuss and explain why the Third Estate felt that it was not being properly represented in the Estates-General and how this led to the Tennis Court Oath.

Advanced High Have students read *Louis XVI Calls the Estates-General*. Then have students prepare a short presentation explaining why the Third Estate felt that it was not being properly represented in the Estates-General. Students should include how this led to the Tennis Court Oath and why it was so important to French citizens.

▶ Differentiate Instruction

Use the Differentiated Instruction notes throughout the lesson plan to support the varied skill sets, levels of readiness, and interests in the mixed-ability classroom.

Challenge These notes include suggestions for expanding the activity for advanced students.

On-Level These notes include suggestions for modifying the activity to address different interests or learning styles.

Extra Support These notes include ideas for providing more scaffolding or reading spuport.

Special Needs These notes provide ideas for adapting instruction to support the needs of various special needs students.

■ NOTES

Topic ⑫ Lesson 6

The French Revolution Begins

Objectives

Objective 1: Describe the social divisions of France's old order.

Objective 2: Trace the causes of the French Revolution.

Objective 3: Identify the reforms enacted by the National Assembly, including the Declaration of the Rights of Man and the Citizen.

LESSON 6 ORGANIZER		PACING: APPROX. 1 PERIOD, .5 BLOCKS			
				RESOURCES	
		OBJECTIVES	**PACING**	**Online**	**Print**
Connect					
DIGITAL START UP ACTIVITY **The Rights of Citizens**			5 min.	●	
Investigate					
DIGITAL TEXT 1 **The Old Regime in France**		Objective 1	10 min.	●	●
INTERACTIVE CARTOON **Characteristics of the Three Estates**			10 min.	●	
DIGITAL TEXT 2 **France's Economic Crisis**		Objective 2	10 min.	●	●
DIGITAL TEXTS 3, 4, AND 5 **Louis XVI Calls the Estates-General, Storming the Bastille, Revolts in Paris and the Provinces**			10 min.	●	●
DIGITAL TEXTS 6 AND 7 **The National Assembly, Reforms of the National Assembly**		Objective 3	10 min.	●	●
INTERACTIVE DOCUMENT **Declaration of the Rights of Man**			10 min.	●	
Synthesize					
DIGITAL ACTIVITY **Events of the French Revolution**			5 min.	●	
Demonstrate					
LESSON QUIZ **Lesson Quiz and Class Discussion Board**			10 min.	●	

PEARSON
realize™
www.PearsonRealize.com

Go online to access additional resources including:
Primary Sources • Biographies • Supreme Court cases •
21st Century Skill Tutorials • Maps • Graphic Organizers.

CONNECT

DIGITAL START UP ACTIVITY
The Rights of Citizens

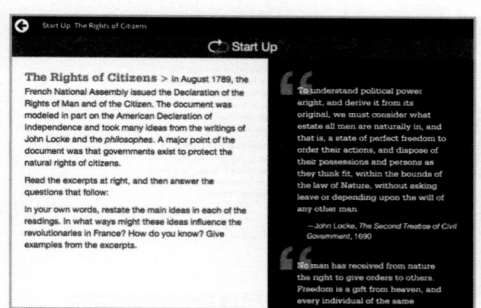

Project the Start Up Activity Ask students to answer the questions as they enter and get settled: In your own words, restate the main ideas in each of the texts. In what ways might these ideas influence the revolutionaries in France? How do you know? Give examples from the excerpts.

Then have students share their ideas with another student, either in class or through a chat room or blog.

Tell students that both authors see individual freedom as a natural right. Such ideas greatly influenced French revolutionaries.

Aa Vocabulary Development: Use the Interactive Reading Notepad to preview the Key Terms and Academic Vocabulary in this Lesson with students.

⇅ FLIP IT!

Assign the Flipped Video for this lesson.

■ STUDENT EDITION PRINT PAGES: 466–474

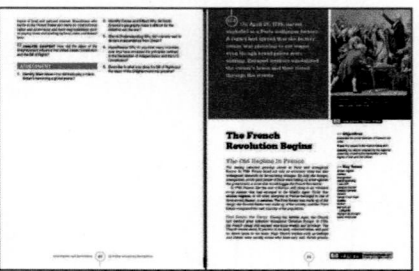

■ INVESTIGATE

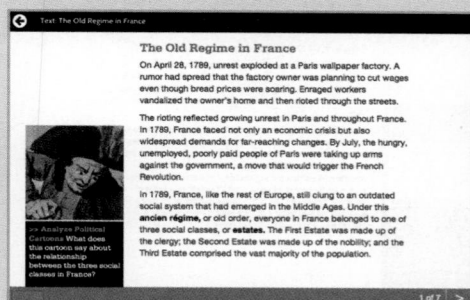

DIGITAL TEXT 1
The Old Regime in France

INTERACTIVE CARTOON
Characteristics of the Three Estates

Objective 1: Describe the social divisions of France's old order.

Quick Instruction
Project the interactive cartoon of the Three Estates on a whiteboard. Click through each hotspot, and read the characteristics of each estate. Have students discuss what these characteristics might mean for French society.

👥 ACTIVE CLASSROOM

Organize students into groups. Have groups look again at the political cartoon of France's Three Estates. Then ask them to create speech bubbles on sticky notes to reflect what each of the characters in the cartoon might be saying. Tell them to post their "graffiti" on the whiteboard, next to the appropriate characters. Tell students to look at each group's work and then discuss the similarities and differences of the captions as a group.

D Differentiate: Challenge/Gifted Using the information contained in the Interactive Cartoon, divide the class into groups representing each of France's pre-revolutionary three estates. Give each group some sticky notes. Have groups spend three minutes writing down their response to this question: What do you think life was like for a member of your group in pre-revolutionary France? Have students post their sticky notes next to the previous exercise on the board. Discuss the similarities and differences among the groups as a class.

ELL Use the ELL activity described in the ELL chart.

Further Instruction
Editable Presentation Use the Editable Presentation to present the main ideas for this Core Text.

Project the questions from the Interactive Reading Notepad. Go through the list of questions, and call on students to answer them.

Summarize Ask students to briefly describe how a desire for equality and greater rights affected France's social classes in the years leading up to the Revolution. (*Students might say that the lower classes suffered the most from the social and economic inequality of pre-Revolutionary France. As a result, they would be in conflict with the upper classes, who generally wanted to continue the status quo.*)

The French Revolution Begins

DIGITAL TEXT 2
France's Economic Crisis

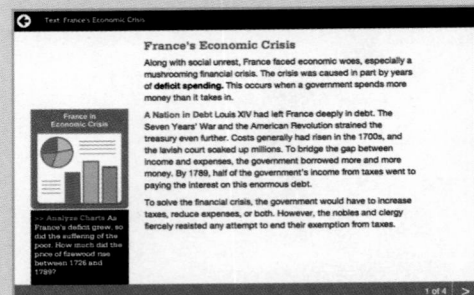

DIGITAL TEXT 3
Louis XVI Calls the Estates-General

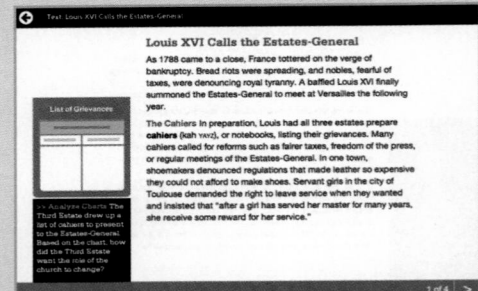

DIGITAL TEXT 4
Storming the Bastille

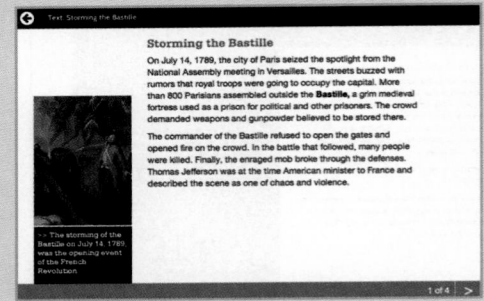

Objective 2: Trace the causes of the French Revolution.

Quick Instruction

Explain to students that France's pre-revolutionary government was deeply in debt due to years of deficit spending. To bridge the gap between income and expenses, the government of King Louis XVI borrowed heavily. The country's economic problems hurt the poor in France the most. Tell students that as the crisis deepened, the public demanded that the king summon the Estates-General in the hope that reforms might be enacted.

Analyze Data Project the chart "France in Economic Crisis." Ask students to study the chart and discuss these questions: How did the cost of certain products and the mounting national debt impact each of the three estates? Why would the French ask King Louis XVI to initiate economic reforms? Which group(s) do you think were impacted the most by rising prices?

Explain that Louis XVI called the Estates-General into session to deal with France's economic crisis. In June 1789, claiming to represent the people of France, members of the Third Estate declared themselves a National Assembly. Tell students that the National Assembly pushed for a just constitution. Explain that the situation in France was so tense that more than 800 Parisians challenged the power of the king when they stormed the Bastille, a prison in Paris.

D Differentiate: Challenge/Gifted Have students work with a partner to outline the main ideas in the texts, Storming the Bastille and Political Crisis and the Great Fear. Ask pairs to write the headings from their outlines on the whiteboard, and discuss the results as a class.

ELL Use the ELL activity described in the ELL chart.

Further Instruction

Discuss What role did taxes play in the discontent among members of French society prior to the Revolution? *(Taxes were mostly spent on debt from the Seven Years' War and the American Revolution, so the government had no money and needed to raise taxes; the nobles and the clergy opposed making them subject to taxes, which Louis XVI's adviser told him to do; those in the Third Estate who paid taxes demanded fairer taxes.)*

DIGITAL TEXT 5

Revolts in Paris and the Provinces

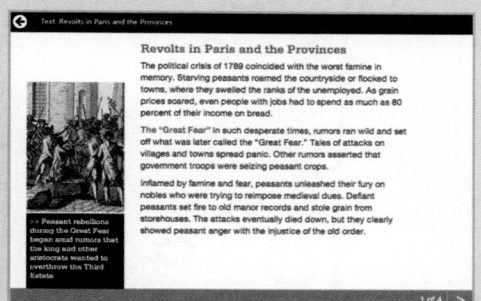

Text: Revolts in Paris and the Provinces

Revolts in Paris and the Provinces

The political crisis of 1789 coincided with the worst famine in memory. Starving peasants roamed the countryside or flocked to towns, where they swelled the ranks of the unemployed. As grain prices soared, even people with jobs had to spend as much as 80 percent of their income on bread.

The "Great Fear" In such desperate times, rumors ran wild and set off what was later called the "Great Fear." Tales of attacks on villages and towns spread panic. Other rumors asserted that government troops were seizing peasant crops.

Inflamed by famine and fear, peasants unleashed their fury on nobles who were trying to reimpose medieval dues. Defiant peasants set fire to old manor records and stole grain from storehouses. The attacks eventually died down, but they clearly showed peasant anger with the injustice of the old order.

>> Peasant rebellions during the Great Fear began amid rumors that the king and other aristocrats wanted to overthrow the Third Estate

1 of 4

Compare and Contrast Compare the crisis in pre-revolutionary France to the crisis in the American colonies prior to the American Revolution. What were the differences? What were the similarities? *(Students might say class divisions were not an issue during the American Revolution, which was based more on abuses of the British monarchy and the desire for self-rule. In France, decades of class division were one of the major reasons for the revolution. Both revolutions were influenced by the Enlightenment.)*

DIGITAL TEXT 6

The National Assembly

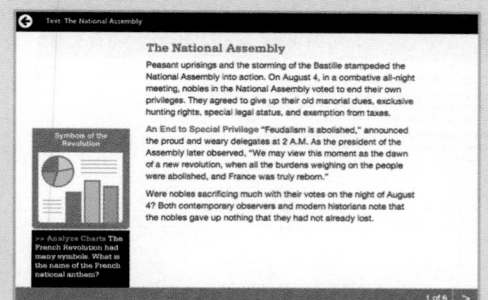

Text: The National Assembly

The National Assembly

Peasant uprisings and the storming of the Bastille stampeded the National Assembly into action. On August 4, in a combative all-night meeting, nobles in the National Assembly voted to end their own privileges. They agreed to give up their old manorial dues, exclusive hunting rights, special legal status, and exemption from taxes.

An End to Special Privilege "Feudalism is abolished," announced the proud and weary delegates at 2 A.M. As the president of the Assembly later observed, "We may view this moment as the dawn of a new revolution, when all the burdens weighing on the people were abolished, and France was truly reborn."

Were nobles sacrificing much with their votes on the night of August 4? Both contemporary observers and modern historians note that the nobles gave up nothing that they had not already lost.

Symbols of the Revolution

>> Analyze Charts The French Revolution had many symbols. What is the name of the French national anthem?

1 of 6

Objective 3: Identify the reforms enacted by the National Assembly, including the Declaration of the Rights of Man and the Citizen.

Quick Instruction

Interactive Document: Declaration of the Rights of Man and the Citizen Project the Interactive Document on the whiteboard. Have students click through the political and legal principles contained in the Declaration. Explain to students that at the height of the French Revolution, the Declaration put into words the Enlightenment ideas of political freedom and equality before the law.

DIGITAL TEXT 7

Reforms of the National Assembly

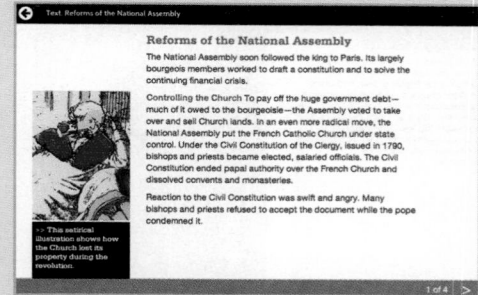

Text: Reforms of the National Assembly

Reforms of the National Assembly

The National Assembly soon followed the king to Paris. Its largely bourgeois members worked to draft a constitution and to solve the continuing financial crisis.

Controlling the Church To pay off the huge government debt—much of it owed to the bourgeoisie—the Assembly voted to take over and sell Church lands. In an even more radical move, the National Assembly put the French Catholic Church under state control. Under the Civil Constitution of the Clergy, issued in 1790, bishops and priests became elected, salaried officials. The Civil Constitution ended papal authority over the French Church and dissolved convents and monasteries.

Reaction to the Civil Constitution was swift and angry. Many bishops and priests refused to accept the document while the pope condemned it.

>> This satirical illustration shows how the Church lost its property during the revolution.

1 of 4

📽 ACTIVE CLASSROOM

Divide the class into equal groups. Have each group discuss and rank what each believes are the most important political and legal ideas contained in the Declaration of the Rights of Man and the Citizen. When they are finished, ask each group to provide a justification for the ranking decisions they made. Poll the class to see if there is agreement.

Identify Central Issues How did the Declaration of the Rights of Man and the Citizen impact the rights of French men? *(It made all male citizens equal before the law.)*

The French Revolution Begins

INTERACTIVE DOCUMENT
Declaration of the Rights of Man

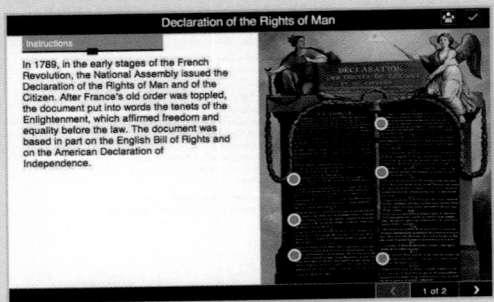

Further Instruction

Compare and Contrast Ask students to recall what they learned about the freedoms protected under the new U.S. Constitution, such as freedom of speech, in the lesson on the American Revolution. Have students review the Text to discern the role religion played in post-revolutionary America versus its role in revolutionary France. How did each government deal with religion in its respective country? Why might these two countries' religious provisions be different? *(Answers will vary, but students might say that the U.S. Constitution's First Amendment prevented the government from supporting a particular religion, while in France, the clergy became employees of the state. The French state wanted to control the influence of religion and even banned public worship, whereas many American colonies were established because colonists were pursuing religious freedom.)*

▮ SYNTHESIZE

DIGITAL ACTIVITY
Events of the French Revolution

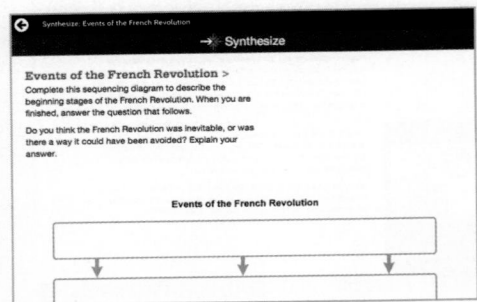

Project the graphic organizer from the Synthesize activity. Fill out the organizer with information as a class. *(The graphic organizer should include these stages: Louis XVI Calls the Estates-General; Tennis Court Oath; Storming the Bastille; Constitution of 1791.)* Ask students the critical-thinking question: Do you think the French Revolution was inevitable, or was there a way it could have been avoided? *(Answers will vary but might mention that if the king had not been ineffective with regard to economic challenges, the outcome might have been different.)*

Ask students to recall the Topic Essential Question, "How much power should the government have?" Project the infographic "Constitution of 1791." Ask students to rank each provision by what they believe is important in relation to government power. Discuss their answers as a class.

▮ DEMONSTRATE

LESSON QUIZ
Lesson Quiz and Class Discussion Board

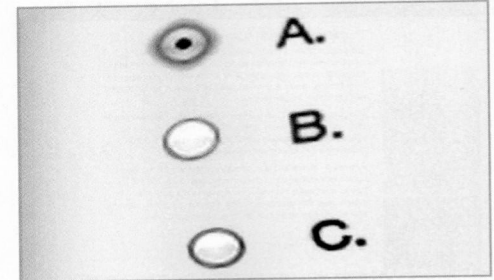

Assign the online Lesson Quiz for this lesson if you haven't already done so. Students will be offered automatic remediation or enrichment based on their score.

Pose these questions to the class on the Discussion Board:

In "The French Revolution," you read about why French revolutionaries wanted to overthrow the old order. You also read how the ideals of the Enlightenment and the American Revolution fueled the rebellion and ultimately changed French society.

Predict Consequences Do think that King Louis XVI could have enacted any social and economic reforms that might have prevented the Revolution? What might those reforms have been? *(Students might say more equitable taxation, equality under the law, and more of a say in the workings of government policy.)*

Summarize What impact did the influence of ideas such as liberty, freedom, human rights, and popular sovereignty have on the French Revolution? What specific role did the American Revolution play in the direction the French Revolution took? *(Students might say that the American Revolution was one of the first times in history that the ideals of the Enlightenment were put into practice. The French witnessed the outcome of the American Revolution, and as a result, they were determined to also create a government based on the ideals of liberty, freedom, and popular sovereignty.)*

Topic Inquiry
Have students continue their investigations for the Topic Inquiry.

A Radical Phase

Supporting English Language Learners

Use with Digital Text 2, **The Monarchy Is Abolished.**

Speaking

Point out that the way we speak changes based on our audience. For example, the way we describe something learned in school to our families is much different from the way we speak when giving a formal presentation to our class.

Beginning Say the following sentences aloud for students. Help students identify which sentences are formal and which are informal. Then work with students to adapt the informal sentences into formal sentences.

On a foggy morning in January 1793, Louis mounted a scaffold in a public square in Paris.

Soldiers beat on the drums.

A couple of minutes later, the king lost his head.

The executioner lifted the king's head by its hair and held it before the crowd.

Intermediate Say the following sentences aloud for students. Have students work in pairs to identify which sentences are formal and which are informal. Then have pairs adapt the informal sentences into formal sentences.

On a foggy morning in January 1793, Louis mounted a scaffold in a public square in Paris.

Soldiers beat on the drums.

A couple minutes later, the king lost his head.

The executioner lifted the king's head by its hair and held it before the crowd.

Advanced Have students read *The Monarchy Is Abolished*. Students should then turn to a partner and use informal language to explain the events surrounding Louis XIV's execution. Then have pairs work together to develop a short, formal summary of the king's death. Guide students' understanding of the difference between formal and informal language by providing support and examples when necessary.

Advanced High Have students read *The Monarchy Is Abolished*. Then have students work in small groups to informally discuss the events surrounding Louis XIV's execution. Ask students to work individually to create a short, formal presentation to describe how Louis XIV was executed. Listening students should provide ideas and support when more formal language is needed. Guide students' understanding of the difference between formal and informal language by providing support and examples when necessary.

Use with Digital Text 3, **The Reign of Terror.**

Reading

Have students work with linguistically accommodating materials and methods to help them in reading *The Reign of Terror*. Then have students summarize what they learned in English.

Beginning Read aloud (or provide) a translated version of the introductory paragraph of *The Reign of Terror* to students. Then read the same paragraph in English. Have students repeat each sentence after you read it aloud. Allow students to use the translation or ask for help to clarify the meanings of challenging vocabulary. Have students summarize the text using a word or phrase in English.

Intermediate Before reading aloud in English, provide students with a translated version of the introductory paragraph of *The Reign of Terror*. Then read the paragraph aloud in English, reading each sentence of the first paragraph of *The Reign of Terror* separately. Allow students to use the translation or ask for help to clarify the meanings of challenging vocabulary. Have students summarize the text in one sentence in English.

Advanced Read aloud the introductory paragraph of *The Reign of Terror*. Then have them read the paragraph aloud together. Have partners take turns reading *The Reign of Terror* aloud. Let students work with bilingual dictionaries to support their understanding of unfamiliar words. Then as a group write a two or three sentence summary of the text.

Advanced High Have students take turns reading *The Reign of Terror* aloud to a partner. Partners should listen to and correct any mistakes in pronunciation and pacing. Let students have access to a bilingual dictionary if needed. Then have partners write a brief summary of the text and read it to the group.

A Radical Phase

Objectives

Objective 1: Explain why the French Revolution entered a more radical phase.

Objective 2: Understand how radicals abolished the French monarchy.

Objective 3: Analyze the causes and course of the Reign of Terror.

Objective 4: Describe France under the Directory.

Objective 5: Identify how the French Revolution changed life in France.

LESSON 7 ORGANIZER		PACING: APPROX. 1 PERIOD, .5 BLOCKS			
				RESOURCES	
		OBJECTIVES	PACING	Online	Print
Connect					
DIGITAL START UP ACTIVITY **Violence in the Name of Revolution**			5 min.	●	
Investigate					
DIGITAL TEXT 1 **Radicals Gain Strength**		Objective 1	10 min.	●	●
DIGITAL TEXT 2 **The Monarchy Is Abolished**		Objective 2	10 min.	●	●
DIGITAL TEXT 3 **The Reign of Terror**		Objective 3	10 min.	●	●
INTERACTIVE GALLERY **The Reign of Terror**			10 min.	●	
DIGITAL TEXT 4 **Reaction and the Directory**		Objective 4	10 min.	●	●
DIGITAL TEXT **The Revolution Transforms France**		Objective 5	10 min.	●	●
INTERACTIVE TIMELINE **The French Revolution Enters a More Radical Phase**			10 min.	●	
Synthesize					
DIGITAL ACTIVITY **The Reign of Terror**			5 min.	●	
Demonstrate					
LESSON QUIZ **Lesson Quiz and Class Discussion Board**			10 min.	●	

CONNECT

DIGITAL START UP ACTIVITY

Violence in the Name of Revolution

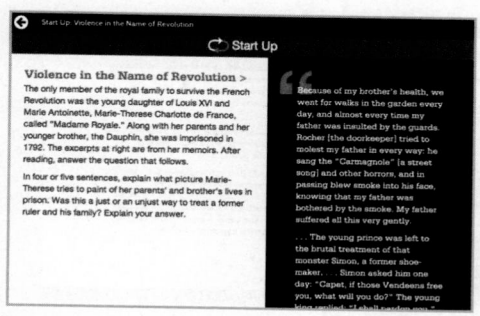

Project the Start Up Activity Ask students to read the writing prompt and question as they enter and get settled: In four or five sentences, explain what picture Marie-Therese tries to paint of her parents' and brother's lives in prison. Was this a just or an unjust way to treat a former ruler and his family? Explain your answer. *(Students' answers will vary, but some might choose to focus on the violence that the king's family faced, while others might focus on the injustices of the absolute monarchy.)*

Then have them share their ideas with another student, either in class or through a chat room or blog.

Aa Vocabulary Development: Use the Interactive Reading Notepad to preview the Key Terms and Academic Vocabulary in this Lesson with students.

⇅ FLIP IT!

Assign the Flipped Video for this lesson.

INVESTIGATE

DIGITAL TEXT 1

Radicals Gain Strength

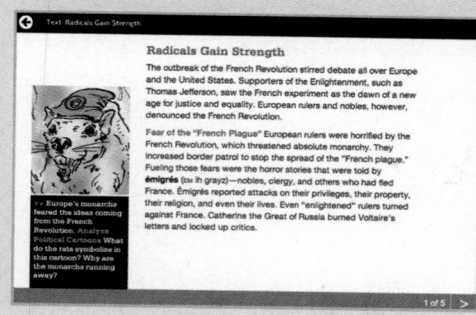

Objective 1: Explain why the French Revolution entered a more radical phase.

Quick Instruction

Explain to students that the French Revolution had taken a more radical turn by the summer of 1791. Tell students that by this time, the Revolution had stirred debate across Europe. While the monarchies of Europe condemned the Revolution, supporters of the Enlightenment applauded its reforms. They saw the French experiment as the dawn of a new age for justice and equality.

D Differentiate: Challenge/Gifted Ask students to act as an American tourist in France during the radical days of the Revolution. Have them write a letter home describing their feelings about what they are witnessing. Have them compare the French Revolution to the American Revolution, listing any differences or similarities.

Further Instruction

Project the questions provided in the Interactive Reading Notepad, and discuss answers to the questions as a class.

Analyze Images Project the "Radical Rats" cartoon from the text. Break the class into groups and have them study the political cartoon. Ask students this question: What was the cartoonist trying to say about the state of affairs in Europe during the radical phase of the French Revolution? *(The rats are marauding revolutionaries who are setting fire to the cities and chasing the monarchs out of power.)*

STUDENT EDITION PRINT
PAGES: 475–481

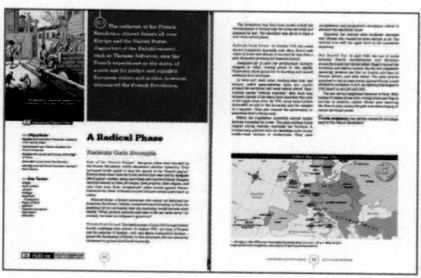

A Radical Phase

DIGITAL TEXT 2
The Monarchy Is Abolished

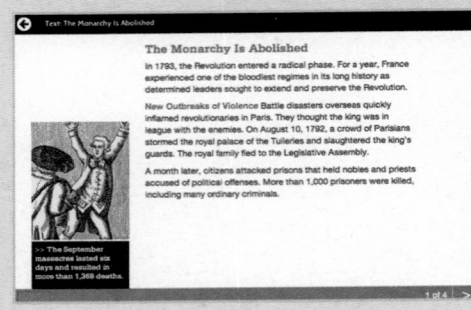

The Monarchy Is Abolished

In 1793, the Revolution entered a radical phase. For a year, France experienced one of the bloodiest regimes in its long history as determined leaders sought to extend and preserve the Revolution.

New Outbreaks of Violence Battle disasters overseas quickly inflamed revolutionaries in Paris. They thought the king was in league with the enemies. On August 10, 1792, a crowd of Parisians stormed the royal palace of the Tuileries and slaughtered the king's guards. The royal family fled to the Legislative Assembly.

A month later, citizens attacked prisons that held nobles and priests accused of political offenses. More than 1,000 prisoners were killed, including many ordinary criminals.

>> The September massacres lasted six days and resulted in more than 1,368 deaths.

DIGITAL TEXT 3
The Reign of Terror

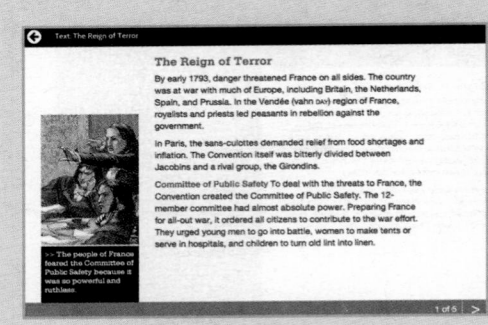

The Reign of Terror

By early 1793, danger threatened France on all sides. The country was at war with much of Europe, including Britain, the Netherlands, Spain, and Prussia. In the Vendée (vahn day) region of France, royalists and priests led peasants in rebellion against the government.

In Paris, the sans-culottes demanded relief from food shortages and inflation. The Convention itself was bitterly divided between Jacobins and a rival group, the Girondins.

Committee of Public Safety To deal with the threats to France, the Convention created the Committee of Public Safety. The 12-member committee had almost absolute power. Preparing France for all-out war, it ordered all citizens to contribute to the war effort. They urged young men to go into battle, women to make tents or serve in hospitals, and children to turn old lint into linen.

>> The people of France feared the Committee of Public Safety because it was so powerful and ruthless.

Objective 2: Understand how radicals abolished the French monarchy.

Quick Instruction
Remind students that the radicals of the French Revolution tried to export the ideals of the Revolution to other countries and attempted to destroy Europe's monarchies. Explain that by 1792, the radicals controlled the National Convention. One of the Convention's first moves was to abolish the monarchy and establish a republic.

ELL Use the ELL activity described in the ELL chart.

Further Instruction
Go through the Interactive Reading Notepad questions and discuss the answers with the class.

Support a Point of View with Evidence Project the image of Marie Antoinette from the text. Ask students to take a stand on the following question: Should France's revolutionaries have executed Louis XVI and his family—yes or no? Ask students to divide into two groups based on their answer and move to separate areas of the classroom. Ask students to talk with each other to compare their reasons for their answer. Ask a representative from each side to present and defend the group's point of view.

Apply Concepts What ideas of the Enlightenment did the National Assembly put into action in 1792? *(Students might answer that the National Assembly extended suffrage and also established a republic.)*

Objective 3: Analyze the causes and course of the Reign of Terror.

Quick Instruction
Project the Interactive Gallery on the whiteboard, and click through all the hotspots so students can become familiar with the Reign of Terror. Explain that in the fall of 1793 and well into 1794, the French Revolution took a radical turn. The Committee of Public Safety rounded up suspected persons, sentencing many to death for being a traitor to the Revolution.

👥 ACTIVE CLASSROOM
Pair students to complete this activity. One student should act as a foreign journalist in France interviewing Robespierre about the Reign of Terror. The other student should act as Robespierre. When the interview is over, have students share the questions and answers with the class.

ELL Use the ELL activity described in the ELL chart.

INTERACTIVE GALLERY

The Reign of Terror

DIGITAL TEXT 4

Reaction and the Directory

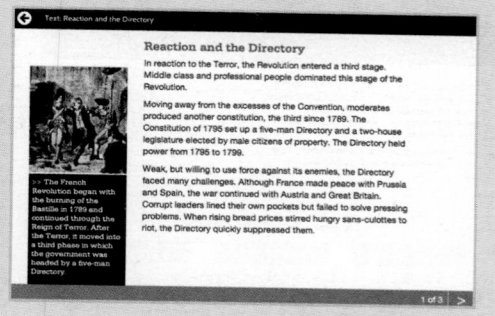

DIGITAL TEXT

The Revolution Transforms France

Further Instruction

Project the questions in the Interactive Reading Notepad. Go through the questions as a class, and have students volunteer answers to each. Discuss their answers as a class.

Identify Cause and Effect Define *nationalism*. Ask students to explain the influence of nationalism on the French Revolution during its most radical phase. (*Nationalism is loyalty to one's country. Nationalism spread as the radicals tried to purify the Revolution, which ultimately led to the Reign of Terror.*)

D Differentiate: Extra Support Project the image of Robespierre going to the guillotine from the text. Write this quote from Robespierre, "Liberty cannot be secured unless criminals lose their heads" on the whiteboard. Ask students: Do you agree that Robespierre eventually became a traitor to the cause of liberty? (*Students might say that Robespierre's actions went against the basic ideals of freedom and liberty that were the cornerstone of the French Revolution.*)

Objective 4: Describe France under the Directory.

Quick Instruction

Explain to students that in 1795 there was a new constitution in France, which set up a five-man Directory. The Directory, however, was weak and corrupt. It faced many internal and external challenges. The Directory's failings eventually led to the rise of Napoleon Bonaparte.

Further Instruction

Project the Interactive Reading Notepad questions and discuss the answers with the class.

Identify Cause and Effect Define *émigré*. Ask students to explain how returning émigrés presented a threat to the Directory. (*Students might say that many émigrés were devout Catholics who resented the measures France's revolutionaries took against the church. As a result, the émigrés wanted the monarchy to return.*)

Objective 5: Identify how the French Revolution changed life in France.

Quick Instruction

Interactive Timeline: The French Revolution Project the Interactive Timeline. Remind students that the French Revolution was a series of events that upended the old order in France. The monarchy was abolished, the French Catholic Church was put under state control, and a republic was established.

🔍 ACTIVE CLASSROOM

List the following changes to French society on the whiteboard: abolishing monarchy; curtailing the power of the church; abolishing the feudal system; creating equality before the law; opening careers to talent; creating a sense of national pride; creating a government based on popular sovereignty. Tell students that they will perform a Rank It activity in which they rank the items listed on the whiteboard based on their importance. Ask students to provide justification for the ranking they made.

Further Instruction

The Revolution Transforms France: Core Text and Interactive Reading Notepad Project the questions provided in the Interactive Reading Notepad, and have students answer the questions by reviewing the text.

Topic ⑫ Lesson 7

A Radical Phase

INTERACTIVE TIMELINE
The French Revolution Enters a More Radical Phase

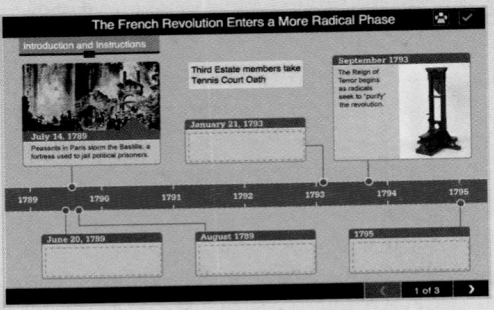

SYNTHESIZE

DIGITAL ACTIVITY
The Reign of Terror

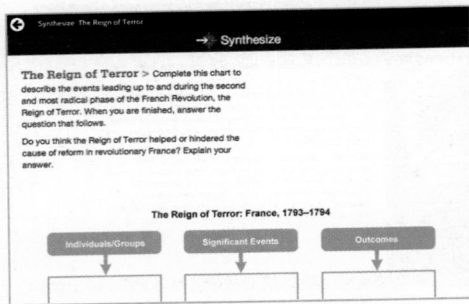

DEMONSTRATE

LESSON QUIZ
Lesson Quiz and Class Discussion Board

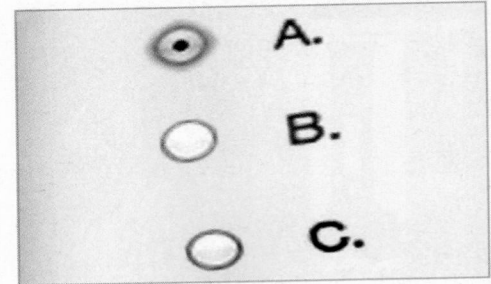

Remind students that the French Revolution came after the American Revolution. The two revolutions had similarities and differences. Both grew out of Enlightenment ideals such as liberty, freedom, and the rights of citizens. Both began with calls for reform but ended up with a complete change of government. In both, people opposed oppressive monarchies and high taxes. Each revolution broke out after years of growing discontent with powerful rulers who imposed their will on the people.

Ask: What kind of government did both countries set up? *(a republican form of government)* How was the American experience with republican government different from that of France? *(In France, the first republic did not last, but in the United States, it has lasted until the present.)* Tell students that the revolutions differed in other ways as well. American colonists saw themselves as citizens of Britain and entitled to the rights guaranteed by the Magna Carta and the Glorious Revolution.

Compare and Contrast How did American and French revolutionaries deal with the role of the church in their respective societies? *(Students might say that Civil Constitution of the Clergy put the French Catholic Church under state control. In America, revolutionary leaders kept the church and state separate, forbidding the state from establishing a church or interfering with freedom of religion.)*

Have students fill out the graphic organizer for the events of the Reign of Terror. *(Possible Answers: **Individuals/Groups:** Robespierre, Jacobins, National Assembly, King Louis XVI, émigrés, sans-culottes, Committee of Public Safety, Directory, bourgeoisie; **Events:** September massacres, execution of Louis XVI and Marie Antoinette, creation of the Committee of Public Safety, soldiers fought wars in other European countries and put down peasant revolts, Robespierre gains power, trials and imprisonment of those considered traitors to the Revolution, execution of those considered traitors to the Revolution; **Outcomes:** Revolution enters a third stage, new constitution sets up five-person Directory, public backlash against the Terror, Robespierre and other radicals lose their heads, the Age of Napoleon begins.)* Then ask them the critical thinking question: Do you think the Reign of Terror helped or hindered the cause of reform in revolutionary France? Explain your answer. *(Answers may vary. Students might say it hindered the cause of reform because of the Reign of Terror's indiscriminate violence. Some students might say it helped the cause because the Reign of Terror resulted in a more reformist constitution.)*

If desired, you can extend this exercise by having students define various individuals and groups that they mentioned in the chart.

Assign the online Lesson Quiz for this lesson if you haven't already done so. Students will be offered automatic remediation or enrichment based on their score.

Pose these questions to the class on the Discussion Board:

In "A Radical Phase," you read about why how the French Revolution took a bloody and violent turn. You also read about how the Revolution changed French society.

Classify List the three most important aspects of the Reign of Terror. Which was most important and why? How did the Reign of Terror lead to the emergence of Napoleon as France's leader? *(Answers will vary, but students may mention the backlash against the Terror and the need for a strong leader amid the chaos.)*

Topic Inquiry
Have students continue their investigations for the Topic Inquiry.

PEARSON realize™

www.PearsonRealize.com
Access your Digital Lesson

The Age of Napoleon

Supporting English Language Learners

Use with Digital Text 2, **Napoleon Reforms France.**

Speaking

Remind students that the way we speak changes based on our audience. For example, we use informal language to speak to our families and friends, but we use formal language to speak to large groups or to teachers.

Beginning Read *Napoleon Reforms France* aloud to students. Demonstrate how to adapt language by adjusting the first sentence in the section to fit an informal conversation. Point out that conversations among people are different from reading. Listeners may ask questions or need clarification as a topic is discussed. Then have students work together to adjust the second sentence of the section for an informal audience. Support their progress and understanding by providing a variety of vocabulary words and sentence structures that reflect an informal style.

Intermediate Read *Napoleon Reforms France* aloud to students. Then have students work together in small groups to develop informal language to describe the content in the first two paragraphs of the section. Remind students that informal speech is different from reading. Guide students' understanding of the difference between formal and informal language by providing support and examples when necessary.

Advanced Have a student volunteer read the first two paragraphs of *Napoleon Reforms France* aloud to the group. Then have pairs of students rework the text of these two paragraphs to suit an informal conversation. Finally, have two sets of pairs join together. Each pair should share their informal explanation of the content with the other pair. Then the second pair should repeat the process. Guide students' understanding of the difference between formal and informal language by providing support and examples when necessary.

Advanced High Have students read *Napoleon Reforms France* and explain the details of the first three paragraphs of the section to a partner in their own words. Then have partners change roles, and ask the second student in each pair to repeat the process for the second three paragraphs of the section. Listening students should provide ideas and support when more informal language is needed. Guide students' understanding of the difference between formal and informal language by providing support and examples when necessary.

Use with Digital Text 6, **The Congress of Vienna.**

Reading

There is more to informational text than the sentences and paragraphs of the narrative. Examining the headings, images, and captions can provide context and visual clues to support student understanding of the content.

Beginning Point out the main head and subheads in the text *The Congress of Vienna*. Have students read the first paragraph of text under each head. Explain how each heading acts provides contextual support for the content that follows. Then ask students to look at the map under the subhead *Successes and Failures*. Point out how this map gives readers a concrete understanding of the national boundaries that were set in place following the Congress of Vienna. Help students recognize how this visual supports the text that explains the new boundaries and why they were set in place.

Intermediate Have students point out the main head and subheads in the text *The Congress of Vienna* and read the content that follows. Explain how each heading acts as a clue to the content underneath it. Then read the subhead *Restoring Peace and Order* and ask students to use the subhead to form a question about the content below. Next, read the section under *Restoring Peace and Order* aloud, and help students answer the question they created. Next, ask students to look at the map under the subhead *Successes and Failures*. Point out how this map gives readers visual support for the section of the text that explains the new boundaries and why they were set in place.

Advanced Have students work in pairs to locate the boldface headings in *The Congress of Vienna* and use them to create questions about the text that follows. Then have students read each subsection, using their questions as a guide. Next, have students examine the map under *Restoring Peace and Order*. Ask students to use the information they gathered from the map to help them understand the corresponding text.

Advanced High Have students work individually to locate the boldface headings in *The Congress of Vienna* and use them to create questions about the text that follows. Then have students read each subsection, and formulate answers for the questions they posed. Next, have students examine the map under *Restoring Peace and Order*. Ask students to explain how they could use the information they gathered from the map to help them understand the corresponding text.

▶ Differentiate Instruction

Use the Differentiated Instruction notes throughout the lesson plan to support the varied skill sets, levels of readiness, and interests in the mixed-ability classroom.

Challenge These notes include suggestions for expanding the activity for advanced students.

On-Level These notes include suggestions for modifying the activity to address different interests or learning styles.

Extra Support These notes include ideas for providing more scaffolding or reading spuport.

Special Needs These notes provide ideas for adapting instruction to support the needs of various special needs students.

■ NOTES

The Age of Napoleon

Objectives

Objective 1: Describe how Napoleon Bonaparte rose to power.

Objective 2: Explain the impact of Napoleon and the Napoleonic Wars.

Objective 3: Identify the reasons for Napoleon's fall from power.

Objective 4: Understand how the Congress of Vienna tried to restore order to Europe.

LESSON 8 ORGANIZER		PACING: APPROX. 1 PERIOD, .5 BLOCKS			
				RESOURCES	
		OBJECTIVES	**PACING**	**Online**	**Print**
Connect					
DIGITAL START UP ACTIVITY **Enter Napoleon Bonaparte**			5 min.	●	
Investigate					
DIGITAL TEXT 1 **Napoleon on the Rise**		Objective 1	10 min.	●	●
DIGITAL TEXTS 2 AND 3 **Napoleon Reforms France, The Napoleonic Wars**		Objective 2	10 min.	●	●
INTERACTIVE MAP **Napoleon's Europe (1804–1815)**			10 min.	●	
DIGITAL TEXTS 4 AND 5 **Challenges to the French Empire, Napoleon Falls from Power**		Objective 3	10 min.	●	●
INTERACTIVE TIMELINE **The Rise and Fall of Napoleon**			10 min.	●	
DIGITAL TEXT 6 **The Congress of Vienna**		Objective 4	10 min.	●	●
Synthesize					
DIGITAL ACTIVITY **The Age of Napoleon**			5 min.	●	
Demonstrate					
LESSON QUIZ **Lesson Quiz and Class Discussion Board**			10 min.	●	

■ CONNECT

DIGITAL START UP ACTIVITY
Enter Napoleon Bonaparte

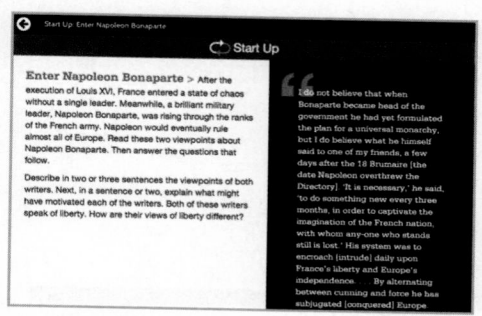

Project the Start Up Activity Ask students to address the writing prompt as they enter and get settled: Describe in two or three sentences the viewpoints of both writers. Next, in a sentence or two, explain what might have motivated each of the writers.

Then have students share their ideas with another student, either in class or through a chat room or blog.

Discuss What does Madame de Staël say are Napoleon's only methods of persuasion? *(To intrude daily on liberty and independence through cunning and force)* What does Marshal Ney say about liberty? *(That through Napoleon's leadership liberty triumphs)*

Aa Vocabulary Development: Use the Interactive Reading Notepad to preview the Key Terms and Academic Vocabulary in this Lesson with students.

N FLIP IT!

Assign the Flipped Video for this lesson.

■ STUDENT EDITION PRINT
PAGES: 482–489

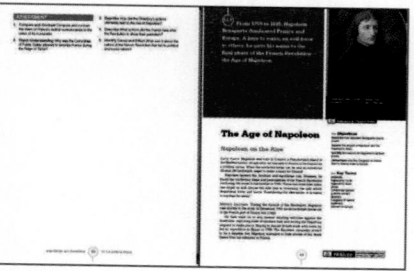

■ INVESTIGATE

DIGITAL TEXT 1
Napoleon on the Rise

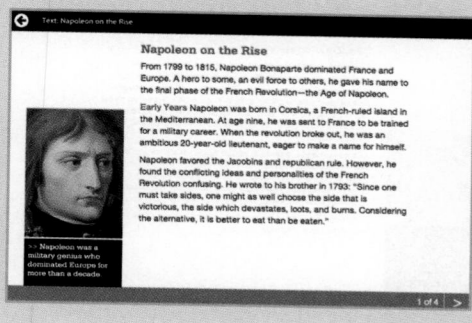

Objective 1: Describe how Napoleon Bonaparte rose to power.

Quick Instruction

Project the image of a young Napoleon from the reading. Explain to students that from 1799 to 1815, Napoleon Bonaparte dominated France and Europe. Tell students that during the French Revolution, Napoleon had become a military hero, ultimately returning to France and crowning himself emperor. Napoleon's rise to power was fueled by his success on the battlefield, personal political ambition, and his popularity with the French people.

Next, project the image of Napoleon dressed in luxurious robes and with a crown on his head. Ask students to describe the differences between the two images.

D Differentiate: Challenge Ask students to write a diary entry from the perspective of a soldier in Napoleon's army about the soldier's feelings regarding Napoleon as emperor of France. Have them describe what Napoleon meant to them on the battlefield and what he could mean to France as its ruler.

Further Instruction

Napoleon on the Rise: Core Text and Interactive Reading Notepad Project the questions in the Interactive Reading Notepad. Ask students to answer the questions using the core reading.

Discuss Have students explain the following quotation Napoleon said after one of his earliest victories in Lodi, Italy: "From that moment, I foresaw what I might be. Already I felt the earth flee from beneath me, as if I were being carried into the sky." *(Students might say that after that victory, Napoleon believed he was destined for great things.)*

The Age of Napoleon

DIGITAL TEXT 2
Napoleon Reforms France

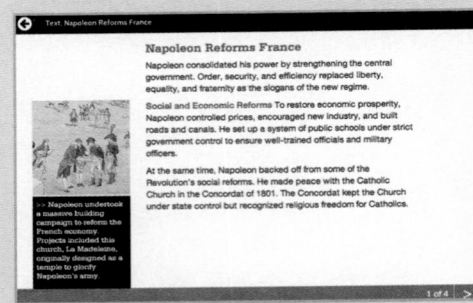

DIGITAL TEXT 3
The Napoleonic Wars

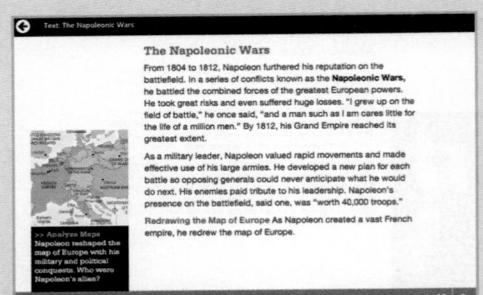

INTERACTIVE MAP
Napoleon's Europe (1804–1815)

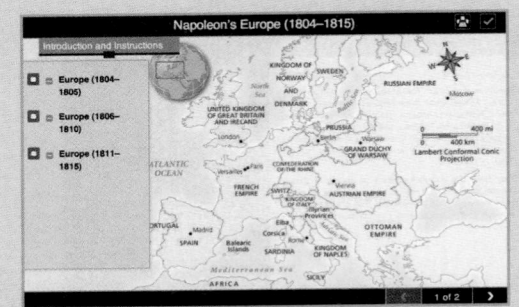

Objective 2: Explain the impact of Napoleon and the Napoleonic Wars.

Quick Instruction

Interactive Map: Napoleon's Europe (1804–1815) Project the map on the whiteboard and click through the hotspots. Introduce the map activity by telling students that while Napoleon undertook social and economic reforms at home, particularly through the Napoleonic Code, he also furthered his reputation on the battlefield in a series of conflicts known as the Napoleonic Wars. Those wars redrew the map of Europe from 1804 to 1812.

👥 ACTIVE CLASSROOM

Project the chart from the reading that outlines some of the aspects of the Napoleonic Code. Divide the class into three or four groups, and give members of each group a sticky note. Ask each member of the groups to come up with a law that embodies the principles of the Enlightenment, including equality of all citizens before the law and religious toleration. Group members should then put their laws together into a "code." Have each group share its code with the rest of the class.

ELL Use the ELL activity described in the ELL chart.

Further Instruction

Project the Interactive Reading Notepad questions and go through them, discussing the answers as a class.

Identify Cause and Effect What impact did the Napoleonic Wars and Napoleon's use of "forceful diplomacy" have on Europe? *(In addition to conquering other nations, Napoleon put relatives and friends on many European thrones. He also forced other countries to sign treaties with France.)*

DIGITAL TEXT 4

Challenges to the French Empire

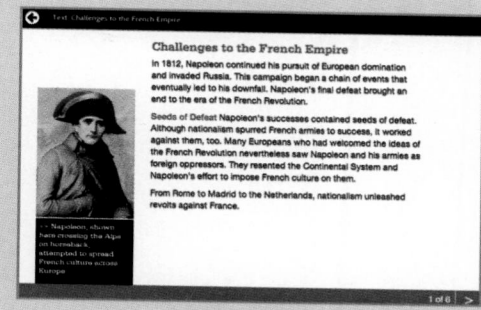

DIGITAL TEXT 5

Napoleon Falls from Power

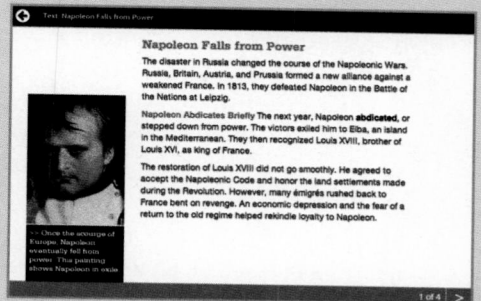

INTERACTIVE TIMELINE

The Rise and Fall of Napoleon

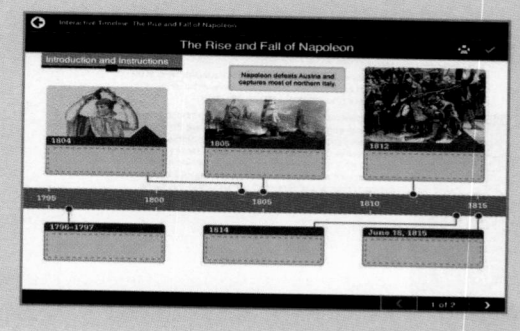

Objective 3: Identify the reasons for Napoleon's fall from power.

Quick Instruction

Interactive Timeline: The Rise and Fall of Napoleon Project the Interactive Timeline on the whiteboard. Introduce the activity by telling students that the end for Napoleon began in 1812 when he invaded Russia.

🗣 ACTIVE CLASSROOM

Have students use the timeline to compare the image of Napoleon being crowned emperor to the image of Napoleon's army retreating from Russia. Have them predict what might happen next after each. Ask students to state what the people in the images might be thinking. Tell them to write a script for each image, and then have volunteers act out their scripts for the class.

D Differentiate: **Challenge** Have students research Napoleon's defeat at the Battle of Waterloo (1815) and produce a battle map showing the movements of allied and French troops. Students should show how elements of each army advanced and/or retreated during the battle.

Further Instruction

Challenges to the French Empire: Core Text and Interactive Reading Notepad Project the questions in the Interactive Reading Notepad. Ask students to answer the questions using the core reading.

The Age of Napoleon

DIGITAL TEXT 6

The Congress of Vienna

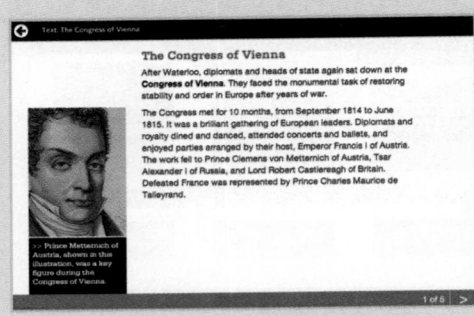

Objective 4: Understand how the Congress of Vienna tried to restore order to Europe.

Quick Instruction

Begin by asking students to summarize and explain the impact of Napoleon Bonaparte on Europe. *(Students might mention the Napoleonic Code, the damage that Napoleon's Continental System did to Europe's economy, and the toppling of many rulers.)* Explain that, after the Battle of Waterloo, the Congress of Vienna met to reestablish stability and order in Europe after years of war. The Congress met for 10 months, from September 1814 to June 1815. The Congress redrew the map of Europe and restored hereditary monarchies that the French Revolution or Napoleon had unseated. Project the map of Europe after the Congress of Vienna from the Text. Explain to students that the Congress kept the peace for nearly 100 years.

ELL Use the ELL activity described in the ELL chart.

Further Instruction

Go through the Interactive Reading Notepad questions and discuss the answers with the class.

Austria, Russia, Prussia, and Great Britain extended their wartime alliance and pledged to act together to maintain the balance of power. The powers also met periodically at the Concert of Europe to discuss any problems affecting peace. Ask students to describe what the shortcomings of the Congress's plans were. *(Answers will vary, but students should mention that the leaders did not anticipate the strength of nationalism.)*

D Differentiate: Challenge Divide the class into five groups and assign each group a country to represent at the Congress of Vienna: Austria, Russia, Prussia, Britain, and France. Ask each group to research (1) Napoleon's impact on the delegate's country; (2) the goals and interests of the country for the Congress; (3) how the country would like to see Europe reorganized. Have each group draw up recommendations on how to achieve a lasting peace. Have a spokesperson for each group present the group's recommendations to the entire Congress. Have the Congress then appoint a committee (one delegate from each nation) to debate a final list for the entire Congress to vote on.

SYNTHESIZE

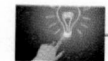

DIGITAL ACTIVITY

The Age of Napoleon

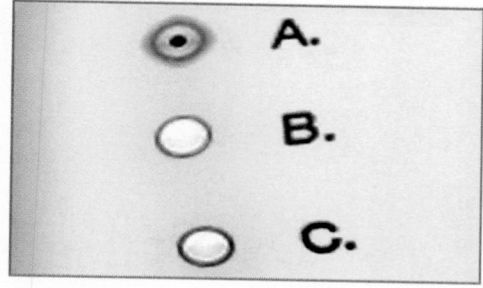

Have students fill out the graphic organizer regarding Napoleon's rise to power. *(Possible Answers: overthrows Directory and crowns himself emperor; reforms France's political and social systems; pursues French military and political domination of Europe; invades Russia in a disastrous campaign; abdicates the throne in 1814 after defeat in the Battle of the Nations at Leipzig; is exiled to Elba; escapes Elba, regains power, and is defeated for good at the Battle of Waterloo in 1815.)*

Then ask them to answer the critical-thinking question: How might Napoleon have avoided his eventual downfall? Tell them to explain their answer. *(Answers may vary and might include such statements as making peace with the allied nations of Europe after returning to France; stopping his quest to dominate Europe; not invading Russia.)*

If desired, you can extend this exercise by having students write a brief summary of each event that they mention in the chart.

DEMONSTRATE

LESSON QUIZ

Lesson Quiz and Class Discussion Board

Assign the online Lesson Quiz for this lesson if you haven't already done so. Students will be offered automatic remediation or enrichment based on their score.

Pose these questions to the class on the Discussion Board:

In "The Age of Napoleon," you read about why how Napoleon changed the face of Europe.

Predict Consequences How might have Napoleon achieved ultimate success in Europe? *(Answers will vary, but students might mention not being too overly ambitious in warfare and territorial expansion.)* How might Europe have looked if Napoleon's conquest of the continent was successful? *(Answers will vary, but students may say that even if he were successful at the time, nationalist movements might still have overthrown his rule at a later date.)*

Topic Inquiry

Have students continue their investigations for the Topic Inquiry.

Absolutism and Revolution

■ SYNTHESIZE

DIGITAL ACTIVITY
Reflect on the Essential Question and Topic

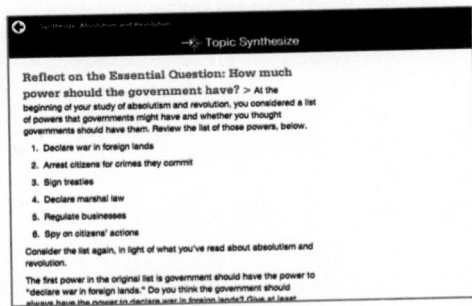

First, ask students to reconsider the Essential Question. Remind students of the questions they answered to try to make predictions about the topic:

- Declare war in foreign lands
- Arrest citizens for crimes they commit
- Sign treaties
- Declare martial law
- Regulate businesses
- Monitor citizens' actions

Ask students, "How many of your predictions were accurate? Did you learn anything that surprised you as you read about this topic?" Have them identify at least one prediction that was correct and one unexpected thing they learned in the chapter.

Next, ask students to reflect on absolutism and revolution as a whole. Tell them to think about how later governments, including that of the United States, began moving away from the idea of absolute power. Write down at least three important observations about why this change came about. If they have difficulty thinking of a response, post the following questions:

- Were most leaders with absolute power fair?
- How did Enlightenment ideas affect people's thinking about government?
- What advantages does limited government bring?

You may ask students to share their questions and answers on the Class Discussion Board.

■ DEMONSTRATE

DIGITAL TOPIC REVIEW AND ASSESSMENT
Absolutism and Revolution

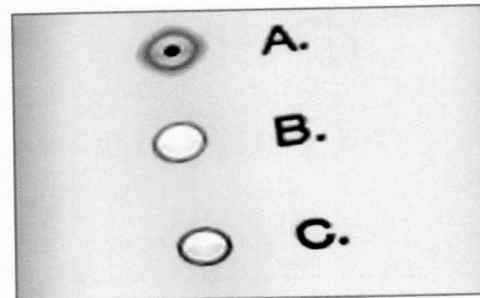

Students can prepare for the Topic Test by answering the questions in the Topic Review and Assessment online or the Assessment questions in the Print Student text. They can also prepare by reviewing their answers to the Interactive Reading Notepad questions or reviewing their notes in the Reading and Notetaking Study Guide.

DIGITAL TOPIC TEST
Absolutism and Revolution

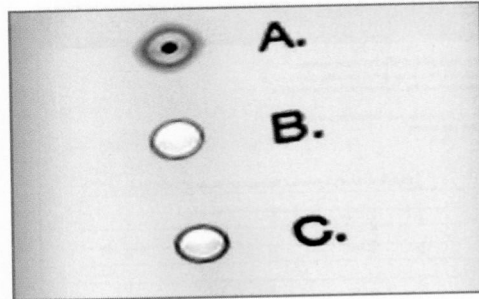

TOPIC TEST
Assign the Topic Test to assess students' understanding of topic content.

BENCHMARK TESTS
Assign these benchmark tests as you complete the relevant topics to monitor student progress toward mastering the course content and as preparation for the End-of-Course Test.

Benchmark Test 1: Topics 1–5

Benchmark Test 2: Topics 6–10

Benchmark Test 3: Topics 11–15

Benchmark Test 4: Topics 16–21

Topic 13

The Industrial Revolution

TOPIC 13 ORGANIZER	PACING: APPROX. 7 PERIODS, 3.5 BLOCKS
	PACING
Connect	1 period
MY STORY VIDEO **Lucy Larcom, Weaving Opportunity**	10 min.
DIGITAL ESSENTIAL QUESTION ACTIVITY **How Do Science and Technology Affect Society?**	10 min.
DIGITAL TIMELINE ACTIVITY **The Industrial Revolution**	10 min.
TOPIC INQUIRY: DOCUMENT-BASED QUESTION **Who Should Control Economic Decisions?**	20 min.
Investigate	2–4 periods
TOPIC INQUIRY: DOCUMENT-BASED QUESTION **Who Should Control Economic Decisions?**	Ongoing
LESSON 1 The Industrial Revolution Begins	30–40 min.
LESSON 2 Social Impact of Industrialism	30–40 min.
LESSON 3 The Second Industrial Revolution	30–40 min.
LESSON 4 Changing Ways of Life and Thought	30–40 min.
Synthesize	1 period
DIGITAL ACTIVITY **Reflect on the Essential Question and Topic**	10 min.
TOPIC INQUIRY: DOCUMENT-BASED QUESTION **Who Should Control Economic Decisions?**	20 min.
Demonstrate	1–2 periods
ONLINE TEST **The Industrial Revolution**	10 min.
TOPIC INQUIRY: DOCUMENT-BASED QUESTION **Who Should Control Economic Decisions?**	20 min.

 **TOPIC INQUIRY: DOCUMENT-BASED QUESTION**

Who Should Control Economic Decisions?

In this Topic Inquiry, students analyze documents to contrast the views of Adam Smith, other laissez-faire economists, Karl Marx, and socialist thinkers. Learning how economists explained the ways the Industrial Revolution affected the economy and society as a whole will contribute to students' understanding of the Topic Essential Question: How do science and technology affect society?

STEP 1: CONNECT
Develop Questions and Plan the Investigation

Launch the DBQ Writing Activity
Display the Winston Churchill quotation, and point out that it mentions two of the economic systems discussed in this topic. Use the questions to lead a class discussion about the quotation, or have students work in pairs to answer the questions.

Suggestion: Give more context for the quotation by explaining that Winston Churchill was one of the most important world leaders of the mid-1900s. He served as British prime minister from 1941 to 1945 and again from 1951 to 1955. During his second term of office, the world experienced a great deal of tension between capitalist Western nations and the communist Soviet Union.

Generate Questions
Divide the class into small groups and have them use the Need-to-Know Questions document to record their questions about how the various economic systems work and who controls economic decisions in each one.

Suggestion: Help students generate questions by reminding them of the five Ws and one H used by journalists: *Who? What? When? Where? Why?* and *How?* Suggest that students take 10 minutes to brainstorm as many questions as possible and then select the ones most relevant to the broader DBQ question.

Resources
- Need-to-Know Questions
- Student Instructions

STEP 2: INVESTIGATE
Apply Disciplinary Concepts and Tools

Analyze the Documents
Have students analyze the six documents to see how they relate to the question, "Who should control economic decisions?" Before students read the documents, you may wish to remind them that Adam Smith and David Ricardo advocated laissez-faire capitalism, Robert Owen is considered a utopian socialist, and Karl Marx's writings are the basis for communism. The photograph is one taken of Moscow shoppers waiting in line to buy produce in 1965. The piece on the mixed economy was published by the State Department and is intended to help people in other countries understand how the U.S. economy works.

Suggestion: You can control the length of the DBQ by having students read just three representative documents: Document A to represent laissez-faire capitalism, Document B to represent utopian socialism, and Document D to represent communism.

Check Understanding
Students should answer the multiple choice and short answer questions that follow each document.

Resources
- Information Organizer

⏻ PROFESSIONAL DEVELOPMENT

Document-Based Question
Be sure to view the Document-Based Question Professional Development resources in the online course.

STEP 3: SYNTHESIZE
Evaluate Sources and
Use Evidence to Formulate Conclusions

Write Your Essay

Have students consider all of the evidence and viewpoints and draw their own conclusions. Using the documents and their knowledge of history, have them write an essay on the following topic: **Who should control economic decisions?**

Remind students that their essays should have the following characteristics: a topic sentence that states their view; evidence from at least *three* of the documents, clearly identified; relevant facts; an explanation and rebuttal of at least one opposing viewpoint; logical organization, including an introduction and a conclusion; and correct spelling, grammar, and punctuation.

Suggestion: If students struggle with organization, review the structure of a five-paragraph essay. The first paragraph is the introduction. The body consists of three paragraphs, each of which explores a key point. The conclusion should restate the main idea and summarizes the key points.

Edit Your Essay

Remind students that they should revise their first draft and create a final draft of their essay before turning it in. You may want to suggest that they ask a classmate to peer-edit their essay.

Resources
• Writing Rubric

STEP 4: DEMONSTRATE
Communicate Conclusions
and Take Informed Action

After students have finished their essays, explain that the work they did on this DBQ will serve as a foundation for the economic understanding they will need as adults. In the future, they may refine or revise the economic ideas they developed here, but they can use a similar process for considering multiple sources of evidence and points of view to form an educated and carefully reasoned opinion.

Suggestion: Help students connect this inquiry to real life by reminding them that the question of who should control economic decisions is still hotly debated today. For example, in the 2012 presidential elections, many campaign issues involved questions of how much the free market should be regulated and whether certain government programs are examples of socialism. This DBQ will help students make informed decisions later in their lives when they have to vote and communicate with elected officials.

INTRODUCTION

The Industrial Revolution (1750–1914)

During the 1700s, life in Europe began to change rapidly. People learned new and better ways of farming, which increased food production and made the population grow. Business owners wanted to find ways to produce more goods. These two trends combined to transform the world's economy. What role did the Industrial Revolution play in creating the world we live in today?

■ CONNECT

MY STORY VIDEO
Lucy Larcom, Weaving Opportunity

Watch a video about Lucy Larcom, a worker in an early 19th century Lowell textile mill.

Check Understanding Where did many of the workers in the early textile mills come from? *(farms)* **Determine Point of View** What may have accounted for the change in Lucy Larcom's view of mill work? *(Once she had grown accustomed to mill work, the novelty of it wore off. She grew to dislike the constant noise, and refused to become a slave to machines. The tedium of the labor and the need constantly to service the machines no doubt accounted for her change in view.)*

⇅ FLIP IT!
Assign the My Story video.

DIGITAL ESSENTIAL QUESTION ACTIVITY
How Do Science and Technology Affect Society?

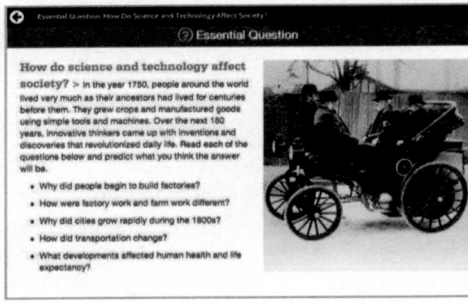

Ask students to think about the Essential Question for this Topic: How do science and technology affect society? New technologies have both positive and negative effects. How can technology have unintended consequences?

If students have not already done so, ask them to make their predictions. Then allow volunteers to share their ideas with the class.

Identify Central Issues What do you expect to be the main areas in which the Industrial Revolution will cause change? *(Sample Response: industry, work, transportation, medicine, city life)*

Predict Consequences What do you think might be some unintended negative consequences of the Industrial Revolution? Explain. *(Sample Response: Unemployment rises as machines throw people out of work; pollution from factory smoke and chemical waste increases.)*

Infer Why do you think the development of industry is called a "revolution"? *(Sample Response: because it overthrew an older way of life or because it radically changed the economy)*

DIGITAL TIMELINE ACTIVITY
The Industrial Revolution

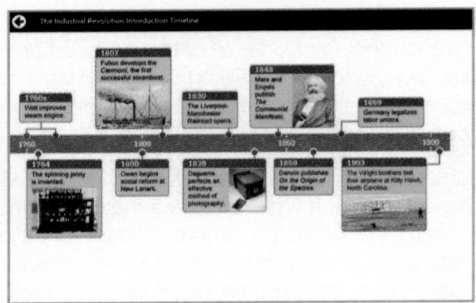

Display the timeline showing the major events in the Industrial Revolution. During the Topic, students will learn about all of these events and many more, but this timeline will provide a framework into which they can place the events they learn about.

D Differentiate: Challenge/Gifted Suggest that students copy the timeline onto their own paper and add entries to it as they read the chapter. Have them make a final, clean copy after they read all four lessons, and discuss the new entries as a class.

Check Understanding About how many years after Watt's invention of the steam engine was the first successful steamboat developed? *(about 40)*

www.PearsonRealize.com
Access your Digital Lesson

The Industrial Revolution Begins

Supporting English Language Learners

Use with Digital Text 5, **Textile Industry Initiates Industrialization.**

Reading

Point out that many of the clothes, tools, and processes that modern humans take for granted were unavailable to people living prior to industrialization. Our clothing, for example, is almost exclusively made by textile machinery. Have students use the three images as they read *Textile Industry Initiates Industrialization* to enhance their understanding of the development of the textile industry.

Beginning Help students locate each of the three images in *Textile Industry Initiates Industrialization*. Explain the term *cottage industry* to students, and make sure to point out that *cottage* is another word for *small house*. Read aloud the text about cottage industry and the factory system. Help students understand how the visuals enhance the concept that the textile industry eventually outgrew homes and needed the larger space that factories provided to fit the new machinery.

Intermediate Ask students to locate each of the three images in *Textile Industry Initiates Industrialization*. Then have students use context clues from the first image to develop a working definition of the term *cottage industry*. Adjust and support student understanding of this term as needed until it is accurate. After they read the text, engage students in a discussion to explain why the textile industry needed more and more space to create cloth from raw cotton. Have students use evidence from the visuals to support their ideas.

Advanced Have pairs of students use context clues from the three images in *Textile Industry Initiates Industrialization* to develop a working definition of the term *cottage industry*. Discuss this definition with students and adjust it as needed until it is accurate. Then ask pairs to use the images and the text to determine why the textile industry needed more and more space to create cloth from raw cotton. Have students share their ideas with the rest of the group.

Advanced High Have students use the three visuals in *Textile Industry Initiates Industrialization* to understand and describe the textile industry's development from cottage industry to a factory-based process with fewer skilled workers. Once students have had a chance to read the text and examine the supporting visuals, have them explain the development of the industry to the rest of the group.

Use with Digital Text 7, **Industrialization Spreads.**

Speaking

The Industrial Revolution did not remain isolated in Britain for long. Have students read *Industrialization Spreads* according to their skill level and respond to the following activities and questions.

Beginning Read the text with students, taking time to examine the map that shows the spread of industrialization to other nations. Help students understand the concept that industrialization began in Britain but soon spread across much of the Western Hemisphere by using the sentence frames that follow to give an oral response.

The British textile industry _____. (began industrialization)

Natural resources in Germany and the United States _____. (helped industrialization develop)

Intermediate Have student volunteers take turns reading the text aloud. Then examine the map that shows the spread of Industrialization with students. Ask students to think about and write down ideas to explain why and how industrialization spread from Britain to other parts of Europe and the United States so quickly. Then guide students in a discussion about this concept. Encourage a spoken response from each student to gauge his or her understanding of the concept.

Advanced Have students read *Industrialization Spreads* aloud in small groups. Then have small groups discuss the reasons why industrialization spread from Britain to other parts of the world. Have students report the main points of their discussions to ensure that they understand the concept.

Advanced High Students should read *Industrialization Spreads*. Then, working with a partner, students should make a list of the many reasons for the spread of the Industrial Revolution and explain how each reason contributed to the rise in industrialization. Each pair should share their list orally with the whole class.

▣ Differentiate Instruction

Use the Differentiated Instruction notes throughout the lesson plan to support the varied skill sets, levels of readiness, and interests in the mixed-ability classroom.

Challenge These notes include suggestions for expanding the activity for advanced students.

On-Level These notes include suggestions for modifying the activity to address different interests or learning styles.

Extra Support These notes include ideas for providing more scaffolding or reading spuport.

Special Needs These notes provide ideas for adapting instruction to support the needs of various special needs students.

■ NOTES

_____

_____

_____

_____

_____

The Industrial Revolution Begins

Objectives

Objective 1: Describe how changes in agriculture helped spark the Industrial Revolution.

Objective 2: Analyze why the Industrial Revolution began in Britain.

Objective 3: Explain the role of steam technology and textile manufacturing in the Industrial Revolution.

Objective 4: Describe how the factory system and transportation revolution advanced industry.

Objective 5: Trace how the Industrial Revolution spread.

LESSON 1 ORGANIZER		PACING: APPROX. 1 PERIOD, .5 BLOCKS			
		OBJECTIVES	PACING	RESOURCES Online	Print
Connect					
	DIGITAL START UP ACTIVITY **Compare Life Before and After Industrialization**		5 min.	●	
Investigate					
	DIGITAL TEXT 1 **New Ways of Working Change Life**	Objective 1	10 min.	●	●
	DIGITAL TEXT 2 **A New Agricultural Revolution**		10 min.	●	●
	DIGITAL TEXT 3 **Coal, Steam, and the Energy Revolution**	Objective 2	10 min.	●	●
	DIGITAL TEXT 4 **Why Did the Industrial Revolution Start in Britain?**		10 min.	●	●
	DIGITAL TEXT 5 **Textile Industry Initiates Industrialization**	Objective 3	10 min.	●	●
	INTERACTIVE GALLERY **The Industrial Revolution and the Textile Industry**		10 min.	●	
	DIGITAL TEXT 6 **A Revolution in Transportation**	Objective 4	10 min.	●	●
	INTERACTIVE MAP **Advances in Transportation in England, 1800s**		10 min.	●	
	DIGITAL TEXT 7 **Industrialization Spreads**	Objective 5	10 min.	●	●
Synthesize					
	DIGITAL ACTIVITY **Causes of the Industrial Revolution**		5 min.	●	
Demonstrate					
	LESSON QUIZ **Lesson Quiz and Class Discussion Board**		10 min.	●	

PEARSON
realize™
www.PearsonRealize.com

Go online to access additional resources including:
Primary Sources • Biographies • Supreme Court cases • 21st Century Skill Tutorials • Maps • Graphic Organizers.

■ CONNECT

DIGITAL START UP ACTIVITY
Compare Life Before and After Industrialization

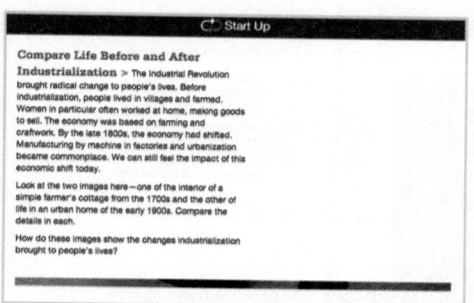

Project the Start Up Activity As students enter and get settled, ask them to look at the photographs on the board and answer the question: How do these images show the changes industrialization brought to people's lives? Then have them share their ideas with another student, either in class or through a chat or blog space.

Discuss What ways of life are shown in the images? How are these ways of life different? *(Students should note that the photos are black and white and show a time of life from centuries ago.)*

Tell students that in this lesson they will learn about the Industrial Revolution and how it changed people's lives.

Aa Vocabulary Development: Use the Interactive Reading Notepad to preview the Key Terms and Academic Vocabulary in this Lesson with students.

↥ FLIP IT!

Assign the Flipped Video for this lesson.

■ STUDENT EDITION PRINT PAGES: 496–503

■ INVESTIGATE

DIGITAL TEXT 1
New Ways of Working Change Life

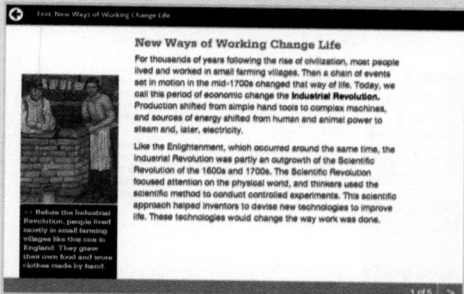

DIGITAL TEXT 2
A New Agricultural Revolution

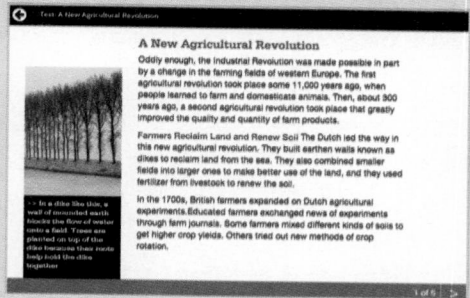

Objective 1: Describe how changes in agriculture helped spark the Industrial Revolution.

Quick Instruction

Remind students about the Scientific Revolution that took place in Europe in the 17th and 18th centuries. Scientists placed a new emphasis on the physical world, on the use of experimentation and the collection of data. Explain how this new attitude encouraged experimentation in scientific agriculture, as well as invention and engineering. This paved the way for the Industrial Revolution. Explain how developments in agriculture were a major cause of the Industrial Revolution. Improvements in farming led to increased food production and population growth. At the same time, farms needed fewer laborers, so this meant workers had to find other kinds of jobs. These developments helped spark the rise of industry.

Analyze Images/Graphs Project the photograph of a dike from the text, along with the table of land enclosures in England as a result of the agricultural revolution. Ask: How do these images relate to changes in agriculture? *(They show more efficient use of land.)* What did the growing population and the loss of farm jobs provide for industry? *(Both changes provided workers for factories.)*

D Differentiate: Extra Support Help students use visuals to support their understanding of the text. For example, have students review the text under "A Rural Way of Life." Prompt them to notice details in the image of a rural setting. Have students compare the details from the visual with the description.

Further Instruction

Editable Presentation Use the Editable Presentation to present the main ideas for this Core Text.

A New Agricultural Revolution: Core Text and Interactive Reading Notepad Project and discuss the Interactive Reading Notepad questions. Use the questions to facilitate class discussion. Review each section of the lesson for the questions students have difficulty answering.

Analyze Images Project the image in the text of a woman buying goods from a grocer. Ask students to describe the goods that they see in the cart. Then, ask them to explain how the agricultural revolution contributed to a healthier population. *(Improvements to agriculture, such as rotating crops, building dikes, experimenting with soil, and enclosing land, provided more and better-quality food and reduced famine, leading to a healthier population.)*

Identify Cause and Effect As students discuss the agricultural revolution, be sure that they identify how agricultural advancements helped lead to industrialization. Once students have an understanding of agriculture's role in industrialization, ask: What was life like before the Industrial Revolution? *(Students may say that life was more rural, and people relied mostly on themselves or their small communities for necessary goods.)*

The Industrial Revolution Begins

DIGITAL TEXT 3

Coal, Steam, and the Energy Revolution

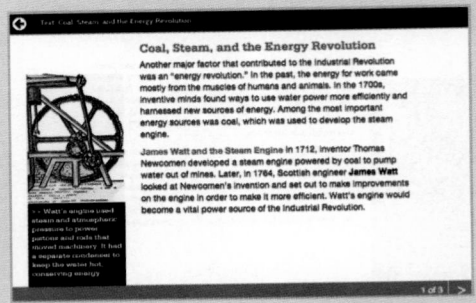

DIGITAL TEXT 4

Why Did the Industrial Revolution Start in Britain?

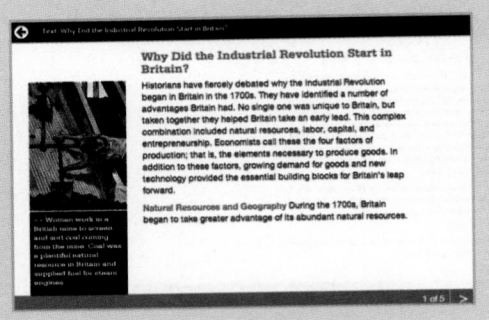

Compare Project the graphic organizer from the Interactive Reading Notepad. Have students use it to compare life before and after industrialization to identify the impact of the Industrial Revolution on humanity. Students should base their answers on the narrative and accompanying images. Suggest that students add to the graphic organizer as they learn more about the living and working conditions brought about by industrialization.

Objective 2: Analyze why the Industrial Revolution began in Britain.

Quick Instruction

Tell students that Great Britain was the first country to industrialize to a significant degree. It had land and resources, labor, capital, and entrepreneurship, all of which businesses need to produce goods and to grow.

Analyze Maps Project the map "Resources and Industry in England, 1750" from the text. Point out the resources available in England in 1750. Discuss how each resource was used for industrialization. *(Iron was used to build machines and rails, coal-powered steam engines, etc.)* Why were resources a factor is Britain's role as the starting point of industrialization? *(Britain had an abundance of natural resources, providing the raw materials needed to industrialize.)*

ACTIVE CLASSROOM

Have students break into groups. Provide the following writing prompt: What might life be like today if James Watt had not invented his steam engine? Have students write as much as they can for a minute, and then pass the paper to the person on their right. The next person should try to improve or elaborate upon the response. Continue to switch until the paper comes back to the first person. The group should then decide which response is the best.

Further Instruction

Coal, Steam, and the Energy Revolution: Core Text and Interactive Reading Notepad Project and discuss the Interactive Reading Notepad questions for this text. Use the questions to spark class discussion about how the innovations of the 1700s revolutionized energy. Make sure students understand that energy sources such as coal and steam provided much more power than the labor of humans and animals.

Why Did the Industrial Revolution Start in Britain? Core Text and Interactive Reading Notepad Project the questions provided in the notepad and have students answer as they progress through the Core Text.

Make sure students understand that the four factors of production are the elements necessary to produce goods. These factors are natural resources, labor, capital, and entrepreneurship. Point out that Britain had the capital, resources, labor, and entrepreneurship needed to spark industrialization. Also, the demand for goods and new technology contributed to Britain's rapid industrialization.

Analyze Images Project the image of the British naval ship from the text. Ask what role the British navy played in Britain's industrialization. *(The navy protected the empire, including shipping and overseas trade routes. This protection further encouraged entrepreneurs to invest in new ventures in Britain.)*

DIGITAL TEXT 5

Textile Industry Initiates Industrialization

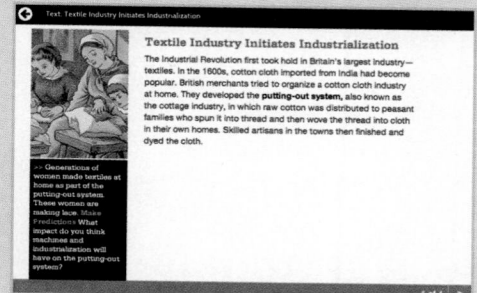

INTERACTIVE GALLERY

The Industrial Revolution and the Textile Industry

DIGITAL TEXT 6

A Revolution in Transportation

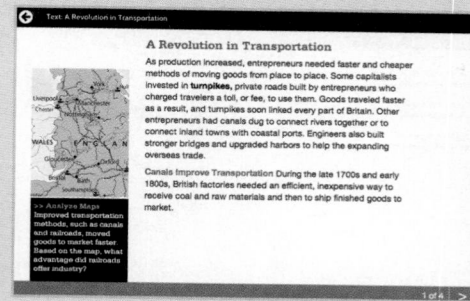

Objective 3: Explain the role of steam technology and textile manufacturing in the Industrial Revolution.

Quick Instruction
Remind students that the Industrial Revolution was a time when new technologies made manufacturing faster and more efficient. The creation of new machinery in the textile industry led to the demise of the putting-out system, in which people manufactured textiles in their homes. Instead, the new factory system brought workers and machines together in one place. The factory system advanced the Industrial Revolution by making manufacturing more efficient.

Interactive Gallery: The Industrial Revolution and the Textile Industry
Project the slideshow. Look at each image individually and then as a whole. Show the diagram of the clothing manufacturing process and the inventions timeline in the gallery. How did advances in one part of the textile process spur other innovations? *(New machines helped weavers make cloth faster, increasing the demand for thread, which created the need for a machine to make thread faster.)*

Draw Conclusions
Have students review the timeline of inventors and inventions and the process of making textiles. Ask: Why were numerous machines invented to improve the textile industry? *(Manufacturing textiles was a complex process that could be simplified and streamlined with machines. A machine that accomplished one aspect of the entire process created demand for more machines to speed up other parts of the process.)*

D **Differentiate: Challenge** Have students suggest other industries that have benefited from new technology. Ask them to break into groups to research more about one of the suggestions. Have groups prepare a short presentation and share their findings with the class.

ELL Use the ELL activity described in the ELL chart.

Further Instruction
Textile Industry Initiates Industrialization: Core Text and Interactive Reading Notepad Next, project and discuss the Interactive Reading Notepad questions for this text. Use the second question to introduce class discussion. Explain that in the American South, the economy relied on cotton, but picking and processing cotton was difficult to do and made processing expensive. Why did Eli Whitney develop the cotton gin? *(To reduce costs and labor in processing cotton.)*

Explain to students that once innovations in technology occurred, each new invention created demand for more innovations. Continue by explaining how that pattern played out in the textile industry. In this way, textile manufacturing initiated the Industrial Revolution.

Identify Cause and Effect Ask students to create a cause-and-effect diagram that demonstrates their understanding of the role of textile manufacturing in initiating the Industrial Revolution.

Make Generalizations Ask: Why is technology developed? Remind students to base their response on what they learned about the development of new textile machines. *(New inventions help solve a problem or make a process easier.)*

Objective 4: Describe how the factory system and transportation revolution advanced industry.

Quick Instruction
Introduce this objective by explaining that the steam engine led to other transportation advances.

Interactive Map: Advances in Transportation in England, 1800s
Project the interactive map. Raw materials and finished goods were transported first on steamships by canal, and then by steam locomotive on railroad tracks. Have students look at the system of canals on the map, and then at the railroads.

Draw Conclusions Describe how transportation improvements helped advance industry. *(Industry relied on transportation to deliver raw materials to make goods and fuel to power the machines. Industries also transported finished goods to market. Steamboats and trains helped transport goods more quickly and cheaply, allowing industry to expand.)*

🖥 ACTIVE CLASSROOM
Ask students to pair with a partner to look at the "Advances in Transportation in England" map. Have them use the map layers on the key to reveal all of the data. Partners should then ask each other: What do you see? What does that make you think? What are you wondering about now that you've seen this? Share responses with the class or by posting the map and comments on Pinterest, Glogster, or Flicker.

The Industrial Revolution Begins

INTERACTIVE MAP
Advances in Transportation in England, 1800s

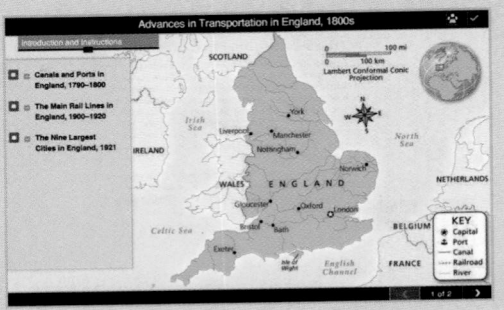

DIGITAL TEXT 7
Industrialization Spreads

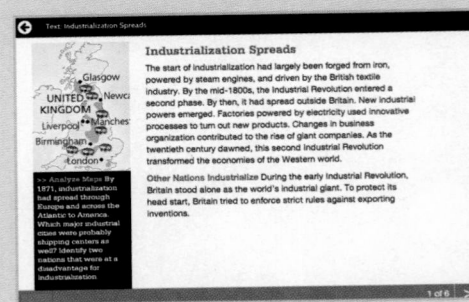

Further Instruction

A Revolution in Transportation: Core Text and Interactive Reading Notepad Use the questions in the notepad to help students demonstrate understanding of this section of the lesson. Be sure that students understand that as production increased, business owners needed to be able to move their goods more quickly and efficiently from place to place. This led to the development of turnpikes, canals, bridges, and railroads.

D Differentiate: Challenge Have students form groups to create and share a presentation about the role of railroads in England. Have members of the group perform different tasks such as providing illustrations, creating maps of specific routes, researching data, etc. If possible, invite other classes to review the presentation.

Objective 5: Trace how the Industrial Revolution spread.

Quick Instruction

Remind students that the Industrial Revolution began in the textile industry in Britain. Explain that it wasn't long before industrialization affected other industries and other countries.

Analyze Maps Project the "Centers of Industry, 1871" map. Ask students to list the centers of industry in Europe. Explain that these cities are where the Industrial Revolution spread. The cities grew as they became economic centers. Then draw students' attention to the inset map of the United States. Point out that when industrialization reached the United States, it took off quickly because of the amount of resources available to fuel industry.

D Differentiate: Extra Support Explain to students why coal and iron are on the map key. Remind them of the importance of these resources to industry. Point out that iron was needed to manufacture machines, rails, and trains. Coal was used to create the steam that worked the machines.

ELL Use the ELL activity described in the ELL chart.

Further Instruction

Industrialization Spreads: Core Text and Interactive Reading Notepad Project and discuss the Interactive Reading Notepad questions for this text. Use the questions and those below to spark class discussion about the spread of the Industrial Revolution.

Predict Consequences Ask students to brainstorm what the result might have been if Britain had been successful at preventing the knowledge about new textile inventions to spread to other countries. (*Answers will vary but students should demonstrate an understanding of the immense economic power Britain wanted to maintain and how some of that power was lost when industrialization spread.*)

Make Generalizations Have students refer to the "Centers of Industry" map and note that the United States is also included. Point out that individual countries in Europe are smaller in size than the United States. Ask students to generalize why land mass and resources in America are important to the discussion of industrialization. (*America's large size means that it may have more resources and labor to fuel its industries and that it also has a huge domestic market. These features give it an economic advantage over smaller countries.*)

▮ SYNTHESIZE

DIGITAL ACTIVITY
Causes of the Industrial Revolution

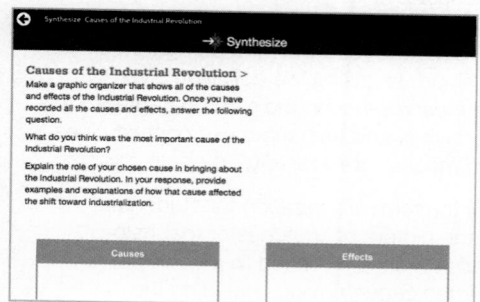

Project the Synthesize Activity Ask students to take turns filling out a class version of the graphic organizer on the whiteboard. Students should add new details to the organizer until it is completed. Have students check their own organizer against the class version to verify they have all the details.

Discuss Ask students to pick one of the causes listed on the board and create an argument for the importance of that cause. Then, conduct a debate in class. After students have had the opportunity to consider all the causes of industrialization and all the arguments for each cause, poll the class to determine if there is a single cause of industrialization that is most important. *(Responses will vary according to the opinions of the class, but encourage students to see how all the causes of the Industrial Revolution worked together to bring about industrialization.)*

▮ DEMONSTRATE

LESSON QUIZ
Lesson Quiz and Class Discussion Board

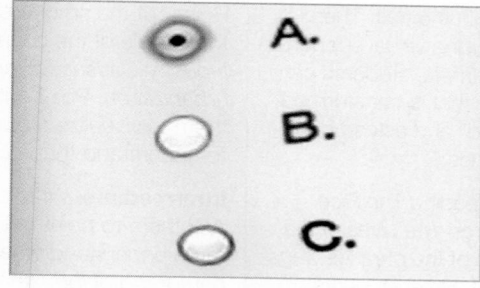

Assign the online Lesson Quiz for this lesson if you haven't already done so. Students will be offered automatic remediation or enrichment based on their score.

Discuss Pose these questions to the class on the Discussion Board:

Cite Evidence Explain the role of transportation technology in advancing the Industrial Revolution. Provide specific examples that illustrate why transportation was vital to industrial growth. *(Transportation allowed raw materials and coal to travel to factories and provided a way to get finished goods to markets. Advances include canals and steam engines for ships and trains. The shipping advances were vital because many industrial processes required material from a wide range of places.)*

Make Predictions Based on what you have learned about the move away from a rural way of life and the subsequent growth of cities, what do you think living and working conditions were like in England in the 1800s? *(Students may have prior knowledge of tenements and slum conditions as well as long work hours and child labor practices. Encourage all suggestions and let students know they will find out about the impact of the Industrial Revolution on humanity in the next lesson.)*

Topic Inquiry
Have students continue their investigations for the Topic Inquiry.

Social Impact of Industrialism

Supporting English Language Learners

Use with Digital Text 2, **The Rise of New Social Classes.**

Speaking

Beginning Read *The Rise of New Social Classes* aloud to students. Then have students focus on *The Lives of the New Middle Class* for this activity. Carefully review the phrase "rags to riches" as it is used in the text. Then have students describe orally what the phrase means, using visual supports to show the meaning of the phrase if necessary. For example, students can draw a "before and after" picture of a person or a home that is transformed from poor to wealthy. Then define the phrase "get ahead" and ask students to explain orally how it relates to the phrase "rags to riches."

Intermediate Ask several student volunteers to share reading *The Rise of New Social Classes* aloud. Then have students focus on *The Lives of the New Middle Class* for this activity. Discuss the meanings of the phrases "rags to riches" and to "get ahead" as they are used in the text. Have students use phrases (including to "get ahead") and complete sentences to describe out loud to the class what it would be like if someone from modern times experienced a "rags to riches" transformation.

Advanced After students have read *The Rise of New Social Classes*, ask them to think about the meaning of the phrase, "rags to riches." Point out that this phrase describes a transition, or change, that a person experiences. It also describes movement. Then have students turn to a partner and explain the meaning of the phrase to "get ahead," which also describes movement. Remind students to use context clues to help them figure out the meanings.

Advanced High After reading *The Rise of New Social Classes*, ask students to discuss the meanings of the phrases "rags to riches" and to "get ahead" with a partner. Point out that these phrases describe movement, and remind students to use context clues to help them figure out the meanings. After the discussion, have students share their ideas with the class.

Use with Digital Text 1, **Industry Causes Urban Growth.**

Reading

Beginning Write and display the term *urbanization* for students. Help students use the picture of Manchester to define what the term means. Point out the smokestacks of the factories and the growth of the city in the middle of the countryside. Proceed to read the third paragraph of *Industry Causes Urban Growth* aloud, stressing the definition given of *urbanization*. Point out the word *mushroomed* in the same paragraph. Ask them to visualize a mushroom growing, and help them use context clues to understand that *mushroomed* means "grew rapidly."

Intermediate Write and display the term *urbanization* for students. Ask them to point out details in the picture of Manchester that help them understand what urbanization means. Proceed to read the third paragraph of *Industry Causes Urban Growth* aloud, including the definition of *urbanization*. Then ask students to use context to create a glossary definition for the term *mushroomed* in the same paragraph, including an illustration.

Advanced Write and display the term *urbanization* for students. Have students independently look at the picture of Manchester and read the third paragraph of *Industry Causes Urban Growth*, focusing on the definition of *urbanization*. Then ask students to use context to create a glossary page for the term *mushroomed*, including a definition, an illustration, and a sentence that uses the term correctly.

Advanced High Have students skim *Industry Causes Urban Growth* and create a list of terms that might be unfamiliar to them or to other students. Then, have students create a pictorial glossary that includes a definition, a sketch, and a sentence for each term on their lists. Have students share their mini-glossaries with the class.

D Differentiate Instruction

Use the Differentiated Instruction notes throughout the lesson plan to support the varied skill sets, levels of readiness, and interests in the mixed-ability classroom.

Challenge These notes include suggestions for expanding the activity for advanced students.

On-Level These notes include suggestions for modifying the activity to address different interests or learning styles.

Extra Support These notes include ideas for providing more scaffolding or reading spuport.

Special Needs These notes provide ideas for adapting instruction to support the needs of various special needs students.

NOTES

PEARSON
realize™
www.PearsonRealize.com

Go online to access additional resources including:
Primary Sources • Biographies • Supreme Court cases •
21st Century Skill Tutorials • Maps • Graphic Organizers.

Objectives

Objective 1: Outline the growth of industrial cities and the emergence of new social classes.

Objective 2: Describe the working conditions in factories and mines.

Objective 3: Analyze the benefits and challenges of industrialism.

Objective 4: Describe the ideas of Adam Smith and other thinkers regarding free enterprise.

Objective 5: Identify the origins and characteristics of socialism and communism.

LESSON 2 ORGANIZER		PACING: APPROX. 1 PERIOD, .5 BLOCKS			
		OBJECTIVES	PACING	RESOURCES	
				Online	Print
Connect					
DIGITAL START UP ACTIVITY **Working Conditions**			5 min.	●	
Investigate					
DIGITAL TEXTS 1 AND 2 **Industry Causes Urban Growth, The Rise of New Social Classes**		Objective 1	10 min.	●	●
DIGITAL TEXT 3 **Harsh Conditions in Factories and Mines**		Objective 2	10 min.	●	●
INTERACTIVE GALLERY **Life of the Working Class**			10 min.	●	
DIGITAL TEXT 4 **Benefits of the Industrial Revolution**		Objective 3	10 min.	●	●
DIGITAL TEXTS 5 AND 6 **Laissez-Faire Economics, Utilitarians Support Limited Government**		Objective 4	10 min.	●	●
DIGITAL TEXTS 7 AND 8 **Socialist Thought Emerges, Marx and the Origins of Communism**		Objective 5	10 min.	●	●
INTERACTIVE CHART **Comparing Economic Systems**			10 min.	●	
Synthesize					
DIGITAL ACTIVITY **Economic Schools of Thought**			5 min.	●	
Demonstrate					
LESSON QUIZ **Lesson Quiz and Class Discussion Board**			10 min.	●	

Social Impact of Industrialism

▮ CONNECT

DIGITAL START UP ACTIVITY
Working Conditions

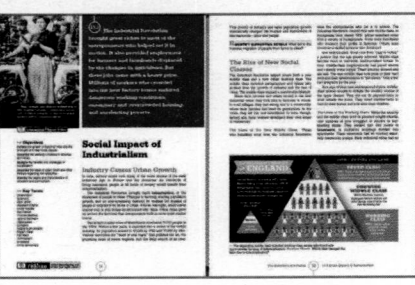

Project the Start Up Activity As students enter and get settled, ask them to look at the photograph on the board. Then have students write their journal entry. Encourage students to share their journals with a partner.

Discuss If you were a teenager in 1850, how would you feel about working a 12-hour day in a factory or coal mine? *(Students will likely respond that it would be difficult and give them little time for doing anything else.)* Why do you think children were expected to work? *(Sample Response: Children worked to help out their families. They earned money to help pay for rent and food.)*

Tell students that in this section they will learn about the social and political effects of the Industrial Revolution.

Aa Vocabulary Development: Use the Interactive Reading Notepad to preview the Key Terms and Academic Vocabulary in this Lesson with students.

⇅ FLIP IT!
Assign the Flipped Video for this lesson.

▮ STUDENT EDITION PRINT PAGES: 504–512

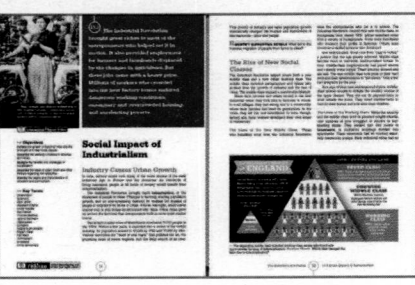

▮ INVESTIGATE

DIGITAL TEXT 1
Industry Causes Urban Growth

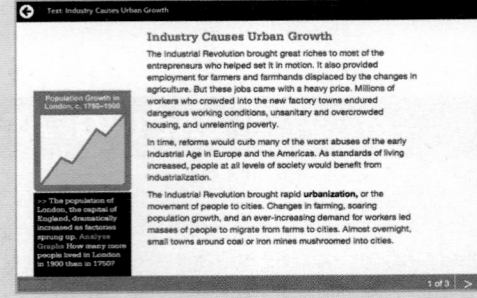

DIGITAL TEXT 2
The Rise of New Social Classes

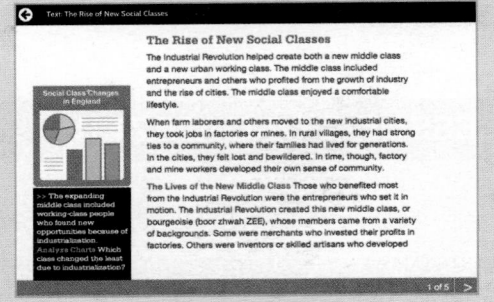

Objective 1: Outline the growth of industrial cities and the emergence of new social classes.

Quick Instruction
Before the Industrial Revolution, European society generally had two classes: the landed nobility and peasants. The economy was based almost entirely on agriculture. The Industrial Revolution changed all that.

Analyze Images Project the Social Class Changes in England infographic. What caused the rise of the middle class? *(New business opportunities and economic growth expanded the middle class.)* Ask students to describe ways that the Industrial Revolution led to social changes in Europe. *(Students should identify how the growing cities differed from rural villages and describe the harsh living and working conditions that industrialization created.)*

D Differentiate: Extra Support Help students understand the differences among the social classes in England at this time. Use a table or chart labeled *Working, Middle,* and *Upper* and have students review the lesson and fill out the table with details from the text and observations from images.

Further Instruction
Editable Presentation Use the Editable Presentation to present the main ideas for these Core Texts.

Industry Causes Urban Growth; The Rise of the New Social Classes: Core Texts and Interactive Reading Notepads Go through the Interactive Reading Notepad questions for both texts and discuss the answers with the class.

Identify Cause and Effect Ask students to describe the major effects of the Industrial Revolution. They should focus on the link between industry and urban growth. *(Cities grew around the factories that entrepreneurs built. Towns near coal and iron mines also expanded as demand for these resources increased.)*

Analyze Images Have students look at the photo of Manchester in the interactive text "Industry Causes Urban Growth." Ask students to describe what life might be like in an urban industrial place like this. *(Students should support their opinion with details from the image.)* Then ask students to identify important changes in human life caused by the Industrial Revolution. If students need help describing the changes, have them compare this urban scene to what they know about life before industrialization. *(Students should identify how rural and urban ways of life differ and describe the harsh living and working conditions that industrialization brought about.)*

DIGITAL TEXT 3

Harsh Conditions in Factories and Mines

INTERACTIVE GALLERY

Life of the Working Class

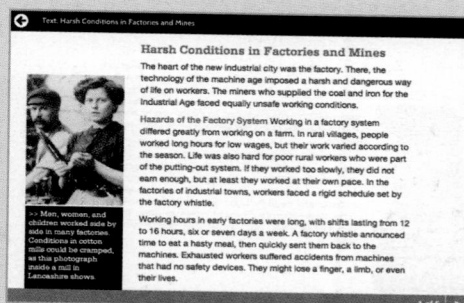

Objective 2: Describe the working conditions in factories and mines.

Quick Instruction

Review that the earliest factories housed machines used to make textiles. One of the most common types of mines in Great Britain was the coal mine.

Interactive Gallery: Life of the Working Class Project the gallery, and click on each of the images. Ask for students' reactions to the images.

Make Generalizations Have students describe the working conditions in factories, basing their responses on the text and the images in the slideshow. Then ask students to explain the role of the factory system in advancing the Industrial Revolution. *(Factories were centers of manufacturing. Using new technology and machines, workers in factories churned out goods. Conditions in factories were often harsh, however. Loud machines ran during the long workdays. Hazards included potential fires and dangerous machines.)*

Formulate Questions Then have students choose an industry's working conditions that they would like to learn more about. Have them write several questions they would like to have answered.

⬛ ACTIVE CLASSROOM

Have students choose an image in the interactive gallery and Cartoon It. Be sure students understand that political cartoons often use exaggeration to emphasize an opinion on a topic. Students should identify a key concept or main idea and emphasize it with their political cartoon. Post their cartoons in the classroom or include them in a class blog on the effects of the Industrial Revolution.

D Differentiate: Challenge Remind students that reformers focused attention on child labor. Have student pairs conduct interviews, with one person in the pair serving as a reform committee member and the other as a child laborer. Then, have them switch roles as interviewer and subject. Tell them they can read first hand accounts of working conditions online to enrich the content of their interviews.

Further Instruction

Harsh Conditions in Factories and Mines: Core Text and Interactive Reading Notepad Project the Interactive Reading Notepad questions, and have students answer as they progress through the text.

Predict Consequences Have students list the working conditions men, women, and children faced due to industrialization. Use this list to discuss the impact of the Industrial Revolution on humanity. *(Students should*

recognize that industrialization brought about intense social change.) Why did children work, too? (Families needed the extra income and children had worked on farms, so it wasn't unusual for them to work.)

Make Decisions Ask students to think about what they would do if faced with similar working conditions. *(Students' answers will vary, but they should demonstrate understanding of the obstacles people faced.)*

Social Impact of Industrialism

DIGITAL TEXT 4

Benefits of the Industrial Revolution

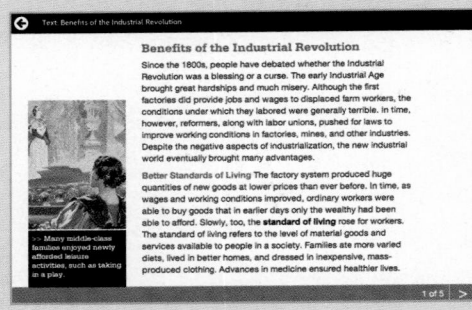

DIGITAL TEXT 5

Laissez-Faire Economics

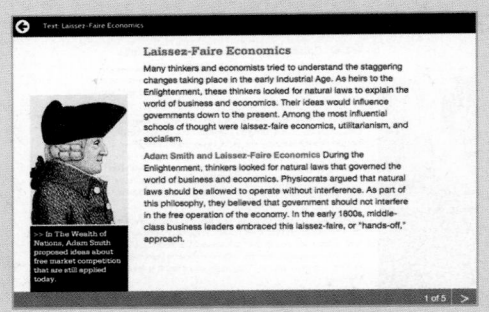

Objective 3: Analyze the benefits and challenges of industrialism.

Quick Instruction

Remind students that they have already learned about some of the negative results of industrialism: workers put in long hours under harsh, sometimes dangerous conditions. Counter this by explaining that industrialism also brought benefits, such as jobs, increased incomes, cheaper goods, and the creation of a middle class.

Project the photograph from the text of a couple enjoying a play, and explain that the emerging middle class had more leisure time and disposable income because of the Industrial Revolution.

Analyze Images What does this photograph reveal about the benefits of industrialization? *(Some people could use their leisure time and disposable income to participate in enjoyable activities.)*

D Differentiate: Challenge Have students present possible solutions to the negative effects of industrialization. Is it possible to have only a positive outcome and no negative results? *(Sample Response: No; there are typically benefits and costs to every decision.)*

Further Instruction

Benefits of the Industrial Revolution: Core Text and Interactive Reading Notepad Use the questions in the Interactive Reading Notepad to review the content of this section.

Harsh Conditions in Factories and Mines: Core Text Review the content in the Core Text to remind students of the challenges of industrialism. Students should then contrast these challenges with the benefits presented in the narrative under "Better Standards of Living" and "New Worlds for Entrepreneurs."

Identify Main Ideas Have students make a table of the challenges and benefits of industrialization in order to evaluate industrialization's effect on society. *(Challenges: long hours, dangerous working conditions, low pay. Benefits: jobs, economic opportunities, cheaper goods, higher standard of living.)*

Make Generalizations Review the negative and positive effects of the Industrial Revolution, and ask students whether they think the benefits of industrialization outweigh the costs. *(Answers will vary, but students should base their opinions on facts and provide details from the lesson to support their point of view. Some might point out that most of the technology we have today wouldn't have been possible without the Industrial Revolution.)*

Objective 4: Describe the ideas of Adam Smith and other thinkers regarding free enterprise.

Quick Instruction

Identify the characteristics of the free enterprise system: a free market with unregulated exchange of goods and services and no government interference in the economy.

Apply Concepts Remind students that according to Enlightenment ideals, "natural law" is a set of principles derived from nature. It is common to and binding upon all human beings. Ask students to explain how natural law relates to free enterprise. *(Free market economists believed that the market operated according to a set of natural laws. Therefore, a free market economy does not need government regulation or interference.)*

D Differentiate: Extra Support Explain that in a free enterprise system, the market—where goods are exchanged between sellers and buyers—determines price. In a free market, buyers use demand to help set prices by purchasing goods at an acceptable cost or by choosing not to purchase goods that are priced too high.

Further Instruction

Laissez-Faire Economics; Utilitarians Support Limited Government: Core Text and Interactive Reading Notepads Go through the Interactive Reading Notepad questions for both texts and discuss the answers with the class.

DIGITAL TEXT 6

Utilitarians Support Limited Government

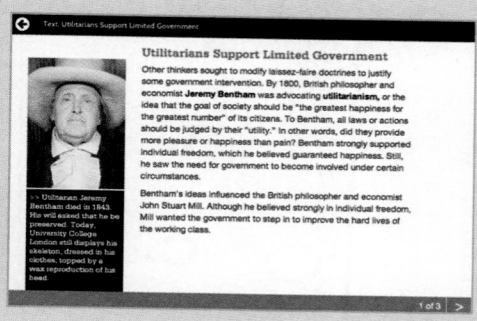

Utilitarians Support Limited Government

Other thinkers sought to modify laissez-faire doctrines to justify some government intervention. By 1800, British philosopher and economist **Jeremy Bentham** was advocating **utilitarianism**, or the idea that the goal of society should be "the greatest happiness for the greatest number" of its citizens. To Bentham, all laws or actions should be judged by their "utility." In other words, did they provide more pleasure or happiness than pain? Bentham strongly supported individual freedom, which he believed guaranteed happiness. Still, he saw the need for government to become involved under certain circumstances.

Bentham's ideas influenced the British philosopher and economist John Stuart Mill. Although he believed strongly in individual freedom, Mill wanted the government to step in to improve the hard lives of the working class.

>> Utilitarian Jeremy Bentham died in 1843. He will asked that he be preserved. Today, University College London still displays his skeleton, dressed in his clothes, topped by a wax reproduction of his head.

1 of 3 >

DIGITAL TEXT 7

Socialist Thought Emerges

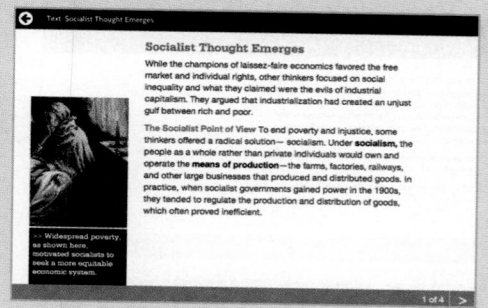

Socialist Thought Emerges

While the champions of laissez-faire economics favored the free market and individual rights, other thinkers focused on social inequality and what they claimed were the evils of industrial capitalism. They argued that industrialization had created an unjust gulf between rich and poor.

The Socialist Point of View To end poverty and injustice, some thinkers offered a radical solution— socialism. Under **socialism**, the people as a whole rather than private individuals would own and operate the **means of production**—the farms, factories, railways, and other large businesses that produced and distributed goods. In practice, when socialist governments gained power in the 1900s, they tended to regulate the production and distribution of goods, which often proved inefficient.

>> Widespread poverty, as shown here, motivated socialists to seek a more equitable economic system.

1 of 4 >

DIGITAL TEXT 8

Marx and the Origins of Communism

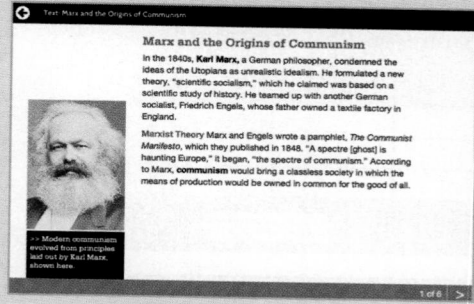

Marx and the Origins of Communism

In the 1840s, **Karl Marx**, a German philosopher, condemned the ideas of the Utopians as unrealistic idealism. He formulated a new theory, "scientific socialism," which he claimed was based on a scientific study of history. He teamed up with another German socialist, Friedrich Engels, whose father owned a textile factory in England.

Marxist Theory Marx and Engels wrote a pamphlet, The Communist Manifesto, which they published in 1848. "A spectre [ghost] is haunting Europe," it began, "the spectre of communism." According to Marx, **communism** would bring a classless society in which the means of production would be owned in common for the good of all.

>> Modern communism evolved from principles laid out by Karl Marx, shown here.

1 of 6 >

Evaluate Sources
Show students the following quotation. Help them with any unfamiliar vocabulary.

"POLITICAL ECONOMY... proposes two distinct objects; first, to provide a plentiful revenue or subsistence for the people, or, more properly, to enable them to provide such a revenue or subsistence for themselves; and, secondly, to supply the state or commonwealth with a revenue sufficient for the public services."
—Adam Smith, *The Wealth of Nations*

Paraphrase
Ask students to restate the purpose of political economy according to Smith. *(The object of political economy is to provide sufficient money or goods for people to live and to provide sufficient revenue for the government to provide public services.)*

Apply Concepts
Ask students to use what they know about laissez-faire economics to explain how a free market fulfills the object of political economy, according to Adam Smith. *(A free market allows people and the state to have sufficient means. Price is determined by the free market, which responds to supply and demand without interference.)*

Objective 5: Identify the origins and characteristics of socialism and communism.

Quick Instruction
Remind students what they have learned about free enterprise, socialism, and communism, and briefly review the definitions of each.

Interactive Chart: Comparing Economic Systems Project the interactive chart on the board. Have volunteers take turns identifying where each statement should be moved.

Analyze Charts When the chart is completed correctly, ask students to compare and contrast the three economic systems to verify their understanding. Because socialism and communism have similarities, make sure students can distinguish between them. *(Capitalism: a free market where individuals own the means of production; Socialism: the community as a whole owns the means of production and cooperates together; Communism: like socialism, the means of production are not individually owned; however, the change to communism is revolution with the workers united to overthrow owners.)*

👥 ACTIVE CLASSROOM

Explain to students that economic systems differ according to who decides what and how much to produce. Group students, and give each a three-column organizer with headings for "Plus," "Minus," and "Interesting."

Ask students to use the organizer to respond to the statement: "Individuals should have the right to own and control the means of production." Have students record their responses by asking: What are the positives about this? What are the negatives about this? What is interesting about this?

D Differentiate: Extra Support This section includes references to economic concepts with which students may not be familiar. Have students write down unfamiliar terms. Have them call out the terms, and others can suggest possible definitions. Clarify the meanings so that students understand the main concepts of this lesson.

Further Instruction
Socialist Thought Emerges; Marx and the Roots of Communism: Core Texts and Interactive Reading Notepads Go through the Interactive Reading Notepad questions for both texts and discuss the answers with the class.

Social Impact of Industrialism

 SYNTHESIZE

 DEMONSTRATE

INTERACTIVE CHART
Comparing Economic Systems

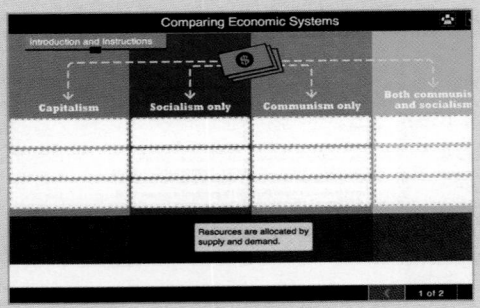

DIGITAL ACTIVITY
Economic Schools of Thought

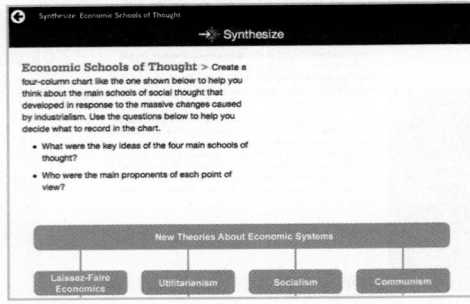

LESSON QUIZ
Lesson Quiz and Class Discussion Board

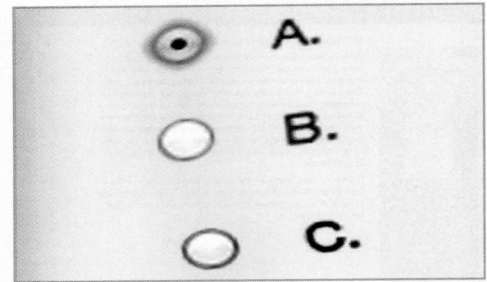

Integrate Information Ask students to summarize how changes to the economy resulting from the Industrial Revolution affected political change. *(The Industrial Revolution quickly expanded the economic power of industrialized countries, leading to new economic theories that eventually drove political decisions.)*

Cite Evidence Have students fill out the following statement three times to identify the historical origin of the three economic systems covered in this lesson. "_____ developed from views about _____." *(Free enterprise: views about laissez-faire economics from Smith, Malthus, and Ricardo; socialism: views about class, injustice, and shared means of production; communism: views about the proletariat rising up to overthrow the bourgeoisie, as predicted by Karl Marx.)*

Compare Points of View Verify that students understand the origins of contemporary economic systems by having them conduct a class debate. Divide the class into three groups and assign an economic system to each group. Groups should research the origins, benefits, and drawbacks of their economic system. Groups can take turns presenting arguments for or against their economic system.

Remind students of the Topic Essential Question: How do science and technology affect society? How does the EQ relate to the development of new ideas about society and the economy? Project the Synthesize Activity. Go through details about the economic systems with students. *(Sample Response: **Laissez-faire** economics are described in Adam Smith's book The Wealth of Nations. Smith believed the free exchange of goods and services would help everyone by producing more goods at lower, more affordable prices. A growing economy would encourage capitalists to reinvest profits in new ventures. **Utilitarians** thought that the government should intervene to improve conditions of the working class. John Stuart Mill thought that the government should step in to prevent harm to others. **Socialists** believed that society as a whole should own the means of production. Some socialists, like Robert Owen, founded communities where the work was shared and all property was owned in common. Karl Marx wrote about **communism** in The Communist Manifesto. He thought that the working class, or proletariat, should unite to overthrow the wealthy class, or bourgeoisie. The result would be a classless society where everyone owned the means of production.)*

Discuss Ask the following for each of the economic systems in the organizer. In what way does _____ address the distribution of wealth brought on by industrialization?

Then ask students to revisit their journal entries from the Connect activity. Have students identify details they would like to change or add to the entry based on what they learned in the lesson.

Assign the online Lesson Quiz for this lesson if you haven't already done so. Students will be offered automatic remediation or enrichment based on their score.

Pose these questions to the class on the Discussion Board:

Make Generalizations Why do historians analyze the Industrial Revolution in terms of positives and negatives? *(The Industrial Revolution created massive social, economic, and political change. As a result, people continue to debate its effects, including its benefits and costs.)*

Apply Concepts Why are economic systems fundamental to studying the Industrial Revolution? *(Industry generated huge profits and produced more wealth than before. Therefore, the Industrial Revolution changed the distribution of wealth and brought attention to class distinctions. New economic systems of thought developed to answer questions about how to distribute the profits from industry. In addition, inequities in society grew, and some thinkers proposed different systems to deal with this change.)*

Topic Inquiry
Have students continue their investigations for the Topic Inquiry.

PEARSON REALIZE™

www.PearsonRealize.com
Access your Digital Lesson

The Second Industrial Revolution

Supporting English Language Learners

Use with Digital Texts 1 and 2, **Advances in Transportation and Communication.**

Learning Strategies, Reading
Write and display each sentence from the second paragraph of this section. Make sure the sentences look as if they stand alone. Do not write them in paragraph form.

Beginning Read the sentences aloud to students. Help students identify which sentence is the most simple and which sentence is the most complex. Explain that the last sentence is more complex than the others because it includes a dependent clause that gives more information about the effects of Henry Ford's use of the assembly line. Underline or circle the dependent clauses in each sentence so students can see how they relate to the rest of the sentence.

Intermediate Have a student volunteer read the sentences aloud to students. Then help students identify the independent and dependent clauses in each sentence. Explain that dependent clauses "lean on" independent clauses. Dependent clauses are also used to add information to the main idea of a sentence.

Advanced Have students read the sentences and number them according to their complexity level, with one being the most simple. Then have students determine the independent and dependent clauses for each sentence by underlining the independent clause twice and underlining the dependent clause twice. Ask students to explain the purpose of a dependent clause to a partner. Support student understanding as necessary.

Advanced High Have students identify the dependent and independent clauses in the paragraph. Then have them compose a sentence about the automobile industry that includes independent and dependent clauses. When they are finished, students should share their sentences with the class.

Use with Digital Text 4, **Better Medicine, Nutrition, and Health.**

Learning Strategies, Speaking
Explain that learning how sounds and letters behave in different English words in the text will help students recognize word patterns in other academic texts.

Beginning Read the first paragraph of *Better Medicine, Nutrition, and Health* aloud to students. Point out the words in the paragraph with a –*tion* ending, including population, distribution, and nutrition. Say each word slowly, focusing on the ending of each word to show the similarities among them. Explain that the –*tion* ending always sounds like "shən." Have students practice these words by listening and repeating them when they are said aloud.

Intermediate Read the first paragraph of *Better Medicine, Nutrition, and Health* aloud with students. Have students point out the words in the paragraph with a –*tion* ending, including *population, distribution,* and *nutrition.* Say *population* slowly, focusing on the –*tion* ending. Then have students repeat *population* while focusing on the –*tion* ending. Explain that the –*tion* ending always sounds like "shən." Then have students practice saying other –*tion* words, including *distribution,* and *nutrition.*

Advanced Have students read the first paragraph of *Better Medicine, Nutrition, and Health* aloud to a partner. Then have them identify and make a list of all the words in this paragraph that contain the word ending –*tion,* including *population, distribution,* and *nutrition.* Have students practice these words by repeating them aloud to a partner.

Advanced High After reading *Better Medicine, Nutrition, and Health* independently, ask students to identify the –*tion* words in the text. Make sure students understand how this suffix sounds and how it changes the meaning of the root word from another part of speech into a noun. For example, *populate,* a verb, becomes *population,* a noun, when –*tion* is added. Have students identify the meaning and part of speech of *distribution,* and *nutrition,* as well as the meaning and part of speech of both root words. If necessary, have them use a dictionary.

▣ Differentiate Instruction

Use the Differentiated Instruction notes throughout the lesson plan to support the varied skill sets, levels of readiness, and interests in the mixed-ability classroom.

Challenge These notes include suggestions for expanding the activity for advanced students.

On-Level These notes include suggestions for modifying the activity to address different interests or learning styles.

Extra Support These notes include ideas for providing more scaffolding or reading spuport.

Special Needs These notes provide ideas for adapting instruction to support the needs of various special needs students.

■ **NOTES**

The Second Industrial Revolution

Objectives

Objective 1: Describe the impact of new technology on industry, transportation, and communication.

Objective 2: Understand how big business emerged.

Objective 3: Summarize the impact of medical advances in the later 1800s.

Objective 4: Describe how cities changed and grew.

Objective 5: Explain how conditions for workers gradually improved.

LESSON 3 ORGANIZER	PACING: APPROX. 1 PERIOD, .5 BLOCKS			
			RESOURCES	
	OBJECTIVES	**PACING**	**Online**	**Print**
Connect				
DIGITAL START UP ACTIVITY **Predict the Future**		5 min.	●	
Investigate				
DIGITAL TEXTS 1 AND 2 **Science and Technology Change Industry, Advances in Transportation and Communication**	Objective 1	10 min.	●	●
INTERACTIVE TIMELINE **Transportation Milestones**		10 min.	●	
DIGITAL TEXT 3 **The Rise of Big Business**	Objective 2	10 min.	●	●
DIGITAL TEXT 4 **Better Medicine, Nutrition, and Health**	Objective 3	10 min.	●	●
INTERACTIVE GALLERY **Advances in Medicine During the Industrial Age**		10 min.	●	
DIGITAL TEXT 5 **City Life Changes**	Objective 4	10 min.	●	●
3-D MODEL **Living in a Tenement**		10 min.	●	
DIGITAL TEXT 6 **The Working Class Wins New Rights**	Objective 5	10 min.	●	●
Synthesize				
DIGITAL ACTIVITY **Birth of the Industrial City**		5 min.	●	
Demonstrate				
LESSON QUIZ **Lesson Quiz and Class Discussion Board**		10 min.	●	

PEARSON
realize™
www.PearsonRealize.com

Go online to access additional resources including:
Primary Sources • Biographies • Supreme Court cases •
21st Century Skill Tutorials • Maps • Graphic Organizers.

CONNECT

DIGITAL START UP ACTIVITY
Predict the Future

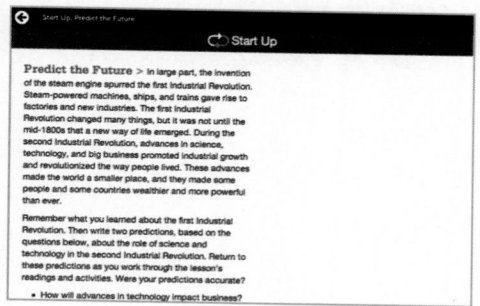

Project the Start Up Activity Ask students to answer the questions from the Start Up Activity as they enter and get settled: How will advances in technology impact business? *(Answers will vary. Students may say that more industries will become mechanized, so that a wider variety of goods become affordable.)* Have students share their ideas with another student, either in class or through a chat room or blog.

Identify Cause and Effect Have students discuss the impact of technology on their lives. Have all of the effects been positive? Explain.

Tell students that in this lesson they will learn about the impact of advances in science, technology, transportation, and communication during the Industrial Revolution.

Aa Vocabulary Development: Use the Interactive Reading Notepad to preview the Key Terms and Academic Vocabulary in this Lesson with students.

⇅ FLIP IT!

Assign the Flipped Video for this lesson.

■ STUDENT EDITION PRINT
PAGES: 513–519

INVESTIGATE

DIGITAL TEXT 1
Science and Technology Change Industry

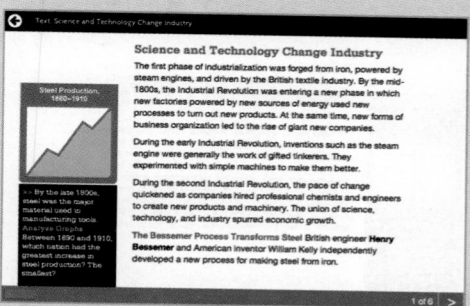

DIGITAL TEXT 2
Advances in Transportation and Communication

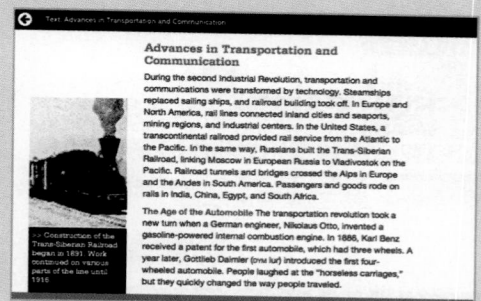

Objective 1: Describe the impact of new technology on industry, transportation, and communication.

Quick Instruction

Interactive Timeline: Transportation Milestones Project the timeline. Introduce the activity by explaining that advances in transportation technology changed the way people traveled and transported goods. These innovations also changed cities by introducing subway systems, elevated trains, paved roads, and bridges. Click through each hot spot on the timeline, and discuss the impact each development had on society and the role it played in advancing the Industrial Revolution.

📽 ACTIVE CLASSROOM

List the following innovations on the board: electricity, dynamo, automobile, airplane, internal combustion engine, radio, telephone, telegraph, interchangeable parts, and assembly line. Ask students to rank them according to which they think had the greatest impact on society and business. Ask students to provide a justification for the ranking based on how each development led to social changes. Then have students work in pairs to share their ideas. *(Answers will vary. Students should provide reasons for their ranking that include specific effects on society, such as greater mobility or instant communications, or improvements in the factory system leading to lower prices for goods.)*

D Differentiate: Challenge/Gifted After students complete their ranking, have them write a short opinion essay explaining the reasons for their top ranking. Remind students to use evidence to support their claim. Have students exchange their essays with a partner and discuss their claim and evidence.

Further Instruction

Editable Presentation Use the Editable Presentation to present the main ideas for these Core Texts.

Science and Technology Change Industry; Advances in Transportation and Communication: Core Texts and Interactive Reading Notepads Project a cause-and-effect graphic organizer. Have students explain the causes and effects of the Industrial Revolution. Fill in the organizer with students' responses. Then project and discuss the Interactive Reading Notepad questions for both core texts. Finally, ask students the following questions:

• Identify the contributions of Thomas Edison and other inventors. How did these inventions advance the Industrial Revolution? *(Sample Response: Edison invented the electric light bulb, which allowed factories to stay open longer and made city streets safer. Faraday invented the dynamo, which was essential for later inventions. Otto invented the internal combustion engine, later used in cars, airplanes, and farming equipment.)*

The Second Industrial Revolution

INTERACTIVE TIMELINE
Transportation Milestones

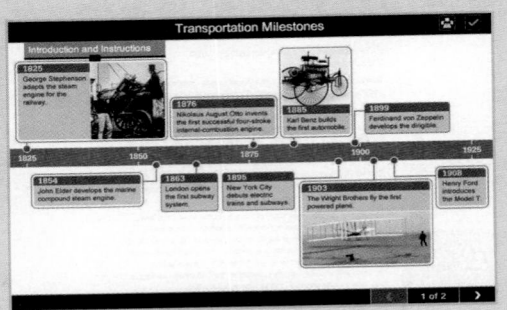

DIGITAL TEXT 3
The Rise of Big Business

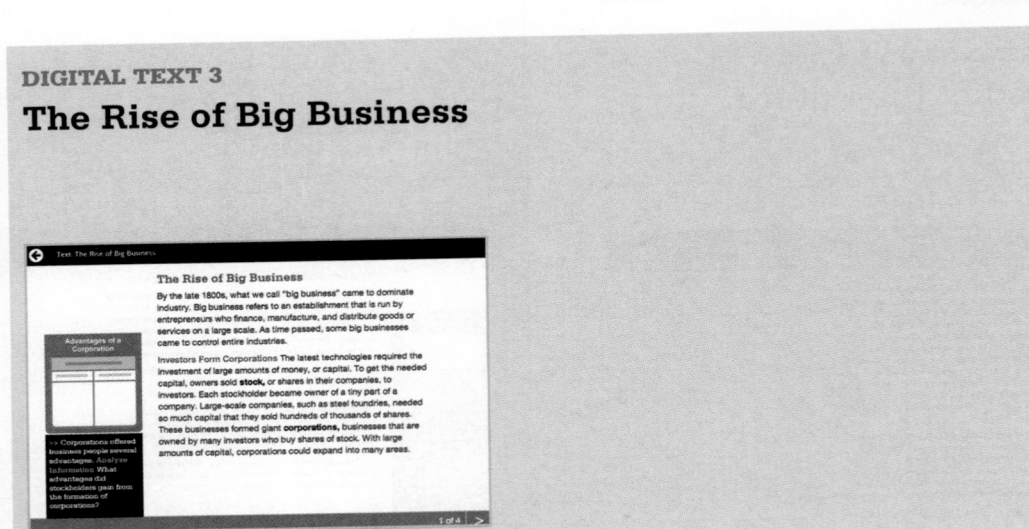

- Explain the global impact of advances in communications and transportation technology and how they led to economic changes. *(Sample Response: Business leaders could communicate more quickly and ship their goods farther, including to foreign countries. New inventions, such as cars, meant more jobs and money because people had to produce the cars.)*

Make Predictions Divide students into small groups and have them write predictions about the additional changes the Industrial Revolution will bring about. Have them explain how these changes will further affect society, business, and the economy. Then discuss their ideas as a class. Have them keep these predictions in mind as they continue reading.

Objective 2: Understand how big business emerged.

Quick Instruction

New technologies and methods of production led to economic changes in Europe and the United States. Entrepreneurs, such as John D. Rockefeller, Alfred Krupp, and Andew Carnegie, formed big businesses and began to finance, manufacture, and distribute goods on a large scale. These big businesses soon dominated industry. In order to get the money they needed, owners began selling stock in their companies. Some powerful leaders created monopolies that controlled entire industries or sectors of the economy.

Analyze Images Project the image of the political cartoon from the text, "The Rise of Big Business." Some critics believed the growth of monopolies had a dangerous effect on society. What does this political cartoon show? Why do you think the cartoonist represented monopolies this way? *(The cartoon shows a monopoly as an octopus-like monster that is taking over businesses. The cartoonist most likely opposed monopolies because they crushed their competitors.)*

D Differentiate: **Challenge/Gifted** Ask students to create their own political cartoons representing big business or monopolies. Remind them that political cartoons express an opinion about an issue. Have students post their cartoons on a Web site or in the classroom.

Further Instruction

To extend the teaching of this objective, have students answer the following question: How did big business, monopolies, and cartels impact the economies of Europe and the United States? *(Monopolies took over whole industries. Cartels were able to fix prices, set production quotas, and control markets. Monopolies and cartels put many small companies out of business. Big business also created the stock market and a new way to invest money.)*

DIGITAL TEXT 4

Better Medicine, Nutrition, and Health

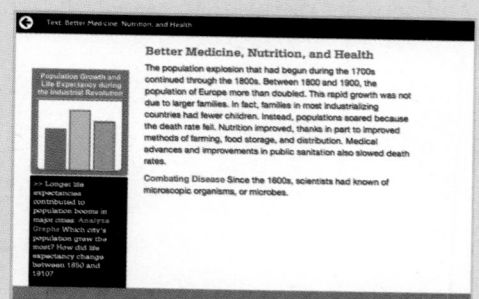

INTERACTIVE GALLERY

Advances in Medicine During the Industrial Age

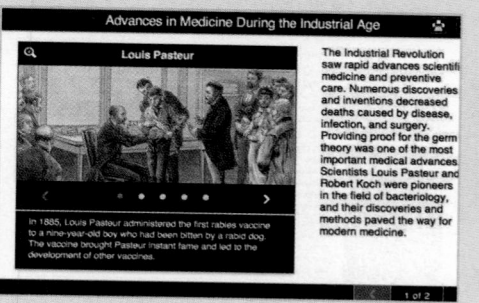

DIGITAL TEXT 5

City Life Changes

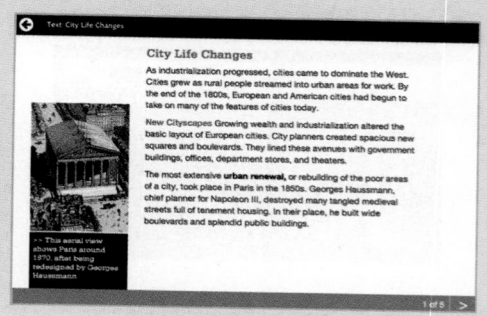

Objective 3: Summarize the impact of medical advances in the later 1800s.

Quick Instruction

The population in Europe exploded during the Industrial Revolution. The rapid increase in population was the direct result of better nutrition and sanitation and major advances in medicine. The discoveries and contributions of many people, such as scientist Louis Pasteur, helped combat disease and create safer, cleaner hospitals.

Interactive Gallery: Advances in Medicine During the Industrial Age Project the slideshow. Look at each image individually and then the collection of images as a whole.

Analyze Images Project the image of Louis Pasteur from the text. What does the image show? How does it help you understand how his contributions improved human life? *(The image shows Pasteur giving vaccinations to people, which kept them from getting different diseases, such as rabies. His contributions lowered the death rate.)*

👥 ACTIVE CLASSROOM

Have students choose two images from the gallery and write headlines that capture the action in each image or the information in the captions. Then divide the class into small groups and have students discuss their headlines. Have groups synthesize their ideas to write a revised headline for each image.

D **Differentiate: Extra Support** Help students understand the different types of medical advances. Explain any terms that might be unfamiliar, such as *vaccines, unsanitary, antiseptics,* and *sterilize.* Ask students why it would be important for doctors to wash their hands and instruments. *(Dirty hands and instruments can lead to infection.)*

ELL Use the ELL activity described in the ELL chart.

Further Instruction

Advances in medicine and science led to important changes in human life. New vaccines and antiseptic operations meant people lived longer than ever before. Improved sanitation in hospitals was particularly important for the poor because they could not afford to be treated at home.

Go through the Interactive Reading Notepad questions and discuss the answers with the class. Then have students work in groups to discuss the following questions:

Express Ideas Clearly Florence Nightingale said that, "The very first requirement in a hospital is that it should do the sick no harm." To what is she referring? What did she believe was necessary in hospitals? Do you agree or disagree with her statement? Does her statement still hold true today? *(Sample Response: She means that the conditions in hospitals and the actions of doctors should not make patients sicker. She believed that proper sanitation could reduce the death rate and prevent the spread of infection. Most students will agree with her statement and say that it is still true today. Hospitals, doctors, and nurses can and should be held accountable for their actions.)*

Objective 4: Describe how cities changed and grew.

Quick Instruction

The Industrial Revolution did not just change the way goods were produced and shipped and the way people communicated and traveled. It also changed the way people lived and the way cities looked. Large cities came to have paved streets lined with electric lights, large buildings, skyscrapers, apartments, and department stores. Sewer systems were installed to improve sanitation and water quality. New forms of transportation, such as trams and electric trains, allowed wealthier people to move away from the city center.

3-D Model: Living in a Tenement Direct students' attention to the image of the tenement. Click at the various locations to reveal what life in a tenement was truly like. For each, ask students to declare whether it shows a positive or a negative aspect of tenement life. Then challenge students to connect that aspect of tenement life to larger social issues affecting women, children, and immigrants caused by rapid urban growth (e.g., sanitation, fire, conflict, etc.).

👥 ACTIVE CLASSROOM

Tell students that they can learn more about life in a tenement if they *Act it Out.* Review the images and information about tenements and tenement living. Then challenge students to create a short sketch that brings the picture to life by depicting appropriate challenges faced by tenement dwellers (e.g., overcrowding, conflict, fetching water, etc.).

The Second Industrial Revolution

3-D MODEL

Living in a Tenement

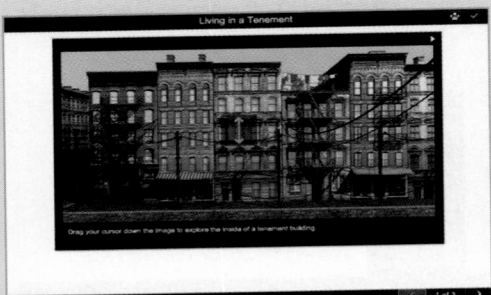

DIGITAL TEXT 6

The Working Class Wins New Rights

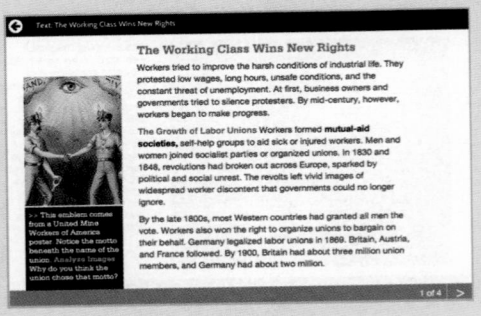

D Differentiate: Challenge/Gifted Have students think about the different people who planned and lived in industrial cities. Have them choose one person, such as a city planner, an architect designing a skyscraper, a police officer, or a factory worker. Have them conduct research, and then create a list of interview questions and the answers they believe the person would give. Finally, have them write a short newspaper article based on the interview.

Further Instruction
Project the Interactive Reading Notepad questions. Discuss the answers with the class. Then ask the following questions:

Analyze Images Project the image of Paris from the text. Why was urban renewal important? How does this image of Paris help you understand urban renewal? *(Urban renewal was the rebuilding of poor areas of a city. The image of Paris shows that it was transformed to create a city center, wide boulevards, and streets lined with buildings. It looks cleaner, more organized, and safer.)*

Compare How do cities during the late Industrial Revolution compare with cities today? *(Early industrial cities like Paris and London look much like cities today. They have skyscrapers, large buildings, public transportation, and wide streets.)*

Objective 5: Explain how conditions for workers gradually improved.

Quick Instruction
One negative effect of the Industrial Revolution and the growth of factories was that factory workers and miners earned low wages and worked long, grueling hours in hazardous conditions. In the late 1800s, many workers joined mutual-aid societies and labor unions and began demanding changes. By the early 1900s, millions of workers in Europe belonged to labor unions. Why did workers join unions? *(Forming unions gave them representation and helped workers strike and demand improvements.)*

Further Instruction
Project the Interactive Reading Notepad questions. Go through the answers with the class.

The Industrial Revolution changed human life for both the better and the worse. Although the Industrial Revolution began in the 1700s, workers had little success organizing until the late 1800s and did not win many rights until the early 1900s. Discuss working conditions and labor unions.

Draw Conclusions Why do you think working conditions were so harsh? *(Sample Response: Some factory and business owners cared more about profit than about employees. Owners wanted to produce as much as possible for as little as possible, which meant low wages, long hours, and little concern for safety.)*

PEARSON • • •
realize™

www.PearsonRealize.com
Access your Digital Lesson

■ SYNTHESIZE

DIGITAL ACTIVITY

Birth of the Industrial City

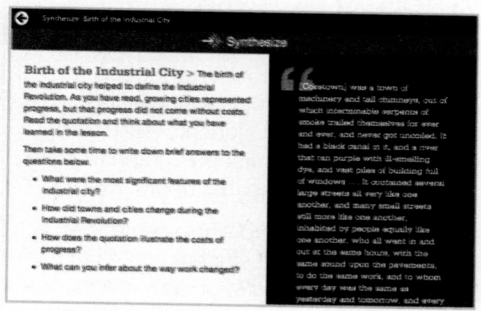

Project and read aloud the quotation by Charles Dickens. Ask students to recall the Topic Essential Question, "How do science and technology affect society?" and consider how Dickens's words respond to or address this question. *(Answers will vary, but students might say that Dickens portrays a negative view of industrial life, in which pollution and monotony characterize every day.)*

Have students take five minutes to answer the questions in the Birth of the Industrial City activity. Then divide the class into small groups, and have each group discuss its responses.

Quick Write Have each group write a short response explaining how Dickens's quotation addresses the Essential Question. Discuss their responses as a class.

■ DEMONSTRATE

LESSON QUIZ

Lesson Quiz and Class Discussion Board

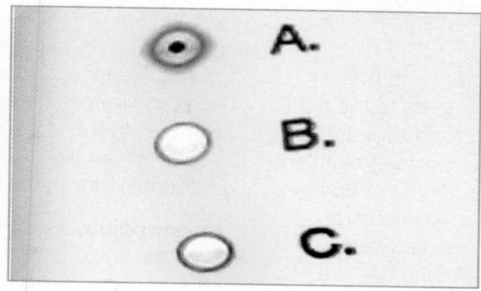

Assign the online Lesson Quiz for this lesson if you haven't already done so. Students will be offered automatic remediation or enrichment based on their score.

Post these questions to the class on the Discussion Board:

In "The Second Industrial Revolution," you read about the ways advances in science, technology, transportation, and communications affected industry and then altered the economy, society, and human life. The changes brought about by the Industrial Revolution continue to affect us today.

Identify Cause and Effect Identify three causes of the Industrial Revolution. Describe three economic or social effects. *(Sample Responses: Causes: growing population, new sources of energy, improved technology, demand for mass-produced goods; Effects: rise of big business, new methods of production, new forms of transportation, urbanization, growing slums)*

Draw Conclusions How does the Industrial Revolution continue to affect the world? *(Sample Responses: The population has continued to grow; more nations have industrialized; new sources of energy have been found; many innovations—such as cars and factories—have polluted the air and water; there is now a global economy.)*

Topic Inquiry

Have students continue their investigations for the Topic Inquiry.

Changing Ways of Life and Thought

Supporting English Language Learners

Use with Digital Text 2, **The Struggle for Women's Rights.**

Reading

Explain that using visuals can help students develop background knowledge on a subject, making it easier to understand the context in which events in history occurred. Have students examine the image of women marching for suffrage in the reading *The Struggle for Women's Rights*.

Beginning Display the term *women's suffrage movement* and break it down into its individual words. Emphasize that *suffrage* refers to the right to vote and *movement* indicates a wide-spread organization. Read the text aloud and have students look at the photo of British women marching for suffrage. Point out details in the picture that help students understand the background of the women's suffrage movement: the women are well-dressed, showing that they are middle-class; the signs advertise a meeting, showing that there is an organized movement; women are bravely marching in front of men who watch from the sidelines.

Intermediate Display the term *women's suffrage movement* and ask students to explain what each individual word means. Have students read the text independently and look at the photo of women marching for suffrage. Ask them to identify details in the photograph that give them information about the background of the women's suffrage movement and what it meant for women to march for suffrage.

Advanced Have pairs of students read the text and discuss the photo to determine how women shared their beliefs on suffrage with others. At the end of the discussion, have pairs of students join into groups of four to discuss how the photo deepens their understanding of the women's suffrage movement. Make sure students understand that using visuals can help them develop a deeper understanding of a topic and the events related to that topic.

Advanced High Ask small groups of students to read the text, examine the photo, and discuss what it reveals about the fight for women's rights. In addition, ask students to discuss why examining photos like this is an important part of the study of history. After the discussion, ask each small group to share a summary of the discussion.

Use with Digital Text 6, **The Romantics Turn from Reason.**

Speaking

Explain that learning how to sound out words in English will help students recognize letter patterns in many different words.

Beginning Read the subsection titled *Romanticism in Music* aloud to students. When you come to the words *audiences*, *laughter*, *passionate*, and *instruments*, pause and slowly demonstrate how to decode these words. Remind students that for words like *laughter*, several letters combine to make a single sound; one that is different from the letters you see. In this case, *ugh* makes the *f* sound. Have students take turns sounding out these words and any others from the first paragraph that are challenging for them. Explain any pronunciation rules that apply.

Intermediate Have different student volunteers read single sentences from the subsection *Romanticism in Music*. When a student comes to a challenging word, like *audiences*, *laughter*, *passionate*, or *instruments*, ask him or her to pause. Then, working with the student, slowly demonstrate how to decode the challenging word(s). Remind students that for words like *laughter*, several letters combine to make a single sound; one that is different from the letters you see. Have students take turns sounding out these words and any others from the first paragraph that are challenging for them. Explain any pronunciation rules that apply.

Advanced Have students take turns reading single sentences from the subsection *Romanticism in Music* to a partner. Tell students to pause when they come to a challenging word, like *audiences*, *laughter*, *passionate*, or *instruments*. Then have partners work together to decode the challenging word(s). Remind students that for words like *laughter*, several letters combine to make a single sound; one that is different from the letters you see. Monitor student progress and correct any misconceptions. Explain any pronunciation rules that apply.

Advanced High Have students silently read the first paragraph from the subsection *Romanticism in Music*. Tell students to pause when they come to a challenging word, like *audiences*, *laughter*, *passionate*, or *instruments*. Then have students indicate which words were the most challenging to them in the paragraph and practice pronouncing those words for the class. Remind students that for words like *laughter*, several letters combine to make a single sound; one that is different from the letters you see. Monitor student progress and correct any misconceptions. Explain any pronunciation rules that apply.

▣ Differentiate Instruction

Use the Differentiated Instruction notes throughout the lesson plan to support the varied skill sets, levels of readiness, and interests in the mixed-ability classroom.

Challenge These notes include suggestions for expanding the activity for advanced students.

On-Level These notes include suggestions for modifying the activity to address different interests or learning styles.

Extra Support These notes include ideas for providing more scaffolding or reading spuport.

Special Needs These notes provide ideas for adapting instruction to support the needs of various special needs students.

▮ NOTES

Objectives

Objective 1: Identify what values shaped the new social order.

Objective 2: Describe how the role of women changed in the Industrial Revolution.

Objective 3: Explain the impact of education, new scientific ideas, and religion.

Objective 4: Analyze how romanticism, realism, and impressionism reflected the culture of the Industrial Age.

LESSON 4 ORGANIZER		OBJECTIVES	PACING	RESOURCES	
				Online	Print
Connect					
	DIGITAL START UP ACTIVITY **Changing Attitudes and Values**		5 min.	●	
Investigate					
	DIGITAL TEXT 1 **The New Social Order**	Objectives 1, 2	10 min.	●	●
	DIGITAL TEXT 2 **The Struggle for Women's Rights**		10 min.	●	●
	INTERACTIVE GALLERY **The New Social Order and Changing Roles of Women**		10 min.	●	
	DIGITAL TEXT 3 **The Rise of Public Education**	Objective 3	10 min.	●	●
	DIGITAL TEXT 4 **New Directions in Science**		10 min.	●	●
	DIGITAL TEXT 5 **The Role of Religion**		10 min.	●	●
	DIGITAL TEXT 6 **The Romantics Turn from Reason**	Objective 4	10 min.	●	●
	DIGITAL TEXT 7 **Artists Represent Real Life**		10 min.	●	●
	DIGITAL TEXT 8 **New Directions in the Visual Arts**		10 min.	●	●
	INTERACTIVE GALLERY **Artistic Movements During the Industrial Revolution**		10 min.	●	
Synthesize					
	DIGITAL ACTIVITY **Art Reflects Culture**		5 min.	●	
Demonstrate					
	LESSON QUIZ **Lesson Quiz and Class Discussion Board**		10 min.	●	

Changing Ways of Life and Thought

■ CONNECT

DIGITAL START UP ACTIVITY
Changing Attitudes and Values

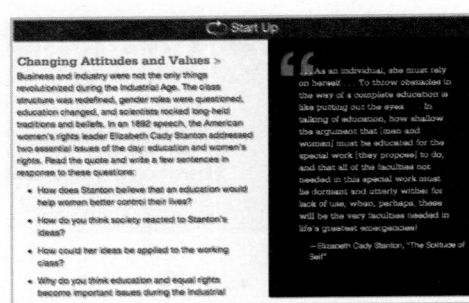

Project the Start Up Activity Ask students to answer the questions as they enter and get settled: How does Stanton believe that an education would help women better control their lives? *(Sample response: It will prepare women to be independent and prepare them to deal with emergencies.)*

Discuss If you were a woman or a member of the working class during the Industrial Revolution, how would you feel about Stanton's ideas? Why? *(Sample Response: I would agree with her because I would want equal rights and a voice in society.)*

Tell students that in this lesson they will be learning how the Industrial Revolution changed the way people lived and thought.

Aa Vocabulary Development: Use the Interactive Reading Notepad to preview the Key Terms and Academic Vocabulary in this Lesson with students.

⇅ FLIP IT!
Assign the Flipped Video for this lesson.

■ STUDENT EDITION PRINT
PAGES: 520–529

■ INVESTIGATE

DIGITAL TEXT 1
The New Social Order

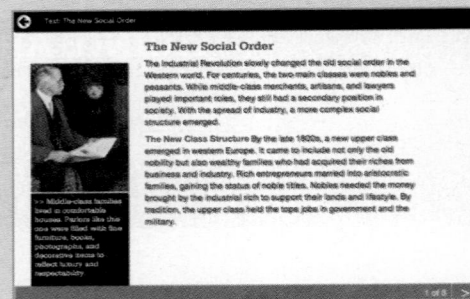

DIGITAL TEXT 2
The Struggle for Women's Rights

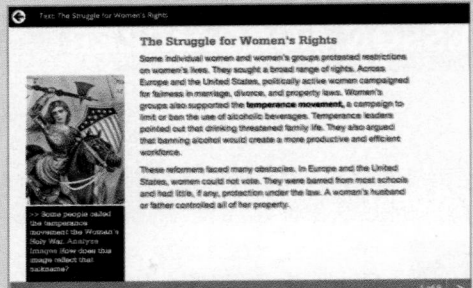

Objectives 1: Identify what values shaped the new social order; 2: Describe how the role of women changed in the Industrial Revolution.

Quick Instruction
Interactive Gallery: The New Social Order and Changing Roles of Women Introduce the activity by reminding students that the Industrial Revolution created new jobs, industries, businesses, and investment prospects. For some people, these new opportunities brought wealth and power. Soon, a new social structure emerged consisting of an upper class, middle class, and working class. The roles of members in a family—particularly women and children—also began to change. Project the image and click through the hot spots on the image. Ask students how the images help them understand what life might have been like for the different classes.

👥 ACTIVE CLASSROOM
Conversation with History Have students select one of the people in one of these images. Ask students to jot down questions they would like to ask that person about his or her life. Then have students work together to write answers to some of their questions.

D Differentiate: Extra Support
Have students work with an on-level partner and create a chart with one column for each social class. Then have students list the types of jobs or roles members of each class might have and describe what their lives might be like.

Further Instruction
Editable Presentation Use the Editable Presentation to present the main ideas for this Core Text.

The New Social Order, The Struggle for Women's Rights: Core Texts and Interactive Reading Notepad Project the Interactive Reading Notepad questions. Go through them and discuss the answers with the class.

The roles of women also changed outside the home. Because most middle-class women did not have to work, they often became involved in charities, religious organizations, and women's groups. Some women became politically active and supported the temperance movement, campaigned for fairness in marriage and property laws, and fought for the right to vote.

Draw Conclusions Why might economic and social changes have encouraged women to fight for political change? *(Sample Response: Women realized that they had important roles in society as mothers, wives, and workers. Women wanted to make sure their voice was heard and that they and their children were protected.)*

INTERACTIVE GALLERY
The New Social Order and Changing Roles of Women

Identify Cause and Effect How did economic freedom improve the human condition? *(Sample Response: Middle- and upper-class women had time to fight for equal rights. Middle-class women were able to spend more time shopping and raising their children because they didn't have to work.)*

ELL Use the ELL activity described in the ELL chart.

DIGITAL TEXT 3
The Rise of Public Education

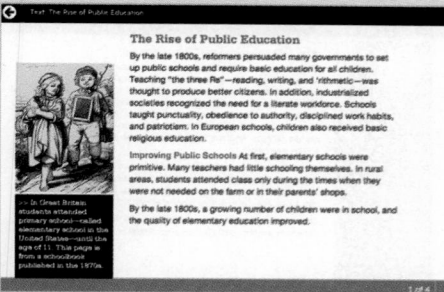

Objective 3: Explain the impact of education, new scientific ideas, and religion.

Quick Instruction

Before 1870, the only formal education available for the majority of British children was in religious schools or "ragged schools," which taught poor children basic skills, such as reading. Schools in other countries were similar in their teaching methods and subjects. The rapid advances in technology and production, as well as new employment opportunities, led to social changes and drastically impacted the education system. In the late 1800s, universities added science and engineering courses to prepare students for life in an industrial world. At the same time, radical new theories in science challenged long-held beliefs. Despite this challenge, religion continued to be an important—and necessary—part of life and society.

Draw Conclusions Have students work in groups to generate a list of reasons why reforms and social services were needed and what religious groups could do to help fill this need. Have student groups share their lists with the class or post them on a blog. *(Sample Response: Reform was needed to help the working poor deal with the harsh realities of industrialization. Religious leaders helped influence political changes. Religious organizations and social services provided charity.)*

DIGITAL TEXT 4
New Directions in Science

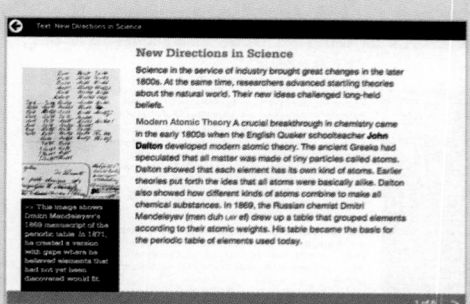

D Differentiate: Challenge/Gifted Review the political cartoon about Darwin's theory. Have students create their own political cartoon based on the debate over his theory. Have them post their cartoons in the class or on a Web site.

Further Instruction

New Directions in Science: Core Text and Interactive Reading Notepad Project and discuss the Interactive Reading Notepad questions. Be sure that students understand the impact new advances and theories in science had on society.

Draw Inferences While these advances had immediate effects, they also had long-term effects. Have students make inferences about the long-term impact of the following: atomic theory, periodic table, geological and archaeological findings and theories, and natural selection. *(Sample Response: Scientists continued to experiment and research to build on these ideas and findings. The atomic theory advanced chemistry, and Mendeleyev's periodic table remains the basis for the modern periodic table. Darwin's theory changed the way people thought about species and led to the study of DNA. Archaeological findings helped scholars develop new ideas about humans and their ancestors.)*

Topic ⑬ Lesson 4

Changing Ways of Life and Thought

DIGITAL TEXT 5

The Role of Religion

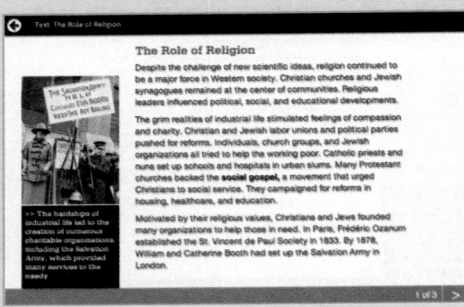

DIGITAL TEXT 6

The Romantics Turn from Reason

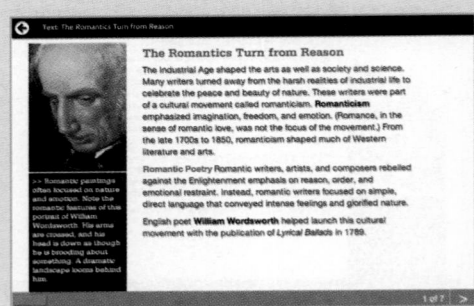

DIGITAL TEXT 7

Artists Represent Real Life

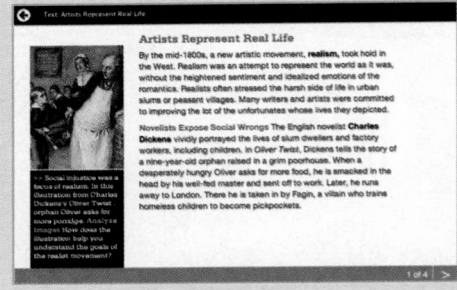

Draw Inferences Tell students that although advances in science and technology were rapidly changing society, many people continued to find comfort in religion and never gave up their beliefs. Priests, rabbis, and other religious leaders formed labor unions and political parties. Protestant churches urged people to provide social services. Why do you think religious leaders became involved in politics? What did they hope to achieve? *(Sample Response: Religious leaders felt it was their duty to represent the poor and to try to help them. The poor did not have a voice in politics, so it was difficult for them to fight for their own rights. Religious leaders hoped they could use their influence and social standing to pressure the government to pass reforms for the working class and improve their housing, health care, and education.)*

Objective 4: Analyze how romanticism, realism, and impressionism reflected the culture of the Industrial Age.

Quick Instruction

Throughout the 1800s, writers, poets, musicians, and painters were influenced by the ways the Industrial Revolution impacted society and human life. Four major movements emerged, each rejecting or reacting to previous artistic movements in order to reflect the culture of the age.

Interactive Gallery: Artistic Movements During the Industrial Revolution Project the interactive activity. Look at each painting and discuss each movement.

Analyze Images Have students analyze each image to identify how the artist's work reflects the culture. They should consider the subject, the colors, and the style when discussing each artist's work. Remind them also to consider the goals of each movement. Does the artist stay true to the movement? How?

ELL Use the ELL activity described in the ELL chart.

🗪 ACTIVE CLASSROOM

Have students form an Opinion Line to answer the following question: Which painting or stylistic movement do you like the best? Romanticism? Realism? Impressionism? Postimpressionism? Once students have found their places in line, ask several to explain their response using details from the images and the text. *(Answers will vary. Students should support their responses with clear explanations and reasons.)*

D Differentiate: Extra Support Redefine each movement. Be sure students understand that romanticism has nothing to do with love or relationships (romance), but rather with a desire to express oneself and idealize nature. To help students understand the difference between the movements, point out various aspects of each painting and compare it to the previous movement. For example, note the difference in subject matter between the realist Courbet and the romantic Constable. Ask students why Courbet might have painted realistic-looking peasants. What does this say about his beliefs or goals in reflecting the Industrial Age? *(He wanted to represent real life and the effects of industrialization rather than an idealized image of life or nature.)*

DIGITAL TEXT 8

New Directions in the Visual Arts

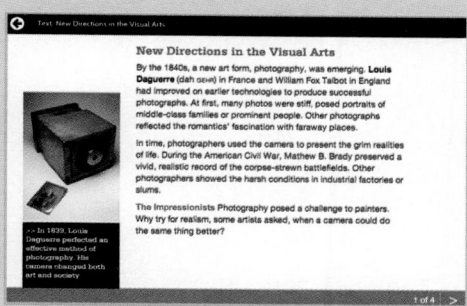

INTERACTIVE GALLERY

Artistic Movements During the Industrial Revolution

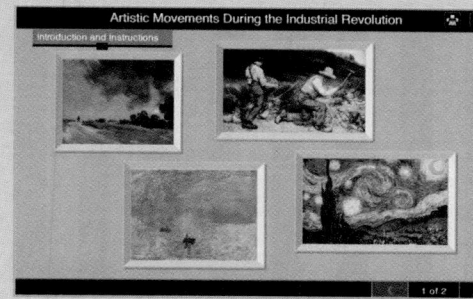

Further Instruction

The Romantics Turn from Reason; Artists Represent Real Life; New Directions in the Visual Arts: Core Texts and Interactive Reading Notepads Project the Interactive Reading Notepad questions. Go through them and discuss the answers with the class.

Remind students that writers and painters were not the only artists to create art that reflected the time. Musicians also composed pieces, such as symphonies and concertos, to convey the times in which they lived. Some musicians, such as Ludwig van Beethoven, composed music that conveyed universal themes that transcended the time and place during which they were created by expressing universal emotions.

Discuss Ask students if they have ever been to the symphony, listened to classical music, or played classical music. Have them discuss how the music stirred their emotions and what themes they felt were expressed in the compositions. If possible, play some of Beethoven's most well-known pieces, such as his Fifth Symphony or Sixth Symphony. Have students listen carefully and then discuss their reaction to the pieces.

Changing Ways of Life and Thought

■ SYNTHESIZE

DIGITAL ACTIVITY
Art Reflects Culture

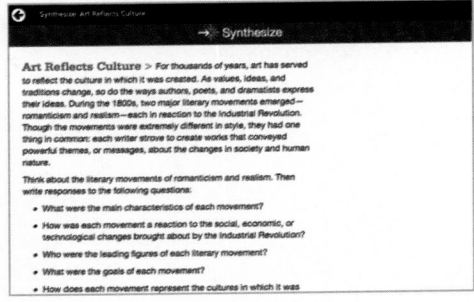

Project the activity Ask students to recall the Topic Essential Question, "How do science and technology affect society?" Remind students that science and technology also affected the arts. Artists focused on different styles and subject matters in response to the changes they witnessed due to the Industrial Revolution.

Have students take five minutes to answer the questions in the Art Reflects Culture activity. Then divide the class into small groups, and have each group discuss its responses.

Discuss Ask students whether they have read books by authors from each literary movement or seen movies or television shows based on those books. Discuss their reactions to these works. Then ask them if they view these works differently or understand them better based on what they have learned in this lesson. Have students explain their responses.

■ DEMONSTRATE

LESSON QUIZ
Lesson Quiz and Class Discussion Board

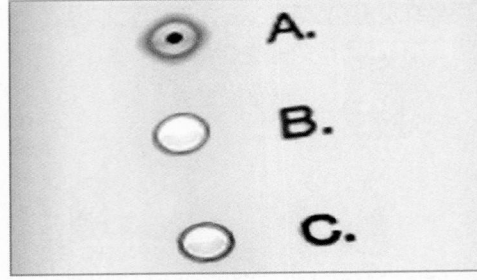

Assign the online Lesson Quiz for this lesson if you haven't already done so. Students will be offered automatic remediation or enrichment based on their score.

Post these questions to the class on the Discussion Board:

In "Changing Ways of Life and Thought," you read about the ways the Industrial Revolution affected human life and society. A new social order emerged, public education was transformed, and scientists introduced radical theories that challenged long-held beliefs. Artists also responded to this changing society and found ways to reflect the culture of the Industrial Age.

Make Connections Some historians have suggested that we are now in the third phase of the Industrial Revolution, characterized by information technology and computers. Do you agree or disagree? How have these advances in technology affected ways of life and thought? How might they continue to change the way we live, work, socialize, and think?

Topic Inquiry
Have students continue their investigations for the Topic Inquiry.

The Industrial Revolution

■ SYNTHESIZE

DIGITAL ACTIVITY
Reflect on the Essential Question and Topic

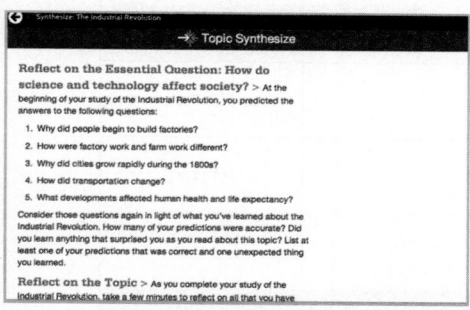

First ask students to reconsider the Essential Question for the Topic: How do science and technology affect society? Remind students of the questions they answered to try to make predictions about the Topic:

- Why did people begin to build factories?
- How were factory work and farm work different?
- Why did cities grow rapidly during the 1800s?
- How did transportation change?
- What developments affected human health and life expectancy?

Ask students, "How many of your predictions were accurate? Did you learn anything that surprised you as you read about this topic?" Have them identify at least one prediction that was correct and one unexpected thing they learned in the chapter.

Next, ask students to reflect on the Industrial Revolution as a whole. Tell them to consider what they would say if they were asked to be an advisor to a country that has not developed much industry yet. If they have difficulty thinking of a response, post the following questions:

- What benefits can my country expect from industrialization?
- What problems can my country expect from industrialization?
- How will industrialization change our traditional way of life?
- How can my country maximize the benefits of industrialization and minimize the problems?

You may ask students to share their questions and answers on the Class Discussion Board.

■ DEMONSTRATE

DIGITAL TOPIC REVIEW AND ASSESSMENT
The Industrial Revolution

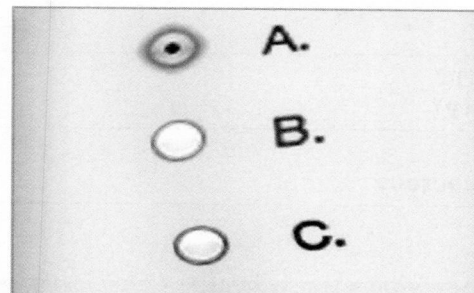

Students can prepare for the Topic Test by answering the questions in the Topic Review and Assessment online or the Assessment questions in the Print Student text. They can also prepare by reviewing their answers to the Interactive Reading Notepad questions or reviewing their notes in the Reading and Notetaking Study Guide.

DIGITAL TOPIC TEST
The Industrial Revolution

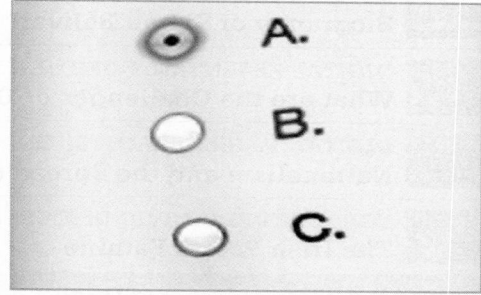

TOPIC TEST
Assign the Topic Test to assess students' understanding of topic content.

BENCHMARK TESTS
Assign these benchmark tests as you complete the relevant topics to monitor student progress toward mastering the course content and as preparation for the End-of-Course Test.

Benchmark Test 1: Topics 1–5
Benchmark Test 2: Topics 6–10
Benchmark Test 3: Topics 11–15
Benchmark Test 4: Topics 16–21

Topic (14)

Nationalism and the Spread of Democracy (1790–1914)

TOPIC 14 ORGANIZER	PACING: APPROX. 11 PERIODS, 5.5 BLOCKS
	PACING
Connect	1 period
MY STORY VIDEO **Biography of Simón Bolívar**	10 min.
DIGITAL ESSENTIAL QUESTION ACTIVITY **What are the Challenges of Diversity?**	10 min.
DIGITAL TIMELINE ACTIVITY **Nationalism and the Spread of Democracy**	10 min.
TOPIC INQUIRY: CIVIC DISCUSSION **The Irish Potato Famine**	20 min.
Investigate	4–8 periods
TOPIC INQUIRY: CIVIC DISCUSSION **The Irish Potato Famine**	Ongoing
LESSON 1 Revolutions Sweep Europe	30–40 min.
LESSON 2 Latin American Nations Win Independence	30–40 min.
LESSON 3 The Unification of Germany	30–40 min.
LESSON 4 The Unification of Italy	30–40 min.
LESSON 5 Democratic Reforms in Britain	30–40 min.
LESSON 6 Divisions and Democracy in France	30–40 min.
LESSON 7 Growth of the United States	30–40 min.
LESSON 8 Nationalism in Eastern Europe and Russia	30–40 min.
Synthesize	1 period
DIGITAL ESSENTIAL QUESTION ACTIVITY **Reflect on the Essential Question and Topic**	10 min.
TOPIC INQUIRY: CIVIC DISCUSSION **The Irish Potato Famine**	20 min.
Demonstrate	1–2 periods
ONLINE TEST **Nationalism and the Spread of Democracy**	10 min.
TOPIC INQUIRY: CIVIC DISCUSSION **The Irish Potato Famine**	20 min.

NOTES

TOPIC INQUIRY: CIVIC DISCUSSION

The Irish Potato Famine

In this Topic Inquiry, students work in teams to examine different perspectives on this issue by analyzing several sources, arguing both sides of a Yes/No question, then developing and discussing their own point of view on the question: **Was the Irish potato famine caused by British policy?**

STEP 1: CONNECT
Develop Questions and Plan the Investigation

Launch the Civic Discussion

Divide the class into groups of four students. Students can access the materials they'll need in the online course or you can distribute copies to each student. Read the main question and introduction with the students.

Have students complete Step 1 by reading the Discussion Launch and filling in Step 1 of the Information Organizer. The Discussion Launch provides YES and NO arguments on the main question. Students should extract and paraphrase the arguments from the reading in Step 1 of their Information Organizers.

Next, students share within their groups the arguments and evidence they found to support the YES and NO positions. The group needs to agree on the major YES and NO points and each student should note those points in their Information Organizer.

Resources
- Student Instructions
- Information Organizer
- Discussion Launch

STEP 2: INVESTIGATE
Apply Disciplinary Concepts and Tools

Examine Sources and Perspectives

Students will examine sources with the goal of extracting information and perspectives on the main question. They analyze each source and describe the author's perspective on the main question and key evidence the author provides to support that viewpoint in Information Organizer Step 2.

Ask students to keep in mind:

- **Author/Creator:** Who created the source? An individual? Group? Government agency?
- **Audience:** For whom was the source created?
- **Date/Place:** Is there any information that reveals where and when the source was created?
- **Purpose:** Why was the source created? Discuss with students the importance of this question in identifying bias.
- **Relevance:** How does the source support one argument or another?

Suggestion: Reading the source documents and filling in Step 2 of the Information Organizer could be assigned as homework.

Resources
- Student Instructions
- Information Organizer
- Source documents

⏻ PROFESSIONAL DEVELOPMENT

Civic Discussion

Be sure to view the Civic Discussion Professional Development resources in the online course.

STEP 3: SYNTHESIZE
Use Evidence to
Formulate Conclusions

Formulate Compelling Arguments with Evidence

Now students will apply perspectives and evidence they extracted from the sources to think more deeply about the main question by first arguing one side of the issue, then the other. In this way students become more prepared to formulate an evidence-based conclusion on their own.

Within each student group, assign half of the students to take the position of YES on the main question and the others to take the position of NO. Students will work with their partners to identify the strongest arguments and evidence to support their assigned YES or NO position.

Present Yes/No Positions

Within each group, those assigned the YES position share arguments and evidence first. As the YES students speak, those assigned NO should listen carefully, take notes to fill in the rest of the Compelling Arguments Chart (Step 3 in Information Organizer) and ask clarifying questions.

When the YES side is finished, students assigned the NO position present while those assigned YES should listen, take notes, and ask clarifying questions. Examples of clarifyin questions are:

- I think you just said [x]. Am I understanding you correctly?
- Can you tell me more about [x]?
- Can you repeat [x]? I am not sure I understand, yet.

Suggestion: You may want to set a 5 minute time limit for each side to present. Provide a two-minute warning so that students make their most compelling arguments within the time frame.

Switch Sides

The students will switch sides to argue the opposite point of view. To prepare to present the other position, partners who first argued YES will use the notes they took during the NO side's presentation, plus add any additional arguments and evidence from the reading and sources. The same for students who first argued the NO position.

STEP 4: DEMONSTRATE
Communicate Conclusions
and Take Informed Action

Individual Points of View

Now the students will have the opportunity to discuss the main question from their own points of view. To help students prepare for this discussion, have them reflect on the YES/NO discussions they have participated in thus far and fill in Step 4 of their Information Organizers.

After all of the students have shared their points of view, each group should list points of agreement, filling the last portion of Step 4 on their Information Organizers.

Reflect on the Discussion

Ask students to reflect on the civic discussion thinking about:

- The value of having to argue both the YES and NO positions.
- If their individual views changed over the course of the discussion and why.
- What they learned from participating in the discussion.

Resources
- Student Instructions
- Information Organizer

INTRODUCTION

Nationalism and the Spread of Democracy (1790–1914)

During the 1800s, nationalism and democratic ideals spread through Europe and Latin America. Nationalism led to the creation of new nation-states and threatened the unity of multinational empires. In Britain and the United States, democracy expanded. In other countries, people used a variety of methods, including revolution, to change their governments and gain democratic rights and freedoms. How did the ideas of nationalism and democracy affect people and their governments in the 1800s?

■ CONNECT

MY STORY VIDEO
Biography of Simón Bolívar

Watch a video about the life of Simón Bolívar.

Check Understanding What was Simón Bolívar's greatest achievement? *(He helped Latin America gain independence from Spain.)*

Identify Central Issues How did Enlightenment ideas influence Bolívar? *(The concepts of liberty, equality, and fraternity, and of representative government were Enlightenment ideas that influenced Bolívar. So too were the examples of the American and French revolutions.)*

⇅ FLIP IT!
Assign the My Story video.

DIGITAL ESSENTIAL QUESTION ACTIVITY
What are the Challenges of Diversity?

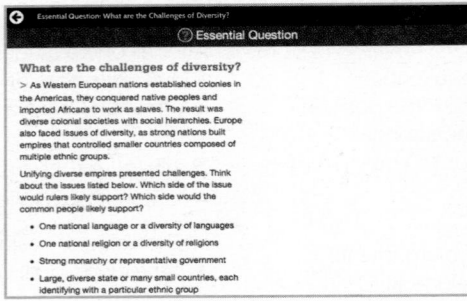

Ask students to think about the Essential Question: What are the challenges of diversity? When people in a society have diverse cultural backgrounds and differing beliefs and ideas, societal challenges can result. Citizens and rulers must make tough choices on difficult issues. Ask students to look at the issues in the Essential Question activity. Which side of an issue would the people support? Which side would rulers support?

Give students a few minutes, then ask volunteers to share their ideas with the class.

Identify Central Issues What ideas challenged monarchs and other rulers? *(Sample Response: democracy, human rights, equality, liberty.)*

Predict Consequences How might nationalism affect empires with people of diverse ethnic and religious backgrounds? *(Sample Response: people from particular groups or regions might want to break away and form independent countries.)*

Identify Cause and Effect Why do you think so many revolutions occurred in the 1800s? *(People wanted more rights, they identified with their own cultural group or region, and they wanted self-government—not to be ruled by a different group or region.)*

DIGITAL TIMELINE ACTIVITY
Nationalism and the Spread of Democracy

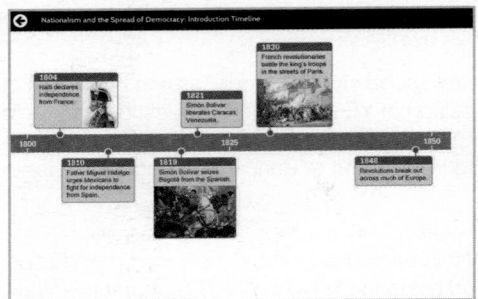

Display the timeline showing the major events having to do with nationalism and the spread of democracy in the 1800s. During this Topic, students will learn about all of these events and many more, but this timeline will provide a framework into which they can place the events they learn about.

D **Differentiate: Extra Support** Suggest that students copy the timeline onto their own paper and add entries to it as they read the chapter. Help students draw the timeline correctly and add years for the late 1800s. Point out to them that some of the events they are seeing on the timeline were directly influenced by an event that happened in their own country—the American Revolution.

Check Understanding Between what years of the mid-1800s did many revolutions occur in Europe? *(between 1830 and 1848)*

Topic Inquiry
Launch the Topic Inquiry with students after introducing the Topic.

Revolutions Sweep Europe

Supporting English Language Learners

Use with Digital Text 3, **Rebellions Erupt in Eastern Europe.**

Reading

Explain to students that languages are written and read in various directions. For example, the Arabic language, which was used by many people in the Ottoman Empire, is written and read from right to left and from top to bottom. Confirm that students understand the directionality of English by using the following strategies.

Beginning Have students point to where they should begin reading the first paragraph of *Rebellions Erupt in Eastern Europe*. Then demonstrate dragging a finger along the words as you read the first sentence aloud. Pause at the end of a line of print and relocate your fingertip at the beginning of the next line. Have students copy your actions. Make sure students' fingers are moving from left to right along the same line that you are reading and moving to the line below once a full line of text is read. Repeat this process until students demonstrate that they understand that English is read from left to right and from the top to the bottom of a page.

Intermediate Have students point to where they should begin reading the first paragraph of *Rebellions Erupt in Eastern Europe*. Then have students drag their fingers along the words as you read the first sentence aloud. Pause at the end of a line of print to make sure that students relocate their fingertips to the beginning of the next line. Confirm that students' fingers are moving from left to right along the same line that is being read and moving to the line below once a full line of text is read. Repeat this process until students can demonstrate that they understand that English is read from left to right and from the top to the bottom of a page.

Advanced Have students point to where they should begin reading the first paragraph of *Rebellions Erupt in Eastern Europe*. Then have students drag their fingers along the words as they read the first two sentences aloud. Confirm that students' fingers are moving from left to right along the same line that is being read and moving to the line below once a full line of text is read.

Advanced High Have students describe the direction in which English text is read. Confirm that students understand that reading should begin at the top left of the page and go from left to right and top to bottom. Ask students to help any of their peers who are having difficulty with this.

Use with Digital Texts 5, 6, and 7, **Demands for Reform Spread.**

Reading

Provide students with your support and/or support from their peers to help them understand the main idea of the text *Demands for Reform Spread*.

Beginning Read *Demands for Reform Spread* aloud to students. Then have students repeat aloud the first two sentences of the first paragraph. Focus on decoding the meaning of the quote "When France sneezes, Europe catches cold." Help them make sense of the analogy and what it says about the influence of France on the rest of Europe. Direct their attention to the two subsidiary headings that follow the heading *Demands for Reform Spread*. Then direct them to the map showing the revolutions of 1830. Ask them to identify the countries that "caught a cold" from France in 1830 and experienced revolutions.

Intermediate Ask students to read *Demands for Reform Spread*. Then have students repeat aloud the first two sentences of the first paragraph. Ask students to explain the meaning of the quote "When France sneezes, Europe catches cold." Help them if needed. Direct their attention to the two subsidiary headings that follow the heading *Demands for Reform Spread*. Then direct them to the map showing the revolutions of 1830. Ask them to identify the countries that "caught a cold" from France in 1830 and what happened in those countries as a result.

Advanced Ask students to read *Demands for Reform Spread*. Remind them to focus on headings and visuals such as maps. Have them work in pairs or groups to explain the meaning of the quote "When France sneezes, Europe catches cold." Ask them to identify the countries that "caught a cold" from France in 1830 and to explain what they mean by that.

Advanced High Ask students to read *Demands for Reform Spread*. Have them work in pairs or groups to explain the meaning of the quote "When France sneezes, Europe catches cold." Ask them to identify the countries that "caught a cold" from France in 1830 and to explain what they mean by that.

▶ Differentiate Instruction

Use the Differentiated Instruction notes throughout the lesson plan to support the varied skill sets, levels of readiness, and interests in the mixed-ability classroom.

Challenge These notes include suggestions for expanding the activity for advanced students.

On-Level These notes include suggestions for modifying the activity to address different interests or learning styles.

Extra Support These notes include ideas for providing more scaffolding or reading spuport.

Special Needs These notes provide ideas for adapting instruction to support the needs of various special needs students.

■ **NOTES**

Revolutions Sweep Europe

Objectives

Objective 1: Compare the goals of conservatives and liberals in 19th century Europe.

Objective 2: Identify the influence of liberty, equality, and nationalism on political revolutions.

Objective 3: Describe the causes and results of the revolutions of 1830 and 1848.

LESSON 1 ORGANIZER		PACING: APPROX. 1 PERIOD, .5 BLOCKS			
				RESOURCES	
		OBJECTIVES	PACING	Online	Print
Connect					
	DIGITAL START UP ACTIVITY **The Revolutions of 1830 and 1848**		5 min.	●	
Investigate					
	DIGITAL TEXT 1 **A Clash of Ideologies**		10 min.	●	●
	DIGITAL TEXT 2 **Liberalism and Nationalism Spur Revolts**	Objective 1	10 min.	●	
	INTERACTIVE CARTOON **Metternich Resists Liberal Ideas**		10 min.	●	
	DIGITAL TEXT 3 **Rebellions Erupt in Eastern Europe**	Objective 2	10 min.	●	●
	DIGITAL TEXT 4 **Revolutions of 1830 and 1848**		10 min.	●	●
	DIGITAL TEXT 5 **Demands for Reform Spread**		10 min.	●	●
	DIGITAL TEXT 6 **The Revolution of 1848 in France**	Objective 3	10 min.	●	
	DIGITAL TEXT 7 **Revolution Spreads Across Europe**		10 min.	●	
	INTERACTIVE MAP **Revolutionary Uprisings, 1830–1848**		10 min.	●	
Synthesize					
	DIGITAL ACTIVITY **"Central Shaft of the Mine"**		5 min.	●	
Demonstrate					
	LESSON QUIZ **Lesson Quiz and Class Discussion Board**		10 min.	●	

PEARSON
realize.™
www.PearsonRealize.com

Go online to access additional resources including:
Primary Sources • Biographies • Supreme Court cases •
21st Century Skill Tutorials • Maps • Graphic Organizers.

■ CONNECT

DIGITAL START UP ACTIVITY
The Revolutions of 1830 and 1848

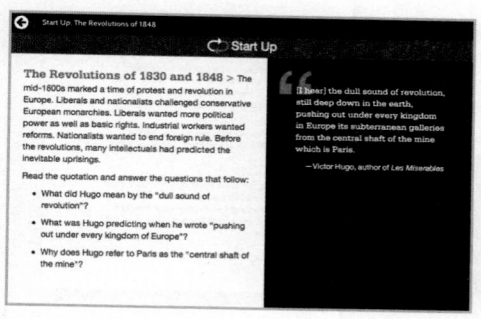

Project the Start Up Activity Ask students to read the quote as they enter and get settled. Have students share their ideas with another student, either in class or through a chat room or blog.

Discuss What do you think Hugo meant by "the dull sound of revolution"? (*Sample Response: He meant that revolution was on the way.*) What was Hugo predicting with his words, "pushing out under every kingdom in Europe"? (*Hugo predicted that revolution would affect all of Europe.*) What do you think were the causes of revolution? (*Sample response: inequality, lack of human rights*)

Tell students that in this lesson they will learn about the causes of the Revolutions of 1848.

Aa Vocabulary Development: Use the Interactive Reading Notepad to preview the Key Terms and Academic Vocabulary in this Lesson with students.

⇅ FLIP IT!

Assign the Flipped Video for this lesson.

■ STUDENT EDITION PRINT PAGES: 536–544

■ INVESTIGATE

DIGITAL TEXT 1
A Clash of Ideologies

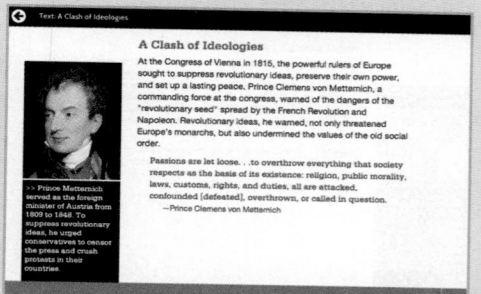

DIGITAL TEXT 2
Liberalism and Nationalism Spur Revolts

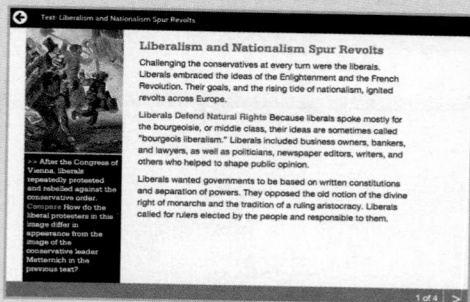

Objective 1: Compare the goals of conservatives and liberals in 19th century Europe.

Quick Instruction

Interactive Cartoon: Metternich Resists Liberal Ideas Project the cartoon on the whiteboard. Explain that Metternich and other conservatives opposed change and wanted to keep the old political order and social structure. They wanted to support the established monarchies and maintain order by using military force to stop nationalist and democratic political revolutions. The liberals and nationalists were influenced by the Enlightenment ideas of liberty, equality, and human rights, and they challenged the conservatives by trying to change the government. The conflict of ideas was a major cause of the political revolutions between 1830 and 1848. Click through the hotspots and ask students to interpret this political cartoon.

💬 ACTIVE CLASSROOM

Have students create a Quickdraw of a banner someone in the crowd might hold to oppose Metternich's ideas. The banner should be of a symbol or a drawing that highlights the ideas of liberals or nationalists between 1815 and 1848. (*Possible symbols: money sign [for free market economy], a written constitution [for constitutional governments], a ballot box [for popular sovereignty and democracy]*)

D Differentiate: Challenge Ask students to draw a new banner representing other aspects of liberal ideology, such as social equality and human rights. Have students write a short opinion essay explaining what the banner represents. Remind students to use evidence to support their claim. Have students exchange their essays with a partner and then discuss their claim and evidence.

Further Instruction

Go through the Interactive Reading Notepad questions and discuss the answers with the class.

Metternich feared that the French Revolution and the Age of Napoleon had planted a seed that would grow into revolution. The seed was fed by ideas about liberty, equality, human rights, democracy, and nationalism. Explain how the ideologies of conservatives clashed with those of liberals and nationalists after the Congress of Vienna. (*Conservatives wanted to keep the social structure and divine-right monarchies in place; liberals wanted governments based on written constitutions and separation of powers; nationalists wanted united, independent nation-states.*)

Revolutions Sweep Europe

   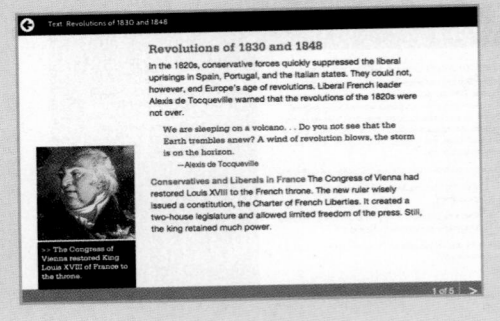

INTERACTIVE CARTOON
Metternich Resists Liberal Ideas

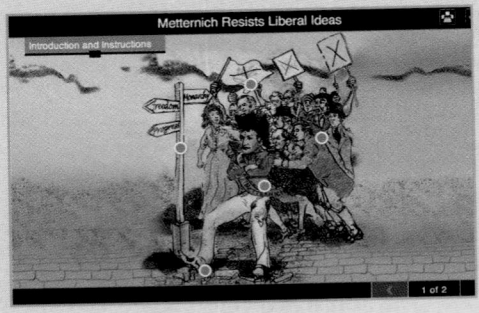

DIGITAL TEXT 3
Rebellions Erupt in Eastern Europe

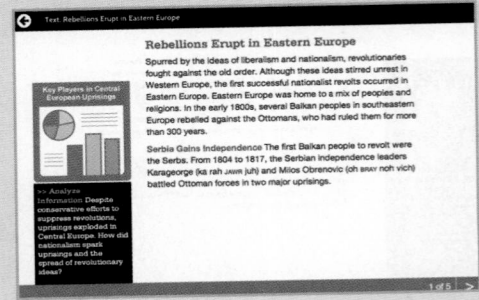

DIGITAL TEXT 4
Revolutions of 1830 and 1848

Identify Supporting Details In a free enterprise system, business owners set prices of goods and services based on supply and demand. Owners have autonomy over pricing and the amount of goods in production. Ask students why liberals might have favored the free enterprise system. *(Liberals saw the free market as a way for people to achieve economic success. The Industrial Revolution and support for free enterprise led to political, economic, and social change.)*

Identify Central Issues Explain the influence of democratic ideas on liberals. *(Liberals wanted separation of powers and the ability to elect people to serve as representatives in a republican form of government.)*

Objective 2: Identify the influence of liberty, equality, and nationalism on political revolutions.

Quick Instruction

Analyze Charts Project the Key Players in Central European Uprisings infographic on the whiteboard. Explain that during the early 1800s the ideas of liberty, equality, and nationalism sparked many revolutions in Europe. For example, Karageorge, a Serbian nationalist, was inspired to liberate Serbia from the Ottoman Empire. In order to "reconquer the rights of individual liberty," Greek rebels won their freedom from the Ottomans. Metternich and other conservative rulers succeeded in stopping most of the uprisings, but not in suppressing the ideas of liberalism and nationalism. Ask: Where did revolutions occur, and why? *(Greece, Serbia, Spain, Portugal, various states in Italy; for rights and freedoms and the nationalist desire for self-rule.)*

D Differentiate: Extra Support Ask students to choose one leader in the infographic, identify whether he favored or opposed revolution, and write one sentence explaining why he favored or opposed revolution.

ELL Use the ELL activity described in the ELL chart.

Further Instruction

Go through the Interactive Reading Notepad questions for the readings, and discuss the answers with the class.

As Metternich predicted, there was an outbreak of rebellions to challenge the old order. Ask students to find examples of how the influence of ideas such as liberty, equality, and nationalism sparked these rebellions. *(Liberals wanted governments based on written constitutions and separation of powers. Nationalists wanted people with a common heritage and culture to have one united homeland.)*

Identify Supporting Details How did the idea of nationalism influence political revolutions? *(The participants wanted to establish independent nation-states with constitutional governments. They wanted to create nations based on shared cultures and identities.)*

DIGITAL TEXT 5

Demands for Reform Spread

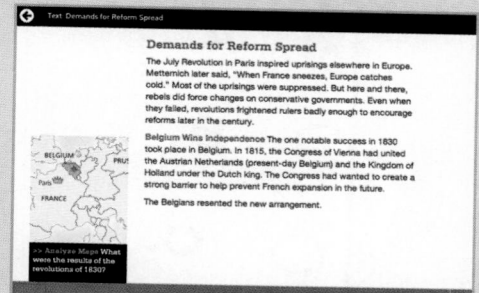

Demands for Reform Spread

The July Revolution in Paris inspired uprisings elsewhere in Europe. Metternich later said, "When France sneezes, Europe catches cold." Most of the uprisings were suppressed. But here and there, rebels did force changes on conservative governments. Even when they failed, revolutions frightened rulers badly enough to encourage reforms later in the century.

Belgium Wins Independence The one notable success in 1830 took place in Belgium. In 1815, the Congress of Vienna had united the Austrian Netherlands (present-day Belgium) and the Kingdom of Holland under the Dutch king. The Congress had wanted to create a strong barrier to help prevent French expansion in the future.

The Belgians resented the new arrangement.

>> Analyze Maps What were the results of the revolutions of 1830?

1 of 4 >

DIGITAL TEXT 6

The Revolution of 1848 in France

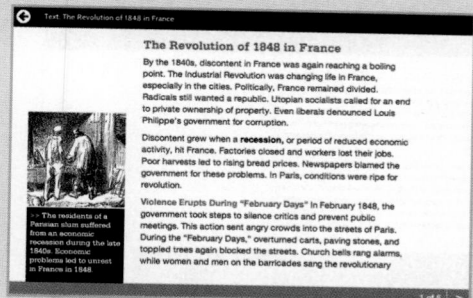

The Revolution of 1848 in France

By the 1840s, discontent in France was again reaching a boiling point. The Industrial Revolution was changing life in France, especially in the cities. Politically, France remained divided. Radicals still wanted a republic. Utopian socialists called for an end to private ownership of property. Even liberals denounced Louis Philippe's government for corruption.

Discontent grew when a **recession**, or period of reduced economic activity, hit France. Factories closed and workers lost their jobs. Poor harvests led to rising bread prices. Newspapers blamed the government for these problems. In Paris, conditions were ripe for revolution.

Violence Erupts During "February Days" In February 1848, the government took steps to silence critics and prevent public meetings. This action sent angry crowds into the streets of Paris. During the "February Days," overturned carts, paving stones, and toppled trees again blocked the streets. Church bells rang alarms, while women and men on the barricades sang the revolutionary

>> The residents of a Parisian slum suffered from an economic recession during the late 1840s. Economic problems led to unrest in France in 1848

1 of 5 >

DIGITAL TEXT 7

Revolution Spreads Across Europe

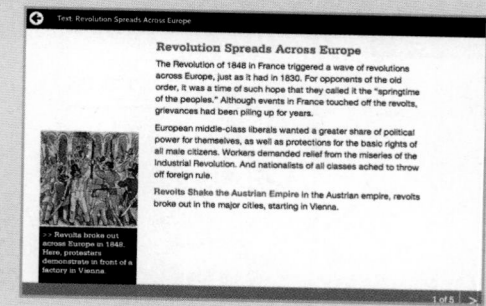

Revolution Spreads Across Europe

The Revolution of 1848 in France triggered a wave of revolutions across Europe, just as it had in 1830. For opponents of the old order, it was a time of such hope that they called it the "springtime of the peoples." Although events in France touched off the revolts, grievances had been piling up for years.

European middle-class liberals wanted a greater share of political power for themselves, as well as protections for the basic rights of all male citizens. Workers demanded relief from the miseries of the Industrial Revolution. And nationalists of all classes ached to throw off foreign rule.

Revolts Shake the Austrian Empire In the Austrian empire, revolts broke out in the major cities, starting in Vienna.

>> Revolts broke out across Europe in 1848. Here, protesters demonstrate in front of a factory in Vienna

1 of 5 >

Objective 3: Describe the causes and results of the revolutions of 1830 and 1848.

Quick Instruction

Interactive Map: Revolutionary Uprisings, 1830–1848 Project the Interactive Map on the whiteboard. Introduce the activity by explaining that the ideals of liberty, equality, and nationalism inspired revolutionaries to revolt in an attempt to change their governments. They opposed conservatives who supported the existing governments. Click on the numbered hotspots to learn more about the revolutions and their results.

📖 ACTIVE CLASSROOM

Organize students into pairs. Have the first student give the second student an Audio Tour of the map, explaining what is shown on the map. *(For example, I see a battle star on Paris.)* Have the second student give the first an explanation of what the different parts of the map mean. *(For example, Paris was the site of uprisings in 1830 and 1848, etc.)*

D **Differentiate: Extra Support** After giving students the instructions for the Active Classroom, allow students five minutes to think about each of the sites on the map. Tell them to write down two details about each location shown on the map. Then continue the group activity.

Further Instruction

Go through the Interactive Reading Notepad questions, and discuss the answers with the class.

The revolutions of 1848, known as "Springtime of the Peoples," were a series of political revolutions. But within a year, conservatives regained control. Why were the revolutions unsuccessful? *(Conservatives took military action against revolutionaries, and the revolutionaries did not have mass public support.)*

Infer Describe how the French people participated in changing their government in 1848. *(The radicals wanted to set up a republic, whereas the moderate liberals insisted on a constitutional monarchy, so they joined forces to overthrow the king and establish the Second Republic.)*

Identify Supporting Details List two reasons why the French working class still wanted change after the "February Days"? *(The working class still demanded better working conditions and was fearful after the liberals shut down the national workshops.)*

Revolutions Sweep Europe

INTERACTIVE MAP

Revolutionary Uprisings, 1830–1848

 **SYNTHESIZE**

DIGITAL ACTIVITY

"Central Shaft of the Mine"

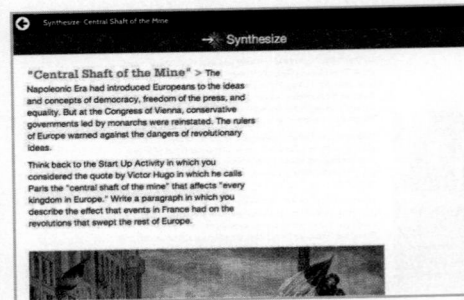

Ask students to take five minutes to share their paragraphs with a partner. Have volunteers read their paragraphs aloud. *(Sample response: The rulers at the Congress of Vienna were trying to put a stop to the spread of revolutionary ideas that started with the French Revolution. Liberals and national groups continued to embrace those ideas, and uprisings began to break out across Europe in the early 1800s. With the July 1830 revolution in France, more revolutions broke out, with limited success. Then, revolution broke out again in France in 1848, triggering yet another wave of revolutions across Europe. Though the revolutions of 1848 didn't instantly change politics in Europe, the seed was planted. Politics in Europe changed forever as a result of the revolutions.)*

Then have students think about the Essential Question: What are the challenges of diversity? How did the events of 1848 portray the challenges of diversity? *(The nationalism among different, diverse groups is what challenged existing governments.)*

Discuss People in Europe were ready for change in 1848. A growing number of people wanted to replace divine-right monarchies with governments based on written constitutions. Even though conservatives regained control of most monarchies, how did the events of 1848 change Europe forever? *(The events of 1848 made the Enlightenment ideals of liberty, equality, and fraternity" common knowledge. Several governments were formed, with elected representatives and written constitutions. The idea of divine-right monarchy weakened and would continue to be challenged by widespread political reform. Citizens recognized the importance of political choices and decisions. They learned that they could shift political thought and change their government.)*

 DEMONSTRATE

LESSON QUIZ

Lesson Quiz and Class Discussion Board

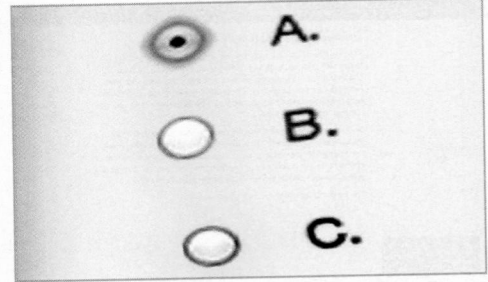

Assign the online Lesson Quiz for this lesson if you haven't already done so. Students will be offered automatic remediation or enrichment based on their score.

Pose these questions to the class on the Discussion Board:

In "Revolutions Sweep Europe," you read about the influences of ideas such as liberty, equality, democracy, and nationalism on the Revolutions of 1848. In most of the revolutions, liberals were fighting for shared rights, nationalists were fighting for united homelands, and the working class was fighting for better working conditions. The economic hardships and political unrest made Europe ripe for revolution.

Draw Conclusions What were the conditions under which the people of France lived that led to revolution rather than peace? *(The people of France lived under absolute rule, government corruption, and extreme poverty.)*

Predict Consequences Based on your knowledge of liberalism and nationalism in Europe, what do you predict will happen in Europe in the late 1800s and beyond? *(Sample Response: Europeans will continue to oppose the old order and seek democratic rights and freedoms, as well as independent, united nation-states. Revolutions and international conflicts will continue in Europe.)*

Topic Inquiry

Have students continue their investigations for the Topic Inquiry.

PEARSON realize™

www.PearsonRealize.com
Access your Digital Lesson

Latin American Nations Win Independence

Supporting English Language Learners

Use with Digital Text 1, **Latin America Ripe for Revolution.**

Reading
Have students skim one or two paragraphs under *The Enlightenment Ideas Reach Latin America* to find sight vocabulary, words that they frequently see and recognize. Then have them say the word and explain its meaning to the group.

Beginning Help students skim the first paragraph under the heading *The Enlightenment Ideas Reach Latin America* and locate each word related to social studies that they recognize. These words should include: *colonist, rule, independence,* and *declaration.* Point to each of these words, say them aloud, and review their purpose or meaning.

Intermediate Ask students to skim the first paragraph under the heading *The Enlightenment Ideas Reach Latin America* and locate each word related to social studies that they automatically recognize. These words should include: *colonist, rule, independence,* and *declaration.* Ask students to point to each of their words, say them aloud, and explain their purpose or meaning.

Advanced Have students skim the content under *The Enlightenment Ideas Reach Latin America* and locate each word related to social studies that they recognize. These words should include: *colonist, rule, independence, declaration, revolution, liberty,* and *equality.* Ask students to point to each of their words, say them aloud, and explain their purpose or meaning.

Advanced High Have students skim the two paragraphs under the *The Enlightenment Ideas Reach Latin America* and locate each word they recognize. Ask students to point to each of these words, say them aloud, and explain their purpose or meaning. Then have students read the paragraphs to themselves, write a one-sentence summary of the content, and share their sentence with the group.

Use with Digital Text 4, **Discontent Sparks Revolts in South America.**

Reading
Have students work with you or other students to build an understanding of descriptive vocabulary that will enhance and confirm their understanding of the text *Discontent Sparks Revolts in South America.* Provide them with a list of key descriptive words, such as *discontent, occupation, republic, toppled, setbacks, daring, gruelling,* and *swooped.* Then continue with one of the following activities.

Beginning Read *Discontent Sparks Revolts in South America* aloud. Help students use printed or online dictionaries to develop a bilingual glossary for the selected vocabulary. Ask pairs to reread *Discontent Sparks Revolts in South America* with those definitions in mind.

Intermediate Help students work with a partner to develop a bilingual glossary for the selected vocabulary, using printed or online dictionaries. Ask them to reread *Discontent Sparks Revolts in South America* with those definitions in mind.

Advanced Have students work in pairs or small groups and use a dictionary to confirm the meaning of each of the descriptive vocabulary words. Ask them to reread the text with those definitions in mind.

Advanced High Have students work in pairs to develop working definitions for each of these terms. Then have pairs reread the text and use context clues to gather more information and confirm the meaning of each term.

▣ Differentiate Instruction

Use the Differentiated Instruction notes throughout the lesson plan to support the varied skill sets, levels of readiness, and interests in the mixed-ability classroom.

Challenge These notes include suggestions for expanding the activity for advanced students.

On-Level These notes include suggestions for modifying the activity to address different interests or learning styles.

Extra Support These notes include ideas for providing more scaffolding or reading spuport.

Special Needs These notes provide ideas for adapting instruction to support the needs of various special needs students.

■ **NOTES**

_____

_____

_____

_____

_____

Latin American Nations Win Independence

Objectives

Objective 1: List the causes of growing discontent in Latin America, including the influence of the Enlightenment.

Objective 2: Trace the influence of the American and French Revolutions on Latin America.

Objective 3: Describe the revolutions in Haiti, Mexico, and Central America.

Objective 4: Explain how South American nations won independence, including the role of Simón Bolívar.

LESSON 2 ORGANIZER		PACING: APPROX. 1 PERIOD, .5 BLOCKS			
				RESOURCES	
		OBJECTIVES	**PACING**	**Online**	**Print**
Connect					
	DIGITAL START UP ACTIVITY **An Oath of Freedom**		5 min.	●	
Investigate					
	DIGITAL TEXT 1 **Latin America Ripe for Revolution**	Objectives 1, 2	10 min.	●	●
	DIGITAL TEXT 2 **Haiti Fights for Freedom**		10 min.	●	●
	DIGITAL TEXT 3 **Revolts in Mexico and Central America**	Objective 3			
	INTERACTIVE GALLERY **Latin American Independence Movements**		10 min.	●	
	DIGITAL TEXT 4 **Discontent Sparks Revolts in South America**	Objective 4	10 min.	●	●
	INTERACTIVE MAP **Latin American Independence**		10 min.	●	
Synthesize					
	DIGITAL ACTIVITY **The "Liberator's" Dream Doesn't Come True**		5 min.	●	
Demonstrate					
	LESSON QUIZ **Lesson Quiz and Class Discussion Board**		10 min.	●	

CONNECT

DIGITAL START UP ACTIVITY
An Oath of Freedom

Project the Start Up Activity Ask students to address the writing stimulus below as they enter and get settled. Have students share their ideas with another student.

Discuss After reading Bolívar's words, explain how the American and French Revolutions inspired him. *(The American Revolution showed it was possible to win independence from colonial control. The French Revolution inspired him with the Enlightenment ideals of natural rights such as liberty and equality.)*

Tell students that in this lesson they will learn about the fight for independence in Latin America.

Aa **Vocabulary Development:** Use the Interactive Reading Notepad to preview the Key Terms and Academic Vocabulary in this Lesson with students.

⇅ FLIP IT!

Assign the Flipped Video for this lesson.

■ STUDENT EDITION PRINT
PAGES: 557–560

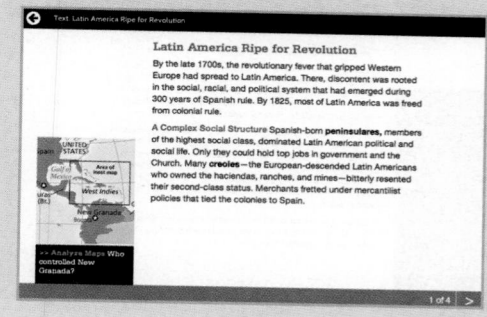

■ INVESTIGATE

DIGITAL TEXT 1
Latin America Ripe for Revolution

Objectives 1: List the causes of growing discontent in Latin America, including the influence of the Enlightenment; 2: Trace the influence of the American and French Revolutions on Latin America.

Quick Instruction
Analyze Maps Project the "Colonial Control in Latin America, Circa 1790" map from the text on the whiteboard. Introduce the activity by explaining that the Spanish controlled most of Latin and South America. Explain that the colonists lived with unfair laws and taxes similar to those of the Americans during the time of the American Revolution. Latin Americans also didn't want to be ruled by a monarchy so far away. Ask students to look at the map and think about how nationalism influenced the Latin American revolutions.

ELL Use the ELL activity described in the ELL chart.

Further Instruction
Go through the Interactive Reading Notepad questions and discuss the answers with the class.

There were many factors that led to the Latin American revolutions. Discontent with the social structure, influences of the Enlightenment ideals, the French and American Revolutions, and the weakening of Spain made Latin America ripe for revolution. Explain the role that liberty and equality had on influencing the Latin American revolutions. *(Liberty and equality inspired creole leaders to fight for independence because they wanted*

to end foreign rule and establish new social structures that allowed more people to own land and participate in the government.)

In the Napoleonic Wars of the early 1800s, Napoleon defeated Spanish armies and put his brother on the Spanish throne. Napoleon's invasion of Spain was a symbol of weakness to Latin American leaders.

Identify Central Issues Explain the impact of Napoleon Bonaparte and the Napoleonic Wars on Latin America. *(Spanish weakness inspired Latin Americans to fight for freedom. Because Spain's military was fighting in Europe, it could not send adequate forces to crush rebellions in Latin America. The weakened Spanish army lacked the strength to put down the revolutions.)*

Express Ideas Clearly Explain the influence of equality on the Latin American revolutions. *(The social structure in Latin America wasn't equal. Many people resented their status and wanted equality.)*

Latin American Nations Win Independence

DIGITAL TEXT 2

Haiti Fights for Freedom

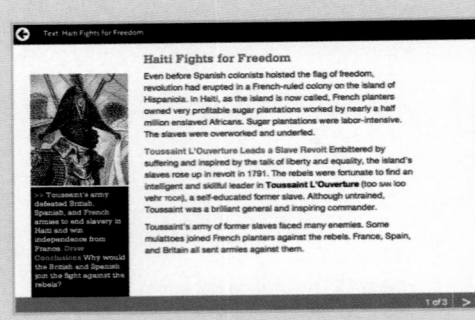

DIGITAL TEXT 3

Revolts in Mexico and Central America

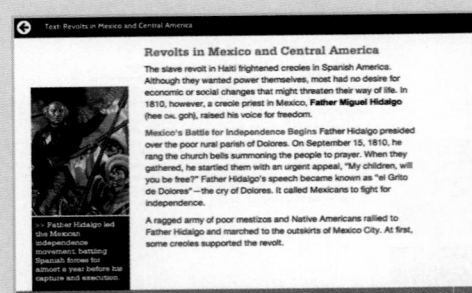

INTERACTIVE GALLERY

Latin American Independence Movements

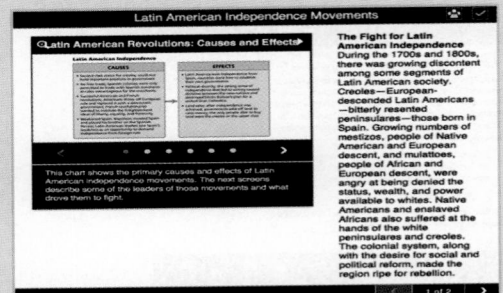

Objective 3: **Describe the revolutions in Haiti, Mexico, and Central America.**

Quick Instruction

Interactive Gallery: Latin American Independence Movements Project the Interactive Gallery on the whiteboard. In the first part of the 1800s, Latin America was still part of Spain's vast empire, but by 1825, it was free. Independence might never have been won without the leadership of those ready to fight for liberty and equality. Click through the gallery to learn more about the liberators of Latin America.

📷 ACTIVE CLASSROOM

Have students choose one of the leaders from the gallery. Ask them to create an analogy using the following prompt: This image shows that _____ is like _____ because _____.

D Differentiate: Extra Support After asking students to choose one of the leaders, have them make a list of words that describe the leader. Then tell them to use their list to think of similar objects in order to create their analogy.

Further Instruction

Go through the Interactive Reading Notepad questions for both of the readings and discuss the answers with the class.

Toussaint L'Ouverture, Father Hidalgo, and Father Morelos led rebellions to obtain equality. They led revolutions to ensure basic human rights were respected. L'Ouverture helped Haitian slaves fight for freedom, while Father Hidalgo and Father Morelos helped poor Mexicans fight for equality. Ask students to find examples of how a desire for equality sparked the rebellions in Haiti and Central America. *(L'Ouverture led an army of slaves to revolt against unfair treatment in Haiti. Father Hidalgo and Father Morelos led a poor army of mestizos and Native Americans to fight for social and political reform.)*

Identify Steps in a Process Describe how the Haitian people and people of Central America participated in changing their governments. *(The Haitian people rose up in revolt until they earned independence and the right to self-rule. Mexicans fought for their independence against the Spanish and stopped the control of creole elites, such as Iturbide, in order to establish independent republics and governments.)*

DIGITAL TEXT 4

Discontent Sparks Revolts in South America

INTERACTIVE MAP

Latin American Independence

Objective 4: Explain how South American nations won independence, including the role of Simón Bolívar.

Quick Instruction

Interactive Map: Latin American Independence Project the Interactive Map on the whiteboard. Remind students that the influence of ideas from the French Revolution, such as liberty, equality, and nationalism, inspired Latin American leaders to fight political revolutions for independence. During the French Revolution, Simón Bolívar traveled through Europe and admired revolutionaries fighting for Enlightenment ideas. Latin American leaders, especially Bolívar, were also inspired by the American Revolution, seeing revolutionaries overthrowing colonial control and creating a government based on a written constitution. Move the slider to compare maps of Latin America before and after the majority of the revolutions.

▣ ACTIVE CLASSROOM

Organize students into pairs. Make sure all students have seen both maps in the interactive map activity. Then ask students to do a See-Think-Wonder activity with the maps. Ask them: What do you see in the maps? What do the changes in the maps make you think? What are you wondering about now that you've seen the two maps? Allow them to discuss their insights with one another, and have a few pairs share with the class.

D **Differentiate: Challenge** After students discuss the map with their partner, have them write a short speech about the map of Latin America in 1845, from the point of view of Simón Bolívar. Remind students that Simon Bolívar's plan was to establish one united nation, Gran Colombia.

ELL Use the ELL activity described in the ELL chart.

Further Instruction

Go through the questions from the Interactive Reading Notepad, and discuss the answers with class.

In the early 1800s, discontent spread across South America. Many of the Latin American Independence leaders were inspired to fight for the ideals fought for during the French Revolution. Leaders, like Simón Bolívar, were inspired and encouraged to fight to gain freedom from colonial control just as the Americans did during the American Revolution. Describe how the liberators of South America participated in changing their governments. *(The liberators were successful in breaking ties to Spain and Portugal. They won independence from foreign monarchs and made it possible for several countries to establish their own governments.)*

Identify Cause and Effect List two causes and two effects of the Latin American revolutions. *(Causes: divided social structure and the weakening of Spain. Effects: creation of independent countries and civil war to create new boundaries.)*

Identify Supporting Details How did the American and French Revolutions influence the Latin American revolutions? *(The ideals of liberty, equality, and fraternity as seen in the French Revolution inspired Latin American leaders, as did the success of Americans in fighting off colonial rule and establishing a democratic republic.)*

Latin American Nations Win Independence

▇ SYNTHESIZE

DIGITAL ACTIVITY
The "Liberator's" Dream Doesn't Come True

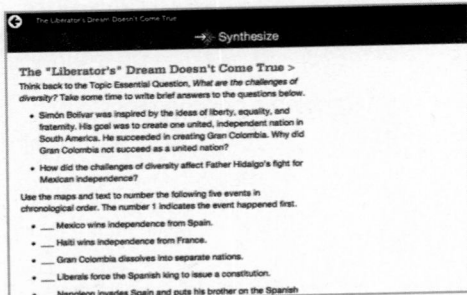

Ask students to recall the Topic Essential Question, "What are the challenges of diversity?" Have them use the Think-Pair-Share strategy to answer the questions in the Liberator's Dream Doesn't Come True activity. Ask them to take five minutes to write down some brief answers to the questions, and then share their answers with a partner. Why do you think Gran Colombia didn't remain a united nation? *(Within the nation of Gran Colombia there were many different groups of people who had their own ideas about government and had their own cultures. Instead of maintaining Gran Colombia, these groups of people waged civil wars that resulted in the formation of other countries.)* How did the challenges of diversity affect Father Hidalgo's fight for Mexican independence? *(Poor mestizos and Native Americans had joined Father Hidalgo's army. Some creoles also supported the revolt. However, the creoles soon rejected Father Hidalgo's calls for an end to slavery and better conditions for Native Americans. They felt these policies would lessen their power.)*

Have students work with their partner to order the events in the activity in chronological order.

Discuss After ordering the events in the Liberator's Dream Doesn't Come True Activity, ask the question, "How do these events portray the challenges of diversity?" *(The events show the struggle that people of different classes and races faced in Latin American society. Some wanted better property rights; others wanted an end to slavery.)*

▇ DEMONSTRATE

LESSON QUIZ
Lesson Quiz and Class Discussion Board

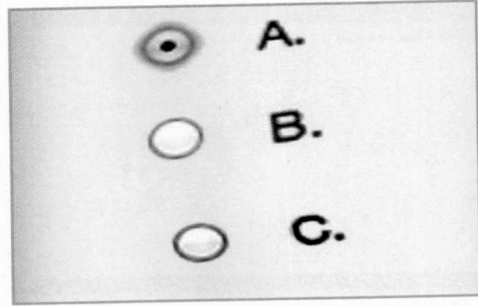

Assign the online Lesson Quiz for this lesson if you haven't already done so. Students will be offered automatic remediation or enrichment based on their score.

Pose the following question to the class on the Discussion Board:

In "Latin American Nations Win Independence," you read about the influences of other revolutions, Enlightenment ideals, and key people who led the fight for independence. The long, bloody battles for independence ended Spanish control in the New World and created several new, independent nations.

Draw Inferences Do you think the tensions between the social classes will dissolve now that the independent nations are free to establish their own governments?

Topic Inquiry
Have students continue their investigations for the Topic Inquiry.

The Unification of Germany

Supporting English Language Learners

Use with Digital Text 1, **Moving Toward a Unified Germany.**

Reading

Tell students that environmental print is the printed material found on signs, catalogs, menus, labels, and more. Show students a U.S. one dollar bill and a quarter. Explain that the United States uses one common system of money, or currency, but that the German states of the 1800s used different currencies. Then use one of the following activities to help students learn about German unification.

Beginning Point out symbols on the currency, including the scales of justice on the front of the dollar bill and the Latin words *E PLURIBUS UNUM* [out of many (states), one (nation)] on the back. Have students read aloud any words on the currency, such as the word *LIBERTY* on the quarter. Explain how one system of currency helps unite a country, and that the symbols and words on the dollar and quarter reflect this unity, as well as some principles of our government. Tell students that different forms of money was just one of the issues preventing German unity. Read *New Efforts to Bring Unity* aloud to students. Ask them to identify and read one or two words or phrases from the text that explain how the *Zollverein* aided German unification. Provide guidance as needed.

Intermediate Ask students to read aloud some of the words on the dollar bill and quarter. Point out some symbols on the currency. Discuss with students the meaning of the scales of justice on the front of the dollar bill, the Latin words *E PLURIBUS UNUM* [out of many (states), one (nation)], and the word *LIBERTY* on the quarter. Explain to students how one system of currency helps to unite a country, and that the symbols and words on our currency reflect this unity, as well as some principles of our government. Tell students that different forms of money was just one of the issues preventing German unity. Then have students read *New Efforts to Bring Unity*. Ask them to explain how the *Zollverein* aided German unification. Provide guidance as needed.

Advanced Ask students to work in small groups to read and discuss the meaning of the words and symbols on the dollar bill and quarter. Point out symbols such as the scales of justice on the dollar bill. Explain how one system of currency benefits a country. Ask students why multiple currencies might be a problem for Germans. Have students read *New Efforts to Bring Unity*. Then ask them to explain how the *Zollverein* helped German unification.

Advanced High Have student pairs read and discuss the meaning of the words and symbols on the dollar bill and quarter. Ask students to write a few sentences explaining how the American currency system benefits our country and how multiple currencies were a problem for Germans. Then have students read *New Efforts to Bring Unity*. Ask students to explain how the *Zollverein* aided German unification.

Use with Digital Text 2, **Bismarck Becomes the Architect of German Unity.**

Reading

Guide students as they create a brief glossary of challenging vocabulary and terms used in the reading *Bismarck Becomes the Architect of German Unity*.

Beginning Ask students to identify three difficult vocabulary and social studies terms from the reading. Help them develop a bilingual glossary for the selected vocabulary. Students should include a basic English and non-English definition for each word.

Intermediate Ask students to identify five difficult vocabulary and social studies terms from the reading. Help them develop a bilingual glossary for the identified vocabulary. Students should include a basic English and non-English definition for each word, as well as an English sentence that uses each word correctly.

Advanced Have students work in groups to make a list of the challenging vocabulary and social studies terms in the reading. Have groups develop a glossary for the identified vocabulary. Students should include the words and definitions in English, plus an English sentence that uses each word correctly.

Advanced High Have students work in pairs to make a list of challenging vocabulary and social studies terms in the reading. Then have students develop a glossary for the identified vocabulary. Students should include the words and definitions in English, plus an English sentence that uses each word correctly.

The Unification of Germany

Objectives

Objective 1: Identify the factors that promoted German nationalism.

Objective 2: Analyze how Bismarck achieved German unification.

Objective 3: Describe the German empire under Bismarck.

Objective 4: Explain the policies of Kaiser William II.

LESSON 3 ORGANIZER		PACING: APPROX. 1 PERIOD, .5 BLOCKS			
		OBJECTIVES	PACING	**RESOURCES**	
				Online	Print
Connect					
DIGITAL START UP ACTIVITY **Nationalist Pride**			5 min.	●	
Investigate					
DIGITAL TEXT 1 **Moving Toward a Unified Germany**		Objective 1	10 min.	●	●
DIGITAL TEXT 2 **Bismarck Becomes the Architect of German Unity**		Objective 2	10 min.	●	●
INTERACTIVE TIMELINE **German Unification**			10 min.	●	
DIGITAL TEXT 3 **Germany Becomes an Industrial Giant**		Objective 3	10 min.	●	●
DIGITAL TEXT 4 **The Iron Chancellor**					
INTERACTIVE CARTOON **A Political Game of Chess**			10 min.	●	
DIGITAL TEXT 5 **Kaiser William II**		Objective 4	10 min.	●	●
Synthesize					
DIGITAL ACTIVITY **The Price of Nationalism**			5 min.	●	
Demonstrate					
LESSON QUIZ **Lesson Quiz and Discussion Board**			10 min.	●	

PEARSON
realize™
www.PearsonRealize.com

Go online to access additional resources including:
Primary Sources • Biographies • Supreme Court cases •
21st Century Skill Tutorials • Maps • Graphic Organizers.

■ CONNECT

DIGITAL START UP ACTIVITY
Nationalist Pride

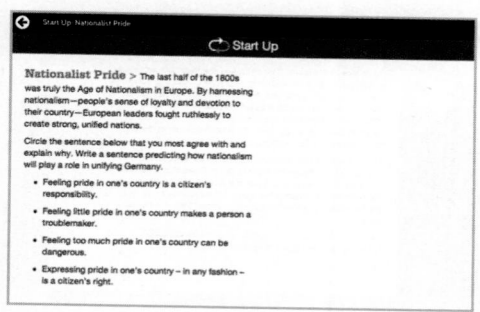

Project the Start Up Activity Ask students to address the writing stimulus as they get settled: Circle the sentence below that you most agree with and explain why.

- Feeling pride in one's country is a citizen's responsibility.
- Feeling little pride in one's country makes a person a troublemaker.
- Feeling too much pride in one's country can be dangerous.
- Expressing pride in one's country—in any fashion—is a citizen's right.

Discuss Write a sentence predicting what role nationalism will play in unifying Germany. *(Sample Response: Strong feelings of nationalism led Germans to demand one unified German state.)*

Aa Vocabulary Development: Use the Interactive Reading Notepad to preview the Key Terms and Academic Vocabulary in this Lesson with students.

⇅ FLIP IT!

Assign the Flipped Video for this lesson.

■ STUDENT EDITION PRINT
PAGES: 550–556

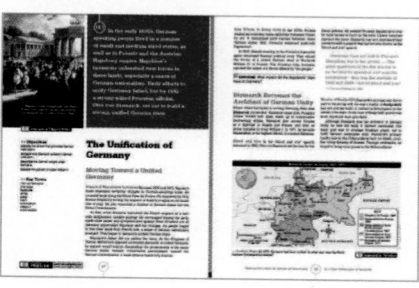

■ INVESTIGATE

DIGITAL TEXT 1
Moving Toward a Unified Germany

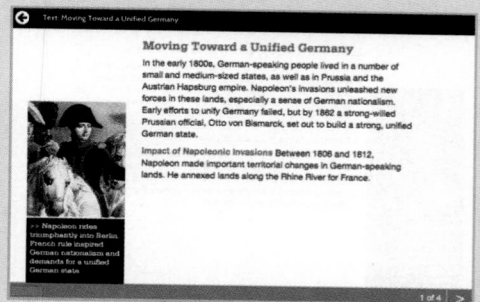

Objective 1: Identify the factors that promoted German nationalism.

Quick Instruction

Project the image of Napoleon riding into Berlin from the text on the whiteboard. Introduce the activity by explaining that German nationalism was a reaction to Napoleon's reorganization of the German states under French control. German-speaking peoples wanted an independent and unified German state. Have students discuss with a partner why the conservatives at the Congress of Vienna didn't create a united Germany.

ELL Use the ELL activity described in the ELL chart.

Further Instruction

Go through the Interactive Reading Notepad questions and discuss the answers with the class.

German-speaking people lived in many small states and several empires. After Napoleon's invasions and the Congress of Vienna, German-speaking people tried unsuccessfully to unify the German states. Explain why it was difficult for the German nationalists to create a unified Germany. *(There were many conservative forces preventing the unification of Germany. Metternich didn't want to dismantle the governments of all the German states, and William IV of Prussia refused the throne.)*

Infer Explain why the Congress of Vienna created the German Confederation, a weak alliance headed by Austria. *(By doing this, the Congress provided some satisfaction to German nationalists without creating a strong united Germany that might threaten Austria, France, and the other powers of Europe.)*

Identify Supporting Details Why did Prussia create the *Zollverein*? *(To promote economic unity between many of the German states)*

DIGITAL TEXT 2
Bismarck Becomes the Architect of German Unity

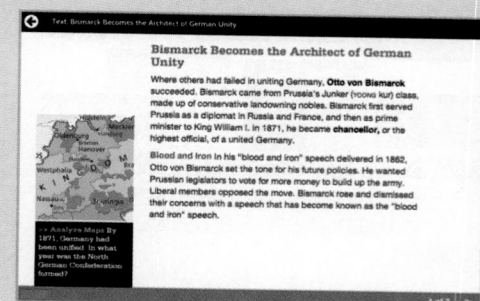

Objective 2: Analyze how Bismarck achieved German unification.

Quick Instruction

Interactive Timeline: German Unification
Project the Interactive Timeline on the whiteboard. Many events contributed to the unification of Germany. Have individual students drag and drop the events into their proper place along the timeline, or call on them to provide the correct answers.

💬 ACTIVE CLASSROOM

Ask students to take a stand on the following question: Do you think Bismarck, the master of Realpolitik, should have changed the telegram that reported on a meeting between King William I and the French ambassador? Yes or no? Then ask students to divide into two groups based on their answer and move to separate areas in the classroom. Ask students to talk with each other to compare their reasons for answering yes or no. Then have a representative from each side present and defend the group's point of view.

D Differentiate: Extra Support After asking students to take a stand, allow students five minutes to think about the question individually. Tell them to write down their response *(yes or no)* and two reasons why they answered that way. Then continue with the group activity.

ELL Use the ELL activity described in the ELL chart.

The Unification of Germany

INTERACTIVE TIMELINE
German Unification

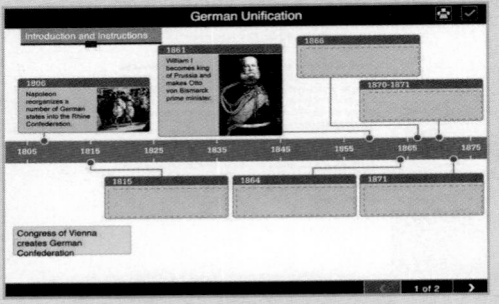

DIGITAL TEXT 3
Germany Becomes an Industrial Giant

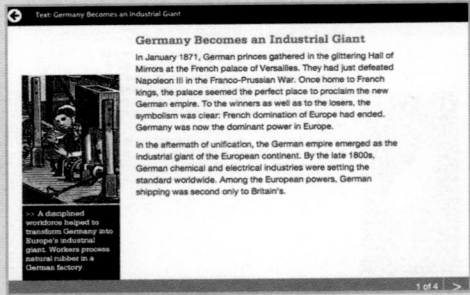

DIGITAL TEXT 4
The Iron Chancellor

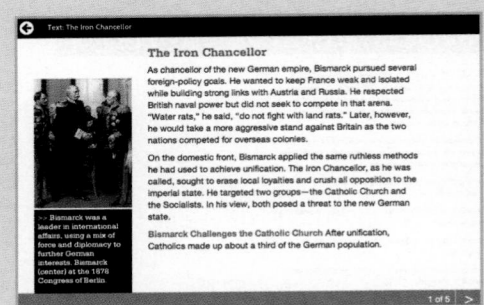

Further Instruction

Go through the Interactive Reading Notepad questions and discuss the answers with the class.

In 1871, German nationalists celebrated the birth of the Second Reich. William I of Prussia took the title of Kaiser and made Bismarck his chancellor. Explain how nationalism played a role in unifying Germany. (*Bismarck used Realpolitik, particularly against foreign powers, to unite the German states. Specifically, he used a war against France to increase nationalism in the southern German states, which led them to unite with Prussia.*)

Identify Supporting Details Describe the importance of the Austro-Prussian War. (*Prussia defeated Austria and annexed several north German states. Bismarck dissolved the Austrian-led German Confederation and created a new confederation under Prussian control.*)

Make sure students understand Bismarck's blood and iron policy and how that was reflected in the three wars Prussia fought prior to German unification.

Objective 3: Describe the German empire under Bismarck.

Quick Instruction

Interactive Cartoon: A Political Game of Chess Project the Interactive Cartoon on the whiteboard. Introduce the activity by explaining that Bismarck implemented a policy known as *Kulturkampf*, or "cultural struggle." This was put in place to reduce the role and power of the Roman Catholic Church in Prussia because Bismarck believed that Germans' loyalty to their nation should come before anything else. Click on each of the hotspots to help students interpret the political cartoon.

👥 ACTIVE CLASSROOM

Have students role-play and engage in an interview with either the pope or Bismarck. Have them write down a question they'd like to ask, and then what either the pope or Bismarck would say in response.

D Differentiate: Extra Support After students choose either the pope or Bismarck, give them five minutes to write a question and an answer that contains two points that either the pope or Bismarck would make about their question. Then continue with the group activity.

Further Instruction

Go through the questions in the Interactive Reading Notepad, and discuss the answers with the class.

Bismarck was known as the Iron Chancellor because he was fierce, and nothing came before his loyalty to Prussia. He was successful in creating a unified Germany, strengthening Germany's economy, and establishing social reform programs. Explain the importance of Bismarck with regard to German unification. (*Bismarck's goal was always to unify Germany, and he began by strengthening the Prussian army, strategically waging three wars, and annexing German states. After Germany's unification, Bismarck established a government where the power seemed shared but primarily was in the hands of the Kaiser and the chancellor.*)

Identify Supporting Details Why did Bismarck attack the Socialists? (*Bismarck was fearful that they would spread ideas of revolution to German workers, and he wanted to keep loyalty to the nation above anything else.*)

INTERACTIVE CARTOON
A Political Game of Chess

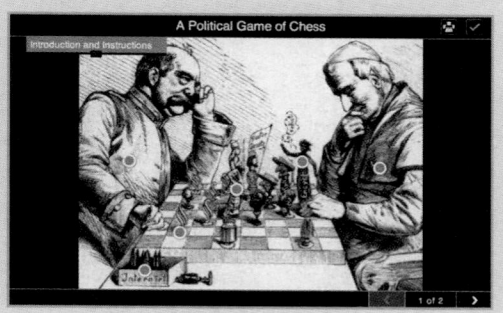

Draw Conclusions How did the Industrial Revolution lead to political changes in Germany? *(The Industrial Revolution led the German government to promote economic development, issue a single currency, reorganize the banking system, coordinate the railroad system, raise tariffs, and enact social reforms such as health, accident, and old-age insurance for the growing working class.)*

DIGITAL TEXT 5
Kaiser William II

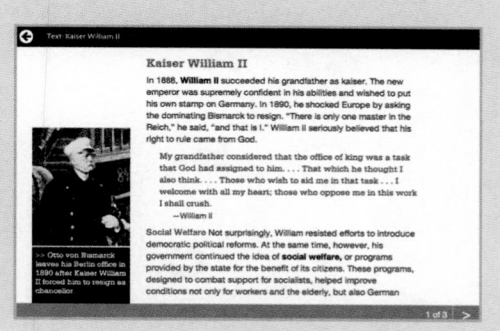

Objective 4: Explain the policies of Kaiser William II.

Quick Instruction

Project the German navy photo from the text on the whiteboard. Introduce the activity by explaining that William II had different views on foreign policy than Bismarck. He forced Bismarck to resign in order to rule Germany single-handedly. William II focused on strengthening the German military, specifically by building a navy that rivaled those of Britain and France. Why do you think William II wanted to strengthen the German navy? *(William II was a nationalist and wanted to show Germany's military strength. He expanded the German navy to win an overseas empire to rival those of France and Britain.)*

Further Instruction

Go through the Interactive Reading Notepad questions. Have students offer answers as a class.

After William II became Kaiser, Bismarck's days of controlling Germany came to an end. William didn't want to share power. He also wanted Germany to be seen as a world power. Why do you think William resisted the efforts to introduce democratic reforms? *(William believed he was given the right to rule from God. Democratic reforms meant that he would have to share his power. As he said, "There is only one master in the Reich, and that is I.")*

Summarize the policies of Kaiser William II. *(Kaiser William II provided social welfare programs, cheap transportation and electricity, and excellent public schools. But his main focus was to strengthen the German navy and military and to make Germany a world power.)*

The Unification of Germany

▮ SYNTHESIZE

DIGITAL ACTIVITY
The Price of Nationalism

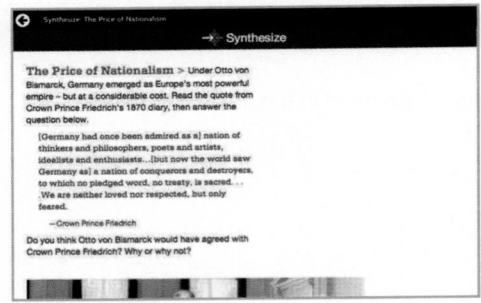

Ask students to recall the Topic Essential Question, "What are the challenges of diversity?" Have them use the Think-Pair-Share strategy to answer the questions in the Price of Nationalism activity. Ask them to take five minutes to write down some brief answers to the questions, and then share their answers with a partner: Do you think Otto von Bismarck would have agreed with Crown Prince Friedrich? Why or Why not?

(Answers may vary. Otto von Bismarck might not agree with Crown Prince Friedrich, but he also believed in the importance of "blood and iron" and thought military and political strength would bring Germany respect. He wanted Germany to be feared in order to be powerful, but he also helped to build Germany as a strong industrial nation, which he thought deserved respect. Otto von Bismarck was known as the Iron Chancellor because he did instill fear, but he also implemented strong policies such as social reform. Therefore, Bismarck would agree that Germany should be feared, but he would also think Germany should be respected.)

Then have students think about the Essential Question and how it affected German unification. Have them work with their partner to list three to four events that portrayed the challenges of diversity in the course of unifying Germany.

Discuss After listing the events, ask the question, "How do these events portray the challenges of diversity?" *(The events show the struggle that different groups, such as German-speaking states, Catholics, and socialists, had in the process of unifying Germany.)*

▮ DEMONSTRATE

LESSON QUIZ
Lesson Quiz and Discussion Board

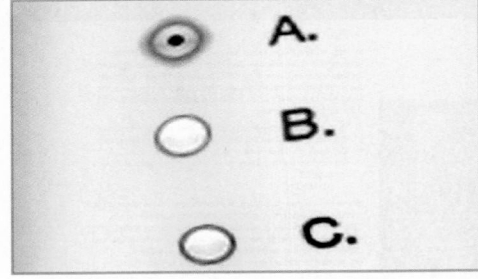

Assign the online Lesson Quiz for this lesson if you haven't already done so. Students will be offered automatic remediation or enrichment based on their score.

Pose the following question to the class on the Discussion Board:

In "The Unification of Germany," you read about the influences of nationalism and the effects of Bismarck's blood and iron philosophy on unifying Germany. Bismarck used Realpolitik in order to accomplish German unification. This can be seen in his use of nonmilitary funds to strengthen the army, his invented reasons to attack Austria, and his deceit to trick Napoleon III into war with Prussia. As a result, Germany emerged as an industrial giant and world power.

Draw Inferences How did Bismarck's government initially hold on to its power in Germany? *(through militarism and diplomacy)*

Topic Inquiry
Have students continue their investigations for the Topic Inquiry.

The Unification of Italy

Supporting English Language Learners

Use with Digital Text 1, **First Steps to Italian Unity.**

Reading

Explain that introductory clauses give background information to help readers understand the main part of a sentence better. Share with students the following sentence from the text: *To nationalists like Mazzini, a united Italy made sense not only because of geography, but also because of a common language and history.* Explain this introductory clause to students. Tell students that in this example, the introductory clause, *to nationalists like Mazzini,* can be moved to almost anywhere in the sentence and the sentence will still make sense. As you guide students through the following activities, share other sentences from the text with introductory clauses, such as: *Over the centuries, ambitious foreign conquerors had turned Italy into a battleground, occupying parts or all of the peninsula.* and *By the early 1800s, nationalism inspired Italian patriots to dream of ousting foreign rulers and reuniting Italy.*

Beginning Select sentences with introductory clauses from the text and identify for students the introductory clause and the main part of the sentence. For the first example above, explain how the introductory clause gives readers the clue that all nationalists in Italy shared a desire for a united Italy. Repeat this technique with additional examples from the text, and ask students to reread the text to find one sentence to do on their own.

Intermediate Have students identify the introductory clause and the main part of the first sentence identified above. Explain how the introductory clause gives readers the clue that all nationalists in Italy shared a desire for a united Italy. Then provide students with several other sentences from the text and ask them to read the sentences and repeat this activity.

Advanced Have students work in small groups. Give each group a few sentences from the text that include introductory clauses. Ask groups to read the sentences and identify the introductory clauses for each one. Then have them explain how each introductory clause helps to make the meaning of each sentence clearer.

Advanced High Have students reread the text and identify sentences that have introductory clauses. Then have them explain how each introductory clause helps to make the meaning of each sentence clearer. Finally, have students write three sentences with introductory clauses about the obstacles that stood in the way of Italian unity.

Use with Digital Text 3, **Italy Faces New Challenges.**

Reading

Work with students to identify and define the following vocabulary words commonly used in social studies texts: unity, nation, regional, culture, population, political. Explain that in social studies classes, these words turn up again and again.

Beginning Help students read and define each word, using bilingual resources as appropriate. Highlight each word in the context of *Italy Faces New Challenges* and have students draw a pictorial representation of each word.

Intermediate Help students read and define each word, using bilingual resources as appropriate. Have students draw or use images in the text to create a pictorial representation of each word. Finally, have students read the text to locate each word in the context of *Italy Faces New Challenges*.

Advanced Ask students to read the text to locate each commonly used word in the context of *Italy Faces New Challenges*. Then have students define each word, using a dictionary or glossary as needed.

Advanced High Ask students to read the text to locate each word in the context of *Italy Faces New Challenges*. Have students define each word, using a dictionary or glossary as needed, and then write an example sentence for each word about the content of the reading.

Ⓓ Differentiate Instruction

Use the Differentiated Instruction notes throughout the lesson plan to support the varied skill sets, levels of readiness, and interests in the mixed-ability classroom.

Challenge These notes include suggestions for expanding the activity for advanced students.

On-Level These notes include suggestions for modifying the activity to address different interests or learning styles.

Extra Support These notes include ideas for providing more scaffolding or reading spuport.

Special Needs These notes provide ideas for adapting instruction to support the needs of various special needs students.

▮ NOTES

_____

_____

_____

_____

_____

Topic (14) Lesson 4

The Unification of Italy

Objectives

Objective 1: List the key obstacles to Italian unity.

Objective 2: Evaluate the roles played by Cavour and Garibaldi in Italian unification.

Objective 3: Describe the challenges that faced the new nation of Italy.

LESSON 4 ORGANIZER		PACING: APPROX. 1 PERIOD, .5 BLOCKS			
				RESOURCES	
		OBJECTIVES	**PACING**	**Online**	**Print**
Connect					
	DIGITAL START UP ACTIVITY **Stirrings of Nationalism**		5 min.	●	
Investigate					
	DIGITAL TEXT 1 **First Steps to Italian Unity**	Objective 1	10 min.	●	●
	INTERACTIVE MAP **Italian Regions Before Unification**		10 min.	●	
	DIGITAL TEXT 2 **The Struggle for Italy**	Objective 2	10 min.	●	●
	INTERACTIVE GALLERY **Leaders of Italian Unification**		10 min.	●	
	DIGITAL TEXT 3 **Italy Faces New Challenges**	Objective 3	10 min.	●	●
Synthesize					
	DIGITAL ACTIVITY **Unity Leads to Turmoil**		5 min.	●	
Demonstrate					
	LESSON QUIZ **Lesson Quiz and Class Discussion Board**		10 min.	●	

CONNECT

DIGITAL START UP ACTIVITY
Stirrings of Nationalism

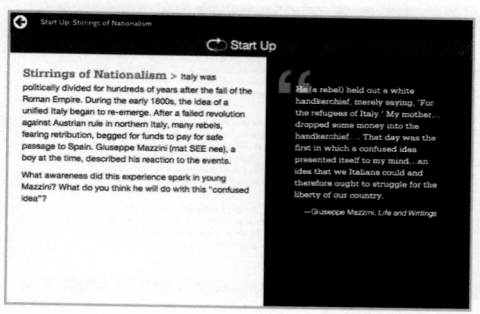

Project the Start Up Activity Ask students to read the quote and answer the questions below as they get settled. Then have them share their ideas with another student.

Discuss What did this experience spark in young Mazzini? *(Sample Response: A belief that Italians should free themselves from foreign rule.)* What do you think he will do with this "confused idea"? *(He will try to unite Italians to create an independent Italy.)* Identify and describe a leader today who is trying to bring about political change. *(Encourage students to think of people in the news.)*

Tell students that in this lesson they will learn how Italians overcame obstacles to build a united, independent Italy.

Aa Vocabulary Development: Use the Interactive Reading Notepad to preview the Key Terms and Academic Vocabulary in this Lesson with students.

↻ FLIP IT!

Assign the Flipped Video for this lesson.

STUDENT EDITION PRINT PAGES: 557–560

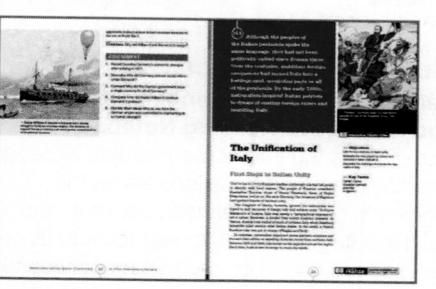

INVESTIGATE

DIGITAL TEXT 1
First Steps to Italian Unity

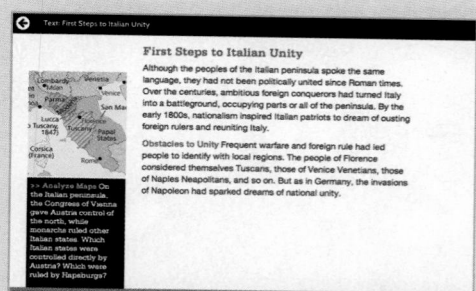

INTERACTIVE MAP
Italian Regions Before Unification

Objective 1: List the key obstacles to Italian unity.

Quick Instruction

Explain that the Italian peninsula had been divided into many small, independent states for centuries. Italy's history was one of succeeding occupations by a number of foreign powers. As a result, people tended to identify with their particular region rather than with the country as a whole. Trying to overcome these obstacles and develop a sense of Italian nationalism was a difficult challenge.

Interactive Map: Italian Regions Before Unification Project the map on the whiteboard. As you click on each area, discuss with students the hurdles that Italian leaders and citizens had to overcome in order to end foreign domination and build a unified Italy.

👥 ACTIVE CLASSROOM

Have students do a Quick Write about the obstacles that impeded Italian nationalism and unification and how individual citizens might participate in changing the governments of Italy. Ask for volunteers to present their Quick Write activities.

Further Instruction

Editable Presentation Use the Editable Presentation to present the main ideas for this Core Text.

Project and discuss the Interactive Reading Notepad questions on the whiteboard.

Explain that even though Mazzini's attempt at revolution failed, he and his followers inspired others because they were willing to fight and die for Italian unity. Italian nationalists struggled to overcome regional loyalties by promoting the unification of the Italian peninsula. Remind students that Italians were united by a common history, language, and culture. In order to succeed, Italian nationalists had to convince specific regions that unification was in their best interests.

Support a Point of View with Evidence Nationalists believed that a united Italy would bring greater economic prosperity than a collection of smaller states. Ask students to support this argument with some potential benefits of economic unity. *(Sample Responses: one common currency, one set of economic regulations, and the removal of tariffs imposed by many states would make it easier and less costly to do business and carry on trade.)*

The Unification of Italy

DIGITAL TEXT 2

The Struggle for Italy

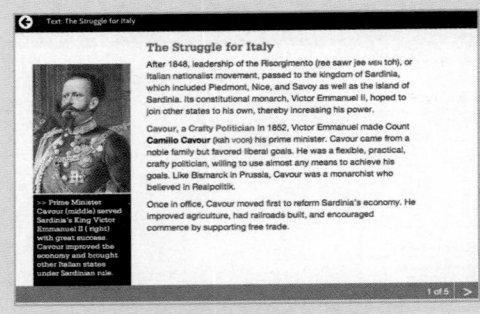

INTERACTIVE GALLERY

Leaders of Italian Unification

DIGITAL TEXT 3

Italy Faces New Challenges

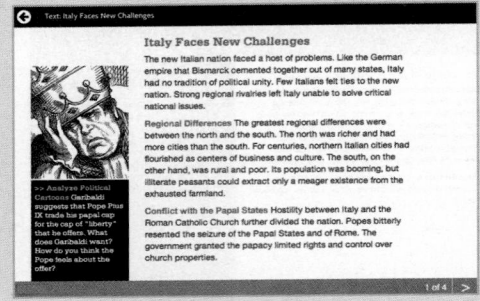

Objective 2: Evaluate the roles played by Cavour and Garibaldi in Italian unification.

Quick Instruction

Introduce the activity by explaining that the success of the Italian unification movement depended on people of many different backgrounds, social statuses, and regions putting aside their differences to make tough political choices and decisions. Nationalist leaders encouraged all Italians to work together to bring about change in their government.

Interactive Gallery: Leaders of Italian Unification Project the Interactive Gallery on the whiteboard. Click on each image and discuss with students how each of these Italian nationalists shifted political thinking in Italy and contributed to the cause of Italian unification.

🖳 ACTIVE CLASSROOM

Use the Conversation with History strategy to have students imagine they are having a conversation with one of the leaders of Italian unification. Ask students to write down a question they would ask this leader, what the leader might say in response, and what they might then reply. Ask volunteers to share their conversations.

D **Differentiate: Extra Support** To help students track the work of different Italian leaders, have them create a two-column chart, labeled *Leader* and *Contribution*. Have them include the names Giuseppe Mazzini, Victor Emmanuel, Camillo Cavour, and Giuseppe Garibaldi. As they read, have them note the way that each person contributed to the unification of Italy.

Further Instruction

Project and discuss the Interactive Reading Notepad questions for this lesson.

Garibaldi and Cavour were worlds apart in terms of social status and training. Cavour was an upper-class nobleman, while Garibaldi was from a family of fishermen and traders. Cavour was the consummate diplomat, whereas Garibaldi was a charismatic and inspirational soldier. Cavour was a monarchist, while Garibaldi was a republican.

Draw Conclusions How did each man's natural ability promote the cause of Italian unification? *(As a diplomat, Cavour was able to develop political alliances, treaties, and agreements that furthered the unification cause. Italy's unification led to armed conflict, and Garibaldi's abilities as a military strategist and leader enabled him to attract volunteers and win key battles.)*

Objective 3: Describe the challenges that faced the new nation of Italy.

Quick Instruction

Eventually, Italy was united, but it faced serious challenges. Regionalism continued, as northern Italy had a prosperous economy based on industry and trade. Southern Italy was poor and rural, with an economy based on agriculture. There was tension between the Italian government and the Catholic Church. Also, socialists and anarchists opposed the conservative constitutional monarchy.

🖳 ACTIVE CLASSROOM

Use the Graffiti Concepts strategy to have students reflect on the meaning of nationalism and then create a visual image and/or phrase that represents nationalism to them. Allow three to five minutes for the thinking and drawing/writing. Ask students to post their graffiti on the board or on chart paper. Then tell them to review the various responses and discuss similarities and differences.

ELL Use the ELL activity described in the ELL chart.

Further Instruction

Italy Faces New Challenges: Core Text and Interactive Reading Notepad Project and discuss the Interactive Reading Notepad Venn diagram and questions about the regional differences between northern and southern Italy. Use whiteboard tools to fill out the diagram based on student responses to the compare and contrast question. Discuss

▌ SYNTHESIZE

DIGITAL ACTIVITY
Unity Leads to Turmoil

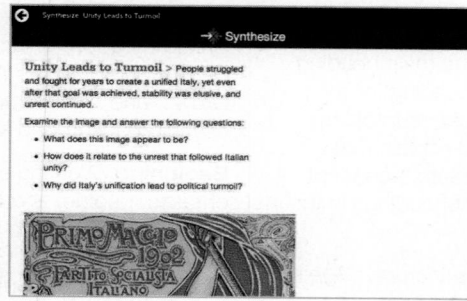

▌ DEMONSTRATE

LESSON QUIZ
Lesson Quiz and Class Discussion Board

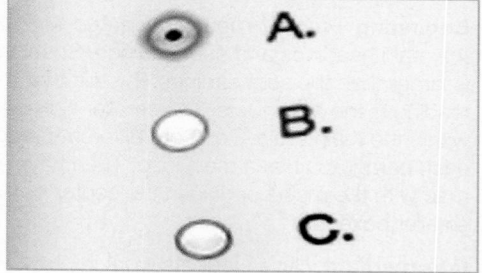

the responses while pointing out that, despite significant differences, northern and southern Italy also shared significant characteristics.

Analyze Information How did the shared characteristics help Italy come together as a nation? *(Shared language and essential cultural history, as well as the economic power of operating as a nation, eventually helped the regions develop a more nationalistic attitude.)*

Ask students to recall the Topic Essential Question, "What are the challenges of diversity?" Have students use the "Think-Pair-Share" strategy to answer the questions in the Unity Leads to Turmoil activity. Ask them to take five minutes to write down some brief answers to the questions, and then share their answers with a partner: What does this image show? *(Sample esponse: It appears to be a political party poster.)* How does it relate to the unrest that followed Italian unity? *(Sample response: In the late 1800s, unrest increased. Socialists organized strikes and demonstrations.)* Why did Italy's unification lead to political turmoil? *(Sample responses: Limited suffrage left people out of the political process, and regional differences left some Italians with local, rather than national, loyalties. People also lived with poverty and poor social conditions caused by industrialization and urbanization, and hostility between Italy and the Catholic Church. Many felt ignored by the conservative government.)*

Then have students think about the Essential Question and how it affected Italian unification. Have them work with their partner to list three to four different examples that portray the challenges of diversity in the course of unifying Italy.

Discuss After listing the examples, ask the question, "How do these examples portray the challenges of diversity?" *(Before unification, there were struggles between the various Italian states. After unification, there were struggles between northern and southern Italy, between the Catholic Church and Italian government, and between those who wanted a conservative constitutional monarchy and others who wanted more liberal or even radical government policies.)*

Assign the online Lesson Quiz for this lesson if you haven't already done so. Students will be offered automatic remediation or enrichment based on their score.

Pose these questions to the class on the Discussion Board:

In "The Unification of Italy," you learned about the challenges facing nationalists working to unite the various regions of Italy into one country, and the challenges that remained even after unification. You read about the key leaders Giuseppe Mazzini, Camillo Cavour, Giuseppe Garibaldi, and Victor Emmanuel II and how their individual contributions unified Italy and changed its government into a constitutional monarchy.

Identify Cause and Effect What did the Italian government do to distract those who opposed the government and to help build Italian prestige and power? *(Italy began to build an overseas empire by trying to colonize Ethiopia.)*

Infer How might the economic problems and population boom in Italy benefit the United States, Canada, and Latin America? *(Sample Response: Many Italians, especially from the poorer south, emigrated from Italy. Italian immigrants contributed to the economies, cultures, and governments of the United States, Canada, and many Latin American countries.)*

Topic Inquiry
Have students continue their investigations for the Topic Inquiry.

Democratic Reforms in Britain

Supporting English Language Learners

Use with Digital Text 2, **The Victorian Age.**

Reading
Show students that understanding the organization of a text can aid in comprehending the information contained in that text.

Beginning Preview *The Victorian Age* with students. Have them read the main headings and subheadings. Show them how the main heading is larger than the subheadings. Explain that the largest heading for the reading is the main topic. The smaller subheadings indicate subtopics within the main topic. Point out different paragraphs and explain that each paragraph has a main idea. Then have students create a concept map with the main heading in the center box and the subheadings in the smaller boxes.

Intermediate Have students work in pairs. Preview *The Victorian Age* by pointing out the reading's main heading, subheadings, and paragraphs. Ask each pair to discuss why the main heading is larger than the subheadings, why most of the content is placed under the subheadings, and why the text is arranged in paragraphs. Then have pairs create short summaries about something specific in the text and share those summaries with the group.

Advanced Have pairs of students preview *The Victorian Age* by paying special attention to the structure of the reading. Ask each pair to identify the reading's main heading, subheadings, and paragraphs. Ask each pair to discuss why the main heading is larger than the subheadings, why most of the content is placed under the subheadings, and why the text is arranged in paragraphs. Then have students create a basic outline of the information they read about the Victorian Age.

Advanced High Have students work individually to preview *The Victorian Age* by paying special attention to the structure of the reading. Ask each pair to use the reading's main heading, subheadings, and paragraphs to create an outline of what they read based on the main heading, subheadings, and paragraphs' main ideas.

Use with Digital Text 7, **The Irish Question.**

Reading
Explain that when classmates and teachers work together to develop background knowledge on a topic, understanding the language used in academic texts becomes easier. Display a historical map of the United Kingdom of Great Britain and Ireland. Also display the headings *Democratic Reforms in Britain*, *The Irish Question*, *Irish Nationalism Grows*, and *Irish Home Rule*. Then use any of the following methods to develop background knowledge on the Irish Question.

Beginning Working as a large group, help students brainstorm words, phrases, people, and things that connect with the topic. Guide the brainstorm session to include information on the historic relationship between Ireland and Great Britain. After the brainstorm is complete, eliminate any irrelevant ideas or words that were written down. Then have students work together to develop background knowledge on the topic of *The Irish Question*. Make sure the background knowledge includes relevant vocabulary that promotes an understanding of the tension between the Irish people and British rule.

Intermediate Divide students into small groups and help students brainstorm words, phrases, people, and things that connect with the topic. After the brainstorm is complete, eliminate any irrelevant ideas or words. Guide students to an understanding of certain terms that will improve their understanding of the reading. Make sure the background knowledge includes an understanding of the tension between the Irish people and British rule.

Advanced Ask students to work in pairs or small groups to brainstorm everything they know about the historic relationship between Ireland and Great Britain. Facilitate as students brainstorm words, phrases, people, and things that connect with the topic. After the brainstorm is complete, have students eliminate any irrelevant ideas or words that were written down. Make sure students' background knowledge includes an understanding of the tension between the Irish people and British rule.

Advanced High Ask students to work in pairs to brainstorm what they know about the historic relationship between Ireland and Great Britain. After the brainstorm is complete, allow students to do quick research to confirm and build their background knowledge. Make sure students come to a basic understanding of the tension between the Irish people and British rule.

◨ Differentiate Instruction

Use the Differentiated Instruction notes throughout the lesson plan to support the varied skill sets, levels of readiness, and interests in the mixed-ability classroom.

Challenge These notes include suggestions for expanding the activity for advanced students.

On-Level These notes include suggestions for modifying the activity to address different interests or learning styles.

Extra Support These notes include ideas for providing more scaffolding or reading spuport.

Special Needs These notes provide ideas for adapting instruction to support the needs of various special needs students.

■ NOTES

PEARSON **realize**™
www.PearsonRealize.com

Go online to access additional resources including:
Primary Sources • Biographies • Supreme Court cases •
21st Century Skill Tutorials • Maps • Graphic Organizers.

Objectives

Objective 1: Understand how political reforms in Britain affected suffrage and the nature of Parliament.

Objective 2: Identify the influence of Queen Victoria and the values she represented.

Objective 3: Describe social and economic reforms enacted by Parliament in the 1800s.

Objective 4: Describe the efforts by British women to win the vote.

Objective 5: Explain the struggle for Irish home rule and the impact of famine on Ireland.

LESSON 5 ORGANIZER

PACING: APPROX. 1 PERIOD, .5 BLOCKS

		OBJECTIVES	PACING	Online	Print
Connect					
DIGITAL START UP ACTIVITY **Harsh Working and Living Conditions Lead to Government Reforms**			5 min.	●	
Investigate					
DIGITAL TEXT 1 **"Two Nations": The Rich and the Poor**		Objective 1	10 min.	●	●
DIGITAL TEXT 2 **The Victorian Age**		Objective 2	10 min.	●	●
DIGITAL TEXTS 3, 4, AND 5 **Reforms Increase Parliamentary Democracy, Economic and Social Reforms, Victories for the Working Class**		Objective 3	10 min.	●	●
INTERACTIVE TIMELINE **Britain Reformed**			10 min.	●	
DIGITAL TEXT 6 **Women Struggle for the Vote**		Objective 4	10 min.	●	●
DIGITAL TEXT 7 **The Irish Question**		Objective 5	10 min.	●	●
INTERACTIVE GALLERY **Famine Changes Ireland**			10 min.	●	
Synthesize					
DIGITAL ACTIVITY **Democratic Transition**			5 min.	●	
Demonstrate					
LESSON QUIZ **Lesson Quiz and Class Discussion Board**			10 min.	●	

Democratic Reforms in Britain

▊ CONNECT

DIGITAL START UP ACTIVITY
Harsh Working and Living Conditions Lead to Government Reforms

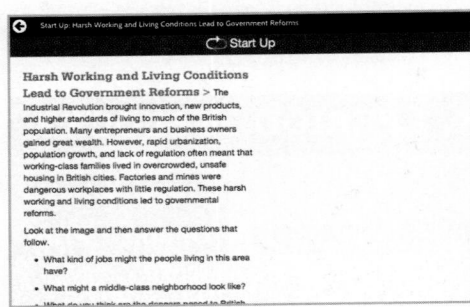

Project the Start Up activity Ask students to answer the questions as they get settled. Then have them share their ideas with another student.

Discuss What kind of jobs might the people living in this area have? *(Answers should include factory workers, laborers, servants, or miners.)* What dangers were posed to British society by the deep divisions between the classes? *(Such divisions could lead to revolution.)* How do you think the British government will resolve these divisions? *(Students may say democratic reforms and better working conditions.)*

Tell students that in this lesson they will learn how the British people gained political, social and economic reforms.

Aa Vocabulary Development: Use the Interactive Reading Notepad to preview the Key Terms and Academic Vocabulary in this Lesson with students.

⇅ FLIP IT!
Assign the Flipped Video for this lesson.

▊ STUDENT EDITION PRINT
PAGES: 561–568

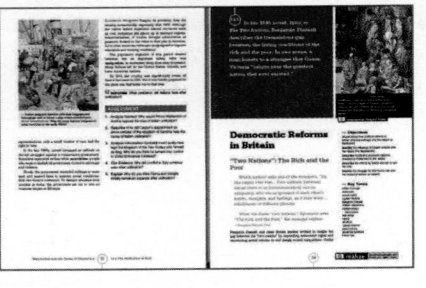

▊ INVESTIGATE

DIGITAL TEXT 1
"Two Nations": The Rich and the Poor

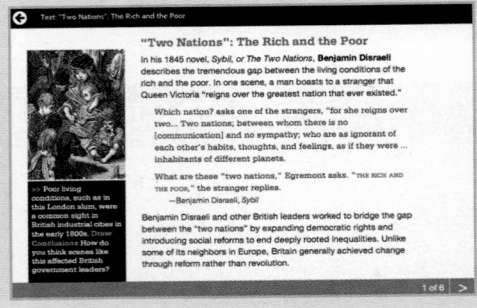

Objective 1: Understand how political reforms in Britain affected suffrage and the nature of Parliament.

Quick Instruction
Project the image of the London urban slum scene. Explain to students that in the early 1800s British government was not fully democratic. Most people could not vote, and the upper-class House of Lords could veto any bill passed by the House of Commons.

Identify Cause and Effect After students have read the text, ask: How did the British people change their government in the 1830s, and what were the effects? *(Sample answers: mostly through peaceful protest and reform law; most men could vote.)*

Further Instruction
Project and discuss the Interactive Reading Notepad questions for "Two Nations: The Rich and the Poor." Explain to students that at the beginning of the 19th century, more than one-fifth of the seats in Parliament were in rotten boroughs. Fifty of the representatives had fewer than 50 voters in their district, while new cities formed by the Industrial Revolution were not allowed any representation. This unfair representation and a lack of a political voice in government led to social instability.

Support Ideas with Evidence Have students list and describe specific reform efforts and laws that extended suffrage, and eliminated rotten boroughs. *(Students should list and describe end of religious restrictions, Reform Act of 1832, Chartist movement.)*

DIGITAL TEXT 2
The Victorian Age

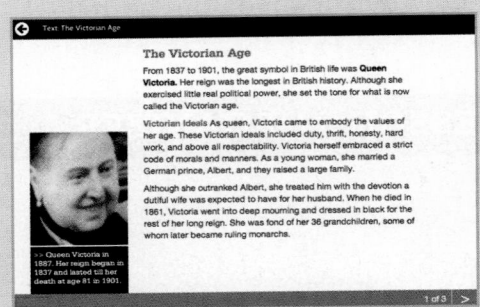

Objective 2: Identify the influence of Queen Victoria and the values she represented.

Quick Instruction
Project the image of Queen Victoria from the text. Explain to students that Queen Victoria and the values she represented had significant influence on British society during her long reign. Be sure students understand that she represented Victorian ideals such as duty, honesty, and hard work; she inspired confidence that British power and wealth would expand; and she favored social reforms for the lower classes.

ELL Use the ELL activity described in the ELL chart.

Further Instruction
Project and discuss the Interactive Reading Notepad questions about Queen Victoria and the Victorian Age. Discuss the Victorian values and ideals that the queen represented, including duty, thrift, honesty, hard work, patriotism, family values, support for the government, strict manners, and respectability. Ask students to keep this in mind while reading the lesson.

Infer During Queen Victoria's reign, Britain's economy, military, and empire all expanded in power. Ask students: How do you think Victorian ideals supported this expansion in power? *(Ideals such as patriotism, duty, and hard work promoted British wealth and power.)*

DIGITAL TEXT 3
Reforms Increase Parliamentary Democracy

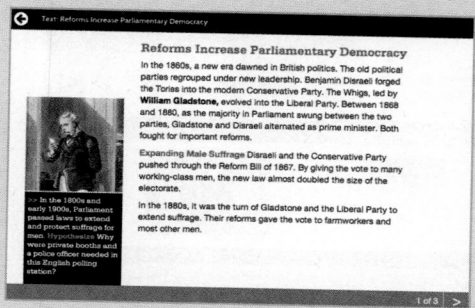

DIGITAL TEXT 4
Economic and Social Reforms

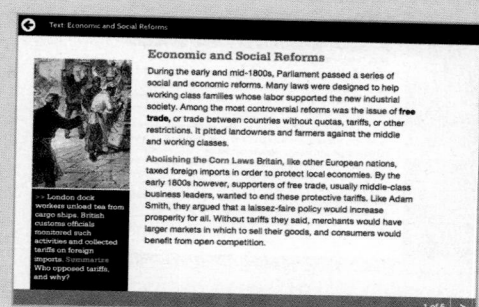

Evaluate Impact Point out Queen Victoria's comment that the lower classes "earn their bread and riches so deservedly that they cannot and ought not to be kept back." Ask students to explain how this comment probably influenced British society. *(Comments like this from the queen encouraged the British people to enact social and economic reforms. Many probably felt this also applied to government and that the working class deserved a political voice. And the working class was more likely to support the government.)*

Objective 3: Describe social and economic reforms enacted by Parliament in the 1800s.

Quick Instruction
Interactive Timeline: Britain Reformed Project the Interactive Timeline on the whiteboard. Using the hotspots for more information, review how reformers changed the British government, and explain how political, social, and economic reforms were interrelated. Ask students to use the text to learn additional details about each of the social and economic reforms on the timeline. Emphasize the tactics people like the abolitionist William Wilberforce used to shift political thought. *(Answers will vary, but students might mention protesting and persistently making your views known in a public setting. William Wilberforce, for example, made speeches to persuade fellow lawmakers in the House of Commons to end the slave trade.)*

👥 ACTIVE CLASSROOM

Have students Make Headlines that summarize the timeline's main idea. Ask: If you were to write a headline that captured the most important aspect of this timeline, what would that headline be? Exchange headlines with a partner for him or her to review and improve.

Further Instruction
Editable Presentation Use the Editable Presentation to present the main ideas for this text.

Democratic Reforms in Britain

DIGITAL TEXT 5

Victories for the Working Class

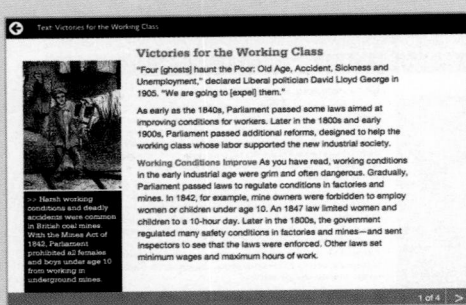

INTERACTIVE TIMELINE

Britain Reformed

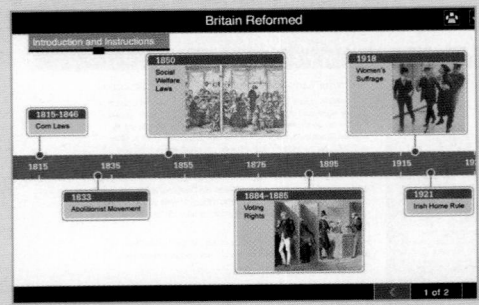

DIGITAL TEXT 6

Women Struggle for the Vote

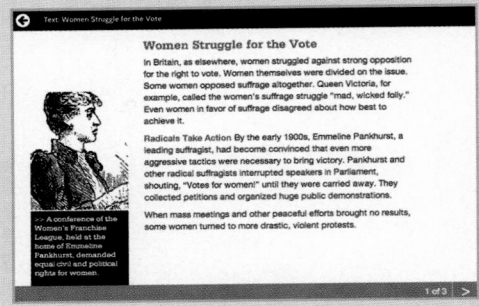

Predict Consequences By the end of the 1800s Britain had universal manhood suffrage. Ask students what this means and what many British might demand next to extend democracy in Britain. *(All adult men could vote; many people might now demand the right to vote for women.)*

Express Ideas Clearly Why did liberals and middle-class business leaders oppose the Corn Laws? *(They believed that a laissez faire, free enterprise system would increase prosperity for all. If tariffs were abolished, merchants would have larger markets in which to sell their goods, and consumers would benefit from open competition and lower prices.)*

D Differentiate: Extra Support To help students explain the argument against the Corn Laws, have them first use the glossary or a dictionary to define *laissez faire, free enterprise system, tariffs*, and any other unfamiliar terms.

Identify Central Issues Project the abolitionist poster from the text. How does this poster provide an example of how people participated in changing the British government? *(The poster is a form of political advertisement or campaigning that citizens and leaders used to promote an end to slavery and other social reforms.)*

Identify Cause and Effect What were some results of interactions between British labor unions, socialists, and government leaders? *(Sample answer: Working conditions improved, and Socialists and union members formed the powerful Labour Party. Because of these reforms, Marxism had only limited appeal to the British working class.)*

Objective 4: Describe the efforts by British women to win the vote.

Quick Instruction

Trace the developments of the women's suffrage movement, and review with students how reformers used increasingly drastic tactics to change their government. Point out that many people did not agree with the idea of women voting. Even those who agreed that women should have the vote did not agree on how to achieve their goals. Emphasize that reformers would not win suffrage for all British women until the mid-1900s.

Further Instruction

Project and discuss the questions from the Interactive Reading Notepad on "Women Struggle for the Vote." Explain that hunger strikes and illegal actions were drastic measures taken by reformers. Discuss reasons why some people felt those actions were required to change their government.

Support a Point of View with Evidence In 1918, Parliament finally granted suffrage to women over the age of 30. If you were a 25-year-old suffragist in 1918, would you support the law passed that year? Use examples from the text to support your opinion. *(Possible Answers: Support—partial suffrage was a first step, similar to the incremental steps towards suffrage for men in the 1800s. Reject—younger women deserved the right to vote just as much as older women, the age limit was arbitrary.)*

Make Generalizations Why would supporters of the women's suffrage movement use hunger strikes as a form of protest? *(Possible answers: Some suffragists concluded that only aggressive actions would help them get the vote. In addition to the hunger strikes, they turned to violence because they believed the government cared more about property than human life. They may have hoped that physically suffering for their cause would garner public sympathy.)*

DIGITAL TEXT 7

The Irish Question

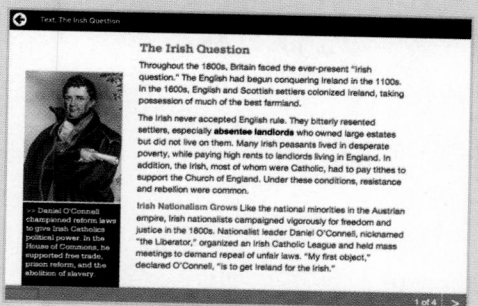

INTERACTIVE GALLERY

Famine Changes Ireland

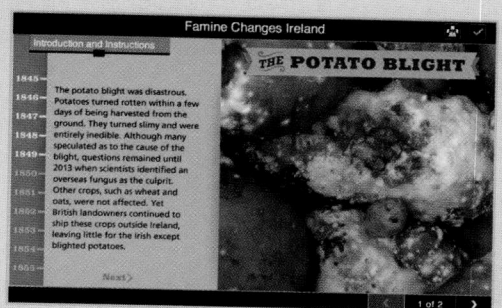

Objective 5: Explain the struggle for Irish home rule and the impact of famine on Ireland.

Quick Instruction

Interactive Gallery: Famine Changes Ireland Project the Interactive Gallery on the whiteboard. Introduce the activity by explaining that the Irish rejected English rule. Ask students to click on the various images to learn more information about the Great Famine and Irish home rule. Introduce the concept of Irish home rule and discuss how absentee landlords charged high rents, allowing little money or food for the Irish families living there. Point out that the Irish Potato Famine further deteriorated the social, economic, and political situation in Ireland.

ACTIVE CLASSROOM

Have students Quick Write short messages, such as those sent via Twitter, that capture the tragedy of the Irish Potato Famine. Ask: If you were to tweet the most important aspect that should be remembered about the Irish Potato Famine, what would your messages be? *(Students should clearly state at least one of the effects of the famine, such as human suffering, or emigration, and show understanding of the lack of help from the British government.)*

ELL Use the ELL activity described in the ELL chart.

Further Instruction

Editable Presentation Use the Editable Presentation to present the main ideas for this text.

The Irish Question: Interactive Reading Notepad Project the questions provided in the Interactive Reading Notepad, and have students answer as they progress through the core text.

Identify Cause and Effect Why did many Irish people mistrust the British after the Great Famine? *(The British continued to export food from Ireland while hundreds of thousands starved. When this situation was combined with harsh British laws, many people were outraged and supported Irish nationalism and independence.)*

Discuss What were some of the ways Irish people attempted to change the British government and achieve Irish home rule? *(Possible answers: The Irish Catholic League held mass meetings to repeal unfair laws; Fenian Brotherhood used force; Irish members of Parliament pressed for home rule.)*

Democratic Reforms in Britain

■ SYNTHESIZE

DIGITAL ACTIVITY
Democratic Transition

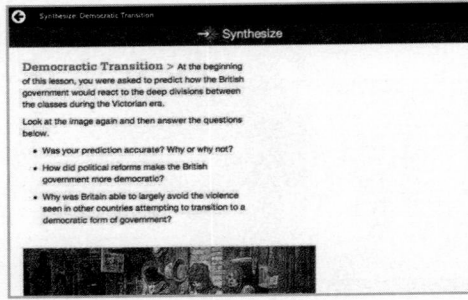

Ask students to recall the Topic Essential Question, "What are the challenges of diversity?" Tell them that at the beginning of this lesson, they were asked to predict how the British government would resolve the deep divisions between the classes during the Victorian era. Ask them to review the Synthesize image and answer these questions: Was your prediction accurate? Why or why not? *(Students should clearly state whether their prediction was accurate and why.)* How did political reforms make the British government more democratic? *(Suffrage was extended to nearly all men and to women over 30. Rotten boroughs were eliminated. The power of the House of Lords was restricted, including their power to veto.)* Why do you think Britain was able to largely avoid the violence seen in other countries attempting to transition to a democratic form of government? *(Students should note that expanding suffrage provided a voice for the people.)*

Next, have students use the "Think-Pair-Share" strategy to answer this question: How did diversity affect democratic reforms in Britain? Ask them to write down some brief answers to the question, and then share their answers with a partner.

Discuss Invite student pairs to share their responses with the class. Encourage students to provide details and examples to support their response. *(Students should mention the interaction between diverse segments of the British population: conservatives and liberals; men and women; upper, middle, and lower classes; capitalists and socialists; laborers and business-owners.)*

■ DEMONSTRATE

LESSON QUIZ
Lesson Quiz and Class Discussion Board

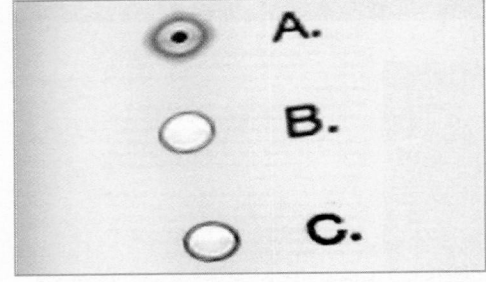

Assign the online Lesson Quiz for this lesson if you haven't already done so. Students will be offered automatic remediation or enrichment based on their score.

Pose these questions to the class on the Discussion Board:

In "Democratic Reforms in Britain," you read about how Britain slowly extended democratic reforms throughout the 19th and early 20th centuries.

Draw Conclusions Identify two examples of key persons who were successful in shifting political thought during the period. Describe how each participated in changing government, and explain why you consider his or her efforts successful. *(Possible answer: William Wilberforce and Emmeline Pankhurst. Wilberforce served in the House of Commons and persistently introduced anti-slavery legislation for 18 years. Pankhurst used radical protest tactics, including violence, to gain attention for the women's suffrage movement. Both would be considered successful because their goals were ultimately achieved.)*

Topic Inquiry
Have students continue their investigations for the Topic Inquiry.

PEARSON realize™

www.PearsonRealize.com
Access your Digital Lesson

Divisions and Democracy in France

Supporting English Language Learners

Use with Digital Text 3, **The Dreyfus Affair.**

Reading
Explain that reading with others can make it easier to understand challenging sentences and difficult vocabulary. Read *The Dreyfus Affair* with students to improve their comprehension of the text.

Beginning Slowly and expressively read one paragraph of *The Dreyfus Affair* to students. Then have the students repeat after you as you read the same paragraph, sentence by sentence. Finally, lead students in a choral reading of the paragraph. At every stage of this process, listen for any issues in pronunciation and correct them before moving on. Reread the paragraph until students are able to pronounce each word successfully. Finally, identify the main idea and details of the paragraph for students. Ask them to summarize the material in their own words in order to demonstrate that comprehension of the text allows you to extract and recall details.

Intermediate Slowly and expressively read one paragraph of *The Dreyfus Affair* to students, carefully sounding out challenging words. Then lead the students in a choral reading of the paragraph. As students read along, listen for any issues in pronunciation and correct them before continuing. Have students reread the paragraph in small groups until they are able to pronounce each word successfully. Finally, help students identify the main idea and details of the paragraph to demonstrate that a clear understanding of the text allows students to extract and recall details.

Advanced Slowly and expressively, read one paragraph of *The Dreyfus Affair* to students. Carefully sound out challenging words. Then have students work in pairs to simultaneously read aloud the paragraph again. As each pair reads, circulate among students, listening for any issues in pronunciation and correct them before continuing. Have pairs continue rereading the paragraph until they are comfortable. Then ask pairs to identify the main idea and details of the paragraph together to check for understanding.

Advanced High Have pairs of students begin by reading the paragraph silently. Then, taking turns, students should read the paragraph aloud, taking care to pronounce each word properly. Students can help one another when they encounter a challenging word. Finally, have pairs identify the main idea and details of the paragraph to check for understanding.

Use with Digital Text 4, **Reforms in France.**

Reading
Guide students in previewing *Reforms in France* by creating a graphic organizer that shows the main idea and details of the text. Then have students read the text and expand and revise their organizers with additional details.

Beginning Help students create a main idea graphic organizer. Preview *Reforms in France* with students and demonstrate how to skim the introductory paragraph for supporting details to put in the organizer. Then with students skim the rest of the reading and add more details to the organizer. Allow students to add drawings for clarity.

Intermediate Have students create a main idea graphic organizer. Help them preview *Reforms in France* by skimming the text for supporting details to put in their\organizers. As students skim the reading, help them identify and define any challenging vocabulary. Remind them to add details in each spoke after they read *Reforms in France*.

Advanced Have pairs preview *French Reforms* and work together to fill in a main idea graphic organizer. Instruct them to skim the text for supporting details to put in the organizer's spokes. As students skim the reading, have them identify and define any challenging vocabulary. Remind them to add details in each spoke after they read *Reforms in France*.

Advanced High Have students preview *French Reforms* and work individually to create a main idea graphic organizer. Have students compare their organizers to a partner's, and correct any errors. Finally, have pairs identify and define any challenging vocabulary. Remind students to add details in each spoke after they read *Reforms in France*.

▣ Differentiate Instruction

Use the Differentiated Instruction notes throughout the lesson plan to support the varied skill sets, levels of readiness, and interests in the mixed-ability classroom.

Challenge These notes include suggestions for expanding the activity for advanced students.

On-Level These notes include suggestions for modifying the activity to address different interests or learning styles.

Extra Support These notes include ideas for providing more scaffolding or reading spuport.

Special Needs These notes provide ideas for adapting instruction to support the needs of various special needs students.

■ NOTES

Divisions and Democracy in France

Objectives

Objective 1: List the domestic and foreign policies of Napoleon III.

Objective 2: Describe the challenges and political reforms of the Third Republic.

Objective 3: Explain how the Dreyfus affair divided France and contributed to the growth of the Zionist movement.

LESSON 6 ORGANIZER		PACING: APPROX. 1 PERIOD, .5 BLOCKS			
				RESOURCES	
		OBJECTIVES	PACING	Online	Print
Connect					
	DIGITAL START UP ACTIVITY **A Different Point of View**		5 min.	●	
Investigate					
	DIGITAL TEXT 1 **Napoleon III and the Second Empire**	Objective 1	10 min.	●	●
	INTERACTIVE GALLERY **The Siege of Paris**		10 min.	●	
	DIGITAL TEXT 2 **The Third Republic Faces New Struggles**	Objective 2	10 min.	●	●
	INTERACTIVE CARTOON **The Boulanger Scandal**		10 min.	●	
	DIGITAL TEXT 3 **The Dreyfus Affair**	Objective 3	10 min.	●	●
	DIGITAL TEXT 4 **Reforms in France**	Objective 2	10 min.	●	●
Synthesize					
	DIGITAL ACTIVITY **The Dreyfus Affair**		5 min.	●	
Demonstrate					
	LESSON QUIZ **Lesson Quiz and Class Discussion Board**		10 min.	●	

CONNECT

DIGITAL START UP ACTIVITY
A Different Point of View

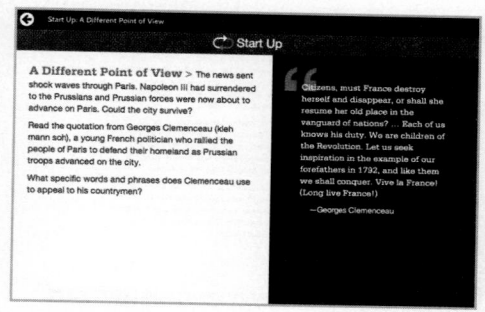

Project the Start Up Activity Ask students to answer the question as they get settled. Then have them share their ideas with another student.

Discuss What words and phrases does Clemenceau use to appeal to his countrymen? *(Sample response: Words and phrases such as "Citizens," "Each of us knows his duty," "We are children of the Revolution," and "Vive la France!")* Do you think Clemenceau's words were effective? *(Sample answer: effective because he used the French Revolution and nationalism to inspire resistance against the Prussians.)*

Tell students that in this lesson they will learn about the Siege of Paris and the challenges that democracy faced in France.

Aa Vocabulary Development: Use the Interactive Reading Notepad to preview the Key Terms and Academic Vocabulary in this Lesson with students.

↰ FLIP IT!

Assign the Flipped Video for this lesson.

■ STUDENT EDITION PRINT
PAGES: 569–573

INVESTIGATE

DIGITAL TEXT 1
Napoleon III and the Second Empire

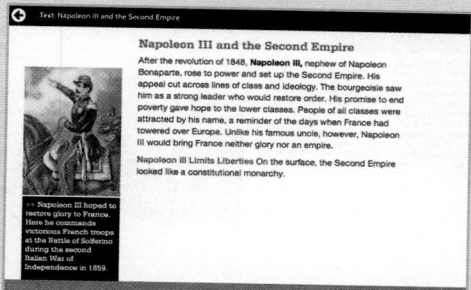

INTERACTIVE GALLERY
The Siege of Paris

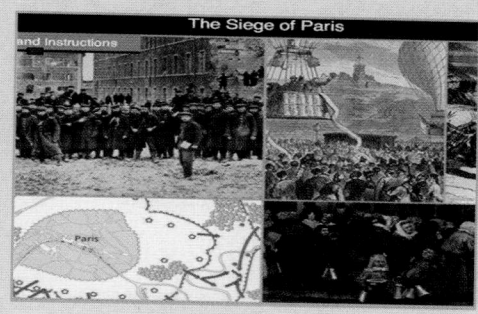

Objective 1: List the domestic and foreign policies of Napoleon III.

Quick Instruction

As leader of France, Napoleon III limited human rights and liberties. He restricted popular sovereignty by appointing legislators and by "fixing" elections. While he promoted economic growth, his ambitious foreign policy led to wars. France suffered a disastrous defeat in the Franco-Prussian War.

Interactive Gallery: The Siege of Paris Project the first screen of the image gallery on the whiteboard. Click through the hot spots on the screen, and discuss each image and what it tells students about the Siege of Paris.

Analyze Images Ask students to describe what they see in these images. Based on these images, how do you think the French people felt about their present and future government? What action might they want to take? *(Possible answers: They blamed Napoleon III for the defeat; they feared they would be ruled by Prussia; they wanted to change their government to make it more democratic.)*

🗣 ACTIVE CLASSROOM

Have students list the major policies of Napoleon III. Use the Rank It strategy to have students review these policies and rank them in order from the most positive effect on France down to the most negative effect on France. Ask students to provide justification for the ranking. Then ask students to work in pairs to share their ideas. Poll the class to see if there is agreement on the rankings.

Further Instruction

Napoleon III and the Second Empire: Core Text and Interactive Reading Notepad Project and discuss the Interactive Reading Notepad questions. Review the government of Napoleon III, its political reforms, and its foreign policy with the class. Have students take notes as you review.

Be sure that students understand the effects of Napoleon's foreign policy on his reign and on France. Discuss the reasons why Napoleon became involved in a war with Prussia. *(France was concerned about the growth of Prussia's power. Bismarck manipulated Napoleon into the war.)*

Predict Consequences Ask students to predict what the new French government, the Third Republic, will be like. Will it benefit the French people? *(Sample response: The Third Republic will be a democracy, and it will help France grow and become a strong nation.)*

Divisions and Democracy in France

DIGITAL TEXT 2

The Third Republic Faces New Struggles

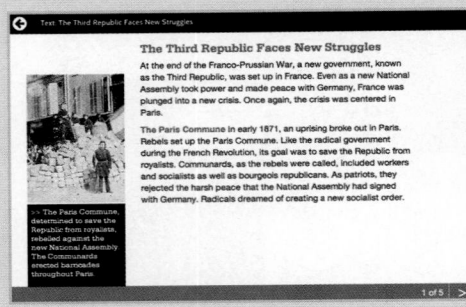

INTERACTIVE CARTOON

The Boulanger Scandal

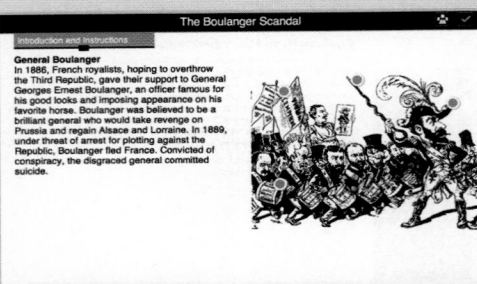

DIGITAL TEXT 3

The Dreyfus Affair

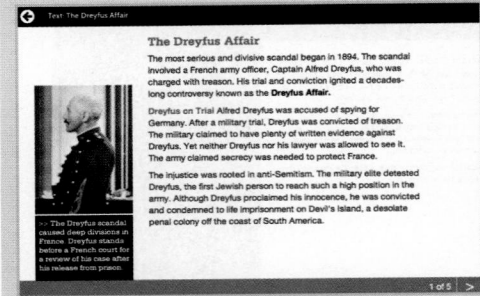

Objective 2: Describe the challenges and political reforms of the Third Republic.

Quick Instruction

The leaders of the Third Republic brought to France a more democratic government that featured a two-house legislature. France had many political parties and they formed coalitions in order to govern. Gradual social reforms benefited workers, women, and children. But the government faced many challenges, including corruption scandals and political divisions.

The Boulanger Scandal: Interactive Cartoon Project the Boulanger political cartoon on the whiteboard. As a class, discuss the details of the Boulanger scandal and how it portrays the corruption and divisions in the French government. Click through the hot spots on the screen, discussing the pop up text and what it tells students about the scandal.

📖 ACTIVE CLASSROOM

Explain that France had an excessive number of political parties, and that during one 10-year period, 50 different coalition governments were formed and fell. Have students use the Cartoon It strategy to create a political cartoon that conveys the instability and confusion resulting from such a political system. Have each student show his or her cartoon to a partner and have the partner decipher its meaning.

D Differentiate: Challenge/Gifted Use the political cartoon as an opportunity to reinforce student understanding of concepts such as irony, metaphor, and hyperbole. Explain to students that a political cartoon is not meant to show a literal event, but to convey an opinion through visual metaphor.

Further Instruction

Go through the Interactive Reading Notepad questions and discuss the answers with the class for "The Third Republic Faces New Challenges."

Compare Have students compare the points of view of the Communards and the National Assembly and examine why their differences led to a civil war. Remind students to keep in mind what they learned about the French Revolution. Discuss why the suppression of the Commune deepened social divisions within France.

Objective 3: Explain how the Dreyfus Affair divided France and contributed to the growth of the Zionist movement.

Quick Instruction

The Dreyfus Affair was a scandal where the French military forged evidence and convicted Captain Alfred Dreyfus of treason in an unfair trial rooted in anti-Semitism. Even after evidence revealed that another man was the spy, Dreyfus was not released from prison. He was finally cleared of all charges in 1906. Review with students the details of the affair, how it revealed French anti-Semitism, and the connection between the affair and the growth of the Zionist movement.

Identify Cause and Effect How did the Dreyfus Affair contribute to the growth of Zionism? *(The Dreyfus Affair convinced Theodor Herzl that only when Jews had their own separate state would they be guaranteed their rights.)*

D Differentiate: Challenge/Gifted Display the political cartoon from Screen 2 and have students research it and its meaning. Challenge students to answer this question: Why is Dreyfus shown as a lindworm? *(In northern European mythology, a lindworm is a dragon or serpent with a poisonous bite. The cartoon uses this image to denounce Dreyfus as a dangerous traitor to France.)*

ELL Use the ELL activity described in the ELL chart.

DIGITAL TEXT 4

Reforms in France

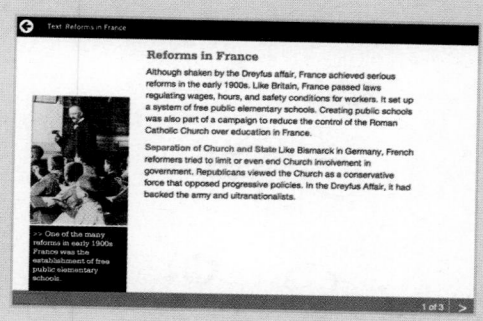

Reforms in France

Although shaken by the Dreyfus affair, France achieved serious reforms in the early 1900s. Like Britain, France passed laws regulating wages, hours, and safety conditions for workers. It set up a system of free public elementary schools. Creating public schools was also part of a campaign to reduce the control of the Roman Catholic Church over education in France.

Separation of Church and State Like Bismarck in Germany, French reformers tried to limit or even end Church involvement in government. Republicans viewed the Church as a conservative force that opposed progressive policies. In the Dreyfus Affair, it had backed the army and ultranationalists.

>> One of the many reforms in early 1900s France was the establishment of free public elementary schools.

1 of 3 >

Further Instruction

Go through the Interactive Reading Notepad questions and discuss the answers with the class. Discuss with students how the Dreyfus Affair revealed anti-Semitism in France.

Infer What were the goals of the Dreyfusards? How could those goals be seen as an attempt to change French government and society? *(Sample response: The Dreyfusards wanted justice and freedom for Alfred Dreyfus. By doing so, the Dreyfusards were challenging their government and attempting to make it and their society more protective of justice and equality.)*

Objective 2: Describe the challenges and political reforms of the Third Republic.

Quick Instruction

Explain to students that France passed major reform laws in the early 1900s. These new laws regulated wages, hours, and safety conditions for workers. They set up a system of free public elementary schools. The government also tried to limit or end Church involvement in government. Ask: why would a government want to end religious influence over its citizens? *(It viewed the Church as a threat to progressive policies.)*

ELL Use the ELL activity described in the ELL chart.

Further Instruction

Go through the Interactive Reading Notepad questions and discuss the answers with the class for Text 4, "Reforms in France." As you work with students, ask them to note how political leaders and the people of France participated in changing their government.

Categorize Based on their reading, ask students to list the reforms that affected workers, women, and children during the Third Republic. *(Suggest to students that a simple two-column chart might help organize their ideas. The first column could be for those affected, and the second column could be for reforms.)*

D **Differentiate: Extra Support** Provide students with a partially completed two-column chart. Prefill the left column with those affected by reforms and insert one of the reforms for one of the groups in the right column. Ask them to complete the missing parts of the chart.

Divisions and Democracy in France

SYNTHESIZE

DIGITAL ACTIVITY
The Dreyfus Affair

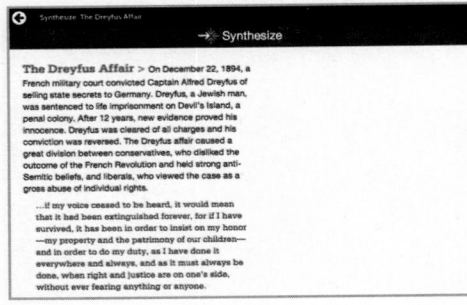

Review the details of the Dreyfus Affair with students. Then move forward to the second and third screens and have a student read each primary source aloud.

Discuss Have the class discuss the different perspectives of Dreyfus and Zola. Explain that even though the writers were on the same side of the issue, they had different points of view. Explain that Dreyfus was the victim of wrongdoing, while Emile Zola was a famous writer expressing his outrage in a public forum.

Analyze Images Move forward to the fourth screen in the Synthesize activity, and work with students to analyze the political cartoon. Discuss with students why the artist chose to use the metaphor of a family dinner and how the political cartoon shows the divisions caused by the Dreyfus Affair. Ask students to relate this cartoon to the Topic Essential Question, "What are the challenges of diversity?"

DEMONSTRATE

LESSON QUIZ
Lesson Quiz and Class Discussion Board

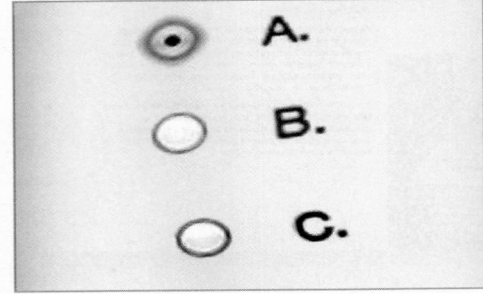

Assign the online Lesson Quiz for this lesson if you haven't already done so. Students will be offered automatic remediation or enrichment based on their score.

During the 1800s, France went from an absolute monarchy to a republic, fought wars, suffered defeats, and survived scandals. But by the end of the 1800s, the French people had made political choices to promote popular sovereignty, expand democratic rights, and extend social reforms for workers, women, and children.

Pose these questions to the class on the Discussion Board:

Predict Consequences The Third Republic ends with the beginning of World War I. How will France's government change after the war? *(Sample answer: France will still be a republic but with a new constitution that stabilizes it and provides more rights for its people.)*

Draw Conclusions During the Second Empire, France had one stable government. During the Third Republic, governing coalitions were unstable, and there were 50 coalition governments in the first 10 years. Does this mean that Napoleon's government was better than the Republic's? Why or why not? *(Sample response: No, having a stable government is not better if that government does not represent the people.)*

Topic Inquiry
Have students continue their investigations for the Topic Inquiry.

Growth of the United States

Supporting English Language Learners

Use with Digital Text 1, **The United States Expands.**

Reading
Read the first introductory paragraph under *The United States Expands.* Ask students to identify the important information in the paragraph, such as political and religious freedom, a growing economy, and so on. Ask students to write a summary sentence for the paragraph using the sentence stem *In the 1800s _____.* Continue with the subsection *Territorial Gains.*

Beginning Read *Territorial Gains* aloud to students. Define challenging terms in the text. Then demonstrate how to summarize by focusing on the first paragraph in that section. Help students retell the details of the second paragraph by asking them to point to three important details that they would include in a summary. Then assist them in combining those details into one or two sentences that summarize the paragraph. Have students read their summaries to the group.

Intermediate Read *Territorial Gains* aloud to students. Help students identify and define challenging terms in the text. Then demonstrate how to summarize by focusing on the first paragraph in that section. Ask students to summarize the second paragraph by telling them to identify three important details. Have students write a sentence that includes those details and summarizes the paragraph. Have students read their sentences to the group.

Advanced Have student pairs read *Territorial Gains* aloud. Pairs should then identify and define challenging terms in the text. Ask one student in each pair to summarize the first paragraph in that section and the second student to summarize the second paragraph. Then have two pairs join together to share their summaries and receive feedback on their work.

Advanced High Have students read *Territorial Gains* independently. After identifying and defining unfamiliar words, have students create a brief summary of the text. Then have students share their summaries with the group.

Use with Digital Text 3, **The Civil War.**

Reading
Read aloud or have students read *The Civil War.* Then use linguistic accommodations to help students understand the content of the text. Have students demonstrate their understanding through answering content-specific questions or writing summaries.

Beginning Read *The Civil War* aloud to students. Then help students develop a list of challenging words from the text, such as *regions*, *division*, *crisis*, and *infringe*. Show students how to locate and define these words using a bilingual dictionary. After defining the words, read the section again. Provide students with sentence stems to help them demonstrate their content comprehension. Allow them to refer to their definitions if needed.

Intermediate Read *The Civil War* aloud to students. Ask students to identify unfamiliar words from the text. Have students use a bilingual dictionary to locate and define these words. Then read the section again. Have students demonstrate comprehension by requiring them to answer who, where, what, why, and how questions in complete sentences. Allow them to refer to their definitions if needed.

Advanced Have student pairs work together to read *The Civil War.* Allow them to use bilingual dictionaries to define unfamiliar words. Have them demonstrate comprehension by requiring them to write answers to who, where, what, why, and how questions in complete sentences.

Advanced High Have pairs work independently to read *The Civil War.* Allow them to use bilingual dictionaries to define unfamiliar words if necessary. Have them demonstrate comprehension by writing a brief paragraph summarizing the issues and events leading up to, during, and following the Civil War.

▣ Differentiate Instruction

Use the Differentiated Instruction notes throughout the lesson plan to support the varied skill sets, levels of readiness, and interests in the mixed-ability classroom.

Challenge These notes include suggestions for expanding the activity for advanced students.

On-Level These notes include suggestions for modifying the activity to address different interests or learning styles.

Extra Support These notes include ideas for providing more scaffolding or reading spuport.

Special Needs These notes provide ideas for adapting instruction to support the needs of various special needs students.

■ NOTES

_____

_____

_____

_____

_____

Growth of the United States

Objectives

Objective 1: Describe the territorial expansion of the United States.

Objective 2: Summarize the causes and effects of the Civil War.

Objective 3: Explain how American democracy grew in the 1800s.

Objective 4: Analyze the impact of economic growth and social reform on the United States.

LESSON 7 ORGANIZER		PACING: APPROX. 1 PERIOD, .5 BLOCKS			
				RESOURCES	
		OBJECTIVES	**PACING**	**Online**	**Print**
Connect					
DIGITAL START UP ACTIVITY **A Shining Beacon**			5 min.	●	
Investigate					
DIGITAL TEXT 1 **The United States Expands**		Objective 1	10 min.	●	●
INTERACTIVE MAP **Expansion of the United States, 1783–1898**			10 min.	●	
DIGITAL TEXT 2 **Expanding Democracy**		Objective 3	10 min.	●	●
INTERACTIVE TIMELINE **The Women's Rights Movement**			10 min.	●	
DIGITAL TEXT 3 **The Civil War**		Objective 2	10 min.	●	●
DIGITAL TEXT 4 **Economic Growth and Reform**		Objective 4	10 min.	●	●
Synthesize					
DIGITAL ACTIVITY **The Growth of the United States**			5 min.	●	
Demonstrate					
LESSON QUIZ **Lesson Quiz and Class Discussion Board**			10 min.	●	

■ CONNECT

DIGITAL START UP ACTIVITY
A Shining Beacon

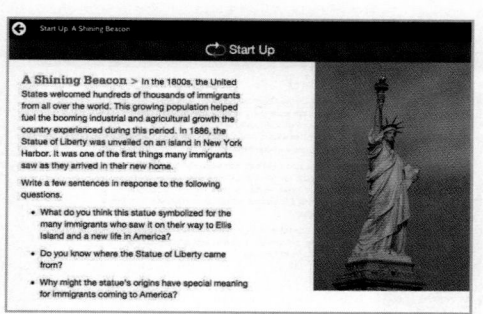

Project the Start Up Activity Ask students to answer the questions as they get settled. Then have them share their ideas with another student.

Discuss What do you think this statue symbolized for immigrants who saw it on the way to America? *(It symbolized freedom or opportunity. Students might say the torch represents light in the darkness, or cite Emma Lazarus's poem that welcomes immigrants.)* Where did the Statue of Liberty come from? *(France)* Why might this have special meaning for immigrants? *(It suggests that the U.S. is a global symbol of liberty.)*

Aa Vocabulary Development: Use the Interactive Reading Notepad to preview the Key Terms and Academic Vocabulary in this Lesson with students.

⚑ FLIP IT!

Assign the Flipped Video for this lesson.

■ STUDENT EDITION PRINT PAGES: 574–578

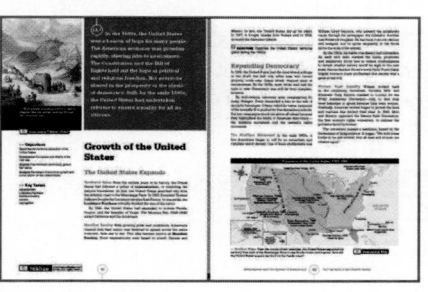

■ INVESTIGATE

DIGITAL TEXT 1
The United States Expands

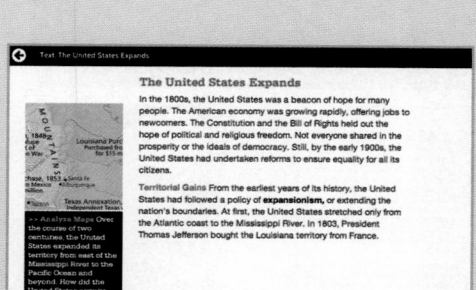

INTERACTIVE MAP
Expansion of the United States, 1783–1898

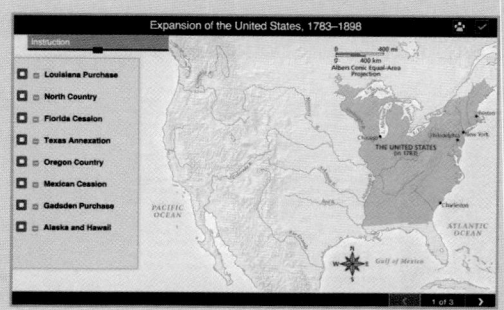

Objective 1: Describe the territorial expansion of the United States.

Quick Instruction

Over the course of the nineteenth century, the United States acquired the territory that makes up the country today.

Interactive Map: The Expansion of the United States, 1783–1898 Project the map on the whiteboard. Click through the key to show the expansion of the United States, and discuss how each section of land was acquired. Relate these discussions to the concept of Manifest Destiny.

👥 ACTIVE CLASSROOM

Have students pair off. Ask each pair to take turns doing a chronological Audio Tour of the map. The first student shows and describes the extent of U.S. territory in 1783. Then the other student shows and describes what territory was added in 1803. Have students continue taking turns in this way until they have covered all of the territories gained by the United States.

ELL Use the ELL activity described in the ELL chart.

Further Instruction

Editable Presentation Use the Editable Presentation to present the main ideas for this text.

The United States Expands: Core Text and Interactive Reading Notepad Project and discuss the Interactive Reading Notepad graphic organizer for this Text. Work with students to begin to fill in Causes and Effects of the territorial growth of the United States.

Be sure that students understand the term *Manifest Destiny*. Discuss with students how the belief in Manifest Destiny might have affected the acquisition of territory. *(Answers will vary but might include that the people of the United States were willing to go to war or pay large sums of money to acquire territory.)*

Infer Engage students in a discussion on how they think the American free enterprise system benefited the development and expansion of the United States. *(Sample responses: Free enterprise promoted entrepreneurship, provided a network of communications and transportation technologies to deliver resources and finished products, and encouraged economic competition and growth.)*

Growth of the United States

DIGITAL TEXT 2

Expanding Democracy

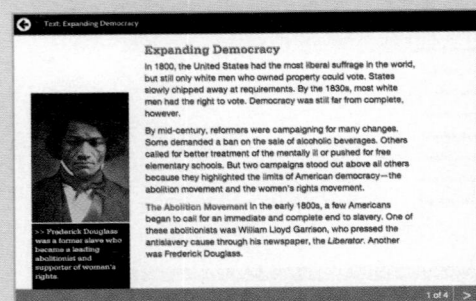

INTERACTIVE TIMELINE

The Women's Rights Movement

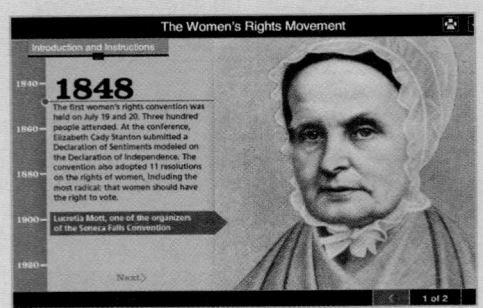

DIGITAL TEXT 3

The Civil War

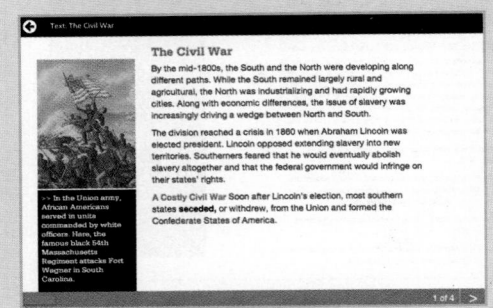

Objective 3: Explain how American democracy grew in the 1800s.

Quick Instruction

In the 1800s, American democracy expanded. Two major movements furthered this development: the anti-slavery, or abolitionist, movement and the women's rights movement. Both of these sought to extend American democratic rights to large portions of the population.

Interactive Timeline: The Women's Rights Movement Project the timeline on the whiteboard. As a class, discuss the role of women in early American society, why the women's rights movement began, and how the movement changed women's roles in society. Engage students in the drag-and-drop activity to connect information on the timeline to information about women's rights in the text.

🎦 ACTIVE CLASSROOM

Use the Conversation with History strategy to engage students in the timeline. Have students imagine that they are having a conversation with one of the people in the timeline. Have them write down a question they'd like to ask, then what that person would say in response, and how they would reply to the response.

Further Instruction

Go through the Interactive Reading Notepad questions and discuss the answers with the class. As you work with students, ask them to keep examining how the people of the United States and their political leaders participated in changing their government.

Hypothesize Have students read the excerpt from Sojourner Truth's speech, "Ain't I a Woman." Ask them to consider how African American women might have been treated in the women's rights movement, and have them give reasons for their opinion. *(Sample response: African American women were probably not treated well in the women's rights movement because discrimination against African Americans was a problem in the United States among women as well as men. Another possible response: African American women were probably welcomed into the women's rights movement because many women in the movement had fought for abolition and knew what it was like to be discriminated against.)*

D Differentiate: Challenge/Gifted Ask students to do some quick online research on this question and report back to the class about the role of black women in the women's rights movement.

Objective 2: Summarize the causes and effects of the Civil War.

Quick Instruction

Abraham Lincoln believed that slavery should not be allowed in new territories. Others said that the citizens of each territory should vote to decide whether or not to allow slavery. They believed in popular sovereignty, the idea that the consent of the people is the true basis of government authority. When Lincoln was elected president, southern states seceded and the Civil War began. The conflict resulted in hundreds of thousands killed and wounded on both sides. But the war also resulted in freedom for millions of enslaved African Americans, the expansion of democracy, and the protection of human rights.

Identify Central Issues Ask students to consider the question: How did the Civil War affect the United States, in the short term and in the long term? What changes were made to government? *(Sample response: In the short term, hundreds of thousands of people were killed, and slavery was abolished. Amendments were added to the U.S. Constitution to guarantee African American rights. The South continued to discriminate against African Americans through segregation laws.)*

Further Instruction

Go through the Interactive Reading Notepad questions and discuss the answers with the class.

ELL Use the ELL activity described in the ELL chart.

DIGITAL TEXT 4

Economic Growth and Reform

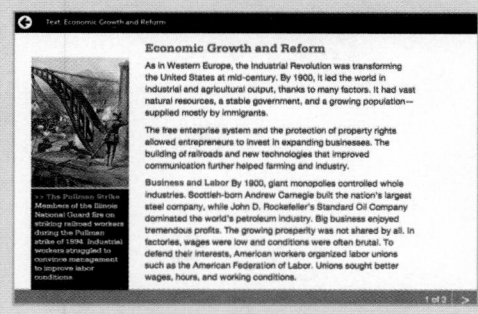

Identify Cause and Effect Have students create their own cause and effect charts to list the causes and effects of the Civil War. *(Causes were differences between the North and South, especially disagreement over economic issues and slavery. The South seceded from the Union in fear that President Lincoln would limit or abolish slavery. Effects included the defeat of the South, abolition of slavery, and political rights for African Americans.)*

Analyze Information Review the infographic on the Civil War amendments to the U.S. Constitution. Engage the class in a discussion about the failures and successes of the amendments. Challenge students with the question: After the Civil War, were African Americans truly free?

Objective 4: Analyze the impact of economic growth and social reform on the United States.

Quick Instruction

After the Civil War the United States became a world economic leader and a destination for millions of immigrants fleeing poverty, war, and persecution around the world.

Discuss Engage students in a discussion about the factors that benefited U.S. economic growth and prosperity. In particular, discuss the benefits of the free enterprise system, such as individual freedom of consumers and producers, variety of goods, and prices that respond to changes in the free market. Point out that anyone can compete in the marketplace, and the profit motive often drives the American entrepreneurial spirit.

Further Instruction

Go through the Interactive Reading Notepad questions. Discuss with students how economic growth prompted social reform. Review the rise of monopolies such as those started by Andrew Carnegie and John D. Rockefeller. Help students understand the effects of monopolies on the market, and why efforts were made to control them.

Express Problems Clearly Ask students to describe working conditions for many industrial workers in the United States and how those conditions led to the push for reform. *(Sample response: Workers were not being paid very much, they had to work very long hours, working conditions were dangerous.)* How did people try to change their situations? *(Sample response: They formed labor unions, they formed political parties, and they fought for voters to have more power.)*

Growth of the United States

■ SYNTHESIZE

DIGITAL ACTIVITY
The Growth of the United States

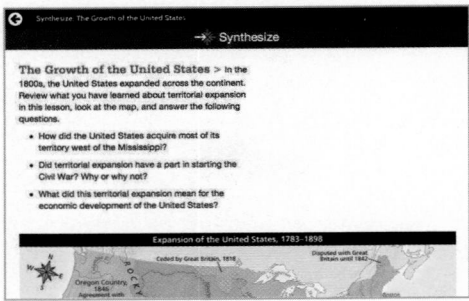

Review the map of territorial expansion with students and how each territory was acquired. Have partners work together to answer the Synthesize questions: How did the United States acquire most of its territory west of the Mississippi? *(Sample response: The United States purchased most of its territory from European countries such as England, France, and Spain.)*

Did territorial expansion have a part in starting the Civil War? Why or why not? *(Sample response: The question of whether new states would be slave or free states increased tensions prior to the Civil War. Fear that President Abraham Lincoln would limit or even abolish slavery was a major cause of secession and the Civil War.)*

Remind students that the Topic Essential Question is "What are the challenges of diversity?" Have them use the Think-Pair-Share strategy to discuss how diversity affected territorial growth and expansion of democracy in the United States. *(Students should discuss various topics, including the women's rights movement, North versus South, slavery versus abolitionism, challenges for African Americans, and tensions between business owners and laborers.)*

■ DEMONSTRATE

LESSON QUIZ
Lesson Quiz and Class Discussion Board

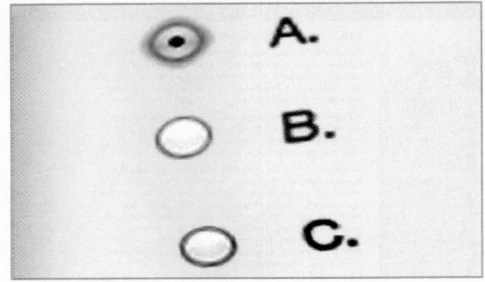

Assign the online Lesson Quiz for this lesson if you haven't already done so. Students will be offered automatic remediation or enrichment based on their score.

Pose these questions to the class on the Discussion Board:

In "Growth of the United States," you read about America's territorial expansion in the 1800s, its violent Civil War, the expansion of its democratic ideals to include more citizens, its economic growth, and the development of social reform.

Make Connections How are these different topics linked? *(Sample response: All of these subjects are linked and influenced by each other. The expansion of the United States was a major cause of the Civil War and is linked to our economic growth. The outcome of the Civil War is linked to the expansion of democratic ideals and to social reforms. The country's economic growth is also linked to social reforms.)*

Hypothesize How would America be different if there hadn't been the extension of democratic ideals or social reform? Why? *(Sample response: America would not be truly free and would not be the world power it is today, because expanding our democratic ideals and instituting social reforms helped build a strong and confident nation, provided people with more economic opportunities and helped ensure equality and human rights.)*

Topic Inquiry
Have students continue their investigations for the Topic Inquiry.

Nationalism in Eastern Europe and Russia

Supporting English Language Learners

Use with Digital Text 3, **The Ottoman Empire Declines.**

Reading

Use the map showing the nationalities and political boundaries of Eastern Europe to help students understand how nationalism challenged Austria and the Ottoman Empire.

Beginning Show students the map showing the nationalities of Eastern Europe in the mid-1800s. Point out that each color represents a different ethnicity in the region. Trace the political boundaries of the Austrian Empire for students. Ask students to identify the number of different ethnicities that lived in the Austrian Empire. Explain that nationalism often kept different ethnic groups from working together. Then ask students to think about what kinds of problems this could cause for the Austrian Empire. Finally, read the section aloud to students, explaining the connections between the map and the text as you read.

Intermediate Examine the map showing the nationalities of Eastern Europe in the mid-1800s with students. Explain that nationalism often kept different ethnic groups from working together. Then have students identify the various ethnicities that lived in the Austrian Empire. Have students think about what kinds of problems this could cause for the Austrian Empire. Finally, read the section aloud. As you read, ask students to explain the connections between the map and the text using simple, short sentences.

Advanced Have students work individually to read the text and examine the map showing the nationalities of Eastern Europe in the mid-1800s. Then have students work in pairs to identify the various ethnicities that lived in the Austrian Empire. Have students think about what kinds of problems this could cause for the Austrian Empire. Finally, have students turn to a partner to share their ideas about how nationalism endangered multinational empires.

Advanced High Have students work with a partner to examine the map. Ask student pairs to predict some of the problems that multinational diversity could cause for aging empires during the mid-1800s. Then instruct pairs to read the text, revise their prediction if needed, and list three supporting details that explain how nationalism threatened the old empires of Eastern Europe.

Use Digital Text 6, **The Beginnings of Industrialization.**

Reading

After reading the text titled *The Beginnings of Industrialization*, have students answer questions about the effects of industrialization in Russia.

Beginning Read *The Beginnings of Industrialization* to students. Define challenging terms in the text. Then assist students as they respond to the following questions using the given sentence frames.

- How did industrialization affect Russian peasants? Industrialization caused Russian peasants to move to cities to get jobs in _____. *(factories)*

- What was the political impact of factory conditions in Russia? Bad conditions in factories caused a rise in _____. *(radicalism)*

Intermediate Read *The Beginnings of Industrialization* with students. Define challenging terms in the text. Then guide students as they respond to the following questions using the given sentence frames.

- How did industrialization affect Russian peasants? Industrialization caused Russian peasants to move to cities because _____. *(They needed jobs.)*

- Why did the ideas of Karl Marx gain support in Russia? A growing number of Russian workers liked the ideas of Karl Marx because _____. *(They were unhappy with working and living conditions.)*

Advanced Have pairs of students read *The Beginnings of Industrialization*. Have students identify and define challenging terms in the text. Then have students respond aloud to the following questions.

- As industrialization began in Russia, where did peasants move and why? *(to the cities for jobs)*

- Why were the areas around slums and factories popular with radicals? *(People were unhappy with their lives and wanted change, which radicals promised.)*

Advanced High Have students read *The Beginnings of Industrialization* independently. Ask them to use a dictionary to define challenging terms from the text. Then have students respond to the following questions. Once students have responded, combine students into small groups to discuss their answers.

- As industrialization began in Russia, where did peasants move and why? *(to the cities for jobs)*

- Why were the areas around slums and factories popular with radicals? *(People were unhappy with their lives and wanted change, which radicals promised.)*

Nationalism in Eastern Europe and Russia

Objectives

Objective 1: Explain how nationalism challenged Austria and the Ottoman Empire.

Objective 2: Summarize major obstacles to progress in Russia.

Objective 3: Describe the cycle of absolutism, reform, and reaction followed by the tsars.

Objective 4: Explain how industrialization contributed to the outbreak of revolution in 1905.

LESSON 8 ORGANIZER	PACING: APPROX. 1 PERIOD, .5 BLOCKS				
		OBJECTIVES	PACING	Online	Print
Connect					
DIGITAL START UP ACTIVITY **Outside Influences**			5 min.	●	
Investigate					
DIGITAL TEXT 1 **Nationalism Endangers Old Empires**		Objective 1	10 min.	●	●
DIGITAL TEXT 2 **The Dual Monarchy**					
DIGITAL TEXT 3 **The Ottoman Empire Declines**					
INTERACTIVE MAP **The Balkan Powder Keg**			10 min.	●	
DIGITAL TEXT 4 **Russia Tries Reform**		Objective 2	10 min.	●	●
INTERACTIVE GALLERY **Tug of War: Reform and Repression by the Russian Tsars**			10 min.	●	
DIGITAL TEXT 5 **Emancipation and Stirrings of Revolution**		Objective 3	10 min.	●	●
DIGITAL TEXT 6 **The Beginnings of Industrialization**		Objective 4	10 min.	●	●
DIGITAL TEXT 7 **The Road to Revolution**			10 min.	●	●
Synthesize					
DIGITAL ACTIVITY **The People Fight Back**			5 min.	●	
Demonstrate					
LESSON QUIZ **Lesson Quiz and Class Discussion Board**			10 min.	●	

PEARSON realize.™
www.PearsonRealize.com

Go online to access additional resources including:
Primary Sources • Biographies • Supreme Court cases •
21st Century Skill Tutorials • Maps • Graphic Organizers.

CONNECT

DIGITAL START UP ACTIVITY
Outside Influences

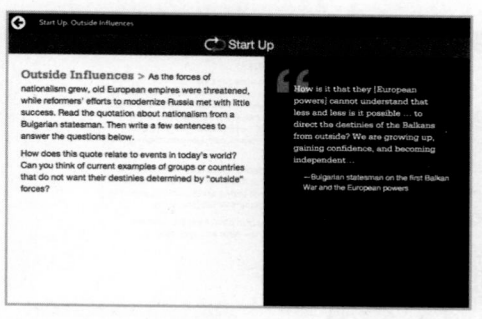

Project the Start Up Activity Ask students to answer the questions below as they enter and get settled. Then have them share their ideas with another student, either in class or through a chat room or blog.

Discuss How does the quote you read relate to events in today's world? Can you think of current examples of groups or countries that do not want their destinies determined by "outside" forces? *(Answers may vary. Students may discuss nationalities struggling to gain independence or independent countries opposing foreign intervention and fighting for self-determination.)*

Tell students that in this lesson they will learn about nationalism in Eastern Europe and the challenges facing the Austrian, Ottoman, and Russian empires.

Aa Vocabulary Development: Use the Interactive Reading Notepad to preview the Key Terms and Academic Vocabulary in this Lesson with students.

↰ FLIP IT!
Assign the Flipped Video for this lesson.

▮ STUDENT EDITION PRINT PAGES: 579–586

INVESTIGATE

DIGITAL TEXT 1
Nationalism Endangers Old Empires

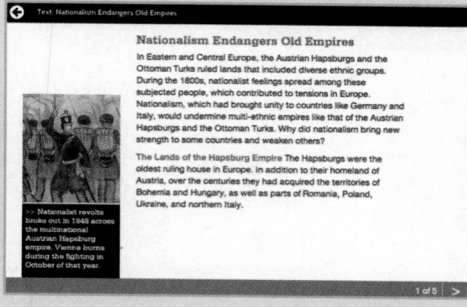

DIGITAL TEXT 2
The Dual Monarchy

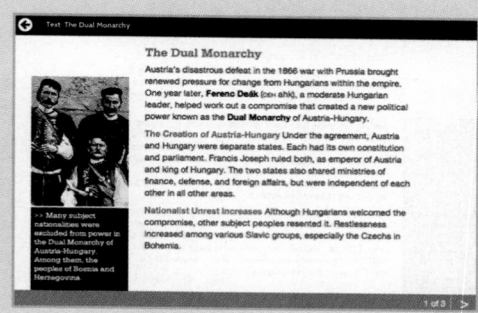

Objective 1: Explain how nationalism challenged Austria and the Ottoman Empire.

Quick Instruction
In the late 1800s and early 1900s nationalism challenged the Austrian and Ottoman empires as various nationalities sought to break away and form their own independent nation-states.

Interactive Map: The Balkan Powder Keg Project the interactive map on the whiteboard. Use the slide to show the political boundaries of the region and the nationalities and ethnic groups that lived within and across these boundaries.

👥 ACTIVE CLASSROOM

Project the ethnicities layer of the interactive map and use a whiteboard tool to divide it into four numbered quadrants. Have students count off 1 to 4 and then study their quadrant. Ask students to note the languages and ethnicities in their quadrant. How do those compare? Engage the slider to show the map's political layer. Have students note which group had political control of their quadrant. Ask students to describe their comparisons and predict the effects of nationalism. *(Political boundaries and ethnic boundaries were quite different. Ethnic groups will use diplomacy and revolution to win their own independent nation-states.)*

Nationalism in Eastern Europe and Russia

DIGITAL TEXT 3

The Ottoman Empire Declines

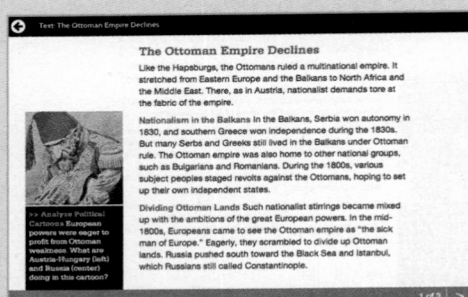

INTERACTIVE MAP

The Balkan Powder Keg

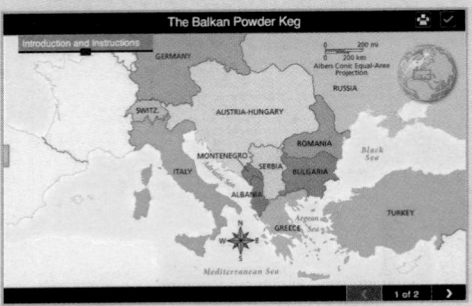

DIGITAL TEXT 4

Russia Tries Reform

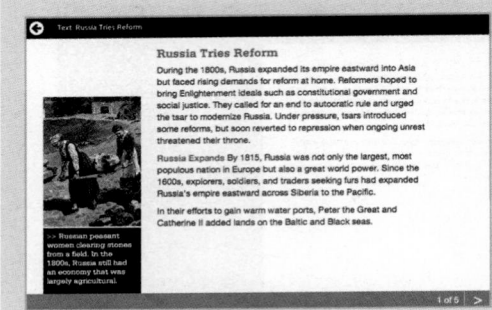

ELL Use the ELL activity described in the ELL chart.

Further Instruction

Go through the Interactive Reading Notepad questions and discuss the answers with the class.

The Dual Monarchy of Austria-Hungary faced continuing unrest. Hungarians welcomed this political compromise but wanted even more power. Czechs, Slovaks, and other groups also had national aspirations. Meanwhile, the Ottoman Empire, the "sick man of Europe," was crumbling as nationalist groups broke away to form their own countries.

Draw Inferences How did the newly independent countries of Serbia and Greece influence nationalism among other subject peoples of the Ottoman Empire? *(Sample response: Other peoples were inspired to fight for their own freedom and independence.)*

Objective 2: Summarize major obstacles to progress in Russia.

Quick Instruction

The Russian empire was huge, stretching from Eastern Europe to the Pacific. The rigid social structure of tsar, nobles, and serfs ensured that reform and progress came slowly, if at all, to Russia.

Interactive Gallery: Tug of War: Reform and Repression by the Russian Tsars Project the image on the whiteboard. Click through the hotspots to show the tug of war between the tsars and the people of Russia. Use the gallery to help students identify the influence of ideas such as human rights on people's efforts for reform.

ACTIVE CLASSROOM

Project the "Tug of War" interactive image gallery. Write down a question you'd like to ask of one of the people in the image gallery visuals or in the lesson text, then what that person might say to you, and what you would say in response.

INTERACTIVE GALLERY

Tug of War: Reform and Repression by the Russian Tsars

Tug of War: Reform and Repression by the Russian Tsars

Introduction and Instructions

1 of 3

DIGITAL TEXT 5

Emancipation and Stirrings of Revolution

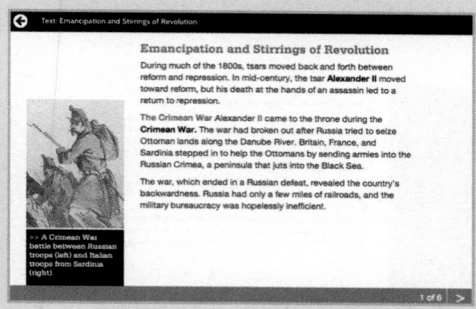

Text: Emancipation and Stirrings of Revolution

Emancipation and Stirrings of Revolution

During much of the 1800s, tsars moved back and forth between reform and repression. In mid-century, the tsar **Alexander II** moved toward reform, but his death at the hands of an assassin led to a return to repression.

The Crimean War Alexander II came to the throne during the **Crimean War.** The war had broken out after Russia tried to seize Ottoman lands along the Danube River. Britain, France, and Sardinia stepped in to help the Ottomans by sending armies into the Russian Crimea, a peninsula that juts into the Black Sea.

The war, which ended in a Russian defeat, revealed the country's backwardness. Russia had only a few miles of railroads, and the military bureaucracy was hopelessly inefficient.

>> A Crimean War battle between Russian troops (left) and Italian troops from Sardinia (right)

1 of 6

Further Instruction

Go through the Interactive Reading Notepad questions and discuss the answers with the class. As you work with students, ask them to explore which factors in Russian society led to its lack of progress.

Compare Remind students that in Western Europe, industrialization, development of free enterprise, and the rise of the middle class all contributed to liberal democratic reforms. Ask students to compare conditions in Russia to those in Western Europe. Why was Russia slow to enact reforms? *(Sample response: The Russian nobles controlled a traditional agricultural economy. The tsars ruled with absolute power. The tsars and nobles were reluctant to allow economic and political reforms. The serfs were not emancipated until 1861.)*

D Differentiate: Extra Support Ask students to create a two-column chart to compare social, economic, and political conditions. In the first column, list conditions in Britain and France, in the second column list conditions in Russia. Fill in some information for them to help them get started.

Objective 3: Describe the cycle of absolutism, reform, and reaction followed by the tsars.

Quick Instruction

The reigns of Alexander II and Alexander III exemplify the tsarist cycle of periods of reform followed by periods of repression.

Identify Patterns Have pairs of students work together to create circular flow charts to show the tsarist cycle of reform and repression. They should fill in the chart with specific details from the text. *(Freedom for serfs led to discontent because serfs were still poor, which led to movement to cities, which led people to drive for further reform; many Russians remained dissatisfied, which led to increased repression by the tsar, especially after the assassination of Alexander II.)*

Draw Conclusions What was the long-term effect of the cycle of repression and reform? *(Sample response: It made people even angrier and more radical as they were given a taste of reform followed by harsh measures of strict repression.)*

Further Instruction

Guide students through these questions:

Identify Cause and Effect How did emancipation affect the serfs? Why? *(Sample response: It made people even angrier and more radical as they were given a taste of reform followed by harsh measures of strict repression.)*

Hypothesize Why did Alexander III think Russification would stifle dissent? *(Alexander's goal was to suppress the cultures of non-Russian peoples in the empire, uniting Russians against these outsiders. His Russification policy did lead to persecution of non-Russians in the empire.)*

Nationalism in Eastern Europe and Russia

DIGITAL TEXT 6
The Beginnings of Industrialization

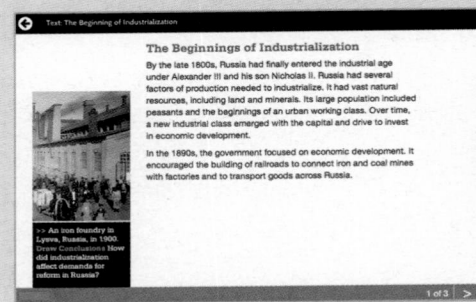

The Beginnings of Industrialization

By the late 1800s, Russia had finally entered the industrial age under Alexander III and his son Nicholas II. Russia had several factors of production needed to industrialize. It had vast natural resources, including land and minerals. Its large population included peasants and the beginnings of an urban working class. Over time, a new industrial class emerged with the capital and drive to invest in economic development.

In the 1890s, the government focused on economic development. It encouraged the building of railroads to connect iron and coal mines with factories and to transport goods across Russia.

>> An iron foundry in Lysva, Russia, in 1900. Draw Conclusions How did industrialization affect demands for reform in Russia?

1 of 3 >

DIGITAL TEXT 7
The Road to Revolution

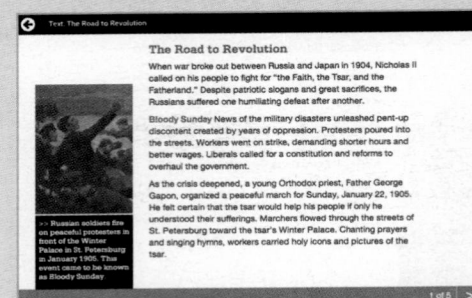

The Road to Revolution

When war broke out between Russia and Japan in 1904, Nicholas II called on his people to fight for "the Faith, the Tsar, and the Fatherland." Despite patriotic slogans and great sacrifices, the Russians suffered one humiliating defeat after another.

Bloody Sunday News of the military disasters unleashed pent-up discontent created by years of oppression. Protesters poured into the streets. Workers went on strike, demanding shorter hours and better wages. Liberals called for a constitution and reforms to overhaul the government.

As the crisis deepened, a young Orthodox priest, Father George Gapon, organized a peaceful march for Sunday, January 22, 1905. He felt certain that the tsar would help his people if only he understood their sufferings. Marchers flowed through the streets of St. Petersburg toward the tsar's Winter Palace. Chanting prayers and singing hymns, workers carried holy icons and pictures of the tsar.

>> Russian soldiers fire on peaceful protesters in front of the Winter Palace in St. Petersburg in January 1905. This event came to be known as Bloody Sunday

1 of 5 >

Objective 4: Explain how industrialization contributed to the outbreak of revolution in 1905.

Quick Instruction

Use the text and image of Russian industrialization to discuss Russia's industrialization. Russia's new class of industrial workers suffered low pay and poor working conditions. Socialists preached the revolutionary ideas of Karl Marx. Liberals called for a constitution and government reforms. Revolution erupted in 1905.

Identify Cause and Effect Work with students to examine the specific causes and effects of the 1905 revolution. *(Sample answers: causes: absolutism, industrialization, years of oppression, Bloody Sunday, inequality, nationalism, appeals of liberalism and socialism, military defeat by Japan; effects: a constitution limiting tsar's power, establishment of an elected legislature, and the protection of basic human rights)*

ELL Use the ELL activity described in the ELL chart.

Further Instruction

Go through the Interactive Reading Notepad questions and discuss the answers with the class.

Hypothesize Why did the attack on the marchers on Bloody Sunday spur people to change their government with the Revolution of 1905? *(Sample response: because it was a peaceful march led by a priest; the excessive violence of the tsar's forces caused outrage and a loss of faith and trust in the tsar.)*

Draw Conclusions How successful were the Russian people in pursuing reform efforts and changing their government? *(Sample response: By striking, protesting, demanding reforms, and revolting, the Russians forced the tsar to agree to a new constitution, but the democratic reforms were largely temporary.)*

SYNTHESIZE

DIGITAL ACTIVITY

The People Fight Back

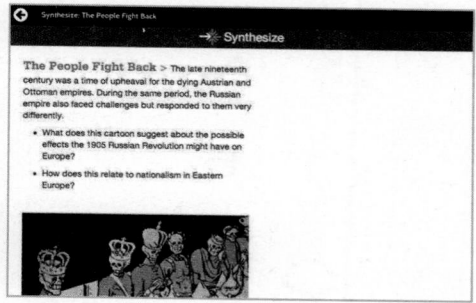

Remind students of the scope and content of this lesson on Eastern Europe and Russia, emphasizing not only the influence of nationalism on political revolutions but also the significance of political choices and decisions, and the ways in which citizens can change their governments through both reform and revolution.

Ask students to recall the Topic Essential Question: What are the challenges of diversity? Ask students to describe how this question relates to the lesson. Have partners work together to answer the Synthesize questions: What is the artist stating with this cartoon about the possible effect the 1905 Revolution might have on monarchies throughout Europe? How does this relate to nationalism in Eastern Europe? *(The artist is showing that the 1905 Revolution would inspire other people to revolt against their kings because they would realize that people could rise up and force a leader to carry out reforms. Many nationalists in Eastern Europe would have looked to the revolution as proof that they could successfully revolt.)* If necessary, help students analyze and decode the political cartoon.

Make Predictions Have students recall conditions in Austria-Hungary, the Ottoman Empire, and the Russian empire. Ask them to predict which of the three empires is most likely to collapse first and why. *(Sample response: the Ottoman Empire, because it was the weakest of the three; nationalism would cause a series of wars in the Balkans, and because European powers sensed the empire's weakness and began to take Ottoman lands.)*

DEMONSTRATE

LESSON QUIZ

Lesson Quiz and Class Discussion Board

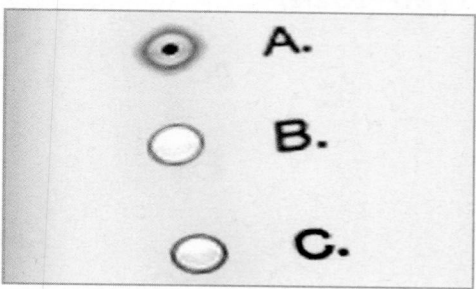

Assign the online Lesson Quiz for this lesson if you haven't already done so. Students will be offered automatic remediation or enrichment based on their score.

Pose these questions to the class on the Discussion Board:

In "Nationalism in Eastern Europe and Russia," you learned about the rise of nationalism in Eastern Europe and the decline of the aging Austrian and Ottoman empires. You also learned about Russia's failed efforts to institute lasting reform. The lesson ends with a powder keg ready to explode in Eastern Europe and a conservative Dumas in Russia.

Draw Conclusions Do you think Russia will finally succeed in instituting democratic reforms? Will the Dumas become more representative of the people? Why or why not? *(Sample response: The Dumas will not become more representative. The cycle of reform and repression is too strong and will be repeated.)* What will happen in the Balkans? Will nationalist groups reach their goals? Why or why not? *(Sample response: Nationalist groups in the Balkans will succeed because the age of empires is ending, and the nationalists will fill the vacuum left when the Austrian and Ottoman empires finally disappear.)*

Topic Inquiry

Have students continue their investigations for the Topic Inquiry.

Nationalism and the Spread of Democracy (1790–1914)

SYNTHESIZE

DIGITAL ESSENTIAL QUESTION ACTIVITY

Reflect on the Essential Question and Topic

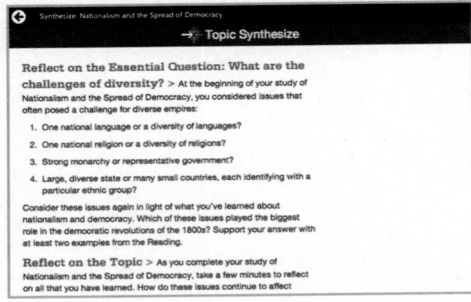

Remind students that at the beginning of their study of Nationalism and the Spread of Democracy, they considered issues that often posed a challenge for diverse empires:

- One national language or a diversity of languages
- One national religion or a diversity of religions
- Strong monarchy or representative government
- Large, diverse state or many small countries, each identifying with a particular ethnic group

Ask students to consider those issues again in light of what they've learned about nationalism and democracy. Which of the issues played the biggest role in the democratic revolutions of the 1800s? Ask them to support their answer with at least two specific examples.

DEMONSTRATE

DIGITAL TOPIC REVIEW AND ASSESSMENT

Nationalism and the Spread of Democracy (1790–1914)

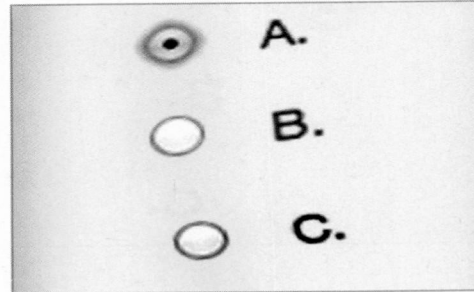

Ask students to reflect on all that they have learned. How do the ideas of nationalism and democracy continue to affect today's world? Write down three important questions about diversity, nationalism, and democracy that challenge the world today. Share these examples if students need help getting started:

- How can a country with a diverse population create a sense of national unity?
- Does every national group have the right to its own country? What are the practical ramifications of that question?
- If a country has a very diverse population, should it move in the direction of greater democracy or greater central control?

Organize students into groups and allow time for them to share their questions and discuss some possible answers. You may ask students to share their questions and answers on the Class Discussion Board.

DIGITAL TOPIC TEST

Nationalism and the Spread of Democracy (1790–1914)

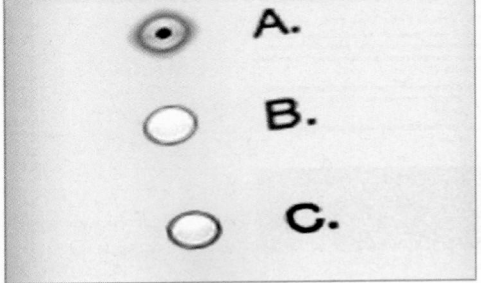

Students can prepare for the Topic Test by answering the questions in the Topic Review and Assessment online or the Assessment questions in the Print Student text. They can also prepare by reviewing their answers to the Interactive Reading Notepad questions or reviewing their notes in the Reading and Notetaking Study Guide.

TOPIC TEST

Assign the Topic Test to assess students' understanding of topic content.

BENCHMARK TESTS

Assign these benchmark tests as you complete the relevant topics to monitor student progress toward mastering the course content and as preparation for the End-of-Course Test.

Benchmark Test 1: Topics 1–5

Benchmark Test 2: Topics 6–10

Benchmark Test 3: Topics 11–15

Benchmark Test 4: Topics 16–21

The Age of Imperialism (1800–1914)

TOPIC 15 ORGANIZER	PACING: APPROX. 11 PERIODS, 5.5 BLOCKS
	PACING
Connect	1 period
MY STORY VIDEO **Menelik II, Independence in the Age of Imperialism**	10 min.
DIGITAL ESSENTIAL QUESTION ACTIVITY **Why Do People Move?**	10 min.
DIGITAL TIMELINE ACTIVITY **The Age of Imperialism**	10 min.
TOPIC INQUIRY: DOCUMENT-BASED QUESTION **What was the Impact of Imperialism on India?**	20 min.
Investigate	4–8 periods
TOPIC INQUIRY: DOCUMENT-BASED QUESTION **What was the Impact of Imperialism on India?**	Ongoing
LESSON 1 The New Imperialism	30–40 min.
LESSON 2 European Colonies in Africa	30–40 min.
LESSON 3 Europe and the Muslim World	30–40 min.
LESSON 4 India Becomes a British Colony	30–40 min.
LESSON 5 China and the West	30–40 min.
LESSON 6 The Modernization of Japan	30–40 min.
LESSON 7 Southeast Asia and the Pacific	30–40 min.
LESSON 8 The Americas in the Age of Imperialism	30–40 min.
Synthesize	1 period
DIGITAL ACTIVITY **Reflect on the Essential Question and Topic**	10 min.
TOPIC INQUIRY: DOCUMENT-BASED QUESTION **What was the Impact of Imperialism on India?**	20 min.
Demonstrate	1–2 periods
DIGITAL TOPIC TEST **The Age of Imperialism**	10 min.
DIGITAL TEKS MASTERY TEST **TEKS Mastery Test**	10 min.
TOPIC INQUIRY: DOCUMENT-BASED QUESTION **What was the Impact of Imperialism on India?**	20 min.

TOPIC INQUIRY: DOCUMENT-BASED QUESTION

What was the Impact of Imperialism on India?

In this Topic Inquiry, students will work individually to analyze six documents describing India under British imperialist rule. Students will reflect on the six documents, draw their own conclusions, and then write an essay on the following question: What was the impact of imperialism on India? Learning about India's experience during the Age of Imperialism will contribute to students' understanding of the Topic Essential Question: Why do people move?

STEP 1: CONNECT
Develop Questions and Plan the Investigation

Launch the DBQ Writing Activity
Have students examine the photograph of the polo team in British India. Explain that polo originated in Persia, but the first Europeans to play the game were the British in Assam, India. This team is made up of British army officers and Indian princes. Discuss the image in class, or have students discuss it with a partner.

Analyze Images What elements of British culture are evident in the photo? *(Sample response: the uniforms and mallets and the British players)* What elements of Indian culture are evident? *(Sample response: the turbans of the Indian players)*

Draw Conclusions What does the photograph tell you about the nature of British rule in India? *(Sample response: The British sometimes cooperated with Indians in positions of power or influence.)*

Generate Questions
Have students examine the question, "What was the impact of imperialism on India?" Ask a volunteer to paraphrase the question. *(Sample response: How did imperialism affect India?)* Then have students work with a partner to make a list of 5-10 questions that could help them answer the essay question. The questions should be specific, such as "How did imperialism affect India's economy?" Encourage students to look for answers to these questions and to add to their list of questions as they examine each document.

Resources
• Student Instructions   • Need-to-Know Questions

STEP 2: INVESTIGATE
Apply Disciplinary Concepts and Tools

Read and Analyze Documents
Tell students that they will read and analyze six documents about India under British rule. Then, they will write an essay and express their own opinions about the impact of imperialism on India. Documents A and B express the views of men who lived in British-ruled India. Document C expresses the view of a British artist of the era about events in India. Documents D and F express the opinions of modern historians, and Document E is a pair of graphs with economic data.

Remind students to read or study each document and make sure they understand what the document says. As part of their analysis, students should determine the point of view of the person who created the document and make a judgment about the reliability of the information.

Suggestion: If possible, encourage students to highlight, circle, or mark the area of each document that helps them answer the essay question.

Check Understanding
After students finish reading each individual document, have them answer the multiple-choice and short-answer questions attached to each document. Review the questions and discuss the answers after students have answered the questions for all the documents.

Resources
• Information Organizer

⏻ PROFESSIONAL DEVELOPMENT

Document-Based Question
Be sure to view the Document-Based Question Professional Development resources in the online course.

STEP 3: SYNTHESIZE
Evaluate Sources and
Use Evidence to Formulate Conclusions

Write Your Essay
Now have students write their essays to express their own opinion about the question: What was the impact of imperialism on India? If students are having trouble getting started, have students begin by writing one or two sentences that give a basic answer to the essay question. Then have them create an outline that expands on that answer and incorporates details from the documents.

Encourage students to include specific historical details and comments about the documents in their essays.

Suggestion: Before students plan and write their essay, review the scoring rubric. Make sure students understand the components of an effective Document-Based Question essay so they can incorporate those elements in their own writing.

Edit Your Essay
Have students read over their first drafts. Suggest they ask themselves these questions: Does it accurately express my viewpoint? Does it need more details? Then have students proofread and edit their essays, revising as needed. If time allows, have students exchange essays for a peer edit.

Suggestion: Have students use a thesaurus to better describe their viewpoint and to make the essay more interesting.

Resources
• Writing Rubric

STEP 4: DEMONSTRATE
Communicate Conclusions
and Take Informed Action

Present Your Essay
Have students make a neat, clean copy of their essays. Then ask volunteers to read their essays aloud to the class.

Suggestion: As an alternative, have students read one or more of their classmates' essays on their own.

Reflect on the Project
Help students go over what they thought went well in their essays and what did not, so they can be even more effective in the future.

Suggestion: As an extension activity, have students research the impact of imperialism on another country, such as Vietnam (Indochina) or Kenya. Ask them to write a three-paragraph essay in which they compare that country's experience with India's. Have volunteers share their comparisons with the class.

The Age of Imperialism

The Industrial Revolution pushed the nations of Europe to move out into the world. Motivated by economic needs, nationalist ambitions, and the desire to spread European culture, Britain, France, and Germany established colonies in Africa and Asia. The United States and Japan quickly followed Europe's example.

▎ CONNECT

MY STORY VIDEO

Menelik II, Independence in the Age of Imperialism

Watch a video about the efforts of Menelik II to maintain his country's independence.

Check Understanding What European country tried to colonize Ethiopia? *(Italy)*

Hypothesize What was the likely reaction to the news that Menelik's forces had defeated a European army in battle? *(Europeans, whose strength had enabled them to divide up most of Africa fairly easily, would have been shocked by news of the battle. Africans would have been encouraged by the news of Italy's failed effort to colonize Ethiopia)*

⇅ FLIP IT!

Assign the Biography video.

DIGITAL ESSENTIAL QUESTION ACTIVITY

Why Do People Move?

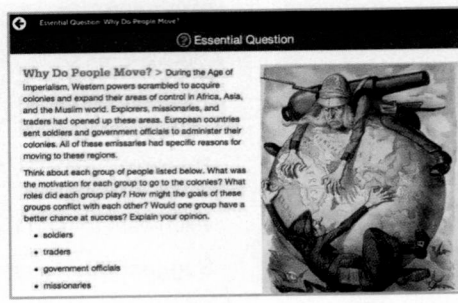

Explain that in this Topic, students will explore the Essential Question, "Why do people move?" People move for many reasons, including economic and political ones.

If students have not already done so, ask them to answer the activity questions. Then discuss student answers as a class.

Hypothesize Think about each of these groups of people: soldiers, traders, government officials, missionaries. What was the motivation for these groups to go to the colonies? What roles did each group play? How might the goals of these groups conflict with one another? Would one group have a better chance at success than the others? Explain your opinion. *(Answers will vary. Students should recognize that each group had different goals, such as making profits for traders and spreading religious ideas for missionaries. Students should also note that these goals could conflict with one another if two groups, such as soldiers and missionaries, tried to accomplish different ends among the same group of people. Students should be able to clearly state an opinion about chances of success and provide examples to support it.)*

DIGITAL TIMELINE ACTIVITY

The Age of Imperialism

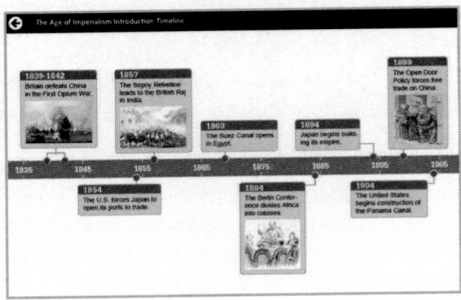

Display the timeline showing important events during the Age of Imperialism. During this Topic, students will learn about these events and many more, but the timeline will provide a framework into which they can place the events they learn about.

Interpret When did the United States force Japan to open to trade? *(1854)* How long after that did Japan begin building its empire? *(40 years)*

Infer The events for the years 1854 and 1899 both use the word *forces*. What does that tell you about the events? *(Sample response: that the events happened against the will or wishes of Japan and China)*

Topic Inquiry

Launch the Topic Inquiry with students after introducing the Topic.

The New Imperialism

Supporting English Language Learners

Use with Digital Text 1, **Motivations for the New Imperialism.**

Reading

Tell students that they will use the visuals in *Motivations for the New Imperialism* to enhance their understanding of the content. Then read *Motivations for the New Imperialism* aloud to students. Instruct students to complete one of the following activities based on their level of English proficiency.

Beginning Focus students' attention on the image of a big European industrial city that appears immediately before the subsection titled "Need for Resources Drives Further Expansion." Read the caption aloud. Explain that this picture shows what an industrialized city in Europe looked like in the late 1800s. Then retell the text of "Need for Resources Drives Further Expansion." Demonstrate how the image can help improve understanding of the content by using a Think Aloud strategy with students.

Intermediate Focus students' attention on the image of a big European industrial city that appears immediately before the subsection titled "Need for Resources Drives Further Expansion." Read the caption aloud. Invite students to describe what they see in this image. Then retell the text of "Need for Resources Drives Further Expansion." Guide a discussion to explore how examining the image helps improve understanding of the content.

Advanced Have students work independently to examine the image of a big European industrial city that appears immediately before the subsection titled "Need for Resources Drives Further Expansion." Invite a volunteer to read the caption aloud, then encourage students to describe what they see in this image. Then have students reread "Need for Resources Drives Further Expansion" independently. After reading, facilitate a discussion to explore how examining the image helps improve understanding of the content.

Advanced High Have small groups of students examine the image of a big European industrial city that appears immediately before the subsection titled "Need for Resources Drives Further Expansion." Instruct small groups to read the caption aloud, then work together to describe what they see in this image. Have small groups reread "Need for Resources Drives Further Expansion." Instruct groups to have a discussion to explore how examining the image helps improve understanding of the content. Circulate among students to support discussions as needed.

Use with Digital Text 3, **Types of Imperial Rule.**

Reading

Read *Types of Imperial Rule* aloud to the class. Have students complete one activity according to their level of English proficiency.

Beginning Reread the subsection "Direct and Indirect Rule" aloud to students. Demonstrate how to take notes on direct rule. Then ask students to help you take notes on indirect rule. Write and display notes for students and instruct them to copy the notes into their notebooks.

Intermediate Reread the subsection "Direct and Indirect Rule" aloud to students. Invite small groups of students to share their ideas for notes on this section with the group. Write and display notes for students to discuss which notes most accurately reflect the information in the text. Once a correct set of notes has been decided upon, instruct students to copy those notes into their notebooks.

Advanced Have students work with a partner to reread and take notes on *Types of Imperial Rule*. Circulate among students to offer support and feedback. Instruct students to make sure their notes accurately reflect the information in the text.

Advanced High Have students reread and take notes on *Types of Imperial Rule*. Circulate among students to offer support and feedback. Then have students share their notes with a partner to ensure accuracy.

▣ Differentiate Instruction

Use the Differentiated Instruction notes throughout the lesson plan to support the varied skill sets, levels of readiness, and interests in the mixed-ability classroom.

Challenge These notes include suggestions for expanding the activity for advanced students.

On-Level These notes include suggestions for modifying the activity to address different interests or learning styles.

Extra Support These notes include ideas for providing more scaffolding or reading spuport.

Special Needs These notes provide ideas for adapting instruction to support the needs of various special needs students.

■ NOTES

The New Imperialism

Objectives

Objective 1: Explain the political, economic, and social causes of European imperialism.

Objective 2: Understand how technology and other factors contributed to the spread of imperialism.

Objective 3: Describe the characteristics of imperial rule.

Objective 4: Summarize the cultural, political, and social effects of imperialism.

LESSON 1 ORGANIZER		PACING: APPROX. 1 PERIOD, .5 BLOCKS			
				RESOURCES	
		OBJECTIVES	PACING	Online	Print
Connect					
DIGITAL START UP ACTIVITY **Empire Builders**			5 min.	●	
Investigate					
DIGITAL TEXT 1 **Motivations for the New Imperialism**		Objective 1	10 min.	●	●
INTERACTIVE MAP **The New Imperialism**			10 min.	●	
DIGITAL TEXT 2 **Western Imperialism Spreads Rapidly**		Objective 2	10 min.	●	●
INTERACTIVE GALLERY **Technology Advances Imperialism**			10 min.	●	
DIGITAL TEXT 3 **Types of Imperial Rule**		Objective 3	10 min.	●	●
DIGITAL TEXT 4 **The Effects of Imperialism**		Objective 4	10 min.	●	●
Synthesize					
DIGITAL ACTIVITY **Imperialism—Different Opinions**			5 min.	●	
Demonstrate					
DIGITAL QUIZ **Lesson Quiz and Class Discussion Board**			10 min.	●	

PEARSON
realize.
www.PearsonRealize.com

Go online to access additional resources including:
Primary Sources • Biographies • Supreme Court cases •
21st Century Skill Tutorials • Maps • Graphic Organizers.

■ CONNECT

DIGITAL START UP ACTIVITY
Empire Builders

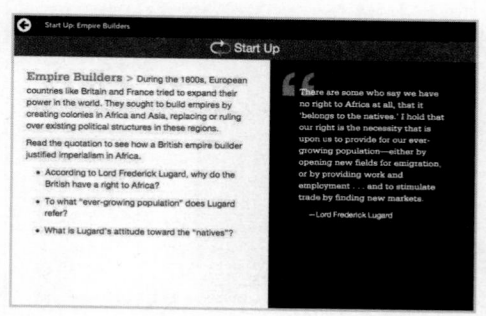

Project the Start Up Activity Ask students to read the quotation and answer the questions as they get settled.

Discuss According to Lord Frederick Lugard, why do the British have a right to Africa? *(Because they need to provide their growing population with new markets, places to live, and jobs.)* To what "ever-growing population" does Lugard refer? *(Lugard refers to the British population.)* What is Lugard's attitude toward the "natives"? *(Lugard's attitude toward natives seems to be that they are less important than the British.)*

Paraphrase Ask students to restate the quotation in their own words. *(People who say that Africa is for Africans are wrong. The British need Africa as a place for its growing population and to help the British economy.)*

Aa Vocabulary Development: Use the Interactive Reading Notepad to preview the Key Terms and Academic Vocabulary in this Lesson with students.

⇅ FLIP IT!
Assign the Flipped Video for this lesson.

■ STUDENT EDITION PRINT PAGES: 592–597

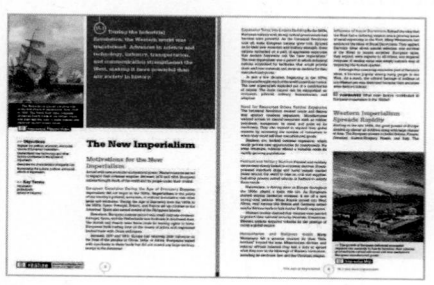

■ INVESTIGATE

DIGITAL TEXT 1
Motivations for the New Imperialism

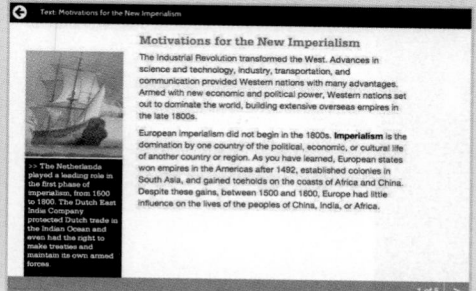

INTERACTIVE MAP
The New Imperialism

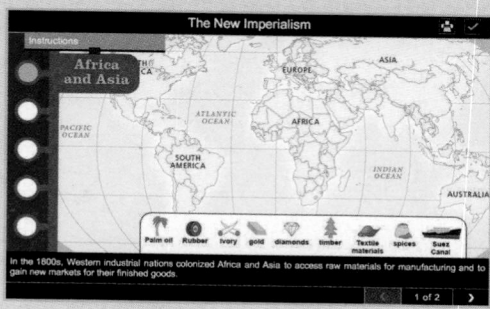

Objective 1: Explain the political, economic, and social causes of European imperialism.

Quick Instruction
Project the image of the Dutch ships from the Text. Ask students which countries were dominant colonial powers in the 1700s. *(Portugal, Spain, Britain, France, the Netherlands)* Ask which nations started out as colonies of European nations. *(The United States, Canada, Mexico, all of South America)* Now, explain that in the 1800s a new, different type of imperialism developed. This imperialism was driven by the advancements of the Industrial Revolution, which created a need for raw materials and new markets. Europeans who believed in their own cultural and racial superiority wanted to spread Western civilization and dominate those they considered weaker races.

Interactive Map: The New Imperialism Now, project the Interactive Map, describing how each layer represents resources sought by imperialist nations in different regions. Have students answer the question at end of the interactive activity.

Summarize What were the motivations of the new imperialism? *(Economic motivations included the need for raw materials for industrial growth, new markets for manufactured goods; humanitarian/religious motives included wanting to spread Christianity; Social Darwinism was also a motivation.)*

■ ACTIVE CLASSROOM
Use the Make Headlines strategy to have students write a headline that captures the new imperialism. Ask: If you were to write a headline that captured the most important aspect about the New Imperialism, what would that headline be? Have them pass their headline to a partner for them to review.

ELL Use the ELL activity described in the ELL chart.

Further Instruction
Editable Presentation Use the Editable Presentation to present the main ideas for this Core Text.

Motivations for the New Imperialism: Core Text and Interactive Reading Notepad Project and discuss the Interactive Reading Notepad questions, including the graphic organizer asking students to identify the causes of the New Imperialism. Review the motivations behind the New Imperialism, filling in the graphic organizer on the whiteboard as you go.

Explore with students the social and political motivations for imperialism, such as nationalism, spreading Christianity, and Social Darwinism. Ask students to give examples of nationalism. *(Sample responses: uniting countries like Germany, fighting wars for expansion, national pride, or patriotism)*

Infer How could nationalism lead to competition and conflict among imperialist powers? *(Sample response: Imperialist powers could fight over a particular colony, especially if that colony were rich in natural resources.)*

The Age of Imperialism

DIGITAL TEXT 2

Western Imperialism Spreads Rapidly

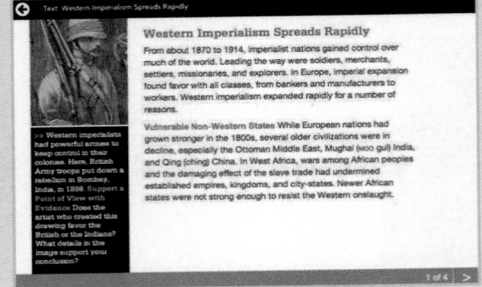

INTERACTIVE GALLERY

Technology Advances Imperialism

Draw Conclusions Westerners often felt that they were protecting and helping their "little brothers." For this reason, they wanted to share their religion. How might native Africans or Asians feel about changing their religion to adapt to the imperial power? *(Sample responses: They would probably be resentful; they may not want to change their religion; alternatively, they might want to convert to another religion because they believe in it.)*

Generate Explanations Some Westerners also believed in Social Darwinism. Explain how Social Darwinism served as a motivation for imperialism. *(Believers in Social Darwinism felt Westerners were superior to non-Westerners and imperial domination of non-Westerners by Westerners was nature's way to improve the human species.)*

Objective 2: Explain the political, economic, and social causes of European imperialism.

Quick Instruction

Remind students that Western imperialism spread very quickly in the years between 1870 to 1914 for a number of reasons, including weaknesses in non-Western states and Western technological advantages.

Interactive Gallery: Technology Advances Imperialism Project the Interactive Gallery. Examine each photo individually and then the gallery as a whole. Have students answer the question at the end, individually, in small groups, or as a class.

ACTIVE CLASSROOM

Ask students to Take a Stand on the following question: Could the New Imperialism have occurred without the advances of the Industrial Revolution? Ask students to divide into two groups based on their answer and move to separate areas of the classroom. Have each group discuss the reasons behind their answer and choose the three to five best details that support their opinion. Ask a representative from each side to present and defend the group's point of view.

Further Instruction

Western Imperialism Spreads Rapidly: Core Text and Interactive Reading Notepad Go through the Interactive Reading Notepad questions and discuss the answers as a class.

Identify Cause and Effect Why did Western imperialism expand as quickly as it did? *Sample response: The West had many technological advantages in medicine, weapons, communications, and transportation. Also, many of the areas that became colonies had been weakened by the slave trade, civil war, or the decline of a ruling empire.)*

Summarize What was the global impact of Western imperialism? *(Sample response: The power of the Western nations grew; Western imperialism continued to spread in Africa and Asia; Western technologies and communications went global; imperialism sparked nationalist movements in the colonized countries.)*

D Differentiate: Challenge/Gifted Direct students' attention to the photo of Mark Twain in the Digital Text. Have them read the caption and then ask them to make a list of questions for Mark Twain about his opposition to imperialism. *(Questions will vary; most students will focus on why he cared about a country so far away from America, why he believed imperialism undermined democracy, and why he thought he might make a difference.)* Have students do research to find the answers.

DIGITAL TEXT 3
Types of Imperial Rule

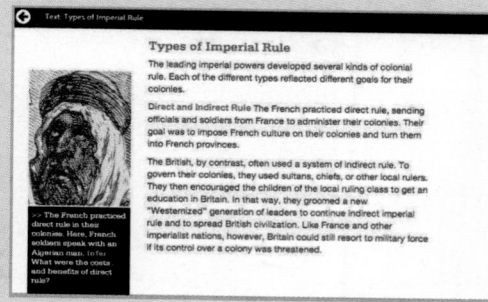

Text: Types of Imperial Rule

Types of Imperial Rule
The leading imperial powers developed several kinds of colonial rule. Each of the different types reflected different goals for their colonies.

Direct and Indirect Rule The French practiced direct rule, sending officials and soldiers from France to administer their colonies. Their goal was to impose French culture on their colonies and turn them into French provinces.

The British, by contrast, often used a system of indirect rule. To govern their colonies, they used sultans, chiefs, or other local rulers. They then encouraged the children of the local ruling class to get an education in Britain. In that way, they groomed a new "Westernized" generation of leaders to continue indirect imperial rule and to spread British civilization. Like France and other imperialist nations, however, Britain could still resort to military force if its control over a colony was threatened.

>> The French practiced direct rule in their colonies. Here, French soldiers speak with an Algerian man. Infer What were the costs and benefits of direct rule?

Objective 3: Describe the characteristics of imperial rule.

Quick Instruction
Under the New Imperialism, European control of colonies took different forms: direct rule *(where officials and soldiers of the imperialist nation rule in the colony)*, indirect rule *(where the imperialist nation allows members of the colonized people to help with the rule)*, protectorate *(where local rulers are left in place but answer to the imperial country)*, and spheres of influence *(where the imperialist country has exclusive trading privileges, but the country remains independent)*. Remind students that the British generally used the indirect form of rule; the French generally used direct rule.

Infer Why might imperialist nations set up protectorates or spheres of influence instead of governing by direct rule? *(Sample response: Protectorates are less expensive to run and don't require as great a military commitment; spheres of influence could be set up because they provide economic benefits without requiring a great political or economic commitment.)*

Analyze Images Project the image of the Shanghai waterfront and have students read the caption. What does the photo tell you about foreigners in China during the Age of Imperialism? *(Sample responses: Foreigners maintained their own businesses and trading houses. Foreigners were more interested in China's trade than in controlling it as a colony.)*

ELL Use the ELL activity described in the ELL chart.

Further Instruction
Types of Imperial Rule: Core Text and Interactive Reading Notepad Go through the Interactive Reading Notepad questions and discuss the answers as a class.

Compare and Contrast Organize students into small groups. Ask students to make a chart of the benefits and potential problems of direct rule, indirect rule, and protectorates. *(Answers will vary. Students might cite the following benefits: direct: more control; indirect: allows locals a role in government; protectorate: less expensive. They might identify these problems: direct: too expensive, not enough people to run government; indirect: fighting between ethnic groups, possible rebellion by locals; protectorate: not enough control [especially military control], rebellion)* Have them share their charts with the class.

Support Ideas with Examples Which form of imperial rule do you think would be most effective? Why? *(Answers will vary. Students should choose one form of imperial rule and support their choice with examples based on what they learned in the lesson thus far.)*

DIGITAL TEXT 4
The Effects of Imperialism

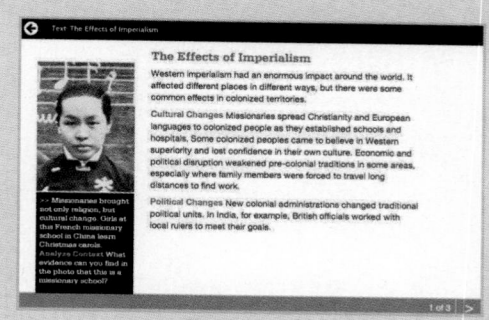

Text: The Effects of Imperialism

The Effects of Imperialism
Western imperialism had an enormous impact around the world. It affected different places in different ways, but there were some common effects in colonized territories.

Cultural Changes Missionaries spread Christianity and European languages to colonized people as they established schools and hospitals. Some colonized peoples came to believe in Western superiority and lost confidence in their own culture. Economic and political disruption weakened pre-colonial traditions in some areas, especially where family members were forced to travel long distances to find work.

Political Changes New colonial administrations changed traditional political units. In India, for example, British officials worked with local rulers to meet their goals.

>> Missionaries brought not only religion, but cultural change. Girls at this French missionary school in China learn Christmas carols. Analyze Context What evidence can you find in the photo that this is a missionary school?

1 of 3 >

Objective 4: Summarize the cultural, political, and social effects of imperialism.

Quick Instruction
Explain to students that imperialism had a huge impact worldwide, including cultural changes such as the spread of Christianity and the loss of older cultures, political changes such as the redrawing of borders without regard for local ethnic situations, and economic changes such as conversion to economies based on cash crops and destruction of local industries.

Infer Project the photo and have students read the caption. If these Chinese girls are learning to play and sing Christmas carols, what are they gaining? *(Sample response: knowledge of the Christian religion and Western music)* What might they be losing? *(Sample response: their traditional religion, traditional Chinese music)*

Further Instruction
The Effects of Imperialism: Core Text and Interactive Reading Notepad Go through the Interactive Reading Notepad questions and discuss the answers as a class.

Classify Review with students the changes that imperialism brought to the world. Have them classify each change as positive or negative. *(Positive: more global communities, including religious communities; imperial powers got very rich and powerful; Western ideas of government were exported; Negative: decline of local cultures; cash crops grown instead of food; local cottage industries declined; workers and resources were exploited for the benefit of imperialist powers.)*

The Age of Imperialism

■ SYNTHESIZE

■ DEMONSTRATE

DIGITAL ACTIVITY

Imperialism—Different Opinions

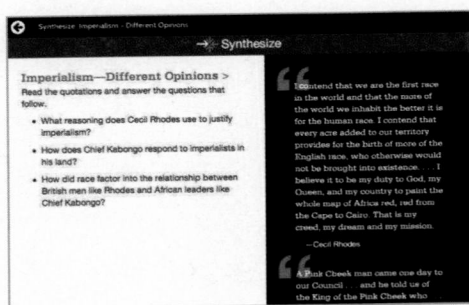

DIGITAL QUIZ

Lesson Quiz and Class Discussion Board

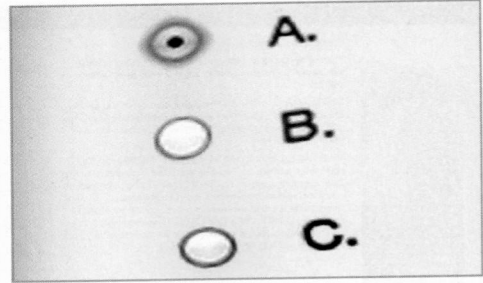

Apply Concepts Organize students into small groups and ask them to answer the following question: How could colonized people use nationalism against their rulers? *(Sample response: If colonized people adapted nationalism, they would work for the independence of their "nation" from the imperialist power.)*

Draw Conclusions Remind students that cash crops are crops grown for export. Then ask: Where would people who are growing cash crops instead of food get food to eat? Would it be more or less expensive than growing food themselves? *(Answers will vary, but most students will say that it would have to be imported and probably by the imperial power; it would probably be more expensive than growing it themselves.)*

Have students read the two quotations and answer the questions.

What reasoning does Cecil Rhodes use to justify imperialism? *(Rhodes uses the idea of Social Darwinism. He believes the English are superior to other races and should spread across the world to improve the world.)* How does Chief Kabongo respond to imperialists in his land? *(Chief Kabongo tells the "Pink Cheek man" that Africans elect their own leaders and make their own rules.)* How did race factor into the relationship between British men like Rhodes and African leaders like Chief Kabongo? *(Sample response: Cecil Rhodes believed that he was part of a superior race and that being part of that race justified imperialism. Chief Kabongo, who refers to a Western visitor as a Pink Cheek man, is angry at the Westerners who seized power from the local people.)*

Assign the online quiz for this lesson if you haven't already done so. Students will be offered automatic remediation or enrichment based on their score.

Pose these questions to the class on the Class Discussion Board:

In "The New Imperialism," you read about the causes and effects of Western imperialism in the 1800s. Driven by economic, political, and social motivations, Europeans brought new political systems, economic systems, and cultural ideas to Africa and Asia, sometimes against the will of those who already lived there.

Predict Consequences What would the world be like if there hadn't been an "Age of Imperialism" in the late 1800s? *(Responses will vary. Students may focus on the lack of unity in the world [languages, religions, etc.]; some students may suggest that African and Asian countries might have become stronger because they didn't lose their independence; some might use China as an example: China was never fully controlled by the West; Western nations had spheres of influence only; and now China is a very strong nation.)*

Topic Inquiry

Have students continue their investigations for the Topic Inquiry.

European Colonies in Africa

Supporting English Language Learners

Use with Digital Text 2, **European Contact Increases.**

Reading

Explain that using the words and phrases around a new vocabulary word can help students understand the meaning of the new word. This is called using the context of a word to improve understanding. Then read *European Contact Increases* aloud to students. Instruct students to complete one of the following activities based on their level of English proficiency.

Beginning Read the following sentences aloud and have students repeat them. Use a Think Aloud to model how to use context clues to determine the meaning of the word *missionaries*.

• Catholic and Protestant missionaries followed the explorers. All across Africa, they sought to win people to Christianity.

Intermediate Read the following sentences aloud and have students repeat them. Lead students through the process of using context clues to determine the meaning of the word *missionaries*.

• Catholic and Protestant missionaries followed the explorers. All across Africa, they sought to win people to Christianity.

Advanced Invite a student volunteer to read the following sentences aloud. Ask small groups of students to work together to develop and explain the steps they took to use context clues to determine the meaning of the word *missionaries*. Then have students share their processes with their peers.

• Catholic and Protestant missionaries followed the explorers. All across Africa, they sought to win people to Christianity.

Advanced High Have a student volunteer read the following sentences aloud. Ask pairs of students to work together to develop and explain the steps they took to use context clues to determine the meaning of the word *missionaries*. Then have pairs share their processes with their peers.

• Catholic and Protestant missionaries followed the explorers. All across Africa, they sought to win people to Christianity.

Use with Digital Text 4, **African Resistance.**

Reading

Have students complete one activity according to their level of English proficiency.

Beginning Explain how to read a text silently. Remind students that when reading silently, they should not move their lips or murmur the words. Read *African Resistance* aloud to students, then instruct students to reread the subsection "Ethiopia Remains Independent" silently. When they are finished, explain any challenging words or concepts to students.

Intermediate Remind students that when reading silently, they should not move their lips or murmur the words. Read *African Resistance* aloud to students, then instruct students to reread the subsections "Ethiopia Remains Independent" and "A New African Elite" silently. When they are finished, review any challenging words or concepts with the class.

Advanced Have students read the subsections "Ethiopia Remains Independent" "A New African Elite" silently. When they are finished, instruct students to ask about any difficult or challenging vocabulary and concepts. Review these as needed.

Advanced High Have students read *African Resistance* silently. When they are finished, instruct students to ask about any difficult or challenging vocabulary and concepts. Review these as needed.

▣ Differentiate Instruction

Use the Differentiated Instruction notes throughout the lesson plan to support the varied skill sets, levels of readiness, and interests in the mixed-ability classroom.

Challenge These notes include suggestions for expanding the activity for advanced students.

On-Level These notes include suggestions for modifying the activity to address different interests or learning styles.

Extra Support These notes include ideas for providing more scaffolding or reading spuport.

Special Needs These notes provide ideas for adapting instruction to support the needs of various special needs students.

■ NOTES

European Colonies in Africa

Objectives

Objective 1: Describe the forces that shaped Africa in the early 1800s.

Objective 2: Explain why European contact with Africa increased.

Objective 3: Analyze how European nations carved up Africa.

Objective 4: Describe African resistance to imperialism.

LESSON 2 ORGANIZER		PACING: APPROX. 1 PERIOD, .5 BLOCKS			
		OBJECTIVES	PACING	Online	Print
Connect					
DIGITAL START UP ACTIVITY **Resisting Imperialism**			5 min.	●	
Investigate					
DIGITAL TEXT 1 **Africa Before Imperialism**		Objective 1	10 min.	●	●
INTERACTIVE MAP **Effects of Imperialism on African Regions**			10 min.	●	
DIGITAL TEXT 2 **European Contact Increases**		Objective 2	10 min.	●	●
DIGITAL TEXT 3 **European Nations Scramble for Colonies**		Objective 3	10 min.	●	●
INTERACTIVE MAP **European Imperialism in Africa**			10 min.	●	
DIGITAL TEXT 4 **African Resistance**		Objective 4	10 min.	●	●
Synthesize					
DIGITAL ACTIVITY **European Domination in Africa**			5 min.	●	
Demonstrate					
DIGITAL QUIZ **Lesson Quiz and Class Discussion Board**			10 min.	●	

PEARSON **realize**™
www.PearsonRealize.com

Go online to access additional resources including:
Primary Sources • Biographies • Supreme Court cases •
21st Century Skill Tutorials • Maps • Graphic Organizers.

▶ CONNECT

DIGITAL START UP ACTIVITY
Resisting Imperialism

Project the Start Up Activity Ask students to read the quotation and answer the questions as they enter and get settled.

Discuss How would you describe the attitude of Chief Machemba toward the German officer? *(Sample response: The chief views the German officer as an equal but he realizes that this officer may try to rule over his people.)* What do you think this chief would have done if Europeans tried to conquer his people? *(The chief would probably have resisted European rule.)*

Predict Consequences How is the German officer likely to respond to Chief Machemba's statement? Why? *(He will likely dismiss the chief's statement and try to dominate the Yao.)*

Aa Vocabulary Development: Use the Interactive Reading Notepad to preview the Key Terms and Academic Vocabulary in this Lesson with students.

⇅ FLIP IT!
Assign the Flipped Video for this lesson.

■ STUDENT EDITION PRINT PAGES: 598–604

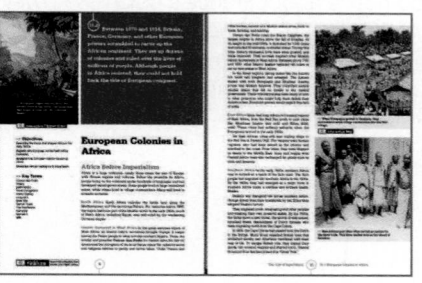

▶ INVESTIGATE

DIGITAL TEXT 1
Africa Before Imperialism

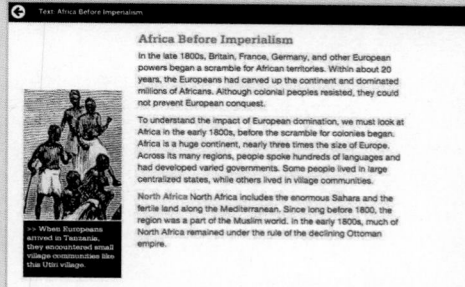

INTERACTIVE MAP
Effects of Imperialism on African Regions

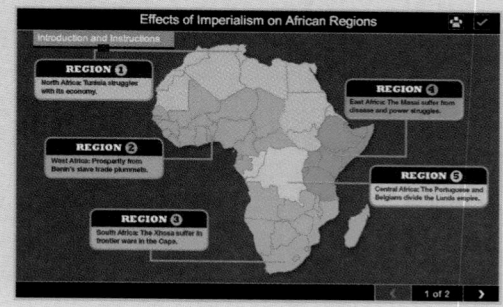

Objective 1: Describe the forces that shaped Africa in the early 1800s.

Quick Instruction

Before the European scramble for African colonies, the continent's population was diverse in language, government, and culture. North Africa was under weakening Muslim rule. Powerful states were emerging in West Africa. South Africa was caught in a series of wars, and the slave trade shaped life in both East and West Africa.

Interactive Map: Effects of Imperialism on African Regions Project the Interactive Map. Click on the different regions, reading about one representative ethnic group from each region and how it was impacted by imperialism. Have students answer the question individually, in small groups or as a class.

Make Generalizations What generalizations can you make about how all the different groups were impacted by imperialism? *(Answers will vary but will typically reflect negative impacts on culture and traditions. Students should be able to support their generalization with specific details from the Interactive Map.)*

🖐 ACTIVE CLASSROOM

Project the image of the Utiri village. Use a whiteboard tool to divide it into four numbered quadrants. Have students count off 1 to 4. Then ask them to take A Closer Look at the part of the image in their quadrant. Have groups make a list of what they see. Then, ask a representative of each group to present the group's findings, either orally or on chart paper. As a class, develop a full description of Utiri village life.

Further Instruction

Editable Presentation Use the Editable Presentation to present the main ideas for this Core Text.

Africa Before Imperialism: Core Text and Interactive Reading Notepad Project and discuss the Interactive Reading Notepad questions.

Summarize the situations in the different regions of Africa in the early 1800s. *(The Ottoman empire was declining in North Africa; in West Africa, Muslims were gaining power; in East Africa, they traded slaves and other goods with India; and in South Africa, the Boers, white settlers who had been in South Africa since the 1600s, were fighting with the Zulus.)*

Predict Consequences The former slaves who were settled in Sierra Leone were from all regions of Africa and had been enslaved all over the world. What are some of the possible outcomes of this action? *(Answers will vary; some students may point to possible tension between different religious and ethnic groups; some may say their skills and abilities would complement each other and build a stronger society.)*

European Colonies in Africa

DIGITAL TEXT 2

European Contact Increases

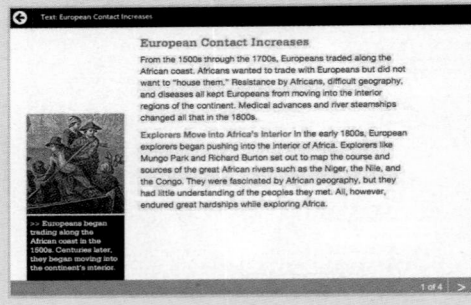

European Contact Increases

From the 1500s through the 1700s, Europeans traded along the African coast. Africans wanted to trade with Europeans but did not want to "house them." Resistance by Africans, difficult geography, and diseases all kept Europeans from moving into the interior regions of the continent. Medical advances and river steamships changed all that in the 1800s.

Explorers Move Into Africa's Interior In the early 1800s, European explorers began pushing into the interior of Africa. Explorers like Mungo Park and Richard Burton set out to map the course and sources of the great African rivers such as the Niger, the Nile, and the Congo. They were fascinated by African geography, but they had little understanding of the peoples they met. All, however, endured great hardships while exploring Africa.

>> Europeans began trading along the African coast in the 1500s. Centuries later, they began moving into the continent's interior.

1 of 4 >

Objective 2: Explain why European contact with Africa increased.

Quick Instruction

Prior to the Age of Imperialism, Europeans traded with Africans but were prevented from moving into Africa's interior by African resistance, geographic obstacles, and disease. Medical advances and river steamships changed all that in the 1800s. The arrival of explorers and Christian missionaries such as Dr. David Livingstone opened the African continent to European imperialism.

Project the image of Henry Stanley meeting Dr. David Livingstone. Remind the students that Livingstone was both an explorer and a missionary. He had not been heard from, so Henry Stanley traveled to Africa to find him.

Contrast How were the motivations different for explorers and missionaries who went to Africa? *(Sample response: Explorers were interested in the geography and the land; missionaries wanted to spread Christianity and Western learning.)*

Generate Explanations Why did explorers like Mungo Park and Richard Burton travel to Africa before most missionaries? *(Sample response: These explorers were fascinated by African geography and wanted to map Africa's major rivers and their sources.)*

ELL Use the ELL activity described in the ELL chart.

Further Instruction

European Contact Increases: Core Text and Interactive Reading Notepad Project the Interactive Reading Notepad questions and discuss the answers with the class.

Categorize Organize students into groups and have each group develop a list of pros and cons for missionaries going to Africa. *(Lists will vary; students will most likely point to missionaries establishing schools and hospitals, along with ending the slave trade, as the pros; cons might include that the local people lost some of their own culture and traditions and that missionaries took a paternalistic attitude toward Africans and treated them like children.)*

D Differentiate: Extra Support Give students a two-column chart to aid them in their Categorize activity. Have them label one column "Pros" and the other "Cons." Make sure students, especially English Language Learners, know what the words *pro* and *con* mean.

Predict Consequences What were some possible long-term benefits of the missionary schools and hospitals for the Africans? *(Sample response: The children educated in missionary schools could go to college and become professionals, serving in government or starting businesses of their own; the hospitals could reduce death rates from disease and injury.)*

DIGITAL TEXT 3

European Nations Scramble for Colonies

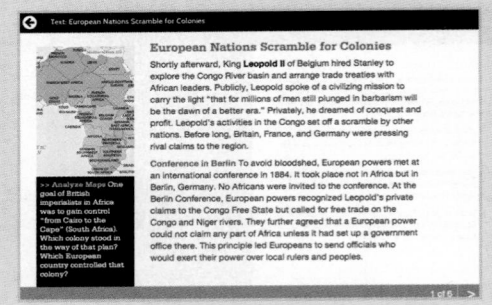

European Nations Scramble for Colonies

Shortly afterward, King **Leopold II** of Belgium hired Stanley to explore the Congo River basin and arrange trade treaties with African leaders. Publicly, Leopold spoke of a civilizing mission to carry the light "that for millions of men still plunged in barbarism will be the dawn of a better era." Privately, he dreamed of conquest and profit. Leopold's activities in the Congo set off a scramble by other nations. Before long, Britain, France, and Germany were pressing rival claims to the region.

Conference in Berlin To avoid bloodshed, European powers met at an international conference in 1884. It took place not in Africa but in Berlin, Germany. No Africans were invited to the conference. At the Berlin Conference, European powers recognized Leopold's private claims to the Congo Free State but called for free trade on the Congo and Niger rivers. They further agreed that a European power could not claim any part of Africa unless it had set up a government office there. This principle led Europeans to send officials who would exert their power over local rulers and peoples.

>> Analyze Maps One goal of British imperialists in Africa was to gain control "from Cairo to the Cape" (South Africa). Which colony stood in the way of that plan? Which European country controlled that colony?

1 of 6 >

Objective 3: Analyze how European nations carved up Africa.

Quick Instruction

The European scramble for African colonies began when King Leopold II of Belgium seized the Congo. He declared that Europeans could bring a civilizing force to Africa and bring Africans out of "barbarism." His actions led to the Berlin Conference, in which European leaders established ground rules for colonizing Africa. They agreed that a European power could not claim any part of Africa unless it had set up a government office there. This principle led Europeans to send officials who would exert their power over local rulers and peoples. France claimed an African empire the size of the United States, while Britain claimed heavily populated regions that were rich in natural resources. Many nations established colonies not only for the resources but also because they wanted to bolster their national image at home.

Interactive Map: European Imperialism in Africa Project the base map (1876) and then slide to the second map (1914).

Analyze Maps Which countries had the most colonies by 1914? *(Britain and France)* What do you notice about France's colonies? *(They are grouped in West Africa.)* What pattern is being established with Britain's colonies? *(The British seem to be trying to establish a north/south corridor.)*

INTERACTIVE MAP
European Imperialism in Africa

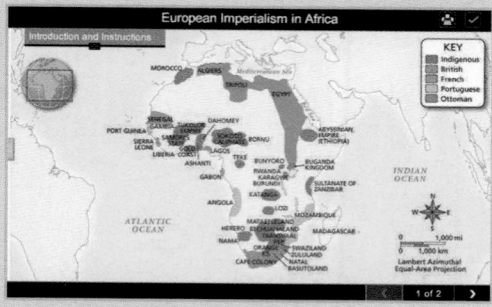

Infer Why did Britain and France have so many more colonies in Africa than other countries? *(Both Britain and France were industrialized and had strong economies and a strong sense of nationalism. Both had advanced militaries. Britain in particular had a large navy.)*

🔲 ACTIVE CLASSROOM

Project the image of the Zulu miners at the Kimberly mine. Ask each student to choose one person from the photo. Then ask them to use the If Photos Could Talk strategy to write a description of what that person had been doing in the 10 minutes before the picture was taken, and what he did in the 10 minutes after it was taken. To extend this, you could ask them to state what their person was thinking.

Further Instruction

European Nations Scramble for Colonies: Core Text and Interactive Reading Notepad Project and discuss the Interactive Reading Notepad questions, including the graphic organizer that asks students to identify causes and effects of the scramble for colonies. Review the events in The Scramble for Africa, filling in the graphic organizer on the whiteboard as you go. *(Causes: France wants to extend its empire in Africa. Rhodes seeks power. British win colonies from Boer rule. Portugal wants to bolster image and*

further economic growth and influence. Italy wants to bolster image and further economic growth and influence. Germany wants to have what other European nations have. Effects: West and Central Africans live under French rule. Rhodesia (now Zimbabwe) is named for Rhodes. Constitution sets up a government run by whites, enforcing segregation. Africans in these regions must live under Portuguese and Italian rule. Regions including Cameroon and Togo become part of newly united German empire. Africans resist imperialism.)

Sequence Events How did Leopold II of Belgium trigger the rush to grab colonies in Africa? *(Leopold II took control of the Congo River basin, making treaties with African leaders. He acquired control of so much territory so quickly that Britain, France, and Germany knew they had to keep up.)*

Contrast Remind students of the unique situation of the Boer settlers in South Africa. How were the Boers different from other European settlers in Africa in the late 1800s? *(Dutch Boer ancestors had farmed in Africa for 300 years. They were not "conquering" Europeans.)*

DIGITAL TEXT 4
African Resistance

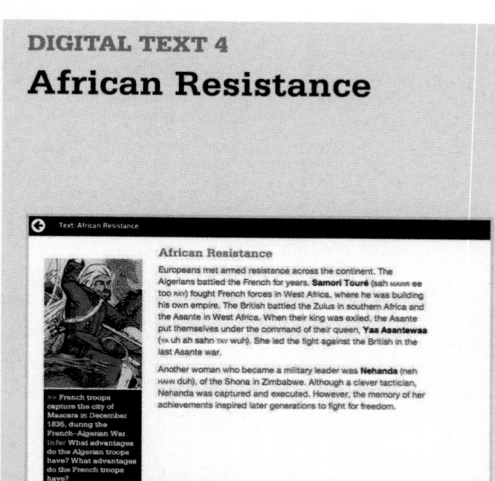

Objective 4: Describe African resistance to imperialism.

Quick Instruction

Many Africans resisted European imperialism, including the Algerians, the Zulus, and the Asante. One kingdom that fought the Europeans was the Ethiopians, who defeated the Italians trying to claim their land. In other parts of Africa, European education helped create an African elite that established nationalist movements to achieve self-determination.

Analyze Images Have students examine the illustration. How might Ethiopia's geography have helped it maintain its independence? *(Sample response: Based on the illustration, Ethiopia had very mountainous terrain. That would have made moving troops and supplies for an invasion difficult and probably gave the Ethiopians an advantage, because they would be familiar with the mountainous terrain.)*

ELL Use the ELL activity described in the ELL chart.

Topic (15) Lesson 2

European Colonies in Africa

Further Instruction

African Resistance: Core Text and Interactive Reading Notepad Project the Interactive Reading Notepad questions and discuss the answers with the class.

Generate Explanations Europeans used their advanced technology to spread imperialism. How did Menelik II use European technology to stop the spread of imperialism in Ethiopia? *(Menelik modernized his country's transportation system with European-built railroads and his army with European weapons and training. He used these modernizations to fight off an Italian invasion.)*

Support an Idea with Examples Which examples in the text support the idea that women played an active role in African resistance to imperialism? *(Queen Yaa Asantewaa led the Asante against the British; Nehanda, a Shona leader, was a clever tactician and military leader.)*

■ SYNTHESIZE

DIGITAL ACTIVITY
European Domination in Africa

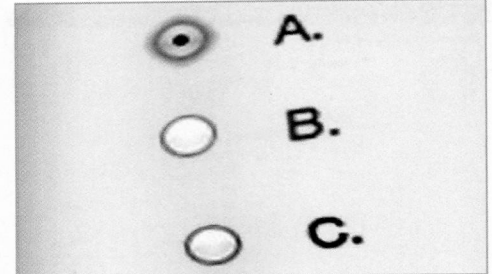

Have students work as a class to brainstorm a list of events in the scramble for African colonies. Then have them work individually to choose the five most important events from the list and write them in the graphic organizer. Ask students to list each event's cause and its effect. *(Sample response: Events: Leopold II of Belgium hires Stanley to arrange treaties with African leaders and claims the Congo for himself; European powers agree to carve up Africa at the Berlin Conference; King Leopold II brutalizes the people of Congo; France conquers Algeria; British form Union of South Africa from Cape Colony and former Boer republics. Causes: Leopold's wish for power and wealth; to avoid bloodshed among European nations; Leopold wants riches of Congo and treats its workers horribly; France wants to establish colonies in Africa; British win colonies from Boer rule. Effects: Other European countries rush to colonize Africa; Africa is partitioned by European nations; international outrage forces Leopold to hand power over Congo to Belgium; Africans in region had direct French rule; constitution sets up a government run by whites and enforcing segregation.)*

Summarize How did imperialist European powers claim control over most of Africa by the end of the 1800s? *(Sample response: King Leopold II of Belgium had the explorer Stanley set up trade agreements with African leaders. Other European nations rushed to take part in African markets, looking for natural resources. They held a meeting in Berlin to decide the rules for dividing the continent. France invaded Algeria in the 1830s and held a large portion of Africa by the end of the 19th century. The British also held important colonies and fought the Boers for control of what became South Africa. Other nations, such as Italy, established their own colonies.)*

■ DEMONSTRATE

DIGITAL QUIZ
Lesson Quiz and Class Discussion Board

Assign the online quiz for this lesson if you haven't already done so. Students will be offered automatic remediation or enrichment based on their score.

Pose these questions on the Class Discussion Board.

In "European Colonies in Africa," you read about how Africa was colonized in the late 1800s by European nations, especially Britain and France. You learned that Africa was carved up by European nations and that Africans resisted being colonized.

Infer Why were no Africans invited to the Berlin Conference? *(Answers will vary. Students may point to a general disregard for Africans' well being or Social Darwinist beliefs that Africans were culturally and racially inferior to Westerners and did not require a place at the table.)*

Predict Consequences What are some potential long-term consequences of African colonization by European nations? *(Answers will vary; sample answers: conflict between European countries over colonies; conflict between different ethnic groups placed together by European-drawn boundaries; continued exploitation of African resources; expense of maintaining colonies; nationalist revolts against colonizers)*

Topic Inquiry

Have students continue their investigations for the Topic Inquiry.

Europe and the Muslim World

Supporting English Language Learners

Use with Digital Text 1, **Unrest in Muslim Regions.**

Reading

Explain the components of complex sentences to students. Then read *Unrest in Muslim Regions* aloud to students. Instruct students to complete one of the following activities based on their level of English proficiency.

Beginning Read the following sentence aloud and have students repeat it. Underline the subordinate clause and circle the independent clause in the sentence. Use a Think Aloud to explain why the subordinate clause cannot stand alone as a complete sentence.

- Although the revolt was put down, *the Wahhabi movement survived*.

Intermediate Read the following sentence aloud and have students repeat it. Instruct students to underline the subordinate clause and circle the independent clause in the sentence. Help students use a Think Aloud to explain why the subordinate clause cannot stand alone as a complete sentence.

- Although the revolt was put down, *the Wahhabi movement survived*.

Advanced Have a student volunteer read the following sentence aloud. Have another volunteer underline the subordinate clause and circle the independent clause in the sentence. Ask a third volunteer use a Think Aloud to explain to the class why the subordinate clause cannot stand alone as a complete sentence.

- Although the revolt was put down, *the Wahhabi movement survived*.

Then have pairs of students review *Unrest in Muslim Regions* to identify other complex sentences. Have pairs repeat the underlining and circling process with the new sentences. Finally, instruct students to share their work with the class.

Advanced High Have a student volunteer read the following sentence aloud, underline the subordinate clause, and circle the independent clause in the sentence. Ask a second volunteer use a Think Aloud to explain to the class why the subordinate clause cannot stand alone as a complete sentence.

- Although the revolt was put down, *the Wahhabi movement survived*.

Then have students work individually to review *Unrest in Muslim Regions* to identify other complex sentences. Have students repeat the underlining and circling process with the new sentences. Finally, instruct students to share their work with a partner.

Use with Digital Text 3, **Modernization in Egypt.**

Reading

Have students complete one activity according to their level of English proficiency.

Beginning Explain how to read a text silently. Remind students that when reading silently, they should not move their lips or murmur the words. Read *Modernization in Egypt* aloud to students, then instruct students to reread the subsection "The Suez Canal" silently. When they are finished, ask leading questions to determine their comprehension of the material. Review any challenging words or concepts with students.

Intermediate Remind students that when reading silently, they should not move their lips or murmur the words. Read *Modernization in Egypt* aloud to students, then instruct students to reread the subsection "The Suez Canal" silently. When they are finished, arrange students in small groups and ask students to share one fact they learned from reading silently. Circulate among students to offer support as needed. Finally, review any challenging words or concepts with the class.

Advanced Have students read *Modernization in Egypt* silently. When they are finished, instruct students to work with a partner to outline the main points of the text. Pairs should share their outlines with the class and make any necessary corrections. Circulate among students to offer support as needed. Finally, review any challenging words or concepts with the class.

Advanced High Have students read *Modernization in Egypt* silently. When they are finished, instruct students to write an outline of the main points of the text. Next, students should share their outlines with a partner and make any necessary corrections. Circulate among students to offer support as needed. Finally, review any challenging words or concepts with the class.

▶ Differentiate Instruction

Use the Differentiated Instruction notes throughout the lesson plan to support the varied skill sets, levels of readiness, and interests in the mixed-ability classroom.

Challenge These notes include suggestions for expanding the activity for advanced students.

On-Level These notes include suggestions for modifying the activity to address different interests or learning styles.

Extra Support These notes include ideas for providing more scaffolding or reading spuport.

Special Needs These notes provide ideas for adapting instruction to support the needs of various special needs students.

■ **NOTES**

Topic (15) Lesson 3

Europe and the Muslim World

Objectives

Objective 1: Explain how internal and external pressures shaped the Muslim world.

Objective 2: Identify the challenges facing the Ottoman empire and Persia.

Objective 3: Describe the ways Egypt tried to modernize, including the opening of the Suez Canal.

LESSON 3 ORGANIZER		PACING: APPROX. 1 PERIOD, .5 BLOCKS			
				RESOURCES	
		OBJECTIVES	**PACING**	**Online**	**Print**
Connect					
	DIGITAL START UP ACTIVITY **The Egyptian Campaign**		5 min.	●	
Investigate					
	DIGITAL TEXT 1 **Unrest in Muslim Regions**	Objective 1	10 min.	●	●
	DIGITAL TEXT 2 **The Ottoman Empire Declines**	Objective 2	10 min.	●	●
	INTERACTIVE GALLERY **European Powers and the Ottoman Empire**		10 min.	●	
	DIGITAL TEXT 3 **Modernization in Egypt**	Objective 3	10 min.	●	●
	INTERACTIVE GALLERY **The Suez Canal**		10 min.	●	
	DIGITAL TEXT 4 **European Imperialism in Persia**	Objective 2	10 min.	●	●
Synthesize					
	DIGITAL ACTIVITY **Effects of Europeans in Muslim Regions**		5 min.	●	
Demonstrate					
	DIGITAL QUIZ **Lesson Quiz and Class Discussion Board**		10 min.	●	

PEARSON
realize™
www.PearsonRealize.com

Go online to access additional resources including:
Primary Sources • Biographies • Supreme Court cases •
21st Century Skill Tutorials • Maps • Graphic Organizers.

CONNECT

DIGITAL START UP ACTIVITY
The Egyptian Campaign

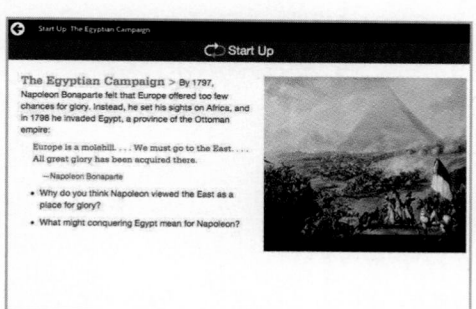

Project the Start up Activity Ask students to answer the questions as they enter and get settled. Then have them share their ideas with another student.

Discuss Why do you think Napoleon viewed the East as a place for glory? *(Sample response: it was the location of previous empires)* What might conquering Egypt mean for Napoleon? *(Napoleon would extend his empire, claim the region before the British, and gain trade routes and resources for France. Also, it would further weaken the Ottoman empire.)*

Tell students that in this lesson they will learn about the decline of the Ottoman empire and how the Europeans took advantage to gain Ottoman territory.

Aa Vocabulary Development: Use the Interactive Reading Notepad to preview the Key Terms and Academic Vocabulary in this Lesson with students.

⇅ FLIP IT!

Assign the Flipped Video for this lesson.

■ STUDENT EDITION PRINT
PAGES: 605–609

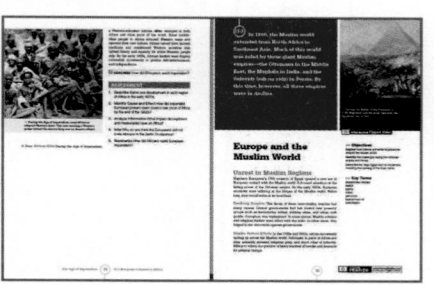

■ INVESTIGATE

DIGITAL TEXT 1
Unrest in Muslim Regions

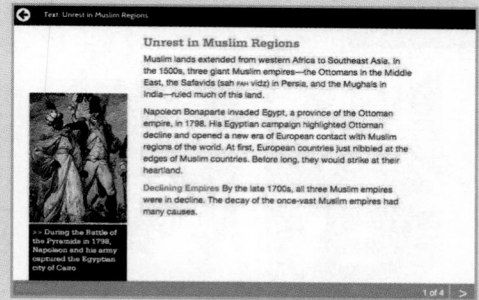

Objective 1: Explain how internal and external pressures shaped the Muslim world.

Quick Instruction

In the 1500s, three giant Muslim empires ruled large areas of the world—the Ottomans in the Middle East, the Safavids in Persia, and the Mughals in India. By the 1700s, all three Muslim empires were in decline, in part because of weakened central governments, corruption and Muslim discontent. Reform movements arose, stressing religious piety and strict rules of behavior. For example, in the Sudan, Muhammad Ahmad announced that he was the Mahdi, the long-awaited savior of the faith. The Mahdi and his followers fiercely resisted British expansion into the region.

Compare and Contrast Project the map from the text. Ask students to compare the size and location of the three empires. Tell them that by the late 1700s, the Ottoman empire was in decline.

Hypothesize Which Muslim empire was first to confront European imperialism? Why? *(Answers will vary. Students will likely choose the Ottoman empire, because of the empire's size, accessible location, and control of territory in southeastern Europe.)*

ELL Use the ELL activity described in the ELL chart.

Further Instruction

Editable Presentation Use the Editable Presentation to present the main ideas for this Core Text.

Unrest in Muslim Regions: Core Text and Interactive Reading Notepad Project and discuss the Interactive Reading Notepad questions, including the graphic organizer asking students to identify causes of unrest in Muslim regions. Review the stresses affecting Muslim empires in the 1700s and 1800s, filling in the graphic organizer on the whiteboard as you go.

Identify Cause and Effect How did these problems destabilize the Ottoman empire? *(Sample response: Corruption allowed provincial rulers to grow powerful, the spread of Western ideas led sultans to reject reform, and European imperialism threatened to compromise Ottoman territory.)*

Identify Central Issues How was Western imperialism a source of stress in Muslim regions of the world? *(Europeans gained better trading terms, demanded special treatment, and interfered in local affairs.)*

Europe and the Muslim World

DIGITAL TEXT 2
The Ottoman Empire Declines

INTERACTIVE GALLERY
European Powers and the Ottoman Empire

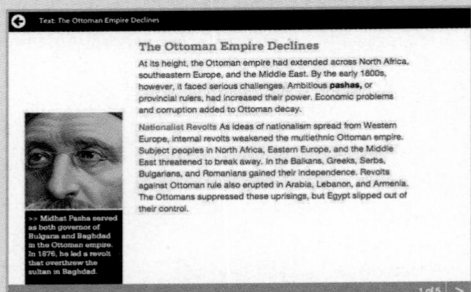

Objective 2: Identify the challenges facing the Ottoman empire and Persia.

Quick Instruction

At its height, the Ottoman empire extended across North Africa, southeastern Europe, and parts of the Middle East. Ambitious pashas, or provincial rulers, and economic problems added to the Ottoman decline. As ideas of nationalism spread from Western Europe, internal revolts by subject peoples weakened the empire. European states took advantage of this weakness to grab Ottoman territory. Some Ottoman leaders saw the need for reform. They looked to the West for ideas on reorganizing the government and its rigid rules. In the early 1700s, they reorganized the bureaucracy and system of tax collection. However, sultans usually rejected reform, adding to the tension. Tension between Ottoman Turkish nationalists and minority groups within the empire led to a brutal genocide of Christian Armenians. Turks accused Christian Armenians of supporting Russia against the Ottoman empire.

Interactive Gallery: European Powers and the Ottoman Empire Project the Image Gallery on the whiteboard. Review the summary of European interests in the Ottoman territory provided by the political cartoonist.

👥 ACTIVE CLASSROOM

Ask students to look closely at the political cartoon and create their own visual concept and/or phrase that represents the same concept. Allow approximately 3–5 minutes. Ask students to post their Graffiti Concepts on the board or chart paper and tell them to look at the various responses. Then, discuss the similarities and differences in the responses as a group.

Further Instruction

Editable Presentation Use the Editable Presentation to present the main ideas for this Core Text.

The Ottoman Empire Declines: Core Text and Interactive Reading Notepad Go through the Interactive Reading Notepad questions and discuss the answers with the class.

Summarize Describe two problems that contributed to Ottoman decline. *(Possible responses: government corruption, nationalist revolts, economic problems, European pressure, efforts to Westernize, the Young Turks movement, problems with Armenians)*

D Differentiate: Challenge/Gifted Ask students to learn more about the Young Turks and their revolutionary movement, including its key leaders, the chronology of events leading up to the overthrow of the sultan, and its main goals. Have them identify another, similar group of individuals in history. Students should then write an editorial for a newspaper or magazine with the information they find.

Tell students that the term *Young Turks* has come to represent individuals or a group inside an organization that tries to take control or pursues liberal or progressive policies or reforms.

Identify Cause and Effect How did the decline of the Ottoman empire encourage Western ambitions in the region? *(European powers saw the decline of the empire as an opportunity to expand their own borders and interests. For example, Russia tried to gain control of the Bosporus and the Dardanelles so that it could have access to the Mediterranean Sea.)*

Sequence Events What events led to the persecution and slaughter of Armenians in the Ottoman empire? *(Muslim Turks accused Christian Armenians of supporting Russia and their plans against the Ottoman empire. When the Armenians protested repressive treatment by the Ottomans, the sultan had tens of thousands of Armenians killed. Even more were killed or died from starvation over the next 25 years.)*

DIGITAL TEXT 3
Modernization in Egypt

Modernization in Egypt

In the early 1800s, Egypt was a semi-independent province of the Ottoman empire, making great strides toward reform. Its success was due to **Muhammad Ali,** an ambitious soldier appointed governor of Egypt by the Ottomans. Ali used the opportunity created by Napoleon's invasion and the civil war that followed to seize power in 1805.

Reform Efforts Muhammad Ali is sometimes called the "father of modern Egypt." He introduced a number of political and economic reforms, including improving tax collection, reorganizing the landholding system, and backing large irrigation projects to increase farm output. By expanding cotton production and encouraging the development of many local industries, Ali increased Egyptian participation in world trade.

>> Muhammad Ali, the Ottoman governor of Egypt, sought to make Egypt a modern state

1 of 4 >

INTERACTIVE GALLERY
The Suez Canal

The Suez Canal

Introduction and Instructions

< 1 of 2 >

DIGITAL TEXT 4
European Imperialism in Persia

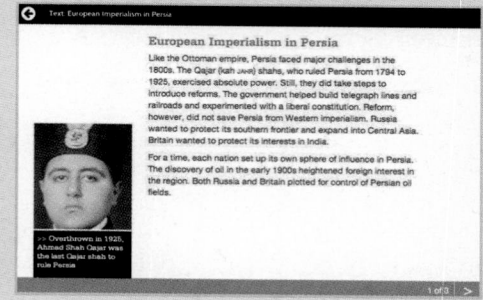

European Imperialism in Persia

Like the Ottoman empire, Persia faced major challenges in the 1800s. The Qajar (kah JAHR) shahs, who ruled Persia from 1794 to 1925, exercised absolute power. Still, they did take steps to introduce reforms. The government helped build telegraph lines and railroads and experimented with a liberal constitution. Reform, however, did not save Persia from Western imperialism. Russia wanted to protect its southern frontier and expand into Central Asia. Britain wanted to protect its interests in India.

For a time, each nation set up its own sphere of influence in Persia. The discovery of oil in the early 1900s heightened foreign interest in the region. Both Russia and Britain plotted for control of Persian oil fields.

>> Overthrown in 1925, Ahmad Shah Qajar was the last Qajar shah to rule Persia

1 of 3 >

Objective 3: Describe the ways Egypt tried to modernize, including the opening of the Suez Canal.

Quick Instruction

In the early 1800s, Egypt was a semi-independent province of the Ottoman empire. Muhammad Ali, the "father of modern Egypt," introduced a number of political and economic reforms. He also conquered the neighboring lands of Arabia, Syria, and Sudan. Before he died in 1849, he had set Egypt on the road to becoming a major Middle Eastern power. His successors were less skilled, however, and in 1882 Egypt became a protectorate of Britain.

Interactive Gallery: The Suez Canal Project the gallery. Have students progress through the images, taking time to read captions and examine each picture. Point out how much time the canal saved on journeys.

Categorize After going through the gallery once, have students review the gallery again and identify the factors that influenced the opening of the Suez Canal. Have them categorize each factor as a human factor or a physical geographic factor. *(Sample response: Human factors: the friendship between de Lesseps and Muhammad Ali and Said Pasha; peasant workers performed labor under slave-like conditions; Physical geographic factors: the Red and Mediterranean seas are at about the same level; dirt and sediment had to be removed as the canal was dug)*

🎥 ACTIVE CLASSROOM

Have students use what they have learned about the Suez Canal to use the Cartoon It strategy to create a political cartoon about one event in the canal's early history. Give students the option of using an image from the Interactive Gallery as the foundation of their cartoon.

ELL Use the ELL activity described in the ELL chart.

Further Instruction

Modernization in Egypt: Core Text and Interactive Reading Notepad Go through the Interactive Reading Notepad questions and discuss the answers with the class.

Generate Explanations How did Britain gain control of the Suez Canal? *(Egypt was unable to repay its loans for the canal, so Britain bought Egypt's shares and gained controlling interest in the canal.)* Point out that European powers often gained control in this way. Explain that in 1882, Britain claimed it intervened to protect its investments in Egypt.

Identify Cause and Effect The Suez Canal allowed European countries to increase trade with the Middle East. Along with increased trade, what problems did the Suez Canal bring to Egypt? *(Sample responses: Egypt was not able to repay loans, and the British gained control of the canal. When Egyptian nationalists revolted against foreign influence, Britain made Egypt a British protectorate.)*

Objective 2: Identify the challenges facing the Ottoman empire and Persia.

Quick Instruction

Like the Ottoman empire, Persia—now Iran—faced major challenges. The Qajar shahs exercised absolute power. Foreign nations, especially Russia and Britain, wanted to control Iran's oil fields, increasing the reach of European imperialism. They were granted concessions and sent troops to protect their interests. These actions outraged Iranian nationalists.

Infer Project the image of the oil well from the text. Have students study the photo and read the caption. Who will most likely gain the greatest benefit from this oil well? *(Russia or Britain)* What details support your answer? *(Britain and Russia both were interested in Persia's oil fields. Both set up spheres of influence in Persia and were granted concessions by the Persian government.)*

Further Instruction

Editable Presentation Use the Editable Presentation to present the main ideas for this Core Text.

European Imperialism in Persia: Core Text and Interactive Reading Notepad Go through the Interactive Reading Notepad questions and discuss the answers with the class.

Europe and the Muslim World

 **SYNTHESIZE**

 DEMONSTRATE

DIGITAL ACTIVITY
Effects of Europeans in Muslim Regions

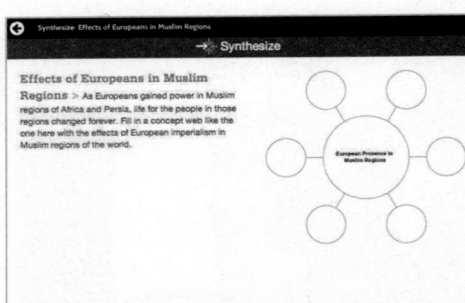

LESSON QUIZ
Lesson Quiz and Class Discussion Board

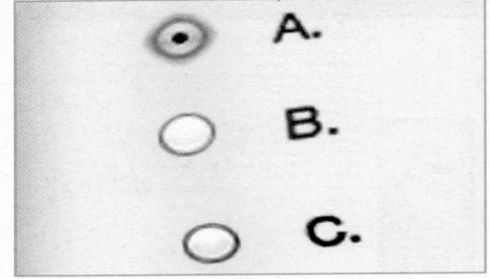

Tell students that countries like Persia did not have the technology or capital to develop their own natural resources or build railways or mines. They granted Europeans concessions, or special rights, so that Europeans could come in and develop Persian industry for them.

Both Westernized Persian nationalists and Muslim nationalists were opposed to the concessions the Persian government granted to allow British and Russian forces into the country. These two groups remain at odds in Iran to this day.

Cite Evidence Why did foreign nations become interested in Persia in the early 1900s? What issues arose from this interest? *(Oil was found in the area, and both Russia and Britain wanted control of the oil fields. Both countries sent troops to the area, causing unrest with Persian nationalists.)*

Analyze Information Why, besides control of Persian oil fields, were Russia and Britain interested in Persia? *(Russia wanted to protect its southern frontier and expand into Central Asia, and Britain wanted to protect its interests in India.)*

Ask students to recall the actions and impact of European imperialists in Muslim regions. Then have them fill in the concept web with six examples of the effects of European imperialism in the Muslim world. *(Sample responses: Europeans intervened in local affairs. Europeans spread Western ideas, such as nationalism, which caused uprisings. Europeans sought power over trade routes to Asia. Germany built a railway to Baghdad; the British took control of the Suez Canal and made Egypt a protectorate. Europeans educated young men, who learned better medicine and farming techniques. This caused overpopulation. Russia's perceived influence over Armenians was one reason for Armenian genocide by nationalist Turks. British and Russian troops in Persia caused nationalist outrage.)*

Compare Think back to the lesson on the causes, characteristics, and effects of European imperialism in Africa. How was European imperialism in the Muslim world similar? *(Sample response: In both places, European imperialism was often motivated by the desire for new resources. In both places, Europeans sought to supplant leaders who were not friendly to their interests, sometimes taking direct control. In both places, nationalist backlashes developed in response to European involvement.)*

Assign the online Lesson Quiz for this lesson if you haven't already done so. Students will be offered automatic remediation or enrichment based on their score.

Pose these questions to the class on the Discussion Board:

In "Europe and the Muslim World," you read about the internal and external pressures that shaped the Muslim world and the challenges faced by the Ottoman empire and Persia from European imperialism. Modernization brought issues as well as greater influence from outside nations.

Express Ideas Clearly How did the modernization of Egypt lead to British rule? *(Muhammad Ali's modernization encouraged Western influence and eventually led to the construction of the Suez Canal, but high-interest loans forced the Egyptian ruler to sell shares of the canal, giving the British a controlling interest. They then made Egypt a British protectorate.)*

Draw Conclusions How did European nations take advantage of stresses in the Muslim world? *(Through diplomacy, economic investments, the introduction of Western ideas, and the threat of force, European nations expanded their control.)*

Topic Inquiry
Have students continue their investigations for the Topic Inquiry.

India Becomes a British Colony

Supporting English Language Learners

Use with Digital Text 2, **India Under British Rule.**

Reading
Remind students that using information already know about a topic can help them learn new information. Read *India Under British Rule* aloud to students. Instruct students to complete one of the following activities based on their level of English proficiency.

Beginning Direct students' attention to the image of Indian cotton workers. Help students use the picture to help them recall what they know about farming and manufacturing. Remind students of the context of the Industrial Revolution and that the textile industry was important to the British economy, making cotton a valuable crop. Then reread "An Unequal Partnership" aloud to students. Help them to use the text, picture, and their prior knowledge to define the term *cash crop*.

Intermediate Direct students' attention to the image of Indian cotton workers. Ask students to use the picture to help them recall what they know about farming and textile manufacturing. Make and display a list of student responses. Then have students independently read "An Unequal Partnership" and use the text, picture, and their prior knowledge to define the term *cash crop*.

Advanced Ask student pairs to examine the image of Indian cotton workers. Have them use the image to make a list of facts and ideas that they already know about farming and manufacturing. Then have pairs reread "An Unequal Partnership"and define the term *cash crop*. Ask partners to share the connections they made between the ideas they listed and the information in the text with the class.

Advanced High Ask small groups of students to use the images in this text to make a list of facts and ideas they already know about imperialism, agriculture, and the Industrial Revolution. Then have students "An Unequal Partnership" and define the term *cash crop*. Ask students to draw conclusions about the link between cash crops and imperialism.

Use with Digital Text 3, **Diverse Views on Culture.**

Reading
Read *Diverse Views on Culture*. Then have students complete one activity according to their level of English proficiency.

Beginning Reread *Diverse Views on Culture* aloud to students and instruct them to carefully follow along in their texts. Demonstrate how to paraphrase the content after you read each paragraph. Then explain how to identify the main idea in the subsection "Indian Attitudes." Assist students in paraphrasing and identifying the main idea in the subsection "Westerner Attitudes."

Intermediate Reread *Diverse Views on Culture* aloud to students and instruct them to carefully follow along in their texts. Demonstrate how to paraphrase the content after you read each paragraph. Then ask students to identify the main idea in the subsection "Indian Attitudes." Support them as they determine the main idea. Then support students as they paraphrase the subsection "Westerner Attitudes" and then identify the main idea.

Advanced Remind students how to paraphrase a text and identify its main idea. Then have students reread *Diverse Views on Culture* with a partner. When they are finished, instruct partners to take turns paraphrasing each subsection and identifying their corresponding main ideas. Circulate among students to offer support as needed. Ask students to share their findings with the class.

Advanced High Ask students to explain how to paraphrase a text and identify its main idea. Then have students reread *Diverse Views on Culture* independently. When they are finished, ask students to paraphrase the text to a partner and identify each subsection's main idea. Circulate among students to offer support as needed. Ask students to share their findings with the class.

▣ Differentiate Instruction

Use the Differentiated Instruction notes throughout the lesson plan to support the varied skill sets, levels of readiness, and interests in the mixed-ability classroom.

Challenge These notes include suggestions for expanding the activity for advanced students.

On-Level These notes include suggestions for modifying the activity to address different interests or learning styles.

Extra Support These notes include ideas for providing more scaffolding or reading spuport.

Special Needs These notes provide ideas for adapting instruction to support the needs of various special needs students.

■ NOTES

India Becomes a British Colony

Objectives

Objective 1: Understand the causes and effects of the Sepoy Rebellion.

Objective 2: Explain the impact of British rule on India.

Objective 3: Describe how the British and Indians viewed one another.

Objective 4: Trace the origins of Indian nationalism.

LESSON 4 ORGANIZER		PACING: APPROX. 1 PERIOD, .5 BLOCKS			
				RESOURCES	
		OBJECTIVES	**PACING**	**Online**	**Print**
Connect					
DIGITAL START UP ACTIVITY **Critical of British Rule**			5 min.	●	
Investigate					
DIGITAL TEXT 1 **The British East India Company**		Objective 1	10 min.	●	●
INTERACTIVE GALLERY **The Sepoy Rebellion**			10 min.	●	
DIGITAL TEXT 2 **India Under British Rule**		Objective 2	10 min.	●	●
INTERACTIVE IMAGE **The Imperial Durbar, 1877**			10 min.	●	
DIGITAL TEXT 3 **Diverse Views on Culture**		Objective 3	10 min.	●	●
DIGITAL TEXT 4 **The Growth of Indian Nationalism**		Objective 4	10 min.	●	●
Synthesize					
DIGITAL ACTIVITY **Positives and Negatives for India**			5 min.	●	
Demonstrate					
LESSON QUIZ **Lesson Quiz and Class Discussion Board**			10 min.	●	

PEARSON **realize**™
www.PearsonRealize.com

Go online to access additional resources including:
Primary Sources • Biographies • Supreme Court cases •
21st Century Skill Tutorials • Maps • Graphic Organizers.

■ CONNECT

DIGITAL START UP ACTIVITY
Critical of British Rule

Project the Start Up Activity Ask students to read the quotation as they get settled. Then have students share their ideas with another student.

Discuss Based on the quote and the image, summarize relations between the British and the Indians during the British rule of India. *(Sample response: The British were in charge.)* What was probably the prevailing opinion of Indians about the British empire? *(Resentment of the "knife of sugar.")*

Make Predictions Ask students to predict some outcomes of British imperialism in India. Would they predict rebellions or peace? Why? *(Students might predict rebellions since the quote shows unhappiness with British rule.)*

Aa Vocabulary Development: Use the Interactive Reading Notepad to preview the Key Terms and Academic Vocabulary in this Lesson with students.

⇄ FLIP IT!

Assign the Flipped Video for this lesson.

■ STUDENT EDITION PRINT
PAGES: 610–614

■ INVESTIGATE

DIGITAL TEXT 1
The British East India Company

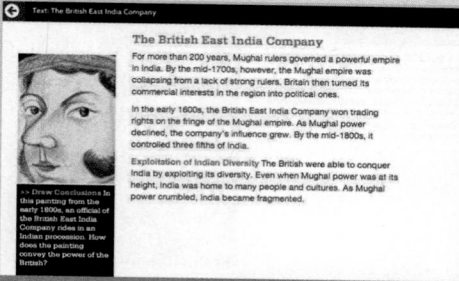

INTERACTIVE GALLERY
The Sepoy Rebellion

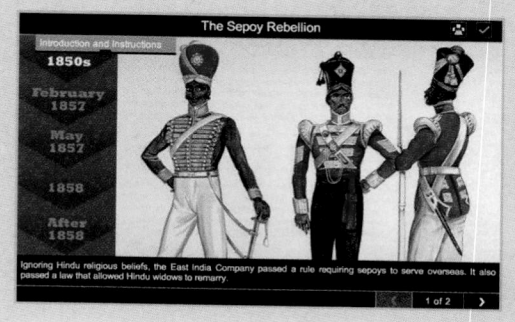

Objective 1: Understand the causes and effects of the Sepoy Rebellion.

Quick Instruction

In the mid-1800s, the British East India Company controlled most of India. Company officials made rules for Indian soldiers, or sepoys, in its service that were not popular with the sepoys. The sepoys rebelled against British officers. The Sepoy Rebellion was eventually put down by England, but it led to reforms and changes in rule: the British government took charge of India.

Interactive Gallery: The Sepoy Rebellion Project the gallery. Have students progress chronologically through the images, taking time to read captions and examine each picture.

👥 ACTIVE CLASSROOM

Use the Make Headlines strategy with the gallery. Have students pick one image to write a headline that would have described and summarized an event that led to or occurred during the Sepoy Rebellion. Students can read their headlines to small or large class groups.

Hypothesize After students have shared their headlines, have them think about the headlines described as causes for the Sepoy Rebellion. Ask students to list some ways the British East India Company **might** have prevented a rebellion of sepoy soldiers. *(Possible Answer: The company **might** have avoided rebellion if it had more respect for Hindu and Muslim traditions. For example, the company could have not required overseas*

travel or the ingesting of animal fat from cartridges. It could have decided against a law allowing Hindu widows to remarry. It might be that none of these practices would have prevented rebellion, since there was general unhappiness with the rule of a foreign power.)

Further Instruction

The British East India Company: Core Text and Interactive Reading Notepad Project and discuss the Interactive Reading Notepad questions, including the graphic organizer asking students to record major causes and effects of British colonial rule in India. Review the causes and effects, filling in the graphic organizer on the whiteboard as you go.

Be sure students understand that some causes of British rule included a weakened Mughal empire, economic motivations to profit from colonies, the exploitation of differences among diverse populations in India, and the transfer of power from the East India Company to the British government after the Sepoy Rebellion. *(The effects of British colonial rule will be completed by students after they have read the other Digital Texts.)*

Summarize What were some effects and outcomes of the Sepoy Rebellion? *(Some effects were a legacy of fear, hatred, and mistrust between the British and Indians. There were also changes in British policy: the British Parliament took over India. More troops were sent to India, and Indians were taxed to pay for troops. There was some easing of rules that had angered and offended Hindus and Muslims.)*

India Becomes a British Colony

DIGITAL TEXT 2

India Under British Rule

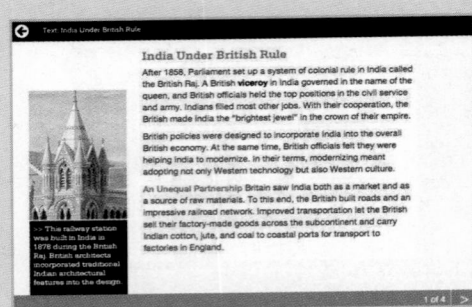

INTERACTIVE IMAGE

The Imperial Durbar, 1877

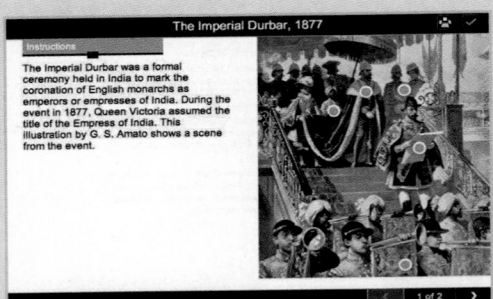

Objective 2: Explain the impact of British rule on India.

Quick Instruction

The impact of British rule on India included some modernizations for India such as improved methods of agriculture, new railways, better healthcare, and improved communication systems, such as the telegraph and a postal system. Most of these changes were to enhance British profits from India, for example, by converting Indian agriculture to the production of more profitable cash crops or having railways to transport Indian raw materials and British goods across India.

Interactive Image: The Imperial Durbar, 1877 Project the illustration. Have students click all the hotspots and learn about the Durbar. Tell them that the British held the Durbar to proclaim and celebrate their queen being named empress of India, and various aspects of British imperialism in India.

⚑ ACTIVE CLASSROOM

Use the Conversation with History strategy. Have each student imagine a conversation with one of the people in the picture. Students can write down a question or two they would like to ask (such as "What was life like under British rule?") and also write what they think the person would reply.

Compare Points of View Although British and Indian people are shown at the Durbar ceremony, how might one compare the probable British and Indian points of view about the occasion at that time? *(Sample response: The British were more likely truly celebrating the declaration of their imperial rule, while Indians would have less reason to celebrate being ruled by a foreign power. Indians may have resented the money being spent on the ceremony during a period of famine in India.)*

ELL Use the ELL activity described in the ELL chart.

Further Instruction

India Under British Rule: Core Text and Interactive Reading Notepad Project and discuss the Interactive Reading Notepad questions.

Be sure students understand that even though the British had economic motives for improving India's infrastructure, some acts such as increased spending on railways and schools did bring benefits for India. However, some British changes in India caused catastrophes; famines and deforestation in India were partly a result of British agricultural changes. In addition, some traditional Indian industries were lost. After the Suez Canal opened in 1869, British trade with India soared. It was an unequal partnership, however, favoring the British. The British flooded India with inexpensive, machine-made textiles, ruining India's once-prosperous hand-weaving industry.

Compare and Contrast What were some ways that British rule affected lower caste members in India? How did British rule affect upper class Indians? *(The lower castes benefited from a British justice system that did not discriminate by class or caste. Lower caste members probably experienced more negative aspects of British rule, however, such as famines. Upper classes in India took advantage of British education, civil service, and military opportunities. Indian landowners and princes grew rich from exporting cash crops.)*

DIGITAL TEXT 3
Diverse Views on Culture

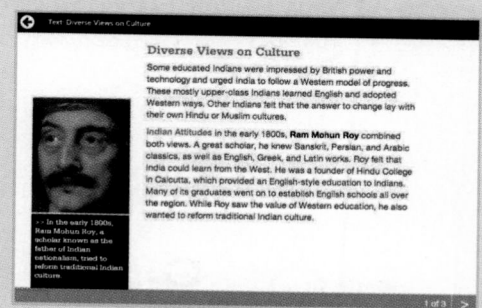

> In the early 1800s, Ram Mohun Roy, a scholar known as the father of Indian nationalism, tried to reform traditional Indian culture

Objective 3: Describe how the British and Indians viewed one another.

Quick Instruction

While under British rule, some Indians (usually from the upper classes) began to adopt Western education and culture, even learning English. Other Indians maintained their own Hindu or Muslim culture while still advocating for some reforms in India. Most British people dismissed Indian culture as inferior, although a few recognized the contributions of the Indian culture in theology, philosophy, classical works, and ancient heritage.

Determine Point of View Project the photo of Thomas Macaulay and read the last sentence under "Diverse Views on Culture." Remind students that the word *arrogant*, used to describe Macaulay's statement, means "full of self-importance." Ask students to explain how this meaning suits Macaulay's quote. *(Answers may vary but can reflect the fact that Macaulay was full of self-importance in judging his own British culture and literary tradition as superior to the Indian culture and literary tradition.)*

ELL Use the ELL activity described in the ELL chart.

Further Instruction

Diverse Views on Culture: Core Text and Interactive Reading Notepad Project and discuss the Interactive Reading Notepad questions.

Compare and Contrast What were Ram Mohun Roy's views about Western culture and Indian culture? *(Ram Mohun Roy saw value in both cultures. He introduced Westernized education in India and knew English, Greek, and Latin. But he also wanted Indians to take pride in their own culture, and he started a type of Indian nationalism. He also believed in reforming less-modern Indian practices such as the caste system, child marriage, sati, and purdah. He knew Sanskrit, Persian, and Arabic classics from his own culture.)*

Predict Consequences Since the British and some Indians promoted a Western-style education system in India, what might one predict about Western-style political values that Indians might embrace? *(Possible response: Democracy, equality, and nationalism were Western-style political values that might be desired by Indians who had been educated in Western-style schools.)*

D Differentiate: Challenge/Gifted British society in the 1800s placed many restrictions on women, as did Indian culture. Some Indian cultural practices such as sati, child marriage, and purdah were even harsher for women, although there were also Indian leaders such as Ram Mohun Roy working to end those practices. Have students research for more information about sati and purdah as practiced in 1800s India and write a short summary to share with the class.

DIGITAL TEXT 4
The Growth of Indian Nationalism

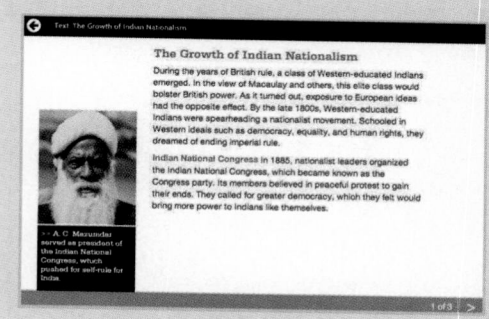

> A. C. Mazumdar served as president of the Indian National Congress, which pushed for self-rule for India

Objective 4: Trace the origins of Indian nationalism.

Quick Instruction

Indians who received a Western-style education came to value Western ideals such as democracy and equality; these Indians formed a nationalist movement to end imperial rule. An Indian National Congress was formed in 1885 to advocate for Indian self-rule. Eventually a Muslim League split off from the Hindu-dominated Indian National Congress.

Analyze Images Project the photo of the Indian National Congress. How does this photograph show a unity of Indians that was not present when the British East India Company first took control of India? *(The congress members are unified in their goal of achieving self-rule for India and in forming a nationalist movement to end imperial rule.)*

Further Instruction

The Growth of Indian Nationalism: Core Text and Interactive Notepad Project and discuss the Interactive Reading Notepad questions.

Analyze Information How can the Indian National Congress be considered an effect of British rule? *(It was an effect of the education system set up by British rule, which promoted Western values such as democracy and equality. It can be considered an effect of British rule because one of its main purposes was to end British rule and promote self-rule in India.)*

India Becomes a British Colony

SYNTHESIZE

DEMONSTRATE

DIGITAL ACTIVITY
Positives and Negatives for India

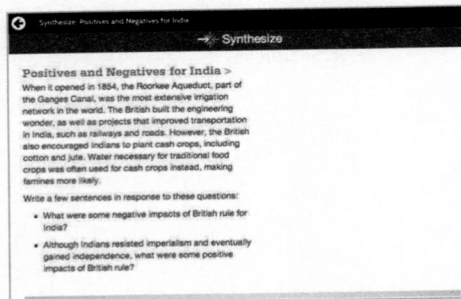

LESSON QUIZ
Lesson Quiz and Class Discussion Board

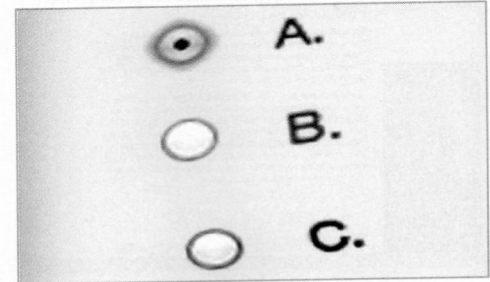

Make Predictions A previous section discussed how British railroads and communication systems modernized and promoted national unity in India. Based on this section's information about the Indian National Congress and Muslim League, what predictions might a reader make about national unity in India? *(Sample response: The Indian National Congress seemed to start out with a strong sense of unifying Indians, but the formation of the Muslim League shows that a reader could safely predict a fracturing of Indian national unity: the Muslim League wanted a "separate Muslim state.")*

Indians resisted British imperialism and eventually gained independence, starting with the formation of the Indian National Congress. But British rule did inadvertently bring some benefits for India's infrastructure, for example the building of roads, railways, irrigation systems, schools, and communication systems. It was always an unequal partnership between the two countries, with England taking more profits and also causing problems in India such as destruction of cottage industries, deforestation, and famines.

Have students review the image for the Synthesize activity and then answer the questions. Ask them to share their answers with a partner. Have students discuss as a group the following question.

Analyze Information If India got some benefits from British rule, why did Indians form the Indian National Congress to end British rule? *(Sample response: Indians formed the Congress partly because they learned Western ideals of democracy and equality. There were also disadvantages of British rule that led them to pursue self-rule. Imperialism was an unequal partnership favoring the British. The quote from the Start Up Activity also summarizes Indian feeling about British rule: imperialism was a "knife of sugar," not overly oppressive, but a "knife" wielded by the British just the same.)*

Assign the online Lesson Quiz for this lesson if you haven't already done so. Students will be offered automatic remediation or enrichment based on their score.

Pose these questions to the class on the Discussion Board: In "India Becomes a British Colony," you read how a British company exploited weaknesses in India's declining Mughal Empire to gain control of India. After a rebellion by Indian sepoys, the British government took over ruling India. There were some benefits of British rule but there were many disadvantages. India pursued self-rule and formed an Indian National Congress.

Analyze Information Indians from different cultures and traditions could not unite to resist British newcomers when the British East India Company took control of India. However, what were some **agreements** between Hindus and Muslims in India before and during the Sepoy Rebellion? *(Possible answer: Hindus and Muslims opposed rules for soldiers made by the British East India Company. Neither group wanted to bite off cartridge tips greased with animal fat for religious reasons. These two groups of sepoys joined forces against the British during the Sepoy Rebellion.)*

Summarize What were some benefits that Indians gained from access to British schools? *(Indians learned English, and some were trained for civil service or military careers. Some established English schools in other parts of India. Indians also learned Western ideals of democracy and equality, leading them to eventually form the Indian National Congress.)*

Topic Inquiry
Have students continue their investigations for the Topic Inquiry.

China and the West

Supporting English Language Learners

Use with Digital Text 1, **Economic Interest in China.**

Reading

Read *Economic Interest in China* aloud to students. Instruct students to complete one of the following activities based on their level of English proficiency.

Beginning Reread *Economic Interest in China* aloud to students. As you read, encourage students to raise their hands when they have questions. Pause in order to allow students to ask their questions. Encourage other students to answer the questions before providing the students with the answers.

Intermediate Instruct small groups of students to reread *Economic Interest in China* aloud. As they read, encourage students to raise their hands when they have questions. Tell students to stop reading in order to allow students to ask their questions. Encourage other students to answer the questions before providing the students with the answers.

Advanced Instruct pairs of students to reread *Economic Interest in China* aloud. As they read, encourage students to ask their partner to stop reading in order for them to ask their questions. Encourage partners to answer the questions before asking for teacher support.

Advanced High Instruct pairs of students to reread *Economic Interest in China* aloud. As they read, encourage students to ask their partner to stop reading in order for them to ask their questions. Tell students to ask both specific and general questions about the topic. Have pairs write down their list of questions. After reading, instruct pairs to use classroom resources and work together to investigate the answers to their questions. Encourage partners to share their questions and answers with their classmates.

Use with Digital Text 3, **Reform Efforts in China.**

Reading

Good readers ask themselves questions as they read to improve their understanding of the material. Read *Reform Efforts in China*. Then have students complete one activity according to their level of English proficiency.

Beginning Reread *Reform Efforts in China* aloud to students and model how to ask questions to improve comprehension as you read. Continue reading but pause frequently to guide students to ask questions about the content as you read aloud.

Intermediate Reread *Reform Efforts in China* aloud to students and model how to ask questions to improve comprehension as you read. Continue reading but pause frequently to offer students the opportunity to ask questions as you read aloud. Encourage students to offer answers to their own questions before continuing to read.

Advanced Discuss how students can practice self-questioning to improve comprehension as they read. Instruct students to read *Reform Efforts in China* with a partner. Have students pause frequently so that their partner can ask questions as they read aloud. Encourage students to offer answers to their own questions before continuing to read.

Advanced High Discuss how students can practice self-questioning to improve comprehension as they read. Instruct students to read *Reform Efforts in China* silently. Have students pause frequently to ask themselves questions about the content. Tell students to write their questions in their notebooks. Encourage students to offer answers to their own questions before continuing to read. Finally, discuss and evaluate this reading method and have students compare questions and answers with each other.

▣ Differentiate Instruction

Use the Differentiated Instruction notes throughout the lesson plan to support the varied skill sets, levels of readiness, and interests in the mixed-ability classroom.

Challenge These notes include suggestions for expanding the activity for advanced students.

On-Level These notes include suggestions for modifying the activity to address different interests or learning styles.

Extra Support These notes include ideas for providing more scaffolding or reading spuport.

Special Needs These notes provide ideas for adapting instruction to support the needs of various special needs students.

■ NOTES

China and the West

Objectives

Objective 1: Describe how Westerners tried to gain trade rights in China.

Objective 2: Explain how reformers tried to strengthen China.

Objective 3: Understand why the Qing dynasty fell.

LESSON 5 ORGANIZER			PACING: APPROX. 1 PERIOD, .5 BLOCKS	
			RESOURCES	
	OBJECTIVES	**PACING**	**Online**	**Print**
Connect				
DIGITAL START UP ACTIVITY **Trading Opium for Tea**		5 min.	●	
Investigate				
DIGITAL TEXT 1 **Economic Interest in China**	Objective 1	10 min.	●	●
INTERACTIVE MAP **Imperialist Spheres of Influence in China**		10 min.	●	
DIGITAL TEXT 2 **The Taiping Rebellion and a Weakened China**	Objective 2	10 min.	●	●
DIGITAL TEXT 3 **Reform Efforts in China**		10 min.	●	●
DIGITAL TEXT 4 **The Fall of the Qing Dynasty**	Objective 3	10 min.	●	●
INTERACTIVE GALLERY **The Boxer Rebellion**		10 min.	●	
Synthesize				
DIGITAL ACTIVITY **The Decline of the Qing Dynasty**		5 min.	●	
Demonstrate				
LESSON QUIZ **Lesson Quiz and Class Discussion Board**		10 min.	●	

PEARSON
realize™
www.PearsonRealize.com

Go online to access additional resources including:
Primary Sources • Biographies • Supreme Court cases •
21st Century Skill Tutorials • Maps • Graphic Organizers.

CONNECT

DIGITAL START UP ACTIVITY
Trading Opium for Tea

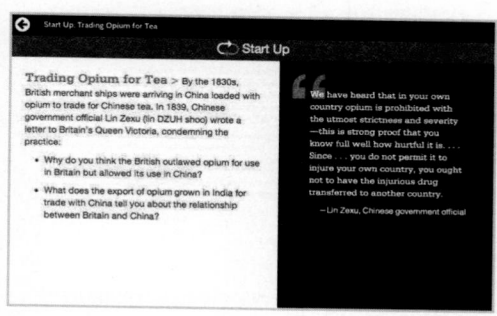

Project the Start Up Activity Ask students to read the quote and answer the question as they get settled.

Discuss What does the export of opium tell you about the relationship between Britain and China? *(Sample response: It shows that Britain did not respect the wishes of China's government or hoped to gain profits by sending a harmful good.)*

Make Predictions Have students predict the consequences of Britain ignoring the Chinese government's rejection of opium. *(Students may predict that China would stop the export of tea to Britain or that the countries would go to war.)*

Aa Vocabulary Development: Use the Interactive Reading Notepad to preview the Key Terms and Academic Vocabulary in this Lesson with students.

⚑ FLIP IT!

Assign the Flipped Video for this lesson.

▉ STUDENT EDITION PRINT
PAGES: 615–619

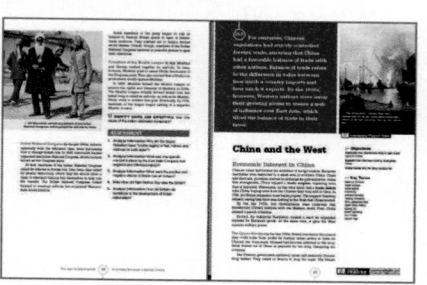

INVESTIGATE

DIGITAL TEXT 1
Economic Interest in China

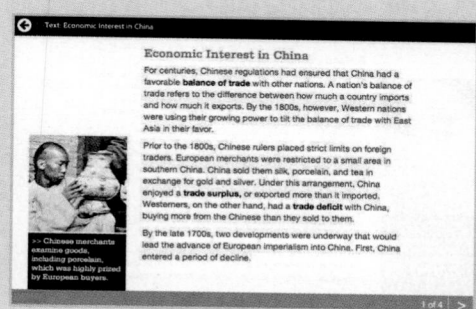

INTERACTIVE MAP
Imperialist Spheres of Influence in China

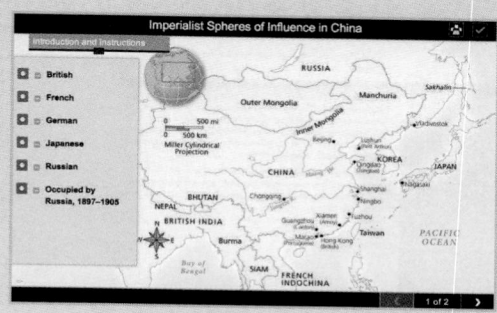

Objective 1: Describe how Westernizers tried to gain trade rights in China.

Quick Instruction

Remind students that China had long resisted trade with the outside world. Because of the country's size and resources, it had managed to be self-sufficient. European countries had economic motivations to gain control of China's resources, goods, and transportation routes.

Interactive Map: Imperialist Spheres of Influence in China Project the map of spheres of influence in China. Remind students that a sphere of influence is a form of imperialism in which an outside power claims exclusive investment or trade privileges in a location. Point out that several European countries and Japan wanted to use their holdings in China to gain economic advantage over one another.

▉▉ ACTIVE CLASSROOM

Project the map and use a whiteboard tool to divide the base layer map of China into four quadrants. Assign quadrants to groups of students. Have students research their regions of China, finding the resources that might have been attractive to imperial powers, and design a piece of Wallpaper about their region. Students can then take a gallery walk and note what others have written about or illustrated.

ELL Use the ELL activity described in the ELL chart.

Further Instruction

Editable Presentation Use the Editable Presentation to present the main ideas for this text.

Economic Interest in China: Core Text and Interactive Reading Notepad Project the Interactive Reading Notepad questions and go over the answers as a class. Use student responses to discuss the causes and effects of European imperialism in China.

Tell students that by the late 1700s, two developments led to the advance of European imperialism into China. First, China entered a period of decline. Second, the Industrial Revolution created a need for expanded markets for European goods and gave the West superior military power. In 1839, Chinese warships clashed with British merchants over the opium trade, triggering the Opium War. British gunboats, equipped with the latest in firepower, easily defeated the Chinese.

Infer The Industrial Revolution was both a motivator for British imperialism and a cause of British control over China. How did it affect China's history? *(Sample response: Because of the Industrial Revolution, Britain had economic motivations to increase its exports, but China did not want many British goods. This gave Britain motivation to exert control over China. Industrialization helped Britain achieve this because advanced military technologies led to an easy victory over China in the Opium War.)*

China and the West

DIGITAL TEXT 2

The Taiping Rebellion and a Weakened China

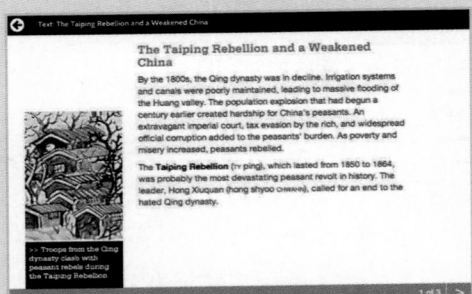

Text: The Taiping Rebellion and a Weakened China

The Taiping Rebellion and a Weakened China

By the 1800s, the Qing dynasty was in decline. Irrigation systems and canals were poorly maintained, leading to massive flooding of the Huang valley. The population explosion that had begun a century earlier created hardship for China's peasants. An extravagant imperial court, tax evasion by the rich, and widespread official corruption added to the peasants' burden. As poverty and misery increased, peasants rebelled.

The **Taiping Rebellion** (ty ping), which lasted from 1850 to 1864, was probably the most devastating peasant revolt in history. The leader, Hong Xiuquan (hong shyoo chwahn), called for an end to the hated Qing dynasty.

>> Troops from the Qing dynasty clash with peasant rebels during the Taiping Rebellion

1 of 3 >

DIGITAL TEXT 3

Reform Efforts in China

Text: Reform Efforts in China

Reform Efforts in China

By the mid-1800s, educated Chinese were divided over the need to adopt Western ways. Most saw no reason for new industries because China's wealth and taxes came from land. Although Chinese merchants were allowed to do business, they were not seen as a source of prosperity.

Scholar-officials also disapproved of the ideas of Western missionaries, whose emphasis on individual choice challenged the Confucian order. They saw Western technology as dangerous, too, because it threatened Confucian ways that had served China successfully for so long.

By the late 1800s, the empress Ci Xi (tsih shih) had gained power. A strong-willed ruler, she surrounded herself with advisors who were deeply committed to Confucian traditions.

Self-Strengthening Movement in the 1860s, reformers launched the "self-strengthening movement." They imported Western technology, setting up factories to make modern weapons.

>> Empress Ci Xi retired as ruler of China in 1889. However, after radical reforms made by the new emperor, her nephew Guang Xu, led to his imprisonment, she once again assumed power

DIGITAL TEXT 4

The Fall of the Qing Dynasty

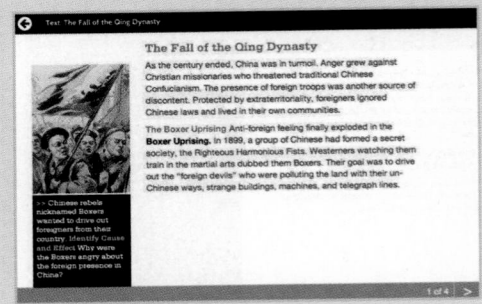

Text: The Fall of the Qing Dynasty

The Fall of the Qing Dynasty

As the century ended, China was in turmoil. Anger grew against Christian missionaries who threatened traditional Chinese Confucianism. The presence of foreign troops was another source of discontent. Protected by extraterritoriality, foreigners ignored Chinese laws and lived in their own communities.

The Boxer Uprising Anti-foreign feeling finally exploded in the **Boxer Uprising**. In 1899, a group of Chinese had formed a secret society, the Righteous Harmonious Fists. Westerners watching them train in the martial arts dubbed them Boxers. Their goal was to drive out the "foreign devils" who were polluting the land with their un-Chinese ways, strange buildings, machines, and telegraph lines.

>> Chinese rebels nicknamed Boxers wanted to drive out foreigners from their country. Identify Cause and Effect Why were the Boxers angry about the foreign presence in China?

1 of 4 >

Objective 2: Explain how reformers tried to strengthen China.

Quick Instruction

Point out that Confucian ideals had shaped Chinese government for approximately 2,000 years. In the 19th century, reformers started to place pressure on Chinese society to modernize by adopting Western technology, philosophies, and practices.

Generate Explanations Why was China so resistant to Western influence? How did European imperialism push China toward reform? *(Sample response: China's system had worked successfully for a very long time; the Chinese did not value new industry or merchants, and individualism and technology threatened Confucian philosophies. Losses in war against Japan and European countries pushed China toward reform, however.)*

ELL Use the ELL activity described in the ELL chart.

Further Instruction

Project the Interactive Reading Notepad questions and use student responses to discuss changes in China after foreign intervention.

Generalize How can interior conflicts such as the Taiping Rebellion make a country vulnerable to another? *(Sample answer: The government's military forces are unavailable to defend against outside attacks, officials are occupied handling discord, resources and funds are used to fix disputes, and destruction and loss of life weakens and separates a population.)*

Analyze a Political Cartoon Project the political cartoon showing guard dogs at the door labeled "China Trade." Read the caption to students. Ask students to explain the figure on the left (Uncle Sam); point out that the figure in the middle is labeled "Japan" and that the figure on the right represents Britain. Ask students to interpret the artist's message about these three countries' intentions toward China. *(Sample response: The artist is showing that these three countries valued Chinese trade so much that they made themselves guardians of its trade policies. Like guard dogs, they made sure that the door to China's exports and imports would always stay open to their countries' interests.)*

D Differentiate: Extra Support Organize students into pairs and ask them to create a timeline of the events in China covered in Digital Texts 2 and 3. They should skim headings for major events and identify dates. After students assemble their timelines, have them discuss possible cause-and-effect connections between the events.

Objective 3: Understand why the Qing dynasty fell.

Quick Instruction

Review with students the events that had already weakened China. Explain that the Boxer Rebellion was an uprising against foreign presence and influence in China. It was the result of many years of European intervention and control.

Interactive Gallery: The Boxer Rebellion Project the interactive gallery. Click through each image, reading the captions. Explain that foreign powers crushed the rebellion, and the defeat led to a spread of Chinese nationalism. This sentiment helped to topple the weakened Qing dynasty.

📷 ACTIVE CLASSROOM

Have students choose an image from the gallery and Make Headlines that capture the action pictured. Ask: If you were to write a headline for this topic that captured the most important aspect about this picture, what would that headline be? Pass your headline to a partner for them to review.

SYNTHESIZE

DEMONSTRATE

INTERACTIVE GALLERY
The Boxer Rebellion

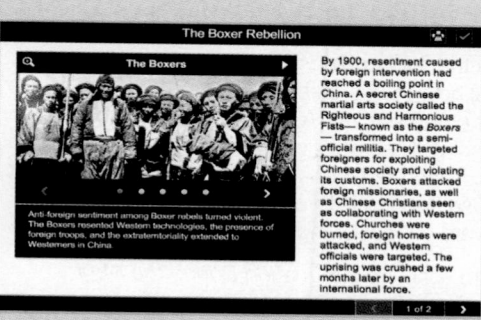

DIGITAL ACTIVITY
The Decline of the Qing Dynasty

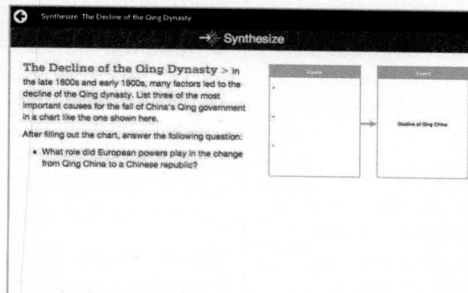

LESSON QUIZ
Lesson Quiz and Class Discussion Board

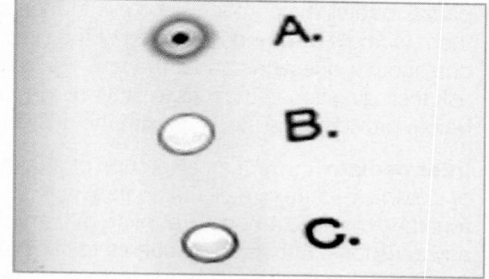

Further Instruction

Project the Interactive Reading Notepad questions and use student responses to discuss the events surrounding the fall of the Qing dynasty.

Identify Cause and Effect How was the Boxer Rebellion an effect of European imperialism? *(The Chinese were rebelling against the effects of European imperialism, including opium addiction, the influence of Christian missionaries, extraterritoriality, foreign control of economic life, and the presence of foreign troops.)*

Apply Concepts How did nationalism contribute to the political revolution that overthrew the Qing dynasty? *(Sample answer: The Qing dynasty had grown increasingly weak, and the Chinese had repeatedly been embarrassed by losses to foreign powers. Nationalists saw the backwards-looking dynasty as a hindrance to modern Chinese identity, unity, and power.)*

Remind students that most of the events discussed in this lesson caused the fall of the Qing dynasty. Project the Graphic Organizer and help students complete it.

Classify The Qing dynasty fell due to both internal and external forces. Classify the causes mentioned in the text as external forces (caused by European or Japanese actions or influence), internal forces (caused by situations within Qing China), or both. Provide an explanation for your classifications. *(Sample responses: The Opium War: both, as Chinese addiction to opium weakened the country economically, and defeat by the British led to loss of territory. The Taiping Rebellion: internal, as the internal rebellion weakened China through death and destruction. The Sino-Japanese War: external, as it led to other countries gaining power within China. Westernization: both, as conflicts with outsiders led to internal rebellions such as the Boxer Uprising. Nationalism: internal, as it led to a call for a republic and chaos caused by placing two-year-old on the throne.)*

Assign the online Lesson Quiz for this lesson if you haven't already done so. Students will be offered automatic remediation or enrichment based on their score.

In this lesson, you have read about the impact of Western imperialism on China and the internal conflicts that led to the fall of the Qing dynasty. Pose this question to the class on the Discussion Board.

Identify Cause and Effect How did European imperialism indirectly cause the fall of the Qing dynasty? *(Sample response: Pressure from wars and foreign control of land weakened the Qing government. The presence of foreigners raised nationalist sympathies among the Chinese, helping to strengthen support for a republic.)*

Topic Inquiry

Have students continue their investigations for the Topic Inquiry.

The Modernization of Japan

Supporting English Language Learners

Use with Digital Text 2, **The Opening of Japan.**

Reading
Read *The Opening of Japan* aloud to students. Instruct students to complete one of the following activities based on their level of English proficiency.

Beginning Reread *The Opening of Japan* aloud to students. As you read, pause to retell the content. Then ask students questions that encourage them to show their understanding of the text. Show students how to ask one another questions about the text. Pause in order to allow students to ask their questions. Encourage other students to answer the questions before providing the students with the answers.

Intermediate Instruct small groups of students to reread *The Opening of Japan* aloud then retell the content in their own words. As they work together, circulate among groups to offer reading support and answer any questions. Encourage students to tell one another when they have questions. Instruct students to pause while reading in order to allow students to ask their questions. Work together with students to find answers to the questions that are asked.

Advanced Invite pairs of students to reread *The Opening of Japan* aloud. As they read, encourage students to ask their partner to stop reading in order for them to ask their questions. Encourage partners to try to answer the questions before asking for teacher support. Tell students to share their most difficult questions with the group.

Advanced High Instruct pairs of students to retell *The Opening of Japan* in their own words. As they retell the content, encourage students discuss the content with their partners in order to elaborate on the text. Tell students to ask both partners and the teacher any questions they have about the topic. Encourage partners to share their questions and answers with their classmates. Students can discuss any especially challenging questions with the group.

Use with Digital Text 3, **Transformation During the Meiji Period.**

Reading
Good readers think about what they are about to read before they begin reading. Often, readers will make predictions by examining the headings and images in a section of text. Have students complete one activity according to their level of English proficiency before reading *Transformation During the Meiji Period*.

Beginning Write and display the subheadings for the text *Transformation During the Meiji Period*. Model how to use these subheadings to make predictions about the content of the section. Ask students to try to make predictions, too. Write and display the predictions and have students copy them in their notebooks. Then read Transformation During the Meiji Period aloud to students. Pause frequently to assess whether or not the predictions that were made were correct or incorrect.

Intermediate Ask students to scan *Transformation During the Meiji Period* and identify its subheadings. Then write and display these subheadings and ask students to copy them into their notebooks. Guide students in a discussion to demonstrate how to use the subheadings to make predictions about the content of the section. Involve students in the process, too, by asking them to make their own predictions. Write and display the predictions and have students copy them in their notebooks. Then read Transformation During the Meiji Period aloud to students. Pause frequently to help students assess whether or not the predictions that were made were correct or incorrect.

Advanced Ask small groups of students to scan *Transformation During the Meiji Period* and identify its subheadings. Instruct them to write these subheadings in their notebooks. Have students discuss how to use the subheadings to make predictions about each subsection. Ask each group to make their own predictions about the text and write them in their notebooks. Then have each small group read Transformation During the Meiji Period aloud. Have students pause frequently to assess whether or not the predictions that were made were correct or incorrect.

Advanced High Ask pairs of students to scan *Transformation During the Meiji Period* and identify its subheadings. Instruct them to write these subheadings in their notebooks. Have students discuss how to use the subheadings to make predictions about each subsection. Ask each pair to make predictions about the text and write them in their notebooks. Then instruct students to read Transformation During the Meiji Period silently. After reading, pairs should assess whether or not the predictions that were made were correct or incorrect.

D Differentiate Instruction

Use the Differentiated Instruction notes throughout the lesson plan to support the varied skill sets, levels of readiness, and interests in the mixed-ability classroom.

Challenge These notes include suggestions for expanding the activity for advanced students.

On-Level These notes include suggestions for modifying the activity to address different interests or learning styles.

Extra Support These notes include ideas for providing more scaffolding or reading spuport.

Special Needs These notes provide ideas for adapting instruction to support the needs of various special needs students.

NOTES

PEARSON
realize™
www.PearsonRealize.com

Go online to access additional resources including:
Primary Sources • Biographies • Supreme Court cases •
21st Century Skill Tutorials • Maps • Graphic Organizers.

Objectives

Objective 1: Identify the problems faced by Tokugawa Japan.

Objective 2: Explain how the United States opened Japan to the outside world.

Objective 3: Analyze the causes and effects of the Meiji Restoration.

Objective 4: Describe how Japan began to build an empire.

LESSON 6 ORGANIZER		PACING: APPROX. 1 PERIOD, .5 BLOCKS			
				RESOURCES	
		OBJECTIVES	**PACING**	**Online**	**Print**
Connect					
DIGITAL START UP ACTIVITY **Adopting Western Ways**			5 min.	●	
Investigate					
DIGITAL TEXT 1 **Unrest in Tokugawa Japan**		Objective 1	10 min.	●	●
DIGITAL TEXT 2 **The Opening of Japan**		Objective 2	10 min.	●	●
INTERACTIVE IMAGE **Commodore Perry's Expedition to Japan**			10 min.	●	
DIGITAL TEXT 3 **Transformation during the Meiji Period**		Objective 3	10 min.	●	●
INTERACTIVE GALLERY **The Meiji Restoration, 1868–1912**			10 min.	●	
DIGITAL TEXT 4 **Japan Builds an Empire**		Objective 4	10 min.	●	●
Synthesize					
DIGITAL ACTIVITY **The Meiji Restoration**			5 min.	●	
Demonstrate					
DIGITAL QUIZ **Lesson Quiz and Class Discussion Board**			10 min.	●	

The Modernization of Japan

■ CONNECT

DIGITAL START UP ACTIVITY
Adopting Western Ways

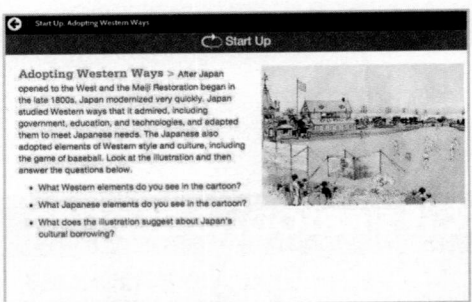

Project the Start Up Activity Ask students to answer the questions as they enter and get settled. Then have them share their ideas with another student.

Analyze Images What Western elements do you see in the image? *(Sample answer: A game similar to baseball is being played. Male spectators wear Western-style clothes.)* What Japanese elements do you see in the image? *(women dressed in kimonos)* What does the illustration suggest about Japan's cultural borrowing? *(Japan adopted the elements of Western culture that it wanted.)*

Tell students that in this lesson they will learn how Japan adapted elements of Western culture to transform itself into a modern industrial and imperialist power.

Aa Vocabulary Development: Use the Interactive Reading Notepad to preview the Key Terms and Academic Vocabulary in this Lesson with students.

⇅ FLIP IT!
Assign the Flipped Video for this lesson.

■ STUDENT EDITION PRINT PAGES: 620–625

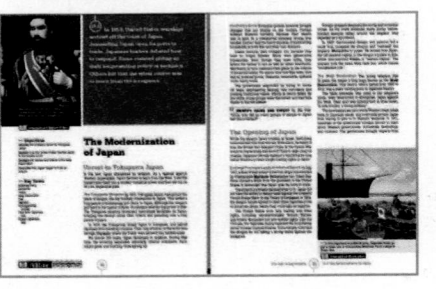

■ INVESTIGATE

DIGITAL TEXT 1
Unrest in Tokugawa Japan

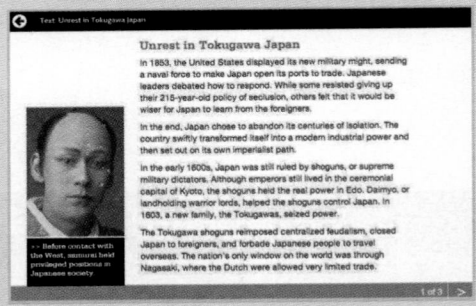

Objective 1: Identify the problems faced by Tokugawa Japan.

Quick Instruction

In the early 1600s, Japan was still ruled by shoguns. In 1603, the Tokugawas took power and brought back centralized feudalism and closed Japan to foreigners. No foreign travel was allowed. For more than 200 years, Japan developed in isolation. Unrest grew among many Japanese as they suffered from financial hardship, no political power, and heavy taxes. The government tried to revive old ways, emphasizing farming over commerce. The shoguns were no longer strong leaders, corruption was common, and the people of Japan were discontented.

Analyze Images Direct students' attention to the photo of the last Tokugawa shogun from the text. Is that what you expect a shogun to look like? Why or why not? *(Answers will vary. Students might say they expected the shogun to look stronger or more militaristic.)*

Generate Explanations How had Japan changed by the time Tokugawa Yoshinobu came to power? *(Japan had developed in virtual isolation and was experiencing internal unrest.)*

Analyze Information Was Tokugawa Japan as completely isolated from the rest of the world as it claimed? Why or why not? *(No, Japan was not completely isolated because it maintained a trading post with the Dutch at Nagasaki.)*

Further Instruction

Editable Presentation Use the Editable Presentation to present the main ideas for this Core Text.

Unrest in Tokugawa Japan: Core Text and Interactive Reading Notepad Project and discuss the Interactive Reading Notepad questions. Project the text describing samurai and the image of samurai, and ask students to compare and contrast the content presented by the two sources. Discuss the information they could draw from each source. *(Answers may vary, but students might mention that both text and illustration represent the emphasis on Japanese tradition of the time period. The photograph shows Samurai using weapons and armor that could have been used in centuries past. They do not look like items imported from the West. The text explains why traditions began to stifle the Japanese.)*

Cite Evidence Identify the pressures faced by the different levels of society in Tokugawa Japan. *(financial hardships of daimyo and lesser samurai; merchants had no political power; peasants were heavily taxed; failure of Tokugawa reform efforts, weakening of shogun's power)*

DIGITAL TEXT 2

The Opening of Japan

INTERACTIVE IMAGE

Commodore Perry's Expedition to Japan

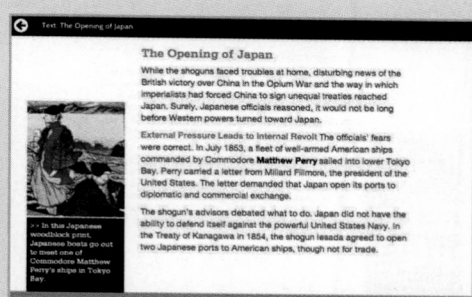

Objective 2: Explain how the United States opened Japan to the outside world.

Quick Instruction

In 1853, a fleet of well-armed U.S. ships led by Commodore Matthew Perry arrived in Japan. Perry demanded that Japan open its ports. Unable to defend itself, Japan was forced to sign treaties giving the United States trading and other rights. Humiliated by the terms of these unequal treaties, discontented daimyo and samurai led a revolt that unseated the shogun and placed the emperor Mutsuhito in power. Mutsuhito began a long reign known as the Meiji Restoration, during which Japan studied Western ways and adapted them to suit Japanese needs.

Interactive Image: Commodore Perry's Expedition to Japan Project the Interactive Image of one of Commodore Perry's warships. Select hotspots on the picture to learn more about the Japanese perspective on Perry's arrival.

📷 ACTIVE CLASSROOM

Have students work with partners and ask pairs to have a Conversation with History between Commodore Perry and a Meiji leader such as Iwakura Tomomi. Have one person in each pair assume the role of Perry, and the other the role of a Meiji leader. Tell them to record the details of their conversation. *(Students' details will vary but should include information from the gallery. They might mention things like aspects of the ship, weapons, or gifts exchanged.)*

D **Differentiate: On-Level** When Commodore Matthew Perry arrived in Japan in July 1853, the Japanese shogun was unsure how to respond, so he sought the recommendations of his advisers. Ask students to conduct further research on Commodore Perry's arrival in Japan. Students should pay attention to the shogun's decision and the factors he had to consider in making it. Then have students re-create a meeting of the shogun and his advisors concerning Perry's arrival. Divide the class into three groups for the discussion: one group will argue for cooperation, one for resistance, and one will represent the shogun and remain undecided. Allow students time to prepare arguments for their position and questions for the other positions, then commence the meeting of the shogun's council.

ELL Use the ELL activity described in the ELL chart.

Further Instruction

Editable Presentation Use the Editable Presentation to present the main ideas for this Core Text.

The Opening of Japan: Core Text and Interactive Reading Notepad Go through the Interactive Reading Notepad questions and discuss the answers with the class.

Draw Conclusions The Japanese adapted many Western ways to the needs of Japan. Why was that important to them? *(By adapting Western ways to Japanese needs, the Japanese could preserve their traditions and retain their identity while still developing as a strong nation.)*

Summarize What caused Japan to end more than 200 years of seclusion? *(a request to open their country to trade, backed up by a display of military power by the United States, along with unrest in the country)*

The Modernization of Japan

DIGITAL TEXT 3

Transformation during the Meiji Period

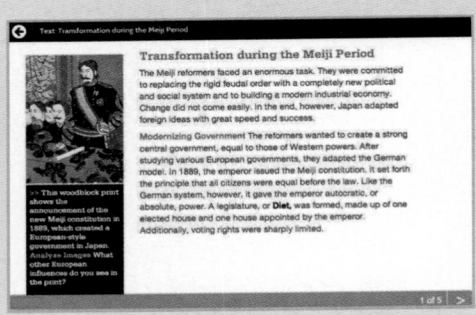

INTERACTIVE GALLERY

The Meiji Restoration, 1868–1912

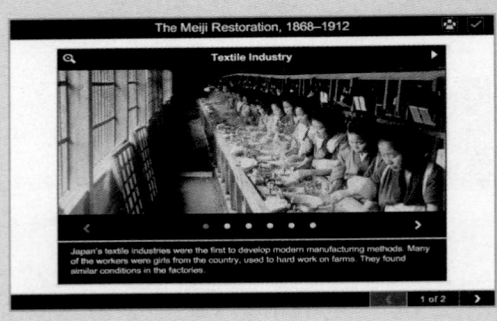

DIGITAL TEXT 4

Japan Builds an Empire

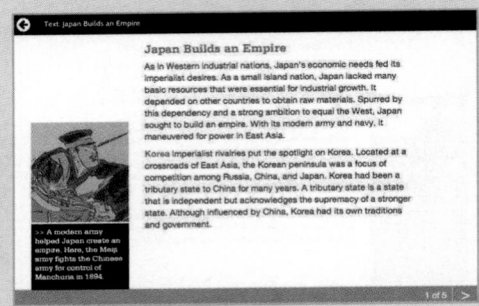

Objective 3: Analyze the causes and effects of the Meiji Restoration.

Quick Instruction

Meiji reformers wanted to create a new political and social system and build a modern industrial economy. The Meiji constitution gave all citizens equality before the law. A legislature, or Diet, was formed, but the emperor held absolute power. With government support, powerful banking and industrial families, known as zaibatsu, soon ruled over their own industrial empires. By the 1890s, industry was booming. Japan modernized with amazing speed and was soon ready to start building its own empire.

Interactive Gallery: The Meiji Restoration, 1868–1912 Project the images showing the modernization of Japan during the Meiji period.

Analyze Images Have students look at the first image in the gallery of a textile factory during the Meiji period. What were the working conditions like for the girls working there? *(Sample answer: Working conditions were difficult as they were in farm life.)*

Categorize Which Meiji reformations contributed the most to Japan's becoming an imperial power? *(Students will likely cite the formation of a national army, industrialization, and the building of railroads.)*

📷 ACTIVE CLASSROOM

Use the Quick Write strategy with students after they review the Image Gallery. Have students share what they now know about the Meiji Restoration. Give them 30 seconds to 1 minute. Challenge them to keep their responses to 140 characters.

ELL Use the ELL activity described in the ELL chart.

Further Instruction

Editable Presentation Use the Editable Presentation to present the main ideas for this Core Text.

Transformation during the Meiji Period: Core Text and Interactive Reading Notepad Go through the Interactive Reading Notepad questions and discuss the answers with the class.

Identify During the Meiji period, Japan's businesses adopted Western methods. Have students list some of the new methods and identify why they were important. *(created modern banking system: allowed saving, lending, and borrowing; built railroads: allowed resources and merchandise to move more quickly around the country; improved ports: increased the ability to ship goods and import goods from other countries; created telegraph and postal system: improved communication)*

Draw Conclusions Part of Japan's success at modernization was due to the fact that it had a homogeneous society. Why was this a factor? *(The Japanese people shared a common language and common culture and therefore had fewer clashes and disruptions during the modernization process.)*

Interpret The motto of the Meiji reformers was "A rich country, a strong military." What do you think was the basis for this motto? *(Japan was humiliated and bitter about the unequal terms of the trade treaties it had to agree to with the United States and European nations. It also did not have a strong enough military to respond to the strength of these nations. Japanese leaders were determined to reverse both of these elements.)*

Objective 4: Describe how Japan began to build an empire.

Quick Instruction

As a small island nation, Japan lacked many resources essential for industry. The need for natural resources and a strong ambition to equal Western imperial nations spurred Japan to build an empire. In 1876, Japan forced Korea to open its ports to Japanese trade. In 1894, competition between Japan and China in Korea led to the First Sino-Japanese War, which Japan easily won. Japan gained ports in China, won control of Taiwan, and joined the West in the race for an empire. Ten years later, Japan defeated Russia in the Russo-Japanese War. By the early 1900s, Japan was the strongest power in Asia.

Analyze Political Cartoons Project the political cartoon and have students answer the question in the caption. Then ask: What was the artist's point of view about Japan? Which details support your conclusion? *(Sample response: The artist disapproved of Japan's actions, as shown by the depiction of Japan as stepping on Korea with a hard expression while Korea and China look shocked.)*

Further Instruction

Editable Presentation Use the Editable Presentation to present the main ideas for this Core Text.

Japan Builds an Empire: Core Text and Interactive Reading Notepad Go through the Interactive Reading Notepad questions and discuss the answers with the class.

Discuss Why did Japan seek greater influence in Korea? *(Japan wanted to create an empire equal to those of Western powers and to gain natural resources.)* How did Japan assert its power in the region? *(through armed warfare, defeating its rivals in the Sino-Japanese War and the Russo-Japanese War)*

Analyze Information How did Korea both benefit and suffer under Japanese rule? *(Korea benefited from the factories, railroads, and communication systems the Japanese built, but the Japanese controlled most of it. Rice production increased dramatically, but most of it went to Japan. Koreans suffered because the Japanese imposed harsh rule and tried to erase the Korean language and national identity.)*

Generate Explanations Why was control of Korea desirable to both China and Japan? *(Korea's location made it a major crossroads for all of East Asia.)*

SYNTHESIZE

The Meiji Restoration

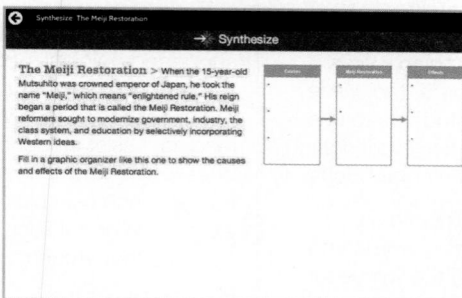

Have students fill in the graphic organizer to show the causes, events, and effects of the Meiji Restoration. *(Causes: Social and economic unrest, foreign pressure, daimyo and samurai revolt; Meiji Restoration: strong central government, businesses adopt Western methods, leaders encourage industrialization, social changes lead to nation building, Effects: builds an empire; extends influence in Korea, conflict with China, defeats Russia)*

Support a Point of View with Evidence Was the Meiji Restoration an example of "enlightened rule"? Why or why not? *(Students might say that the Meiji Restoration was enlightened because of the dramatic changes it brought to Japan; others might say it was not enlightened because Japan copied what had already been done in the West.)*

DEMONSTRATE

Lesson Quiz and Class Discussion Board

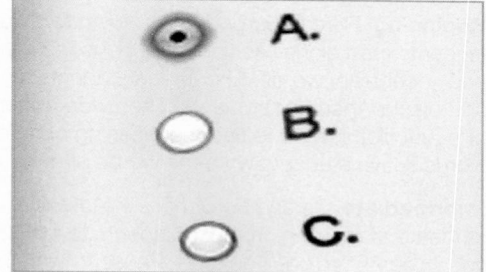

Assign the online Lesson Quiz for this lesson if you haven't already done so. Students will be offered automatic remediation or enrichment based on their score.

Pose these questions to the class on the Discussion Board.

In "The Modernization of Japan" you read about how feudal, isolated Japan modernized to become an industrial and imperialist power.

Summarize How did Japan change course in the late 1800s? *(Japan went from isolation and a rigid feudal order to a modern industrial economy and new political and social system, with a central government and a democratic constitution.)*

Identify Cause and Effect By the 1890s, how had the more modernized Japan changed its relationship with the West? *(In 1853, the United States forced Japan from its isolation; by the 1890s, Japan had become more powerful and started acquiring its own empire and revising unequal treaties.)*

Topic Inquiry

Have students continue their investigations for the Topic Inquiry.

Southeast Asia and the Pacific

Supporting English Language Learners

Use with Digital Texts 4 and 5, **Europeans in Australia.**

Reading
Read *Europeans in Australia* aloud to students. Instruct students to complete one of the following activities based on their level of English proficiency.

Beginning Reread *Europeans in Australia* aloud to students and as students read along. As you read, pause to identify challenging words and vocabulary words. Encourage students to identify words, too. Write and display them for students. Then work together with students to use bilingual dictionaries to find the meaning of no more than five challenging words. Have students write the words and meanings in their notebooks.

Intermediate Reread *Europeans in Australia* aloud to students as students read along. Instruct students to identify challenging words and vocabulary words as you read. Pause to write and display the words for students. Then work together with students to use dictionaries to find the meaning of no more than five challenging words. Have students write the words and meanings in their notebooks.

Advanced Have small groups of students reread *Europeans in Australia* aloud. Instruct students to identify challenging words and vocabulary words as they read. Tell them to pause to write the words in their notebooks. Then small groups should use dictionaries and other classroom resources to find the meaning of each word. Have students write the meaning for each word in their notebooks.

Advanced High Have pairs of students reread *Europeans in Australia* aloud. Instruct students to identify challenging words and vocabulary words as they read. Tell them to pause to write the words in their notebooks. Then pairs should use dictionaries and other classroom resources to find the meaning of each word. Have students write the meaning for each word in their notebooks.

Use with Digital Text 2, **Military Might and the Philippines.**

Reading
Read Military Might and the Philippines aloud to students. Then have students complete one of the following activities according to their language proficiency.

Beginning Tell students that it is critical for them to evaluate (develop supported opinions about) what they read and learn. Ask them to listen as you retell *Military Might and the Philippines* and think about their opinion of the actions of the United States after the Spanish-American War. After reading, assist students in expressing their opinions by asking guiding questions and writing and displaying students' responses. Use sentences frames, such as, I believe _____., to support students' formation and expression of opinions. Model how to use textual evidence to support opinions that students share.

Intermediate Tell students that it is critical for them to evaluate (develop supported opinions about) what they read and learn. Ask them to listen as you retell *Military Might and the Philippines* and think about their evaluation of the actions of the United States after the Spanish-American War. After reading, instruct students to express their evaluations. Write and display these for students to examine as a group. Discuss each evaluation in turn with the class and model how to use textual evidence to support ideas that students share. Encourage students to do the same.

Advanced Lead students in a discussion of the importance of formulating evaluations of what they read and learn. Then instruct pairs of students to reread *Military Might and the Philippines* and think about their evaluation of the actions of the United States after the Spanish-American War. After reading, instruct students to share their evaluations with their partner. Have pairs discuss each evaluation and identify textual evidence to support their ideas. Finally, have pairs share their evaluations and evidence with their classmates.

Advanced High Facilitate a discussion of the importance of formulating evaluations of what they read and learn. Then instruct students to reread *Military Might and the Philippines* independently and think about their evaluation of the actions of the United States after the Spanish-American War. After reading, instruct students to write a paragraph to explain their evaluation. Remind students to identify textual evidence to support their ideas. Finally, have students share their paragraphs with their classmates.

▣ Differentiate Instruction

Use the Differentiated Instruction notes throughout the lesson plan to support the varied skill sets, levels of readiness, and interests in the mixed-ability classroom.

Challenge These notes include suggestions for expanding the activity for advanced students.

On-Level These notes include suggestions for modifying the activity to address different interests or learning styles.

Extra Support These notes include ideas for providing more scaffolding or reading spuport.

Special Needs These notes provide ideas for adapting instruction to support the needs of various special needs students.

■ NOTES

Objectives

Objective 1: Describe how Europe and the United States built colonies in Southeast Asia.

Objective 2: Explain how imperialism spread to the islands of the Pacific.

Objective 3: Analyze how Australia and New Zealand achieved self-rule.

LESSON 7 ORGANIZER		PACING: APPROX. 1 PERIOD, .5 BLOCKS			
				RESOURCES	
		OBJECTIVES	**PACING**	**Online**	**Print**
Connect					
DIGITAL START UP ACTIVITY **Europeans in Southeast Asia**			5 min.	●	
Investigate					
DIGITAL TEXT 1 **European Imperialism in Southeast Asia**			10 min.	●	●
DIGITAL TEXT 2 **Military Might and the Philippines**		Objective 1	10 min.	●	
INTERACTIVE MAP **Imperialism in Southeast Asia, 1900**			10 min.	●	
DIGITAL TEXT 3 **Strategic Holdings in the Pacific Islands**		Objective 2	10 min.	●	●
DIGITAL TEXT 4 **Europeans in Australia**			10 min.	●	●
DIGITAL TEXT 5 **New Zealand's Story**		Objective 3	10 min.	●	
INTERACTIVE CHART **Colonization of Australia and New Zealand**			10 min.	●	
Synthesize					
DIGITAL ACTIVITY **The United States and the Philippines**			5 min.	●	
Demonstrate					
DIGITAL QUIZ **Lesson Quiz and Class Discussion Board**			10 min.	●	

Southeast Asia and the Pacific

◼ CONNECT

DIGITAL START UP ACTIVITY
Europeans in Southeast Asia

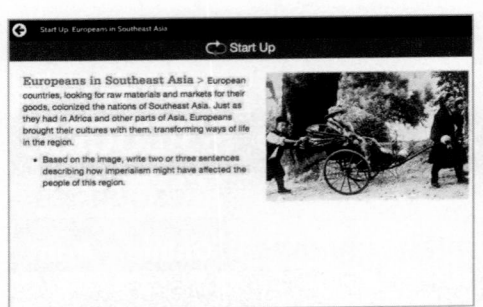

Project the Start Up Activity Ask students to look at the image and answer the questions as they enter and get settled.

Identify Cause and Effect Based on the image, write two or three sentences describing how imperialism might have affected the people of this region. *(Answers will vary. Students might say that the colonized peoples of Southeast Asia had to serve the Europeans. These people did the manual labor for industries that benefited Europeans, and the Europeans grew wealthy.)*

Connect How does the image connect to your knowledge of Westerners' role in other regions, such as Africa or India? *(Students should draw a connection to Westerners' dominant economic, political, and cultural roles in colonized lands.)*

Aa Vocabulary Development: Use the Interactive Reading Notepad to preview the Key Terms and Academic Vocabulary in this Lesson with students.

⇅ FLIP IT!
Assign the Flipped Video for this lesson.

◼ STUDENT EDITION PRINT PAGES: 626–631

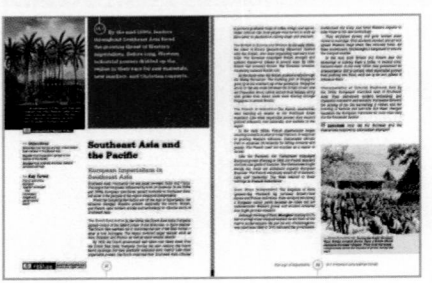

◼ INVESTIGATE

DIGITAL TEXT 1
European Imperialism in Southeast Asia

Objective 1: Describe how Europe and the United States built colonies in Southeast Asia.

Quick Instruction

Remind students that imperialism involves economic, political, and cultural control of a region or country by another country. Point out that imperialism is caused by the ruling country pursuing economic, political, and/or social gains. The nations of Southeast Asia were especially attractive to European rulers because of their rich natural resources, which were even easier to access after the opening of the Suez Canal in 1860.

Interactive Map: Imperialism in Southeast Asia, 1900 Display the Interactive Map and click on the different layers, identifying the Western countries that held control in Southeast Asia. Name some of the modern-day countries that fall under this territory, such as Vietnam (French Indochina), Malaysia (Malaya), and Indonesia (the Dutch East Indies).

DIGITAL TEXT 2
Military Might and the Philippines

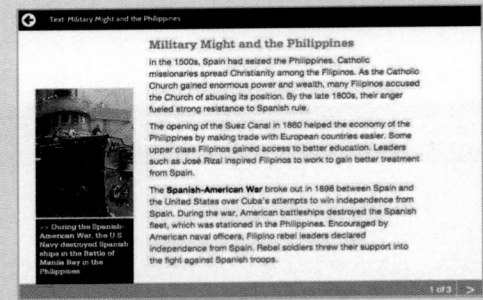

👥 ACTIVE CLASSROOM

Have student pairs do an Audio Tour of the map. Have the first student give the second a verbal "tour" of the map, pointing out the information communicated through the layers. Have the second student give the first an explanation of the map's purpose.

ELL Use the ELL activity described in the ELL chart.

INTERACTIVE MAP

Imperialism in Southeast Asia, 1900

DIGITAL TEXT 3

Strategic Holdings in the Pacific Islands

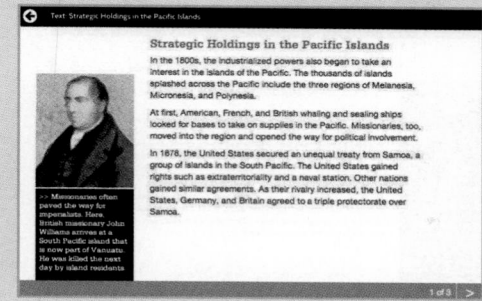

Further Instruction

Editable Presentation Use the Editable Presentation to present the main ideas for these texts.

Project the Interactive Reading Notepad questions and use student responses to discuss the causes of Western imperialism in Southeast Asia. Economic motivations for Western imperialism included access to natural resources, new markets and transportation hubs, and a cheap labor force; political motivations included access to tactical military locations; social motivations included the desire to convert native populations to Christianity.

Classify Give examples from the Text of causes for Western imperialism in Southeast Asia. Classify the examples as political, economic, or social motivations. *(Sample answer: Economic: The Dutch profited from coffee, indigo, and spices from the Dutch East Indies; the British benefited from Singapore's port. Social: France supported Catholic missionaries in their work to spread Christianity in French Indochina, as did Spain in the Philippines; Political: The United States took over the Philippines after defeating Spain in the Spanish-American War.)*

D Differentiate: Extra Support Students may need further explanation of political, economic, and social motivations. Explain that two countries can clash over reasons that fall into one of the categories. A political conflict could involve the location of a border, for example. An economic conflict could involve trade restrictions one country places on another. A social conflict could refer to religious or ethnic disputes.

Objective 2: Explain how imperialism spread to the islands of the Pacific.

Quick Instruction

Explain that the Philippines and the small islands of the Pacific had strategic benefits for the United States, allowing expansion of an American military presence, with the islands serving as military bases. Even if the islands did not produce large amounts of natural resources, their role as transportation, whaling, and sealing bases also provided economic motivation for Western control. And, as in Southeast Asia, Christian missionaries wished to minister to island populations.

Analyze Images Project the image of British missionary John Williams arriving at a South Pacific island from the Text. Tell students the title of the painting: *The Return of the Rev. John Williams at Tanna in the South Seas, the Day Before He Was Massacred.* Ask students to interpret what Williams's posture and appearance say about his motives. *(Sample response: He seems to have grand plans for helping the people of the island. He is approaching them as if he is their leader.)* How do the islanders in the image seem to receive him? *(Sample response: They seem to accept his arrival, though they are not doing anything especially welcoming. They do not seem to view him as an immediate threat.)* As the title of the painting reveals, the people of the island killed Williams. Ask: what conclusions can you draw about Christian missionaries and these faraway cultures? *(Sample response: Some*

people of the South Pacific may have viewed missionaries as either threatening or insulting. Williams may have approached the people's culture in an offensive way, or the people may have viewed outside interference in their lives as sinister. Either way, some missionaries were not welcomed.)

Further Instruction

Project the Interactive Reading Notepad questions, and use student responses to discuss the causes of Western imperialism's spread to the Pacific Islands. Review the details of the opening of the Suez Canal and point out that additional sea routes to Asia aided and motivated imperialist governments' maneuvers for control in the Pacific.

Remind students that the United States destroyed the Spanish fleet that was stationed in the Philippines during the Spanish-American War and took control of the Philippines. Discuss with students the role of the U.S. military and transportation technologies in initiating and advancing imperialist goals.

Draw Conclusions How would advanced military and transportation technologies help extend the United States' reach in the Pacific? *(Sample response: The small islands of the Pacific, including Hawaii, would not have the means to defend against or resist the American military. The Pacific islands are spread over a vast area, far from other nations, so the United States would have needed reliable transportation methods to reach and rule over the people there.)*

Southeast Asia and the Pacific

DIGITAL TEXT 4
Europeans in Australia

DIGITAL TEXT 5
New Zealand's Story

INTERACTIVE CHART
Colonization of Australia and New Zealand

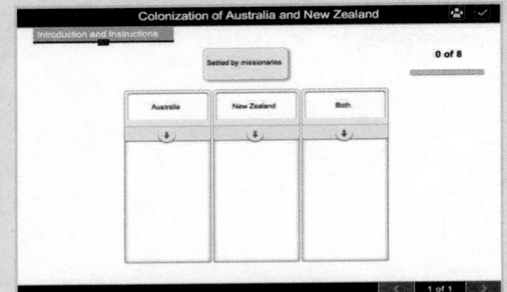

Objective 3: Analyze how Australia and New Zealand achieved self-rule.

Quick Instruction

European colonization of Australia and New Zealand eventually led to the creation of self-ruled nations with strong ties to Britain. The stories of Australia and New Zealand differs from that of Southeast Asian countries because they developed into nations with large English-speaking populations with European ancestry. By the time that these countries had gained independence from Britain, their indigenous populations were minorities.

Interactive Chart: Colonization of Australia and New Zealand Display the Interactive Chart and explain to students that they will work with a partner to drag and drop the characteristics of colonization to the correct nation. There is one characteristic that applies to both nations.

👥 ACTIVE CLASSROOM

Consider posting the text from the Interactive Chart in different parts of the room to create a Walking Tour of the activity. Partners can visit each country's passage, discussing and summarizing it before investigating another.

ELL Use the ELL activity described in the ELL chart.

Further Instruction

Project the Interactive Reading Notepad questions and go over the answers as a class. Use student responses to compare and contrast the road from colonization to self-rule in Australia and New Zealand.

Analyze Information Britain was responsive to Australian self-rule because it feared the interference of other European powers. Analyze the economic motivations for imperialism in Australia and New Zealand against the difficulties of maintaining power over these lands. *(Sample response: Britain benefited from wool, wheat, beef, and other farm products by keeping control of the land. Because of the distance between Britain and Australia and New Zealand, however, transportation, military, and administrative costs might not have been worth the trouble. Governing people so far away would have been difficult, especially in the case of Australia, where Europeans had settled all over a vast continent.)*

■ SYNTHESIZE

DIGITAL ACTIVITY
The United States and the Philippines

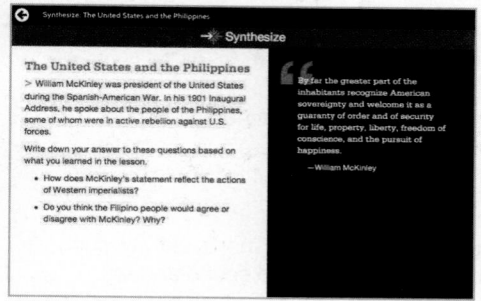

Remind students of the benefits Europeans and Americans derived from their imperialist holdings in Southeast Asia. These economic, political, and social benefits served as powerful motivators for initiating and advancing their power in the region. Though the new rulers made improvements in areas like infrastructure and education, the effects of imperialism on native populations was not always positive.

Display the Synthesize screen and review the questions. Have students cite examples from the text to answer the first question. To answer the second question, have students recall the hopes of Filipino rebels after the Spanish-American War.

Discuss Have students discuss how a justification like McKinley's could have prompted the general rise of imperialism. *(Answers will vary. Students may interpret the quote as well meaning, with leaders such as McKinley truly thinking they were helping by stepping in with a strong government and organization. Students may also note that imperialists with such attitudes reflected Social Darwinism and felt that the people in other lands were weak and in need of their leadership.)*

■ DEMONSTRATE

LESSON QUIZ
Lesson Quiz and Class Discussion Board

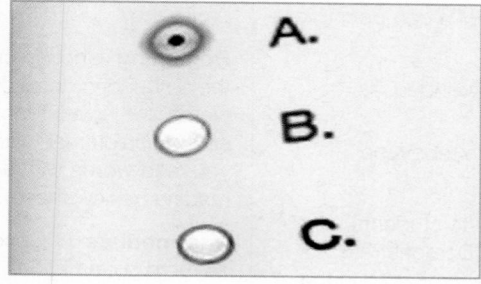

Assign the online Lesson Quiz for this lesson if you haven't already done so. Students will be offered automatic remediation or enrichment based on their score.

In this lesson you have read about European and American imperialism in the nations of Southeast Asia, the Pacific Islands, Australia, and New Zealand. Pose the question below to the class on the Discussion Board.

Generate Explanations Of the countries mentioned in this lesson, only Siam remained independent in this time period. How did Siam resist European imperialism and thrive? *(The king of Siam understood the Western countries. Instead of rebelling, he was willing to sign unequal treaties in order to avoid European control. At the same time, he modernized his country, which allowed his government to slowly do away with the unequal treaties.)*

Topic Inquiry
Have students continue their investigations for the Topic Inquiry.

The Americas in the Age of Imperialism

Supporting English Language Learners

Use with Digital Text 2, **Mexico's Search for Stability.**

Reading

Read *Mexico's Search for Stability* aloud to students. Instruct students to complete one of the following activities based on their level of English proficiency. When helping students to find an example of a compound sentence, use the following examples from the text:

- Still, Juárez was elected president in 1861 and he expanded his reforms.
- Wages remained low, and workers were rarely able to repay the hacienda owner.

Beginning Reread *Mexico's Search for Stability* aloud to students. Identify a compound sentence in the text for students. Demonstrate how to identify the independent clauses and the connecting word in the sentence. Then repeat the process with a complex sentence from the text. Help students examine the text for another example of each type of sentence. Repeat the process of examining the clauses and connecting words for each sentence.

Intermediate Reread *Mexico's Search for Stability* aloud to students. Help students identify a compound sentence in the text. Guide students to identify the independent clauses and the connecting word in the sentence. Then repeat the process with a complex sentence from the text. Challenge students to examine the text for another example of each type of sentence. Repeat the process of examining the clauses and connecting words for each sentence.

Advanced Have small groups of students reread *Mexico's Search for Stability* aloud. Instruct students to identify one compound and one complex sentence from the text. Small groups should identify the clauses in each sentence. Have students write their sentences in their notebooks and share them with their classmates.

Advanced High Have pairs of students reread *Mexico's Search for Stability* aloud. Instruct students to identify two compound and two complex sentences from the text. Pairs should identify the clauses in each sentence then write them in their notebooks and share them with the class.

Use with Digital Text 1, **Political Problems Linger.**

Writing

Read *Political Problems Linger* aloud to students. Then have students complete one of the following activities according to their language proficiency.

Beginning Choose one letter sound to highlight in this activity, such as the d sound in despite and democracy. Say the d sound and the example words and have students repeat them. Instruct students to listen for this sound as you read. Reread *Political Problems Linger* aloud. Each time you read words with the d sound, write and display it for students. After reading, review these words with the students.

Intermediate Choose one letter sound to highlight in this activity, such as the d sound in despite and democracy. Say the d sound and the example words and have students repeat them. Instruct students to listen for this sound as you read and raise their hands when they hear it. Reread *Political Problems Linger* aloud. Each time you read a word with the d sound, pause to write and display it for students. After reading, review these words with students, challenging them to sound out each word with support from you.

Advanced Choose one letter sound to highlight in this activity, such as the d sound in despite and democracy. Have students say the d sound and the example words aloud. Instruct pairs of students to read *Political Problems Linger* aloud. Each time pairs read words with the d sound, instruct them to pause to write the words in their notebooks. After reading, have two sets of partners work together to compare their lists and review the words. Students should practice sounding out each word with support from their peers.

Advanced High Choose one vowel sound to highlight in this activity, such as the long i sound in despite and bright. Have students say the long i sound and the example words aloud. Instruct pairs of students to read *Political Problems Linger* aloud. Each time pairs read words with the long i sound, instruct them to pause to write the words in their notebooks. After reading, have two sets of partners work together to compare their lists and identify the different letter patterns that produce the long i sound. Students should practice sounding out each word with support from their peers.

◩ Differentiate Instruction

Use the Differentiated Instruction notes throughout the lesson plan to support the varied skill sets, levels of readiness, and interests in the mixed-ability classroom.

Challenge These notes include suggestions for expanding the activity for advanced students.

On-Level These notes include suggestions for modifying the activity to address different interests or learning styles.

Extra Support These notes include ideas for providing more scaffolding or reading spuport.

Special Needs These notes provide ideas for adapting instruction to support the needs of various special needs students.

■ NOTES

PEARSON
realize™
www.PearsonRealize.com

Go online to access additional resources including:
Primary Sources • Biographies • Supreme Court cases •
21st Century Skill Tutorials • Maps • Graphic Organizers.

Objectives

Objective 1: Identify the political problems faced by new Latin American nations.

Objective 2: Describe Mexico's struggle to achieve stability.

Objective 3: Explain why Latin America entered a cycle of economic dependence.

Objective 4: Analyze the influence of the United States on Latin America, including the opening of the Panama Canal.

Objective 5: Analyze how Canada achieved self-rule.

LESSON 8 ORGANIZER		PACING: APPROX. 1 PERIOD, .5 BLOCKS			
		OBJECTIVES	**PACING**	**RESOURCES**	
				Online	**Print**
Connect					
DIGITAL START UP ACTIVITY **The United States and Latin America**			5 min.	●	
Investigate					
DIGITAL TEXT 1 **Political Problems Linger**		Objective 1	10 min.	●	●
DIGITAL TEXT 2 **Mexico's Search for Stability**		Objective 2	10 min.	●	●
DIGITAL TEXT 3 **The Economics of Latin America's Dependence**		Objective 3	10 min.	●	●
DIGITAL TEXT 4 **The United States Wields Power and Influence**			10 min.	●	●
INTERACTIVE CARTOON **Uncle Sam Takes Off—United States Imperialism**		Objective 4	10 min.	●	
INTERACTIVE GALLERY **The Panama Canal**			10 min.	●	
DIGITAL TEXT 5 **Canada Achieves Self-Rule**		Objective 5	10 min.	●	●
Synthesize					
DIGITAL ACTIVITY **Canada and Latin America**			5 min.	●	
Demonstrate					
LESSON QUIZ **Lesson Quiz and Class Discussion Board**			10 min.	●	

The Americas in the Age of Imperialism

CONNECT

DIGITAL START UP ACTIVITY
The United States and Latin America

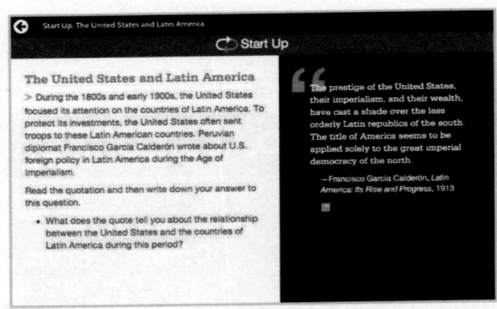

Project the Start Up Activity Ask students to read the quote as they get settled. Then have them share their ideas with another student.

Discuss What does the quote tell you about the relationship between the *U.S.* and the countries of Latin America? *(Students should note an unequal relationship as the U.S. pursued imperialist goals. Latin Americans resented U.S. involvement.)*

Make Predictions Based on your knowledge of Latin American history, what might you predict were causes of disorder in Latin America? *(Students may predict that colonialism and the unequal social structure contributed to political instability.)*

Aa Vocabulary Development: Use the Interactive Reading Notepad to preview the Key Terms and Academic Vocabulary in this Lesson with students.

↑↓ FLIP IT!
Assign the Flipped Video for this lesson.

▮ STUDENT EDITION PRINT
PAGES: 632–640

INVESTIGATE

DIGITAL TEXT 1
Political Problems Linger

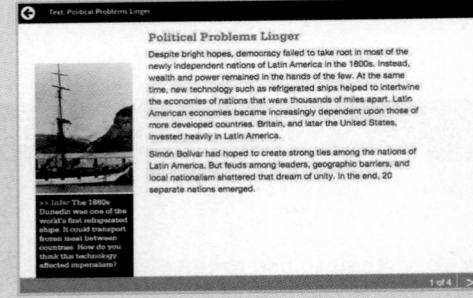

Objective 1: Identify the political problems faced by new Latin American nations.

Quick Instruction

Many Latin American countries gained independence in the 1800s but had a hard time establishing democratic governments. The legacy of colonialism contributed to lingering political problems; the colonial system favored a wealthy elite over the majority of people. Inequalities remained, voting rights were limited, and there was still some racial prejudice. Dictators arose in some countries, while conservatives and liberals vied for power in other countries.

Identify Cause and Effect Project the image of the caudillo. Ask: What was a consequence of the rise of caudillos? *(government funds taken for personal use, power struggles, and frequent revolts, with privileged elites retaining power)*

ELL Use the ELL activity described in the ELL chart.

Further Instruction

Editable Presentation Use the Editable Presentation to present the main ideas for this Core Text.

Political Problems Linger: Core Text and Interactive Reading Notepad Project and discuss the Interactive Reading Notepad questions.

Analyze Information How was regionalism linked to the rise of caudillos? *(Regionalism was loyalty to a local area, rather than to a central government. Caudillos were locally based strongmen with private armies. Caudillos used their armies to resist the central government. Sometimes caudillos became national dictators themselves.)*

Cite Evidence The reading states that "many of the problems in the new nations had their origins in colonial rule." Cite evidence from the text to support this statement. *(Evidence includes facts about how the colonial social and political hierarchy remained the same; the Roman Catholic Church kept a privileged position, controlling much of the land; remaining inequalities; limits on voting rights; racial prejudices; property owned by a privileged few; and peasants working land in a peonage system.)*

DIGITAL TEXT 2

Mexico's Search for Stability

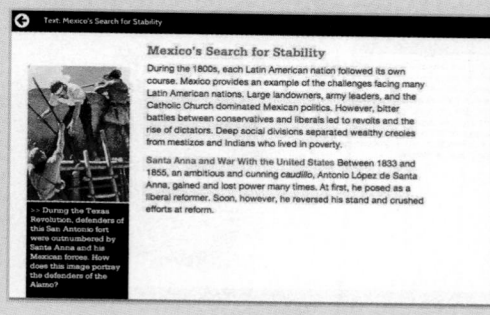

Mexico's Search for Stability

During the 1800s, each Latin American nation followed its own course. Mexico provides an example of the challenges facing many Latin American nations. Large landowners, army leaders, and the Catholic Church dominated Mexican politics. However, bitter battles between conservatives and liberals led to revolts and the rise of dictators. Deep social divisions separated wealthy creoles from mestizos and Indians who lived in poverty.

Santa Anna and War With the United States Between 1833 and 1855, an ambitious and cunning caudillo, Antonio López de Santa Anna, gained and lost power many times. At first, he posed as a liberal reformer. Soon, however, he reversed his stand and crushed efforts at reform.

>> During the Texas Revolution, defenders of this San Antonio fort were outnumbered by Santa Anna and his Mexican forces. How does this image portray the defenders of the Alamo?

Objective 2: Describe Mexico's struggle to achieve stability.

Quick Instruction

Mexico struggled for stability as conservatives and liberals battled for control of the country. Mexico's war with the United States over Texas territory exacerbated debate among Mexicans. Liberals tried to bring reform to Mexico, while conservatives and some dictators (like General Porfirio Díaz) extended colonial-type systems such as peonage, where hacienda owners could extract more work from low-paid Indians and mestizos.

Hypothesize Project the photo of Benito Juárez from the Text. How do you think that Juárez's Zapotec heritage (Zapotecs were Native Americans in Mexico) influenced Juárez's politics? *(His heritage probably contributed to his sympathy for the problems and issues faced by poorer Native Americans and mestizos in Mexico and contributed to his efforts to bring about political and economic reforms to help those communities.)*

ELL Use the ELL activity described in the ELL chart.

Further Instruction

Editable Presentation Use the Editable Presentation to present the main ideas for this Core Text.

Mexico's Search for Stability: Core Text and Interactive Reading Notepad Project and discuss the Interactive Reading Notepad questions.

Summarize What struggles did Mexico experience while trying to achieve stability in the 1800s? *(Answers will vary but should include a few of the following: losing a war with the United States over territory in Texas and then losing territory, social and economic inequalities, civil war, war with France, living under the dictatorship of General Díaz.)*

D Differentiate: Extra Support For students who need extra help with Mexican history, have them create a chart titled "Factors Contributing to Instability in Mexico." Give them three column headings, explaining that these were factors in Mexico's instability: "Territory Disputes with the United States," "Foreign Intervention," and "Inequality of the Lower Class." Help them read the section for one example of each factor to put under the headings. *(The war with the United States for Texas could go under the first column; Europe's intervention in Mexico's civil war could go under the second column; and the peonage system of poor workers forced by debts to work on haciendas for low pay could go under the third column heading.)*

DIGITAL TEXT 3

The Economics of Latin America's Dependence

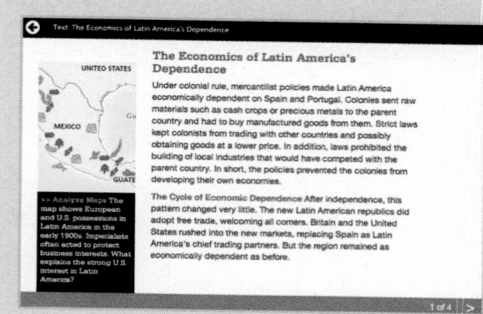

The Economics of Latin America's Dependence

Under colonial rule, mercantilist policies made Latin America economically dependent on Spain and Portugal. Colonies sent raw materials such as cash crops or precious metals to the parent country and had to buy manufactured goods from them. Strict laws kept colonists from trading with other countries and possibly obtaining goods at a lower price. In addition, laws prohibited the building of local industries that would have competed with the parent country. In short, the policies prevented the colonies from developing their own economies.

>> Analyze Maps The map shows European and U.S. possessions in Latin America in the early 1900s. Imperialists often acted to protect business interests. What explains the strong U.S. interest in Latin America?

The Cycle of Economic Dependence After independence, this pattern changed very little. The new Latin American republics did adopt free trade, welcoming all comers. Britain and the United States rushed into the new markets, replacing Spain as Latin America's chief trading partners. But the region remained as economically dependent as before.

Objective 3: Explain why Latin America entered a cycle of economic dependence.

Quick Instruction

Under colonial rule, Latin American countries generated profits for European countries without much chance to develop their own economies. This pattern did not change greatly after independence. Free trade, foreign investment, technological developments, and migration did help Latin American economies make some advances, but only a few elites and a small middle class benefitted. A majority of Latin American people remained poor.

Interpret Project the map of Imperialism in Latin America. According to the map, what were some natural resources that Latin America had that attracted the interest of U.S. imperialists? *(According to the purple areas on the map showing U.S. possessions in Latin America, the United States was interested in bananas, cacao, coffee, fishing, sugar, and timber.)*

The Americas in the Age of Imperialism

DIGITAL TEXT 4
The United States Wields Power and Influence

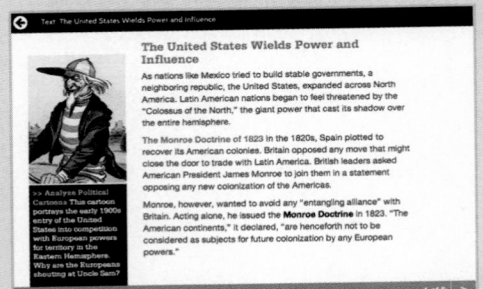

INTERACTIVE CARTOON
Uncle Sam Takes Off— United States Imperialism

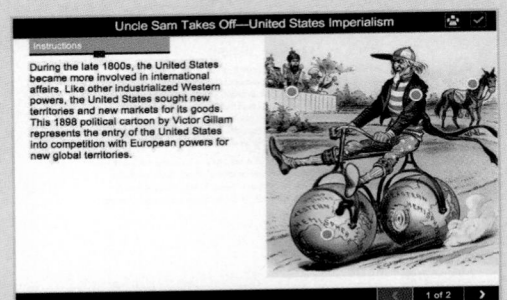

Further Instruction

Editable Presentation Use the Editable Presentation to present the main ideas for this Core Text.

The Economics of Latin America's Dependence: Core Text and Interactive Reading Notepad Project and discuss the Interactive Reading Notepad questions.

Analyze Information During the 1800s, the United States stepped up its trade with, and investment in, Latin America. While this brought some benefits for Latin America, how did it also contribute to growing United States imperialism toward Latin America? *(It contributed to a growing imperialism because Americans felt their investments gave them the right to interfere in Latin American politics to protect those investments. U.S. investors pressured their own government to take action if Latin American political events or reform movements threatened U.S. investors' interests.)*

Objective 4: Analyze the influence of the United States on Latin America, including the opening of the Panama Canal.

Quick Instruction

In 1823, American president James Monroe issued the Monroe Doctrine, discouraging European powers from establishing colonies in the American continents. While this doctrine protected Latin America from European colonization, the United States became more imperialistic toward Latin American countries, especially when it wanted to build a canal across Panama to cut sea travel time between American coasts.

Interactive Cartoon: Uncle Sam Takes Off—United States Imperialism Project the cartoon. Have students click each hotspot to learn about aspects of the Monroe Doctrine. Tell them that this 1896 political cartoon shows Uncle Sam representing the United States, a bicycle with tires representing the Eastern and Western hemispheres, a horse with no rider representing the Monroe Doctrine, and angry European powers in the background.

🎥 ACTIVE CLASSROOM

Use the If Images Could Talk strategy with the cartoon. Have students pick either a European power or Uncle Sam in the cartoon and then write some dialogue for that character. What are the character's motivations? Why does he want to be involved in Latin America? What is the European shouting at Uncle Sam, or Uncle Sam to the European? Have students read their finished dialogues aloud.

Identify Cause and Effect What was a cause of the Monroe Doctrine, and what was an effect? *(The Monroe Doctrine was caused by American concern that Europeans would try to establish or regain colonies in Latin America, jeopardizing British and U.S. trade with Latin America. An effect of the doctrine was to help discourage European interference in Latin America.)*

Interactive Gallery: The Panama Canal Project the gallery. Have students progress chronologically through the images, taking time to read captions and examine each picture.

🎥 ACTIVE CLASSROOM

Use the Quick Write strategy with this gallery. Give students a short period (30 seconds to 1 minute) to answer one of the following question prompts: How did the desire for a canal influence U.S. imperialism in Latin America? What is the connection between Latin American geography and the building of the Panama canal?

Infer What help did the United States need to build the Panama Canal? *(The United States needed help from Panama to get the rights to the land and to build the canal. They needed help fighting diseases such as malaria and yellow fever. They needed help with the engineering and construction of the canal.)*

INTERACTIVE GALLERY

The Panama Canal

DIGITAL TEXT 5

Canada Achieves Self-Rule

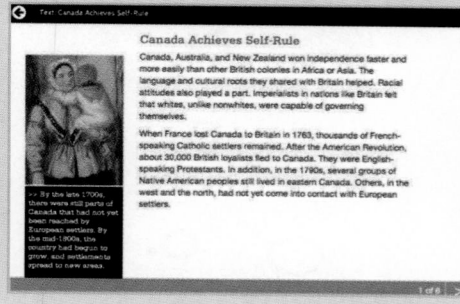

Further Instruction

Editable Presentation Use the Editable Presentation to present the main ideas for this Core Text.

The United States Wields Power and Influence: Core Text and Interactive Reading Notepad Project and discuss the Interactive Reading Notepad questions.

Be sure students understand that the Roosevelt Corollary to the Monroe Doctrine was created by the United States in 1904 to give it "international police power" in the Western Hemisphere. The United States used this corollary to send troops to several Latin American countries in order to protect its investments in these countries. This economic imperialism made the United States a target of resentment by Latin Americans.

Support Ideas with Examples What is one example that supports the idea that the United States acted like an imperialist power in Cuba after the Spanish-American War? *(The example supporting this idea is the fact that in 1901, the United States forced Cuba to add the Platt Amendment to the Cuban constitution. The Platt Amendment allowed the United States to set up naval bases in Cuba and the right to intervene in Cuban affairs.)*

Objective 5: Analyze how Canada achieved self-rule.

Quick Instruction

Canada, a British colony, gained independence and became a **dominion**, or self-governing nation, in 1867. While Canada had been a colony like Latin American countries, there had not been a colonial legacy of racial prejudice or economic injustice to overcome, as there was for Latin American countries. Canada also did not experience imperialism from the United States, as Latin American countries did.

Analyze Maps Project the map of Canada, 1867–1914, from the text. What were some natural resources in British Columbia that were not found in the interior province of Saskatchewan? Ask: Why might these resources have partly motivated the building of the Canadian Pacific Railway to reach as far west as British Columbia? *(British Columbia had some resources not found in Saskatchewan, such as silver, copper, and fish. Some of these items could have been sent by railway to the interior province.)*

Further Instruction

Canada Achieves Self-Rule: Core Text and Interactive Reading Notepad Project and discuss the Interactive Reading Notepad questions, including the graphic organizer, and ask students to record the sequence of events leading up to Canada's self-rule. Review the sequence of events, filling in the graphic organizer on the whiteboard as you go.

Be sure that students understand other events leading to Canada's self-rule, such as the division into two provinces: English-speaking Upper Canada and French-speaking Lower Canada. Both Upper and Lower Canada led rebellions against British rule. Britain responded to rebellions with experience gained from the American Revolution, and Britain maintained partial control over Canada for a period. Canada unified its provinces in the mid-1880s and then effectively advocated for self-rule as one united country.

Summarize Although Canada had fewer ethnic differences with Britain than Latin American countries had with their colonizers, Canada did experience ethnic tensions. What were some of those ethnic tensions? *(The ethnic tensions in Canada included those between French and English speaking settlers and those between European settlers, Native Americans, and métis.)*

The Americas in the Age of Imperialism

SYNTHESIZE

DIGITAL ACTIVITY
Canada and Latin America

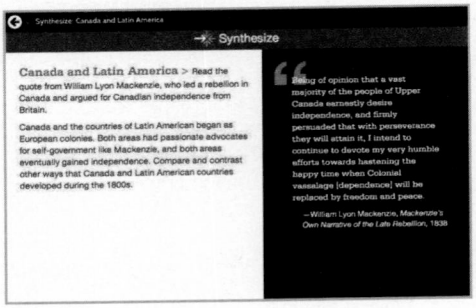

Both Canada and Latin American countries began as colonies of European countries. Both areas had passionate advocates for self-government. Both areas eventually gained independence from Europe, although Latin American countries had more struggles to surmount on the path to self-rule, such as U.S. imperialism, civil wars, economic and social inequality, and a cycle of economic dependence.

Have students answer the question in this activity, then share their answers with a partner. Have students discuss as a group the following question.

Contrast Contrast some characteristics of Latin American countries with Canadian characteristics that might help explain why Canada did not experience imperialism from the United States as much as Latin America did. *(Canada was a former British colony that had native English speakers, making it similar to the United States. Also, Canada had strong, close ties to Britain, which would limit U.S. opportunities for imperialism. Canada did not have an isthmus providing an ideal shipping channel, as in Panama, which inspired U.S. imperialism and canal building. Latin America had other European powers interested in colonizing its countries; the United States involved itself in Latin American politics before, during, and after European colonization.)*

DEMONSTRATE

LESSON QUIZ
Lesson Quiz and Class Discussion Board

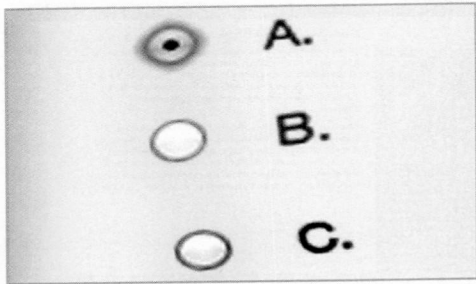

Assign the online Lesson Quiz for this lesson if you haven't already done so. Students will be offered automatic remediation or enrichment based on their score.

Pose this question to the class on the Discussion Board: In "The Americas in the Age of Imperialism," you read about political problems in Latin American nations after colonization, including Mexico's struggle for stability. Latin American countries entered a cycle of economic dependence with their trading partners, England and the United States, who replaced the previous European colonizers. The United States influenced the development of Latin America, fighting a war against Mexico for territory, and wars against Spain and Colombia to liberate Cuba and Panama. Canada's achievement of self-rule occurred with less imperialist interference and less economic instability.

Compare What are some similarities when comparing Benito Juárez of Mexico to John Macdonald and George-Etienne Cartier of Canada? *(All three were men trying to unify and gain self-rule for their countries. Juárez did help unite Mexico, while Macdonald and Cartier helped Canada achieve confederation, a type of unification.)*

Topic Inquiry
Have students continue their investigations for the Topic Inquiry.

The Age of Imperialism (1800–1914)

■ SYNTHESIZE

DIGITAL ACTIVITY
Reflect on the Essential Question and Topic

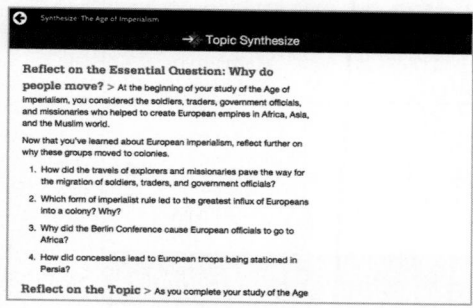

Remind students of the Essential Question for the Topic: Why do people move?

Discuss Now that you've learned about European imperialism, reflect further on why these groups moved to the colonies.

- How did explorers and missionaries pave the way for the migration of Europeans? *(Explorers and missionaries were often the first to travel to a region. Government officials then used the information provided by explorers to gain control of the region.)*

- Which form of imperialist rule led to the greatest influx of Europeans into a colony? Why? *(Direct rule, because Europeans administered the colony themselves and moved there to serve as government officials and soldiers.)*

- Why did the Berlin Conference cause European officials to go to Africa? *(The Berlin Conference set the rules for claiming colonies in Africa. European countries had to set up offices in Africa to claim colonies.)*

- How did concessions lead to European troops in Persia? *(Britain and Russia gained oil concessions and then sent troops to Persia to protect their oil resources.)*

Next ask students to reflect on the Topic before posing and answering three questions related to what they learned. Share these examples:

- What effects did European rule have on Africa and India?

- How do the imperialist policies of the 1800s influence the world you live in today?

Topic Inquiry
Have students complete Step 3 of their DBQ Inquiry.

■ DEMONSTRATE

DIGITAL TOPIC REVIEW AND ASSESSMENT
The Age of Imperialism (1800–1914)

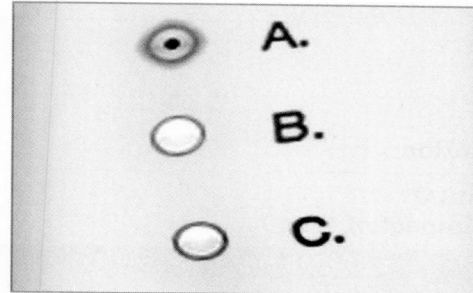

Students can prepare for the Topic Test by answering the questions in the Topic Review and Assessment online or the Assessment questions in the Print Student text. They can also prepare by reviewing their answers to the Interactive Reading Notepad questions or reviewing their notes in the Reading and Notetaking Study Guide.

DIGITAL TOPIC TEST
The Age of Imperialism (1800–1914)

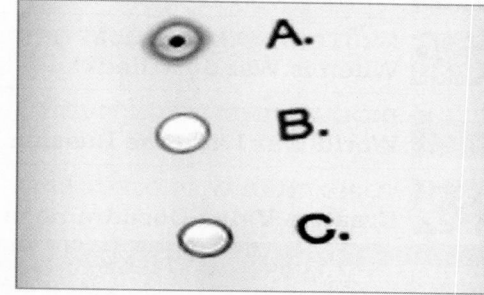

TOPIC TEST
Assign the Topic Test to assess students' understanding of topic content.

BENCHMARK TESTS
Assign these benchmark tests as you complete the relevant topics to monitor student progress toward mastering the course content and as preparation for the End-of-Course Test.

Benchmark Test 1: Topics 1–5
Benchmark Test 2: Topics 6–10
Benchmark Test 3: Topics 11–15
Benchmark Test 4: Topics 16–21

Topic (16)

World War I and the Russian Revolution (1914–1924)

TOPIC 16 ORGANIZER	PACING: APPROX. 7 PERIODS, 3.5 BLOCKS	
		PACING
Connect		1 period
MY STORY VIDEO **Wilfred Owen, A Poet in the Trenches**		10 min.
DIGITAL ESSENTIAL QUESTION ACTIVITY **When is War Justified?**		10 min.
DIGITAL TIMELINE ACTIVITY **World War I and the Russian Revolution**		10 min.
TOPIC INQUIRY: PROJECT-BASED LEARNING **Create a Video Docudrama on The Impact of War**		20 min.
Investigate		2–4 periods
TOPIC INQUIRY: PROJECT-BASED LEARNING **Create a Video Docudrama on The Impact of War**		Ongoing
LESSON 1 World War I Begins		30–40 min.
LESSON 2 Fighting the Great War		30–40 min.
LESSON 3 World War I Ends		30–40 min.
LESSON 4 Revolution in Russia		30–40 min.
Synthesize		1 period
DIGITAL ACTIVITY **Reflect on the Essential Question and Topic**		10 min.
TOPIC INQUIRY: PROJECT-BASED LEARNING **Create a Video Docudrama on The Impact of War**		20 min.
Demonstrate		1–2 periods
DIGITAL TOPIC TEST **World War I and the Russian Revolution**		10 min.
DIGITAL TEKS MASTERY TEST **TEKS Mastery Test**		10 min.
TOPIC INQUIRY: PROJECT-BASED LEARNING **Create a Video Docudrama on The Impact of War**		20 min.

TOPIC INQUIRY: PROJECT-BASED LEARNING

Create a Video Docudrama on The Impact of War

In this Topic Inquiry, students work in teams to create video docudramas telling the story of how World War I impacted the lives of civilians, soldiers, and leaders. Learning how war affects the lives of people will contribute to students' understanding of the Topic Essential Question: When is war justified?

STEP 1: CONNECT
Develop Questions and Plan the Investigation

Launch the Project and Generate Questions
Display the Entry Event, which is a fictional assignment from a movie studio. Direct students to the key points in the invitation. Now, display the Video Docudrama Rubric, and use it to discuss the essential elements of a docudrama. Finally, tell students that in this project, they will learn about civilians, soldiers, and leaders during World War I, and each team will create a docudrama video to capture and convey how the war impacted one of these groups. Answer any questions students might have.

Plan the Investigation
Divide students into teams and assign each team one of the three groups: civilians, soldiers, or leaders. Have them learn or review the essentials of working as a team by taking a tutorial and signing the Project Contract. Display the Project Roles document and review with students. Guide students as they complete the *Need-to-Know Questions* for their assigned World War I group.

Suggestion: To control the length of this project, set parameters for how long you want student videos to run and how many days you will allow for video production. To reduce the length of the project, you can also decide to focus students on specific *Need-to-Know Questions* of your choosing.

Resources
- Project Launch
- Project Contract
- Need-to-Know Questions
- Student Instructions
- Video Docudrama Rubric

STEP 2: INVESTIGATE
Apply Disciplinary Concepts and Tools

Conduct Research
Assign team member roles or allow teams time to assign roles. To control the length of this project, you may wish to have all students conduct research.

Remind students to focus their research on the *Need-to-Know Questions.* Guide research by directing students to helpful sections of the digital text. You may wish to recommend specific books or specific websites such as PBS, the Library of Congress, or the Imperial War Museum. Help students begin to fill out the *Information Organizer.*

Suggestion: If your class has limited access to online resources, here are some books that they might find helpful: *The First World War* by John Keegan, *A World Undone: The Story of the Great War, 1914 to 1918,* by G. J. Meyer, and *World War I,* by H. P. Willmott.

Write and Edit Docudrama
Guide students as they develop their video docudrama's story, characters, script, and images. Remind students to refer to the various project roles and to keep their script focused on the *Need-to-Know Questions* about their group of people in World War I. Encourage students to mix dramatic reenactment and dialogue with historical images and firsthand accounts.

Resources
- Project Roles
- Project Tracker
- Information Organizer

⏻ PROFESSIONAL DEVELOPMENT

Project-Based Learning
Be sure to view the Project-Based Learning Professional Development resources in the online course.

STEP 3: SYNTHESIZE
Evaluate Sources and
Use Evidence to Formulate Conclusions

Create Your Video Docudrama

Now, allow students time to put together their video docudrama. Students may use software or a website of their or your choosing. Remind them to refer to the *Project Launch* and *Video Docudrama Rubric* as a reminder of the desired elements and qualities of an instructional video docudrama.

Suggestion: Before students get into these final stages, you may wish to show them some finished videos created by your students of previous years. You could also refer them to World War I videos or other student-generated videos on the Internet.

Add an Informative Conclusion to Your Video

Teams should be sure that they have a powerful conclusion that makes a clear statement on the impact of World War I on their assigned group of participants. Tell students that they might even go beyond this to make a comment about the continuing impact of wars today.

Review and Edit Your Video

Ask teams to review and do final edits on their docudrama. They should be sure that they have satisfied the requirements in the project launch documents. Stress that their goal is to excel in each area of the project rubric: Purpose, Content Accuracy, Artistic Creativity, Technology, and Delivery.

Resources
- Project Rubric
- Software or website for creating docudrama

STEP 4: DEMONSTRATE
Communicate Conclusions
and Take Informed Action

Present Your Video Docudrama

You may wish students to refer to *21st Century Skill Tutorials: Give an Effective Presentation.* Have students present their video docudramas to the class or a larger audience. Allow time for comments, questions, and answers after each presentation.

Reflect on the Project

After students have finished creating and presenting their docudramas, provide your assessment, and help them go over what worked well and what did not work well so they they can improve their results on the next project.

Suggestion: As an extension activity, invite students to find a recent news video clip reporting on the human impact of an international conflict, civil war, or terrorist attack. Have them present it to the class and draw comparisons between World War I and the news story.

Resources
- Video Docudrama Rubric
- 21st Century Skill Tutorials: Give an Effective Presentation
- Self-Assessment

World War I and the Russian Revolution (1914–1924)

In the early 1900s, powerful forces were pushing Europe toward war. These forces included nationalism, militarism, imperialism, and alliance systems. Meanwhile, in Russia, discontent with tsarist rule, peasant unrest, and economic challenges set the stage for revolution. The results were World War I and the Russian Revolution. These upheavals would leave Europe in turmoil and give rise to the Communist Soviet Union.

■ CONNECT

MY STORY VIDEO

Wilfred Owen, A Poet in the Trenches

Watch a video about Wilfred Owen's experiences in World War I.

Check Understanding What accounts for Wilfred Owen's change of opinion about fighting in World War I? *(His enthusiasm for the war changed after he witnessed first-hand the horrors of modern combat.)*

Determine Author's Purpose What did Wilfred Owen hope to convey through his poetry? *(He wanted to describe the grim reality of combat and the disillusionment he felt about war.)*

DIGITAL ESSENTIAL QUESTION ACTIVITY

When is War Justified?

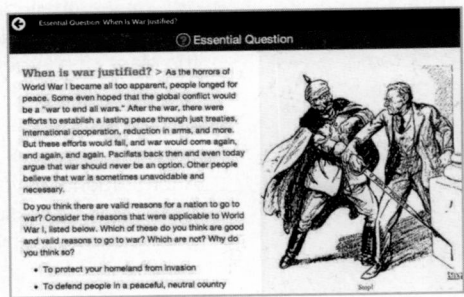

Ask students to think about the Essential Question for this Topic: When is war justified?

If students have not already done so, ask them to respond to the Activity questions about the causes of World War I. Then review the questions and ask for some student responses.

Check Understanding Go through each of these causes of World War I and ask students to explain them in their own words. Provide further explanation as needed.

Generate Explanations For each of these causes, poll students on whether or not they think it was a good and valid reason for going to war. Ask them to explain the reasons for their opinions.

DIGITAL TIMELINE ACTIVITY

World War I and the Russian Revolution

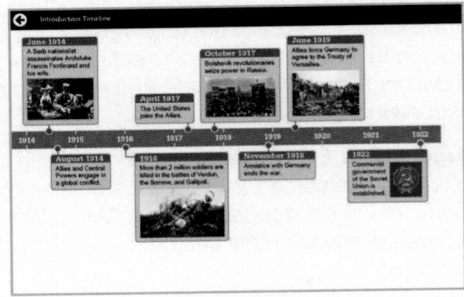

Display the timeline showing some key events of World War I and the Russian Revolution. During this Topic, students will learn about all of these events and many more, but this timeline will provide a framework into which they can place the events they learn about.

D Differentiate: Extra Support Ask students which events pertain mostly to the Russian Revolution rather than to World War I. *(Bolshevik revolutionaries in 1917 and Communist government in 1922)*

Check Understanding How long did World War I last? *(a little more than four years, from August 1914 to November 1918)*

World War I Begins

Supporting English Language Learners

Use with Digital Text 1, **European Powers Form Alliances.**

Learning Strategies

Explain that using personal experiences and information students already know can help them more easily understand what they are reading in their academic classes. Using this kind of information is called "accessing background knowledge." Before reading, ask students to think about their friendships. In most cases, students will have friendships with others that overlap. If students feel hurt by a friend, others may take sides. Calling out these complexities in relationships should make it easier to understand the alliance system that created a global conflict situation during the early years of World War I. Ask students to listen carefully to *European Powers Form Alliances* as you read aloud. Then have students complete the following activities according to their English proficiency.

Beginning Model developing a friendship web for students. Ask a student volunteer to share a list of friends' names. Write the volunteer's name in the center and the names of the friends around the center. Draw connecting lines from the volunteer's name to each friend's name. Then have the student volunteer indicate which friends are also friends with each other. Draw connecting lines between those friends' names, too. Then point out that if two of these friends had a disagreement, the balance of these relationships could change. Model making the connection between this friendship web and the alliance system of World War I. Create a second web to show the relationships among European nations and how they eventually took sides in the war.

Intermediate Help students develop their own friendship webs by having them write their names on a piece of paper and as many friends' names as possible around the rest of the page. Then instruct students to draw connecting lines from their name to each friend's name. Ask students to draw connecting lines between the friends who also know one another. Ask students to think about what might happen if two of the friends in their webs had a disagreement. Then have them turn to a partner to share their thoughts. Ask pairs to consider how their friendship webs resemble the relationships among European nations around WWI. Help students create another web to show the relationships among the nations of Europe and how they eventually took sides in the war.

Advanced Have students work with a partner to create a single friendship web to show how they and their friends are connected. Then instruct pairs to talk about what could happen if two individuals in their webs had a disagreement. Then ask pairs to consider how their friendship webs resemble the relationships among European nations around WWI. Facilitate a discussion in which students work together as a class to create another web showing the relationships among the nations of Europe and how they eventually took sides in the war.

Advanced High Have students create a friendship web to show how they and their friends are connected. Then instruct students to consider what could happen if two individuals in their webs had a disagreement. Have students write down their ideas. Then ask students to create another web to show the alliances among European nations. Have students consider how their friendship webs resemble the relationships among European nations around WWI.

Use with Digital Text 2, **Major Causes of World War I.**

Learning Strategies

Read *Major Causes of World War I* aloud to the class. After students listen to the text, have them complete one of the following activities depending on their level of English proficiency.

Beginning Help students practice using basic vocabulary in their writing by helping them complete the following sentences frames. If students need extra support, define each of the word choices to improve their understanding of the vocabulary words.

- France and Germany were competing for _____ in Morocco. (control, gold, resources)

- Austria-Hungary and Ottoman Turkey were afraid of the _____ of nationalism. (pride, growth, decline)

Intermediate Have students practice using basic vocabulary in their writing by helping them complete the following sentences frames. If students need extra support, have them define each of the word choices to improve their understanding of the vocabulary words.

- France and Germany were competing for _____ in Morocco. (control, gold, resources)

- Austria-Hungary and Ottoman Turkey were afraid of the _____ of nationalism. (pride, growth, decline)

Advanced Have students practice using basic vocabulary in their writing by having them work with a partner to write three sentences about the major causes of World War I. If students need extra support, provide them with bilingual dictionaries and other resources. Circulate among students to offer support as needed.

Advanced High Have students practice using basic vocabulary in their writing by having them write five sentences about the major causes of World War I. If students need extra support, provide them with bilingual dictionaries and other resources. Circulate among students to offer support as needed.

World War I Begins

Objectives

Objective 1: Describe how imperialism, nationalism, and militarism pushed Europe closer to war.

Objective 2: Identify the key event that sparked World War I.

Objective 3: Trace how the alliance system drew nations into the war.

LESSON 1 ORGANIZER		PACING: APPROX. 1 PERIOD, .5 BLOCKS			
		OBJECTIVES	PACING	Online	Print
Connect					
DIGITAL START UP ACTIVITY **The Balkan Powder Keg**			5 min.	●	
Investigate					
DIGITAL TEXT 1 **European Powers Form Alliances**		Objective 3	10 min.	●	●
INTERACTIVE CHART **Alliances and World War I**			10 min.	●	
DIGITAL TEXT 2 **Major Causes of World War I**		Objective 1	10 min.	●	●
INTERACTIVE CARTOON **Nationalist Struggles in the Balkans**			10 min.	●	
DIGITAL TEXT 3 **The Balkan Powder Keg Explodes**		Objective 2	10 min.	●	●
DIGITAL TEXT 4 **The Alliance System Leads to War**			10 min.	●	●
Synthesize					
DIGITAL ACTIVITY **Causes of World War I**			5 min.	●	
Demonstrate					
DIGITAL QUIZ **Lesson Quiz and Class Discussion Board**			10 min.	●	

PEARSON realize™
www.PearsonRealize.com

Go online to access additional resources including:
Primary Sources • Biographies • Supreme Court cases •
21st Century Skill Tutorials • Maps • Graphic Organizers.

CONNECT

DIGITAL START UP ACTIVITY
The Balkan Powder Keg

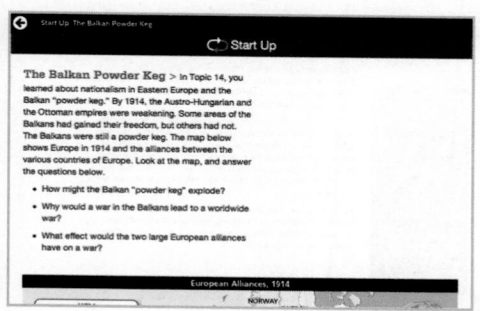

Project the Start Up Activity Ask students to examine the political cartoon and answer the questions as they enter and get settled: How might the Balkan "powder keg" explode? *(Answers will vary. Students might write about an event sparked by the nationalist aspirations of people in the smaller countries of the Balkans such as Serbia, Montenegro, Rumania, and Bulgaria that would be a threat to the dying Austro-Hungarian and Ottoman empires.)* Why would a war in the Balkans lead to a worldwide war? *(Answers will vary. Students might deduce from the map that there were two major alliances in Europe at the time and that those alliances would pull various countries into a war. Other students might hypothesize that major European countries would want to have power in the Balkans.)*

Aa Vocabulary Development: Use the Interactive Reading Notepad to preview the Key Terms and Academic Vocabulary in this lesson with students.

⚡ FLIP IT!

Assign the Flipped Video for this lesson.

▪ STUDENT EDITION PRINT PAGES: 646–651

INVESTIGATE

DIGITAL TEXT 1
European Powers Form Alliances

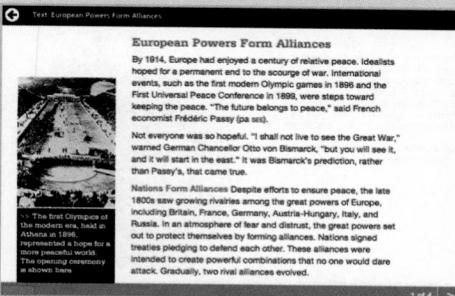

INTERACTIVE CHART
Alliances and World War I

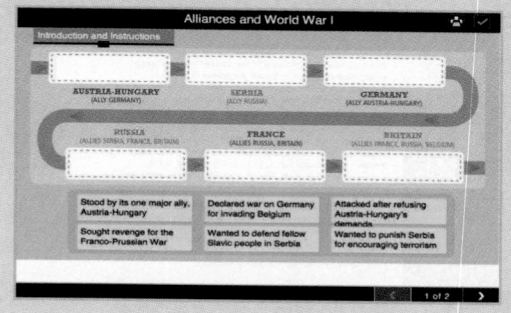

Objective 3: Trace how the alliance system drew nations into the war.

Quick Instruction

The alliance system was a major cause of World War I. Increased tensions and suspicions led nations to form alliances, agreeing to defend each other in case of attack. In August and September 1914, Europe went to war. One by one, the countries of Europe honored their alliances and declared war on each other.

Interactive Chart: Alliances and World War I
Project the Interactive Chart drag-and-drop activity. Work as a class to drag each reason for going to war to the appropriate country.

👥 ACTIVE CLASSROOM

Use the Take a Stand strategy to engage students. Have them take a stand on the following statement: Did the alliance system make World War I inevitable? Yes or no? Have a class debate where students on either side of the issue defend their positions.

Further Instruction

Go through the Interactive Reading Notepad questions and discuss the answers with the class for Text 1, "The Alliance System Threatens Peace." As you work with students, ask them to note the importance of the alliance system in causing World War I and involving many countries in the war.

Analyze Information How did the alliances created at the end of the nineteenth century (Triple Alliance and Triple Entente) relate to the alliances that formed during World War I? *(Answers may vary. Sample response: The alliances created in the nineteenth century were the basis for the alliances during World War I. The Triple Alliance became the Central Powers and the Triple Entente became the Allies.)*

Identify Causes and Effects Why did the alliance system develop, and why did it result in war rather than peace? *(Sample response: The nations of Europe did not trust each other and wanted to check each other's power. When the crisis occurred, some countries used it as an opportunity to gain power or land.)*

World War I Begins

DIGITAL TEXT 2

Major Causes of World War I

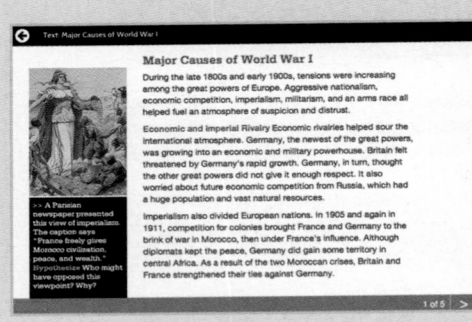

INTERACTIVE CARTOON

Nationalist Struggles in the Balkans

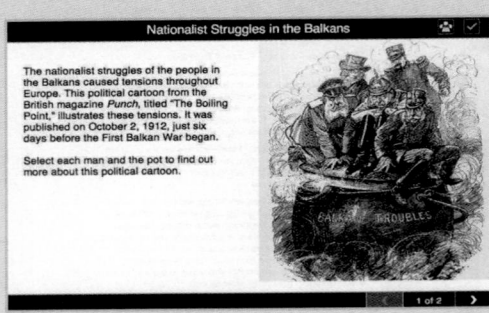

DIGITAL TEXT 3

The Balkan Powder Keg Explodes

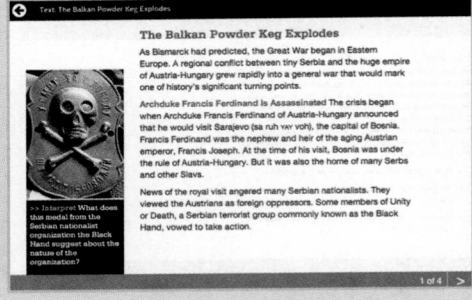

Objective 1: Describe how imperialism, nationalism, and militarism pushed Europe closer to war.

Quick Instruction

Imperialism, militarism, and nationalism were all major causes of World War I, a cataclysm that would mark an historical turning point. Imperialism in the form of rivalries and disputes over colonial territories increased tensions between nations. Militarism made countries more prepared for and more willing to go to war. Nationalism threatened old empires and fed desires to redress perceived wrongs.

Interactive Cartoon: Nationalist Struggles in the Balkans Project the Interactive Cartoon on the whiteboard. As a class, discuss the situation in the Balkans in the early twentieth century. Click through the hotspots on the screen, discussing the pop-up text and what it tells students about the cartoon.

> **📹 ACTIVE CLASSROOM**
>
> Before going through the cartoon with the class, use the Closer Look strategy to have pairs of students closely examine the static cartoon and interpret the visual elements in their sections. Ask students to present their conclusions to the class.

Analyze Visuals Why did the cartoonist represent the Balkans in this way? *(Answers will vary. Students should show a clear understanding that the metaphor of the boiling cauldron represents nationalist desires and conflicts that built pressure and tension in the region.)*

D Differentiate: Extra Support Help students understand the concepts of the political cartoon by explicitly explaining the central metaphor of the cartoon, the bubbling cauldron. Tell students to think about what happens when water simmers or boils on the stove. Point out to students that in this case, the cauldron could be said to represent the term *simmering tensions*.

ELL Use the ELL activity described in the ELL chart.

Further Instruction

Project and discuss the Interactive Reading Notepad questions. Be sure that students understand that imperialism, militarism, and nationalism were all major causes of World War I.

Synthesize How were economic rivalries connected to imperialism in Europe before World War I? *(Sample response: European countries gained economically from the resources provided by their colonies. As a result, the country with the most colonies would have access to the most resources. This created a rivalry for colonies and increased tensions.)*

Connect How were the following major causes of World War I, imperialism, nationalism, and militarism, interconnected? *(Responses may vary. Sample response: International tensions led to increases in military spending and militarism, and militarism led to increased nationalism, which in turn led to imperialism.)*

Objective 2: Identify the key event that sparked World War I.

Quick Instruction

On June 28, 1914, a Serbian nationalist named Gavrilo Princip assassinated the Austria-Hungarian Archduke Francis Ferdinand and his wife, Sophie, in Sarajevo. This event started World War I. Nationalism wasn't just one of many causes of World War I; it was also the immediate cause, the spark that exploded the powder keg. Then, the carefully planned alliances that had developed in the decades before the assassination plunged the world into deeper conflict, as members of each side leaned on their allies for support.

As a class, examine the medal of the Black Hand terrorist organization and discuss its effect on the viewer. Was it intended to intimidate? Why would the organization have wanted such a visual? How might this visual have made an Austrian audience feel? *(Sample response: The skull and crossbones are symbols of violence and death, meant to convey to the Austrian government that the Serb nationalists were willing to kill to achieve their goals. Such symbols would still be frightening to viewers today.)*

Analyze Points of View Why were Serbian nationalists upset that Archduke Francis Ferdinand was coming to Sarajevo? *(Sample response: The nationalists felt that Austrians were foreign oppressors.)* Why did some in Austria blame Serbia for the assassination? *(Sample response: Some in Austria thought people in the Serbian government were*

SYNTHESIZE

DEMONSTRATE

DIGITAL TEXT 4

The Alliance System Leads to War

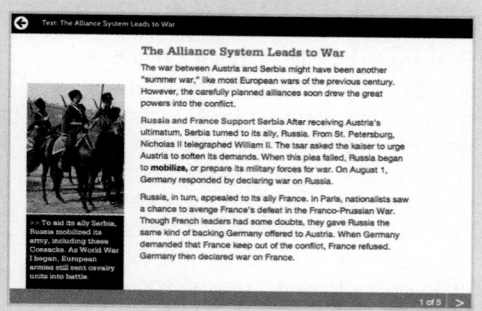

DIGITAL ACTIVITY

Causes of World War I

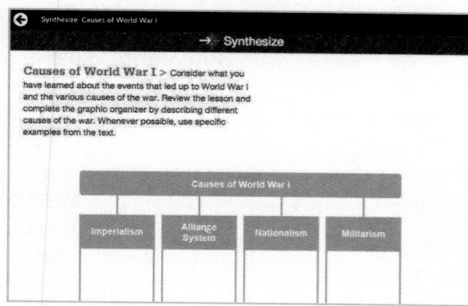

DIGITAL QUIZ

Lesson Quiz and Class Discussion Board

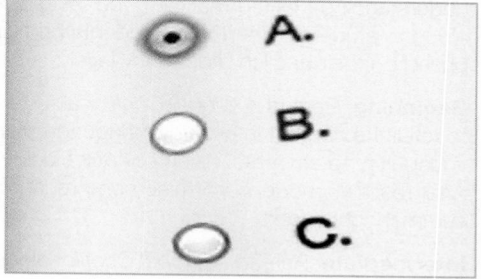

involved in the assassination. Serbia also allowed anti-Austrian agitation within its borders.)

D Differentiate: **Challenge/Gifted**
Challenge students to research the Black Hand, Gavrilo Princip, and Princip's trial, and present their findings to the class.

Further Instruction

Project and discuss the Interactive Reading Notepad questions for the texts "The Balkan Powder Keg Explodes" and "The Alliance System Leads to War." Help students understand the connection between the assassination of Francis Ferdinand, nationalism, and alliances as causes of World War I.

Identify Cause and Effect How was the assassination of Francis Ferdinand the spark that exploded the powder keg and therefore a cause of World War I? *(Sample response: The assassination gave Austria the excuse to declare war on Serbia, whose nationalist ambitions threatened the empire.)*

Identify Cause and Effect Explain why a global conflict developed after the assassination, and describe the sequence of events. *(Because of the alliance system; Russia threatened Austria and then mobilized troops because Serbia was its ally; Germany declared war on Russia because it had risen up against Austria; Russia appealed to its ally France, and so Germany declared war on France. When German troops marched through Belgium to attack France, Britain (which had guaranteed Belgian neutrality and was a French ally) declared war on Germany.)*

Remind students of the scope and content of this lesson on the causes of World War I and the events leading up to the war, emphasizing the importance of the alliance system as well as imperialism, nationalism, and militarism. Help students complete the graphic organizer and remind them to include specific examples from the text.

Remind students of the Topic Essential Question: When is war justified? Engage them in a discussion about whether they believe World War I was justified and why.

Make Predictions Tell students that many people at the start of the war thought it would be over quickly. Have students recall the attitude of many Europeans toward the war, and ask them to predict what will happen. Will the war end quickly? Who will win the war? *(Answers may vary. Some students might think that Germany is so well prepared that the war will end quickly. Others might think that the alliance of Britain, Russia, and France surrounds Germany and Austria, and therefore the war will end quickly, but the Allies will win. Still others might think that the war will last longer than anyone expects because both sides will be unwilling to give up.)*

Assign the online Lesson Quiz for this lesson if you haven't already done so. Students will be offered automatic remediation or enrichment based on their score.

Alliances created at the end of the nineteenth century as well as increasing nationalism, imperialism, and militarism among rival countries in Europe all set the stage for one act to trigger a war that changed the world forever. Pose these questions to the class on the Discussion Board.

Evaluate Arguments Was Austria-Hungary justified in going to war against Serbia? Why or why not? *(Answers may vary. Some students might respond that the act of terrorism was enough to warrant declaring war. Others might respond that Serbia gave in to most of Austria-Hungary's demands and therefore Austria-Hungary was not justified.)*

Connect How does nationalism still threaten peace in the world today? *(Answers may vary. Students may consider nationalities seeking fully independent countries of their own such as Palestinians or Kurds, or Muslim groups in Russia. They might think of international rivalries, such as between Israel and Iran, or between North Korea and South Korea.)*

Topic Inquiry

Have students continue their investigations for the Topic Inquiry.

Fighting the Great War

Supporting English Language Learners

Use with Digital Text 4, **A Global Conflict.**

Learning Strategies

Remind students that active reading—pausing to ask questions, rephrasing information, and thinking aloud while reading—can make understanding the information in the text easier. Read *A Global Conflict* aloud to students. Then have students participate in the activities below based on their English proficiency level.

Beginning Reread *A Global Conflict* aloud to students. Model pausing to retell the content in everyday language. Explain new or challenging vocabulary to students, using context clues from the text when possible. After reading, model confirming comprehension by giving students a brief summary of the text.

Intermediate Reread *A Global Conflict* aloud to students. After reading the first two sentences, pause to model retelling the content in everyday language. Continue reading but ask students to take turns retelling the content after you pause. Help students understand new or challenging vocabulary by using context clues from the text when possible.

Advanced Have students take turns rereading *A Global Conflict* aloud to the group, pausing to retell the information in their own words. Challenge students to define any difficult words by using context clues as a guide.

Advanced High Have students take turns rereading *A Global Conflict* aloud to a partner, pausing to retell the information in their own words. Challenge students to define any difficult words by using context clues as a guide. Ask students to explain how shared reading helped them understand the text better.

Use with Digital Text 2, **Modern Military Technology.**

Learning Strategies

Read *Modern Military Technology* aloud to the class. After students listen to the text, have them complete one of the following activities depending on their level of English proficiency.

Beginning Create a word wall with students that includes the content-based vocabulary from this section. Distribute sheets of paper among students and review the text together. When you encounter a content-based vocabulary word, pause and ask one student to write that word on a sheet of paper. Then provide the student with a definition for that word, which should be written in smaller print below the vocabulary word. Continue with the activity until each student has written at least one word and definition. Display the words in a prominent position in the classroom. After the word wall is complete, help students write one sentence about the text using content-area vocabulary correctly.

Intermediate Create a word wall with students that includes the content-based vocabulary from this section. Distribute sheets of paper among students and assign each student one of the vocabulary words listed below. Then review the text together. When you encounter a content-based vocabulary word, pause and ask the student assigned to that word to write it down. Then help that student look up and write the definition for that word, which should be written in smaller print below the vocabulary word. Continue with the activity until each student has written at least one word and definition. Display the words in a prominent position in the classroom. After the word wall is complete, instruct students to write two sentences about the text using content-area vocabulary correctly. Circulate among students to offer support as needed.

Advanced Have students work in small groups to create a word wall for the content-based vocabulary from this section. Distribute sheets of paper among groups and have students review the text together. Instruct groups to pause when they encounter a content-based vocabulary word, write it down, and look up the definition in a dictionary or glossary. Tell students to write the definition in smaller print below the vocabulary word. When students complete this activity for the text, have them display their words in a prominent position in the classroom. After the word wall is complete, instruct groups to work together to write a paragraph summarizing the text, using content-area vocabulary correctly. Circulate among students to offer support as needed.

Advanced High Have students read and review *Modern Military Technology* to make a list of content-based vocabulary words. Instruct students to create a glossary for the terms they find, using classroom resources and context clues to develop their definitions. Then have students write a paragraph to summarize the text using the content-based vocabulary that they found in their writing. Circulate among students to offer support as needed.

PEARSON
realize™
www.PearsonRealize.com

Go online to access additional resources including:
Primary Sources • Biographies • Supreme Court cases •
21st Century Skill Tutorials • Maps • Graphic Organizers.

Objectives

Objective 1: Understand how trench warfare led to a stalemate on the Western Front.

Objective 2: Identify and describe the impact of modern military technology on the fighting.

Objective 3: Outline the course of the war on multiple European fronts.

Objective 4: Explain how World War I was a global conflict.

LESSON 2 ORGANIZER		OBJECTIVES	PACING	RESOURCES	
				Online	Print
Connect					
DIGITAL START UP ACTIVITY **In Flanders Fields**			5 min.	●	
Investigate					
DIGITAL TEXT 1 **A New Kind of War**		Objective 1	10 min.	●	●
INTERACTIVE MAP **Europe in World War I, 1914–1918**			10 min.	●	
3-D MODEL **Trench Warfare**			10 min.	●	
DIGITAL TEXT 2 **Modern Military Technology**		Objective 2	10 min.	●	●
INTERACTIVE GALLERY **Military Technology in World War I**			10 min.	●	
DIGITAL TEXT 3 **Other European Fronts**		Objective 3	10 min.	●	●
DIGITAL TEXT 4 **A Global Conflict**		Objective 4	10 min.	●	●
Synthesize					
DIGITAL ACTIVITY **Defining Characteristics**			5 min.	●	
Demonstrate					
DIGITAL QUIZ **Lesson Quiz and Class Discussion Board**			10 min.	●	

PACING: APPROX. 1 PERIOD, .5 BLOCKS

Fighting the Great War

■ CONNECT

DIGITAL START UP ACTIVITY
In Flanders Fields

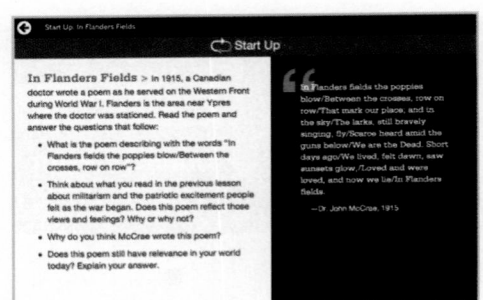

Project the Start Up Activity Ask students to answer the questions as they enter and get settled: What is the poem describing with the words "In Flanders fields the poppies blow/Between the crosses, row on row"? *(Answers will vary. Students should show an understanding that these lines are describing a cemetery filled with men killed by the war.)* Think about what you read in the previous lesson about militarism and the patriotic excitement people felt as the war began. Does this poem reflect those views and feelings? Why or why not? *(Answers will vary. Students should show an understanding that the reality of war as expressed in the poem is different from the romantic view of war described in the previous lesson.)* Why do you think McCrae wrote this poem? *(Answers will vary. Most students will probably reflect on the sadness in the poem and relate it to the carnage a doctor on the front lines would be seeing.)*

⚑ FLIP IT!
Assign the Flipped Video for this lesson.

■ STUDENT EDITION PRINT
PAGES: 652–657

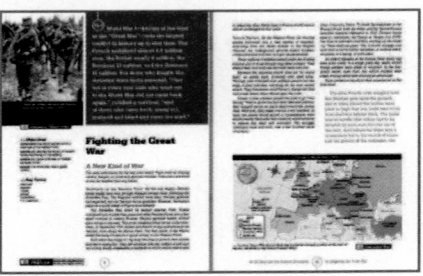

■ INVESTIGATE

DIGITAL TEXT 1
A New Kind of War

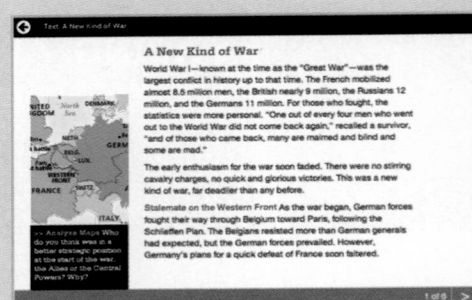

INTERACTIVE MAP
Europe in World War I, 1914–1918

Objective 1: Understand how trench warfare led to a stalemate on the Western Front.

Quick Instruction
During World War I, the war on the Western Front was characterized by trench warfare and a stalemate with neither side able to make significant advances. The stalemate, coupled with deadly new weapons, contributed to high casualty rates as each side launched massive offensives in an attempt to break the stalemate.

Interactive Map: Europe in World War I, 1914–1918 Project the map on the whiteboard. Click through the key to show how the war progressed on the Western Front each year. Help students see that the front lines moved very little from year to year. Help students connect this to these major characteristics of World War I: trench warfare, stalemate, and high casualty rates.

👥 ACTIVE CLASSROOM
Have students use the Make Headlines strategies to write headlines that capture the changes depicted by the Interactive Map. Ask: If you were to write a headline capturing the most important main idea that should be remembered, what would that headline be? Exchange your headline with a partner and try to edit and improve each other's headline.

3-D Model: Trench Warfare Project the 3-D Model and click on the red circles to reveal information about the experience of soldiers in World War I trenches. Discuss each aspect of the trench experience. Challenge students to explain how technological innovations made defenses such as trenches necessary. *(The introduction of deadly machine guns and artillery required much stronger and better defensive positions, like the trench.).* Invite students to compare and contrast World War I trench warfare with modern-day warfare. *(Modern warfare does not utilize trenches. Much of warfare today is done remotely, either by long-range missiles or drones. Airplanes and naval vessels with long-rang weapons are also important.)*

👥 ACTIVE CLASSROOM
Ask students to have a "Conversation with a World War I soldier." Tell students to imagine that they are having a conversation with a soldier who has been living in a World War I trench for several months. Direct each student to write down a question he or she would like to ask, then how the soldier would respond, and then what the student would say in response.

Integrate Information How do the map, model, and photo visually express the characteristics of trench warfare? *(Sample response: In the map, the front lines barely move over the course of the war. This shows that the trench warfare of the Western Front led to a stalemate, where neither side won decisive victories. The flipbook shows how difficult it would be for soldiers to advance without being*

3-D MODEL

Trench Warfare

DIGITAL TEXT 2

Modern Military Technology

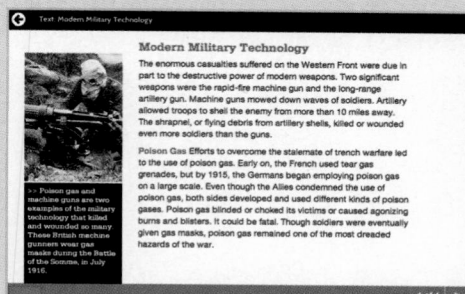

INTERACTIVE GALLERY

Military Technology in World War I

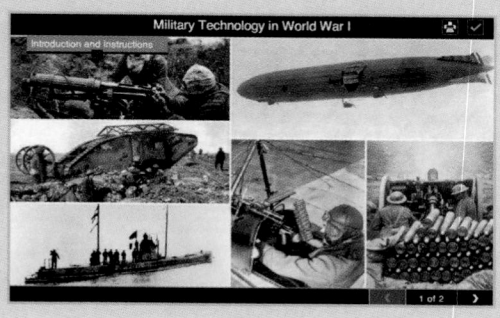

killed by the enemy. This illustrates why there were such high casualty rates. The photo provides an example of the wounds and suffering that casualties experienced.)

Further Instruction

Project the Interactive Reading Notepad questions and use student responses to discuss the causes and effects of trench warfare.

Identify Cause and Effect Ask students to explain why the German Schlieffen Plan failed, and what happened as a result. (*Russia armed more quickly than the Germans expected, and German troops had to be reassigned to the east. As a result, in the west the two sides became bogged down in trench warfare. This contributed to high casualty rates.*)

Compare and Contrast Project the poem, "Flanders Field" from the Start Up activity and the quote by Schmieder from the text. Have students compare and contrast the two pieces. (*Answers will vary. Students might point out that both texts contrast death with bird songs, both texts represent war in a negative light, or that the texts have similar perspectives even though they were written by people from opposing sides.*)

D Differentiate: **Gifted/Challenge** Have students research other quotes, poems, or songs that were written during or about World War I. As a class, discuss the content and point of view of each.

Objective 2: **Identify and describe the impact of modern military technology on the fighting.**

Quick Instruction

Modern military technology was a major characteristic of World War I. Discuss with students the effects of new military technologies on the war.

Interactive Gallery: Military Technology in World War I Project the first image of the gallery on the whiteboard. Click through the images and discuss how each technology affected the war. Discuss how this technology helped cause the trench warfare, stalemate, and high casualties that occurred on the Western Front and other fronts of the war.

🎬 ACTIVE CLASSROOM

Use the Ranking atrategy to have students go through the technologies in the gallery and rank which ones they believe had the greatest impact on World War I. Poll the class to see if there is agreement on the rankings. Discuss the results.

D Differentiate: **On Level** Extend the activity by having students rank the World War I technology that has the greatest impact on warfare today. Be prepared to help students link the older technology shown here to current equivalents.

ELL Use the ELL activity described in the ELL chart.

Further Instruction

Project and discuss the Interactive Reading Notepad questions, including the concept web graphic organizer, asking students to summarize technologies used in the war. Fill in the graphic organizer on the whiteboard as you go.

Compare and Contrast Have small groups of students choose two technologies (try to ensure that groups compare different technologies from each other) and compare and contrast their effect on the war, particularly trench warfare and high casualty rates.

D Differentiate: **Special Needs** Provide students with a simple two-column chart that already has two very different technologies at the head of each column. Ask students to go through the text and write down characteristics of each type of technology. Then help students compare the two.

Topic ⑯ Lesson 2

Fighting the Great War

DIGITAL TEXT 3
Other European Fronts

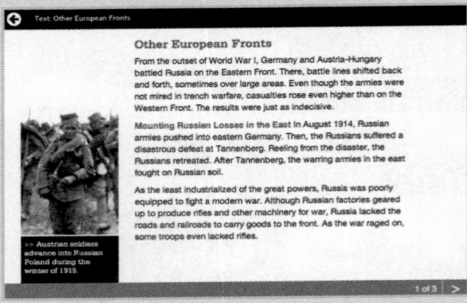

DIGITAL TEXT 4
A Global Conflict

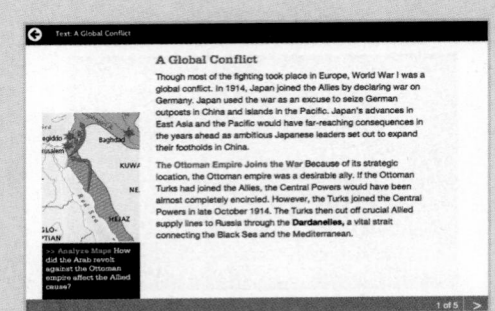

Objective 3: Outline the course of the war on multiple European fronts.

Quick Instruction

Introduce students to the other European fronts of World War I. Explain that high casualty rates were a characteristic of the Eastern Front as well as the Western Front.

Interactive Map: Europe in World War I, 1914–1918 Project the interactive map on the whiteboard again. Click through the key to show how the war progressed on the Eastern and Italian fronts each year. Help students see that the Eastern Front line move dramatically from year to year.

📖 ACTIVE CLASSROOM

Use the See, Think, Wonder strategy with this map. Pair students with a partner. Ask them: What do you see on the Eastern Front? What does that make you think? What are you wondering about now that you've seen this? Share insights with the class.

Further Instruction

Editable Presentation Use the Editable Presentation to present the main ideas for this text.

Draw Conclusion What effect did major new military technologies have on the Eastern Front? *(Answers may vary. Sample response: The Germans had a greater amount of modern military technology than the Russians. Some Russian soldiers didn't even have adequate rifles. As a result, the German army penetrated far into Russia as the Russian army retreated and suffered very high casualties.)*

Make Inferences If it was so poorly equipped, why did Russia not lose to Germany early in the war? *(Answers may vary. Sample response: Early in the war, Germany did not have enough troops on the Eastern Front. Also, while Russia did not have enough technology, it had the manpower, as the text notes: "Russian commanders continued to send masses of soldiers into combat.")*

D Differentiate: Challenge/Gifted Have students do research on the Russian defeat at Tannenberg and the Italian defeat at Caporetto. Ask them to compare the causes and effects of these important battles of World War I.

Objective 4: Explain how World War I was a global conflict.

Quick Instruction

Remind students that World War I was a truly global war fought in Europe, the Middle East, Africa, and Asia. Use the map of the Ottoman empire to discuss the importance of the battle at Gallipoli and the Arab revolt against Ottoman rule. Use the photo of Armenian refugees to introduce the topic of politically motivated mass murders in Armenia. Use the photo of colonial soldiers to introduce the impact of the war on Europe's colonies.

Summarize What was the status of the Armenians in the Ottoman empire? *(Sample response: The Armenians were a minority people without equal rights in the Ottoman empire. During World War I, the Ottoman government considered them a threat. The Ottoman government deported Armenians from their land. During the deportation, more than a million Armenians died as a result of mass murder, mistreatment, and starvation. Many of the survivors fled to other countries.)*

D Differentiate: Challenge/Gifted Many Armenians argue today that the deportation of the Armenian people during World War I was a planned genocide. Invite students to do additional research and write essays on the issue.

ELL Use the ELL activity described in the ELL chart.

Further Instruction

Editable Presentation Use the Editable Presentation to present the main ideas for this text.

SYNTHESIZE

DEMONSTRATE

DIGITAL ACTIVITY

Defining Characteristics

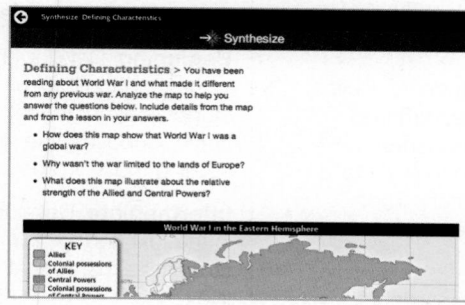

DIGITAL QUIZ

Lesson Quiz and Class Discussion Board

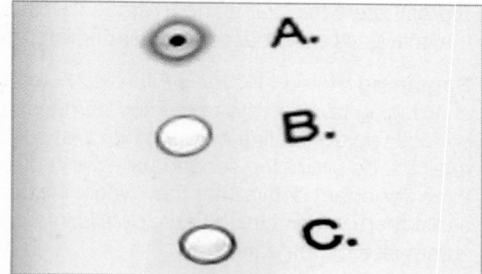

Project and discuss the Interactive Reading Notepad questions to cover more information about the role of the Ottoman empire, Arabs, Armenians, and European colonies in World War I.

Draw Inferences Project the map of the Ottoman empire during World War I. Why did Arabs fight against the Ottoman empire during World War I? *(Sample response: Arabs, driven by a spirit of nationalism, wanted to rule their own lands and be free from Ottoman rule.)*

Identify Cause and Effect How were the European colonies affected by World War I? What were the expectations of some colonial peoples as a result of their involvement in the war? *(Sample response: European colonies were affected by World War I because they provided not only supplies and labor, but also troops during World War I. Some colonial peoples hoped that their efforts in World War I would be rewarded by citizenship or independence.)*

D **Differentiate: Extra Support** Help students visualize the war as a global event by showing them a world map with the various countries involved in the war highlighted in different colors. Point out the European colonies in Asia and Africa.

Remind students of the main issues connected to the lesson and the fighting of World War I. Project the first Synthesize screen.

Discuss Lead a class discussion on the effects of major new military technology on the war. Have students examine the photograph and identify the modern military technology in it. Ask them to identify how that technology shows that World War I was a new kind of war. Connect this new technology to other key characteristics of the war, including trench warfare and high casualty rates.

Connect Is there something comparable in today's world, such as a new technology or type of warfare, that is changing how wars are fought or may be fought in the future? *(Answers may vary. Some students might talk about the modern use of unmanned drones, the threat of dirty bombs, or the spread of terrorist activities.)*

Draw Conclusions Project the second Synthesize screen and discuss how World War I was a global war. Ask: Do we fight global wars today? *(Answers may vary. Some students may be aware of the international nature of the wars in Afghanistan and Iraq, while others might not.)*

Assign the online Lesson Quiz for this lesson if you haven't already done so. Students will be offered automatic remediation or enrichment based on their score.

In this lesson, you have read about how World War I was fought and how modern technology and trench warfare resulted in high casualty rates.

Generate Explanations World War I was also called the Great War. Why do you think it was called that? *(Answers will vary, but might include the wide geographic scope of the war and/or its high casualty rate. It was the largest war the world had seen up to that time.)*

Predict Consequences How do you think the nature of World War I affected international politics after the war? *(Answers will vary. Sample responses: Countries will want revenge and remain militaristic, or countries will want to avoid war and become pacifists; countries will avoid alliances, or countries will make new alliances; European colonies will want independence; international organizations will try to prevent another war like World War I.)*

Topic Inquiry

Have students continue their investigations for the Topic Inquiry.

World War I Ends

Supporting English Language Learners

Use with Digital Text 3, **The United States Enters the War.**

Reading

Remind students that retelling what they have read in their own words is a good way to make sure they understand the content. Read *The United States Enters the War* aloud to students. Then have students participate in the activities below based on their English proficiency level.

Beginning Reread *Wilson's Fourteen Points* aloud to students. Define challenging terms in the text. Then demonstrate how to summarize by focusing on the first paragraph in that section. Help students retell the details of the second paragraph by asking them to point to three important details that they would include in a summary. Then assist them in combining those details into one or two sentences that summarize the paragraph.

Intermediate Reread *Wilson's Fourteen Points* aloud to students. Help students identify and define challenging terms in the text. Then demonstrate how to summarize by focusing on the first paragraph in that section. Ask students to summarize the second paragraph by telling them to identify three important details. Have students write a sentence that includes those details and summarizes the paragraph.

Advanced Have students pairs silently reread *Wilson's Fourteen Points.* Pairs should then identify and define challenging terms in the text. Ask one student in each pair to summarize the first paragraph in that section and the second student to summarize the second paragraph. Then have two pairs join together to share their summaries and receive feedback on their work.

Advanced High Have students silently reread *Wilson's Fourteen Points.* Then have students work independently to write a short summary of the paragraph. Circulate among students to provide support as needed.

Use with Digital Text 4, **The Great War Ends.**

Writing

Read *The Great War Ends* aloud to the class. After students listen to the text, have them complete one of the following activities depending on their level of English proficiency.

Beginning Develop a list of commonly misspelled words that appear in the text and explain the spelling of each word to students. Have the students either repeat the correct spelling aloud or write each word five times. Choose three words on which to focus and continue practice spelling those words until students consistently spell them correctly.

Intermediate Develop a list of commonly misspelled words that appear in the text and explain the spelling of each word to students. Have the students either repeat the correct spelling aloud or write each word five times. Then give students a simple spelling test to gauge their understanding of how to spell the words.

Advanced Have students skim the text to develop a list of commonly misspelled words. Discuss the spelling of each word to students. Have the students study the list of words with a partner. Then give students a simple spelling test to gauge their understanding of how to spell the words. Circulate among students to offer support as needed.

Advanced High Have students skim the text to develop a list of commonly misspelled words. Ask students to look up each word to confirm the correct spelling, definition, and part of speech. Then have the students study the list of words with a partner. Ask partners to quiz each other to make sure they know the spelling of each word. Circulate among students to offer support as needed.

▣ Differentiate Instruction

Use the Differentiated Instruction notes throughout the lesson plan to support the varied skill sets, levels of readiness, and interests in the mixed-ability classroom.

Challenge These notes include suggestions for expanding the activity for advanced students.

On-Level These notes include suggestions for modifying the activity to address different interests or learning styles.

Extra Support These notes include ideas for providing more scaffolding or reading spuport.

Special Needs These notes provide ideas for adapting instruction to support the needs of various special needs students.

▪ NOTES

PEARSON
realize ™
www.PearsonRealize.com

Go online to access additional resources including:
Primary Sources • Biographies • Supreme Court cases •
21st Century Skill Tutorials • Maps • Graphic Organizers.

Objectives

Objective 1: Describe how World War I became a total war.

Objective 2: Explain how U.S. entry into the war led to an Allied victory.

Objective 3: List the effects of World War I in terms of financial costs, high casualty rates, and political impact.

Objective 4: Describe the issues at the Paris Peace Conference and the impact of Woodrow Wilson's Fourteen Points.

Objective 5: Summarize the terms and impact of the Treaty of Versailles.

LESSON 3 ORGANIZER		PACING: APPROX. 1 PERIOD, .5 BLOCKS			
		OBJECTIVES	PACING	RESOURCES Online	RESOURCES Print
Connect					
DIGITAL START UP ACTIVITY **An Uneasy Peace?**			5 min.	●	
Investigate					
DIGITAL TEXT 1 **Governments Direct Total War**		Objective 1	10 min.	●	●
DIGITAL TEXT 2 **Morale Breaks Down**		Objective 1	10 min.	●	●
INTERACTIVE GALLERY **World War I Propaganda Posters**			10 min.	●	
DIGITAL TEXT 3 **The United States Enters the War**		Objective 2	10 min.	●	●
DIGITAL TEXT 4 **The Great War Ends**		Objective 3	10 min.	●	●
DIGITAL TEXTS 5 AND 6 **Making the Peace, Effects of the Peace Settlements**		Objectives 4, 5	10 min.	●	●
INTERACTIVE MAP **Europe in 1914 and 1920**			10 min.	●	
Synthesize					
DIGITAL ACTIVITY **The Treaty of Versailles**			5 min.	●	
Demonstrate					
DIGITAL QUIZ **Lesson Quiz and Class Discussion Board**			10 min.	●	

World War I Ends

■ CONNECT

DIGITAL START UP ACTIVITY
An Uneasy Peace?

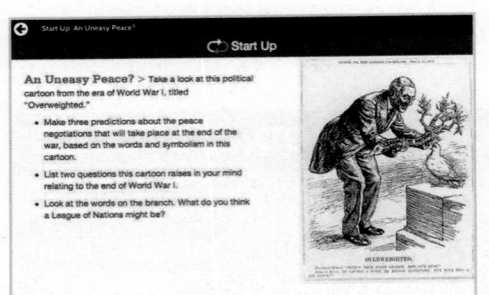

Project the Start Up Activity Ask students to answer the writing stimuli as they enter and get settled: Make three predictions about the peace negotiations that will take place at the end of the war. *(Answers will vary, but students may say that Wilson believes that something called the League of Nations will bring or keep the peace. It won't be easy, or perhaps even possible, to please everyone in the peace negotiations. Wilson's peace proposals will be too difficult to implement.)* List two questions this cartoon raises in your mind about the end of World War I. *(Sample responses: What is the League of Nations? Why is it, in the cartoonist's opinion, "overweighted"? Why is President Wilson getting involved in a peace process for this war?)*

Aa Vocabulary Development: Use the Interactive Reading Notepad to preview the Key Terms and Academic Vocabulary in this lesson with students.

⇅ FLIP IT!
Assign the Flipped Video for this lesson.

■ STUDENT EDITION PRINT PAGES: 658–666

■ INVESTIGATE

DIGITAL TEXT 1
Governments Direct Total War

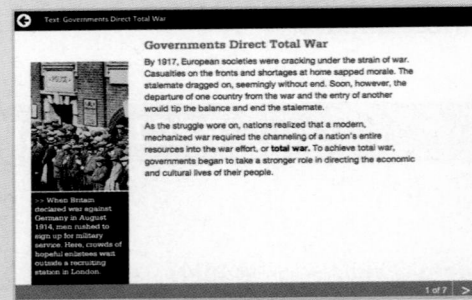

DIGITAL TEXT 2
Morale Breaks Down

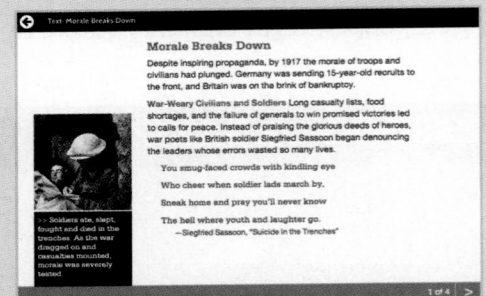

Objective 1: Describe how World War I became a total war.

Quick Instruction
World War I became a total war as nations directed all resources to the war effort. Governments exerted more control over people's lives by requiring military service, rationing food and other necessities, raising money through taxes and bonds, and controlling information, media, and public opinion. As the economic impact and casualty rates dramatically increased, morale sank. In Russia, revolution erupted.

Interactive Gallery: World War I Propaganda Posters Project the gallery. Begin by reminding students that during the time of World War I, there was no Internet or television. Explain that posters hanging in public areas were a common and effective way to convey information and influence public opinion. Make sure students understand the meaning of the word *propaganda* and that government propaganda was one aspect of total war.

🎭 ACTIVE CLASSROOM
Break students into six teams, one for each propaganda poster in the Interactive Gallery. Have each team use the Act It Out strategy to present its propaganda poster as if it were a TV commercial. Ask students to "bring the poster to life." Their commercial should clearly represent the message of their propaganda poster.

Further Instruction
Project the Interactive Reading Notepad questions for these texts. Be sure students understand the concept of total war *(channeling of a nation's entire resources into a war effort)*. Discuss with students how economic warfare and women's contributions to the war effort were both examples of total war.

Identify Cause and Effect How did total war cause soldiers' and civilians' morale to collapse? *(Sample response: Morale collapsed because of food shortages, economic decline, high taxes, and the high number of solders killed, wounded, or captured.)* What were some effects of the decline in morale? *(Sample response: calls for leaders to end the war, ant-war literature, soldiers mutinying and deserting, revolution in Russia)* What impact did the February and October revolutions in Russia have on the war? *(Sample response: The February revolution encouraged the Allies that Russia would become a strong democratic ally. But the October revolution led to Russia's withdrawal from the war, and allowed the Central Powers to focus on the Western Front.)*

INTERACTIVE GALLERY

World War I Propaganda Posters

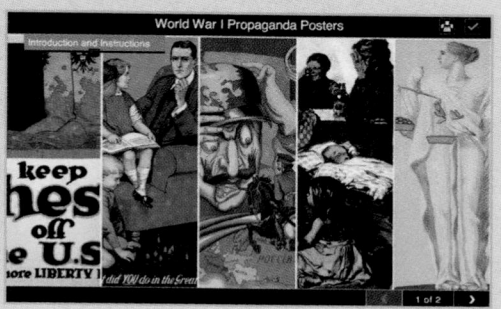

Draw Inferences Why might citizens of warring nations be willing to give up some of their individual freedoms and accept a more limited standard of living? *(Sample response: They might fear for their future if their country does not win the war; they might want to do what is necessary to help the troops and not want to feel guilty about not actively supporting their country.)*

DIGITAL TEXT 3

The United States Enters the War

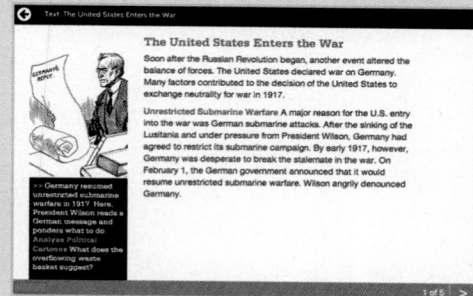

Objective 2: Explain how U.S. entry into the war led to an Allied victory.

Quick Instruction

The United States remained neutral during the war's early years. But after Germany's resumption of unrestricted submarine warfare and the release of the Zimmermann note, the United States declared war on Germany in 1917. The entry of the United States into the war brought fresh troops, money, and vigor to the Allies' cause. It broke the stalemate, revived morale, and ultimately led to Allied victory. President Wilson began to work for a just and lasting peace.

Analyze Information Project the chart on the Fourteen Points, and read through the summaries of Wilson's ideas. To help students understand the political impact of the Fourteen Points, ask them to explain how the Fourteen Points would lead to the creation of new independent countries and the breakup of empires. *(Points 10 thru 13 call for various nationalities to have autonomy or independence. Carrying out these ideas would lead to the breakup of empires and the creation of new independent countries.)*

ELL Use the ELL activity described in the ELL chart.

Further Instruction

Editable Presentation Use the Editable Presentation to present the main ideas from this text.

Make Generalizations Tell students that Wilson's Fourteen Points were welcomed by some but criticized by others. Who, in general, would probably support Wilson's Fourteen Points? *(Sample response: those who favored international cooperation and peace, nationalists who wanted independent countries, colonial people who wanted rights and freedoms)* Who, in general, would oppose the Fourteen Points? *(Sample response: militarists, imperialists, rulers of empires)*

D Differentiate: Extra Support Ask students to work in small groups to identify key terms in the Fourteen Points that they do not fully understand. Have them use a dictionary to define those terms. Then invite them to explain the terms' importance in the Fourteen Points.

World War I Ends

DIGITAL TEXT 4
The Great War Ends

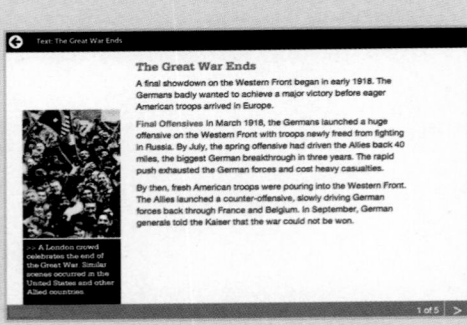

The Great War Ends

A final showdown on the Western Front began in early 1918. The Germans badly wanted to achieve a major victory before eager American troops arrived in Europe.

Final Offensives In March 1918, the Germans launched a huge offensive on the Western Front with troops newly freed from fighting in Russia. By July, the spring offensive had driven the Allies back 40 miles, the biggest German breakthrough in three years. The rapid push exhausted the German forces and cost heavy casualties.

By then, fresh American troops were pouring into the Western Front. The Allies launched a counter-offensive, slowly driving German forces back through France and Belgium. In September, German generals told the Kaiser that the war could not be won.

>> A London crowd celebrates the end of the Great War. Similar scenes occurred in the United States and other Allied countries.

1 of 5 >

DIGITAL TEXTS 5 AND 6
Making the Peace, Effects of the Peace Settlements

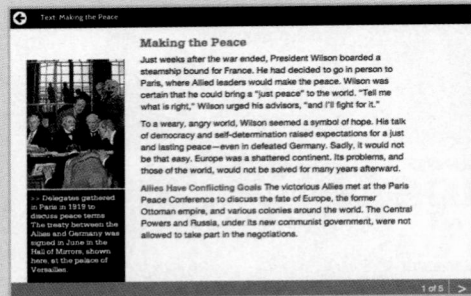

Making the Peace

Just weeks after the war ended, President Wilson boarded a steamship bound for France. He had decided to go in person to Paris, where Allied leaders would make the peace. Wilson was certain that he could bring a "just peace" to the world. "Tell me what is right," Wilson urged his advisors, "and I'll fight for it."

To a weary, angry world, Wilson seemed a symbol of hope. His talk of democracy and self-determination raised expectations for a just and lasting peace—even in defeated Germany. Sadly, it would not be that easy. Europe was a shattered continent. Its problems, and those of the world, would not be solved for many years afterward.

Allies Have Conflicting Goals The victorious Allies met at the Paris Peace Conference to discuss the fate of Europe, the former Ottoman empire, and various colonies around the world. The Central Powers and Russia, under its new communist government, were not allowed to take part in the negotiations.

>> Delegates gathered in Paris in 1919 to discuss peace terms. The treaty between the Allies and Germany was signed in June in the Hall of Mirrors, shown here, at the palace of Versailles.

1 of 5 >

Objective 3: List the effects of World War I in terms of financial costs, high casualty rates, and political impact.

Quick Instruction

The war finally ended, leaving Europe in shambles. More than 8.5 million soldiers had died in battle. Millions of civilians also lost their lives. The economic impact was staggering, with the war costing countries billions of dollars. The governments of several empires collapsed. In other countries, political radicals pushed for extreme change.

Analyze Data Project the chart detailing the costs of World War I. Ask students to spend three minutes jotting down their response to these two questions on sticky notes: "Which two countries suffered the greatest losses in World War I?" "In what ways?" Ask students to pair up or turn to an assigned partner and share their responses. Poll the class to see if there is general agreement. Discuss the results.

D **Differentiate: Extra Support** Make sure students understand the difference between numbers and percentages, both of which are presented in the graphic. Also point out to students the precise difference between millions and billions.

Further Instruction

The Great War Ends: Core Text and Interactive Reading Notepad Project the Interactive Reading Notepad questions for this text. Be sure students understand how the destruction of World War I led to political turmoil and uncertainty.

Compare Points of View After the war, there was disagreement on the issue of reparations. Ask students to identify and compare two different viewpoints that leaders had. Have them express their own opinions on whether reparations were useful and fair. *(Sample response: Many Allied leaders favored reparations so that the defeated countries could pay for the war damages. Many leaders of the Central Powers felt that the costs of war should be shared by all participating countries, not just the defeated ones. Students' opinions should be supported by sound reasoning.)*

ELL Use the ELL activity described in the ELL chart.

Objectives 4: Describe the issues at the Paris Peace Conference and impact of the Treaty of Versailles; 5: Summarize the terms and impact of the Treaty of Versailles.

Quick Instruction

After compromising on conflicting goals, the leaders at the Paris Peace Conference drew up the Treaty of Versailles. It violated several of the Fourteen Points and imposed harsh terms on Germany. As a result of it and other peace settlements, political boundaries changed. Empires broke up, and new nations were created. The mandate system granted Britain and France control over former German colonies and Ottoman territories. The system provided economic benefits to Britain and France but denied self-determination to the people living in the mandates.

Interactive Map: Europe in 1914 and 1920 Project the map activity. Move the slider to compare the two maps of Europe and read the text aloud, or ask a student to do so. Have students answer the questions in the activity.

INTERACTIVE MAP

Europe in 1914 and 1920

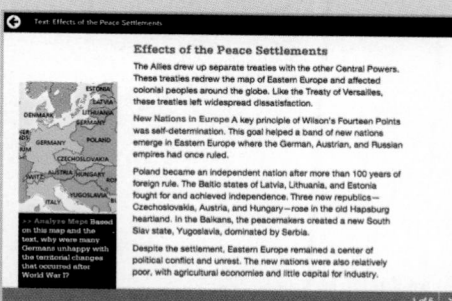

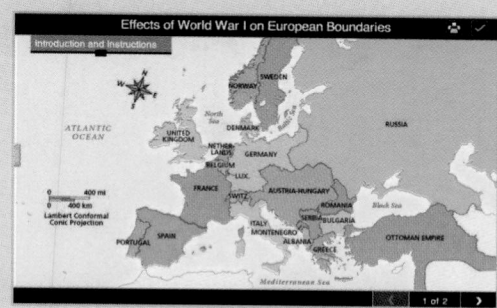

ACTIVE CLASSROOM

How did the Treaty of Versailles impact the lives of people in Europe? Pair students. Have the first student give the second an Audio Tour of the map, explaining what it shows. Have the second student give the first an explanation of what it means. How did the boundary changes benefit some, but not others? *(Some new nations were created in Europe, but many colonies remained under foreign control.)*

Further Instruction

Project the Interactive Reading Notepad questions for this text and discuss the political and economic impact of the Treaty of Versailles.

Summarize Ask students to summarize the main goals and weaknesses of the League of Nations. *(Goals: international cooperation for negotiation of disputes, collective security and preservation of peace; Weaknesses: Not all countries were members, the powerful United States did not join, the League could not enforce its will on nonmember states)*

Draw Inferences How did the Treaty of Versailles and changes in boundaries impact the economies of Europe? *(Sample response: Allied powers gained reparations that helped them repair war damage and rebuild their economies. Germany's economy suffered because it had to pay high reparations and lost valuable territory, including land along the Baltic Sea. The new nations created in Eastern Europe were poor, rural, and had little capital to develop industry.)*

Identify Central Ideas Britain and France treated their new mandates in the Middle East and elsewhere like colonies. What was the political and economic impact of the mandate system on Britain, France, and the mandates? *(Answers will vary. Sample response: Britain and France used the mandates as markets for their goods and sources of raw materials. The mandates were denied self-government and remained under the political and economic control of European powers; they felt betrayed.)*

World War I Ends

■ SYNTHESIZE

■ DEMONSTRATE

DIGITAL ACTIVITY

The Treaty of Versailles

DIGITAL QUIZ

Lesson Quiz and Class Discussion Board

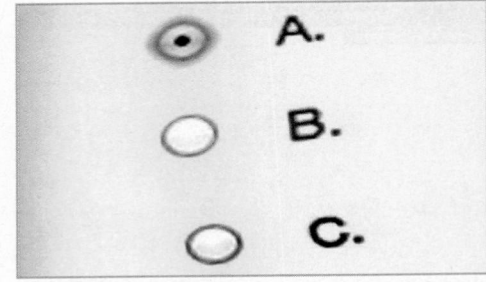

Ask students to recall the Topic Essential Question: When is war justified? Have them use the Think-Pair-Share strategy to answer the questions in the Synthesize activity on the Treaty of Versailles: What is the German newspaper's opinion of the Treaty of Versailles? *(It is obviously angry and opposed to the treaty, and urges the German people to undo it and seek revenge on the Allies who forced Germany to accept it.)* Based on what you have learned in this lesson, do you agree or disagree with this newspaper's viewpoint? *(Answers may vary. Students may cite evidence that the treaty was unjustly harsh on Germany and violated Wilson's Fourteen Points. Other students may say that Germany was in large part responsible for the war, had lost, and therefore should suffer the consequences.)* Do you think the tone of this article reflects President Wilson's hope that World War I would be the "war to end all wars?" *(Answers may vary. But students should recognize that the treaty was imperfect and extremely harsh on Germany. Rightly or wrongly, the German people were likely to go to war again. World War I would not be the war to end all wars, as Wilson had hoped.)*

Discuss Have pairs think about the following question: Do you think most Germans after World War I would favor pacifism or militarism? Why? Have pairs share their answers with the class. *(Sample responses: pacifism, because most Germans will be against war because they don't want to experience terrible losses again; or militarism, because most Germans will want to regain what their country lost and get revenge on the Allies who forced the Treaty of Versailles on them)*

Assign the online Lesson Quiz for this lesson if you haven't already done so. Students will be offered automatic remediation or enrichment based on their score. Pose these questions to the class on the Discussion Board:

In "World War I Ends," students learned about total war, the war's high human and economic costs, and the effects of the war's peace treaties. Pose these questions to the class on the Discussion Board:

Hypothesize Do you think the world is better off because of international organizations like the League of Nations and the United Nations? Why? *(Sample response: Yes, the world is better off because such an organization requires greater accountability and responsibility for all nations.)*

Predict Consequences How might World War I and its peace settlements have future consequences for the world as a whole? *(Answers will vary; some students may know that hostility regarding the peace settlements would eventually contribute to the outbreak of another world war.)*

Topic Inquiry

Have students continue their investigations for the Topic Inquiry.

Revolution in Russia

Supporting English Language Learners

Use with Digital Text 2, **Lenin Leads the Bolsheviks.**

Reading

Read *Lenin Leads the Bolsheviks* aloud to students. Then have students answer questions below based on their English proficiency level.

Beginning Ask students the following questions. Students may answer by pointing to or reciting specific information in the text.

- Who influenced Lenin the most? [Karl Marx]
- What does the name Bolsheviks mean? [majority]

Intermediate Ask students to answer the following questions using complete sentences. Allow students to refer to the text for support as needed.

- How did Lenin and Krupskaya influence political thought in Russia?
- How did Lenin adjust Marxist ideas to encourage a political revolution in Russia?

Advanced Ask students to answer the following questions using complete sentences. Allow students to refer to the text for support as needed.

- How did the death of Lenin's older brother influence his future political career?
- Do you think the creation of the Bolsheviks is a true reflection of Marxist ideals? Why or why not?

Advanced High Ask students to use the following questions to begin a discussion of the revolution in Russia. Allow students to refer to the text for support as needed.

- How did the death of Lenin's older brother influence his future political career?
- Do you think the creation of the Bolsheviks is a true reflection of Marxist ideals? Why or why not?
- How is the impending Russian revolution similar to other revolutions you have studied?

Use with Digital Text 1, **Causes of the February Revolution.**

Writing

Read *Causes of the February Revolution* aloud to the class. After students listen to the text, have them complete one of the following activities depending on their level of English proficiency.

Beginning Write and display the following words from the text: *Eastern*, *year*, and *appearance*. Show students the spelling pattern by underlining *ea* in each of the words and saying the letter blend aloud. Tell them that *ea* makes the long e sound in certain English words. Then show students other words that share the same pattern, such as *near*, *steal*, and *weak*.

Intermediate Write and display the word *revolution* for students. Explain the *-tion* pattern to students, focusing on the sound that those letters make in a word. Help them review the text to find other words that share the same spelling pattern. Students should be able to find the following words: *transportation*, *constitution*, and *ammunition*. Practice saying and spelling these words aloud with students.

Advanced Write and display the word *revolution* for students. Ask a student volunteer to explain the *-tion* pattern to the class. Then have students work with a partner to review the text to find other words that share the same spelling pattern. Students should be able to find the following words: *transportation*, *constitution*, and *ammunition*. Partners should practice saying and spelling these words aloud to each other.

Advanced High Write and display the words *influence* and *revolution* for students. Ask two student volunteers to explain the *-ence* and *-tion* spelling patterns to the class. Then have students work with a partner to review the text to find other words that share the same spelling pattern. Students should be able to find the following words: *confidence*, *transportation*, *constitution*, and *ammunition*. Have partners add other words that share the same spelling patterns to each list. Then ask them to practice saying and spelling these words aloud to each other.

D Differentiate Instruction

Use the Differentiated Instruction notes throughout the lesson plan to support the varied skill sets, levels of readiness, and interests in the mixed-ability classroom.

Challenge These notes include suggestions for expanding the activity for advanced students.

On-Level These notes include suggestions for modifying the activity to address different interests or learning styles.

Extra Support These notes include ideas for providing more scaffolding or reading spuport.

Special Needs These notes provide ideas for adapting instruction to support the needs of various special needs students.

■ NOTES

_____

_____

_____

_____

_____

_____

Revolution in Russia

Objectives

Objective 1: Explain the causes of the February (March) Revolution.

Objective 2: Describe the goals of Lenin and the Bolsheviks in the October Revolution.

Objective 3: Summarize the outcome of the civil war in Russia.

Objective 4: Analyze how Lenin built a Communist state in the Soviet Union.

LESSON 4 ORGANIZER	PACING: APPROX. 1 PERIOD, .5 BLOCKS				
				RESOURCES	
		OBJECTIVES	PACING	Online	Print
Connect					
DIGITAL START UP ACTIVITY **"End the War and Its Bloodshed"**			5 min.	●	
Investigate					
DIGITAL TEXT 1 **Causes of the February Revolution**		Objective 1	10 min.	●	●
DIGITAL TEXT 2 **Lenin Leads the Bolsheviks**			10 min.	●	●
DIGITAL TEXT 3 **Revolution Brings the Bolsheviks to Power**		Objective 2	10 min.	●	●
INTERACTIVE CHART **1917—Revolutions in Russia**			10 min.	●	
DIGITAL TEXT 4 **Civil War Erupts in Russia**		Objective 3	10 min.	●	●
DIGITAL TEXT 5 **The Communist Soviet Union Emerges**			10 min.	●	●
INTERACTIVE MAP ACTIVITY **From Russian Empire to Soviet Union, 1914–1923**		Objective 4	10 min.	●	
Synthesize					
DIGITAL ACTIVITY **End the War and Its Bloodshed**			5 min.	●	
Demonstrate					
DIGITAL QUIZ **Lesson Quiz and Class Discussion Board**			10 min.	●	

Go online to access additional resources including:
Primary Sources • Biographies • Supreme Court cases •
21st Century Skill Tutorials • Maps • Graphic Organizers.

 CONNECT

DIGITAL START UP ACTIVITY
"End the War and Its Bloodshed"

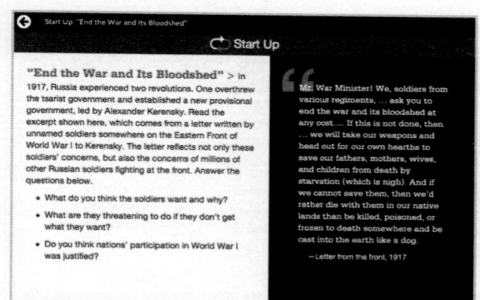

Project the Start Up Activity Have students read the excerpt from the Russian soldiers' letter and answer the questions as they enter and get settled: What do the soldiers want and why? *(They want Russia to get out of the war. They want to go home to help their starving families.)* What are they threatening to do if they don't get what they want? *(They threaten to desert and go home without the government's permission.)* Do you think nations' participation in World War I was justified? *(Answers will vary, but some students may point out that it depends on which nations you're talking about. Some may say that going to war over alliances is not a good enough reason to go to war.)*

Tell students that in this lesson they will learn about revolutions in Russia, the Russian Civil War, and the establishment of the Union of Soviet Socialist Republics.

Aa Vocabulary Development: Use the Interactive Reading Notepad to preview the Key Terms and Academic Vocabulary in this lesson with students.

STUDENT EDITION PRINT PAGES: 667–672

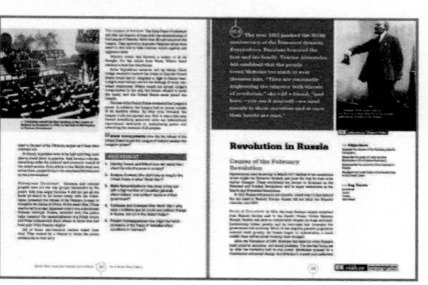

 INVESTIGATE

DIGITAL TEXT 1
Causes of the February Revolution

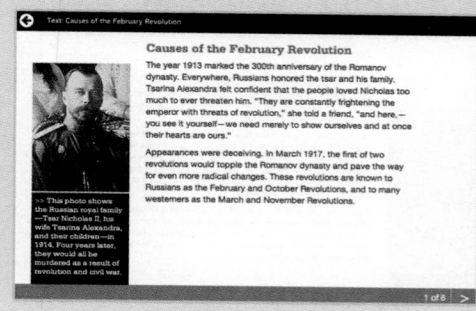

Objective 1: Explain the causes of the February (March) Revolution.

Quick Instruction
As World War I was raging in 1917, Russia suffered from great social inequality and many economic problems. Tsar Nicholas II continued to use force to limit representative government and deny individual freedoms. The inadequately supplied and poorly led Russian army suffered massive defeats and millions of casualties. At home, food and fuel shortages added to the misery. All these factors caused a revolution that forced the tsar to abdicate.

Analyze Images Ask students to compare the text photo of the peasants with that of the tsar. How do the images suggest some of the causes of the February Revolution? *(Sample response: The peasants were poor workers with little hope for advancement. The tsar, in military uniform, used force to control Russia. He also led Russian soldiers to defeat in World War I.)*

Further Instruction
Editable Presentation Use the Editable Presentation to present the main ideas for this text.

Project and discuss the Interactive Reading Notepad questions. Be sure students understand how World War I and the actions of the tsar and tsarina were causes of revolution in Russia.

Solve Problems Divide students into groups. Ask each group to recall the problems that led to the February Revolution and then work together to devise a plan of action that might

have solved the problems and delayed or prevented revolution. *(Answers will vary. Sample responses: withdraw from World War I, give the Duma more democratic power, provide land to the peasants and food to the needy, urge the tsar to reduce his power and rule as a constitutional monarch)*

D Differentiate: Challenge/Gifted Ask students to do research to learn more about the influence of the monk Gregory Rasputin over the tsar's family and how that contributed to the February Revolution. Have them write a brief, three-paragraph report on their findings.

Revolution in Russia

DIGITAL TEXT 2

Lenin Leads the Bolsheviks

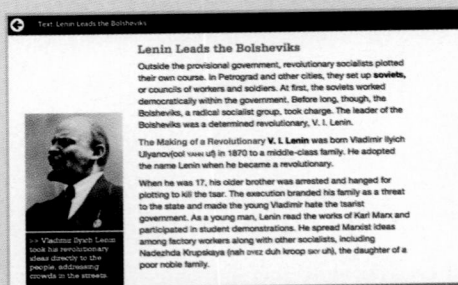

DIGITAL TEXT 3

Revolution Brings the Bolsheviks to Power

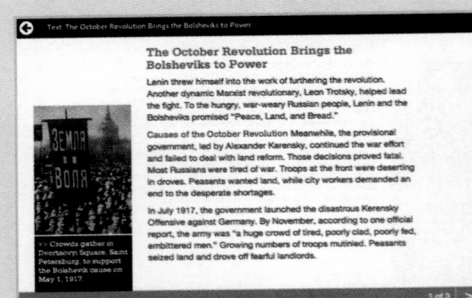

INTERACTIVE CHART

1917—Revolutions in Russia

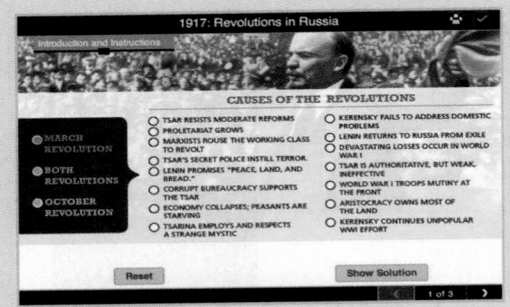

Objective 2: Describe the goals of Lenin and the Bolsheviks in the October Revolution.

Quick Instruction

Following the February Revolution, Russia's provisional government implemented few reforms and continued the war effort. Vladimir Lenin adapted Marx's ideas to fit conditions in Russia. With promises of "Peace, Land, and Bread," Lenin's Bolsheviks led workers and soldiers in the October Revolution that overthrew the provisional government. Lenin then distributed land to peasants, gave workers control of the factories, and established a socialist state.

Interactive Chart: 1917—Revolutions in Russia Project the chart and explain to students that they will decide if each item was a cause of the February Revolution, the October Revolution, or both revolutions. Invite students or pairs to take turns categorizing and explaining each cause.

📷 ACTIVE CLASSROOM

Use the Act It Out strategy to have students stage a TV round-table news show. One student acts as the moderator/interviewer. Other students assume various roles such as Tsar Nicholas II, Kerensky, Lenin, a soldier, a peasant, and a factory worker. The focus of the discussion should be whether or not revolution is necessary, and why or why not. Students may wish to record their show and present it as an online video.

ELL Use the ELL activity described in the ELL chart.

Further Instruction

Editable Presentation Use the Editable Presentation to present the main ideas for this text.

Project and discuss the Interactive Reading Notepad questions. Be sure students understand how the ideas of Karl Marx and Vladimir Lenin shifted political thought and brought about a communist revolution in Russia.

Identify Cause and Effect Ask students why they think Lenin was so successful in winning support from many Russians. *(Answers will vary. Sample response: Lenin promised people what they wanted and needed, such as withdrawing Russia from World War I, providing land to the peasants, food for the starving, and workers' control of factories.)*

Compare and Contrast Ask: How did Lenin's ideas differ from those of Karl Marx and those of moderate socialists like the Mensheviks? *(Marx predicted the proletariat would revolt and overthrow capitalism. But Russia lacked a large proletariat, so Lenin used a small elite group to lead revolution. Moderate socialists favored gradual moderate reforms such as higher wages and social welfare programs. Lenin wanted radical change through revolution.)*

DIGITAL TEXT 4
Civil War Erupts in Russia

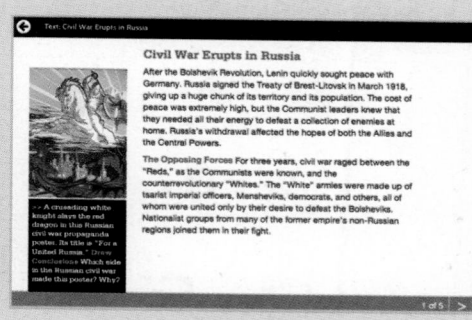

Civil War Erupts in Russia

After the Bolshevik Revolution, Lenin quickly sought peace with Germany. Russia signed the Treaty of Brest-Litovsk in March 1918, giving up a huge chunk of its territory and its population. The cost of peace was extremely high, but the Communist leaders knew that they needed all their energy to defeat a collection of enemies at home. Russia's withdrawal affected the hopes of both the Allies and the Central Powers.

The Opposing Forces For three years, civil war raged between the "Reds," as the Communists were known, and the counterrevolutionary "Whites." The "White" armies were made up of tsarist imperial officers, Mensheviks, democrats, and others, all of whom were united only by their desire to defeat the Bolsheviks. Nationalist groups from many of the former empire's non-Russian regions joined them in their fight.

↑↑ A crusading white knight slays the red dragon in this Russian civil war propaganda poster. Its title is "For a United Russia." **Draw Conclusions** Which side in the Russian civil war made this poster? Why?

1 of 5 >

DIGITAL TEXT 5
The Communist Soviet Union Emerges

Text: The Communist Soviet Union Emerges

The Communist Soviet Union Emerges

Russia was in chaos. Millions of people had died since the beginning of World War I. Millions more perished from famine and disease. Lenin faced the enormous problem of rebuilding a shattered state and economy.

New Government, Old Problems In 1922, Lenin's Communist government united much of the old Russian empire into the Union of Soviet Socialist Republics (USSR), or Soviet Union. The Communists produced a constitution that seemed both democratic and socialist. It set up an elected legislature, later called the Supreme Soviet, and gave all citizens over 18 the right to vote. All political power, resources, and means of production would belong to workers and peasants. The Soviet Union was a multinational state made up of European and Asian peoples. In theory, all the member republics shared certain equal rights.

↑↑ **Analyze Maps** Russia was by far the largest of the various republics that made up the Soviet Union. How do you think nationalism affected the Soviet Union?

1 of 5 >

Objective 3: Summarize the outcome of the civil war in Russia.

Quick Instruction

From 1918 to 1921, civil war raged in Russia with Lenin's Communist "Reds" fighting the counterrevolutionary "Whites." The Whites consisted of Mensheviks, democrats, non-Russian nationalists, and others opposed to the Communists. The Whites were supported by British, French, and American forces, but the Red Army, under the command of the brilliant strategist Leon Trotsky, was ultimately triumphant. That victory paved the way for the establishment of the Communist Soviet Union.

Draw Conclusions Ask: Why were the Reds able to defeat the Whites? *(Answers will vary. Sample response: The Reds won popular support by appealing to Russian nationalism. They had excellent leadership and training and used terror against their own people and against the Whites. They used "war communism" to seize property and food for the Red Army. Geography aided the Reds because they controlled the center of Russia, while the Whites were scattered about.)*

Further Instruction

Compare and Contrast Compare Russia's civil war with its involvement in World War I. Ask students, How were both wars alike? How were they different? *(Answers will vary. Sample response: Both wars were alike in that they killed millions of people, caused starvation and suffering for the Russian people, and involved the incursion of foreign forces on Russian soil. They were different in that World War I was fought by Russians against an external foe, while the civil war pitted Russians against Russians as they fought to decide the kind of government Russia would have.)*

Sequence Events Have students work in groups to create a graphic organizer, such as a flow chart, to show the sequence of the major events during the Russian Civil War.

Objective 4: Analyze how Lenin built a Communist state in the Soviet Union.

Quick Instruction

Lenin's Communists won the civil war and established the Union of Soviet Socialist Republics, also called the Soviet Union. Russia, the largest republic, controlled the other republics in this multinational state. The Communist party, not the people, reigned supreme and used the military to enforce its will. But to spur economic improvement, Lenin's New Economic Policy retreated from war communism and allowed some limited capitalism.

Interactive Map: From Russian Empire to Soviet Union, 1914–1923 Tell students that world war, revolution, and civil war transformed the tsarist Russian empire into the communist Soviet Union. Point out on the first layer of the Interactive Map that the western border of Russia formed the Eastern Front of World War I. Then tell them that Russia lost lands when it left the war. Show them the lands lost on the map. Then, conclude by showing them how Russia, the Ukraine, Belarus, and the Transcaucasus section of the former Ottoman empire eventually became the Soviet Union.

📖 ACTIVE CLASSROOM

Have students Write Headlines, one for each layer of the map. Each headline should capture one of the main ideas of the map layer Ask: If you were to write a headline for this map that conveyed the most important change to be remembered, what would that headline be? Pass your headline to a partner for him or her to review and to improve, if he or she can.

Revolution in Russia

 **SYNTHESIZE** **DEMONSTRATE**

INTERACTIVE MAP ACTIVITY
From Russian Empire to Soviet Union, 1914–1923

DIGITAL ACTIVITY
End the War and Its Bloodshed

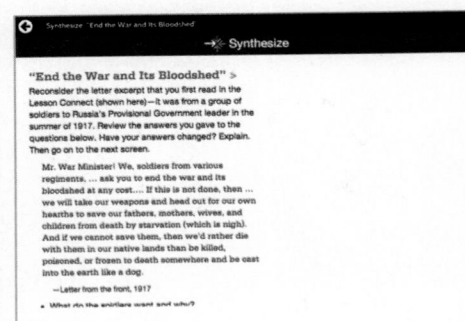

DIGITAL QUIZ
Lesson Quiz and Class Discussion Board

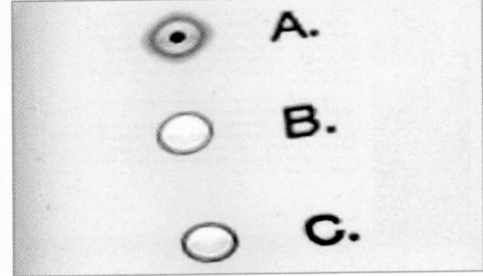

Further Instruction

Editable Presentation Use the Editable Presentation to present the main ideas for this text.

Project and discuss the Interactive Reading Notepad questions. Be sure students understand how Lenin's Communists established the Soviet Union and that they can describe the structure and polices of the new government.

Identify Cause and Effect Ask: Why did Lenin allow some capitalism in his New Economic Plan? *(War communism had greatly damaged the economy. To renew productivity, Lenin allowed small businesses to operate for private profit and peasants to sell some of their crops for profit.)*

Summarize Ask students to summarize the struggle for power that occurred after Lenin's death. *(Summaries should include profiles of Stalin and Trotsky and how Stalin forced Trotsky out of the country and then had him murdered.)*

D **Differentiate: Extra Support** To help students master vocabulary, ask them to make a list of economic terms that may be new to them. Ask students to make flashcards and to quiz each other using the flashcards.

Project the letter from Russian soldiers to Kerensky from the Start Up Activity. Then ask students to reconsider their previous answers to the questions in light of what they have learned in this lesson. *(Some answers might change based on the information they have learned. Other answers may not change, but now students should be able to support their previous opinions with evidence from the lesson.)*

The Essential Question for this topic, "When is war justified?" can be modified slightly to apply to what students have learned about the Russian Revolution. Ask students the following questions:

Synthesize In your view, were the two revolutions in Russia justified? Why or why not? *(Answers will vary. Students might say "yes," because millions of Russians were dying from the war and starvation. Others might say "no," because they should have used peaceful protest and reform efforts. Another possibility is to say that the first revolution against the tsar was justified but that the second against the provisional government was not, because people did not give the new government enough time to bring about change.)*

Support a Point of View with Evidence Once students have shared their answers to the Essential Question, divide them into teams of like-minded peers (assuming students have differing opinions). Conduct a debate between the teams. Select any undecided students to act as judges. After the debate, ask students if their peers' arguments have caused them to change their own opinions, and if so, why?

Assign the online Lesson Quiz for this lesson if you haven't already done so. Students will be offered automatic remediation or enrichment based on their score.

Post these questions to the class on the Discussion Board:

Identify Main Ideas What are the basic characteristics of communism? *(Answers will vary. Sample responses: All assets of the state are owned jointly by the people, private ownership is forbidden; the government—in the name of the people—owns all means of production, banks, and property; in theory, wealth is distributed evenly among the people.)*

Identify Supporting Ideas In general, do you think the people of Russia will end up better or worse following the revolutions? Why? *(Answers will vary. Some might say that any government would be better than the tsarist government; others may know that the Soviet government was just as dictatorial and harsh as the tsarist government.)*

Topic Inquiry
Have students continue their investigations for the Topic Inquiry.

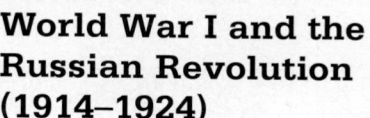
World War I and the Russian Revolution (1914–1924)

◼ SYNTHESIZE

DIGITAL ACTIVITY

Reflect on the Essential Question and Topic

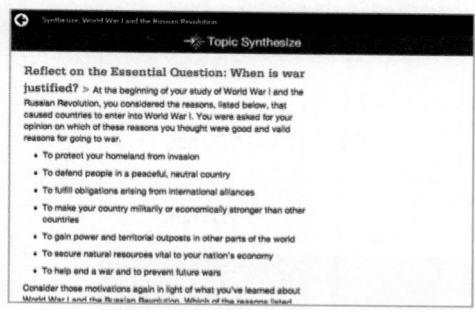

Ask students to again recall the Topic Essential Question: When is war justified? Have them rank the causes listed in the Synthesize activity in order of which causes they think are most justifiable for going to war down to those that they think are the least justifiable.

- To protect your homeland from invasion
- To defend people in a peaceful, neutral country
- To fulfill obligations arising from international alliances
- To make your country militarily or economically stronger than other countries
- To gain power and territorial outposts in other parts of the world
- To secure natural resources vital to your nation's economy
- To stop a warring country from sinking the ships of neutral countries
- To help other countries that share your country's culture, language, or values
- To help end a war and to prevent future wars

Ask students to provide a brief explanation for the ranking decisions they made. Then ask students to work in pairs to share their rankings and justifications. Poll the class to see if there is agreement on the rankings.

Discuss Discuss with students one recent international conflict. How are the causes similar to or different from the causes of World War I?

Topic Inquiry

Have students complete the Topic Inquiry.

◼ DEMONSTRATE

DIGITAL TOPIC REVIEW AND ASSESSMENT

World War I and the Russian Revolution (1914–1924)

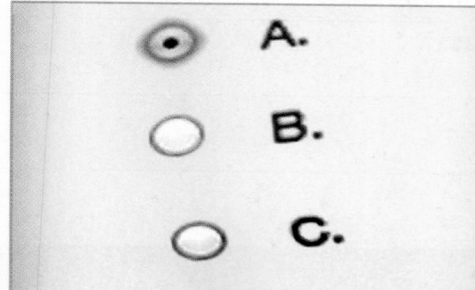

Students can prepare for the Topic Test by answering the questions in the Topic Review and Assessment online or the Assessment questions in the Print Student text. They can also prepare by reviewing their answers to the Interactive Reading Notepad questions or reviewing their notes in the Reading and Notetaking Study Guide.

DIGITAL TOPIC TEST

World War I and the Russian Revolution (1914–1924)

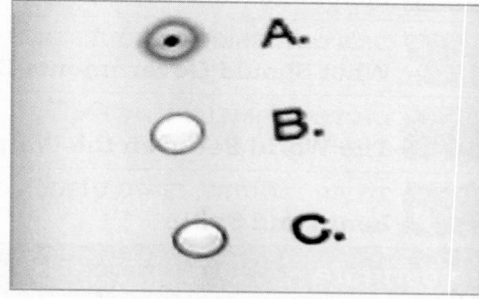

TOPIC TEST

Assign the Topic Test to assess students' understanding of topic content.

BENCHMARK TESTS

Assign these benchmark tests as you complete the relevant topics to monitor student progress toward mastering the course content and as preparation for the End-of-Course Test.

Benchmark Test 1: Topics 1–5
Benchmark Test 2: Topics 6–10
Benchmark Test 3: Topics 11–15
Benchmark Test 4: Topics 16–21

The World Between the Wars (1910–1939)

TOPIC 17 ORGANIZER	PACING: APPROX. 11 PERIODS, 5.5 BLOCKS	
		PACING
Connect		1 period
MY STORY VIDEO **Mohandas Gandhi, The Power of Nonviolence**		10 min.
DIGITAL ESSENTIAL QUESTION ACTIVITY **What Should Governments Do?**		10 min.
DIGITAL TIMELINE ACTIVITY **The World Between the Wars**		10 min.
TOPIC INQUIRY: CIVIC DISCUSSION **Lenin and Stalin**		20 min.
Investigate		4–8 periods
TOPIC INQUIRY: CIVIC DISCUSSION **Lenin and Stalin**		Ongoing
LESSON 1 Revolution and Nationalism in Latin America		30–40 min.
LESSON 2 Nationalist Movements in Africa and the Middle East		30–40 min.
LESSON 3 India Seeks Self-Rule		30–40 min.
LESSON 4 New Forces in China and Japan		30–40 min.
LESSON 5 The West After World War I		30–40 min.
LESSON 6 Fascism Emerges in Italy		30–40 min.
LESSON 7 The Soviet Union Under Stalin		30–40 min.
LESSON 8 The Rise of Nazi Germany		30–40 min.
Synthesize		1 period
DIGITAL ACTIVITY **Reflect on the Essential Question and Topic**		10 min.
TOPIC INQUIRY: CIVIC DISCUSSION **Lenin and Stalin**		20 min.
Demonstrate		1–2 periods
DIGITAL TOPIC TEST **The World Between the Wars**		10 min.
TOPIC INQUIRY: CIVIC DISCUSSION **Lenin and Stalin**		20 min.

TOPIC INQUIRY: CIVIC DISCUSSION

Lenin and Stalin

In this Topic Inquiry, students work in teams to examine different perspectives on this issue by analyzing several sources, arguing both sides of a Yes/No question, then developing and discussing their own point of view on the question: **Did Lenin sow the seeds of Stalinism?**

STEP 1: CONNECT
Develop Questions and Plan the Investigation

Launch the Civic Discussion

Divide the class into groups of four students. Students can access the materials they'll need in the online course or you can distribute copies to each student. Read the main question and introduction with the students.

Have students complete Step 1 by reading the Discussion Launch and filling in Step 1 of the Information Organizer. The Discussion Launch provides YES and NO arguments on the main question. Students should extract and paraphrase the arguments from the reading in Step 1 of their Information Organizers.

Next, students share within their groups the arguments and evidence they found to support the YES and NO positions. The group needs to agree on the major YES and NO points and each student should note those points in their Information Organizer.

Resources
- Student Instructions
- Information Organizer
- Discussion Launch

⏻ PROFESSIONAL DEVELOPMENT

Civic Discussion

Be sure to view the Civic Discussion Professional Development resources in the online course.

STEP 2: INVESTIGATE
Apply Disciplinary Concepts and Tools

Examine Sources and Perspectives

Students will examine sources with the goal of extracting information and perspectives on the main question. They analyze each source and describe the author's perspective on the main question and key evidence the author provides to support that viewpoint in Information Organizer Step 2.

Ask students to keep in mind:

- **Author/Creator:** Who created the source? An individual? Group? Government agency?
- **Audience:** For whom was the source created?
- **Date/Place:** Is there any information that reveals where and when the source was created?
- **Purpose:** Why was the source created? Discuss with students the importance of this question in identifying bias.
- **Relevance:** How does the source support one argument or another?

Suggestion: Reading the source documents and filling in Step 2 of the Information Organizer could be assigned as homework.

Resources
- Student Instructions
- Information Organizer
- Source documents

STEP 3: SYNTHESIZE
Use Evidence to Formulate Conclusions

Formulate Compelling Arguments with Evidence

Now students will apply perspectives and evidence they extracted from the sources to think more deeply about the main question by first arguing one side of the issue, then the other. In this way students become more prepared to formulate an evidence-based conclusion on their own.

Within each student group, assign half of the students to take the position of YES on the main question and the others to take the position of NO. Students will work with their partners to identify the strongest arguments and evidence to support their assigned YES or NO position.

Present Yes/No Positions

Within each group, those assigned the YES position share arguments and evidence first. As the YES students speak, those assigned NO should listen carefully, take notes to fill in the rest of the Compelling Arguments Chart (Step 3 in Information Organizer) and ask clarifying questions.

When the YES side is finished, students assigned the NO position present while those assigned YES should listen, take notes, and ask clarifying questions. Examples of clarifyin questions are:

- I think you just said [x]. Am I understanding you correctly?
- Can you tell me more about [x]?
- Can you repeat [x]? I am not sure I understand, yet.

Suggestion: You may want to set a 5 minute time limit for each side to present. Provide a two-minute warning so that students make their most compelling arguments within the time frame.

Switch Sides

The students will switch sides to argue the opposite point of view. To prepare to present the other position, partners who first argued YES will use the notes they took during the NO side's presentation, plus add any additional arguments and evidence from the reading and sources. The same for students who first argued the NO position.

STEP 4: DEMONSTRATE
Communicate Conclusions and Take Informed Action

Individual Points of View

Now the students will have the opportunity to discuss the main question from their own points of view. To help students prepare for this discussion, have them reflect on the YES/NO discussions they have participated in thus far and fill in Step 4 of their Information Organizers.

After all of the students have shared their points of view, each group should list points of agreement, filling the last portion of Step 4 on their Information Organizers.

Reflect on the Discussion

Ask students to reflect on the civic discussion thinking about:

- The value of having to argue both the YES and NO positions.
- If their individual views changed over the course of the discussion and why.
- What they learned from participating in the discussion.

Resources
- Student Instructions
- Information Organizer

INTRODUCTION

The World Between the Wars

In the wake of World War I, people around the world questioned their old assumptions. Some protested colonial rule, while others led revolutions against their governments. The Great Depression began in the United States and spread hardship to other lands. In many nations, people looked to strong, authoritarian governments to solve their problems.

◼ CONNECT

MY STORY VIDEO
Mohandas Gandhi, The Power of Nonviolence

Watch a video about the efforts of Mohandas Gandhi to win independence for India.

Check Understanding What was Gandhi's concept of satyagraha? *(an approach for winning rights through nonviolent means)*

Identify Patterns How was Gandhi able to influence the civil rights movement in the United States? *(American civil rights leaders recognized the moral power of using nonviolent protests to gain rights and employed many of the same tactics that Gandhi had used in winning independence from Great Britain.)*

⟳ FLIP IT!

Assign the My Story Video.

DIGITAL ESSENTIAL QUESTION ACTIVITY
What Should Governments Do?

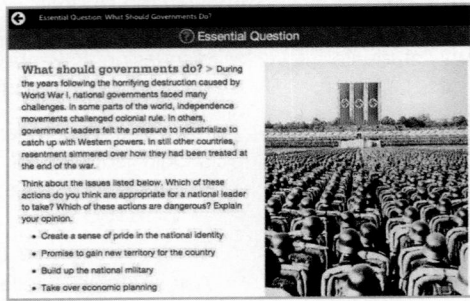

Ask students to think about the Essential Question for this topic: What should governments do? Government actions can influence a large number of people both inside and outside a country's borders. What do students believe are the duties of government?

Categorize What types of government actions do you think are generally positive? What types of actions are negative? *(Answers will vary. Many students will say that defending the nation and keeping order are generally positive. Some will have a negative view of taxation, while others may explain that taxes are necessary to pay for services. Students may take a similarly divided view of regulation.)*

Compare Points of View What is an example of a government action that might be viewed negatively by one group and positively by a different group? *(Sample response: Environmentalists would view stricter pollution controls as a positive action, while factory owners might view them as a negative action.)*

Hypothesize Under what circumstances might a head of government pursue a course of action that runs contrary to the accepted role of government? *(Sample response: A head of government might seize more power than is considered acceptable if he or she decides to become a dictator. Governments may assume greater powers during a war or other emergency.)*

DIGITAL TIMELINE ACTIVITY
The World Between the Wars

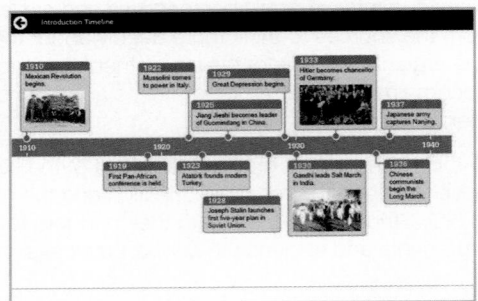

Display the timeline showing the major events that occurred between the two world wars. During this Topic, students will learn about all of these events and many more, but this timeline will provide a framework into which they can place the events they learn about.

D Differentiate: Extra Support Explain to students that this topic covers many different regions around the world. Ask them to name the different regions or countries they see listed on the timeline. Alert students to the need to pay close attention to which region is being discussed at all times.

Check Understanding Which event deals with the overthrow of a government? *(Mexican Revolution)*

Predict What area do you think Stalin was trying to improve by implementing a five-year plan? *(Sample responses: economic growth; military strength)*

Topic Inquiry
Launch the Topic Inquiry with students after introducing the topic.

Revolution and Nationalism in Latin America

Supporting English Language Learners

Use with Digital Text 3, **Nationalism Spreads in Latin America.**

Reading

Read *Nationalism Spreads in Latin America* aloud to students. Then have students follow the activities below based on their English proficiency level.

Beginning Read "Economic Nationalism" aloud. Model taking notes on the content by stopping whenever you need to write down a key idea or word. Write and display the notes for students to see.

Intermediate Reread "Economic Nationalism" and "Political Nationalism" aloud to students. Then have students work together in small groups to take notes on these two subsections. Encourage students to discuss and debate which pieces of information are important enough to be included in the groups' notes. Circulate among students and offer help as needed.

Advanced Have students work with a partner to take notes on *Nationalism Spreads in Latin America*. When partners are finished taking notes, have them review their notes and make corrections. Then have two pairs convene and share and compare their notes on the text.

Advanced High Have students take notes on *Nationalism Spreads in Latin America*. When they are finished taking notes, have them review their notes and make corrections. Then have students turn to a partner and share and compare their notes on the text.

Use with Digital Text 1, **The Mexican Revolution.**

Writing

Read *The Mexican Revolution* aloud to the class. After students listen to the text, have them complete one of the following activities depending on their level of English proficiency.

Beginning Write and display the following words from the text: *ruled* and *rippled*. Explain the rule that controls the spelling of the past tense of verbs that end in the letter *e*. Show students how to form the past tense by writing and displaying the following: *rule + -ed = ruled* and *ripple + -ed = rippled*. Explain that when changing a verb that ends in e to past tense, the e on the end of the base word is dropped, and -ed is added.

Intermediate Write and display the words *reelection* and *discontent* for students. Help students underline the base word and circle the prefix for each word. Then explain the spelling rule: When adding a prefix to a word, the spelling of the base word does not change, even if the first letter of the base word and the last letter of the prefix are the same, as in *re- + election = reelection*. Help students skim the rest of the text to look for other words with prefixes. Examples include *unrest*, *reformer*, and *resigned*.

Advanced Write and display *re- + election = _____* for students. Then ask students to work in small groups to fill in the blank and explain the rule that controls the spelling of reelection. Discuss the rule with the class to make sure that every student understands. Then have pairs skim the rest of the text to make a list of other words with prefixes. Finally, have students divide each word into a base word and its prefix.

Advanced High Facilitate a discussion in which students share spelling rules with one another. Make sure that the rule governing the spelling of words with prefixes and how to add -ed to change a verb's tense to past tense are included in the discussion. Then have students skim the text to find other words with prefixes and verbs in the past tense with -ed. Instruct students to divide each word into its word parts. Finally, have students turn to a partner to check their work.

▣ Differentiate Instruction

Use the Differentiated Instruction notes throughout the lesson plan to support the varied skill sets, levels of readiness, and interests in the mixed-ability classroom.

Challenge These notes include suggestions for expanding the activity for advanced students.

On-Level These notes include suggestions for modifying the activity to address different interests or learning styles.

Extra Support These notes include ideas for providing more scaffolding or reading spuport.

Special Needs These notes provide ideas for adapting instruction to support the needs of various special needs students.

▮ NOTES

_____

_____

_____

_____

_____

Revolution and Nationalism in Latin America

Objectives

Objective 1: Identify causes and effects of the Mexican Revolution.

Objective 2: Analyze the effects of economic and political nationalism on Latin America.

Objective 3: Trace the changing relationship between Latin America and the United States.

LESSON 1 ORGANIZER	PACING: APPROX. 1 PERIOD, .5 BLOCKS				
		OBJECTIVES	PACING	RESOURCES	
				Online	Print
Connect					
	DIGITAL START UP ACTIVITY **Comparing Experiences of the Mexican Revolution**		5 min.	●	
Investigate					
	DIGITAL TEXT 1 **The Mexican Revolution**	Objective 1	10 min.	●	●
	INTERACTIVE GALLERY **The Mexican Revolution**		10 min.	●	
	DIGITAL TEXT 2 **Economic and Social Reforms**	Objective 2	10 min.	●	●
	DIGITAL TEXT 3 **Nationalism Spreads in Latin America**	Objective 3	10 min.	●	●
	INTERACTIVE GALLERY **Revolutionary Art**		10 min.	●	
Synthesize					
	DIGITAL ACTIVITY **Mexico's Revolutionary Leaders**		5 min.	●	
Demonstrate					
	LESSON QUIZ **Lesson Quiz and Class Discussion Board**		10 min.	●	

■ CONNECT

DIGITAL START UP ACTIVITY

Comparing Experiences of the Mexican Revolution

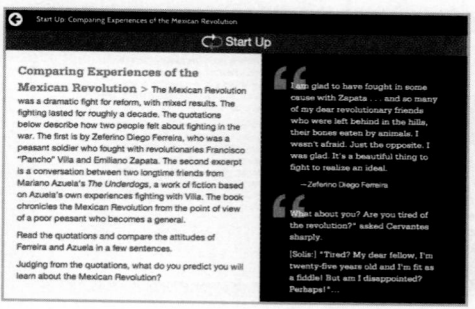

Project the Start up Activity Ask students to compare the quotations and answer the question as they enter and get settled: Judging from the quotations, what do you predict you will learn about the Mexican Revolution? *(Sample answers: Ferreira was proud to serve with Zapata and Villa and was not afraid. He believed the ideals were worth fighting for. Azuela felt that the revolution had disastrous effects on the common people and that their ideals were never realized. I will learn that people had different viewpoints about fighting and that the results were not necessarily what people had hoped for.)*

Tell students that in this lesson they will learn about the causes and effects of the Mexican Revolution and nationalism in Latin America.

Aa Vocabulary Development: Use the Interactive Reading Notepad to preview the Key Terms and Academic Vocabulary in this Lesson with students.

⇅ FLIP IT!

Assign the Flipped Video for this lesson.

■ STUDENT EDITION PRINT PAGES: 678–683

■ INVESTIGATE

DIGITAL TEXT 1
The Mexican Revolution

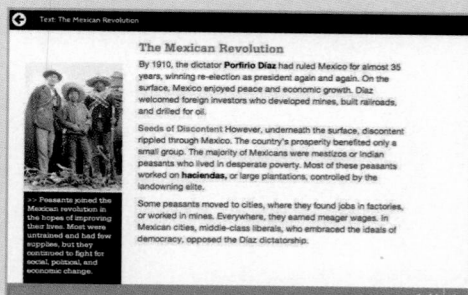

Objective 1: Identify causes and effects of the Mexican Revolution.

Quick Instruction

People from every social class opposed Mexican President Porfirio Díaz's dictatorship and supported a political revolution. However, each class generally had different reasons for that support. The peasants wanted social reform and better wages. The middle class wanted democracy, and the elite wanted to take back control of the economy from foreign companies. In 1910, the unrest boiled over into a revolution that lasted for more than a decade.

Interactive Gallery: The Mexican Revolution Project the gallery. Begin by reviewing the timeline of major events during the Mexican Revolution. Then look at each image individually. Ask students how the images and the information help them understand the complex nature of the revolution. Students should know that different groups were fighting for different beliefs and that many leaders were overthrown or assassinated during this long war.

🖼 ACTIVE CLASSROOM

Use the Ranking Strategy to have students go through the timeline and images and rank which events seemed to advance the revolution and which seemed to be setbacks. Have students explain the reasons for their choices.

INTERACTIVE GALLERY
The Mexican Revolution

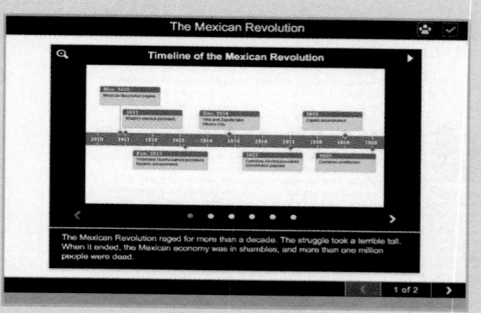

Further Instruction

Editable Presentation Use the Editable Presentation to present the main ideas for the core reading.

The Mexican Revolution: Core Text and Interactive Reading Notepad Project and discuss the Interactive Reading Notepad questions.

Be sure students understand the causes that led to the Mexican Revolution and the differing motives of each group. For example, Venustiano Carranza wanted political reforms, but he opposed the idea of redistributing land.

Infer During the war, several revolutionary leaders were overthrown or assassinated by other leaders. Why do you think the leaders turned on each other? Use evidence to support your response. *(Sample response: Some of the leaders didn't trust each other; many of them had different goals and beliefs; and some, like Huerta, wanted power and control. For example, Carranza did not trust Zapata or Villa, and he was fighting for democratic reform, not social reform like giving peasants land. He turned on them so he could take power.)*

Sequence Events Have students work in groups to create a graphic organizer, such as a flow chart, to show the sequence of the major events during the Mexican Revolution and the relationship between the leaders.

Topic ⟨17⟩ Lesson 1

Revolution and Nationalism in Latin America

DIGITAL TEXT 2
Economic and Social Reforms

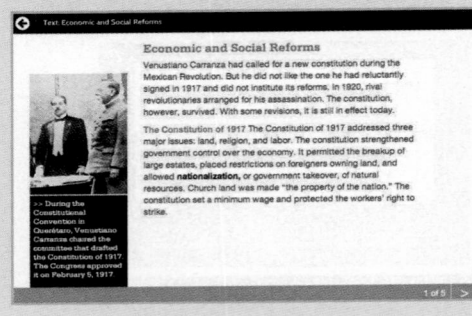

>> During the Constitutional Convention in Querétaro, Venustiano Carranza chaired the committee that drafted the Constitution of 1917. The Congress approved it on February 5, 1917.

DIGITAL TEXT 3
Nationalism Spreads in Latin America

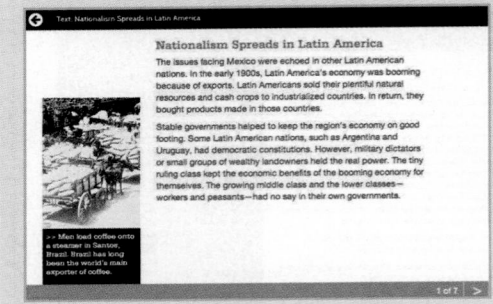

>> Men load coffee onto a steamer in Santos, Brazil. Brazil has long been the world's main exporter of coffee.

Objective 2: Analyze the effects of economic and political nationalism on Latin America.

Quick Instruction

Although the Constitution of 1917 addressed land, religion, and labor reform, Carranza was slow to make changes. Three years after signing the constitution, Carranza was overthrown.

In 1929, the government organized the Institutional Revolutionary Party (PRI). The party made some changes, but it kept the real power. The PRI dominated politics until 2000.

Further Instruction

Economic and Social Reforms: Core Text and Interactive Reading Notepad Project and discuss the Interactive Reading Notepad.

Analyze Charts Project the chart "Land Distribution in Mexico by President, 1915–1940." Explain that one of the goals of the Constitution of 1917 was the redistribution of land. Ask the following questions: What does this map tell you about the Mexican presidents and the government during these years? *(It shows that, even though the constitution addressed land reform and redistribution, Carranza and many of the following presidents did not pass reforms.)* Why do you think Carranza distributed only 1 percent of the millions of acres? *(Carranza did not fight for social reform. He was a wealthy land owner and probably did not want to give up his land or force his supporters to give up their lands.)* How does it help you understand why fighting continued throughout the 1920s? *(The revolutionaries were not ready to give up. They wanted the government to take the actions that were promised in the constitution.)*

D **Differentiate: Extra Support** Help students understand the pie chart. Remind them that a pie chart is a visual representation of statistics. Have students work in pairs to interpret the pie chart. Then create another graphic that represents the same information, such as a table or bar graph. Have pairs present their graphics. Discuss which is the most helpful. Creating different types of graphics will help them understand the different ways they can present statistics or information.

Express Problems Clearly Organize students to debate whether PRI control was good or bad for Mexico. Have them consider the goals of the revolution, the importance of stability, and the location of power. *(Answers will vary. The group for the PRI may say that the PRI created a stable government and passed many of the reforms. The group opposed to the PRI may say that while the PRI passed some reforms, it kept most of the power for itself.)*

Identify Main Ideas Ask students whether the aims of the groups who fought in the revolution had been fulfilled by the 1930s. *(Answers will vary. Students may say that the peasants did get some land redistributed and that wages were increased, especially for women. However, not all the reforms were passed. The middle class did achieve a democracy, but one party retained control. The wealthy did not achieve all their goals because much of their land was redistributed.)*

Objective 3: Trace the changing relationship between Latin America and the United States.

Quick Instruction

The end of World War I and the Great Depression affected Latin American economies. Mexico's growing spirit of economic, political, and cultural nationalism spread throughout Latin America.

Interactive Image: Revolutionary Art Work through the Interactive Image with students. Point out that it shows the history of Mexico, beginning with the Aztec through the Mexican Revolution and to the present. Ask students what they find most interesting about the mural and why they think Rivera included so much of Mexico's history. What was he trying to achieve? *(Sample response: Rivera wanted to provide perspective for the revolution and also give Mexicans a sense of pride in their history.)*

🎭 ACTIVE CLASSROOM

Have students plan and create a Graffiti Concepts that represents their culture. They should consider what traditions and aspects of their culture they think are the most important to include and how best to illustrate them. Allow students time to find or draw images. Ask students to post their "graffiti" on the board and to look at the various responses. Discuss some of the "graffiti" and why students chose to include certain things.

INTERACTIVE GALLERY

Revolutionary Art

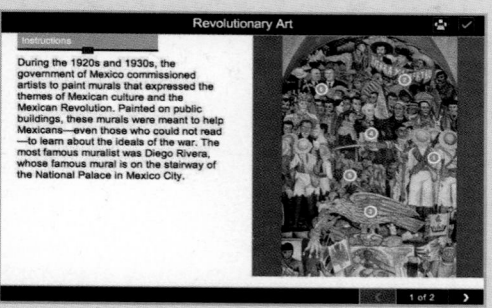

D **Differentiate: Extra Support** Have students work with a partner to create a chart showing the political, economic, and cultural effects of Latin American nationalism. Discuss their charts to make sure they understand the causes and effects.

ELL Use the ELL activity described in the ELL chart.

Further Instruction

Nationalism Spreads in Latin America: Core Text and Interactive Reading Notepad Project and discuss the Interactive Reading Notepad questions.

Analyze Cartoons Project the political cartoon from the section, "Economic Nationalism." Some people believed that nationalizing oil and other resources and industries was a positive thing. However, nationalizing industry was not entirely successful. Some nations boycotted Mexican oil. Ask students what this political cartoon shows. Why do you think the cartoonist represented nationalizing oil this way? *(The cartoon shows Mexican President Cárdenas standing on a pile of oil barrels with a "For Sale" sign. It looks like he is begging people to buy Mexican oil. The cartoonist most likely opposed nationalizing oil because it negatively impacted economic development as many nations began boycotting Mexican oil.)*

Remind students that the Good Neighbor Policy was a pledge by the United States to lessen its interference in the affairs of Latin American nations.

Analyze Charts Project the table that identifies the instances of U.S. intervention in Latin America. Ask students how this table helps them understand the relationship between the United States and Latin America. Why did the United States act this way? *(The United States regularly occupied land in Latin America and sent in troops to support different sides in rebellions. The United States most likely did this to protect its economic interests in the areas.)*

Analyze Images Then project the poster depicting the Good Neighbor Policy. Ask students why they think Roosevelt passed the Good Neighbor Policy. What does the poster show? Why were posters created about the policy? *(Roosevelt wanted to improve relations with Latin America. The poster shows peace and friendship. The posters were meant to persuade people that the policy was a good idea and that the United States and Latin America could be good allies.)*

Revolution and Nationalism in Latin America

SYNTHESIZE

DIGITAL ACTIVITY
Mexico's Revolutionary Leaders

Project the graphic organizer. Have students take five minutes to sketch out and complete the organizer on their own paper. Then divide the class into small groups, and have each group discuss members' responses. Remind students to consider what they read in the digital texts and what they learned in the interactive activities. Instruct students to record any details they missed on their individual graphic organizers. Fill in the projected graphic organizer as a class.

☞ ACTIVE CLASSROOM

Have students complete a Quick Write short paragraph explaining why they think so many Mexican leaders came to violent ends. Have groups share their responses with the class.

DEMONSTRATE

LESSON QUIZ
Lesson Quiz and Class Discussion Board

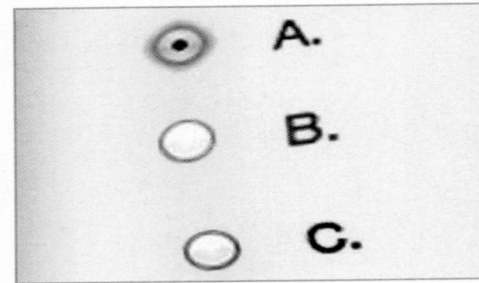

Assign the online Lesson Quiz for this lesson if you haven't already done so. Students will be offered automatic remediation or enrichment based on their score.

Remind students that the Great Depression triggered political and economic changes in Latin America. Post these questions to the class on the Discussion Board:

Identify Cause and Effect Have students make a two-column chart labeled causes and effects. Ask: What were the causes and effects of economic nationalism in Latin America? *(Sample response: Global events like World War I and the Great Depression caused prices for Latin American exports to plunge and the cost of imported goods to rise. As a result, Latin American economies declined. These events created a tide of economic nationalism. Latin Americans built factories. The governments raised tariffs and invested in local businesses. The drive for economic nationalism was not entirely successful because wealth was unequally distributed, which held back economic development.)*

Identify Main Ideas How did the relationship between Latin America and the United States change during the first three decades of the 20th century? What were the effects of these changes? *(Sample response: In the 1910s and 1920s, the United States regularly interfered in Latin American affairs. The relationship between Latin American countries and the United States deteriorated. In the 1930s, President Franklin Roosevelt decided to improve relations by passing the Good Neighbor Policy, which stated that the United States would lessen its interference in Latin America. The Good Neighbor Policy strengthened Latin American nationalism and improved relations between the United States and Latin America.)*

Topic Inquiry
Have students continue their investigations for the Topic Inquiry.

Nationalist Movements in Africa and the Middle East

Supporting English Language Learners

Use with Digital Text 2, **A Rising Tide of African Nationalism.**

Learning Strategies

Read *A Rising Tide of African Nationalism* aloud to students. Then complete one of the activities below based on their English proficiency level.

Beginning Have students read the first paragraph of *A Rising Tide of African Nationalism* silently. Provide students with bilingual dictionaries to support their understanding of the text. Circulate among students as they read to offer support and answer questions. When students are finished reading, review the paragraph by asking simple questions to gauge their understanding. If necessary, retell the text in accessible language so that students are sure to understand.

Intermediate Have students silently read *A Rising Tide of African Nationalism* one paragraph at a time. After each paragraph, help students retell what they read. Write and display important information and provide them with bilingual dictionaries to support their comprehension of the text.

Advanced Have students silently read *A Rising Tide of African Nationalism* one paragraph at a time. After each paragraph, have students turn to a partner and explain what they read. Give pairs bilingual dictionaries to support their comprehension of the text. Circulate among pairs to offer help as needed.

Advanced High Have students read *A Rising Tide of African Nationalism* silently. When they are finished, students should write a brief summary of the text and share it a partner. Partners should compare summaries to make sure that they contain accurate information.

Use with Digital Text 1, **Africans Protest Colonial Rule.**

Learning Strategies

Read *Africans Protest Colonial Rule* aloud to the class. Write and display the following sentences for students to use with the activities below. Have them complete one activity according to their level of English proficiency.

- Africans feels inspired by President Wilson's call for self-determination.
- Racial segregation separate white people from black people.
- The African National Congress demand rights for black South Africans.

Beginning Write and display the sentences above. Have students copy them. Then read the sentences aloud to students and underline the subject and circle the verb in each. Review the subject-verb agreement and make the appropriate corrections for students. Explain the rule that if the subject is singular, the *-s* form of the verb is used. Correct the sentences for students to see and then have students copy the correct version into their notes. Circulate among students to offer support as necessary.

Intermediate Write and display the sentences above. Have students copy them. Then read the sentences aloud to students and help them identify the subject-verb agreement errors in each. Correct the sentences for students to see and then have students copy the correct version into their notes. Circulate among students to offer support as necessary.

Advanced Write and display the sentences above. Have students copy them, identify the subject-verb agreement errors in each, and rewrite the sentence correctly. Circulate among students to offer support as necessary. Then review each sentence with the class and have students check their work.

Advanced High Write and display the sentences above. Have students copy them, identify the subject-verb agreement errors in each, and rewrite the sentences correctly. Then have students turn to a partner to check their work. Circulate among students to offer support as necessary.

▣ Differentiate Instruction

Use the Differentiated Instruction notes throughout the lesson plan to support the varied skill sets, levels of readiness, and interests in the mixed-ability classroom.

Challenge These notes include suggestions for expanding the activity for advanced students.

On-Level These notes include suggestions for modifying the activity to address different interests or learning styles.

Extra Support These notes include ideas for providing more scaffolding or reading spuport.

Special Needs These notes provide ideas for adapting instruction to support the needs of various special needs students.

■ NOTES

Topic ⑰ Lesson 2

Nationalist Movements in Africa and the Middle East

Objectives

Objective 1: Explain how Africans resisted colonial rule.

Objective 2: Describe the rise of nationalism in Africa.

Objective 3: Describe how Turkey and Persia modernized.

Objective 4: Understand how the mandate system contributed to Arab nationalism and to conflict between Jews and Arabs.

LESSON 2 ORGANIZER		PACING: APPROX. 1 PERIOD, .5 BLOCKS			
				RESOURCES	
		OBJECTIVES	**PACING**	**Online**	**Print**
Connect					
DIGITAL START UP ACTIVITY **Impact of World War I**			5 min.	●	
Investigate					
DIGITAL TEXT 1 **Africans Protest Colonial Rule**		Objective 1	10 min.	●	●
INTERACTIVE MAP **African Resistance to Colonial Rule**			10 min.	●	
DIGITAL TEXT 2 **A Rising Tide of African Nationalism**		Objective 2	10 min.	●	●
INTERACTIVE GALLERY **Writers of the Négritude Movement**			10 min.	●	
DIGITAL TEXT 3 **Modernization of Turkey and Persia**		Objective 3	10 min.	●	●
DIGITAL TEXT 4 **Nationalism and Conflict in the Middle East**		Objective 4	10 min.	●	●
Synthesize					
DIGITAL ACTIVITY **Nationalist Movements in Africa and the Middle East**			5 min.	●	
Demonstrate					
LESSON QUIZ **Lesson Quiz and Class Discussion Board**			10 min.	●	

PEARSON realize™
www.PearsonRealize.com

Go online to access additional resources including:
Primary Sources • Biographies • Supreme Court cases •
21st Century Skill Tutorials • Maps • Graphic Organizers.

CONNECT

DIGITAL START UP ACTIVITY
Impact of World War I

Project the Start Up Activity Ask students to write their predictions and answer the questions as they enter and get settled: How will the people who thought they would gain independence react to foreign control? What future problems might result from those actions? *(Sample responses: They will fight to rule themselves. Conflicts between the people who fought for independence may result after they have won their freedom from foreign rulers because rival groups may claim the same lands.)*

Tell students that in this lesson they will learn about nationalist movements in African colonies, Turkey, Persia, and Arab lands.

Aa Vocabulary Development: Use the Interactive Reading Notepad to preview the Key Terms and Academic Vocabulary in this Lesson with students.

⚡ FLIP IT!
Assign the Flipped Video for this lesson.

■ STUDENT EDITION PRINT
PAGES: 684–690

INVESTIGATE

DIGITAL TEXT 1
Africans Protest Colonial Rule

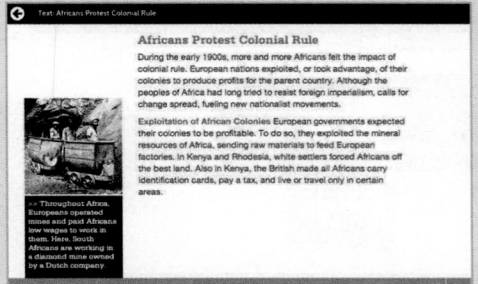

INTERACTIVE MAP
African Resistance to Colonial Rule

Objective 1: **Explain how Africans resisted colonial rule.**

Quick Instruction
More than one million Africans fought in World War I. When the Axis powers lost the war, people in the African colonies thought that their service in the war would lead to their gaining more rights. This did not happen. Many Africans began protesting colonial rule and fighting to gain independence.

Interactive Map: African Resistance to Colonial Rule Project the map. First, point out the key and have students identify German colonies that were given to other European powers. Then, look at each colony separately. Have students identify the different ways people resisted colonial rule. *(squatting on land, holding protests, forming labor unions, developing political organizations)*

👥 ACTIVE CLASSROOM
Ask students to use the Rank It strategy to rank the examples of resistance in the order of their effectiveness. Have students provide a justification for the decisions they made. Then have students discuss their ideas with a partner. Finally, take a poll to see if there any disagreements about the ranking.

D Differentiate: Challenge/Gifted Have students further research one of the events or people featured in the map and write a short newspaper article or blog post about their topic. Have students share their articles or posts.

Further Instruction
Editable Presentation Use the Editable Presentation to present the main ideas for the core reading.

Africans Protest Colonial Rule: Core Text and Interactive Reading Notepad Project and discuss the Interactive Reading Notepad questions.

Identify Main Ideas Ask students to describe the conditions in colonial Africa during the early 1900s. Record their ideas. *(Sample response: The conditions for black Africans were extremely bad. They lived on the worst land and help the lowest paying jobs. They were segregated from whites and had no economic or political control.)* Then have them review the list and describe ways that Africans responded to these conditions. Ask: How did colonial abuses and African resistance play out in South Africa? *(Sample response: Whites instituted a repressive system of segregation called apartheid. Black South Africans resisted by forming a political party to protest apartheid by legal means.)*

Nationalist Movements in Africa and the Middle East

DIGITAL TEXT 2

A Rising Tide of African Nationalism

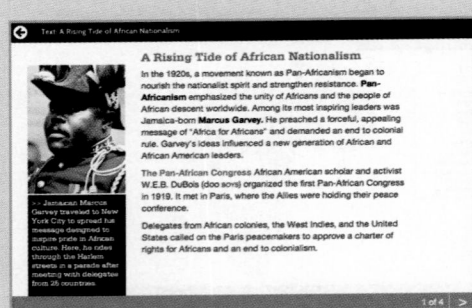

INTERACTIVE GALLERY

Writers of the Négritude Movement

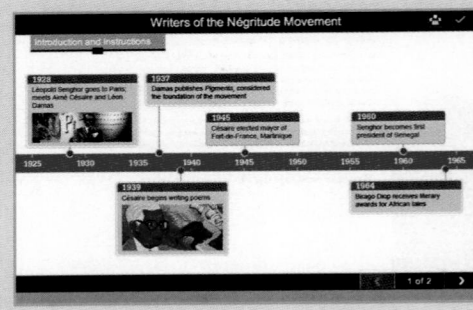

Objective 2: Describe the rise of nationalism in Africa.

Quick Instruction

In the 1920s, Pan-Africanism strengthened the nationalist movement and resistance to colonial rule. Leaders like Marcus Garvey and W. E. B. DuBois led movements to improve the rights of Africans.

Interactive Gallery: Writers of the Négritude Movement Project the gallery. Look at each image individually. Then discuss the négritude movement. Remind students that the movement developed during the 1930s and continued into the 1950s. Writers protested the mistreatment of Africa and Africans by colonial powers. The writers' work inspired a sense of pride and self-confidence in Africans and strengthened nationalist movements. Senghor inspired many writers, including David Diop, Jacques Rabemananjara, Mongo Beti, Ferdinand Oyone, and Tchicaya U Tam'si. Their writings transcended their time, however. Long after the end of colonialism, they continue to inspire pride in African cultural achievements and convey universal themes such as the desire of all people for freedom and respect.

👥 ACTIVE CLASSROOM

Ask students to reflect on the Négritude movement and design a piece of "Wallpaper" that encapsulates key learnings about the movement. Wallpaper should be posted in the classroom so students can take a gallery/"wisdom" walk and note what others have written/illustrated. Suggest that they jot down ideas that occur to them.

D Differentiate: On-Level Obtain copies of the poem "Prayer to the Masks" by Leopold Senghor. To help students better understand how the négritude movement inspired pride in African accomplishments, pass out the poem. Divide the class into small groups and assign a section of the poem to each one. Have groups discuss their selection, particularly focusing on how Africans might have felt about it. Then have them present their ideas to the class.

ELL Use the ELL activity described in the ELL chart.

Further Instruction

A Rising Tide of African Nationalism: Core Text and Interactive Reading Notepad Project and discuss the Interactive Reading Notepad questions.

Identify Main Ideas Ask students to define the key term *Pan-Africanism* and explain the slogan "Africa for Africans." How did the movement and phrase strengthen the spirit of nationalism? *(Sample response: Pan-Africanism encouraged Africans to work together because of their common heritage, and the slogan emphasized that Africans should rule themselves and their homeland.)*

Compare Remind students that Egyptians held protests, strikes, and riots after World War I. They finally won independence from Britain in 1922. How did Egyptian nationalists' tactics compare to those of nationalists in South Africa? *(Sample response: Many young Egyptian nationalists joined the Muslim Brotherhood, which rejected Western culture and the existing Egyptian government. In South Africa, the ANC tried to fight injustice*

using protest and the political system, which didn't have an immediate effect but did lead to political action later.) Do you think other African nations would have gained their independence sooner if they had followed the Egyptian nationalists' example? *(Answers will vary. Some students may say that more strikes, revolts, and protests might have won other countries their independence sooner because their foreign rulers could not control them.)*

DIGITAL TEXT 3

Modernization of Turkey and Persia

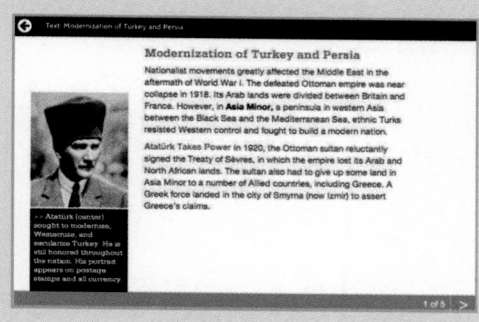

DIGITAL TEXT 4

Nationalism and Conflict in the Middle East

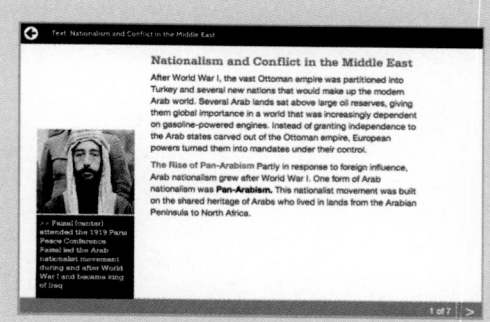

Objective 3: Describe how Turkey and Persia modernized.

Quick Instruction

World War I greatly impacted the Middle East and Arab lands were divided among Allied nations. Led by Mustafa Kemal—who later called himself Atatürk—the Turks resisted Western control and fought to build a modern nation.

Persian nationalists resented the British and Russians, who had influence over Persia. Inspired by Atatürk's success, Persian nationalists fought to change their government and finally overthrew the shah and began to modernize the nation.

Identify Main Ideas Why did Mustafa Kemal change his name? What does his name mean? *(He ordered all Turkish people to take on surnames, a Western custom. His name means "Father of the Turks.")* What were Atatürk main goals for Turkey? *(He wanted to strengthen Turkey as a nation and modernize and westernize it.)*

Further Instruction

Modernization of Turkey and Persia: Core Text and Interactive Reading Notepad Project and discuss the Interactive Reading Notepad questions, including the graphic organizer. Have students compare and contrast Reza Khan and Atatürk. Fill in the graphic organizer on the whiteboard as you go.

Treaty of Sèvres Remind students that the Ottoman sultan signed the Treaty of Sèvres in 1920. Then ask: What were the terms of the treaty, and why did the sultan sign it?

What was the significance of this treaty? *(The Ottoman empire was near collapse. The treaty forced the sultan to give up some land in Asia Minor to a number of Allied countries, including Greece.)*

Identify Cause and Effect What were some long-term results of the treaty? *(Sample response: Greek forces landed in Smyrna to claim their land. Turk nationalists fought to remove foreign influences and change their government. They overthrew the sultan and defeated the Greeks. Then a new treaty was signed that called for more than a million Greeks to leave Turkey. Nearly 400,000 Turks left Greece.)*

Remind students that Atatürk is considered "Father of the Turks." To modernize Turkey, he ruled with an iron hand. Discuss some of the following reforms. Ask students what possible effects they had, why he might have made these reforms, and what his reforms are modeled on.

- Replaced Muslim calendar with Western (Christian) calendar
- Moved day of rest from Friday to Sunday
- Closed religious schools and opened state schools
- Forced people to wear Western-style clothes
- Replaced Arabic alphabet with Latin alphabet
- Gave women the right to vote and to work outside the home

After discussing the reforms, ask students what arguments people might have made against some of these reforms.

Objective 4: Understand how the mandate system contributed to Arab nationalism and to conflict between Jews and Arabs.

Quick Instruction

The Middle East underwent many changes after World War I. Two of the biggest changes were the discovery of large oil fields and the creation of European-controlled mandates in Syria, Lebanon, Palestine, and Iraq by the Treaty of Versailles. These foreign influences helped give rise to a nationalistic movement called Pan-Arabism and caused long-standing conflicts between the Arabs and Jews in Palestine Mandate.

Analyze Data Project the infographic "The Changing Middle East." Review the information presented. Then ask the following questions:

Draw Conclusions Who discovered the first oil field? Why is this significant? *(Sample response: The first oil field was discovered by a British businessman. This is significant because it shows that foreign companies were already searching for oil in the area and wanted to be the first to find and control this important resource.)*

Identify Cause and Effect What effect do you think the discovery of oil had on the region? *(The discovery of oil caused foreign companies to begin moving to the Middle East to exploit the resources.)*

Nationalist Movements in Africa and the Middle East

Analyze Data How did the population change between 1919 and 1940? *(1.3 million Greeks migrated from Turkey; 400,000 Turks migrated from Greece; 340,000 Jews and almost 500,000 Muslims migrated to Palestine Mandate.)*

Draw Conclusions How do you think this population shift affected Palestine Mandate? *(It caused conflict over land and resources. Each group wanted to control the area and wanted to be the majority.)*

D **Differentiate: Challenge/Gifted** Have students find news articles about current conflicts or problems in the Middle East. Ask them to consider whether any of these problems stem from events that occurred after World War I. Have them write a short essay expressing their opinion. Allow students time to share their findings with the class.

Further Instruction

Nationalism and Conflict in the Middle East: Core Text and Interactive Reading Notepad Project and discuss the Interactive Reading Notepad questions.

Identify Cause and Effect How did the Paris Peace Conference affect Arabs? *(The Treaty of Versailles was drafted and signed at the Paris Peace Conference. Among other things, the treaty created the League of Nations, which gave Ottoman lands to Allied nations in the form of mandates.)*

Analyze Maps Project the map "The Middle East, 1920s." Ask students what this map shows. *(It shows the land that was mandated to Britain and France; the location of Jewish settlements; the population movement of Greeks and Turks; oil discoveries)* How does this map help you understand the conditions in the Middle East in the 1920s? *(The map shows the many changes the area underwent—different groups were migrating, Britain and France took control of Arab lands, oil was discovered. All of these changes caused instability and tension.)* Where are the Jewish settlements located? Why do you think there are so many Jewish settlements? *(The settlements are located in Palestine Mandate. The Jews believed the land they called Zion was their ancestral homeland. They wanted to return to it and also escape anti-Semitism in Europe.)*

Analyze Documents Project the Balfour Declaration, and zoom in so students can read it. Ask the following questions:

Identify Central Ideas What is the main point this document makes about the Jewish Zionists and the British government? *(It says the British government "views with favour the establishment in the Palestine Mandate of a national home for the Jewish people.")*

Interpret How did many people interpret this document? Was this interpretation accurate? *(Sample response: Many people interpreted this document to mean the British government was announcing that it was going to establish a homeland for Jews. In fact, the Balfour Declaration never explicitly says that.)*

Infer Why do you think it was interpreted this way? What was the result? *(Sample response: It might have been misinterpreted because the Jews were hoping Britain or another country would step in and help them establish a homeland. The letter caused a lot of tension and conflict between the Arabs and Jews because the Arabs thought the British had promised them their own land, which included Palestine Mandate.)*

Synthesize How did the Balfour Declaration and Jewish immigration further undermine Pan-Arabism? *(Sample response: The Balfour Declaration weakened Pan-Arabism because it set forth the goal of a Jewish homeland in the midst of Arab lands. The influx of Jews to Palestine Mandate weakened Pan-Arab goals because Jewish immigrants purchased increasing amounts of land and established their own military defense force.)*

Tell students that in the early 1900s, many Jewish settlers in Palestine Mandate wanted to develop a new way of life. They organized collective farms, called *kibbutzim*. Members shared belongings, labor, and proceeds. Together, these settlers introduced new techniques of drainage and irrigation. They grew grain, fruit trees, and vegetables, and raised chickens and cows for meat. What long-term effect do you think their work had? *(Sample response: Their efforts probably helped the future nation of Israel improve its agricultural production.)*

■ SYNTHESIZE

DIGITAL ACTIVITY

Nationalist Movements in Africa and the Middle East

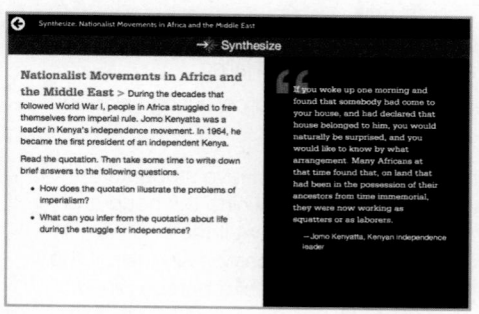

Have students use the Think Pair Share strategy to answer the questions in the "Nationalist Movements in Africa and the Middle East" Synthesize activity. Ask them to take five minutes to write down some brief answers to the questions. Then discuss their responses as a class.

Quick Write Have students read the quotation again and think of a question they would like to ask Jomo Kenyatta or one of the other nationalists they read about. Have them think about what they learned in the Core Texts, particularly why about why people wanted to change their government. Then have students write how they think the person would respond. Discuss their questions and answers as a class.

■ DEMONSTRATE

LESSON QUIZ

Lesson Quiz and Class Discussion Board

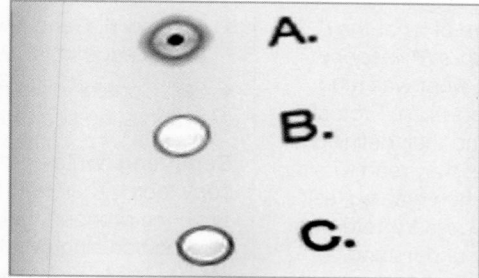

Assign the online Lesson Quiz for this lesson if you haven't already done so. Students will be offered automatic remediation or enrichment based on their score.

Pose these questions to the class on the Discussion Board:

Identify Main Ideas Describe the rise of nationalism in Africa and the Middle East. In what ways did people fight to change their governments?

Identify Cause and Effect How did World War I affect Africa and the Middle East? How did the effects contribute to nationalism and conflict?

Topic Inquiry

Have students continue their investigations for the Topic Inquiry.

India Seeks Self-Rule

Supporting English Language Learners

Use with Digital Text 2, **Gandhi's Philosophy of Civil Disobedience.**

Learning Strategies
Read *Gandhi's Philosophy of Civil Disobedience* aloud to students. Then have students complete one of the activities below based on their English proficiency level.

Beginning Encourage students to try to make a picture of what they are reading as they listen to the first paragraph of *Gandhi's Philosophy of Civil Disobedience* as it is read aloud. Model retelling what was read. Then have students read the next paragraph under "Nonviolent Protest." Assist students by making a list of challenging words and their definitions available as students read. Circulate among students as they read to offer support and answer questions. When students are finished reading, ask simple questions to gauge student understanding. If necessary, retell the text in accessible language so that students are sure to understand.

Intermediate Instruct students to read *Gandhi's Philosophy of Civil Disobedience* silently. Tell students to visualize what they read—to make a picture in their mind of what they are reading. Allow students to use bilingual dictionaries or other language supports as they read. After each paragraph, guide students to retell what they read. Write and display any important information.

Advanced Remind students to use visualization when they read. Have students silently read *Gandhi's Philosophy of Civil Disobedience*. After reading, have students turn to a partner and explain what they read. Give pairs bilingual dictionaries to support their comprehension of the text. Circulate among pairs to offer help as needed.

Advanced High Remind students to use visualization when they read. Have students read *Gandhi's Philosophy of Civil Disobedience* silently. When they are finished, students should share their visualization of the text with a partner. Together, pairs will write a brief summary of the text and share it with the class.

Use with Digital Text 3, **Gandhi Takes a Stand.**

Learning Strategies
Read *Gandhi Takes a Stand* aloud to the class. Write and display the following sentences for students to use with the activities below. Have them complete one activity according to their level of English proficiency.

- On April 6, Gandhi waded into the surf and picked up a lump of sea salt by the edge of the water. I was soon arrested and jailed.
- Still, Coastal villagers followed his lead. He started collecting salt and evaporating seawater to make them.

Beginning Write and display the sentences above. Have students copy them. Then read the sentences aloud and underline the noun and circle the pronoun that replaces it. Explain the rule that if the noun is third person singular, the pronoun will also be third person singular; if the noun is third person plural, the pronoun will also be third person plural. Model making the appropriate corrections to the sentences for students and have students copy the correct sentences into their notes. Circulate among students to offer support as necessary.

Intermediate Write and display the sentences above. Have students copy them. Then read the sentences aloud to students and help them identify the pronoun in each set of sentences and the noun that is replaced by it. Help students make the appropriate corrections to the sentences and have them copy the correct sentences into their notes. Circulate among students to offer support as necessary.

Advanced Write and display the sentences above. Have students copy them and identify the noun-pronoun relationship in each set of sentences. Instruct students to make the appropriate corrections to the sentences and then copy the correct sentences into their notes. Circulate among students to offer support as necessary. Then review each sentence with the class and have students check their work.

Advanced High Write and display the sentences above. Have students copy them, identify and correct the errors in the noun-pronoun relationships in each set of sentences. Then have students turn to a partner to check their work. Circulate among students to offer support as necessary.

▣ Differentiate Instruction

Use the Differentiated Instruction notes throughout the lesson plan to support the varied skill sets, levels of readiness, and interests in the mixed-ability classroom.

Challenge These notes include suggestions for expanding the activity for advanced students.

On-Level These notes include suggestions for modifying the activity to address different interests or learning styles.

Extra Support These notes include ideas for providing more scaffolding or reading spuport.

Special Needs These notes provide ideas for adapting instruction to support the needs of various special needs students.

■ NOTES

Objectives

Objective 1: Explain the impact of World War I and the Amritsar massacre on Indian nationalism.

Objective 2: Evaluate the ideas of Mohandas Gandhi.

Objective 3: Analyze how Gandhi led resistance to political oppression in India.

LESSON 3 ORGANIZER		PACING: APPROX. 1 PERIOD, .5 BLOCKS			
				RESOURCES	
		OBJECTIVES	**PACING**	**Online**	**Print**
Connect					
DIGITAL START UP ACTIVITY **Gandhi Pushes for Independence**			5 min.	●	
Investigate					
DIGITAL TEXT 1 **India's Struggle for Independence Begins**		Objective 1	10 min.	●	●
DIGITAL TEXT 2 **Gandhi's Philosophy of Civil Disobedience**		Objective 2	10 min.	●	●
INTERACTIVE GALLERY **Influences of Gandhi**			10 min.	●	
DIGITAL TEXT 3 **Gandhi Takes a Stand**		Objective 3	10 min.	●	●
Synthesize					
INTERACTIVE GRAPHIC ORGANIZER **Causes and Effects of Events in the Indian Independence Movement**			5 min.	●	
Demonstrate					
LESSON QUIZ **Lesson Quiz and Class Discussion Board**			10 min.	●	

India Seeks Self-Rule

■ CONNECT

DIGITAL START UP ACTIVITY

Gandhi Pushes for Independence

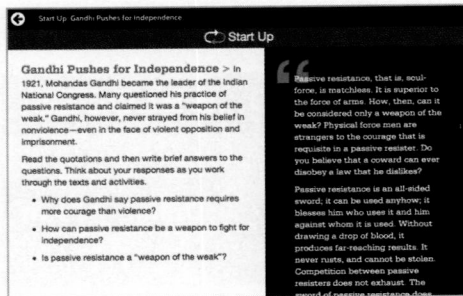

Project the Start Up Activity Ask students to read the quotations and answer the questions as they enter and get settled: Why does Gandhi say passive resistance requires more courage than violence? *(Sample response: It is harder to believe in yourself and maintain control when faced with violence or imprisonment. It is human nature, or basic instinct, to fight back when attacked.)* How can passive resistance be a weapon to fight for independence? *(Sample response: If the other person has a basic sense of decency, he or she may feel ashamed of using violence against someone who does not resist.)*

Tell students that in this lesson they will learn about India's struggle for independence and the role Mohandas Gandhi played in the struggle.

Aa Vocabulary Development: Use the Interactive Reading Notepad to preview the Key Terms and Academic Vocabulary in this Lesson with students.

⟳ FLIP IT!

Assign the Flipped Video for this lesson.

■ STUDENT EDITION PRINT PAGES: 691–694

■ INVESTIGATE

DIGITAL TEXT 1

India's Struggle for Independence Begins

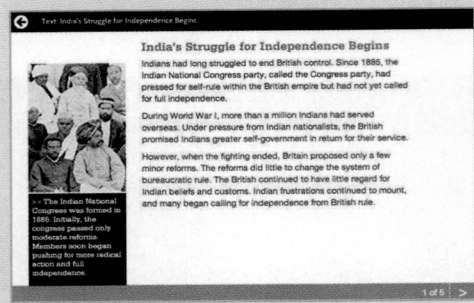

Objective 1: **Explain the impact of World War I and the Amritsar massacre on Indian nationalism.**

Quick Instruction

The National Congress party began pressing for self-rule after 1885. However, after World War I and the 1919 Amritsar massacre, the Congress party and other Indians were finally convinced that they needed full independence.

Analyze Images Project the painting of the Amritsar massacre from the text, India's Struggle for Independence Begins. Tell students that this massacre began as a peaceful protest against the Rowlatt Acts. The massacre was a turning point for many people. What does this image show? How does it help you understand the event and why it caused many Indians to want full independence? *(Sample response: It shows British soldiers shooting into a crowd of protesters. There are hundreds of people on the ground. The massacre convinced many Indians that the British didn't care about their rights or their lives. The massacre gave Indians even more incentive to want the British gone.)*

Further Instruction

Editable Presentation Use the Editable Presentation to present the main ideas for this Core Text.

India's Struggle for Independence: Core Text and Interactive Reading Notepad Project and discuss the Interactive Reading Notepad questions, including the cause-and-effect graphic organizer. Complete the graphic organizer as a class to show how World War I started a chain of events that led to the Congress party's call for independence. Fill in the organizer with students' responses.

D Differentiate: Extra Support Help students understand the causes and effects of World War I and the Amritsar massacre. Remind students that a cause is the reason something happens. A cause can have more than one effect, or it can create a chain of causes and effect. In a chain, each effect becomes the cause that then leads to the next effect. Explain that the events surrounding the war is an example of a cause-and-effect chain. *(Sample chain: Many Indians fought in World War I. Because Indians served, nationalists demanded greater self-government. When Indians did not get reforms, nationalists began protesting and demanding full independence. These protests caused the British government to pass new laws. These laws led to more protests. One protest led to a massacre. This massacre made many people join the independence movement.)*

Recall What were the Rowlatt Acts? *(Laws passed by the British government that allowed British officials to arrest and imprison any Indian citizen suspected of sedition.)*

Draw Conclusions Why might these Acts have been passed? *(Events after World War I sparked discontent and many protests. The British were probably trying to gain more control and stop Indians from protesting.)*

Identify Supporting Details Why did British Commander General Reginald Dyer order 50 soldiers to fire into the crowd at the Amritsar protest? *(He had banned public meetings. The crowd ignored this order. He ordered his soldiers to fire to disband the crowd.)*

DIGITAL TEXT 2

Gandhi's Philosophy of Civil Disobedience

INTERACTIVE GALLERY

Influences of Gandhi

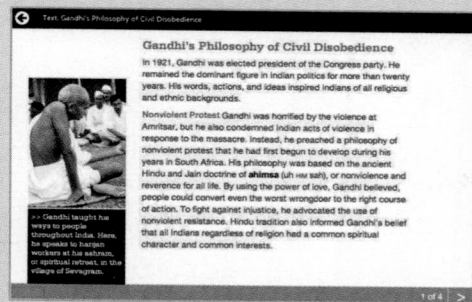

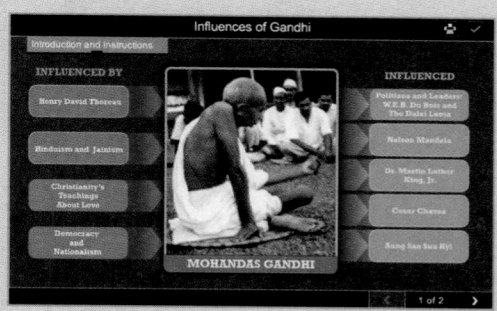

Objective 2: Evaluate the ideas of Mohandas Gandhi.

Quick Instruction

Gandhi became the leader of the Congress party in 1920. His words, actions, and ideas inspired people of all religions and backgrounds, and they helped to shift political thought.

Interactive Gallery: Influences of Gandhi Project the image gallery and explain that Gandhi's beliefs were inspired by different people and traditions. In turn, his actions and ideas influenced independence and civil rights leaders around the world. First, look at the overall image showing what ideas and thinkers influenced Gandhi and who he influenced. Before looking at each individual image, ask: Are you familiar with any of these people and their work? What do you know about them? *(Answers will vary. Some students may be familiar with Thoreau, King, and Mandela and their work. Ask them to summarize their work for those students who are not, or be prepared to do so yourself.)* Which of these people or traditions surprise you the most? Why? *(Answers will vary. Students may say that they were surprised to see Christian beliefs and democratic and nationalist ideas listed because Gandhi was a Hindu.)*

Then look at each image individually. Ask students what they learned about the people.

📖 ACTIVE CLASSROOM

Ask students to conduct a Conversation with History. Tell them to write down a question they would like to ask one of the people that Gandhi influenced. Then ask students to write down how they think the person they chose would reply. Ask students to explain how they would respond in turn. Then tell them to share their questions and answers with a partner.

ELL Use the ELL activity described in the ELL chart.

Further Instruction

Gandhi's Philosophy of Civil Disobedience: Core Text and Interactive Reading Notepad Project the Interactive Reading Notepad questions. Discuss the answers with the class.

Analyze Images Project the image of Gandhi teaching. Have students describe the scene. How does this image help you understand Gandhi and his influence over people? *(Sample Response: Gandhi is sitting cross-legged on a platform surrounded by people. The scene looks serene, and the people seem very interested; they are leaning in to hear him. It does not look like a typical protest meeting or rally. It seems almost like a classroom. His peaceful nature and belief in love seem evident in the way people are acting. It seems like they are trying to be like him.)*

Make Predictions Why did the Muslim League and the Congress party begin to diverge? What does this division help you understand about the independence movement? What do you predict will happen between these groups? *(Sample Responses: Each organization wanted to make sure that the interests of its members were promoted. It shows the struggle was complicated because the different religious groups did not necessarily want the same thing from independence and that each group wanted power and protection for its own interests. I predict that the differences between the groups will lead to major problems and possibly conflicts.)*

India Seeks Self-Rule

DIGITAL TEXT 3
Gandhi Takes a Stand

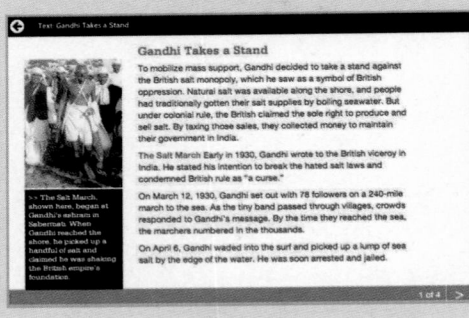

Gandhi Takes a Stand

To mobilize mass support, Gandhi decided to take a stand against the British salt monopoly, which he saw as a symbol of British oppression. Natural salt was available along the shore, and people had traditionally gotten their salt supplies by boiling seawater. But under colonial rule, the British claimed the sole right to produce and sell salt. By taxing those sales, they collected money to maintain their government in India.

The Salt March Early in 1930, Gandhi wrote to the British viceroy in India. He stated his intention to break the hated salt laws and condemned British rule as "a curse."

On March 12, 1930, Gandhi set out with 78 followers on a 240-mile march to the sea. As the tiny band passed through villages, crowds responded to Gandhi's message. By the time they reached the sea, the marchers numbered in the thousands.

On April 6, Gandhi waded into the surf and picked up a lump of sea salt by the edge of the water. He was soon arrested and jailed.

>> The Salt March, shown here, began at Gandhi's ashram in Sabermati. When Gandhi reached the shore, he picked up a handful of salt and claimed he was shaking the British empire's foundation.

1 of 4

Objective 3: Analyze how Gandhi led resistance to political oppression in India.

Quick Instruction

Gandhi viewed the British government's law that Indians buy salt from the British salt monopoly as another example of oppression. In April, 1930, Gandhi decided to take a stand by leading some of his followers on a 240-mile march to the sea. The march grew as people from the towns and villages Gandhi passed through joined him. Once at the shore, Gandhi and the Indians picked up lumps of salt. Later, he, and thousands of others, were arrested. Why did people join Gandhi? Why were Gandhi and the protesters arrested? *(The march was a symbol of their struggle for independence. People believed in Gandhi and his ways. The British arrested them to show that they were in power.)*

D Differentiate: Challenge/Gifted Have students write a short opinion essay explaining which event they think was more significant in the struggle for independence, the Salt March or the Amritsar massacre. Remind students to use evidence to support their claim. Have students exchange their essays with a partner and discuss their claim and evidence.

ELL Use the ELL activity described in the ELL chart.

Further Instruction

Gandhi Takes a Stand: Core Text and Interactive Reading Notepad Project and discuss the Interactive Reading Notepad questions.

Be sure students understand the effects of the Salt March. The British reaction to the Salt March garnered media attention around the world and put India and Gandhi in the spotlight. Many people were horrified by the government's reaction, and the negative publicity eventually forced the British to give in to some of the Indians' demands.

Draw Conclusions Have students work in groups to write a paragraph evaluating Gandhi's ideas and the ways he was able to shift political thought. Discuss their responses as a class.

Sequence Events After India won independence from Britain, what new conflict arose? What previous events indicated that there might be problems in India even after it was free? *(Sample response: A conflict between Hindus and Muslims ensued because Muslims feared a Hindu majority. The split of the Muslim League and the Congress party indicated that there would be conflict between the groups for years to come.)*

SYNTHESIZE

INTERACTIVE GRAPHIC ORGANIZER

Causes and Effects of Events in the Indian Independence Movement

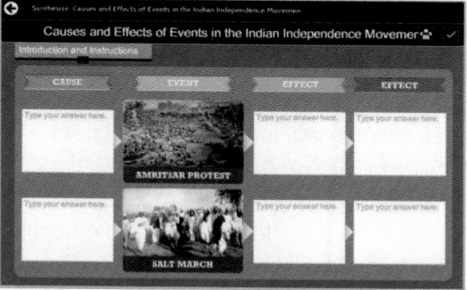

Interactive Graphic Organizer: Causes and Effects of Events in the Indian Independence Movement Project the interactive organizer. Have students take five minutes to complete the organizer with the causes and effects of each event listed in the organizer. Then divide the class into small groups, and have each group discuss member responses. During this discussion, students should add any details they left out.

📷 ACTIVE CLASSROOM

If you were to write Make Headlines about the Salt March right now that captured the most important aspects of the event or its effects, what would that headline be? Discuss the headlines as a class.

DEMONSTRATE

LESSON QUIZ

Lesson Quiz and Class Discussion Board

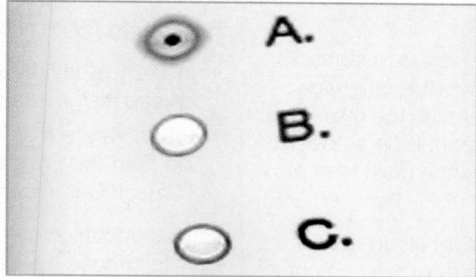

Assign the online Lesson Quiz for this lesson if you haven't already done so. Students will be offered automatic remediation or enrichment based on their score.

Pose these questions to the class on the Discussion Board: In "India Seeks Self-Rule," you read about how World War I and the Amritsar massacre led to Indian nationalism.

Identify Main Ideas Explain how Gandhi led the nationalist movement and the effect he had on people of many religions and beliefs. *(Sample answer: Gandhi led boycotts and nonviolent protests and resistance. His beliefs in love and reverance for all life inspired people around the world. Because his values embraced both Christian and Hindu traditions and ideas, he appealed to a variety of people.)*

Express Ideas Clearly Which of Gandhi's ideas and actions do you think were most effective, and why? *(Sample answer: His belief in civil disobedience and the Salt March were the most effective. The Salt March received international attention, which eventually forced Britain to grant some reforms.)*

Topic Inquiry

Have students continue their investigations for the Topic Inquiry.

New Forces in China and Japan

Supporting English Language Learners

Use with Digital Text 3, **China Faces Japanese Imperialism.**

Learning Strategies
Read *China Faces Japanese Imperialism* aloud to students. Then have students complete one of the activities below based on their English proficiency level.

Beginning Reread *China Faces Japanese Imperialism* aloud to students. Pause after each paragraph to retell the content in accessible language for English language learners. Then help students determine the main idea of the text by underlining the main idea of each paragraph. Help students take those three main ideas and use them to determine the main idea of the whole text.

Intermediate Reread *China Faces Japanese Imperialism* aloud to students. Pause after each paragraph to help students retell the content in everyday language. Then ask students to underline the main idea of each paragraph. Guide students to take those three main ideas and use them to determine the main idea of the whole text.

Advanced Have students reread *China Faces Japanese Imperialism*. Then lead a class discussion and ask students to retell the content in their own words and highlight the main idea of each paragraph. Have students use the three main ideas to determine the main idea of the whole text. Have students write the main idea and share it with the rest of the class. As a group, refine and clarify the main idea of the text and have students write it in their notes.

Advanced High Have students reread *China Faces Japanese Imperialism*. Then ask students to retell the content in their own words to a partner. Pairs should then highlight the main idea of each paragraph. Have pairs use the three main ideas to determine and write down the main idea of the whole text. Pairs should share their work with another pair to refine and clarify the main idea of the text.

Use with Digital Text 2, **Nationalists and Communists.**

Learning Strategies
Read *Nationalists and Communists* aloud to the class. Have students complete the activities below according to their level of English proficiency.

Beginning Write and display the following sentences.

- In 1921, Sun (plans/planned) to raise an army, defeat the warlords, and spread his government's rule over all of China.
- When Western democracies (refuses/refused) to help, Sun accepted aid from the Soviet Union and joined forces with the small group of Chinese Communists.

Have students copy them. Then read the first sentence aloud and model how to choose the correct verb tense. Remind students that because these events occurred in the past, the past tense is almost always used. Assist students as they complete the second sentence on their own. Circulate among students to offer support as necessary.

Intermediate Reread *Nationalists and Communists* aloud to students. Work together with students to write about the conflict between the Guomindang and Chinese Communists. Make sure the three verb tenses—past, present, and future—are included in students' writing.

Advanced Have students reread *Nationalists and Communists* with a partner. Then instruct pairs to work together to write about the conflict between the Guomindang and Chinese Communists. Make sure the three verb tenses—past, present, and future—are included in students' writing. Have each pair share their writing with the class. Have students correct any errors as necessary.

Advanced High Have students silently reread *Nationalists and Communists*. Then have students write a paragraph describing the conflict between the Guomindang and Chinese Communists. Make sure the three verb tenses—past, present, and future—are included in students' writing. Have each student turn to a partner to share the paragraphs. Encourage students to point out each other's errors and make any corrections as necessary.

▶ Differentiate Instruction

Use the Differentiated Instruction notes throughout the lesson plan to support the varied skill sets, levels of readiness, and interests in the mixed-ability classroom.

Challenge These notes include suggestions for expanding the activity for advanced students.

On-Level These notes include suggestions for modifying the activity to address different interests or learning styles.

Extra Support These notes include ideas for providing more scaffolding or reading spuport.

Special Needs These notes provide ideas for adapting instruction to support the needs of various special needs students.

■ NOTES

PEARSON

realize™
www.PearsonRealize.com

Go online to access additional resources including:
Primary Sources • Biographies • Supreme Court cases •
21st Century Skill Tutorials • Maps • Graphic Organizers.

Objectives

Objective 1: Explain the key challenges faced by the Chinese republic in the early 1900s.

Objective 2: Analyze the struggle between nationalists and Communists in China.

Objective 3: Summarize the effects of liberal changes in Japan in the 1920s.

Objective 4: Describe the rise of extreme nationalism and militarism in Japan.

Objective 5: Describe the impact of the Japanese invasion of China.

LESSON 4 ORGANIZER		PACING: APPROX. 1 PERIOD, .5 BLOCKS			
		OBJECTIVES	PACING	**RESOURCES** Online	Print
Connect					
DIGITAL START UP ACTIVITY **China Resists Japan's Expanding Empire**			5 min.	●	
Investigate					
DIGITAL TEXT 1 **Trouble in the Chinese Republic**		Objective 1	10 min.	●	●
DIGITAL TEXT 2 **Nationalists and Communists**		Objective 2	10 min.	●	●
INTERACTIVE CHART **Communism vs. Guomindang**			10 min.	●	
DIGITAL TEXT 3 **China Faces Japanese Imperialism**		Objectives 2, 5	10 min.	●	●
DIGITAL TEXT 4 **Conflicting Forces in Japan**		Objective 3	10 min.	●	●
DIGITAL TEXT 5 **The Ultranationalist Reaction**		Objective 4	10 min.	●	●
DIGITAL TEXT 6 **Militarists Gain Power**		Objectives 4, 5	10 min.	●	●
INTERACTIVE GALLERY **Revival of Japanese Glory**			10 min.	●	
Synthesize					
DIGITAL ACTIVITY **Nationalism in China and Japan**			5 min.	●	
Demonstrate					
LESSON QUIZ **Lesson Quiz and Class Discussion Board**			10 min.	●	

New Forces in China and Japan

■ CONNECT

DIGITAL START UP ACTIVITY
China Resists Japan's Expanding Empire

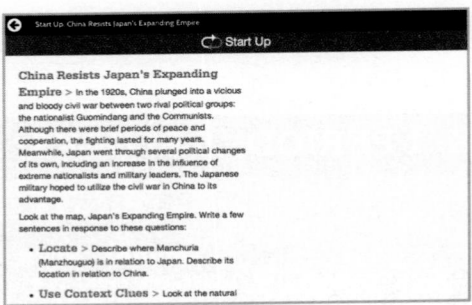

Project the Start Up Activity and the map depicting Japanese expansion from the text. Ask students to review the map and answer the questions as they enter and get settled: Describe where Manchuria (Manzhouguo) is in relation to Japan. Describe its location in relation to China. *(It is west of Japan, and in the northeast part of China.)* Look at the natural resources listed on the map. What might Japan gain by invading mainland Asia? *(Sample response: Japan could gain access to coal, petroleum, iron, copper, bauxite, and gold.)* Then have them share their ideas with another student, either in class or through a chat or blog space.

Discuss Why did the Japanese public push for territorial expansion? *(Sample response: pressures from the Great Depression)* What natural resources did Japan lack? *(Sample response: coal, petroleum, iron, copper, bauxite, and gold)*

Aa Vocabulary Development: Use the Interactive Reading Notepad to preview the Key Terms and Academic Vocabulary in this Lesson with students.

ℕ FLIP IT!
Assign the Flipped Video for this lesson.

■ STUDENT EDITION PRINT PAGES: 695–701

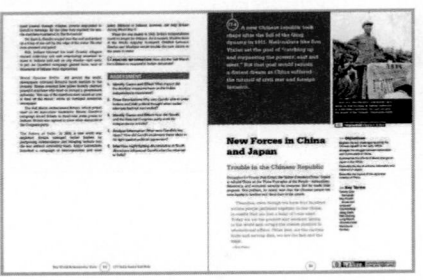

■ INVESTIGATE

DIGITAL TEXT 1
Trouble in the Chinese Republic

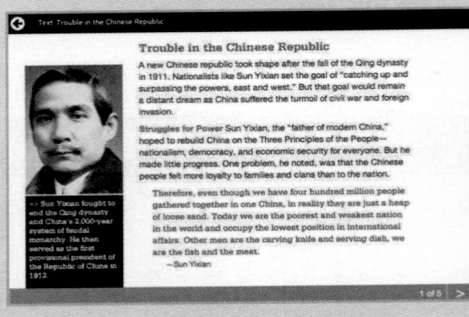

Objective 1: Explain the key challenges faced by the Chinese republic in the early 1900s.

Quick Instruction
The Republic of China was founded after the Qing dynasty fell in 1911. Nationalists like Sun Yixian wanted to rebuild China and make it a world power. Ask: What did Sun Yixian mean when he said: "Other men are the carving knife and serving dish, we are the fish and the meat"? *(that China will be left behind and taken advantage of by other more powerful nations if no changes are made)*

China faced two challenges, however: internal conflict and foreign influence. In the provinces, local warlords fought each other. Foreign influence included imperialists that dominated Chinese ports, and Japan, which sought to make China a Japanese protectorate with the Twenty-One Demands.

Further Instruction
Editable Presentation Use the Editable Presentation to present the main ideas for this Core Text.

Go through the Interactive Reading Notepad questions and discuss the answers with the class.

Be sure students understand how the Twenty-One Demands and the Paris Peace Conference affected Chinese interests. Ask students what common effect they had on China. *(Sample response: Both led to a loss of Chinese control over its own affairs and/or territory.)*

Project the image of the May Fourth Movement from the text. Explain that the May Fourth Movement and the birth of the Chinese Communist Party were both reactions to the internal problems and foreign aggression that China faced. Students should also understand that both movements shared the goal of "catching up" to the West.

Infer Why would women have been interested in the May Fourth Movement? Cite evidence to support your answer. *(Sample response: In traditional Chinese society, women held a subservient role. Women may have believed that the Western ideas that influenced the movement would help them gain more freedom. This can be seen in their effort to overthrow traditions like foot binding.)*

Contrast In what ways were the goals of the May Fourth Movement and Chinese Communists in conflict? *(Sample response: The May Fourth Movement wanted to adopt Western ways. The goal of Communists was a revolution that would overthrow some of the very institutions—like democratic government—that the May Fourth Movement wanted to establish in China.)*

Nationalists and Communists

Communism vs. Guomindang

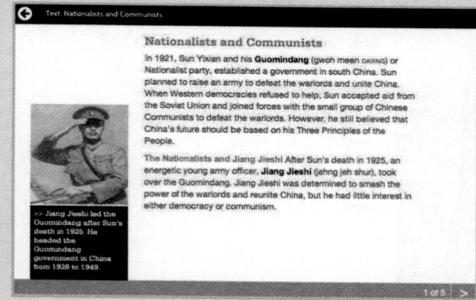

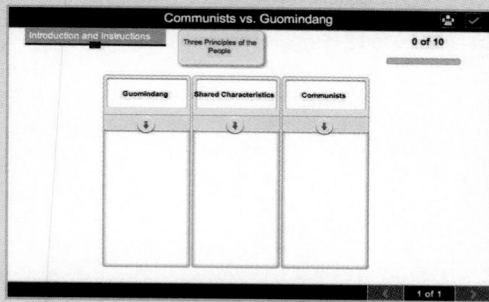

Objective 2: Analyze the struggle between nationalists and Communists in China.

Quick Instruction

After Sun Yixian's death, Jiang Jieshi took over the Nationalist party, or Guomindang. Jiang cooperated with the Communists in the Northern Expedition to conquer warlords and capture Beijing. Then Jiang turned against the Communists and sent troops to slaughter them. The Communists, led by Mao Zedong, retreated during the Long March. The Communists won peasant support by redistributing land and by showing courage.

Interactive Chart: Communism vs. Guomindang Project the chart. Verify student understanding through review of the tiles listed. Ask students to place the tiles into one of three categories: Guomindang, Communists, or Shared Characteristics. *(Sample response: Guomindang: Sun Yixian; Jiang Jieshi; Three Principles of the People; Campaign to exterminate rivals. Communists: Mao Zedong; Supported by large peasant masses; The Long March; Advocated the writings of Carl Marx. Shared: Worked to oppose Japanese invasion; Established totalitarian government; Northern Expedition Victory.)*

🗣 ACTIVE CLASSROOM

Ask the students to break into groups to answer the following: "Which group was more 'revolutionary' in the sense that it would bring broad changes?" Have students conduct a Circle Write in which they write as much as they can for one minute, then switch with the person on their right. The next person tries to improve or elaborate the response where the other person left off. Continue to switch until the paper comes back to the first person. The group then decides which is the best response and shares that with the larger group. *(Sample response: The Communists were more revolutionary because they wanted to empower peasants, the largest group of people.)*

Compare and Contrast Look at the completed chart. Summarize how the Communists were radically different from the Guomindang. *(Sample response: The Communists were supported by the enormous peasant masses and, theoretically, gave the peasants political power.)*

Further Instruction

Natonalists and Communists: Core Text and Interactive Reading Notepad Project and discuss the Interactive Reading Notepad questions. Be sure that students understand that Jiang Jieshi had little interest in democracy. He opposed the Communists primarily because he saw them as a threat to his own power. Review the violent tactics used by the Guomindang to rid China of Communists and how these policies led to the Long March.

Analyze Maps Project the map depicting the Long March from the Digital Text. Explain to students that Mao's Communist forces faced nearly daily attacks, forcing them to flee from the Guomindang across the nation. Review the movement of the Communists and the natural features of the land that caused difficulties along their journey.

Sequence Events Briefly list the changes in the relationship between the Guomindang and the Communists from 1926 to 1935, in order. *(Sample response: In 1926, they combined forces to defeat the local warlords. In 1927, civil war began between the two groups, and between 1934–1935, the Communists retreated during the Long March.)*

Predict Consequences How might the great hardships experienced during the Long March actually have strengthened the Communist cause? *(Sample response: The Communists showed discipline, loyalty, and bravery during the Long March. These qualities won them respect from the peasants in the long term.)*

New Forces in China and Japan

DIGITAL TEXT 3
China Faces Japanese Imperialism

> **China Faces Japanese Imperialism**
> While Jiang was pursuing the Communists across China, the country faced another danger. In 1931, Japan invaded Manchuria in northeastern China, adding it to the growing Japanese empire. As Japanese aggression increased, some of Jiang's generals pushed him to form a united front with the Communists against Japan.
>
> In 1937, the Japanese struck again, starting what became the Second Sino-Japanese War. Airplanes bombed Chinese cities, and Japanese troops overran eastern China, including Beijing and Guangzhou. Jiang Jieshi and his government retreated to the interior and set up a new capital at Chongqing (chawng chihg).
>
> After a lengthy siege, Japanese troops marched into the city of Nanjing (nahn jihg) on December 13. Nanjing was an important cultural center and had been the Guomindang capital before Chongqing. After the city's surrender, the Japanese killed hundreds of thousands of soldiers and civilians and brutalized still more. The cruelty and destruction became known as the "Rape of Nanjing."
>
> >> The national capital at Nanjing surrendered to the Japanese on December 13, 1937. The Japanese army brutally murdered members of the Chinese Army and abused Chinese citizens
>
> 1 of 3 >

Objectives 2: Analyze the struggle between nationalists and Communists in China; 5: Describe the impact of the Japanese invasion of China.

Quick Instruction
Tell students that as the Guomindang chased the Communists across China, Japanese forces took advantage of the situation and invaded. Explain that Japan captured the city of Nanjing and committed countless atrocities upon its citizens. Project the image of the Rape of Nanjing from the Text. Ask students: "How was China able to fight off Japanese invasions?" *(Sample response: The Guomindang and the Communists united to fight the Japanese invaders.)*

Further Instruction
Project and discuss the Interactive Reading Notepad questions. Although the Japanese had hoped the chaos from China's internal fighting would aid their invasion, that didn't happen. The Communists and the Guomindang temporarily put aside their differences and cooperated to resist Japanese aggression.

Explain to students that after the city of Nanjing surrendered, Japanese forces ruthlessly killed and brutalized hundreds of thousands of Chinese. The atrocities committed were so horrendous, the event became known throughout the world as the Rape of Nanjing.

Identify Cause and Effect How did domestic unrest in China lead to an increase in foreign imperialism? *(Sample response: The warlord uprisings weakened China. Because of this, there was no central force to block Japanese encroachment on Chinese possessions.)*

Hypothesize How do you think the Rape of Nanjing affected Japan's reputation around the world? *(Sample response: It probably caused distrust and anger toward the Japanese.)*

Identify Patterns The Communists and Guomindang united for the Northern Expedition and during the Japanese invasion. What did those two events have in common? *(Sample response: The opposing groups united against a common enemy in both cases.)*

ELL Use the ELL activity described in the ELL chart.

DIGITAL TEXT 4
Conflicting Forces in Japan

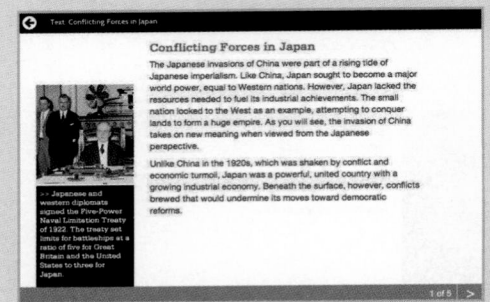

> **Conflicting Forces in Japan**
> The Japanese invasions of China were part of a rising tide of Japanese imperialism. Like China, Japan sought to become a major world power, equal to Western nations. However, Japan lacked the resources needed to fuel its industrial achievements. The small nation looked to the West as an example, attempting to conquer lands to form a huge empire. As you will see, the invasion of China takes on new meaning when viewed from the Japanese perspective.
>
> Unlike China in the 1920s, which was shaken by conflict and economic turmoil, Japan was a powerful, united country with a growing industrial economy. Beneath the surface, however, conflicts brewed that would undermine its moves toward democratic reforms.
>
> >> Japanese and western diplomats signed the Five-Power Naval Limitation Treaty of 1922. The treaty set limits for battleships at a ratio of five for Great Britain and the United States to three for Japan.
>
> 1 of 5 >

Objective 3: Summarize the effects of liberal changes in Japan in the 1920s.

Quick Instruction
Explain to students that the Japanese economy experienced enormous growth during World War I. After the war, the nation cut back on expansionist policies to focus on business relationships with the West and moved toward more widespread democracy at home. Review the tensions and unrest that became more evident during the 1920s, such as governmental corruption and rejection of tradition. Ask students to describe the problem of governmental corruption and how it affected Japanese society in the 1920s. *(Sample response: Military officers and conservatives resented government corruption. They accused officials of receiving payoffs from powerful zaibatsu, or influential banking and industrial Japanese families who sought to buy government favor though political donations. These families pushed for policies that favored international trade and aligned with their own financial interests.)*

Further Instruction
Project and discuss the Interactive Reading Notepad questions. Ask students to discuss what they know about Japan from the Digital Text so far. *(Sample response: So far, the text has focused on China and Japan's role as an aggressive imperialist and invader.)* Explain to students that the upcoming Digital Texts will review the events from a Japanese perspective.

DIGITAL TEXT 5

The Ultranationalist Reaction

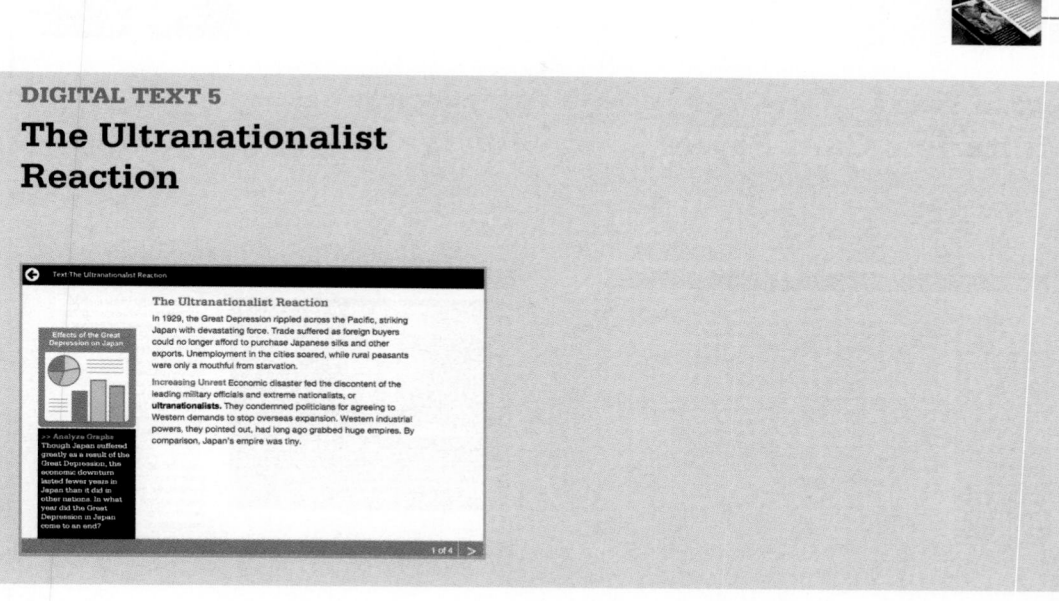

Objective 4: Describe the rise of extreme nationalism and militarism in Japan.

Quick Instruction

Explain to students that militarists came into power due to high public support. Project the infographic showing the effects of the Great Depression on Japan and other nations. Tell students that during the 1930s, the Great Depression devastated the Japanese economy and many people were fed up with the increasing political instability. Foreign conquests appeared as a solution to the issues facing the Japan.

Further Instruction

Project and discuss the map of Japanese Expansion from the Digital Text and the Interactive Reading Notepad questions. Explain to students that the high unemployment of the 1930s fed Japanese discontent with the government. Many people supported the militarists' aggressive imperialism as a solution to domestic problems. During the 1930s, Japan built up its military and repeatedly attempted to invade other nations throughout southeast Asia. The League of Nations failed to take military action, and the world watched as Japan built up its territory and military despite objections. Make sure students understand that the Manchurian incident was a military plot to provide an excuse to seize the Chinese territory of Manchuria.

Be sure students understand that Japan's economy boomed during World War I, and it was based primarily upon production of goods that were exported to the West. Japan reined in imperialist goals following the war and focused on developing business relationships with the West.

Remind students that Japan also faced serious issues following World War I. Despite government moves toward more widespread democracy, the zaibatsu remained very powerful domestically. Military leaders accused government officials of corruption and condemned the rejection of traditional ideals for Western modernity.

Summarize Describe the tensions between the military and the government of Japan during the 1920s. *(Sample response: The military blasted government corruption and condemned Western influences on Japanese culture.)*

Determine Point of View Why did conservatives resent Western influences? *(Sample response: They believed Western influences were undermining basic Japanese values of obedience and respect for authority.)*

D Differentiate: Extra Support To help visual learners, ask students to work in pairs and create a timeline of the events in the 1920s. Have students categorize each event as positive or negative and make a mark above the timeline for a positive event, below the timeline for a negative event. Then have them connect the dots and describe the pattern. Make sure that students understand that Japan's behavior zigzagged between two opposite extremes during this period.

Analyze Maps Look at the map of "Japan's Expanding Empire" from the Digital Text. Which territories did Japan add by 1918? *(Sample response: Taiwan, Korea, and part of the island directly to the north)*

Identify Cause and Effect Explain how the Great Depression affected Japan. *(Sample response: Foreign buyers were no longer able to purchase Japanese exports, causing unemployment in cities, and near starvation in rural areas.)*

Summarize Describe the state of Manzhouguo and its relationship with Japan. *(Sample response: The area was the state of Manchuria. It was a puppet state set up by Japanese forces after the Manchurian incident. The Japanese brought in Puyi to act as a puppet government for Japan's interests.)*

New Forces in China and Japan

DIGITAL TEXT 6
Militarists Gain Power

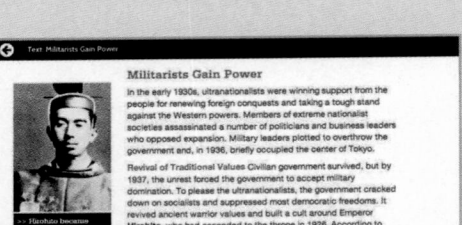

INTERACTIVE GALLERY
Revival of Japanese Glory

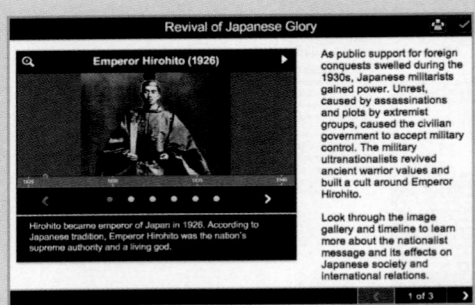

Objectives 4: Describe the rise of extreme nationalism and militarism in Japan; **5:** Describe the impact of the Japanese invasion of China.

Quick Instruction

Explain to students that ultranationalists revived ancient warrior values and built a cult around Emperor Hirohito. Japan's military expected to complete its conquest of China within a few years. As World War II broke out in Europe, the conflict quickly spread to Asia, with Japan joining the Axis powers of Germany and Italy.

Interactive Gallery: Revival of Japanese Glory Project the image of Emperor Hirohito from the Interactive Gallery. Review each image and discuss where it falls on the timeline. Examine the timeline as a whole, and ask students to discuss the relationships between events on the timeline.

📷 ACTIVE CLASSROOM

Have students make the images in the gallery come to life with the Act It Out strategy. After reviewing the images, ask students what happens next in the image and what happened before. Students can act out a scene from the images, bringing to life what those people are thinking. Or, choose one image and ask students to write a conversation that could have occurred between the people in that image.

Support Ideas with Examples What are some examples of nationalism in Japan during the 1930s? *(Sample response: the cult of Hirohito; the revival of Japanese warrior values; public support for military ultranationalists; public pressure for territorial expansion; use of schools to spread nationalistic message to children)*

Further Instruction

Militarists Gain Power: Core Text and Interactive Reading Notepad Project and discuss the Interactive Reading Notepad questions. Ask students to think of reasons why ultranationalists might gain support during difficult times, such as the Great Depression.

Remind students that Japan wanted to take advantage of unrest in China and invaded while the Guomindang and Communists were fighting a civil war. Be sure students understand the importance of Japan's alliance with Germany and Italy. Explain that this alliance, along with increased Japanese territorial conquests, directly led to fighting throughout Asia and the Pacific during World War II.

Summarize The changes militarists made when they came into power. *(Sample response: They restricted freedoms and imposed traditional Japanese culture on the people. They also attempted to expand farther into China.)*

SYNTHESIZE

DIGITAL ACTIVITY
Nationalism in China and Japan

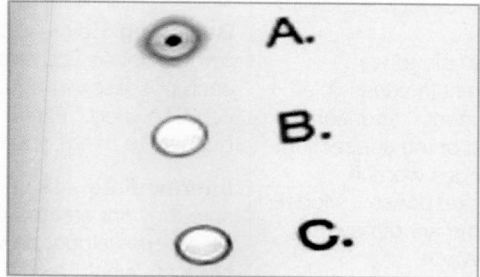

Project the graphic organizer from the Synthesize Digital Activity. Discuss how the concept of nationalism grew around the world during the early part of the 20th century. Remind students that both China and Japan experienced the growing trend of nationalism in different ways. Explore the relationship between anti-Western sentiments and the expression of nationalism. After the discussion, ask students to use the graphic organizer to compare the goals of nationalism in each country and how those goals were expressed. *(Sample response: China—Goals of Nationalism: To lessen foreign domination of China. Effects of Nationalism: Resistance to Japanese invasions; attempts to strengthen China; new intellectual movements and political parties to address perceived problems. Japan—Goals of Nationalism: to build a Japanese empire in Asia. Effects of Nationalism: issuing the Twenty-One Demands; repeated invasions of China; ultranationalists and militarists invoke symbols to inspire service and obedience to the emperor and the state. Both—Goals of Nationalism: to be treated as equals and with respect by Western nations. Effects of Nationalism: created a sense of unity and national identity in each country)*

Make Generalizations What were some characteristics of nationalism that were shared by both China and Japan? *(Sample response: Both shared the goal of being treated as equals and with respect by Western nations. And nationalism created a sense of national identity in each country, although Japan became more unified than China did.)*

DEMONSTRATE

LESSON QUIZ
Lesson Quiz and Class Discussion Board

Assign the online Lesson Quiz for this lesson if you haven't already done so. Students will be offered automatic remediation or enrichment based on their score.

Pose these questions to the class on the Discussion Board:

Identify Cause and Effect Why were Jiang Jieshi's attempts to exterminate Chinese Communists unsuccessful? *(Sample response: The Communists retreated more than 6,000 miles across the country to escape the Guomindang. Many peasants supported the Communists, who treated them fairly and paid for food, in contrast to the Guomindang who had treated peasants badly. The peasant support gave the Communists much strength.)*

Cite Evidence How did China respond to the challenges of internal division and foreign imperialism during the early 1900s? *(Sample response: After a period of upheaval, two main parties emerged: the Guomindang and the Communists. The two united against local warlord uprisings, but the Guomindang soon turned against the Communists and civil war ensued for years. Fighting ceased again when the two groups reunited to block Japanese invasions during the 1930s.)*

Identify Central Issues Why did Japan draw back from its imperialist goals during the 1920s? Why did Japan return to aggressive territorial expansion in the 1930s? *(Sample response: Japan drew back to strengthen its trade relationships with foreign countries. The Great Depression hit the Japanese economy hard during the 1930s because foreign trade dwindled. Out of desperation and fear, the Japanese public pressured for foreign invasion to provide the natural resources and space necessary to fuel the economy and feed the population.)*

Topic Inquiry
Have students continue their investigations for the Topic Inquiry.

The West After World War I

Supporting English Language Learners

Use with Digital Text 1, **Social Change After World War I.**

Learning Strategies
Read *Social Change After World War I* aloud to students. Then have students complete one of the activities below based on their English proficiency level.

Beginning Reread the subsection "Women's Progress" aloud to students. Pause after each paragraph to retell the content in accessible language for English language learners. Then direct students' attention to the image of women performing various jobs at the end of the subsection. Ask students to brainstorm words to describe the changes women experienced during this time. Write and display student responses. Model how to take those responses and work them into a summary of how a woman's role in Western society changed after World War I.

Intermediate Reread the subsection "Women's Progress" aloud to students. Pause after each paragraph and ask students to take turns retelling the content in their own words. Then direct students' attention to the image of women performing various jobs at the end of the subsection. Ask students to brainstorm words to describe the changes women experienced during this time. Write and display student responses. Help students take those responses and work them into a summary of how a woman's role in Western society changed after World War I.

Advanced Have students reread the subsection "Women's Progress." Ask students to work in small groups to take turns retelling the text in their own words. Then have students examine the image of women performing various jobs at the end of the subsection. Have groups discuss the changes women experienced during this time and then share their ideas with the rest of the class.

Advanced High Have students reread the subsection "Women's Progress" and examine the image of women performing various jobs at the end of the subsection. Have pairs of students discuss the changes women experienced during this time and then share their ideas with the rest of the class.

Use with Digital Text 2, **Scientific Discoveries.**

Learning Strategies
Read *Scientific Discoveries* aloud to the class. Have students complete the activities below according to their level of English proficiency.

Beginning Before reading, remind students that possessive case shows ownership. As you reread *Scientific Discoveries* to students, underline each possessive noun. Ask students what Freud, Einstein, Curie, and Fermi "owned." Explain that ownership applies not only to physical items but also to things you cannot see or touch, like ideas and feelings.

Intermediate Ask students to explain the possessive case. Make sure they understand that it shows ownership. As you reread *Scientific Discoveries* aloud, have students underline each possessive noun. Ask students what Freud, Einstein, Curie, and Fermi "owned." Explain that ownership does apply not only to physical items but also to things you cannot see or touch, like ideas and feelings.

Advanced Ask students to explain the possessive case to a partner. Then have pairs take turns rereading *Scientific Discoveries* aloud. Have students underline each possessive noun. Then have pairs discuss what Freud, Einstein, Curie, and Fermi "owned." Have each pair team up with another pair to share the main points of their discussion. As a class, guide students to the understanding that ownership applies not only to physical items but also to intangible things, like ideas and feelings.

Advanced High Have students reread *Scientific Discoveries* and underline each possessive noun. Then instruct students to write a few notes about what Freud, Einstein, Curie, and Fermi "owned." Have each student join a small group of three or four students to share and discuss their ideas. Finally, have groups share their ideas and consider the concept that ownership applies not only to physical items but also to intangible things, like ideas and feelings.

D Differentiate Instruction

Use the Differentiated Instruction notes throughout the lesson plan to support the varied skill sets, levels of readiness, and interests in the mixed-ability classroom.

Challenge These notes include suggestions for expanding the activity for advanced students.

On-Level These notes include suggestions for modifying the activity to address different interests or learning styles.

Extra Support These notes include ideas for providing more scaffolding or reading spuport.

Special Needs These notes provide ideas for adapting instruction to support the needs of various special needs students.

■ NOTES

PEARSON
realize™
www.PearsonRealize.com

Go online to access additional resources including:
Primary Sources • Biographies • Supreme Court cases •
21st Century Skill Tutorials • Maps • Graphic Organizers.

Objectives

Objective 1: Analyze how Western society and culture changed after World War I.

Objective 2: Identify the contributions of modern scientists such as Marie Curie and Albert Einstein.

Objective 3: Summarize the domestic and foreign policy issues that the Western democracies faced after World War I.

Objective 4: Describe how the global depression began and spread.

Objective 5: Explain the responses of Britain, France, and the United States to the Great Depression.

LESSON 5 ORGANIZER		PACING: APPROX. 1 PERIOD, .5 BLOCKS			
				RESOURCES	
		OBJECTIVES	**PACING**	**Online**	**Print**
Connect					
DIGITAL START UP ACTIVITY **Life During the Great Depression**			5 min.	●	
Investigate					
DIGITAL TEXT 1 **Social Change After World War I**		Objective 1	10 min.	●	●
DIGITAL TEXT 2 **Scientific Discoveries**		Objective 2	10 min.	●	●
DIGITAL TEXT 3 **Literature Reflects New Perspectives**			10 min.	●	●
DIGITAL TEXT 4 **Modern Art and Architecture**		Objective 1	10 min.	●	●
INTERACTIVE GALLERY **Modern Art Develops**			10 min.	●	
DIGITAL TEXT 5 **Postwar Politics in the West**			10 min.	●	●
DIGITAL TEXT 6 **International Relations**			10 min.	●	●
INTERACTIVE GALLERY **League of Nations Fails to Stop Aggression**		Objective 3	10 min.	●	
DIGITAL TEXT 7 **Economics in the Postwar Era**			10 min.	●	●
DIGITAL TEXT 8 **The Great Depression**		Objective 4	10 min.	●	●
DIGITAL TEXT 9 **Western Democracies React to the Depression**		Objective 5	10 min.	●	●
Synthesize					
DIGITAL ACTIVITY **Worldwide Economic Crisis**			5 min.	●	
Demonstrate					
LESSON QUIZ **Lesson Quiz and Class Discussion Board**			10 min.	●	

The West After World War I

◼ CONNECT

DIGITAL START UP ACTIVITY

Life During the Great Depression

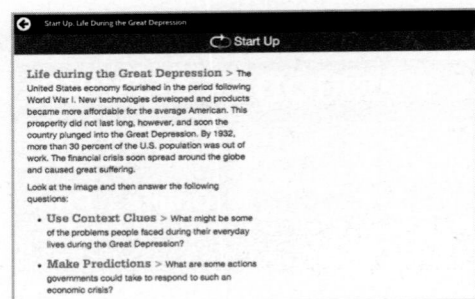

Project the Start Up Activity Ask students to look at the image to gain a better understanding of what life was like during the Great Depression. Have them answer the questions as they enter and get settled: What might be some of the problems people faced during their everyday lives during the Great Depression? *(Sample response: People struggled to find work and to feed their families.)* What are some actions governments could take to respond to such an economic crisis? *(Sample response: The government could institute employment programs, establish soup kitchens, and set controls on the financial market.)* Then have them share their ideas with another student, either in class or through a chat or blog space.

⇅ FLIP IT!

Assign the Flipped Video for this lesson.

◼ STUDENT EDITION PRINT PAGES: 702–712

◼ INVESTIGATE

DIGITAL TEXT 1

Social Change After World War I

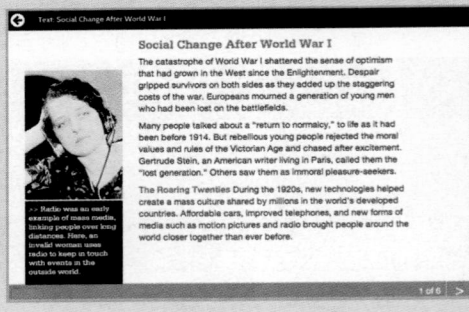

Objective 1: Analyze how Western society and culture changed after World War I.

Quick Instruction

Remind students that during the 1920s, Western nations were recovering from the horrific effects of the world war. Many people in those countries threw off the constraints of the past and embraced a popular culture that celebrated freedom and experimentation. This booming era in the United States was known as the Jazz Age.

Ask students: How did the Jazz Age reflect the effects of World War I on society? *(Answers will vary but students may say that it expressed a new willingness to experiment and a rebellion against old moral values.)*

Further Instruction

Editable Presentation Use the Editable Presentation to present the main ideas for this Core Text.

Social Change After World War I: Core Text and Interactive Reading Notepad Project and discuss the Interactive Reading Notepad questions and the image of the flapper from the Digital Text. Explain to students that technology and society experienced rapid changes after World War I. Tell students that innovations in mass communication allowed a mass culture to develop. Ask them to think about the term *mass culture* and discuss a definition for what it means today. *(Sample response: shared interest in music, fashion, movies, television, online videos, celebrities, etc. Students should also note that these interests are constantly changing.)* How do people learn about the latest fashion trends,

celebrity romances, musicians, artists, etc. today? *(Sample response: websites, fashion shows, blogs, video websites, television, friends, etc.)*

Explain that during the Jazz Age, the Victorian morals that had been so fundamental in pre-war Western culture no longer seemed relevant. Describe the characteristics of the Jazz Age and how flappers embodied society's rejection of Victorian ideals. Be sure students understand that certain groups did not embrace the new jazz culture. Some Americans joined a strong Christian fundamentalist movement and helped enact Prohibition in the United States.

Identify Cause and Effect How did new technologies affect American society during the 1920s? *(Sample response: They helped to spread popular American culture. Labor-saving devices became more common in middle-class homes, enabling more women to work outside the home.)*

DIGITAL TEXT 2
Scientific Discoveries

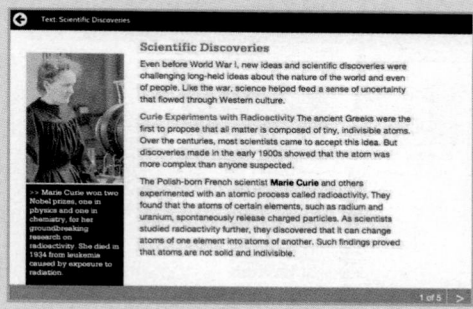

DIGITAL TEXT 3
Literature Reflects New Perspectives

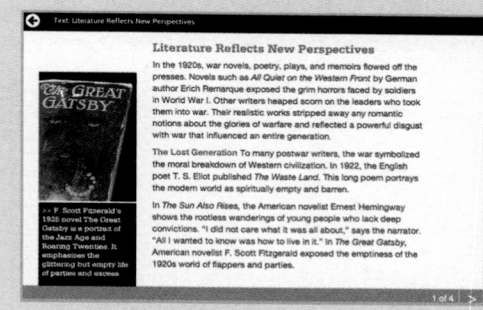

Objective 2: Identify the contributions of modern scientists such as Marie Curie and Albert Einstein.

Quick Instruction

Project the image of Marie Curie from the Text. Explain that new scientific findings, such as the discovery of radioactivity and the theory of relativity, challenged long-held beliefs. These theories reinforced the sense that the old world was falling apart. Be sure students understand that scientists such as Marie Curie and Albert Einstein impacted society beyond their fields of study. Ask: How did the work of Curie and Einstein affect the work of Enrico Fermi and other scientists? *(Their theories led to the discovery of atomic fission.)*

ELL Use the ELL activity described in the ELL chart.

Further Instruction

Scientific Discoveries: Core Text and Interactive Reading Notepad Project and discuss the Interactive Reading Notepad and the image of Albert Einstein from the Digital Text. Trace the discoveries of Marie Curie and her ground-breaking work in the field of radioactivity. Discuss Einstein's theories of relativity. Ask students why his complex scientific theories challenged traditional perspectives of how the universe works. *(Sample response: Einstein's ideas raised questions about Newtonian science, which described the universe as a predictable machine. As a result, people began to feel that old certainties were falling apart and the universe was beyond human understanding.)*

Discuss how the work of Sigmund Freud also challenged people's faith in reason. Ask students to define the term *subconscious mind*. *(Sample response: The subconscious is the part of the mind that influences actions that we are not consciously aware of.)* Explain that Freud's theories influenced popular culture of the time. Authors and artists explored the subconscious mind, creating new works that are considered masterpieces today.

Generate Explanations Why were Marie Curie's achievements unique for her time? *(Sample response: Pursuing a career in science and making ground-breaking discoveries were not traditional expectations for a woman of that period.)*

Identify Patterns How did Einstein's theories embody the feelings of uncertainty in the future and distrust of tradition that many felt during the postwar period? *(Sample response: Einstein proposed that the universe did not operate like a machine according to absolute laws. Instead, he theorized that measurements of space and time were determined by the relative position of the observer.)*

Objective 1: Analyze how Western society and culture changed after World War I.

Quick Instruction

Project the image of the book cover of *The Great Gatsby.* Explain to students that literature during this time was often bleak and pessimistic. Many authors were reacting to the atrocities experienced during the war and the lingering effects after the fighting ended. Some writers explored new styles of writing to express themselves. Ask: How did the war impact many postwar writers' work? *(They wrote pieces reflecting a lack of connection with the modern world.)*

Further Instruction

Project and discuss the Interactive Reading Notepad questions. Explain to students that many authors and thinkers expressed disgust with modern warfare and the futility of war.

Remind students of Freud's theories about the subconscious mind, and tell them that they influenced Virginia Woolf and James Joyce, who explored the subconscious in their works. Discuss nihilism, a movement represented by Friedrich Nietzsche that held that traditional values were unfounded and human existence was meaningless. Explain that Nietzsche's work reflected the dark outlook on life of the postwar years.

Tell students that another movement during the 1920s was the Harlem Renaissance. In this literary and artistic movement, African Americans expressed pride in their unique culture.

The West After World War I

DIGITAL TEXT 4

Modern Art and Architecture

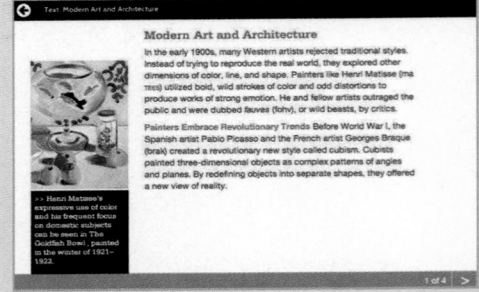

INTERACTIVE GALLERY

Modern Art Develops

Make Generalizations Describe the literature of the postwar period. *(Sample response: Many works of literature reflected a sense of uncertainty, of civilization falling apart. Works of the Harlem Renaissance reflected pride in African American culture.)*

Contrast In what way were the authors of the Harlem Renaissance different from many other writers of the postwar period? *(Sample response: Instead of portraying the horrors of war, Harlem Renaissance writers explored aspects of African American culture and the African American experience.)*

Objective 1: Analyze how Western society and culture changed after World War I.

Quick Instruction

Explain to students that many visual artists, like musicians and writers, rejected traditional values and styles after World War I. Some created art to shock the viewer, others rejected representation and explored line, shape, and color, and still others used art to interpret some of the new scientific theories.

Interactive Gallery: Modern Art Develops Project the image gallery. Look at each image individually and discuss how each style reflected a new, modern perspective. Clarify for students that, in this context, the word *modern* refers to art that broke from the traditions of the past, rather than meaning "contemporary" as it often does in daily speech.

👥 ACTIVE CLASSROOM

Post images from the Interactive Image Gallery on individual pages around the room. Ask the students to break into groups to tour the room and Make Headlines for each image. Ask each group to present its summary to the class.

Make Generalizations Review the image gallery. How would you define "modern art" to someone who has never seen an example before? *(Sample response: It encompasses a variety of styles and techniques used to present artistic expression in a nontraditional way.)*

Further Instruction

Ask if any students have been to an art museum or art gallery. Ask volunteers to describe different styles and types of artwork they saw there.

Modern Art and Architecture: Core Text and Interactive Reading Notepad Project and discuss the Interactive Reading Notepad questions and the image of the Salvador Dali painting from the Interactive Image Gallery. Tell students that these works rejected traditional styles and Victorian values. Ask them to study the image of the painting by Dali. Discuss how Dali and other artists were influenced by stream-of-consciousness literature and Freud's exploration of the unconscious mind. Ensure students understand that many artists chose to reject realistic representations of their world. Explain that through artistic techniques such as cubism, these artists rejected traditional ways of representing objects in a natural or realistic way.

Categorize Give an example of modern art or architecture that emphasized the importance of technology in the 20th century. *(Sample response: The Bauhaus school in Germany blended science and technology with design. Bauhaus buildings feature glass, steel, and concrete but have little ornamentation.)*

Draw Conclusions How did cubism reflect some artists' feelings about what was happening to their culture and society after the war? *(Sample response: In cubism, artists portrayed their subjects as fragmented pieces with sharp angles and planes instead of as solid objects. This reflected the belief that the war had shattered old certainties and values.)*

DIGITAL TEXT 5

Postwar Politics in the West

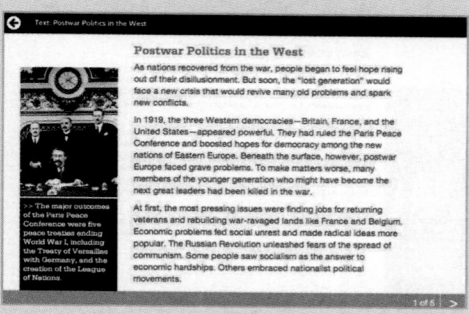

>> The major outcomes of the Paris Peace Conference were five peace treaties ending World War I, including the Treaty of Versailles with Germany, and the creation of the League of Nations

DIGITAL TEXT 6

International Relations

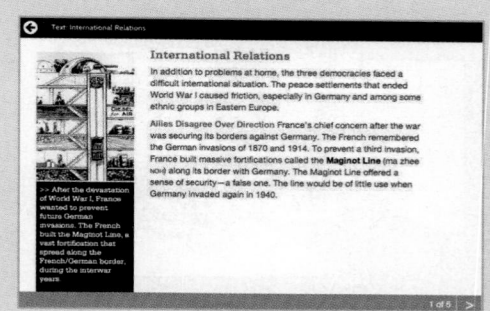

>> After the devastation of World War I, France wanted to prevent future German invasions. The French built the Maginot Line, a vast fortification that spread along the French/German border, during the interwar years

Objective 3: Summarize the domestic and foreign policy issues that the Western democracies faced after World War I.

Quick Instruction

Project the image of the delegates at the Paris Peace Conference. Remind students that Western democracies emerged victorious from World War I and appeared powerful. However, both Britain and France faced political unrest as rival parties—some conservative, some socialist or even communist—competed for power. Britain also had to answer Irish calls for independence. The United States faced its own political unrest, particularly a fear of immigrants and radicals.

Further Instruction

Project and discuss the Interactive Reading Notepad questions and the image of the Easter Rising from the Digital Text. This uprising in Ireland was an example of the domestic political instability that troubled Britain, France, and the United States following the war. After the brutal fighting of World War I, people hoped for peaceful democratic solutions rather than violent revolution. However, economic problems fed social unrest during the postwar period, and many began to search for radical solutions to society's problems.

Compare the limitations on workers' rights in Britain with the limitations on immigration in the United States. Point out how both are examples of balancing national needs with civil liberties. Tell students that the United States tried to balance national security with limitations on civil liberties during the "Red Scare" of the 1920s. Ask students to offer

examples of this struggle today. *(Sample responses: limitations on strikes for public safety officers; video surveillance in public places; airport screenings; government surveillance of cell phone calls)*

Summarize How did the British and Irish compromise to achieve Irish independence? *(Sample response: Most of Ireland became the self-governing Irish Free State, while the largely Protestant counties in the north remained under British rule.)*

Draw Conclusions How did the "Red Scare" feed growing demands to limit immigration to the United States? *(Sample response: Some native-born Americans sought to exclude foreign immigrants. They used the Red Scare to expel foreign-born people and to impose immigration limitations.)*

Objective 3: Summarize the domestic and foreign policy issues that the Western democracies faced after World War I.

Quick Instruction

Remind students that once World War I's brutal fighting ended, Western nations focused on global peace. However, each nation wanted to ensure domestic security also. This led to the pursuit of contradictory policies such as disarmament on one hand but building up fortifications like the Maginot Line on the other.

Interactive Gallery: League of Nations Fails to Stop Aggression Project the political cartoon from the Interactive Gallery. Ask students to click on the numbered hotspots to learn more about each part of the political cartoon. Review each hotspot individually, and then view the cartoon as a whole.

👥 ACTIVE CLASSROOM

Break up the students into pairs. Ask the first student give the second a verbal Audio Tour of the political cartoon, describing what it shows. Have the second student give the first an explanation of what the cartoon means.

Further Instruction

International Relations: Core Text and Interactive Reading Notepad Project and discuss the Interactive Reading Notepad questions. Remind students how devastating the war was, both in lives lost and in the high economic cost. Politicians and diplomats

The West After World War I

INTERACTIVE GALLERY
League of Nations Fails to Stop Aggression

DIGITAL TEXT 7
Economics in the Postwar Era

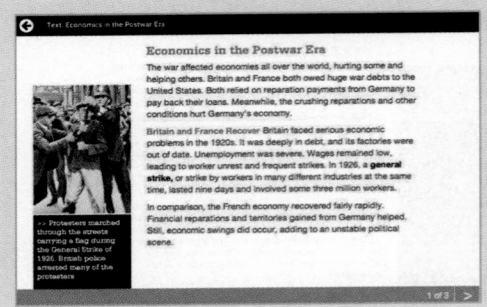

wanted to attain a lasting global peace after the war to ensure such a global conflict would never happen again. Ask students to speculate on policies that might guarantee lasting peace. *(Sample response: international treaties; global military force instead of national ones; disarmament)*

Use the political cartoon from the Interactive Image to start a class discussion of the political climate during the postwar period. Explain that each nation was focused on its own security and defensive capabilities. Review the developments in Britain and France intended to maintain peace within their borders. Tell students that France wanted a strict interpretation of the Versailles Treaty to check German aggression and built the Maginot Line in an effort to protect the French border. However, Britain feared the increasing power of the Soviet Union and France and preferred to relax the treaty's harshest conditions.

Discuss the international efforts towards peace during the 1920s. Tell them that the treaties of Locarno and the Kellogg-Briand Pact are examples of this international effort and cooperation. Explain that international treaties had to balance global peace with each nation's interest in its own national security. Remind students that the United States did not join the League of Nations, limiting the power of the organization. Tell students the League was further limited by the unwillingness of member-nations to stand up to aggressors during the 1930s, such as Germany, Italy, and Japan. Ensure students understand that the intense international focus

on maintaining global peace caused many to dismiss aggressive acts perpetrated by increasingly radical nations. These acts would eventually lead to another global conflict.

Identify Central Issues How did the League of Nations respond when Japan invaded Manchuria in 1931? *(Sample response: It condemned Japan's actions but did nothing to stop it.)*

Make Generalizations Why were the Locarno treaties important? Explain. *(Sample response: The treaties settled the disputed borders of Germany. They symbolized a new era of global peace.)*

Objective 3: Summarize the domestic and foreign policy issues that the Western democracies faced after World War I.

Quick Instruction

Project the image of the American parking lot filled with cars. Remind students that World War I was economically devastating for many European countries. Following the war, much of Europe relied heavily upon loans and investments from the United States. Be sure students understand that a significant portion of the globe depended upon the economic prosperity of the United States.

Further Instruction

Project and discuss the Interactive Reading Notepad questions. Remind students that many countries spent staggering amounts of money to fund World War I and were forced to take out loans to cover the enormous costs. Discuss the general strike in Britain during 1926 and how such enormous disruptions in labor fed the cycle of economic instability.

Tell students that the United States was economically prosperous during the Jazz Age, and Europe depended on American financing during the postwar era. Explain that although the economies of Britain and France eventually began to recover and stabilize, the entire global economy relied upon the wealth of the United States. Ask students to predict what the repercussions of a financial crisis in the United States would be. *(Sample response: European countries would lack the financing needed to continue recovering and rebuilding. The United States would no longer purchase many of the goods produced in foreign countries.)*

DIGITAL TEXT 8

The Great Depression

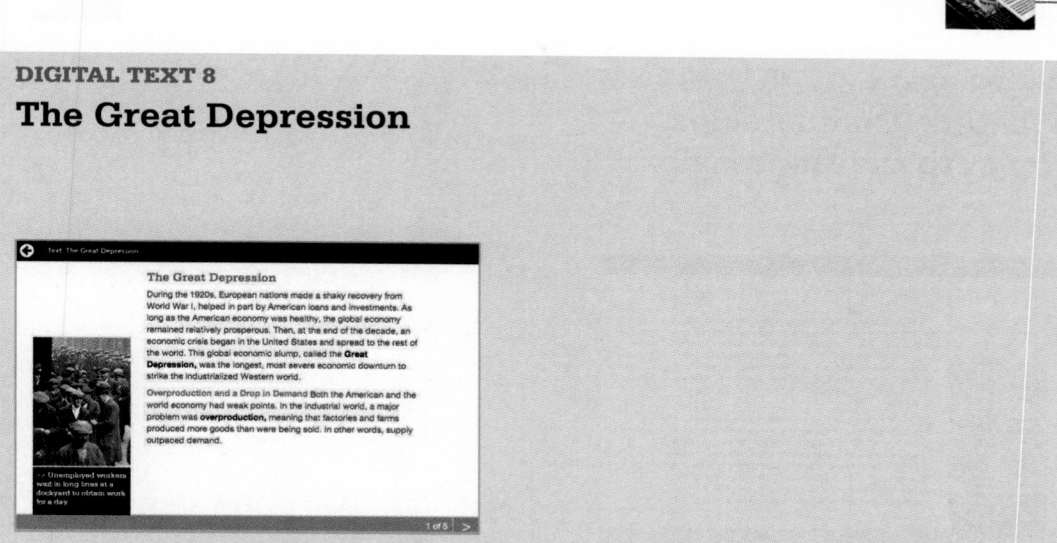

The Great Depression

During the 1920s, European nations made a shaky recovery from World War I, helped in part by American loans and investments. As long as the American economy was healthy, the global economy remained relatively prosperous. Then, at the end of the decade, an economic crisis began in the United States and spread to the rest of the world. This global economic slump, called the **Great Depression,** was the longest, most severe economic downturn to strike the industrialized Western world.

Overproduction and a Drop in Demand Both the American and the world economy had weak points. In the industrial world, a major problem was **overproduction,** meaning that factories and farms produced more goods than were being sold. In other words, supply outpaced demand.

→ Unemployed workers wait in long lines at a dockyard to obtain work for a day

1 of 8 >

Compare and Contrast How was the standard of living of the U.S. middle class during the 1920s different from that of Europe? Explain. *(Sample response: The European economy took longer to recover and was more unstable than that of the United States. Middle class families in the United States benefited by having a higher standard of living.)*

Identify Patterns What economic problem did Britain and France share following World War I? *(Sample response: They both owed money to the United States.)*

Objective 4: Describe how the global depression began and spread.

Quick Instruction

Project the image of the lines of unemployed workers from the Digital Text. Ask students to look for the key term *Great Depression* in the Digital Text and explain its meaning. *(a painful time of global economic collapse, starting in 1929 and lasting until about 1939)* Explain that the economic crisis developed in the United States and spread around the world because countries were linked through international loans and finance. Political reactions, such as the decision by the United States to raise tariffs and the resulting retaliation by other nations, deepened the depression by dampening trade.

Further Instruction

Project and discuss the Interactive Reading Notepad questions. Identify the developments leading up to the Great Depression, including the role of overproduction, the stock market crash, and the policies of the Federal Reserve. Explain that a vicious cycle developed: people stop buying products, creating a surplus of supply, which caused companies to lay off workers to save money, reducing the income of many families, who then reduced purchases. To check for understanding, ask students to identify three effects of the Great Depression. *(Sample response: unemployment; families unable to afford food; loss of faith in capitalism and democracy)*

Make sure students understand that the U.S. economy was central to the international network of trade and finance. When the U.S. economy faltered, it set off a downward spiral of motion that encompassed much of the world. Production in the United States plummeted, which meant Americans had little or no money to invest abroad. Without this money, Europeans could no longer afford American goods and they were unable to pay back loans from the United States.

Sequence Events Describe how the Great Depression began in the United States. *(Sample response: The price of raw materials and agricultural products plummeted following the war. The lower prices meant workers were paid less. They could not afford to buy products, leading to a slump in demand. Coupled with new technology, the reduced demand led to overproduction, causing factories to cut back production and workers to lose their jobs. A stock market crash aggravated the decline.)*

Identify Cause and Effect Why did the Great Depression spread from the United States, eventually affecting world markets? *(Sample response: The U.S. economy was part of an international network of trade and finance; as its economy faltered, the economies that relied on it faltered, too.)*

The West After World War I

DIGITAL TEXT 9

Western Democracies React to the Depression

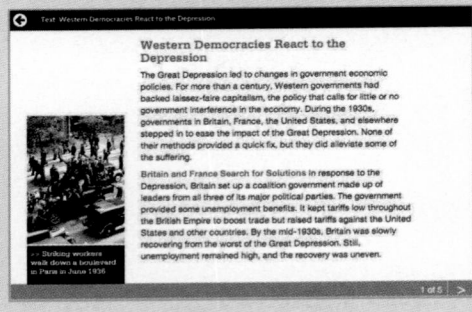

Objective 5: **Explain the responses of Britain, France, and the United States to the depression.**

Quick Instruction

Britain and France were hit especially hard by the Great Depression. Both countries instituted some policies to provide relief, but their governments hesitated to make radical changes. The U.S. government originally took limited measures, but then Franklin Delano Roosevelt became president. Ask: What was the New Deal? *(a package of economic and social programs proposed by President Roosevelt to combat the Depression more aggressively)*

Further Instruction

Western Democracies React to the Depression: Core Text and Interactive Reading Notepad Project and discuss the Interactive Reading Notepad questions. Remind students how world payments created a vicious cycle and helped spread the Great Depression from the United States to Europe. Trace the developments and policies each of the Western powers adopted in an effort to lift the Depression. Tell students that the governments of Britain and France lacked strong, decisive action.

Explain how the Dust Bowl was an ecological disaster that exacerbated the financial crisis in the United States. Ask students to speculate on how the Dust Bowl effected the entire country. *(Sample response: Farmers could*

not produce food; dust blew east across the nation; massive waves of immigration to unaffected states, most notably in California.) Tell students that the massive package of economic and social programs implemented by President Roosevelt, known as the New Deal, greatly expanded the government's role in the daily lives of Americans.

Summarize Briefly summarize Western countries' attempts to end the Great Depression. *(Sample response: They put into place programs that lessened suffering but did not solve the problems.)*

Identify Patterns As the world struggled to react to the global depression, what unifying political force was lacking in both Britain and France? *(Sample response: They both lacked strong leadership capable of taking decisive action.)*

D **Differentiate:** **Challenge** Remind students how FDR's New Deal programs expanded the role of government in the daily lives of Americans. Explain that many Americans disliked this trend, and it remains a central debate in American politics. Ask students to break into groups and stage a classroom debate on this question. Have one side defend the New Deal and the other argue against it.

■ SYNTHESIZE

DIGITAL ACTIVITY
Worldwide Economic Crisis

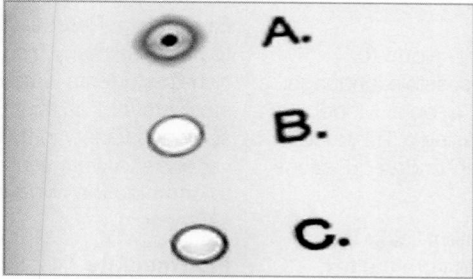

Project the image from the Synthesize Digital Activity. Explain to students that the effects of the Great Depression lasted for many years. Review some of the immediate effects and how those policies had effects far into the future. Ask students to review the readings in the Digital Text to identify examples of those effects. *(Sample responses: Economic Effects: Vast unemployment and misery; Protective tariffs imposed; Countries abandon gold standard; Political Effects: Governments set up some relief programs; loss of faith in capitalism and democracy; authoritarian leaders emerge. Social Effects: Soup kitchens; migration away from the Dust Bowl.)*

Draw Conclusions Do you think the Great Depression still has effects today? Explain. *(Sample response: Yes. Social Security is an example of a policy implemented during the Great Depression that is a standard feature of life today.)*

■ DEMONSTRATE

LESSON QUIZ
Lesson Quiz and Class Discussion Board

Assign the online Lesson Quiz for this lesson if you haven't already done so. Students will be offered automatic remediation or enrichment based on their score.

Pose these questions to the class on the Discussion Board:

Draw Conclusions Why was the United States able to become a leading economic power in the world during the 1920s? *(Sample response: After World War I, the United States fared better economically than Europe. Much of Europe had suffered devastating damage during the war. Both Britain and France were heavily in debt to the United States after the war. Also, the United States made significant investments in the recovery and rebuilding that was needed in Europe after World War I.)*

Identify Central Issues How did the Great Depression lay the foundation for the rise of radical extremists? *(Sample response: It created misery and hopelessness. Governments failed to take decisive action. People were desperate for change.)*

Topic Inquiry
Have students continue their investigations for the Topic Inquiry.

Fascism Emerges in Italy

Supporting English Language Learners

Use with Digital Text 1, **The Rise of Mussolini.**

Learning Strategies
Read *The Rise of Mussolini* aloud to students. As they listen, have them follow along in their texts. Ask them to think about the reasons behind the anger of Italians following World War I.

Beginning Reread the subsection "Postwar Discontent" aloud to students. Then retell the information from the text in accessible language. Explain that predicting is one way to think ahead about a topic. Model making a prediction about what will happen in Italy by using a Think Aloud strategy to show students how to use self-talk and open-ended questions to make predictions.

Intermediate Reread the subsection "Postwar Discontent" aloud to students. Support students as they retell the information from the text in everyday language. Explain that predicting is one way to think ahead about a topic. Model making a prediction about what will happen in Italy by using a Think Aloud strategy for the first paragraph of the text to show students how to use self-talk and open-ended questions to make predictions. Then have students repeat this procedure for the second paragraph of the text.

Advanced Have students reread the subsection "Postwar Discontent" aloud to a partner. Remind students that predicting is one way to think ahead about a topic. Ask students to make predictions about what will happen in Italy by using a Think Aloud strategy. One partner should read and make predictions using the first paragraph of the text, and the other partner should repeat the procedure for the second paragraph of the text. Then have pairs share their predictions with the whole class.

Advanced High Have students reread the subsection "Postwar Discontent." Ask students to use a Think-Pair-Share to make predictions about what will happen in Italy. Have pairs discuss their predictions and choose their best one to share with the class.

Use with Digital Text 3, **Characteristics of Fascism.**

Learning Strategies
Read *Characteristics of Fascism* aloud to the class. Have students complete the activities below according to their level of English proficiency.

Beginning Reread *Characteristics of Fascism* for students. Ask students to name as many features of fascism as possible. Then use those features to help students write two simple sentences to describe fascism. Explain to students that as they become better writers, they will want to include sentence variety in their writing. Tell them that one way to include sentence variety is to write sentences of different lengths. Then demonstrate how to combine the two simple sentences you wrote into a single, compound sentence.

Intermediate Reread *Characteristics of Fascism* for students. Ask students to name as many features of fascism as possible. Then have students use those features to write two simple sentences to describe fascism. Remind them that sentence variety, including writing sentences of different lengths, makes writing more interesting to read. Then assist students as they combine the two simple sentences you wrote into a single compound sentence.

Advanced Have students reread *Characteristics of Fascism*. Ask students to work with a partner to name as many features of fascism as possible. Then have students use those features to write four simple sentences to describe fascism. Remind them that sentence variety, including writing sentences of different lengths, makes writing more interesting to read. Then instruct pairs to combine their four simple sentences into two compound sentences. Have pairs share their sentences with the class.

Advanced High Have students reread *Characteristics of Fascism*. Ask students to write down as many features of fascism as possible. Then have students use those features to write four to six simple sentences to describe fascism. Remind them that sentence variety, including writing sentences of different lengths, makes writing more interesting to read. Then instruct students to combine their four simple sentences into two compound sentences. Have students share their sentences with a partner.

D Differentiate Instruction

Use the Differentiated Instruction notes throughout the lesson plan to support the varied skill sets, levels of readiness, and interests in the mixed-ability classroom.

Challenge These notes include suggestions for expanding the activity for advanced students.

On-Level These notes include suggestions for modifying the activity to address different interests or learning styles.

Extra Support These notes include ideas for providing more scaffolding or reading spuport.

Special Needs These notes provide ideas for adapting instruction to support the needs of various special needs students.

NOTES

PEARSON
realize™
www.PearsonRealize.com

Go online to access additional resources including:
Primary Sources • Biographies • Supreme Court cases •
21st Century Skill Tutorials • Maps • Graphic Organizers.

Objectives

Objective 1: Describe the rise of Mussolini.

Objective 2: Summarize Mussolini's policies as leader of Italy.

Objective 3: Identify the characteristics of totalitarianism and fascism.

LESSON 6 ORGANIZER		PACING: APPROX. 1 PERIOD, .5 BLOCKS			
				RESOURCES	
		OBJECTIVES	PACING	Online	Print
Connect					
DIGITAL START UP ACTIVITY **Children and Totalitarianism**			5 min.	●	
Investigate					
DIGITAL TEXT 1 **The Rise of Mussolini**		Objective 1	10 min.	●	●
DIGITAL TEXT 2 **Mussolini's Totalitarian Rule**		Objectives 2, 3	10 min.	●	●
INTERACTIVE GALLERY **The Makings of an Italian Totalitarian State**			10 min.	●	
DIGITAL TEXT 3 **Characteristics of Fascism**		Objective 3	10 min.	●	●
INTERACTIVE CHART **Communism vs. Fascism**			10 min.	●	
Synthesize					
DIGITAL ACTIVITY **The Economics of Totalitarian Governments**			5 min.	●	
Demonstrate					
LESSON QUIZ **Lesson Quiz and Class Discussion Board**			10 min.	●	

Fascism Emerges in Italy

▮ CONNECT

DIGITAL START UP ACTIVITY

Children and Totalitarianism

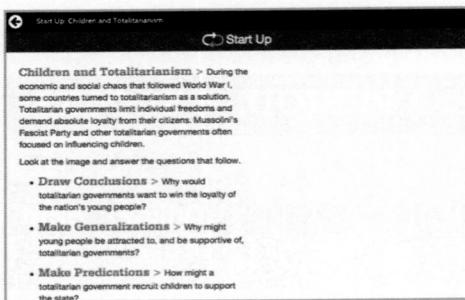

Project the Start Up Activity and the image of the Young Fascists from the Digital Text. Ask students to look at the image and answer the questions as they enter and get settled: Why would totalitarian governments want to win the loyalty of the nation's young people? *(Sample response: Young people are the nation's future. Winning them over creates a constant flow of people who will serve the interests of the government without question.)* Why might young people be attracted to, and be supportive of, totalitarian governments? *(Sample response: because they trusted the adults who taught them and did not know any different forms of government; because totalitarian governments offer a very clear-cut view of the world)* How might a totalitarian government recruit children to support the state? *(Sample response: by incorporating totalitarian beliefs into school curriculums and forming youth groups that pass on ideology)*

⬆ FLIP IT!

Assign the Flipped Video for this lesson.

▮ STUDENT EDITION PRINT PAGES: 713–716

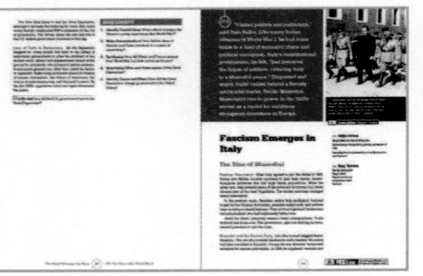

▮ INVESTIGATE

DIGITAL TEXT 1

The Rise of Mussolini

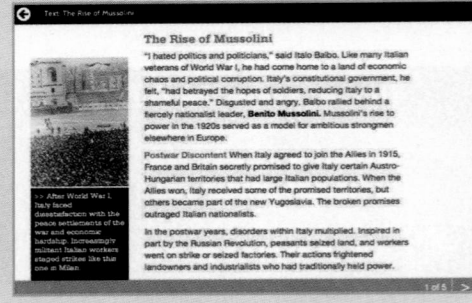

Objective 1: Describe the rise of Mussolini.

Quick Instruction

Project the image of the general strike in Italy in 1920. Explain to students that Italy was in a state of turmoil after World War I. Many felt cheated by the broken promises made by the Allies. In addition, veterans returned home to economic chaos. When Italians felt they had no strong political leadership to turn to, Benito Mussolini stepped up, offering hope and stability to the Italian people.

Further Instruction

Editable Presentation Use the Editable Presentation to present the main ideas for this Core Text.

The Rise of Mussolini: Core Text and Interactive Reading Notepad Project and discuss the Interactive Reading Notepad questions and the image of the Fascists' March on Rome in 1922. Remind students that Mussolini promised to restore the greatness of Italy, reminiscent of the days of the Roman empire. Have students identify and define the key term *Black Shirts* from the Digital Text. Ask students to list the ways in which Mussolini and the fascists drew upon the history of ancient Rome. *(Sample response: Fascists took their name from the fasces, which was a symbol of authority in ancient Rome; Mussolini promised to turn the Mediterranean into a "Roman lake.")*

Summarize Summarize the situation in Italy following World War I that led people to support Mussolini. *(Sample response: Italy had massive unemployment and strikes, rising taxes, and declining trade. The country lacked political unity. Italians desperately desired a new, more effective government. Nationalists resented the broken promises made by the Allies. Mussolini was making big promises to the Italian people but used terror and intimidation to gain political power.)*

D Differentiate: Extra Support To help students practice previewing, ask them to skim headings, images, and boldface key terms before they read the section. Tell them that the subject of the section shifts from a specific topic (Mussolini's rule in Italy) to a broader concept (the nature of fascism) part way through. Based on their previewing, ask them to pinpoint when this shift occurs.

DIGITAL TEXT 2

Mussolini's Totalitarian Rule

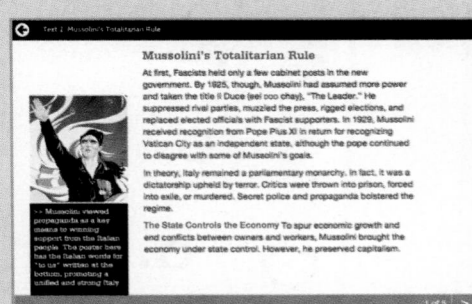

INTERACTIVE GALLERY

The Makings of an Italian Totalitarian State

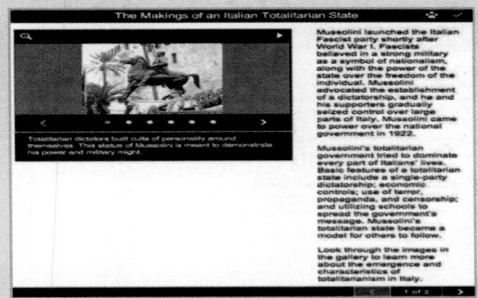

DIGITAL TEXT 3

Characteristics of Fascism

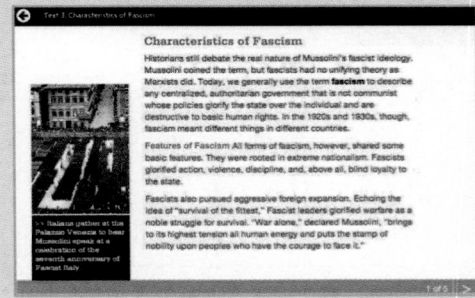

Objectives 2: Summarize Mussolini's policies as leader of Italy; 3: Identify the characteristics of totalitarianism and fascism.

Quick Instruction

Remind students how Mussolini gained power. Explain that Mussolini's Italy was a dictatorship upheld by terror. Mussolini held absolute power and controlled Italian society, economics, and politics.

Interactive Gallery: The Makings of an Italian Totalitarian State Project the first image from the Interactive Gallery. Review each image individually. Ask: What does each of these images suggest about how Mussolini tried to use his own image as a tool to promote his message? (Answers will vary but students may point out all of the images suggest that Mussolini wanted to be sure that everyday citizens were aware of his power and his personal desire to return Italy to greatness.)

👥 ACTIVE CLASSROOM

Ask students to review the information they have learned. Have each student design a piece of Wallpaper that encapsulates key learnings about characteristics of Mussolini's totalitarian state. Post the wallpaper around the room. Ask students to tour the room and note what others have written or illustrated. Students can use the information to develop their notes.

Infer Why did Mussolini build a cult of personality around himself? (Sample response: He wanted to gain and keep total control over the actions, thoughts, and hearts of the Italian people.)

Further Instruction

Mussolini's Totalitarian Rule: Core Text and Interactive Reading Notepad Project and discuss the Interactive Reading Notepad questions. Discuss the ways in which Mussolini gained his power. Ask students to speculate as to why it was important for Mussolini to have the support of the pope. (Sample response: because many Italians were Roman Catholic and looked to the pope's leadership) Explain that Mussolini brought the economy under the control of the state, but he preserved capitalism. Point out that this is a significant difference between communism and fascism. Ensure students understand that the priority of fascism was the success and glory of the state over the interests of the individual. Ask students to think about why people would be willing to relinquish their individual rights. (Sample response: They did so because people had lost faith in constitutional government after experiencing the chaos following World War I.)

Make Generalizations Briefly summarize the characteristics of a totalitarian state. (Sample response: Some basic characteristics of a totalitarian state include a single-party dictatorship; state-controlled economy; use of terror, secret police, and spies; government-sponsored propaganda and strict censorship of the media; use of schools to spread their message.)

Compare and Contrast Did the lives of women improve under Mussolini's rule? Explain. (Sample response: No. Women were pushed out of paying jobs and pressured to stay home to raise children.)

Objective 3: Identify the characteristics of totalitarianism and fascism.

Quick Instruction

Explain that totalitarian governments take different forms and that fascism was only one type of totalitarian government. Both fascists and communists established totalitarian governments in which a centralized state controlled all aspects of society.

Interactive Chart: Communism vs. Fascism Project the Interactive Chart. Explain to students that the tiles contain key nations, major ideas, and leaders of communism and fascism during the 1930s. Review the tiles to ensure student understanding. Ask students to place the tiles into the appropriate area: Communism, Fascism, or Both.

👥 ACTIVE CLASSROOM

Ask students to perform a Write 1-Get 3 activity in which they answer the question: "What are four key characteristics of fascism?" Have students take a piece of paper and fold it into quarters and write down one response in the first box. Then have students move around the classroom asking to hear other responses. Instruct students to evaluate whether a response is correct and write a correct response in each box until all four boxes are filled. Ask students to share their filled pages with the class.

ELL Use the ELL activity described in the ELL chart.

Fascism Emerges in Italy

INTERACTIVE CHART
Communism vs. Fascism

Draw Conclusions How are fascist governments destructive to basic human rights? *(Sample response: Individual rights are ignored for the supremacy of the state. Authoritarian dictators use violence and terror to gain power.)*

Further Instruction

Project and discuss the Interactive Reading Notepad questions. Explain to students that Mussolini's fascism served as a model for other totalitarian states. Remind students of the chaotic situation in Italy after World War I. Discuss the struggles people faced on a daily basis. Ask students, "What kind of emotions do you think people were feeling during this unstable period?" *(Sample response: desperation from hunger, frustration due to unemployment, resentment of broken promises during the war, fear for the future)* Explain that fascism often used propaganda to illicit an emotional response from the people.

Use Context Clues What are some of the emotions fascists might use to control people? Explain. *(Sample response: Fascists could use propaganda to scare the population into believing their only option was an authoritarian state.)*

SYNTHESIZE

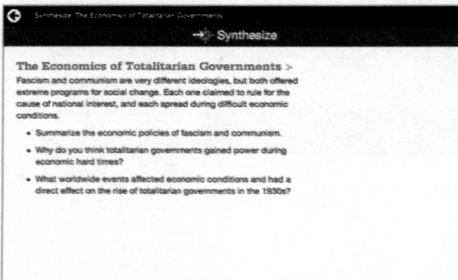

DIGITAL ACTIVITY
The Economics of Totalitarian Governments

Project the Synthesize activity, and ask students to answer the questions: Summarize the economic policies of fascism and communism. *(Sample response: Fascism: brought the economy under state control but preserved capitalism; supported by business leaders, wealthy landowners, and the lower middle class; Communism: advocated a classless society and complete state control over the economy; supported by urban and agricultural workers)* Why do you think totalitarian governments gained power during economic hard times? *(Sample response: Because people were tired of economic instability and the social unrest it caused; democracies move slowly and tend to offer incremental changes; however, people had been suffering for many years and wanted immediate and drastic action to be taken for improving the economic situation)* What worldwide events affected economic conditions and had a direct effect on the rise of totalitarian governments in the 1930s? *(Sample response: the economic conditions created during and after WWI and then the Great Depression)*

Remind students that fascism as practiced in Italy and Germany and communism as practiced in the Soviet Union were different types of totalitarian government. Review the key features of fascism and communism. Explain that devastating economic conditions helped lay the foundation for totalitarian governments to rise to power.

Hypothesize Do you think fascism could rise as a political force in the world today? Explain. *(Sample response: Yes. A nation experiencing devastating economic conditions and lacking strong, centralized political leadership could find the ideology appealing.)*

DEMONSTRATE

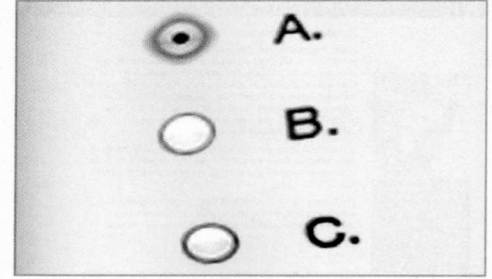

LESSON QUIZ
Lesson Quiz and Class Discussion Board

Assign the online Lesson Quiz for this lesson if you haven't already done so. Students will be offered automatic remediation or enrichment based on their score.

Pose these questions to the class on the Discussion Board:

Draw Conclusions How and why did fascism rise in Italy? *(Sample response: The fascists, led by Mussolini, took advantage of Italy's postwar turmoil to seize control of the nation.)*

Predict Consequences During the 1930s, nations, such as Japan and Germany, adopted increasingly aggressive foreign policies. How do you think Mussolini will react? *(Sample response: He could make alliances and join forces with Germany.)*

Topic Inquiry

Have students continue their investigations for the Topic Inquiry.

The Soviet Union Under Stalin

Supporting English Language Learners

Use with Digital Text 3, **Stalin Builds a Totalitarian State.**

Learning Strategies

Read *Stalin Builds a Totalitarian State* aloud to students. As they listen, have them follow along in their texts. Ask them to think about their opinions of how Stalin attempted to control the ideas and feelings of Soviet citizens.

Beginning Reread the subsection "Propaganda and the 'Cult of Personality'" aloud to students. Then retell the information from the text in accessible language. Explain that it is important to form opinions about events in history. One way to do this is to evaluate the actions of a historical figure. Model how to evaluate the actions of Stalin by summarizing the subsection, then responding to it with simple sentences that show a judgment of Stalin's actions and reasons to support that judgment. Invite students to share their opinions by asking open-ended questions that guide them to an evaluation of Stalin's actions and goals.

Intermediate Reread the subsection "Propaganda and the 'Cult of Personality'" aloud to students. Help students paraphrase the text in everyday language. Lead a brief discussion on the importance of forming opinions about events in history. Invite students to evaluate Stalin's use of propaganda to control Soviets. Ask open-ended questions that guide them to an evaluation of Stalin's actions and goals. Provide support and definitions of any challenging words or concepts as needed.

Advanced Have students reread the subsection "Propaganda and the 'Cult of Personality.'" Lead a brief discussion on the importance of forming opinions about events in history. Invite students to evaluate and discuss Stalin's use of propaganda to control Soviets. Encourage students to ask one another questions about their opinions, allowing them to refine their logic and identify the best sources of factual support. Offer support as needed.

Advanced High Have students reread the subsection "Propaganda and the 'Cult of Personality.'" Divide students into small groups of four or five students. Instruct students to discuss the importance of forming opinions about events in history. Then have groups evaluate and discuss Stalin's use of propaganda to control Soviets. Encourage students to ask one another questions about their opinions, challenging them to refine their logic and identify the best sources of factual support. Circulate among groups and offer support as needed.

Use with Digital Text 4, **Soviet Society Under Stalin.**

Learning Strategies

Review sentence patterns with students. Then read *Soviet Society Under Stalin* aloud to the class. Have students complete the activities below according to their level of English proficiency.

Beginning Reread *Soviet Society Under Stalin* for students, having them follow along in their texts. Then retell the content in accessible language, using bilingual dictionaries and other language supports to be sure students understand the information in the text. Tell students that they will be writing a simple sentence about what they learned from this section. Explain that a simple sentence includes a noun and a verb, in that order. Model writing two or three simple sentences for students and then instruct them to try writing their own. Circulate among students to offer support and guidance as needed.

Intermediate Reread *Soviet Society Under Stalin* for students, having them follow along in their texts. Help students retell the content in their own words, using bilingual dictionaries and other language supports as needed. Then tell students that they will be writing two sentences that should include a subject, verb, and an object. The sentences should be about what they learned from this section. Ask for volunteers to share with the class. Write and display the sentences students share.

Advanced Have students reread *Soviet Society Under Stalin*. Instruct pairs of students to write three sentences, each with a subject, verb, indirect object, and a direct object or a subject, verb, and a complement. Then have two pairs of students work together, share their sentences, and choose two of the four sentences to share with the class.

Advanced High Have students reread *Soviet Society Under Stalin*. Instruct students to write four or five sentences about Soviet society. Each sentence should include a subject, verb, indirect object, and a direct object or a subject, verb, object, and complement. Have students share their work with the class.

▶ Differentiate Instruction

Use the Differentiated Instruction notes throughout the lesson plan to support the varied skill sets, levels of readiness, and interests in the mixed-ability classroom.

Challenge These notes include suggestions for expanding the activity for advanced students.

On-Level These notes include suggestions for modifying the activity to address different interests or learning styles.

Extra Support These notes include ideas for providing more scaffolding or reading spuport.

Special Needs These notes provide ideas for adapting instruction to support the needs of various special needs students.

■ NOTES

The Soviet Union Under Stalin

Objectives

Objective 1: Explain how Stalin built a command economy in the Soviet Union.

Objective 2: Describe how Stalin used terror to build a totalitarian state.

Objective 3: Analyze Stalin's use of propaganda to control thought and the arts.

Objective 4: Summarize the characteristics of Soviet society under Stalin.

Objective 5: Understand the goals of Soviet foreign policy.

LESSON 7 ORGANIZER	OBJECTIVES	PACING	RESOURCES Online	Print
PACING: APPROX. 1 PERIOD, .5 BLOCKS				
Connect				
DIGITAL START UP ACTIVITY **Stalin Leads the Soviet Union**		5 min.	●	
Investigate				
DIGITAL TEXT 1 **Stalin Builds a Command Economy**	Objectives 1, 2	10 min.	●	●
DIGITAL TEXT 2 **Control through Terror**	Objective 2	10 min.	●	●
DIGITAL TEXT 3 **Stalin Builds a Totalitarian State**	Objectives 2, 3	10 min.	●	●
INTERACTIVE GALLERY **Art as Propaganda**		10 min.	●	
DIGITAL TEXT 4 **Soviet Society Under Stalin**	Objective 4	10 min.	●	●
DIGITAL TEXT 5 **Soviet Foreign Policy**	Objective 5	10 min.	●	●
INTERACTIVE GRAPHIC ORGANIZER **Characteristics of Stalin's Rule**		10 min.	●	
Synthesize				
DIGITAL ACTIVITY **Stalin's Soviet Union**		5 min.	●	
Demonstrate				
LESSON QUIZ **Lesson Quiz and Class Discussion Board**		10 min.	●	

■ CONNECT

DIGITAL START UP ACTIVITY
Stalin Leads the Soviet Union

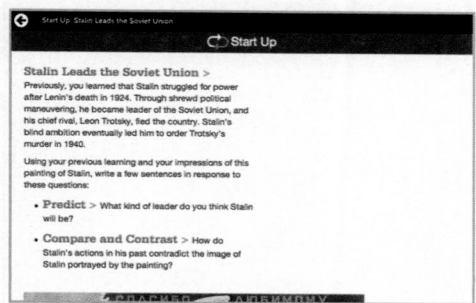

Project the Start Up Activity and the image of a fatherly Stalin with children. Ask students to look at the image and read the information about Stalin and Trotsky. Have them answer the questions as they enter and get settled: What kind of national leader do you think Stalin will be? *(Sample response: Based on his past actions against Trotsky, Stalin might be ruthless and cunning, pursuing and silencing critics and potential rivals. Based on the painting, Stalin wants the people to view him as the ideal leader.)* How do Stalin's actions toward his rival compare to the image of Stalin portrayed by the painting? *(Sample response: Stalin used political maneuvering to isolate his chief rival and strip him of party membership. In contrast, the painting portrays Stalin as a loving, all-powerful, and adored father figure.)* Then have them share their ideas with another student, either in class or through a chat or blog space.

⚡ FLIP IT!

Assign the Flipped Video for this lesson.

■ STUDENT EDITION PRINT PAGES: 717–724

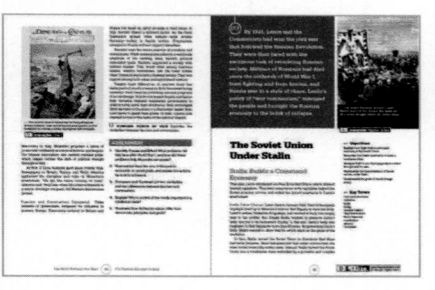

■ INVESTIGATE

DIGITAL TEXT 1
Stalin Builds a Command Economy

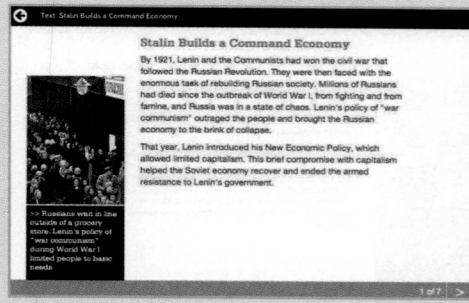

Objectives 1: Explain how Stalin built a command economy in the Soviet Union; 2: Describe how Stalin used terror to build a totalitarian state.

Quick Instruction
Remind students that Lenin founded the Soviet state. He and the Communists had were then faced with the enormous task of rebuilding Russian society after World War I. Millions of Russians had died since the outbreak of the war, from fighting and from famine, and Russia was in a state of chaos. Lenin's policy of "war communism" outraged the people and brought the Russian economy to the brink of collapse. After Lenin died in 1924, Stalin took power. Discuss Stalin's five-year plans and explain that the government decided what would be produced, how it would be produced, and to whom products and services would be distributed. In other words, it was the government that "commanded" the economy. Ask: What were the goals of Stalin's five-year plans? *(to build up heavy industry, improve transportation, and increase farm output)*

Further Instruction
Editable Presentation Use the Editable Presentation to present the main ideas for this Core Text.

Stalin Builds a Command Economy: Core Text and Interactive Reading Notepad Project and discuss the Interactive Reading Notepad questions and the image of the Soviet collective from the Digital Text. Tell students that many Westerners suffering the effects of the Great Depression pointed to the industrial growth of the Soviet Union during this period as proof that Stalin's

economic policies were successful. Point out that the results were mixed, however. Explain that forced collectivization of peasant farms resulted in a drastic decline in agricultural production. Staggering numbers of people starved, an event later known as the Terror Famine. Have students examine the image and ask, "Do you think this image is an accurate portrayal of life on a Soviet collective? Explain." *(Sample response: No. Life on a Soviet collective was harsh, and people were starving. These people look well fed and vigorous.)* Why did the Soviet Union keep inaccurate population records and offer false images of life in the Soviet Union? *(Sample response: to glorify communism and project a positive image to the Russian people and the international community)*

Cite Evidence What evidence from the image supports the idea that collectivization was successful during Stalin's five-year plan? Is that evidence credible? Explain. *(Sample response: The people look happy and healthy; there is food being produced; everyone seems to be working together. Even without outside data to compare this image to, it does not seem credible because it is so idealized.)*

Generate Explanations Why did Stalin believe peasant-owned farms were a threat to state power? *(Sample response: The state could not control the production of peasant-owned farms. Stalin wanted to ensure that the state controlled all production and strictly controlled access to resources.)*

The Soviet Union Under Stalin

DIGITAL TEXT 2

Control through Terror

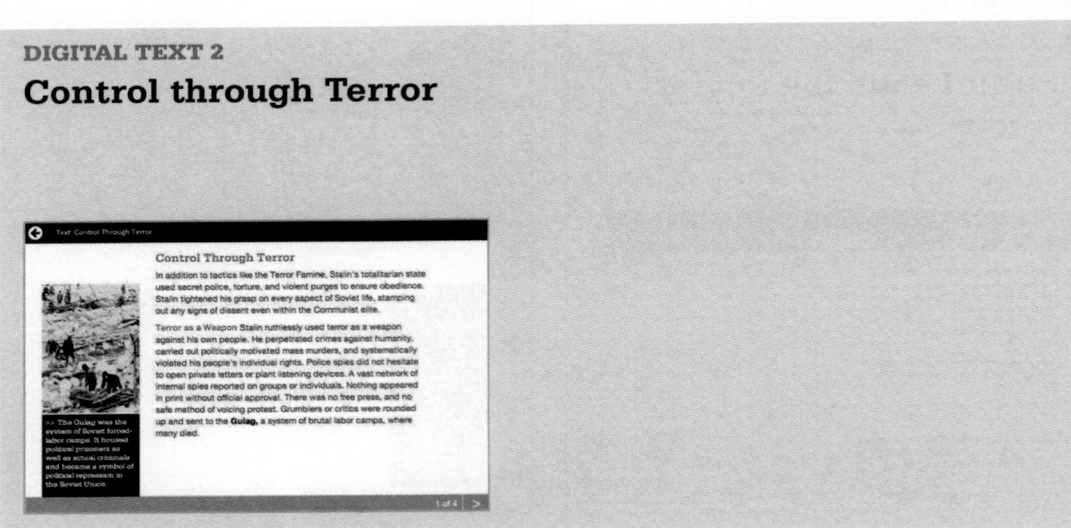

Then, tell students that Stalin created support for his policies through propaganda and by stifling artistic expression that didn't conform to the principles of socialist realism. He required artists to follow this official style for painting, sculpture, music, drama, and literature.

Explain What happened to artists and writers who didn't adhere to the guidelines of socialist realism? *(They were imprisoned and exiled or sent to a labor camp.)*

Objective 2: Describe how Stalin used terror to build a totalitarian state.

Quick Instruction

Project the image of the Soviet Gulag labor camp. Explain to students that Stalin used the threat of labor camps such as these to control life in the Soviet Union. Ask students to think of other ways Stalin may have enforced control over everyday life. *(Sample response: seizing church property, government propaganda)* Tell students that Stalin used secret police, torture, and violent purges to ensure absolute obedience. The police monitored private communications, and the government controlled the press.

Further Instruction

Control Through Terror: Core Text and Interactive Reading Notepad Project and discuss the Interactive Reading Notepad questions. Discuss the Great Purge that began in 1934 and Stalin's staged "show trials." Ask, "If Stalin had absolute control, why do you think he would bother with a public display of justice?" *(Sample response: to give the public the perception that the trials were legitimate and to display the consequences for disloyalty)* Explain that the Soviet Union lost many of its top experts, writers, thinkers, and military leaders during the Great Purge. Project the image of the map of the Soviet Union. Point out the different republics of the Soviet Union and the regions of forced labor camps.

Infer Look at the map again. What does the number of labor camps in the Soviet Union indicate about Stalin's rule? *(Sample response: There were many labor camps because Stalin needed the threat of imprisonment to guarantee his dominance.)*

Synthesize Why did Stalin target Old Bolsheviks during the Great Purge? *(Sample response: They were possible rivals for power.)*

DIGITAL TEXT 3

Stalin Builds a Totalitarian State

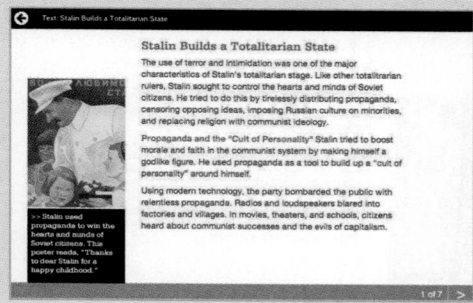

INTERACTIVE GALLERY

Art as Propaganda

Objectives 2: Describe how Stalin used terror to build a totalitarian state; 3: Analyze Stalin's use of propaganda to control thought and the arts.

Quick Instruction

Project the image of the painting of Stalin with children from the Interactive Gallery "Art as Propaganda." Remind students that the Communist Party under Stalin had complete control over the arts and media. Explain that it was Stalin's goal to control the hearts and minds of the Soviet people. He used art, music, literature, film, and the media to craft an image of a caring, protective, all-powerful leader of the Soviet Union. Point out that Stalin's use of propaganda and strict censorship of the media are key features of a totalitarian state.

Interactive Gallery: Art as Propaganda Project the Interactive Gallery. Remind students that Soviet culture was influenced by the art, literature, music, and films that were popular during the time. Stalin's strict censorship was an effort to control that influence. Ask students to review each image individually, keeping in mind that each image is meant to portray a specific message to the audience. Ask: Why might Stalin portray himself as providing children with a "happy childhood"? *(Answers will vary but students may say that Stalin wanted to foster support for his regime from a very early age.)*

🖥 ACTIVE CLASSROOM

Have students review the Interactive Gallery. Ask students to Take a Stand on the following question: Is propaganda an effective tool for public persuasion? Ask students to divide into two groups based on whether they answer yes or no, and then move to separate areas of the classroom. Have each group discuss their reasons for answering yes or no. Ask a representative from each side to present and defend the group's point of view.

Determine Point of View How do you think Soviet people felt about the art and film produced as Soviet propaganda? *(Sample response: They might have felt pride in the artistic achievement but doubted the accuracy of the representation.)*

ELL Use the ELL activity described in the ELL chart.

Further Instruction

Project and discuss the Interactive Reading Notepad questions. Discuss the all-encompassing nature of Stalin's propaganda. Tell students that the Soviet people were unable to escape the constant barrage of loudspeakers, billboards, films, artwork, music, and posters. Tell students that authors, musicians, and artists faced dire consequences if they failed to conform to and meet Stalin's expectations. Remind students of the forced labor camps Stalin used to terrify the Soviet people into total obedience. Explain that fear for their own safety and the safety of

their loved ones motivated artists to produce works that would please Stalin.

Remind students how Stalin attempted to remove religious institutions and replace them with communist ideology. Ensure students understand that the Soviet Union under Stalin is an example of a totalitarian state. Point out that the efforts of the Communists to control every aspect of the daily lives of Soviet people is another feature of a totalitarian state.

Compare and Contrast Do you think the constant Communist propaganda in the Soviet Union is similar to advertising in America today? Explain. *(Sample response: No. People can choose to ignore advertisements without the fear of physical harm.)*

Generate Explanations Briefly explain Stalin's policy of russification. *(Sample response: Russification was an attempt to unify the diverse peoples of the Soviet Union through the adoption of Russian culture. Russia was only one republic in the Soviet Union, but it was the most powerful. Stalin wanted to replace regional cultural identities with a universal Russian identity.)*

The Soviet Union Under Stalin

DIGITAL TEXT 4
Soviet Society Under Stalin

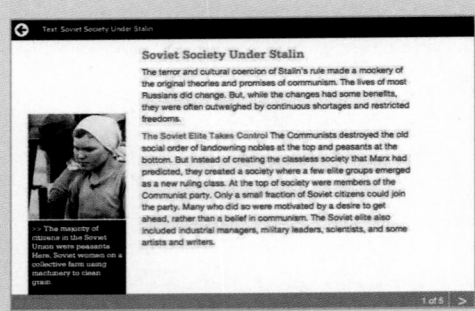

DIGITAL TEXT 5
Soviet Foreign Policy

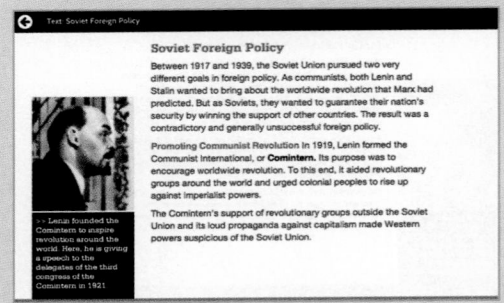

Objective 4: Summarize the characteristics of Soviet society under Stalin.

Quick Instruction
Explain to students that the Communists created a society where a few elite groups had complete government control. Those able to join the party usually did so to gain power and access to special treatment, such as the best housing and finest foods. The majority of the population gained few benefits and lacked adequate housing and many basic foods.

Further Instruction
Soviet Society Under Stalin: Core Text and Interactive Reading Notepad Project and discuss the Interactive Reading Notepad questions. Detail the benefits and drawbacks of living in the Soviet Union under Stalin. Explain that the state provided free medical care, day care, subsidized housing, and public recreation. However, adequate housing was scarce, and foods such as meat and fresh fruit were limited.

Project the image of the women factory workers. Explain that women gained equality under the law when the Communists came to power. Women worked alongside men as equals, in factories, in construction, on collectives, in engineering, and in the sciences.

Identify Central Issues How was the Soviet Union similar to the system of government prior to the revolution? *(Sample response: The Communists replaced the landowning nobles with elite party members as the ruling class.)*

Compare Did the lives of women improve under the Communists? Explain. *(Sample response: No. Both women and men were paid low wages under the Communists, were forced to work in harsh conditions, and lacked adequate housing or readily available food.)*

ELL Use the ELL activity described in the ELL chart.

Objective 5: Understand the goals of Soviet foreign policy.

Quick Instruction
Have students identify and define the key term *Comintern*. Explain to students that the Soviet Union actively encouraged the worldwide revolution predicted by Marx. However, the Communists also wanted the support of other countries to ensure the security and power of the Soviet Union.

Interactive Graphic Organizer: Characteristics of Stalin's Rule Project the Interactive Graphic Organizer. Remind students that Stalin initiated policies designed to control every aspect of the lives of the Soviet people. Ask students to use the graphic organizer to list these characteristics under political, economic, and social headings. Be sure students understand there is no "right answer" for many characteristics and some can be categorized under more than one heading. *(Sample response: (Row 1: "What were Stalin's goals in this area?" Political: totalitarian state; Economic: Collectivization and state control of agriculture; Social: Absolute control of cultural expression and thought. Row 2: "What policies did Stalin implement in this area?" Political: Gulags, secret police, and purges; Economic: Command economy; Five-Year plans; Social: Propaganda and censorship. Row 3: "What was the impact on Soviet life?" Political: New elite in control of governmental power; Economic: Poor agricultural output led to famine; Social: Women gain equal rights; Low standard of living.)*

INTERACTIVE GRAPHIC ORGANIZER

Characteristics of Stalin's Rule

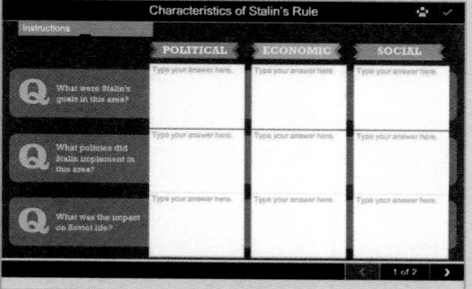

🗪 ACTIVE CLASSROOM

Have students list the characteristics of Stalin's rule, and write their suggestions on the board. Ask students to conduct the Rank It strategy to rank the characteristics from most significant to least significant. Students should find evidence from the Digital Text to support their decisions.

Draw Conclusions Which of Stalin's policies do you think was most effective in maintaining control over the Soviet Union? Why? *(Sample response: The policy of using secret police to spy on people and then send dissenters to the Gulag was probably the most effective because anyone who opposed Stalin risked losing everything.)*

Further Instruction

Project and discuss the Interactive Reading Notepad questions. Lead a discussion of the two foreign policy goals of the Communists and why they were incompatible. Remind students of the "Red Scare" in the United States during the 1920s. Ask students why the U.S. government would be afraid of Communist supporters. *(Sample response: The Comintern encouraged violent revolution and political destabilization of capitalist nations.)*

Discuss the Interactive Graphic Organizer "Characteristics of Stalin's Rule." Ask students to share their completed charts to ensure student understanding. Be sure students understand that Stalin built a totalitarian regime based on terror.

Express Problems Clearly Briefly summarize why the two foreign policy goals of the Soviet Union were contradictory. *(Sample response: Both Lenin and Stalin supported communist revolutionaries in foreign nations while simultaneously looking to those nations for international recognition and trade relationships.)*

Then, tell students that by the late 1930s, Stalin feared a growing threat from Nazi Germany and suggested that Russia, France, and Britain form an alliance against Germany, but these nations did not act because they feared Soviet intentions. Then, Stalin made an about-face and signed an alliance with Nazi Germany.

Hypothesize What do you think the outcome of such an alliance might be? *(Students' answers will vary but they might mention that this alliance could threaten world peace.)*

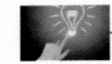
The Soviet Union Under Stalin

■ SYNTHESIZE

DIGITAL ACTIVITY
Stalin's Soviet Union

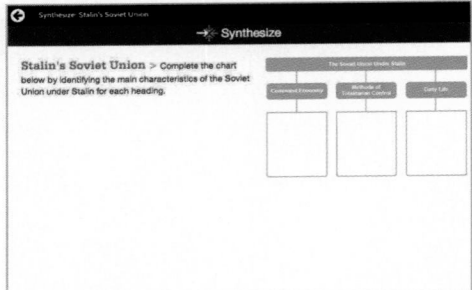

Project the image from the Synthesize Digital Activity. Review the main headings from the lesson. Explain that each heading details an important aspect or characteristic of the Soviet Union during this time period. Ask students to use the graphic organizer to list the main ideas under each heading, and have them reflect on the Topic Essential Question: What should governments do? Have them respond to the question based on what they have learned about the Soviet Union. *(Sample response: Students may point out that governments should benefit their citizens, offer a certain level of personal freedom, and not force citizens to live in constant fear of punishment.)*

Explain How did the Communists try to control the lives of children? *(Sample response: Soviet schools taught students to worship Stalin, to believe in falsely reported benefits of collectivization, and to obey the state blindly.)*

■ DEMONSTRATE

LESSON QUIZ
Lesson Quiz and Class Discussion Board

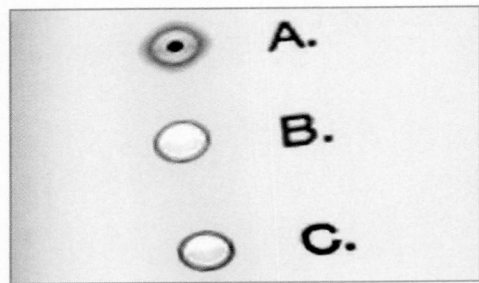

Assign the online Lesson Quiz for this lesson if you haven't already done so. Students will be offered automatic remediation or enrichment based on their score.

Pose these questions to the class on the Discussion Board:

Summarize Briefly summarize the goals and the outcomes of Stalin's five-year plans. *(Sample response: The goal was to build up heavy industry, improve transportation, and increase agricultural output. The outcome was mixed. Industry saw some growth, but there were tremendous shortages in agriculture.)*

Recall Describe Stalin's "show trials." Who did he target for elimination? *(Sample response: Stalin orchestrated public trials to intimidate the Soviet population while under the guise of a legitimate trial. Stalin targeted anyone he saw as a threat to his power.)*

Topic Inquiry
Have students continue their investigations for the Topic Inquiry.

The Rise of Nazi Germany

Supporting English Language Learners

Use with Digital Text 2, **Hitler Leads the Nazi Party.**

Speaking

Provide students with a select list of content-related words from *Hitler Leads the Nazi Party.* Assist them in understanding their meaning and using the terms as they communicate concepts related to the content covered in the text.

Beginning Select and display up to seven content-related words from *Hitler Leads the Nazi Party* on the board. Have students repeat after you as you read each aloud. Discuss their meanings using visuals as support. Use the words to ask questions and provide sentence stems for students to use in their response.

Intermediate Select and display up to seven content-related words from *Hitler Leads the Nazi Party* on the board. Have students repeat after you as you read each aloud. Discuss their meanings using visuals as support. Using the words in your queries, ask questions that require a response that uses the words in phrases or short sentences.

Advanced Select and display up to ten content-related words from *Hitler Leads the Nazi Party* on the board. Discuss their meanings with the group. Guide the student in writing two questions using the words or that require the words in their answers. Have pairs ask and answer each other's questions.

Advanced High Select and display up to ten content-related words from *Hitler Leads the Nazi Party* on the board. Have students look up the definitions of the words in a dictionary. The ask students to write a short paragraph using the words. Have students read their paragraphs to the group.

Use with Digital Text 4, **Authoritarian Rule in Eastern Europe.**

Reading

Review how to decode challenging words with students. Then read *Authoritarian Rule in Eastern Europe* aloud to the class. Have students complete the activities below according to their level of English proficiency.

Beginning Reread the first sentence of *Authoritarian Rule in Eastern Europe* for students and sound out each word. Choose three or four words in the sentence and have students repeat after you sound them out. Then continue with the other sentences in the paragraph, allowing students to practice sounding out words whenever possible.

Intermediate Reread the first sentence of *Authoritarian Rule in Eastern Europe* for students and sound out each word. Then assist a student volunteer as he or she rereads the second sentence independently. Continue allowing each student to read one sentence from the paragraph so that each student is able to practice sounding out words whenever possible.

Advanced Have students reread *Authoritarian Rule in Eastern Europe* aloud to a partner. Instruct students to circle each difficult word and return to it to be sure it is pronounced correctly. Offer pronunciation support as needed to all student pairs.

Advanced High Have students reread *Authoritarian Rule in Eastern Europe* aloud to a partner. Instruct students to circle each difficult word and return to it to be sure it is pronounced correctly. Then have students write down each challenging word and use an English dictionary to find its meaning and review the pronunciation for each entry. Offer support as needed to all students.

▷ Differentiate Instruction

Use the Differentiated Instruction notes throughout the lesson plan to support the varied skill sets, levels of readiness, and interests in the mixed-ability classroom.

Challenge These notes include suggestions for expanding the activity for advanced students.

On-Level These notes include suggestions for modifying the activity to address different interests or learning styles.

Extra Support These notes include ideas for providing more scaffolding or reading spuport.

Special Needs These notes provide ideas for adapting instruction to support the needs of various special needs students.

■ NOTES

The Rise of Nazi Germany

Objectives

Objective 1: Summarize the political and economic problems faced by the Weimar Republic.

Objective 2: Analyze Hitler's rise to power.

Objective 3: Describe the political, social, economic, and cultural policies of Nazi Germany.

Objective 4: Explain why Eastern Europe turned to authoritarian rule.

LESSON 8 ORGANIZER	PACING: APPROX. 1 PERIOD, .5 BLOCKS		RESOURCES	
	OBJECTIVES	PACING	Online	Print
Connect				
DIGITAL START UP ACTIVITY **Hitler's Rise to Power**		5 min.	●	
Investigate				
DIGITAL TEXT 1 **The Weimar Republic**	Objective 1	10 min.	●	●
DIGITAL TEXT 2 **Hitler Leads the Nazi Party**	Objective 2	10 min.	●	●
INTERACTIVE TIMELINE **The Rise and Fall of the Weimar Republic**		10 min.	●	
DIGITAL TEXT 3 **The Third Reich**	Objective 3	10 min.	●	
INTERACTIVE GALLERY **Growing Up in Nazi Germany**		10 min.	●	
DIGITAL TEXT 4 **Authoritarian Rule in Eastern Europe**	Objective 4	10 min.	●	●
Synthesize				
DIGITAL ACTIVITY **Nazi Propaganda**		5 min.	●	
Demonstrate				
LESSON QUIZ **Lesson Quiz and Class Discussion Board**		10 min.	●	

PEARSON
realize™
www.PearsonRealize.com

Go online to access additional resources including:
Primary Sources • Biographies • Supreme Court cases •
21st Century Skill Tutorials • Maps • Graphic Organizers.

CONNECT

DIGITAL START UP ACTIVITY
Hitler's Rise to Power

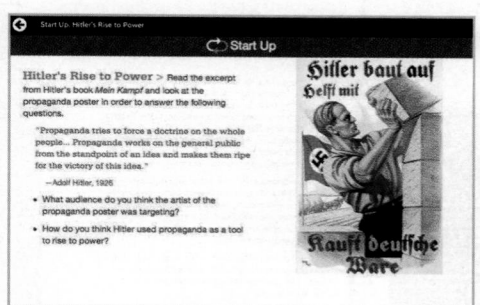

Project the Start Up Activity Ask students to answer the questions as they enter and get settled: What audience do you think the artist of the propaganda poster was targeting? *(The artist is targeting a working-class audience because its members are suffering from economic hardship and would benefit most from a leader who would create more jobs and support the middle class.)* How do you think Hitler used propaganda as a tool to rise to power? *(Hitler's words show that he would use propaganda to create hope or interest in an idea. In this scenario, he was targeting the working class with a propaganda poster about the future of Germany, and he promoted himself as the last hope.)*

Tell students that in this lesson they will be learning about the rise and fall of the Weimar Republic, including Hitler's rise to power.

↯ FLIP IT!
Assign the Flipped Video for this lesson.

■ STUDENT EDITION PRINT PAGES: 725–730

INVESTIGATE

DIGITAL TEXT 1
The Weimar Republic

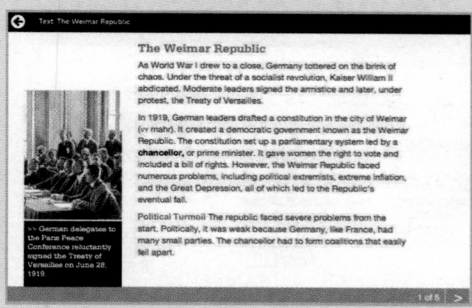

Objective 1: Summarize the political and economic problems of the Weimar Republic.

Quick Instruction
Analyze Political Cartoons Project the political cartoon portraying the controversy of the Versailles Treaty on the whiteboard. Introduce the cartoon by reminding students that the signing of the Treaty of Versailles in 1919 officially ended World War I. However, the treaty brought about new problems for Germany. Besides losing territory, Germany was forced to take the entire blame for World War I and was forced to pay reparation payments. As a result, Germany's new government, the Weimar Republic, suffered from economic hardships.

Further Instruction
Editable Presentation Use the Editable Presentation to present the main ideas for this Core Text.

The Weimar Republic: Core Text and Interactive Reading Notepad Project and discuss the Interactive Reading Notepad questions and answers.

The Weimar Republic faced political and economic hardships from its creation. Many Germans blamed the delegates for the hated Versailles Treaty and rejected the government from the start. The reparations payments were extremely high, and the German government made poor decisions while paying them, actions that eventually

contributed to a period of hyperinflation. The German people were in need of a strong leader. Ask students to predict how someone like Hitler might take advantage of the weaknesses of the Weimar Republic to rise to power. *(Sample response: Hitler might strongly criticize the government's weaknesses to encourage people to turn against it even more, and he might promise to be the strong leader they desired.)*

Identify Cause and Effect How did the onset of the Great Depression affect the Weimar Republic? *(Sample response: The Great Depression brought back fears of 1924, the time of hyperinflation, so Germans lost faith in their government. Political parties were divided, and the government had little to no support.)*

Tell students that in spite of these problems, music and the arts flourished during the Weimar Republic. New cultural movements, such as dadaist art and Bauhaus architecture, developed. Germany's struggles during the period were often depicted in these new works. For example, the German playwright Bertolt Brecht sharply criticized middle-class values with *The Three-Penny Opera*. The artist George Grosz, through scathing drawings and paintings, blasted the failings of the Weimar Republic.

Hypothesize How might works that are critical of the government affect some Germans' opinion of their leaders? *(Sample response: Some people might begin to view their government with distrust.)*

The Rise of Nazi Germany

DIGITAL TEXT 2
Hitler Leads the Nazi Party

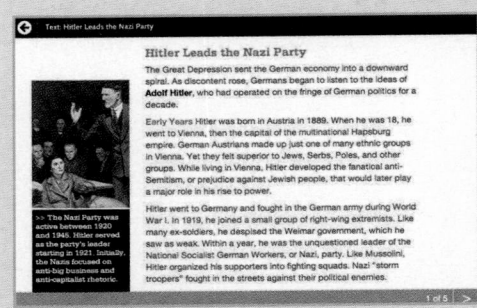

INTERACTIVE TIMELINE
The Rise and Fall of the Weimar Republic

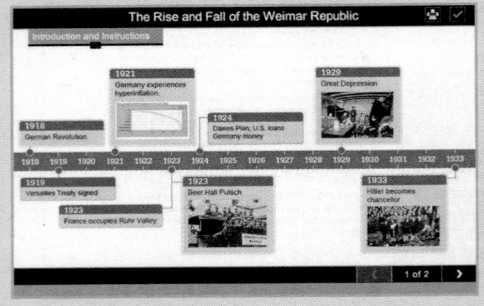

DIGITAL TEXT 3
The Third Reich

Objective 2: Analyze Hitler's rise to power.

Quick Instruction

Because of the instability of the postwar years, the German people desired change. This created an opportunity for Adolf Hitler and the Nazi Party to rise to power. Hitler blamed the Weimar government, Jews, and Marxists for Germany's problems and promised that a strong leader could restore Germany to greatness.

Interactive Timeline: The Rise and Fall of the Weimar Republic Project the timeline. Click on each hotspot to learn more about the events that contributed to Hitler's rise in power. Focus on the Beer Hall Putsch, and discuss how Hitler's imprisonment as a result helped him in his rise to power. *(Sample response: Hitler's imprisonment helped his rise to power by bringing attention to him and his ideologies.)*

ACTIVE CLASSROOM

Ask students to Make Headlines for one of the events from the timeline. Once they make their headline, have them share it with a partner to review and revise if necessary. Allow students to share a few with the class.

D Differentiate: Challenge/Gifted Ask students to do additional research on one of the events on the timeline. Then have students write a newspaper article to accompany their headline.

ELL Use the ELL activity described in the ELL chart.

Further Instruction

Hitler Leads the Nazi Party: Core Text and Interactive Reading Notepad Project and discuss the Interactive Reading Notepad questions and answers.

Be sure students understand that Hitler was able to rise to power as an effect of the political and economic weaknesses during the Weimar Republic. Towards the end of the 1920s, especially after the Great Depression, the Nazi Party began to gain more control in the Reichstag. The president of the Weimar Republic asked Hitler to be chancellor as a way to command the legislative majority. Discuss how the Great Depression was a contributing factor in Hitler's rise to power. *(Sample response: Because of the economic hardship, people began to lose faith in their government and turn towards extremist parties, such as the Nazi Party.)*

Draw Inferences What impact did the German political system have on the rise of the Nazi Party? *(Sample response: The German government was paralyzed by political divisions, which helped the rise of the Nazi Party. The president of the Weimar Republic needed to make Hitler chancellor to check Communist influence and to gain more control over the Reichstag. That position gave the Nazi Party an opportunity to take full control.)*

Objective 3: Describe the political, social, economic, and cultural policies of Nazi Germany.

Quick Instruction

After Hitler was appointed chancellor, he quickly destroyed the Weimar Republic and established the Third Reich. Hitler created a totalitarian state and passed anti-Semitic laws. The Nazis indoctrinated children to help change political thought in Germany.

Interactive Gallery: Growing Up in Nazi Germany Project the images in the gallery. Look at each image individually and then discuss the pressures all children must have felt growing up in Nazi Germany. Make sure students understand that Hitler viewed Aryans, or Germans, as a "master race." Point out the picture of the young Jewish boy, and compare it to the girls lining up to march. Tell students that indoctrination into the Nazis' racist ideals began at a very early age.

Draw Inferences Why would Nazi Germany create posters with young, Aryan children on them? *(Sample response: The Nazis wanted to promote their view of the master race, and pictures of blond, blue-eyed children helped spread Nazi ideology.)*

INTERACTIVE GALLERY

Growing Up in Nazi Germany

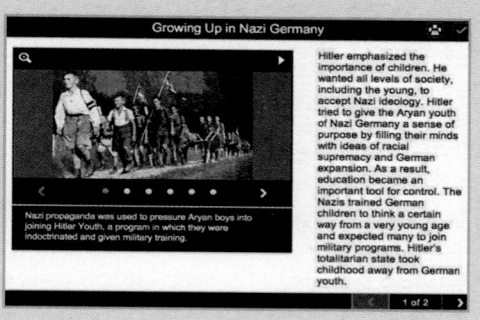

DIGITAL TEXT 4

Authoritarian Rule in Eastern Europe

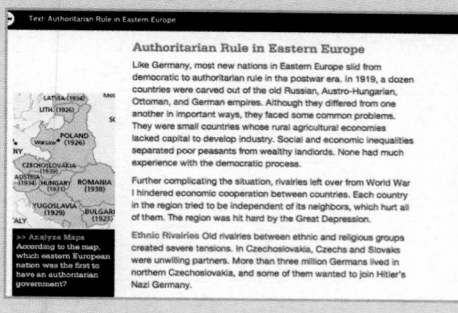

ACTIVE CLASSROOM

Ask students to spend three minutes jotting down a response to the following question on Sticky Notes: Viewed together, what do these images tell you about life for children in Nazi Germany? *(Sample response: The photos show the importance of children in Hitler's totalitarian state. It also shows how youth had many responsibilities and were expected to contribute to society as well.)*

Further Instruction

The Third Reich: Core Text and Interactive Reading Notepad Project and discuss the Interactive Reading Notepad questions. Be sure students understand the emergence and characteristics of totalitarianism, including the role Hitler played in ensuring that only people with similar ideologies held positions of power. Discuss how Hitler's totalitarian state and propaganda were tools to help the Nazis shift political thought and spread anti-Semitic beliefs.

Identify Steps in a Process Explain the steps that the Nazis took to spread their anti-Semitic beliefs and make them official. *(Sample response: Hitler blamed the Jewish people for Germany's problems and then started propaganda campaigns to depict Jews as an inferior race. The Nazis implemented laws against Jews, and eventually the anti-Semitism escalated into violent acts.)*

Objective 4: Explain why Eastern Europe turned to authoritarian rule.

Quick Instruction

Analyze Maps Project the map on the whiteboard. Introduce the map by reminding students that after World War I several of the Eastern European states were newly created. The new countries had racial tensions and faced some common problems. They were small countries whose rural agricultural economies lacked capital for industry. Social and economic inequalities separated poor peasants from the wealthy. In addition, rivalries leftover from World War I prevented economic cooperation between countries. As a result, the area was weak, and it was easier for dictators to rise to power. Ask students to explain the impact of World War I on the rise of authoritarian power in Eastern Europe. *(Sample response: World War I impacted the rise of authoritarian power because it created smaller countries in Eastern Europe but didn't take in to consideration the differences in racial and ethnic groups within them and throughout the region. Weak governments made it easier for dictators to rise to power by promising reform.)*

ELL Use the ELL activity described in the ELL chart.

Further Instruction

Authoritarian Rule in Eastern Europe: Core Text and Interactive Reading Notepad Project and discuss the Interactive Reading Notepad questions and answers. Be sure that students understand the impact of

World War I on Eastern Europe. Discuss how weak governments made the region ripe for the rise of authoritarian rule.

Identify Cause and Effect How did economics affect the political situation in Eastern Europe? *(Sample response: Most Eastern European countries lacked capital to industrialize, so they had agricultural economies. Poverty and the lack of economic progress contributed to the political instability.)*

Draw Inferences Why did Eastern Europeans prefer the rise of authoritarian rule over democracies in the mid to late 1920s? *(Sample response: Eastern Europeans had little experience with democracy, so when there were problems in the postwar period, they turned to the political model they knew best—authoritarian rule.)*

The Rise of Nazi Germany

SYNTHESIZE

DEMONSTRATE

DIGITAL ACTIVITY
Nazi Propaganda

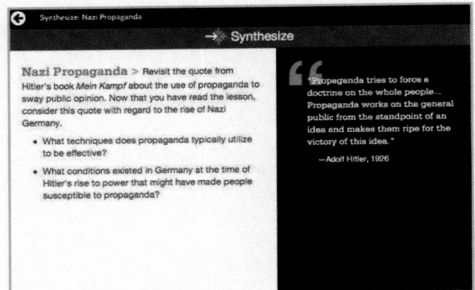

LESSON QUIZ
Lesson Quiz and Class Discussion Board

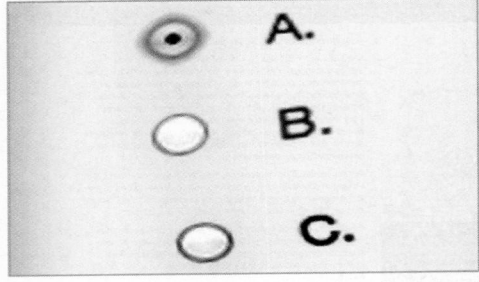

Hitler came to power when the Great Depression was causing hardship around the world. Have the class read the quote from Hitler's book *Mein Kampf* again. Ask students to use the information from the text to think of reasons why the German people might have been particularly susceptible to Nazi propaganda during the 1930s. Then tell them to take one minute to do a quick write on this topic, and exchange papers with a classmate to compare ideas. *(Sample response: The German people felt demoralized because they were forced to bear the entire blame for World War I and because they had experienced economic hardship during the 1920s. Their hurt pride and bleak outlook probably made them vulnerable to Nazi propaganda about being a master race and Nazi promises of a return to German glory.)*

Discuss Ask students to think about the propaganda posters they viewed during this lesson. Ask if they think Hitler would have had as many followers if he hadn't used propaganda in the early 1930s. *(Answers will vary but some students may say yes, because Hitler had a forceful personality that inspired many, while others will say no, that the propaganda brainwashed people into following him.)*

Assign the online Lesson Quiz for this lesson if you haven't already done so. Students will be offered automatic remediation or enrichment based on their score.

Pose these questions to the class on the Discussion Board:

In "The Rise of Nazi Germany," you read about the rise and fall of the Weimar Republic resulting in the rise of Hitler and the Nazi Party. Economic hardships and political strife allowed Hitler to take control of the government and implement a totalitarian state. Other Eastern European countries also fell into the hands of authoritarian rule.

Synthesize How do you think the Treaty of Versailles impacted the rise of authoritarian rule in Eastern Europe?

Topic Inquiry
Have students continue their investigations for the Topic Inquiry.

The World Between the Wars (1910–1939)

■ SYNTHESIZE

DIGITAL ACTIVITY

Reflect on the Essential Question and Topic

Ask students to recall the Topic Essential Question, "What should governments do?" Remind students of the reasons they considered at the start of the Topic. For example,

- Create a sense of pride in the national identity
- Promise to gain new territory for the country
- Build up the national military
- Take over economic planning
- Protect individual rights
- Preserve order
- Promote education
- Provide a social safety net
- Overthrow old traditions to modernize the country

Have students use the Think Pair Share strategy to revisit those questions. They should take five minutes to list an example of each of those types of actions from the Topic. Instruct them to circle government actions that they think caused problems and to underline government actions that they think helped to solve problems. Then they should share their answers with a talking partner. Finally, have the partners work together to fill out the graphic organizer comparing the three totalitarian governments.

You may ask students to share their lists of government actions or their completed graphic organizers on the Class Discussion Board.

Topic Inquiry

Have students complete Step 3 of the Topic Inquiry.

■ DEMONSTRATE

DIGITAL TOPIC REVIEW AND ASSESSMENT

The World Between the Wars (1910–1939)

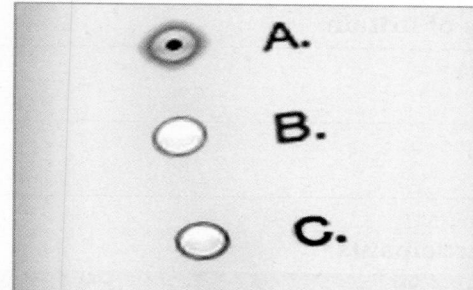

Students can prepare for the Topic Test by answering the questions in the Topic Review and Assessment online or the Assessment questions in the Print Student text. They can also prepare by reviewing their answers to the Interactive Reading Notepad questions or reviewing their notes in the Reading and Notetaking Study Guide.

DIGITAL TOPIC TEST

The World Between the Wars (1910–1939)

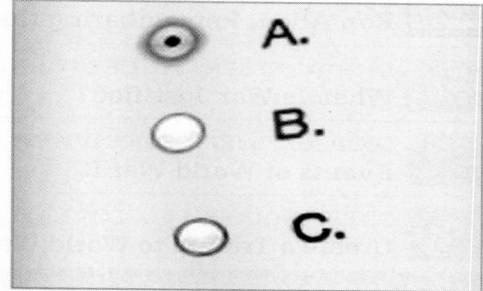

TOPIC TEST

Assign the Topic Test to assess students' understanding of topic content.

BENCHMARK TESTS

Assign these benchmark tests as you complete the relevant topics to monitor student progress toward mastering the course content and as preparation for the End-of-Course Test.

Benchmark Test 1: Topics 1–5
Benchmark Test 2: Topics 6–10
Benchmark Test 3: Topics 11–15
Benchmark Test 4: Topics 16–21

World War II (1930–1945)

TOPIC 18 ORGANIZER	PACING: APPROX. 8 PERIODS, 4 BLOCKS
	PACING
Connect	1 period
MY STORY VIDEO **Ron Allen, Remembering the Battle of Britain**	10 min.
DIGITAL ESSENTIAL QUESTION ACTIVITY **When Is War Justified?**	10 min.
DIGITAL TIMELINE ACTIVITY **Events of World War II**	10 min.
TOPIC INQUIRY: PROJECT-BASED LEARNING **Create a Tribute to World War II Participants**	20 min.
Investigate	2–5 periods
TOPIC INQUIRY: PROJECT-BASED LEARNING **Create a Tribute to World War II Participants**	Ongoing
LESSON 1 Aggression, Appeasement, and War	30–40 min.
LESSON 2 Axis Powers Advance	30–40 min.
LESSON 3 The Holocaust	30–40 min.
LESSON 4 The Allies Turn the Tide	30–40 min.
LESSON 5 Victory for the Allies	30–40 min.
Synthesize	1 period
DIGITAL ACTIVITY **Reflect on the Essential Question and Topic**	10 min.
TOPIC INQUIRY: PROJECT-BASED LEARNING **Create a Tribute to World War II Participants**	20 min.
Demonstrate	1–2 periods
DIGITAL TOPIC TEST **World War II**	10 min.
TOPIC INQUIRY: PROJECT-BASED LEARNING **Create a Tribute to World War II Participants**	20 min.

 TOPIC INQUIRY: PROJECT-BASED LEARNING

Create a Tribute to World War II Participants

In this Topic Inquiry, students work in teams to research and create a multimedia tribute to those who fought in or experienced World War II and to their friends and relatives. Learning how war impacts people will contribute to students' understanding of the Topic Essential Question: When Is War Justified?

STEP 1: CONNECT
Develop Questions and Plan the Investigation

Launch the Project, Generate Questions, and Examine Existing War Memorials and Tributes

Display the Project Launch letter from a committee formed to create a tribute for local participants in World War II. Have students work with a team partner to make a list of things to include in a memorial or tribute. Have them refer to the list as they discuss memorials and other tributes with the team. Have them review the *Rubric for a World War II Tribute* to establish expectations.

Then turn to the bulleted list about what makes a tribute effective:

- Its subject must be clear.
- It must present information in a stimulating, memorable way.
- Its design should encourage people to think about the person, event, or experience.
- It should communicate important ideas about the person, event, or experience.
- It can appeal to different senses, such as sight, sound, or touch.

Suggestion: Ask students to explain each point and give an example of a tribute or memorial they feel reflects the bullet point. Share this example: The Vietnam Memorial in Washington, D.C., is effective because it appeals to both sight and touch. People want to look at it, but they also want to touch the carved names of loved ones who died in the war.

Plan the Investigation

Help the class decide what form its tribute will take. Form students into teams. Have students sign the *Project Contract*, and assign team roles using the *Project Tracker*. Give students more examples of how to break down the Driving Question to begin the *Need-to-Know Questions*.

Suggestion: You can control the length of the project by limiting the complexity and number of different media used in the tribute.

Resources
- Project Launch
- Project Contract
- Need-to-Know Questions
- Student Instructions
- Project Tracker
- Tribute Rubric

⏻ PROFESSIONAL DEVELOPMENT

Project-Based Learning
Be sure to view the Project-Based Learning Professional Development resources in the online course.

STEP 2: INVESTIGATE
Apply Disciplinary Concepts and Tools

Examine Your Contribution

Before students begin their investigation, have them review the Skills Tutorial, *Work In Teams*.

Teams will learn how to assign tasks and monitor their work with the *Project Tracker*. They will brainstorm how to approach their segment of the tribute, keeping in mind the Driving Question: How can we create something that will help people remember the contributions of World War II participants?

To guide their research, teams will create a list of *Need-to-Know Questions* about their segment of the tribute. Help students begin to fill out the *Information Organizer*.

Suggestion: The wide choice of possible media may overwhelm some teams, while others may settle on a plan that is too ambitious for the available time and resources. Be prepared to step in with suggestions on how each team can accomplish its goals without taking on insurmountable technical challenges or tasks that will consume too much time.

Conduct Research

The many possible components of the research phase of this inquiry may call for careful monitoring. Check to see that each team has allocated research tasks fairly and efficiently. If necessary, remind teams that mastering the technology needed to create the tribute may need as much attention as gathering the information to present.

Suggestion: You may want to monitor teams' contacts with local veterans organizations and government offices so that contacts are not duplicated unnecessarily. If needed, also provide assistance with Internet contacts with non-local groups and organizations.

Write, Edit, and Assemble Your Tribute

The teams should plan how to present the information they have gathered. Next, students should write their presentation and create any visual, sound, or kinetic elements, as well as live performances. When students do peer review of their work, remind them to offer detailed, constructive criticism.

Resources
- Student Instructions
- Project Tracker
- Information Organizer
- Need-to-Know Questions

STEP 3: SYNTHESIZE
Evaluate Sources and Use
Evidence to Formulate Conclusions

Create Your Part of the World War II Tribute

Now have students get together to create their presentation. If students are having trouble sharing the work on this part of the project, remind them to review their *Roles for a Group Presentation* in the *Project Tracker*. Review the teams' progress on their presentations to make sure they are on track.

Suggestion: For a less technology-dependent end product, have students restrict media to printed text, photos, and other illustrations, and live kinetic elements.

Review Your Part of the World War II Tribute

Have students review each other's work and offer suggestions and edits to improve the text, visuals, and other media of the tribute. Be prepared to offer advice on how to improve the teams' products.

State Conclusions about the Driving Question

Have students write a conclusion about the Driving Question based on their work on the tribute. To help teams start, ask them to think about how social studies ideas can be communicated using visuals and text in a multimedia format. Have each team member write down his or her answer and share those answers with the team.

Resources
• Model Tribute   • Project Tracker

STEP 4: DEMONSTRATE
Communicate Conclusions
and Take Informed Action

Combine Portions to Create the Class Tribute

Have teams merge their tribute elements, then set up the tribute. Depending on the audience you have chosen to view the tribute, you may need to make arrangements for visitors to your classroom or to transport the tribute.

Present Your World War II Tribute

Have presenters work through the Give an Effective Presentation Skills Tutorial and plan how to best present the tribute. Make sure teams have practiced presenting the combined elements of the complete tribute so that they fit together smoothly and efficiently. After practicing the complete tribute, remind students to think of ways to improve the presentation.

After the presentation, invite the audience to examine the visual elements of the tribute. Have team members make themselves available to answer questions and explain their findings and conclusions.

Reflect on the Project

After students have finished their Team Assessments, help them go over what they thought went well and what did not, so they can be even more effective in the future.

Suggestion: As an extension activity, have students contact and interview a current member of the military or his or her family to learn how the experiences of military families today are similar to and different from the people they have learned about in researching this tribute.

Resources
• Tribute Rubric   • Self-Assessment

World War II (1930–1945)

In the years following World War I, many nations suffered from heavy debt, destruction, loss of life, and other ills that the war had brought upon them. In some places, citizens became dissatisfied with postwar life, and they looked to new leaders to bring change. Dictators gained power in countries in Europe and Asia and soon took aggressive action to gain more territory. This aggression sparked World War II. In the war's early years, Germany and Japan overran most of Europe and the Pacific. Neutral at first, the United States eventually entered the war. After more than six years of war, destruction, and unspeakable horror, the dictators were defeated. What kind of world would the war's survivors inherit?

■ CONNECT

MY STORY VIDEO
Ron Allen, Remembering the Battle of Britain

Watch a video in which a student interviews a survivor of the London blitz.

Check Understanding What was the Battle of Britain? *(the German attack on Britain during World War II)*

Hypothesize Why was the effort to break the will of the British people so ineffective? *(The Germans attacked cities in Britain by dropping bombs during the Blitz and, later, by launching V2 rockets. Despite the damage caused and the lives lost, the will of the British people was not broken. Students may hypothesize that people adjust to the horrors of warfare and remain strong in their determination to carry on their daily lives. They may also mention Britain's need to continue the fight against Nazism and to resist any German threat of invasion.)*

> **⚞ FLIP IT!**
> Assign the My Story Video.

DIGITAL ESSENTIAL QUESTION ACTIVITY
When Is War Justified?

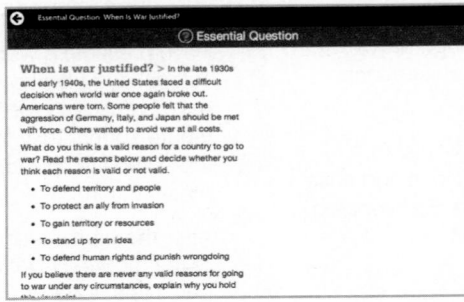

Ask students to think about the Essential Question for this Topic: When Is War Justified? Going to war is always a serious matter with far-reaching consequences for all involved. What circumstances justify the decision to go to war?

If they have not already done so, have students read the list of justifications for war and decide which they feel are valid.

Support a Point of View with Evidence Choose one of the justifications you feel is valid. What are the reasons you feel this way? What are the reasons you rejected one of the justifications?

Identify Central Issues For what ideas might a country be willing to fight? *(Possible response: human rights, democracy, freedom, religion)*

Identify Cause and Effect For what resources might a country fight? Why? *(Possible response: water, fertile soil, oil, coal; to increase its wealth, gain a source of energy to fuel its factories, economy, feed its people)*

DIGITAL TIMELINE ACTIVITY
Events of World War II

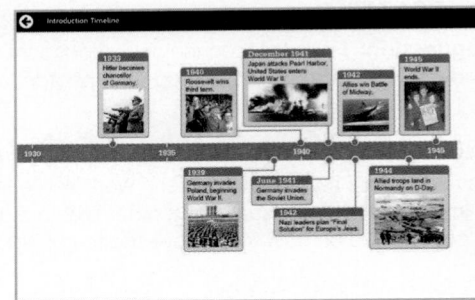

Display the timeline showing the major events leading up to and during World War II. In this Topic, students will learn about all of these events and many more, but this timeline will provide a framework into which they can place the events they learn about.

D Differentiate: Extra Support How many years passed between Adolf Hitler taking power in Germany and the start of the war? *(6; Hitler took power in 1933; war began in September 1939)*

Check Understanding In which years was the United States at war during World War II? *(1941 through 1945)* How many years had the war been going on before the United States entered the fighting? *(2; the war began in 1939; the United States entered the war in 1941)*

Topic Inquiry
Launch the topic inquiry with students after introducing the topic.

Aggression, Appeasement, and War

Supporting English Language Learners

Use with Digital Text 2, **The Spanish Civil War.**

Learning Strategies

Read *The Spanish Civil War* aloud to students. As they listen, have them follow along in their texts. Then have students complete one of the following activities according to their level of English proficiency.

Beginning Reread the first paragraph of *The Spanish Civil War* aloud to students. Then write and display the letter p. Make the *p* sound and have students repeat it. Review the text, word by word, looking for words that begin with the *p* sound. Underline these words. Review the pronunciation of each one, having students repeat each word. Then call on student volunteers to try pronouncing the words on their own. Continue practicing until students feel comfortable with the words. If time allows, continue the activity with words that begin with the letter *c*.

Intermediate Reread *The Spanish Civil War* aloud to students. Ask students to search for and underline words that contain the letter combination *con-*. Write and display each of these words and practice pronouncing them with students. Then have students work in small groups to write two sentences. Each sentence should be about the topic and contain one of the con- words identified in the text.

Advanced Have students take turns rereading paragraphs of *The Spanish Civil War* aloud to a partner. Have partners support each other as they pronounce challenging words. Instruct pairs to write down the words that were difficult to pronounce and share them with the class. Review these words with all the students, having student volunteers attempt to offer the correct pronunciation. Provide pronunciation support for challenging words.

Advanced High Have students reread *The Spanish Civil War* quietly to themselves. Instruct students to write down the words that were difficult to pronounce and share them with a partner. Have partners review these words and practice pronouncing them correctly. Provide pronunciation support for challenging words as needed.

Use with Digital Text 4, **World War II Begins.**

Learning Strategies

Review sentence patterns with students. Then read *World War II Begins* aloud to the class. Have students complete the activities below according to their level of English proficiency.

Beginning Reread *World War II Begins* for students, having them follow along in their texts. Display the following sentence for students and help them use different connecting words to combine two sentences at a time into a single sentence.

- In March 1939, Hitler broke his promises. Germany took control of Czechoslovakia. Hitler feared communism. Stalin feared fascism.

Intermediate Reread *World War II Begins* for students, having them follow along in their texts. Display the following sentence for students:

- The pact was based not on friendship or respect, but it was based on mutual need.

Explain that this is a compound sentence, or two independent clauses joined by a comma and a connecting word, or conjunction. Help students create two complete sentences from this compound sentence. Then provide them with two more simple sentences about the topic and help them combine them using *and*, *or*, *but*, or;.

Advanced Have students reread *World War II Begins* with a partner and work together to identify all the compound sentences in the text. Instruct pairs to underline each compound sentence and circle the connecting words in each compound sentence. Then ask pairs of students to write three compound sentences about how WWII began.

Advanced High Have students reread *World War II Begins* independently and identify all the compound sentences in the text. Instruct students to underline each compound sentence and circle the connecting words in each compound sentence. Then ask students to write three compound sentences about how WWII began. Have students choose their best sentence to share with the class.

▣ Differentiate Instruction

Use the Differentiated Instruction notes throughout the lesson plan to support the varied skill sets, levels of readiness, and interests in the mixed-ability classroom.

Challenge These notes include suggestions for expanding the activity for advanced students.

On-Level These notes include suggestions for modifying the activity to address different interests or learning styles.

Extra Support These notes include ideas for providing more scaffolding or reading spuport.

Special Needs These notes provide ideas for adapting instruction to support the needs of various special needs students.

▮ NOTES

Aggression, Appeasement, and War

Objectives

Objective 1: Describe how the Western democracies responded to aggression.

Objective 2: Explain the significance of the Spanish Civil War.

Objective 3: Understand how German aggression led Europe into World War II.

LESSON 1 ORGANIZER		PACING: APPROX. 1 PERIOD, .5 BLOCKS			
				RESOURCES	
		OBJECTIVES	PACING	Online	Print
Connect					
DIGITAL START UP ACTIVITY **Aggression Leads to War**			5 min.	●	
Investigate					
DIGITAL TEXT 1 **A Pattern of Aggression**		Objective 1	10 min.	●	●
INTERACTIVE CARTOON **Hitler's March to European Domination**			10 min.	●	
DIGITAL TEXT 2 **The Spanish Civil War**		Objective 2	10 min.	●	●
DIGITAL TEXT 3 **German Aggression Continues**			10 min.	●	●
DIGITAL TEXT 4 **World War II Begins**		Objective 3	10 min.	●	●
INTERACTIVE GALLERY **Axis Aggression**			10 min.	●	
Synthesize					
DIGITAL ACTIVITY **Aggression Leads to War**			5 min.	●	
Demonstrate					
LESSON QUIZ **Lesson Quiz and Class Discussion Board**			10 min.	●	

PEARSON
realize™
www.PearsonRealize.com

Go online to access additional resources including:
Primary Sources • Biographies • Supreme Court cases •
21st Century Skill Tutorials • Maps • Graphic Organizers.

CONNECT

DIGITAL START UP ACTIVITY
Aggression Leads to War

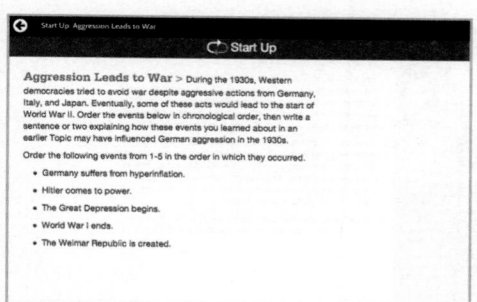

Project the Start Up Activity Ask students to answer the question as they get settled.

Discuss Remind students that Germany struggled politically and economically during the Weimar Republic and hoped for positive change when Hitler became chancellor. Hitler quickly turned Germany into a totalitarian state.

Predict Consequences Predict the aggressive actions Germany might take to protest the Versailles Treaty. *(Sample response: Germany will want to rebuild its military power, recover lost land and restore national pride.)*

Aa **Vocabulary Development:** Use the Interactive Reading Notepad to preview the Key Terms and Academic Vocabulary in this lesson with students.

↯ FLIP IT!

Assign the Flipped Video for this lesson.

STUDENT EDITION PRINT PAGES: 738–743

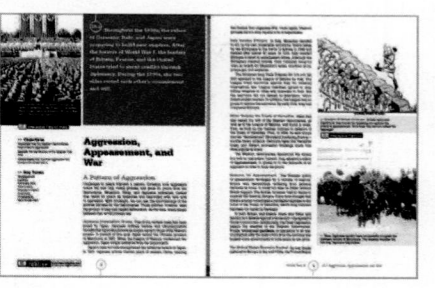

INVESTIGATE

DIGITAL TEXT 1
A Pattern of Aggression

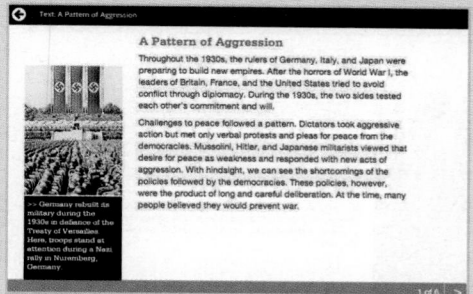

INTERACTIVE CARTOON
Hitler's March to European Domination

Objective 1: Describe how the Western democracies responded to aggression.

Quick Instruction
Interactive Political Cartoon: Hitler's March to European Domination Project the political cartoon. Look carefully at the text in the cartoon and discuss the message the cartoonist is trying to portray. Especially note Hitler's mannerisms as taunting the "weak" democratic leaders. Discuss the policy of appeasement and how it contributed to the road to World War II.

🖳 ACTIVE CLASSROOM

Ask students to create a My Simile activity based on the content of the political cartoon. Give them the following prompt to complete: This cartoon shows that _____ is like _____ because _____.

D **Differentiate: Extra Support** After asking students to think of a simile, allow students five minutes to brainstorm different things to which they can compare appeasement or Chamberlain. Tell them to use their comparison to help with the simile. Then continue with the group activity.

Further Instruction
A Pattern of Aggression: Core Text and Interactive Reading Notepad Project and discuss the Interactive Reading Notepad questions and answers, including the graphic organizer asking students to sequence the

acts of aggression in the 1930s. Review the sequence of events with the class and fill in the table as you go.

Analyze Timelines Project the timeline from the Text on the whiteboard. Introduce the timeline by reminding students that Italy, Germany, and Japan created an alliance known as the Axis. Walk through the events on the timeline together, focusing on the 1930s. Point out to students that there were more acts of aggression in the mid-to-late 1930s than before. Japan seized the Chinese province of Manchuria in 1931. In 1937, Japanese armies overran much of eastern China. In 1935, Italy invaded Ethiopia and conquered it in 1936. Hitler built up the German military, and in 1936, he sent troops into the "demilitarized" Rhineland bordering France.

Be sure that students understand that the acts of aggression were an effect of the policy of appeasement. The Axis powers viewed appeasement as weak. Discuss why the Western powers thought the policy of appeasement was the best way to maintain peace.

Synthesize Explain the significance of the League of Nations to the Axis in the 1930s. *(Sample response: To the Axis powers, the League of Nations was insignificant because it didn't follow through with consequences designed to make the aggressive nations stop. Japan simply dropped out of the League and continued its invasion of China after the League of Nations spoke out against Japanese imperialism.)*

Aggression, Appeasement, and War

DIGITAL TEXT 2

The Spanish Civil War

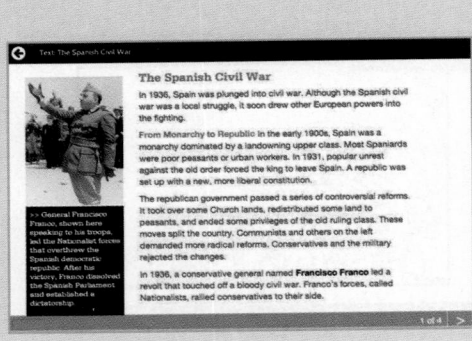

DIGITAL TEXT 3

German Aggression Continues

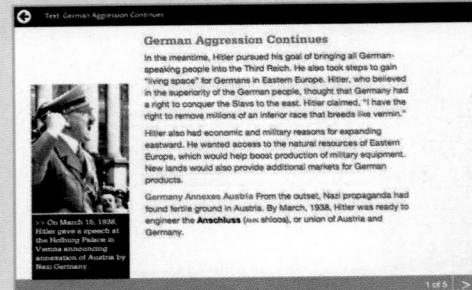

DIGITAL TEXT 4

World War II Begins

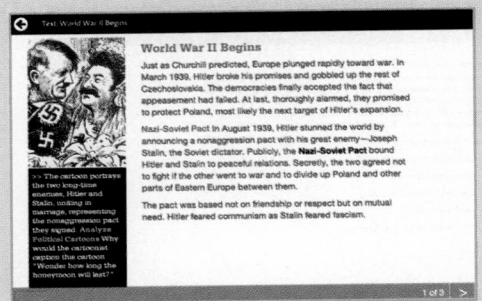

Objective 2: Explain the significance of the Spanish Civil War.

Quick Instruction

The Spanish Civil War was another step in the march towards world war. The civil war was fought between the Republicans, loyal to the established Spanish Republic, and the Nationalists, led by Francisco Franco. The Spanish Civil War is known for the political division it created throughout Europe. Both Hitler and Mussolini were supporters of the Nationalists. The Germans used the war as a way to showcase their advanced military weaponry and as a way to warn the rest of the world of Germany's new power.

ELL Use the ELL activity described in the ELL chart.

Further Instruction

Go through the Interactive Reading Notepad questions and discuss the answers as a class.

Hitler and Mussolini saw supporting Franco and the Nationalists during the Spanish Civil War as a way to spread fascist and Nazi ideology. Ask students to think of German advantages in assisting the Nationalists during the Spanish Civil War. *(Sample response: Franco was a fascist and anticommunist, and it would benefit Hitler and Mussolini to have another political ally in Europe. Hitler was also able to test his new military equipment and techniques.)*

Objective 3: Understand how German aggression led Europe into World War II.

Quick Instruction

Axis aggression refers to the violent attacks and invasions by Germany, Italy, and Japan prior to and during World War II. Hitler's aggressive acts broke several terms in the Versailles treaty by the time he annexed Austria and claimed the Sudetenland, Western powers decided to meet with the German leader. British Prime Minster Chamberlain thought he was bringing "peace to our time" by forging an agreement to let Hitler have a section of Czechoslovakia. But Hitler shattered hopes for peace with the invasion of Poland. This invasion marked the beginning of World War II, a turning point in history. Discuss with students why the invasion of Poland was a major cause of World War II. (The invasion proved the failure of appeasement. Britain and France finally realized they had to take a stand against German aggression and declared war on Germany.)

Interactive Gallery: Axis Aggression
Project the gallery. Look at the pictures showing examples of the Axis powers forcefully taking over smaller, independent nations in order to expand their own empires.

Notice the roles of the Axis powers leaders, specifically Hitler and Mussolini as they led aggressive acts against other countries in order to expand territory for their countries.

ACTIVE CLASSROOM

Ask students to select an image from the Interactive Gallery and "Cartoon It." Instruct them to create a quick copy of one compelling image from the gallery onto a piece of paper. Then, tell students to turn their drawing into a political cartoon that illustrates either appeasement or aggression.

ELL Use the ELL activity described in the ELL chart.

Further Instruction

German Aggression Continues and World War II Begins: Core Text and Interactive Reading Notepad Project and discuss the questions and answers from the Interactive Reading Notepad, including the graphic organizer, asking students to sequence the acts of German aggression. Review the acts of German aggression with students, and discuss the role of Adolf Hitler prior to the start of World War II.

INTERACTIVE GALLERY
Axis Aggression

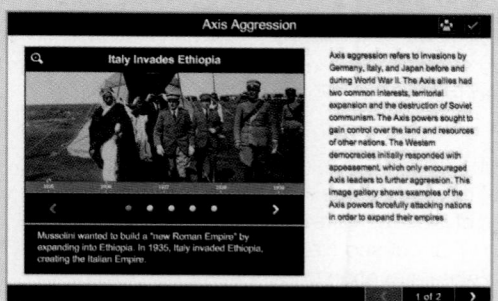

Compare and Contrast After the Munich Agreement, Churchill gave a speech to the House of Commons. Contrast Chamberlain's views on appeasement with Churchill's. *(Sample response: Chamberlain believed by giving Hitler the Sudetenland he was bringing "peace to our time," but Churchill thought it was the beginning of the road to war; he felt Hitler wouldn't stop until he was forced to stop.)*

■ SYNTHESIZE

DIGITAL ACTIVITY
Aggression Leads to War

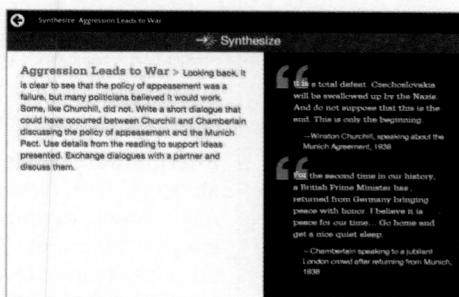

Ask students to recall the Topic Essential Question, "When is war justified?" Have them use the Think Pair strategy to answer the questions in the Digital Activity. Ask them to reread the quotes from Chamberlain and Churchill. Then have students write a short dialogue that could have occurred between the two British politicans discussing the policy of appeasement and the Munich Pact. Remind students to use details from the text to support their ideas. *(Sample response: Dialogue from Churchill should speak out against the Munich Pact and the policy of appeasement. Dialogue from Chamberlain should support appeasement because he thought it would stop aggressive actions without a war.)*

Have partners think about the following question: Do you think Churchill was justified in speaking out against the policy of appeasement to the House of Commons? *(Answers will vary, but many students may say yes, in light of the war that followed.)* Have pairs share their answers with the class.

■ DEMONSTRATE

LESSON QUIZ
Lesson Quiz and Class Discussion Board

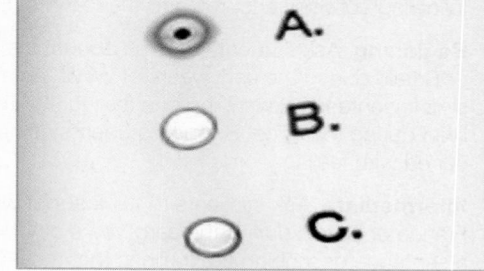

Assign the online Lesson Quiz for this lesson if you haven't already done so. Students will be offered automatic remediation or enrichment based on their score.

Pose the following question to the class on the Discussion Board:

In "Aggression, Appeasement, and War" you read about the events that led to the beginning of World War II and learned that the policy of appeasement was not successful in stopping the aggressive actions of the Axis powers.

Summarize List three main causes that led to World War II. *(Sample response: Germany's aggressive actions, policy of appeasement, Nazi-Soviet Pact providing that Germany and Soviet Union wouldn't go to war once Germany invaded Poland)*

Evaluate Data Considering what you have learned in this lesson, do you think World War II could have been avoided if the leaders and nations involved had made different decisions? Why or why not? *(Answers will vary. Students who believe World War II could have been avoided will discuss more aggressive actions from the Allied Powers and the League of Nations once Germany began violating the terms of the Versailles treaty. Students who believe World War II could not have been avoided will discuss the unfair terms in the Versailles treaty and the control Hitler and other dictators had over their citizens, leading to radical thinking and extreme actions.)*

Topic Inquiry
Have students continue their investigations for the Topic Inquiry.

Axis Powers Advance

Supporting English Language Learners

Use with Digital Text 1, **Axis Domination of Europe.**

Learning Strategies
Read *Axis Domination of Europe* aloud to students. As they listen, have them follow along in their texts. Then have students complete one of the following activities according to their level of English proficiency.

Beginning Ask students to think about what it was like to live in France or Britain during the early years of WWII. As a group, help students write a simple sentence describing one feeling that they may have had if they had lived during that time. Support students as needed by providing images paired with feeling words.

Intermediate Ask students to think about what it was like to live in France or Britain during the early years of WWII. Instruct students to write a sentence describing the feelings that they may have had if they had lived during that time. Support students as needed by providing images paired with feeling words and bilingual dictionaries to help them in their writing.

Advanced Ask students to think about what it was like to live in France or Britain during the early years of WWII. Instruct students to write a few sentences describing the feelings that they may have had if they had lived during that time. Allow students to use language supports like bilingual dictionaries to help them in their writing. Then have students share their sentences with the class. Correct any errors as needed.

Advanced High Ask students to think about what it was like to live in France or Britain during the early years of WWII. Instruct students to write paragraph describing the feelings that they may have had if they had lived during that time. Allow students to use language supports like bilingual dictionaries to help them in their writing. Then have students share their paragraphs with a partner. Students should critique and edit their partner's work. Partners should correct any errors as needed, then share their paragraphs with the class.

Use with Digital Text 2, **Nazis Attack the Soviet Union.**

Learning Strategies
Read *Nazis Attack the Soviet Union* aloud to the class. Have students complete the activities below according to their level of English proficiency.

Beginning Retell the information in the subsection "German Advance Stalls" to students. Then have students draw a series of pictures to tell the story of how Germany invaded the Soviet Union and what caused Nazi troops to stop their advance.

Intermediate Reread the subsection "German Advance Stalls" to students. Then have students retell what was read in their own words. Ask students to draw a series of pictures to tell the story of how Germany invaded the Soviet Union and what caused Nazi troops to stop their advance. Instruct students to write a caption under each to explain the action in the pictures.

Advanced Have students reread the subsection "German Advance Stalls." Then have students write a paragraph to tell the story of how Germany invaded the Soviet Union and what caused Nazi troops to stop their advance. Students may enhance their writing with pictures if time allows. Then have students share their work with a partner.

Advanced High Have students reread the subsection "German Advance Stalls." Then have students write a paragraph from the perspective of a Nazi soldier to tell the story of how Germany invaded the Soviet Union and what caused Nazi troops to stop their advance. Students may enhance their writing with pictures if time allows. Then have students share their work with the rest of the class.

▶ Differentiate Instruction

Use the Differentiated Instruction notes throughout the lesson plan to support the varied skill sets, levels of readiness, and interests in the mixed-ability classroom.

Challenge These notes include suggestions for expanding the activity for advanced students.

On-Level These notes include suggestions for modifying the activity to address different interests or learning styles.

Extra Support These notes include ideas for providing more scaffolding or reading spuport.

Special Needs These notes provide ideas for adapting instruction to support the needs of various special needs students.

■ NOTES

Objectives

Objective 1: Trace the course of German aggression and British resistance in Europe.

Objective 2: Describe the Nazi invasion of the Soviet Union.

Objective 3: Explain how Japanese imperialism and the attack on Pearl Harbor brought the United States into the war.

LESSON 2 ORGANIZER		PACING: APPROX. 1 PERIOD, .5 BLOCKS			
				RESOURCES	
		OBJECTIVES	PACING	Online	Print
Connect					
DIGITAL START UP ACTIVITY **Axis Powers Advance**			5 min.	●	
Investigate					
DIGITAL TEXT 1 **Axis Domination of Europe**		Objective 1	10 min.	●	●
INTERACTIVE GALLERY **London Blitz**			10 min.	●	
DIGITAL TEXT 2 **Nazis Attack the Soviet Union**		Objective 2	10 min.	●	●
INTERACTIVE MAP **Axis Aggression**			10 min.	●	
DIGITAL TEXT 3 **U.S Involvement in the War**		Objective 3	10 min.	●	●
Synthesize					
DIGITAL ACTIVITY **Axis Powers Advance**			5 min.	●	
Demonstrate					
LESSON QUIZ **Lesson Quiz and Class Discussion Board**			10 min.	●	

Axis Powers Advance

▮ CONNECT

DIGITAL START UP ACTIVITY
Axis Powers Advance

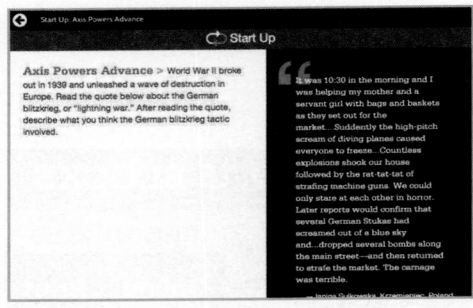

Project the Start Up Activity Ask students to read the quote as they get settled. Then have them share their ideas with another student.

Discuss Ask students what tactics they think were used by Germany in its "lightning war"? *(Possible answers: heavy aerial bombing of military and civilian targets, invasions by fast-moving tanks and troops)*

Tell students that in this lesson they will read about the beginning of World War II and the dominance of the Axis powers. They will learn how combatants and civilians from many countries were affected by the war.

Aa Vocabulary Development: Use the Interactive Reading Notepad to preview the Key Terms and Academic Vocabulary in this lesson with students.

▮ FLIP IT!

Assign the Flipped Video for this lesson.

▮ STUDENT EDITION PRINT PAGES: 744–749

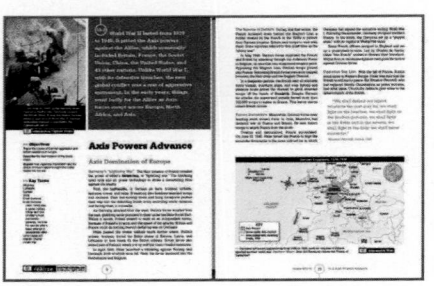

▮ INVESTIGATE

DIGITAL TEXT 1
Axis Domination of Europe

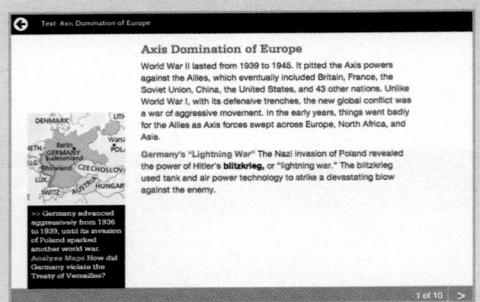

INTERACTIVE GALLERY
London Blitz

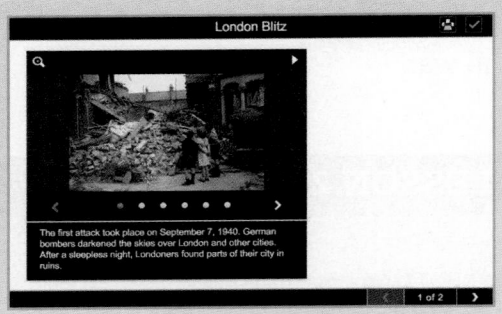

Objective 1: Trace the course of German aggression and British resistance in Europe.

Quick Instruction
Interactive Gallery: London Blitz Project the gallery on the whiteboard and click through the images in the gallery. Introduce the gallery by telling students that for eight consecutive months, the German air force bombed London and other major industrial British cities every night. The British did not lose hope but continued to persevere despite the gains the Axis powers had made throughout Europe.

▮ ACTIVE CLASSROOM

Have students use the See-Think-Wonder strategy with a partner. Ask students to select one image from the gallery. Then ask: *What do you see? What does that make you think? What are you wondering about now that you've seen this?* Give students time to discuss with a partner, then share insights with the class.

D Differentiate: Challenge Ask students to do additional research on the London Blitz and present their findings. During the Blitz, the British persevered and kept their spirits high in order to support the war effort. Churchill gave many speeches and used propaganda effectively to keep the British morale as high as possible throughout the war.

Discuss Examine the importance of high morale for people on the home front during wartime. Ask: What might happen if morale drops? *(Answers will vary, but students might say that enlistment and fundraising for the war effort might also drop, which would hurt success.)*

Further Instruction
Go through the Interactive Reading Notepad questions and answers with the class.

The ruthless efficiency of Germany's "lightning war" surprised many countries, and most of Europe fell into the control of the Axis powers before 1941. However, Germany was unable to subdue Great Britain. Italy played a smaller role, but Mussolini sent troops to support the invasion of France and ordered invasions of Greece and Egypt.

Sequence The Axis powers were able to take control of most of Europe before 1941. Which country was the first to fall to Axis aggression in September 1939? *(Poland)*

DIGITAL TEXT 2

Nazis Attack the Soviet Union

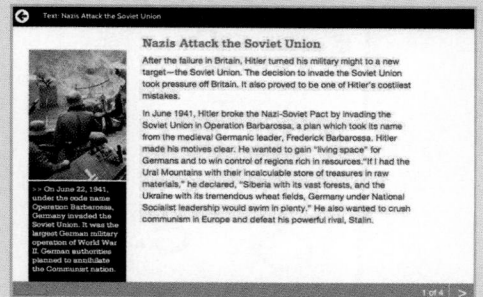

INTERACTIVE MAP

Axis Aggression

DIGITAL TEXT 3

U.S Involvement in the War

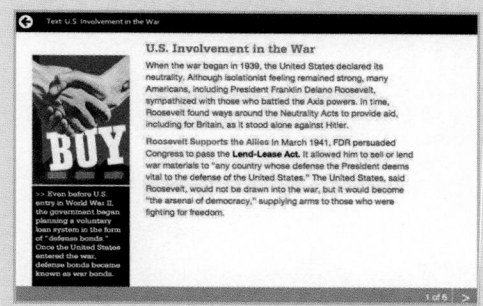

Objective 2: Describe the Nazi invasion of the Soviet Union.

Quick Instruction

Interactive Map: Axis Aggression Project the map on the whiteboard and click through the multiple layers of the map. Introduce the map activity by reminding students of the domination of the Axis powers throughout Europe. Before the invasion of Poland, Hitler and Stalin agreed to the Nazi-Soviet Pact, as they agreed to support and not oppose each other as they expanded their territory in Eastern Europe. Hitler broke the terms of the Nazi-Soviet Pact when he invaded the Soviet Union. His goals were to stop the spread of communism and gain control of the Soviet Union's natural resources.

🎥 ACTIVE CLASSROOM

Have students form an Opinion Line to answer the following question: Was Hitler's decision to invade the Soviet Union successful? Yes or No? *(Sample responses: Yes: it allowed Germany to weaken an enemy to the east and take control of useful resources. No: it created another enemy on the eastern border of Germany.)*

D **Differentiate: Extra Support** After asking students to take a stand, allow students five minutes to think about the question individually. Tell them to write down their response (yes or no) and two reasons why they answered that way. Then continue with the group activity.

ELL Use the ELL activity described in the ELL chart.

Further Instruction

Go through the Interactive Reading Notepad and discuss the questions and answers with the class.

The German army successfully advanced into the Soviet Union until winter arrived, when it became unable to continue its offensive. Discuss why the German invasion of the Soviet Union was a major turning point of World War II. *(Sample response: The invasion of the Soviet Union was a major turning point because Hitler broke an agreement when invading, and it led the Soviet Union to form an alliance with the Allied powers.)*

Objective 3: Explain how Japanese imperialism and the attack on Pearl Harbor brought the United States into the war.

Quick Instruction

The United States was trying to avoid direct involvement in the war but continued to support the Allied forces, specifically the British. Roosevelt and Churchill met to discuss the Atlantic Charter, a statement of common goals for the war. Roosevelt also pushed Congress to adopt the Lend-Lease Act and banned the sale of war materials to Japan, to stop Japanese imperialism. As a result, Japan bombed the American naval fleet in the Pacific at Pearl Harbor, Hawaii. Ask: Why was Roosevelt concerned about the actions of militarists such as Hideki Tojo prior to war? *(Tojo had supported the invasion of China and the formation of the Axis alliance.)* Do you think Roosevelt was justified in calling for a declaration of war after the attack on Pearl Harbor? *(Answers may vary, but some may say that Roosevelt was justified because the United States was physically attacked, and it was important to protect American assets and lives. The American people were directly affected by the attack; therefore, the United States declared war on Japan.)*

Axis Powers Advance

SYNTHESIZE

DIGITAL ACTIVITY

Axis Powers Advance

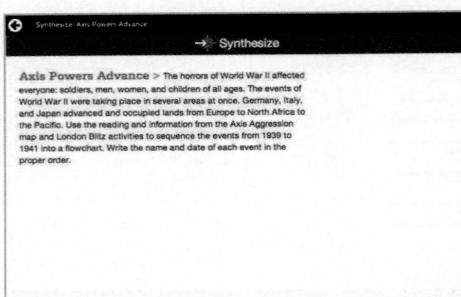

DEMONSTRATE

LESSON QUIZ

Lesson Quiz and Class Discussion Board

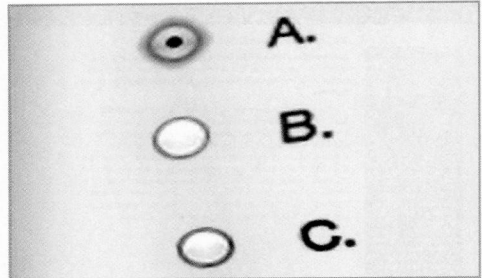

Further Instruction

Go through the Interactive Reading Notepad questions and answers with the class. Then tell students that President Roosevelt believed supporting the Allies was important for protecting democracy. Ask students how the bombing of Pearl Harbor shifted American thought about entering World War II and how this helped the Allies. *(Sample response: Americans were outraged at the bombing, and the country entered the war, greatly increasing the potential military and industrial strength of the Allies.)*

Ask students to recall the Topic Essential Question, "When is war justified?" Have students think about the horrors of World War II and how it affected everyone involved—men, women, and children of all ages. Remind students about the aggressive actions of the Germans, Italians, Japanese, and Soviets. Allow students time to sequence events from 1939 to 1941 into a flowchart, writing the name and date of each event in the proper order. *(Sept 1939: Germany invades Western Poland, Soviets invade Eastern Poland; Winter 1939: Soviets invade Estonia, Latvia, and Lithuania; April 1940: Germany invades Norway, Denmark, Netherlands, Belgium; June 1940: France surrenders to Germany; August 1940: Battle of Britain; Sept 1940: Italy and Germany invade North Africa and Balkans; Oct 1940: Italy and Germany invade Greece and Yugoslavia; Fall 1940: Japan invades French Indochina and Dutch East Indies; June 1941: Germany invades Soviet Union: 1941: Japan takes Hong Kong, Burma, and Malaya; Dec 1941: Japan attacks the United States)*

Discuss Then have students think about the following questions: What roles did Roosevelt, Hitler, Churchill, Stalin, and Tojo play during World War II? *(Answers will vary. Roosevelt tried to keep the U.S. out of World War II while aiding Britain, until the attack on Pearl Harbor. Roosevelt then led the U.S. into war with Japan. Hitler was the aggressor, determined to conquer Europe. Churchill led Britain and kept his country strong during Germany's attacks. Stalin protected the interests of the Soviet Union initially by forming an alliance with Germany and then by joining the Allied Powers. Tojo wanted to expand Japan's empire and power.)*

Assign the online Lesson Quiz for this lesson if you haven't already done so. Students will be offered automatic remediation or enrichment based on their score.

Pose the following question to the class on the Discussion Board:

In "Axis Powers Advance," you read about the early period of World War II and how, as most of Europe fell under the Nazis' control, Great Britain held out alone.

Draw Inferences Why do you think the British were able to withstand the German pressure? *(Answers will vary, but may include experience with opposing threats from outside and strong leadership from Churchill, the royal family, and others.)*

Draw Conclusions Although the United States remained officially neutral before the bombing of Pearl Harbor in December 1941, how did the Lend-Lease Act show the true sympathies of the Roosevelt administration? *(Sample response: Roosevelt's true sympathies lay with the defenders of democracy and against the fascist powers, and the Lend-Lease Act demonstrates that he found a way to aid Britain while still remaining officially neutral, avoiding upsetting Americans opposed to any involvement in the war.)*

Topic Inquiry

Have students continue working on their assignments for the Topic Inquiry.

The Holocaust

Supporting English Language Learners

Use with Digital Text 1, **The Nazi Campaign Against the Jews.**

Learning Strategies
Read *The Nazi Campaign Against the Jews* aloud to students. As they listen, have them follow along in their texts. Then have students complete one of the following activities according to their level of English proficiency.

Beginning Help students create a list of vocabulary words from the text. Make sure the following terms are included: *genocide, concentration camps, anti-Semitism, Holocaust,* and *crematorium*. Using context clues and bilingual dictionaries, help students write the definitions for each of the words in the list. Then model writing a sentence that relates to the text for each word.

Intermediate Write and display this list of vocabulary words from the text: *genocide, concentration camps, anti-Semitism, Holocaust,* and *crematorium*. Then show students how to skim the text and underline each word. Help students develop definitions for each word by using context clues and bilingual dictionaries. Then have students write a sentence that relates to the text for each word. Have students share their sentences with the class.

Advanced Ask pairs of students to review the text and create a list of important vocabulary terms. Tell students to make sure they include all the bolded terms in the text. Then have pairs use context clues to develop a working definition for each word. After this, pairs should compare their definitions to the dictionary definition for each word. Finally, have pairs write sentences for each vocabulary word on the list and share them with their partners.

Advanced High Ask students to review the text and create a list of important vocabulary terms. Tell students to make sure they include all the bolded terms in the text. Then have students use context clues to develop a working definition for each word. After this, have students compare their definitions to the dictionary definition for each word. Finally, have students write sentences for each vocabulary word on the list and share them with the class.

Use with Digital Text 2, **Jewish Resistance.**

Learning Strategies
Read *Jewish Resistance* aloud to the class. Have students complete the activities below according to their level of English proficiency.

Beginning Reread *Jewish Resistance* to students. Retell the content in accessible language for Beginning English speakers. Then ask students to think about the ways that Jews resisted persecution during WWII. Instruct students to participate in a group writing activity in which they brainstorm details to include in a sentence that describes one way that Jews resisted the Nazis.

Intermediate Reread *Jewish Resistance* to students. Help students retell the content in the text in their own words. Then ask students to think about the ways that Jews resisted persecution during WWII. Instruct students to work in pairs to write two sentences that describe one way that Jews resisted the Nazis.

Advanced Have students reread *Jewish Resistance*. Ask students to think about the ways that Jews resisted persecution during WWII. Instruct students to work in pairs to write a brief paragraph that describes two ways that Jews resisted the Nazis.

Advanced High Have students reread *Jewish Resistance*. Ask students to think about the ways that Jews resisted persecution and the ways that others assisted the Jews during WWII. Instruct students to write a well-developed paragraph that describes how the Jews resisted the Nazis and how other Europeans assisted the Jews during WWII.

◨ Differentiate Instruction

Use the Differentiated Instruction notes throughout the lesson plan to support the varied skill sets, levels of readiness, and interests in the mixed-ability classroom.

Challenge These notes include suggestions for expanding the activity for advanced students.

On-Level These notes include suggestions for modifying the activity to address different interests or learning styles.

Extra Support These notes include ideas for providing more scaffolding or reading spuport.

Special Needs These notes provide ideas for adapting instruction to support the needs of various special needs students.

■ NOTES

The Holocaust

Objectives

Objective 1: Identify the roots of Nazi persecution of the Jews.

Objective 2: Describe how the Nazis carried out a program of genocide.

Objective 3: Describe the various acts of Jewish resistance.

Objective 4: Summarize the response of the Allies to the Holocaust.

LESSON 3 ORGANIZER		PACING: APPROX. 1 PERIOD, .5 BLOCKS			
				RESOURCES	
		OBJECTIVES	PACING	Online	Print
Connect					
	DIGITAL START UP ACTIVITY **The Holocaust**		5 min.	●	
Investigate					
	DIGITAL TEXT 1 **The Nazi Campaign Against the Jews**	Objectives 1, 2	10 min.	●	●
	INTERACTIVE MAP **Life in the Concentration Camps**		10 min.	●	
	DIGITAL TEXT 2 **Jewish Resistance**	Objective 3	10 min.	●	●
	DIGITAL TEXT 3 **The Allies Respond to the Holocaust**	Objective 4	10 min.	●	●
	INTERACTIVE GALLERY **Remembering the Holocaust**		10 min.	●	
Synthesize					
	DIGITAL ACTIVITY **Speaking Up**		5 min.	●	
Demonstrate					
	LESSON QUIZ **Lesson Quiz and Class Discussion Board**		10 min.	●	

PEARSON
realize™
www.PearsonRealize.com

Go online to access additional resources including:
Primary Sources • Biographies • Supreme Court cases •
21st Century Skill Tutorials • Maps • Graphic Organizers.

■ CONNECT

DIGITAL START UP ACTIVITY
The Holocaust

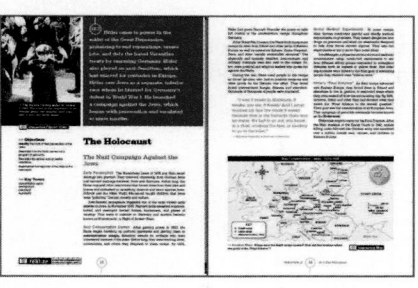

Project the Start Up Activity Ask students to write their responses as they get settled. Then have them share their writing with another student.

Discuss Write a short poem or paragraph describing the Start Up image. *(Responses will vary. Writings will probably focus on the sense of fear, the lack of understanding of what is happening, leaving a life behind, and other emotional issues.)*

Tell students that in this lesson they will learn about how the Nazis committed genocide and the horrors of the Holocaust.

Aa Vocabulary Development: Use the Interactive Reading Notepad to preview the Key Terms and Academic Vocabulary in this Lesson with students.

↻ FLIP IT!
Assign the Flipped Video for this lesson.

■ STUDENT EDITION PRINT
PAGES: 750–755

■ INVESTIGATE

DIGITAL TEXT 1
The Nazi Campaign Against the Jews

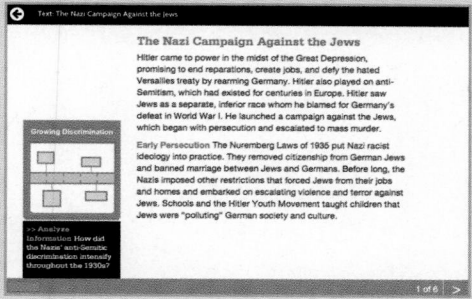

INTERACTIVE MAP
Life in the Concentration Camps

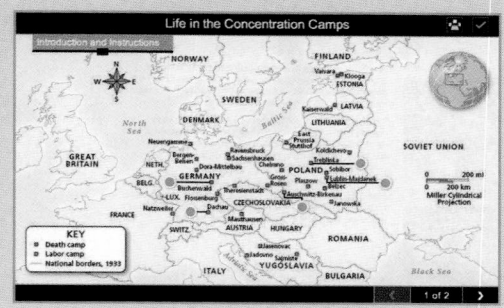

Objectives 1: **Identify the roots of Nazi persecution of the Jews;** 2: **Describe how the Nazis carried out a program of genocide.**

Quick Instruction

Interactive Map: Concentration Camps Project the map on the whiteboard, and click through the hotspots on the map. Introduce the map activity by telling students that Hitler originally implemented the concentration camp system for political prisoners or people who spoke out against the Nazi Party. Eventually, Hitler created the "Final Solution" as a way to rid the world of cultures the Nazis considered racially inferior and created extermination camps for the purpose of killing. Over 6 million Jews were killed in Nazi concentration and extermination camps as a result of anti-Semitism in Nazi Germany.

👥 ACTIVE CLASSROOM

Have students use the Sticky Notes strategy. Ask them to jot down questions, comments, or observations on Sticky Notes about what they noticed or thought while looking at the images of the concentration camps. Have them post the notes on the classroom wall. Sort and discuss questions as a group.

Further Instruction

Project and discuss the Interactive Reading Notepad questions and discuss the answers with the class. Be sure that students understand the Holocaust was an act of genocide, stemming from Hitler's ideology that Jews were an inferior race.

Hitler's anti-Semitism grew into a systematic policy of genocide as he devised a plan for the "Final Solution of the Jewish question," a plan to exterminate European Jews. Discuss how anti-Semitism grew into genocide throughout World War II.

Synthesize Explain the roots of Hitler's anti-Semitism. *(Sample response: Hitler believed that Jews were the reason Germany lost World War I. He also believed in the idea of a master race, and Jews, Slavs, Roma, and other ethnic groups were seen as inferior compared to Hitler's own "Aryan race.")*

The Holocaust

DIGITAL TEXT 2
Jewish Resistance

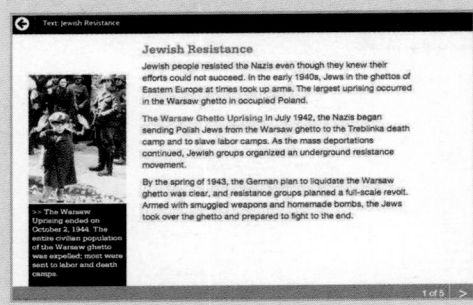

Jewish Resistance

Jewish people resisted the Nazis even though they knew their efforts could not succeed. In the early 1940s, Jews in the ghettos of Eastern Europe at times took up arms. The largest uprising occurred in the Warsaw ghetto in occupied Poland.

The Warsaw Ghetto Uprising In July 1942, the Nazis began sending Polish Jews from the Warsaw ghetto to the Treblinka death camp and to slave labor camps. As the mass deportations continued, Jewish groups organized an underground resistance movement.

By the spring of 1943, the German plan to liquidate the Warsaw ghetto was clear, and resistance groups planned a full-scale revolt. Armed with smuggled weapons and homemade bombs, the Jews took over the ghetto and prepared to fight to the end.

>> The Warsaw Uprising ended on October 2, 1944. The entire civilian population of the Warsaw ghetto was expelled; most were sent to labor and death camps.

Objective 3: Describe the various acts of Jewish resistance.

Quick Instruction

Project the photo from the Warsaw ghetto uprising. Introduce the text by telling students that although 6 million Jews died during the Holocaust, many Jews resisted against Hitler and the Nazis.

Synthesize How did other countries react to Hitler's persecution of the Jews in the 1930s and 40s? *(Sample response: Many countries didn't provide aid or help to the Jews and blocked immigration, and some even became Nazi collaborators.)*

ELL Use the ELL activity described in the ELL chart.

Further Instruction

Project and discuss the Interactive Reading Notepad questions and answers. Remind students that although many resistance movements were unsuccessful, they offered hope to many of the people suffering from persecution. There were some instances of armed revolts, such as the Warsaw Ghetto uprising. Jews also engaged in spiritual resistance by preserving their culture and traditions.

DIGITAL TEXT 3
The Allies Respond to the Holocaust

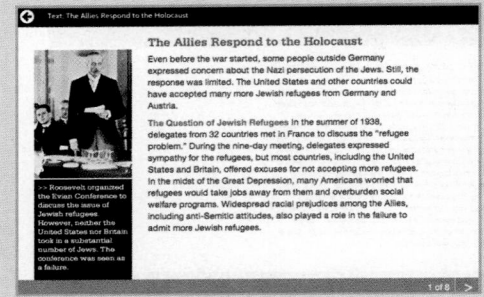

The Allies Respond to the Holocaust

Even before the war started, some people outside Germany expressed concern about the Nazi persecution of the Jews. Still, the response was limited. The United States and other countries could have accepted many more Jewish refugees from Germany and Austria.

The Question of Jewish Refugees In the summer of 1938, delegates from 32 countries met in France to discuss the "refugee problem." During the nine-day meeting, delegates expressed sympathy for the refugees, but most countries, including the United States and Britain, offered excuses for not accepting more refugees. In the midst of the Great Depression, many Americans worried that refugees would take jobs away from them and overburden social welfare programs. Widespread racial prejudices among the Allies, including anti-Semitic attitudes, also played a role in the failure to admit more Jewish refugees.

>> Roosevelt organized the Evian Conference to discuss the issue of Jewish refugees. However, neither the United States nor Britain took in a substantial number of Jews. The conference was seen as a failure.

Objective 4: Summarize the response of the Allies to the Holocaust.

Quick Instruction

Interactive Gallery: Remembering the Holocaust Project the Interactive Gallery on the whiteboard and click through the museum exhibits that showcase life inside the concentration camps. Point out that, while numbers and statistics are often used to describe the Holocaust, it is important to look at individual stories of survivors and victims and remember the people who lived through the Holocaust. These images help remind us that Holocaust victims were more than just numbers. Look again at the image of the toy exhibit from the Yad Vashem Museum and reread how the Bucci sisters recounted their days in Auschwitz. Discuss the importance of imagination, especially for children, in order to survive the everyday horrors of the concentration camps.

🎥 ACTIVE CLASSROOM

Have students form a Word Wall. Ask them to chose one of the vocabulary terms for the lesson and create a visual image with a definition. Allow 3-5 minutes. Ask students to post their words and images on the board, then ask students to discuss similarities and differences in the responses as a group.

SYNTHESIZE

DEMONSTRATE

INTERACTIVE GALLERY
Remembering the Holocaust

D **Differentiate: Extra Support** After asking students to choose a vocabulary word, allow students five minutes to think about synonyms for the word or a list of adjectives to describe the word. Tell them to use the synonyms and adjectives to help create a visual image for the word. Then continue with the group activity.

Further Instruction

Go through the Interactive Reading Notepad questions and discuss the answers with the class. Discuss how people from the liberating countries may have felt after learning the extent of the Holocaust, knowing that their countries may have supported policies to turn away Jewish refugees. Ask: Do you think other countries could have done more to stop Nazi genocide before it was too late? *(Students' answers will vary, but most will say yes, countries should have done more.)* Discuss the responsibility of countries to protect basic human rights around the world. Ask: What obligation do other nations have to protect people in another country from genocide? *(Sample response: If a country's leaders know that another country's leaders have engaged in the systematic elimination of an entire race of people, then they have a moral obligation to try to stop it.)*

DIGITAL ACTIVITY
Speaking Up

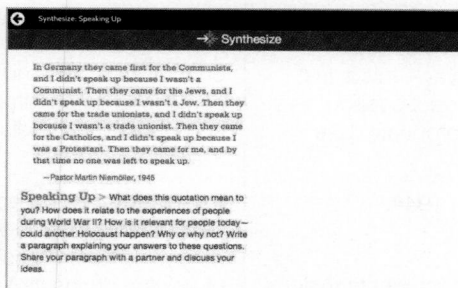

Ask students to recall the Topic Essential Question, "When is War Justified?" Reread and discuss with students the meaning behind Niemöller's quote. Discuss how the statement was aimed at all people for allowing such a terrible event to happen. Next, discuss the importance of memorials and museums for honoring victims and survivors and for educating the world about the horrors of genocide.

Instruct students to look back in the text to the picture of the delegates at the Evian Conference. More than 32 representatives were there in the late 1930s to discuss the Jewish refugee problem. Although delegates expressed their sympathies for the Jewish community, nobody opened their doors to the refugees because of economic hardships due to the Great Depression and feelings of anti-Semitism. Do you think the countries who met at the Evian Conference in France share some guilt for the Holocaust? Why or why not? Have pairs share their answers with the class. *(This is an opinion question, so answers will vary. Some students might think that the countries were not aware of the mistreatment and were only looking out for the people of their own country. Others will think that the countries were aware of the laws against the Jews and the escalation of mistreatment and they should be held responsible for not defending the human rights of others.)*

LESSON QUIZ
Lesson Quiz and Class Discussion Board

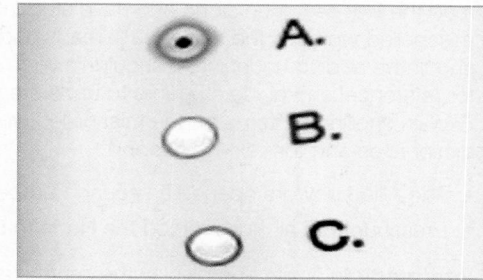

Assign the online Lesson Quiz for this lesson if you haven't already done so. Students will be offered automatic remediation or enrichment based on their score.

Pose this question to the class on the Discussion Board:

In "The Holocaust," you read about Hitler's attempted systematic elimination of European Jews and how the survivors were finally liberated.

Identify Cause and Effect How did the creation of Israel result from the Holocaust? *(Sample response: As the horrors of the Holocaust became evident, many believed the Jewish people deserved a homeland and that creating one might prevent or mitigate future manifestations of anti-Semitism.)*

The Allies Turn the Tide

Supporting English Language Learners

Use with Digital Text 3, **A Second Front in Europe.**

Learning Strategies
Read *A Second Front in Europe* aloud to students. As they listen, have them follow along in their texts. Then have students complete one of the following activities according to their level of English proficiency.

Beginning Write and display the sentences below for students. Then read the first sentence aloud and have students repeat. Underline the misspelled words in the sentence [already underlined, but instructor should be adding underline; it shouldn't go to print this way—this is just for reference] and guide students to understand their correct spelling. Explain spelling patterns for the misspelled words as appropriate. Use dictionaries and the text for support.

- The Allied powors opened a secund European front in 1944.
- Presshur from all sides forced the Nazis to retreete.

Intermediate Write and display the sentences below for students. Ask student volunteers to read the sentences aloud, then have all students read them chorally. Ask student volunteers to identify and underline the misspelled words in the sentence [already underlined, but instructor should be adding underline; it shouldn't go to print this way—this is just for reference]. Encourage students to offer the correct spelling of each misspelled word and provide students with spelling patterns as appropriate. Use dictionaries and the text for support.

- The Allied powors opened a secund European front in 1944.
- Presshur from all sides forced the Nazis to retreete.

Advanced Working in groups of three, ask students to review the text and create a list of everyday words that are a challenge to spell correctly. Instruct groups to think about why each word on the list is difficult to spell. Then have groups write the correct spelling and definition of each word using dictionaries or glossaries for support. Finally, have each group share their list with the rest of the class.

Advanced High Working independently, ask students to review the text and create a list of everyday words that are a challenge to spell correctly. Ask students to think about why each word on the list is difficult to spell. Then instruct students to write the correct spelling and definition of each word using dictionaries or glossaries for support. Finally, have students turn to a partner to share their list.

Use with Digital Text 2, **Progress on Three Fronts.**

Learning Strategies
Read *Progress on Three Fronts* aloud to the class. Have students complete the activities below according to their level of English proficiency.

Beginning Reread the subsection "'Big Three' Strategize" to students. Tell students that explaining a topic requires communicating information in a way that makes it easier to understand. Describe how to compare and contrast something. Then retell the content in everyday language, focusing on the similarities and differences among the "Big Three" leaders. Model comparing and contrasting by explaining, then writing, how Churchill's and Roosevelt's goals for Europe were both the same and different from Stalin's.

Intermediate Reread the subsection "'Big Three' Strategize" to students. Tell students to review the information in the text with a partner to determine how Churchill and Roosevelt shared goals and had differences of opinion during WWII. Remind students how to compare and contrast information. Then ask pairs to write several sentences comparing and contrasting Churchill's and Roosevelt's goals with Stalin's goals for Europe.

Advanced Instruct pairs of students to reread the subsection "'Big Three' Strategize" aloud to each other. Tell students to take notes on how Churchill and Roosevelt shared goals and had differences of opinion during WWII. Remind students how to compare and contrast information. Then ask pairs to write several sentences comparing and contrasting Churchill's and Roosevelt's goals with Stalin's goals for Europe.

Advanced High Instruct students to reread the subsection "'Big Three' Strategize" aloud to each other. Tell students to take notes on how Churchill and Roosevelt shared goals and had differences of opinion during WWII. Then ask students to write a paragraph to compare and contrast Churchill's and Roosevelt's with Stalin's goals for Europe.

D Differentiate Instruction

Use the Differentiated Instruction notes throughout the lesson plan to support the varied skill sets, levels of readiness, and interests in the mixed-ability classroom.

Challenge These notes include suggestions for expanding the activity for advanced students.

On-Level These notes include suggestions for modifying the activity to address different interests or learning styles.

Extra Support These notes include ideas for providing more scaffolding or reading spuport.

Special Needs These notes provide ideas for adapting instruction to support the needs of various special needs students.

■ NOTES

PEARSON
realize™
www.PearsonRealize.com

Go online to access additional resources including:
Primary Sources • Biographies • Supreme Court cases •
21st Century Skill Tutorials • Maps • Graphic Organizers.

Objectives

Objective 1: Understand how nations committed all of their resources to fighting World War II.

Objective 2: Explain how the Allies began to push back the Axis powers in Europe and the Pacific.

Objective 3: Describe the Normandy landings and the Allied advance toward Germany.

LESSON 4 ORGANIZER — PACING: APPROX. 1 PERIOD, .5 BLOCKS

	OBJECTIVES	PACING	RESOURCES Online	Print
Connect				
DIGITAL START UP ACTIVITY **Exit the Axis**		5 min.	●	
Investigate				
DIGITAL TEXT 1 **A Commitment to Total War**	Objective 1	10 min.	●	●
DIGITAL TEXT 2 **Progress on Three Fronts**	Objective 2	10 min.	●	●
INTERACTIVE CHART **European Turning Points in World War II—Causes and Effects**		10 min.	●	
DIGITAL TEXT 3 **A Second Front in Europe**	Objective 3	10 min.	●	●
INTERACTIVE MAP **World War II in Europe, 1942–1945**		10 min.	●	
3-D MODEL **The B-24 Liberator**		10 min.	●	
Synthesize				
DIGITAL ACTIVITY **Factors: Turning the Tide**		5 min.	●	
Demonstrate				
LESSON QUIZ **Lesson Quiz and Class Discussion Board**		10 min.	●	

The Allies Turn the Tide

■ CONNECT

DIGITAL START UP ACTIVITY
Exit the Axis

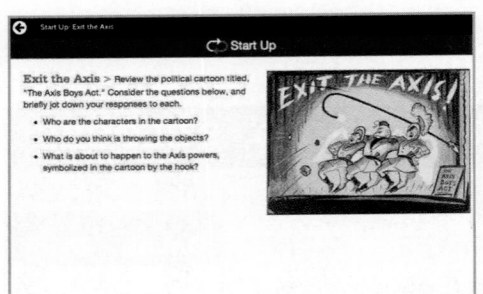

Project the Start Up Activity Have students answer the questions as they enter and get settled. Have students share their ideas with another student.

Discuss Who are the characters in the cartoon? *(Sample response: They are the Axis leaders: Tojo, Mussolini, and Hitler.)* Who do you think is throwing the objects? *(Students may say that conquered peoples are throwing the objects, or that Allied forces are throwing the objects.)* What is about to happen to the Axis powers? *(The Allied leaders are about to yank the Axis leaders and end their performance.)*

Aa Vocabulary Development: Use the Interactive Reading Notepad to preview the Key Terms and Academic Vocabulary in the Lesson with students.

⇅ FLIP IT!
Assign the Flipped Video for this lesson.

■ STUDENT EDITION PRINT
PAGES: 756–761

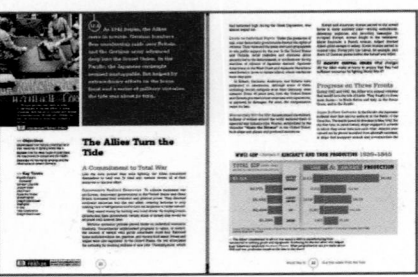

■ INVESTIGATE

DIGITAL TEXT 1
A Commitment to Total War

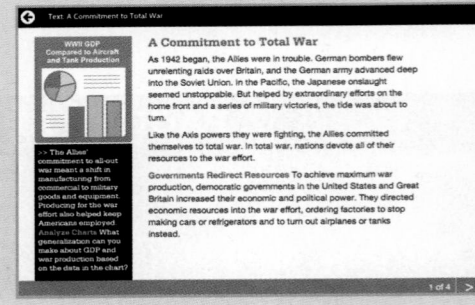

Objective 1: Understand how nations committed all of their resources to fighting World War II.

Quick Instruction
Remind students that the Allies were on the defensive in early 1942. They were being attacked by Japan in the Pacific, and Germany was bombing Britain and gaining ground in the Soviet Union. The Allies needed to manufacture as much military equipment as possible to out-produce the Axis. They waged total war, the dedication of all a country's varied resources to producing war materials. Governments implemented programs to ration the amount of certain vital goods consumers could buy, and prices and wages were regulated. In the United States, the war stimulated the economy by creating millions of new jobs. Unemployment, which had remained high during the Great Depression, was almost wiped out.

Analyze Images Project on the whiteboard the image of the women putting the finishing touches on a British tank. Discuss the image as a class. Then ask the students how the world political situation has changed since the photograph was taken. *(Answers will vary, but students may say that in World War II, the Soviets were Allies. After the war, that alliance broke apart. Today, the Russians, who used to be part of the Soviet Union, are frequently at odds with both the United States and Britain. In this photograph, the British are manufacturing tanks for the Soviets, an act that, most likely, would not take place today.)*

D Differentiate: Challenge/Gifted Ask students to do further research on the restrictions of civil liberties imposed by the Allied governments on their citizens at home. Have them write a brief essay in which they describe their findings and whether or not they believe these restrictions were justified.

Further Instruction
A Commitment to Total War: Core Reading and Interactive Reading Notepad Project and discuss the Interactive Reading Notepad questions and answers.

Summarize Why did U.S. and Canadian citizens of Japanese descent lose their jobs, have their property seized, and then get sent to internment camps? *(Sample response: Those citizens of Japanese descent were considered by the American and Canadian governments as a security risk based solely on their ethnicity.)*

DIGITAL TEXT 2

Progress on Three Fronts

INTERACTIVE CHART

European Turning Points in World War II—Causes and Effects

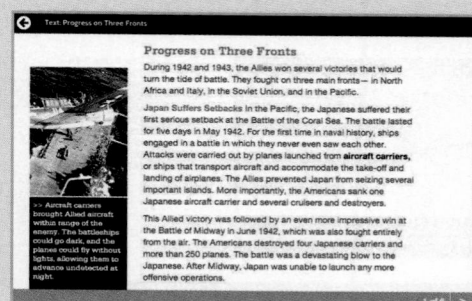

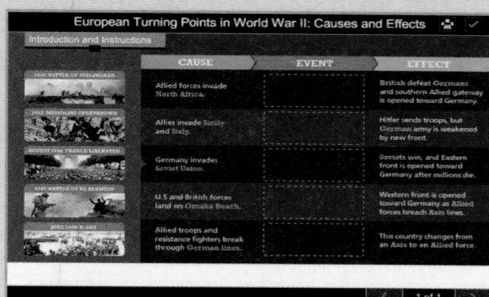

Objective 2: Explain how the Allies began to push back the Axis powers in Europe and the Pacific.

Quick Instruction

Interactive Chart: European Turning Points in World War II: Causes and Effects Project the gallery on the whiteboard. Click on the various moveable tiles to show students how to drag. Introduce the gallery by telling students that more than one front, which included many battles, was necessary to win World War II, and the Allies engaged the Axis in both Europe and the Pacific. After several years with few notable successes, 1942–1943 saw the tide beginning to turn for America, Britain, and the Soviet Union. Successes on three different fronts–the Pacific, North Africa and Italy, and the Soviet Union–gave the Allies cause for cautious hope.

📷 ACTIVE CLASSROOM

Introduce students to the Act It Out strategy by dividing the room into three groups: Great Britain, the Soviet Union, and the United States. Ask students to portray the leaders of these countries– Churchill, Stalin, and Roosevelt–and their advisors. Tell students they will be in an Allied situation room strategizing their campaigns in Europe against the Axis countries. Ask students to include the battles in the North African desert, and in the Soviet Union. *(Possible dialogues: Germany is in the middle of Europe. The best offensive is to move in toward Germany from every direction. If troops enter North Africa, they can defeat the German army there and invade Europe through the boot of Italy. At the same, the Allies could overthrow Mussolini, liberate Italy, and gain more resources. The Soviets will hold their own against the Germans entering the Soviet Union unless they ask for Allied help. Their goal will be to push the Germans west and back into Germany.)*

ELL Use the ELL activity described in the ELL chart.

Further Instruction

Progress on Three Fronts: Core Text and Interactive Reading Notepad Go through the Interactive Reading Notepad and discuss the answers with the class.

Draw Conclusions Why was it important that the Allies continue constant aerial bombings on Germany when the ground troops were already making progress from all directions? *(Sample response: The aerial attacks were a demoralizing factor in addition to preventing the Germans from manufacturing military products.)*

Discuss Historians have studied World War II for more than 50 years and some still disagree on important issues. Ask students how impressions they had before they began studying the war have changed. *(Responses will vary, but should reflect knowledge of the facts about the war incuded in these texts.)*

The Allies Turn the Tide

DIGITAL TEXT 3

A Second Front in Europe

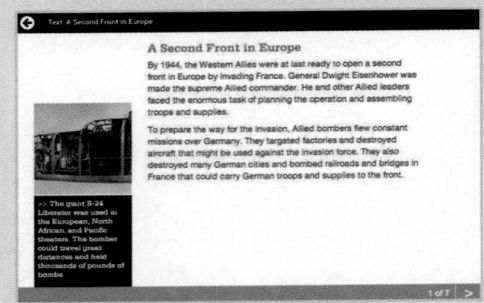

INTERACTIVE MAP

World War II in Europe, 1942–1945

3-D MODEL

The B-24 Liberator

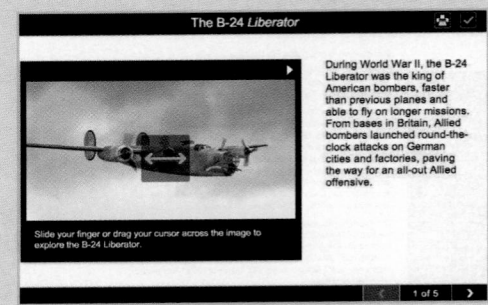

Objective 3: Describe the Normandy landings and the Allied advance toward Germany.

Quick Instruction

Combined military fronts enabled the Allies to turn the tide on the Axis. From the west, the British, Canadians, and Americans landed at Normandy and advanced toward Germany. Allied forces battled in North Africa, aiming for Europe through southern Italy. Stalin engaged the Germans on Soviet soil and then pushed the Germans west, back to Germany. The location of Germany was a weakness that Hitler could not overcome, and as the war progressed, Nazi Germany found itself surrounded by enemies.

Interactive Map: World War II in Europe, 1942–1945 Project the map on the whiteboard. There are four layers, one each for the years 1942–1945. The single layers show the status of the Allies and the Axis for a particular year. As the years progressed, the Allies switched from defensive to offensive positions. What specific events changed the course of the war in Europe? (*Answers will vary, but may include Battle of the Bulge, D-Day invasion of Normandy, Battle at Stalingrad, Battle of El-Alamein, and Allied bombing of German factories and military arsenals.*)

📷 ACTIVE CLASSROOM

Employ the Make Headlines strategy and have students write a headline that describes the content of the interactive map. Ask students this question: If you were to write a headline for this topic right now that captured the map's most important aspect, what would that headline be? (*Answers will vary, but may include "Allies Land at Omaha Beach," "Allies Liberate France," "Desert Fox Loses at El Alamein," "Mussolini Overthrown," "Germans Retreat from Soviet Union."*) Pass your headline to a partner for him or her to review.

3-D Model: The B-24 Liberator Work through The B-24 Liberator Activity with students. Tell students that the B-24 Liberator was faster than previous American bombers and able to carry a heavy load of bombs on long missions. How do you think this air war affected the outcome of World War II? How do you think it affected Europe in terms of lives lost and rebuilding after the war? (*The air war had an important impact on World War II in Europe, relieving pressure on the Soviet Union, harming Germany's ability to make war, and making it possible for an all-out Allied offensive in France. The bombing likely killed many people and made the postwar rebuilding process more challenging.*)

📷 ACTIVE CLASSROOM

Conduct a Thumbs Up When Ready activity. Ask students to think about this statement: "True or false: By the end of 1943, the Allies were poised for final victory in World War II." Ask students to put their thumbs up to indicate that they have finished their thinking. When all have responded, ask them to share their thoughts in pairs or in small groups.

ELL Use the ELL activity described in the ELL chart.

Further Instruction

A Sceond Front in Europe: Core Text and Interactive Reading Notepad Go through the Interactive Reading Notepad questions and discuss the answers with the class.

Predict Consequences Ask students to write "yes" and "no" answers to the following question: Do you think that if Hitler had kept his aggression to a one-country-at-a-time strategy, he would have been successful in gaining European domination? (*Sample response: "pro" side: if the United States and Soviet Union had not joined World War II, it could have been a possibility; Hitler made gains with Austria, Czechoslovakia, Poland, and France; "con" side: while Hitler formed alliances with various European countries such as Italy, they were not under German control and may have fought against him if they believed his strategy was to annex them as a German possession.*)

SYNTHESIZE

DEMONSTRATE

DIGITAL ACTIVITY
Factors: Turning the Tide

LESSON QUIZ
Lesson Quiz and Class Discussion Board

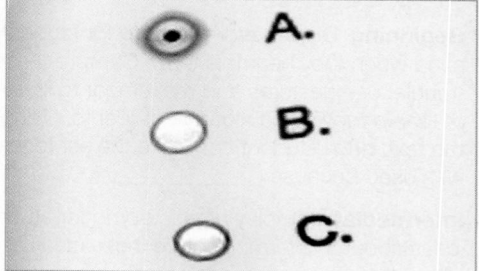

Evaluate Impact Who were the French Resistance? Why were they so important to the French people and the Allies? *(Sample response: The French Resistance was an underground army that opposed the Germans' occupation of France.)*

Discuss Historians have studied World War II for more than 50 years and some still disagree on important issues. Ask students how impressions they had before they began studying the war have changed. *(Responses will vary, but should reflect knowledge of the facts about the war included in these texts.)*

Have students use the Pair Share Activity to answer the question in Factors: Turning the Tide in the Synthesize Activity. Ask them to take five minutes to write down some brief answers to the question: Which factors do you think played the most important role in turning the tide against Germany, Japan, and Italy? *(Responses will vary. Many students will cite the increased economic power of the post-Great Depression U.S. fully engaged in winning the war as unstoppable, as well as invulnerable since Hitler could not attack the U.S. forces. Others may argue that Germany's geographical position doomed it once the Soviet Union opened the Eastern Front.)* Have them share their answers with their talking partner.

Now, ask partners to think about the following questions: What significance do you think the French Resistance had in liberating France? What did many members of this organization do once their country was no longer under the control of the Nazis? Have pairs share their answers with the class.

Discuss Have students describe what they believe the post-liberation French government did to assist in bringing the war in Europe to an end. *(Answers may vary. After France was liberated, the country changed from Axis to Allied. The new government committed military support in joining the Allies. Civilians, including some of those who were members of the French Resistance, either joined the French army or supported the war effort at home.)*

Assign the online Lesson Quiz if you have not already done so. Students will be offered automatic remediation or enrichment based on their score.

Pose these questions to the class on the Discussion Board:

Recognize Cause and Effect How did the Allied victories in the European front affect the economic systems of these countries? *(Answers will vary. The war decimated the factories, communities, industries, and infrastructure of the European countries. The rebuilding put people to work and created jobs.)*

Draw Conclusions What do you think would have happened if the Soviets had lost the Battle of Stalingrad? *(Sample response: The Allied strategy to stop Hitler's war machine was based on encircling Germany and pushing in from the west via Britain, across the channel through France, the south from North Africa through Italy, and the east from the Soviet Union. Without winning the Battle of Stalingrad, there was the possibility that the Germans could have taken control of the Soviet Union. This would have created a much larger German power and an adversary that would have caused the Allies to need to regroup.)*

Topic Inquiry
Have students continue their investigations for the Topic Inquiry.

Victory for the Allies

Supporting English Language Learners

Use with Digital Text 3, **End of the War in the Pacific.**

Learning Strategies
Have students use their prior knowledge to reflect on the atomic bomb, then read *End of War in the Pacific* aloud. Explain that using what they already know can help them make connections with new information.

Beginning Display *atomic bomb* for students. Ask them what comes to mind when they hear this term. Capture these ideas. If students are having trouble, use gestures and movement to illustrate the term. Then read *End of War in the Pacific* aloud to students. Using the ideas on the board and the text, have student complete the sentence frame: The atomic bomb was used because _____.

Intermediate Display *atomic bomb* for students. Ask them to brainstorm ideas about this term. Capture these ideas. If students are having trouble, show them the image in the text. As a group, write a few sentences summarizing what students know about the atomic bomb. Then read *End of War in the Pacific* aloud to students. Have the group select the sentence on the board that best connects with why the atomic bomb was used.

Advanced Have students work in small groups to use their prior knowledge to brainstorm ideas about the atomic bomb. Instruct each group to write a few sentences summarizing what they already know. Then have each group read *End of War in the Pacific* aloud. Ask groups to make one connection between the information that they brainstormed and the text.

Advanced High Using their prior knowledge, have students work individually to brainstorm ideas about the term *atomic bomb.* With a partner, have them combine their ideas and write a few sentences summarizing what they already know. Then have them read *End of War in the Pacific* independently. Then have partners discuss two connections between the information that they brainstormed and the text.

Use with Digital Text 1, **End of the War in Europe.**

Writing
Explain to students that recognizing spelling patterns can help them prevent spelling errors in their writing. Read *End of the War in Europe* aloud to the class. Have students complete the activities below according to their level of English proficiency.

Beginning Explain that the long *e* sound can be made using several different spelling patterns. Two of these spelling patterns are *ee* and *ea*. Review *End of the War in Europe* with students. Locate the following words that show these spelling patterns: *nearing, see, east, defeat,* and *meanwhile.* Underline the long *e* sound in each word, say each word, and have students repeat the words. Brainstorm other words with the same spelling pattern with students.

Intermediate Write and display the words *read* and *free.* Point out that the long *e* sound in these four words is either spelled with *ee* and *ea.* Review *End of the War in Europe* with students. As you reread the text, instruct students to raise their hands when they encounter a word with the long *e* sound spelled *ee* or *ea.* Make sure to locate the following words that show these spelling patterns: *nearing, see, east, defeat,* and *meanwhile.* Write and display these words, say each word, and have students repeat the words. Have students work in small groups to brainstorm other words with the same spelling pattern.

Advanced Instruct pairs of students to reread the subsection *End of the War in Europe* aloud to each other. Tell students to look for and underline words with the long *e* sound spelled *ee* or *ea.* Make sure pairs locate the following words that show these spelling patterns: *nearing, see, east, defeat,* and *meanwhile.* Write and display these words, say each word, and have students repeat the words. Then ask pairs to write a sentence using each long *e* word correctly.

Advanced High Instruct students to reread the subsection *End of the War in Europe.* As they read, have students to look for and underline words with the long *e* sound spelled *ee* or *ea.* Make sure students locate the following words that show these spelling patterns: *nearing, see, east, defeat,* and *meanwhile.* Ask students to practice saying these words correctly. Offer pronunciation assistance as needed. Then ask students to write a sentence using each long *e* word correctly.

▣ Differentiate Instruction

Use the Differentiated Instruction notes throughout the lesson plan to support the varied skill sets, levels of readiness, and interests in the mixed-ability classroom.

Challenge These notes include suggestions for expanding the activity for advanced students.

On-Level These notes include suggestions for modifying the activity to address different interests or learning styles.

Extra Support These notes include ideas for providing more scaffolding or reading spuport.

Special Needs These notes provide ideas for adapting instruction to support the needs of various special needs students.

▮ NOTES

_____

_____

_____

_____

_____

_____

PEARSON •••
realize™
www.PearsonRealize.com

Go online to access additional resources including:
Primary Sources • Biographies • Supreme Court cases •
21st Century Skill Tutorials • Maps • Graphic Organizers.

Objectives

Objective 1: Understand the reasons for the final defeat of the Nazis.

Objective 2: Describe how the Allies began to push back the Japanese in the Pacific.

Objective 3: Explain how the dropping of the atomic bombs ended the war.

Objective 4: Describe the aftermath of World War II and the founding of the United Nations.

LESSON 5 ORGANIZER		PACING: APPROX. 1 PERIOD, .5 BLOCKS			
		OBJECTIVES	**PACING**	**RESOURCES**	
				Online	Print
Connect					
💿	DIGITAL START UP ACTIVITY **Hitler's Vision**		5 min.	●	
Investigate					
📄	DIGITAL TEXT 1 **End of the War in Europe**	Objective 1	10 min.	●	●
📄	DIGITAL TEXT 2 **Battles in the Pacific**	Objective 2	10 min.	●	●
🗺️	INTERACTIVE MAP **World War II in the Pacific, 1942–1945**		10 min.	●	
📄	DIGITAL TEXT 3 **End of the War in the Pacific**	Objective 3	10 min.	●	●
📄	DIGITAL TEXT 4 **Aftermath of the War**	Objective 4	10 min.	●	●
📄	DIGITAL TEXT 5 **The United Nations Is Formed**		10 min.	●	●
📊	INTERACTIVE TIMELINE **Key Events of World War II in Europe and the Pacific**		10 min.	●	
Synthesize					
💡	DIGITAL ACTIVITY **Victory in the Pacific**		5 min.	●	
Demonstrate					
☑	LESSON QUIZ **Lesson Quiz and Classroom Discussion Board**		10 min.	●	

Victory for the Allies

■ CONNECT

DIGITAL START UP ACTIVITY
Hitler's Vision

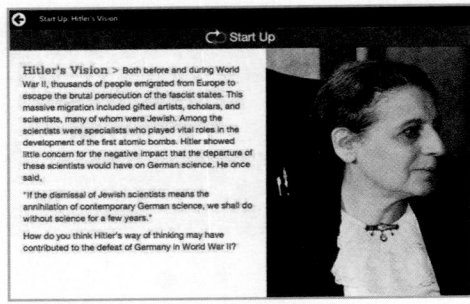

Project the Start Up Activity Ask students to answer the question as they enter and get settled. Then have them share their ideas with another student.

Discuss How do you think Hitler's way of thinking may have contributed to Germany's defeat in World War II? *(Students should point out that these scientists brought their knowledge, including weapons technology, to the Allies.)* If you had taken part in the fighting against Germany, how would you have felt about your contribution to the Allied victory? *(Answers will vary, but should include a sense of accomplishment and pride in contributing to the defeat of fascism.)*

Aa Vocabulary Development: Use the Interactive Reading Notepad to preview the Key Terms and Academic Vocabulary in this Lesson with students.

⇅ FLIP IT!
Assign the Flipped Video for this lesson.

■ STUDENT EDITION PRINT
PAGES: 762–768

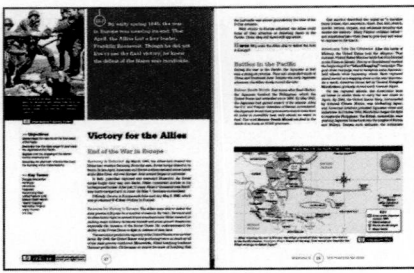

■ INVESTIGATE

DIGITAL TEXT 1
End of the War in Europe

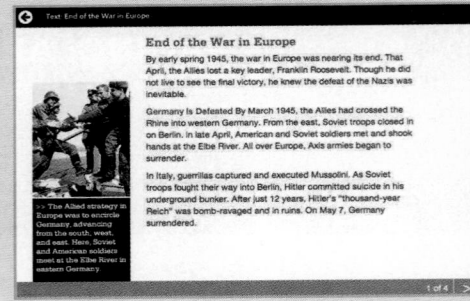

Objective 1: Understand the reasons for the final defeat of the Nazis.

Quick Instruction
Project the image of U.S. and Soviet soldiers shaking hands at the Elbe River. Remind students that the Soviet and U.S. troops were on the side of the Allies. Also project the image of the formal signing of Germany's unconditional surrender. Explain to students that this signified that World War II had ended in Europe.

Further Instruction
Project and discuss the questions from the Interactive Reading Notepad for the reading "End of the War in Europe." Ask students to think about the causes and effects of the decisions by Roosevelt, Stalin, Churchill, and Hitler that led to the end of the war in Europe.

Make Generalizations What symbolic message does the photograph of the American and Soviet troops shaking hands at the Elbe River communicate? *(Sample response: The Allied military strategies of Roosevelt, Stalin, and Churchill were to surround Germany and push Hitler's troops into retreat from the west and east. This photo shows how that goal was met, with the Soviets advancing from the east and the Americans from the west.)*

Draw Conclusions Why did the Allies believe it important that Germany sign an "unconditional," or total, surrender? *(Sample response: It was important to each of the Allied countries that they stand united and that Germany be unable to reach different surrender agreements with the Allied countries.)*

DIGITAL TEXT 2
Battles in the Pacific

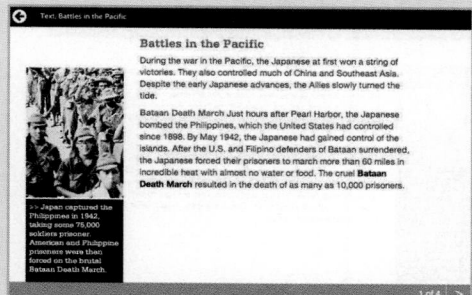

INTERACTIVE MAP
World War II in the Pacific, 1942–1945

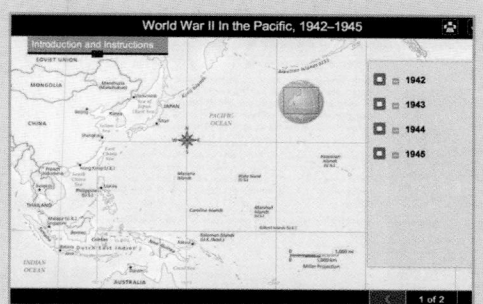

DIGITAL TEXT 3
End of the War in the Pacific

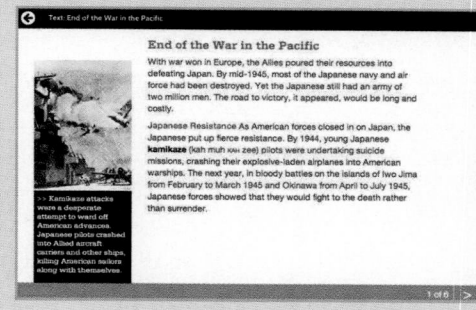

Objective 2: Describe how the Allies began to push back the Japanese in the Pacific.

Quick Instruction

Interactive Map: World War II in the Pacific Project the interactive map on the whiteboard. Introduce the activity by explaining that there was an Allied military presence in the Pacific while the Allies were fighting on the European front. Once the European front had been won by the Allies, their focus turned to the Pacific theater until Japan was defeated. Click through the various layers of the map showing the students that they can isolate the activity occurring in the Pacific by year from 1942 to 1945. The last layer will reveal all Allied military activity in one map for those same years.

👥 ACTIVE CLASSROOM

Use the Quickdraw strategy and pair students. Give students a short period to share what they know by writing with symbols or drawings. Have the first students tell their partner what they are going to draw or symbolize. Then, have the second students prepare the symbols or drawing. Use a document camera, if available, to scan drawings to add to the class blog.

D Differentiate: Challenge/Gifted While viewing the map, point out that Allied offensives in the Pacific theater extended beyond the island-hopping of the Philippines.

Ask students to list two areas of the Pacific front named on the map where Allied troops won battles and moved toward Japan from those positions. *(Manchuria, Burma)*

Further Instruction

Editable Presentation Use the Editable Presentation to present the main ideas for this Core Text.

Battles in the Pacific: Core Text and Interactive Reading Notepad Project the questions provided in the Interactive Reading Notepad, and have students answer as they move through the core text.

Interactive Map: World War II in the Pacific Project the interactive map of the battles in the Pacific again, and ask students to describe how it was possible that the Allied forces were able to surround Japan. Be sure that students understand the geography and what types of military weapons were necessary to win the battles in the Pacific. Ask students to list two Allied offensive locations and the type of battles and weapons used to secure these locations in the advancement toward Japan. *(Answers will vary, but may include battles on land such as those in Manchuria and Burma. The weapons used in these locations were land combat weapons such as tanks. The advancements from the Kuril Islands, the Hawaiian Islands, the Philippine Islands, and Borneo were a combination of land, sea, and air battles where hand-to-hand combat, weapons, tanks, aircraft carriers, fighter planes, and battleships were used.)*

Objective 3: Explain how the dropping of the atomic bombs ended the war.

Quick Instruction

Project the image of the aftermath of the atomic bomb. Explain to students that the dropping of the two atomic bombs finally ended the war. Explain that by mid-1945, even though most of the Japanese navy and air force had been destroyed, Japan still had an army of two million men, and the road to victory was predicted to be long and costly. Review the results of the Manhattan Project and how President Truman decided that using atomic weapons would shorten the war and save many American lives. Finally, discuss the results of the attacks on Hiroshima and Nagasaki.

ELL Use the ELL activity described in the ELL chart.

Further Instruction

Project and discuss the questions from the Interactive Reading Notepad for "End of the War in the Pacific." Ask students to think about the causes and effects that led to the decision to use an atomic bomb on Nagasaki and Hiroshima.

Make Predictions If the atomic bombs had not been not dropped, what do you think would have happened on the Pacific front? *(Answers will vary. Most students will say that the war would have continued for an indefinite period of time, and many more American, and possibly Japanese, lives would have been lost.)*

Victory for the Allies

DIGITAL TEXT 4
Aftermath of the War

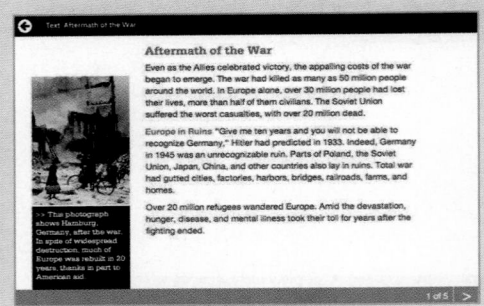

DIGITAL TEXT 5
The United Nations Is Formed

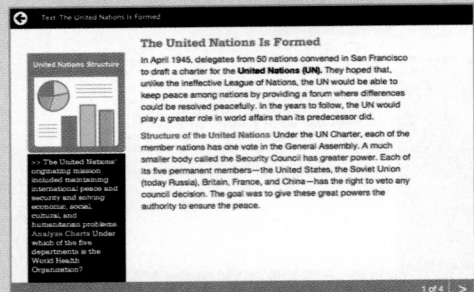

Paraphrase Explain how kamikaze pilots delayed the ending of the war in the Pacific. *(Kamikaze pilots, as suicide bombers, were on a mission to destroy the Allies at all costs. Their crashing of bomb-laden planes into Allied aircraft carriers and battleships killed many people and destroyed many ships, delaying the end of the war.)*

Draw Comparisons In what ways did the European and Pacific fronts differ? *(Answers will vary. The European front was fought mostly on land. The Pacific theater was predominantly fought from the sea and the air. The European front did not have kamikaze pilots, and the Pacific did.)*

Analyze Context The text states that President Truman may have been thinking about post-war relations with the Soviet Union when he made the decision to drop the atomic bombs on Japan. What about the relationship of the United States and the Soviet Union might have concerned Truman? *(Possible response: He was aware of profound differences between the values of the West and of the communist Soviet Union and probably foresaw future conflicts.)* What message may he have been trying to communicate to Stalin and other Soviet leaders? *(Possible response: that the U.S. possessed a powerful new weapon it was prepared to use to defend its interests against an enemy)*

Objective 4: Describe the aftermath of World War II and the founding of the United Nations.

Quick Instruction
Interactive Timeline: Key Events of World War II in Europe and the Pacific Project the timeline on the whiteboard and click through the draggable tiles. Introduce the timeline by telling students that key events, known as turning points, were significant events that changed the direction of the war in favor of the Allies. Ask students to match the draggable tiles with their correct place in history on the timeline.

📺 ACTIVE CLASSROOM
Have students us the Wallpaper strategy to review the information they have learned. Each student should design a piece of "wallpaper" that encapsulates key learnings. The wallpaper is posted. Students then take a gallery/"wisdom" walk and note what others have written/illustrated. Students can jot down ideas as they occur. A video can be made of the wisdom walk and posted on YouTube.

Further Instruction
Analyze Information Why was the United Nations established? How do the original mission of the United Nations and its mission today differ? *(Sample response: The original purpose of the United Nations in 1945 was to maintain peace. As the number of members increased, the UN's mission expanded to include preventing the outbreak of disease, improving education, protecting refugees, and helping nations manage their new independence and develop economically.)*

Synthesize Why are there only five permanent member countries on the United Nations Security Council? Why were these nations chosen? Would these same five nations be chosen today? Why or why not? *(Sample response: The five nations that sit on the Security Council are the United States, Soviet Union (now Russia), Britain (now United Kingdom), France, and China. These members were the victors in World War II and key in the creation of the United Nations. It was also thought they would be helpful in maintaining international peace and security. Some students will note that Britain and France are no longer as powerful as they were following the war and could be replaced by Japan and Germany, or by other large developing countries such as Brazil or India.)*

INTERACTIVE TIMELINE
Key Events of World War II in Europe and the Pacific

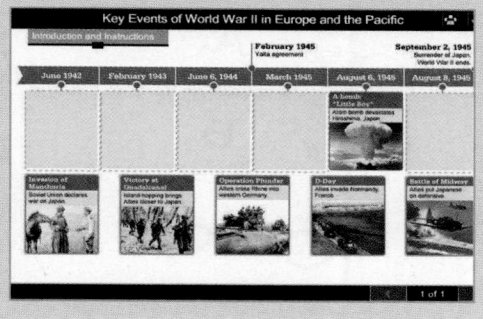

SYNTHESIZE

DIGITAL ACTIVITY
Victory in the Pacific

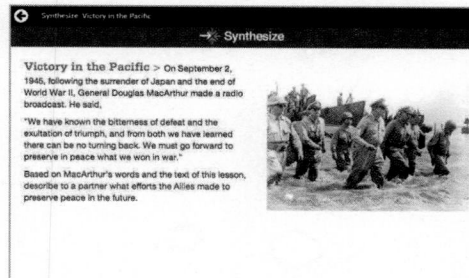

Have students form small groups to answer the question in the Victory in the Pacific activity. Ask them to brainstorm and take five minutes to write down brief answers to the following questions:

Do you think the creation of the United Nations will contribute to a more stable world? What approach do you think war-ravaged countries will take to rebuild their social, economic, and political structures? Have the groups present their answers to the class.

Discuss Have students describe what they believe governments can do to promote peace among nations. *(Answers may vary, but students may say that governments need good government officials to be role models, need to address people's needs, and need to establish policies that promote peace.)*

DEMONSTRATE

LESSON QUIZ
Lesson Quiz and Classroom Discussion Board

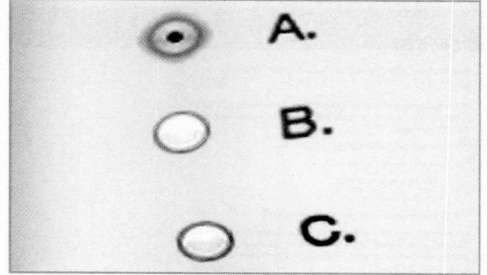

Assign the online Lesson Quiz for this lesson if you have not already done so. Students will be offered automatic remediation or enrichment based on their score.

In Victory for the Allies, you learned that to win World War II, it took an all-out commitment of resources and strategies. The timeline describes some key events of the war in the Pacific, but there are other notable events. It took two years from the time Japan attacked Pearl Harbor to the significant turning point in the Pacific, defeating the Japanese at Guadalcanal. The small advances of the island-hopping strategy brought the Allies within range of Japan.

Pose the question below to the class on the Discussion Board.

Predict Consequences Consider what you have read about World War II. Do you believe that after the war's end, the Allies will continue to be allies? Or will differences in values and goals cause them to break apart? Give reasons for your answer. *(Answers will vary, but most students will be aware that significant social, political, and economic differences between the United States and the Soviet Union led to the Cold War.)*

Topic Inquiry
Have students continue their investigations for the Topic Inquiry.

World War II (1930–1945)

◼ SYNTHESIZE

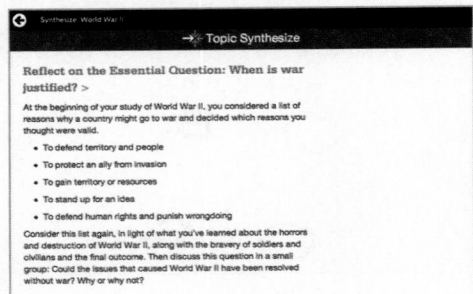

DIGITAL ACTIVITY

Reflect on the Essential Question and Topic

Ask students to recall the Topic Essential Question, "When Is War Justified?" Remind students of the justifications for war they considered at the start of the Topic.

- To defend territory and people
- To fulfill obligations to allies
- To gain territory or resources
- To defend human rights and punish wrongdoing

Ask students to consider this list again, in light of what they've learned about the causes that led to the war, the human toll, and the final outcome. Then have small groups discuss this question: Could the issues that caused World War II have been resolved without war? Why or why not?

Ask them to give at least three reasons to support their position. Discuss their answers as a class.

Next, ask students to reflect on the Topic as a whole. Have them review the list of reasons why a country might go to war. Ask them to choose one of the main combatants in the war (the U.S., Great Britain, France, Germany, the Soviet Union, or Japan) and write a paragraph explaining which reason(s) applies to the country's entry into the war. Share this example: Japan went to war to ensure a supply of vital natural resources for its industrial development. Japan's military leader also believed that Japan should rule an empire in East Asia and the Pacific.

Have volunteers share their paragraphs with the class, focusing on as many of the combatants as possible. Discuss issues that arise from the paragraphs.

Topic Inquiry

Have students complete Step 3 of the Topic Inquiry.

◼ DEMONSTRATE

DIGITAL TOPIC REVIEW AND ASSESSMENT

World War II (1930–1945)

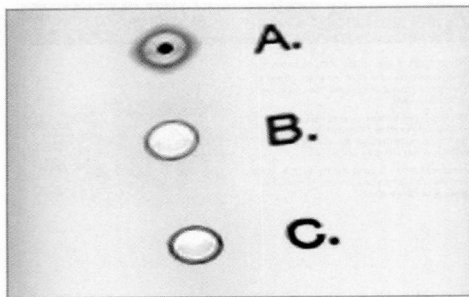

Students can prepare for the Topic Test by answering the questions in the Topic Review and Assessment online or the Assessment questions in the Print Student text. They can also prepare by reviewing their answers to the Interactive Reading Notepad questions or reviewing their notes in the Reading and Notetaking Study Guide.

DIGITAL TOPIC TEST

World War II (1930–1945)

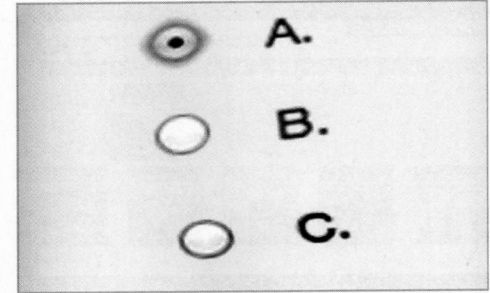

TOPIC TEST

Assign the Topic Test to assess students' understanding of topic content.

BENCHMARK TESTS

Assign these benchmark tests as you complete the relevant topics to monitor student progress toward mastering the course content and as preparation for the End-of-Course Test.

Benchmark Test 1: Topics 1–5

Benchmark Test 2: Topics 6–10

Benchmark Test 3: Topics 11–15

Benchmark Test 4: Topics 16–21

The Cold War Era (1945–1991)

TOPIC 19 ORGANIZER	PACING: APPROX. 8 PERIODS, 4 BLOCKS	
		PACING
Connect		1 period
 **MY STORY VIDEO** Gabriele Hayes, Remembering the Cold War		10 min.
DIGITAL ESSENTIAL QUESTION ACTIVITY How Should We Handle Conflict?		10 min.
DIGITAL TIME LINE ACTIVITY The Cold War Era		10 min.
TOPIC INQUIRY: CIVIC DISCUSSION The Cold War		20 min.
Investigate		2–5 periods
TOPIC INQUIRY: CIVIC DISCUSSION The Cold War		Ongoing
LESSON 1 A New Global Conflict		30–40 min.
LESSON 2 The Western Democracies and Japan		30–40 min.
LESSON 3 Communism in East Asia		30–40 min.
LESSON 4 War in Southeast Asia		30–40 min.
LESSON 5 The Cold War Ends		30–40 min.
Synthesize		1 period
DIGITAL ACTIVITY Reflect on the Essential Question and Topic		10 min.
TOPIC INQUIRY: CIVIC DISCUSSION The Cold War		20 min.
Demonstrate		1–2 periods
DIGITAL TOPIC TEST The Cold War Era		10 min.
TOPIC INQUIRY: CIVIC DISCUSSION The Cold War		20 min.

TOPIC INQUIRY: CIVIC DISCUSSION

The Cold War

In this Topic Inquiry, students work in teams to examine different perspectives on this issue by analyzing several sources, arguing both sides of a Yes/No question, then developing and discussing their own point of view on the question: **Did the end of the Cold War make the world safer?**

STEP 1: CONNECT
Develop Questions and Plan the Investigation

Launch the Civic Discussion

Divide the class into groups of four students. Students can access the materials they'll need in the online course or you can distribute copies to each student. Read the main question and introduction with the students.

Have students complete Step 1 by reading the Discussion Launch and filling in Step 1 of the Information Organizer. The Discussion Launch provides YES and NO arguments on the main question. Students should extract and paraphrase the arguments from the reading in Step 1 of their Information Organizers.

Next, students share within their groups the arguments and evidence they found to support the YES and NO positions. The group needs to agree on the major YES and NO points and each student should note those points in their Information Organizer.

Resources
• Student Instructions   • Information Organizer   • Discussion Launch

⏻ PROFESSIONAL DEVELOPMENT

Civic Discussion
Be sure to view the Civic Discussion Professional Development resources in the online course.

STEP 2: INVESTIGATE
Apply Disciplinary Concepts and Tools

Examine Sources and Perspectives

Students will examine sources with the goal of extracting information and perspectives on the main question. They analyze each source and describe the author's perspective on the main question and key evidence the author provides to support that viewpoint in Information Organizer Step 2.

Ask students to keep in mind:

• **Author/Creator:** Who created the source? An individual? Group? Government agency?
• **Audience:** For whom was the source created?
• **Date/Place:** Is there any information that reveals where and when the source was created?
• **Purpose:** Why was the source created? Discuss with students the importance of this question in identifying bias.
• **Relevance:** How does the source support one argument or another?

Suggestion: Reading the source documents and filling in Step 2 of the Information Organizer could be assigned as homework.

Resources
• Student Instructions   • Information Organizer   • Source documents

STEP 3: SYNTHESIZE
Use Evidence to Formulate Conclusions

Formulate Compelling Arguments with Evidence

Now students will apply perspectives and evidence they extracted from the sources to think more deeply about the main question by first arguing one side of the issue, then the other. In this way students become more prepared to formulate an evidence-based conclusion on their own.

Within each student group, assign half of the students to take the position of YES on the main question and the others to take the position of NO. Students will work with their partners to identify the strongest arguments and evidence to support their assigned YES or NO position.

Present Yes/No Positions

Within each group, those assigned the YES position share arguments and evidence first. As the YES students speak, those assigned NO should listen carefully, take notes to fill in the rest of the Compelling Arguments Chart (Step 3 in Information Organizer) and ask clarifying questions.

When the YES side is finished, students assigned the NO position present while those assigned YES should listen, take notes, and ask clarifying questions. Examples of clarifyin questions are:

- I think you just said [x]. Am I understanding you correctly?
- Can you tell me more about [x]?
- Can you repeat [x]? I am not sure I understand, yet.

Suggestion: You may want to set a 5 minute time limit for each side to present. Provide a two-minute warning so that students make their most compelling arguments within the time frame.

Switch Sides

The students will switch sides to argue the opposite point of view. To prepare to present the other position, partners who first argued YES will use the notes they took during the NO side's presentation, plus add any additional arguments and evidence from the reading and sources. The same for students who first argued the NO position.

STEP 4: DEMONSTRATE
Communicate Conclusions and Take Informed Action

Individual Points of View

Now the students will have the opportunity to discuss the main question from their own points of view. To help students prepare for this discussion, have them reflect on the YES/NO discussions they have participated in thus far and fill in Step 4 of their Information Organizers.

After all of the students have shared their points of view, each group should list points of agreement, filling the last portion of Step 4 on their Information Organizers.

Reflect on the Discussion

Ask students to reflect on the civic discussion thinking about:

- The value of having to argue both the YES and NO positions.
- If their individual views changed over the course of the discussion and why.
- What they learned from participating in the discussion.

Resources

- Student Instructions
- Information Organizer

INTRODUCTION

The Cold War Era

Following the Allied victory in World War II, conflicts quickly increased among some of the victors. The rivalry between the United States and Soviet Union turned into a "cold war" in which the two superpowers and their allies competed for global influence. Communism and political oppression spread, nuclear arsenals grew, and actual wars broke out, notably in Korea and Vietnam. All played a role in raising tensions. Finally, however, the Cold War ended in 1989 with the collapse of the Soviet Union and the breakup of its empire.

■ CONNECT

MY STORY VIDEO

Gabriele Hayes, Remembering the Cold War

Watch a video where a former resident of East Germany tells about life behind the Iron Curtain during the Cold War.

Check Understanding What is the goal of the museum where Gabriele Hayes works? *(The museum is dedicated to the study of the Cold War.)*

Apply Concepts What was the symbolic importance of the destruction of the Berlin Wall? *(The Berlin Wall had symbolized the divide between the communist East and the democratic West during the Cold War. Its destruction signaled the end of the Cold War.)*

↑↓ FLIP IT!

Assign the My Story video.

DIGITAL ESSENTIAL QUESTION ACTIVITY

How Should We Handle Conflict?

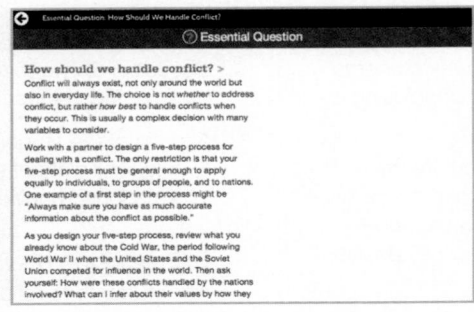

Ask students to think about the Essential Question for this Topic: How should we handle conflict? If students have not already done so, ask them to finalize their five-step processes. Then have volunteers read their steps. Discuss the results as a class.

Predict Consequences How would your five-step process work in action? Predict what might happen if two people, groups, or nations found themselves in a conflict. *(Answers will vary, but should show an understanding of both the five-step-process students have created and the ways people would likely react in a conflict situation.)*

Compare and Contrast Exchange your process with another pair. Discuss how your processes are alike and how they are different. Would a conflict likely be resolved in the same way using these two processes, or would a different result be probable? *(Discussions will vary. Pairs may find that some steps are similar while others are different; it is possible that students will find that similar outcomes will result from different five-step processes.)*

Support Ideas with Evidence How would you test the effectiveness of your five-step process for resolving conflict? *(Suggestions will vary; most students will offer a testing scenario involving individuals or local groups.)*

DIGITAL TIMELINE ACTIVITY

The Cold War Era

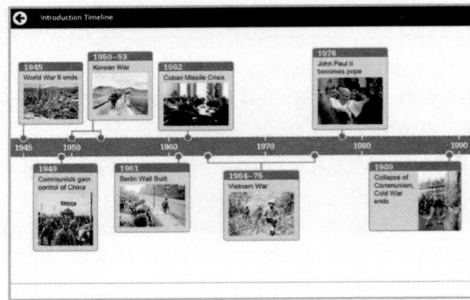

Display the time line showing the major events of the Cold War era. In this topic, students will learn about all of these events and many more, but this time line will provide a framework into which they can place the events they learn about.

D Differentiate: Extra Support Ask a volunteer to point out the time intervals on the time line and the overall range of time covered. *(1945–1989, 44 years)* Ask: How many years are there between John Paul II becoming pope and the fall of communism? *(11)*

Check Understanding In what year did the Korean War end? *(1953)*

Topic Inquiry

Launch the Topic inquiry with students after introducing the Topic.

A New Global Conflict

Supporting English Language Learners

Use with Digital Text 1, **Wartime Alliance Breaks Apart.**

Learning Strategies
Help students use their own prior experiences about relationships to help them understand how the relationships among world leaders changed following WWII.

Beginning Ask students to recall a time when their relationship with someone changed. Explain that when world leaders begin to disagree, their relationships change. Then read *Wartime Alliance Breaks Apart* aloud to students and have them follow along in their texts as you read. Ask students to complete the following: Similar to _____ my relationship changed because of _____.

Intermediate Ask students to recall a time when their relationship with someone changed and share their experience with a small group. Ask them to speculate about the types of relationships that world leaders have with one another. Read *Wartime Alliance Breaks Apart* aloud to students and have them follow along in their texts as you read. Then ask students to name any similarities between their own experiences and those of Stalin, Churchill, and Roosevelt.

Advanced Ask students to recall a time when one of their relationships changed and share their experience with a partner. Have them speculate about the types of relationships that world leaders have with one another. Then have pairs read *Wartime Alliance Breaks Apart* together. Ask students to discuss how their own relationship experiences are similar to those of Stalin, Churchill, and Roosevelt.

Advanced High Ask students to write about a time when one of their relationships changed. Then have students add on to their writing by speculating about the types of relationships that world leaders have with one another. Have pairs read *Wartime Alliance Breaks Apart* together. Facilitate a large group discussion about why relating to historical figures can improve their ability to understand historical events.

Use with Digital Text 3, **Two Opposing Sides in Europe.**

Writing
Explain to students that recognizing and using spelling rules can help them prevent spelling errors in their writing. Read *Two Opposing Sides in Europe* aloud to the class. Have students complete the activities below according to their level of English proficiency.

Beginning Explain that adding a suffix to a base word follows certain spelling rules. In some cases, the base word remains unchanged, as in *power-ful* and *prosper-ity*. In other cases, however, the spelling of the base word must change when a suffix is added, as in *early + -est = earliest*. Explain that adding a suffix that begins with a vowel to a word that ends in *y* requires that the *y* be changed to an *i* before the suffix is added. Help students come up with other words that fit this rule.

Intermediate Explain that adding a suffix to a base word follows certain spelling rules. In some cases, the base word remains unchanged, as in power-ful and prosper-ity. In other cases, however, the spelling of the base word must change when a suffix is added. Show students the word earliest and ask them to underline the base word and circle the suffix. Then show them this expression: *early + -est = earliest*. Make sure they understand that the *y* was changed to an *i* before the suffix *-est* was added. Help students come up with other words that fit this rule.

Advanced Have students work in pairs to explain how to add a suffix to a word. Ask pairs to skim *Two Opposing Sides in Europe* to look for words with suffixes. Have pairs list these words, then separate them into their base words and suffixes. Ask pairs write a set of rules for adding suffixes to words. Finally, instruct students to work together to combine pairs' rules into a single set of rules for adding suffixes.

Advanced High Have students skim the text to make a list of words with suffixes. Have students separate the words into their base words and suffixes. Ask students to write a set of rules for adding suffixes to words. Finally, instruct students to work together to combine pairs' rules into a single set of rules for adding suffixes.

▣ Differentiate Instruction

Use the Differentiated Instruction notes throughout the lesson plan to support the varied skill sets, levels of readiness, and interests in the mixed-ability classroom.

Challenge These notes include suggestions for expanding the activity for advanced students.

On-Level These notes include suggestions for modifying the activity to address different interests or learning styles.

Extra Support These notes include ideas for providing more scaffolding or reading spuport.

Special Needs These notes provide ideas for adapting instruction to support the needs of various special needs students.

■ NOTES

A New Global Conflict

Objectives

Objective 1: Summarize how the outcome of World War II contributed to the development of the Cold War.

Objective 2: Identify continuing Cold War conflicts in Germany and Eastern Europe.

Objective 3: Explain the growth of the nuclear arms race.

Objective 4: Analyze how the Cold War became a global conflict.

Objective 5: Compare the United States and the Soviet Union in the Cold War.

LESSON 1 ORGANIZER	PACING: APPROX. 1 PERIOD, .5 BLOCKS			
			RESOURCES	
	OBJECTIVES	PACING	Online	Print
Connect				
DIGITAL START UP ACTIVITY **The Berlin Wall**		5 min.	●	
Investigate				
DIGITAL TEXT 1 **Wartime Alliance Breaks Apart**	Objective 1	10 min.	●	●
DIGITAL TEXT 2 **Soviet Aggression Grows**	Objective 2	10 min.	●	●
DIGITAL TEXT 3 **Two Opposing Sides in Europe**		10 min.	●	●
DIGITAL TEXT 4 **The Nuclear Arms Race**	Objective 3	10 min.	●	●
INTERACTIVE GALLERY **Cold War Technologies**		10 min.	●	
DIGITAL TEXT 5 **The Cold War Around the World**	Objective 4	10 min.	●	●
INTERACTIVE GALLERY **The Cuban Missile Crisis**		10 min.	●	
DIGITAL TEXT 6 **The Soviet Union During the Cold War**	Objective 5	10 min.	●	●
DIGITAL TEXT 7 **The United States in the Cold War**		10 min.	●	●
Synthesize				
DIGITAL ACTIVITY **Actions and Consequences of the Cold War**		5 min.	●	
Demonstrate				
DIGITAL QUIZ **Lesson Quiz and Class Discussion Board**		10 min.	●	

PEARSON realize™
www.PearsonRealize.com

Go online to access additional resources including:
Primary Sources • Biographies • Supreme Court cases •
21st Century Skill Tutorials • Maps • Graphic Organizers.

■ CONNECT

DIGITAL START UP ACTIVITY
The Berlin Wall

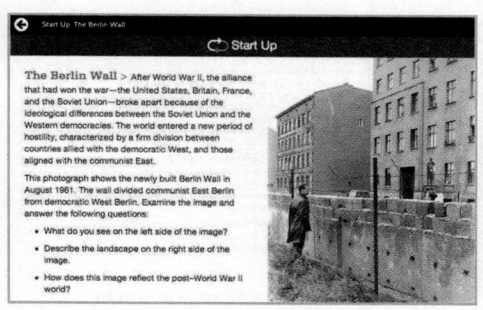

Project the Start Up Activity Ask students to answer the questions as they get settled. Then have students share their ideas with another student.

Discuss Why do you think the East Berlin government wanted to separate East Berlin from West Berlin? What do you think it would be like to live in a city that was suddenly separated by barbed wire, concrete walls, and guard posts? Are there any circumstances in which a separation would be justified? *(Sample responses: 1) to keep people from interacting or escaping; 2) Difficult. The wall could cut you off from friends and relatives like living in a war zone; 3) if people on one side were going to get hurt by people on the other)*

Aa **Vocabulary Development:** Use the Interactive Reading Notepad to preview the Key Terms and Academic Vocabulary in this lesson with students.

⇅ FLIP IT!
Assign the Flipped Video for this lesson.

■ STUDENT EDITION PRINT
PAGES: 774–782

■ INVESTIGATE

DIGITAL TEXT 1
Wartime Alliance Breaks Apart

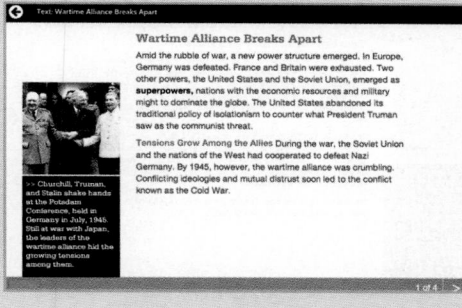

Objective 1: Summarize how the outcome of World War II contributed to the development of the Cold War.

Quick Instruction
Project the image of the Big Three (WWII Allied leaders) at Potsdam. Ask students what they remember about the Soviet Union's system of government. *(communist dictatorship)* How is that different from the system in the United States? *(representative democracy).* Ask students what kept the alliance together during WWII. *(unity against the Nazis)* Then project the map of the Warsaw Pact and NATO alliances. Ask students to list NATO and Warsaw Pact countries, either orally as a class or in group work.

Infer Ask students to answer this question in small groups: Was the Cold War inevitable? *(Answers will vary, but most students will say yes, based on the differences in the governmental systems and strategic goals.)*

ELL Use the ELL activity described in the ELL chart.

Further Instruction
Ask students to answer question 2 in the Interactive Reading Notepad: How did Stalin make sure that the eastern part of Europe came under Soviet influence? *(by leaving Soviet armies as occupying forces in Eastern European countries after the war)* Then, break students into small groups and ask them to address this question: Did Stalin's approach with Eastern European nations fit with his earlier policies? *(Answers will vary, but students should mention his purges, his treatment of the peasants, his imprisonment of opponents, and other actions.)*

Editable Presentation Use the Editable Presentation to present the main ideas for this Core Text.

A New Global Conflict

DIGITAL TEXT 2

Soviet Aggression Grows

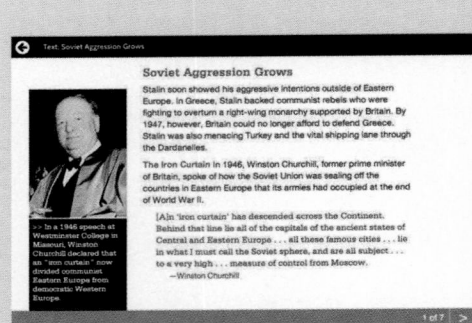

DIGITAL TEXT 3

Two Opposing Sides in Europe

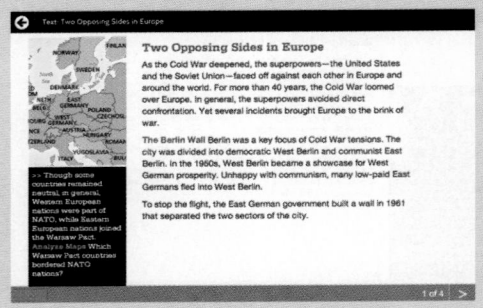

DIGITAL TEXT 4

The Nuclear Arms Race

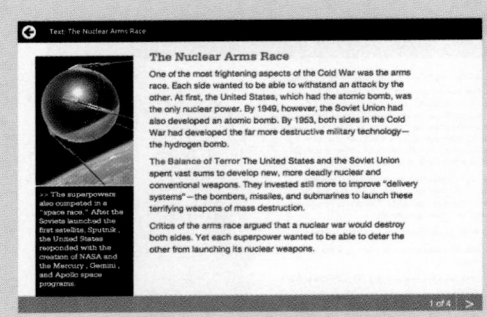

Objective 2: Identify continuing Cold War conflicts in Germany and Eastern Europe.

Quick Instruction

Project the map of NATO and Warsaw Pact countries. Ask students why they think Winston Churchill called the division of Europe the "Iron Curtain," and what the symbolism of each of those words might be. *(iron for force; curtain for dividing; Eastern Europe was now shut off from the rest of the world)* Remind students of the way the Soviets had taken control of the countries behind the Iron Curtain. *(by force)* How do you think the Soviets will continue to keep control of these countries? *(by force)*

Analyze Information Remind students of the countries that resisted Soviet rule in the 1950s and 1960s. *(East Germany, Hungary, Czechoslovakia)* Then, ask students to fill out the graphic organizer in question 8 of the IRN. *(East Germany, Reaction: Workers confronted Red Army street demonstrations in cities of East Germany; Soviet Response: Soviet Army tanks. Hungary, Reaction: Imre Nagy ended communist one-party rule. Threatened to pull out of Warsaw Pact; Soviet Response: Massive military assault. Czechoslovakia, Reaction: Freedoms introduced by Czechoslovakian government; Soviet Response: Massive military assault.)*

ELL Use the ELL activity described in the ELL chart.

Further Instruction

Project and discuss the Interactive Reading Notepad questions. Then, remind students of the events of the Berlin Airlift. List these on the board. Ask students to answer questions 5 and 6 in the IRN. *(Sample response: 5. The Soviet Union cut off all roads and railroads through East Germany to West Berlin. This isolated the residents of West Berlin. The United States and its allies responded by airlifting supplies to West Berlin. The Soviets ended the blockade after a year. 6. They closed off the road through East Germany that connected West Germany to West Berlin.)* Ask students to write a short paragraph describing what it would have been like to live in Berlin during the airlift. Have them share their paragraphs with the class.

Infer Ask students to answer the following question: Why do you think the Eastern Europeans continued to resist communist rule? *(Answers will vary; most students will conclude that Eastern Europeans wanted more freedom, both economic and political, and didn't want to be ruled by another country.)*

Objective 3: Explain the growth of the nuclear arms race.

Quick Instruction

Interactive Gallery: Cold War Technologies Project the Interactive Gallery, and have students read the captions as a class. Tell them that the competition between the two superpowers during the Cold War resulted in many advances in technology, including military technology. Explain that many of these changes still affect our daily lives.

ACTIVE CLASSROOM

Review the gallery images, and then project the infographic on the arms race. Have students break into groups, and provide a key question based on information in the table. Have students use the Circle Write strategy to write as much as they can for one minute, and then switch with the person on their right. The next person tries to improve or elaborate on the response where the other person left off. Continue to switch until the paper comes back to the first person. The group then decides which is the best composition (or response) and shares that with the larger group. Break students into pairs, and ask each student to write a question based on the data in the table. Have partners trade questions with each other and then answer them.

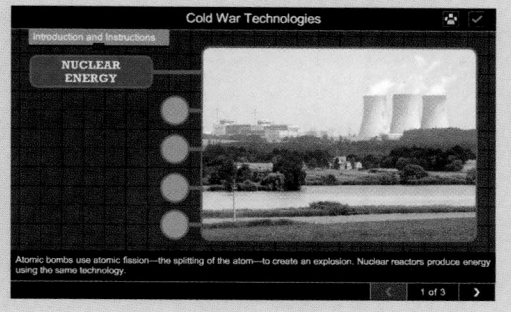

INTERACTIVE GALLERY
Cold War Technologies

DIGITAL TEXT 5
The Cold War Around the World

INTERACTIVE GALLERY
The Cuban Missile Crisis

Further Instruction

Ask students which of the inventions in the Interactive Gallery they believe had the greatest impact and have them explain why. Group students by which invention they thought was most influential. Have students meet in their groups and write a group statement, combining the ideas of each student. Tell them to select one student to present their statement to the class. After all presentations, discuss the inventions as a class.

Objective 4: Explain how the Cold War became a global conflict.

Quick Instruction

Ask students to define the term "Cold War." *(a war between two superpowers who never faced each other directly, only indirectly through local allies)* Tell them that they will be studying times when the Cold War got "hot" later in the topic, but that during the Cuban Missile Crisis, the two superpowers came closest to direct conflict with each other.

Interactive Gallery: The Cuban Missile Crisis Project the Interactive Gallery and go through the events as a class. Tell students that for one week, a tense confrontation brought the world to the brink of nuclear war. Ask students to answer the question for the activity either as a class, in small groups, or individually.

👥 ACTIVE CLASSROOM

Break students into groups and have them use the Graffiti Concepts strategy. Ask them to reflect on the meaning of the Cuban Missile Crisis and create a visual image and/or phrase that represents that event. Allow approximately three to five minutes. Have students post their "graffiti" on the board or on chart paper, and ask them to look at the various responses. Then discuss similarities and differences in the responses as a group.

D Differentiate: Challenge/Gifted Ask students to write a series of diary entries of a character they create who was living in the United States, Europe, or Cuba during the Cuban Missile Crisis. Tell them to use the events in the Interactive Gallery and think about how the character they create would have reacted to these events.

Further Instruction

The Cold War Spreads: Core Text and Interactive Reading Notepad Project and discuss the Interactive Reading Notepad questions, including the graphic organizer asking students to identify Cold War hotspots. Review the hotspots with the class and fill in the graphic organizer on the whiteboard as you go.

Summarize Why did the Cold War go global? *(The two superpowers were competing with each other; if one superpower gained influence, the other wanted to counter that influence.)*

A New Global Conflict

DIGITAL TEXT 6

The Soviet Union During the Cold War

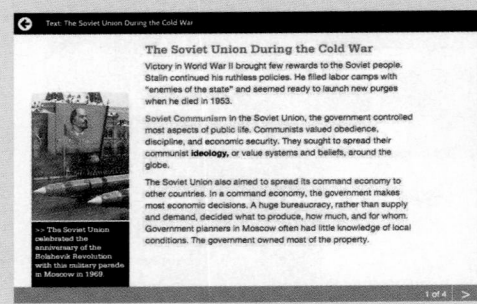

The Soviet Union During the Cold War

Victory in World War II brought few rewards to the Soviet people. Stalin continued his ruthless policies. He filled labor camps with "enemies of the state" and seemed ready to launch new purges when he died in 1953.

Soviet Communism In the Soviet Union, the government controlled most aspects of public life. Communists valued obedience, discipline, and economic security. They sought to spread their communist **ideology**, or value systems and beliefs, around the globe.

The Soviet Union also aimed to spread its command economy to other countries. In a command economy, the government makes most economic decisions. A huge bureaucracy, rather than supply and demand, decided what to produce, how much, and for whom. Government planners in Moscow often had little knowledge of local conditions. The government owned most of the property.

>> The Soviet Union celebrated the anniversary of the Bolshevik Revolution with the military parade in Moscow in 1969

1 of 4 >

DIGITAL TEXT 7

The United States in the Cold War

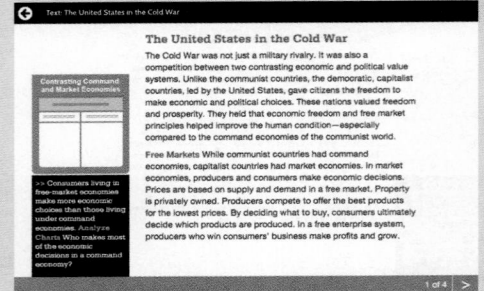

The United States in the Cold War

The Cold War was not just a military rivalry. It was also a competition between two contrasting economic and political value systems. Unlike the communist countries, the democratic, capitalist countries, led by the United States, gave citizens the freedom to make economic and political choices. These nations valued freedom and prosperity. They held that economic freedom and free market principles helped improve the human condition—especially compared to the command economies of the communist world.

Free Markets While communist countries had command economies, capitalist countries had market economies. In market economies, producers and consumers make economic decisions. Prices are based on supply and demand in a free market. Property is privately owned. Producers compete to offer the best products for the lowest prices. By deciding what to buy, consumers ultimately decide which products are produced. In a free enterprise system, producers who win consumers' business make profits and grow.

>> Consumers living in free-market economies make more economic choices than those living under command economies. **Analyze Charts** Who makes most of the economic decisions in a command economy?

1 of 4 >

Objective 5: Compare the United States and the Soviet Union in the Cold War.

Quick Instruction

Project the image of a military parade in Red Square from the text. Ask students to remember how the Soviets gained power in Eastern Europe. *(by force)* Ask: How did the United States support its allies after WWII? *(through the Marshall Plan and other economic support)* Ask them to list Eastern European revolts against the Soviets. *(East Germany, 1954; Hungary, 1956; Czechoslovakia, 1968)* How did the Soviets keep the members of the Warsaw Pact loyal? *(through force, threats of force, and intimidation)* Explain to students that the difference between the Soviet Union's political system *(communist dictatorship)* and the system in the United States *(representative democracy)* dictated the different ways in which the two superpowers dealt with their allies. Ask students to formulate generalizations about how economic freedom helped improve the human condition. *(It allowed people choice and provided opportunity, both in the economic and political realms. It promoted prosperity and growth. It rewarded effort and success.)*

Further Instruction

Project an image of the HUAC hearings. Break students into small groups. Assign half of the groups to write a short summary of how the United States acted during the Cold War. Assign the other half to write a short summary of how the Soviet Union acted during the Cold War. Make sure summaries address domestic and foreign actions. As a class, discuss this question: How were the United States and the Soviet Union similar in their actions during the Cold War? *(Both spied on one another; both sent disloyal people to prison; both stockpiled nuclear weapons; both sought allies all over the world and countered the other's gains.)* How were they different? (Make sure that students understand that dissidents like Andrei Sakharov faced punishment when the criticized the Soviet government.) *(The Soviet Union didn't allow people to speak freely and imprisoned people for years for speaking out; it also repressed any revolt against communist governments; the United States had greater freedoms and supported its allies with economic aid.)*

■ SYNTHESIZE

DIGITAL ACTIVITY
Actions and Consequences of the Cold War

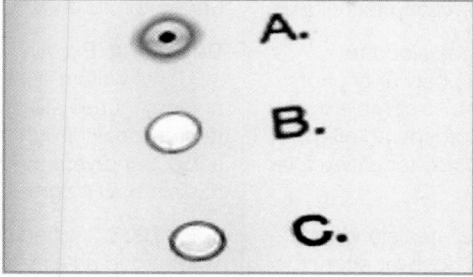

Ask students to fill in the graphic organizer on Cold War actions and consequences. Time constraints will limit the number of answers students can list. Answers to the question will vary. Students should use the evidence from their table.

Interpret Ask students to answer this question: Who benefited most from the events of the Cold War? Why? Cite evidence from the chart. *(Answers will vary. Students may suggest the U.S., Soviet Union, Eastern Europe, or Western Europe, but should support their answers with evidence from the text.)*

■ DEMONSTRATE

DIGITAL QUIZ
Lesson Quiz and Class Discussion Board

Assign the online quiz for this lesson if you haven't already done so. Students will be offered automatic remediation or enrichment based on their score.

In "A New Global Conflict," you read about the tensions that drove the World War II allies apart and led to the beginning of the Cold War. The Cold War was rooted in the competing value systems and world views of the United States and the Soviet Union and their allies. Pose these questions on the Class Discussion Board.

Support a Point of View with Evidence
Was the United States right to try to contain communism? Why or why not?

Analyze Information Were arms control agreements necessary? Were they successful in meeting their goals?

Topic Inquiry
Have students continue their investigations for the Topic Inquiry.

The Western Democracies and Japan

Supporting English Language Learners

Use with Digital Text 1, **Postwar Prosperity in the United States.**

Learning Strategies

Read aloud or have students read *Postwar Prosperity in the United States.* Then have them describe American prosperity in their own words, helping them improve their speaking skills by practicing self-correcting techniques.

Beginning Read *Postwar Prosperity in the United States* aloud to students. Then create a concept web on the American postwar economy. Ask students to use the information on the concept web to complete the following sentence frame: The American economy prospered after World War II because _____. Support students by repeating their answers back to them and correcting any errors.

Intermediate Read *Postwar Prosperity in the United States* aloud to students. Then create a concept web on the American postwar economy. Ask students to explain why the United States became an economic leader after WWII. Support students by repeating their answers back to them, then correcting their errors.

Advanced Have students read *Postwar Prosperity in the United States.* Ask students to explain why the United States became an economic leader after WWII to a partner. Have partners repeat answers back to each other, correcting any speaking or grammatical errors.

Advanced High Have students read *Postwar Prosperity in the United States.* Ask them to work in small groups to discuss why the United States became an economic leader after WWII. Instruct group members to correct others' grammatical pronunciation, and word use errors. Circulate among students to offer support.

Use with Digital Text 2, **The United States Responds to New Challenges.**

Writing

Read *The United States Responds to New Challenges* aloud to the class. Have students complete the activities below according to their level of English proficiency.

Beginning Explain that the subject and verb in each sentence that students write must follow a pattern of agreement. The subject-verb agreement rule still applies when a sentence uses helping verbs in the past tense. Highlight the following examples from the text. Underline the subject and verb in each sentence. Help students circle the helping verb. Explain how it agrees with the subject.

- By 1956, a gifted preacher, Dr. Martin Luther King, Jr., had/have emerged as a leader of the civil rights movement.
- However, some was/were elected to political office or gained top jobs in business or the military.

Intermediate Explain that the subject and verb in each sentence that students write must follow a pattern of agreement. Review the subject-verb agreement rule and apply it to sentences written in the past tense that also use helping verbs. Highlight the following examples from the text. Have students underline the subject and verb in each sentence. Then have students circle the correct helping verb. Explain how it agrees with the subject.

- By 1956, a gifted preacher, Dr. Martin Luther King, Jr., had/have emerged as a leader of the civil rights movement.
- However, some was/were elected to political office or gained top jobs in business or the military.

Advanced Explain that the subject and verb in each sentence that students write must follow a pattern of agreement. Review the subject-verb agreement rule and apply it to sentences written in the past tense that also use helping verbs. Have pairs of students locate examples in the text. Pairs should write out their example sentences and underline the subject and verb in each sentence. Then have pairs explain how the verb agrees with the subject.

Advanced High Remind students that the subject and verb in each sentence must follow a pattern of agreement. Review the subject-verb agreement rule and apply it to sentences written in the past tense that also use helping verbs. Have students locate examples of past tense subject-verb agreement in the text. Students should write out their example sentences and underline the subject and verb in each sentence. Then have students to explain how the verb agrees with the subject.

PEARSON realize.
www.PearsonRealize.com

Go online to access additional resources including:
Primary Sources • Biographies • Supreme Court cases •
21st Century Skill Tutorials • Maps • Graphic Organizers.

Objectives

Objective 1: Analyze the postwar American economy.

Objective 2: Identify developments in American society and government.

Objective 3: Explain how Western Europe rebuilt and moved toward greater unity.

Objective 4: Describe how Japan changed after World War II.

LESSON 2 ORGANIZER		PACING: APPROX. 1 PERIOD, .5 BLOCKS			
				RESOURCES	
		OBJECTIVES	**PACING**	**Online**	**Print**
Connect					
DIGITAL START UP ACTIVITY **Historical Connections**			5 min.	●	
Investigate					
DIGITAL TEXT 1 **Postwar Prosperity in the United States**		Objective 1	10 min.	●	●
INTERACTIVE GALLERY **Suburbanization in Postwar America**			10 min.	●	
DIGITAL TEXT 2 **The United States Responds to New Challenges**		Objective 2	10 min.	●	●
DIGITAL TEXT 3 **Rebuilding Western Europe**		Objective 3	10 min.	●	●
INTERACTIVE CHART **Free Market Economy v. Command Economy**			10 min.	●	
DIGITAL TEXT 4 **Japan Is Transformed**		Objective 4	10 min.	●	●
Synthesize					
DIGITAL ACTIVITY **Rebuilding West Germany and Japan**			5 min.	●	
Demonstrate					
DIGITAL QUIZ **Lesson Quiz and Class Discussion Board**			10 min.	●	

The Western Democracies and Japan

▪ CONNECT

DIGITAL START UP ACTIVITY
Historical Connections

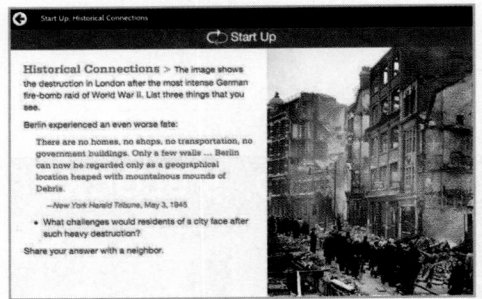

Project the Start Up Activity Ask students to answer the question as they get settled. Then have students share their ideas with another student.

Discuss What challenges would residents of a city face after such heavy destruction? *(Answers will vary. Bombed-out abandoned buildings; piles of rubble; no services)*

Aa Vocabulary Development: Use the Interactive Reading Notepad to preview the Key Terms and Academic Vocabulary in this lesson with students.

> ⇅ **FLIP IT!**
> Assign the Flipped video for this lesson.

▪ STUDENT EDITION PRINT PAGES: 783–790

▪ INVESTIGATE

DIGITAL TEXT 1
Postwar Prosperity in the United States

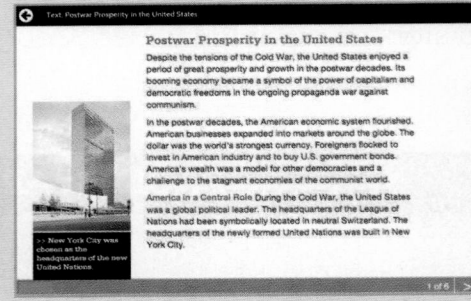

INTERACTIVE GALLERY
Suburbanization in Postwar America

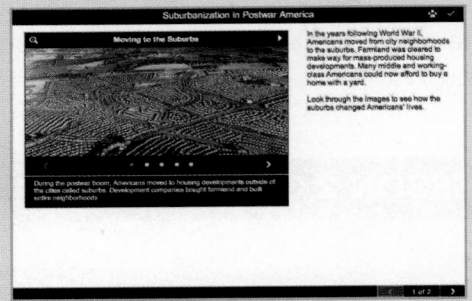

Objective 1: Analyze the postwar American economy.

Quick Instruction

Interactive Gallery: Suburbanization in Postwar America Project the Interactive Gallery, and run through the images. Have students read the captions. Ask them to answer the question as a class, in small groups, or individually. Ask students to discuss how the images represent developments in American society and government in the post-World War II era, such as the growth of suburbs, the desire to escape crowded and unhealthy city neighborhoods, the expansion of the highway system, the growing dependence on cars for transportation rather than public transportation, and the growth of large shopping centers.

> **👥 ACTIVE CLASSROOM**
>
> Use the Take a Stand strategy. Ask students to take a stand on the following statement: American society was changed for the better during the 1950s. Have students divide into two groups based on their position and move to separate areas of the classroom. Tell them to talk with each other to compare their reasons for their position. Ask a representative from each side to present and defend the group's point of view.

ELL Use the ELL activity described in the ELL chart.

Further Instruction

Editable Presentation Use the Editable Presentation to present the main ideas for this Core Text.

Project the image of the UN building from the text. Ask students to give some examples of the new role for the United States after WWII. *(The UN, the World Bank, and the International Monetary Fund [IMF] were all headquartered in the United States. The United States played a leading economic role in the postwar period.)* Break students into small groups. Ask them to think about the role the United States plays in the world now. Ask each group to come up with a list of positive effects of our leadership role in the world and a list of negative effects. *(Answers will vary, but positives will include strong alliances, strong military, strong role in policy making for the world; negatives might include terrorist attacks and the cost of having to intervene all over the world as in Iraq and Afghanistan.)* List positives and negatives on the board and discuss them as a class.

DIGITAL TEXT 2

The United States Responds to New Challenges

>> Segregated drinking fountain were a common sight in the southern states.

DIGITAL TEXT 3

Rebuilding Western Europe

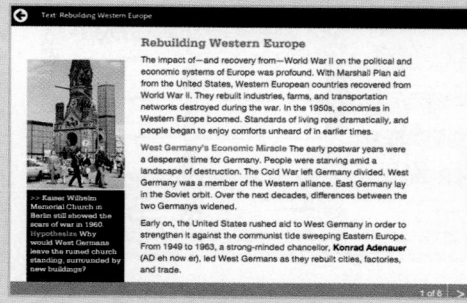

>> Kaiser Wilhelm Memorial Church in Berlin still showed the scars of war in 1960. Hypothesize Why would West Germans leave the ruined church standing, surrounded by new buildings?

Objective 2: Identify developments in American society and government.

Quick Instruction

Analyze Images Project the image of the civil rights march from the text. Draw a T-chart on the whiteboard. Ask students what people in these marches were protesting for? *(voting rights, equal pay, end to discrimination, end to segregation)* List these issues under Civil Rights on one side of the T-chart. Ask students if they know of any other protest movements. *(They may mention women's rights, women's suffrage, Latino rights, or other social movements. As an example, list Women's Rights on the other side of the T-chart.)* Remind students that women also fought for the vote in the early 20th century, and for equal pay and an end to discrimination in the 1970s. Add this information to the T-chart.

D Differentiate: **Challenge/Gifted** Have students read the "Letter from Birmingham Jail," the "I Have a Dream" speech, and the biography of Dr. Martin Luther King, Jr. Ask them to write a question they would've liked to ask King. As part of a class discussion, have the class answer the questions written by the students.

ELL Use the ELL activity described in the ELL chart.

Further Instruction

The United States Responds to New Challenges Core Text and Interactive Reading Notepad Project and discuss the Interactive Reading Notepad questions. Ask students to answer question 4 in the IRN. What is the difference between discrimination and segregation? *(Segregation is a form of legal discrimination involving separation of the races, such as in education or housing. Discrimination on its own is unfair or unequal treatment, or barriers.)* Divide students into small groups. Ask each group to brainstorm about other groups that experienced discrimination. *(Latinos, Asians, people with disabilities, Native Americans)* Ask groups to come up with two different ways in which people could protest against discrimination today, besides protest marches. *(Answers will vary, but students may come up with using boycotts, social media, and other ways of raising awareness.)*

Objective 3: Explain how Western Europe rebuilt and moved toward greater unity.

Quick Instruction

Interactive Chart: Free Market Economy v. Command Economy Ask students what type of economy we have in the United States. *(free market, free enterprise, capitalism)* Then, ask them what type of economy existed in communist countries. *(command economy)* Project the infographic on life in East Germany versus West Germany. On the whiteboard, make a T-chart. List characteristics of a free-enterprise economic system. *(Individuals own businesses; there is competition and choice; the free market decides prices; the economy can have recessions; there are no guaranteed jobs.)* Next, list characteristics of command economic systems. *(Government makes most economic decisions, there are guaranteed jobs, no private property.)* Project the Interactive Chart, Free-Market Economy v. Command Economy. Perform the activity as a class, and then ask students to answer the question as a class, in small groups, or individually.

The Western Democracies and Japan

INTERACTIVE CHART
Free Market Economy v. Command Economy

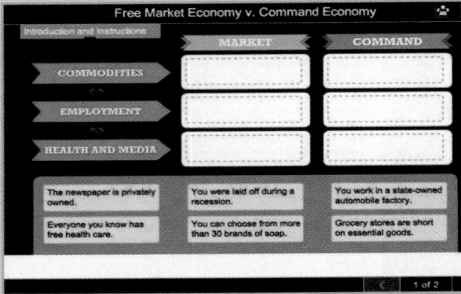

DIGITAL TEXT 4
Japan Is Transformed

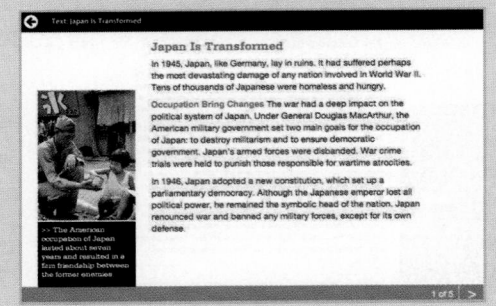

☙ ACTIVE CLASSROOM

Use the Circle Write strategy. Project the images of the suburban house and the council estate housing in the UK from the text. Break students into groups of four and ask them to sit in a circle. One student will respond to this prompt: America's rebuilding after WWII was different from Western Europe's rebuilding because _____. Have students write as much as they can for one minute, and then switch papers with the person on their right. The next person tries to improve or elaborate on the response where the other person left off. Continue to switch until the paper comes back to the first person. The group can then decide which is the best composition (or response) and share it with the larger group.

Further Instruction

Project the Interactive Reading Notepad questions. Remind students of the goals of the welfare state. *(to give aid to the poor and needy and to provide an economic cushion to help people get through difficult times)* Ask students to answer question 11 in the IRN. In the graphic organizer, list the services provided by the welfare state and the costs of those services. *(Welfare State Services: national health care, unemployment insurance, old-age pensions; Welfare State Costs: high taxes, government regulation of private enterprise)*

Next, tell students that by 1979, Britain and the rest of Europe faced economic hard times. Britain's Conservative party, led by Margaret Thatcher, won power and set out to roll back the welfare state by privatizing industries, cutting back on services, and reducing the size of government. Ask: Why would Thatcher make these choices? *(to cut back on government spending)* Then, ask students to write a paragraph summarizing the positive and negative aspects of the welfare state. *(Paragraphs will vary, but may mention free or low-cost services and high tax rates.)*

Objective 4: Describe how Japan changed after the war.

Quick Instruction

Project the image of Japanese factory workers from the text. Ask students how World War II ended in Asia. *(with the dropping of atomic bombs on Hiroshima and Nagasaki)* Explain that the United States then helped rebuild Japan during the occupation and helped set up a democratic political system and a free-enterprise economic system. Next, ask students what Japan manufactures today. *(Most students will say cars and motorcycles; some will say TVs, other electronics, or movies.)*

Further Instruction

Project the Interactive Reading Notepad questions. Ask students to answer questions 12 and 13. *(Answers: 12. education for all, equality for women, land reform, rebuilding cities and industry; 13. low cost of defense, efficient factories, skilled workforce, high tariffs)* Break students into pairs. Ask one student in each pair to brainstorm benefits to the Japanese of the rebuilding after World War II. *(new factories, democratic systems, rights for women)* Ask the other to brainstorm benefits of the continuing relationship with the United States. *(supplying defense, markets for their products)* Ask each pair to answer the following question: How did Japan change after the war?

SYNTHESIZE

DIGITAL ACTIVITY

Rebuilding West Germany and Japan

Have students fill out the graphic organizer with details of how the United States helped rebuild West Germany and Japan after WWII. Then discuss the following questions.

Draw Conclusions What were the benefits to the United States in helping West Germany and Japan rebuild after WWII? What were some disadvantages? *(Benefits: creating new markets for U.S. trade goods, creating strong allies against the Soviet bloc, promoting democracy; Disadvantages: creating formidable trade rivals, taking on the cost of defending these nations)*

DEMONSTRATE

DIGITAL QUIZ

Lesson Quiz and Class Discussion Board

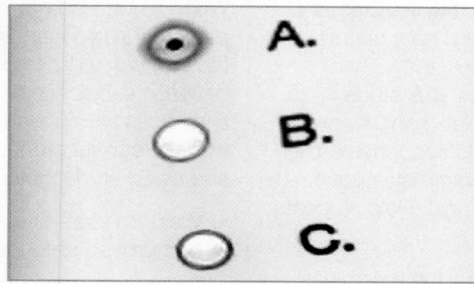

Assign the online quiz for this lesson if you haven't already done so. Students will be offered automatic remediation or enrichment based on their score. Pose these questions to the class on the Class Discussion Board:

Synthesize What are the strengths and weaknesses of the welfare state?

Evaluate Is Japan right to keep high tariffs on imported goods?

Topic Inquiry

Have students continue their investigations for the Topic Inquiry.

Communism in East Asia

Supporting English Language Learners

Use with Digital Text 3, **The Two Koreas.**

Learning Strategies

Read *The Two Koreas*. Then help students improve their writing skills by using the steps of the writing process to write about the relationship between North and South Korea.

Beginning Before beginning this activity, list and display the five stages of the writing process for students. Explain each stage and tell students that they will practice the first stage of the process in this activity. Then retell *The Two Koreas* in accessible language for students. Ask students to participate in brainstorming ideas for writing about the relationship between North Korea and South Korea. Write and display students' responses. Then review the list and have students vote on their favorite topic. Ask students to identify which stage of the writing process should come next. Help students develop an introductory sentence for their chosen topic.

Intermediate Before beginning this activity list and display the five stages of the writing process for students. Guide students as they explain each stage. Tell students that they will work in small groups to complete the first three stages of the process in this activity. Then reread *The Two Koreas* for students. Ask small groups to brainstorm how to write about the relationship between North Korea and South Korea. Have one student in each group write down students' responses and ask students to review and vote on their favorite topic. Monitor small groups as they organize and write a draft for their paragraphs. Then instruct each small group to trade paragraphs with another small group to review the drafts that have been written. After paragraphs have been reviewed and returned to their original group, have students make revisions to their first drafts. Support students throughout this process by circulating among groups to offer writing support whenever necessary.

Advanced Working in pairs, have students brainstorm, draft, revise, edit and proofread, and publish a paragraph or two on the relationship between North Korea and South Korea. Pairs can compare and contrast North and South Korea with East and West Germany or simply compare and contrast North Korea and South Korea. Instruct pairs to keep a record of each stage of the writing process to turn in with their final, published paragraph.

Advanced High Have students brainstorm, draft, revise, edit and proofread, and publish a paragraph or two on the relationship between North Korea and South Korea. Students can compare and contrast North and South Korea with East and West Germany or simply compare and contrast North Korea and South Korea. Instruct students to keep a record of each stage of the writing process to turn in with their final, published paragraph.

Use with Digital Text 2, **China and the Cold War.**

Writing

Read *China and the Cold War* aloud to the class. Have students complete the activities below according to their level of English proficiency.

Beginning Explain to students that pronouns take the place of nouns. When a noun is singular, the pronoun is singular. When a noun is in the first person, the pronoun will also be in the first person. If a noun is possessive, the pronoun will also be possessive. Make sure to explain the differences between subject and object pronouns. Write and display the following sentences for students. Show them how to replace the underlined nouns with the correct pronoun. Then repeat the procedure with new sentences and assist students as they replace nouns with correct pronouns.

- Western fears of a strong alliance between the Soviet Union and China had proved unfounded.
- Jiang Jieshi's government continued to rule Taiwan under martial law as a one-party dictatorship.

Intermediate Remind students of the rules that govern pronoun use in English. Then write and display the following sentences for students. Help them replace the underlined nouns with the correct pronoun. Then repeat the procedure with new sentences.

- Western fears of a strong alliance between the Soviet Union and China had proved unfounded.
- Jiang Jieshi's government continued to rule Taiwan under martial law as a one-party dictatorship.

Advanced Remind students of the rules that govern pronoun use in English. Then ask students to work in pairs to write two sentences about China's role in the Cold War. Once the sentences have been written, have students replace the nouns in the sentences with the correct pronoun. Have each pair join with another pair to check their work.

Advanced High Remind students of the rules that govern pronoun use in English. Then ask students to write four sentences about China's role in the Cold War. Once the sentences have been written, have students replace the nouns in the sentences with the correct pronoun. Have students turn to a partner to share their sentences and check their work.

◨ Differentiate Instruction

Use the Differentiated Instruction notes throughout the lesson plan to support the varied skill sets, levels of readiness, and interests in the mixed-ability classroom.

Challenge These notes include suggestions for expanding the activity for advanced students.

On-Level These notes include suggestions for modifying the activity to address different interests or learning styles.

Extra Support These notes include ideas for providing more scaffolding or reading spuport.

Special Needs These notes provide ideas for adapting instruction to support the needs of various special needs students.

◼ NOTES

Objectives

Objective 1: Analyze how Mao Zedong turned China into a communist state.

Objective 2: Describe China's role in the Cold War.

Objective 3: Explain the causes and impact of the Korean War.

LESSON 3 ORGANIZER	PACING: APPROX. 1 PERIOD, .5 BLOCKS			
			RESOURCES	
	OBJECTIVES	PACING	Online	Print
Connect				
DIGITAL START UP ACTIVITY **Defining Governments**		5 min.	●	
Investigate				
DIGITAL TEXT 1 **The Chinese Communist Victory**	Objective 1	10 min.	●	●
INTERACTIVE GALLERY **Communism in China**		10 min.	●	
DIGITAL TEXT 2 **China and the Cold War**	Objective 2	10 min.	●	●
DIGITAL TEXT 3 **The Two Koreas**	Objective 3	10 min.	●	●
INTERACTIVE MAP **The Korean War**		10 min.	●	
Synthesize				
DIGITAL ACTIVITY **Who Benefits from a People's Republic?**		5 min.	●	
Demonstrate				
DIGITAL QUIZ **Lesson Quiz and Class Discussion Board**		10 min.	●	

Communism in East Asia

■ CONNECT

DIGITAL START UP ACTIVITY
Defining Governments

Project the Start Up Activity Ask students to answer the questions as they get settled. Then have students share their ideas with another student.

Discuss What do you think a "People's Republic" would be? Give an example of a policy from a "People's Republic." *(Answers will vary. They should include the participation of the people in the government (elections making of laws and policies). A "People's Republic" should include policies that benefit all the people, including human and political rights.)*

Aa Vocabulary Development: Use the Interactive Reading Notepad to preview the Key Terms and Academic Vocabulary in this lesson with students.

⮌ FLIP IT!
Assign the Flipped Video for this lesson.

■ STUDENT EDITION PRINT
PAGES: 791–795

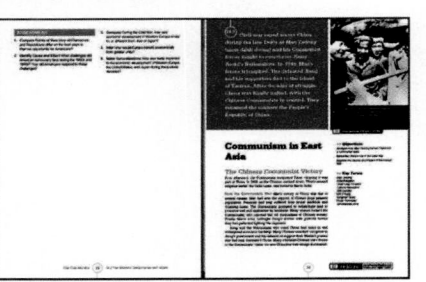

■ INVESTIGATE

DIGITAL TEXT 1
The Chinese Communist Victory

INTERACTIVE GALLERY
Communism in China

Objective 1: Analyze how Mao Zedong turned China into a communist state.

Quick Instruction
Project the Interactive Gallery and have students read the captions as a class. Ask students to answer the two questions as a class, in small groups, or individually. Make sure students understand that Mao had won the support of China's huge peasant population. Nationalist policies had led to widespread economic hardship. Many Chinese people also resented corruption in Jiang's government and the government's reliance on support from Western "imperialist" powers.

📽 ACTIVE CLASSROOM
Use the Make Headlines strategy. Project images from the Interactive Gallery of the Cultural Revolution poster and the poster revering Mao. Divide students into pairs. Have students write a headline that captures the main idea in one of the posters. Ask: If you were to write a headline for this topic right now that captures the most important aspect that should be remembered, what would that headline be? Pass your headline to a partner for him or her to review.

D Differentiate: Extra Support What do you think the word *commune* means in this sentence? "In an attempt to make agriculture more efficient, he created communes." Ask students to think of other words that sound like *commune*. *(community, common)* Have them discuss the meanings of similar words and then figure out the meaning of *commune*.

Further Instruction
Editable Presentation Use the Editable Presentation to present the main ideas for this Core Text.

Discuss Project the Interactive Reading Notepad questions. Break students up into small groups. Have them answer question 2 from the IRN: "What happened to opponents of the Communist Party in China?" *(They were persecuted, accused of being "counter-revolutionary," sent to labor camps, and/or killed.)* Make sure students recognize that communist leaders committed politically motivated mass murder in China. Now, ask them to remember back to earlier in this topic and other topics, and have them answer the following question: "What happened to opponents of the Communist Party in the Soviet Union?" Bring the class together to discuss the question, "What do our observations of the Soviet Union and China show us about communist states?"

DIGITAL TEXT 2
China and the Cold War

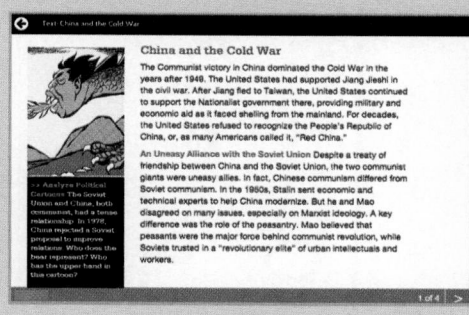

Objective 2: Describe China's role in the Cold War.

Quick Instruction
Project the image of Nixon in China from the text. Ask students to recall the U.S. position on the spread of communism. (The Truman Doctrine said that the United States should oppose communism and support anti-communist movements around the world; the United States supported NATO governments economically to resist communism in Western Europe, and it opposed the Cuban communist revolution.) "Ask them why they think the United States would engage with a communist country." Remind them of the phrase, "my enemy's enemy is my friend." Then, explain that in the 1970s, the United States backed China against the Soviet Union because U.S. leaders felt the Soviets were a greater threat.

ELL Use the ELL activity described in the ELL chart.

Further Instruction
Make Decisions Remind students of the complex relationship between China and the Soviet Union. (ancient territorial disputes; Soviet Union provided economic and technical aid to China, but disputes led to estrangement) Remind students also how communism in China differed from communism in the Soviet Union. (Mao and Stalin differed ideologically over the role of the peasantry, whom Mao trusted, compared to urban intellectuals, whom Stalin believed would propel the revolution.) Now, ask students to characterize the U.S. relationship with the Soviet Union. (Responses will vary, but most students will say the nations distrusted each other.) Ask them why they think the United States would engage with a communist country. Remind them of the phrase, "my enemy's enemy is my friend." (The United States engaged with the Chinese against the Soviets, who were a greater threat; the United States benefited from the friction between China and the Soviet Union and considered China "the enemy of my enemy," therefore a possible friend.) Break students into small groups and ask them to discuss the following question: Do you agree with the U.S. decision to recognize China and bring it into the UN? Remind them to reflect on China's history. If time allows, bring the class together for a group discussion.

DIGITAL TEXT 3
The Two Koreas

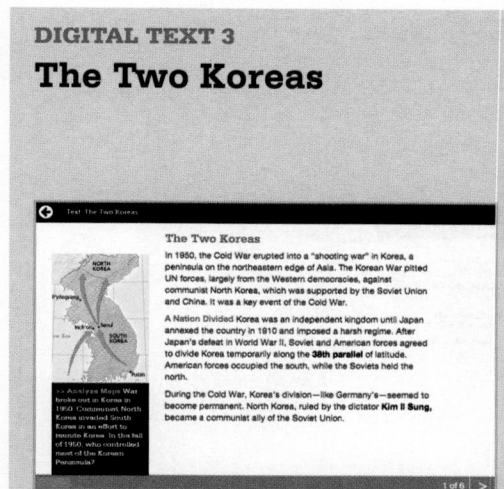

Objective 3: Explain the causes and impact of the Korean War.

Quick Instruction
Interactive Map: The Korean War Make sure students understand that the Korean War was a key event of the Cold War. Project the Interactive Map and run through the layers as a class, asking students to read the captions. Then, have them answer the question as a class, in small groups, or individually. What risk did the UN forces run when they invaded North Korea in 1950? (They risked that China, newly communist, would invade if they got too close to the Yalu River, the Korean border with China; the Chinese did invade, supporting the North Koreans and prolonging the war.)

📷 ACTIVE CLASSROOM

Use the Make Headlines strategy. Project the image of North Korea at night and the image of Seoul at night. Have students write a headline that captures the most important aspect that should be remembered for each. Have them present their headlines to the class. As a class, discuss what the images represent about the differences between the communist/command and democratic/capitalist systems.

ELL Use the ELL activity described in the ELL chart.

Communism in East Asia

 **SYNTHESIZE** **DEMONSTRATE**

INTERACTIVE MAP

The Korean War

DIGITAL ACTIVITY

Who Benefits from a People's Republic?

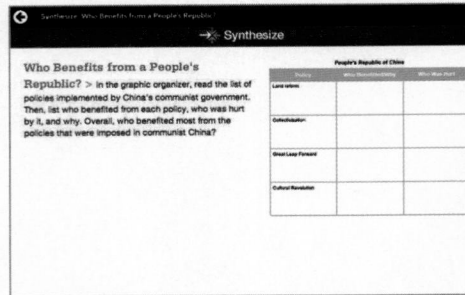

DIGITAL QUIZ

Lesson Quiz and Class Discussion Board

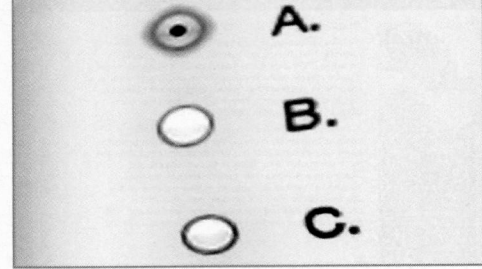

Further Instruction

Compare Ask students to answer question 8 in the IRN: How would you describe Kim Il Sung as a leader? Give specific evidence from the text. *(Answers will vary, but students might say words like "stubborn" [stuck with communism], "full of himself", "prideful" [glorified himself], or "self-absorbed" [built a personality cult around himself].).* Now, ask: How is he similar to Mao Zedong? *(Both were revered by their people, and both were dictators and very self-absorbed.)*

Have students fill out the graphic organizer, listing specific policies of Communist China, who benefited from the policies, and who was hurt by them.

Explain Who benefited from the policies in North Korea? Who was hurt? *(The leaders benefited; the people were hurt.)*

Make Generalizations Based on this example, who benefits most from communism? *(the party and the leaders, not the people)*

Assign the online quiz for this lesson if you haven't already done so. Students will be offered automatic remediation or enrichment based on their score. Pose these questions to the class on the Class Discussion Board:

Make Generalizations Were Mao Zedong's initial goals of the Communist Revolution in China fulfilled? *(Answers will vary, but students may say yes, because Mao won the support of the large peasant population by redistributing land and ending oppression by landlords.)*

Cite Evidence Was the United Nations' intervention in Korea worthwhile? Explain your answer with information from the text. *(Answers will vary, but students may say no, because North Korea is still communist and poses a threat to the United States today. Or they may answer yes, because the UN intervention kept communism out of South Korea.)*

Topic Inquiry

Have students continue their investigations for the Topic Inquiry.

War in Southeast Asia

Supporting English Language Learners

Use with Digital Text 2, **The United States Enters the War.**

Learning Strategies

Read aloud or have students read *The United States Enters the War*. Then have students learn how to use a strategic learning technique by creating a concept map of the U.S. involvement in Vietnam.

Beginning Write "U.S. involvement in the Vietnam War" in the center circle of a concept map on the board. Then reread the text aloud to students and model identifying important details to add to the concept map. Add these details and connect them to the main circle with lines. Then have students provide additional details for the map as you continue reading the text.

Intermediate Write "U.S. involvement in the Vietnam War" in the center circle of a concept map on the board. Then reread the text aloud to students and have students identify important details to add to the concept map. Add these details and connect them to the main circle with lines.

Advanced Have students work with a partner to develop a concept map of U.S. involvement in the Vietnam War. Instruct them to write "U.S. involvement in the Vietnam War" in the center circle of their concept map. Have pairs reread the text and identify important details to include in their maps. When student pairs have completed the maps, have them share them with the group.

Advanced High Tell students that they will develop a concept map of U.S. involvement in the Vietnam War. Instruct them to write "U.S. involvement in the Vietnam War" in the center circle of their concept map. Have students review the text and identify important details to include in their maps. When students have completed the maps, have them share them with a partner and add any missing information as needed.

Use with Digital Text 1, **The Road to War in Southeast Asia.**

Writing

Read *The Road to War in Southeast Asia* aloud to the class. Have students complete the activities below according to their level of English proficiency.

Beginning Explain to students that verb tenses let a reader know when an action is occurring: in the past, present, or future. Point out that in history texts, much of the writing is in the past tense. It is important for verb tenses to agree within a sentence. Help students choose the best verb tense in the sentences below.

- The French (conquered / conquered / will conquer) Indochina during the 1800s.
- Southeast Asia (played / plays / will play) an important role in the Cold War.

Intermediate Remind students that verb tenses let a reader know when an action is occurring: in the past, present, or future. Point out that in history texts, much of the writing is in the past tense. It is important for verb tenses to agree within a sentence. Work in small groups with students to write two sentences about *The Road to War in Southeast Asia* using the past tense.

Advanced Remind students that verb tenses let a reader know when an action is occurring: in the past, present, or future. Ask students to identify the verb tense that is used most in *The Road to War in Southeast Asia*. Make sure students notice that most of the writing in the text is in the past tense. Have students work with a partner to write three sentences about *The Road to War in Southeast Asia* using the past tense.

Advanced High Ask students to explain the purpose of using different verb tenses in different situations. Then ask students to identify the verb tense that is used most in *The Road to War in Southeast Asia*. Make sure students notice that most of the writing in the text is in the past tense. Have students write a short paragraph about *The Road to War in Southeast Asia* using the past tense.

▣ Differentiate Instruction

Use the Differentiated Instruction notes throughout the lesson plan to support the varied skill sets, levels of readiness, and interests in the mixed-ability classroom.

Challenge These notes include suggestions for expanding the activity for advanced students.

On-Level These notes include suggestions for modifying the activity to address different interests or learning styles.

Extra Support These notes include ideas for providing more scaffolding or reading spuport.

Special Needs These notes provide ideas for adapting instruction to support the needs of various special needs students.

▮ NOTES

_____

_____

_____

_____

_____

War in Southeast Asia

Objectives

Objective 1: Describe events in Indochina after World War II.

Objective 2: Explain how the United States became involved in the Vietnam War.

Objective 3: Explore the end of the Vietnam War.

Objective 4: Summarize the impact of the war on Vietnam and Cambodia.

LESSON 4 ORGANIZER			PACING: APPROX. 1 PERIOD, .5 BLOCKS		
				RESOURCES	
		OBJECTIVES	PACING	Online	Print
Connect					
DIGITAL START UP ACTIVITY **Fighting Communism in Vietnam**			5 min.	●	
Investigate					
DIGITAL TEXT 1 **The Road to War in Southeast Asia**		Objectives 1	10 min.	●	●
DIGITAL TEXT 2 **The United States Enters the War**		Objective 2	10 min.	●	●
INTERACTIVE TIMELINE **Vietnam, 1945–1965—From Independence Struggle to Cold War Battleground**			10 min.	●	
DIGITAL TEXT 3 **The Vietnam War Ends**		Objective 3	10 min.	●	●
INTERACTIVE GALLERY **Fighting a Different War**			10 min.	●	
Synthesize					
DIGITAL ACTIVITY **President Johnson's 1965 Defense of Involvement**			5 min.	●	
Demonstrate					
DIGITAL QUIZ **Lesson Quiz and Class Discussion Board**			10 min.	●	

■ CONNECT

DIGITAL START UP ACTIVITY

Fighting Communism in Vietnam

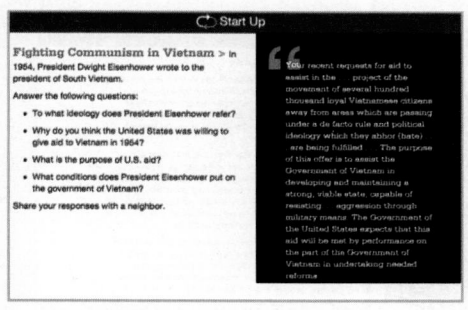

Project the Start Up Activity Ask students to answer the questions as they enter and get settled. Then have them share their ideas with another student.

Discuss To what ideology do you think President Eisenhower is referring? *(communism)* Why do you think the U.S. is willing to give aid to Vietnam in 1954? *(To contain the spread of communism.)* What is the purpose of U.S. aid? *(to develop a strong state that can resist communism)* What conditions does President Eisenhower put on the government of Vietnam? *(He requires them to enact reforms.)*

Aa Vocabulary Development: Use the Interactive Reading Notepad to preview the Key Terms and Academic Vocabulary in this Lesson with students.

⟲ FLIP IT!

Assign the Flipped Video for this lesson.

■ STUDENT EDITION PRINT
PAGES: 796–800

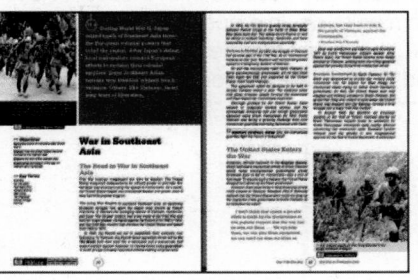

■ INVESTIGATE

DIGITAL TEXT 1

The Road to War in Southeast Asia

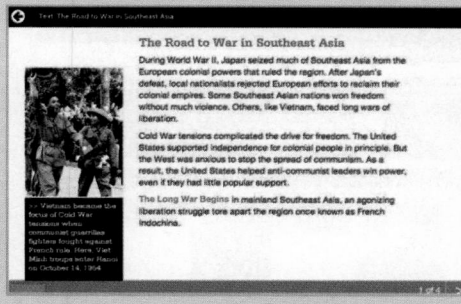

Objective 1: Describe events in Indochina after World War II.

Quick Instruction

Project the image of the Viet Minh fighters. Ask students what were the motivations behind the Russian, Chinese, and Cuban communist revolutions they have learned about? *(land, better living conditions, more responsive government, less power to a small elite)* Explain to them that the origins of the Vietnamese struggle were very different. *(The Vietnamese wanted their French colonial rulers to leave Vietnam and they wanted to be an independent nation.)*

ELL Use the ELL activity described in the ELL chart.

Further Instruction

Editable Presentation Use the Editable Presentation to present the main ideas for this Core Text.

Tell students that the struggle that became the Vietnam War was one of the key events of the Cold War. Remind students how this conflict started. Ask students why the French were in Indochina. *(It was part of their colonial empire.)* Now ask them, how would you categorize the conflict between the French and the Vietnamese? *(independence struggle)* Ask them for another example of such a conflict. *(Answers will vary but students might mention independence struggles in Africa or Latin America or the American colonists' conflict with the British.)* Now, divide students into small groups and have them brainstorm ways in which other colonial relationships might be similar to the

relationship between the relationship of the French and the Vietnamese. *(Responses will vary, but students may identify the long war, the fact that other nations got involved, that the Vietnamese lacked resources, and that the Vietnamese fought with guerrilla tactics; many of these conditions are similar to those in other independence struggles around the world.)*

War in Southeast Asia

The United States Enters the War

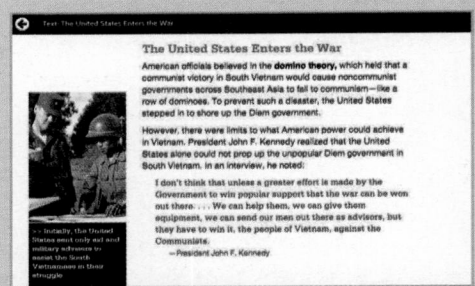

Vietnam, 1945–1965—From Independence Struggle to Cold War Battleground

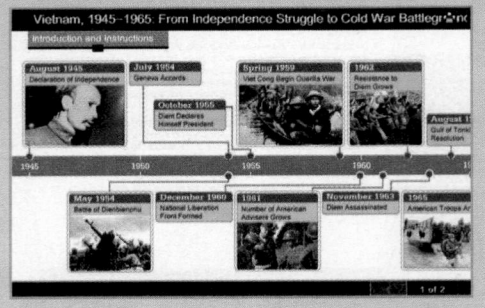

The Vietnam War Ends

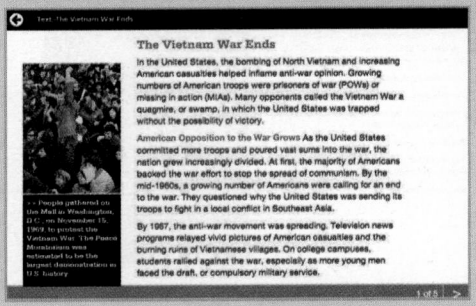

Objective 2: Explain how the United States became involved in the Vietnam War.

Quick Instruction

Interactive Timeline: Vietnam, 1945-1965—From Independence Struggle to Cold War Battleground Project the Interactive Timeline. Click through the timeline, reading the captions aloud. Have students answer the question as a class, in small groups, or individually.

> **📷 ACTIVE CLASSROOM**
>
> Ask students to Take a Stand on the following question: Should the United States get involved in the Vietnam War? Organize them into two groups based on their answer, and have them move to separate areas of the classroom. Ask students to talk with each other to compare their reasons for answering yes or no. Ask a representative from each side to present and defend the group's point of view.

ELL Use the ELL activity described in the ELL chart.

Further Instruction

Ask students to answer question 3 in the IRN: What events led to the American involvement in Vietnam? *(The United States supported the anticommunist Diem even though he was unpopular; U.S. leaders were responding to the domino theory; they sent in military supplies and advisers to help the South Vietnamese; after a U.S. ship was attacked in the Gulf of Tonkin, the president was authorized to commit ground troops)* Then, ask them to select one event they feel was the most important in the U.S. movement toward involvement in the Vietnam War and why. Ask them to share their response with a classmate.

Objective 3: Explore the end of the Vietnam War.

Quick Instruction

Interactive Gallery: Fighting a Different War Project the Interactive Gallery. Click through the images and have students read the captions. Ask students to answer the question as a class, in small groups, or individually. Have students respond to the following question: How did the challenges of fighting a war in Southeast Asia help the United States decide to leave Vietnam? *(Answers may mention that the Viet Cong's tactics, the terrain, and a seeming lack of progress all contributed to the decision to end the war.)* Then ask them to identify other factors that put pressure on U.S. leaders to end American involvement in the war. *(rising death toll, media coverage of casualties, the antiwar movement and domestic protests against the war, doubts about the justness of the war)*

> **📷 ACTIVE CLASSROOM**
>
> Use the Speaking with History strategy. Ask students to imagine they are having a conversation with one of the people in the visuals or text covered in this lesson. Have them write down a question they'd like to ask, then what that person would answer, and what students would say in response.

INTERACTIVE GALLERY
Fighting a Different War

D **Differentiate: Extra Support** Ask: what does the word *terminate* mean in the sentence: Johnson's successor, President Nixon, came under increasing pressure to terminate American involvement? Note that the word is a verb. Ask students what actions President Nixon was being pressured to take. Use this strategy to help students figure out what *terminate* means.

Further Instruction

Analyze Information Remind students of the situation in Vietnam in 1968. *(The Tet Offensive had changed the war.)* Now remind students of other events in 1968 in the United States. *(assassinations of Martin Luther King Jr. and Robert Kennedy; stormy Democratic National Convention)* List these on the board. Now, have students fill out the graphic organizer in question 6 in the IRN. Have them answer the question: "Do you think the United States made the right decision when it pulled out of Vietnam? Give at least two reasons for your answer. *(Answers will vary; evidence should come from the graphic organizer responses.)*

Cite Evidence Project the image of Khmer Rouge fighters. Explain to the students that these children were fighting in Cambodia and that the communist revolution in that country turned into a bloodbath, in which more than one million Cambodians were killed. Now, project image of the boat people. Ask students

if they know anyone of Vietnamese heritage. Explain that the boat people were Vietnamese who fled their country after the communists came to power, looking for freedom, safety, and economic opportunities. Ask students this question: What were the effects of the war in Southeast Asia on the people of that region? *(Some benefitted, such as those who supported the communists, but many did not or were very poor and fled to other countries to start a new life. Others had to endure harsh communist regimes.)*

Compare and Contrast Remind students of the background of the war in Cambodia *(The Ho Chi Minh Trail had run through Cambodia; the United States had bombed Cambodia to stop supplies from getting to the Viet Cong; later, Vietnam invaded Cambodia to prevent more atrocities by the Khmer Rouge.)* Explain that the mass murder committed by Pol Pot and the Khmer Rouge was politically motivated. Divide students into small groups and ask them to generate a list of the ways in which the experiences of the Cambodians and Vietnamese were similar. *(They both had communist regimes take over their countries; many of them fled to other countries; war left both countries desolated.)* How did they differ? *(The Khmer Rouge starved and tortured its own people and killed over one million of them; the Vietnamese fought a long civil war to liberate their country, with outside countries helping.)*

War in Southeast Asia

■ **SYNTHESIZE**

DIGITAL ACTIVITY

President Johnson's 1965 Defense of Involvement

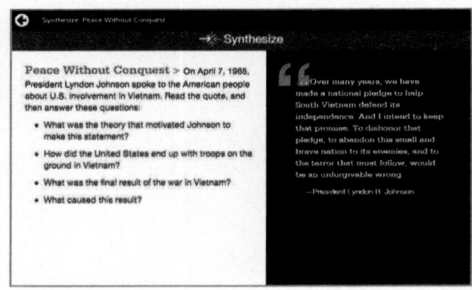

Project the Synthesize Activity and have students answer the questions.

Discuss What pressures for and against continued involvement did President Johnson face? *(Sample responses may point out that domestic factors such as the rising death toll, media coverage of casualties, war protests, and increasing doubts about the justness of the war pressured Johnson and American leaders to end U.S. involvement in the war, while loyalty to allies, fear of appearing weak toward communists, and domestic political pressures not to end involvement provided reasons to continue fighting.)*

■ **DEMONSTRATE**

DIGITAL QUIZ

Lesson Quiz and Class Discussion Board

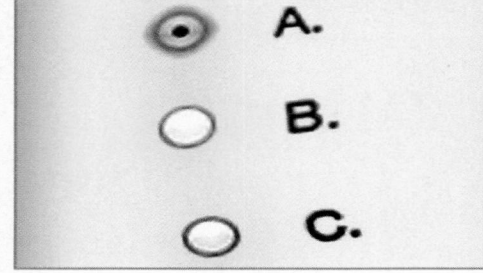

Assign the online quiz for this lesson if you haven't already done so. Students will be offered automatic remediation or enrichment based on their score. Pose these questions to the class on the Class Discussion Board:

Generate Explanations What did the United States gain or lose through its involvement in the Vietnam War? *(Sample response: It gained nothing and lost many soldiers.)*

Evaluate Arguments Should the United States have intervened when the Khmer Rouge gained power in Cambodia? *(Sample response: At the time, it needed to end its involvement in Southeast Asia. However, some might say that the Khmer Rouge was committing atrocities and should have been stopped for moral reasons.)*

Topic Inquiry
Have students continue their investigations for the Topic Inquiry.

The Cold War Ends

Supporting English Language Learners

Use with Digital Text 3, **Eastern Europe Transformed.**

Learning Strategies
Read aloud to students or have them read *Eastern Europe Transformed*. Have them identify unfamiliar words. Then have students use synonyms to help them understand how Eastern Europe changed in the late 20th century.

Beginning Reread the first paragraph of *Eastern Europe Transformed* aloud. Have students identify words they do not know, by completing the following: I'm not sure what _____ means. Use gestures or movements to illustrate the word so that students can come up with a synonym. Have students replace the unfamiliar word with the synonym to see if they now understand the meaning of the word.

Intermediate Reread the first paragraph of *Eastern Europe Transformed* aloud. Have students identify words they do not know and list them on the board. Have students work in small groups to use thesauruses or other resources to find as many synonyms for each word. Ask small groups to replace each target word with any of its synonyms, and discuss whether the meaning of the sentence remains the same.

Advanced Instruct pairs of students to reread *Eastern Europe Transformed* to identify words they do not know. Have pairs use their own vocabularies, thesauruses, or other resources to find as many synonyms for each word as possible. Ask pairs to replace each target word with any of its synonyms, and discuss whether the meaning of the sentence remains the same.

Advanced High Instruct students to reread *Eastern Europe Transformed* to identify words they do not know. Have students use their own vocabularies, thesauruses, or other resources to find as many synonyms for each word as possible. Then with a partner, have them share and compare lists. Ask them to replace each target word with its synonyms, and discuss its effect on the meaning of the sentence.

Use with Digital Text 1, **The Soviet Union Declines.**

Writing
Read *The Soviet Union Declines* aloud to the class. Have students complete the activities below according to their level of English proficiency.

Beginning Explain to students that there are more verb tenses than just past, present, and future. One such tense is the progressive verb tense. Explain that the past progressive tense lets a reader know that an action was in progress over a period of time. Use the following two sentences to demonstrate the difference between the simple past tense and the past progressive tense. Underline the verbs in both sentences and explain the difference between the two verb forms for students.

The arms race put an additional strain on the Soviet economy. By the 1980s, both superpowers were spending massive sums on costly weapons systems.

Intermediate Explain to students that the past progressive tense lets a reader know that an action that occurred in the past was in progress over a period of time. Use the following two sentences to demonstrate the difference between the simple past tense and the past progressive tense. Have students underline the verbs in both sentences. Help them identify and explain the difference between the two verb forms.

The arms race put an additional strain on the Soviet economy. By the 1980s, both superpowers were spending massive sums on costly weapons systems.

Advanced Remind students that the past progressive tense lets a reader know that an action that occurred in the past was in progress over a period of time. Have students work in small groups to review *The Soviet Union Declines*. Students should work together to find sentences in the past progressive tense. Have students write these sentences in their notes and underline the verb forms in each one. After they have identified these verb forms, have each group write two sentences of their own about the weaknesses of the Soviet Union using the past progressive tense. Then have small groups reconvene to discuss the sentences they found with the class.

Advanced High Remind students that the past progressive tense lets a reader know that an action that occurred in the past was in progress over a period of time. Have students work in pairs to review *The Soviet Union Declines*. Students should work together to find sentences in the past progressive tense. Have pairs write these sentences in their notes and underline the verb forms in each one. After they have identified these verb forms, have them write two sentences of their own about the weaknesses of the Soviet Union using the past progressive tense. Then have pairs reconvene to discuss the sentences they found with the class.

▣ Differentiate Instruction

Use the Differentiated Instruction notes throughout the lesson plan to support the varied skill sets, levels of readiness, and interests in the mixed-ability classroom.

Challenge These notes include suggestions for expanding the activity for advanced students.

On-Level These notes include suggestions for modifying the activity to address different interests or learning styles.

Extra Support These notes include ideas for providing more scaffolding or reading spuport.

Special Needs These notes provide ideas for adapting instruction to support the needs of various special needs students.

▮ NOTES

_____

_____

_____

_____

_____

The Cold War Ends

Objectives

Objective 1: Understand why the Soviet Union declined.

Objective 2: Identify the reforms introduced by Mikhail Gorbachev.

Objective 3: Describe the collapse of communism in Eastern Europe and the Soviet Union.

Objective 4: Evaluate how the end of the Cold War affected the remaining communist nations and the United States.

LESSON 5 ORGANIZER	PACING: APPROX. 1 PERIOD, .5 BLOCKS			
	OBJECTIVES	PACING	Online	Print
Connect				
DIGITAL START UP ACTIVITY **The Decline of the Soviet Union**		5 min.	●	
Investigate				
DIGITAL TEXT 1 **The Soviet Union Declines**	Objective 1	10 min.	●	●
INTERACTIVE MAP **The Fall of the Soviet Union**		10 min.	●	
DIGITAL TEXT 2 **The Soviet Union Collapses**	Objective 2	10 min.	●	●
DIGITAL TEXT 3 **Eastern Europe Transformed**	Objective 3	10 min.	●	●
INTERACTIVE TIME LINE **Fall of Communism in Soviet Bloc**		10 min.	●	
DIGITAL TEXT 4 **Communism Declines Around the World**	Objective 4	10 min.	●	●
DIGITAL TEXT 5 **The Post-Cold War World**		10 min.	●	●
Synthesize				
DIGITAL ACTIVITY **Pro-Reform and Anti-Reform Leaders**		5 min.	●	
Demonstrate				
DIGITAL QUIZ **Lesson Quiz and Classroom Discussion Board**		10 min.	●	

PEARSON realize™
www.PearsonRealize.com

Go online to access additional resources including:
Primary Sources • Biographies • Supreme Court cases •
21st Century Skill Tutorials • Maps • Graphic Organizers.

■ CONNECT

DIGITAL START UP ACTIVITY

The Decline of the Soviet Union

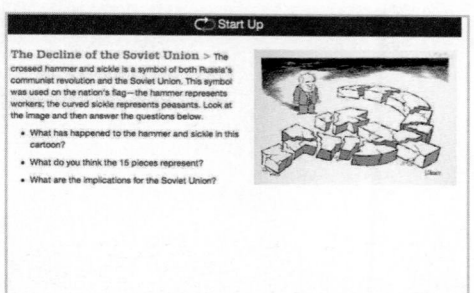

Project the Start Up Activity Ask students to answer the question and writing prompt as they enter and get settled. Then have students share their ideas with another student.

Discuss Explain that the hammer and sickle was the symbol of the Soviet Union. The hammer represents workers; the sickle represents farmers. What has happened to the hammer and sickle in this cartoon? What do you think this represents? What are the implications for the Soviet Union? *(The hammer and sickle are broken; the Soviet Union is breaking up; the Soviet Union would lose power in the world.)*

Aa Vocabulary Development: Use the Interactive Reading Notepad to preview the Key Terms and Academic Vocabulary in this lesson with students.

⬆⬇ FLIP IT!

Assign the Flipped Video for this lesson.

■ STUDENT EDITION PRINT PAGES: 801–806

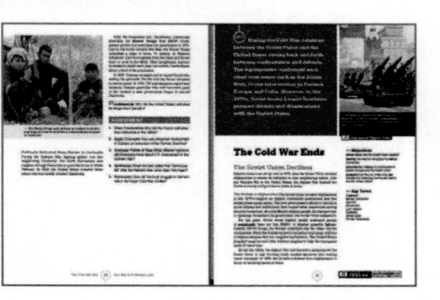

■ INVESTIGATE

DIGITAL TEXT 1

The Soviet Union Declines

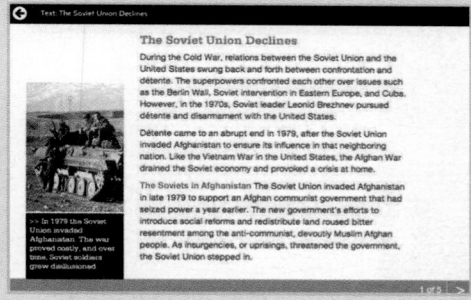

Objective 1: Understand why the Soviet Union declined.

Quick Instruction

Interactive Map: The Fall of the Soviet Union Project the Interactive Map. Point out that the Soviet Union reaches from the Black and Baltic Seas in the west, to the Pacific Ocean in the east and south, to its borders with Afghanistan and China. Then, slide to the second map (1992). Ask students to list all the countries that used to be part of the Soviet Union. Explain that the Soviet Union broke up because of political repression, the stagnation of the command economy, rebellions against Soviet domination of Eastern Europe, extensive military commitments, and failure to win a war in Afghanistan. Point out how geography—for example, the sheer size of the Soviet Union—contributed to its collapse. *(The vast area included people of many different ethnic groups and interests, who desired self-determination and rebelled against authoritarian rule.)*

Draw Conclusions Ask students to identify elements of the command economy. *(The state makes all the economic decisions and owns businesses; lack of consumer choice, guaranteed jobs.)* Why might this system become stagnant? *(Sample response: It does not meet consumer needs; state may make bad economic decisions; workers have no incentive to improve quality of products.)*

INTERACTIVE MAP

The Fall of the Soviet Union

👥 ACTIVE CLASSROOM

Use the Rank It strategy. Put four pieces of chart paper on the wall that list the four main reasons the Soviet Union declined (Repression, Stagnation of command economy, Extensive military commitments, Afghanistan). Form students into small groups. Ask the groups to select the one issue they think is most significant and to come up with reasons for their choice. Then, ask representatives from each group to write the reason on their event's chart paper. Discuss as a class.

D Differentiate: Challenge/Gifted Have a group of students research and present for the class a "You Are There" news report about the fall of communism in Eastern Europe and the Soviet Union. If available, use video/audio equipment to record the presentation or incorporate video into it.

ELL Use the ELL activity described in the ELL chart.

Further Instruction

Remind students of the relationship of the individual and the state in the Soviet Union. *(history of oppression, including purges, not an elected government, few civil rights, no free speech)* Ask students to answer question 1 in the IRN.

The Cold War Ends

DIGITAL TEXT 2

The Soviet Union Collapses

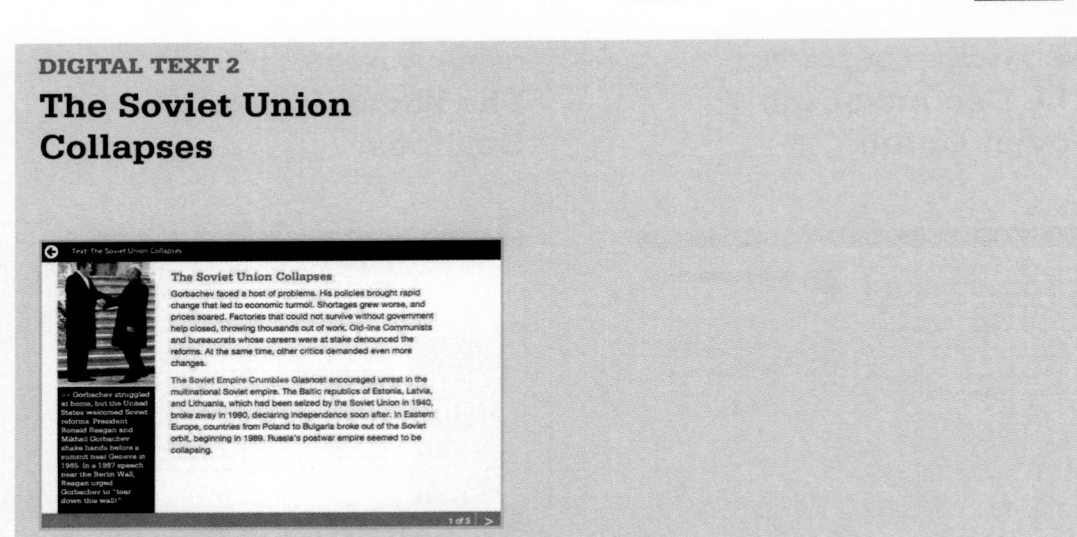

Compare Remind students of the differences between the free-enterprise economy and the command economy. *(Free-enterprise: producers and consumers make economic decisions: Command economy: government makes economic decisions)* Explain that in competition with the free market economies of the West, the communist command economies collapsed at the end of the 20th century. They could not match the West in its production of military hardware or consumer goods. Then ask students to answer question 2 in the IRN: How did the arms race put pressure on the Soviet economy? *(The economy had stagnated and was very inefficient; the Soviets didn't have the money to produce an ever-increasing number of weapons.)*

Objective 2: Identify the reforms introduced by Mikhail Gorbachev.

Quick Instruction

Project the image of Reagan and Gorbachev. Ask students to summarize the Cold War relationship between the United States and the Soviet Union. *(They competed in the arms race; they took opposite sides in conflicts all over the world.)* Explain to them that during the 1980s, a new leader, Mikhail Gorbachev, emerged in the Soviet Union who saw reform as the only option. Point out that Reagan and Gorbachev met many times during the 1980s to negotiate new arms treaties. Explain that Gorbachev proposed two types of reform: *glasnost* ("openness"), which created greater freedom of expression, and *perestroika*, which reformed the government and economy.

Predict Consequences What are some of the possible results of glasnost reforms? *(People could start to speak out against the government, loosening the tight control that the Soviet Union had over its people and the people in the communist countries of Eastern Europe.)* Then, tell students that *glasnost* enabled Natan Sharansky, a Soviet scientist and human rights activist who had been imprisoned for 10 years for treason to emigrate to Israel.

Further Instruction

Remind students of the economic challenges to the Soviet Union in the 1980s. *(Gorbachev's reforms led to economic turmoil: shortages increased, prices soared, and factories closed down, leading to high unemployment.)* Now remind them of the political challenges they faced. *(People had no political freedoms, political opponents were imprisoned, Eastern European satellite states wanted to break away.)* Now, ask students to complete the graphic organizer about the goals of glasnost and perestroika in the Interactive Reading Notepad.

Infer Remind students of the benefits of the command economy to workers. *(guaranteed employment and health care)* Have students answer question 6 in the Interactive Reading Notepad: Why did Gorbachev's reforms cause economic turmoil in the Soviet Union? *(Shortages grew; factories closed; unemployment soared; population was divided on whether to continue, or even accelerate, the reforms.)*

DIGITAL TEXT 3

Eastern Europe Transformed

INTERACTIVE TIME LINE

Fall of Communism in Soviet Bloc

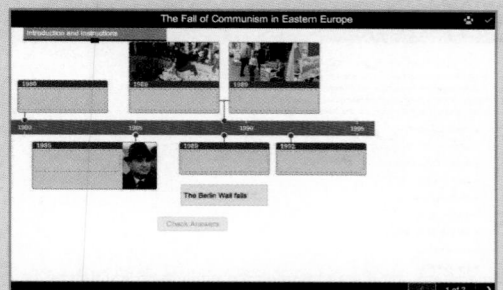

DIGITAL TEXT 4

Communism Declines Around the World

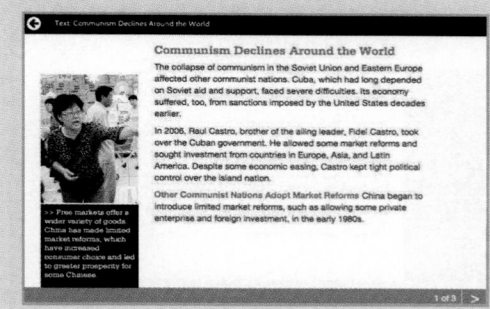

Objective 3: Describe the collapse of communism in Eastern Europe and the Soviet Union.

Quick Instruction

Interactive Time Line: Collapse of Communism Project the Interactive Time Line. Divide students into groups and jigsaw the text: Group 1: first paragraph and Poland Struggles Toward Democracy; Group 2: Revolution and Freedom; Group 3: Ethnic Tensions in Eastern Europe and The Breakup of Yugoslavia. Then, together as a class, go through the Interactive Time Line and sort the tiles into the correct positions.

Analyze Information Which of the events of 1989 was the most important in leading to the collapse of communism? Why? (*Answers will vary. Students may cite the fall of Berlin Wall, but answers should reflect information in the text and time line activity.*)

ACTIVE CLASSROOM

Use the If Photos Could Talk strategy. Break students into small groups. Ask each group to create a question to ask one of the people pictured in photographs in this text. Then, ask them to trade questions with another group and answer the question.

ELL Use the ELL activity described in the ELL chart.

Further Instruction

Project the Interactive Reading Notepad questions and go over the answers as a class. Remind students that Lech Walesa was the

leader of the Solidarity Union in Poland. Have students answer question 8 in the IRN: Explain Lech Walesa's role in the Polish people's fight against their communist government and his role in the collapse of communism in Eastern Europe. (*He was a leader of the Solidarity labor union that had millions of members; he led strikes and was arrested; he visited the pope, who was a Pole and was critical of communism.*)

Discuss also the role of Pope John Paul II in the collapse of communism in Eastern Europe. Explain the significance of his resistance to communist rule.

Determine Central Ideas Ask students to characterize the Soviet response to Eastern European resistance in the 1950s and 1960s. (*repressive, violent*) Have students answer question 9 in the IRN: Why were Eastern European reforms allowed to happen in the late 1980s? What had happened before when Eastern Europeans attempted reform? (*because Gorbachev said he wouldn't intervene if Eastern European governments introduced reforms; all other times [1953, 1956, 1986, 1980] the Soviets had sent in tanks and troops*)

Have students answer question 10 in the IRN: How did the East Germans put an end to their communist government? (*They protested in huge numbers; eventually, when no Soviet tanks came to put them down, the gates of the Berlin Wall were opened.*) Then, break students into small groups. Have them write a letter (dated late November 1989) from an East German citizen to Mikhail Gorbachev. Tell them to be sure to include reasons for East Germans' demands for a new government.

Objective 4: Evaluate how the end of the Cold War affected the remaining communist nations and the United States.

Quick Instruction

Project the infographic on China's Changing Economy. Ask students to remember what type of government China had. (*communist dictatorship*) Ask them what type of economy it had. (*command economy*) Go through the charts and answer the questions. Explain that since the fall of the Soviet Union, communism has declined around the world. China and Vietnam have embraced aspects of capitalism, although they are still politically repressive. Cuba and North Korea are the only communist countries left that have command economies. Explain also that the United States is the sole remaining superpower.

Hypothesize Why do you think the Chinese economy has changed so dramatically? (*Answers will vary, but most students will note that economic reforms have led China to become a major producer of consumer goods and created an economic boom. It now meets the needs of its huge population more efficiently.*)

Further Instruction

Cite Evidence Project the infographic. Remind students of China's history in the 1950s and 1960s. (*It was a communist dictatorship; the government made all of the economic decisions, some of them, such as the Great Leap Forward, were catastrophic.*) Ask students to answer question 11 in the IRN: Using the charts from the infographic, provide evidence that China's economy is becoming more capitalistic. (*Between 1978 and 1996, there is much more*

The Cold War Ends

 **SYNTHESIZE**

 DEMONSTRATE

DIGITAL TEXT 5

The Post-Cold War World

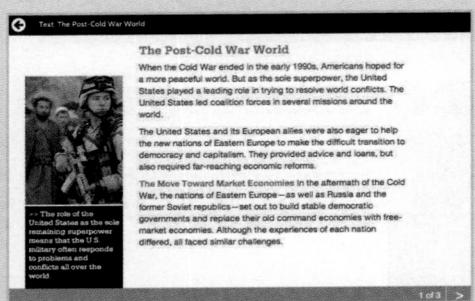

individual-owned industry and fewer state-owned businesses; between 1990 and 2008, more people owned cars; between 2001 and 2004, unemployment went up sharply.)

Predict Consequences What are some possible negative results of the United States becoming the world's remaining superpower? *(Answers will vary; some students will cite the expense of keeping armies to intervene in conflicts around the world; some will point to possible resentment from local citizens when the United States intervenes.)*

DIGITAL ACTIVITY

Pro-Reform and Anti-Reform Leaders

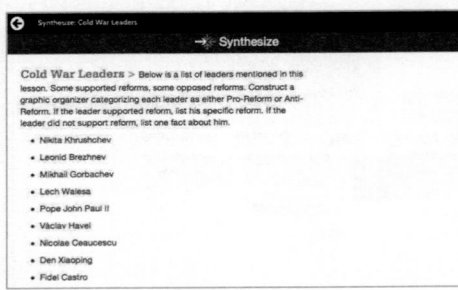

Ask students to construct a graphic organizer with the leaders provided. Have them categorize each leader as either Pro-Reform or Anti-Reform. If the leader supports reform, ask students to list his specific reform (or area of reform). If the leader does not support reform, have them list one fact about him.

Why do you think North Korea and Cuba have remained repressive communist states with command economies? *(Answers will vary but may include that the people are too afraid to pressure the governments to change because of greater repression.)*

DIGITAL QUIZ

Lesson Quiz and Classroom Discussion Board

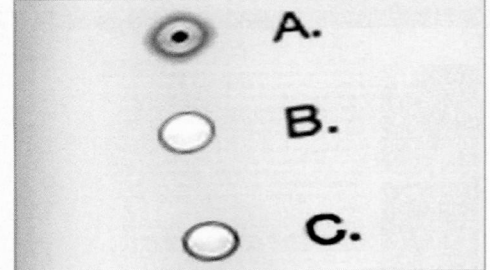

Assign the online quiz if you haven't already done so. Students will be offered automatic remediation or enrichment based on their score. Pose these questions to the class on the Class Discussion Board:

Hypothesize Was the fall of communism inevitable? Support your answer with evidence.

Identify Central Issues Will the United States continue to be the world's sole superpower? Why or why not?

Topic Inquiry

Have students continue their investigations for the Topic Inquiry.

The Cold War Era (1945–1991)

■ SYNTHESIZE

DIGITAL ACTIVITY

Reflect on the Essential Question and Topic

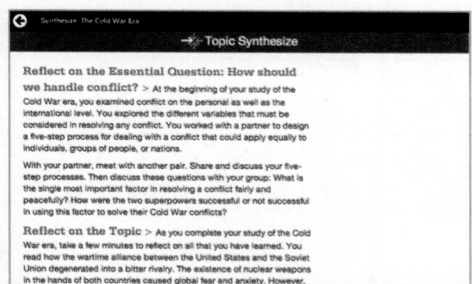

First ask students to reconsider the Essential Question: How should we handle conflict? Remind students that they examined conflict on a personal and international level. They explored the different variables that have to be considered in resolving any conflict. They worked with a partner to design a five-step process for dealing with conflict that could apply equally to individuals, groups, or countries. They also exchanged processes and critiqued them.

Have students take out their processes and critique notes from the opening activity. As a class, discuss this question: What is the single most important factor in resolving a conflict peaceably and equitably? If necessary, share this example: The most important factor in resolving a conflict is for both sides to genuinely want to solve the problem.

Have volunteers make suggestions and discuss issues raised, or ask students to post their comments on the Class Discussion Board.

Discuss Next, ask students to reflect on the topic as a whole, focusing on whether the world was safer during the Cold War era than it is today. Ask them to think about specific events from the Cold War that posed great danger and how they were resolved. How might similar events be resolved today? Who would help to resolve them? How might an act of terrorism have been handled during the Cold War? End the discussion by having students vote on which era was safer, or have students respond to a poll on the Class Discussion Board.

Topic Inquiry

Have students complete step 3 of the Topic Inquiry.

■ DEMONSTRATE

DIGITAL TOPIC REVIEW AND ASSESSMENT

The Cold War Era (1945–1991)

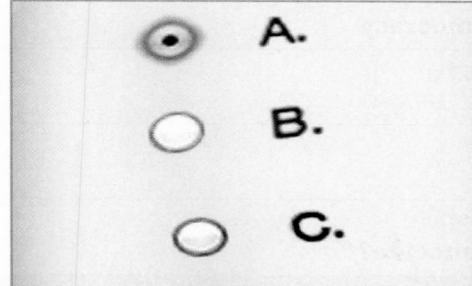

Students can prepare for the Topic Test by answering the questions in the Topic Review and Assessment online or the Assessment questions in the Print Student text. They can also prepare by reviewing their answers to the Interactive Reading Notepad questions or reviewing their notes in the Reading and Notetaking Study Guide.

DIGITAL TOPIC TEST

The Cold War Era (1945–1991)

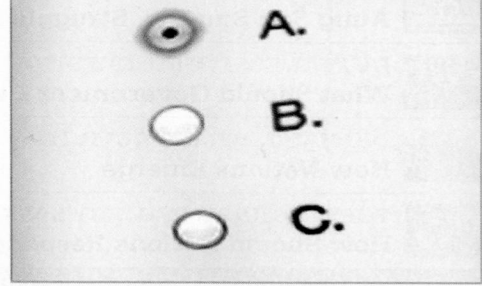

TOPIC TEST

Assign the Topic Test to assess students' understanding of topic content.

BENCHMARK TESTS

Assign these benchmark tests as you complete the relevant topics to monitor student progress toward mastering the course content and as preparation for the End-of-Course Test.

Benchmark Test 1: Topics 1–5

Benchmark Test 2: Topics 6–10

Benchmark Test 3: Topics 11–15

Benchmark Test 4: Topics 16–21

New Nations Emerge (1945–Present)

TOPIC 20 ORGANIZER	PACING: APPROX. 7 PERIODS, 3.5 BLOCKS
	PACING
Connect	1 period
MY STORY VIDEO **Aung San Suu Kyi, Struggle for Democracy**	10 min.
DIGITAL ESSENTIAL QUESTION ACTIVITY **What Should Government Do?**	10 min.
DIGITAL TIMELINE ACTIVITY **New Nations Emerge**	10 min.
TOPIC INQUIRY: PROJECT-BASED QUESTION **How Should Nations Respond to Genocide?**	20 min.
Investigate	2–4 periods
TOPIC INQUIRY: DOCUMENT-BASED QUESTION **How Should Nations Respond to Genocide?**	Ongoing
LESSON 1 New Nations in South Asia and Southeast Asia	30–40 min.
LESSON 2 African Nations Win Independence	30–40 min.
LESSON 3 The Modern Middle East Takes Shape	30–40 min.
LESSON 4 Conflicts in the Middle East	30–40 min.
Synthesize	1 period
DIGITAL ACTIVITY **Reflect on the Essential Question and Topic**	10 min.
TOPIC INQUIRY: DOCUMENT-BASED QUESTION **How Should Nations Respond to Genocide?**	20 min.
Demonstrate	1–2 periods
DIGITAL TOPIC TEST **New Nations Emerge**	10 min.
TOPIC INQUIRY: DOCUMENT-BASED QUESTION **How Should Nations Respond to Genocide?**	20 min.

NOTES

Topic (20)

How Should Nations Respond to Genocide?

In this Topic Inquiry, students work individually to analyze six documents that address in different ways the problem of genocide and how nations should respond to it. The documents include a first-person narrative, a photograph, a cartoon, and three essay excerpts from articles. Students will answer questions about each document, reflect on the ideas, draw their own conclusions, and then write an essay on the following question: **How Should Nations Respond to Genocide?** Learning how nations might choose to respond to genocide will contribute to students' understanding of the Topic Essential Question: What should governments do?

STEP 1: CONNECT
Develop Questions and Plan the Investigation

Launch the DBQ Writing Activity

Begin this activity by reminding students that genocide is defined as "a deliberate attempt to destroy an entire religious or ethnic group." Then ask students to work with a partner to discuss and write a list of five principles the world community should follow to decide if it should intervene to prevent or stop genocide. Have a volunteer read the examples. Suggest that they keep this list handy as they read the documents, answer the questions, and write their essays.

Suggestion: Have volunteers read their lists, and ask the rest of the class to discuss them. Ask: What are some risks a nation might face in intervening in another country's genocide?

Generate Questions

Divide the class into small groups and have them record their questions about whether nations should intervene to prevent or stop genocide.

Suggestion: Help students generate questions by asking them to think of genocides they have read about, such as the Holocaust. Ask them to consider what the United States or other nations did, did not do, or could have done to prevent or stop this genocide.

Resources
- Student Instructions
- Need-to-Know Questions

STEP 2: INVESTIGATE
Apply Disciplinary Concepts and Tools

Analyze the Documents

Have students analyze the six documents to see how they relate to the question: How should nations respond to genocide? Then, have them write an essay expressing their own opinions about this difficult question. Document A is the story of a survivor of the genocide in Rwanda, told on the CBS news program *60 Minutes.* Document B is a photograph of a moment in the lives of refugees at a refugee camp in South Sudan. In Documents C and D, two commentators debate in the *Chicago Tribune* whether the United States should intervene in the Bosnian genocide of the 1990s. Document E is a political cartoon addressing world inaction in cases of genocide. Document F is an excerpt from an article about a soldier who led the United Nations intervention in Bosnia and how the assignment affected him.

Suggestion: You can control the length of the DBQ by having students read just the two documents that focus on Bosnia (C and D) and the cartoon (E), or the three that focus on African problems (A, B, and F) and the cartoon (E).

Check Understanding

After students finish reading each individual document, have them answer the multiple-choice and short-answer questions attached to each document. Review the questions and discuss the answers after students have answered the questions for all the documents.

Resources
- Information Organizer

⏻ PROFESSIONAL DEVELOPMENT

Document-Based Question
Be sure to view the Document-Based Question Professional Development resources in the online course.

STEP 3: SYNTHESIZE
Evaluate Sources and
Use Evidence to Formulate Conclusions

Write Your Essay

Have students consider all of the evidence and viewpoints and draw their own conclusions. Using the documents and their knowledge of history, have them write an essay on the following topic: **How should nations respond to genocide?**

Remind students that their essays should have the following characteristics: a topic sentence that states their views; evidence from at least *three* of the documents, clearly identified; relevant facts; an explanation and rebuttal of at least one opposing viewpoint; logical organization, including an introduction and a conclusion; and correct spelling, grammar, and punctuation.

Suggestion: Remind students that they need to anticipate disagreements readers may have with the points they make. Anticipating readers' objections will help them strengthen their own arguments and evidence.

Edit Your Essay

Remind students that they should revise their first draft and create a final draft of their essay before turning it in. You may want to suggest that they ask a classmate to peer edit their essay.

Resources
• Writing Rubric

STEP 4: DEMONSTRATE
Communicate Conclusions
and Take Informed Action

Present Your Essay

Have students make a neat, clean copy of their essays. Then ask volunteers to read their essays aloud to the class.

Suggestion: As an alternative, have students publish their essays on a class website, bulletin board, or other online vehicle.

Reflect on the Project

Have students briefly discuss what they found challenging in their essays and what they feel they did well. Encourage them to use the lessons they learned writing this essay so they can write even more effectively in future writing projects.

Suggestion: As an extension activity, have students research a specific genocide situation, either one studied in this activity or one they have read about. Ask them to write a three-paragraph essay in which they describe how different countries actually responded to the situation. Have students share their descriptions with the class.

INTRODUCTION

New Nations Emerge

As European imperial powers declined after World War II, colonies in Africa and Asia gained independence. Some nations achieved independence peacefully, while others had to fight for their freedom. The legacy of colonialism had serious effects even many years after independence, as ethnic and religious conflict plagued many parts of the world, including the Middle East, South Asia, Rwanda, Darfur, and Sri Lanka.

▮ CONNECT

MY STORY VIDEO
Aung San Suu Kyi, Struggle for Democracy

Watch a video about Aung San Suu Kyi's efforts to bring democracy to her homeland of Myanmar.

Check Understanding What price did Aung San Suu Kyi pay for her struggle for human rights? *(She was placed under house arrest for 15 years.)*

Determine Point of View What does Aung San Suu Kyi mean when she says she made a choice and not a sacrifice in her life? *(She chose to fight for human rights and suffer the consequences, but her family, from who she was separated, had to sacrifice.)*

⟲ FLIP IT!
Assign the My Story video.

DIGITAL ESSENTIAL QUESTION ACTIVITY
What Should Government Do?

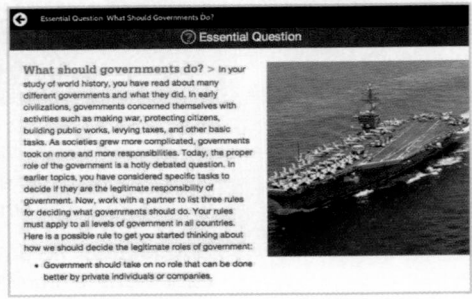

Ask students to think about the Essential Question for this Topic: What should government do? What activities are legitimate roles for government to play? Which roles should government not take on? How should we decide?

If students have not already done so, ask them to list their three rules from the Essential Question activity. Then allow volunteers to share their answers with the class.

Support a Point of View with Evidence Why did you choose these three rules? Explain your answer. *(Answers will vary. Students should be able to offer valid reasons for their choices; evidence may include philosophical or moral reasons, evidence of what governments did in the past, and references to current government roles.)*

Connect Is there a role you think government should take on that it does not do now? What is one government role that you feel it should give up? Explain. *(Answers will vary, but students may mention government roles in healthcare, education, economic regulations, or social services, as well as taxation.)*

DIGITAL TIMELINE ACTIVITY
New Nations Emerge

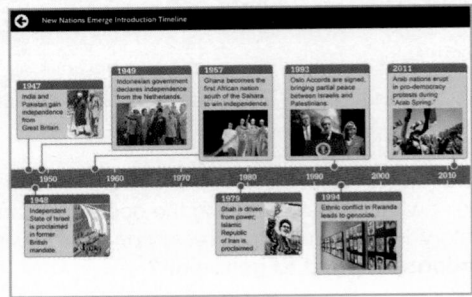

Display the timeline showing the major events concerning new nations in the second half of the 20th century. During the Topic, students will learn about all of these events and many more, but this timeline will provide a framework into which they can place the events they learn about.

▯ Differentiate: Challenge/Gifted Suggest that students copy the timeline onto their own paper and add entries to it as they read the chapter. Have them make a final, clean copy after they read all four lessons, and discuss the new entries as a class.

Check Understanding About how many years after the founding of Israel was a partial agreement signed between Israelis and Palestinians? *(45)*

Topic Inquiry
Launch the Topic Inquiry with students after introducing the Topic.

New Nations in South Asia and Southeast Asia

Supporting English Language Learners

Use with Digital Text 2, **Challenges to Modern India.**

Learning Strategies
Read *Challenges to Modern India* aloud to students. Then instruct students to complete one of the following activities based on their level of English proficiency.

Beginning Write and display the words think, read, and discuss for students. Read the words aloud and have students repeat them. Begin by using each word in a basic sentence to demonstrate how these words are used daily. Then guide students to use the information in *Challenges to Modern India* to compose short phrases or sentences using these words. Have students write the words and phrases in their notebooks.

Intermediate Write and display the words think, read, and discuss for students. Read the words aloud and have students repeat them. Help students develop basic sentences for each word to demonstrate how these words are used daily. Then support students as they use the information in *Challenges to Modern India* to compose short phrases or sentences using these words. Have students write the words and phrases in their notebooks.

Advanced Write and display the words leadership and modern. Use these words in a group discussion about some aspect of daily life. Use informal assessment to make sure all students understand the meanings of the two words. Then have students work with a partner to create sentences about the information in *Challenges to Modern India* for each word. Pairs should write their sentences in their notebooks and then share them with the class.

Advanced High Write and display the words leadership and modern. Have students talk to a partner about some aspect of daily life, using these words in their conversation. Then have students create sentences about the information in *Challenges to Modern India* for each word. Students should write their sentences in their notebooks and then share them with the class.

Use with Digital Text 7, **Struggle for Democracy in the Philippines.**

Learning Strategies
Read *Struggle for Democracy in the Philippines* aloud to the class. Have students complete one activity according to their level of English proficiency.

Beginning Write and display several simple sentences about the progression of democracy in the Philippines. Show students how to add descriptive words to lengthen their sentences and make them more interesting. Finally, provide students with cloze sentences and instruct them to add a descriptive word to improve each sentence. For example:

- A growing population is a strain on _____ resources.

Intermediate Write and display several simple sentences about the progression of democracy in the Philippines. Use one or two of the example sentences to show students how to add descriptive words to lengthen their sentences and make them more interesting. Then ask student volunteers to contribute descriptive words to the remaining example sentences. Rewrite the sentences with the additional descriptive words. Read them aloud and have students repeat them.

Advanced Instruct students to work in pairs to write several sentences about the development of democracy in the Philippines. Remind students to use descriptive clauses and phrases to make their writing more interesting and accurate. Then have two pairs of students come together to create a group of four. Instruct small groups to share their sentences and give one another feedback on their writing.

Advanced High Instruct students write several sentences about the development of democracy in the Philippines. Remind students to use descriptive clauses and phrases to make their writing more interesting and accurate. Then have students turn to a partner to share their sentences and give each other feedback on their writing.

▣ Differentiate Instruction

Use the Differentiated Instruction notes throughout the lesson plan to support the varied skill sets, levels of readiness, and interests in the mixed-ability classroom.

Challenge These notes include suggestions for expanding the activity for advanced students.

On-Level These notes include suggestions for modifying the activity to address different interests or learning styles.

Extra Support These notes include ideas for providing more scaffolding or reading spuport.

Special Needs These notes provide ideas for adapting instruction to support the needs of various special needs students.

■ NOTES

_____

_____

_____

_____

_____

New Nations in South Asia and Southeast Asia

Objectives

Objective 1: Explain how independence led to the partition of India.

Objective 2: Describe the national development of India, Pakistan, and Bangladesh.

Objective 3: Define the role of South Asia in the Cold War.

Objective 4: Explain the impact of independence on nations of Southeast Asia.

LESSON 1 ORGANIZER		PACING: APPROX. 1 PERIOD, .5 BLOCKS			
				RESOURCES	
		OBJECTIVES	PACING	Online	Print
Connect					
DIGITAL START UP ACTIVITY **The Struggle for Unity**			5 min.	●	
Investigate					
DIGITAL TEXT 1 **Independence and Partition in South Asia**		Objective 1	10 min.	●	●
INTERACTIVE GALLERY **Indian Independence and Partition**			10 min.	●	
DIGITAL TEXTS 2 AND 3 **Challenges to Modern India, Pakistan and Bangladesh Separate**		Objective 2	10 min.	●	●
INTERACTIVE MAP **South Asian Borders**			10 min.	●	
DIGITAL TEXT 4 **South Asia in the Cold War**		Objective 3	10 min.	●	●
DIGITAL TEXTS 5 AND 6 **Independent Nations in Southeast Asia, Populous Indonesia Faces Challenges**		Objective 4	10 min.	●	●
DIGITAL TEXT 7 **Struggle for Democracy in the Philippines**			10 min.	●	●
Synthesize					
DIGITAL ACTIVITY **Independence in Southeast Asia**			5 min.	●	
Demonstrate					
LESSON QUIZ **Lesson Quiz and Class Discussion Board**			10 min.	●	

PEARSON
realize™
www.PearsonRealize.com

Go online to access additional resources including:
Primary Sources • Biographies • Supreme Court cases •
21st Century Skill Tutorials • Maps • Graphic Organizers.

CONNECT

DIGITAL START UP ACTIVITY
The Struggle for Unity

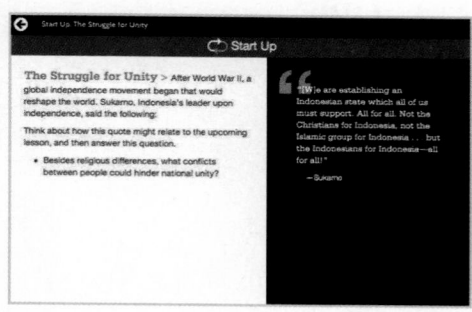

Project the Start Up Activity Ask students
to read the explanation and quotation and
answer the question as they get settled:
Besides religious differences, what conflicts
could hinder national unity? *(Students could
mention differences in race, ethnicity, political
opinions, or wealth. Conflicts could also
develop over control of resources and land.)*

Hypothesize What extra challenges might
face a new nation that had been under colonial
control? *(Colonial rulers may have united
groups that had traditionally been in conflict
Such groups might have trouble working
together.)*

Aa Vocabulary Development: Use the
Interactive Reading Notepad to preview the
Key Terms and Academic Vocabulary in this
lesson with students.

⇅ FLIP IT!
Assign the Flipped Video for this lesson.

■ STUDENT EDITION PRINT
PAGES: 812–820

■ INVESTIGATE

DIGITAL TEXT 1
Independence and
Partition in South Asia

INTERACTIVE GALLERY
Indian Independence
and Partition

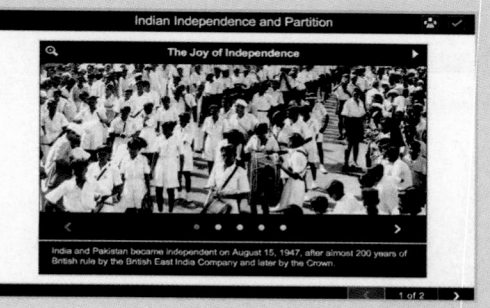

Objective 1: Explain how independence led to the partition of India.

Quick Instruction

Tell students that at the beginning of the Cold
War, a global independence movement started
to reshape the world. The European colonial
powers, especially Britain and France, had been
weakened by World War II. Their military and
financial resources were exhausted. Nationalists in
the colonies were ready to fight for their freedom,
and many Europeans had no desire for further
conflict. Among the first new nations to win
independence were the former British colonies of
South Asia, or the Indian subcontinent.

Review the events surrounding British colonial
rule of India and the independence movement
led by Mohandas Gandhi. Explain that the British
granted India self-rule in 1947, but the region
was partitioned into Hindu-dominated India and
Muslim-dominated East and West Pakistan.

**Interactive Gallery: Indian Independence and
Partition** Project the gallery and click through
the images, reading the captions. Ask students
to consider that British rule had united diverse
kingdoms containing different religious and ethnic
groups. Along with the joy of independence
came the reality that some of the groups did not
want to create a new nation together.

▶▶ ACTIVE CLASSROOM

Ask students to create a quick copy of
an image from the gallery on a piece of
paper. Have them Cartoon It into a political
cartoon that illustrates a key concept or
main idea from Digital Text 1.

Further Instruction

Editable Presentation Use the Editable
Presentation to present the main ideas for this
Core Text.

Project the Interactive Reading Notepad
questions and use student responses to
discuss the causes and effects of South Asian
partition. Make sure students understand that
the Muslim minority in South Asia wanted
its own nation, which was carved from the
northeast and northwest of India. As Hindus
and Muslims moved over the borders, violence
erupted.

Sequence Events Name major events
that led from British rule over India to armed
conflict in Kashmir. *(Sample response: The
independence movement in India let to Britain
granting the country self-rule. One condition
of self-rule was the partition between India
and East and West Pakistan. The region
of Kashmir had a Hindu ruler but a Muslim
majority, and both nations wanted to claim it.
The region is still under dispute, and Muslim
separatists clash with Indian troops.)*

New Nations in South Asia and Southeast Asia

DIGITAL TEXT 2
Challenges to Modern India

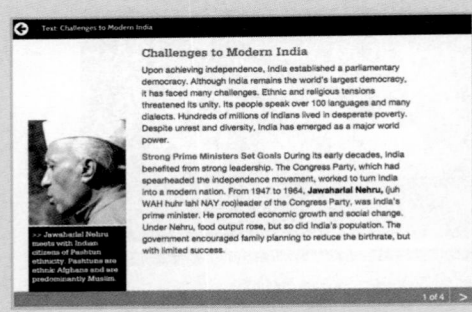

DIGITAL TEXT 3
Pakistan and Bangladesh Separate

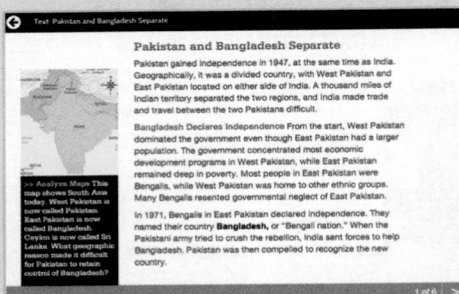

INTERACTIVE MAP
South Asian Borders

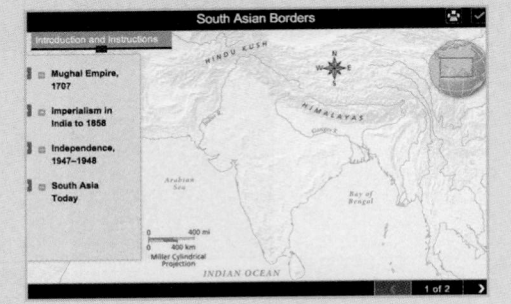

Objective 2: Describe the national development of India, Pakistan, and Bangladesh.

Quick Instruction

Explain that a series of strong prime ministers, including Jawaharlal Nehru, his daughter Indira Gandhi, and her son Rajiv Gandhi, contributed significantly to developing a modern India. Indira Gandhi also had significant influence in her role as one of the world's few female leaders. Religious conflicts are still an ongoing problem, however. Ethnic and economic differences between West and East Pakistan caused the rise of an independence movement in East Pakistan, leading to the formation of Bangladesh.

Interactive Map: South Asian Borders Project the map, and click through the sequence, pointing out the differences in national borders through time. Students should notice that borders between the 1947 and present-day maps do not change, but East and West Pakistan became the nations of Bangladesh and Pakistan, while Ceylon became the nation of Sri Lanka.

ACTIVE CLASSROOM

Distribute sticky notes to use for the Sticky Notes strategy. Give students three minutes to write their comments or observations about the changes in South Asian nations from 1947 to today. Have them consider positive and negative aspects of those changes. Then ask students to post their sticky notes on the board, and have them look at the various responses. Discuss similarities and differences in the responses.

ELL Use the ELL activity described in the ELL chart.

Further Instruction

Project the Interactive Reading Notepad questions, and use student responses to summarize ongoing conflicts in South Asia.

Summarize Describe the ongoing South Asian conflicts and issues mentioned in the text. *(Sample response: India and Pakistan dispute ownership of the Kashmir region. Tamil rebels in Sri Lanka call for independence from the nation's majority Sinhalese. India's religious diversity sometimes leads to violence between groups. Pakistan's government is often unstable because of the conflicts between different ethnic groups, military and civilian leaders, and Islamic fundamentalists and other Pakistanis. Additionally, Taliban supporters have been hiding in Pakistan. Bangladesh faces crippling poverty and recurring natural disasters.)*

DIGITAL TEXT 4

South Asia in the Cold War

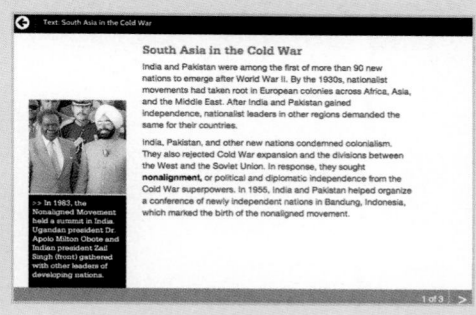

Text: South Asia in the Cold War

South Asia in the Cold War

India and Pakistan were among the first of more than 90 new nations to emerge after World War II. By the 1930s, nationalist movements had taken root in European colonies across Africa, Asia, and the Middle East. After India and Pakistan gained independence, nationalist leaders in other regions demanded the same for their countries.

India, Pakistan, and other new nations condemned colonialism. They also rejected Cold War expansion and the divisions between the West and the Soviet Union. In response, they sought **nonalignment**, or political and diplomatic independence from the Cold War superpowers. In 1955, India and Pakistan helped organize a conference of newly independent nations in Bandung, Indonesia, which marked the birth of the nonaligned movement.

>> In 1983, the Nonaligned Movement held a summit in India. Ugandan president Dr. Apolo Milton Obote and Indian president Zail Singh (front) gathered with other leaders of developing nations.

1 of 3 >

Objective 3: Define the role of South Asia in the Cold War.

Quick Instruction

Review the goals of the United States and the Soviet Union during the Cold War. Explain that emerging nations such as India and Pakistan were wary of picking sides in the global conflict.

Project the image of the Nonaligned Movement summit. In 1955, India and Pakistan helped organize a conference of new nations, marking the start of the nonaligned movement. The group's conferences, which still occur, consist of leaders from countries that achieved independence in the 20th century. Discuss with students how the concerns of developing nations would differ from those of the superpowers involved in the Cold War.

Further Instruction

Project the Interactive Reading Notepad questions and use student responses to summarize the nonalignment movement.

Analyze Why were the goals of the Cold War superpowers at odds with the goals of newly independent nations? *(During the Cold War, the United States and Soviet Union wanted to increase their territory and attract allies for military advantages over each other. Nations like India and Pakistan, recently free from more powerful nations controlling their land, were wary of these tactics.)*

D **Differentiate: Challenge/Gifted** The Nonaligned Movement summit still exists. Have students research the organization today and find out how its goals have changed since the end of the Cold War. Ask students to share their findings about what changes have occurred in the movement now that its original reason for existing, the Cold War, has ended.

DIGITAL TEXT 5

Independent Nations in Southeast Asia

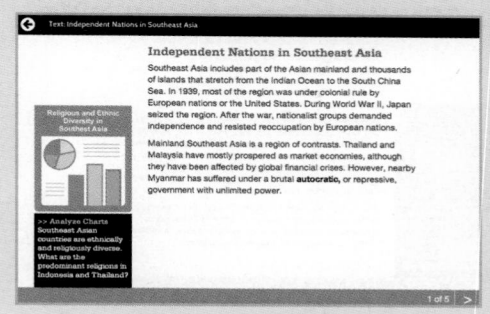

Text: Independent Nations in Southeast Asia

Independent Nations in Southeast Asia

Southeast Asia includes part of the Asian mainland and thousands of islands that stretch from the Indian Ocean to the South China Sea. In 1939, most of the region was under colonial rule by European nations or the United States. During World War II, Japan seized the region. After the war, nationalist groups demanded independence and resisted reoccupation by European nations.

Mainland Southeast Asia is a region of contrasts. Thailand and Malaysia have mostly prospered as market economies, although they have been affected by global financial crises. However, nearby Myanmar has suffered under a brutal **autocratic**, or repressive, government with unlimited power.

>> Analyze Charts Southeast Asian countries are ethnically and religiously diverse. What are the predominant religions in Indonesia and Thailand?

1 of 5 >

Objective 4: Explain the impact of independence on nations of Southeast Asia.

Quick Instruction

Have students recall the role of imperialism in Southeast Asia. Explain that after South Asian nations achieved independence, the nations of Southeast Asia followed. As in South Asia, some of the new countries faced challenges relating to national identity and unity among diverse groups. Relatively equal distribution of wealth and peace among ethnic groups has helped Malaysia reach prosperity, but Myanmar, Indonesia, and the Philippines have all struggled with internal conflict.

ELL Use the ELL activity described in the ELL chart.

New Nations in South Asia and Southeast Asia

DIGITAL TEXT 6

Populous Indonesia Faces Challenges

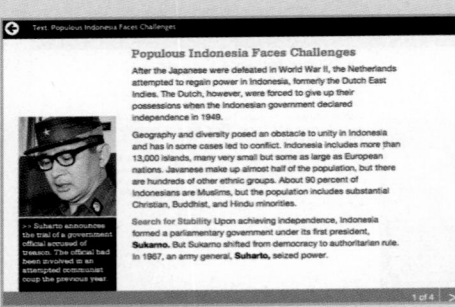

Populous Indonesia Faces Challenges

After the Japanese were defeated in World War II, the Netherlands attempted to regain power in Indonesia, formerly the Dutch East Indies. The Dutch, however, were forced to give up their possessions when the Indonesian government declared independence in 1949.

Geography and diversity posed an obstacle to unity in Indonesia and has in some cases led to conflict. Indonesia includes more than 13,000 islands, many very small but some as large as European nations. Javanese make up almost half of the population, but there are hundreds of other ethnic groups. About 90 percent of Indonesians are Muslims, but the population includes substantial Christian, Buddhist, and Hindu minorities.

Search for Stability Upon achieving independence, Indonesia formed a parliamentary government under its first president, **Sukarno.** But Sukarno shifted from democracy to authoritarian rule. In 1967, an army general, **Suharto,** seized power.

>> Suharto announces the trial of a government official accused of treason. The official had been involved in an attempted communist coup the previous year

1 of 4 >

DIGITAL TEXT 7

Struggle for Democracy in the Philippines

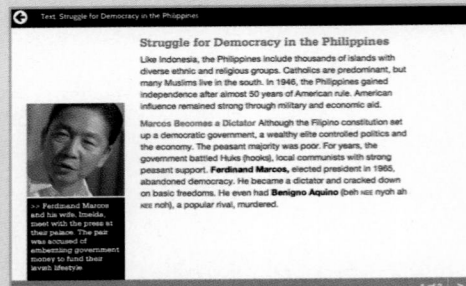

Struggle for Democracy in the Philippines

Like Indonesia, the Philippines include thousands of islands with diverse ethnic and religious groups. Catholics are predominant, but many Muslims live in the south. In 1946, the Philippines gained independence after almost 50 years of American rule. American influence remained strong through military and economic aid.

Marcos Becomes a Dictator Although the Filipino constitution set up a democratic government, a wealthy elite controlled politics and the economy. The peasant majority was poor. For years, the government battled Huks (hooks), local communists with strong peasant support. **Ferdinand Marcos,** elected president in 1965, abandoned democracy. He became a dictator and cracked down on basic freedoms. He even had **Benigno Aquino** (beh NEE nyoh ah KEE nohj, a popular rival, murdered.

>> Ferdinand Marcos and his wife, Imelda, meet with the press at their palace. The pair was accused of embezzling government money to fund their lavish lifestyle

1 of 3 >

Further Instruction

Project the Interactive Reading Notepad questions, and use student responses to describe the path of Southeast Asia after independence.

Analyze Information How do autocratic rulers stunt the growth of nations in Southeast Asia and elsewhere? *(Autocratic rulers in countries such as Myanmar, Indonesia, and the Philippines have hurt their countries through limitations in foreign trade, the silencing or murder of dissenters, and economic policies that benefited only them and their supporters.)*

■ SYNTHESIZE

DIGITAL ACTIVITY

Independence in Southeast Asia

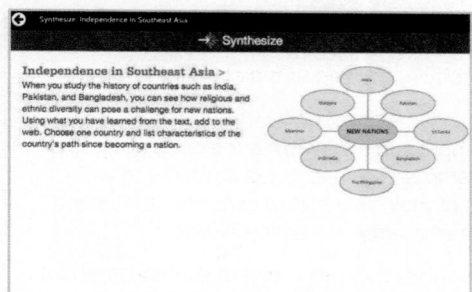

Remind students that the diverse nature of nations in South and Southeast Asia often causes marginalized groups to develop independence or separatist movements. The movements sometimes result in the formation of strong nations, but other effects include ongoing conflicts within and between nations. Project the Synthesize graphic organizer and help students complete it.

Identify Patterns Some South and Southeast Asian nations had similar struggles with building new nations. Name some common problems that occurred across the region. *(Sample responses: minority groups' desire for independence, power struggles between military and civilian government structures, oppression from religious fundamentalists, the rise of dictators, setbacks from natural disasters)*

■ DEMONSTRATE

LESSON QUIZ

Lesson Quiz and Class Discussion Board

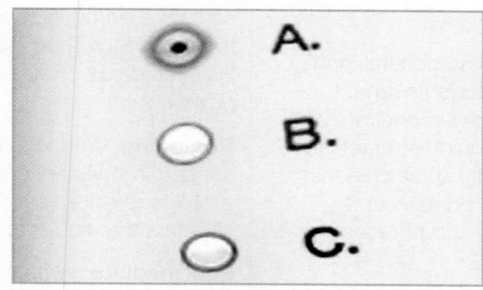

Assign the online Lesson Quiz for this lesson if you haven't already done so. Students will be offered automatic remediation or enrichment based on their score.

In this lesson, you learned about independence movements in South and Southeast Asia, starting with India gaining independence from the British. India's independence was accompanied by partition, eventually leading to the nations of Pakistan and Bangladesh. Nations across Southeast Asia also gained independence, with varying results.

Generate Explanations How has geography had a similar impact on the development of Indonesia and the Philippines as nations? *(Sample response: Both countries include large groups of islands. The distance between the islands and the differences among the people who live on them make it difficult to achieve national unity. The isolation of some of the islands might also complicate government business.)*

Topic Inquiry

Have students continue their investigations for the Topic Inquiry.

African Nations Win Independence

Supporting English Language Learners

Use with Digital Text 1, **The New Nations of Africa.**

Learning Strategies
Read The New Nations of Africa aloud to students. Then instruct students to complete one of the following activities based on their level of English proficiency.

Beginning Write and display the words continent, forest, coastal, and desert for students. Read the words aloud and have students repeat them. Begin by using each word in a basic sentence to demonstrate how these words are used in everyday conversation. Then guide students to use the information in *The New Nations of Africa* to write short phrases or sentences using these words. Write and display the phrases and sentences for students and have them write the words and phrases in their notebooks.

Intermediate Write and display the words continent, forest, coastal, and desert for students. Read the words aloud and have students repeat them. Help students develop basic sentences for each word to demonstrate how these words are used in everyday conversation. Then support students as they use the information in *The New Nations of Africa* to write short phrases or sentences using these words. Have students write the words and phrases in their notebooks, then invite them to share their work with the class.

Advanced Write and display the words continent, forest, coastal, and desert. Use these words in a general group discussion about geography. Use informal assessment to make sure all students understand the meanings of the two words. Then have students work with a partner to write sentences about the information in *The New Nations of Africa* for each word. Pairs should write their sentences in their notebooks and then share them with the class.

Advanced High Write and display the words continent, forest, coastal, and desert. Have students talk to a partner about geography, using these words in their conversation. Then have students write sentences about the information in *The New Nations of Africa* for each word. Students should write their sentences in their notebooks and then share them with the class.

Use with Digital Text 2, **A Variety of New Governments.**

Learning Strategies
Review sentence patterns with students. Explain that all sentences must have a subject + verb to be complete. Demonstrate how to add additional sentence elements, object, direct object, indirect object, and complement, to add variety. Then read *A Variety of New Governments* aloud to the class. Have students complete one activity according to their level of English proficiency.

Beginning Write and display simple subject + verb sentences about the content in *A Variety of New Governments*. Then guide students to write simple subject + verb sentences of their own in their notebooks. Remind students that subjects are nouns and verbs are action words.

Intermediate Write and display subject + verb + object sentences about the content in *A Variety of New Governments*. Then guide students to write simple subject + verb + object sentences of their own in their notebooks. Invite student volunteers to share their sentences with the class.

Advanced Write and display an example subject + verb + indirect object + direct object and a subject + verb + complement sentence about the content in *A Variety of New Governments*. Then have students work with a partner to write two of each variety in their notebooks. Ask pairs to share their sentences with the class.

Advanced High Write and display an example subject + verb + object + complement sentence about the content in *A Variety of New Governments*. Then have students work independently to write three sentences with the same sentence pattern in their notebooks. Ask students to turn to a partner and share their sentences.

D Differentiate Instruction

Use the Differentiated Instruction notes throughout the lesson plan to support the varied skill sets, levels of readiness, and interests in the mixed-ability classroom.

Challenge These notes include suggestions for expanding the activity for advanced students.

On-Level These notes include suggestions for modifying the activity to address different interests or learning styles.

Extra Support These notes include ideas for providing more scaffolding or reading spuport.

Special Needs These notes provide ideas for adapting instruction to support the needs of various special needs students.

■ NOTES

Objectives

Objective 1: Summarize how African nations won independence.

Objective 2: Analyze the issues facing new African nations and the different paths they took.

Objective 3: Identify examples of and summarize the reasons for ethnic conflict and genocide in African nations.

LESSON 2 ORGANIZER		PACING: APPROX. 1 PERIOD, .5 BLOCKS			
				RESOURCES	
		OBJECTIVES	**PACING**	**Online**	**Print**
Connect					
DIGITAL START UP ACTIVITY **Challenges of Independence**			5 min.	●	
Investigate					
DIGITAL TEXT 1 **The New Nations of Africa**		Objective 1	10 min.	●	●
DIGITAL TEXT 2 **A Variety of New Governments**		Objective 2	10 min.	●	●
INTERACTIVE MAP **Imperialism and Independence in Africa**			10 min.	●	
DIGITAL TEXT 3 **Case Studies: Five African Nations**		Objective 2	10 min.	●	●
INTERACTIVE GALLERY **Independence in Congo**			10 min.	●	
DIGITAL TEXT 4 **The Wars of Southern Africa**		Objective 3	10 min.	●	●
DIGITAL TEXT 5 **Ethnic Conflict and Genocide**			10 min.	●	●
Synthesize					
DIGITAL ACTIVITY **Addressing the Challenges of Independence**			5 min.	●	
Demonstrate					
DIGITAL QUIZ **Lesson Quiz and Class Discussion Board**			10 min.	●	

African Nations Win Independence

■ CONNECT

DIGITAL START UP ACTIVITY
Challenges of Independence

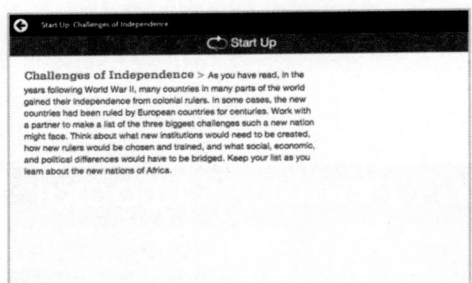

Project the Start Up Activity After students enter and get settled, ask them to work with a partner to make their lists of the three biggest challenges a newly independent nation might face. You might prompt students' thinking by asking these questions: What do you know about Africa's colonial past? How might this past present challenges to newly independent countries? Would any countries have an advantage over others because of their colonial past? Why or why not? (*Students' lists will vary, but will probably focus on creating economic, social, and political institutions, forming an effective government, establishing foreign relations, and dealing with conflicts left over from the colonial period.*)

Aa Vocabulary Development: Use the Interactive Reading Notepad to preview the Key Terms and Academic Vocabulary in this lesson with students.

⇅ FLIP IT!
Assign the Flipped Video for this lesson.

■ STUDENT EDITION PRINT
PAGES: 821–828

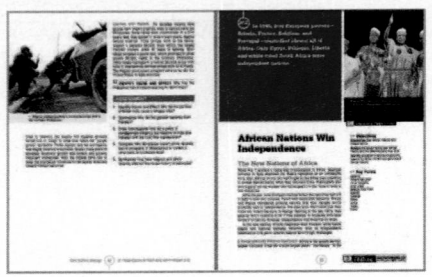

■ INVESTIGATE

DIGITAL TEXT 1
The New Nations of Africa

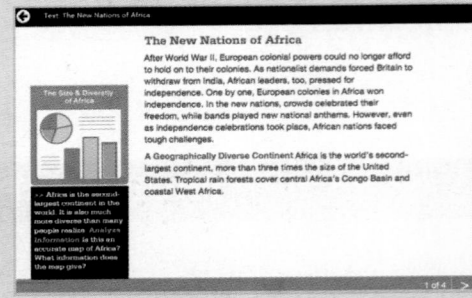

INTERACTIVE MAP
Imperialism and Independence in Africa

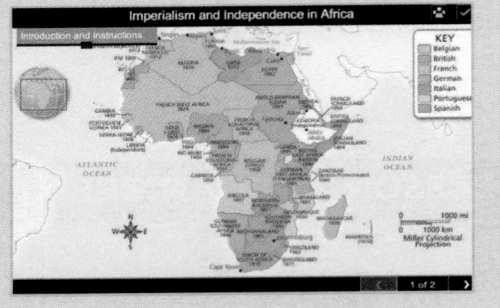

Objective 1: Summarize how African nations won independence.

Quick Instruction

After World War II, European colonial powers could no longer afford to hold onto their colonies. As nationalist demands forced Britain to withdraw from India, African leaders, too, pressed for independence. One by one, European colonies in Africa won independence. Remind students that the nations of Africa won independence over a long period, but that most African countries gained independence after World War II, during the 1950s and 1960s.

Interactive Map: Imperialism and Independence in Africa Display the interactive map, focusing students' attention on the second layer that shows the dates of African independence.

Generalize Work with students to tabulate which decades African countries became independent. The point of the exercise is to numerically show the number of countries that became independent in the 1950s and 1960s. Discuss why so many independence movements in Africa were successful during this period.

📖 ACTIVE CLASSROOM

Have students engage in the My Metaphor strategy by completing the following sentence: This map shows that _____ is like _____ because _____.

ELL Use the ELL activity described in the ELL chart.

Further Instruction

Editable Presentation Use the Editable Presentation to present the main ideas for these texts.

Project the Interactive Reading Notepad questions and use student responses to discuss how the many nations of Africa became independent. Review the information in the text about the geography of Africa. Remind students of the impact of the independence movements of Africa and help students summarize the rise of those movements. Explain that some movements were violent, while others were relatively peaceful.

Generalize What effect did World War II have on the independence of African nations and why? (*Sample response: World War II depleted European energies and resources, giving independence movements in Africa the opportunity to grow and achieve success.*)

D Differentiate: Challenge/Gifted Invite students to compare and contrast the independence of the United States with a particular nation in Africa. How were their paths to independence similar, and how were they different? How were the post-independence periods similar and different?

DIGITAL TEXT 2

A Variety of New Governments

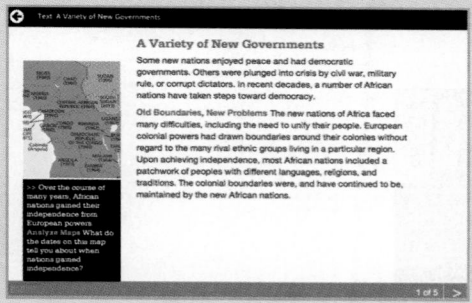

INTERACTIVE MAP

Imperialism and Independence in Africa

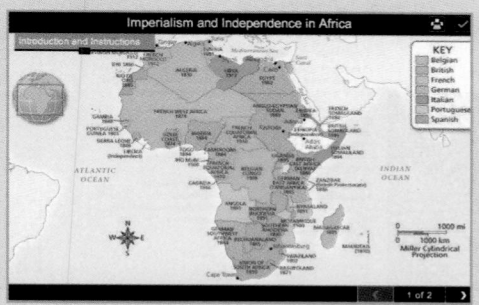

DIGITAL TEXT 3

Case Studies: Five African Nations

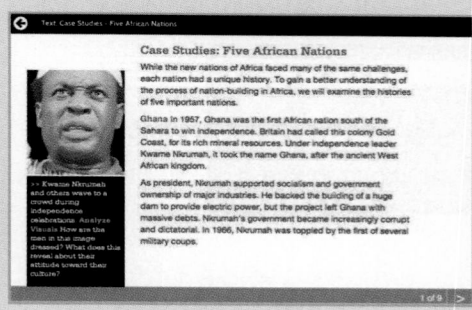

Objective 2: Analyze the issues facing new African nations and the different paths they took.

Quick Instruction

After independence, African nations followed many different paths but also faced many challenges and ongoing conflicts.

Interactive Map: Imperialism and Independence in Africa Project the Interactive Map on the whiteboard again. Use the slider to show how the new nations' boundaries usually maintained the boundaries established by the European colonial powers. Engage students in a discussion about the effect this might have had.

📷 ACTIVE CLASSROOM

Have students engage in the Take a Stand activity by answering the question: Should the newly independent nations of Africa have changed their borders from the ones established by the colonial powers? Why or why not? Why might this have been difficult?

ELL Use the ELL activity described in the ELL chart.

Further Instruction

Project the Interactive Reading Notepad questions and use student responses to discuss the new governments that arose among the newly independent African nations.

Summarize What do you think are the main reasons for ongoing ethnic conflicts in Africa? *(Sample response: loyalty to tribe or ethnic group before country; because in some countries, several ethnic groups are competing for power and resources)*

Discuss Have a class discussion about the effect of one-party governments on various states in Africa. What was frequently the reason for the one-party state? *(Sample response: Leaders argued that multiple parties would lead to disunity.)* Does this reason have any merit? Why or why not? *(Answers may vary. Some students might argue that the leaders only wanted power. Others might point out that leaders had a legitimate concern that ethnic groups could form parties, which would result in conflict and civil war.)* What was the result? *(Students' answers should show an understanding that the one-party system often led to dictatorships and military coups.)*

D Differentiate: Extra Support Some students might have difficulty understanding the reasons for the ongoing conflict among groups in Africa and the effect of national boundaries on those conflicts. Engage those students in a discussion about groups in their own community or school. Are there long-standing conflicts? What would happen if two rival high schools were combined into one building?

Objective 2: Analyze the issues facing new African nations and the different paths they took.

Quick Instruction

Remind students of the five African nations profiled: Ghana, Kenya, Algeria, Democratic Republic of Congo, and Nigeria.

Interactive Gallery: Independence in Congo Project the Interactive Gallery on the whiteboard. Click through each image, and discuss the story that is revealed from viewing all the images. Ask: How does the gallery add to your knowledge of the Democratic Republic of Congo? Does the information provided in these images change your perception of Congo? Why or why not? *(Answers may vary. Some students will identify specific details from the images as increasing their knowledge. Others might point to the emotional impact of some of the photos as changing their perception of the country, possibly making it more "real" to them.)*

📷 ACTIVE CLASSROOM

Use the "See-Think-Wonder" strategy with this map. Pair students with a partner. Ask: What story is revealed through this gallery of images? Why do you think that? How does this compare to the other African nations you have learned about? Share insights with the class.

African Nations Win Independence

INTERACTIVE GALLERY	DIGITAL TEXT 4	DIGITAL TEXT 5
Independence in Congo	**The Wars of Southern Africa**	**Ethnic Conflict and Genocide**

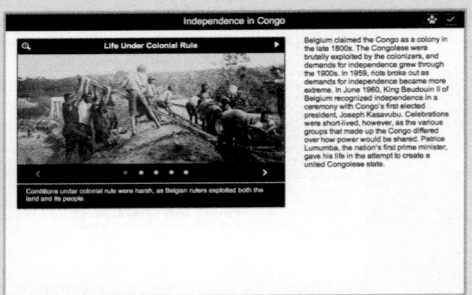

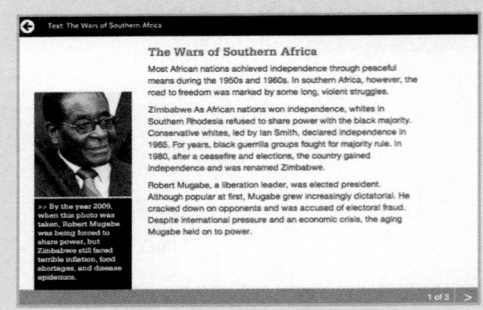

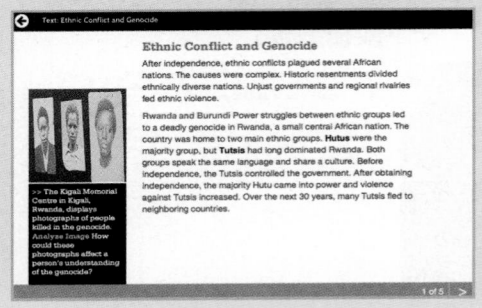

Further Instruction

Project the Interactive Reading Notepad questions and use student responses to discuss the five case studies and the different paths to and from independence by the five detailed nations. Help students identify and summarize the reasons for ongoing conflicts in Africa.

Compare and Contrast Work with students to compare and contrast the five nations profiled. Create a table with five columns, one for each nation. The table should have three rows. The first row should be labeled "Independence," where major points about the countries' independence can be recorded. The second row might be labeled "Country Details" for details about whether the countries had a large variety of ethnic groups, whether they had access to valuable resources, etc. The third row should be labeled "Post-Independence," where major points about what happened after independence can be recorded. Points might include the type of government established, whether countries suffered from a civil war, and whether dictatorships developed or military coups occurred.

D Differentiate: Extra Support Help students complete the table by having groups review the text and highlight portions they think might be relevant. Then have groups share and compare their findings with the rest of the class. Finally, complete the table as a class.

Objective 3: Identify examples of and summarize reasons for ethnic conflict and genocide in African nations.

Quick Instruction

Ethnic tensions and power struggles led to genocide in the nations of Rwanda and Sudan. Work with students to review the material.

Analyze Images Project the image from Screen 1 of the text. Explore with students what the image shows and read the caption. Discuss whether or how it illustrates the effects of ethnic violence and genocide. Ask: Is this an effective memorial? Why or why not? *(Answers may vary. Some students may feel that showing photographs of victims does not effectively convey the violence done to them, while others might feel that the images of the victims the genocide more 'real.')*

Further Instruction

Project the Interactive Reading Notepad questions, and use student responses to discuss instances of ethnic violence and genocides that have occurred in some countries in Africa. Review how the Cold War rivalry between the United States and the Soviet Union led to ongoing conflict in the southern African nations of Zimbabwe, Angola, and Mozambique. Help students understand why the events in Darfur and Rwanda are examples of genocide.

Cite Evidence Display for students a definition of *genocide*. Then have students review the text to find evidence that shows that the events in Rwanda and Darfur are examples of genocide and why. *(Answers may vary, but should show an understanding that people in Rwanda and Darfur were killed solely because of their political affiliation or their ethnic group.)*

■ SYNTHESIZE

DIGITAL ACTIVITY

Addressing the Challenges of Independence

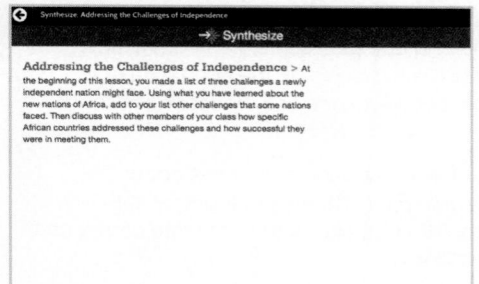

Remind students of the scope and content of this lesson on the history of independence movements in Africa and the challenges faced by the newly independent nations. At the beginning of this lesson, they made a list of three challenges a newly independent nation might face. Using what they have learned about the new nations of Africa, have them add to their lists other challenges that some nations faced. Then discuss with the class how specific African countries addressed these challenges and how successful they were in meeting them.

Compare Points of View What was your point of view about African nations before the lesson? Has it changed based on what you have learned about how these nations addressed the challenges of independence? *(Students' answers will vary, but they should be able to identify specific details from the lesson that either confirmed their point of view or changed it.)*

■ DEMONSTRATE

LESSON QUIZ

Lesson Quiz and Class Discussion Board

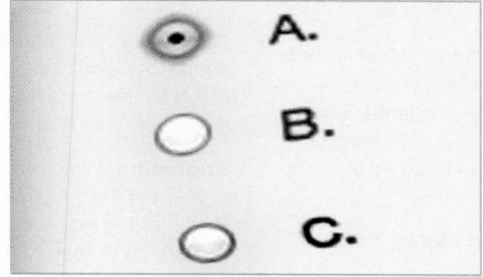

Assign the online Lesson Quiz for this lesson if you haven't already done so. Students will be offered automatic remediation or enrichment based on their score.

Pose these questions to the class on the Discussion Board. In this lesson, you have read about how the nations of Africa gained independence and the challenges faced and successes achieved post-independence.

Generate Explanations What were the most important reasons that the new nations of Africa faced such struggles after their independence? *(Answers may vary. Students might point out the influence of Cold War rivalries on newly struggling nations, ethnic tensions in many African nations, struggles over resources, or corrupt governments and poverty.)*

Make Predictions The lesson points out some positive signs for the future. Do these positive signs indicate that the many nations of Africa are facing a more peaceful and prosperous future? Why or why not? *(Answers may vary. Some students may feel that poverty and corruption are too entrenched, and most African nations will not be able to overcome those problems. Others might point to the rise in democratic governments, the end of several long-running civil wars in southern Africa, or the growing prosperity in nations such as Ghana as signs that the future will be brighter for many African nations.)*

Topic Inquiry

Have students continue their investigations for the Topic Inquiry.

The Modern Middle East Takes Shape

Supporting English Language Learners

Use with Digital Text 2, **The Founding of Israel.**

Learning Strategies
Read *The Founding of Israel* aloud to students. Then instruct students to complete one of the following activities based on their level of English proficiency.

Beginning Write and display the word *kibbutz* for students. Read *kibbutz* aloud and have students repeat the word. Show students a visual of a kibbutz and give students a simple definition. Then have students write the word and definition in their notebooks. Guide students in a discussion of the implications of Jews from around the world returning to Israel to work on kibbutzim.

Intermediate Write and display the word *kibbutz* for students. Read *kibbutz* aloud and have students repeat the word. Show students a visual of a kibbutz and assist students in developing a simple definition for the term. Then have students write the word and definition in their notebooks. Ask students to work in small groups to discuss the implications of Jews from around the world returning to Israel to work on kibbutzim. Circulate among students to offer support as needed.

Advanced Write and display the word *kibbutz* for students. Read *kibbutz* aloud and have students repeat the word. Show students a visual of a kibbutz and instruct students to develop a definition for the term using the visual and the text. Then have students write the word and definition in their notebooks. Ask students to work in pairs to discuss the implications of Jews from around the world returning to Israel to work on kibbutzim. Circulate among students to offer support as needed.

Advanced High Have students reread *The Founding of Israel* and focus on key academic terms in the subsection "The Growth of Israel." Instruct students to develop definitions for the key term using appropriate visuals and the text and write them in their notebooks. Ask students to work in small groups to discuss the implications of Jews from around the world returning to Israel after 1950. Circulate among students to offer support as needed.

Use with Digital Text 3, **New Nations in the Middle East.**

Learning Strategies
Review compound and complex sentences with students. Explain that all sentences must include an independent clause, which includes a *subject + verb*. Demonstrate how to use connecting words and punctuation to create compound and complex sentences from simple sentences and phrases. Then read *New Nations in the Middle East* aloud to the class. Have students complete one activity according to their level of English proficiency.

Beginning Write and display simple compound sentences about the content in *New Nations in the Middle East*. Then work together with students to use connecting words like but, and, and or to write compound sentences of their own in their notebooks.

Intermediate Write and display simple compound sentences about the content in *New Nations in the Middle East*. Then guide students to use connecting words like but, and, and or to write compound sentences of their own in their notebooks. Invite student volunteers to share their sentences with the class.

Advanced Write and display one compound and one complex sentence about the content in *New Nations in the Middle East*. Then instruct student to work with a partner to write one complex and two compound sentences of their own in their notebooks. Ask pairs to share their sentences with the class.

Advanced High Have students work independently to write a brief paragraph using a variety of compound and complex sentences about *New Nations in the Middle East*. Have students write their paragraphs in their notebooks. Ask students to turn to a partner and share their paragraphs.

◫ Differentiate Instruction

Use the Differentiated Instruction notes throughout the lesson plan to support the varied skill sets, levels of readiness, and interests in the mixed-ability classroom.

Challenge These notes include suggestions for expanding the activity for advanced students.

On-Level These notes include suggestions for modifying the activity to address different interests or learning styles.

Extra Support These notes include ideas for providing more scaffolding or reading spuport.

Special Needs These notes provide ideas for adapting instruction to support the needs of various special needs students.

■ NOTES

_____

_____

_____

_____

_____

PEARSON
realize™
www.PearsonRealize.com

Go online to access additional resources including:
Primary Sources • Biographies • Supreme Court cases • 21st Century Skill Tutorials • Maps • Graphic Organizers.

Objectives

Objective 1: Analyze the development of modern nations in the Middle East.

Objective 2: Describe the founding of Israel and the impact of the Arab rejection of Israel.

Objective 3: Understand how oil has affected nations of the Middle East.

Objective 4: Examine the impact of Islam on government, law, and the lives of women.

Objective 5: Define the "Arab Spring."

LESSON 3 ORGANIZER		PACING: APPROX. 1 PERIOD, .5 BLOCKS			
				RESOURCES	
		OBJECTIVES	PACING	Online	Print
Connect					
DIGITAL START UP ACTIVITY **Ties to the Land**			5 min.	●	
Investigate					
DIGITAL TEXT 1 **The Challenges of Diversity**		Objective 1	10 min.	●	●
INTERACTIVE MAP **Religious Diversity in the Middle East**			10 min.	●	
DIGITAL TEXT 2 **The Founding of Israel**		Objective 2	10 min.	●	●
INTERACTIVE CHART **Birth of Israel**			10 min.	●	
DIGITAL TEXT 3 **New Nations in the Middle East**		Objectives 1, 5	10 min.	●	●
DIGITAL TEXT 4 **The Importance of Oil in the Middle East**		Objective 3	10 min.	●	●
DIGITAL TEXT 5 **Islam and the Modern World**		Objective 4	10 min.	●	●
Synthesize					
DIGITAL ACTIVITY **The Changing Middle East**			5 min.	●	
Demonstrate					
DIGITAL QUIZ **Lesson Quiz and Class Discussion Board**			10 min.	●	

The Modern Middle East Takes Shape

■ CONNECT

DIGITAL START UP ACTIVITY
Ties to the Land

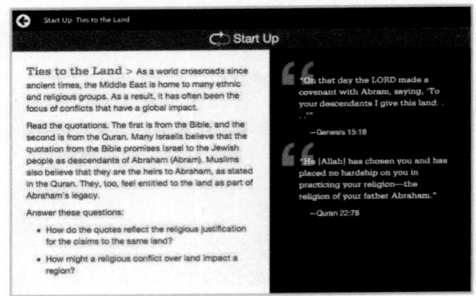

Project the Start Up Activity as the students enter and get settled. Have them read the quotes and answer the following questions: How do the quotes reflect the religious justification for the claims to the same land? *(Each quote gives the justification that God (Allah) has provided the right to the land based on being descendants of Abraham.)*

Connect Ask students to think about a disagreement they have had with a friend or family member. How was the disagreement settled? Was a compromise reached in which each party had to give up something in order to resolve the disagreement?

Aa Vocabulary Development: Use the Interactive Reading Notepad to preview the Key Terms and Academic Vocabulary in this lesson with students.

⇅ FLIP IT!
Assign the Flipped Video for this lesson.

■ STUDENT EDITION PRINT PAGES: 829–836

■ INVESTIGATE

DIGITAL TEXT 1
The Challenges of Diversity

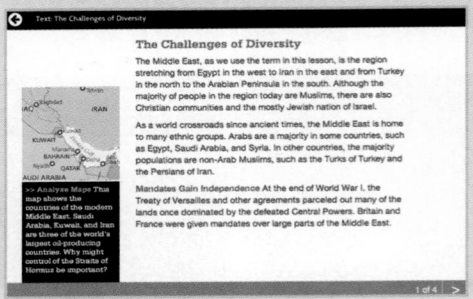

INTERACTIVE MAP
Religious Diversity in the Middle East

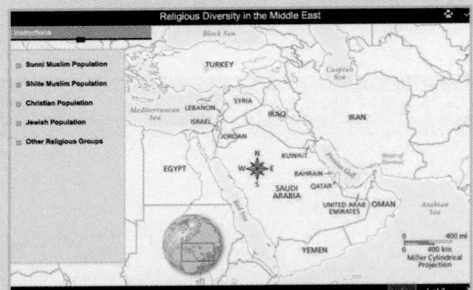

Objective 1: Analyze the development of modern nations in the Middle East.

Quick Instruction
Interactive Map: Religious Diversity in the Middle East Project the interactive map showing religious diversity in the Middle East. Click through the layers and have students read the captions aloud. Ask students to answer the question individually, in small groups, or as a class.

Analyze Maps Which country has the largest Shiite majority? *(Iran)* Which country has the largest population of Christians? *(Lebanon)*

👥 ACTIVE CLASSROOM
Organize students into pairs to work on the See-Think-Wonder strategy. Project the different layers of the map in sequence. Allow students to look at the map quietly for two minutes. Ask them: What do you see? What does that make you think? What are you wondering about now that you've seen this? Repeat with the other layers. Have students share their insights first with their partner, and then with the class.

D Differentiate: Extra Support What do you think the word *mandates* means? Based on this meaning, what does it mean when the text states: "Britain and France were given mandates over large parts of the Middle East?" *(Sample response: In this example, the word "mandate" means "a territory given to a European country to administer following World War I." The mandates were given to*

Britain and France to administer territories that were taken from the defeated Ottoman empire and transferred to Europeans to run.)

Further Instruction
The Challenges of Diversity: Core Text and Interactive Reading Notepad Project and discuss the Interactive Reading Notepad questions.

Remind students that much of the modern Middle East had been part of the Ottoman empire. These became part of the mandate system as a result of the Treaty of Versailles and other agreements that followed World War I, giving Britain and France control over much of the region. The people who lived in these areas resisted these developments, and independence movements grew.

Connect How did the mandate system, set in place after World War I, contribute to violence in the Middle East? *(Sample response: The mandates increased tension between Arabs and Jews because both groups wanted to establish independent nations in the Palestine Mandate. The mandates were eventually divided into Iraq, Syria, Lebanon, Jordan, and Israel. However, the borders of these nations grouped together diverse ethnic and religious communities, creating further tension).*

Hypothesize What negative effects can a diverse population have? *(Sample response: If there isn't enough national spirit and cohesiveness holding people together, there can be conflict between different ethnic or religious groups.)* What positive results can grow out of diversity? *(Society can become rich through its multiculturalism.)*

DIGITAL TEXT 2

The Founding of Israel

INTERACTIVE CHART

Birth of Israel

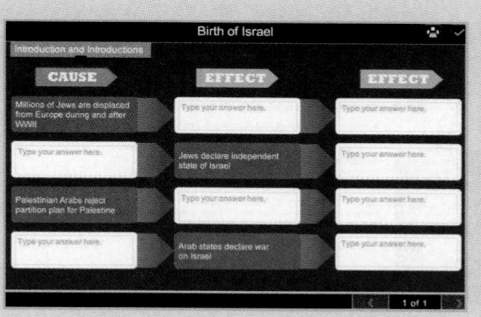

Express Ideas Clearly Were you surprised by any information on the diversity map? Be specific. *(Responses will vary. Students may be surprised that there are as many Christians and Christian sects; some may be surprised that Shiites are a small minority in most Muslim countries.)*

Objective 2: Describe the founding of Israel and the impact of the Arab rejection of Israel.

Quick Instruction

Ask students what they remember about the treatment of Jews in Europe. *(Most students will remember the Holocaust; others might remember the pogroms in Russia or laws passed about where Jews could live and what they could do.)* Tell them that the State of Israel was created out of the British Mandate of Palestine as a safe haven for the Jews after World War II. In 1947, the United Nations drew up a plan to divide the Palestine Mandate into a Palestinian state and a Jewish state. The Israelis accepted the plan; the Palestinian Arabs rejected it. In 1948, the State of Israel was declared.

Interactive Chart: Birth of Israel Have students read "The Founding of Israel." Then, have them complete the Interactive Chart, either individually, in small groups, or as a class.

Express Problems Clearly How has the Arab rejection of Israel led to continued conflict? *(Immediately after the State of Israel was formed in 1948, neighboring Arab states declared war on Israel; many Palestinians who had fled Israel lived in refugee camps for decades; students may also include additional information such as the terrorism used by some radical Palestinian groups and the refusal of most Arab states to recognize the existence of Israel.)*

👥 ACTIVE CLASSROOM

Use the If Photos Could Talk strategy. Project the image of Palestinian refugees. Ask each student to pick one figure from the photo. Have them imagine the 30 minutes before this photo was taken and the 30 minutes after. (Some questions to pose: Where are they coming from? Where are they headed? Who or what have they left behind?) Ask students to write down a description of both before and after. Students can then meet together with others who selected the same figure and compare notes.

ELL Use the ELL activity described in the ELL chart.

Further Instruction

The Founding of Israel: Core Text and Interactive Reading Notepad Project and discuss the Interactive Reading Notepad questions. Mention to students that Israel has become a Western-style, multiparty democracy, one of the only democratic countries in the Middle East.

Ask: What is the purpose of a kibbutz, and how was it used in Israel to further development? *(It is a collective farm and was used to produce crops for export.)*

Explain How did Golda Meir contribute to the founding of Israel? *(Golda Meir grew up in the United States and emigrated to Palestine in the 1920s. She worked for Israeli independence and became one of its prime ministers.)*

The Modern Middle East Takes Shape

DIGITAL TEXT 3

New Nations in the Middle East

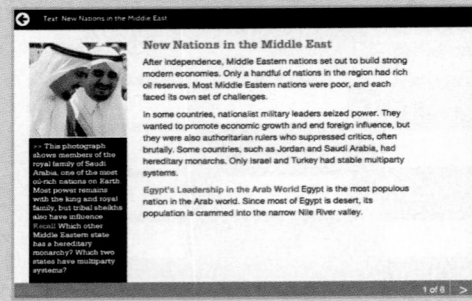

Objectives 1: Analyze the development of modern nations in the Middle East; 5: Define the "Arab Spring."

Quick Instruction

Project the map of the modern Middle East from the first Text. Remind students that many nations of the Middle East had been part of European empires and, later, the mandate system set up after World War I. *(Egypt had been a British colony; Lebanon and Syria were part of the French mandate; Palestine was part of the British mandate.)* After independence, some of these nations set up military governments. Others had hereditary monarchies. Turkey and Israel set up multiparty democracies.

Tell students that one of the countries that had a hereditary monarchy was Iran. The shah, or king, of Iran was allied during the Cold War with the United States. He westernized and modernized Iran. Islamic fundamentalists overturned the shah in 1979 and established the Islamic Republic of Iran, a theocracy (government where religious leaders are in charge), led by the Ayatollah Khomeini until his death in 1989. Project the image of the Ayatollah.

Refer back to the map of the modern Middle East. Tell students that Egypt, the most populous nation in the Middle East, is important because it controls the Suez Canal. Ask: Why would the Suez Canal be important? *(It is the*

water passage between the Mediterranean Sea and the Red Sea, which flows into the Indian Ocean.)* Point out that Egypt also shares a long border with Israel. Tell them that Egypt has gone to war twice with Israel, but signed a peace treaty in 1979. Project the image showing the "Arab Spring." Tell students that Egypt also played an important role in this pro-democracy movement, which started in Tunisia in the spring of 2011. In Egypt, pro-democracy demonstrators forced their president, Hosni Mubarak, to resign.

ELL Use the ELL activity described in the ELL chart.

Further Instruction

Project and discuss the Interactive Reading Notepad questions.

Many of the countries in this lesson have gone through major changes since the end of World War II. Iran has gone from being an ally of the United States to being one of its most vocal critics. Egypt was once allied with the Soviet Union. Saudi Arabia's oil wealth has made it important on the world stage.

Identify Steps in a Process How did the Iranian Revolution occur? *(Islamic clergy saw the shah as corrupt and disliked the secular Western state Iran had become; the clergy accused him of violating Islamic law; Ayatollah Khomeini and his followers drove the shah from power and established the Islamic Republic of Iran, a theocracy in which the Islamic clergy ruled.)*

Compare and Contrast How were the Islamic Revolution and the "Arab Spring" alike? *(In both, the people changed their government because they thought it was corrupt.)* How were they different? *(The "Arab Spring" was a pro-democracy movement in which people wanted a greater say in their government; the Islamic Revolution's goal was to set up an Islamic state run by Muslim clerics according to Sharia law.)*

Summarize Describe the "Arab Spring" and its effects. *(Sample response: The "Arab Spring" refers to a period of political unrest in the Middle East. The movement began in 2011, as people in various Arab countries across the Middle East became frustrated with corrupt and dictatorial governments. The movement led to massive protests and has forced some officials, such as Egypt's Hosni Mubarak, to step down.)*

Ask: How has the "Arab Spring" changed women's lives in the Middle East? *(The "Arab Spring" has led to a renewed hope among many women in the Middle East that they will receive the same treatment, rights, and opportunities as men.)*

DIGITAL TEXT 4

The Importance of Oil in the Middle East

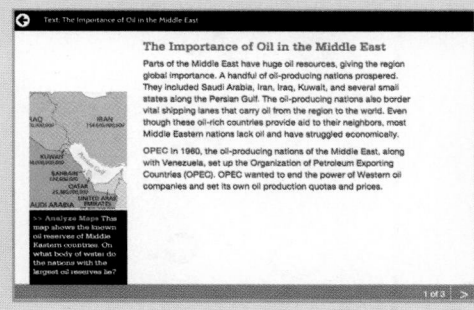

The Importance of Oil in the Middle East

Parts of the Middle East have huge oil resources, giving the region global importance. A handful of oil-producing nations prospered. They included Saudi Arabia, Iran, Iraq, Kuwait, and several small states along the Persian Gulf. The oil-producing nations also border vital shipping lanes that carry oil from the region to the world. Even though these oil-rich countries provide aid to their neighbors, most Middle Eastern nations lack oil and have struggled economically.

OPEC In 1960, the oil-producing nations of the Middle East, along with Venezuela, set up the Organization of Petroleum Exporting Countries (OPEC). OPEC wanted to end the power of Western oil companies and set its own oil production quotas and prices.

DIGITAL TEXT 5

Islam and the Modern World

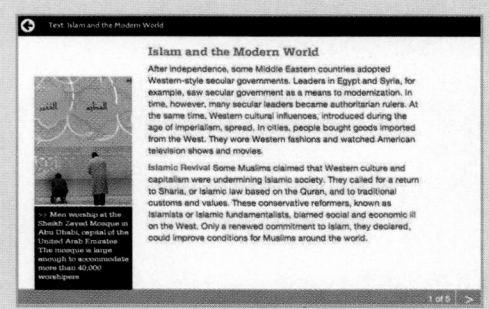

Islam and the Modern World

After independence, some Middle Eastern countries adopted Western-style secular governments. Leaders in Egypt and Syria, for example, saw secular government as a means to modernization. In time, however, many secular leaders became authoritarian rulers. At the same time, Western cultural influences, introduced during the age of imperialism, spread. In cities, people bought goods imported from the West. They wore Western fashions and watched American television shows and movies.

Islamic Revival Some Muslims claimed that Western culture and capitalism were undermining Islamic society. They called for a return to Sharia, or Islamic law based on the Quran, and to traditional customs and values. These conservative reformers, known as Islamists or Islamic fundamentalists, blamed social and economic ill on the West. Only a renewed commitment to Islam, they declared, could improve conditions for Muslims around the world.

Objective 3: Understand how oil has affected nations of the Middle East.

Quick Instruction

Project the map of oil reserves from the text. Have students list the five Middle Eastern countries with the greatest oil reserves and locate them on the map. *(Saudi Arabia, Oman, Kuwait, Iraq, Iran)* Explain that OPEC (Organization of Petroleum Exporting Countries) was set up in 1960 to end the power of Western nations to set oil prices. Project the infographic chart on OPEC nations. Have students list those that are in the Middle East. *(Iran, Iraq, Kuwait, Qatar, Saudi Arabia, United Arab Emirates)*

Project the chart on oil production. Ask the students to list the top five oil-producing nations. *(Saudi Arabia, United States, Russia, China, Canada)* Which of those countries is in the Middle East? *(Saudi Arabia)*

Further Instruction

The Importance of Oil in the Middle East: Core Text and Interactive Reading Notepad Project and discuss the Interactive Reading Notepad questions. Review with students that even though some of the oil-producing nations are not in the Middle East, many of the largest producers are. Therefore, the oil economy has a great impact on the region, and the region has a great impact on the oil economy.

Integrate Information Have students review the Text, "The Importance of Oil in the Middle East," and look at the map of oil-producing states in the Middle East.

Based on both the text and the map, what is one of the main economic contrasts between countries in the Middle East? *(Sample response: Only a handful of nations in the Middle East have prosperous oil-producing economies. These include Saudi Arabia, Iran, Iraq, Kuwait, and some small states along the Gulf. The oil-rich countries do provide some aid to those countries that are not prosperous oil producers. However, there is a definite economic disconnect between those countries that produce oil and those that do not.)*

Infer Read the information about the Organization of Petroleum Exporting Countries (OPEC). Based on what you've read, what is the effect of OPEC's production quotas on the global economy? *(Sample answer: Since OPEC controls a large amount of the world's oil resources, the setting of production quotas by OPEC has major consequences for the global economy. If OPEC lowers production quotas, there is a projected lack of oil resources, and the cost of oil goes up. If OPEC raises production quotas, or keeps them steady, there will be a perceived increase in resources, and the cost of oil should remain steady or go down. Fluctuating oil prices have a large effect on the buying power of the global economy.)*

Explain How did the OPEC nations use oil as a political weapon in 1973? *(As a response to the Arab-Israeli War and U.S. support of Israel, the OPEC nations stopped oil shipments to the United States and other Israeli allies, triggering a worldwide recession.)*

Objective 4: Examine the impact of Islam on government, law, and the lives of women.

Quick Instruction

Tell students that many people of the Middle East saw modern Western secularism as a threat to their Islamic identity. Some rulers, such as Nasser in Egypt, embraced secularism, but in other countries Western secularism was associated with corrupt rulers, such as the shah of Iran. These Islamists (or Islamic fundamentalists) called for a return to Sharia law, based on the Quran. In Iran, they overthrew the shah and established an Islamic republic, a theocracy (government headed by religious leaders). Project the image of women wearing the hejab. Ask students if they know why Muslim women cover their heads. *(as a sign of their faith)* Tell students that conditions for women differ greatly throughout the Middle East. In some countries women have full rights, but in other, more conservative countries, their activities are restricted.

Infer The word *fundamental* means *serving as a foundation*; what does *fundamentalist* mean? *(returning to the foundations, in this case the foundations of the religion of Islam)*

Further Instruction

Project and discuss the Interactive Reading Notepad questions.

Remind students that one important belief of Islamic fundamentalism is that Sharia law, the law based on the Quran, should be the law of the land in Muslim countries.

The Modern Middle East Takes Shape

SYNTHESIZE

DEMONSTRATE

DIGITAL ACTIVITY
The Changing Middle East

DIGITAL QUIZ
Lesson Quiz and Class Discussion Board

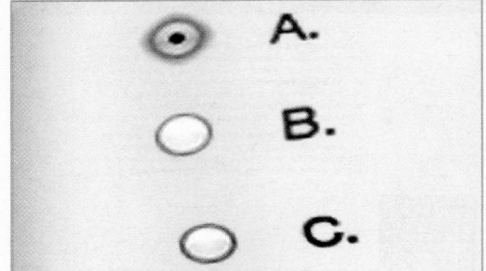

Cite Evidence Based on the text, what is the relationship between the Islamic religion and the various governments in the Middle East? Cite evidence from the text to support your answer. *(Sample response: In response to the influence of Western culture on some Middle Eastern countries, Islamic fundamentalists began to blame social and economic ills in the Middle East on the influence of the West. This led to a renewed commitment to the tenets of Islam amongst fundamentalist extremists. These fundamentalists have worked to overthrow many of the westernized secular governments, creating theocracies in some countries. Conflict between those that believe in more moderate Islam and fundamentalists has led to violence in the region and elsewhere.)*

In this lesson, students have learned about factors that have influenced the development of the modern Middle East. Have students fill out the graphic organizer itemizing changes to Israel, Egypt, Iran, and Turkey over the last 65 years.

Support Ideas with Examples Religion has been an important part of many developments in the Middle East. Cite examples from Israel, Egypt, Iran, and Turkey in which religion played an important role in events. *(Sample answer: Israel: desire to create a safe haven for Jews; Egypt: election of Muhammed Morsi; Iran: Islamic Revolution; Turkey: clashes between Islamists and supporters of individual freedoms)*

Assign the online Lesson Quiz for this lesson if you haven't already done so. Students will be offered automatic remediation or enrichment based on their score.

Pose these questions to the class on the Class Discussion Board:

Ask: How do religious and ethnic differences affect the Middle East? *(Different ethnic and religious groups are often in conflict with each other over land and self-determination.)*

Identify Cause and Effect What were some of the causes of the declaration of the State of Israel? *(The exodus of Jews from Europe following the Holocaust; the Balfour Declaration; the break-up of the mandate system; the UN partition plan)* What were some of the effects? *(Arab rejection of the State of Israel; creation of Jewish and Palestinian refugees; the 1948 Arab-Israeli War)*

Topic Inquiry
Have students continue their investigations for the Topic Inquiry.

Conflicts in the Middle East

Supporting English Language Learners

Use with Digital Text 4, **Warfare in Iraq.**

Learning Strategies
Read *Warfare in Iraq* aloud to students. Then instruct students to complete one of the following activities based on their level of English proficiency.

Beginning Write and display the bolded terms from *Warfare in Iraq* for students. Read each term aloud and have students repeat the words. Use appropriate visuals and accessible language to support and increase students' understanding. Then have students write the word and definition in their notebooks. Work together with students to use each term correctly in a sentence.

Intermediate Write and display the bolded terms from *Warfare in Iraq* for students. Read each term aloud and have students repeat the words. Use appropriate visuals and accessible language to support and increase students' understanding. Then have students write the word and definition in their notebooks. Ask students to work in small groups to write a sentence for each term. Invite small groups to share their work with the class. Circulate among students to offer support as needed.

Advanced Have students work with a partner to reread *Warfare in Iraq* and focus on key academic terms in the text. Instruct students to create a list of bolded terms and write their definitions in their notebooks. Then have partners work together to write a summary of the text, making sure to include the bolded terms. Circulate among students to offer support as needed.

Advanced High Have students reread *Warfare in Iraq* and focus on key academic terms in the text. Instruct students to create a list of bolded terms and write their definitions in their notebooks. Then have students write a summary of the text, making sure to include the bolded terms in their writing. Circulate among students to offer support as needed.

Use with Digital Text 1, **Israel and Palestine.**

Learning Strategies
Read *Israel and Palestine* aloud to the class. Have students complete one activity according to their level of English proficiency.

Beginning Retell the content of *Israel and Palestine* in accessible language. Then tell students that you will be working together to develop a narrative about the life of Palestinian leader Yasser Arafat. Use information from the text and the glossary to develop a basic narrative about Arafat's political life.

Intermediate Reread *Israel and Palestine* aloud for students and ask them to follow along in their texts. Then tell students they will be working together in small groups to develop a narrative about the life of Palestinian leader Yasser Arafat. Use information from the text and the glossary to develop a basic narrative about Arafat's political life.

Advanced Instruct students to reread *Israel and Palestine*. Then tell students they will be working with a partner to develop a narrative about the life of Palestinian leader Yasser Arafat. Instruct students to use information from the text, the glossary, and other classroom resources to develop a basic narrative about Arafat's political life. Invite partners to share their narratives with the class.

Advanced High Instruct students to reread *Israel and Palestine*. Then tell students they will be developing a narrative about the life of Palestinian leader Yasser Arafat. Instruct students to use information from the text, the glossary, and other classroom resources to develop a basic narrative about Arafat's political life. Invite students to share their narratives with the class.

▶ Differentiate Instruction

Use the Differentiated Instruction notes throughout the lesson plan to support the varied skill sets, levels of readiness, and interests in the mixed-ability classroom.

Challenge These notes include suggestions for expanding the activity for advanced students.

On-Level These notes include suggestions for modifying the activity to address different interests or learning styles.

Extra Support These notes include ideas for providing more scaffolding or reading spuport.

Special Needs These notes provide ideas for adapting instruction to support the needs of various special needs students.

▮ NOTES

Conflicts in the Middle East

Objectives

Objective 1: Explain the ongoing Israeli-Palestinian conflict and the obstacles to peace.

Objective 2: Explain the causes and effects of conflicts in Lebanon and Syria.

Objective 3: Understand why Iraq became a battleground.

LESSON 4 ORGANIZER		PACING: APPROX. 1 PERIOD, .5 BLOCKS			
				RESOURCES	
		OBJECTIVES	**PACING**	**Online**	**Print**
Connect					
	DIGITAL START UP ACTIVITY **Independence and Violence**		5 min.	●	
Investigate					
	DIGITAL TEXT 1 **Israel and Palestine**		10 min.	●	●
	DIGITAL TEXT 2 **The Difficult Road to Peace**	Objective 1	10 min.	●	●
	INTERACTIVE MAP **Changing Boundaries of the State of Israel**		10 min.	●	
	DIGITAL TEXT 3 **Conflict in Lebanon and Syria**	Objective 2	10 min.	●	●
	DIGITAL TEXT 4 **Warfare in Iraq**	Objective 3	10 min.	●	●
	INTERACTIVE TIMELINE **Conflicts in the Middle East**		10 min.	●	
Synthesize					
	DIGITAL ACTIVITY **Independence and Unrest**		5 min.	●	
Demonstrate					
	DIGITAL QUIZ **Lesson Quiz and Class Discussion Board**		10 min.	●	

PEARSON
realize™
www.PearsonRealize.com

Go online to access additional resources including:
Primary Sources • Biographies • Supreme Court cases •
21st Century Skill Tutorials • Maps • Graphic Organizers.

▪ CONNECT

DIGITAL START UP ACTIVITY
Independence and Violence

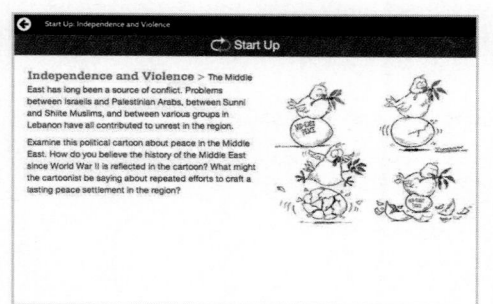

Project the Start Up Activity Ask students to answer the question as they enter and get settled: What is the cartoonist saying about the prospects for peace in the Middle East? *(Every time it seems like peace is about to "hatch," another egg appears.)* Then have them share their ideas with another student, either in class or through a chat or blog space.

Discuss How do you believe the history of the Middle East since World War II is reflected in the cartoon? *(The cartoon reflects the difficulty of finding a permanent solution to conflict in the Middle East.)*

Tell students that in this lesson they will be learning about the conflicts in the Middle East.

Aa **Vocabulary Development:** Use the Interactive Reading Notepad to preview the Key Terms and Academic Vocabulary in this lesson with students.

⇅ FLIP IT!
Assign the Flipped Video for this lesson.

▪ STUDENT EDITION PRINT PAGES: 837–843

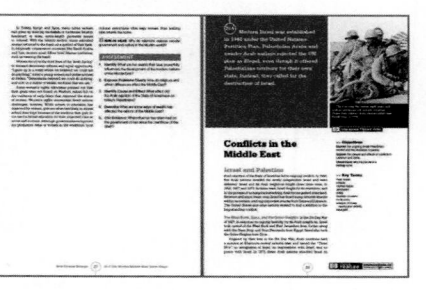

▪ INVESTIGATE

DIGITAL TEXT 1
Israel and Palestine

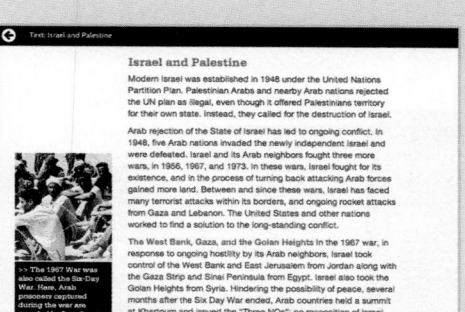

>> The 1967 War was also called the Six-Day War. Here, Arab prisoners captured during the war are...

DIGITAL TEXT 2
The Difficult Road to Peace

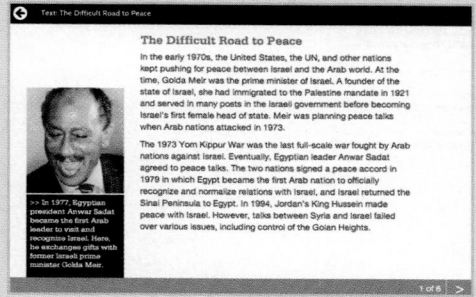

>> In 1977, Egyptian president Anwar Sadat became the first Arab leader to visit and recognize Israel. Here, he exchanges gifts with former Israeli prime minister Golda Meir.

Objective 1: Explain the ongoing Israeli-Palestinian conflict and the obstacles to peace.

Quick Instruction

Modern Israel was established in 1948 under the United Nations Partition Plan. Palestinian Arabs and nearby Arab nations rejected the UN plan as illegal, even though it offered Palestinians territory for a Palestinian state. Instead, they called for the destruction of Israel. Arab rejection of the State of Israel has led to ongoing conflict. In 1948, Arab nations invaded the newly independent Israel and were defeated. Israel and its Arab neighbors fought three more wars, in 1956, 1967, and 1973. In these wars, Israel not only turned back attacking Arab forces but also gained more land. Since these wars, Israel has continued to face terrorist attacks from Palestinians and radical fundamentalist Islamists. The United States and other nations have worked to find a solution to the long-standing conflict.

Interactive Map: Changing Boundaries of the State of Israel Project the Interactive Map. Click through the map layers to show the changes in Israel's borders over time.

🎬 ACTIVE CLASSROOM

Use the Make Headlines strategy to have students write a headline that captures the action in one layer of the Interactive Map. Students should create a headline that captures the most important aspect of the time represented on the map that should be remembered. Have students pass their headline to a partner for review.

ELL Use the ELL activity described in the ELL chart.

Further Instruction

Editable Presentation Use the Editable Presentation to present the main ideas for this Core Text.

Project and discuss the Interactive Reading Notepad questions for the texts, including the graphic organizer summarizing the causes and effects of the longstanding conflict between Israelis and Palestinians. *(**Causes:** United Nations Partition Plan; Arab nations invade Israel between 1948 and 1973; 1967 war; 1973 Yom Kippur War **Effects:** establishes Israel as a separate state; Israel takes control of the West Bank, East Jerusalem, Gaza Strip, Golan Heights, and Sinai Peninsula; Arabs fail to regain occupied territories)*

Remind students that Jerusalem is a city holy to Jews, Christians, and Muslims. The disputed status of the city has added to the conflict.

In the wars of 1967 and 1973, Israel gained more land. Israel took the West Bank, East Jerusalem, and the Gaza Strip, as well as the Sinai Peninsula and the Golan Heights. These territories are referred to by Palestinians as the occupied territories. The Palestine Liberation Organization, led by Yasir Arafat, sought to destroy Israel and establish a Palestinian state.

Attempts toward forging peace have been made over the years. Still, conflicts have continued. The most recent peace talks occurred in the aftermath of the Arab Spring. Little progress was made.

Conflicts in the Middle East

Changing Boundaries of the State of Israel

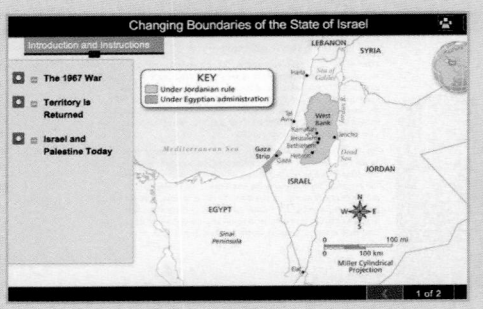

Conflict in Lebanon and Syria

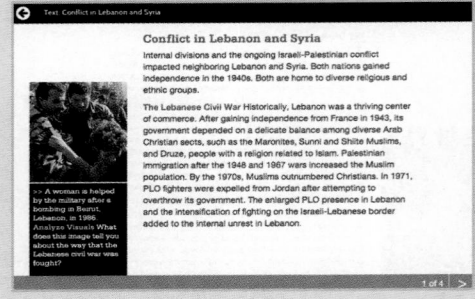

Have students identify the three main obstacles to peace between Israel and Palestine and identify why each is an issue. *(1. land claims—Palestinians want to reclaim their lands taken by Israel. 2. Jewish settlements in the West Bank—Palestinians want Jewish settlers to leave the West Bank as they have left Gaza. 3. Jerusalem—Palestinians want East Jerusalem as the capital of any Palestinian state.)*

Tell students that Israel's first female prime minister, Golda Meir, was elected in March 1969 and was planning peace talks in 1973 when Arab nations attacked Israel. She resigned as prime minister in 1974 following the Yom Kippur War. She was succeeded by Yitzhak Rabin.

Predict Consequences Christians, Jews, and Muslims all have strong feelings about the holy city of Jerusalem. How might these feelings affect the conflict over the area? *(Possible answer: Because people care deeply about their religion, they may be less likely to compromise on any issues related to key religious sites.)*

D Differentiate: Challenge/Gifted
To challenge students to solve historical problems, have them use the Internet to research Palestinian claims to land within Israel and Israeli claims to land within the disputed areas. Have them create a list of arguments both for and against Palestinian claims to a right of return. Then have them write a letter to the editor on this issue. Their letters should propose a solution and use arguments based on their research. Letters can be posted to the class Web site.

Objective 2: Explain the causes and effects of conflicts in Lebanon and Syria.

Quick Instruction
Project the text image of the woman being helped by the military after a bombing in Beirut, Lebanon. Tell students that Lebanon is home to diverse ethnic and religious groups. There is a delicate balance among Arab Christians, Sunni Muslims, Shiite Muslims, and Druze. In 1975, civil war broke out, and eventually Israel and Syria were drawn into the fighting. In 2006, a radical group backed by Iran and Syria, called Hezbollah, launched attacks against Israel from Lebanon. In response, Israel invaded Lebanon. In 2012, a civil war in Syria caused a huge number of refugees to flee to Lebanon, straining the small country's resources.

Further Instruction
Project the Interactive Reading Notepad questions, and discuss answers as a class.

Be sure students understand that the Israeli-Palestinian conflict has consequences for other countries in the area. Palestinians moved to Lebanon, disrupting the Muslim-Christian balance. Muslims outnumbered Christians. Attacks on Israel from Lebanon brought counterattacks from Israel. Israel attacked bases in Lebanon that it saw as a threat.

Predict Consequences Why would one conflict in a region with diverse groups living in close contact fuel other conflicts so easily? *(Sample response: People with strong beliefs have a hard time separating one issue from another. One area of conflict can easily be tied to another.)*

Identify Patterns How is the Lebanese civil war similar to civil wars in other countries you have read about? *(People of different ethnicities and religions fought over access to power.)*

DIGITAL TEXT 4

Warfare in Iraq

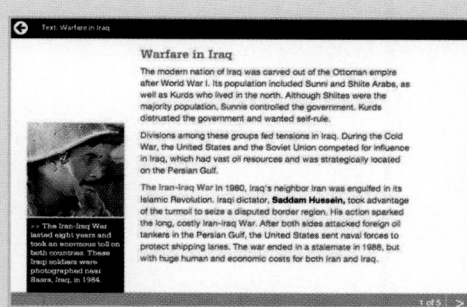

INTERACTIVE TIMELINE

Conflicts in the Middle East

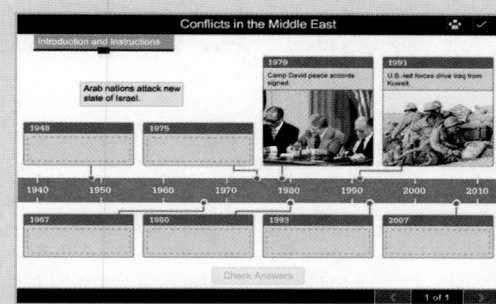

Objective 3: Understand why Iraq became a battleground.

Quick Instruction

Conflicts were also an issue in Iraq. Iraq's Sunni Arab minority had long dominated the country. Iraq's Kurdish minority and Shiite majority were mostly excluded from power. In 1979, Saddam Hussein took power as a dictator. In the 1980s, he fought with Iran, and in 1990, Iraq invaded Kuwait. In response, the United States led a coalition that liberated Kuwait and crushed Iraqi forces in 1991. This conflict was known as the Gulf War. In 2003, the United States led a coalition that invaded Iraq again and overthrew Saddam Hussein. Hussein was later tried for war crimes by an elected Iraqi government. He was found guilty and executed in 2006.

Interactive Timeline: Conflicts in the Middle East Project the Interactive Timeline on the whiteboard and challenge students to correctly match the events to the conflicts in the Middle East. Discuss the length of the timeline and review the issues that caused the history of conflict in the area.

👥 ACTIVE CLASSROOM

Ask students to Take a Stand on the following question: Should the United States and international forces have invaded Iraq and removed Saddam Hussein from power? Yes or no? Organize students into two groups based on their answer, and have each group move to separate areas of the classroom. Have each group discuss its arguments, and then have a representative present and defend the group's point of view. Each group could create a blog entry and have the other group post comments on the entry.

ELL Use the ELL activity described in the ELL chart.

Further Instruction

Project the Interactive Reading Notepad questions and go through the answers with the class.

Be sure students understand that ethnic and religious differences in Iraq are a major cause of the fighting in Iraq. Differences between the Shiites and Sunnis continue to cause conflict. Rebels on both sides have targeted civilian and government workers with guerilla attacks and suicide bombings.

Cite Evidence Identify several of the negative consequences of continued internal conflict in Iraq. *(The economy has been hurt due to the destruction of its oil fields, and corruption and sabotage have also slowed oil exports. Millions of Iraqis fled the country and are not willing to return until safety and stability are established.)*

Identify Cause and Effect How did Saddam Hussein's policies cause suffering for Iraqis? *(He treated his opponents, ethnic Kurds, and Shiites brutally, and his attacks on neighboring countries led to deadly wars and sanctions that caused great suffering for Iraqis.)*

Conflicts in the Middle East

■ **SYNTHESIZE**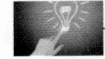

DIGITAL ACTIVITY

Independence and Unrest

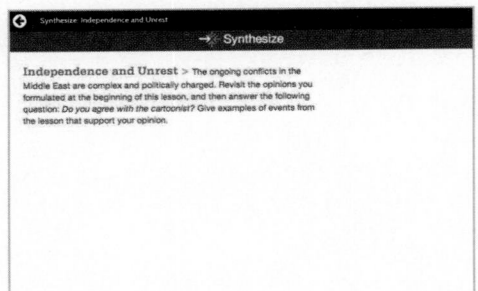

Ask the students to revisit the opinion they formulated at the beginning of this lesson based on the political cartoon and answer the following questions: Do you agree with the cartoonist? Give examples of events from the lesson that support your opinion. *(Answers will vary but may mention that the conflicts have been going on for many years, and that there is still no peace, in spite of many agreements drafted to establish it. If they agree, students should provide evidence from the text to substantiate that the path to peace in the Middle East has been elusive.)*

Discuss As a class, discuss students' responses to the questions. Discuss reasons why students may have determined that their earlier analysis was correct or incorrect.

■ **DEMONSTRATE**

DIGITAL QUIZ

Lesson Quiz and Class Discussion Board

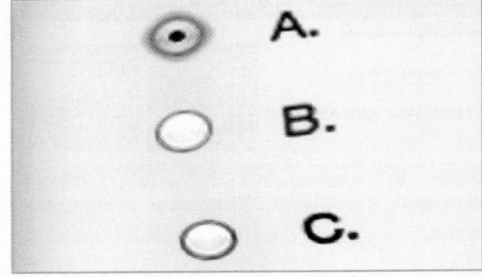

Assign the online Lesson Quiz for this lesson if you haven't already done so. Students will be offered automatic remediation or enrichment based on their scores.

Pose these questions to the class on the Discussion Board:

In "Conflicts in the Middle East," you read about the causes of the ongoing Israeli-Palestinian conflict and the obstacles to peace, including the disagreements over Jerusalem, a city holy to Jews, Christians, and Muslims. You also read about the causes and effects of the conflicts in Lebanon and Syria, the wars in Iraq, and the invasion that overthrew Saddam Hussein.

Draw Conclusions Why has the Arab-Israeli conflict been difficult to solve? *(Both sides feel very strongly about their land claims. They also both consider Jerusalem a holy city, and both want to control it.)*

Generate Explanations What were the causes of Lebanon's civil war? *(An influx of Muslim Palestinian refugees upset Lebanon's ethnic and religious balance of power.)*

Topic Inquiry

Have students continue their investigations for the Topic Inquiry.

New Nations Emerge (1945–Present)

■ SYNTHESIZE

DIGITAL ACTIVITY
Reflect on the Essential Question and Topic

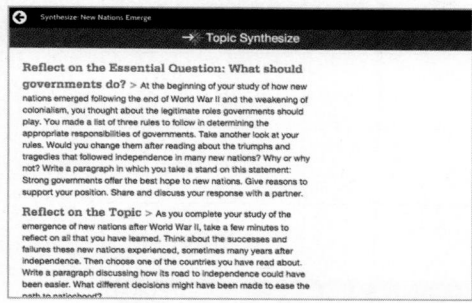

First ask students to reconsider the Essential Question for the Topic: What should governments do? Remind students of the rules they formulated about what governments should do. Ask them if they would make any changes in light of what they have learned about the struggles of newly independent nations. Discuss whether the role of government differs depending on the country. Then have them write paragraphs in response to the statement: Strong governments offer the best hope to new nations. After students have discussed their response with a partner, ask volunteers to share theirs with the class. Discuss issues that arise.

Next, ask students to reflect on the Topic as a whole. Ask volunteers to share their paragraphs about how the road to independence might have been easier if different decisions had been made by both former colonial rulers and the new leaders of the independent nations. Remind students of the three rules they wrote at the beginning of the Topic. Ask them if their rules would now be different.

Next, ask students to reflect on the Topic as a whole and jot down one to three questions they've thought about during the Topic. Share these examples if students need help getting started:

- What happens when a country gains independence from a colonial power?
- What problems might occur during the movement toward independence?
- How do decisions made by "outsiders" have long-term effects?
- What are the sources of conflict around the world?

You may ask students to share their paragraphs on the Class Discussion Board.

■ DEMONSTRATE

DIGITAL TOPIC REVIEW AND ASSESSMENT
New Nations Emerge (1945–Present)

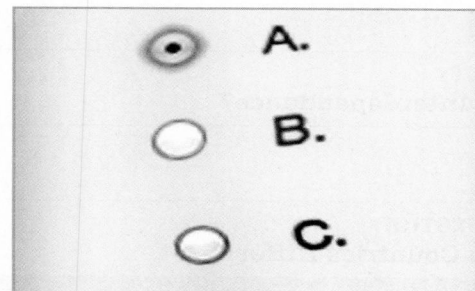

Students can prepare for the Topic Test by answering the questions in the Topic Review and Assessment online or the Assessment questions in the Print Student text. They can also prepare by reviewing their answers to the Interactive Reading Notepad questions or reviewing their notes in the Reading and Notetaking Study Guide.

DIGITAL TOPIC TEST
New Nations Emerge (1945–Present)

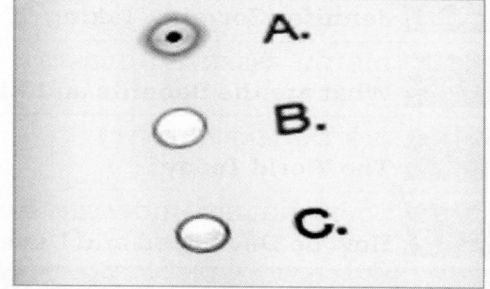

TOPIC TEST
Assign the Topic Test to assess students' understanding of topic content.

BENCHMARK TESTS
Assign these benchmark tests as you complete the relevant topics to monitor student progress toward mastering the course content and as preparation for the End-of-Course Test.

Benchmark Test 1: Topics 1–5
Benchmark Test 2: Topics 6–10
Benchmark Test 3: Topics 11–15
Benchmark Test 4: Topics 16–21

Topic ㉑

The World Today (1980–Present)

TOPIC 21 ORGANIZER	PACING: APPROX. 11 PERIODS, 5.5 BLOCKS
	PACING
Connect	1 period
MY STORY VIDEO **Jennifer Correiro, Taking IT Global**	10 min.
DIGITAL ESSENTIAL QUESTION ACTIVITY **What are the Benefits and Risks of Interdependence?**	10 min.
DIGITAL MAP ACTIVITY **The World Today**	10 min.
TOPIC INQUIRY: DOCUMENT-BASED QUESTION **How do Developed and Developing Countries Differ?**	20 min.
Investigate	4–9 periods
TOPIC INQUIRY: DOCUMENT-BASED QUESTION **How do Developed and Developing Countries Differ?**	Ongoing
LESSON 1 Challenges of Development	30–40 min.
LESSON 2 Challenges for African Nations	30–40 min.
LESSON 3 Rapid Development in China and India	30–40 min.
LESSON 4 Latin American Nations Move Toward Democracy	30–40 min.
LESSON 5 The Industrialized World	30–40 min.
LESSON 6 Globalization and Trade	30–40 min.
LESSON 7 Social and Environmental Issues	30–40 min.
LESSON 8 Terrorism and International Security	30–40 min.
LESSON 9 Advances in Science and Technology	30–40 min.
Synthesize	1 period
DIGITAL ACTIVITY **Reflect on the Essential Question and Topic**	10 min.
TOPIC INQUIRY: DOCUMENT-BASED QUESTION **How do Developed and Developing Countries Differ?**	20 min.
Demonstrate	1–2 periods
DIGITAL TOPIC TEST **The World Today**	10 min.
TOPIC INQUIRY: DOCUMENT-BASED QUESTION **How do Developed and Developing Countries Differ?**	20 min.

Topic 21

How do Developed and Developing Countries Differ?

In this Topic Inquiry, students work individually to analyze five documents that address in different ways the differences between developed and developing countries. The documents are in the form of charts, graphs, maps, models, and charts, all compiled from raw data from various international sources. Students will answer questions about each document, analyze and compare geographic patterns and distributions, draw their own conclusions, and then write an essay on the following question: **What are the differences between developed and developing countries?**

STEP 1: CONNECT
Develop Questions and Plan the Investigation

Launch the DBQ Writing Activity
Have students make their lists of the characteristics of developed nations and developing nations. If necessary, remind students that developed countries are those with highly developed industrial and service economies, high standards of living, and high per capita gross domestic products. Developing countries are those that are working toward higher levels of development. Suggest they keep these definitions in mind as they read the documents, answer the questions, and write their essays.

Suggestion: Have volunteers read their lists and have the rest of the class discuss them. Ask: What are some countries that fit each of your definitions? Why do you categorize them in this way?

Generate Questions
Divide the class into small groups and have them record their questions about the differences between developed nations and developing nations.

Professional Development
Document Based Questions
Be sure to view the Document Based Questions resources in the online course.

Resources
- Student Instructions
- Need-to-Know Questions

STEP 2: INVESTIGATE
Apply Disciplinary Concepts and Tools

Analyze the Documents
Have students analyze the five documents to see how they relate to the question, What are the differences between developed and developing countries? Then, ask them to write an essay and express their own opinions about what these differences are. Document A is a line graph that tracks global population growth since 1950 in developed and developing countries. Document B is a bar graph that shows per capita GDP, the most widely accepted measure of national wealth, in selected countries in 1900 and today. Document C is a model showing electricity usage in the world today. Document D is a map that shows the per capita gross domestic product of the world's nations. Document E reveals how the rankings of the world's largest cities have—and have not—changed since 1900.

Ask students to describe how they have become aware of the differences between developed and developing countries in their own lives. What current events, media, or personal experiences have made impressions on them? How have these impressions shaped their understanding of the differences between developed and developing countries? Point out that these documents tell the same story using charts, graphs, maps, and models.

Suggestion: You can control the length of the DBQ by having students examine just the documents A and E, which focus on demographic changes, or those that focus on economic changes, B, C, and D.

Check Understanding
After students finish reading each individual document, have them answer the multiple-choice and short-answer questions attached to each document. Review the questions and discuss the answers after students have answered the questions for all the documents.

Resources
- Information Organizer

⏻ PROFESSIONAL DEVELOPMENT

Document-Based Question
Be sure to view the Document-Based Question Professional Development resources in the online course.

STEP 3: SYNTHESIZE
Evaluate Sources and
Use Evidence to Formulate Conclusions

Write Your Essay

Have students consider all of the evidence and draw their own conclusions, then write their essays to express their own opinion about the question: **What are the differences between developed and developing countries?** If students are having trouble getting started, remind them to look at their list of questions.

Remind students that their essays should have the following characteristics: a topic sentence that states their view; evidence from at least *three* of the documents, clearly identified; relevant facts; an explanation and rebuttal of at least one opposing viewpoint; logical organization, including an introduction and a conclusion; and correct spelling, grammar, and punctuation.

Suggestion: If students struggle with content, ask pairs to take turns explaining to each other what each document shows. For example, a student might explain Document A in this way: *This is really two line graphs in one. The top line shows the growth of the world population over time. The big section is the part of that growth that comes from less-developed countries. The smaller section shows how much of total world population growth comes from developed countries. You can tell that almost all the growth is coming from poorer countries.*

Edit Your Essay

Have students read over their first drafts. Suggest they ask themselves these questions: Does it state what I think is the main idea about the differences between developed and developing countries? Does it need more details to support the main idea? Is my point of view clear? What can I do to make it clearer? Then have students proofread and edit their essays, revising as needed, and create a final draft of their essay before turning it in. You may want to suggest that they ask a classmate to peer edit their essay.

Resources

• Writing Rubric

STEP 4: DEMONSTRATE
Communicate Conclusions
and Take Informed Action

Present Your Essay

Have students make a neat, clean copy of their essays. Then ask volunteers to read their essays aloud to the class.

Suggestion: As an alternative, have students publish their essays on a class website, bulletin board, or other online vehicle.

Reflect on the Project

Have students briefly discuss what they found challenging in their essays and what they feel they did well. Encourage them to use the lessons they learned writing this essay so they can write even more effectively in future writing projects.

Suggestion: As an extension activity, have students present their essays to the class using presentation software, with illustrations added.

Topic ㉑

INTRODUCTION

The World Today (1980–Present)

In the world today, great differences exist in the economic, political, social, and religious spheres, with a wide gap between the developed world and the developing world. Globalization, created by modern technology, free-trade agreements, and international organizations, has changed the balance in some ways. Many challenges remain, however, including fighting poverty, protecting human rights and the environment, and defeating terrorism. Will the nations of the world be able to work together to address such problems?

▮ CONNECT

MY STORY VIDEO	DIGITAL ESSENTIAL QUESTION ACTIVITY	DIGITAL MAP ACTIVITY

Jennifer Correiro, Taking IT Global

What are the Benefits and Risks of Interdependence?

The World Today

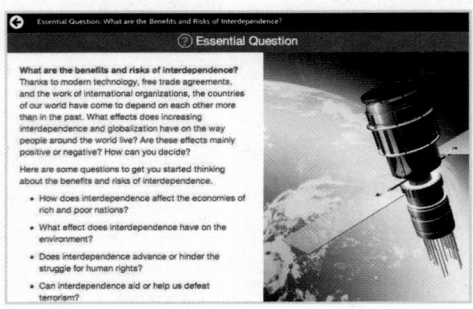

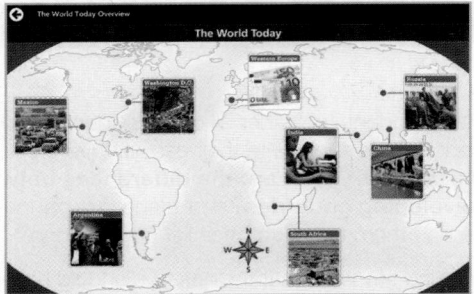

Watch a video about Jennifer Correiro's new technology-based organization.

Check Understanding What is the goal of Taking It Global? *(to empower young people around the world, through technology, to connect and take action on social issues)*

Compare and Contrast How has technology changed the way people around the world can communicate today, as opposed to 50 years ago? *(Today communication can be instantaneous as compared to the recent past when people communicated by mail or telephone or had to travel long distances for face-to-face contact.)*

↑↓ FLIP IT!

Assign the My Story video.

Ask students to think about the Essential Question for this Topic: What are the benefits and risks of interdependence?

If students have not already done so, ask them to answer the questions. Then allow volunteers to share their answers with the class.

Identify Main Ideas Do you think interdependence can help the world address such problems as the struggle for human rights, destruction of the environment, and terrorism? Why or why not? *(Some students may say that these problems are so challenging that only international cooperation can overcome them, while others may argue that many countries cannot or will not aid in addressing these challenges.)*

Connect How do you think increasing interdependence will affect your life? Explain. *(Answers will vary. Some students will forecast positive changes, such as growing cooperation to address problems, while others may be more pessimistic and predict greater social, economic, and environmental problems in our own country and abroad.)*

Display the world map showing sites of important events and places of today. During this Topic, students will learn about all of these events and places, but this map will provide a framework into which they can place what they learn. Ask students to use the map to point out ways the countries and people of the world have become more closely connected.

D Differentiate: Extra Support What advantage does Mexico possess over India and China in trading with the United States? *(It is much closer.)*

Analyze Maps Look at the map. Think about what you already know about the world today, and point out to a partner ways the countries and people of the world have become more closely connected and interdependent in the 21st century. *(Responses will vary. Students may point out that Russia, since the end of the Cold War and the fall of communism, has joined the world community, or that China and India have become economic superpowers.)*

Topic Inquiry

Launch the Topic Inquiry with students after introducing the Topic.

PEARSON
realize™

www.PearsonRealize.com
Access your Digital Lesson

Challenges of Development

Supporting English Language Learners

Use with Digital Text 1, **Working Toward Development.**

Learning Strategies
Review with students the key terms included in *Working Toward Development.* Guide students to use accessible words to learn these new terms by completing graphic organizers.

Beginning Using visuals where possible as support, discuss the meaning of each of the key terms in *Working Toward Development* with students. Display a short definition for each word. Then as a group create a graphic organizer for each key term by completing it with its actual definition and a definition created by students with accessible words.

Intermediate Using visuals where possible as support, discuss the meaning of each of the key terms in *Working Toward Development* with students. Have small groups create a graphic organizer for the key terms, including the actual definition and their own accessible word definition. Have each group share their work with the entire group.

Advanced Have partners look up the key words in *Working Toward Development* in the glossary or dictionary. Using these definitions, have them come up with their own definitions with accessible words and complete a graphic organizer with these and the actual definitions. Have them share their definitions with the group.

Advanced High Working independently, have students look up the key words in *Working Toward Development* in the glossary or dictionary. Using these definitions, ask them to come up with their own definitions with accessible words and complete a graphic organizer with these definitions compared to the actual definitions. Have them share their definitions with the group.

Use with Digital Text 2, **Challenges to Development.**

Writing
Read *Challenges to Development* aloud to students. Then have students complete one of the following activities according to their language proficiency.

Beginning Review the different challenges facing underdeveloped nations. Have students choose one challenge and draw a picture to describe the challenge. Then work with students individually to examine the drawing and the text and find words to describe the challenge they chose. Use those words to help students write a few sentences to describe the challenge of their choice.

Intermediate Review the different challenges facing underdeveloped nations. Have students choose one challenge and draw a picture to describe the challenge. Then instruct students to review the text to find words to describe the challenge they chose. Have students use those words to write a few sentences to describe the challenge of their choice. Circulate among students to provide support as necessary.

Advanced Have students work in small groups to review the different challenges facing underdeveloped nations. Students should then choose one of the challenges and write a short paragraph to describe it. Students may enhance their descriptive paragraphs with drawings or diagrams if time allows. Circulate among students to provide support as necessary.

Advanced High Have students work independently to review the different challenges facing underdeveloped nations. Students should then choose one of the challenges and write a descriptive paragraph to describe it. Students may enhance their descriptive paragraphs with drawings or diagrams if time allows. Circulate among students to provide support as necessary.

▣ Differentiate Instruction

Use the Differentiated Instruction notes throughout the lesson plan to support the varied skill sets, levels of readiness, and interests in the mixed-ability classroom.

Challenge These notes include suggestions for expanding the activity for advanced students.

On-Level These notes include suggestions for modifying the activity to address different interests or learning styles.

Extra Support These notes include ideas for providing more scaffolding or reading spuport.

Special Needs These notes provide ideas for adapting instruction to support the needs of various special needs students.

■ NOTES

Challenges of Development

Objectives

Objective 1: Understand how nations in the developing world have tried to build strong economies.

Objective 2: Describe obstacles to development in the global South.

Objective 3: Explain how development is changing patterns of life in the developing world.

LESSON 1 ORGANIZER		PACING: APPROX. 1 PERIOD, .5 BLOCKS		
			RESOURCES	
	OBJECTIVES	PACING	Online	Print
Connect				
DIGITAL START UP ACTIVITY **The Developing World**		5 min.	●	
Investigate				
DIGITAL TEXT 1 **Working Toward Development**	Objective 1	10 min.	●	●
DIGITAL TEXT 2 **Challenges to Development**	Objective 2	10 min.	●	●
INTERACTIVE MAP **Global Population Growth**		10 min.	●	
DIGITAL TEXT 3 **Development Brings Social Change**	Objective 3	10 min.	●	●
INTERACTIVE GALLERY **Children of the Developing World**		10 min.	●	
Synthesize				
DIGITAL ACTIVITY **The Risks and Benefits of Global Development**		5 min.	●	
Demonstrate				
DIGITAL QUIZ **Lesson Quiz and Class Discussion Board**		10 min.	●	

■ CONNECT

DIGITAL START UP ACTIVITY
The Developing World

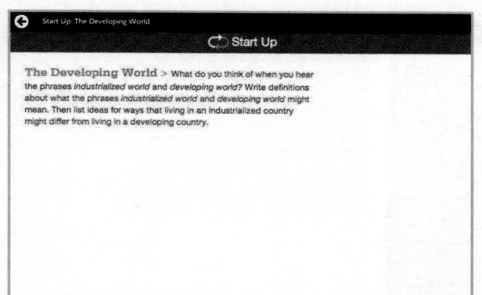

Project the Start Up Activity Ask students to brainstorm on the term *developing world* as they get settled for class. Then have them share their ideas with another student, either in class or through a chat or blog space.

Discuss Think about what the phrase *developing world* might mean, and brainstorm some ideas on how you would define the term. Then, brainstorm ideas on what it might mean to live in the developing world.

Tell students that in this lesson they will learn about the developing world—nations that are working toward creating a more advanced economy and higher living standards.

Aa Vocabulary Development: Use the Interactive Reading Notepad to preview the Key Terms and Academic Vocabulary in this Lesson with students.

⇅ FLIP IT!
Assign the Flipped Video for this lesson.

■ STUDENT EDITION PRINT
PAGES: 850–854

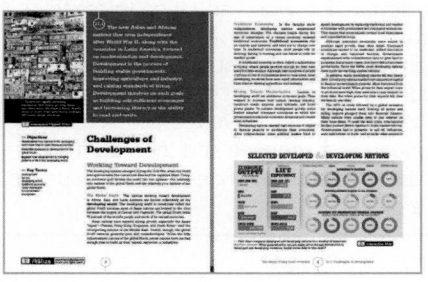

■ INVESTIGATE

DIGITAL TEXT 1
Working Toward Development

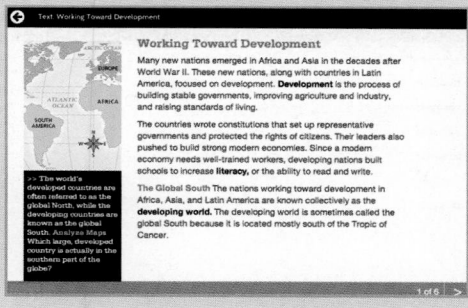

Objective 1: Understand how nations in the developing world have tried to build strong economies.

Quick Instruction
Project the map from the Text of the Global North and Global South. Tell students that many new nations emerged in Africa and Latin America after World War II. These nations focused on development—the building of stable governments, improving agriculture and industry, and raising the standard of living. Most of these areas are located in what is sometimes known as the global South because the areas are mostly south of the Tropic of Cancer. Investment in developing countries by the global North and improved seeds, fertilizers, and farm equipment increased farm output.

ELL Use the ELL activity described in the ELL chart.

Further Instruction
Editable Presentation Use the Editable presentation to present the main ideas in this Core Text.

Working Toward Development: Core Text and Interactive Reading Notepad Project and discuss the Interactive Reading Notepad questions. Discuss how the Green Revolution increased farm output but hurt smaller farmers. *(Sample response: As food production increased, prices for crops dropped. Only big land owners who could afford the new tools and methods could survive the drop in crop prices. The smaller farmers could not, and had to sell their farms.)*

Trace the path developing nations have taken from traditional to market economies. Ask: What are the main features of a traditional economy? *(Sample response: property owned by families or ethnic groups; economic activity and consumer choice limited by custom; production limited to fulfilling the needs of the group)* Review the definition of *market economy* with students. *(A market economy is an economic system in which decisions on production and consumption of goods and services are based on voluntary exchanges in markets according to the laws of supply and demand.)*

Be sure students understand how countries that adopted a command economy suffered. Governments seized land and businesses and created problems for the economic base of the country. Land redistribution gave people land, but there was little incentive to expand crop and livestock production because prices were limited by the government.

Identify Cause and Effect During the Green Revolution, many small farmers had to sell their farms and move to cities. What hardships might they have faced in the city? *(Possible response: lack of housing, not trained for available jobs)*

Challenges of Development

DIGITAL TEXT 2

Challenges to Development

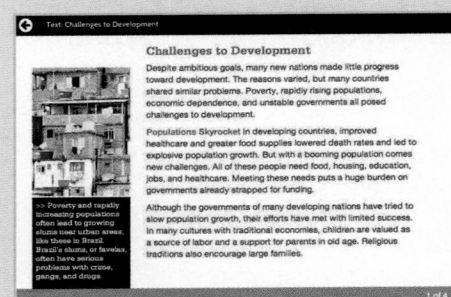

INTERACTIVE MAP

Global Population Growth

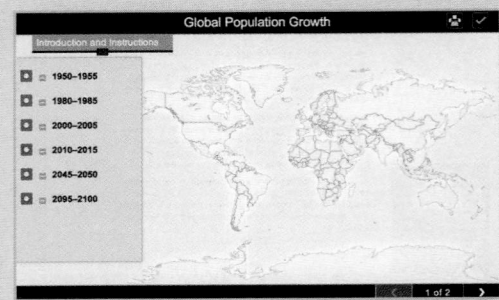

DIGITAL TEXT 3

Development Brings Social Change

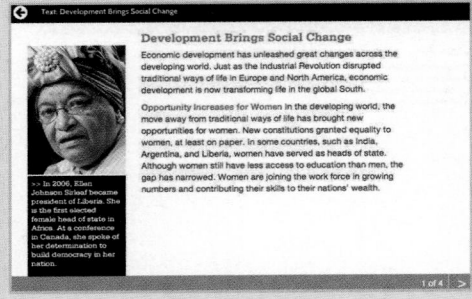

Objective 2: **Describe obstacles to development in the global South.**

Quick Instruction

Population growth was explosive in many parts of the developing world due to improved healthcare and greater food supplies. The increased population stressed governments already strapped for funding. Many nations also remained economically dependent on their former colonial rulers.

Interactive Map: Global Population Growth Tell students that the world's population has experienced dramatic growth in the last half century. However, not all regions of the world have the same growth rates. Click the layers of the map, explaining that the United Nations predicts the world population to be more than 9 billion by 2050. Growth will likely stabilize in much of the world; however, African nations will likely still show a high rate of growth.

👥 ACTIVE CLASSROOM

Have students Make Headlines about population growth based on what they learned in the Interactive Map. Ask: If you were to write a headline about predicted population growth right now, what would that headline be? Tell them to pass their headlines to a partner for them to review.

D **Differentiate: Extra Support** Have students write one cause-and-effect statement for each heading in the reading. Discuss with students how, if at all, each cause could be modified to improve the outcome or effect.

ELL Use the ELL activity described in the ELL chart.

Further Instruction

Challenges to Development: Core Text and Interactive Reading Notepad Project and discuss the answers to the Interactive Reading Notepad questions. Review the issues surrounding colonialism in developing countries.

Summarize Ask students to write a few sentences explaining the issues surrounding expanding populations in developing countries. Tell them to trade their papers with a partner and then read the summaries aloud to one another. *(Sample response: The growing population needs food, housing, education, jobs, and healthcare. Lack of money and resources leads to a cycle of poverty.)*

Make Generalizations Some developing countries have a one-crop economy. How can this hinder the economic stability of the country? What could be done to create a more stable economy for the country? *(Sample response: The country must reduce its dependence on one crop. By diversifying the products the country produces, it can weather fluctuations in global demand.)*

Objective 3: **Explain how development is changing patterns of life in the developing world.**

Quick Instruction

Economic development is dramatically changing life in the global South, especially for women and children. New constitutions have granted equality to women, and in some countries women have served as heads of state. Women are joining the workforce in growing numbers. Children in traditional economies worked on the family farm with parents. In the new economies, many children work in factories for low wages to help the family survive.

Interactive Gallery: Children of the Developing World Click through the images of the gallery, pausing to read the captions for each one. Ask: what is one of the challenges children in the developing world face on a daily basis? *(Sample response: gaining access to clean water, acquiring life-threatening diseases)*

👥 ACTIVE CLASSROOM

Ask students to use the Graffiti Concepts strategy to reflect on life for children in the developing world and then to create a phrase that represents that concept. Allow approximately 3-5 minutes, and then ask students to post their "graffiti" on the board or on chart paper. Have them look at all the various responses and then discuss similarities and differences in the responses as a group.

INTERACTIVE GALLERY
Children of the Developing World

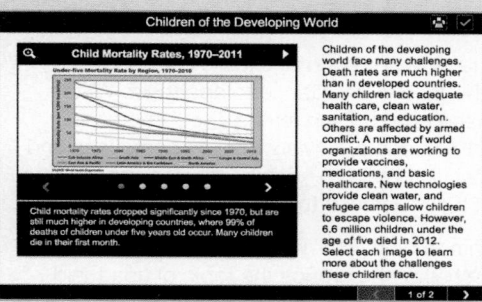

Further Instruction

Development Brings Social Change: Core Text and Interactive Reading Notepad Project and discuss the Interactive Reading Notepad questions, including the graphic organizer asking students to explain the effects of economic development in the developing world. Review the effects with the class and fill in the graphic organizer on the whiteboard as you go.

Discuss how repressive governments place economic development over the rights of citizens. Many developing nations also face religious fundamentalists trying to take power in their countries.

Identify Cause and Effect Children have to work in many developing countries to help support the family. What long-term effects might there be for countries with high child labor rates in the future? *(Possible response: Since so many children work, they are not in school. This will lead to a shortage of educated workers for the future and ensures that poverty continues.)*

Compare and Contrast How might city life compare to rural life in the global South? *(Possible response: For many, city life involves serious poverty and hardship. Since so many people choose city life, poverty and living conditions are probably even worse in rural areas.)*

■ SYNTHESIZE

DIGITAL ACTIVITY
The Risks and Benefits of Global Development

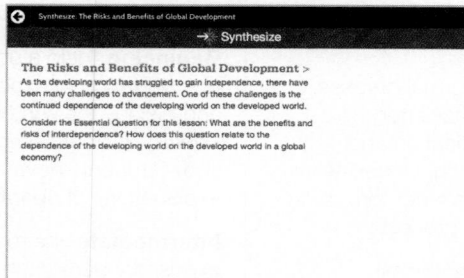

Ask students to recall the Topic Essential Question, *"What are the benefits and risks of interdependence?"* How does this relate to the dependence of the developing world on the developed world in a global economy? Have students take a few minutes to write down some brief answers to these questions, then share them with a talking partner. *(Answers will vary. Students should think about the attempts of developing nations to remove themselves from their former colonial rulers. Students should also consider how effective these attempts have been, in light of the interdependence between the labor force and industrialization in the developed and developing world.)*

■ DEMONSTRATE

DIGITAL QUIZ
Lesson Quiz and Class Discussion Board

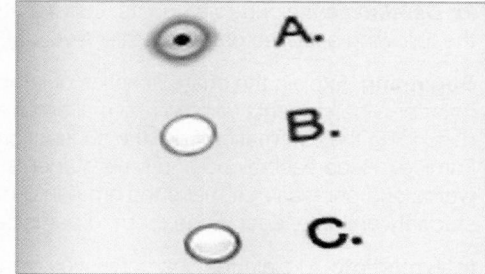

Assign the online Lesson Quiz for this lesson if you haven't already done so. Students will be offered automatic remediation or enrichment based on their score.

Pose these questions to the class on the Discussion Board.

In "Challenges of Development," you read about the economic challenges developing countries face as they industrialize and urbanize. Poverty and a gap between the rich and poor are problems along with the lack of resources for healthcare, education, and nutrition. The roles of women and children have changed in developing countries. Women have gained rights, while children have had to go to work in factories earning low wages.

Predict Consequences How do you think increased social and economic roles for women and better educational prospects for children will affect developing countries? *(Sample response: Possible response: Living standards will rise as women assume greater roles in the economy and children are able to receive more education.)*

Identify Central Issues How has rapid population growth affected developing nations? *(Sample response: It has put pressure on local and national governments to try to provide public services and has led to poverty and high unemployment.)*

Topic Inquiry
Help students continue their investigations for the Topic Inquiry.

Challenges for African Nations

Supporting English Language Learners

Use with Digital Text 3, **Continuing Challenges for Development.**

Learning Strategies
Explain that knowing when to use formal or informal English is an important skill for communicating properly. Read *Continuing Challenges for Development* aloud to students. Instruct students to complete one of the following activities based on their level of English proficiency.

Beginning Explain the characteristics of informal and formal phrases. Then provide students with an informal email and a formal letter describing the information from the subsection "Desertification and Famine." Read each aloud and have students follow along. Underline key words and phrases that make the email informal and the letter formal. If students are able, encourage them to participate in this process.

Intermediate Explain the characteristics of informal and formal phrases. Then provide students with an informal email and a formal letter describing the information from the subsection "Desertification and Famine." Read each aloud and have students follow along. Have students identify and underline key words and phrases that make the email informal and the letter formal. Review students' work with the whole class to check for accuracy and understanding.

Advanced Lead a discussion about the characteristics of informal and formal phrases. Then provide students with an informal email and a formal letter describing the information from the subsection "Desertification and Famine." Instruct pairs of students to read each aloud. Then have pairs identify and underline key words and phrases that make the email informal and the letter formal. Review students' work with the whole class to check for accuracy and understanding.

Advanced High Have students discuss the characteristics of informal and formal phrases in small groups. Then provide students with an informal email and a formal letter describing the information from the subsection "Desertification and Famine." Instruct students to independently read each passage. Then have students identify and underline key words and phrases that make the email informal and the letter formal. Ask students to review their work with their small groups to check for accuracy and understanding.

Use with Digital Text 1, **The Struggle for Equality in South Africa.**

Writing
Read *The Struggle for Equality in South Africa* aloud to students. Then have students complete one of the following activities according to their language proficiency.

Beginning Help students write one sentence to explain apartheid and one sentence to explain South Africans' resistance to apartheid. Write and display the sentences on the board. Then reread *The Struggle for Equality in South Africa* aloud to students. Review the two sentences and show students how to add specific details to each in order to improve the explanations of apartheid and the resistance to it.

Intermediate Instruct students to work in small groups to write expository paragraphs. Assign half of the groups the topic of apartheid and the other half the topic of the resistance. If needed, reread *The Struggle for Equality in South Africa* aloud to students. Then have groups write their expository paragraphs, using specific details from the text. Pair up the groups so that one apartheid group and one resistance group are working together. Ask groups to share their paragraphs within the newly formed larger groups. Circulate among students to offer support as needed.

Advanced Have students work in pairs to write a short expository essay explaining apartheid and the ways black South Africans resisted it. Encourage students to use specific details from *The Struggle for Equality in South Africa* to support the main ideas of their essays. If possible, pairs should use other classroom resources to enrich their understanding of the topic.

Advanced High Have students write a short expository essay explaining apartheid and the ways black South Africans resisted it. Encourage students to use specific details to support the main ideas of their essays. If possible, students should use other classroom resources to enrich their understanding of the topic.

▷ Differentiate Instruction

Use the Differentiated Instruction notes throughout the lesson plan to support the varied skill sets, levels of readiness, and interests in the mixed-ability classroom.

Challenge These notes include suggestions for expanding the activity for advanced students.

On-Level These notes include suggestions for modifying the activity to address different interests or learning styles.

Extra Support These notes include ideas for providing more scaffolding or reading spuport.

Special Needs These notes provide ideas for adapting instruction to support the needs of various special needs students.

■ NOTES

PEARSON
realize™
www.PearsonRealize.com

Go online to access additional resources including:
Primary Sources • Biographies • Supreme Court cases •
21st Century Skill Tutorials • Maps • Graphic Organizers.

Objectives

Objective 1: Summarize the struggle for equality in South Africa and identify how Nelson Mandela led resistance efforts.

Objective 2: Describe choices African nations had to make as they developed their economies.

Objective 3: Understand the challenges African nations face.

LESSON 2 ORGANIZER			PACING: APPROX. 1 PERIOD, .5 BLOCKS		
				RESOURCES	
		OBJECTIVES	**PACING**	**Online**	**Print**
Connect					
DIGITAL START UP ACTIVITY **Nelson Mandela**			5 min.	●	
Investigate					
DIGITAL TEXT 1 **The Struggle for Equality in South Africa**		Objective 1	10 min.	●	●
INTERACTIVE TIME LINE **The Struggle Against Apartheid**			10 min.	●	
DIGITAL TEXT 2 **African Nations Face Economic Choices**		Objective 2	10 min.	●	●
DIGITAL TEXT 3 **Continuing Challenges to Development**		Objective 3	10 min.	●	●
INTERACTIVE GALLERY **Environmental Challenges in Africa**			10 min.	●	
Synthesize					
DIGITAL ACTIVITY **Glory and Hope**			5 min.	●	
Demonstrate					
LESSON QUIZ **Lesson Quiz and Class Discussion Board**			10 min.	●	

Topic ⟨21⟩ Lesson 2

Challenges for African Nations

■ CONNECT

DIGITAL START UP ACTIVITY
Nelson Mandela

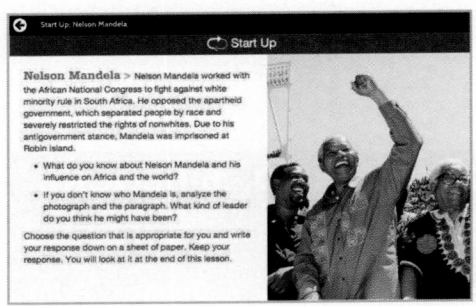

Project the Start Up Activity Ask students to examine the photograph and answer the questions as they enter the classroom and get settled: What do you know about Nelson Mandela? *(Sample response: Nelson Mandela changed South Africa by working to end apartheid. He worked with his former opponents to bring peace and racial equality to South Africa.)*

Discuss Engage the class in a discussion about people who have stood up against injustice or helped change the world, their society, or their community. Remind students about leaders in previous lessons and topics. Who would students name? How did they change their world?

Aa Vocabulary Development: Use the Interactive Reading Notepad to preview the Key Terms and Academic Vocabulary in this lesson with students.

⇅ FLIP IT!

Assign the Flipped Video for this lesson.

■ STUDENT EDITION PRINT
PAGES: 855–860

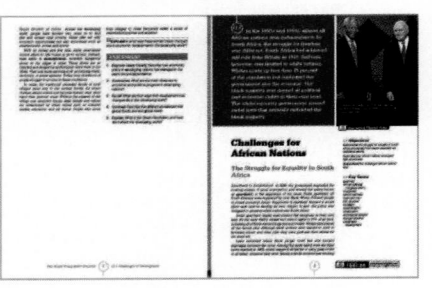

■ INVESTIGATE

DIGITAL TEXT 1
The Struggle for Equality in South Africa

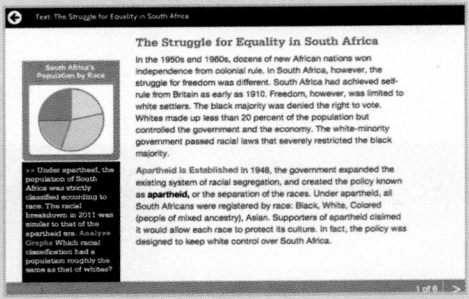

INTERACTIVE TIME LINE
The Struggle Against Apartheid

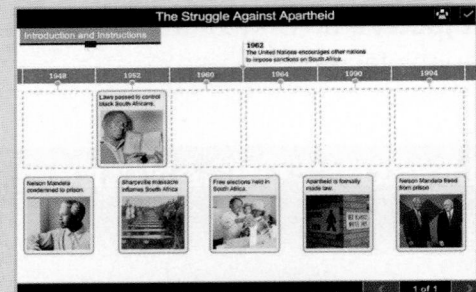

Objective 1: Summarize the struggle for equality in South Africa and identify how Nelson Mandela led resistance efforts.

Quick Instruction

From 1948 to 1994, the system of apartheid segregated blacks and whites in South Africa. Laws were put in place to make sure that people classified as blacks, coloreds, and Asians were kept in positions inferior to whites. Throughout this period, people in South Africa fought against apartheid. The most famous is Nelson Mandela, who was imprisoned for 27 years, yet still led the fight, and ultimately became the president of a free and democratic South Africa. Help students identify why Nelson Mandela was a key individual in the resistance to political oppression.

Interactive Time Line: The Struggle Against Apartheid Project the drag and drop time line and work with students to correctly position each event, from the beginning of apartheid to free elections in 1994. Remind students that every event in the time line is detailed in the text.

🖳 ACTIVE CLASSROOM

Have students use the Make Headlines strategy to write headlines that capture the conditions depicted by the time line. Ask: If you were to write a headline capturing the most important main idea of the struggle against apartheid, what would the headline be? Exchange your headline with a partner and try to edit and improve each other's headlines.

Integrate Information As students complete drag and drop items in the time line, extend the discussion about each event. Why were the pass book laws one of the most hated restrictions? *(Answers will vary. Some students might point out that restricting freedom of movement affects people economically. Others might point out that it takes away their dignity.)* What effect did Sharpeville have on Nelson Mandela, and why? *(The Sharpeville massacre radicalized Mandela, and he shifted from a policy of non-violence to believing that armed struggle was necessary.)* Why did the Nobel committee believe that both de Klerk and Mandela deserved the Nobel Peace Prize? *(Sample response: The conflict required both sides to cooperate in order to reach a peaceful resolution to the problem.)*

ELL Use the ELL activity described in the ELL chart.

Further Instruction

Editable Presentation Use the Editable Presentation to present the main ideas for these texts.

Project the Interactive Reading Notepad questions. Use student responses to discuss how people in South Africa struggled for equality and how Nelson Mandela serves as an example of individuals who led resistance to political oppression.

Help students understand how apartheid became a more restrictive and violent system. Increasingly, laws were passed that segregated restaurants, beaches, and schools. Other laws restricted where people could live and banned marriages between the

DIGITAL TEXT 2

African Nations Face Economic Choices

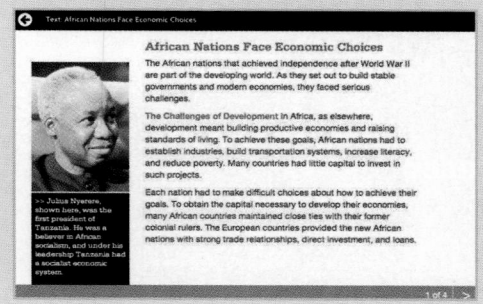

African Nations Face Economic Choices

The African nations that achieved independence after World War II are part of the developing world. As they set out to build stable governments and modern economies, they faced serious challenges.

The Challenges of Development In Africa, as elsewhere, development meant building productive economies and raising standards of living. To achieve these goals, African nations had to establish industries, build transportation systems, increase literacy, and reduce poverty. Many countries had little capital to invest in such projects.

Each nation had to make difficult choices about how to achieve their goals. To obtain the capital necessary to develop their economies, many African countries maintained close ties with their former colonial rulers. The European countries provided the new African nations with strong trade relationships, direct investment, and loans.

>> Julius Nyerere, shown here, was the first president of Tanzania. He was a believer in African socialism, and under his leadership Tanzania had a socialist economic system.

1 of 4 >

races. As apartheid became more restrictive, the resistance movement was forced to go underground, and it became more militant.

Analyze Graphs Project the graph from Screen 1. How does the graph illustrate why apartheid developed? *(Sample response: The graph shows that whites were a very small minority in South Africa. This minority developed apartheid because people were afraid of losing power if the majority had rights.)*

Draw Conclusions How did Nelson Mandela shift political thought in his own country and around the world? *(Sample response: Nelson Mandela never gave up, and through his example, he convinced people that blacks in South Africa deserved justice. He also served as an example for people around the world who were struggling against injustice.)*

Objective 2: **Describe choices African nations had to make as they developed their economies.**

Quick Instruction

After independence, the newly independent African nations developed different economic systems. Some chose socialism and others chose capitalism. Another huge economic issue was the reliance on a single main cash crop or commodity. Help students identify the characteristics of socialism in Africa. *(African nations hoped to reduce dependence on their former colonial rulers and end the inequalities between rich and poor. To regulate the economy, socialism relied on large, generally inefficient bureaucracies.)*

Open the class up to a discussion about why some countries came to rely on cash crops or commodities *(to raise funds for development)* and the effect this reliance had *(puts economies at the mercy of sudden price changes in the market.)*

Identify Steps in a Process How could the reliance on cash crops potentially lead to an economic deficit for a country rather than a benefit? What would have to happen for the cash crop to be an economic benefit? *(Answers will vary, but students should show an understanding of the steps in this process: cash crops mean less land for growing food, which leads to the need to import food, which leads to money spent on food and food subsidies rather than on development. For a cash crop to be an economic benefit, the government would have to make more from the crop than it spent on importing food.)*

Further Instruction

Project the Interactive Reading Notepad questions, and use student responses to discuss how African nations developed economically. Make sure students understand the difference between socialism and communism. Also point out that, despite sometimes severe challenges, some African nations were making important strides toward prosperity.

Compare Points of View As a class, examine the differences between capitalism and socialism. Extend the compare and contrast exercise in the Interactive Reading Notepad by having a discussion about why certain choices were made. Why did some leaders believe socialism was the best economic choice? *(Sample response: They thought that socialism would help reduce inequality.)* Why did others hope capitalism was the best economic choice? *(Sample response: They thought capitalism would promote foreign lending and lead to more development.)*

Analyze Context Help students make inferences about how the past influenced the present. How might the history of the continent have influenced some leaders' decisions? *(Answers may vary, but students should show an understanding that some leaders might have felt anger toward their former rulers and wanted to distance their countries from them, while others did not.)*

D **Differentiate: Challenge/Gifted** Have students learn more about African socialism. Who were its proponents? Why was it developed? Did it succeed? Why or why not? How was it different from other forms of socialism around the world?

Topic ㉑ Lesson 2

Challenges for African Nations

DIGITAL TEXT 3

Continuing Challenges to Development

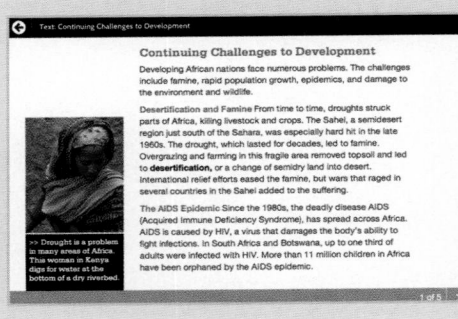

INTERACTIVE GALLERY

Environmental Challenges in Africa

Objective 1: Understand the challenges African nations face.

Quick Instruction

Africa faces many challenges, not the least of which are the environmental problems caused by deforestation and desertification. Help students understand how these two problems are linked and why they are occurring in Africa. How might these issues contribute to ongoing conflict in Africa?

Interactive Drill Down: Environmental Challenges in Africa Project the drill down and take students through the items in it. Analyze the maps and the graphs and explore their meaning with students. Show students a physical map of Africa. Work with them to connect the physical map with the areas of deforestation and desertification. What countries are most affected? Why? How will deforestation and desertification affect these countries' futures? Help students understand that desertification and deforestation are linked. Ask students to consider what they have learned about the economic needs of African nations and the benefits of logging, mining, and agriculture. Then have them consider the dangers of deforestation and desertification.

📷 ACTIVE CLASSROOM

Ask students to Take a Stand on the following question: Do the economic needs of Africa outweigh the risks and drawbacks of development? Ask students to divide into two groups based on their answer and move to separate areas of the classroom. Ask students to talk with each other to compare their reasons for answering yes or no. Ask a representative from each side to present and defend the group's point of view.

ELL Use the ELL activity described in the ELL chart.

Further Instruction

Project the Interactive Reading Notepad graphic organizer and work as a class to complete it. Use students' responses to extend the discussion about the challenges faced by African countries. Help students summarize how these challenges are among the reasons there are ongoing conflicts in Africa.

Compare and Contrast Is the urbanization of Africa similar in any way to industrialization in Europe and North America? Why or why not? *(Answers will vary. Some students may point out similarities such as the transfer of populations from rural to urban and the great overcrowding and poverty of the cities in both situations. Others may point out that the lack of industrialization or stable governments in Africa makes the two situations very different.)*

D **Differentiate: Special Needs** Help students with special needs understand how deforestation leads to desertification by setting up a science experiment in the classroom. In two trays plant fast-growing seedlings. Water both trays sufficiently for healthy growth. Once the seedlings are growing, cut all the seedlings in one tray, leaving only tiny stubs. Then stop or significantly lower the amount of watering of both trays. Have students witness that the soil with the growing seedlings stays moist longer than the tray with the exposed soil.

■ SYNTHESIZE

■ DEMONSTRATE

DIGITAL ACTIVITY

Glory and Hope

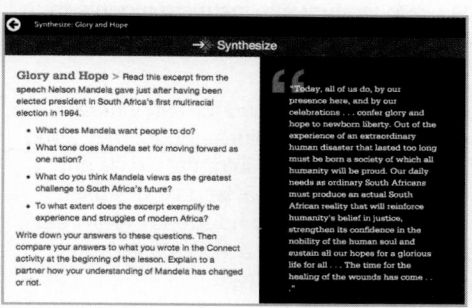

LESSON QUIZ

Lesson Quiz and Class Discussion Board

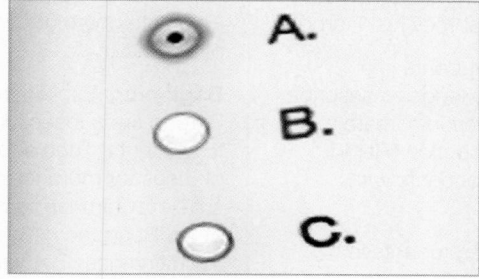

Remind students of the main issues connected to the lesson and the challenges faced by Africa as it moves to modernize. Project the Synthesize screen, and have students read the excerpt.

Discuss Before students answer the questions, lead a class discussion on what Mandela is saying in this speech. Are there any underlying meanings? What does Mandela mean by "the healing of the wounds"? What does he mean by "there is no easy road to freedom"? Why does he talk of "national reconciliation"?

Analyze a Primary Source Do you find this speech moving? Why or why not? Is this the speech Mandela should have given on this occasion? Why or why not? Is this speech an example of how Mandela was successful in shifting political thought? If so, how? If not, why not? *(Answers may vary, but students should be able to justify their answer with specific explanations and reasoning.)*

Assign the online Lesson Quiz for this lesson if you haven't already done so. Students will be offered automatic remediation or enrichment based on their score.

In this lesson you have read about how African nations are moving to modernize and how Nelson Mandela successfully led the resistance to political oppression in South Africa. You have read about the challenges facing many of the countries of Africa and some of its successes.

Predict Consequences What do you think will happen in Africa in the next 50 years and why? Will South Africa become the country Mandela spoke of in his speech? Why or why not? *(Answers will vary. Some students may believe that the problems facing the nations of Africa will lead to a bleak future for the continent. Other students may point to positive shifts in African economics and politics as well as inspirational figures such as Mandela and Maathai.)*

Topic Inquiry

Launch the Topic Inquiry with students after introducing the Topic.

Rapid Development in China and India

Supporting English Language Learners

Use with Digital Text 2, **Reforms Bring Growth and Challenges.**

Learning Strategies
Have students use their prior knowledge to create a concept web on industrialization. After reading "Rapid Industrialization", help them identify connections between what they already know and what they just learned.

Beginning Display the word *industrialization*. Guide students in a brainstorming activity in which they use their prior knowledge to describe what comes to mind when they think about *industrialization*. Create a word web for student responses. Then reread the subsection "Rapid Industrialization" aloud and pause whenever the text connects with information in the word web.

Intermediate Display the word *industrialization*. Guide students in a brainstorming activity in which they use their prior knowledge to describe what comes to mind when they think about *industrialization*. Have students create a word web for their responses. Then reread the subsection "Rapid Industrialization" aloud and invite students to identify connections between the text and the information in the concept web.

Advanced Display the word *industrialization*. Have small groups work together to create a word web that describes what they know about *industrialization*. Have each group reread the subsection "Rapid Industrialization" and identify connections between the text and the information in their concept web. Have students take notes on their connections and share them with the entire group.

Advanced High Have partners work together to create a word web to describe what they know about *industrialization*. Instruct pairs to reread the subsection "Rapid Industrialization" and identify connections between the text and the information in their concept web. Have partners take notes on their connections and share them with the group.

Use with Digital Text 1, **Reform and Repression in China.**

Learning Strategies
Explain the characteristics of formal or informal English again. Read *Reform and Repression in China* aloud to students. Instruct students to complete one of the following activities based on their level of English proficiency.

Beginning Explain the characteristics of informal and formal phrases. Reread the subsection "A New Approach to the Chinese Economy" aloud to students. Then show students how to substitute informal words and phrases for more formal ones. Point out that informal language is best suited for familiar communication between people who already know each other. Read the new, informal sentences aloud and ask students about the differences between the two sentences they hear.

Intermediate Provide students with a brief, formal essay about the modern Chinese economy. The subsection "A New Approach to the Chinese Economy" may also be used. Read the essay aloud and then guide students to rewrite the essay using informal language. Ask a student volunteer to read the new, informal essay aloud to the class. Support student pronunciation as needed.

Advanced Provide students with a brief, formal essay about the modern Chinese economy. Instruct students to work in small groups to read the essay then rewrite the essay using informal language. Finally, have small groups share their rewritten essays with the class. Invite the class to listen and evaluate their classmates' use of informal language and suggest appropriate changes.

Advanced High Provide students with a brief, formal essay about the modern Chinese economy. Instruct students to read the essay with a partner then rewrite the essay using informal language. Finally, have two pairs join together to create a small group of four students. Instruct small groups to share their writing and evaluate the transition from formal to informal language.

⧉ Differentiate Instruction

Use the Differentiated Instruction notes throughout the lesson plan to support the varied skill sets, levels of readiness, and interests in the mixed-ability classroom.

Challenge These notes include suggestions for expanding the activity for advanced students.

On-Level These notes include suggestions for modifying the activity to address different interests or learning styles.

Extra Support These notes include ideas for providing more scaffolding or reading spuport.

Special Needs These notes provide ideas for adapting instruction to support the needs of various special needs students.

◼ NOTES

_____

_____

_____

_____

_____

Objectives

Objective 1: Describe how China has moved toward a free market economy without allowing democratic reform.

Objective 2: Identify continuing challenges that China faces.

Objective 3: Explain how India has built its economy.

Objective 4: Summarize social reforms in modern India.

LESSON 3 ORGANIZER		PACING: APPROX. 1 PERIOD, .5 BLOCKS			
				RESOURCES	
		OBJECTIVES	**PACING**	**Online**	**Print**
Connect					
DIGITAL START UP ACTIVITY **"Made in China"**			5 min.	●	
Investigate					
DIGITAL TEXT 1 **Reform and Repression in China**		Objective 1	10 min.	●	●
INTERACTIVE GALLERY **Protests in Tiananmen Square**			10 min.	●	
DIGITAL TEXT 2 **Reforms Bring Growth and Challenges**		Objective 2	10 min.	●	●
DIGITAL TEXT 3 **India Builds a Modern Economy**		Objective 3	10 min.	●	●
DIGITAL TEXT 4 **Social Reform in India**		Objective 4	10 min.	●	●
INTERACTIVE GALLERY **India on the Rise**			10 min.	●	
Synthesize					
DIGITAL ACTIVITY **The Economies of China and India**			5 min.	●	
Demonstrate					
DIGITAL QUIZ **Lesson Quiz and Class Discussion Board**			10 min.	●	

Rapid Development in China and India

■ CONNECT

DIGITAL START UP ACTIVITY
"Made in China"

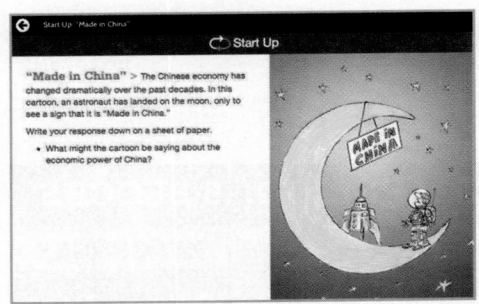

Project the Start-Up Activity Ask students to choose a partner, review the cartoon, and answer the question after they enter the classroom and get settled: What might the cartoon be saying about the economic power of China? *(Sample response: In the cartoon, an astronaut lands on the moon, only to see a sign that it is "Made in China." This shows the economic power of China's economy and workforce. Things that people buy all around the world are made there.)* Students should then share their ideas with another group of students and compare their answers.

Aa Vocabulary Development: Use the Interactive Reading Notepad to preview the Key Terms and Academic Vocabulary in this Lesson with students.

⇗ FLIP IT!
Assign the Flipped Video for this lesson.

■ STUDENT EDITION PRINT
PAGES: 861–865

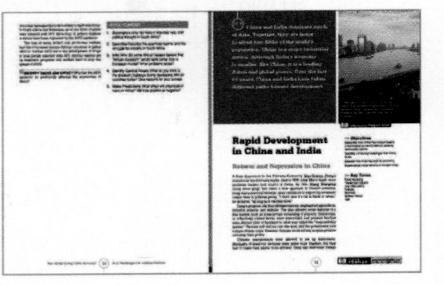

■ INVESTIGATE

DIGITAL TEXT 1
Reform and Repression in China

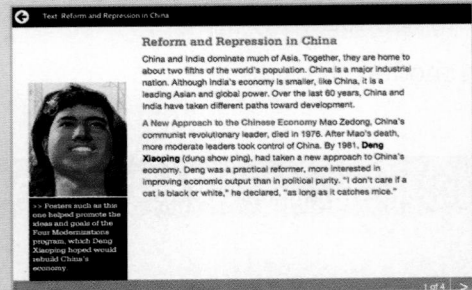

INTERACTIVE GALLERY
Protests in Tiananmen Square

Objective 1: **Describe how China has moved toward a free market economy without allowing democratic reform.**

Quick Instruction

China is a leading Asian and global power. Mao Zedong, China's leading communist leader, died in 1976 and was replaced by a more moderate leader, Deng Xiaoping. Deng's main interest was in improving the economy in China. His Four Modernizations focused on agriculture, industry, science, and defense. Collectively owned farms were dismantled. Deng welcomed foreign capital and technology as well as foreign investors from Japan, Hong Kong, Taiwan, and Western nations.

Interactive Gallery: Protests in Tiananmen Square Economic reforms brought a surge of growth and increased contact with the West. This encouraged some Chinese citizens to seek greater political freedoms. The Communist government cracked down on all protests for democracy, unwilling to give up control. Project the gallery on the whiteboard and review each image. Have students describe what the protesters might have been thinking or feeling.

🖥 ACTIVE CLASSROOM

Use the See-Think-Wonder strategy with students as they review the gallery of the protest in Tiananmen Square. Ask them to talk about the following questions: What do you see? What does that make you think? What are you wondering about now that you've seen this? Have groups discuss their answers with others in the class. *(Possible responses: the images show anger, passion, and fear. Students may wonder about the lives of the protesters, and what their lives are like without the freedoms offered in other countries.)*

ELL Use the ELL activity described in the ELL chart.

Further Instruction

Editable Presentation Use the Editable presentation to present the main ideas for this Core Text.

Reform and Repression in China: Core Text and Interactive Reading Notepad Project the Interactive Reading Notepad questions.

Be sure students understand that while Chinese leaders wanted economic expansion, they did not want an expansion in personal freedoms for the country. Deng and other Chinese leaders refused democratic reforms. The thousands of demonstrators in Tiananmen Square, many of them students, were killed or wounded for protesting for democracy. The Communist government was determined to keep control.

DIGITAL TEXT 2

Reforms Bring Growth and Challenges

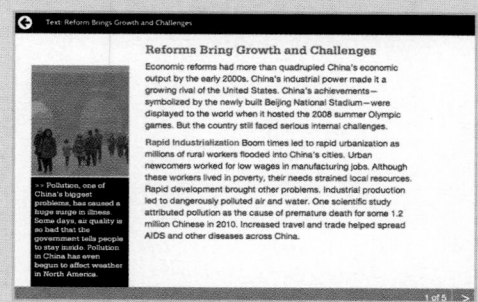

Reforms Bring Growth and Challenges

Economic reforms had more than quadrupled China's economic output by the early 2000s. China's industrial power made it a growing rival of the United States. China's achievements—symbolized by the newly built Beijing National Stadium—were displayed to the world when it hosted the 2008 summer Olympic games. But the country still faced serious internal challenges.

Rapid Industrialization Boom times led to rapid urbanization as millions of rural workers flooded into China's cities. Urban newcomers worked for low wages in manufacturing jobs. Although these workers lived in poverty, their needs strained local resources. Rapid development brought other problems. Industrial production led to dangerously polluted air and water. One scientific study attributed pollution as the cause of premature death for some 1.2 million Chinese in 2010. Increased travel and trade helped spread AIDS and other diseases across China.

>> Pollution, one of China's biggest problems, has caused a huge surge in illness Some days, air quality is so bad that the government tells people to stay inside. Pollution in China has even begun to affect weather in North America.

Tell students that Tiananmen Square is located in the center of Beijing, China. It is more than 100 acres in size and was the site of several important political events and protests over the years.

D Differentiate: Challenge/Gifted Have students find out more about the history of Tiananmen Square and create an infographic using charts and/or a timeline to present the information.

Identify Cause and Effect How did the economic changes in China lead to the conflict in Tiananmen Square in 1989? *(They led to demands for greater freedom by many, such as those of the students protesting in Tiananmen Square.)*

Predict Consequences Do you think that China can continue to develop economically without making political reforms? Explain. *(Possible response: No, a lack of democratic rights will lead to political unrest that will hurt economic development. Yes, as long as economic development continues, the government will be able to avoid political reforms.)*

Objective 2: Identify continuing challenges that China faces.

Quick Instruction

Economic reforms quadrupled China's economic output by the early 2000s. This growth led to rapid urbanization, as many rural workers moved to China's cities. Many people in the cities worked for low wages in manufacturing jobs and lived in poverty. Industry created pollution, and increased travel spread diseases across China. Human rights abuses continued in China, and many trading partners called for an end to them. In 2013, some political and social reforms were enacted, including a new policy allowing parents to have a second child, a change from China's earlier one-child policy.

ELL Use the ELL activity described in the ELL chart.

Further Instruction

Go through the Interactive Reading Notepad questions and discuss the answers with the class.

Ask students: Why did China's government want to limit population growth? *(Leaders believed that population growth could damage economic development.)* Have students think about how limiting population size too much could have negative consequences in the future.

Ask student to define "human rights" in their own words and identify some important human rights. Compile a list of the rights students identified. Be sure students understand that while China's economy grew dramatically, its record on human rights remained poor.

Predict Consequences Air and water pollution remains a problem in China. What are possible consequences if the amount of pollution is not lowered? *(Possible answer: continued premature deaths due to poor air and water quality, more illness due to pollution, less productivity, and a slowing of the economy)*

Identify Cause and Effect A global recession in 2008 slowed the economy in China. What were the results for the population? *(Possible answer: Many factory jobs were lost, unemployment rose, people left the cities for rural areas, the government was forced to provide a stimulus package to keep the economy going.)*

Rapid Development in China and India

DIGITAL TEXT 3
India Builds a Modern Economy

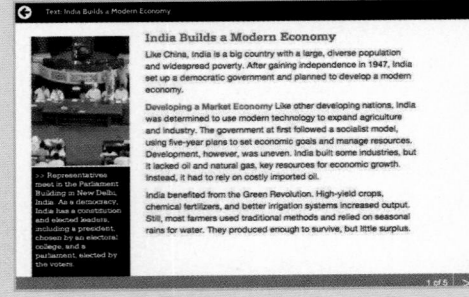

DIGITAL TEXT 4
Social Reform in India

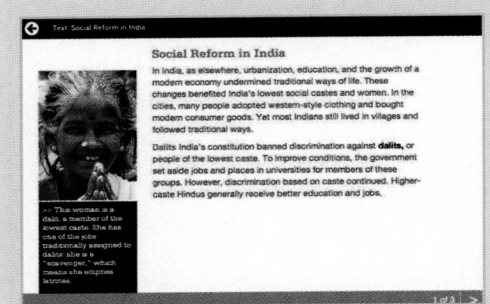

Objective 3: Explain how India has built its economy.

Quick Instruction

In 1947, India gained its independence. It set up a democratic government and planned to develop a modern economy by expanding agriculture and industry. India initially adopted a socialist model but was pushed to a market economy during an economic slowdown in the 1980s. In the 1990s, Indian textiles, technology and some other industries began to expand, and by 2000, India was a leader in information technology, providing computer software services to the world. Rapid population growth hurt efforts to improve living conditions. Many Indians migrated to cities, but there were not enough jobs to support all, and basic services such as water and sewage systems were not available. Many lived in poverty. Mother Teresa, a Roman Catholic nun, founded the Missionaries of Charity in Calcutta to provide medicine and food to those in need.

Further Instruction

India Builds a Modern Economy: Core Text and Interactive Reading Notepad Project and discuss the Interactive Reading Notepad questions, including the Venn diagram, asking students to compare and contrast the challenges faced by India and China. Review the challenges and issues with the class as you complete the Venn diagram on the whiteboard. Be sure students understand that India first used socialist elements such as five-year plans. It later shifted to a free-market system.

Cite Evidence How did the booming technology industry in India lead to social change? *(Possible response: It led to increased education and mobility that led to a change in traditional ways of life for many people.)*

Objective 4: Summarize social reforms in modern India.

Quick Instruction

In India, as in other developing countries, urbanization, education, and the growth of a modern economy undermined traditional ways of life. Those individuals in the lowest social castes and women benefited the most from these changes. The government banned discrimination against dalits and also granted equal rights to women.

Interactive Gallery: India on the Rise Project the images and charts one at a time on the whiteboard. Have students make note of the percentage of GNP each area claims for each year. Ask: About how many people work in Indian call centers, servicing U.S. customers? *(around 350,000)*

📷 ACTIVE CLASSROOM

Use the Sticky Notes strategy with students. Ask students to spend three minutes jotting down their response to this question on sticky notes: What do these graphs tell you about the economy of India? Have students turn to a partner and share their responses. *(The services area of the GNP is growing, while agriculture and industry are staying relatively the same.)*

SYNTHESIZE

DEMONSTRATE

INTERACTIVE GALLERY

India on the Rise

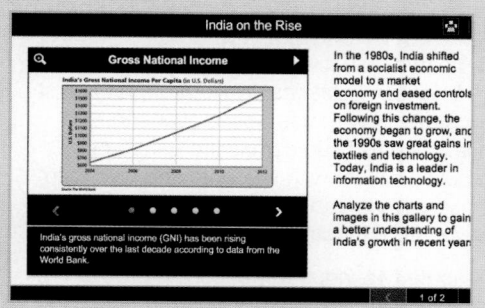

DIGITAL ACTIVITY

The Economies of China and India

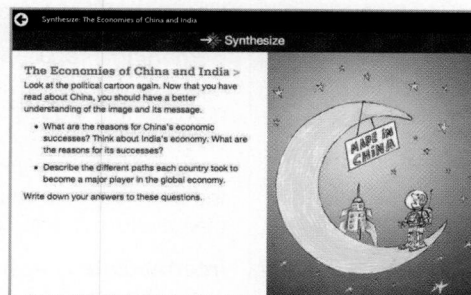

DIGITAL QUIZ

Lesson Quiz and Class Discussion Board

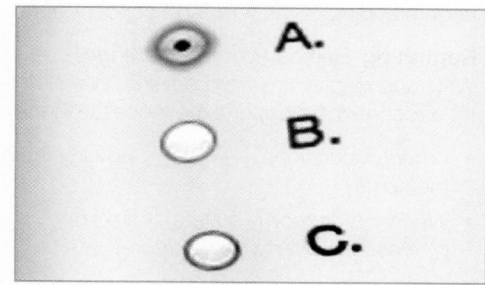

Further Instruction

Go through the Interactive Reading Notepad questions and discuss the answers as a class.

Make Generalizations Mother Teresa's mission helped fight poverty but did not end it in India. What government actions were taken to end poverty in India? *(Possible answer: banning the caste system and discrimination against people of the lowest class, providing jobs and education to the poorest groups)*

Look at the political cartoon again. Now that you have read about China, you should have a better understanding of the image and its message. What are the reasons for China's economic successes? What are the reasons for India's successes? *(China and India have been successful economically because they moved towards free-market economies.)* Describe the different paths each country took to become dominant in the global economy. *(China allowed for privatization of businesses and land ownership. Foreign investment was encouraged. Economic reforms brought growth. India followed a socialist model, but then switched to a market economy. Industries were privatized, and foreign investment was broadened. Some industries, like information technology, saw rapid expansion.)* Write down your answers to these questions.

Assign the online Lesson Quiz for this lesson if you haven't already done so. Students will be offered automatic remediation or enrichment based on their scores.

Pose these questions to the class on the Discussion Board:

In "Rapid Development in China and India," you read about the problems faced by both China and India as their populations grew and developed as nations. Together, they are home to about 40 percent of the world's population. Both countries have issues with large populations and poverty. China and India each took a different path toward development. China remains a communist nation and limits human rights. India began with a socialist model but moved to a free-market economy.

Draw Conclusions Which problem facing India or China do you think is the most important one for the country to solve? Explain your answer. *(Responses may refer to any of the major problems discussed, such as poverty, population growth, debt, human rights, economic and political reform, or environmental damage. They should be well reasoned and supported with facts.)*

Make Generalizations How has rapid population growth affected India and China? *(It put pressure on local and national governments to try to provide public services and has led to poverty and high unemployment.)*

Topic Inquiry

Have students continue their investigations for the Topic Inquiry.

Latin American Nations Move Toward Democracy

Supporting English Language Learners

Use with Digital Text 1, **Poverty Challenges Latin America.**

Learning Strategies
Read *Poverty Challenges Latin America* aloud to students. Then have students use their personal experiences to help them enhance their understanding of the term and concept of poverty.

Beginning Reread *Poverty Challenges Latin America* aloud to students. Write and display the word *poverty*. Use simple cloze sentences to help them connect their prior experiences with the concept of poverty, such as:

- When populations _____, poverty increases. (grow quickly/stay the same
- When the economy suffers, there are _____ jobs; this can cause an increase in poverty. (fewer/more)

Intermediate Reread *Poverty Challenges Latin America* aloud to students. Write and display the word *poverty*. Ask students questions that will help them make connections between their prior experiences, in class and in life, with the concept of poverty. Questions can tap into students' experiences of observing poverty in their local communities and the issues related to poverty that they have previously learned about in the class.

Advanced Instruct small groups to reread *Poverty Challenges Latin America* aloud together. Instruct the groups to discuss the connections between their prior experiences, in class and in life, with the concept of poverty. Students can discuss their personal experiences of observing poverty in their local communities and the issues related to poverty that they have previously learned about in the class.

Advanced High Instruct pairs of students to reread *Poverty Challenges Latin America* aloud together. Have partners discuss the connections between their prior experiences, in class and in life, with the concept of poverty. Students can discuss their personal experiences of observing poverty in their local communities and the issues of poverty that they have previously learned about in the class.

Use with Digital Text 3, **U.S.-Latin American Relations.**

Learning Strategies
Review how to reason inductively with students. Then read *U.S.-Latin American Relations* aloud to students. Have students complete one of the following activities according to their language proficiency.

Beginning Prepare and distribute two inductive reasoning problems about the content in *U.S.-Latin American Relations*. Walk through the first problem with students to demonstrate how to use observations to lead students to a general idea or rule, such as Drug cartels are dangerous groups. Then walk through the next problem with students and give them the opportunity to share their observations and assist you in determining the general rule that can be derived from those observations.

Intermediate Prepare and distribute two inductive reasoning problems about the content in *U.S.-Latin American Relations*. Walk through the first problem with students to demonstrate how to use observations to lead students to a general idea or rule, such as Drug cartels are dangerous groups. Then support students as they work through the next problem. Offer observations if students become stuck and support their formulation of a general rule to apply to their observations.

Advanced Prepare and distribute two inductive reasoning problems about the content in *U.S.-Latin American Relations*. Instruct pairs of students to use observations to support a general idea or rule. Use examples to help students as necessary. Offer observations if students become stuck and support their formulation of a general rule to apply to their observations. Finally, ask pairs to share their observations and rules with the rest of the class.

Advanced High Prepare and distribute two inductive reasoning problems about the content in *U.S.-Latin American Relations*. Instruct students to use observations to support a general idea or rule. Use examples to help students as necessary. Offer observations if students become stuck and support their formulation of a general rule to apply to their observations. Finally, ask students to share their observations and rules with a partner.

◨ Differentiate Instruction

Use the Differentiated Instruction notes throughout the lesson plan to support the varied skill sets, levels of readiness, and interests in the mixed-ability classroom.

Challenge These notes include suggestions for expanding the activity for advanced students.

On-Level These notes include suggestions for modifying the activity to address different interests or learning styles.

Extra Support These notes include ideas for providing more scaffolding or reading spuport.

Special Needs These notes provide ideas for adapting instruction to support the needs of various special needs students.

◼ NOTES

_____

_____

_____

_____

_____

_____

PEARSON **realize**™
www.PearsonRealize.com

Go online to access additional resources including:
Primary Sources • Biographies • Supreme Court cases •
21st Century Skill Tutorials • Maps • Graphic Organizers.

Objectives

Objective 1: Analyze how Latin America has grappled with poverty.

Objective 2: Describe the struggles of Latin American nations to build democratic governments.

Objective 3: Explain the struggle between repression and freedom in Argentina.

LESSON 4 ORGANIZER		PACING: APPROX. 1 PERIOD, .5 BLOCKS			
				RESOURCES	
		OBJECTIVES	**PACING**	**Online**	**Print**
Connect					
	DIGITAL START UP ACTIVITY **Fighting Poverty**		5 min.	●	
Investigate					
	DIGITAL TEXT 1 **Poverty Challenges Latin America**	Objective 1	10 min.	●	●
	INTERACTIVE MAP **Economic Activities in Latin America**		10 min.	●	
	DIGITAL TEXT 2 **Dictatorships and Civil War**	Objective 2	10 min.	●	●
	DIGITAL TEXT 3 **U.S.–Latin American Relations**	Objective 2	10 min.	●	●
	DIGITAL TEXT 4 **The Long Road to Democracy in Argentina**	Objective 3	10 min.	●	●
	INTERACTIVE GALLERY **Argentina's Long Road to Democracy**		10 min.	●	
Synthesize					
	DIGITAL ACTIVITY **The Poor in Latin America**		5 min.	●	
Demonstrate					
	DIGITAL QUIZ **Lesson Quiz and Class Discussion Board**		10 min.	●	

Latin American Nations Move Toward Democracy

■ CONNECT

DIGITAL START UP ACTIVITY
Fighting Poverty

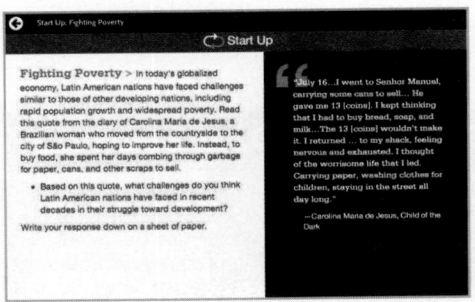

Project the Start Up Activity Ask students to read the quote and answer the question as they enter and get settled: *(Sample response: Based on this quote, I think Latin American nations have struggled with urbanization. Many poor, rural people moved to large cities, hoping to improve their lives, but there were not enough jobs for everyone. The government does not have the resources to help its poor people meet the basic requirements of food and shelter.)* Have students share their ideas with another student, either in class or through a chat or blog space.

Tell students that in this lesson they will be learning about Latin America's road to democracy and the struggles along the way.

Aa Vocabulary Development: Use the Interactive Reading Notepad to preview the Key Terms and Academic Vocabulary in this Lesson with students.

⇅ FLIP IT!
Assign the Flipped Video for this lesson.

■ STUDENT EDITION PRINT PAGES: 866–872

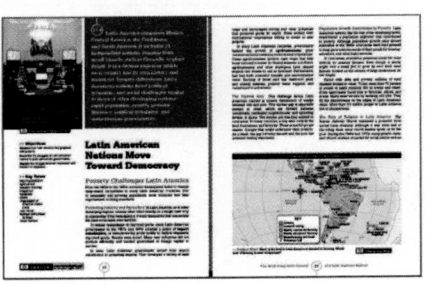

■ INVESTIGATE

DIGITAL TEXT 1
Poverty Challenges Latin America

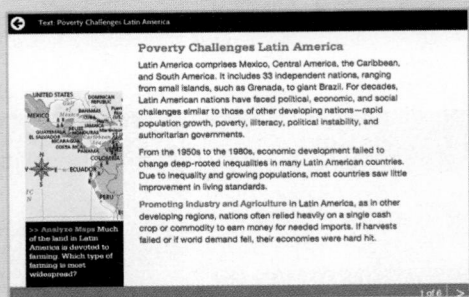

INTERACTIVE MAP
Economic Activities in Latin America

Objective 1: Analyze how Latin America has grappled with poverty.

Quick Instruction

For decades, Latin American nations have faced political, economic, and social challenges similar to those in other developing nations. These challenges include rapid population growth, poverty, illiteracy, political instability, and authoritarian governments. Many Latin American nations depended on a single cash crop or commodity to import needed products. If the crop failed or demand fell, the economy was hit hard.

Interactive Map: Economic Activities in Latin America Project the Interactive Map, and click through all of the layers. Point out to students that South America has become a major agricultural contributor to the world market. Commercial farms own much of the land and control a large labor force.

👥 ACTIVE CLASSROOM

Pair students. Have the first student give the second an Audio Tour of the map. What does the map show? What different economic activities are prominent in Latin America? Have the second student give the first an explanation of what it means.

D Differentiate: Challenge/Gifted Many Latin American countries have a diverse mixture of ethnic groups, which often enriches the country's culture, but sometimes leads to discrimination and political conflict. Have students choose one of the countries of Latin America and investigate the ethnic makeup of its people and the impact of that ethnic makeup of its people on the country. Students should create an infographic, including a graph, showing the share of different ethnic backgrounds in the overall population, a timeline detailing the important events in ethnic relations, and other visuals that help demonstrate the role that ethnic differences play in the country they choose to investigate.

ELL Use the ELL activity described in the ELL chart.

Further Instruction

Editable Presentation Use the Editable Presentation to present the main ideas for the Core Text.

Poverty Challenges Latin America: Core Text and Interactive Reading Notepad Project and discuss the Interactive Reading Notepad questions, including the graphic organizer, asking students to provide details about the population explosion in Latin America and how it has contributed to poverty. *(Possible response: Supporting Detail 1: More people made life hard for rural peasant farmers, Supporting Detail 2: Millions of people moved to cities, Supporting Detail 3: Shanty towns on the edges of cities are huge.)*

DIGITAL TEXT 2

Dictatorships and Civil War

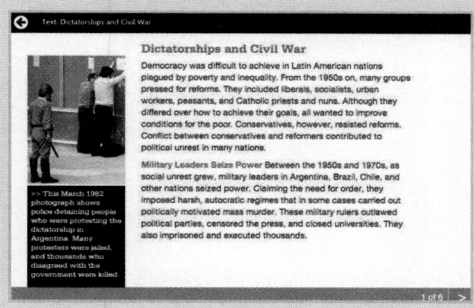

Dictatorships and Civil War

Democracy was difficult to achieve in Latin American nations plagued by poverty and inequality. From the 1950s on, many groups pressed for reforms. They included liberals, socialists, urban workers, peasants, and Catholic priests and nuns. Although they differed over how to achieve their goals, all wanted to improve conditions for the poor. Conservatives, however, resisted reforms. Conflict between conservatives and reformers contributed to political unrest in many nations.

Military Leaders Seize Power Between the 1950s and 1970s, as social unrest grew, military leaders in Argentina, Brazil, Chile, and other nations seized power. Claiming the need for order, they imposed harsh, autocratic regimes that in some cases carried out politically motivated mass murder. These military rulers outlawed political parties, censored the press, and closed universities. They also imprisoned and executed thousands.

>> This March 1982 photograph shows police detaining people who were protesting the dictatorship in Argentina. Many protesters were jailed, and thousands who disagreed with the government were killed.

Summarize Why has the gap between rich and poor grown in Latin America? What steps could be taken to change this inequality? *(Sample response: Most benefits of economic growth went to the wealthy elite, who in turn discouraged reforms that might spread these benefits to all. The problem might be helped by the government stepping in to create policies to support the smaller farmers and business owners.)*

Analyze Data Analyze the infographic on Brazil's efforts to combat poverty. How did Brazil's economic output change from 1970 to 2002? How did this change help Brazilians move out of poverty? *(The economy steadily increased. The improved economy created more jobs and educational opportunities.)*

Objective 2: Describe the struggles of Latin American nations to build democratic governments.

Quick Instruction

Democracy was difficult for Latin American nations plagued by poverty and inequality. Many pushed to improve conditions for the poor, while conservatives resisted reforms. Between the 1950s and 1970s, as social unrest grew, military leaders in several nations seized power. Leftist guerrillas battled repressive governments and pushed socialism.

Civil wars shook parts of Central America. In Guatemala, the military targeted the indigenous populations and slaughtered thousands of Native Americans. Archbishop Oscar Romero was assassinated in El Salvador for preaching liberation theology. When socialist rebels, called Sandinistas, came to power in Nicaragua, the United States supported the contras, guerrillas who fought the Sandinistas. By the 1990s, democratic reforms led to free elections in many countries.

Further Instruction

Remind students that military leaders enforced strict rules restricting rights, outlawed political parties, censored the press, closed universities, and imprisoned or murdered thousands of political opponents. One example of a person killed for speaking out against military rule was Archbishop Oscar Romero in El Salvador. He was shot while saying mass in 1980.

Draw Conclusions Why would a military regime close universities? *(Sample response: Authoritarian leaders have more power over uneducated people. They also did not want groups of young people meeting and discussing ideas.)*

Summarize What countries in Central America were torn by civil wars? Why did they start? *(Guatemala, El Salvador, and Nicaragua were three. These wars started when revolutionaries fought against authoritarian, military governments.)*

Latin American Nations Move Toward Democracy

DIGITAL TEXT 3

U.S.–Latin American Relations

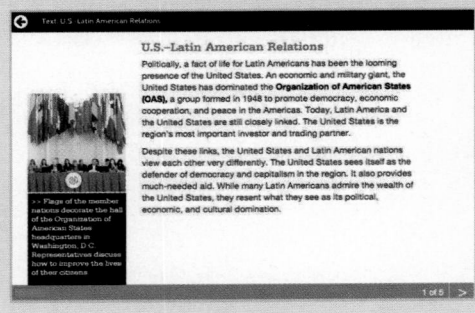

DIGITAL TEXT 4

The Long Road to Democracy in Argentina

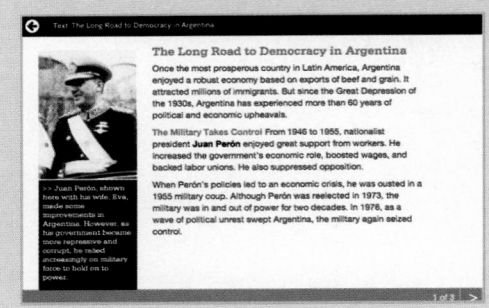

Objective 2: Describe the struggles of Latin American nations to build democratic governments.

Quick Instruction

The United States has had a powerful influence on Latin America. It has dominated the Organization of American States (OAS). During the Cold War, the United States backed dictators who were anti-communist. The United States has also pressed Latin American governments to help stop the drug trade. Many Latin Americans alleged that the problem was not in Latin America but rather in the United States, where the demand for drugs was high.

ELL Use the ELL activity described in the ELL chart.

Further Instruction

Editable Presentation Use the Editable Presentation to present the main ideas for this Core Text.

Go through the Interactive Reading Notepad questions and answers with the class.

Discuss the power struggle that has raged in much of Latin America. Have students identify the different participants, and explain their views. Then ask: How did Latin America's political struggles evolve in the 1990s and early 2000s? *(Several nations, such as El Salvador, have moved toward greater democracy.)* Why does the United States have such strong views about events in Latin America? *(These nations are just to the south of the United States, so events there can affect citizens here.)*

Identify Cause and Effect How did the Cold War affect U.S. relations with Latin American nations? *(In order to prevent the Soviet Union from gaining allies in Latin America, the United States intervened when it believed that revolutions might bring socialist governments into power or when it wanted to help topple socialist leaders.)*

Objective 3: Explain the struggle between repression and freedom in Argentina.

Quick Instruction

Argentina was once the most prosperous country in Latin America. Its economy was based on exports of beef and grain. Its problems began during the Great Depression in the 1930s and continued for decades.

Interactive Gallery: Argentina's Long Road to Democracy Click through the gallery images. Explain to students that Juan Perón was a nationalist president from 1946 to 1955. His policies eventually led to an economic crisis, and he was ousted in 1955 in a military coup. The military was in and out of control of Argentina for two decades. They tortured and murdered their own citizens for political reasons. As many as 20,000 people were kidnapped by the government and disappeared. The Mothers of the Plaza de Mayo marched every week, demanding to know what happened to the missing. By 1983, civilian rule was restored, and the military was forced to allow elections.

🖳 ACTIVE CLASSROOM

Have students use the Act It Out strategy on one of the Interactive Gallery images. Have students make the picture come to life. Tell them to explain what happens next in the image, and what happened before. Tell them to imitate the characters in the image and become a living tapestry, using a script that they have written.

SYNTHESIZE

DEMONSTRATE

INTERACTIVE GALLERY
Argentina's Long Road to Democracy

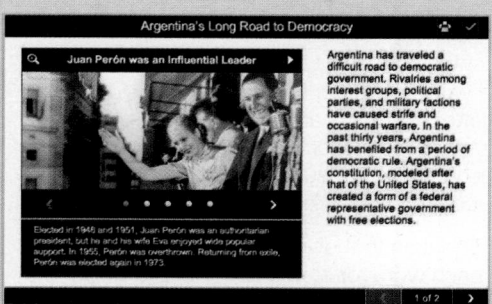

Further Instruction
The Long Road to Democracy in Argentina: Core Text and Interactive Reading Notepad Project and discuss the Interactive Reading Notepad questions. Then project the image of the Mothers of the Plaza de Mayo. Discuss the information that is conveyed by the text and image with students. *(The text explains that the women march each week because they want to find out what happened to their missing sons and daughters during the "dirty war," when tens of thousands of people disappeared. The image shows the women packed into a square holding signs. They are protesting peacefully, but clearly they want answers.)*

Identify Central Issues How are the words *military* and *oppression* connected in Latin American politics? *(Military leadership often involves oppression.)*

Draw Conclusions How might military control have limited Argentina's economic development? *(The violence and unrest that often accompany oppression make it hard to do business.)*

DIGITAL ACTIVITY
The Poor in Latin America

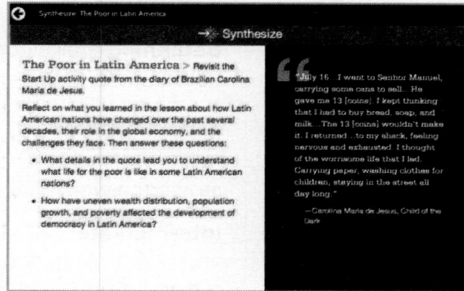

Have students reread the quote from the diary of Carolina Maria de Jesus from the Start Up Activity. Discuss the details in the quote that illustrate life in poverty. *(selling cans, not having enough coins to buy basic items, living in a shack)* Ask: How have uneven wealth distribution, population growth, and poverty affected the development of democracy in Latin America? *(Uneven wealth distribution and poverty have affected the development of democracy in Latin America by causing political unrest. The population explosion contributed to poverty. Many political groups wanted to help the poor, but they differed in their methods to achieve a more equitable society. This led to social unrest and propelled military dictators into power. Before civilian rule was restored, many countries suffered through civil wars.)*

DIGITAL QUIZ
Lesson Quiz and Class Discussion Board

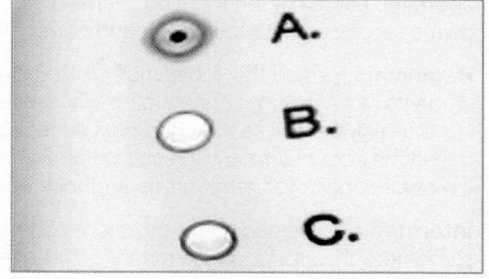

Assign the online Lesson Quiz for this lesson if you haven't already done so. Students will be offered automatic remediation or enrichment based on their score.

Pose these questions to the class on the Discussion Board:

In "Latin American Nations Move Toward Democracy," you read about the difficulties faced by Latin American nations in overcoming poverty and in gaining democratic governments. Many Latin American countries suffered from oppressive governments and civil war.

Predict Consequences Many developing nations are ruled by dictators or one party. What do you think could be the consequences of this type of rule on the economy of the country? *(Possible response: People can become disgruntled with a government that does not listen to their needs, which can cause unrest and hurt economic growth. Too many limits can be placed on individuals by an unchallenged government.)*

Topic Inquiry
Have students continue their investigations for the Topic Inquiry.

The Industrialized World

Supporting English Language Learners

Use with Digital Text 1, **A New Europe.**

Learning Strategies

Read aloud or have students read "A Reunited Germany." Then have students practice their oral language production by answering questions about the effects of reunification. Remind students that listening to their own speech can help them hear and correct their own mistakes.

Beginning Reread the subsection "A Reunited Germany" aloud to students. As a group, create a cause-and-effect chart on the board. Have the students use the chart as a springboard to answer some simple questions about Germany's reunification. When they make errors, repeat their words back to them and correct their mistakes.

Intermediate Reread the subsection "A Reunited Germany" aloud to students. As a group, create a cause-and-effect chart on the board. Have the students use the chart as a springboard to answer some simple questions about Germany's reunification. When they make errors, repeat their words back to them and ask them leading questions to enable them to identify their mistakes. Then help them correct their mistakes.

Advanced Instruct students to reread the subsection "A Reunited Germany." Have students work in small groups and take turns asking one another questions about Germany's reunification so they can practice speaking in English about the content. Have students help one another identify and correct their mistakes.

Advanced High Instruct students to reread the subsection "A Reunited Germany." Have students work with a partner and take turns asking one another questions about Germany's reunification so they can practice speaking in English about the content. Have students help one another identify and correct their mistakes.

Use with Digital Text 2, **Shifts in Global Power.**

Listening

Read *Shifts in Global Power* aloud to students. Then have students complete one of the following activities according to their language proficiency.

Beginning Call students' attention to the vocabulary words surplus and deficit. Write and display each word for students like this: *s-u-r-p-l-u-s* and *d-e-f-i-c-i-t*. Sound out each letter of surplus and have students repeat the sounds after you. Point out that in this word, each word corresponds to its own sound. Then say the whole word, surplus, and have students repeat the word. Repeat the same process with deficit.

Intermediate Call students' attention to the vocabulary words surplus and deficit. Write and display each word for students like this: *s-u-r-p-l-u-s* and *d-e-f-i-c-i-t*. Sound out each letter of surplus and have students repeat the sounds after you. Point out that in this word, each word corresponds to its own sound. Then say the whole word, surplus, and have students repeat the word. Invite student volunteers to repeat the same process with deficit. Assist with pronunciation as needed.

Advanced Have students work with a partner to skim the text to look for words that are difficult to pronounce. Instruct pairs to make a list of these difficult words. Then instruct each pair to join with another pair to make a group of four students. As a group, have students work on pronouncing each word correctly. Circulate among groups to offer pronunciation support as needed.

Advanced High Have students skim the text to look for words that are difficult to pronounce. Instruct students to make a list of these difficult words. Then have students turn to a partner to work on pronouncing each word correctly. Circulate among pairs to offer pronunciation support as needed.

▶ Differentiate Instruction

Use the Differentiated Instruction notes throughout the lesson plan to support the varied skill sets, levels of readiness, and interests in the mixed-ability classroom.

Challenge These notes include suggestions for expanding the activity for advanced students.

On-Level These notes include suggestions for modifying the activity to address different interests or learning styles.

Extra Support These notes include ideas for providing more scaffolding or reading spuport.

Special Needs These notes provide ideas for adapting instruction to support the needs of various special needs students.

■ NOTES

PEARSON
realize™
www.PearsonRealize.com

Go online to access additional resources including:
Primary Sources • Biographies • Supreme Court cases •
21st Century Skill Tutorials • Maps • Graphic Organizers.

Objectives

Objective 1: Examine social, political, and economic trends in Europe since the Cold War.

Objective 2: Describe how the breakup of Yugoslavia led to war and genocide.

Objective 3: Analyze the challenges facing Russia since the end of the Soviet Union.

Objective 4: Summarize economic developments in Asia.

LESSON 5 ORGANIZER		PACING: APPROX. 1 PERIOD, .5 BLOCKS			
				RESOURCES	
		OBJECTIVES	PACING	Online	Print
Connect					
DIGITAL START UP ACTIVITY **Russia's GDP**			5 min.	●	
Investigate					
DIGITAL TEXT 1 **A New Europe**		Objective 1	10 min.	●	●
INTERACTIVE MAP **Evolution of the European Union**			10 min.	●	
DIGITAL TEXT 2 **Shifts in Global Power**		Objective 3	10 min.	●	●
DIGITAL TEXT 3 **The Former Soviet Republics**			10 min.	●	●
DIGITAL TEXT 4 **War in Yugoslavia**		Objective 2	10 min.	●	●
INTERACTIVE TIMELINE **War in Bosnia**			10 min.	●	
DIGITAL TEXT 5 **A New Role for Asia**		Objective 4	10 min.	●	●
Synthesize					
DIGITAL ACTIVITY **Post–Cold War World**			5 min.	●	
Demonstrate					
DIGITAL QUIZ **Lesson Quiz and Class Discussion Board**			10 min.	●	

The Industrialized World

■ CONNECT

DIGITAL START UP ACTIVITY
Russia's GDP

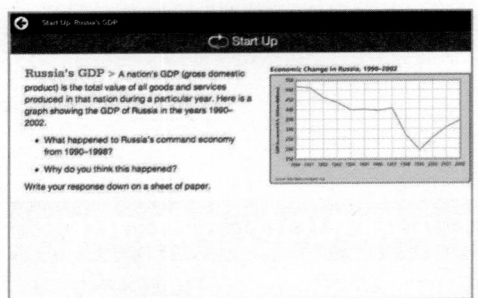

Project the Start Up Activity while students enter and get settled. Have students look at the graph and answer the following questions: What happened to Russia's economy from 1990 to 1998? (*Sample response: The value of Russia's economy was falling between 1990 and 1998. The GDP dips from 100 to around 55, indicating that the economy was in trouble. People were also using less electricity and consuming less. This is probably because they had less money to spend.*) Why do you think this happened? (*Sample response: This might have happened because the country was struggling to develop a market economy after the breakup of the Soviet Union and the collapse of the command economy.*)

Aa **Vocabulary Development:** Use the Interactive Reading Notepad to preview the Key Terms and Academic Vocabulary in this Lesson with students.

⇅ FLIP IT!

Assign the Flipped Video for this lesson.

■ STUDENT EDITION PRINT
PAGES: 873–880

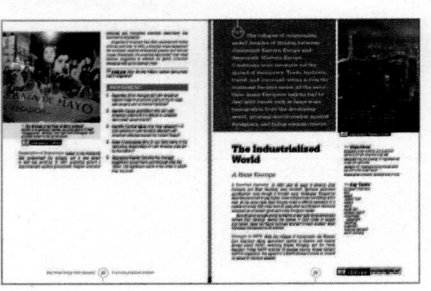

■ INVESTIGATE

DIGITAL TEXT 1
A New Europe

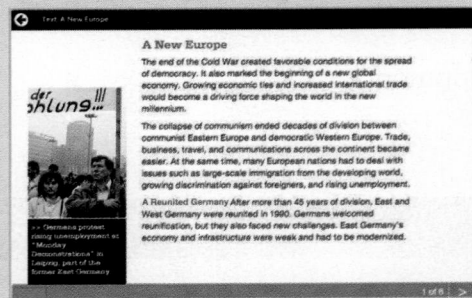

INTERACTIVE MAP
Evolution of the European Union

Objective 1: Examine social, political, and economic trends in Europe since the Cold War.

Quick Instruction

Interactive Map: Evolution of the European Union Project the interactive multilayer map of Europe. Start with the 1952 map. Ask students to remember what was happening in Europe, the United States, and the Soviet Union in the 1950s. (*Sample response: height of the Cold War, rebellions from Warsaw Pact countries, Western Europe is rebuilding from destruction of World War II*) Point out the name of the international organization on the map. (*Sample response: European Coal and Steel Community*) Explain that its function was to make sure that one country didn't rearm and develop its military without the other countries knowing about it. Now, go through the other layers, and have students read the caption material. Note the dates when each country joined (Britain was not part of the EEC until 1973). When you come to the 2004 map, ask students what region most of the new member countries are in. (*Eastern Europe, former Warsaw Pact countries*) Remind them what happened in the early 1990s in Europe. (*fall of the Soviet Union*)

Hypothesize Ask students: Why do you think it took until 2004 for most of the former Warsaw Pact countries to join the EU? (*Answers will vary. Some students will remember the Start Up Activity and see that it takes a several years to make the transition from a command economy to a free-market economy.*)

📷 ACTIVE CLASSROOM

Have students Write Headlines that capture the action in the maps of the growing European Union. If you were to write a headline or a slogan that captured the most important aspect that should be remembered, what would that headline be? Ask them to pass their headline to a partner to review. Then, ask them to share their headlines with the class.

ELL Use the ELL activity described in the ELL chart.

Further Instruction

Editable Presentation Use the Editable Presentation to present the main ideas for this Core Text.

A New Europe: Core Text and Interactive Reading Notepad Project and discuss the Interactive Reading Notepad questions as a class.

Review with students the changes to NATO membership. (*NATO extended, like the EU, to include many former Warsaw Pact countries and has always included Turkey.*) Review the challenges to German reunification. (*It was difficult economically, because the East German economy was inefficient, and socially, because there was a resurgence in neo-Nazi activity.*)

Infer Despite the challenges, what enabled Germany to successfully reunite in spite of the difficult challenges? (*Sample response: Germans were able to reunite because the German people welcomed the idea.*)

DIGITAL TEXT 2

Shifts in Global Power

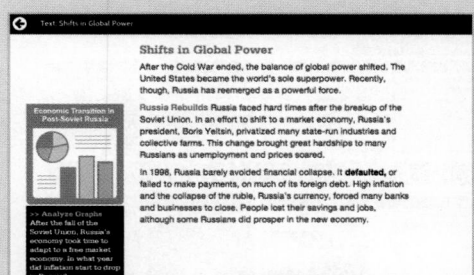

DIGITAL TEXT 3

The Former Soviet Republics

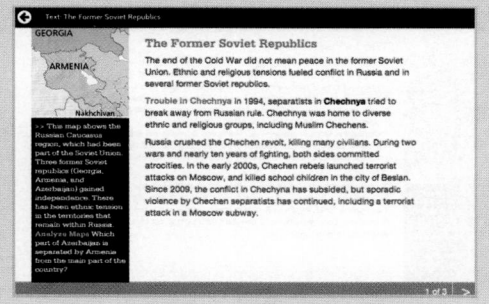

Cite Evidence Why is Turkey's membership in the European Union controversial? Cite evidence from the text to support your answer. *(Sample response: Some people think Turkey should have full membership in the EU because it is a part of NATO. Other people think that Turkey should not be admitted as a full member to the EU because they believe it has a poor record on human rights and may not share European traditions and values.)*

Objective 3: Analyze the challenges facing Russia since the end of the Soviet Union.

Quick Instruction

Ask students to describe the relationship between the United States and the Soviet Union during the Cold War. *(Sample response: They were enemies who divided the world into two different influence areas.)* Project the picture of Vladimir Putin and Barack Obama. Explain to students that as the Cold War ended and the Soviet Union shrank to become just Russia, the relationship between the two countries changed. Russia experienced hard times economically in the 1990s and has lost much of its territory, but it is still important. It is a large oil producer, a member of the UN Security Council, and a member of the G-8 (organization of the eight largest economies in the world).

Identify Steps in a Process What early steps in shifting to a market economy did Boris Yeltsin take? What was the effect? *(Sample response: Boris Yeltsin privatized state-run industries and collective farms in an effort to shift to a market economy. The change brought hardships to many Russians because unemployment and prices soared.)*

Summarize How did Vladimir Putin help Russia? What do his critics think of his leadership? *(Sample response: Vladimir Putin helped Russia by rebuilding the economy. His critics think that he is corrupt and that under his control the central government took too much power at the expense of civil liberties.)*

Analyze Maps Project the map of the Russian Caucasus. Remind students of the developments in the former Soviet Union in the early 1990s. *(Sample response: Many of the former Soviet Republics were breaking away and declaring independence; by 1991, many of the more populous and wealthy former republics were independent.)* Why would Russia want to hold on to Chechnya? *(Answers will vary. Chechnya may have oil wealth like Azerbaijan, Russia might be afraid that the example of a breakaway Chechnya would encourage other parts of Russia to seek independence.)*

ELL Use the ELL activity described in the ELL chart.

Further Instruction

Project and discuss as a class the Interactive Reading Notepad questions for the Core Texts.

Remind students that as the world's only superpower, the United States has a great deal of military and political influence. After terrorist attacks on the United States in September 2001, President George W. Bush declared a "war on terror." In 2002, the United States sent forces first to Afghanistan and the next year to Iraq. American involvement in Iraq ended in August 2010. In May 2011, American forces killed Osama bin Laden, the architect of the September 2001 attack. Ask: Why might some Americans believe a strong show of force is necessary to fight terrorism? *(Sample response: They believe that the United States has to be willing to stand up to acts of terror and show that it has the strength and the willingness to fight back.)*

The Industrialized World

DIGITAL TEXT 4

War in Yugoslavia

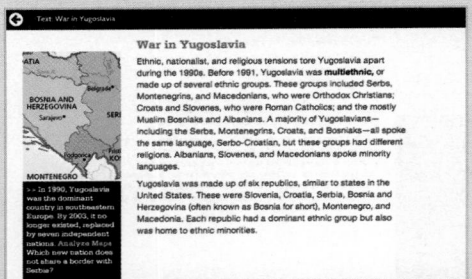

INTERACTIVE TIMELINE

War in Bosnia

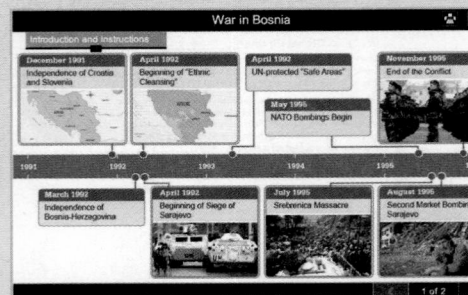

Objective 2: Describe how the breakup of Yugoslavia led to war and genocide.

Quick Instruction

Interactive Timeline: War in Bosnia Project the Interactive Timeline of the Bosnian conflict. Go through the events and have students (or teacher) read the captions. Ask students to answer the question at the end.

Project the map of southeastern Europe from the Text. Ask students to locate Srebrenica on the map. Ask them: Why do you think the Serbs wanted Srebrenica? *(It is located very close to Serbia and is surrounded by areas that have a Serb majority.)*

⬛ ACTIVE CLASSROOM

Use the Rank It strategy. List the following events on the whiteboard: Independence of Slovenia/Croatia; Beginning of Ethnic Cleansing; Beginning of Siege of Sarajevo; Srebrenica Massacre; NATO Bombing; 2nd Market Bombing. Ask students to rank them from most to least influential. Ask students to provide a justification for the ranking decisions they made. Then ask students to work in pairs to share their rankings and justifications. Poll the class to see if there is agreement on the ranking.

D Differentiate: Extra Support Have students look up *genocide* in the glossary. *(deliberate attempt to destroy an entire religious or ethnic group)* Ask them to come up with an example of genocide. *(Most will say the Holocaust.)* Ask them if they think that ethnic cleansing in Yugoslavia should be considered genocide. *(Responses will vary, but it fits the definition because it targeted a specific ethnic group.)*

Further Instruction

War in Yugoslavia: Core Text and Interactive Reading Notepad Project and discuss the Interactive Reading Notepad questions.

Review the issues surrounding the disintegration of Yugoslavia in the 1990s. *(Sample response: ethnic, nationalist, and religious tensions between people who had been forced to live with each other in a state assembled without taking into account these differences)*

Identify Central Issues What tensions were at the root of the problems in Yugoslavia during the 1990s? *(Sample response: Ethnic, nationalist, and religious tensions were the root of the problems in Yugoslavia during the 1990s. The multiethnic country had people of different religions who identified more closely with their own regional or ethnic group than with their national government.)*

Analyze Interactions Why do you think Serbs wanted to create areas that were purely Serbian and drive people of other ethnicities away? *(Sample response: Serbs wanted to create purely Serbian areas to focus their control. If people of other ethnicities did not live there, the Serbs could live as they wanted.)*

Integrate Information Read the second paragraph of "War in Kosovo." Then look at the picture showing members of the Kosovo Liberation Army. What do the text and the illustration convey about the people on both sides of the war? What different information about the fighters can you draw from these two sources? *(Sample response: The text says that Serbs were oppressing Kosovo Albanians, so a small guerilla force of Albanians emerged to fight the Serbs. The image shows fighters with guns. People on both sides of the war were fighting for their own ethnic group.)*

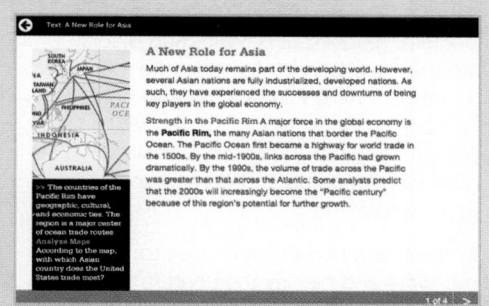

DIGITAL TEXT 5
A New Role for Asia

DIGITAL ACTIVITY
Post–Cold War World

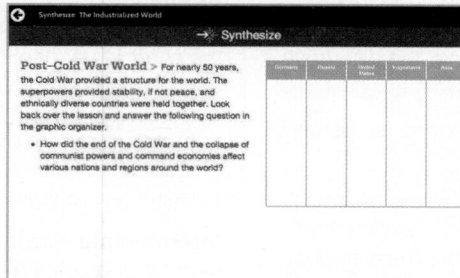

DIGITAL QUIZ
Lesson Quiz and Class Discussion Board

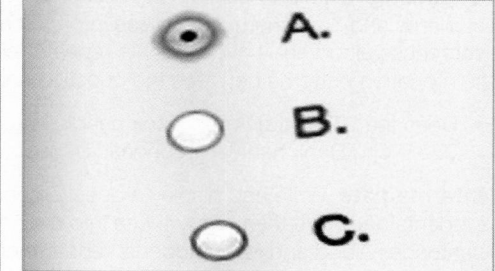

Objective 4: Summarize economic developments in Asia.

Quick Instruction

Project the map of the Pacific Rim from the Text. Have students name the most economically important countries (the ones with the most trade routes) on the map. *(United States, Australia, Japan, Singapore, China)* Ask them if they've ever heard the term *Asian Tigers*. Explain that the Asian Tigers are four Asian countries with very strong economies that are growing rapidly due to low wages, long hours, and other worker sacrifices. Each stressed education as a way to increase worker productivity. The countries have export-driven economies and dominate the electronics and other industries.

Infer Why might the 21st century be called the "Pacific Century"? *(Sample response: because of the region's economic dominance and potential for growth)*

Further Instruction

A New Role for Asia: Core Text and Interactive Reading Notepad Project and discuss the Interactive Reading Notepad questions.

Cite Evidence Why are nations in the Pacific well poised to take a leading role in trade? Cite evidence from the Text to support your answer. *(Sample response: Nations in the Pacific are well poised to take a leading role in trade because the Pacific Ocean is the "highway" for world trade. The volume of trade across the Pacific is greater than that of the Atlantic. The area has enormous potential for future growth.)*

Ask students to reflect on the lesson and answer the following question: How did the end of the Cold War and of communism affect various nations and regions around the world? *(Sample response: Germany: Brought about the reunification of East and West Germany. Russia: Struggled to forge a market economy. United States: Became the world's only superpower. Yugoslavia: Was torn apart by ethnic, nationalist, and religious tensions once the Communist Party no longer held the country together. Asia: Experienced successes and downturns of global economy)*

Assign the online quiz for this lesson if you haven't already done so. Students will be offered automatic remediation or enrichment based on their score.

Pose these questions to the class on the Class Discussion Board.

Predict Consequences Which country or countries will dominate the global economy in the coming years? Why do you think so? *(Sample response: I think the United States will dominate the global economy in the coming years. The recession seems to be nearing an end, and we do not face some of the challenges of India and China. Germany and the Asian Tigers will also probably continue to play leading roles in the global economy. They are strong countries that are industrialized and have productive workers.)*

Topic Inquiry

Have students continue their investigations for the Topic Inquiry.

Globalization and Trade

Supporting English Language Learners

Use with Digital Text 2, **Global Organizations and Trade Agreements.**

Listening
Read *Global Organizations and Trade Agreements* aloud to students. Then have students complete one of the following activities according to their language proficiency.

Beginning Write and display a question and answer about the text for students and have them copy these into their notebooks. Then say the sentences aloud and have students repeat them. Point out the difference in intonation patterns between the question and the answer. For example:

- Does the UN or the World Bank handle international economic issues? The World Bank handles economic issues.

Intermediate Write and display a question and answer about the text for students and have them copy these into their notebooks. Then say the sentences aloud and have students repeat them. Point out the difference in intonation patterns between the question and the answer. For example:

- Does the UN or the World Bank handle international economic issues? The World Bank handles economic issues.

Then have students ask questions and make statements about the text. Make sure their intonation is correct. Point out how to improve intonation if necessary.

Advanced Have students practice using proper intonation by working with a small group to ask questions and make statements about the text. Instruct group members to provide intonation support to one another as much as possible. Circulate among students to offer teacher support as well.

Advanced High Have students practice using proper intonation by working with a partner to ask and answer questions about the text. Instruct partners to provide intonation support to one another as much as possible. Circulate among partners to offer teacher support as well.

Use with Digital Text 3, **Benefits and Costs of Globalization.**

Learning Strategies
Read *Benefits and Costs of Globalization* aloud to students. Instruct students to complete one of the following activities based on their level of English proficiency.

Beginning Work together with students to develop a two-column chart to show the benefits and costs of globalization. Write and display the chart for students to copy into their notebooks. As you write the benefits and costs in the chart, point out challenging words and phrases and explicitly explain how to spell them. Then write two sentences, one to explain a benefit of globalization and another to explain a cost of globalization. Review the sentences with students and demonstrate how to make revisions and edits to your own writing.

Intermediate Guide students to develop a two-column chart to show the benefits and costs of globalization. Write and display the chart for students to copy into their notebooks. As the benefits and costs are written in the chart, point out challenging words and phrases and explicitly explain how to spell them. Then have students work together as a group to write two sentences, one to explain a benefit of globalization and another to explain a cost of globalization. Review the sentences with students and demonstrate how to make revisions and edits to your own writing.

Advanced Instruct pairs of students to develop a two-column chart to show the benefits and costs of globalization. As students work on their charts, encourage them to ask for help in pronouncing and writing any challenging words and phrases. Then have pairs write two sentences, one to explain a benefit of globalization and another to explain a cost of globalization. Guide students to review their sentences and demonstrate how to make revisions and edits to their writing.

Advanced High Instruct students to develop a two-column chart to show the benefits and costs of globalization. As students work on their charts, encourage them to ask for help in pronouncing and writing any challenging words and phrases. Then have students write two sentences, one to explain a benefit of globalization and another to explain a cost of globalization. Have students review their own writing first and make notes on what they want to revise. Then students should share their writing with a partner to review their sentences and suggest any revisions and edits to their writing. Give students time to make any necessary changes to their writing before presenting the final product to the class.

◱ Differentiate Instruction

Use the Differentiated Instruction notes throughout the lesson plan to support the varied skill sets, levels of readiness, and interests in the mixed-ability classroom.

Challenge These notes include suggestions for expanding the activity for advanced students.

On-Level These notes include suggestions for modifying the activity to address different interests or learning styles.

Extra Support These notes include ideas for providing more scaffolding or reading spuport.

Special Needs These notes provide ideas for adapting instruction to support the needs of various special needs students.

▮ NOTES

PEARSON **realize**™
www.PearsonRealize.com

Go online to access additional resources including:
Primary Sources • Biographies • Supreme Court cases •
21st Century Skill Tutorials • Maps • Graphic Organizers.

Objectives

Objective 1: Summarize the impact of globalization on the modern world.

Objective 2: Describe the role of international organizations and treaties in expanding trade.

Objective 3: Analyze the costs and benefits of globalization.

LESSON 6 ORGANIZER		PACING: APPROX. 1 PERIOD, .5 BLOCKS			
				RESOURCES	
		OBJECTIVES	**PACING**	**Online**	**Print**
Connect					
DIGITAL START UP ACTIVITY **The Beginnings of Globalization**			5 min.	●	
Investigate					
DIGITAL TEXT 1 **Global Interdependence**		Objective 1	10 min.	●	●
INTERACTIVE GALLERY **Aspects of Globalization**			10 min.	●	
DIGITAL TEXT 2 **Global Organizations and Trade Agreements**		Objective 2	10 min.	●	●
DIGITAL TEXT 3 **Benefits and Costs of Globalization**		Objective 3	10 min.	●	●
INTERACTIVE GALLERY **Smart Phones—American-Made?**			10 min.	●	
Synthesize					
DIGITAL ACTIVITY **Globalization**			5 min.	●	
Demonstrate					
DIGITAL QUIZ **Lesson Quiz and Class Discussion Board**			10 min.	●	

Globalization and Trade

▮ CONNECT

DIGITAL START UP ACTIVITY
The Beginnings of Globalization

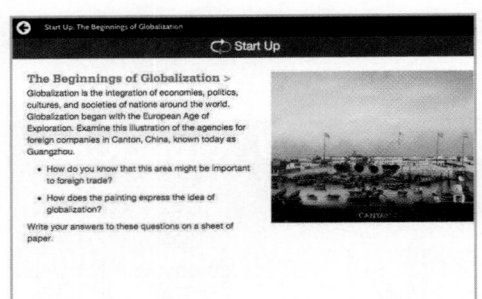

Project the Start Up Activity Ask students to answer the questions as they enter and get settled: How does the painting express the idea of globalization? *(Sample response: The flags flying over the buildings are from countries other than China, and they are flying over a building that appears to be on a harbor with large ships in it. These elements suggest that this is an early trading center in China and that other countries from around the globe have established a presence in China.)* Then have them share their ideas with another student, either in class or through a chat or blog space.

Tell students that in this lesson they will be learning about modern globalization.

Aa Vocabulary Development: Use the Interactive Reading Notepad to preview the Key Terms and Academic Vocabulary in this Lesson with students.

⟳ FLIP IT!
Assign the Flipped Video for this Lesson.

▮ STUDENT EDITION PRINT PAGES: 881–885

▮ INVESTIGATE

DIGITAL TEXT 1
Global Interdependence

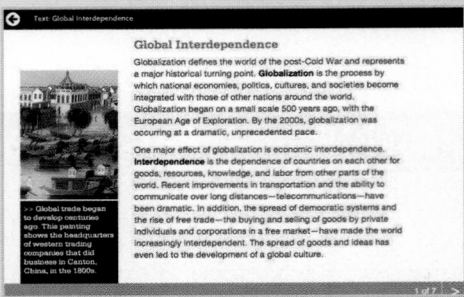

INTERACTIVE GALLERY
Aspects of Globalization

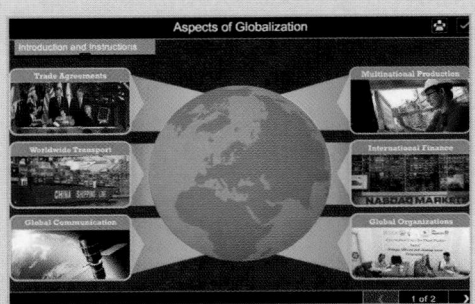

Objective 1: Summarize the impact of globalization on the modern world.

Quick Instruction
Tell students that improvements in transportation and communication, the spread of democratic systems, and the rise of free trade—the buying and selling of goods by private individuals and corporations in a free market—have made the world increasingly interdependent. The spread of goods and ideas has even led to the development of a global culture. The rapid pace and dramatic impact of these developments in recent times make globalization an historical turning point.

Interactive Gallery: Aspects of Globalization
Project the globe on the whiteboard. Click through the images and discuss different aspects of globalization with students. Students will gain information on transportation, telecommunications, production, finance, and global organizations.

Globalization defines the post–Cold War world. It is the process by which national economies, politics, and cultures become integrated with those of other nations. One effect of globalization is increased economic interdependence. This means that countries depend on one another for goods, resources, knowledge, and labor.

👥 ACTIVE CLASSROOM
Have students form groups. Give them this question, "Explain the importance of global communication to the world economy." Have students write as much as they can for one minute, then switch with the person to their right. The next person tries to improve or elaborate on the response where the other person left off. Continue to switch until the paper comes back to the first person. The group then decides which is the best response and shares with the larger group. *(Students' responses may contain details on the fact that globalization would not be possible without modern communication technology.)*

D Differentiate: Extra Support Have students work in pairs to define *interdependence*. Ask them how nations that are oil consumers and nations with oil reserves are interdependent. Have them discuss the advantages and disadvantages of interdependence as it relates to oil.

Further Instruction
Editable Presentation Use the Editable Presentation to present the main ideas of this Core Reading.

Global Interdependence: Core Reading and Interactive Reading Notepad Project and discuss the Interactive Reading Notepad questions, including the graphic organizer, asking students to identify the causes and effects of the global economic downturn in the 2000s. Review the causes and effects with the class and fill in the graphic organizer as you go.

Global Organizations and Trade Agreements

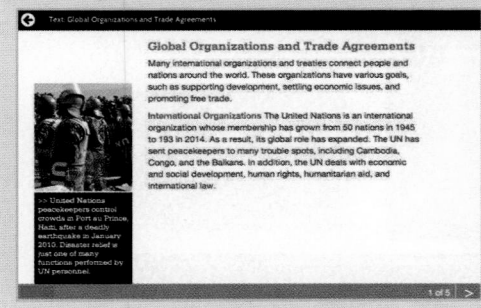

Text: Global Organizations and Trade Agreements

Global Organizations and Trade Agreements

Many international organizations and treaties connect people and nations around the world. These organizations have various goals, such as supporting development, settling economic issues, and promoting free trade.

International Organizations The United Nations is an international organization whose membership has grown from 50 nations in 1945 to 193 in 2014. As a result, its global role has expanded. The UN has sent peacekeepers to many trouble spots, including Cambodia, Congo, and the Balkans. In addition, the UN deals with economic and social development, human rights, humanitarian aid, and international law.

>> United Nations peacekeepers control crowds in Port au Prince, Haiti, after a deadly earthquake in January 2010. Disaster relief is just one of many functions performed by UN personnel.

1 of 5   >

Summarize How has debt harmed the developing world? *(Sample response: Developing countries had to borrow heavily to modernize. When the demand for their goods fell, they had difficulty repaying the loans, stalling development in their country.)*

Identify Central Issues Describe the role of energy resources in the global economy. Why could a change in the global oil supply have a global impact? *(Sample response: Energy in the form of oil is critical for transportation and industry. Limiting supplies or raising prices can hurt economies around the world.)*

Compare Points of View Multinational corporations typically invest heavily in the developing world. What is their rationale for this strategy? Why are some people critical of multinational corporations? *(Sample response: The corporations will say they brought new technologies, provided jobs, and improved transportation in developing countries. The critics say they have taken large profits out of developing nations, paid low wages, and caused environmental damage.)*

Objective 2: Describe the role of international organizations and treaties in expanding trade.

Quick Instruction

Many international organizations and treaties make global trade possible. The United Nations deals with a broad range of issues. The World Bank gives loans and advice to developing nations. The International Monetary Fund promotes global economic growth. The World Trade Organization (WTO) tries to ensure that trade flows smoothly and freely. It opposes protectionism—the use of tariffs to protect a country's industries from competition. Regional trade blocs, such as the EU in Europe, NAFTA in North America, and APEC in Asia, promote trade within regions.

ELL Use the ELL activity described in the ELL chart.

Further Instruction

Editable Presentation Use the Editable Presentation to present the main ideas for this Core Reading.

Go through the Interactive Reading Notepad questions and discuss the answers with the class.

Discuss Have students predict ways that regional and national global trade organizations might respond to global interdependence. What goals might they have? What problems might they face?

Using the Numbered Heads strategy, have students list each global organization or treaty on the board or on chart paper. For each, have students describe the organization or treaty and explain its impact on globalization. Discuss the goals of each as well as any problems that have resulted. Ask students how their reading confirmed to or revised their prediction about the goals and problems of trade organizations.

Be sure students understand that the United Nations is an international organization that primarily works to keep or regain peace in troubled areas as well as provides aid for economic and social development, human rights, humanitarian aid, and international law. It is not a trade organization.

Compare and Contrast How does the work of the World Bank differ from the World Trade Organization? *(Sample response: The World Bank offers loans and technical advice to developing nations. The World Trade Organization monitors trade to ensure that it flows smoothly and opposes tariffs and other restrictions. The World Bank supports development, while the World Trade Organization promotes free trade.)*

Globalization and Trade

DIGITAL TEXT 3

Benefits and Costs of Globalization

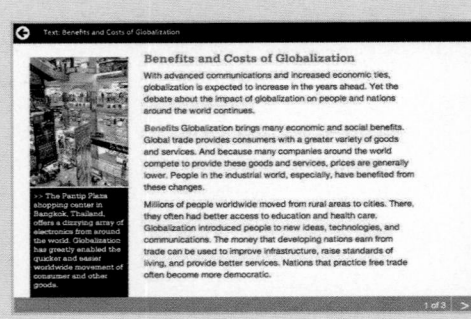

INTERACTIVE GALLERY

Smart Phones— American-Made?

Objective 3: Analyze the cost and benefits of globalization.

Quick Instruction

Global trade has many social and economic benefits and costs. It brings consumers a greater variety of goods and services. It generally keeps prices lower. It also exposes people to new ideas and technology. However, some people oppose globalization of trade. They claim that rich countries exploit poor countries and that the emphasis on profits encourages too-rapid development. This endangers sustainability, thereby threatening future generations.

Interactive Gallery: Smart Phones— American-Made? Step through the hotspots on the smart phone with students to learn how this technology is truly a global technology. Ask students, "Do you think it is more efficient to manufacture products all in one country or to spread the process across the world? Why?"

ACTIVE CLASSROOM

Have students write a headline that captures the key point of the Interactive Gallery. Ask: If you were to write a headline for this topic right now that captured the most important aspect that should be remembered, what would that headline be?

ELL Use the ELL activity described in the ELL chart.

Further Instruction

Go through the Interactive Reading Notepad questions and discuss with the class.

Create two columns on the board, labeled *Costs* and *Benefits*. Have students list the costs or benefits of globalization in the appropriate column. Encourage them to include both social and economic effects. Discuss how, if at all, each item differs for developed and developing nations.

Support Ideas with Evidence How has globalization improved the lives of people around the world? Give a specific example. *(Sample response: Global trade brings a variety of goods to consumers, generally at low prices. It improves technology and communications. Sometimes it raises people's standard of living and provides better services.)*

Make Predictions Do you think that increased globalization is inevitable? Explain. *(Sample response: Yes, because technology has created ties among nations. No, because there will always be opposition by some groups.)*

SYNTHESIZE

DIGITAL ACTIVITY
Globalization

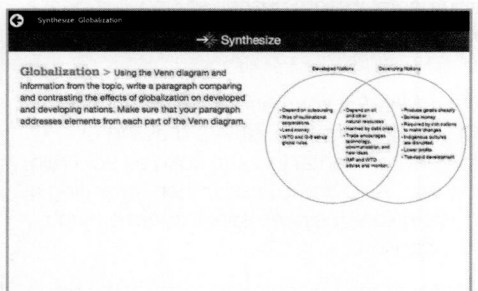

Ask students to study the Venn diagram on globalization and then write a paragraph comparing and contrasting the effects of globalization on developed and developing nations. *(Paragraphs should include some of the following information: Globalization affects developed and developing nations differently. Developing nations produce goods and services cheaply. Consumers in developed nations are therefore able to buy goods at reduced rates. However, many jobs are outsourced in order to keep prices low. Developing nations often need to borrow money from developed nations to boost their economies, which, in turn, allows developed nations to exert some control over them. Multinational corporations from developed nations take some profits from developing nations. Indigenous cultures in developing nations are often disrupted by industrialization. Urbanization and other forms of too-rapid development can cause many challenges for developing countries. Both developing and developed countries rely on oil and other natural resources, so many trade relationships revolve around these items. Globalization benefits people by spreading technology, communication, and new ideas around the globe, but the economies of countries become tied together. If one country has a financial crisis, it now spreads around the world, causing economic downturns in other countries as well.)*

DEMONSTRATE

DIGITAL QUIZ
Lesson Quiz and Class Discussion Board

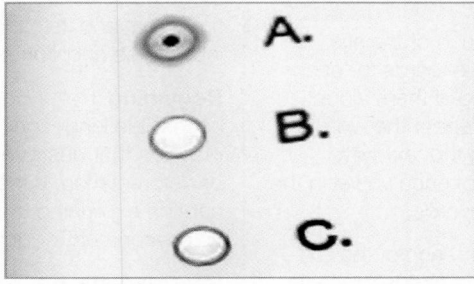

Assign the online Lesson Quiz for this lesson if you haven't already done so. Students will be offered remediation or enrichment based on their score.

Pose these questions to the class on the Discussion Board:

In "Globalization and Trade," you read about the impact of globalization on the modern world. You also read about how the agencies developed to deal with the issues surrounding globalization and the costs and benefits.

Identify Cause and Effect How does outsourcing jobs affect both the home country and the country where the jobs are outsourced? *(Sample response: Outsourcing creates jobs in the country where the jobs are outsourced and eliminates some jobs in the home country.)*

Summarize Summarize the benefits and costs of globalization. *(Sample response: Globalization has exposed people to new ideas and technologies. However, it may allow rich nations to exploit poorer nations, and it could lead to increased economic imbalances.)*

Topic Inquiry
Have students continue their investigations for the Topic Inquiry.

Social and Environmental Issues

Supporting English Language Learners

Use with Digital Text 1, **Global Challenges.**

Listening
Read *Global Challenges* aloud to students. Then have students complete one of the following activities according to their language proficiency.

Beginning Explain long and short vowel sounds for each of the six vowels in the alphabet (*a, e, i, o, u,* and *y*). Find example words for each vowel sound in the text. Write and display the words, read them aloud, and underline the vowel in each word. Have students repeat the words after they hear them spoken aloud. Continue reviewing the text with students, inviting them to identify additional examples of each vowel in the text. Repeat the same process with the new example words.

Intermediate Review long and short vowel sounds for each of the six vowels in the alphabet (*a, e, i, o, u,* and *y*). Find example words for each vowel sound in the text. Write and display the words, read them aloud, and underline the vowel in each word. Then invite student volunteers to locate additional examples of each vowel in the text, write them for other students, and underline the vowel. Help students pronounce each word correctly.

Advanced Have pairs of students scan *Global Challenges* for three examples of each short vowel and each long vowel. Students should create a two-column, six-row chart to accommodate these example words. Then have pairs work with another pair of students to share their lists. Circulate among students to offer support as needed.

Advanced High Have students scan *Global Challenges* for three examples of each short vowel and each long vowel. Students should create a two-column, six-row chart to accommodate these example words. Then have students turn to a partner to share their lists. Circulate among students to offer support as needed.

Use with Digital Text 3, **Development and the Environment.**

Learning Strategies
Retell or have students reread *Development and the Environment*. Have students select one of the environmental threats described and illustrate the threat and its effects in a drawing or diagram, including captions or labeling as appropriate.

Beginning Retell *Development and the Environment* to students using accessible language. Then work with students to create a drawing or diagram that illustrates one of the environmental threats, such as acid rain or deforestation, described in the text. As a group, assist them in writing a caption explaining the diagram. Make sure they use specific terms, such as environment or pollution, in the caption.

Intermediate Retell *Development and the Environment* to students using accessible language. Then have students create a drawing or diagram to explain one environmental threat, such as acid rain or deforestation, described in the text. When students are finished, instruct them to write a caption to explain their work. Make sure students use specific terms, such as environment or pollution, in their captions.

Advanced Instruct students to reread *Development and the Environment* independently. Then have students create a diagram illustrating one of the environmental threats, such as acid rain or deforestation, described in the text. Instruct students to label their diagrams and write a caption. Then have students show and explain their diagrams to a partner.

Advanced High Instruct students to reread *Development and the Environment* independently. Then have students create a diagram illustrating one of the environmental threats, such as acid rain or deforestation, described in the text. Instruct students to label their diagrams. Ask students to write a paragraph to explain their work.

▣ Differentiate Instruction

Use the Differentiated Instruction notes throughout the lesson plan to support the varied skill sets, levels of readiness, and interests in the mixed-ability classroom.

Challenge These notes include suggestions for expanding the activity for advanced students.

On-Level These notes include suggestions for modifying the activity to address different interests or learning styles.

Extra Support These notes include ideas for providing more scaffolding or reading spuport.

Special Needs These notes provide ideas for adapting instruction to support the needs of various special needs students.

■ NOTES

PEARSON
realize™
www.PearsonRealize.com

Go online to access additional resources including:
Primary Sources • Biographies • Supreme Court cases •
21st Century Skill Tutorials • Maps • Graphic Organizers.

Objectives

Objective 1: Explain the impact of poverty, disasters, and disease on nations around the world.

Objective 2: Describe global efforts to protect human rights.

Objective 3: Evaluate the environmental challenges facing the world.

LESSON 7 ORGANIZER		PACING: APPROX. 1 PERIOD, .5 BLOCKS			
				RESOURCES	
		OBJECTIVES	**PACING**	**Online**	**Print**
Connect					
	DIGITAL START UP ACTIVITY **Global Challenges**		5 min.	●	
Investigate					
	DIGITAL TEXT 1 **Global Challenges**	Objective 1	10 min.	●	●
	DIGITAL TEXT 2 **Human Rights**	Objective 2	10 min.	●	●
	INTERACTIVE GALLERY **Women's Lives in the 21st Century**		10 min.	●	
	DIGITAL TEXT 3 **Development and the Environment**	Objective 3	10 min.	●	●
	INTERACTIVE MAP **Global Environmental Challenges**		10 min.	●	
Synthesize					
	DIGITAL ACTIVITY **"The Same Boat"**		5 min.	●	
Demonstrate					
	DIGITAL QUIZ **Lesson Quiz and Class Discussion Board**		10 min.	●	

Social and Environmental Issues

■ CONNECT

DIGITAL START UP ACTIVITY
Global Challenges

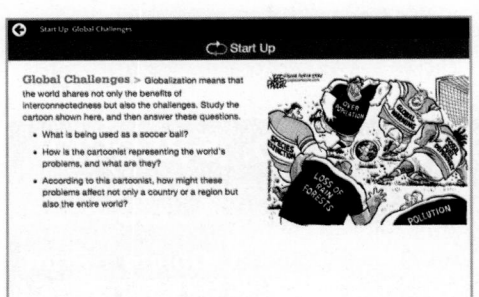

Project the Start Up Activity Ask students to answer the questions as they enter and get settled: What is being used as a soccer ball? *(the Earth)* How is the cartoonist representing the world's problems? *(They are the soccer players kicking Earth.)* According to this cartoonist, how might these problems affect not only a country or a region but also the entire world? *(Sample response: Problems like these impact Earth as a whole, not just a particular region.)* Then have them share their ideas with another student, either in class or through a chat or blog space.

Discuss Discuss what other "soccer players" might be kicking this "ball" around.

Aa Vocabulary Development: Use the Interactive Reading Notepad to preview the academic vocabulary and key terms in this lesson with students.

⇅ FLIP IT!
Assign the Flipped Video for this lesson.

■ STUDENT EDITION PRINT
PAGES: 886–893

■ INVESTIGATE

DIGITAL TEXT 1
Global Challenges

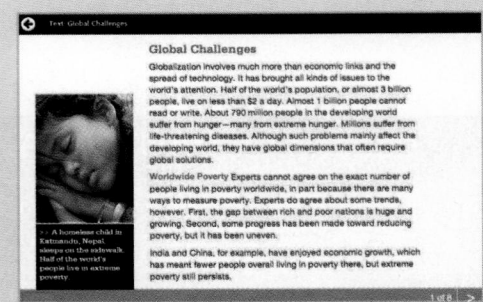

Objective 1: Explain the impact of poverty, disasters, and disease on nations around the world.

Quick Instruction
Explain that poverty, disasters, and disease have always been part of the human experience. The difference is that today's world is interconnected in unprecedented ways. Today, these problems have a far-reaching social and economic impact.

Analyze Maps Project the world map from Text 1, Screen 2. Explain that it shows the relative wealth and poverty of nations according to their GDP per capita. Briefly explain gross domestic product. It is an economic term that measures a country's output, or production—that is, the total value of the goods and services it produces in a certain time period, usually a year. Per capita is a Latin phrase that means "per head," or "per person." The GDP per capita is a statistic that divides the GDP by the number of people in the country. It is not a measure of individual income. Rather, it is a formula for measuring a nation's average standard of living.

Discuss Ask students to use their prior knowledge to identify some of the world's wealthiest nations *(U.S., Canada, Australia, Norway, Sweden)* and poorest nations *(Afghanistan, Ethiopia, Somalia, Myanmar, Zimbabwe)*. Have them identify patterns of wealth and poverty according to continents or other geographical areas. Ask how other global challenges might relate to this distribution of wealth and poverty: environmental problems, hunger and famine, natural disasters, education and human rights.

ELL Use the ELL activity described in the ELL chart.

Further Instruction
Analyze Charts Project the infographic found on Screen 6. Point out the various reasons why people leave their homeland and migrate to other countries. Call attention to the Top Five lists of countries that people leave (Countries of Origin) and countries they move to (Destination Countries). Notice which country is on both lists. Ask, Why might this be the case? *(The people migrating to a certain country are not the same ones who are leaving it, and the two groups may have different reasons for migrating—mostly economic in one case, and mostly political in another, for example.)*

Draw Inferences Ask: How does international migration influence globalization? *(As people move from one country to another, they bring their language and customs with them, which adds diversity to the population of the host country. Those migrants often send money home to family members left behind, which adds to the economy in the home country.)* Alternatively, how does globalization influence migration? *(Advances in global communication and technology make it easier than ever for people to share information, transfer money, and travel from one place to another. Multinational corporations need workers from a wide variety of national backgrounds.)*

DIGITAL TEXT 2
Human Rights

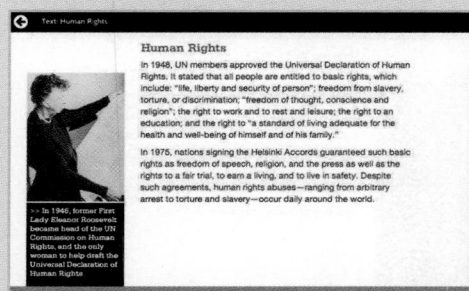

INTERACTIVE GALLERY
Women's Lives in the 21st Century

D **Differentiate: Challenge/Gifted** Have students do additional research on the complex interaction between globalization and human mobility. Ask them to answer the question, How and why does the United States both encourage and discourage immigration? *(There are many factors. Certain industries, such as agriculture, are dependent on the cheap labor provided by unskilled migrants, while other industries, such as technology companies, are in need of highly educated, skilled workers from abroad. Factors that discourage immigration include complex and controversial U.S. immigration laws, and the fears of some Americans that the cultural and political identity of the American people will change if the country allows too many foreigners to immigrate.)*

Objective 2: Describe global efforts to protect human rights.

Quick Instruction

What are human rights? From their study of American history, students are probably familiar with the phrase from the Declaration of Independence: "We hold these truths to be self-evident, that all men are created equal, that they are endowed by their Creator with certain unalienable Rights, that among these are Life, Liberty and the pursuit of Happiness." Explain that other nations and cultures hold both similar and dissimilar views of the "unalienable rights" of human beings. In 1948, on the heels of World War II, the United Nations set out to list and define those rights to which are all people are entitled. Certain groups of people have historically been denied equal human rights. Legal and cultural discrimination has been aimed at women, children, indigenous people, as well as people of certain races, religions, and other categories.

Interactive Gallery: Women's Lives in the 21st Century Project the slideshow. Look at each image individually and then at the collection of images as a whole. What are students' overall impressions of the status of women around the world?

Analyze Images Focus on the third image in the gallery, showing a billboard in China. What is the intent of that billboard? *(to solicit support for China's one-child policy)*

■ ACTIVE CLASSROOM

Using the "Cartoon It" activity, have each student draw a quick copy of one compelling image from this lesson. The image can be from the Interactive Gallery, "The Lives of Women Around the World," or the Digital Text, "Human Rights." Then have students turn their drawings into political cartoons that illustrate a key concept or main idea.

Further Instruction

Remind students that the human rights of women and children are often connected. Why is that? Countries that value individual human rights are usually the same countries that value women's rights and those of children. Nevertheless, discrimination against various groups exists in most countries.

Explain What is the basis for discrimination, and why does discrimination exist in the 21st century? *(The basis of discrimination is the idea that people are not equal, but that some people, by virtue of their gender, social position, religion, ethnicity, race, or other characteristics, are better than others. Discrimination exists because it benefits the people in power, who enjoy privileges at the expense of those who are discriminated against.)*

Social and Environmental Issues

DIGITAL TEXT 3

Development and the Environment

INTERACTIVE MAP

Global Environmental Challenges

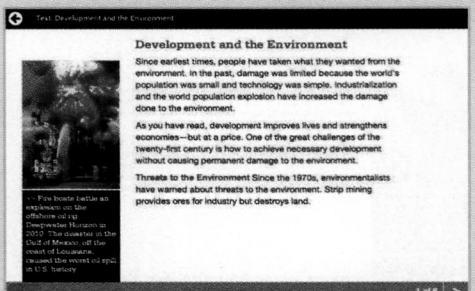

Evaluate Impact Break students into six teams. Assign each team five consecutive articles of the Universal Declaration of Human Rights. Have the teams investigate their assigned rights and report back to the class in the following manner: briefly explain the meaning of each article, state whether everyone on the team agrees with its content, and give an illustration of how a particular country either recognizes or fails to recognize that universal right.

Objective 3: Evaluate the environmental challenges facing the world.

Quick Instruction

Globalization has contributed to environmental problems around the world. Ask students to list different types of environmental concerns. *(air, water, and soil pollution and the varieties of pollution: radiation, chemical, toxic waste, litter; habitat encroachment and species extinctions; climate and land use concerns: deforestation, desertification, climate change/global warming)*

Identify Cause and Effect Break students into teams, and have each team choose one of the environmental concerns listed above. Have each team identify the causes of the problem and its effects on the environment.

Interactive Map: Global Environmental Challenges Project the Interactive Map activity and view each hot spot while a student reads the text aloud. Have the students write their answer to the follow-up question.

🐾 ACTIVE CLASSROOM

Use the Ranking strategy with the Interactive Map. Have students rank the environmental challenges shown on the map according to how critical each one is to solve immediately.

Drawing Conclusions In the course of doing the Active Classroom activity, students might conclude that it is not possible or realistic to rank the environmental challenges, as all are interconnected and all are critical. However, the act of ranking will force students to consider which challenges have the most widespread or influential effects on human lives.

ELL Use the ELL activity described in the ELL chart.

Further Instruction

Have students debate the pros and cons of the Kyoto Protocol. Assemble two teams, one in favor of the protocol and one opposed. In addition, choose a team of judges. Have each team choose three students who will be the debaters, while the remaining team members contribute research. All students should research the topic in order to develop informed opinions. The students chosen as judges should review the rules of debate. Finally, hold the debate in class and have the judges decide a winner.

■ SYNTHESIZE

■ DEMONSTRATE

DIGITAL ACTIVITY
"The Same Boat"

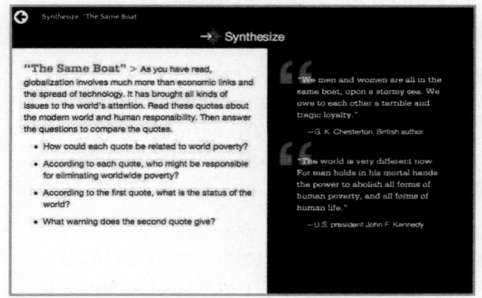

DIGITAL QUIZ
Lesson Quiz and Class Discussion Board

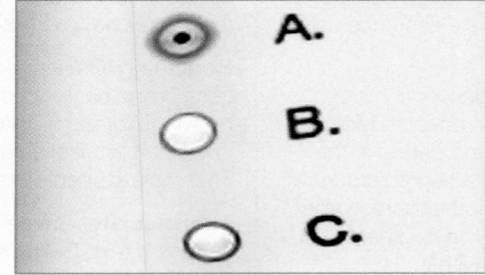

Project the two quotes from the Digital Activity, "The Same Boat." Ask students to write their answers to the questions. Have students pair with a partner and share their answers. Have partners compare and contrast the two quotes—how are they the same, and how are they different? Ask: What did Kennedy mean when he said, "Things are different now"? Different from when? Different how?

Discuss Ask students to recall the Topic Essential Question, "What are the benefits and risks of interdependence?" How do the two quotes above relate to the question?

Assign the online lesson quiz for this lesson if you haven't already done so. Students will be offered automatic remediation or enrichment based on their score.

Post these questions to the class on the Discussion Board: What are the benefits of globalization? What are the drawbacks? Explain why some aspects of globalization can fall into both categories.

Topic Inquiry
Have students continue their investigations for the Topic Inquiry.

Terrorism and International Security

Supporting English Language Learners

Use with Digital Text 2, **The Growing Threat of Terrorism.**

Listening
Use content from *The Growing Threat of Terrorism* to help students hear the difference between a fragment and a complete sentence. Then guide them in how to recognize the two and to write a complete sentence using the content of the text.

Beginning Display: *greater international cooperation between governments*. Say the phrase aloud and have students repeat it. Model how to create a complete sentence using this phrase and details in the text. Read the phrase and then the complete sentence aloud so students can hear the difference between the two. Then read another phrase from the text aloud and have students determine whether it is a fragment or a sentence, then help them create a complete sentence with it.

Intermediate Display: *The spread of terrorism has led to greater international cooperation between governments in an effort to prevent further attacks*. Say the phrase aloud and have students repeat it. Model how to create a complete sentence using this phrase and details in the text. Read the phrase and then the complete sentence aloud so students can hear the difference between the two. Then read another phrase from the text aloud and have students determine whether it is a fragment or a sentence, Have the group work together to make it a complete sentence.

Advanced Have pairs of students write three complete sentences and three fragments about the content in *The Growing Threat of Terrorism*. Ask pairs to read their sentences and fragments aloud to the group and have the group categorize each as either a sentence or fragment.

Advanced High Have student write three complete sentences and three fragments about the content in *The Growing Threat of Terrorism*. Ask students to read their sentences and fragments aloud to a partner, who should categorize each as either a sentence or fragment and explain their reasoning behind each categorization.

Use with Digital Text 3, **The U.S. Response to Terrorism.**

Learning Strategies
Using lists of terms and synonyms from *The U.S. Response to Terrorism*, have students match the two. Then have them revisit the sentences in the text to see how a synonym helps them understand the content.

Beginning Create a list of words from *The U.S. Response to Terrorism* text. Define each word as it relates to the text. Have students suggest drawings for each definition. Then display a list of synonyms for words in the first list. Define each word in the second list and include drawings. Then help students match each word to its synonym.

Intermediate Create a list of words from *The U.S. Response to Terrorism* text. Define each word as it relates to the text. Then display a list of synonyms for words in the first list. Define each word in the second list. Have students work together to match each word to its synonym. Ask them to return to the sentences in the text and reread each aloud using the applicable word's synonym.

Advanced Create a list of words from *The U.S. Response to Terrorism* text. Have students define each word as it relates to the text. Then display a list of synonyms for words in the first list. Have students work with a partner to match each word to its synonym. Then have pairs return to the sentences in the text and reread each aloud using the applicable word's synonym.

Advanced High Create a list of words from *The U.S. Response to Terrorism* text. Have students use context clues to define each word. Then have them find a synonym for each word on the list. Have students turn to a partner to discuss the meanings of each word, explain the synonyms, and reread each sentence aloud using the synonyms they found.

◨ Differentiate Instruction

Use the Differentiated Instruction notes throughout the lesson plan to support the varied skill sets, levels of readiness, and interests in the mixed-ability classroom.

Challenge These notes include suggestions for expanding the activity for advanced students.

On-Level These notes include suggestions for modifying the activity to address different interests or learning styles.

Extra Support These notes include ideas for providing more scaffolding or reading spuport.

Special Needs These notes provide ideas for adapting instruction to support the needs of various special needs students.

■ NOTES

_____

_____

_____

_____

_____

PEARSON
realize.
www.PearsonRealize.com

Go online to access additional resources including:
Primary Sources • Biographies • Supreme Court cases •
21st Century Skill Tutorials • Maps • Graphic Organizers.

Objectives

Objective 1: Explain how nuclear, biological, and chemical weapons threaten international security.

Objective 2: Analyze the growth of terrorist groups such as al Qaeda.

Objective 3: Explain how the United States and other nations have responded to terrorism from September 11, 2001, to the present.

LESSON 8 ORGANIZER		PACING: APPROX. 1 PERIOD, .5 BLOCKS			
		OBJECTIVES	PACING	**RESOURCES**	
				Online	Print
Connect					
DIGITAL START UP ACTIVITY **Looking Back—September 11, 2001**			5 min.	●	
Investigate					
DIGITAL TEXT 1 **The Threat of New Weapons**		Objective 1	10 min.	●	●
DIGITAL TEXT 2 **The Growing Threat of Terrorism**		Objective 2	10 min.	●	●
INTERACTIVE MAP **Terrorism Around the World**			10 min.	●	
DIGITAL TEXT 3 **The U.S. Response to Terrorism**		Objective 3	10 min.	●	●
INTERACTIVE GALLERY **September 11, 2001**			10 min.	●	
Synthesize					
DIGITAL ACTIVITY **Taken by Surprise**			5 min.	●	
Demonstrate					
DIGITAL QUIZ **Lesson Quiz and Class Discussion Board**			10 min.	●	

Terrorism and International Security

▮ CONNECT

DIGITAL START UP ACTIVITY

Looking Back— September 11, 2001

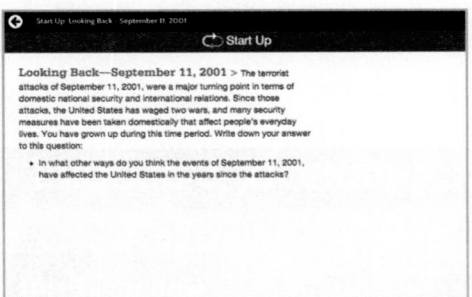

Project the Start Up Activity Ask students to answer the questions as they enter and get started: In what other ways do you think the events of September 11, 2001, have affected the United States in the years since the attacks? *(Sample response: the events of September 11 affected the country by destroying many people's sense of safety. National security and personal privacy have often come into conflict.)*

Discuss Ask: Do your parents or older siblings ever mention the events of September 11, 2001? If so, what stories do they tell? Point out that in the days immediately following the attacks, Americans of different political and regional backgrounds united in solidarity and much of the world showed great support for the United States.

> **⇅ FLIP IT!**
> Assign the Flipped Video for this Lesson.

Aa Vocabulary Development: Use the Interactive Reading Notepad to preview the Key Terms and Academic Vocabulary in this Lesson with students.

▮ STUDENT EDITION PRINT PAGES: 894–899

▮ INVESTIGATE

DIGITAL TEXT 1

The Threat of New Weapons

Objective 1: **Explain how nuclear, biological, and chemical weapons threaten international security.**

Quick Instruction

Over the course of the 20th century, nations developed new kinds of weaponry capable of quickly killing masses of people. The creation of these weapons of mass destruction brought a new urgency to international negotiations— cooperation in detering the use of such weapons. Nuclear, biological, and chemical weapons work in different ways, but all have the same goal. Controlling access to them, preventing the spread and use of them, and even eliminating them has become a focus of 21st-century diplomacy.

Further Instruction

Ask students to review the lesson coverage of the Nuclear Nonproliferation Treaty (NPT). Remind them that the treaty, signed in 1968, allows for five countries to have nuclear weapons—the United States, Russia, the United Kingdom, France, and China. They are known in the treaty as the nuclear states. The treaty stipulates that countries without nuclear weapons agree not to acquire them. However, those countries are allowed to develop nuclear programs for peaceful domestic power uses. To date, 190 countries have signed. Three countries that have not signed—India, Pakistan, and Israel. All have developed nuclear weapons. North Korea, which had originally signed, has withdrawn and is suspected of having a program to develop nuclear weapons.

Support a Point of View with Evidence
Ask students to take a stand on the following questions, and to argue their opinion in class: Does the NPT make sense as an international agreement? Is it fair of the five nuclear states to forbid the remaining countries to develop such weapons? *(Some students may assert that the NPT is not fair, and that each country should have the right to determine its own defense needs. Other students may argue that the danger of nuclear weapons is so dire that the global community must agree to limit proliferation for the good of all. By the time the NPT was drawn up, those five nations already had the weapons, and the intent of the agreement was and is to prevent further expansion of such arsenals.)*

DIGITAL TEXT 2

The Growing Threat of Terrorism

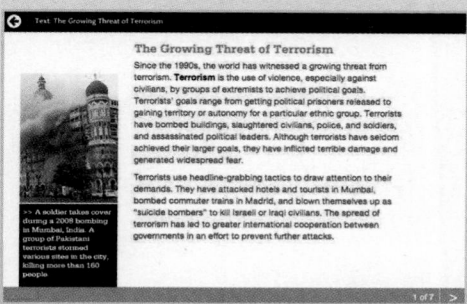

INTERACTIVE MAP

Terrorism Around the World

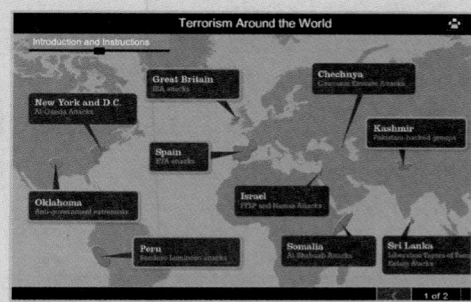

Objective 2: Analyze the growth of terrorist groups such as al Qaeda.

Quick Instruction

Remind students that terrorism has existed for centuries. However, it has taken on new dimensions in recent decades. The growth of international terrorist groups with the strength, scope, and financial backing of al Qaeda is a relatively new phenomenon. Such groups often recruit members from the dissatisfied youth of impoverished or war-torn nations and seem to offer them a sense of purpose. September 11 proved that a terror network can take on an international superpower.

Interactive Map: Terrorism Around the World Project the Interactive Map. Point out that terror is (or has been) practiced by various groups around the world and is not unique to Middle Eastern or Islamic cultures.

🖳 ACTIVE CLASSROOM

Introduce the Write 1 Get 3 activity. Ask the question, "What are four key characteristics of terrorism?" *(Possible responses include using the element of surprise, political goals, use of violence to achieve goals, targeting of civilians, destruction of life and property, creation of fear and panic, secret networks, desire for media attention.)*

ELL Use the ELL activity described in the ELL chart.

Further Instruction

Tell students that by the 1980s, Islamic fundamentalism—often referred to as Islamism—was on the rise. This conservative reform movement wanted to revive Islamic values and install governments that strictly followed Islamic law, or Sharia. The Islamist movement was partly a response to the rise of secular governments in many Muslim nations and the impact of Western culture. It was also a backlash against foreign support for Israel and the presence of foreign powers in the Middle East. Not all Islamists support terrorism, but in many places, the movement has fed the growth of terrorism.

Provide students with examples of regional terrorism from various points in history: a Serbian terrorist group played a key role in the outbreak of World War I; from the 1960s to the 1990s, the Irish Republican Army (IRA) used terrorist tactics to force Britain out of Northern Ireland; the ETA, a Basque terrorist group, wants the Spanish government to grant independence to the Basque region in northern Spain.

In recent years, much attention has been focused on Islamist terrorist groups, particularly al Qaeda. The founder and leader of al Qaeda was Osama bin Laden, a wealthy Saudi businessman. Al Qaeda built a global network to train and finance terrorist activities. Al Qaeda has struck numerous times, but the major blow came when al Qaeda attacked

the United States. On September 11, 2001, the Al Qaeda Islamic terrorist group hijacked four commercial passenger airplanes and crashed two of them into the World Trade Center in New York City and one into the Pentagon in northern Virginia. A fourth plane, aimed at the White House, crashed into a Pennsylvania field after passengers rushed the hijackers in the cockpit. Nearly 3,000 people died in the attacks. The swift U.S. response to the terror attacks would have far-reaching consequences in the United States and overseas.

Hypothesize How might Americans' confidence in their own safety on American soil have been shaken by 9-11? *(Sample response: No attack of this scale had ever taken place on American soil. Many Americans became very fearful that the next attack was just around the corner.)*

Terrorism and International Security

DIGITAL TEXT 3

The U.S. Response to Terrorism

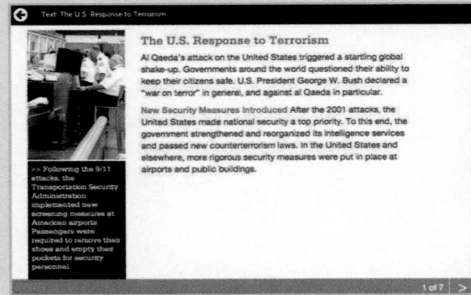

INTERACTIVE GALLERY

September 11, 2001

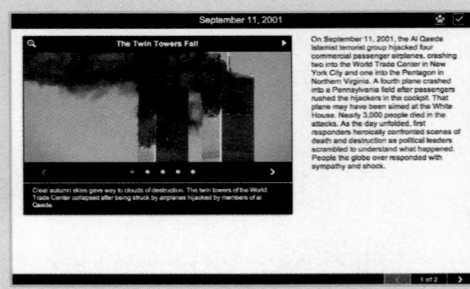

Objective 3: **Explain how the United States and other nations have responded to terrorism from September 11, 2001, to the present.**

Quick Instruction

To help students understand the significance of September 11, 2001, set the stage. On September 10 of that year, the United States was at peace. Terrorism was not something Americans worried about very much. For the most part, terrorist attacks were things that happened in other countries, to other people. There had been terrorist strikes before in the United States, but they seemed to be the acts of a few isolated individuals. The September 11 strikes were the kind of attacks no one had imagined.

Interactive Gallery: September 11, 2001
Project the Interactive Gallery and have students view the images and respond to the question.

Analyze Images Look at the second image of the firemen at the scene in New York. Discuss the role of the first responders that day. Ask: What kinds of challenges did the first responders face on September 11? (Sample response: rescuing people, communicating effectively, deciding whether to enter the buildings, crowd control, evacuations, not knowing if more attacks were imminent)

⟦🗪⟧ ACTIVE CLASSROOM

Break students into groups and introduce the Circle Write activity. Remind students of the images they just saw in the Interactive Gallery, "September 11, 2001." Have them begin with a writing prompt of your choice, or use this one: "September 11, 2001, began as a beautiful day with bright blue skies. No one expected it would become one of the most important days in American history. But then, ... "

ELL Use the ELL activity described in the ELL chart.

Further Instruction
Days after the Sept. 11 attacks, President George W. Bush announced a "war on terror." He said, "Our war on terror begins with al-Qaeda, but it does not end there. It will not end until every terrorist group of global reach has been found, stopped, and defeated."

Compare and Contrast How is America's war on terror similar to a conventional war? How is it different? (Sample response: The war on terror is a war against a concept, rather than a war against a nation. It is a war against an unclear enemy. The political goals of the enemy may be unclear, since the enemy is not one centralized power, but one certain goal is terror itself. Therefore, the war on terror is

unlike conventional wars. However, it does include the use of U.S. military forces, who suffer casualties as in conventional wars. And, similarly, innocent civilians are often caught up in the fighting. However, unlike in most conventional wars, civilians are often the targets of terrorist actions.)

Evaluate Arguments Point out that some Americans believe the federal government is using the threat of terrorism to increase its power and violate the constitutional rights and freedoms of its citizens. Ask students if they agree with this charge. Have them support their opinions with evidence from current and recent events.

■ SYNTHESIZE

DIGITAL ACTIVITY

Taken by Surprise

First, project the image from the Connect activity that students considered at the introduction to this lesson. Ask them to recall their responses and share them with the class. Next, project the quote from the Synthesize activity, "Taken by Surprise." Tell students that this quote reflects journalist George Packer's response to the same question they considered in the Connect activity. Ask students to read Packer's thoughts and write their answers to the questions.

Discuss Ask: Now that you have learned more about terrorism and international security, reconsider your answers to the original Connect Activity. How did the events of September 11, 2001, change the United States? Has your understanding expanded or changed? If so, how? *(Answers will vary, but might include that the events of September 11, 2001, caused the country to institute greater security measures at airports and other public places, prompted the country to go to war in Afghanistan, and changed Americans' perceptions about their relative safety from terror incidents compared to those in other countries.)*

■ DEMONSTRATE

DIGITAL QUIZ

Lesson Quiz and Class Discussion Board

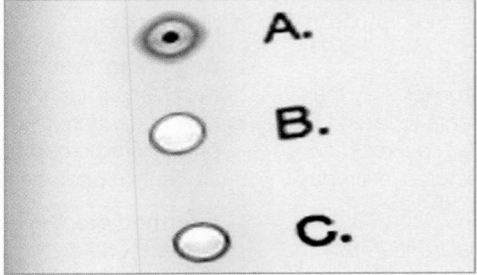

Assign the online lesson quiz for this lesson if you haven't already done so. Students will be offered automatic remediation or enrichment based on their score.

Post these questions to the class on the Discussion Board:

In "Terrorism and International Security," you have read that terrorism is a global concern that is not limited to the Middle East. Nevertheless, the Middle East is a region where centuries-old conflicts have proven extremely difficult, if not impossible, to solve. The recent rise of Islamic fundamentalism has only exacerbated that problem.

Identify Central Issues What is the relationship between Islamists and terrorism? *(Sample response: Not all Islamists support terrorism, but some Islamist governments have provided financial support for terrorist organizations.)*

Draw Conclusions Why might a "war on terror" sometimes be controversial? *(Sample response: It is sometimes unclear what is an actual terrorist threat versus what is a potential or presumed terrorist threat.)*

Topic Inquiry

Have students continue their investigations for the Topic Inquiry.

Advances in Science and Technology

Supporting English Language Learners

Use with Digital Text 1, **Space Exploration.**

Listening

Read or have students read the second paragraph of *Space Exploration* aloud. Have students listen for the use of the expression "the final frontier" as you read. Guide students as they determine and discuss the expression's meaning.

Beginning Display the following expression: *the final frontier*. Say the expression aloud and have students repeat it. Tell students to listen for the expression as you read the second paragraph under *Space Exploration* aloud. Help students understand its meaning, using gestures, everyday examples, and the text.

Intermediate Display the following expression: *the final frontier*. Say the expression aloud and have students repeat it. Tell students to listen for the expression as you read the second paragraph under *Space Exploration* aloud. Discuss its meaning with students, using everyday examples and the text. Then repeat the activity with the expression *secret weapon.*

Advanced Display the following expression: *final frontier*. Have small groups listen for the expression as a member reads the second paragraph under *Space Exploration* aloud. Then have groups work together to explain its meaning, using everyday examples and examples from the text. Then have groups repeat the activity with the expression *secret weapon.*

Advanced High Have pairs of students skim *Space Exploration* for two expressions: *final frontier* and *secret weapon*. Tell pairs to listen for the expression as each reads the paragraphs with one of the expressions aloud. Have pairs discuss the meanings of both expressions, using everyday examples and examples from the text. Invite pairs to share the main points of their discussions with the rest of the group.

Use with Digital Text 2, **The Computer Revolution.**

Learning Strategies

Read *The Computer Revolution* aloud to students. Instruct students to complete one of the following activities based on their level of English proficiency.

Beginning Write and display the words *computer* and *Internet* from the text. Use bilingual dictionaries to define each word for students to ensure their understanding. Then help students create meaningful sentences or phrases using *computer* and *Internet*. Say the sentences aloud and have students repeat them.

Intermediate Write and display the words *computer* and *Internet* from the text. Use dictionaries to define each word for students to ensure their understanding. Then ask students to compose meaningful sentences or phrases using *computer* and *Internet*. Invite student volunteers to read the sentences and phrases aloud.

Advanced Instruct pairs of students to define the words *computer* and *Internet* using context clues in the text. Then have pairs write a short paragraph using the two words correctly. Encourage pairs of students to make their paragraphs meaningful and personal. Have pairs share their work with the rest of the class.

Advanced High Instruct students to define the words *computer* and *Internet* using context clues in the text. Then have pairs write a short paragraph using the two words correctly. Encourage students to make their paragraphs meaningful and personal. Then have students share their work with a partner.

D Differentiate Instruction

Use the Differentiated Instruction notes throughout the lesson plan to support the varied skill sets, levels of readiness, and interests in the mixed-ability classroom.

Challenge These notes include suggestions for expanding the activity for advanced students.

On-Level These notes include suggestions for modifying the activity to address different interests or learning styles.

Extra Support These notes include ideas for providing more scaffolding or reading spupport.

Special Needs These notes provide ideas for adapting instruction to support the needs of various special needs students.

NOTES

PEARSON
realize™
www.PearsonRealize.com

Go online to access additional resources including:
Primary Sources • Biographies • Supreme Court cases •
21st Century Skill Tutorials • Maps • Graphic Organizers.

Objectives

Objective 1: Describe the exploration of space and the innovations that have resulted.

Objective 2: Analyze the development and impact of computer technology and telecommunications.

Objective 3: Summarize key advancements in medicine and biotechnology.

LESSON 9 ORGANIZER

PACING: APPROX. 1 PERIOD, .5 BLOCKS

		OBJECTIVES	PACING	RESOURCES Online	RESOURCES Print
Connect					
	DIGITAL START UP ACTIVITY **Instant Communication**		5 min.	●	
Investigate					
	DIGITAL TEXT 1 **Space Exploration**	Objective 1	10 min.	●	●
	INTERACTIVE TIMELINE **The Age of Space Exploration**	Objective 1	10 min.	●	
	DIGITAL TEXT 2 **The Computer Revolution**	Objective 2	10 min.	●	●
	DIGITAL TEXT 3 **Breakthroughs in Medicine and Biotechnology**	Objective 3	10 min.	●	●
	INTERACTIVE TIMELINE **Medical Milestones**	Objective 3	10 min.	●	
Synthesize					
	DIGITAL ACTIVITY **Advances in Science and Technology**		5 min.	●	
Demonstrate					
	DIGITAL QUIZ **Lesson Quiz and Class Discussion Board**		10 min.	●	

Advances in Science and Technology

■ CONNECT

DIGITAL START UP ACTIVITY
Instant Communication

Project the Start Up Activity Ask students to answer the question as they enter and get settled. Then have them share their answers with another student, either in class or through a chat or blog space.

Discuss What is the cartoonist saying about technology and social media in our world? *(Possible answers: People communicate via digital devices rather than talking directly. People just repeat or "parrot" what they hear.)* Discuss the benefits and drawbacks of instant communications.

Tell students that in this lesson they will be learning about space exploration, computers, and advancements in medicine.

Aa Vocabulary Development: Use the Interactive Reading Notepad to preview the Key Terms and Academic Vocabulary in this Lesson with students.

⇌ FLIP IT!
Assign the Flipped Video for this lesson.

■ STUDENT EDITION PRINT
PAGES: 900–904

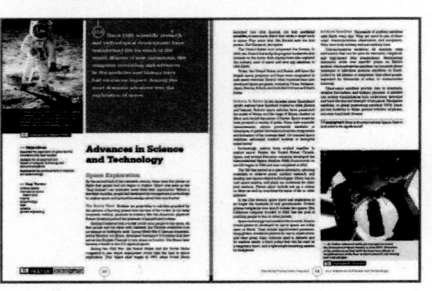

■ INVESTIGATE

DIGITAL TEXT 1
Space Exploration

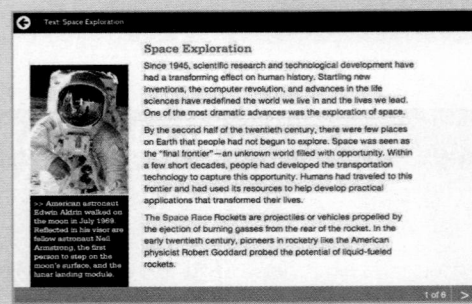

INTERACTIVE TIMELINE
The Age of Space Exploration

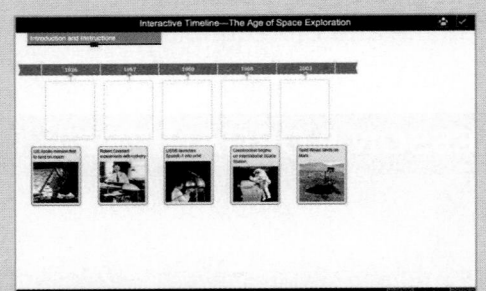

Objective 1: Describe the exploration of space and the innovations that have resulted.

Quick Instruction

Since 1945, scientific research and technological developments have transformed human existence. One example is the exploration of space. During the Cold War, the United States and the Soviet Union competed in a "space race." This began in 1957 when the Soviet Union launched Sputnik, the first artificial satellite. By 1969, the United States had landed the first human on the moon. Both superpowers explored military uses of space and sent spy satellites to orbit Earth. However, since the end of the Cold War, nations have worked in space together. For example, several countries are involved in the International Space Station (ISS). Thousands of artificial satellites belonging to many countries now orbit Earth. They are used for communication, observation, and navigation.

Interactive Timeline: The Age of Space Exploration Have students consider the space race of the 1990s. Ask: Why did nations throughout history find it important to explore new frontiers? *(access to new resources and new areas of influence)*

👥 ACTIVE CLASSROOM

Use the Conversation with History strategy. Have students imagine they are having a conversation with one of the people mentioned in the reading about space exploration. They could choose Neil Armstrong, Robert Goddard, or another famous astronaut or scientist from the early space program. Have them write down a question, then a possible response from the person. Tell them to share their dialogues with a partner.

ELL Use the ELL activity described in the ELL chart.

Further Instruction

Editable Presentation Use the Editable Presentation to present the main ideas for this Core Text.

Go through the Interactive Reading Notepad questions and discuss the answers with the class.

DIGITAL TEXT 2

The Computer Revolution

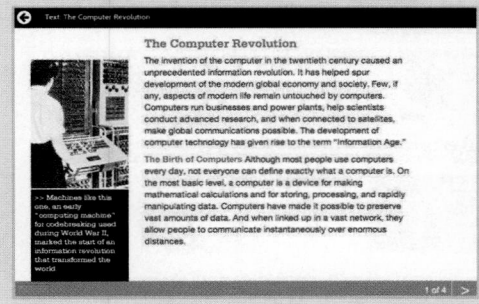

Review the different ways nations have explored space. Write the term *space race* on the board, and ask students to define and describe it. Then discuss how interaction between nations about the use of space has changed since the end of the Cold War.

Summarize Considering the history of the Cold War, explain why the United States and Russia competed against each other to achieve dominance in the space race. *(Each nation felt that winning the space race would show the superiority of its political system. In addition, domination in space could play a role in the arms race.)*

Make Predictions How do you think the International Space Station will help advance science? *(Possible answer: Scientists from many different countries sharing ideas can develop new technologies faster.)*

Objective 2: Analyze the development and impact of computer technology and telecommunications.

Quick Instruction

An important technological development was the invention of the computer. It has led to the "Information Age." Personal computers, or PCs, have replaced typewriters and account books in homes and businesses. Factories now use computerized robots, and computers remotely control satellites and probes in space. The Internet links computer systems worldwide and allows people to communicate instantly around the globe. It also allows people to access vast storehouses of information that were unavailable before and is an essential part of the modern global economy and society.

ELL Use the ELL activity described in the ELL chart.

Further Instruction

Editable Presentation Use the Editable Presentation to present the main ideas for this Core Text.

Go through the Interactive Reading Notepad questions and discuss the answers with the class.

Trace the changes that have occurred since computers were invented. Ask: How has life changed since the invention of personal computers? *(Personal computers enable people to access information, create and revise documents, and perform complex and elaborate tasks for work and personal use rapidly and easily.)*

Make Predictions Predict the future of the Internet. What advantages and disadvantages come with this technology? *(Possible response: The Internet will continue to grow and become accessible to more people. Advantages: access to information anytime and any place; fast, easy communication, e-commerce, and entertainment. Disadvantages: personal information theft, lack of privacy, plagiarism, over-reliance on the Internet for ideas, spam, inappropriate content, isolation, lack of physical exercise)*

Advances in Science and Technology

DIGITAL TEXT 3

Breakthroughs in Medicine and Biotechnology

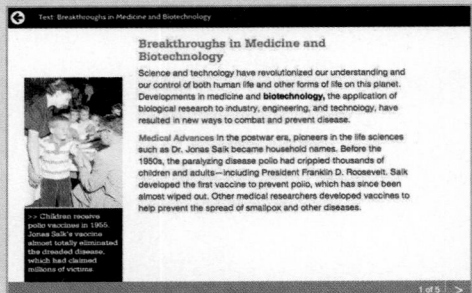

INTERACTIVE TIMELINE

Medical Milestones

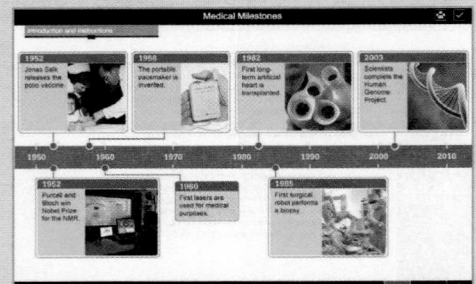

Objective 3: Summarize key advancements in medicine and biotechnology.

Quick Instruction

Important developments have occurred in medicine and biotechnology—the application of biological research to industry, engineering, and technology. Vaccines have been developed that help prevent the spread of diseases. In the 1970s, surgeons learned to transplant human organs. Lasers have made many types of surgery safer and more precise. Computers and other technologies have helped doctors diagnose and treat diseases. The fields of genetics and genetic engineering have made dramatic advances.

Interactive Timeline: Medical Milestones
Project the timeline on the whiteboard and quickly review the medical advancements made over the years. Have students form six groups. Have each group choose one of the advancements on the timeline and find out more details about it. Have each group present its information to the class.

⬛ ACTIVE CLASSROOM

Have students write a headline that captures one key concept in this Core Text. Ask: If you were to write a headline for this topic or issue right now that captured the most important aspect that should be remembered, what would the headline be? Have students trade headlines with a partner to review and discuss.

Further Instruction

Editable Presentation Use the Editable Presentation to present the main ideas for this Core Text.

Go through the Interactive Reading Notepad questions and discuss the answers with the class.

Ask students to notice the key term *biotechnology*. What do they think biotechnology is? Clarify that *bio* means "life." Discuss other types of technology that students have read about. Ask students to suggest ways that technology could affect life.

Make Generalizations How have scientific advances affected people's standard of living? What challenges are brought about by these advances? *(Scientific advances have improved many people's standard of living by increasing agricultural output and reducing the impact of disease. Genetic engineering of food organisms has raised questions about the role of science in creating and changing life. Safety questions about use of genetically engineered organisms as food have also been raised. Overpopulation, corrupt governments, pollution, and natural disasters are all global problems that will need to be solved with technology and other tools.)*

Express Problems Clearly Biotechnology has provided many benefits, but many people worry about its long-term effects. Explain why this is so. *(Some people fear that biotechnology will change food in unsafe ways; some also fear that it could give people dangerous power to create or change life.)*

■ SYNTHESIZE

DIGITAL ACTIVITY

Advances in Science and Technology

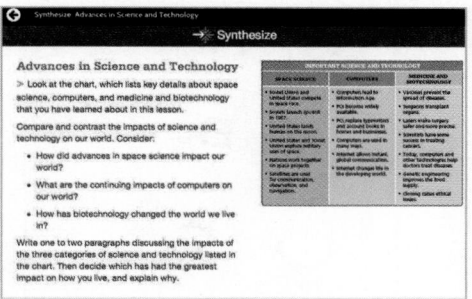

The chart lists key details about space, science, computers, medicine, and biotechnology from the lesson. Have students write one or two paragraphs discussing the impacts of the three categories of science and technology listed in the chart. Then have them decide which has had the greatest impact on how they live, and explain why. *(Sample response: Space science, computers, and medicine and biotechnology are three categories of science and technology that have greatly impacted our world. Because of the space race, humans have walked on the moon, and artificial satellites have been developed. Computers have made work more productive and allowed people to have instant communication around the world. The field of biotechnology has also impacted our world. Vaccines are used to prevent the spread of diseases, and surgeries have become more complex and safer at the same time. Genetic engineering will most likely continue to develop in order to produce more food for all of the people around the world.)*

Discuss Lead a discussion about the impacts of science and technology on our world. Consider the following questions.

• How did advances in space impact our world?

• What is the continuing impact of computers on our world?

• How has biotechnology changed the world we live in?

■ DEMONSTRATE

DIGITAL QUIZ

Lesson Quiz and Class Discussion Board

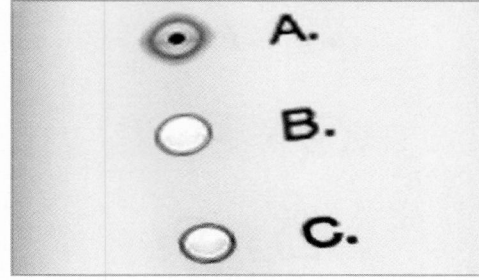

Assign the online Lesson Quiz for this lesson if you haven't done so already. Students will be offered automatic remediation or enrichment based on their scores.

Pose these questions to the class on the Discussion Board:

In "Advances in Science and Technology," you read about space exploration, the birth and explosion of computers in the workplace and in homes around the world. You also read about advances in medicine and biotechnology

Identify Cause and Effect What impact has the computer had on globalization? *(It has brought nations into closer contact and allowed individuals access to global information and the ability to communicate and trade globally.)*

Summarize Summarize the impact of science and technology on modern life. *(Space exploration has led to new knowledge and advances in communications technology. Computers link people to each other and to information, speeding up many business processes.)*

Topic Inquiry

Have students continue their investigations for the Topic Inquiry.

The World Today (1980–Present)

■ SYNTHESIZE

DIGITAL ACTIVITY
Reflect on the Essential Question and Topic

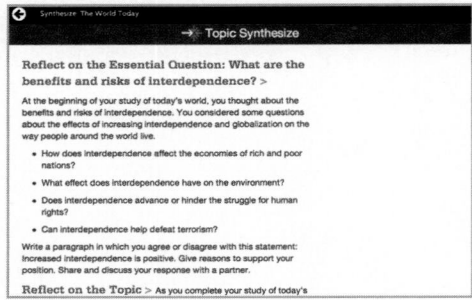

At the beginning of their study of the world today, students thought about the benefits and risks of interdependence. They considered some questions about the effects of increasing interdependence and globalization on the way people around the world live.

- How does interdependence affect the economies of rich and poor nations?
- What effect does interdependence have on the environment?
- Does interdependence advance or hinder the struggle for human rights?
- Can interdependence help us defeat terrorism?

Have students write paragraphs responding to the statement: Increased interdependence is positive. Suggest they start by making a list of some effects of increased interdependence.

Have volunteers read their letters that they wrote for the Synthesize activity and discuss issues raised, or ask students to post their responses on the Class Discussion Board.

Topic Inquiry
As time allows, discuss these and other questions:

- What factors will help determine if interdependence and globalization continue to increase?
- What major changes do you expect to see in your lifetime?
- Which time in the past that you have read about in this course most resembles our world today? Why?

■ DEMONSTRATE

DIGITAL TOPIC REVIEW AND ASSESSMENT
The World Today (1980–Present)

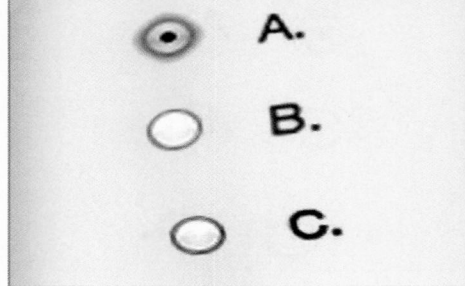

Students can prepare for the Topic Test by answering the questions in the Topic Review and Assessment online or the Assessment questions in the Print Student text. They can also prepare by reviewing their answers to the Interactive Reading Notepad questions or reviewing their notes in the Reading and Notetaking Study Guide.

DIGITAL TOPIC TEST
The World Today (1980–Present)

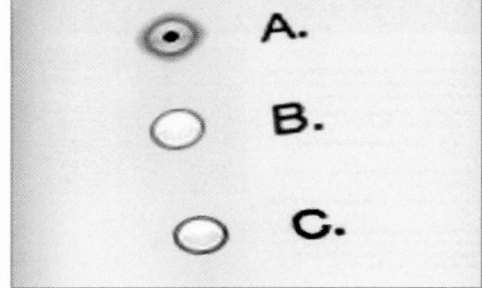

TOPIC TEST
Assign the Topic Test to assess students' understanding of topic content.

BENCHMARK TESTS
Assign these benchmark tests as you complete the relevant topics to monitor student progress toward mastering the course content and as preparation for the End-of-Course Test.

Benchmark Test 1: Topics 1–5
Benchmark Test 2: Topics 6–10
Benchmark Test 3: Topics 11–15
Benchmark Test 4: Topics 16–21

End-of-Course Tests
Assign End-Of-Course Test 1 or 2 to measure students' progress in mastering the course content.